Hoover's Handbook of

Emerging Companies

2008

HOOVERS™

A D&B COMPANY

Austin, Texas

Hoover's Handbook of Emerging Companies 2008 is intended to provide readers with accurate and authoritative information about the enterprises covered in it. Hoover's asked all companies and organizations profiled to provide information. Many did so; a number did not. The information contained herein is as accurate as we could reasonably make it. In many cases we have relied on third-party material that we believe to be trustworthy, but were unable to independently verify. We do not warrant that the book is absolutely accurate or without error. Readers should not rely on any information contained herein in instances where such reliance might cause loss or damage. The publisher, the editors, and their data suppliers specifically disclaim all warranties, including the implied warranties of merchantability and fitness for a specific purpose. This book is sold with the understanding that neither the publisher, the editors, nor any content contributors are engaged in providing investment, financial, accounting, legal, or other professional advice.

The financial data (Historical Financials sections) in this book are from a variety of sources. EDGAR Online provided selected data for the Historical Financials sections of publicly traded companies. For private companies and for historical information on public companies prior to their becoming public, we obtained information directly from the companies or from trade sources deemed to be reliable. Hoover's, Inc., is solely responsible for the presentation of all data.

Many of the names of products and services mentioned in this book are the trademarks or service marks of the companies manufacturing or selling them and are subject to protection under US law. Space has not permitted us to indicate which names are subject to such protection, and readers are advised to consult with the owners of such marks regarding their use. Hoover's is a trademark of Hoover's, Inc.

10 9 8 7 6 5 4 3 2 1

Publishers Cataloging-in-Publication Data

Hoover's Handbook of Emerging Companies 2008

    Includes indexes.

    ISBN 978-1-57311-123-2

    ISSN 1069-7519

    1. Business enterprises — Directories. 2. Corporations — Directories.

HF3010 338.7

Hoover's Company Information is also available on the Internet at Hoover's Online (www.hoovers.com). A catalog of Hoover's products is available on the Internet at www.hooversbooks.com.

The Hoover's Handbook series is produced for Hoover's Business Press by:

Sycamore Productions, Inc.
5808 Balcones Drive, Suite 205
Austin, Texas 78731
info@sycamoreproductions.com

Cover design is by John Baker. Electronic prepress and printing are by R.R. Donnelley, Owensville, Missouri.

U.S. AND WORLD BOOK SALES

Hoover's, Inc.
5800 Airport Blvd.
Austin, TX 78752
Phone: 512-374-4500
Fax: 512-374-4538
e-mail: orders@hoovers.com
Web: www.hooversbooks.com

EUROPEAN BOOK SALES

William Snyder Publishing Associates
5 Five Mile Drive
Oxford OX2 8HT
England
Phone & fax: +44-186-551-3186
e-mail: snyderpub@aol.com

Hoover's, Inc.

Founder: Gary Hoover
President: David Mather
VP Sales and Operations: Jim Currie
Finance Leader: Michael (Mike) Clark
EVP Internet Product Development and Interim Technology Leader: Jeffrey (Jeff) Guillot
EVP Customer Experience and International: Russell Secker
VP Program and Process Management: Shannon Kovar
VP Product Development and Management: Chris Warwick

EDITORIAL

Managing Editor: Margaret C. Lynch
Senior Editors: Kathleen Kelly, Barbara Redding, Dennis Sutton
Team Leads: Larry Bills, Kathleen Cottay, Zack Gonzales, Nancy Kay, Greg Perliski
Editors: Sally Alt, Adam Anderson, Jenn Barnier, Victoria Bernard, Alex Biesada, Joe Bramhall, James Bryant, Anthony Buchanan, Ryan Caione, Jason Cella, Catherine Colbert, Danny Cummings, Jennifer DeShaw, Jeff Dorsch, Bobby Duncan, Lesley Epperson, Rachel Gallo, Stuart Hampton, Jim Harris, Dan Hayes, Chris Huston, Donna Iroabuchi, Jessica Jimenez, Linnea Anderson Kirgan, Julie Krippel, Anne Law, Josh Lower, John MacAyeal, Rebecca Mallett, Erin McInnis, Barbara Murray, Nell Newton, Lynett Oliver, Kristi Park, Peter Partheymuller, Tracey Panek, David Ramirez, Melanie Robertson, Patrice Sarath, Matt Saucedo, Amy Schein, Seth Shafer, Paula Smith, Anthony Staats, Diane Stimets, Barbara Strickland, Tracy Uba, Vanessa Valencia, Ryan Wade, Tim Walker, Kathi Whitley, Randy Williams, David Woodruff
QA Editors: Jason Cother, Carrie Geis, Rosie Hatch, Diane Lee, John Willis
Project Analyst: Tara LoPresti
Editorial Customer Advocates: Adi Anand, Kenny Jones

HOOVER'S BUSINESS PRESS

Senior Director: Jim Currie
Distribution Manager: Rhonda Mitchell
Customer Support and Fulfillment Manager: Michael Febonio

ABOUT HOOVER'S, INC. – THE BUSINESS INFORMATION AUTHORITY™

Hoover's, a D&B company, gives its customers a competitive edge with insightful information about industries, companies, and key decision makers. Hoover's provides this updated information for sales, marketing, business development, and other professionals who need intelligence on U.S. and global companies, industries, and the people who lead them. This information, along with powerful tools to search, sort, download, and integrate the content, is available through Hoover's (www.hoovers.com), the company's premier online service. Hoover's business information is also available through corporate intranets and distribution agreements with licensees, as well as via Hoover's books. The company is headquartered in Austin, Texas.

Abbreviations

AFL-CIO – American Federation of Labor and Congress of Industrial Organizations

AMA – American Medical Association

AMEX – American Stock Exchange

ARM – adjustable-rate mortgage

ASP – application services provider

ATM – asynchronous transfer mode

ATM – automated teller machine

CAD/CAM – computer-aided design/computer-aided manufacturing

CD-ROM – compact disc – read-only memory

CD-R – CD-recordable

CEO – chief executive officer

CFO – chief financial officer

CMOS – complimentary metal oxide silicon

COO – chief operating officer

DAT – digital audiotape

DOD – Department of Defense

DOE – Department of Energy

DOS – disk operating system

DOT – Department of Transportation

DRAM – dynamic random-access memory

DSL – digital subscriber line

DVD – digital versatile disc/digital video disc

DVD-R – DVD-recordable

EPA – Environmental Protection Agency

EPROM – erasable programmable read-only memory

EPS – earnings per share

ESOP – employee stock ownership plan

EU – European Union

EVP – executive vice president

FCC – Federal Communications Commission

FDA – Food and Drug Administration

FDIC – Federal Deposit Insurance Corporation

FTC – Federal Trade Commission

FTP – file transfer protocol

GATT – General Agreement on Tariffs and Trade

GDP – gross domestic product

HMO – health maintenance organization

HR – human resources

HTML – hypertext markup language

ICC – Interstate Commerce Commission

IPO – initial public offering

IRS – Internal Revenue Service

ISP – Internet service provider

kWh – kilowatt-hour

LAN – local-area network

LBO – leveraged buyout

LCD – liquid crystal display

LNG – liquefied natural gas

LP – limited partnership

Ltd. – limited

mips – millions of instructions per second

MW – megawatt

NAFTA – North American Free Trade Agreement

NASA – National Aeronautics and Space Administration

Nasdaq – National Association of Securities Dealers Automated Quotations

NATO – North Atlantic Treaty Organization

NYSE – New York Stock Exchange

OCR – optical character recognition

OECD – Organization for Economic Cooperation and Development

OEM – original equipment manufacturer

OPEC – Organization of Petroleum Exporting Countries

OS – operating system

OSHA – Occupational Safety and Health Administration

OTC – over-the-counter

PBX – private branch exchange

PCMCIA – Personal Computer Memory Card International Association

P/E – price to earnings ratio

RAID – redundant array of independent disks

RAM – random-access memory

R&D – research and development

RBOC – regional Bell operating company

RISC – reduced instruction set computer

REIT – real estate investment trust

ROA – return on assets

ROE – return on equity

ROI – return on investment

ROM – read-only memory

S&L – savings and loan

SCSI – Small Computer System Interface

SEC – Securities and Exchange Commission

SEVP – senior executive vice president

SIC – Standard Industrial Classification

SOC – system on a chip

SVP – senior vice president

USB – universal serial bus

VAR – value-added reseller

VAT – value-added tax

VC – venture capitalist

VoIP – Voice over Internet Protocol

VP – vice president

WAN – wide-area network

WWW – World Wide Web

Contents

Companies Profiled

Companies Profiled (continued)

Companies Profiled (continued)

About Hoover's Handbook of Emerging Companies 2008

Finding value in today's marketplace is a daunting task, and so we are particularly pleased to present the 2008 edition of *Hoover's Handbook of Emerging Companies* — the result of a search of our extensive database of business information for companies with demonstrated growth and the potential for future gains. *Hoover's Handbook of Emerging Companies* is in its 15th year as one of America's premier sources of business information on younger, growth-oriented enterprises.

The 600 companies in this book were chosen from the universe of public US companies with sales between $10 million and $1 billion. Their selection was based primarily on sales growth and profitability, although in a few cases we made some rather subjective decisions about which companies we chose to include. They all have reported at least three years of sales and have sustained annualized sales growth of more than 15% during that time. Also, they are profitable (through year-end September 2007).

HOOVER'S ONLINE FOR BUSINESS NEEDS

In addition to the 2,550 companies featured in our handbooks, comprehensive coverage of more than 40,000 business enterprises is available in electronic format on our Web site, Hoover's Online (www.hoovers.com). Our goal is to provide one site that offers authoritative, updated intelligence on US and global companies, industries, and the people who shape them. Hoover's has partnered with other prestigious business information and service providers to bring you all the right business information, services, and links in one place.

Hoover's Handbook of Emerging Companies is one of our four-title series of handbooks that covers, literally, the world of business. The series is available as an indexed set, and also includes *Hoover's Handbook of American Business*, *Hoover's Handbook of World Business*, and *Hoover's Handbook of Private Companies*. This series brings you information on the biggest, fastest-growing, and most influential enterprises in the world.

We believe that anyone who buys from, sells to, invests in, lends to, competes with, interviews with, or works for a company should know as much as possible about that enterprise. Taken together, *Hoover's Handbook of Emerging Companies 2008* and the other Hoover's products represent the most complete source of basic corporate information readily available to the general public.

HOW TO USE THIS BOOK

This book has four sections:

1. "Using Hoover's Handbooks" describes the contents of our profiles.

2. "A List-Lover's Compendium" contains lists of the fastest-growing and most profitable companies. The lists are based on the information in our profiles, or compiled from well-known sources.

3. The company profiles section makes up the largest and most important part of the book — 600 profiles arranged alphabetically. Each profile features an overview of the company; some larger and more visible companies have an additional History section. All companies have up to five years of financial information, product information where available, and a list of company executives and key competitors.

4. At the end of this volume are the combined indexes from our 2008 editions of all Hoover's Handbooks. The information is organized into three separate sections. The first sorts companies by industry groups, the second by headquarters location. The third index is a list of all the executives found in the Executives section of each company profile. For a more thorough description of our indexing style, see page xiv.

As always, we hope you find our books useful. We invite your comments via phone (512-374-4500), fax (512-374-4538), mail (5800 Airport Boulevard, Austin, Texas 78752), or e-mail (custsupport@hoovers.com).

The Editors
Austin, Texas
March 2008

Using Hoover's Handbooks

ORGANIZATION

The profiles in this volume are presented in alphabetical order. This alphabetization is generally word by word, which means that CAS Medical Systems precedes Cascade Bancorp. You will find the commonly used name of the enterprise at the beginning of the profile; the full, legal name is found in the Locations section. If a company name is also a person's name, such as Bill Barrett Corporation, it will be alphabetized under the first name; if the company name starts with initials, such as A.D.A.M., Inc. or U.S. Auto Parts Network, look for it under the combined initials (in the above example, ADAM and US, respectively).

Basic financial data is listed under the heading Historical Financials; also included is the exchange on which the company's stock is traded, the ticker symbol used by the stock exchange, and the company's fiscal year-end. The annual financial information contained in the profiles is current through fiscal year-ends occurring as late as September 2007. We have included certain nonfinancial developments, such as officer changes, through January 2008.

OVERVIEW

In the first section of the profile, we have tried to give a thumbnail description of the company and what it does. The description will usually include information on the company's strategy, reputation, and ownership. We recommend that you read this section first.

HISTORY

This extended section, which is available for some of the larger and more well-known companies, reflects our belief that every enterprise is the sum of its history and that you have to know where you came from in order to know where you are going. While some companies have limited historical awareness and were unable to help us much and other companies are just plain boring, we think the vast majority of the enterprises in this book have colorful backgrounds. We have tried to focus on the people who made the enterprises what they are today. We have found these histories to be full of twists and ironies; they make fascinating reading.

EXECUTIVES

Here we list the names of the people who run the company, insofar as space allows. In the case of public companies, we have shown the ages and pay of key officers. The published data is for the previous fiscal year, although the company may have announced promotions or retirements since year-end. The pay represents cash compensation, including bonuses, but excludes stock option programs.

Although companies are free to structure their management titles any way they please, most modern corporations follow standard practices. The ultimate power in any corporation lies with the shareholders, who elect a board of directors, usually including officers or "insiders" as well as individuals from outside the company. The chief officer, the person on whose desk the buck stops, is usually called the chief executive officer (CEO). Often, he or she is also the chairman of the board.

As corporate management has become more complex, it is common for the CEO to have a "right-hand person" who oversees the day-to-day operations of the company, allowing the CEO plenty of time to focus on strategy and long-term issues. This right-hand person is usually designated the chief operating officer (COO) and is often the president of the company. In other cases one person is both chairman and president.

A multitude of other titles exists, including chief financial officer (CFO), chief administrative officer, and vice chairman. We have always tried to include the CFO, the chief legal officer, and the chief human resources or personnel officer. Our best advice is that officers' pay levels are clear indicators of who the board of directors thinks are the most important members of the management team.

The people named in the Executives section are indexed at the back of the book.

The Executives section also includes the name of the

company's auditing (accounting) firm, where available.

LOCATIONS

Here we include the company's full legal name and its headquarters, street address, telephone and fax numbers, and Web site, as available. The back of the book includes an index of companies by headquarters locations.

In some cases we have also included information on the geographic distribution of the company's business, including sales and profit data. Note that these profit numbers, like those in the Products/Operations section below, are usually operating or pretax profits rather than net profits. Operating profits are generally those before financing costs (interest income and payments) and before taxes, which are considered costs attributable to the whole company rather than to one division or part of the world. For this reason the net income figures (in the Historical Financials section) are usually much lower, since they are after interest and taxes. Pretax profits are after interest but before taxes.

PRODUCTS/OPERATIONS

This section lists as many of the company's products, services, brand names, divisions, subsidiaries, and joint ventures as we could fit. We have tried to include all its major lines and all familiar brand names. The nature of this section varies by company and the amount of information available. If the company publishes sales and profit information by type of business, we have included it.

COMPETITORS

In this section we have listed companies that compete with the profiled company. This feature is included as a quick way to locate similar companies and compare them. The universe of competitors includes all public companies and all private companies with sales in excess of $500 million. In a few instances we have identified smaller private companies as key competitors.

HISTORICAL FINANCIALS

Here we have tried to present as much data about each enterprise's financial performance as we could compile in the allocated space. Although the information varies somewhat from industry to industry, the following is generally present.

A five-year table, with relevant annualized compound growth rates, covers:

- Sales — fiscal year sales (year-end assets for most financial companies)
- Net income — fiscal year net income (before accounting changes)

- Net profit margin — fiscal year net income as a percent of sales (as a percent of assets for most financial firms)
- Employees — fiscal year-end or average number of employees
- Stock price — the fiscal year closing price
- P/E — high and low price/earnings ratio
- Earnings per share — fiscal year earnings per share (EPS)
- Dividends per share — fiscal year dividends per share
- Book value per share — fiscal year-end book value (common shareholders' equity per share)

The information on the number of employees is intended to aid the reader interested in knowing whether a company has a long-term trend of increasing or decreasing employment. As far as we know, we are the only company that publishes this information in print format.

The numbers on the left in each row of the Historical Financials section give the month and the year in which the company's fiscal year actually ends. Thus, a company with a September 30, 2007, year-end is shown as 9/07.

In addition, we have provided in graph form a stock price history for each company. The graphs, covering up to five years, show the range of trading between the high and the low price, as well as the closing price for each fiscal year.

Key year-end statistics in this section generally show the financial strength of the enterprise, including:

- Debt ratio (long-term debt as a percent of shareholders' equity)
- Return on equity (net income divided by the average of beginning and ending common shareholders' equity)
- Cash and cash equivalents
- Current ratio (ratio of current assets to current liabilities)
- Total long-term debt (including capital lease obligations)
- Number of shares of common stock outstanding
- Dividend yield (fiscal year dividends per share divided by the fiscal year-end closing stock price)
- Dividend payout (fiscal year dividends divided by fiscal year EPS)
- Market value at fiscal year-end (fiscal year-end closing stock price multiplied by fiscal year-end number of shares outstanding)
- Research and development as a percentage of sales
- Advertising as a percentage of sales

Per share data has been adjusted for stock splits. The data for public companies has been provided to us by EDGAR Online. Other public company information was compiled by Hoover's, which takes full responsibility for the content of this section.

Using the Index to Hoover's Handbooks

PAGE NUMBERS

The letter preceding each page number of an index entry indicates the handbook volume that is being referenced:

A=American Business
E=Emerging Companies
P=Private Companies
W=World Business

(For convenience, this list of handbook titles and the corresponding letters are also included at the top of every index page.)

ALPHABETIZATION

English-language articles (a, an, the) are ignored when they appear at the beginning of a company name, but foreign articles are not ignored and are alphabetized as they appear. Ampersands are treated as though they are spelled out, as are the abbreviations Ft., Mt., and St.

If a company name is also a person's name, such as Edward J. DeBartolo or Mary Kay, it will be alphabetized under the first name; if the company name starts with initials, for example, L.L. Bean or S.C. Johnson, look for it under the combined initials (in the above examples, LL and SC, respectively).

Initials or words indicating limited liability appearing at the beginning of international company names (AB, A/S, NV, P.T., S.A., AS, Industrias, Gesellschaft, Koninklijke, Kongl, and Oy) are ignored and the company is sorted on the following word. Similarly, foreign-language words (Grupo, Gruppo, Compagnie, Sociedad, etc.) that begin foreign company names are ignored and the names are sorted by the key word that follows.

INDUSTRY INDEX

Companies are listed alphabetically within industry types. Similar types are grouped under industry categories. For example, Appliances and Housewares are found under the category Consumer Products Manufacturers, while Dairy Products and Fish & Seafood are found under the category Food. For your convenience, a listing of Hoover's industry categories and the pages on which each begins can be found on page 384.

Hoover's Handbook of

Emerging Companies

A List-Lover's Compendium

The Top 100 Companies in Five-Year Sales Growth
in *Hoover's Handbook of Emerging Companies 2008*

Rank	Company	Five-Year Annualized Sales Growth (%)	Rank	Company	Five-Year Annualized Sales Growth (%)	Rank	Company	Five-Year Annualized Sales Growth (%)
1	Aircastle Limited	4,250.9	36	Petrohawk Energy	112.1	71	SiRF Technology	75.0
2	Specialty Underwriters' Alliance	1,877.4	37	Limco-Piedmont Inc.	104.6	72	Targacept, Inc.	74.5
3	Hercules Technology Growth Capital	1,114.5	38	Atlas Pipeline Partners	104.2	73	CKX, Inc.	74.2
4	Genco Shipping and Trading	737.3	39	Heelys, Inc.	103.9	74	Tennessee Commerce Bancorp	71.8
5	Concho Resources	642.2	40	DivX, Inc.	97.5	75	Under Armour	71.7
6	Airvana, Inc.	587.8	41	True Religion Apparel	97.2	76	Home BancShares	71.7
7	Patriot Capital Funding	365.7	42	DealerTrack Holdings	96.2	77	Medifast, Inc.	71.5
8	Linn Energy	286.9	43	Home Solutions of America	96.0	78	Ceradyne, Inc.	71.0
9	VeraSun Energy	252.8	44	Trimeris, Inc.	95.4	79	Ultra Petroleum	70.4
10	First Solar	248.1	45	United Therapeutics	94.7	80	Allion Healthcare	70.2
11	Darwin Professional Underwriters	231.1	46	Diamond Hill Investment Group	92.7	81	First Advantage	70.0
12	Syntax-Brillian	225.8	47	WSB Financial Group	91.5	82	Sport Supply Group	69.6
13	Bronco Drilling	209.9	48	MVC Capital	90.9	83	Allegiant Travel	69.5
14	Acme Packet	194.3	49	NeuroMetrix, Inc.	90.5	84	GeoMet, Inc.	69.2
15	Duff & Phelps	191.6	50	Rackable Systems	90.1	85	Penn Virginia Resource Partners	69.1
16	I-trax, Inc.	190.7	51	WPCS International	89.7	86	Mellanox Technologies	68.2
17	Arena Resources	188.3	52	WPT Enterprises	89.6	87	Netflix, Inc.	67.4
18	Approach Resources	186.2	53	Rex Energy	89.1	88	OSG America	67.2
19	Atheros Communications	178.5	54	iRobot Corporation	89.0	89	LoopNet, Inc.	66.4
20	Force Protection	177.1	55	NutriSystem, Inc.	88.6	90	Starent Networks	65.6
21	SunPower Corporation	175.6	56	salesforce.com	85.9	91	ValueClick, Inc.	64.8
22	EXCO Resources	159.3	57	Sirona Dental Systems	85.8	92	Vineyard National Bancorp	64.0
23	Franklin Bank	158.5	58	Delta Petroleum	85.3	93	Synchronoss Technologies	63.7
24	optionsXpress Holdings	145.8	59	First Marblehead Corporation	84.4	94	ExlService Holdings	63.6
25	Sucampo Pharmaceuticals	143.6	60	Occam Networks	84.4	95	Superior Well Services	63.5
26	NetLogic Microsystems	140.4	61	The Bank Holdings	83.2	96	Bank of Florida	63.1
27	Illumina, Inc.	136.4	62	Techwell, Inc.	82.9	97	Travelzoo Inc.	62.2
28	Allis-Chalmers Energy	129.8	63	ImClone Systems	82.8	98	Boardwalk Pipeline Partners	62.0
29	Prospect Capital	124.2	64	ShoreTel, Inc.	81.0	99	IPG Photonics	62.0
30	GeoEye, Inc.	120.8	65	Masimo Corporation	79.8	100	NGAS Resources	61.8
31	VAALCO Energy	120.2	66	VMware, Inc.	79.4			
32	Bill Barrett Corporation	119.7	67	Vanguard Natural Resources	78.9			
33	ViroPharma Incorporated	117.9	68	Cbeyond, Inc.	78.6			
34	Williams Partners	116.4	69	Pinnacle Financial Partners	76.1			
35	InnerWorkings, Inc.	114.8	70	Rodman & Renshaw Capital Group	75.0			

Note: These rates are compounded annualized increases in sales growth for the most current fiscal years and may have resulted from acquisitions or one-time gains. If the company has been public for less than six years, sales growth is for the years available.

SOURCE: HOOVER'S, INC., DATABASE, FEBRUARY 2008

The Top 100 Companies in One-Year Sales Growth
in *Hoover's Handbook of Emerging Companies 2008*

Rank	Company	One-Year Sales Growth (%)	Rank	Company	One-Year Sales Growth (%)	Rank	Company	One-Year Sales Growth (%)
1	Airvana, Inc.	7,304.3	36	Smith Micro Software	168.5	71	Prospect Capital	92.0
2	BioSante Pharmaceuticals	4,700.0	37	NutriSystem, Inc.	167.4	72	Flotek Industries	90.2
3	Targacept, Inc.	2,191.7	38	PowerSecure International	154.5	73	Simclar, Inc.	90.2
4	EXCO Resources	1,507.8	39	Illumina, Inc.	151.2	74	Intevac, Inc.	89.4
5	Williams Partners	987.6	40	Pinnacle Financial Partners	142.7	75	Allscripts Healthcare Solutions	89.1
6	M & F Worldwide	494.7	41	Rudolph Technologies	142.7	76	Neutral Tandem	88.9
7	Ambassadors International	436.8	42	VeraSun Energy	136.0	77	ICF International	87.0
8	Aircastle Limited	425.8	43	Epoch Holding	134.3	78	Home Solutions of America	86.8
9	MVC Capital	407.6	44	Avici Systems	134.2	79	Limco-Piedmont Inc.	86.1
10	Vanguard Natural Resources	357.1	45	Tidelands Bancshares	134.0	80	Superior Well Services	85.7
11	Heelys, Inc.	327.7	46	Hallmark Financial Services	133.0	81	Entegris, Inc.	84.9
12	Force Protection	294.4	47	Acme Packet	133.0	82	Medifast, Inc.	84.8
13	Specialty Underwriters' Alliance	288.4	48	Omrix Biopharmaceuticals	132.0	83	Mercer Insurance	84.4
14	Linn Energy	284.5	49	Arena Resources	131.8	84	Beach First National Bancshares	84.1
15	GeoEye, Inc.	271.5	50	OMNI Energy Services	128.6	85	Allegiant Travel	83.7
16	Bronco Drilling	266.9	51	Ultra Clean Technology	128.6	86	Community Bancorp	83.3
17	Syntax-Brillian	261.5	52	Petrohawk Energy	127.8	87	The Bank Holdings	82.7
18	Concho Resources	261.2	53	Cal Dive International	127.3	88	Cascade Bancorp	82.5
19	Lakes Entertainment	248.7	54	Patriot Capital Funding	126.1	89	VMware, Inc.	81.8
20	Diamond Hill Investment Group	246.7	55	Tessera Technologies	120.4	90	Stratus Properties	81.8
21	Duff & Phelps	231.6	56	TGC Industries	119.4	91	Union Drilling	81.4
22	Mariner Energy	230.2	57	Gulfport Energy	118.8	92	Ceradyne, Inc.	80.0
23	Boots & Coots	228.8	58	Rodman & Renshaw Capital Group	118.4	93	DivX, Inc.	79.7
24	Crocs, Inc.	226.6	59	EPIQ Systems	110.9	94	ValueClick, Inc.	79.5
25	SunPower Corporation	200.5	60	InnerWorkings, Inc.	108.7	95	Cherokee, Inc.	79.4
26	Versar, Inc.	199.4	61	Masimo Corporation	107.9	96	OSG America	78.5
27	InterDigital, Inc.	194.6	62	GAINSCO, INC.	107.3	97	Bank of Florida	78.0
28	Delta Petroleum	193.5	63	Venoco, Inc.	103.3	98	Kowabunga, Inc.	78.0
29	Allis-Chalmers Energy	191.8	64	Intercontinental-Exchange	101.3	99	FNB United Corp.	77.6
30	ATP Oil & Gas	186.2	65	U.S. Auto Parts Network	101.2	100	Gateway Financial	77.0
31	Quicksilver Gas Services	183.7	66	LaBranche & Co	98.1			
32	First Solar	180.7	67	Eastern Insurance Holdings	97.7			
33	Hercules Technology Growth Capital	175.7	68	Hecla Mining	97.3			
34	Rex Energy	174.2	69	Oplink Communications	96.2			
35	Sigma Designs	173.9	70	Trimeris, Inc.	93.7			

Note: These rates are for sales growth for the most current fiscal year and may have resulted from acquisitions or one-time gains.

SOURCE: HOOVER'S, INC., DATABASE, FEBRUARY 2008

The Top 100 Companies in Five-Year Net Income Growth
in *Hoover's Handbook of Emerging Companies 2008*

Rank	Company	Five-Year Net Income Growth (%)	Rank	Company	Five-Year Net Income Growth (%)	Rank	Company	Five-Year Net Income Growth (%)
1	Genco Shipping and Trading	740.0	36	RELM Wireless	102.4	71	ICF International	70.5
2	Rodman & Renshaw Capital Group	663.8	37	MedAssets, Inc.	102.4	72	Bridge Capital Holdings	69.3
3	Houston Wire & Cable	435.4	38	OSG America	101.3	73	Blue Nile	69.2
4	VeraSun Energy	401.6	39	Hansen Natural	100.8	74	Titan Machinery	68.7
5	ITC Holdings	257.3	40	Ceradyne, Inc.	100.1	75	Pioneer Drilling	68.0
6	Diodes Incorporated	243.9	41	First Marblehead Corporation	98.0	76	First State Financial	67.7
7	Hologic, Inc.	242.7	42	Hecla Mining	97.5	77	DXP Enterprises	67.6
8	Rex Energy	208.2	43	MarkWest Energy Partners	93.3	78	American Medical Alert	67.0
9	EXCO Resources	198.9	44	Under Armour	93.2	79	Willamette Valley Vineyards	67.0
10	Heelys, Inc.	198.3	45	The Middleby Corporation	92.6	80	Zumiez Inc.	66.8
11	NYMEX Holdings	194.4	46	LHC Group	91.5	81	Ultra Petroleum	66.8
12	First Advantage	187.0	47	GeoMet, Inc.	90.6	82	Life Time Fitness	66.1
13	FormFactor, Inc.	185.8	48	Amtech Systems	88.8	83	First Community Bancorp	65.6
14	Consumer Portfolio Services	165.5	49	Layne Christensen	88.7	84	Beach First National Bancshares	65.5
15	Tower Group	147.0	50	Technitrol, Inc.	87.0	85	First Community Bank	65.3
16	American Equity Investment Life	142.5	51	WSB Financial Group	86.6	86	Super Micro Computer	64.5
17	Duff & Phelps	141.5	52	Central European Distribution	85.9	87	Omni Financial Services	64.2
18	PAB Bankshares	132.9	53	The Bancorp, Inc.	83.8	88	Brooke Corporation	64.1
19	Euronet Worldwide	131.3	54	American Ecology	81.8	89	Bare Escentuals	62.0
20	NutriSystem, Inc.	130.8	55	Hittite Microwave	81.0	90	Arrhythmia Research Technology	61.5
21	InnerWorkings, Inc.	128.0	56	Deckers Outdoor	80.4	91	Home BancShares	61.1
22	VMware, Inc.	126.1	57	Natural Gas Services	80.2	92	LKQ Corporation	60.3
23	Avatar Holdings	125.4	58	Bank of the Carolinas	78.4	93	Websense, Inc.	59.6
24	Vanguard Natural Resources	124.0	59	PetMed Express	78.3	94	Stratus Properties	59.5
25	Cal Dive International	122.8	60	Penson Worldwide	77.2	95	Umpqua Holdings	57.9
26	Venoco, Inc.	121.3	61	SandRidge Energy	76.7	96	Mariner Energy	57.8
27	Versar, Inc.	121.2	62	Commonwealth Bankshares	75.9	97	Superior Well Services	56.6
28	SeaBright Insurance	114.7	63	Basic Energy Services	75.1	98	FPB Bancorp	56.5
29	Travelzoo Inc.	111.2	64	Vineyard National Bancorp	75.0	99	Temecula Valley Bancorp	56.5
30	AeroVironment, Inc.	111.1	65	Crescent Financial	74.8	100	CAS Medical Systems	55.2
31	MSCI Inc.	108.9	66	Tennessee Commerce Bancorp	74.7			
32	LoopNet, Inc.	108.9	67	First Regional Bancorp	74.0			
33	Williams Partners	108.3	68	Copano Energy	73.8			
34	Limco-Piedmont Inc.	107.4	69	North American Galvanizing	71.9			
35	Boardwalk Pipeline Partners	106.3	70	Emergent BioSolutions	71.8			

Note: These rates are compounded annualized increases in net income for the most current fiscal years and may have resulted from acquisitions or one-time gains. If the company has been public for less than six years, net income growth is for the years available.

SOURCE: HOOVER'S, INC., DATABASE, FEBRUARY 2008

The Top 100 Companies in One-Year Net Income Growth
in *Hoover's Handbook of Emerging Companies 2008*

Rank	Company	One-Year Net Income Growth (%)	Rank	Company	One-Year Net Income Growth (%)	Rank	Company	One-Year Net Income Growth (%)
1	Aircastle Limited	25,500.0	36	The Female Health Company	466.7	71	Shuffle Master	221.6
2	VeraSun Energy	25,133.3	37	Masimo Corporation	444.3	72	Chart Industries	220.2
3	EXCO Resources	15,333.3	38	Hercules Technology Growth Capital	442.9	73	Bitstream Inc.	220.0
4	Ciena Corporation	13,700.0	39	PowerSecure International	408.7	74	Cal Dive International	216.7
5	Sirona Dental Systems	6,962.5	40	MEMSIC, Inc.	400.0	75	Palomar Medical Technologies	202.9
6	Williams Partners	2,960.4	41	Allis-Chalmers Energy	394.4	76	Mariner Energy	200.0
7	MarkWest Energy Partners	2,820.8	42	NeuroMetrix, Inc.	377.8	77	Aehr Test Systems	200.0
8	Neutral Tandem	2,650.0	43	Stratus Properties	374.1	78	Techwell, Inc.	193.3
9	GSI Commerce	1,888.9	44	Aspect Medical Systems	336.5	79	Intevac, Inc.	190.1
10	Rochester Medical	1,600.0	45	Darwin Professional Underwriters	332.4	80	Cuisine Solutions	183.8
11	Pinnacle Entertainment	1,160.7	46	Gaiam, Inc.	330.8	81	K12 Inc.	178.6
12	Sonus Networks	1,123.8	47	DealerTrack Holdings	328.9	82	AZZ incorporated	176.9
13	Benjamin Franklin Bancorp	1,075.0	48	ImClone Systems	328.6	83	Avatar Holdings	176.9
14	Bronco Drilling	1,072.5	49	InterDigital, Inc.	311.7	84	ARRIS Group	176.3
15	Consumer Portfolio Services	1,064.7	50	NutriSystem, Inc.	305.2	85	Ceradyne, Inc.	174.4
16	Website Pros	975.0	51	AeroCentury Corp.	300.0	86	Central European Distribution	173.4
17	Concho Resources	885.0	52	Community Capital Bancshares	300.0	87	K-Sea Transportation	167.8
18	COMSYS IT Partners	854.5	53	Boots & Coots	300.0	88	NATCO Group	167.6
19	Penson Worldwide	744.8	54	Starent Networks	300.0	89	Genesee & Wyoming	167.5
20	Coeur d'Alene Mines	734.9	55	IPG Photonics	294.6	90	TETRA Technologies	167.5
21	Ultra Clean Technology	715.0	56	Rodman & Renshaw Capital Group	288.9	91	Dril-Quip, Inc.	166.6
22	Eastern Insurance Holdings	654.5	57	OSG America	285.0	92	Kenexa Corporation	160.7
23	North American Galvanizing	650.0	58	Crocs, Inc.	278.8	93	Bill Barrett Corporation	160.5
24	Hungarian Telephone and Cable	627.6	59	Versar, Inc.	278.6	94	Astronics Corporation	159.1
25	DivX, Inc.	613.0	60	LaBranche & Co	264.8	95	Gulfport Energy	155.0
26	Oplink Communications	594.7	61	Intercontinental-Exchange	254.7	96	Rudolph Technologies	154.0
27	Numerex Corp.	583.3	62	Jones Soda	253.8	97	Home Solutions of America	148.6
28	Heelys, Inc.	579.1	63	TransDigm Group	253.0	98	Kadant Inc.	147.8
29	Entegris, Inc.	575.5	64	Hologic, Inc.	245.3	99	Alkermes, Inc.	147.4
30	Concur Technologies	533.3	65	Superior Well Services	235.8	100	Houston Wire & Cable	145.6
31	CommVault Systems	495.4	66	Radiant Systems	228.6			
32	ICF International	495.0	67	Life Partners Holdings	227.3			
33	The Knot, Inc.	485.0	68	Sigma Designs	226.3			
34	Brooks Automation	484.9	69	Newport Corporation	222.4			
35	Union Drilling	469.6	70	Simclar, Inc.	222.2			

Note: These rates are for net income for the most current fiscal year and may have resulted from acquisitions or one-time gains.

SOURCE: HOOVER'S, INC., DATABASE, FEBRUARY 2008

The Top 100 Companies in Five-Year Employment Growth
in *Hoover's Handbook of Emerging Companies 2008*

Rank	Company	Five-Year Annualized Employment Growth (%)	Rank	Company	Five-Year Annualized Employment Growth (%)	Rank	Company	Five-Year Annualized Employment Growth (%)
1	Crocs, Inc.	336.3	36	Prospect Capital	58.3	71	TGC Industries	40.1
2	Website Pros	292.0	37	Medifast, Inc.	55.7	72	New Century Bancorp	39.9
3	Allis-Chalmers Energy	266.7	38	Allegiant Travel	54.8	73	Providence Service	38.5
4	Cathay General Bancorp	222.8	39	GeoEye, Inc.	54.6	74	Specialty Underwriters' Alliance	38.3
5	Tidelands Bancshares	187.2	40	Under Armour	53.8	75	Goodrich Petroleum	37.6
6	Caraco Pharmaceutical	164.0	41	Hercules Technology Growth Capital	53.7	76	SI International	37.6
7	Sirona Dental Systems	154.1	42	Pinnacle Financial Partners	53.7	77	Netflix, Inc.	37.6
8	Evercore Partners	105.8	43	EXCO Resources	52.8	78	Hologic, Inc.	37.5
9	The Bank Holdings	105.1	44	InnerWorkings, Inc.	52.7	79	K-Sea Transportation	37.4
10	Atheros Communications	101.8	45	Greenfield Online	52.6	80	Radiation Therapy Services	36.8
11	Beach First National Bancshares	101.6	46	Atlas America	52.1	81	SandRidge Energy	36.8
12	SunPower Corporation	94.4	47	Bare Escentuals	49.8	82	Ceradyne, Inc.	36.6
13	InfoSonics Corporation	85.7	48	First Community Bancorp	48.3	83	Waccamaw Bankshares	36.5
14	Genco Shipping and Trading	84.2	49	MEMSIC, Inc.	48.0	84	BNC Bancorp	35.9
15	Gulfport Energy	81.2	50	ShoreTel, Inc.	47.5	85	Central European Distribution	35.5
16	Arena Resources	79.6	51	Hansen Natural	47.3	86	Range Resources	35.5
17	Kenexa Corporation	76.0	52	Community Bancorp	47.0	87	Amedisys, Inc.	35.3
18	Petrohawk Energy	75.7	53	Bronco Drilling	46.4	88	optionsXpress Holdings	34.6
19	Rackable Systems	74.3	54	Western Alliance Bancorporation	46.2	89	VeraSun Energy	34.5
20	True Religion Apparel	71.6	55	ExlService Holdings	46.2	90	FormFactor, Inc.	34.2
21	Linn Energy	69.2	56	Sonic Solutions	46.0	91	Rainmaker Systems	33.7
22	Sport Supply Group	69.2	57	Synchronoss Technologies	45.3	92	Gateway Financial	33.5
23	Tessera Technologies	67.3	58	LoopNet, Inc.	43.5	93	Greenhill & Co	33.1
24	Appalachian Bancshares	66.9	59	Volcom, Inc.	43.1	94	Pioneer Drilling	32.9
25	Superior Well Services	65.3	60	Parallel Petroleum	42.4	95	First National Bancshares	32.5
26	Sun American Bancorp	64.9	61	WebMD Health	42.4	96	Zumiez Inc.	32.2
27	NeuStar, Inc.	63.7	62	Hiland Partners	41.8	97	GSI Commerce	32.1
28	M & F Worldwide	63.5	63	Dreams, Inc.	41.7	98	Vineyard National Bancorp	32.0
29	Home Solutions of America	62.8	64	Syntax-Brillian	41.5	99	Sciele Pharma	32.0
30	ITC Holdings	62.8	65	Copano Energy	41.2	100	iRobot Corporation	31.7
31	Flotek Industries	61.1	66	The Knot, Inc.	41.2			
32	Williams Partners	59.2	67	NGAS Resources	41.0			
33	salesforce.com	58.7	68	Smith & Wesson	40.9			
34	Perficient, Inc.	58.6	69	Delta Petroleum	40.9			
35	ValueClick, Inc.	58.5	70	GMX Resources	40.6			

Note: These rates are compounded annualized increases in employment growth for
the most current fiscal years and may have resulted from acquisitions or one-time gains.
If the company has been public for less than six years, employment growth is for the
years available.

SOURCE: HOOVER'S, INC., DATABASE, FEBRUARY 2008

The Top 40 Companies in Five-Year Stock Appreciation
in *Hoover's Handbook of Emerging Companies 2008*

Rank	Company	Five-Year Annualized Stock Appreciation (%)	Rank	Company	Five-Year Annualized Stock Appreciation (%)	Rank	Company	Five-Year Annualized Stock Appreciation (%)
1	Cbeyond, Inc.	197.0	16	Angeion Corporation	99.3	31	Ultra Petroleum	73.3
2	Intercontinental-Exchange	196.8	17	Atlas America	87.4	32	Kowabunga, Inc.	72.7
3	NutriSystem, Inc.	182.9	18	TransDigm Group	87.2	33	PetMed Express	71.4
4	Hansen Natural	130.3	19	j2 Global Communications	85.5	34	Boardwalk Pipeline Partners	71.4
5	Health Grades	129.8	20	Diamond Hill Investment Group	83.7	35	Dawson Geophysical	71.4
6	Bankrate, Inc.	125.6	21	Concur Technologies	82.4	36	LCA-Vision Inc.	71.0
7	Medifast, Inc.	124.6	22	The Middleby Corporation	81.9	37	Perficient, Inc.	70.2
8	US Global Investors	114.4	23	Jones Soda	81.8	38	Dynamic Materials	70.0
9	True Religion Apparel	114.1	24	Brooke Corporation	80.6	39	Smith Micro Software	68.3
10	The Knot, Inc.	112.9	25	salesforce.com	78.9	40	Southwestern Energy	68.2
11	Palomar Medical Technologies	111.8	26	Arrhythmia Research Technology	75.8			
12	GlobalSCAPE, Inc.	109.9	27	Epoch Holding	75.7			
13	Deckers Outdoor	105.8	28	Continucare Corporation	74.7			
14	Ceradyne, Inc.	100.9	29	LivePerson, Inc.	73.8			
15	DXP Enterprises	99.8	30	TGC Industries	73.5			

Note: These rates are compounded annualized increases based on fiscal year-end closing prices. If the company has been public for less than six years, stock appreciation is for the years available.

SOURCE: HOOVER'S, INC., DATABASE, FEBRUARY 2008

The Top 40 Companies in Market Value
in *Hoover's Handbook of Emerging Companies 2008*

Rank	Company	Market Value ($ mil.)	Rank	Company	Market Value ($ mil.)	Rank	Company	Market Value ($ mil.)
1	Celgene Corporation	21,633	16	ResMed Inc.	3,202	31	First Solar	2,158
2	NYMEX Holdings	11,121	17	F5 Networks	3,138	32	TransDigm Group	2,150
3	Akamai Technologies	8,515	18	Hansen Natural	3,033	33	Greenhill & Co	2,101
4	Ultra Petroleum	7,247	19	FactSet Research Systems	2,898	34	St. Mary Land & Exploration	2,026
5	Intercontinental-Exchange	6,272	20	Quicksilver Resources	2,839	35	Sirona Dental Systems	1,953
6	Southwestern Energy	5,922	21	Bare Escentuals	2,775	36	Petrohawk Energy	1,938
7	salesforce.com	5,020	22	SunPower Corporation	2,596	37	Tessera Technologies	1,905
8	Red Hat, Inc.	4,330	23	Atwood Oceanics	2,425	38	Morningstar, Inc.	1,902
9	Ciena Corporation	4,152	24	NeuStar, Inc.	2,412	39	Investment Technology Group	1,879
10	Range Resources	3,815	25	ValueClick, Inc.	2,349	40	Illumina, Inc.	1,842
11	First Marblehead Corporation	3,607	26	Boardwalk Pipeline Partners	2,316			
12	Intuitive Surgical	3,557	27	ImClone Systems	2,288			
13	The Corporate Executive Board	3,416	28	NutriSystem, Inc.	2,274			
14	Hologic, Inc.	3,358	29	Digital River	2,257			
15	Denbury Resources	3,339	30	East West Bancorp	2,176			

Note: These values are based on the latest available fiscal year-end stock price and the number of shares outstanding.

SOURCE: HOOVER'S, INC., DATABASE, FEBRUARY 2008

The Top 40 Companies with the Highest Profit Margin
in *Hoover's Handbook of Emerging Companies 2008*

Rank	Company	Profit Margin (%)	Rank	Company	Profit Margin (%)	Rank	Company	Profit Margin (%)
1	Rochester Medical	104.0	16	Golden Star Resources	45.0	31	Pope Resources	37.6
2	Capital Southwest	98.4	17	Airvana, Inc.	43.5	32	Asta Funding	37.1
3	Masimo Corporation	81.1	18	CommVault Systems	42.6	33	Sonus Networks	36.8
4	MVC Capital	70.0	19	First Marblehead Corporation	42.2	34	Sucampo Pharmaceuticals	36.8
5	Stratus Properties	63.0	20	Palomar Medical Technologies	41.9	35	Somanetics Corporation	36.2
6	ImClone Systems	54.7	21	Linn Energy	41.4	36	Omrix Biopharmaceuticals	36.2
7	Patriot Capital Funding	51.5	22	Prospect Capital	41.0	37	BreitBurn Energy Partners	36.2
8	Vanguard Natural Resources	48.9	23	VAALCO Energy	41.0	38	CREDO Petroleum	35.9
9	Genco Shipping and Trading	47.7	24	Coeur d'Alene Mines	40.9	39	GulfMark Offshore	35.8
10	InterDigital, Inc.	46.9	25	Aspect Medical Systems	40.6	40	Concur Technologies	35.2
11	United Therapeutics	46.4	26	ViroPharma Incorporated	39.9			
12	Gulfport Energy	46.0	27	Ultra Petroleum	39.0			
13	Intercontinental-Exchange	45.7	28	Arena Resources	39.0			
14	Cherokee, Inc.	45.4	29	Hercules Technology Growth Capital	38.6			
15	Approach Resources	45.4	30	optionsXpress Holdings	38.1			

Note: These values are based on the latest available fiscal year-end net income and sales.

SOURCE: HOOVER'S, INC., DATABASE, FEBRUARY 2008

The Top 40 Companies with the Highest Return on Equity
in *Hoover's Handbook of Emerging Companies 2008*

Rank	Company	Return on Equity (%)	Rank	Company	Return on Equity (%)	Rank	Company	Return on Equity (%)
1	Caraco Pharmaceutical	1,028.7	16	Houston Wire & Cable	74.5	31	First Marblehead Corporation	52.3
2	HFF, Inc.	655.3	17	ImClone Systems	73.3	32	Diamond Hill Investment Group	51.7
3	eHealth, Inc.	187.9	18	Cal Dive International	71.2	33	Omrix Biopharmaceuticals	51.0
4	Vanguard Natural Resources	146.8	19	Techwell, Inc.	69.6	34	Miller Industries	50.9
5	Bidz.com, Inc.	126.9	20	Palomar Medical Technologies	62.7	35	Grey Wolf	48.7
6	Cherokee, Inc.	117.7	21	The Middleby Corporation	56.9	36	optionsXpress Holdings	47.9
7	Rodman & Renshaw Capital Group	115.4	22	Heelys, Inc.	56.9	37	True Religion Apparel	47.5
8	InterDigital, Inc.	100.1	23	Crocs, Inc.	56.7	38	Concur Technologies	46.2
9	OMNI Energy Services	88.5	24	Greenhill & Co	56.0	39	Dynamic Materials	45.0
10	Evercore Partners	85.0	25	Hansen Natural	55.8	40	Transcend Services	43.3
11	Thomas Group	84.9	26	Life Partners Holdings	55.6			
12	Williams Partners	82.3	27	Cuisine Solutions	55.4			
13	Rochester Medical	77.6	28	IPG Photonics	54.5			
14	VMware, Inc.	77.0	29	US Global Investors	53.4			
15	NutriSystem, Inc.	75.9	30	Boots & Coots	53.1			

Note: These values are based on the latest available fiscal year-end net income and average total equity.

SOURCE: HOOVER'S, INC., DATABASE, FEBRUARY 2008

The Top 40 Companies with the Highest P/E Ratios
in *Hoover's Handbook of Emerging Companies 2008*

Rank	Company	P/E High	Rank	Company	P/E High	Rank	Company	P/E High
1	Delta Petroleum	3,068	16	Alkermes, Inc.	253	31	Allscripts Healthcare Solutions	133
2	NetLogic Microsystems	1,501	17	Toreador Resources	230	32	Cbeyond, Inc.	128
3	Novatel Wireless	1,318	18	Mac-Gray Corporation	225	33	NeuroMetrix, Inc.	125
4	WebMD Health	1,183	19	Cutera, Inc.	214	34	Resource America	124
5	SiRF Technology	1,063	20	Synergetics USA	198	35	SunPower Corporation	122
6	Vocus, Inc.	605	21	CKX, Inc.	198	36	Sigma Designs	121
7	Unica Corporation	504	22	I-trax, Inc.	196	37	Red Hat, Inc.	112
8	First Solar	429	23	Ultimate Software	180	38	CAS Medical Systems	107
9	Opnext, Inc.	399	24	Akamai Technologies	167	39	Packeteer, Inc.	103
10	ADA-ES, Inc.	363	25	ANSYS, Inc.	157	40	Entertainment Distribution	100
11	Celgene Corporation	334	26	LivePerson, Inc.	157			
12	Atlas Energy Resources	286	27	LOUD Technologies	152			
13	Sapient Corporation	279	28	Rackable Systems	140			
14	iRobot Corporation	271	29	NGAS Resources	137			
15	Alliance Fiber Optic	270	30	Dreams, Inc.	134			

Note: These values are based on the latest available fiscal year earnings per share and the highest stock price for that fiscal year.

SOURCE: HOOVER'S, INC., DATABASE, FEBRUARY 2008

The Top 40 Companies with the Lowest P/E Ratios
in *Hoover's Handbook of Emerging Companies 2008*

Rank	Company	P/E Low	Rank	Company	P/E Low	Rank	Company	P/E Low
1	Force Protection	2	16	US Global Investors	5	31	VSE Corporation	6
2	Rochester Medical	3	17	GulfMark Offshore	5	32	Grey Wolf	6
3	Avatar Holdings	3	18	Versar, Inc.	6	33	Bronco Drilling	6
4	Consumer Portfolio Services	3	19	Avici Systems	6	34	VAALCO Energy	6
5	North American Galvanizing	3	20	Pope Resources	6	35	Commercial Vehicle Group	6
6	OMNI Energy Services	4	21	Trio-Tech International	6	36	BankUnited Financial	6
7	LaBranche & Co	4	22	AZZ incorporated	6	37	ImClone Systems	6
8	Cal-Maine Foods	4	23	KSW, Inc.	6	38	Swift Energy	6
9	Stratus Properties	4	24	Allis-Chalmers Energy	6	39	FirstFed Financial	6
10	Miller Industries	4	25	AeroCentury Corp.	6	40	Trico Marine Services	7
11	InterDigital, Inc.	4	26	Intevac, Inc.	6			
12	MVC Capital	4	27	Genco Shipping and Trading	6			
13	Syntax-Brillian	4	28	Corus Bankshares	6			
14	Universal Stainless	5	29	Brooks Automation	6			
15	Boots & Coots	5	30	Cal Dive International	6			

Note: These values are based on the latest available fiscal year earnings per share and the lowest stock price for that fiscal year.

SOURCE: HOOVER'S, INC., DATABASE, FEBRUARY 2008

BusinessWeek 100 Hot Growth Companies

Rank	Company	Three-Year Sales Increase (%)	Rank	Company	Three-Year Sales Increase (%)	Rank	Company	Three-Year Sales Increase (%)
1	Heelys	104.1	36	Kinetic Concepts	21.6	71	Universal Stainless & Alloy Products	43.2
2	Bare Escentuals	63.0	37	Metretek Technologies	44.4	72	Ventiv Health	51.3
3	TGC Industries	98.0	38	Bucyrus International	29.5	73	FLIR Systems	20.8
4	VASCO Data Security International	52.3	39	Select Comfort	21.0	74	DSW	17.5
5	Titanium Metals	45.0	40	Eagle Materials	25.2	75	Tidewater	20.6
6	Applix	23.6	41	Arena Resources	158.3	76	LSB Industries	15.1
7	Under Armour	53.2	42	Korn/Ferry International	22.2	77	Smith & Wesson Holding	20.6
8	Dynamic Materials	41.7	43	Jos. A. Bank Clothiers	22.4	78	Magellan Midstream Partners	38.6
9	Flotek Industries	93.9	44	Gulfport Energy	52.0	79	Concur Technologies	20.4
10	Houston Wire & Cable	28.9	45	ITT Educational Services	13.0	80	Balchem	18.3
11	Hittite Microwave	44.2	46	Tempur-Pedic International	25.1	81	Comtech Telecommunications	31.7
12	Mannatech	29.3	47	Reliv' International	15.3	82	Actuant	27.8
13	Cal Dive International	57.7	48	Mariner Energy	75.5	83	Cybex International	12.0
14	Alliance Resource Partners	21.9	49	Diodes	33.7	84	NETGEAR	23.5
15	Cognizant Technology Solutions	56.4	50	Pioneer Drilling	54.1	85	Teledyne Technologies	19.4
16	Atlas Energy Resources	43.5	51	A.M. Castle	29.1	86	RBC Bearings	16.7
17	Ceradyne	85.3	52	Penn Virginia Resource Partners	133.2	87	Tween Brands	13.7
18	Liquidity Services	32.8	53	Middleby	18.3	88	MICROS Systems	19.6
19	Quality Systems	28.3	54	Sotheby's	25.0	89	Knight Transportation	25.3
20	Tessera Technologies	72.1	55	Raven Industries	15.7	90	Cascade	17.1
21	Zumiez	36.0	56	Ventana Medical Systems	21.5	91	Trimble Navigation	19.8
22	Huron Consulting Group	41.6	57	ExlService Holdings	41.9	92	Microchip Technology	13.7
23	Guess?	24.0	58	Lufkin Industries	32.8	93	Genesco	19.9
24	Immucor	23.9	59	Labor Ready	15.2	94	Covance	13.5
25	Ansoft	15.8	60	Cabot Oil & Gas	15.7	95	Rofin-Sinar Technologies	17.6
26	Morningstar	30.7	61	Pharmaceutical Product Development	20.1	96	VCA Antech	22.0
27	Emergent BioSolutions	35.3	62	GulfMark Offshore	26.6	97	Wabtec	15.9
28	Super Micro Computer	29.8	63	Portfolio Recovery Associates	30.5	98	K-Tron International	15.0
29	Smith Micro Software	91.2	64	DXP Enterprises	22.1	99	Copart	14.9
30	Unit	58.4	65	Amedisys	57.2	100	EZCORP	14.9
31	Grey Wolf	50.4	66	Acme United	17.3			
32	Ruth's Chris Steak House	18.8	67	Gymboree	11.4			
33	Sun Hydraulics	25.9	68	Meridian Bioscience	17.9			
34	Aéropostale	24.4	69	Forward Air	13.5			
35	VSE	38.3	70	Altera	15.3			

Ranked by composite score based on sales and earnings growth and average return on capital over a three-year period.

SOURCE: *BUSINESSWEEK*, JUNE 4, 2007

FORTUNE 100 Fastest-Growing Companies

Rank	Company	Three-Year EPS Annual Growth Rate (%)	Rank	Company	Three-Year EPS Annual Growth Rate (%)	Rank	Company	Three-Year EPS Annual Growth Rate (%)
1	NutriSystem	433	36	Valero Energy	87	71	Southwestern Energy	37
2	Hansen Natural	145	37	General Cable	76	72	Lam Research	132
3	Arena Resources	140	38	Hologic	74	73	Penn National Gaming	81
4	Intuitive Surgical	123	39	Lufkin Industries	98	74	Jones Lang Lasalle	73
5	Titanium Metals	151	40	American Science & Engineering	169	75	Radiant Systems	115
6	Apple	149	41	Joy Global	141	76	Steel Dynamics	66
7	RTI International Metals	225	42	Range Resources	66	77	Oil States International	71
8	Dynamic Materials	127	43	Palomar Medical Technologies	119	78	Layne Christensen	76
9	Southern Copper	83	44	Patterson-UTI Energy	136	79	Pinnacle Financial Partners	46
10	Global Industries	159	45	Unit	91	80	Concur Technologies	165
11	Frontier Oil	291	46	Netflix	180	81	Avatar Holdings	82
12	Allegheny Technologies	250	47	Gardner Denver	59	82	inVentiv Health	57
13	Ceradyne	105	48	Akamai Technologies	123	83	Noble Energy	58
14	VASCO Data Security International	75	49	Psychiatric Solutions	76	84	A.M. Castle	74
15	Perficient	59	50	F5 Networks	69	85	Encore Wire	84
16	Holly	89	51	Rowan Cos.	532	86	Commercial Metals	63
17	SEACOR Holdings	198	52	RPC	106	87	American Capital Strategies	31
18	Pioneer Drilling	262	53	Atwood Oceanics	155	88	Team	35
19	Freeport-McMoRan Copper & Gold	127	54	Superior Energy Services	87	89	WMS Industries	109
20	Kansas City Southern	178	55	W-H Energy Services	100	90	First Advantage	43
21	Ladish	198	56	First Marblehead	83	91	Deckers Outdoor	47
22	Grey Wolf	248	57	TETRA Technologies	75	92	OYO Geospace	56
23	Allscripts Healthcare Solutions	138	58	Cognizant Technology Solutions	55	93	Pantry	101
24	XTO Energy	83	59	Cleveland-Cliffs	72	94	Cameron International	70
25	Grant Prideco	300	60	ImClone Systems	87	95	Jackson Hewitt Tax Services	61
26	Hornbeck Offshore Services	157	61	ValueClick	47	96	Dress Barn	100
27	Dawson Geophysical	97	62	Allis-Chalmers Energy	54	97	World Fuel Services	32
28	National Oilwell Varco	69	63	Nucor	118	98	Regal Beloit	55
29	Helmerich & Payne	202	64	Chesapeake Energy	58	99	Swift Energy	64
30	Dril-Quip	116	65	Celgene	33	100	Berry Petroleum	46
31	Knot	155	66	Tesoro	82			
32	First Acceptance	105	67	Precision Castparts	73			
33	CB Richard Ellis Group	88	68	Miller Industries	145			
34	Gulfmark Offshore	306	69	Oneok	34			
35	Helix Energy Solutions Group	96	70	Reliance Steel & Aluminum	75			

Ranked by composite score based on profit and sales growth and three-year total return.

SOURCE: *FORTUNE*, SEPTEMBER 17, 2007

Forbes 200 Best Small Companies

Rank	Company	Five-Year Average ROE (%)	Rank	Company	Five-Year Average ROE (%)	Rank	Company	Five-Year Average ROE (%)
1	Hansen Natural	40	51	Balchem	19	101	Eastern	11
2	NutriSystem	39	52	Gen-Probe	13	102	Red Robin Gourmet Burgers	14
3	Under Armour	48	53	Lifeway Foods	14	103	Atwood Oceanics	8
4	VSE	17	54	Jos. A. Bank Clothiers	23	104	Ladish	7
5	Quality Systems	27	55	Hornbeck Offshore Services	18	105	SurModics	9
6	PetMed Express	53	56	American Reprographics	94	106	Monarch Casino & Resort	25
7	LHC	48	57	Ansys	18	107	Cascade	15
8	Dynamic Materials	28	58	II-VI	13	108	Universal Electronics	9
9	Deckers Outdoor	15	59	Radiation Therapy Services	32	109	ADDvantage Technologies	23
10	Bolt Technology	12	60	Rocky Mountain Chocolate Factory	23	110	Graham	7
11	Abaxis	20	61	National Presto Industries	7	111	GulfMark Offshore	9
12	Ceradyne	22	62	ArthroCare	3	112	Dionex	23
13	Avatar	16	63	MicroStrategy	25	113	Acme United	19
14	Healthways	17	64	Tyler Technologies	11	114	Neogen	11
15	Middleby	58	65	Dialysis Corp. of America	13	115	Bright Horizons Family Solutions	17
16	Diodes	18	66	Carbo Ceramics	16	116	Span-America Medical Systems	11
17	Ventana Medical Systems	12	67	Syntel	25	117	Royal Gold	11
18	Cherokee	120	68	Dril-Quip	10	118	Dynamex	17
19	K-Tron International	16	69	ATMI	5	119	PolyMedica	16
20	Citi Trends	28	70	Twin Disc	11	120	Pre-Paid Legal Services	113
21	Blackbaud	24	71	OYO Geospace	5	121	National Instruments	11
22	Strayer Education	70	72	Lufkin Industries	12	122	L.B. Foster	3
23	Build-A-Bear Workshop	21	73	Miller Industries	19	123	Sonic	21
24	Daktronics	19	74	Knight Transportation	17	124	Interactive Data	10
25	Psychemedics	38	75	Spartan Motors	14	125	Rofin-Sinar Technologies	12
26	United Industrial	63	76	North American Galvanizing & Coating	6	126	infoUSA	16
27	Buffalo Wild Wings	12	77	Almost Family	15	127	CRA International	13
28	Euronet Worldwide	18	78	Lo-Jack	20	128	Bovie Medical	9
29	Ambassadors Group	36	79	Sciele Pharma	7	129	American Medical Alert	4
30	Dolby Laboratories	23	80	Comtech Telecommunications	18	130	KMG Chemicals	9
31	Cutera	13	81	G-III Apparel	8	131	Sykes Enterprises	5
32	Amedisys	17	82	Quidel	10	132	United-Guardian	19
33	Portfolio Recovery Associates	23	83	Ixia	6	133	AAON	19
34	Ansoft	17	84	Medical Action Industries	17	134	Prestige Brands Holdings	6
35	Synaptics	15	85	Raven Industries	26	135	Cymer	7
36	Team	16	86	Multi-Color	22	136	Denbury Resources	18
37	Flir Systems	28	87	Inter Parfums	13	137	Power Integrations	7
38	Sun Hydraulics	16	88	Green Mountain Coffee Roasters	19	138	Atlantic Tele-Network	13
39	DXP Enterprises	29	89	Techne	22	139	EMS Technologies	7
40	RPC	19	90	ViaSat	6	140	Copart	14
41	Stratasys	11	91	Metalico	19	141	Macrovision	7
42	Texas Roadhouse	30	92	Universal Stainless & Alloy Products	10	142	Nathan's Famous	11
43	Gulf Island Fabrication	12	93	Rimage	16	143	CCA Industries	21
44	Houston Wire & Cable	177	94	Air Methods	12	144	Anaren	5
45	FactSet Research Systems	29	95	AMCOL International	14	145	Tennant	10
46	Advisory Board	39	96	Foundry Networks	8	146	California Pizza Kitchen	10
47	Ultra Clean	13	97	Chattem	25	147	Heartland Express	18
48	Natural Gas Services	12	98	Healthcare Services	12	148	T-3 Energy Services	6
49	Hibbett Sports	22	99	Boston Beer	16	149	Micrel	5
50	Bio-Reference Laboratories	21	100	Littelfuse	8	150	MGP Ingredients	8

Ranked by composite score based on growth in sales, earnings, and ROE for the past five years and the latest 12 months.

SOURCE: *FORBES*, OCTOBER 11, 2007

Forbes 200 Best Small Companies (continued)

Rank	Company	Five-Year Average ROE (%)
151	Standard Microsystems	4
152	Digi International	4
153	Heico	8
154	Matthews International	20
155	Manhattan Associates	10
156	Buckle	15
157	Tessco Technologies	8
158	Rosetta Resources	7
159	AZZ	12
160	Supertex	8
161	Chase	14
162	LSI Industries	9
163	Steven Madden	15
164	Charlotte Russe	12
165	Landauer	42
166	ICU Medical	12
167	OPNET Technologies	4
168	Gentex	15
169	J&J Snack Foods	12
170	Amsurg	12

Rank	Company	Five-Year Average ROE (%)
171	Circor International	7
172	Movado	10
173	Jackson Hewitt Tax Service	12
174	Tech/Ops Sevcon	5
175	Helen of Troy	15
176	MTS Systems	17
177	Courier	17
178	Methode Electronics	8
179	American Dental Partners	10
180	Exponent	11
181	Books-A-Million	8
182	Kaydon	13
183	RF Industries	8
184	Gorman-Rupp	10
185	Century Casinos	10
186	E-Z-EM	6
187	Kadant	5
188	Espey Manufacturing & Electronics	5
189	Intersil	3
190	National Beverage	15

Rank	Company	Five-Year Average ROE (%)
191	Noven Pharmaceuticals	11
192	Shoe Carnival	11
193	Dover Downs Gaming & Entertainment	25
194	Vital Signs	12
195	Ducommun	9
196	Oil-Dri Corp. of America	5
197	Preformed Line Products	6
198	Waste Industries USA	10
199	CSS Industries	11
200	Met-Pro	10

Forbes Fastest-Growing Tech Companies

Rank	Company	Industry	Five-Year Annualized Sales Growth (%)
1	Google	Online search engine, Web portal	155
2	Salesforce.com	Sales management software	85
3	Ceradyne	Aerospace, defense ceramics	75
4	Euronet Worldwide	Banking software	69
5	FalconStor Software	Archive, backup software	58
6	Cognizant Technology Solutions	Consulting	53
7	Celgene	Biotechnology	53
8	LifeCell	Biotechnology	48
9	Martek Biosciences	Nutritional supplements	42
10	j2 Global Communications	Internet telecom services	42
11	Red Hat	Linux software	41
12	Digital River	E-commerce services	41
13	Genentech	Biotechnology	41
14	DRS Technologies	Aerospace, defense ceramics	39
15	L-3 Communications Holdings	Communications equipment	38
16	Vocus	Public relations management software	37
17	CommVault Systems	Archive, backup software	37
18	FARO Technologies	Measuring equipment	35
19	Comtech Telecommunications	Telecommunications equipment	31
20	Network Appliance	Data storage hardware, software	30
21	NII Holdings	Latin America wireless telecom	30
22	Diodes	Semiconductors	28
23	Dolby Laboratories	Audio technology	23
24	Gen-Probe	DNA diagnostic technology	23
25	Adobe Systems	Imaging software	23

SOURCE: *FORBES*, JANUARY 24, 2008

Hoover's Handbook of

Emerging Companies

The Companies

Abaxis, Inc.

Abaxis makes a praxis of producing what the facts is, when analyzing patients' blood. Its point-of-care blood analyzers can perform more than 20 types of tests on animals and humans. The analyzers are designed to be portable, require little training, provide on-the-spot results, and offer built-in quality control and calibration. They come with reagent discs for performing common blood tests. Abaxis markets the system under the name VetScan in the veterinary market and Piccolo in the human medical market. It is developing a wider range of tests to better penetrate the human diagnostic market. Abaxis sells its products to veterinarians, hospitals, managed care organizations, and the military.

Most of the company's sales (about 75%) are to veterinarians. To expand its foothold in the human diagnostics market, Abaxis has been developing oncology-related tests, including ones that analyze liver function in patients undergoing chemotherapy.

In 2007 the company introduced next-generation versions of its blood analyzers, branded VetScan VS2 and Piccolo xpress.

EXECUTIVES

Chairman, President, and CEO: Clinton H. Severson, age 59, $867,000 pay
VP Finance and CFO: Alberto R. Santa Ines, age 60, $484,000 pay
VP Government Affairs and Marketing, Pacific Rim: Vladimir E. Ostoich, age 61, $504,000 pay
VP Marketing and Sales, Domestic Medical Market: Christopher M. (Chris) Bernard, age 38
VP Research and Development: Kenneth P. Aron, age 54, $494,000 pay
VP Operations: Donald P. (Don) Wood, age 55
Director, Customer Relations: Ken Murchison
Auditors: Burr, Pilger & Mayer LLP

LOCATIONS

HQ: Abaxis, Inc.
3240 Whipple Rd., Union City, CA 94587
Phone: 510-675-6500   **Fax:** 510-441-6150
Web: www.abaxis.com

2007 Sales

	$ mil.	% of total
North America	72.0	84
Europe	10.4	12
Asia/Pacific & other	3.8	4
Total	**86.2**	**100**

PRODUCTS/OPERATIONS

2007 Sales

	$ mil.	% of total
Reagent discs & kits	50.7	59
Instruments	28.9	34
Other products	4.8	5
Development & licensing	1.8	2
Total	**86.2**	**100**

2007 Sales by Customer Group

	$ mil.	% of total
Veterinary market	63.8	74
Medical market	17.5	20
Other	4.9	6
Total	**86.2**	**100**

COMPETITORS

Abbott Labs
Beckman Coulter
Hemagen Diagnostics
Heska
IDEXX Labs
Immucor
Johnson & Johnson
Quidel
Roche Diagnostics

HISTORICAL FINANCIALS

Company Type: Public

Income Statement

FYE: March 31

	REVENUE ($ mil.)	NET INCOME ($ mil.)	NET PROFIT MARGIN	EMPLOYEES
3/07	86.2	10.1	11.7%	265
3/06	68.9	7.5	10.9%	217
3/05	52.8	4.8	9.1%	184
3/04	46.9	24.0	51.2%	—
3/03	34.8	1.6	4.6%	—
Annual Growth	**25.5%**	**58.5%**	**—**	**20.0%**

2007 Year-End Financials

Debt ratio: —
Return on equity: 12.7%
Cash ($ mil.): 45.2
Current ratio: 6.85
Long-term debt ($ mil.): —
No. of shares (mil.): 21.2
Dividends
Yield: —
Payout: —
Market value ($ mil.): 516.8
R&D as % of sales: —
Advertising as % of sales: —

Stock History

NASDAQ (GS): ABAX

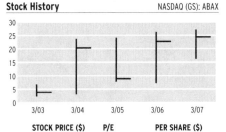

	STOCK PRICE ($) FY Close	P/E High/Low	PER SHARE ($) Earnings	Dividends	Book Value
3/07	24.37	58 36	0.46	—	4.14
3/06	22.68	74 21	0.35	—	3.53
3/05	8.85	108 36	0.22	—	3.10
3/04	20.32	20 3	1.16	—	2.80
3/03	3.81	328 125	0.02	—	1.32
Annual Growth	**59.0%**	**— —**	**119.0%**	**—**	**33.0%**

Abigail Adams National Bancorp

Abigail Adams National is sure to "remember the ladies." The holding company owns The Adams National Bank, which was founded in 1977 as the first federally chartered bank owned and operated by women. With six branches in the Washington, DC, area, it targets women, minorities, small businesses, and not-for-profit organizations. Subsidiary Consolidated Bank & Trust (acquired in 2005) operates three branches in Virginia's Richmond and Hampton Roads areas. The banks' offerings include such standard retail products as checking and savings accounts, money markets, IRAs, and loans and mortgages. Director Marshall T. Reynolds (chairman of Champion Industries) and his family control about 20% of Abigail Adams National.

Like its bigger sister bank, Consolidated Bank & Trust also has a page in the history books: It was founded in 1903 by a woman of color, Maggie Lena Walker, and claims to be the US' oldest bank continuously operated by African-Americans.

The Adams National Bank originates primarily commercial real estate loans, which account for about 45% of a lending portfolio that also includes construction loans (about 25%) and residential mortgages (nearly 20%).

EXECUTIVES

Chairwoman, President, and CEO, Abigail Adams National and The Adams National Bank: Jeanne Delaney Hubbard, age 59, $134,812 pay
SVP and CFO, Abigail Adams National Bancorp and The Adams National Bank: Karen E. Troutman, age 60, $166,250 pay
SVP Operations and Compliance, The Adams National Bank: Betty J. Serrano, age 57, $122,708 pay
SVP and Chief Lending Officer, The Adams National Bank: John P. Shroads Jr., age 47, $137,500 pay
SVP Retail Administration, Marketing, and Business Development, The Adams National Bank: David M. Glaser, age 47
Secretary: Lorel D. Scott
Human Resources Manager: Everett Hitchner
Auditors: McGladrey & Pullen, LLP

LOCATIONS

HQ: Abigail Adams National Bancorp, Inc.
1130 Connecticut Ave. NW, Ste. 200, Washington, DC 20036
Phone: 202-772-3600   **Fax:** 202-835-3871
Web: www.adamsbank.com

Abigail Adams National Bancorp has operations in Hampton, Virginia; Richmond, Virginia; Silver Spring, Maryland; and Washington, DC.

PRODUCTS/OPERATIONS

2006 Sales

	$ mil.	% of total
Interest		
Loans	22.7	80
Securities & other	3.6	13
Service charges on deposit accounts	1.4	5
Other	0.7	2
Total	**28.4**	**100**

2006 Sales By Subsidiary

	$ mil.	% of total
The Adams National Bank	22.9	81
Consolidated Bank & Trust	5.5	19
Total	**28.4**	**100**

COMPETITORS

Bank of America
BB&T
Chevy Chase Bank
Citibank
Greater Atlantic Financial
IBW Financial
Independence Federal
PNC Financial
SunTrust
Virginia Commerce Bancorp
Wachovia

HISTORICAL FINANCIALS

Company Type: Public

Income Statement

FYE: December 31

	ASSETS ($ mil.)	NET INCOME ($ mil.)	INCOME AS % OF ASSETS	EMPLOYEES
12/06	405.5	3.7	0.9%	108
12/05	343.0	3.3	1.0%	103
12/04	251.2	3.6	1.4%	—
12/03	231.9	3.2	1.4%	—
12/02	204.9	3.4	1.7%	55
Annual Growth	18.6%	2.1%	—	18.4%

2006 Year-End Financials

Equity as % of assets: 7.4%
Return on assets: 1.0%
Return on equity: 12.7%
Long-term debt ($ mil.): 6.3
No. of shares (mil.): 3.5
Market value ($ mil.): 46.2

Dividends
  Yield: 3.7%
  Payout: 46.7%
Sales ($ mil.): 28.4
R&D as % of sales: —
Advertising as % of sales: —

Stock History

NASDAQ (GM): AANB

	STOCK PRICE ($) FY Close	P/E High/Low	PER SHARE ($) Earnings	Dividends	Book Value
12/06	13.35	14 12	1.07	0.50	8.72
12/05	14.00	20 14	0.98	0.38	8.10
12/04	19.31	19 12	1.08	2.44	7.45
12/03	17.29	19 13	0.95	0.45	7.59
12/02	13.64	14 10	1.03	2.21	7.05
Annual Growth	(0.5%)	— —	1.0%	(31.0%)	5.4%

Acme Packet

Acme Packet aims for the top. The company makes communications equipment designed to route voice and data over Internet Protocol (IP) networks. Acme's family of Net-Net session border controllers are routers used at the network edge to help communications service providers build networks capable of handling interactive services including Voice over IP, videoconferencing, and PBX. The company has established sales and distribution partnerships with other manufacturers including Sonus Networks and Sumitomo. Acme was founded in 2000. Menlo Ventures owns a 29% stake in the company.

Session border controllers (SBCs) are typically deployed at the borders between IP networks, such as when the networks of two service providers meet or at the intersection of a service provider's network and its business, residential, and mobile customers. SBCs integrate the control of signaling messages and media flows, complementing the functionality and effectiveness of routers, softswitches, and firewalls that reside within the network.

EXECUTIVES

President, CEO, and Director: Andrew (Andy) Ory, age 41, $260,000 pay
CFO and Treasurer: Keith Seidman, age 52, $297,000 pay
CTO and Director: Patrick J. MeLampy, age 47, $260,000 pay
VP Marketing and Product Management: Seamus Hourihan, age 54, $185,000 pay
VP Professional Services: Erin Medeiros, age 34
VP Product Management: Kevin Klett
VP Sales and Business Development: Dino DiPalma, age 40, $355,338 pay
VP Engineering: David C. Hunter, age 52
Chief Software Architect: Bob Penfield
Auditors: Ernst & Young LLP

LOCATIONS

HQ: Acme Packet, Inc.
  71 3rd Ave., Burlington, MA 01803
Phone: 781-328-4400   **Fax:** 781-425-5077
Web: www.acmepacket.com

2006 Sales

	$ mil.	% of total
US & Canada	48.0	57
Other countries	36.1	43
Total	**84.1**	**100**

PRODUCTS/OPERATIONS

2006 Sales

	$ mil.	% of total
Products	71.8	85
Services	12.3	15
Total	**84.1**	**100**

COMPETITORS

ADC Telecommunications
AudioCodes
Cisco Systems
Ditech
Juniper Networks
Nortel Networks
Sonus Networks

HISTORICAL FINANCIALS

Company Type: Public

Income Statement

FYE: December 31

	REVENUE ($ mil.)	NET INCOME ($ mil.)	NET PROFIT MARGIN	EMPLOYEES
12/06	84.1	28.9	34.4%	247
12/05	36.1	0.0	—	—
12/04	16.0	(7.0)	—	—
12/03	3.3	(7.5)	—	—
Annual Growth	194.3%	—	—	—

2006 Year-End Financials

Debt ratio: —
Return on equity: 38.9%
Cash ($ mil.): 118.9
Current ratio: 6.43
Long-term debt ($ mil.): —
No. of shares (mil.): 58.6

Dividends
  Yield: —
  Payout: —
Market value ($ mil.): 1,208.8
R&D as % of sales: —
Advertising as % of sales: —

Stock History

NASDAQ (GM): APKT

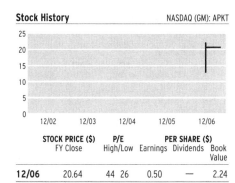

	STOCK PRICE ($) FY Close	P/E High/Low	PER SHARE ($) Earnings	Dividends	Book Value
12/06	20.64	44 26	0.50	—	2.24

ADA-ES, Inc.

Coal: not just for the 19th century anymore. ADA-ES tries to make coal an economically and environmentally viable energy option once again. The company (which was spun off from Earth Sciences in 2003) makes environmental technology systems and specialty chemicals that reduce emissions at coal-burning power plants. It offers integrated mercury control systems, as well as flue gas conditioning and combustion aid chemicals. ADA-ES also provides consulting and testing services and mercury measurement equipment. In 2006 ADA-ES set up a joint venture with NexGen Refined Coal, LLC, to market proprietary coal technology which reduces emissions of nitrogen oxides and mercury from some treated coals.

EXECUTIVES

President, CEO, and Director:
  Michael D. (Mike) Durham, age 57
COO: C. Jean Bustard, age 49
SVP, CFO, Secretary, and Director: Mark H. McKinnies, age 55
VP Sales and Marketing: Jonathan S. (Jon) Barr, age 49
VP Business Development, Utility Systems:
  Richard L. Miller, age 53
VP Contract Research and Development:
  Richard J. Schlager, age 55
VP Technology: Sharon Sjostrom, age 40
Human Resources Manager: Beth Turner-Graziano
Manager Financial Reporting: Derrick Moss

LOCATIONS

HQ: ADA-ES, Inc.
  8100 SouthPark Way, Unit B, Littleton, CO 80120
Phone: 303-734-1727   **Fax:** 303-734-0330
Web: www.adaes.com

PRODUCTS/OPERATIONS

2006 Sales

	$ mil.	% of total
Mercury emission control	13.6	88
Flue gas conditioning & other	1.9	12
Total	**15.5**	**100**

COMPETITORS

Calgon Carbon
Donaldson Company
Ebara
Marsulex

Wahlco
Wheelabrator
Woodward

HISTORICAL FINANCIALS
Company Type: Public

Income Statement
FYE: December 31

	REVENUE ($ mil.)	NET INCOME ($ mil.)	NET PROFIT MARGIN	EMPLOYEES
12/06	15.5	0.4	2.6%	42
12/05	11.0	0.7	6.4%	32
12/04	8.4	0.3	3.6%	—
12/03	5.9	0.4	6.8%	—
12/02	5.7	0.5	8.8%	—
Annual Growth	28.4%	(5.4%)	—	31.3%

2006 Year-End Financials

Debt ratio: —
Return on equity: 1.5%
Cash ($ mil.): 18.6
Current ratio: 5.77
Long-term debt ($ mil.): —
No. of shares (mil.): 5.6
Dividends
 Yield: —
 Payout: —
Market value ($ mil.): 91.3
R&D as % of sales: —
Advertising as % of sales: —

Stock History
NASDAQ (CM): ADES

	STOCK PRICE ($) FY Close	P/E High/Low	PER SHARE ($) Earnings	Dividends	Book Value
12/06	16.20	363 156	0.07	—	4.90
12/05	18.24	241 104	0.13	—	4.61
12/04	24.01	353 83	0.08	—	2.50
12/03	7.10	67 17	0.12	—	0.83
Annual Growth	31.6%	— —	(16.4%)	—	80.9%

A.D.A.M., Inc.

A.D.A.M. (formerly adam.com) has prescribed itself a healthy dose of information distribution. The company provides interactive health and medical content and applications to a variety of customers in media ranging from the Internet to newsletters and CD-ROMs. Web sites, media companies, health care companies, hospitals, students, and consumers use the company's library, which features such content as 40,000 medical illustrations, color graphics, animation, 3D models, video content, and printed reference guides. A.D.A.M. also provides a Web-based HR benefits management product, Benergy, to health care providers.

A.D.A.M. (which stands for Animated Dissection of Anatomy for Medicine) was started in 1990 to cater to the educational market, but then expanded into consumer and business-to-business distribution.

Chairman Robert S. Cramer Jr. owns 12% of the company.

EXECUTIVES

Chairman: Robert S. Cramer Jr., age 46, $175,000 pay
President, CEO, and Director: Kevin S. Noland, age 44, $238,125 pay
CFO and Secretary: Mark B. Adams, age 55, $134,635 pay
SVP Product Development: Greg Juhn
SVP Sales: John H. George
VP Education Sales: Shannon H. McGuire
VP Engineering: Tony Lynn
VP Internet and Product Design: Kyle A. McNeir
VP Production: Meredith Nienkamp
VP Sales: James L. (Jim) Retel, age 53, $128,529 pay
Chief Medical Officer: Alan Greene
President, Online Benefits: Alan Cohen, age 40, $112,500 pay
Auditors: Tauber & Balser, P.C.

LOCATIONS

HQ: A.D.A.M., Inc.
 1600 RiverEdge Pkwy., Ste. 100, Atlanta, GA 30328
Phone: 770-980-0888 **Fax:** 770-955-3088
Web: www.adam.com

PRODUCTS/OPERATIONS

2006 Sales

	$ mil.	% of total
Licensing	13.8	84
Product	1.6	10
Professional services & other	1.1	6
Total	**16.5**	**100**

Selected Products

A.D.A.M. Health Management Platform
 Health Illustrated Encyclopedia
 In-Depth Medical Reports
 Symptom Navigator
 Wellness Assessments
Benefit Management Platform
 Benergy

COMPETITORS

AMA
Cerner
Essential Group
GE Healthcare
HealthGate Data
Healthline
HealthStream
HLTH Corp.
McKesson
Medem
Medsite
PRIMEDIA

HISTORICAL FINANCIALS
Company Type: Public

Income Statement
FYE: December 31

	REVENUE ($ mil.)	NET INCOME ($ mil.)	NET PROFIT MARGIN	EMPLOYEES
12/06	16.5	2.5	15.2%	108
12/05	10.1	7.1	70.3%	40
12/04	8.4	1.6	19.0%	—
12/03	7.9	0.6	7.6%	—
12/02	8.9	(1.5)	—	38
Annual Growth	16.7%	—	—	29.8%

2006 Year-End Financials

Debt ratio: 103.0%
Return on equity: 12.3%
Cash ($ mil.): 9.4
Current ratio: 1.28
Long-term debt ($ mil.): 24.2
No. of shares (mil.): 9.1
Dividends
 Yield: —
 Payout: —
Market value ($ mil.): 55.4
R&D as % of sales: —
Advertising as % of sales: —

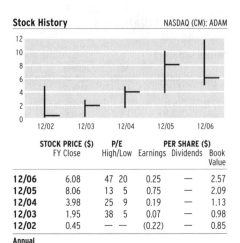

Stock History
NASDAQ (CM): ADAM

	STOCK PRICE ($) FY Close	P/E High/Low	PER SHARE ($) Earnings	Dividends	Book Value
12/06	6.08	47 20	0.25	—	2.57
12/05	8.06	13 5	0.75	—	2.09
12/04	3.98	25 9	0.19	—	1.13
12/03	1.95	38 5	0.07	—	0.98
12/02	0.45		(0.22)	—	0.85
Annual Growth	91.7%	— —	—	—	31.8%

Advanced Environmental Recycling

It may not turn straw into gold, but Advanced Environmental Recycling Technologies (AERT) does practice a kind of alchemy by turning recycled plastics and wood filler into building materials for windows, doors, floors, and decks. AERT plants recycle waste plastics and plastic byproducts of paper recycling mills; the recycled plastic material then goes to AERT manufacturing plants, where it is combined with cedar or hardwood fiber to create composite building materials.

AERT markets its products under such names as MoistureShield, ChoiceDek, CornerLoc, and LifeCycle. Weyerhaeuser is AERT's largest customer (some 80% of sales). The founding Brooks family controls AERT.

AERT's agreement with Weyerhauser has the manufacturer providing Weyerhauser with decking products that are sold exclusively through Lowe's stores under the Weyerhauser ChoiceDek brand.

EXECUTIVES

Chairman, President, and Co-CEO: Joe G. Brooks, age 51, $335,625 pay
Vice Chairman: Sal Miwa, age 50
Co-CEO and Director: Stephen W. Brooks, age 50, $151,423 pay
SVP and CFO: Robert A. Thayer, age 55, $217,500 pay
SVP Administration: Alford Drinkwater, age 55, $107,000 pay
SVP: J. Douglas Brooks, age 47, $117,500 pay
SVP Sales and Marketing: James (Jim) Precht, age 61, $192,500 pay
Secretary, Treasurer, and Director: Marjorie S. Brooks, age 71
Controller and Chief Accounting Officer: Eric E. Barnes, age 33
Auditors: Tullius Taylor Sartain & Sartain LLP

LOCATIONS

HQ: Advanced Environmental Recycling
  Technologies, Inc.
  914 N. Jefferson St., Springdale, AR 72764
Phone: 479-756-7400   **Fax:** 479-756-7410
Web: www.aertinc.com

Advanced Environmental Recycling Technologies has manufacturing plants in Springdale, Lowell, and Tontitown, Arkansas; Junction, Texas; and Alexandria, Louisiana.

PRODUCTS/OPERATIONS

Selected Product Applications

Commercial and residential decking components
Exterior door and window components
Exterior housing trim
Fencing

COMPETITORS

CertainTeed
Louisiana-Pacific
NEW Plastics
Plastic Lumber
TAMKO
Trex Company

HISTORICAL FINANCIALS

Company Type: Public

Income Statement

	REVENUE ($ mil.)	NET INCOME ($ mil.)	NET PROFIT MARGIN	EMPLOYEES
12/06	97.8	1.8	1.8%	664
12/05	87.3	7.8	8.9%	670
12/04	63.6	1.3	2.0%	—
12/03	43.5	2.3	5.3%	—
12/02	41.4	1.2	2.9%	410
Annual Growth	24.0%	10.7%	—	12.8%

FYE: December 31

2006 Year-End Financials

Debt ratio: 61.1%
Return on equity: 7.4%
Cash ($ mil.): 3.0
Current ratio: 0.87
Long-term debt ($ mil.): 16.8
No. of shares (mil.): 43.0
Dividends
  Yield: —
  Payout: —
Market value ($ mil.): 86.9
R&D as % of sales: —
Advertising as % of sales: —

Stock History

NASDAQ (CM): AERT

	STOCK PRICE ($) FY Close	P/E High/Low	Earnings	Dividends	Book Value
12/06	2.02	93 37	0.04	—	0.64
12/05	1.79	10 6	0.19	—	0.56
12/04	1.27	57 33	0.03	—	0.37
12/03	1.57	26 14	0.07	—	0.31
12/02	1.20	137 55	0.02	—	0.20
Annual Growth	13.9%	— —	18.9%	—	33.2%

Aehr Test Systems

Aehr Test Systems' products don't test air, but rather silicon. Aehr (pronounced "air") makes gear that tests logic and memory semiconductors to weed out defective devices. Its burn-in systems test chips' reliability under stress by exposing them to high temperatures and voltages. Aehr also makes massively parallel test systems for handling thousands of chips simultaneously, die carriers for testing unpackaged chips, custom-designed fixtures for test equipment, and other memory test products. Top customers include Spansion (about 39% of sales) and Texas Instruments (nearly 23%). Aehr gets about 80% of its business from the US.

CEO and founder Rhea Posedel (who reversed his first name to create the company's moniker) owns about 14% of Aehr.

Private Capital Management holds nearly 17% of the company. The State of Wisconsin Investment Board has an equity stake of about 15%. RGM Capital owns 5%.

EXECUTIVES

Chairman and CEO: Rhea J. Posedel, age 66, $220,590 pay
VP Finance and CFO: Gary L. Larson, age 57, $177,053 pay
VP Contactor Business Group: Carl N. Buck, age 55, $159,093 pay
VP Engineering: David S. Hendrickson, age 50, $185,330 pay
VP Worldwide Sales and Service:
  Gregory M. (Greg) Perkins, age 52, $160,952 pay
VP of Operations: Joel Bustos
President, Aehr Test Systems Japan: Kunio Sano, age 51
Secretary and Director: Mario M. Rosati, age 61
Director, Marketing: Bill Barraclough
Auditors: KPMG

LOCATIONS

HQ: Aehr Test Systems
  400 Kato Terrace, Fremont, CA 94539
Phone: 510-623-9400   **Fax:** 510-623-9450
Web: www.aehr.com

Aehr Test Systems has operations in Japan, Germany, Taiwan, and the US.

2007 Sales

	$ mil.	% of total
US	24.9	82
Asia/Pacific	4.1	14
Europe	1.2	4
Adjustments	(2.8)	—
Total	**27.4**	**100**

PRODUCTS/OPERATIONS

Products

Burn-in test systems (MAX)
Die carriers and test fixtures (DiePak)
Full wafer contact test systems (FOX)
Massively parallel test systems (MTX)

COMPETITORS

Advantest	Mirae
Aetrium	Reliability Incorporated
Cascade Microtech	Teradyne
Hitachi	Tokyo Electron
KLA-Tencor	Trio-Tech
Matsushita Electric	Yokogawa Electric

HISTORICAL FINANCIALS

Company Type: Public

Income Statement

	REVENUE ($ mil.)	NET INCOME ($ mil.)	NET PROFIT MARGIN	EMPLOYEES
5/07	27.4	2.4	8.8%	108
5/06	23.8	0.8	3.4%	—
5/05	16.1	(4.9)	—	—
5/04	15.8	(4.0)	—	—
5/03	15.1	(4.5)	—	—
Annual Growth	16.1%	—	—	—

FYE: May 31

2007 Year-End Financials

Debt ratio: —
Return on equity: 11.6%
Cash ($ mil.): 9.6
Current ratio: 4.50
Long-term debt ($ mil.): —
No. of shares (mil.): 7.8
Dividends
  Yield: —
  Payout: —
Market value ($ mil.): 47.3
R&D as % of sales: —
Advertising as % of sales: —

Stock History

NASDAQ (GM): AEHR

	STOCK PRICE ($) FY Close	P/E High/Low	Earnings	Dividends	Book Value
5/07	6.05	37 15	0.30	—	2.90
5/06	6.43	63 23	0.11	—	2.47
5/05	3.02	— —	(0.66)	—	2.33
5/04	4.11	— —	(0.55)	—	3.00
5/03	2.87	— —	(0.63)	—	3.54
Annual Growth	20.5%	— —	—	—	(4.9%)

AeroCentury Corp.

With a high-flyin' inventory, AeroCentury leases used turboprop aircraft and engines to regional airlines and other commercial customers. The company often buys equipment from an airline, then leases it back to the seller, usually for a term of three to five years. AeroCentury also buys assets already under lease. The company only makes a purchase when it has a customer committed to a lease. Typically, lessees are responsible for any maintenance costs. AeroCentury owns about 30 aircraft, mainly de Havilland and Fokker models. The majority of the company's lease revenues come from airlines headquartered outside the US.

The company was formed by the consolidation of the aircraft equipment leasing and management partnerships JetFleet Aircraft and JetFleet Aircraft II.

AeroCentury is managed by JetFleet Management, which in turn is overseen by AeroCentury officers. Chairman and president Neal Crispin and SVP Toni Perazzo each own 21% of AeroCentury.

EXECUTIVES

Chairman and President: Neal D. Crispin, age 60, $1 pay
SVP, COO, and Director: Marc J. Anderson, age 70
SVP, CFO, Secretary, and Director: Toni M. Perazzo, age 60
SVP: John S. Myers, age 61
VP, Controller: Glenn Roberts, age 42
VP, Finance: Harold M. Lyons, age 48
VP, Aircraft Remarketing: Steven H. Wallace, age 61
VP, Corporate Development: Brian J. Ginna, age 38
VP, Maintenance: Jack Humphreys, age 59
General Counsel: Christopher B. Tigno, age 45
Auditors: BDO Seidman, LLP

LOCATIONS

HQ: AeroCentury Corp.
1440 Chapin Ave., Ste. 310, Burlingame, CA 94010
Phone: 650-340-1888   **Fax:** 650-696-3929
Web: www.aerocentury.com

COMPETITORS

AAR
AIG
Aviation Capital
Boeing Capital
Bombardier
CIT Group
EADS
GE Commercial Aviation Services
ILFC
Jetscape
Saab AB
Willis Lease

HISTORICAL FINANCIALS

Company Type: Public

Income Statement

FYE: December 31

	REVENUE ($ mil.)	NET INCOME ($ mil.)	NET PROFIT MARGIN	EMPLOYEES
12/06	18.3	0.8	4.4%	0
12/05	13.5	0.2	1.5%	0
12/04	10.9	0.3	2.8%	—
12/03	8.9	(1.3)	—	—
12/02	8.8	1.0	11.4%	—
Annual Growth	20.1%	(5.4%)	—	—

2006 Year-End Financials

Debt ratio: —
Return on equity: 4.1%
Cash ($ mil.): 3.4
Current ratio: 0.05
Long-term debt ($ mil.): —
No. of shares (mil.): 1.6
Dividends
  Yield: —
  Payout: —
Market value ($ mil.): 10.4
R&D as % of sales: —
Advertising as % of sales: —

Stock History

AMEX: ACY

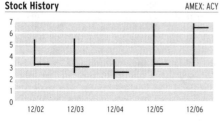

	STOCK PRICE ($) FY Close	P/E High/Low	PER SHARE ($) Earnings	Dividends	Book Value
12/06	6.46	13 6	0.53	—	12.67
12/05	3.29	52 18	0.13	—	11.82
12/04	2.57	— —	0.00	—	11.70
12/03	3.05	— —	—	—	11.53
12/02	3.27	— —	—	—	12.37
Annual Growth	18.6%	— —	—	—	0.6%

AeroVironment, Inc.

AeroVironment is giving US soldiers their own birds-eye view. The company designs, manufactures, and supports a variety of small unmanned aircraft systems (UAS) for the Department of Defense and its component military branches. Small enough for one-man transport, launchable by a single person, and operated through a hand-held control unit, AeroVironment's aircraft can provide intelligence, surveillance, and reconnaissance for small tactical units or individual soldiers. The company also makes fast-charge systems for industrial vehicle batteries under the PosiCharge brand, and makes power processing test equipment through its Energy Technology Center business segment.

AeroVironment's PosiCharge products help clients recharge vehicle batteries 16 times faster than traditional methods, improving productivity and safety by preventing the need for frequent and labourous battery changes. Customers of the company's PosiCharge products include Ford, IKEA, and SYSCO.

Although AeroVironment's primary customer for its UAS is the US military (about 56% of sales in 2007), the company is angling to add militaries from allied nations, and US non-military businesses to its customer list.

EXECUTIVES

Chairman, President, and CEO: Timothy E. Conver, age 64, $1,608,461 pay
EVP and General Manager, Unmanned Aircraft Systems: John F. Grabowsky, age 61, $305,150 pay
VP Finance, CFO, and Secretary: Stephen C. Wright, age 51, $289,674 pay
VP Administration: Cathleen Cline, age 49
VP and General Manager, PosiCharge Systems: Patrick R. Dellario, age 51, $267,781 pay
VP and General Manager, Energy Technology Center: Joseph S. Edwards, age 60
VP Unmanned Aircraft Systems Logistics: Daniel H. Stone
VP International Initiatives: Ilker (Ike) Bayraktar
Auditors: Ernst & Young LLP

LOCATIONS

HQ: AeroVironment, Inc.
181 W. Huntington Dr., Ste. 202, Monrovia, CA 91016
Phone: 626-357-9983   **Fax:** 626-359-9628
Web: www.avinc.com

PRODUCTS/OPERATIONS

2007 Sales

	$ mil.	% of total
UAS	146.5	84
PosiCharge	17.6	10
Energy Technology Center	9.6	6
Total	**173.7**	**100**

Selected Unmanned Aircraft Systems

Dragon Eye (3.8 foot wingspan, 5.9 lbs, 3 mile range, 60 minute flight time)
Puma (8.5, 12.5, 6, 240)
Raven (4.5, 4.2, 6, 90)
Swift (3.8, 5.9, 3, 60)
Wasp II (1.3, 0.6, 2.4, 30)
Wasp III (2.4, 1.0, 5.0, 45)

COMPETITORS

AAI Corporation
Edison International
Elbit Systems
L-3 Communications
Lockheed Martin
Northrop Grumman

HISTORICAL FINANCIALS

Company Type: Public

Income Statement

FYE: April 30

	REVENUE ($ mil.)	NET INCOME ($ mil.)	NET PROFIT MARGIN	EMPLOYEES
4/07	173.7	20.7	11.9%	495
4/06	139.4	11.4	8.2%	—
4/05	105.2	14.7	14.0%	—
4/04	47.7	2.2	4.6%	—
Annual Growth	53.8%	111.1%	—	—

2007 Year-End Financials

Debt ratio: —
Return on equity: 24.3%
Cash ($ mil.): 109.6
Current ratio: 5.16
Long-term debt ($ mil.): —
No. of shares (mil.): 18.9
Dividends
  Yield: —
  Payout: —
Market value ($ mil.): 403.9
R&D as % of sales: —
Advertising as % of sales: —

Stock History

NASDAQ (GM): AVAV

	STOCK PRICE ($) FY Close	P/E High/Low	PER SHARE ($) Earnings	Dividends	Book Value
4/07	21.40	21 17	1.22	—	7.23

Aircastle Limited

Not to be confused with the inflatable palaces parents rent for their for kids' birthday parties, Aircastle Limited is an aircraft leasing concern. The company owns a portfolio of jet aircraft which it leases to passenger and cargo airlines. Aircastle boasts a portfolio of 69 aircraft which are leased to 32 different lessees. The lessees of Aircastle's aircraft are responsible for maintaining the planes as well as paying operational and insurance expenses. The company's leases are managed from offices in Ireland, Singapore, and the US. Aircastle also invests in debt securities secured by commercial jet aircraft. Chairman Wesley R. Edens, through Fortress Investment Group, has a controlling stake in Aircastle.

Aircastle's customers include US Airways (22% of sales) and Hainan Airlines (8%).

Lifted on the wings of an improving global economy and the increasing significance of emerging markets, worldwide air travel is on the rise. Amid the high costs associated with updating and expanding airline fleets and brutal competition for low fares, outsourcing aircraft ownership is a strategy that can help an airline stay aloft.

EXECUTIVES

Chairman: Wesley R. (Wes) Edens, age 46
CEO: Ron Wainshal, age 43, $580,000 pay
COO and General Counsel: David Walton, age 45, $505,000 pay
CFO: Mark S. Zeidman, age 55, $750,000 pay
EVP, Marketing: Peter Chang
EVP, Technical: Joseph Schreiner, age 49, $380,000 pay
Chief Investment Officer: Michael Platt
Chief Technology Officer: Jonathan Lang, age 38
Auditors: Ernst & Young LLP

LOCATIONS

HQ: Aircastle Limited
300 First Stamford Place, 5th Fl.,
Stamford, CT 06902
Phone: 203-504-1020   **Fax:** 203-504-1021
Web: www.aircastle.com

PRODUCTS/OPERATIONS

2006 Sales

	$ mil.	% of total
Lease rentals	180.1	95
Interest income	9.0	5
Other	0.2	—
Total	**189.3**	**100**

COMPETITORS

AerCap
Aviation Capital
Babcock & Brown
Boeing Capital
CIT Group
GE Commercial Aviation Services
ILFC
Royal Bank of Scotland

HISTORICAL FINANCIALS
Company Type: Public

Income Statement
FYE: December 31

	REVENUE ($ mil.)	NET INCOME ($ mil.)	NET PROFIT MARGIN	EMPLOYEES
12/06	189.3	51.2	27.0%	45
12/05	36.0	0.2	0.6%	—
12/04	0.1	(1.5)	—	—
Annual Growth	**4,250.9%**	**—**	**—**	**—**

2006 Year-End Financials

Debt ratio: 158.5%
Return on equity: 9.8%
Cash ($ mil.): 164.2
Current ratio: 0.91
Long-term debt ($ mil.): 1,010.1
No. of shares (mil.): 51.6
Dividends
Yield: 2.1%
Payout: 56.8%
Market value ($ mil.): 1,522.8
R&D as % of sales: —
Advertising as % of sales: —

Stock History
NYSE: AYR

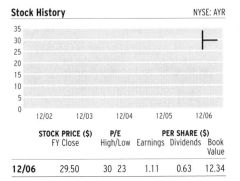

	STOCK PRICE ($) FY Close	P/E High/Low		PER SHARE ($) Earnings	Dividends	Book Value
12/06	29.50	30	23	1.11	0.63	12.34

Airvana, Inc.

Airvana can help you rock out to Nirvana. The company makes mobile broadband infrastructure products for wireless carriers. Its products enable wireless networks to deliver broadband multimedia services — such as Internet access, e-mail, music downloads, and video streaming — to cell phones, laptops, and other mobile devices. Airvana sells its software and hardware to service providers such as Verizon Wireless in the US, TELUS in Canada, Telstra in Australia, Israel's Pelephone, and Eurotel in the Czech Republic; however, most of its revenue (some 95% in 2006) is derived from Nortel Networks. Founded in 2000, Airvana operates offices in China, India, Japan, South Korea, the UK, and the US.

The company plans to use IPO proceeds for working capital and other general expenses, including product development, sales and marketing, and capital expenditures. It may use some of the money to expand through strategic alliances with or acquisitions of complementary businesses, products, and technologies, though no deals are currently in the works. Director Paul Ferri controls about a third of Airvana.

EXECUTIVES

President, CEO, and Director: Randall S. Battat, age 47, $269,808 pay
VP Finance and Operations: David P. Gamache, age 40
VP Worldwide Sales and Services: Luis J. Pajares, age 46, $212,771 pay
VP and General Counsel: Peter C. Anastos, age 44
VP and CFO: Jeffrey D. (Jeff) Glidden, age 56, $256,726 pay
VP Marketing and Product Management: David J. Nowicki, age 41
VP, CTO, and Director: Vedat M. Eyuboglu, age 51, $225,420 pay
VP Engineering: Mark W. Rau, age 48, $225,739 pay
VP Marketing and Business Development and Director: Sanjeev Verma, age 43
Auditors: Ernst & Young LLP

LOCATIONS

HQ: Airvana, Inc.
19 Alpha Rd., Chelmsford, MA 01824
Phone: 978-250-3000   **Fax:** 978-250-3910
Web: www.airvana.com

PRODUCTS/OPERATIONS

2006 Sales

	$ mil.	% of total
Product	145.8	86
Service	24.5	14
Total	**170.3**	**100**

COMPETITORS

Alcatel-Lucent
Cisco Systems
Ericsson
Hitachi
Huawei Technologies
Samsung Group

HISTORICAL FINANCIALS
Company Type: Public

Income Statement
FYE: Sunday nearest December 31

	REVENUE ($ mil.)	NET INCOME ($ mil.)	NET PROFIT MARGIN	EMPLOYEES
12/06	170.3	74.1	43.5%	491
12/05	2.3	(63.0)	—	—
12/04	3.6	(29.1)	—	—
Annual Growth	**587.8%**	**—**	**—**	**—**

2006 Year-End Financials

Debt ratio: —
Return on equity: —
Cash ($ mil.): 160.1
Current ratio: 1.01
Long-term debt ($ mil.): —

Net Income History
NASDAQ (GM): AIRV

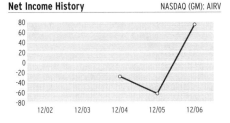

Akamai Technologies

Akamai Technologies wasn't content to confine itself to the delivery business. The company's EdgePlatform technology enables companies and government agencies to deliver Web content and applications, such as ads, video, and other high-bandwidth content. Through its network of some 15,000 servers in nearly 70 countries, Akamai's services analyze and manage Web traffic, transmitting content from the server geographically closest to the end user. The company serves more than 1,800 customers, including Airbus, Apple, Best Buy, FedEx, Microsoft, MTV Networks, Sony Ericsson Mobile Communications, the US Department of Defense, the US Department of Labor, Victoria's Secret, and XM Satellite Radio.

The company also offers audio and video streaming services, business intelligence and content targeting applications, and pay-as-you-go extra capacity on demand to avoid network congestion during periodic spikes in traffic through a partnership with IBM. Akamai's Web Application Accelerator service speeds up applications based on the Web and Internet protocol by compression, connection optimization, dynamic caching, and routing. The service is tailored for such online applications as airline reservation systems, course planning tools, customer order processing, and human resources.

In 2005 Akamai acquired archrival Speedera Networks for approximately 12 million shares of Akamai common stock, valued at about $130 million. As part of the merger agreement, Akamai and Speedera agreed to dismiss all pending litigation between the two companies. Late in 2006 Akamai purchased Nine Systems, a provider of rich media production and publishing tools, for about $160 million. Early in 2007 the company purchased application delivery service provider Netli.

EXECUTIVES

Chairman: George H. Conrades, age 69
President, CEO, and Director: Paul L. Sagan, age 49, $402,854 pay
EVP Global Sales, Services, and Marketing:
Robert W. (Bob) Hughes, age 40, $351,954 pay
EVP Technology and Networks: Chris Schoettle, age 43, $300,990 pay
CFO: J. Donald (J. D.) Sherman, age 42, $304,010 pay
VP Public Sector: Betsy Appleby
VP and General Counsel: Melanie Haratunian, age 47, $210,770 pay
VP Business Development: Robert Wood
CTO: Michael M. (Mike) Afergan
Chief Human Resources Officer: Cathy Welsh, age 55
Chief Scientist and Director:
F. Thomson (Tom) Leighton, age 50
Chief Security Architect: Andy Ellis
Director, Investor Relations: Sandy Smith
Director, Corporate Communications: Jeff Young
Auditors: PricewaterhouseCoopers LLP

LOCATIONS

HQ: Akamai Technologies, Inc.
8 Cambridge Center, Cambridge, MA 02142
Phone: 617-444-3000   **Fax:** 617-444-3001
Web: www.akamai.com

2006 Sales

	% of total
US	78
Europe	18
Other regions	4
Total	**100**

PRODUCTS/OPERATIONS

Selected Services

Business intelligence
Content and application delivery
Edge processing and content targeting
EdgeSuite content delivery network
Geolocation services
Internet traffic monitoring
Streaming media

COMPETITORS

Akimbo Systems	On2 Technologies
Anystream	Onstream Media
Blue Coat	Propel Software
Brilliant Digital	Radiance Technologies
Entertainment	RealNetworks
Chyron	Resonate, Inc.
Cisco Systems	SAVVIS
Google	Sorenson Media
Intraware	Teknowledge
Level 3 Communications	VeriSign
Limelight	Virage
Mirror Image Internet	Yahoo!
NetApp	

HISTORICAL FINANCIALS

Company Type: Public

Income Statement

FYE: December 31

	REVENUE ($ mil.)	NET INCOME ($ mil.)	NET PROFIT MARGIN	EMPLOYEES
12/06	428.7	57.4	13.4%	1,058
12/05	283.1	328.0	115.9%	784
12/04	210.0	34.4	16.4%	—
12/03	161.3	(29.3)	—	—
12/02	145.0	(204.4)	—	567
Annual Growth	**31.1%**	**—**	**—**	**16.9%**

2006 Year-End Financials

Debt ratio: 20.9%	Dividends	
Return on equity: 7.3%	Yield: —	
Cash ($ mil.): 269.8	Payout: —	
Current ratio: 4.20	Market value ($ mil.): 8,515.1	
Long-term debt ($ mil.): 200.0	R&D as % of sales: —	
No. of shares (mil.): 160.3	Advertising as % of sales: —	

Stock History

NASDAQ (GS): AKAM

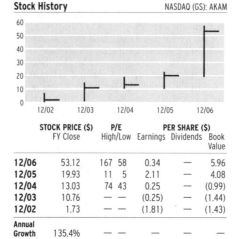

	STOCK PRICE ($) FY Close	P/E High/Low		PER SHARE ($) Earnings	Dividends	Book Value
12/06	53.12	167	58	0.34	—	5.96
12/05	19.93	11	5	2.11	—	4.08
12/04	13.03	74	43	0.25	—	(0.99)
12/03	10.76	—	—	(0.25)	—	(1.44)
12/02	1.73	—	—	(1.81)	—	(1.43)
Annual Growth	**135.4%**	**—**	**—**	**—**	**—**	**—**

Alkermes, Inc.

Alkermes, whose name is Arabic for "magic potion," is working some biotech alchemy. The firm uses its proprietary drug-delivery systems to make fragile biotech compounds that require less frequent dosing or provide more targeted delivery. It has a couple of drugs on the market that use its injectable extended-release technology, which lets patients take a drug once or twice a month, rather than once or twice a day. One such drug is Risperdal Consta, a long-acting version of Janssen's schizophrenia medication Risperdal. Another is Vivitrol, a treatment for alcohol dependence that partner Cephalon markets in the US. Alkermes is working with Eli Lilly on an inhaled insulin, using its inhaler-based technology AIR.

The company's AIR Insulin product is in the later stages of clinical development, as is its Exenatide LAR, a long-acting injectable version of Amylin Pharmaceuticals' diabetes drug Byetta.

Compounds at earlier stages of development include inhalable treatments for chronic obstructive pulmonary disease (with Indevus) and osteoporosis (with Eli Lilly), as well as orally administered medications for addiction.

Alkermes' development partner for Risperdal Consta, Janssen, has worldwide marketing rights to the drug. Alkermes manufactures the drug and gets royalties on sales.

HISTORY

Floyd Bloom, Alexander Rich, Paul Schimmel, and Michael Wall founded Alkermes in 1987. The company targeted the development of diagnostic and therapeutic agents for central nervous system diseases. It went public in 1991.

The next year Alkermes created a separate partnership to fund development of Cereport technology, and in the mid-1990s it branched out into other types of delivery systems and forged alliances with major drug companies to adapt its technologies to their products.

In the late 1990s Alkermes began collaborations with Johnson & Johnson to develop erythropoietin blood booster Procrit with ProLease and with Genentech to develop Nutropin Depot, a sustained-release formulation of Genentech's human growth hormone.

In 1999 Alkermes bought AIR (Advanced Inhalation Research), its pulmonary drug delivery unit. In 2004 the company ceased making its first FDA-approved product, Nutropin Depot.

EXECUTIVES

Chairman: Richard F. Pops, age 46
President and CEO: David A. Broecker, age 46
SVP and COO: Gordon G. Pugh, age 50
SVP, CFO, and Treasurer: James M. (Jim) Frates, age 40
SVP, General Counsel, and Secretary:
Kathryn L. (Kathy) Biberstein, age 48
SVP Corporate Development: Michael J. (Mike) Landine, age 53
SVP Science and Development and Chief Medical Officer: Elliot W. Ehrich, age 49
VP Corporate Communications: Rebecca Peterson
VP Human Resources: Madeline D. Coffin
VP Medical Affairs: David R. Gastfriend
VP Research and Development:
Richard P. (Rick) Batycky
VP Sales and Marketing and Chief Commercial Officer:
F. Ken Andrews
Associate, Corporate Communications: Debra Koufos
Auditors: Deloitte & Touche LLP

LOCATIONS

HQ: Alkermes, Inc.
88 Sidney St., Cambridge, MA 02139
Phone: 617-494-0171   **Fax:** 617-494-9263
Web: www.alkermes.com

Alkermes has facilities in Massachusetts and Ohio.

PRODUCTS/OPERATIONS

2007 Sales

	$ mil.	% of total
Manufacturing	105.4	44
Collaborative R&D agreements	74.5	31
Collaborative profits (Vivitrol)	36.9	15
Royalties (Risperdal Consta)	23.2	10
Total	**240.0**	**100**

Selected Products

Marketed
Risperdal Consta (long-acting Risperdal for schizophrenia, with Janssen)
Vivitrol (extended-release naltrexone for alcohol dependence, with Cephalon)
In development
AIR Insulin (inhalable insulin, with Eli Lilly)
AIR parathyroid hormone (inhalable treatment for osteoporosis, with Eli Lilly)
ALKS 27 (inhalable treatment for chronic obstructive pulmonary disease, with Indevus Pharmaceuticals)
ALKS 29 (oral medication for alcohol dependence)
Exenatide LAR (long-acting exenatide for type 2 diabetes, with Amylin Pharmaceuticals)

COMPETITORS

ALZA	Forest Labs
Barr Pharmaceuticals	Johnson & Johnson
Biovail	Nektar Therapeutics
Bristol-Myers Squibb	NPS Pharmaceuticals
DrugAbuse Sciences	Penwest Pharmaceuticals
DURECT	Pfizer
Eli Lilly	SkyePharma
Emisphere	

HISTORICAL FINANCIALS

Company Type: Public

Income Statement

FYE: March 31

	REVENUE ($ mil.)	NET INCOME ($ mil.)	NET PROFIT MARGIN	EMPLOYEES
3/07	240.0	9.4	3.9%	830
3/06	166.6	3.8	2.3%	760
3/05	76.1	(73.9)	—	528
3/04	39.0	(102.4)	—	—
3/03	47.3	(106.9)	—	—
Annual Growth	50.1%	—	—	25.4%

2007 Year-End Financials

Debt ratio: 77.1%
Return on equity: 7.9%
Cash ($ mil.): 351.6
Current ratio: 6.98
Long-term debt ($ mil.): 156.9
No. of shares (mil.): 100.7

Dividends
  Yield: —
  Payout: —
Market value ($ mil.): 1,555.2
R&D as % of sales: 48.9%
Advertising as % of sales: —

Stock History

NASDAQ (GS): ALKS

	STOCK PRICE ($) FY Close	P/E High/Low	PER SHARE ($) Earnings	Dividends	Book Value
3/07	15.44	253 142	0.09	—	2.02
3/06	22.05	670 242	0.04	—	0.36
3/05	10.38	— —	(0.82)	—	0.05
3/04	15.99	— —	(1.25)	—	0.85
3/03	9.07	— —	(1.66)	—	(0.08)
Annual Growth	14.2%	— —	—	—	—

Allegiant Travel

Allegiant Travel pledges to serve the vacation needs of residents of more than 45 small US cities. Through Allegiant Air, the company provides nonstop service to tourist destinations such as Las Vegas and Orlando, Florida, from places such as Abilene, Texas; Fargo, North Dakota; and Toledo, Ohio. It maintains a fleet of about 25 MD80 series aircraft. Besides scheduled service, Allegiant Air offers charter flights for casino operator Harrah's and other customers. Sister company Allegiant Vacations works with partners to allow customers to book hotel rooms and rental cars with their airline tickets.

The company hopes to thrive by sticking to what it believes to be an underserved niche: Allegiant Air is the only provider of nonstop service to Las Vegas or Orlando in most of the markets where it operates. Allegiant Travel has identified more than 50 additional small cities in the US and Canada as candidates for its services. The company also plans to add vacation spots elsewhere in the US to its route map, and it is considering offering service to Mexico and the Caribbean, as well.

Allegiant Travel believes the diversity of its revenue mix will help ensure the company's suc-

cess. The long-term, fixed-fee contract with Harrah's is a useful supplement to its scheduled airline service. Besides the fees it collects when customers arrange lodging and ground transportation via the Allegiant Air Web site, the company charges for services such as advance seat assignments and in-flight food and beverages.

Allegiant Travel plans to use the proceeds of its 2006 IPO to buy more aircraft in order to expand services on existing routes and add new markets. The company's chosen MD80 models, formerly an industry mainstay, are more expensive to operate than new planes but cheaper to obtain.

Just as the company's aircraft have been tested, so has Allegiant Travel's management team. This isn't the first go-round in the airline industry for CEO Maurice Gallagher and director Robert Priddy, who helped found low-fare carrier ValuJet (now AirTran). Allegiant Travel's board also includes Declan Ryan, a co-founder and former CEO of European low-fare carrier Ryanair.

Gallagher owns 23% of Allegiant Travel. Private equity firm ComVest, which is represented on the company's board by Priddy and Michael Falk, owns about 10%.

The original Allegiant Air was founded in 1997. That company filed for Chapter 11 bankruptcy protection in 2000 and emerged from its reorganization in 2002 under new ownership and management, led by Gallagher. Allegiant Travel was formed in 2005 as a holding company for Allegiant Air and Allegiant Vacations.

EXECUTIVES

Chairman, President, and CEO:
  Maurice J. (Maury) Gallagher Jr., age 57
CFO: Andrew C. Levy, age 37, $249,349 pay
SVP, Operations: Michael P. Baxter, age 64, $251,726 pay
VP, Flight Operations: James R. Carr
Managing Director, Marketing and Sales:
  M. Ponder Harrison, age 45, $251,726 pay
Director, Corporate Communications: Tyri Squyres
Director, Sales: Eric Woodson
Principal Accounting Officer: Scott Sheldon
Auditors: Ernst & Young LLP

LOCATIONS

HQ: Allegiant Travel Company
  3301 N. Buffalo Dr., Ste. B-9, Las Vegas, NV 89129
Phone: 702-851-7300   **Fax:** 702-256-7209
Web: www.allegiantair.com

PRODUCTS/OPERATIONS

2006 Sales

	$ mil.	% of total
Scheduled service	178.4	73
Charter service	33.7	14
Other	31.3	13
Total	**243.4**	**100**

COMPETITORS

AirTran Holdings
AMR Corp.
Continental Airlines
Delta Air Lines
Frontier Airlines
JetBlue
Midwest Air
Northwest Airlines
Southwest Airlines
UAL
US Airways

HISTORICAL FINANCIALS

Company Type: Public

Income Statement

FYE: December 31

	REVENUE ($ mil.)	NET INCOME ($ mil.)	NET PROFIT MARGIN	EMPLOYEES
12/06	243.4	8.7	3.6%	1,046
12/05	132.5	7.3	5.5%	—
12/04	90.4	9.1	10.1%	—
12/03	50.0	4.3	8.6%	282
Annual Growth	69.5%	26.5%	—	54.8%

2006 Year-End Financials

Debt ratio: 37.7%
Return on equity: 10.4%
Cash ($ mil.): 144.7
Current ratio: 1.92
Long-term debt ($ mil.): 57.9
No. of shares (mil.): 19.8

Dividends
  Yield: —
  Payout: —
Market value ($ mil.): 555.5
R&D as % of sales: —
Advertising as % of sales: —

Stock History

NASDAQ (GM): ALGT

	STOCK PRICE ($) FY Close	P/E High/Low	PER SHARE ($) Earnings	Dividends	Book Value
12/06	28.06	55 46	0.52	—	7.75

Alliance Bankshares

Alliance Bankshares has enjoyed a healthy partnership with mortgages since 1996. The financial institution is the holding company for Alliance Bank and its mortgage subsidiary Alliance Home Funding. Alliance Bankshares operates branches and loan production offices in the DC suburbs of northern Virginia. The bank offers such services as checking and savings accounts, CDs, corporate credit cards, and cash management. Its lending activities mainly consist of residential and commercial mortgages, with business and consumer loans rounding out its portfolio.

In 2005 Alliance Bank acquired Danaher Insurance Agency, a Virginia company dating back to 1963. It sells commercial and personal lines of insurance and other financial services. The agency was renamed Alliance Insurance Corporation.

Vice chairman George Webb owns about 6% of Alliance Bankshares; directors and executive officers collectively own 21% of the company.

EXECUTIVES

Chairman Emeritus: Thomas P. Danaher, age 80
Chairman: Harvey E. Johnson Jr., age 69
President, CEO, and Director; President and CEO, Alliance Bank: Thomas A. Young Jr., age 55, $264,718 pay

EVP, CFO, and Secretary; EVP and CFO, Alliance Bank: Paul M. Harbolick Jr., age 47, $175,989 pay
EVP: Frank H. Grace III, age 48
EVP Residential Real Estate Finance: Craig W. Sacknoff, age 56
SVP and Chief Credit Officer, Alliance Bankshares and Alliance Bank: John B. (Jack) McKenney III, age 53, $133,639 pay
SVP and Director of Commercial Banking, Alliance Bank: Michael C. O'Grady
President, Alliance Insurance Agency: Thomas P. Danaher, age 48, $156,733 pay
Auditors: Yount, Hyde & Barbour, P.C.

LOCATIONS

HQ: Alliance Bankshares Corporation
  14200 Park Meadow Dr., Ste. 200 South, Chantilly, VA 20151
Phone: 703-814-7200   **Fax:** 703-378-7210
Web: www.alliancebankva.com

PRODUCTS/OPERATIONS

2006 Sales

	$ mil.	% of total
Interest		
Loans	29.5	65
Investment securities	9.8	21
Federal funds sold	0.5	1
Noninterest		
Gain on sale of loans	4.1	9
Insurance commissions	1.6	3
Deposit account service charges	0.2	1
Other operating income	0.2	—
Net gain (loss) on sale of securities	(0.2)	—
Total	**45.7**	**100**

COMPETITORS

Access National
Bank of America
BB&T
Cardinal Financial
Chevy Chase Bank
Greater Atlantic Financial
Millennium Bankshares
Provident Bankshares
SunTrust
United Bankshares
United Financial Banking
Wachovia

HISTORICAL FINANCIALS

Company Type: Public

Income Statement
FYE: December 31

	ASSETS ($ mil.)	NET INCOME ($ mil.)	INCOME AS % OF ASSETS	EMPLOYEES
12/06	644.4	4.5	0.7%	115
12/05	611.5	4.1	0.7%	115
12/04	479.7	2.8	0.6%	—
12/03	356.7	4.0	1.1%	—
12/02	280.6	2.4	0.9%	—
Annual Growth	**23.1%**	**17.0%**	**—**	**0.0%**

2006 Year-End Financials

Equity as % of assets: 8.5%
Return on assets: 0.7%
Return on equity: 8.7%
Long-term debt ($ mil.): 10.3
No. of shares (mil.): 5.6
Market value ($ mil.): 86.9
Dividends
  Yield: —
  Payout: —
Sales ($ mil.): 45.7
R&D as % of sales: —
Advertising as % of sales: —

Alliance Fiber Optic

Alliance Fiber Optic Products (AFOP) unites with light. Communications equipment manufacturers incorporate AFOP's fiber-optic components into products used to build networks that connect cities, regions within cities, and telecom service providers with their individual customers. Its optical path integration and optical fiber amplifier components, which include attenuators, couplers, depolarizers, multiplexers, and splitters, account for most of sales.

The company sells directly to telecom equipment makers, primarily in North America. Foxconn Holding/Hon Hai Precision Industry owns about 20% of AFOP.

About 70% of sales are in North America. AFOP has more than 200 customers.

CEO Peter Chang owns nearly 16% of Alliance Fiber Optic Products, including stock options. Investor Lloyd I. Miller III holds around 5% of the company.

EXECUTIVES

Chairman, CEO, President, and Secretary: Peter C. Chang, age 50, $200,000 pay
Acting CFO and Controller: Anita K. Ho, age 61, $130,000 pay
SVP Product Development: Wei-shin Tsay, age 56, $150,000 pay
VP Sales and Marketing: David A. Hubbard, age 47, $150,000 pay
Press Relations: Helen Chan
Auditors: Stonefield Josephson, Inc.

LOCATIONS

HQ: Alliance Fiber Optic Products, Inc.
  275 Gibraltar Dr., Sunnyvale, CA 94089
Phone: 408-736-6900   **Fax:** 408-736-4882
Web: www.afop.com

Alliance Fiber Optic Products has offices and manufacturing plants in China, Taiwan, and the US.

2006 Sales

	$ mil.	% of total
North America	18.6	70
Asia	6.3	23
Europe	1.9	7
Total	**26.8**	**100**

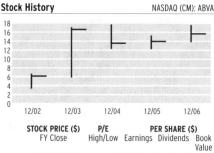

	STOCK PRICE ($) FY Close	P/E High/Low		PER SHARE ($) Earnings	Dividends	Book Value
12/06	15.65	23	18	0.76	—	9.84
12/05	13.92	22	18	0.70	—	10.10
12/04	13.52	35	25	0.50	—	9.73
12/03	16.57	17	6	0.99	—	5.97
12/02	6.12	10	5	0.64	—	8.31
Annual Growth	**26.5%**	**—**	**—**	**4.4%**	**—**	**4.3%**

PRODUCTS/OPERATIONS

2006 Sales

	$ mil.	% of total
Optical path management products	16.4	61
Dense wave division multiplexers	10.4	39
Total	**26.8**	**100**

Selected Products

Advanced optical devices
  All-fiber optical depolarizer
  Automatic variable optical attenuator
  Switchable optical drop/add module
Optical path management
  Amplifiers
  Couplers and splitters
  Customized integrated modules
  Optical interconnect devices
Wavelength management
  Fused fiber WDM couplers
  Multiplexing components and modules

COMPETITORS

Avago Technologies
Avanex
Bookham
Cisco Systems
Covega
DiCon Fiberoptics
Finisar
Gemfire
JDS Uniphase
Kotura
Oplink Communications
Optical Communication Products
Tyco Electronics

HISTORICAL FINANCIALS

Company Type: Public

Income Statement
FYE: December 31

	REVENUE ($ mil.)	NET INCOME ($ mil.)	NET PROFIT MARGIN	EMPLOYEES
12/06	26.8	0.7	2.6%	684
12/05	21.0	(2.6)	—	581
12/04	14.6	(9.3)	—	—
12/03	11.5	(8.5)	—	—
12/02	13.1	(18.3)	—	307
Annual Growth	**19.6%**	**—**	**—**	**22.2%**

2006 Year-End Financials

Debt ratio: 1.4%
Return on equity: 1.9%
Cash ($ mil.): 31.2
Current ratio: 6.87
Long-term debt ($ mil.): 0.5
No. of shares (mil.): 40.5
Dividends
  Yield: —
  Payout: —
Market value ($ mil.): 82.7
R&D as % of sales: —
Advertising as % of sales: —

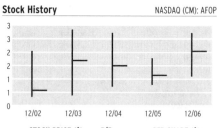

	STOCK PRICE ($) FY Close	P/E High/Low		PER SHARE ($) Earnings	Dividends	Book Value
12/06	2.04	270	112	0.01	—	0.93
12/05	1.14	—	—	(0.07)	—	0.91
12/04	1.50	—	—	(0.24)	—	0.99
12/03	1.69	—	—	(0.24)	—	1.16
12/02	0.57	—	—	(0.53)	—	1.38
Annual Growth	**37.5%**	**—**	**—**	**—**	**—**	**(9.2%)**

Alliance Resource Partners

Coal is the main resource of Alliance Resource Partners. The company has eight coal mining complexes (seven underground, one surface) in Illinois, Indiana, Kentucky, Maryland, Pennsylvania, and West Virginia. Alliance controls 633.9 million tons of reserves. The company produces about 20 million tons of coal annually, nearly all of which is sold to electric utilities. Two customers — Synfuel Solutions Operating and the Tennessee Valley Authority — account for just about a third of sales. Alliance bought out River View Coal in early 2006, giving it 100 million more tons of high-sulfur coal reserves. President and CEO Joseph Craft III controls a 44% stake in Alliance Resource Partners.

Craft, a coal industry veteran, owns his stake in Alliance Resource Partners through Alliance Holdings GP, a company he controls that went public in 2006.

EXECUTIVES

Chairman: John P. Neafsey, age 67
President, CEO, and Director: Joseph W. Craft III, age 57, $534,828 pay
EVP Marketing and Strategic Development: Robert G. Sachse, age 59
SVP and CFO: Brian L. Cantrell, age 48
SVP Operations: Charles R. Wesley, age 54, $480,857 pay
SVP General Counsel and Corporate Secretary: R. Eberley Davis, age 51
Auditors: Deloitte & Touche LLP

LOCATIONS

HQ: Alliance Resource Partners, L.P.
1717 S. Boulder Ave., Ste. 600, Tulsa, OK 74119
Phone: 918-295-7600   **Fax:** 918-295-7358
Web: www.arlp.com

COMPETITORS

Alpha Natural Resources	International Coal Group
Arch Coal	James River Coal
CONSOL Energy	Massey Energy
Drummond Company	Peabody Energy

HISTORICAL FINANCIALS

Company Type: Public

Income Statement

FYE: December 31

	REVENUE ($ mil.)	NET INCOME ($ mil.)	NET PROFIT MARGIN	EMPLOYEES
12/06	967.6	172.9	17.9%	2,500
12/05	838.7	160.0	19.1%	2,300
12/04	653.3	76.6	11.7%	—
12/03	542.8	47.9	8.8%	—
12/02	517.7	36.3	7.0%	1,745
Annual Growth	16.9%	47.7%	—	9.4%

2006 Year-End Financials

Debt ratio: 51.3%
Return on equity: 85.5%
Cash ($ mil.): 37.0
Current ratio: 1.28
Long-term debt ($ mil.): 127.5
No. of shares (mil.): 36.4
Dividends
  Yield: 5.6%
  Payout: 63.4%
Market value ($ mil.): 1,257.2
R&D as % of sales: —
Advertising as % of sales: —

Allion Healthcare

Allion Healthcare is a specialty drug distributor focusing on patients with HIV and AIDS. Through its subsidiary MOMS Pharmacy, the company fulfills prescriptions for necessary medications at nearly a dozen distribution centers and delivers them to patients, doctors' offices, and clinics nationwide. Allion also provides ancillary drugs and nutritional supplies, and it offers special software and packaging of drug orders — pre-filled pill boxes, for instance — that are intended to help patients stick with their medication regimens. Most of Allion's customers rely on Medicaid or state programs such as the AIDS Drug Assistance Program for payment of their prescriptions.

EXECUTIVES

Chairman, President, and CEO: Michael P. Moran, age 47, $375,000 pay
VP Pharmacy Operations: Robert E. Fleckenstein, age 54, $165,000 pay
VP Oris Health and HIV Sales: Anthony D. Luna, age 38
Director, Finance, Interim CFO, Secretary, and Treasurer: Stephen A. Maggio, age 58
Auditors: BDO Seidman, LLP

LOCATIONS

HQ: Allion Healthcare, Inc.
1660 Walt Whitman Rd., Ste. 105, Melville, NY 11747
Phone: 631-547-6520   **Fax:** 631-249-5863
Web: www.allionhealthcare.com

Allion Healthcare's distribution centers are located in California, Florida, New York, and Washington.

2006 Sales

	$ mil.	% of total
California	138.3	66
New York	65.2	31
Seattle	3.9	2
Florida	2.1	1
Total	**209.5**	**100**

Stock History

NASDAQ (GS): ARLP

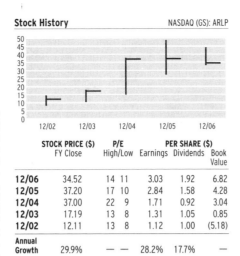

	STOCK PRICE ($) FY Close	P/E High/Low		Earnings	PER SHARE ($) Dividends	Book Value
12/06	34.52	14	11	3.03	1.92	6.82
12/05	37.20	17	10	2.84	1.58	4.28
12/04	37.00	22	9	1.71	0.92	3.04
12/03	17.19	13	8	1.31	1.05	0.85
12/02	12.11	13	8	1.12	1.00	(5.18)
Annual Growth	29.9%	—	—	28.2%	17.7%	—

COMPETITORS

BioScrip
Cardinal Health
Caremark Pharmacy Services
Critical Care Systems International
Express Scripts
McKesson
Medco Health

HISTORICAL FINANCIALS

Company Type: Public

Income Statement

FYE: December 31

	REVENUE ($ mil.)	NET INCOME ($ mil.)	NET PROFIT MARGIN	EMPLOYEES
12/06	209.5	3.2	1.5%	222
12/05	123.1	(1.0)	—	170
12/04	60.1	(2.7)	—	—
12/03	42.5	(3.0)	—	—
Annual Growth	70.2%	—	—	30.6%

2006 Year-End Financials

Debt ratio: 0.0%
Return on equity: 3.8%
Cash ($ mil.): 23.5
Current ratio: 2.61
Long-term debt ($ mil.): 0.1
No. of shares (mil.): 16.2
Dividends
  Yield: —
  Payout: —
Market value ($ mil.): 116.0
R&D as % of sales: —
Advertising as % of sales: —

Stock History

NASDAQ (GM): ALLI

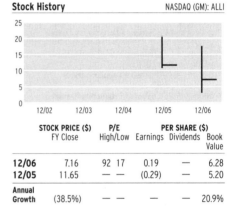

	STOCK PRICE ($) FY Close	P/E High/Low		Earnings	PER SHARE ($) Dividends	Book Value
12/06	7.16	92	17	0.19	—	6.28
12/05	11.65	—	—	(0.29)	—	5.20
Annual Growth	(38.5%)	—	—	—	—	20.9%

Allis-Chalmers Energy

This company knows the drill. Allis-Chalmers Energy provides drilling and oil field services to oil and gas exploration companies operating primarily in the western and southern US. It installs casing and tubing and provides drilling and workover services. Its Strata Directional Technology subsidiary offers drilling services to clients in Texas and Louisiana. Through its AirComp unit, Allis-Chalmers operates a fleet of more than 175 compressors used for well production enhancement and completion. Moving into the tool rental field, the company acquired Safco-Oil Field Products in 2004 and Delta Rental Service in 2005. In 2006 it acquired Oil & Gas Rental Services for about $342 million in cash and stock.

Allis-Chalmers, through its AirComp subsidiary, has expanded its drilling technology products business through the 2004 acquisition of Diamond Air. The acquisition also included Diamond Air's Marquis Bit subsidiary. It has also acquired Texas-based oil and gas field services provider Downhole Injection Systems for $1 million.

In 2005 the company acquired $15 million in used casing and tubing installation equipment from Patterson Services, Inc., a subsidiary of RPC, Inc. It also acquired Target Energy Inc., the US measurement-while-drilling (MWD) operations of UK-based Target Energy Group. Continuing its acquisition streak into 2006, Allis-Chalmers acquired Specialty Rental Tools Inc. for about $90 million, and bought Rogers Oil Tool Services for about $14 million. That year it also acquired Petro Rentals for $29.78 million.

In 2007 the company acquired Diamondback Oilfield Services for $22 million. In 2008 Allis-Chalmers agreed to buy Bronco Drilling for $437.8 million. It also announced that it would spend $40 million for a minority stake in BCH Ltd., a Canadian company that operates drilling rigs in Brazil.

EXECUTIVES

Chairman and CEO: Munawar H. (Micki) Hidayatallah, age 62
Vice Chairman: Leonard Toboroff
CFO: Victor M. Perez, age 54
SVP Oilfield Services: Terrence P. (Terry) Keane, age 55
SVP Rental Services: Mark Patterson
VP and Corporate Controller: Bruce Sauers, age 43
General Counsel and Secretary: Theodore F. Pound III, age 52
President and CEO, Strata Directional: David K. Bryan, age 50
President, Allis-Chalmers Rental Tools: James Davey, age 53
President, Allis-Chalmers Tubular Services: Gary Edwards, age 55
President, Allis-Chalmers Production Services: Steven Collins, age 55
Auditors: UHY LLP

LOCATIONS

HQ: Allis-Chalmers Energy Inc.
   5075 Westheimer, Ste. 890, Houston, TX 77056
Phone: 713-369-0550   **Fax:** 713-369-0555

Allis-Chalmers provides services to customers operating in the US (in the West and the Gulf of Mexico), Argentina, and Mexico.

2006 Sales

	$ mil.	% of total
US	228.2	74
Other countries	79.1	26
Total	**307.3**	**100**

PRODUCTS/OPERATIONS

2006 Sales

	$ mil.	% of total
Directional drilling services	72.8	24
International drilling	69.5	23
Rental tools	51.5	17
Casing & tubing services	50.9	16
Compressed air drilling services	43.0	14
Production services	19.6	6
Total	**307.3**	**100**

COMPETITORS

Boots & Coots
Cudd Pressure Control
Eaton Oil Tools
GulfMark Offshore
Trico Marine
Weatherford International

HISTORICAL FINANCIALS

Company Type: Public

Income Statement

FYE: December 31

	REVENUE ($ mil.)	NET INCOME ($ mil.)	NET PROFIT MARGIN	EMPLOYEES
12/06	307.3	35.6	11.6%	2,567
12/05	105.3	7.2	6.8%	700
12/04	47.7	0.9	1.9%	—
12/03	32.7	2.9	8.9%	—
12/02	18.0	(4.0)	—	—
Annual Growth	**103.3%**	**—**	**—**	**266.7%**

2006 Year-End Financials

Debt ratio: 221.1%
Return on equity: 22.6%
Cash ($ mil.): 39.7
Current ratio: 2.50
Long-term debt ($ mil.): 561.5
No. of shares (mil.): 28.2
Dividends
   Yield: —
   Payout: —
Market value ($ mil.): 650.5
R&D as % of sales: —
Advertising as % of sales: —

Stock History

AMEX: ALY

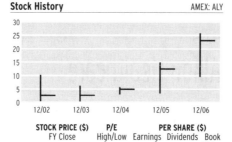

	STOCK PRICE ($) FY Close	P/E High/Low		PER SHARE ($) Earnings	Dividends	Book Value
12/06	23.04	15	6	1.66	—	8.99
12/05	12.47	33	8	0.44	—	3.61
12/04	4.90	60	36	0.09	—	2.53
12/03	2.60	—	—	(0.01)	—	0.23
12/02	2.55	—	—	(1.15)	—	0.05
Annual Growth	**73.4%**	**—**	**—**	**—**	**—**	**263.6%**

Allscripts Healthcare Solutions

Jokes about doctors' handwriting may go the way of house calls thanks to Allscripts Healthcare — a provider of clinical software and information systems for doctors. The company sells prescription-management software and services that let doctors enter prescription information over computer networks, including tools that give doctors access (via desktop or wireless handheld devices) to patient drug history, drug interactions, and generic alternatives. Other services include electronic document imaging and scanning and physician feedback services. Allscripts bought ChannelHealth from IDX Systems, adding thousands of physicians to its clientele. IDX Systems owns about 20% of Allscripts.

Allscripts also provides medication repackaging services for physicians through its Medication Services Group. The company acquired A4 Health Systems, which offers practice management and electronic health record services, in 2006.

EXECUTIVES

Chairman and CEO: Glen E. Tullman, age 47, $487,647 pay
President and Secretary: Lee A. Shapiro, age 51, $412,099 pay
COO: Benjamin Bulkley, age 43
CFO: William J. (Bill) Davis, age 39, $379,847 pay
Management Team Assistant: Joseph E. Carey, age 49, $378,072 pay
EVP Development: Jeff Amrein
SVP Corporate Business Development: Steven P. Schwartz
SVP Deployment Management: Karl L. Greiter II
SVP Product Management: Mike Gluth
VP and General Counsel: Brian D. Vandenberg
VP Human Resources: Bonnie Schirato
Chief Medical Officer: Douglas A. (Doug) Gentile
Chief Marketing Officer: Dan Michelson
President, ePrescribing: T. Scott Leisher, age 47, $315,839 pay
President, Clinical Solutions Group: Laurie A. S. McGraw, age 43, $285,021 pay
President, Medication Services Group: John G. Cull, age 46
President, Physicians Interactive: Donato J. Tramuto, age 50
President, Healthmatics: David A. Bond, age 50
Auditors: Grant Thornton LLP

LOCATIONS

HQ: Allscripts Healthcare Solutions, Inc.
   222 Merchandise Mart Plaza, Ste. 2024, Chicago, IL 60654
Phone: 312-506-1200   **Fax:** 312-506-1201
Web: www.allscripts.com

PRODUCTS/OPERATIONS

2006 Sales

	$ mil.	% of total
Software & related services	173.5	76
Prepackaged medications	43.7	19
Information services	10.8	5
Total	**228.0**	**100**

Selected Products

AIC — Electronic document imaging & scanning solutions
Physicians Interactive — doctor feedback solutions
TouchWorks — Electronic medical record & clinical information solutions

COMPETITORS

BioScrip
Cardinal Health
Caremark Pharmacy Services
HLTH Corp.
McKesson
ProxyMed

HISTORICAL FINANCIALS

Company Type: Public

Income Statement

FYE: December 31

	REVENUE ($ mil.)	NET INCOME ($ mil.)	NET PROFIT MARGIN	EMPLOYEES
12/06	228.0	11.9	5.2%	914
12/05	120.6	9.7	8.0%	386
12/04	100.8	3.1	3.1%	—
12/03	85.8	(5.0)	—	—
12/02	78.8	(15.2)	—	304
Annual Growth	**30.4%**	**—**	**—**	**31.7%**

2006 Year-End Financials

Debt ratio: 27.0%
Return on equity: 5.7%
Cash ($ mil.): 57.0
Current ratio: 2.15
Long-term debt ($ mil.): 85.4
No. of shares (mil.): 54.4

Dividends
 Yield: —
 Payout: —
Market value ($ mil.): 1,467.1
R&D as % of sales: 4.7%
Advertising as % of sales: —

Stock History   NASDAQ (GS): MDRX

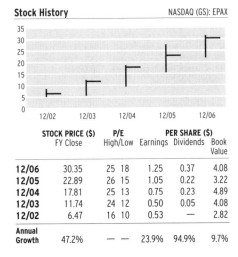

	STOCK PRICE ($) FY Close	P/E High/Low		PER SHARE ($) Earnings	Dividends	Book Value
12/06	26.99	133	61	0.22	—	5.82
12/05	13.40	83	39	0.23	—	2.41
12/04	10.67	163	75	0.07	—	1.96
12/03	5.32	—	—	(0.13)	—	2.14
12/02	2.39	—	—	(0.40)	—	2.23
Annual Growth	83.3%	—	—	—	—	27.1%

Ambassadors Group

Ambassadors Group's educational travel programs provide students and professionals with opportunities to meet their counterparts overseas. Most trips are organized under contracts with the People to People organization, which was founded by President Eisenhower in 1956 as a way to promote world peace. Ambassadors Group markets trips using the People to People name and makes travel arrangement for participants. Specialized People to People offerings allow student athletes to participate in international sports programs and enable student leaders to meet one another. The organization's Professional Ambassador trips offer meetings and seminars involving people from different countries who work in similar fields.

EXECUTIVES

Chairman: John A. Ueberroth, age 63
President, CEO, and Director: Jeffrey D. (Jeff) Thomas, age 40, $1,183,000 pay
CFO and Secretary: Chadwick J. Byrd, age 35, $232,500 pay
CFO, Ambassador Programs: Colleen K. McCann-Lillie, age 40
EVP; President and COO, Ambassador Programs: Margaret M. (Peg) Thomas, age 40, $600,000 pay
Investor Relations: Julie Strugar
Auditors: BDO Seidman, LLP

LOCATIONS

HQ: Ambassadors Group, Inc.
 Dwight D. Eisenhower Bldg., 110 S. Ferrall St.,
 Spokane, WA 99202
Phone: 509-534-6200   **Fax:** 509-534-5245
Web: www.ambassadorsgroup.com

2006 Sales

	% of total
Europe	43
South Pacific (primarily Australia & New Zealand)	26
US	13
Asia (primarily China)	13
Other	5
Total	**100**

COMPETITORS

American Express
BCD Travel
Carlson Wagonlit
Expedia
Orbitz Worldwide
Travelocity
University of Pennsylvania

HISTORICAL FINANCIALS

Company Type: Public

Income Statement   FYE: December 31

	REVENUE ($ mil.)	NET INCOME ($ mil.)	NET PROFIT MARGIN	EMPLOYEES
12/06	89.0	26.7	30.0%	273
12/05	69.3	22.4	32.3%	234
12/04	51.8	15.6	30.1%	—
12/03	37.7	10.1	26.8%	—
12/02	36.1	10.8	29.9%	153
Annual Growth	25.3%	25.4%	—	15.6%

2006 Year-End Financials

Debt ratio: 0.2%
Return on equity: 35.5%
Cash ($ mil.): 133.1
Current ratio: 2.01
Long-term debt ($ mil.): 0.2
No. of shares (mil.): 20.6

Dividends
 Yield: 1.2%
 Payout: 29.6%
Market value ($ mil.): 625.2
R&D as % of sales: —
Advertising as % of sales: —

Stock History   NASDAQ (GS): EPAX

	STOCK PRICE ($) FY Close	P/E High/Low		PER SHARE ($) Earnings	Dividends	Book Value
12/06	30.35	25	18	1.25	0.37	4.08
12/05	22.89	26	15	1.05	0.22	3.22
12/04	17.81	25	13	0.75	0.23	4.89
12/03	11.74	24	12	0.50	0.05	4.08
12/02	6.47	16	10	0.53	—	2.82
Annual Growth	47.2%	—	—	23.9%	94.9%	9.7%

Ambassadors International

Ambassadors International represents itself around the world in the cruise, marina, and travel and events businesses. The company provides river and coastal cruises in North America via its Majestic America Line unit, which operates seven vessels. Ambassadors International's three-vessel Windstar Cruises unit operates in the Mediterranean and the Caribbean. In addition, Ambassadors International designs and builds marinas worldwide and operates marinas in the US and Japan. The company's travel and events businesses focus on making arrangements for conventions and trade shows. Ambassadors International also helps companies develop performance improvement programs that use travel awards as incentives.

Ambassadors International has been expanding its cruise operations via acquisitions, and the company plans to continue to look for complementary cruise businesses. In 2007 it bought Windstar Cruises from Holland America Line, a unit of industry leader Carnival.

The Windstar deal followed Ambassadors International's 2006 purchase of Delta Queen Steamboat, a three-vessel cruise line owned by Delaware North. That acquisition doubled Ambassadors' fleet of cruise vessels and added the Mississippi River region to its list of destinations, which had focused on the Pacific Northwest and Alaska. Ambassadors International subsequently combined Delta Queen Steamboat with its American West Steamboat unit under the Majestic America Line brand.

Along with its travel-related units, Ambassadors International operates a reinsurance business (insurance for insurance companies), but it has been scaling back those operations.

Ambassadors International chairman, president, and CEO Joseph Ueberroth and his father, company director and former Major League Baseball commissioner Peter Ueberroth, own about 20% of the company.

EXECUTIVES

Chairman, President, and CEO; Interim President, Ambassadors Cruise Group: Joseph J. (Joe) Ueberroth, age 38, $585,000 pay (prior to title change)
CFO: Blake T. Barnett, age 45
VP and Chief Accounting Officer: Laura L. Tuthill, age 29, $140,000 pay
VP Corporate Development and General Counsel: Joseph G. McCarthy, age 35, $208,333 pay
VP Human Resources: Tricia Mora
VP Information Technology: Brett Jones
President and COO, Ambassadors Cruise Group: David A. Giersdorf, age 50, $435,000 pay
President and COO, Ambassadors: Jerry G. McGee, age 36, $210,000 pay
EVP Marketing and Sales, Reservations/Guest Services, and Customer Relations, Ambassadors Cruise Group: Diane Moore
Auditors: Ernst & Young LLP

LOCATIONS

HQ: Ambassadors International, Inc.
   1071 Camelback St., Newport Beach, CA 92660
Phone: 949-759-5900   **Fax:** 949-759-5901
Web: www.ambassadors.com

Ambassadors International has operations in Australia, France, Mexico, New Zealand, Spain, the UK, and the US.

PRODUCTS/OPERATIONS

2006 Sales

	$ mil.	% of total
Cruise	75.8	53
Marine	46.6	32
Travel & events	13.1	9
Insurance	8.9	6
Total	**144.4**	**100**

COMPETITORS

American Express
BCD Travel
Carlson Wagonlit
Carnival Corporation
NCL
Royal Caribbean Cruises
Sekisui House
The Trump Organization

HISTORICAL FINANCIALS

Company Type: Public

Income Statement

FYE: December 31

	REVENUE ($ mil.)	NET INCOME ($ mil.)	NET PROFIT MARGIN	EMPLOYEES
12/06	144.4	5.6	3.9%	765
12/05	26.9	3.1	11.5%	157
12/04	18.7	(1.9)	—	132
12/03	13.7	(1.0)	—	—
12/02	14.7	1.6	10.9%	147
Annual Growth	**77.0%**	**36.8%**	**—**	**51.0%**

2006 Year-End Financials

Debt ratio: 62.0%
Return on equity: 5.0%
Cash ($ mil.): 57.2
Current ratio: 1.76
Long-term debt ($ mil.): 71.8
No. of shares (mil.): 10.8

Dividends
   Yield: 0.9%
   Payout: 81.6%
Market value ($ mil.): 494.4
R&D as % of sales: —
Advertising as % of sales: —

Stock History

NASDAQ (GM): AMIE

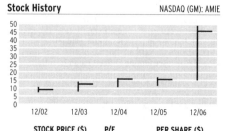

	STOCK PRICE ($) FY Close	P/E High/Low		PER SHARE ($) Earnings	Dividends	Book Value
12/06	45.62	99	32	0.49	0.40	10.68
12/05	15.50	55	40	0.30	0.40	10.39
12/04	15.73	—	—	(0.20)	0.40	10.51
12/03	12.55	—	—	(0.10)	0.20	11.30
12/02	8.99	68	52	0.15	17.27	11.60
Annual Growth	**50.1%**	**—**	**—**	**34.4%**	**(61.0%)**	**(2.0%)**

Amedisys, Inc.

Because the last thing you want to do when you're sick is drive to a doctor's office, Amedisys has decided to bring health care to you. The company's home health care segment comprises skilled nursing and home health aide services, as well as programs focused on disease management including diabetes, wound care, and geriatric surgical recovery. Amedisys also provides terminal illness hospice care and therapy staffing services. The company operates through more than 250 agencies and facilities offices located in nearly 20 states. The company derives more than 90% of its revenues from Medicare reimbursements.

The company's locations have primarily been located in southern and eastern states, but it has entered new markets, including Missouri and Arizona through acquisitions.

In 2007, as part of its acquisition strategy, it bought privately held IntegriCare, which operates home health care and hospice operations in nine states, eight of which are new markets for Amedisys. IntegriCare's nearly 20 agencies are located in Alaska, Colorado, Idaho, Kansas, New Hampshire, Oregon, Washington, West Virginia, and Wyoming. Late in the same year it expanded its operations in Georgia and South Carolina with the purchase of six home health agencies. And early in 2008 it acquired an agency in Puerto Rico, its first in that market.

The company also has plans to develop additional specialized disease management programs and services.

EXECUTIVES

Chairman and CEO: William F. (Bill) Borne, age 48, $582,701 pay
President and COO: Larry R. Graham, age 40, $364,855 pay
CFO: Dale E. Redman, age 59
CIO: Alice Ann Schwartz, age 39, $169,803 pay
SVP and Principal Accounting Officer and Treasurer: Don Loverich, $155,385 pay
SVP, Business Development: William Mayes
SVP, Compliance and Corporate Counsel: Jeffrey D. Jeter, age 33, $124,935 pay
SVP, Human Resources: Cindy L Phillips
SVP, Marketing: Patty Graham
SVP, Finance and Acquisitions: Tom Dolan
Auditors: KPMG LLP

LOCATIONS

HQ: Amedisys, Inc.
   5959 S. Sherwood Forest Blvd.,
   Baton Rouge, LA 70816
Phone: 225-292-2031   **Fax:** 225-292-8163
Web: www.amedisys.com

PRODUCTS/OPERATIONS

2006 Sales

	% of total
Medicare	
Home health agencies	87
Hospice agencies	6
Non-Medicare	
Home health agencies	6
Hospice agencies	1
Total	**100**

Selected Services

Disease management
Home health aides
Infusion therapy
Occupation therapy
Pain management
Patient education
Physical therapy
Psychiatric services
Skilled nursing
Social services
Speech therapy
Wound management

COMPETITORS

Almost Family
Apria Healthcare
Coram
Gentiva
Girling Health Care
Home Health Corporation of America
Home Instead
National HealthCare
Option Care
Pediatric Services of America
Tender Loving Care
VITAS Healthcare

HISTORICAL FINANCIALS

Company Type: Public

Income Statement

FYE: December 31

	REVENUE ($ mil.)	NET INCOME ($ mil.)	NET PROFIT MARGIN	EMPLOYEES
12/06	541.2	38.3	7.1%	6,892
12/05	381.6	30.1	7.9%	6,206
12/04	227.1	20.5	9.0%	—
12/03	142.5	8.4	5.9%	—
12/02	129.4	0.8	0.6%	2,237
Annual Growth	**43.0%**	**163.0%**	**—**	**32.5%**

2006 Year-End Financials

Debt ratio: 1.9%
Return on equity: 13.8%
Cash ($ mil.): 89.0
Current ratio: 2.19
Long-term debt ($ mil.): 7.1
No. of shares (mil.): 25.8

Dividends
   Yield: —
   Payout: —
Market value ($ mil.): 848.0
R&D as % of sales: —
Advertising as % of sales: —

Stock History

NASDAQ (GS): AMED

	STOCK PRICE ($) FY Close	P/E High/Low		PER SHARE ($) Earnings	Dividends	Book Value
12/06	32.87	20	13	1.72	—	14.11
12/05	31.69	25	14	1.41	—	12.13
12/04	24.30	24	9	1.13	—	9.70
12/03	11.37	20	5	0.62	—	4.32
12/02	4.53	150	54	0.06	—	1.85
Annual Growth	**64.1%**	**—**	**—**	**131.4%**	**—**	**66.2%**

AMEN Properties

AMEN Properties' prayers are being answered with power. Subsidiary W Power, formed in 2004, provides retail electricity services in West Texas. W Power (a venture made possible when the state deregulated the wholesale electricity market) now accounts for the bulk of AMEN Properties' sales. Its Priority Power subsidiary (acquired in 2006) has current or previous business activities in 22 states including Texas. These activities include electricity load aggregation, natural gas and electricity procurement, energy risk management, and energy consulting. AMEN Properties' Amen Delaware subsidiary invests in commercial real estate in secondary markets; Amen Minerals invests in oil and gas royalties.

AMEN Properties once wanted to guide Web users to a spiritual life. The company previously operated one of the largest Christian-oriented Web portals in the US; in 2002 the company sold its Crosswalk.com site and e-mail business to Salem Communications for $4.1 million.

EXECUTIVES

Chairman: Eric L. Oliver, age 49
CEO and Director: Jon M. Morgan, age 49
COO: Kevin Yung
CFO: Kris Oliver
Auditors: Johnson, Miller & Co.

LOCATIONS

HQ: AMEN Properties, Inc.
303 W. Wall St., Ste. 2300, Midland, TX 79701
Phone: 432-684-3821   **Fax:** 432-685-3143
Web: amenproperties.com

PRODUCTS/OPERATIONS

2006 Sales

	$ mil.	% of total
Retail electric	10.5	69
Rental revenue	2.4	16
Energy management fees	2.2	15
Total	**15.1**	**100**

Selected Subsidiaries

Amen Delaware, L.P.
Amen Minerals, L.P. (gas and oil royalty interests)
NEMA Properties, LLC
Priority Power Management, Ltd.
W Power and Light, L.P. (retail electric provider)

COMPETITORS

AEP Texas North
Constellation NewEnergy
Direct Energy
Energy Future
Equity Office Properties
First Choice Power
Green Mountain Energy
Highwoods Properties
Reliant Energy
Sabine Royalty Trust
Strategic Energy

HISTORICAL FINANCIALS

Company Type: Public

Income Statement

FYE: December 31

	REVENUE ($ mil.)	NET INCOME ($ mil.)	NET PROFIT MARGIN	EMPLOYEES
12/06	15.1	2.2	14.6%	11
12/05	10.2	(0.7)	—	11
12/04	2.5	0.8	32.0%	—
12/03	4.3	0.4	9.3%	—
12/02	1.1	(2.2)	—	10
Annual Growth	**92.5%**	**—**	**—**	**2.4%**

2006 Year-End Financials

Debt ratio: 31.5%
Return on equity: 29.8%
Cash ($ mil.): 4.5
Current ratio: 3.41
Long-term debt ($ mil.): 2.7
No. of shares (mil.): 2.3
Dividends
 Yield: —
 Payout: —
Market value ($ mil.): 13.1
R&D as % of sales: —
Advertising as % of sales: —

Stock History

NASDAQ (CM): AMEN

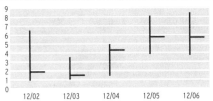

	STOCK PRICE ($) FY Close	P/E High/Low	PER SHARE ($) Earnings	Dividends	Book Value
12/06	5.71	15 7	0.56	—	3.77
12/05	5.75	— —	(0.32)	—	2.78
12/04	4.30	19 6	0.26	—	2.19
12/03	1.50	27 8	0.13	—	1.82
12/02	1.88	— —	(1.08)	—	1.64
Annual Growth	**32.0%**	**—**	**—**	**—**	**23.1%**

American Ecology

American Ecology and its US Ecology subsidiary help keep a lid on hazardous waste, industrial waste, and low-level radioactive waste. The company handles hazardous and nonhazardous waste at sites in Texas, Nevada, and Idaho, and it operates a low-level radioactive waste facility in Washington state. In 2006 Honeywell International and the US Army Corps of Engineers accounted for 38% and 27% of sales, respectively. Other customers include nuclear plants, steel mills, petrochemical facilities, and academic and medical institutions. American Ecology retains interests in several nonoperating waste disposal facilities.

The company sold its low-level radioactive waste processing facility in Oak Ridge, Tennessee in 2004.

EXECUTIVES

Chairman: Kenneth Ch'uan-k'ai (Ken) Leung, age 63
President, CEO, COO, and Director:
 Stephen A. Romano, age 53, $245,577 pay
CFO: Jeffrey R. (Jeff) Feeler, age 38
VP and CIO: John M. Cooper, age 53, $124,694 pay
VP Sales and Marketing: Steven D. (Steve) Welling, age 49, $128,750 pay
VP and General Manager, US Ecology (Washington):
 Thomas (Tom) Hayes
VP Hazardous Waste Operations: Simon G. Bell, age 36, $125,000 pay
Director, Marketing and External Affairs: Chad Hyslop
Director, Human Resources: Betsy Sterk
Auditors: Moss Adams, LLP

LOCATIONS

HQ: American Ecology Corporation
 300 E. Mallard Dr., Ste. 300, Boise, ID 83706
Phone: 208-331-8400   **Fax:** 208-331-7900
Web: www.americanecology.com

American Ecology has disposal facilities in Idaho, Nevada, Texas, and Washington.

PRODUCTS/OPERATIONS

Selected Subsidiaries

Texas Ecologists, inc.
US Ecology, Inc.
US Ecology Idaho, Inc.
US Ecology Nevada, Inc.
US Ecology Texas, L.P.
US Ecology Washington, Inc.

COMPETITORS

Clean Harbors
EnergySolutions
Heritage Environmental Services
Perma-Fix Environmental
Safety-Kleen
Shaw Group
Stericycle
Valhi
Waste Management

HISTORICAL FINANCIALS

Company Type: Public

Income Statement

FYE: December 31

	REVENUE ($ mil.)	NET INCOME ($ mil.)	NET PROFIT MARGIN	EMPLOYEES
12/06	116.8	15.9	13.6%	226
12/05	79.4	15.4	19.4%	214
12/04	54.2	23.4	43.2%	—
12/03	57.0	(8.6)	—	—
12/02	46.8	18.8	40.2%	199
Annual Growth	**25.7%**	**(4.1%)**	**—**	**3.2%**

2006 Year-End Financials

Debt ratio: 0.0%
Return on equity: 23.2%
Cash ($ mil.): 9.9
Current ratio: 2.33
Long-term debt ($ mil.): 0.0
No. of shares (mil.): 18.2
Dividends
 Yield: 0.8%
 Payout: 17.2%
Market value ($ mil.): 336.4
R&D as % of sales: —
Advertising as % of sales: —

Stock History

	STOCK PRICE ($) FY Close	P/E High/Low		PER SHARE ($) Earnings	Dividends	Book Value
12/06	18.51	32	16	0.87	0.15	4.04
12/05	14.43	23	12	0.86	0.45	3.60
12/04	11.97	10	5	1.32	—	2.96
12/03	8.20	—	—	(0.52)	—	2.13
12/02	2.79	4	1	1.15	—	3.16
Annual Growth	60.5%	—	—	(6.7%)	(66.7%)	6.3%

American Equity Investment Life

Seeking to save? American Equity Investment Life Holding Company issues and administers fixed rate, index, and variable annuities through subsidiaries American Equity Investment Life Insurance and American Equity Investment Life Insurance Company of New York. Licensed in 49 states and the District of Columbia, the company sells its products through more than 52,000 independent agents and 70 national marketing associations. American Equity Investment Life targets individuals between the ages of 45 to 75. The company also offers a variety of whole, term, and universal life insurance products.

The top five states bringing income to American Equity Investment Life's business together account for more than 35% of premiums.

In early 2008 American Equity Investment Life Insurance settled a class-action suit brought by the Minnesota State Attorney General. The suit alleged that the subsidiary had engaged in improper sales techniques, particularly with regard to senior citizens, including violation of a law requiring insurance companies to ensure that an annuity is appropriate for the person to whom it is sold. Without admitting any liability or acknowledging the lawsuit's validity, American Equity has agreed to accept and review claims for refunds on annuities sold to senior citizens using improper sales tactics.

EXECUTIVES

Chairman, President, CEO, and Treasurer; Chairman, American Equity Life: David J. (D.J.) Noble, age 75, $60,000 pay
Vice Chairman: John M. Matovina, age 52, $198,675 pay
President, American Equity Life and Director: Kevin R. Wingert, age 49, $265,105 pay
CFO and General Counsel American Equity Life: Wendy L. Carlson, age 46, $265,105 pay
SVP, Director and Secretary: Debra J. Richardson, age 50, $265,105 pay
VP Accounting: Ted M. Johnson
Auditors: KPMG LLP

LOCATIONS

HQ: American Equity Investment Life Holding Company
5000 Westown Pkwy., Ste. 440,
West Des Moines, IA 50266
Phone: 515-221-0002   **Fax:** 515-221-9947
Web: www.american-equity.com

PRODUCTS/OPERATIONS

2006 Sales

	$ mil.	% of total
Net investment income	677.6	74
Change in fair value of derivatives	183.8	20
Annuity & single premium universal life product charges	39.5	4
Traditional life, accident & health insurance premiums	13.6	2
Other	1.4	—
Total	**915.9**	**100**

COMPETITORS

AEGON USA	Lincoln Financial Group
AIG	MetLife
AIG Retirement Services	MetLife of Connecticut
Allianz Life	Midland National Life
Aviva	Nationwide
ERC	Northwestern Mutual
FBL Financial	OM Financial
The Hartford	Prudential
ING	Union Central
Kansas City Life	

HISTORICAL FINANCIALS
Company Type: Public

Income Statement
FYE: December 31

	ASSETS ($ mil.)	NET INCOME ($ mil.)	INCOME AS % OF ASSETS	EMPLOYEES
12/06	14,990.1	75.5	0.5%	280
12/05	14,042.8	43.0	0.3%	270
12/04	11,087.3	29.3	0.3%	—
12/03	8,989.2	25.4	0.3%	—
12/02	6,042.3	14.2	0.2%	—
Annual Growth	25.5%	51.8%	—	3.7%

2006 Year-End Financials

Equity as % of assets: 4.0%
Return on assets: 0.5%
Return on equity: 13.5%
Long-term debt ($ mil.): 534.9
No. of shares (mil.): 53.5
Market value ($ mil.): 697.1
Dividends
 Yield: 0.4%
 Payout: 3.9%
Sales ($ mil.): 915.9
R&D as % of sales: —
Advertising as % of sales: —

Stock History

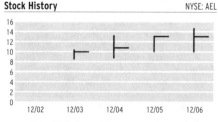

	STOCK PRICE ($) FY Close	P/E High/Low		PER SHARE ($) Earnings	Dividends	Book Value
12/06	13.03	11	8	1.27	0.05	11.12
12/05	13.05	13	10	0.99	0.04	9.35
12/04	10.77	19	12	0.71	0.02	7.96
12/03	9.97	9	7	1.21	0.01	7.47
Annual Growth	9.3%	—	—	12.2%	71.0%	20.0%

American Medical Alert

It's like having a guardian angel hovering above, but without the wings. With personal emergency response systems from American Medical Alert, the disabled, elderly, or infirm can press a button to speak to a dispatcher who will send help or contact relatives. The company also offers medication dispensing devices and online physician referrals, appointment confirmation, and lab results. Its products are sold to health care facilities and to consumers. In addition, American Medical Alert offers telephone-answering services for health professionals and security monitoring systems for pharmacies (SafeCom).

American Medical Alert operates call centers in the Northeast that support both its emergency response systems and its telephone-answering operations.

The company has a deal with Walgreen Co. to provide its personal emergency response systems under the Walgreen brand.

Chairman Howard Siegel owns about 12% of the company; investor Gregory Fortunoff owns about 8%.

EXECUTIVES

Chairman: Howard M. Siegel, age 73
President, CEO, and Director: Jack Rhian, age 52
CFO: Richard Rallo, age 43
EVP and Director: Frederic S. Siegel, age 37
SVP Marketing and Program Development: Randi Baldwin, age 38
VP Field Operations and Secretary: John Rogers, age 60
VP, MD On Call and Capitol Medical Bureau: Louis Shapiro
President, ACT Teleservices: Thomas Gelbach
President, North Shore Answering Service: Mel Roberts
Auditors: Margolin, Winer & Evens LLP

LOCATIONS

HQ: American Medical Alert Corp.
3265 Lawson Blvd., Oceanside, NY 11572
Phone: 516-536-5850   **Fax:** 516-536-5276
Web: www.amacalert.com

PRODUCTS/OPERATIONS

COMPETITORS

ADT Worldwide
Health Watch
Napco Security

HISTORICAL FINANCIALS
Company Type: Public

Income Statement
FYE: December 31

	REVENUE ($ mil.)	NET INCOME ($ mil.)	NET PROFIT MARGIN	EMPLOYEES
12/06	30.8	1.3	4.2%	531
12/05	22.5	0.9	4.0%	389
12/04	19.1	0.4	2.1%	—
12/03	16.6	0.6	3.6%	—
12/02	14.8	0.2	1.4%	194
Annual Growth	20.1%	59.7%	—	28.6%

2006 Year-End Financials

Debt ratio: 26.9%
Return on equity: 6.5%
Cash ($ mil.): 0.9
Current ratio: 1.79
Long-term debt ($ mil.): 5.8
No. of shares (mil.): 9.2
Dividends
 Yield: —
 Payout: —
Market value ($ mil.): 61.5
R&D as % of sales: 0.8%
Advertising as % of sales: —

Stock History

NASDAQ (CM): AMAC

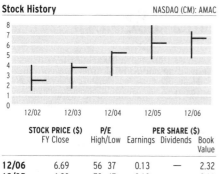

	STOCK PRICE ($) FY Close	P/E High/Low		PER SHARE ($) Earnings	Dividends	Book Value
12/06	6.69	56	37	0.13	—	2.32
12/05	6.20	79	47	0.10	—	2.11
12/04	5.22	107	60	0.05	—	1.90
12/03	3.75	59	24	0.07	—	1.78
12/02	2.46	197	74	0.02	—	1.69
Annual Growth	28.4%	—	—	59.7%	—	8.3%

American Pacific

American Pacific knows how to have a blast. The company's products launch rockets, propel missiles, deploy airbags, and suppress fires. Its largest unit also makes active pharmaceutical ingredients. American Pacific's specialty chemicals include ammonium perchlorate (AP), a rocket fuel oxidizer; sodium azide, an airbag deployment chemical also used in pharmaceuticals; and Halotron, an ozone-friendly fire suppressant. The company also makes commercial packaged explosives, aerospace propulsion equipment for satellites, and environmental protection products. American Pacific relies heavily on a few customers, with its five largest accounting for more than two-thirds of sales; Alliant Techsystems accounts for 15%.

The company is the only commercial producer of ammonium perchlorate in the US. Specialty chemicals used to account for nearly 80% of American Pacific's sales, with perchlorate chemicals alone accounting for about half. Other AP customers include commercial satellite launchers and contractors participating in NASA and Department of Defense programs.

The company has a 50% stake in Energetic Systems, a commercial packaged explosives producer. It acquired Atlantic Research, an in-space propulsion (ISP) business, from Aerojet-General (a subsidiary of GenCorp) in 2004. The following year, American Pacific purchased pharmaceutical ingredient manufacturer Aerojet Fine Chemicals from GenCorp. Atlantic Research is now named Ampac ISP, and Aerojet Fine Chemicals is named Ampac Fine Chemicals (AFC).

In its first full year with the business AFC quickly became American Pacific's largest segment. Its sales account for more than half of the company's total figure.

EXECUTIVES

Chairman and CEO: John R. Gibson, age 70
President, COO, and Director: Joseph (Joe) Carleone, age 60
VP, CFO, and Treasurer: Dana M. Kelley, age 44, $164,000 pay
VP and CTO: Jeffrey M. Gibson
VP Administration and Assistant Secretary: Linda G. Ferguson, age 65

VP Engineering: Dirk Venderink
VP Ampac-ISP Operations: Robert Huebner, age 54, $180,800 pay
Administrator, Investor Relations: Deanna Riccardi
President, Ampac Fine Chemicals: Aslam Malik, age 48, $437,688 pay
Auditors: Deloitte & Touche LLP

LOCATIONS

HQ: American Pacific Corporation
3770 Howard Hughes Pkwy., Ste. 300,
Las Vegas, NV 89169
Phone: 702-735-2200   **Fax:** 702-735-4876
Web: www.apfc.com

American Pacific operates manufacturing facilities in both the UK and the US.

PRODUCTS/OPERATIONS

2007 Sales

	$ mil.	% of total
Fine Chemicals	104.4	57
Specialty Chemicals	57.1	31
Aerospace Equipment	17.3	9
Other	5.1	3
Total	**183.9**	**100**

Selected Products

Fine chemicals (pharmaceutical ingredients; Ampac Fine Chemicals)
Specialty chemicals
  Ammonium perchlorate (oxidizing agent for solid fuel rockets; Western Electrochemical)
  Commercial explosives (Energetic Systems, 50%)
  Halotron (fire extinguisher; Halotron)
  Sodium azide (airbag chemical; American Azide Corporation)
Aerospace equipment (propulsion systems, thrusters, and propellant tanks; Ampac-ISP)
Other operations
  Environmental protection equipment (Pepcon Systems)
    ChlorMaster system (disinfects wastewater, brine and sea water)
    OdorMaster system (controls noxious odors)
  Real estate development (Ampac Development)

COMPETITORS

APi Group
Arch Chemicals
Austin Chemical
Cambrex
Daicel Chemical
DuPont
Evonik Degussa Corporation
Nippon Kayaku
Orica
SNPE

HISTORICAL FINANCIALS
Company Type: Public

Income Statement
FYE: September 30

	REVENUE ($ mil.)	NET INCOME ($ mil.)	NET PROFIT MARGIN	EMPLOYEES
9/07	183.9	5.0	2.7%	487
9/06	141.9	(3.9)	—	—
9/05	83.3	(9.7)	—	254
9/04	59.5	(0.4)	—	—
9/03	68.9	9.4	13.6%	—
Annual Growth	27.8%	(14.6%)	—	38.5%

2007 Year-End Financials

Debt ratio: 145.8%	Dividends
Return on equity: 6.8%	Yield: —
Cash ($ mil.): 21.4	Payout: —
Current ratio: 2.70	Market value ($ mil.): 116.0
Long-term debt ($ mil.): 110.4	R&D as % of sales: —
No. of shares (mil.): 7.4	Advertising as % of sales: —

Stock History

NASDAQ (GM): APFC

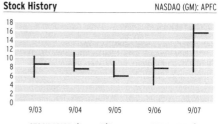

	STOCK PRICE ($) FY Close	P/E High/Low		PER SHARE ($) Earnings	Dividends	Book Value
9/07	15.62	26	10	0.67	—	10.19
9/06	7.66	—	—	(0.53)	—	9.81
9/05	5.92	—	—	(1.33)	—	10.23
9/04	7.47	—	—	(0.05)	0.42	11.63
9/03	8.48	8	4	1.27	—	11.71
Annual Growth	16.5%	—	—	(14.8%)	—	(3.4%)

American Public Education

American Public Education promotes military intelligence. The company offers online postsecondary educations to those in the military and public service sector through the American Military University and American Public University. Together these two schools make up the American Public University System which offers 50 degree programs and nearly as many certificate programs in such disciplines as business, criminal justice, intelligence, liberal arts, military studies, and national security. Enrollment consists of about 25,000 part-time students hailing from all 50 states and about 135 foreign countries, more than 80% of whom serve in the US military.

Most of the system's other students are public service professionals, including law enforcement personnel and other first responders.

American Public Education has an open enrollment system, accepting all applicants with a high school diploma or equivalent. Tuition is $250 per credit hour; tuition assistance programs offered by the US Armed Forces constitute more than two-thirds of the company's annual revenues.

The company is using funds from its 2007 IPO to pay a special stockholder distribution.

Director Timothy Weglicki owns about 42% of American Public Education through his affiliation with ABS Capital Partners.

EXECUTIVES

Chairman: Phillip A. (Phil) Clough, age 46
EVP and CFO: Harry T. Wilkins, age 51
President, CEO, and Director: Wallace E. Boston Jr., age 53

EVP and Provost: Frank B. McCluskey, age 58
SVP and Chief Administrative Officer:
 Peter W. Gibbons, age 54
SVP Marketing: Carol S. Gilbert, age 48
SVP and CIO: Marl L. Leuba, age 51
Auditors: McGladrey & Pullen, LLP

LOCATIONS

HQ: American Public Education, Inc.
 111 W. Congress St., Charles Town, WV 25414
Phone: 304-724-3700   **Fax:** 304-724-3780
Web: www.apus.edu

HISTORICAL FINANCIALS
Company Type: Public

Income Statement
FYE: December 31

	REVENUE ($ mil.)	NET INCOME ($ mil.)	NET PROFIT MARGIN	EMPLOYEES
12/06	40.0	2.5	6.3%	660
12/05	28.2	1.4	5.0%	—
12/04	23.1	2.3	10.0%	—
Annual Growth	**31.6%**	**4.3%**	**—**	**—**

2006 Year-End Financials

Debt ratio: 11.6%   Current ratio: 1.62
Return on equity: 16.0%   Long-term debt ($ mil.): 1.9
Cash ($ mil.): 11.7

Net Income History   NASDAQ (GM): APEI

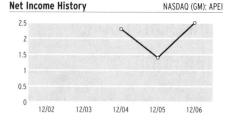

American Railcar Industries

American Railcar Industries doesn't make the little engine that could or the little red caboose — just the cars that go in between. The company is a leading manufacturer of covered hopper cars, used for dry bulk commodities, and tank cars, used for liquid and compressed bulk commodities. American Railcar Industries also makes railcar components and offers railcar maintenance and fleet management services. It operates two manufacturing facilities in Arkansas; manufacturing operations account for more than 90% of the company's sales. The company's main customers are railcar leasing companies, rail shippers, and railroads. Financier Carl Icahn controls about a 53% stake in American Railcar Industries.

Icahn also controls railcar lessors ACF Industries and American Railcar Leasing, the latter of which accounted for about 11% of American Railcar Industries' sales in 2006. Lessor CIT Group, which accounted for about 41% of sales in 2006, has agreed to buy at least 9,000 railcars from the company by the end of 2008.

American Railcar Industries moved to expand in 2006 when it bought Custom Steel, a subsidiary of Steel Technologies. Custom Steel makes fabricated parts that are used in American Railcar Industries' railcar manufacturing operations.

EXECUTIVES

Chairman: Carl C. Icahn, age 71
President, CEO, and Director: James J. Unger, age 59
EVP and COO: James A. (Jim) Cowan, age 49
SVP, CFO, and Treasurer: William P. Benac, age 61
SVP Sales, Marketing and Services: Alan C. Lullman, age 51
VP Engineering and Manufacturing:
 Michael R. Williams, age 45
Director Railcar Manufacturing: Jackie R. Pipkin, age 56
Auditors: Grant Thornton LLP

LOCATIONS

HQ: American Railcar Industries, Inc.
 100 Clark St., St. Charles, MO 63301
Phone: 636-940-6000   **Fax:** 636-940-6030
Web: www.americanrailcar.com

PRODUCTS/OPERATIONS

2006 Sales

	$ mil.	% of total
Manufacturing operations	597.9	93
Railcar services	48.1	7
Total	**646.0**	**100**

COMPETITORS

Greenbrier	Miner Enterprises
Meridian Rail Acquisition	Trinity Industries
Millennium Rail	Union Tank Car

HISTORICAL FINANCIALS
Company Type: Public

Income Statement
FYE: December 31

	REVENUE ($ mil.)	NET INCOME ($ mil.)	NET PROFIT MARGIN	EMPLOYEES
12/06	646.0	35.2	5.4%	2,575
12/05	608.2	14.8	2.4%	2,425
12/04	355.1	1.9	0.5%	2,372
12/03	218.0	1.1	0.5%	—
12/02	168.8	(3.9)	—	—
Annual Growth	**39.9%**	**—**	**—**	**4.2%**

2006 Year-End Financials

Debt ratio: 0.0%   Dividends
Return on equity: 25.6%   Yield: 0.3%
Cash ($ mil.): 40.9   Payout: 5.4%
Current ratio: 2.78   Market value ($ mil.): 721.9
Long-term debt ($ mil.): 0.0   R&D as % of sales: —
No. of shares (mil.): 21.2   Advertising as % of sales: —

Stock History   NASDAQ (GS): ARII

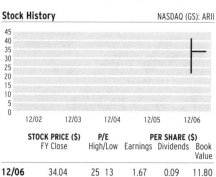

	STOCK PRICE ($) FY Close	P/E High/Low		PER SHARE ($) Earnings	Dividends	Book Value
12/06	34.04	25	13	1.67	0.09	11.80

Ameris Bancorp

Ameris Bancorp (formerly ABC Bancorp) is the holding company of Ameris, a community bank serving Alabama, Georgia, South Carolina, and northern Florida from 45 branch locations. Ameris offers standard deposit products and services, including checking and savings accounts, money market accounts, and NOW accounts; it also provides credit card, trust, and brokerage services. Commercial mortgages make up about 30% of its loan portfolio, which also includes residential mortgages (about 25%) and business loans (about 10%).

Previously organized under about a dozen separate charters, Ameris Bancorp combined its subsidiaries into a single entity in 2005. Heritage Community Bank in Brooks County, Georgia; Merchants & Farmers Bank in Seminole County, Georgia; and Tri-County Bank in Gilchrist County, Florida, were among the banking subsidiaries that were merged into Ameris.

The company expanded into Florida's Wakulla County in 2004 with its acquisition of Citizens Bancshares, Inc., and acquired First National Banc, which has five branches in Florida and Georgia, in 2005.

The bank moved into South Carolina in 2007 with the acquisition of Islands Bancorp.

EXECUTIVES

Chairman: Kenneth J. (Jack) Hunnicutt, age 70
President, CEO, and Director:
 Edwin W. (Ed) Hortman Jr., age 54, $604,867 pay
EVP and Director of Credit Administration:
 Jon S. Edwards, age 45, $239,622 pay
EVP and CFO: Dennis J. Zember Jr., age 37, $336,500 pay
EVP, Chief Administrative Officer, and Corporate Secretary: Cindi H. Lewis, age 53
EVP and South Regional Executive: Johnny R. Myers, age 57, $232,050 pay
SVP and Director of Automation and Operations: Marc E. DeMott
SVP and Director of Internal Audit:
 Charles A. Robinson
SVP and Director of Retail Banking:
 Michael F. McDonald
SVP and CIO: Gregory H. Walls
Auditors: Mauldin & Jenkins, LLC

LOCATIONS

HQ: Ameris Bancorp
 24 2nd Ave. SE, Moultrie, GA 31768
Phone: 229-890-1111   **Fax:** 229-890-2235
Web: www.amerisbank.com

PRODUCTS/OPERATIONS

2006 Sales

	$ mil.	% of total
Interest		
Loans	107.6	75
Securities	12.7	9
Other	3.9	3
Noninterest		
Service charges on deposit accounts	11.5	8
Mortgage origination fees	2.2	1
Other service charges, commissions & fees	1.0	1
Other	4.8	3
Total	**143.7**	**100**

COMPETITORS

Bank of America
Capital City Bank
Colonial BancGroup
Colony Bankcorp
Community Capital
Compass Bancshares
First South Bancorp (NC)

PAB Bankshares
Regions Financial
Southwest Georgia
 Financial
SunTrust
Thomasville Bancshares
Wachovia

HISTORICAL FINANCIALS
Company Type: Public

Income Statement — FYE: December 31

	ASSETS ($ mil.)	NET INCOME ($ mil.)	INCOME AS % OF ASSETS	EMPLOYEES
12/06	2,047.5	22.1	1.1%	600
12/05	1,697.2	13.7	0.8%	585
12/04	1,268.0	13.1	1.0%	—
12/03	1,168.0	12.0	1.0%	—
12/02	1,192.5	10.4	0.9%	500
Annual Growth	14.5%	20.7%	—	4.7%

2006 Year-End Financials

Equity as % of assets: 8.7%
Return on assets: 1.2%
Return on equity: 13.5%
Long-term debt ($ mil.): 117.8
No. of shares (mil.): 13.5
Market value ($ mil.): 381.2

Dividends
 Yield: 2.0%
 Payout: 33.3%
Sales ($ mil.): 143.7
R&D as % of sales: —
Advertising as % of sales: —

Stock History
NASDAQ (GS): ABCB

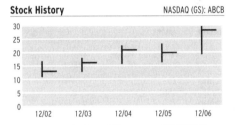

	STOCK PRICE ($) FY Close	P/E High/Low	PER SHARE ($) Earnings	Dividends	Book Value
12/06	28.18	17 12	1.68	0.56	13.21
12/05	19.84	20 14	1.14	1.48	11.48
12/04	20.91	20 14	1.11	0.42	10.28
12/03	16.10	17 13	1.02	0.52	11.61
12/02	12.95	19 13	0.88	0.48	11.00
Annual Growth	21.5%	— —	17.5%	3.9%	4.7%

Amtech Systems

Amtech Systems furnishes fabs with furnaces and more. The company's Tempress Systems subsidiary makes diffusion furnaces for semiconductor fabrication and for precision thermal processing — including annealing, brazing, silvering, sealing, and soldering — of electronic devices, including optical components and solar cells. Its P.R. Hoffman Machine Products subsidiary makes equipment used to polish such items as silicon wafers, precision optics, ceramic components, and disk media. Amtech Systems gets about half of its sales from the Asia/Pacific region, primarily from China and Taiwan.

Amtech was one of the first suppliers of semiconductor production equipment to provide equipment for making photovoltaic solar cells, which are mainly fabricated in a process similar to semiconductor manufacturing on silicon wafers. The company has been supplying Tempress diffusion furnaces for solar-cell manufacturing since the early 21st century, a move that has since been emulated by Applied Materials and other big vendors of semiconductor equipment. Business in this segment doubled for Amtech from 2005 to 2006 and nearly quintupled from 2006 to 2007, to more than one-quarter of sales.

In late 2007 the company acquired R2D Ingenierie, a French supplier of automation equipment for making semiconductors and solar cells. Amtech paid about $6 million to buy R2D and provided a working capital infusion of $1 million. R2D Ingenierie posted 2006 sales of nearly $5 million, with operating income of around $800,000.

Amtech's other products include the Atmoscan, a controlled environment system that loads silicon wafers into diffusion furnaces, and systems for handling and storing wafers during the manufacturing process.

In 2004 the company acquired the Bruce Technology Inc. (BTI) unit of Japan-based Kokusai Semiconductor Equipment Corporation for about $4 million, expanding its line of horizontal diffusion furnaces. Amtech, which also purchased rights to the brand name, operates the businesses under the Bruce Technologies moniker.

AWM Investment owns about 12% of Amtech Systems. Tontine Capital Partners holds 10% of the company.

EXECUTIVES

Chairman, President, and CEO: Jong S. Whang, age 62, $275,361 pay
VP Finance, CFO, Treasurer, and Secretary: Bradley C. Anderson, age 46, $91,015 pay (partial-year salary)
Chief Accounting Officer: Robert T. Hass, age 57, $116,885 pay
General Manager, P. R. Hoffman Machine Products: John Albright
General Manager, Tempress Systems: Fokko Pentinga
Director Human Resources: Katherine Burgess
Auditors: Mayer Hoffman McCann P.C.

LOCATIONS

HQ: Amtech Systems, Inc.
131 S. Clark Dr., Tempe, AZ 85281
Phone: 480-967-5146   **Fax:** 480-968-3763
Web: www.amtechsystems.com

Amtech Systems has operations in Arizona, Massachusetts, and Pennsylvania, and in the Netherlands.

2007 Sales

	% of total
Asia/Pacific	52
North America	28
Europe	20
Total	**100**

PRODUCTS/OPERATIONS

2007 Sales

	$ mil.	% of total
Semiconductor & solar equipment	37.7	82
Polishing supplies	8.3	18
Total	**46.0**	**100**

Products

Atmoscan (controlled-environment wafer processing systems)
Diffusion furnaces (horizontal and conveyor diffusion furnace systems)
Double-sided precision lapping and polishing machines
 Carriers
 Plates, gears, and other parts
 Polishing templates
Individual boats with automated loading (IBAL) systems and modules
 IBAL Butler (wafer transferring device)
 IBAL Queue (staging area and automated boat loading)
 IBAL Trolley (automatic boat placement, used with Atmoscan)
Load stations (mounting for IBAL systems or diffusion furnaces)

COMPETITORS

Applied Materials
ASML
Asyst Technologies
Aviza Technology
Brooks Automation
CVD Equipment
Entegris
ESEC
GT Solar
Jenoptik

Koyo Lindberg
Mattson Technology
MRL Industries
Novellus
OTB Group
Rohm and Haas
Singulus
Tokyo Electron
Ultratech

HISTORICAL FINANCIALS
Company Type: Public

Income Statement — FYE: September 30

	REVENUE ($ mil.)	NET INCOME ($ mil.)	NET PROFIT MARGIN	EMPLOYEES
9/07	46.0	2.4	5.2%	165
9/06	40.4	1.3	3.2%	153
9/05	27.9	(0.3)	—	144
9/04	19.3	(3.2)	—	132
9/03	19.4	(0.1)	—	106
Annual Growth	24.1%	—	—	11.7%

2007 Year-End Financials

Debt ratio: —
Return on equity: 8.9%
Cash ($ mil.): 18.8
Current ratio: 3.60
Long-term debt ($ mil.): —
No. of shares (mil.): 6.5

Dividends
 Yield: —
 Payout: —
Market value ($ mil.): 83.6
R&D as % of sales: —
Advertising as % of sales: —

Stock History
NASDAQ (GM): ASYS

	STOCK PRICE ($) FY Close	P/E High/Low	PER SHARE ($) Earnings	Dividends	Book Value
9/07	12.82	32 14	0.44	—	5.86
9/06	6.65	27 14	0.38	—	4.49
9/05	5.75	— —	(0.12)	—	4.87
9/04	4.28	— —	(1.17)	—	4.31
9/03	5.20	— —	(0.04)	—	5.37
Annual Growth	25.3%	— —	—	—	2.2%

Angeion Corporation

Angeion Corporation didn't have the heart to continue making implantable cardioverter defibrillators (ICDs). It sold all its licenses to patents and its intellectual property rights relating to ICDs. Angeion now focuses on designing products that diagnose heart and lung disease through its Medical Graphics subsidiary. Products include testing systems for asthma and emphysema, as well as cardiopulmonary exercise systems. Its Personal Digital Coach is an exercise device that provides verbal feedback to the user. Angeion's products are sold under the MedGraphics and New Leaf brand names.

EXECUTIVES

Chairman; CEO and President, Northcott Hospitality International: Arnold A. Angeloni, age 65
President, CEO, and Director: Rodney A. Young, age 52, $538,942 pay
CFO: Dale H. Johnson, age 63, $219,194 pay
Auditors: KPMG LLP

LOCATIONS

HQ: Angeion Corporation
  350 Oak Grove Pkwy., St. Paul, MN 55127
Phone: 651-484-4874   **Fax:** 651-379-8227
Web: www.angeion.com

2007 Sales

	$ mil.	% of total
US	29.0	75
Other countries	9.6	25
Total	**38.6**	**100**

COMPETITORS

Axis-Shield
Cambridge Heart
Cardinal Health
Cybex International
diaDexus
Jenny Craig
Thermo Fisher Scientific
Weight Watchers

HISTORICAL FINANCIALS

Company Type: Public

Income Statement   FYE: October 31

	REVENUE ($ mil.)	NET INCOME ($ mil.)	NET PROFIT MARGIN	EMPLOYEES
10/07	38.6	1.1	2.8%	140
10/06	33.7	1.4	4.2%	155
10/05	23.8	(0.9)	—	127
10/04	20.7	(2.3)	—	—
10/03	18.7	(2.8)	—	—
Annual Growth	**19.9%**	**—**	**—**	**5.0%**

2007 Year-End Financials

Debt ratio: —
Return on equity: 6.9%
Cash ($ mil.): 6.9
Current ratio: 3.23
Long-term debt ($ mil.): —
No. of shares (mil.): 4.1
Dividends
  Yield: —
  Payout: —
Market value ($ mil.): 32.1
R&D as % of sales: —
Advertising as % of sales: —

Stock History   NASDAQ (CM): ANGN

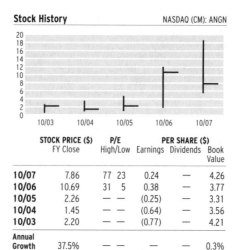

	STOCK PRICE ($) FY Close	P/E High/Low		PER SHARE ($) Earnings	Dividends	Book Value
10/07	7.86	77	23	0.24	—	4.26
10/06	10.69	31	5	0.38	—	3.77
10/05	2.26	—	—	(0.25)	—	3.31
10/04	1.45	—	—	(0.64)	—	3.56
10/03	2.20	—	—	(0.77)	—	4.21
Annual Growth	**37.5%**	**—**	**—**	**—**	**—**	**0.3%**

ANSYS, Inc.

ANSYS helps design engineers around the world hook up and get physical. With the company's software, developers and engineers can create computerized models of their designs and analyze the models' responses to combinations of such physical variables as stress, pressure, impact, temperature, and velocity. The company also offers related services, such as customization, implementation, support, and maintenance. Customers have included Boeing, Cummins, and Motorola. ANSYS sells its products through independent distributors in about 40 countries.

In early 2005 the company purchased Century Dynamics, a provider of CFD software and services, for about $5 million in cash.

The company acquired Aavid Thermal Technologies in 2006 for about $565 million in cash and stock, and kept Aavid's Fluent software business following the transaction.

EXECUTIVES

Chairman: Peter J. Smith, age 62
President, CEO, and Director:
  James E. (Jim) Cashman III, age 53, $1,087,106 pay
VP Finance and Administration and CFO:
  Maria T. Shields, age 42, $346,630 pay
VP, General Counsel, and Secretary: Sheila S. DiNardo
VP; General Manager, Fluids Business Unit:
  Hasan Ferit Boysan, age 59
VP Marketing: J. Christopher (Chris) Reid, age 52, $460,525 pay
VP Sales and Support: Joseph C. (Joe) Fairbanks Jr., age 52, $401,480 pay
Chief Technologist: Joseph S. (Joe) Solecki
Treasurer and Investor Relations: Lisa M. O'Connor
VP Human Resources: Elaine Keim
Auditors: Deloitte & Touche LLP

LOCATIONS

HQ: ANSYS, Inc.
  275 Technology Dr., Canonsburg, PA 15317
Phone: 724-746-3304   **Fax:** 724-514-9494
Web: www.ansys.com

PRODUCTS/OPERATIONS

Selected Software

Customer- and industry-specific engineering simulation (AI*Solutions)
Design simulation and virtual prototyping (ANSYS Software Suite)
Geometry-integrated mesh generation and post-processing tools (ICEM CFD Suite)
Product simulation (DesignSpace Software Suite)

Selected Services

Customization
Implementation
Integration
Training

COMPETITORS

Altair Engineering	Moldflow
Ansoft	MSC.Software
Autodesk	Parametric Technology
Bentley Systems	SIMULIA
Cadence Design	SofTech
Cimatron	SolidWorks
Dassault	think3
Delcam	UGS PLM Software
FARO Technologies	Vero International
Kubotek USA	Software
MathWorks	Z Corp
Mentor Graphics	

HISTORICAL FINANCIALS

Company Type: Public

Income Statement   FYE: December 31

	REVENUE ($ mil.)	NET INCOME ($ mil.)	NET PROFIT MARGIN	EMPLOYEES
12/06	263.6	14.2	5.4%	1,400
12/05	158.0	43.9	27.8%	600
12/04	134.5	34.6	25.7%	550
12/03	113.5	21.3	18.8%	—
12/02	91.0	19.0	20.9%	470
Annual Growth	**30.5%**	**(7.0%)**	**—**	**31.4%**

2006 Year-End Financials

Debt ratio: 20.5%
Return on equity: 3.7%
Cash ($ mil.): 104.5
Current ratio: 1.20
Long-term debt ($ mil.): 109.4
No. of shares (mil.): 38.6
Dividends
  Yield: —
  Payout: —
Market value ($ mil.): 839.2
R&D as % of sales: —
Advertising as % of sales: —

Stock History   NASDAQ (GS): ANSS

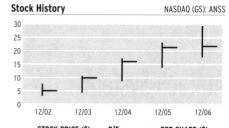

	STOCK PRICE ($) FY Close	P/E High/Low		PER SHARE ($) Earnings	Dividends	Book Value
12/06	21.75	157	97	0.19	—	13.86
12/05	21.34	35	22	0.65	—	6.97
12/04	16.03	32	17	0.52	—	5.59
12/03	9.93	31	14	0.34	—	8.32
12/02	5.05	24	11	0.31	—	6.27
Annual Growth	**44.1%**	**—**	**—**	**(11.5%)**	**—**	**21.9%**

Appalachian Bancshares

Appalachian Bancshares doesn't make mountains out of molehills, but it does make money at banking. The holding company owns Appalachian Community Bank, which serves several north Georgia counties, as well as nearby areas in North Carolina and Tennessee, from about a dozen locations. The bank, which operates as Gilmer County Bank in some locations, offers such products and services as checking and savings accounts, credit and debit cards, money market accounts, and loans. The company's lending activities are focused on real estate; construction loans make up about half of the portfolio and other real estate loans contribute nearly 40%. The bank also originates business loans and consumer loans.

Appalachian Bancshares also in 2007 launched a thrift (Appalachian Community Bank, F.S.B.) and converted former loan offices in North Carolina and Tennessee loan offices to banking offices under the thrift's charter.

EXECUTIVES

Chairman: J. Ronald Knight, age 64
Vice Chairman: Charles A. Edmondson, age 59
President, CEO and Director; CEO and President, Appalachian Community Bank: Tracy R. Newton, age 51, $321,097 pay
EVP and COO: J. Keith Hales, age 49
EVP and CFO: Danny F. Dukes, age 47
Secretary and Director: Joseph C. Hensley, age 49
Investor Relations: Cathy Hillebert
Media Relations: Cathy Murphy
Auditors: Mauldin & Jenkins, LLC

LOCATIONS

HQ: Appalachian Bancshares, Inc.
822 Industrial Blvd., Ellijay, GA 30540
Phone: 706-276-8000   **Fax:** 706-276-8010
Web: www.appalachianbank.com

Appalachian Bancshares has operations in Georgia's Dawson, Fannin, Gilmer, Murray, and Union counties; in North Carolina's Cherokee County, and in Tennessee's Polk County.

PRODUCTS/OPERATIONS

2006 Sales

	$ mil.	% of total
Interest		
Loans	49.9	87
Securities & other	3.4	6
Customer service fees	1.6	3
Mortgage origination commissions	1.3	2
Other	1.0	2
Total	**57.2**	**100**

COMPETITORS

BB&T
Chestatee Bancshares
Cornerstone Bancshares
Regions Financial
United Community Banks

HISTORICAL FINANCIALS

Company Type: Public

Income Statement

FYE: December 31

	ASSETS ($ mil.)	NET INCOME ($ mil.)	INCOME AS % OF ASSETS	EMPLOYEES
12/06	758.2	6.0	0.8%	262
12/05	592.6	5.1	0.9%	157
12/04	472.8	4.1	0.9%	—
Annual Growth	26.6%	21.0%	—	66.9%

2006 Year-End Financials

Equity as % of assets: 8.8%
Return on assets: 0.9%
Return on equity: 9.5%
Long-term debt ($ mil.): 6.2
No. of shares (mil.): 5.2
Market value ($ mil.): 100.2
Dividends
 Yield: —
 Payout: —
Sales ($ mil.): 57.2
R&D as % of sales: —
Advertising as % of sales: —

Stock History

NASDAQ (GM): APAB

	STOCK PRICE ($) FY Close	P/E High/Low		PER SHARE ($) Earnings	Dividends	Book Value
12/06	19.25	21	15	1.14	—	12.83
12/05	18.11	15	13	1.21	—	11.62
Annual Growth	6.3%	—	—	(5.8%)	—	10.4%

Approach Resources

Approach Resources takes a different approach to natural gas and oil exploration, development, and production. Specializing in finding and exploiting unconventional reservoirs, the company operates primarily in West Texas' Ozona Northeast field, while developing its operations in Western Kentucky and Northern New Mexico. The company's unconventional designation results from a focus on developing natural gas reserves in tight gas sands and shale areas, necessitating a reliance on advanced completion, fracturing, and drilling techniques. Approach Resources has proved reserves of approximately 149 billion cu. ft. of oil equivalent, with a reserve life index of about 19 years.

All of the company's proved reserves and production have so far been limited to its West Texas operations and consists primarily of natural gas. The company has one key customer, Ozona Pipeline Energy Company that accounts for almost 90% of sales. Yorktown Energy Partners controls the company.

EXECUTIVES

Chairman: Bryan H. Lawrence, age 65
President, CEO, and Director: J. Ross Craft, age 50
EVP and General Counsel: J. Curtis Henderson, age 44
EVP and CFO: Steven P. Smart, age 52
SVP Operations: Glenn W. Reed, age 55
SVP Land: Ralph P. Manoushagian, age 56

LOCATIONS

HQ: Approach Resources Inc.
6300 Ridglea Place, Ste. 1107,
Fort Worth, TX 76116
Phone: 817-989-9000   **Fax:** 817-989-9001

Areas of Operation

West Texas
 Ozona Northeast field (Canyon Sands)
 Cinco Terry project (Wolfcamp, and Canyon Sands, and Ellenburger)
Western Kentucky
 Boomerang prospect(New Albany Shale)
Northern New Mexico
 El Vado East prospect (Mancos Shale)

COMPETITORS

Anadarko Petroleum
Ascent Energy
Chesapeake Energy
Parallel Petroleum
Quicksilver Resources

HISTORICAL FINANCIALS

Company Type: Public

Income Statement

FYE: December 31

	REVENUE ($ mil.)	NET INCOME ($ mil.)	NET PROFIT MARGIN	EMPLOYEES
12/06	46.7	21.2	45.4%	16
12/05	43.3	12.1	27.9%	—
12/04	5.7	(0.3)	—	—
Annual Growth	186.2%	—	—	—

2006 Year-End Financials

Debt ratio: 68.4%
Return on equity: 38.8%
Cash ($ mil.): 4.9
Current ratio: 1.17
Long-term debt ($ mil.): 47.6

Net Income History

NASDAQ (GM): AREX

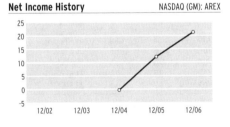

Arena Resources

Independent energy company Arena Resources battles with the big boys in the arena of oil and gas exploration and production. The company operates in Kansas, New Mexico, Oklahoma, and Texas, and has proved reserves of 43.1 million barrels of oil equivalent. Its assets in Oklahoma and Texas account for the bulk of the company's proved reserves. Arena Resources had an average daily production of 3,700 barrels of oil equivalent in 2004. Navajo Refining accounted for 82% of the company's revenues in 2006. The company purchased a second drilling rig in 2007. President and CEO Lloyd Rochford holds a 7% stake in Arena Resources.

Arena Resources was founded in 2000. The exploration and production independent drilled its first successful well (in Oklahoma) in 2001. It expanded its operations that year by acquiring assets in Texas. In 2005 the company acquired the Parrish Lease located in Andrews County, Texas for a price of $1.2 million. The deal added 945,000 barrels of oil equivalent to Arena Resources' proved reserves.

In 2007 the company acquired two oil and gas properties in Texas for $49 million.

EXECUTIVES

Chairman and Secretary: Stanley M. McCabe, age 75
CEO: Lloyd T. (Tim) Rochford, age 61
President and COO: Phillip (Phil) Terry, age 59
VP and CFO: William Randall (Randy) Broaddrick, age 27, $55,667 pay
VP Operations: David D. Ricks
VP and Manager, Investor Relations: William (Bill) Parsons, age 58
VP Land Department: Thomas W. Wahl
VP Geology and Exploration: Patric R. McConn
Auditors: Hansen, Barnett & Maxwell

LOCATIONS

HQ: Arena Resources, Inc.
4290 S. Lewis Ave., Ste. 107, Tulsa, OK 74105
Phone: 918-747-6060 **Fax:** 918-747-7620
Web: www.arenaresourcesinc.com

COMPETITORS

Anadarko Petroleum
Apache
Cabot Oil & Gas
Chesapeake Energy
Key Energy
Pioneer Natural Resources

HISTORICAL FINANCIALS

Company Type: Public

Income Statement
FYE: December 31

	REVENUE ($ mil.)	NET INCOME ($ mil.)	NET PROFIT MARGIN	EMPLOYEES
12/06	59.8	23.3	39.0%	52
12/05	25.8	9.5	36.8%	22
12/04	8.5	2.5	29.4%	—
12/03	3.7	0.8	21.6%	—
12/02	1.7	0.4	23.5%	5
Annual Growth	143.5%	176.3%	—	79.6%

2006 Year-End Financials
Debt ratio: 16.4%
Return on equity: 26.1%
Cash ($ mil.): 4.9
Current ratio: 0.98
Long-term debt ($ mil.): 19.7
No. of shares (mil.): 14.7
Dividends
  Yield: —
  Payout: —
Market value ($ mil.): 313.3
R&D as % of sales: —
Advertising as % of sales: —

Stock History
NYSE: ARD

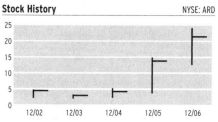

	STOCK PRICE ($) FY Close	P/E High/Low		PER SHARE ($) Earnings	Dividends	Book Value
12/06	21.35	31	17	0.77	—	8.18
12/05	13.80	39	11	0.38	—	4.48
12/04	4.25	34	17	0.15	—	2.28
12/03	3.03	56	41	0.05	—	1.13
12/02	4.50	—	—	(0.05)	—	0.82
Annual Growth	47.6%	—	—	—	—	78.0%

Arrhythmia Research Technology

It's all about heart for Arrhythmia Research Technology (ART). The company offers signal-averaging electrocardiographic (SAECG) software that collects data and analyzes electrical impulses of the heart in an effort to detect potentially lethal heart arrhythmias. The company plans to sell the products through licensing agreements with equipment makers. Until it finds a marketing partner, however, ART is relying on sales from its Micron Products subsidiary, which makes snaps and sensors used in the manufacture and operation of disposable electrodes for electrocardiographic (ECG) equipment. Micron Products has acquired assets of several companies that enhance its metal and plastics molding capabilities.

EXECUTIVES

Chairman: E. P. Marinos, age 66
President, CEO, and Director: James E. Rouse, age 53, $187,100 pay
EVP Finance and CFO: David A. Garrison, age 39, $125,000 pay
COO Micron Products, Inc: Michael F. Nolan
Auditors: Carlin, Charron & Rosen LLP

LOCATIONS

HQ: Arrhythmia Research Technology, Inc.
25 Sawyer Passway, Fitchburg, MA 01420
Phone: 978-345-5000 **Fax:** 978-342-0168
Web: www.arthrt.com

2006 Sales

	$ mil.	% of total
US	9.3	48
Canada	5.8	30
Europe	3.4	18
Pacific Rim	0.4	2
Other	0.4	2
Total	19.3	100

PRODUCTS/OPERATIONS

2006 Sales

	$ mil.	% of total
Sensors	10.8	56
Other molded products	6.9	36
Snaps & snap machines	0.5	3
Other products	1.1	5
Total	19.3	100

COMPETITORS

Criticare
Merit Medical Systems
Spacelabs Healthcare

HISTORICAL FINANCIALS

Company Type: Public

Income Statement
FYE: December 31

	REVENUE ($ mil.)	NET INCOME ($ mil.)	NET PROFIT MARGIN	EMPLOYEES
12/06	19.3	2.2	11.4%	100
12/05	12.9	1.6	12.4%	75
12/04	11.1	1.6	14.4%	—
12/03	7.7	1.3	16.9%	—
12/02	7.2	0.8	11.1%	46
Annual Growth	28.0%	28.8%	—	21.4%

2006 Year-End Financials
Debt ratio: —
Return on equity: 16.6%
Cash ($ mil.): 2.5
Current ratio: 4.58
Long-term debt ($ mil.): —
No. of shares (mil.): 2.7
Dividends
  Yield: 0.2%
  Payout: 7.5%
Market value ($ mil.): 65.8
R&D as % of sales: 0.3%
Advertising as % of sales: —

Stock History
AMEX: HRT

	STOCK PRICE ($) FY Close	P/E High/Low		PER SHARE ($) Earnings	Dividends	Book Value
12/06	24.33	38	10	0.80	0.06	5.33
12/05	8.80	38	15	0.59	0.12	4.51
12/04	21.09	80	12	0.60	0.11	3.96
12/03	31.43	85	5	0.48	0.05	3.37
12/02	2.55	13	9	0.26	—	2.95
Annual Growth	75.8%	—	—	32.4%	6.3%	16.0%

ARRIS Group

ARRIS brings the idea of broadband home. The company makes communications equipment and components used to enable voice and data transmission in high-speed networks and to build television broadcast networks. ARRIS' products include cable network headend gear, IP switching systems, modems and other consumer premises products, and associated software. The company also sells such related hardware as cable, connectors, and other supplies used for mounting and installation. ARRIS primarily serves cable operators; other clients include local and long distance carriers.

ARRIS's largest customers — Comcast, Cox Communications, Liberty Media, and Time Warner Cable — collectively account for more than 65% of the company's sales.

After a failed bid to acquire TANDBERG Television, ARRIS purchased network distribution equipment maker C-COR for $730 million in 2007. After the acquisition ARRIS announced a new organizational structure that includes three units: Broadband Communications Group; Access, Transport, and Supplies Group; and Media and Communications Systems Group.

HISTORY

Formed as a division of Anixter Bros. (now Anixter International) in 1969, ANTEC became a wholly owned subsidiary of that company in 1993 and went public later that year. The company made several strategic acquisitions in 1994, including broadband consulting company Electronic System Products, broadband power supply manufacturer Power Guard, and telecommunications equipment maker Keptel.

In 1995 ANTEC and Northern Telecom (now Nortel Networks) created a joint venture called Arris Interactive to sell voice and Internet access equipment to cable operators. ANTEC also opened a research and development facility near Atlanta that year.

When cable giant — and major customer — TCI stopped its capital spending in 1996, ANTEC's sales and profits suffered into the next year. The company in 1997 acquired optical node and distribution amplifier maker TSX. The next year Anixter sold its stake in the company.

In 1999 Nortel's broadband operations (formerly LANcity) became part of Arris Interactive, reducing ANTEC's stake in the joint venture from 25% to 19%. That year the company moved its headquarters from Illinois to Georgia.

In early 2000 John Egan, who had joined ANTEC in 1973 and served as CEO since 1980, passed the torch on to president and COO Robert Stanzione; Egan remained chairman. Later that year the company laid off workers when AT&T Broadband, its largest customer, began canceling orders.

Amid continued slowing sales of telecom gear the company announced in 2001 that it would continue cutting staff. Also that year ANTEC increased its stake in Arris Interactive, from 19% to 51%. ANTEC effectively became a subsidiary of the combined company, which changed its name to ARRIS Group. The company bought privately held cable modem termination system maker Cadant in 2002, and network traffic flow specialist Atoga in 2003. The company also bought assets of cable modem termination systems maker Com21 and sold its engineering services product line in 2003.

Early in 2007 ARRIS reached an agreement to acquire TANDBERG Television for about $1.2 billion, but it was eventually outbid by Ericsson for the company.

EXECUTIVES

Chairman and CEO: Robert J. (Bob) Stanzione, age 60, $1,800,000 pay
EVP, CFO, and CIO: David B. (Dave) Potts, age 51, $509,500 pay
EVP Strategic Planning and Administration, Chief Counsel, and Secretary: Lawrence A. (Larry) Margolis, age 60, $765,550 pay
SVP, Asia Sales: George Fletcher
SVP, Sales Engineering: Richard Rommes
SVP, International Sales: Claudio Cerioli
VP and Treasurer: Marc S. Geraci, age 53
VP and Controller: Daniel G. Owens, age 36
President, Broadband: James D. Lakin, age 65, $524,323 pay
President, New Business Ventures: Bryant K. Isaacs, age 47
President, TeleWire Supply: Robert (Bob) Puccini, age 45
President, Worldwide Sales: Ronald M. (Ron) Coppock, age 54, $449,050 pay
Investor Relations Contact: James A. Bauer
Auditors: Ernst & Young LLP

LOCATIONS

HQ: ARRIS Group, Inc.
3871 Lakefield Dr., Suwanee, GA 30024
Phone: 770-622-8400   **Fax:** 770-622-8770
Web: www.arrisi.com

2006 Sales

	$ mil.	% of total
North America		
US	668.1	75
Canada	53.9	6
Europe	75.0	8
Asia/Pacific	52.8	6
Latin America	41.7	5
Total	**891.5**	**100**

PRODUCTS/OPERATIONS

2006 Sales

	$ mil.	% of total
Customer premise equipment & supplies	527.3	59
Broadband	364.2	41
Total	**891.5**	**100**

Selected Products and Services

Broadband
Headend equipment
    Constant bit rate host digital terminals (Cornerstone Voice)
    Voice over IP and data cable modem termination systems (Cornerstone Cadant)
Subscriber premises
    Cable modems (Touchstone)
    Network interface units (Voice Port)
    Services (systems integration and operations center design, installation, activation, and traffic planning)
Optical transmission
    Amplifiers
    Block converters
    DWDM transport systems (Transplex)
    Element management software
    Receivers (Laser Link)
    Routers (Optical Application Routers)
    Transmitters (Laser Link)
Interconnectivity
    Connectors (Digicon)
    Demarcation housings
    Optical entrance enclosures
    Outside plant fiber optics
    Splice closures (LightGuard)
    Transmission equipment
Supplies
    Conduit
    Galvanized steel cables and strand
    Pedestals
    Power protection materials
    Test equipment
    Tools
    Underground vaults

COMPETITORS

ADC Telecommunications	JDS Uniphase
Alcatel-Lucent	Juniper Networks
Aurora Networks	Motorola, Inc.
BigBand Networks	Philips Electronics
Cisco Systems	Scientific-Atlanta
CommScope	Siemens AG
Fujitsu	Tellabs
Harmonic	Vyyo

HISTORICAL FINANCIALS

Company Type: Public

Income Statement

FYE: December 31

	REVENUE ($ mil.)	NET INCOME ($ mil.)	NET PROFIT MARGIN	EMPLOYEES
12/06	891.5	142.3	16.0%	781
12/05	680.4	51.5	7.6%	732
12/04	490.0	(28.4)	—	728
12/03	434.0	(47.3)	—	—
12/02	651.9	(191.2)	—	959
Annual Growth	**8.1%**	—	—	**(5.0%)**

2006 Year-End Financials

Debt ratio: 46.4%
Return on equity: 27.9%
Cash ($ mil.): 552.3
Current ratio: 6.44
Long-term debt ($ mil.): 276.0
No. of shares (mil.): 107.9
Dividends
  Yield: —
  Payout: —
Market value ($ mil.): 1,349.8
R&D as % of sales: —
Advertising as % of sales: —

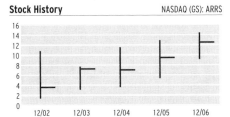

Stock History

NASDAQ (GS): ARRS

	STOCK PRICE ($) FY Close	P/E High/Low		Earnings	PER SHARE ($) Dividends	Book Value
12/06	12.51	11	7	1.30	—	5.52
12/05	9.47	25	10	0.52	—	4.03
12/04	7.04	—	—	(0.33)	—	3.21
12/03	7.24	—	—	(0.62)	—	2.88
12/02	3.57	—	—	(2.33)	—	4.29
Annual Growth	**36.8%**	—	—	—	—	**6.5%**

ArthroCare Corporation

With the wave of a wand, ArthroCare makes tissue disappear. The company's proprietary Coblation technology uses radio frequency energy to remove soft tissue from the body. Its Arthroscopic Surgery System lets surgeons use specialized wands to focus the energy and minimize damage to nearby healthy tissue, simultaneously sealing small, bleeding vessels. First used in arthroscopic procedures to repair joints, the electrosurgery system product line now includes equipment used in ear, nose, and throat procedures; spinal and neurological surgery; cardiology and gynecology; and cosmetic surgery.

ArthroCare plans to continue to expand its product line and develop strategic partnerships. The company also intends to focus on the sale of disposable devices.

EXECUTIVES

President, CEO, and Director: Michael A. Baker, age 48, $599,575 pay
SVP and CFO: Michael Gluk, age 49
SVP Operations: Richard A. (Rich) Christensen, age 47, $319,293 pay
SVP; General Manager, Strategic Business Units: John T. Raffle, age 38
SVP; President, Sports Medicine: John H. (Jack) Giroux, age 62, $346,353 pay
VP Corporate Development and Chief Medical Officer: Norman R. (Norm) Sanders
VP, CTO, and Chief Scientific Officer: Jean A. Woloszko, age 49
VP Sales: Ross Beam
VP Legal Affairs: Richard Rew II
Auditors: PricewaterhouseCoopers LLP

LOCATIONS

HQ: ArthroCare Corporation
7500 Rialto Blvd., Bldg. 2, Ste. 100,
Austin, TX 78735
Phone: 512-391-3900   **Fax:** 512-391-3901
Web: www.arthrocare.com

2006 Sales

	% of total
Americas	80
UK	5
Germany	4
Rest of world	11
Total	**100**

PRODUCTS/OPERATIONS

2006 Sales

	$ mil.	% of total
Sports medicine products	166.7	63
Ear, nose & throat products	59.9	23
ArthroCare Spine products	26.6	10
Coblation Technology products	0.2	—
Royalties, fees & other	9.6	4
Total	**263.0**	**100**

COMPETITORS

Arthrex	Johnson & Johnson
C. R. Bard	Karl Storz
Cardinal Health	Medtronic Sofamor Danek
Codman & Shurtleff	Radionics
CONMED Corporation	Smith & Nephew
Cook Incorporated	St. Jude Medical
Covidien	Stryker
DePuy Mitek	Synthes
DePuy Spine	Trimedyne
Edwards Lifesciences	Urologix
Gyrus ACMI	Zimmer Holdings

HISTORICAL FINANCIALS

Company Type: Public

Income Statement — FYE: Saturday nearest December 31

	REVENUE ($ mil.)	NET INCOME ($ mil.)	NET PROFIT MARGIN	EMPLOYEES
12/06	263.0	31.7	12.1%	881
12/05	214.3	23.5	11.0%	1,324
12/04	154.1	(26.2)	—	—
12/03	118.8	7.5	6.3%	—
12/02	88.8	1.1	1.2%	498
Annual Growth	31.2%	131.7%	—	15.3%

2006 Year-End Financials

Debt ratio: —
Return on equity: 11.5%
Cash ($ mil.): 30.8
Current ratio: 3.29
Long-term debt ($ mil.): —
No. of shares (mil.): 27.4

Dividends
Yield: —
Payout: —
Market value ($ mil.): 1,093.6
R&D as % of sales: —
Advertising as % of sales: —

Stock History

NASDAQ (GS): ARTC

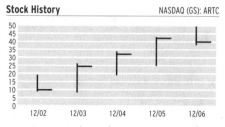

	STOCK PRICE ($) FY Close	P/E High/Low	PER SHARE ($) Earnings	Dividends	Book Value
12/06	39.92	43 34	1.14	—	11.77
12/05	42.14	48 28	0.89	—	9.06
12/04	32.06	— —	(1.21)	—	7.28
12/03	24.50	76 25	0.34	—	5.71
12/02	9.85	374 183	0.05	—	5.58
Annual Growth	41.9%	— —	118.5%	—	20.5%

Aspect Medical Systems

"Frère Jacques. Frère Jacques. Dormez-vous?" Aspect Medical Systems can give you the answer. The company makes the BIS System, which can assess consciousness levels during surgery. The system is based on its Bispectral Index technology, which measures the effects of anesthetics on the brain. The BIS is designed to prevent surgical awareness, wherein patients become conscious during surgery though they appear anesthetized and are unable to communicate. Aspect Medical Systems markets the product in the US and abroad through direct sales and distribution agreements.

Aspect Medical Systems generates most of its revenue through the sale of BIS sensors, which are disposable single-patient use products. The company plans to expand its operations in international markets.

Aspect Medical Systems is investigating other uses of its BIS technology, including diagnosis and treatment of neurological diseases.

The company had been collaborating with medical device maker Boston Scientific to develop brain monitors for use in diagnosing and treating neurological diseases. But in 2007 the two companies ended the partnership. Prior to the breakup, Boston Scientific owned more than 25% of the company, but Aspect Medical has bought back most of those shares, leaving Boston Scientific with a less than 10% stake.

EXECUTIVES

Chairman: J. Breckenridge Eagle, age 57
President, CEO, and Director: Nassib G. Chamoun, age 44, $272,416 pay
EVP Worldwide Sales and Marketing: William H. (Bill) Floyd, age 50, $220,096 pay
VP, CFO, and Secretary: Michael Falvey, age 48, $220,000 pay
VP Clinical, Regulatory, and Quality Assurance: Paul J. Manberg, age 52
VP Corporate Communications: Emily Anderson
VP Engineering: Marc Davidson, age 43
VP Manufacturing: John Coolidge, age 46
VP and General Manager, Neuroscience: Philip H. Devlin, age 50
VP and Medical Director: Scott D. Kelley, age 48, $244,227 pay
Director Human Resources: Margery Ahearn, age 44
Auditors: Ernst & Young LLP

LOCATIONS

HQ: Aspect Medical Systems, Inc.
1 Upland Rd., Norwood, MA 02062
Phone: 617-559-7000   **Fax:** 617-559-7400
Web: www.aspectms.com

2006 Sales

	$ mil.	% of total
US	70.7	77
International	20.6	23
Total	**91.3**	**100**

PRODUCTS/OPERATIONS

2006 Sales

	$ mil.	% of total
Products	85.0	93
Strategic alliance	6.3	7
Total	**91.3**	**100**

Selected Products

A-2000 BIS Monitor
BIS Module Kit
BIS sensors
BIS XP System
Zipprep EEG Electrode

COMPETITORS

Bio-logic
Criticare
Somanetics

HISTORICAL FINANCIALS

Company Type: Public

Income Statement — FYE: December 31

	REVENUE ($ mil.)	NET INCOME ($ mil.)	NET PROFIT MARGIN	EMPLOYEES
12/06	91.3	37.1	40.6%	288
12/05	77.0	8.5	11.0%	258
12/04	55.6	0.3	0.5%	—
12/03	44.1	(6.5)	—	—
12/02	39.8	(15.3)	—	205
Annual Growth	23.1%	—	—	8.9%

2006 Year-End Financials

Debt ratio: —
Return on equity: 42.0%
Cash ($ mil.): 56.6
Current ratio: 6.51
Long-term debt ($ mil.): —
No. of shares (mil.): 22.4

Dividends
Yield: —
Payout: —
Market value ($ mil.): 421.7
R&D as % of sales: —
Advertising as % of sales: —

Stock History

NASDAQ (GM): ASPM

	STOCK PRICE ($) FY Close	P/E High/Low	PER SHARE ($) Earnings	Dividends	Book Value
12/06	18.81	23 9	1.59	—	4.87
12/05	34.35	111 56	0.35	—	3.03
12/04	24.46	2,596 1,110	0.01	—	2.19
12/03	11.43	— —	(0.34)	—	1.59
12/02	3.39	— —	(0.83)	—	1.90
Annual Growth	53.5%	— —	—	—	26.6%

Asta Funding

Say "hasta luego" to unpaid receivables. Asta Funding buys, sells, services, and collects unpaid credit card debts and consumer loans. The company buys discount, primarily delinquent accounts directly from the credit grantors as well as indirectly through auctions and brokers. It buys credit card charge-offs from Visa, MasterCard, private labels, and banks in addition to telecom and other industry charge-offs. The company then collects on its debt balances either internally or with an outsourced agency. Asta Funding also invests in semi-performing and non-delinquent receivables.

38   HOOVER'S HANDBOOK OF EMERGING COMPANIES 2008

Chairman Arthur Stern and his family control some 47% of the company.

In 2007 Asta Funding more than doubled its assets by purchasing a portfolio of credit card receivables valued at $6.9 billion for some $300 million plus a percentage of future payments. The acquisition was one of the largest such deals in industry history. Sellers included Great Seneca Financial, Platinum Financial Services, and Monarch Capital. With the purchase, however, the company also inherited additional risk: Collections initially fell behind schedule.

Asta Funding acquired bankruptcy and deceased account recovery provider VATIV Recovery Solutions in 2006.

EXECUTIVES

Chairman and EVP: Arthur Stern, age 86, $401,923 pay
President, CEO, and Director: Gary Stern, age 54, $638,462 pay
COO: Cameron E. (Bill) Williams, age 61
CFO and Secretary: Mitchell M. Cohen, age 51, $276,923 pay
SVP, Operations: Mary Curtin
VP, Business Development: Rob Knight
VP and National Sales Manager: Nan Beilinson
Director, Human Resources: Gihan Elsmira
Auditors: Eisner LLP

LOCATIONS

HQ: Asta Funding, Inc.
210 Sylvan Ave., Englewood Cliffs, NJ 07632
Phone: 201-567-5648   **Fax:** 201-569-4595
Web: www.astafunding.com

COMPETITORS

The Aegis Consumer Funding Group, Inc.
Applied Card Systems
Arrow Financial Services
Asset Acceptance
Encore Capital Group, Inc.
FirstCity Financial
Genesis Financial Solutions
NCO Portfolio Management
Outsourcing Solutions
Performance Capital Management
Plaza Associates
Portfolio Recovery
Rampart Capital

HISTORICAL FINANCIALS

Company Type: Public

Income Statement

	REVENUE ($ mil.)	NET INCOME ($ mil.)	NET PROFIT MARGIN	EMPLOYEES
9/07	140.8	52.3	37.1%	172
9/06	102.0	45.8	44.9%	166
9/05	69.5	31.0	44.6%	—
9/04	51.2	22.2	43.4%	—
9/03	34.9	11.6	33.2%	—
Annual Growth	41.7%	45.7%	—	3.6%

FYE: September 30

2007 Year-End Financials

Debt ratio: 137.4%
Return on equity: 24.8%
Cash ($ mil.): 10.2
Current ratio: —
Long-term debt ($ mil.): 326.5
No. of shares (mil.): 13.9
Dividends
 Yield: 0.4%
 Payout: 4.5%
Market value ($ mil.): 533.3
R&D as % of sales: —
Advertising as % of sales: —

Astronics Corporation

Lights in the sky that aren't UFOs or shooting stars may well be the work of Astronics. The company makes external and internal lighting systems, as well as power generation and distribution technology, for commercial, general aviation, and military aircraft. Products include cabin emergency lighting systems (floor and seat escape path markers, exit locators), cockpit lighting systems (avionics keyboards, ambient light sensors, annunciator panels, electronic dimmers), and formation lighting systems (external lights). Astronics' lighting systems are made by the company's Luminescent Systems unit.

In 2005 sales to commercial aviation customers (41% of sales) surpassed those to military customers (37%). The trend continued in 2006 with commercial and military customers accounting for 55% and 23% of sales, respectively. The US government, once the company's largest customer, is becoming less critical to the company's success. Sales to the US government have gradually dwindled over time; the US government accounted for less than 7% of sales in 2006 compared to 10% in 2005, 19% in 2004, 26% in 2003, and 37% in 2002.

Astronics entered the market for electrical power generation, control, and distribution systems for aircraft in 2005 by buying the assets of Airborne Electronics Systems from a unit of General Dynamics. Astronics paid $13 million for Airborne Electronics Systems, which had revenue of about $25 million in 2004.

Chairman Kevin Keane controls a 5% equity stake and a 37% voting stake in Astronics.

HISTORY

Founded in 1968, Astronics was originally involved in electroluminescent products until it began to diversify into the packaging and printing industries. The company acquired MOD-PAC, a maker of paperboard packaging, in 1972, and Krepe-Kraft, a specialized printing company, in 1987.

In 1995 Astronics bought Loctite Luminescent Systems and integrated it with E-L FlexKey Technologies, which specialized in components

used in the aerospace and military electronics industries. Later renamed Luminescent Systems, the division was awarded two high-dollar Canadian contracts the following year. One contract was for cockpit lighting systems for Bombardier's long-range business jets; the other was for ruggedized keyboards for the control room of a Canadian nuclear power plant.

The US Air Force awarded Astronics a contract to manufacture night-vision lighting for the F-16 aircraft in 1998. The next year the company was awarded an additional contract that almost doubled the number of units it would provide for F-16s. Astronics' aerospace and electronics segment doubled its manufacturing capabilities with the addition of two new facilities.

Astronics further enhanced its ability to fulfill its F-16 contract with the acquisition of Canada-based CRL Technologies (lighted keyboards) in 2000. Also that year the company acquired illuminated indicators for use in aircraft cockpits from Aerospace Avionics. In late 2001 the company was awarded a contract from the US government to provide lighted control panels for the Bradley M2A3 infantry fighting vehicle. The following year Astronics received a contract from the US Air Force valued at up to $30 million to develop spare parts for the F-16.

Astronics discontinued its electroluminescent lamp business in 2002 and spun off MOD-PAC in 2003.

EXECUTIVES

Chairman: Kevin T. Keane, age 75
President, CEO, and Director: Peter J. Gundermann, age 45, $331,000 pay
EVP, Advanced Electronics Systems: Mark Peabody
VP, CFO, Treasurer, and Secretary: David C. Burney, age 43, $210,000 pay
VP, Luminescent Systems: Frank G. Johns III
VP, Luminescent Systems: James S. (Jim) Kramer
VP, Luminescent Systems, Inc.: Richard C. (Rick) Miller
Manager, Human Resources: Jill Draper
Auditors: Ernst & Young LLP

LOCATIONS

HQ: Astronics Corporation
130 Commerce Way, East Aurora, NY 14052
Phone: 716-805-1599   **Fax:** 716-805-1286
Web: www.astronics.com

Astronics has operations in Canada and the US.

2006 Sales

	$ mil.	% of total
North America	89.1	80
Europe	13.7	12
Asia	7.3	7
South America	0.5	1
Other regions	0.2	—
Total	**110.8**	**100**

PRODUCTS/OPERATIONS

2006 Sales by Customer

	% of total
Commercial transport	55
Military	23
Business jet	21
Other	1
Total	**100**

COMPETITORS

Ducommun	Key Tronic
Goodrich Corporation	Lumen Technologies, Inc.
Honeywell Aerospace	Ultra Electronics
Indel	

Stock History

NASDAQ (GS): ASFI

	STOCK PRICE ($) FY Close	P/E High/Low		PER SHARE ($) Earnings	Dividends	Book Value
9/07	38.32	13	8	3.56	0.16	17.07
9/06	37.49	14	7	3.13	0.56	13.40
9/05	30.36	15	7	2.15	0.14	10.68
9/04	16.19	13	8	1.57	0.09	8.52
9/03	12.99	13	4	1.13	0.03	13.84
Annual Growth	31.1%	—	—	33.2%	52.0%	5.4%

Income Statement
FYE: December 31

	REVENUE ($ mil.)	NET INCOME ($ mil.)	NET PROFIT MARGIN	EMPLOYEES
12/06	110.8	5.7	5.1%	787
12/05	74.3	2.2	3.0%	700
12/04	34.7	(0.7)	—	—
12/03	33.2	1.1	3.3%	—
12/02	42.9	4.6	10.7%	412
Annual Growth	26.8%	5.5%	—	17.6%

2006 Year-End Financials
Debt ratio: 30.1%
Return on equity: 20.1%
Cash ($ mil.): 0.2
Current ratio: 1.51
Long-term debt ($ mil.): 9.4
No. of shares (mil.): 6.5
Dividends
  Yield: —
  Payout: —
Market value ($ mil.): 111.8
R&D as % of sales: —
Advertising as % of sales: —

Stock History
NASDAQ (GM): ATRO

	STOCK PRICE ($) FY Close	P/E High/Low	PER SHARE ($) Earnings	Dividends	Book Value
12/06	17.13	26 14	0.69	—	4.80
12/05	10.75	39 17	0.28	—	4.04
12/04	5.10	— —	(0.09)	—	3.87
12/03	4.97	43 21	0.14	—	4.03
12/02	5.55	19 8	0.55	—	7.48
Annual Growth	32.5%	— —	5.8%	—	(10.5%)

Atheros Communications

Atheros Communications builds high-speed connections right through the ether. Its radio-frequency transceiver chipsets combine features such as a radio, power amplifier, low-noise amplifier, and a media access control (MAC) processor onto just two or three chips, eliminating the need for bulkier components in wireless networking equipment. The company's customers include Apple, Cisco Systems, Dell, Fujitsu, Hewlett-Packard, Hon Hai Precision Industry (20% of sales), IBM, Microsoft, QUALCOMM, Sony, Toshiba, and UTStarcom (10%). The fabless semiconductor company was started by faculty members from Stanford and Berkeley. Nearly all sales are to customers in Asia, principally in Taiwan and China.

Late in 2007 Atheros acquired the assets and certain liabilities of u-Nav Microelectronics for about $54 million in cash and stock, specifically $15.4 million in cash and 1.28 million shares of common stock. u-Nav is a developer of Global Positioning Systems (GPS) chipsets and software for mobile location-based products and services. The In-Stat market research firm forecasts the number of GPS-enabled mobile devices to grow from 180 million units in 2007 to 720 million units in 2011. More and more chip makers are adding GPS and other location capabilities to their products to answer demand from not only suppliers of navigation devices, but manufacturers of mobile handsets and other portable electronics.

In 2006 the company acquired ZyDAS Technology, a Taiwan-based designer of chips for wireless networks used in embedded, mobile, and PC applications. Atheros paid around $23 million in cash and stock for ZyDAS, and more than 70 employees of the privately held Taiwanese company joined Atheros following the acquisition.

Also that year Atheros acquired Attansic Technology, a developer of networking semiconductors, for more than $71 million in cash and stock. Attansic was a subsidiary of ASUSTek Computer, the PC motherboard and modem manufacturer.

Atheros contracts out manufacturing of its chips to such silicon foundries as Taiwan Semiconductor Manufacturing, Semiconductor Manufacturing International, Tower Semiconductor, and United Microelectronics. Semiconductor packaging and testing chores are done for the company by Amkor Technology, ASAT, Siliconware Precision Industries, and STATS ChipPAC, among others.

FMR (Fidelity Investments) owns nearly 13% of Atheros Communications. Capital Research & Management holds around 7% of the company. All officers and directors as a group own nearly 12% of Atheros.

EXECUTIVES

Chairman: John L. Hennessy, age 54
President, CEO, and Director: Craig H. Barratt, age 45, $291,200 pay
VP, CFO, and Secretary: Jack R. Lazar, age 42, $272,500 pay
VP and CTO: William J. (Bill) McFarland
VP and Chief Accounting Officer: Dave D. Torre
VP, General Counsel, and Assistant Secretary: Adam H. Tachner, age 41
VP Engineering: Richard G. (Rick) Bahr, age 53, $272,500 pay
VP, Global Human Resources: Edward L. Martin
VP Marketing: Todd D. Antes, $226,160 pay
VP, Software Engineering: Kenneth P. (Ken) McKeithan
VP Worldwide Sales: Gary L. Szilagyi, $279,300 pay
Senior Corporate Communications Manager: Dakota Lee
Auditors: Deloitte & Touche LLP

LOCATIONS

HQ: Atheros Communications, Inc.
  5480 Great America Pkwy., Santa Clara, CA 95054
Phone: 408-773-5200   **Fax:** 408-773-9940
Web: www.atheros.com

Atheros Communications has operations in China, Hong Kong, India, Japan, South Korea, Taiwan, and the US.

2006 Sales

	% of total
Taiwan	53
China	35
US	1
Other countries	11
Total	**100**

COMPETITORS

Bandspeed	Motia
Broadcom	National Semiconductor
Conexant Systems	NXP
Freescale Semiconductor	QUALCOMM
Intel Corporation	RF Micro Devices
Intellon	Texas Instruments
Intersil	Toshiba Semiconductor
Marvell Technology	WAV, Inc.
Metalink	

HISTORICAL FINANCIALS
Company Type: Public

Income Statement
FYE: December 31

	REVENUE ($ mil.)	NET INCOME ($ mil.)	NET PROFIT MARGIN	EMPLOYEES
12/06	301.7	18.7	6.2%	660
12/05	183.5	16.7	9.1%	327
12/04	169.6	10.8	6.4%	—
12/03	87.4	(13.2)	—	—
12/02	22.2	(22.4)	—	—
Annual Growth	92.0%	—	—	101.8%

2006 Year-End Financials
Debt ratio: —
Return on equity: 7.8%
Cash ($ mil.): 185.9
Current ratio: 4.20
Long-term debt ($ mil.): —
No. of shares (mil.): 54.3
Dividends
  Yield: —
  Payout: —
Market value ($ mil.): 1,157.8
R&D as % of sales: —
Advertising as % of sales: —

Stock History
NASDAQ (GS): ATHR

	STOCK PRICE ($) FY Close	P/E High/Low	PER SHARE ($) Earnings	Dividends	Book Value
12/06	21.32	85 37	0.34	—	5.17
12/05	13.00	45 21	0.31	—	3.96
12/04	10.25	93 30	0.21	—	3.61
Annual Growth	44.2%	— —	27.2%	—	19.7%

Atlantic BancGroup

Even in Florida you can't always bank on sunshine, so Atlantic BancGroup urges you to save for a rainy day. Atlantic BancGroup is the holding company for Oceanside Bank, a community bank serving Florida's Duval and St. John's counties from a a handful of banking locations. The locally operated institution targets individuals and small to midsized businesses, offering deposit products such as checking and savings accounts, IRAs, and CDs. Loans include real estate mortgages, commercial loans, and consumer loans. About 90% of the company's loan portfolio is secured by real estate mortgages.

Director Gordon Watson owns 6% of Atlantic BancGroup; directors and executive officers collectively own about 20% of the company.

EXECUTIVES

Chairman: Donald F. Glisson Jr., age 47
President, CEO, and Director; Chairman, President, and CEO, Oceanside Bank: Barry W. Chandler, age 56, $244,640 pay
EVP, CFO, and Corporate Secretary; EVP and CFO, Oceanside Bank: David L. Young, age 61, $140,096 pay
VP, Special Projects: June I. Williams
EVP and Senior Lending Officer, Oceanside Bank: Grady R. Kearsey, age 62, $169,942 pay
Assistant VP and Branch Manager, Neptune Beach, Oceanside Bank: Gwen Dasher
Branch Manager, Jacksonville, Oceanside Bank: Julie Markus
Auditors: Mauldin & Jenkins, LLC

LOCATIONS

HQ: Atlantic BancGroup, Inc.
1315 S. 3rd St., Jacksonville Beach, FL 32250
Phone: 904-247-9494   **Fax:** 904-247-9402
Web: www.oceansidebank.com

PRODUCTS/OPERATIONS

2006 Sales

	$ mil.	% of total
Interest		
Interest & fees on loans	13.6	82
Taxable interest income on investment securities & interest bearing deposits in banks	1.3	8
Tax-exempt interest income on investment securities	0.4	2
Interest on federal funds sold	0.3	2
Noninterest		
Fees & service charges on deposit accounts	0.6	4
Other fee income for banking services	0.2	1
Mortgage banking fees	0.1	1
Income from bank-owned life insurance	0.1	1
Total	**16.6**	**100**

COMPETITORS

Bank of America
Compass Bancshares
First Citizens BancShares
Jacksonville Bancorp (FL)
Regions Financial
SunTrust
VyStar Credit Union
Wachovia

HISTORICAL FINANCIALS

Company Type: Public

Income Statement

	ASSETS ($ mil.)	NET INCOME ($ mil.)	INCOME AS % OF ASSETS	EMPLOYEES
12/06	243.5	1.9	0.8%	51
12/05	213.9	1.5	0.7%	47
12/04	184.3	1.2	0.7%	—
12/03	145.6	1.0	0.7%	—
12/02	112.3	0.9	0.8%	—
Annual Growth	21.3%	20.5%	—	8.5%

2006 Year-End Financials

Equity as % of assets: 7.1%
Return on assets: 0.8%
Return on equity: 11.7%
Long-term debt ($ mil.): 5.4
No. of shares (mil.): 1.2
Market value ($ mil.): 41.6
Dividends
Yield: —
Payout: —
Sales ($ mil.): 16.6
R&D as % of sales: —
Advertising as % of sales: —

Stock History

NASDAQ (CM): ATBC

	STOCK PRICE ($) FY Close	P/E High/Low	Earnings	Dividends	Book Value
12/06	33.35	27 16	1.54	—	13.83
12/05	29.05	25 20	1.18	—	12.21
12/04	27.07	31 19	0.93	—	11.25
12/03	18.49	37 14	0.79	2.20	10.36
12/02	10.83	13 12	0.87	—	11.69
Annual Growth	32.5%	— —	15.3%	—	4.3%

Atlantic Tele-Network

The Big Banana in Guyana's rain forests is Atlantic Tele-Network (ATN). The company owns 80% of incumbent carrier Guyana Telephone & Telegraph (GT&T). GT&T operates more than 120,000 fixed access lines and has about 270,000 cellular subscribers. About 16% of the company's revenue comes from international traffic from US-based carrier Verizon Communications; GT&T has agreements with other carriers including IDT Corporation. ATN also owns Choice Communications, which provides Internet access and wireless cable TV services in the US Virgin Islands. In 2006 ATN purchased Vermont-based communications provider SoVerNet. Chairman Cornelius Prior owns 40% of the firm.

Other holdings include 43% of wireless company Bermuda Digital. It has also acquired Commnet Wireless LLC, which provides roaming services to other mobile carriers; Commnet operates networks in rural areas of 12 states.

ATN has ceased its paging and dispatch operation in Haiti.

EXECUTIVES

Chairman; Chairman, Guyana Telephone and Telegraph: Cornelius B. Prior Jr., age 73, $306,000 pay
President and CEO: Michael T. Prior, age 42, $393,000 pay
CFO and Treasurer: Justin D. Benincasa, age 45, $132,000 pay (partial-year salary)
SVP Corporate Development: William F. (Bill) Kreisher
VP Financial Analysis and Planning: John P. Audet, age 49, $150,000 pay
VP, General Counsel, and Secretary: Douglas J. Minster, age 46
Chief Accounting Officer: Andrew S. Fienberg, age 39
CEO, Guyana Telephone and Telegraph: Sonita Jagan, age 40
Auditors: PricewaterhouseCoopers LLP

LOCATIONS

HQ: Atlantic Tele-Network, Inc.
10 Derby Sq., Salem, MA 01970
Phone: 978-619-1300   **Fax:** 978-744-3951
Web: www.atni.com

Atlantic Tele-Network has operations in Bermuda, Guyana, the US, and the US Virgin Islands.

PRODUCTS/OPERATIONS

2006 Sales

	% of total
Wireless	40
International long distance	30
Local telephone & data	28
Other	2
Total	**100**

Selected Services

Local telephone access
National and international interconnections
Public phones
Wireless communications

Selected Subsidiaries and Affiliates

Bermuda Digital Communications, Ltd. (Cellular One, 43%, competitive PCS and cellular services)
Choice Communications, LLC (ISP and wireless TV provider, US Virgin Islands)
Commnet Wireless, LLC (95%, wireless roaming provider)
Guyana Telephone and Telegraph Company Limited (GT&T, 80%, local and long-distance phone services)
SoVerNet, Inc. (96%, facilities-based voice and data services)

COMPETITORS

AT&T Mobility
Cellco
Sprint Nextel
Verizon

HISTORICAL FINANCIALS

Company Type: Public

Income Statement

FYE: December 31

	REVENUE ($ mil.)	NET INCOME ($ mil.)	NET PROFIT MARGIN	EMPLOYEES
12/06	155.4	23.5	15.1%	852
12/05	102.3	13.6	13.3%	853
12/04	89.3	12.1	13.5%	700
12/03	83.3	12.2	14.6%	—
12/02	74.7	9.5	12.7%	817
Annual Growth	20.1%	25.4%	—	1.1%

2006 Year-End Financials

Debt ratio: 28.0%
Return on equity: 16.0%
Cash ($ mil.): 60.5
Current ratio: 2.60
Long-term debt ($ mil.): 50.0
No. of shares (mil.): 15.2
Dividends
Yield: 1.4%
Payout: 23.3%
Market value ($ mil.): 444.5
R&D as % of sales: —
Advertising as % of sales: —

Stock History

NASDAQ (GM): ATNI

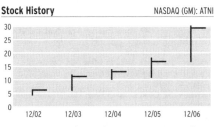

	STOCK PRICE ($) FY Close	P/E High/Low	Earnings	Dividends	Book Value
12/06	29.30	17 10	1.72	0.40	11.78
12/05	16.76	17 10	1.09	—	9.28
12/04	13.00	14 11	0.96	—	21.61
12/03	11.22	12 6	0.97	—	20.30
12/02	6.20	8 6	0.75	—	18.87
Annual Growth	47.4%	— —	23.1%	—	(11.1%)

Atlas America

Atlas America's production map can be found on the page titled Appalachia. The independent energy company is engaged in the development, production, and transportation of natural gas (and some oil) primarily in the Appalachian Basin. The company, which drills through partnerships, has proved reserves of 180.9 billion cu. ft. of natural gas equivalent. Atlas America has interests in 7,252 gross producing wells. Its natural gas transportation business is conducted through 15%-owned Atlas Pipeline Partners, which operates 3,265 miles of intrastate natural gas gathering systems in New York, Ohio, Oklahoma, Pennsylvania, and Texas. In 2007 the company agreed to buy DTE Gas & Oil for $1.2 billion.

The acquisition would give Atlas America entry into Michigan, where DTE has interests in some 2,150 producing natural gas wells.

Resource America owned 80% of Atlas America before spinning it off in 2005. Resource America's stake was distributed to its shareholders.

In 2004, Atlas Pipeline Partners acquired Spectrum Field Services, Inc., for $142.4 million. The acquisition greatly increased Atlas Pipeline's size and expanded the natural gas supply basins in which it operates.

Atlas America announced in November 2005 that it was forming a subsidiary to hold its ownership stake in the general partner of Atlas Pipeline Partners; the company filed for an IPO of the new company (Atlas Pipeline Holdings, L.P.) in 2006.

In 2006 Atlas America formed Atlas Energy Resources to operate its oil and gas business.

EXECUTIVES

Chairman, CEO, and President: Edward E. Cohen, age 68, $2,000,000 pay
Vice Chairman: Jonathan Z. Cohen, age 37, $1,400,000 pay
CFO: Matthew A. Jones, age 43, $1,050,000 pay
EVP: Frank P. Carolas, age 47
EVP: Freddie M. Kotek, age 50, $650,000 pay
EVP: Jeffrey C. Simmons, age 48
EVP: Michael L. Staines
SVP and Chief Accounting Officer: Nancy J. McGurk, age 51
VP Investor Relations: Brian J. Begley
VP Marketing: Marci F. Bleichmar, age 33
VP Public Relations and Investor Relations Contact: Pamela Schreiber
President and COO, Atlas Energy; President and COO, Atlas Energy Management: Richard D. (Rich) Weber, age 43, $1,001,923 pay
President and COO, Atlas Pipeline Mid-Continent; President and COO, Atlas Pipeline Holdings: Robert R. Firth, age 52
Secretary and Chief Legal Officer: Lisa Washington, age 39
Auditors: Grant Thornton LLP

LOCATIONS

HQ: Atlas America, Inc.
311 Rouser Rd., Moon Township, PA 15108
Phone: 412-262-2830   **Fax:** 412-262-7430
Web: www.atlasamerica.com

PRODUCTS/OPERATIONS

2006 Sales

	$ mil.	% of total
Gathering, transmission & processing	437.6	58
Well construction & completion	198.6	27
Gas & oil production	88.4	12
Well services	12.9	2
Other	11.8	1
Total	**749.3**	**100**

COMPETITORS

Anadarko Petroleum
Belden & Blake
Cabot Oil & Gas
Dominion Resources
Petroleum Development
Range Resources

HISTORICAL FINANCIALS

Company Type: Public

Income Statement
FYE: December 31

	REVENUE ($ mil.)	NET INCOME ($ mil.)	NET PROFIT MARGIN	EMPLOYEES
12/06*	749.3	45.8	6.1%	517
9/05	474.5	32.9	6.9%	340
9/04	180.9	21.2	11.7%	—
9/03	105.7	13.9	13.2%	—
9/02	99.3	7.2	7.3%	—
Annual Growth	**65.7%**	**58.8%**	**—**	**52.1%**

*Fiscal year change

2006 Year-End Financials

Debt ratio: 119.4%
Return on equity: 23.4%
Cash ($ mil.): 185.4
Current ratio: 1.33
Long-term debt ($ mil.): 324.0
No. of shares (mil.): 19.3
Dividends
  Yield: —
  Payout: —
Market value ($ mil.): 657.5
R&D as % of sales: —
Advertising as % of sales: —

Stock History
NASDAQ (GS): ATLS

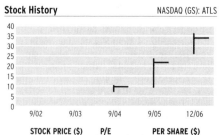

	STOCK PRICE ($) FY Close	P/E High/Low		PER SHARE ($) Earnings	Dividends	Book Value
12/06*	33.98	16	12	2.27	—	14.02
9/05	21.71	21	9	1.09	—	9.03
9/04	9.68	13	9	0.80	—	6.83
Annual Growth	**87.4%**	**—**	**—**	**68.4%**	**—**	**43.3%**

*Fiscal year change

Atlas Energy Resources

Atlas Energy Resources has its fingers in lots of oily pies. The company, through interests in more than 90 investment partnerships, drills for and produces natural gas and oil in the Appalachian Basin, which is known for its high yields that require little or no processing. It has a nearly 100% success rate with its 7,252 wells on about 548,000 acres; about 61% of the acreage is undeveloped. In 2006 Atlas Energy reported proved reserves of 180.9 billion cu. ft. of natural gas equivalent. The company was formed in 2006 to manage the natural gas and oil holdings of parent Atlas America, which retains an 80% interest in the company.

In 2007 the company agreed to buy DTE Energy's Michigan Antrim Shale gas exploration and production assets for $1.2 billion.

EXECUTIVES

Chairman and CEO: Edward E. Cohen, age 68, $27,391 pay
Vice Chairman: Jonathan Z. Cohen, age 37
President, COO, and Director: Richard D. (Rich) Weber, age 43, $15,217 pay
CFO and Director: Matthew A. Jones, age 43, $13,696 pay
Chief Accounting Officer: Nancy J. McGurk, age 51
Chief Legal Officer and Secretary: Lisa Washington, age 39
VP Completion Technology: Henry Jacot
Auditors: Grant Thornton LLP

LOCATIONS

HQ: Atlas Energy Resources, LLC
311 Rouser Rd., Moon Township, PA 15108
Phone: 412-262-2830
Web: www.atlasenergyresources.com

PRODUCTS/OPERATIONS

2006 Sales

	$ mil.	% of total
Partnership management		
Well construction & completion	198.6	62
Well services	13.0	4
Administration & oversight	11.8	4
Gathering	9.2	3
Gas & oil production	88.4	27
Total	**321.0**	**100**

COMPETITORS

Belden & Blake
EOG
Equitable Resources
EV Energy
EXCO Resources
Penn Virginia
Petroleum Development
Range Resources
Seneca

HISTORICAL FINANCIALS

Company Type: Public

Income Statement
FYE: December 31

	REVENUE ($ mil.)	NET INCOME ($ mil.)	NET PROFIT MARGIN	EMPLOYEES
12/06*	321.0	51.8	16.1%	0
9/05	212.0	41.4	19.5%	0
9/04	148.0	27.6	18.6%	—
9/03	103.1	15.9	15.4%	—
Annual Growth	**46.0%**	**48.2%**	**—**	**—**

*Fiscal year change

2006 Year-End Financials

Debt ratio: 0.0%	Dividends
Return on equity: 28.9%	Yield: —
Cash ($ mil.): 36.5	Payout: —
Current ratio: 0.45	Market value ($ mil.): 830.3
Long-term debt ($ mil.): 0.0	R&D as % of sales: —
No. of shares (mil.): 36.6	Advertising as % of sales: —

Stock History

NYSE: ATN

9/02   9/03   9/04   9/05   12/06

	STOCK PRICE ($) FY Close	P/E High/Low	PER SHARE ($) Earnings	Dividends	Book Value
12/06	22.67	286 272	0.08	—	5.81

Atlas Pipeline Partners

Atlas Pipeline Partners shoulders the burden of getting natural gas from wellheads to major gas utilities such as Peoples Natural Gas, National Fuel Gas, and East Ohio Gas. Atlas Pipeline operates about 3,265 miles of natural gas gathering systems in Arkansas, southeastern Missouri, eastern Ohio, southern Oklahoma, western New York, western Pennsylvania, and northern Texas. The company was formed to buy the gas gathering systems of its former owners Atlas America and Resource Energy. In 2006 Atlas America filed an IPO for subsidiary Atlas Pipeline Holdings L.P. to hold its ownership stake in the general partner of Atlas Pipeline.

In 2004 Atlas Pipeline acquired Spectrum Field Services, which added more than 1,900 miles of natural gas pipelines and a gas processing facility to Atlas Pipeline's asset base, for about $142 million. In an effort to further expand its geographical reach, Atlas Pipeline planned to acquire SEMCO Energy's Alaska Pipeline subsidiary for $95 million. Alaska Pipeline owns a 354-mile natural gas transmission pipeline that delivers gas to customers in Anchorage. SEMCO Energy terminated the deal in 2004.

In 2005 Atlas Pipeline acquired the Oklahoma gathering, treating, and processing assets of Energy Transfer Partners for $192 million. It also bought OGE Energy's 75% stake in NOARK Pipeline System for $173 million.

In 2007 it acquired Anadarko Petroleum's stakes in the Chaney Dell and Midkiff-Benedum natural gas gathering and processing systems for about $1.9 billion.

EXECUTIVES

Chairman and CEO Atlas Pipeline GP: Edward E. Cohen, age 68, $542,500 pay
Vice Chairman Atlas Pipeline GP: Jonathan Z. Cohen, age 37
President, COO, and Director: Michael L. Staines, $350,000 pay
CFO Atlas Pipeline GP: Matthew A. Jones, age 43
VP Investor Relations: Brian J. Begley
VP Corporate Development: Daniel C. Herz, age 29

Chief Accounting Officer: Sean McGrath
Chief Legal Officer and Secretary: Lisa Washington, age 39
President and CEO, Atlas Pipeline Mid-Continent LLC: Robert R. Firth, age 52
Auditors: Grant Thornton LLP

LOCATIONS

HQ: Atlas Pipeline Partners, L.P.
311 Rouser Rd., Moon Township, PA 15108
Phone: 412-262-2830   **Fax:** 412-262-2820
Web: www.atlaspipelinepartners.com/home.html

PRODUCTS/OPERATIONS

2006 Sales

	$ mil.	% of total
Natural gas & liquids	391.4	84
Transportation	60.9	13
Other	12.4	3
Total	**464.7**	**100**

COMPETITORS

Belden & Blake
Cabot Oil & Gas
Dominion Resources
Duke Energy
Equitable Resources
MarkWest Hydrocarbon
ONEOK

HISTORICAL FINANCIALS

Company Type: Public

Income Statement

FYE: December 31

	REVENUE ($ mil.)	NET INCOME ($ mil.)	NET PROFIT MARGIN	EMPLOYEES
12/06	464.7	33.7	7.3%	188
12/05	371.5	25.8	6.9%	210
12/04	91.3	18.3	20.0%	—
12/03	15.8	9.6	60.8%	—
12/02	10.7	5.4	50.5%	—
Annual Growth	**156.7%**	**58.1%**	**—**	**(10.5%)**

2006 Year-End Financials

Debt ratio: 87.7%	Dividends
Return on equity: 9.5%	Yield: 7.0%
Cash ($ mil.): 7.2	Payout: 265.4%
Current ratio: 1.02	Market value ($ mil.): 627.9
Long-term debt ($ mil.): 332.5	R&D as % of sales: —
No. of shares (mil.): 13.1	Advertising as % of sales: —

Stock History

NYSE: APL

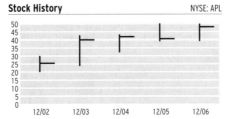

12/02   12/03   12/04   12/05   12/06

	STOCK PRICE ($) FY Close	P/E High/Low	PER SHARE ($) Earnings	Dividends	Book Value
12/06	48.00	39 31	1.27	3.37	28.98
12/05	40.60	27 21	1.84	2.33	26.26
12/04	41.90	17 13	2.60	2.67	24.57
12/03	40.00	20 11	2.17	2.38	16.31
12/02	25.40	19 13	1.54	2.13	12.15
Annual Growth	**17.2%**	**— —**	**(4.7%)**	**12.2%**	**24.3%**

ATP Oil & Gas

ATP Oil & Gas looks for its revenues where others have shelved their operations. The company's strategy is to exploit continental shelf assets that are being sold by larger oil companies searching for higher returns in deeper waters. It explores and develops natural gas and oil properties primarily on the outer continental shelf of the Gulf of Mexico (where it has interests in 72 offshore blocks, 44 platforms, and 112 wells) and in the Southern Gas Basin of the UK's North Sea. Its proved reserves total 636.9 billion cu. ft. of natural gas equivalent; natural gas makes up the bulk of the reserves. Founder and CEO Paul Bulmahn owns about 24% of ATP Oil & Gas.

ATP Oil & Gas was founded in Texas in 1991. In 1995 ATP pioneered the use of offshore horizontal drilling in the Gulf of Mexico at its South Timbalier 30 block. In 2005 the company acquired the Rowan-Midland mobile offshore drilling unit from an operating subsidiary of Rowan Companies.

EXECUTIVES

Chairman and President: T. Paul Bulmahn, age 63, $1,470,000 pay
COO: Leland E. Tate, age 57, $381,819 pay
CFO and Treasurer: Albert L. Reese Jr., age 57, $251,551 pay
SVP International and General Counsel: John E. Tschirhart, age 56
Chief Accounting Officer: Keith R. Godwin, age 39, $236,441 pay
Chief Communications Officer and Secretary: Isabel M. Plume, age 46
VP Acquisitions: George R. Morris
VP Engineering: G. Ross Frazer
VP Production Operations: Mickey W. Shaw
VP Projects: Robert M. Shivers III
Auditors: Deloitte & Touche LLP

LOCATIONS

HQ: ATP Oil & Gas Corporation
4600 Post Oak Place, Ste. 200, Houston, TX 77027
Phone: 713-622-3311   **Fax:** 713-622-5101
Web: www.atpog.com

2006 Proved Reserves

	% of total
Gulf of Mexico	56
North Sea	44
Total	**100**

2006 Sales

	$ mil.	% of total
Gulf of Mexico	327.6	78
North Sea	92.2	22
Total	**419.8**	**100**

COMPETITORS

Apache
BP
Comstock Resources
Devon Energy
Eni
Forest Oil
McMoRan Exploration
Meridian Resource
Murphy Oil
Newfield Exploration
Petsec Energy
Royal Dutch Shell

HISTORICAL FINANCIALS

Company Type: Public

Income Statement
FYE: December 31

	REVENUE ($ mil.)	NET INCOME ($ mil.)	NET PROFIT MARGIN	EMPLOYEES
12/06	419.8	6.9	1.6%	59
12/05	146.7	(2.7)	—	48
12/04	116.1	1.4	1.2%	—
12/03	70.2	(50.8)	—	—
12/02	94.4	(4.7)	—	53
Annual Growth	45.2%	—	—	2.7%

2006 Year-End Financials

Debt ratio: 2,957.8%
Return on equity: 20.1%
Cash ($ mil.): 211.3
Current ratio: 1.31
Long-term debt ($ mil.): 1,062.4
No. of shares (mil.): 30.2
Dividends
Yield: —
Payout: —
Market value ($ mil.): 1,194.9
R&D as % of sales: —
Advertising as % of sales: —

Stock History
NASDAQ (GS): ATPG

	STOCK PRICE ($) FY Close	P/E High	P/E Low	Earnings	Dividends	Book Value
12/06	39.57	—	—	(1.33)	—	1.19
12/05	37.01	—	—	(0.43)	—	7.30
12/04	18.59	383	94	0.05	—	1.97
12/03	6.28	—	—	(2.21)	—	0.18
12/02	4.07	—	—	(0.23)	—	1.90
Annual Growth	76.6%	—	—	—	—	(11.1%)

Atwood Oceanics

Atwood Oceanics is at work at sea all over the world. An offshore oil and gas drilling contractor, the firm owns eight drilling rigs, including four semisubmersible rigs, two jack-ups, one submersible, and one semisubmersible tender assist vessel (which places drilling equipment on permanent platforms). In 2007 some 93% of sales came from international operation. Its customers include Woodside Energy (17% of sales) BHP Billiton Petroleum Pty (13%), and Sarawak Shell Bhd. (13%). The company, which also operates in the Gulf of Mexico, is expanding its operations to include offshore Japan. Fellow drilling contractor Helmerich & Payne owns 13% of Atwood Oceanics.

Founded in 1970, the company has conducted drilling operations in most of the world's major offshore oil patches, including in the Arabian Gulf and the Red Sea, Australia, East and West Africa, Southeast Asia, Papua New Guinea, India, the Mediterranean Sea, Central and South America, and the Gulf of Mexico.

In 2005 Atwood Oceanics sold a spare blowout preventer stack to a Norwegian company for $15 million. In 2007 the company announced that its ATWOOD SOUTHERN CROSS semisubmersible had been awarded a contract by ENI's AGIP Exploration & Production division to drill two wells plus options for two additional wells.

EXECUTIVES

President, CEO, and Director: John R. Irwin, age 62, $666,448 pay
SVP, CFO, and Secretary: James M. (Jim) Holland, age 62, $343,027 pay
SVP Marketing and Administration: Glen P. Kelley, age 59, $337,174 pay
VP Engineering: Alan Quintero, age 44
VP Operations: Darryl R. Smith, age 62
General Counsel: Rodney Mallams
General Manager, Administrative Services: Randal F. Presley
General Manager, Financial Services: Michael A. (Mike) Campbell
Manager, Human Resources: James E. Gillenwater
Auditors: PricewaterhouseCoopers LLP

LOCATIONS

HQ: Atwood Oceanics, Inc.
15835 Park Ten Place Dr., Houston, TX 77084
Phone: 281-749-7800 **Fax:** 281-492-7871
Web: www.atwd.com

COMPETITORS

Diamond Offshore
ENSCO
Nabors Industries
Noble
Oceaneering International
Parker Drilling
Pride International
Saipem
Schlumberger
Transocean Inc.

HISTORICAL FINANCIALS

Company Type: Public

Income Statement
FYE: September 30

	REVENUE ($ mil.)	NET INCOME ($ mil.)	NET PROFIT MARGIN	EMPLOYEES
9/07	403.0	139.0	34.5%	900
9/06	276.6	86.1	31.1%	—
9/05	176.2	26.0	14.8%	1,100
9/04	163.4	7.6	4.7%	—
9/03	144.8	(12.8)	—	—
Annual Growth	29.2%	—	—	(9.5%)

2007 Year-End Financials

Debt ratio: —
Return on equity: 25.9%
Cash ($ mil.): 100.4
Current ratio: 3.75
Long-term debt ($ mil.): —
No. of shares (mil.): 31.7
Dividends
Yield: —
Payout: —
Market value ($ mil.): 2,425.0
R&D as % of sales: —
Advertising as % of sales: —

Stock History
NYSE: ATW

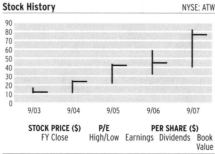

	STOCK PRICE ($) FY Close	P/E High	P/E Low	Earnings	Dividends	Book Value
9/07	76.56	19	9	4.37	—	19.44
9/06	44.97	21	12	2.74	—	14.78
9/05	42.10	52	27	0.83	—	23.61
9/04	23.77	90	43	0.27	—	19.58
9/03	11.99	—	—	(0.46)	—	19.02
Annual Growth	59.0%	—	—	—	—	0.6%

Avatar Holdings

Avatar aspires to be the embodiment of retirement living. The company develops residential communities in the popular retirement destinations of central Florida and Arizona; amenities include golf courses, restaurants, and fitness centers. The company owns some 32,000 acres in Florida and Arizona of developable land, and wetlands and other open space. To focus on its core operations, Avatar Holdings has sold its cable TV holdings, mini-storage, and shopping center in Poinciana, Florida; its Harbor Island marina in Hollywood, Florida; and its utility operations in Arizona. The company also continues to purchase more land in Florida with an eye on future developments.

Chairman Joshua Nash and his father, Jack, control more than 25% of Avatar Holdings' stock.

EXECUTIVES

Chairman: Joshua Nash, age 45
Vice Chairman, President, and CEO: Gerald D. Kelfer, age 61, $5,500,000 pay
EVP and CFO: Randy L. Kotler, age 42
EVP and General Counsel: Patricia K. Fletcher, age 49
VP and Secretary: Juanita I. Kerrigan, age 60
President, Avatar Properties: Jonathan Fels, age 54, $900,000 pay
President, South Florida Homebuilding Operations, Avatar Properties: Steven Knot
EVP and COO, Avatar Properties: Michael Levy, age 48, $900,000 pay
Controller and Chief Accounting Officer: Michael P. Rama
Auditors: Ernst & Young LLP

LOCATIONS

HQ: Avatar Holdings Inc.
201 Alhambra Cir., Coral Gables, FL 33134
Phone: 305-442-7000 **Fax:** 305-448-9927
Web: www.avatarhomes.com

PRODUCTS/OPERATIONS

2006 Sales

	$ mil.	% of total
Real estate revenues	829.6	99
Interest income & other	5.5	1
Total	**835.1**	**100**

Selected Subsidiaries

Avatar Properties, Inc.
Banyan Bay Corporation Florida
Dorten, Inc.
Harbor Islands Realty, Inc.
Poinciana New Township, Inc.
Prominent Title Insurance Agency, Inc. Florida
Rio Rico Properties Inc.

COMPETITORS

ACTS
John Wieland Homes
Lennar
Pulte Homes
The Ryland Group
Toll Brothers
WCI Communities

HISTORICAL FINANCIALS

Company Type: Public

Income Statement

FYE: December 31

	REVENUE ($ mil.)	NET INCOME ($ mil.)	NET PROFIT MARGIN	EMPLOYEES
12/06	835.1	174.7	20.9%	483
12/05	516.8	63.1	12.2%	585
12/04	337.4	29.6	8.8%	—
12/03	253.0	18.5	7.3%	—
12/02	190.3	5.6	2.9%	351
Annual Growth	44.7%	136.3%	—	8.3%

2006 Year-End Financials

Debt ratio: 27.1%
Return on equity: 42.7%
Cash ($ mil.): 207.4
Current ratio: 2.75
Long-term debt ($ mil.): 136.9
No. of shares (mil.): 8.2

Dividends
Yield: —
Payout: —
Market value ($ mil.): 662.5
R&D as % of sales: —
Advertising as % of sales: —

Stock History

NASDAQ (GS): AVTR

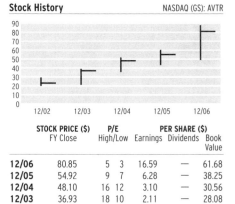

	STOCK PRICE ($) FY Close	P/E High/Low		PER SHARE ($) Earnings	Dividends	Book Value
12/06	80.85	5	3	16.59	—	61.68
12/05	54.92	9	7	6.28	—	38.25
12/04	48.10	16	12	3.10	—	30.56
12/03	36.93	18	10	2.11	—	28.08
12/02	23.00	45	32	0.64	—	26.07
Annual Growth	36.9%	—	—	125.6%	—	24.0%

Avici Systems

Avici has chosen a new route. The company has traditionally developed core network routers. Its Terabit Switch Router (TSR), which is used to prioritize, manage, and transmit large volumes of data over core fiber-optic communications networks, has made a small dent in the high-end market dominated by Cisco Systems and Juniper Networks. The company also makes stackable (SSR) and compact (QSR) models of its router for use in lower volume networks such as metropolitan areas. In 2007 Avici announced plans to phase out development of its core router products in order to focus on its Soapstone Networks business, which develops network management software.

Avici sells to telecommunications service providers. AT&T accounted for 94% of Avici's revenues in 2006.

In an effort to cut costs, Avici announced restructuring plans in 2006 that included laying off 45% of its workforce; the company has also considered strategic alternatives including a sale or merger.

EXECUTIVES

Chairman: Richard T. (Dick) Liebhaber, age 71
President, CEO and Director: William J. Leighton, age 56, $259,471 pay
SVP Finance, CFO, Treasurer, and Secretary: William J. (Bill) Stuart, age 57
VP Marketing: Esmeralda Swartz
VP Finance and Principal Accounting Officer: T.S. Ramesh, age 41
Director Investor Relations: Inna Vyadro
CTO: Larry Dennison
Auditors: Ernst & Young LLP

LOCATIONS

HQ: Avici Systems Inc.
101 Billerica Ave., Bldg. 2,
North Billerica, MA 01862
Phone: 978-964-2000   **Fax:** 978-964-2100
Web: www.avici.com

2006 Sales

	% of total
North America	95
Europe	5
Total	**100**

PRODUCTS/OPERATIONS

2006 Sales

	$ mil.	% of total
Products	76.4	92
Services	6.4	8
Adjustments	(0.6)	—
Total	**82.2**	**100**

Products

Non-stop routers with backup route controller that enables service/reconfiguration during use (NSR)
Quarter-rack switch routers for metropolitan and smaller service carriers (QSR)
Stackable switch routers for metropolitan networks (SSR)
Terabit switch routers for core networks (TSR)

COMPETITORS

Alcatel-Lucent
Cisco Systems
Juniper Networks
Nortel Networks
Redback Networks
Sycamore Networks
Tellabs

HISTORICAL FINANCIALS

Company Type: Public

Income Statement

FYE: December 31

	REVENUE ($ mil.)	NET INCOME ($ mil.)	NET PROFIT MARGIN	EMPLOYEES
12/06	82.2	8.3	10.1%	170
12/05	35.1	(24.6)	—	206
12/04	24.5	(35.4)	—	—
12/03	39.4	(37.0)	—	—
12/02	33.1	(64.8)	—	230
Annual Growth	25.5%	—	—	(7.3%)

2006 Year-End Financials

Debt ratio: —
Return on equity: 14.0%
Cash ($ mil.): 61.3
Current ratio: 3.85
Long-term debt ($ mil.): —
No. of shares (mil.): 13.9

Dividends
Yield: —
Payout: —
Market value ($ mil.): 107.6
R&D as % of sales: —
Advertising as % of sales: —

Stock History

NASDAQ (GM): AVCI

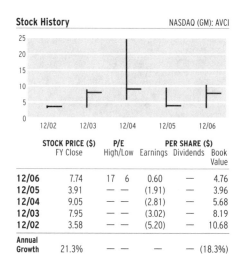

	STOCK PRICE ($) FY Close	P/E High/Low		PER SHARE ($) Earnings	Dividends	Book Value
12/06	7.74	17	6	0.60	—	4.76
12/05	3.91	—	—	(1.91)	—	3.96
12/04	9.05	—	—	(2.81)	—	5.68
12/03	7.95	—	—	(3.02)	—	8.19
12/02	3.58	—	—	(5.20)	—	10.68
Annual Growth	21.3%	—	—	—	—	(18.3%)

Axsys Technologies

Precision products are precisely Axsys Technologies' business. The company makes optical systems used in fighter planes, tanks, and other military and commercial applications. Offerings include precision metal optical, infrared optical, and motion control products, along with precision machined lightweight structures. The aerospace and defense market accounts for a majority of the company's sales; BAE Systems accounts for more than 12%. Other customers include companies in the graphic arts, medical imaging, and semiconductor equipment industries. Axsys has divested its business that distributed precision ball bearings, spherical bearings, and bushings. Chairman and CEO Stephen Bershad owns 18% of Axsys.

Axsys' Optical Systems unit is made up of the company's former Aerospace and Defense and Commercial Products divisions. Axsys is expanding the Optical Systems unit through acquisitions. In 2004 the company acquired Telic Optics, a maker of infrared optical products, and the next year Axsys bought Diversified Optical Products (DiOp), a maker of thermal surveillance camera systems and lenses.

Axsys has sold its automation group, which was made up of its Fiber Automation Division and Automation Engineering, Inc. Axsys has also divested its interest in Teltrac, a manufacturer of spin stands used to test data storage recording heads, to Colorado-based Storage Test Solutions. As a result of the sales, Axsys closed its Santa Monica manufacturing facility and moved its laser interferometer and autofocus operations to its imaging systems facility in Rochester Hills, Michigan.

In 2007 Axsys also sold its AST Bearings division to an affiliate of Tonka Bay Equity Partners for about $15.5 million. At the time of the sale, Axsys also reorganized its operations into two, market-focused divisions: Surveillance Systems Group and Imaging Systems Group. Surveillance Systems will focus on infrared cameras and gyro-stabilized camera systems, while Imaging Systems will concentrate on optical and motion control sub-systems including infrared lenses and positioning systems.

EXECUTIVES

Chairman, President, and CEO: Stephen W. Bershad, age 65, $380,000 pay
President and COO: Scott B. Conner, age 39, $210,000 pay
VP, CFO, and Treasurer: David A. Almeida, age 47, $237,077 pay
Group President, Surveillance Systems Group: Randy Moore
President, Motion Control Business: Chalmers (Bud) Jenkins
President, Commercial Products Group: Gary G. Wagner
President, Imaging Systems Group: James W. Howard
Manager, Human Resources: Lynn Kerley
Director, Investor Relations: Geoffrey Ling
Secretary: Cynthia J. McNickle
Auditors: Ernst & Young LLP

LOCATIONS

HQ: Axsys Technologies, Inc.
175 Capital Blvd., Ste. 103, Rocky Hill, CT 06067
Phone: 860-257-0200   **Fax:** 860-594-5750
Web: www.axsys.com

Axsys Technologies operates facilities in Alabama, California, Michigan, New Hampshire, and New Jersey.

2006 Sales

	% of total
US	91
Europe	6
Other regions	3
Total	**100**

PRODUCTS/OPERATIONS

2006 Sales

	% of total
Optical Systems	83
Distributed Products	17
Total	**100**

COMPETITORS

Aeroflex
Allied Motion Technologies
Applied Industrial Technologies
Carbone Lorraine
Carl Zeiss
CST
Danaher
EOS
Excel Technology
FLIR
JDS Uniphase
Methode Electronics
Mikron Infrared
NN Inc.
Rotork
SAFRAN
SatCon Technology
Servotronics
Spirent
Valeo

HISTORICAL FINANCIALS

Company Type: Public

Income Statement

FYE: December 31

	REVENUE ($ mil.)	NET INCOME ($ mil.)	NET PROFIT MARGIN	EMPLOYEES
12/06	156.4	10.3	6.6%	765
12/05	133.5	7.3	5.5%	69
12/04	103.5	8.7	8.4%	—
12/03	85.1	5.0	5.9%	—
12/02	79.6	(7.1)	—	557
Annual Growth	**18.4%**	**—**	**—**	**8.3%**

2006 Year-End Financials

Debt ratio: —
Return on equity: 8.2%
Cash ($ mil.): 6.0
Current ratio: 2.17
Long-term debt ($ mil.): —
No. of shares (mil.): 10.6
Dividends
  Yield: —
  Payout: —
Market value ($ mil.): 187.0
R&D as % of sales: —
Advertising as % of sales: —

Stock History

NASDAQ (GS): AXYS

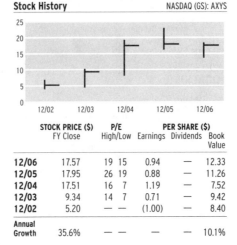

	STOCK PRICE ($) FY Close	P/E High/Low		PER SHARE ($) Earnings	Dividends	Book Value
12/06	17.57	19	15	0.94	—	12.33
12/05	17.95	26	19	0.88	—	11.26
12/04	17.51	16	7	1.19	—	7.52
12/03	9.34	14	7	0.71	—	9.42
12/02	5.20	—	—	(1.00)	—	8.40
Annual Growth	**35.6%**	**—**	**—**	**—**	**—**	**10.1%**

AZZ incorporated

When companies need to power up or get that "zinc-ing" feeling, they call AZZ incorporated (formerly Aztec Manufacturing). The company has two business segments: electrical and industrial products and galvanizing services. Through its subsidiaries, AZZ makes lighting fixtures, bus duct electrical distribution systems, and electrical power distribution centers and assemblies. Industrial, petrochemical, and power-generation and -transmission industries use the company's products. To protect steel from corrosion, the galvanizing services unit dips it into baths of molten zinc for companies in the highway construction, electrical utility, transportation, and water-treatment industries.

AZZ provides galvanizing services from 14 plants across the southern and southwestern US.

In late 2006 the company acquired the assets of three galvanizing plants in Indiana and Ohio from Witt Industries, a privately held, Cincinnati-based firm. The move extends the geographic reach of AZZ's galvanizing business.

EXECUTIVES

Chairman: H. Kirk Downey, age 64
President, CEO, and Director: David H. Dingus, age 59, $390,000 pay
SVP Finance, CFO, Secretary, and Director: Dana L. Perry, age 58, $218,400 pay
SVP Operations, Galvanizing Services: Fred L. Wright Jr., age 66, $198,000 pay
SVP Operations, Electrical Products: John V. Petro, age 61, $198,000 pay
VP and Corporate Controller: Richard W. Butler, age 41
VP Business and Manufacturing Systems: James C. (Jim) Stricklen, age 58
VP Sales, Electrical Products: Clement H. Watson, age 60, $175,000 pay
VP Human Resources: Robert D. Ruffin, age 66
VP Operations, Galvanizing Services Segment: Tim E. Pendley, age 45
Auditors: BDO Seidman, LLP

LOCATIONS

HQ: AZZ incorporated
1300 S. University Dr.,
University Centre 1, Ste. 200,
Fort Worth, TX 76107
Phone: 817-810-0095   **Fax:** 817-336-5354
Web: www.azzincorporated.com

AZZ operates electrical and galvanizing facilities in Alabama, Arizona, Arkansas, Indiana, Kansas, Louisiana, Massachusetts, Mississippi, Missouri, Ohio, Oklahoma, South Carolina, and Texas.

PRODUCTS/OPERATIONS

2007 Sales

	$ mil.	% of total
Electrical & industrial products	150.2	58
Galvanizing services	110.1	42
Total	**260.3**	**100**

COMPETITORS

Chamberlin & Hill
Earle M. Jorgensen
Eaton
Energy Focus
Friedman Industries
GE
Gewiss
Jarden
Legrand
LSI Industries
North American Galvanizing & Coatings
Powell Industries
SPX

HISTORICAL FINANCIALS

Company Type: Public

Income Statement

FYE: Last day in February

	REVENUE ($ mil.)	NET INCOME ($ mil.)	NET PROFIT MARGIN	EMPLOYEES
2/07	260.3	21.6	8.3%	1,301
2/06	187.2	7.8	4.2%	1,019
2/05	152.4	4.8	3.1%	—
2/04	136.2	4.3	3.2%	—
2/03	183.4	8.6	4.7%	—
Annual Growth	**9.1%**	**25.9%**	**—**	**27.7%**

2007 Year-End Financials

Debt ratio: 31.7%
Return on equity: 21.8%
Cash ($ mil.): 1.7
Current ratio: 2.25
Long-term debt ($ mil.): 35.2
No. of shares (mil.): 11.7
Dividends
  Yield: —
  Payout: —
Market value ($ mil.): 236.0
R&D as % of sales: —
Advertising as % of sales: —

Stock History

NYSE: AZZ

	STOCK PRICE ($) FY Close	P/E High/Low		PER SHARE ($) Earnings	Dividends	Book Value
2/07	20.25	15	6	1.82	—	9.54
2/06	11.40	18	11	0.69	—	15.20
2/05	8.10	19	15	0.44	—	13.69
2/04	8.00	22	11	0.40	—	12.79
2/03	5.72	12	7	0.81	—	11.99
Annual Growth	**37.2%**	**—**	**—**	**22.4%**	**—**	**(5.6%)**

The Bancorp, Inc.

The Bancorp is The Holding Company for The Bancorp Bank, which provides services on both the local and national level in the virtual world. On its home turf of the Philadelphia-Wilmington metropolitan area, The Bancorp Bank offers deposit, lending, and similar services, targeting the wealthy individuals and small to midsized businesses it believes are underserved by larger banks in the market. Nationally, The Bancorp provides private-label online banking services for affinity groups and performs merchant card-processing services. The Bancorp's services are provided via the Internet. The bank does not have a branch system; it does have three loan offices in its home market.

The Bancorp also has offices in Alabama, Florida, and Maryland related to an auto-leasing business it acquired in 2005. The company bought Stored Value Solutions, the prepaid card business of South Dakota-based Bank First, in 2007.

Commercial real estate and business loans dominate The Bancorp's loan portfolio.

CEO and founder Betsy Cohen and other family members own some 15% of The Bancorp.

EXECUTIVES

Chairman; Vice Chairman, The Bancorp Bank: Daniel G. Cohen, age 38, $196,154 pay
CEO and Director; Chairman and CEO, The Bancorp Bank: Betsy Z. Cohen, age 65, $371,154 pay
President, COO, and Director, The Bancorp, Inc. and The Bancorp Bank: Frank M. Mastrangelo, age 39, $253,846 pay
Secretary; SVP and CFO, The Bancorp, Inc. and The Bancorp Bank: Martin F. (Marty) Egan, age 39, $169,085 pay
EVP and Chief Lending Officer, The Bancorp, Inc. and The Bancorp Bank: Scott R. Megargee, age 55, $179,462 pay
EVP, Commercial Loans, The Bancorp, Inc. and The Bancorp Bank: Arthur M. Birenbaum, age 50, $327,691 pay
EVP and Chief Credit Officer, The Bancorp, Inc. and The Bancorp Bank: Donald F. (Don) McGraw Jr., age 50
CTO: John Marino
Chief Risk Officer: James Hilty
Auditors: Grant Thornton LLP

LOCATIONS

HQ: The Bancorp, Inc.
405 Silverside Rd., Wilmington, DE 19809
Phone: 302-385-5000   **Fax:** 302-385-5194
Web: www.thebancorp.com

PRODUCTS/OPERATIONS

2006 Sales

	$ mil.	% of total
Interest		
Loans	71.3	83
Securities & other	9.7	11
Leasing income	1.4	2
Merchant credit card deposit fees	1.1	1
Service fees on deposit accounts	0.8	1
Other	1.7	2
Total	**86.0**	**100**

COMPETITORS

Citizens Financial Group	Republic First
Commerce Bancorp	Royal Bancshares
E*TRADE Bank	Sovereign Bancorp
EverBank Financial	Sun Bancorp (NJ)
ING DIRECT	Wachovia
Lydian	Wilmington Trust
PNC Financial	WSFS Financial

HISTORICAL FINANCIALS

Company Type: Public

Income Statement

FYE: December 31

	ASSETS ($ mil.)	NET INCOME ($ mil.)	INCOME AS % OF ASSETS	EMPLOYEES
12/06	1,334.8	12.5	0.9%	181
12/05	917.5	7.4	0.8%	150
12/04	576.3	3.7	0.6%	—
Annual Growth	**52.2%**	**83.8%**	**—**	**20.7%**

2006 Year-End Financials

Equity as % of assets: 11.2%
Return on assets: 1.1%
Return on equity: 8.8%
Long-term debt ($ mil.): —
No. of shares (mil.): 13.7
Market value ($ mil.): 406.2
Dividends
  Yield: —
  Payout: —
Sales ($ mil.): 86.0
R&D as % of sales: —
Advertising as % of sales: —

Stock History

NASDAQ (GM): TBBK

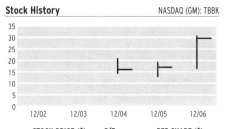

	STOCK PRICE ($) FY Close	P/E High	P/E Low	Earnings	Dividends	Book Value
12/06	29.60	35	19	0.86	—	10.85
12/05	17.00	40	27	0.48	—	9.89
12/04	16.00	86	60	0.24	—	10.21
Annual Growth	**36.0%**	**—**	**—**	**89.3%**	**—**	**3.1%**

The Bank Holdings

You can probably guess what The Bank Holdings does. Where they do it is out west. As the holding company for Nevada Security Bank, the company operates branches in the northern portion of the state. Nevada Security Bank offers typical deposit products, such as checking and savings accounts, as well as CDs and IRAs. Commercial real estate loans make up about 40% of the bank's loan portfolio, which also includes construction/development loans, consumer loans, residential mortgages, and business loans (including SBA loans). The Bank Holdings moved into California through its 2004 purchase of CNA Trust Corporation of Costa Mesa. The California branch (now located in Roseville) operates as Silverado Bank.

EXECUTIVES

Chairman and CEO; CEO and Director, Nevada Security Bank: Harold G. (Hal) Giomi, age 64, $408,000 pay
President and Director; SEVP, Marketing and Sales, and Director, Nevada Security Bank: Joseph P. (Joe) Bourdeau, age 53, $165,000 pay
CFO; EVP and CFO, Nevada Security Bank: Jack B. Buchold, age 63, $196,000 pay
EVP and Chief Credit Officer, The Bank Holdings and Nevada Security Bank: John N. Donovan, age 58, $211,000 pay
Director; President and Director, Nevada Security Bank: David A. Funk, age 63, $205,000 pay
Corporate Secretary and Director; Director, Nevada Security Bank: Edward Coppin, age 67
Auditors: Moss Adams, LLP

LOCATIONS

HQ: The Bank Holdings
9990 Double R Blvd., Reno, NV 89521
Phone: 775-853-8600   **Fax:** 775-853-2068
Web: www.thebankholdings.com

The Bank Holdings has locations in Reno and Incline Village, Nevada, and in Roseville, California.

PRODUCTS/OPERATIONS

2006 Sales

	$ mil.	% of total
Interest		
Loans	25.9	79
Securities & other	5.1	15
Noninterest		
Exchange fee income	0.5	2
Unrealized gain on trading securities	0.4	1
Service charges	0.3	1
Other	0.5	2
Total	**32.7**	**100**

COMPETITORS

American River Bankshares
Bank of America
Bank of the West
First Northern
U.S. Bancorp
Wells Fargo

HISTORICAL FINANCIALS

Company Type: Public

Income Statement

FYE: December 31

	ASSETS ($ mil.)	NET INCOME ($ mil.)	INCOME AS % OF ASSETS	EMPLOYEES
12/06	651.5	2.1	0.3%	121
12/05	384.6	1.4	0.4%	59
12/04	246.8	0.3	0.1%	—
12/03	166.1	(0.6)	—	—
Annual Growth	**57.7%**	**—**	**—**	**105.1%**

2006 Year-End Financials

Equity as % of assets: 11.3%
Return on assets: 0.4%
Return on equity: 4.1%
Long-term debt ($ mil.): 28.9
No. of shares (mil.): 5.8
Market value ($ mil.): 105.5
Dividends
  Yield: —
  Payout: —
Sales ($ mil.): 32.7
R&D as % of sales: —
Advertising as % of sales: —

Stock History

| | STOCK PRICE ($) | P/E | | PER SHARE ($) | | |
	FY Close	High/Low	Earnings	Dividends	Book Value
12/06	18.09	42 34	0.47	—	12.62
12/05	17.95	45 34	0.41	—	9.19
12/04	18.78	207 133	0.09	—	9.21
Annual Growth	(1.9%)	— —	128.5%	—	17.0%

Bank of Commerce

Bank of Commerce Holdings is where Northern California commerce banks. Formerly Redding Bancorp, Bank of Commerce Holdings provides traditional banking services through subsidiary Redding Bank of Commerce and its divisions, Roseville Bank of Commerce and Sutter Bank of Commerce. It targets small to midsized businesses and medium to high net worth individuals in the California counties of El Dorado, Placer, Sacramento, and Shasta. Through its handful of branches the company provides savings accounts, deposit accounts, and loans. It provides single- and multifamily residential financing, refinancing, and equity lines of credit through subsidiary Bank of Commerce Mortgage (formerly RBC Mortgage Services).

Director Harry Grashoff Jr. and former chairman Robert Anderson each own more than 6% of the company; director John Fitzpatrick controls nearly 7%.

EXECUTIVES

Chairman: Kenneth R. Gifford Jr., age 62
President and CEO: Patrick J. (Pat) Moty, age 50, $160,000 pay
EVP and CFO, Bank of Commerce Holdings, Redding Bank of Commerce, and Bank of Commerce Mortgage: Linda J. Miles, age 54, $195,000 pay
Regional President, Roseville Bank of Commerce: Randall S. (Randy) Eslick, age 50, $150,000 pay (prior to title change)
SVP and CIO, Redding Bank of Commerce: Caryn A. Blais, age 56
SVP and Senior Loan Officer: John C. Rainey
SVP and Senior Loan Officer: Dennis E. Lee
SVP and Regional Credit Manager, Roseville Bank of Commerce: Robert J. O'Neil, age 52, $140,000 pay
SVP and Administrative Operations Officer: Debra A. Sylvester, age 49
VP and Controller: David J. Gonzales
Corporate Secretary and Director: David H. Scott, age 63
Auditors: Moss Adams, LLP

LOCATIONS

HQ: Bank of Commerce Holdings
1951 Churn Creek Rd., Redding, CA 96002
Phone: 530-224-3333 **Fax:** 530-224-3337
Web: www.reddingbankofcommerce.com

COMPETITORS

Bank of America
North Valley Bancorp
Plumas Bancorp
U.S. Bancorp
Wells Fargo

HISTORICAL FINANCIALS

Company Type: Public

Income Statement

FYE: December 31

	ASSETS ($ mil.)	NET INCOME ($ mil.)	INCOME AS % OF ASSETS	EMPLOYEES
12/06	583.4	6.6	1.1%	115
12/05	511.6	6.3	1.2%	125
12/04	438.5	5.0	1.1%	—
12/03	401.2	4.2	1.0%	—
12/02	367.4	3.7	1.0%	—
Annual Growth	12.3%	15.6%	—	(8.0%)

2006 Year-End Financials

Equity as % of assets: 7.5%
Return on assets: 1.2%
Return on equity: 15.9%
Long-term debt ($ mil.): 15.5
No. of shares (mil.): 8.8
Market value ($ mil.): 106.1
Dividends
  Yield: 2.5%
  Payout: 40.5%
Sales ($ mil.): 39.7
R&D as % of sales: —
Advertising as % of sales: —

Stock History

| | STOCK PRICE ($) | P/E | | PER SHARE ($) | | |
	FY Close	High/Low	Earnings	Dividends	Book Value
12/06	11.99	17 12	0.74	0.30	4.96
12/05	10.10	18 13	0.71	0.26	4.52
12/04	12.35	30 18	0.57	—	4.15
12/03	8.42	18 11	0.50	—	11.26
12/02	6.78	18 15	0.43	—	10.47
Annual Growth	15.3%	— —	14.5%	15.4%	(17.0%)

Bank of Florida

Bank of Florida (formerly Bancshares of Florida) is the holding company for its eponymous Bank of Florida subsidiaries, which operate about ten branches in southeastern and southwestern portions of the state, as well as the Tampa Bay area. Subsidiary Bank of Florida Trust offers trust, estate planning, and investment management services. The bank and the trust company cater to professionals, entrepreneurs, and small to midsized businesses, providing personalized deposit, lending, and investment services that larger banks in their market often do not. In 2007 Bank of Florida bought Old Florida Bankshares, the holding company for Old Florida Bank. The company bought Bristol Bank, a single-branch institution in Dade County, Florida, in 2006.

Bank of Florida's loan portfolio is primarily composed of real estate construction loans (almost 40% of all loans), followed by commercial real estate loans (around 30%). Other loan offerings include residential mortgages, business loans, consumer loans, and lines of credit. The bank also offers deposit accounts, credit cards, and merchant services.

EXECUTIVES

Chairman: Michael T. Putziger, age 61
Vice Chairman; Chairman, Bank of Florida Trust Corporation; Director, Bank of Florida — Southwest: Joe B. Cox, age 67
President, CEO, and Director: Michael L. McMullan, age 52, $352,000 pay
President and CEO, Southeast: John S. Chaperon, age 58
SEVP, Chief Administrative Officer, and Director: John B. James, age 65, $200,000 pay
EVP and CFO: Tracy L. Keegan, age 41, $197,500 pay
EVP and Chief Risk Manager: Thomas M. (Tom) Whelan, age 53
EVP and Director, Bank Operations and Technology: David W. Taylor, age 59
SVP and Chief Accounting Officer: Sharon I. Hill, age 49
VP, Marketing: Sara Dewberry
Corporate Secretary: Arlette Yassa
Director; Chairman, Bank of Florida: Harry K. Moon, age 57
CEO, Bank of Florida Trust Company: Julie W. Husler, $210,000 pay
EVP and Chief Lending Officer; President and CEO, Bank of Florida — Southwest: Craig D. Sherman, age 49, $197,950 pay (prior to promotion)
Auditors: Hacker, Johnson & Smith PA

LOCATIONS

HQ: Bank of Florida Corporation
1185 Immokalee Rd., Naples, FL 34103
Phone: 239-254-2100 **Fax:** 239-254-2107
Web: www.bankoffloridaonline.com

Bank of Florida has branches in Aventura, Boca Raton, Bonita Springs, Coral Gables, Fort Lauderdale (2), Naples (2), and Tampa, Florida.

PRODUCTS/OPERATIONS

2006 Sales

	$ mil.	% of total
Interest		
Loans, including fees	49.0	86
Federal funds sold	1.6	3
Securities & other	1.8	3
Noninterest		
Trust fees	2.6	5
Service charges & fees	1.2	2
Net gain on sales of loans	0.4	1
Total	**56.6**	**100**

COMPETITORS

Bank of America
BankUnited
Colonial BancGroup
Fifth Third
First Citizens BancShares
F.N.B. (PA)
Home BancShares
Northern Trust
Regions Financial
SunTrust
Wachovia

HISTORICAL FINANCIALS
Company Type: Public

Income Statement
FYE: December 31

	ASSETS ($ mil.)	NET INCOME ($ mil.)	INCOME AS % OF ASSETS	EMPLOYEES
12/06	883.1	2.3	0.3%	200
12/05	569.8	4.9	0.9%	153
12/04	420.8	(2.9)	—	—
12/03	222.6	(2.7)	—	—
12/02	144.5	(2.6)	—	—
Annual Growth	57.2%	—	—	30.7%

2006 Year-End Financials
Equity as % of assets: 15.3%
Return on assets: 0.3%
Return on equity: 2.4%
Long-term debt ($ mil.): 11.0
No. of shares (mil.): 9.6
Market value ($ mil.): 196.2
Dividends
  Yield: —
  Payout: —
Sales ($ mil.): 56.6
R&D as % of sales: —
Advertising as % of sales: —

Stock History
NASDAQ (GM): BOFL

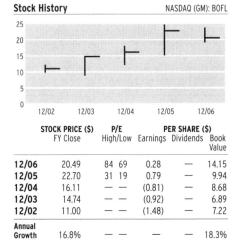

	STOCK PRICE ($) FY Close	P/E High/Low	Earnings	Dividends	Book Value
12/06	20.49	84 69	0.28	—	14.15
12/05	22.70	31 19	0.79	—	9.94
12/04	16.11	— —	(0.81)	—	8.68
12/03	14.74	— —	(0.92)	—	6.89
12/02	11.00	— —	(1.48)	—	7.22
Annual Growth	16.8%	— —	—	—	18.3%

Bank of South Carolina

What, were you expecting something different? The Bank of South Carolina Corporation is the holding company for The Bank of South Carolina. The bank operates four branches in and around Charleston. Targeting individuals and small to midsized business customers, the bank offers such standard retail services as checking and savings accounts, credit cards, and money market accounts. The bank focuses on commercial lending. Real estate loans make up more than 60% of the bank's loan portfolio, which also includes commercial (around one-third) and personal loans. President Hugh Lane and his family control about 20% of the company.

EXECUTIVES
President, CEO, and Director, Bank of South Carolina Corporation and Bank of South Carolina:
  Hugh C. Lane Jr., age 59, $191,600 pay
EVP, Treasurer, and Director, Bank of South Carolina Corporation and Bank of South Carolina:
  William L. (Bill) Hiott Jr., age 62, $168,600 pay
EVP and Director: Fleetwood S. Hassell, age 47, $121,600 pay
Secretary and Director: Richard W. Hutson Jr., age 49

Human Resources Director, Bank of South Carolina:
  Mindy Buhrmaster
Network Administrator, Bank of South Carolina:
  Bret Roesner
Auditors: KPMG LLP

LOCATIONS
HQ: Bank of South Carolina Corporation
  256 Meeting St., Charleston, SC 29401
Phone: 843-724-1500   **Fax:** 843-724-1513
Web: www.banksc.com

PRODUCTS/OPERATIONS
2006 Sales

	$ mil.	% of total
Interest		
Loans, including fees	13.4	76
Securities	1.8	10
Other	1.0	6
Noninterest		
Service charges, fees & commissions	0.9	5
Mortgage banking & other	0.6	3
Total	**17.7**	**100**

COMPETITORS
Bank of America
BB&T
Coastal Banking Company
First Citizens Bancorporation
First Financial Holdings
SCBT Financial
South Financial
Wachovia

HISTORICAL FINANCIALS
Company Type: Public

Income Statement
FYE: December 31

	ASSETS ($ mil.)	NET INCOME ($ mil.)	INCOME AS % OF ASSETS	EMPLOYEES
12/06	243.5	3.9	1.6%	69
12/05	222.5	3.2	1.4%	65
12/04	201.2	1.9	0.9%	—
12/03	187.3	1.9	1.0%	—
12/02	169.5	1.9	1.1%	69
Annual Growth	9.5%	19.7%	—	0.0%

2006 Year-End Financials
Equity as % of assets: 9.7%
Return on assets: 1.7%
Return on equity: 17.3%
Long-term debt ($ mil.): —
No. of shares (mil.): 3.9
Market value ($ mil.): 61.9
Dividends
  Yield: 4.1%
  Payout: 64.0%
Sales ($ mil.): 17.7
R&D as % of sales: —
Advertising as % of sales: —

Stock History
NASDAQ (CM): BKSC

	STOCK PRICE ($) FY Close	P/E High/Low	Earnings	Dividends	Book Value
12/06	15.75	18 14	1.00	0.64	6.02
12/05	15.24	19 12	0.82	2.08	6.96
12/04	9.74	22 17	0.48	0.24	7.13
12/03	10.18	23 15	0.49	1.76	7.00
12/02	7.33	22 15	0.48	0.25	7.57
Annual Growth	21.1%	— —	20.1%	26.5%	(5.6%)

Bank of the Carolinas

It would be more accurate to call it Bank of the North Carolina. Bank of the Carolinas Corporation was formed in 2006 to be the holding company for Bank of the Carolinas, which provides traditional deposit and lending services to individuals and businesses through about 10 branches in central North Carolina. Deposit services include checking, savings, and money market accounts; IRAs; and CDs. The bank's lending activities include credit cards, business and consumer loans, mortgages, equity lines of credit, and overdraft checking credit. However, commercial real estate loans account for the largest portion of the company's loan portfolio.

EXECUTIVES
Chairman, President, and CEO: Robert E. Marziano, age 59
Vice Chairman: Stephen R. (Steve) Talbert
EVP: George Edward (Ed) Jordan
EVP: Harry E. Hill
EVP: Robin H. Smith
SVP and CFO: John A. (Jack) Bush
SVP and Senior Loan Officer: Doc T. Twiford
SVP, Harrisburg: Dana Ritchie
Auditors: Dixon Hughes PLLC

LOCATIONS
HQ: Bank of the Carolinas Corporation
  135 Boxwood Village Dr., Mocksville, NC 27028
Phone: 336-751-5755   **Fax:** 336-751-4222
Web: www.bankofthecarolinas.com

PRODUCTS/OPERATIONS
2006 Sales

	$ mil.	% of total
Interest		
Loans, including fees	26.7	82
Investment securities	2.2	7
Other	0.4	1
Noninterest		
Gain on sale of branch	1.8	5
Customer service fees	0.9	3
Other	0.7	2
Total	**32.7**	**100**

COMPETITORS
Bank of America
Bank of Oak Ridge
BB&T
NewBridge Bancorp
Piedmont Federal
RBC Centura Banks
Southern Community Financial
SunTrust
Wachovia

HISTORICAL FINANCIALS
Company Type: Public

Income Statement
FYE: December 31

	ASSETS ($ mil.)	NET INCOME ($ mil.)	INCOME AS % OF ASSETS	EMPLOYEES
12/06	454.6	3.5	0.8%	101
12/05	390.2	2.3	0.6%	—
12/04	292.1	1.1	0.4%	72
Annual Growth	24.8%	78.4%	—	18.4%

2006 Year-End Financials

Equity as % of assets: 8.3%
Return on assets: 0.8%
Return on equity: 9.7%
Long-term debt ($ mil.): —
No. of shares (mil.): 3.8
Market value ($ mil.): 56.5

Dividends
Yield: 0.7%
Payout: 11.4%
Sales ($ mil.): 32.7
R&D as % of sales: —
Advertising as % of sales: —

Stock History

NASDAQ (GM): BCAR

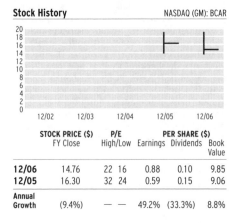

	STOCK PRICE ($) FY Close	P/E High/Low		PER SHARE ($) Earnings	Dividends	Book Value
12/06	14.76	22	16	0.88	0.10	9.85
12/05	16.30	32	24	0.59	0.15	9.06
Annual Growth	(9.4%)	—	—	49.2%	(33.3%)	8.8%

Bank of the Ozarks

Bank of the Ozarks is the holding company for the bank of the same name, which operates in northern, central, and western Arkansas and in Texas and North Carolina. The bank has around 70 branch locations and loan production offices; individuals and small to midsized businesses are its primary clientele. Services include traditional banking and loan offerings; trust and cash management and equipment leasing services are also available. Commercial mortgages make up nearly 30% of a loan portfolio that also includes residential mortgages and business, agricultural, consumer, and construction loans. CEO George Gleason owns around 23% of the company.

Bank of the Ozarks has expanded by opening new branches in targeted areas. At first, the bank began slowly expanding into smaller communities, but has since turned its sights on bigger game after tasting success in Little Rock and Fort Smith. The company opened 10 new branches during 2004 and, upon acquiring a Texas bank charter, converted its Texas loan production offices into bank branches.

EXECUTIVES

Chairman and CEO, Bank of the Ozarks, Inc. and Bank of the Ozarks: George G. Gleason, age 53, $570,577 pay
Vice Chairman, President, and COO, Bank of the Ozarks, Inc. and Bank of the Ozarks: Mark Ross, age 51, $239,423 pay
CFO and Chief Accounting Officer, Bank of the Ozarks, Inc. and Bank of the Ozarks: Paul Moore, age 60, $174,450 pay
EVP, Bank of the Ozarks, Inc. and Bank of the Ozarks: Dan Rolett, age 44
SVP Human Resources: Diane Hilburn
President, Central Division, Bank of the Ozarks: Darrel Russell, age 53, $170,585 pay
President, Leasing Division, Bank of the Ozarks: Scott Hastings, age 49
President, Mortgage Division, Bank of the Ozarks: Gene Holman, age 59, $192,074 pay
CIO: Ron Kuykendall
Auditors: Ernst & Young LLP

LOCATIONS

HQ: Bank of the Ozarks, Inc.
12615 Chenal Pkwy., Little Rock, AR 72231
Phone: 501-978-2265   **Fax:** 501-978-2350
Web: www.bankozarks.com

PRODUCTS/OPERATIONS

2006 Sales

	$ mil.	% of total
Interest		
Loans & leases	121.5	68
Securities & other	33.7	19
Noninterest		
Service charges on deposit accounts	10.2	6
Gains on sales of investment securities	3.9	2
Mortgage lending	2.9	2
Trust income	2.0	1
Bank-owned life insurance	1.8	1
Other	2.4	1
Total	**178.4**	**100**

COMPETITORS

Arvest Holdings
BancorpSouth
BOK Financial
First Federal Bancshares of Arkansas
First Horizon
Home BancShares
IBERIABANK
Regions Financial
Simmons First

HISTORICAL FINANCIALS

Company Type: Public

Income Statement

FYE: December 31

	ASSETS ($ mil.)	NET INCOME ($ mil.)	INCOME AS % OF ASSETS	EMPLOYEES
12/06	2,529.4	31.7	1.3%	699
12/05	2,134.9	31.5	1.5%	629
12/04	1,726.8	25.9	1.5%	—
12/03	1,386.5	20.2	1.5%	—
12/02	1,035.8	14.4	1.4%	382
Annual Growth	25.0%	21.8%	—	16.3%

2006 Year-End Financials

Equity as % of assets: 6.9%
Return on assets: 1.4%
Return on equity: 19.6%
Long-term debt ($ mil.): 259.6
No. of shares (mil.): 16.7
Market value ($ mil.): 553.6

Dividends
Yield: 1.2%
Payout: 21.2%
Sales ($ mil.): 178.4
R&D as % of sales: —
Advertising as % of sales: —

Stock History

NASDAQ (GS): OZRK

	STOCK PRICE ($) FY Close	P/E High/Low		PER SHARE ($) Earnings	Dividends	Book Value
12/06	33.06	20	16	1.89	0.40	10.43
12/05	36.90	21	16	1.88	0.29	8.97
12/04	34.03	24	13	1.56	0.15	7.36
12/03	22.53	20	9	1.24	0.23	6.07
12/02	11.72	14	7	0.92	0.16	9.41
Annual Growth	29.6%	—	—	19.7%	25.7%	2.6%

Bankrate, Inc.

Bankrate knows there's life after budget-cutting. The firm's Bankrate.com provides personal finance information on more than 300 products including mortgages, credit cards, money market accounts, certificates of deposit, and home equity loans. Its Interest.com publishes financial rates and information connecting consumers with lenders, and its FastFind sells consumer leads to lenders for mortgages, home-equity loans, auto financing, and online education. Bankrate also has print publications, such as its *Mortgage Guide*, a weekly newspaper-advertising table consisting of product and rate information from local mortgage companies and financial institutions. Director and former CEO Peter Morse owns 26% of Bankrate.

Companies such as AOL, Yahoo!, CNN, MSN, Internet Broadcasting System, and USA Today drive traffic to Bankrate.com.

The company reduced staff, sold a number of assets (including CPNet.com and Pivot.com), and shut down others (ilife.com, Consejero.com, and Garzarelli.com) to survive the dot-com crash. In 2006 Bankrate purchased a group of assets that include three Web sites — Mortgage-calc.com, Mortgagecalc.com, and Mortgagemath.com — for about $4 million in cash. The acquired sites were integrated into the company's online publishing segment.

EXECUTIVES

President, CEO, and Director: Thomas R. Evans, age 52, $365,385 pay
SVP, CFO, and Secretary: Edward J. (Ed) DiMaria, age 41, $215,000 pay
SVP and CTO: Daniel P. Hoogterp, age 47
SVP and Chief Communications/Marketing Officer: Bruce J. Zanca, age 46, $210,000 pay
SVP and Chief Revenue Officer: Donaldson M. Ross, age 43
SVP and Publisher: Lynn Varsell, age 46
SVP Finance: Robert J. (Bob) DeFranco, age 50, $210,000 pay
SVP Product and Business Development: Steven L. Horowitz, age 35, $210,000 pay
SVP Consumer Marketing: Michael Ricciardelli
Director Corporate Communications: Kayleen Keneally
Auditors: KPMG LLP

LOCATIONS

HQ: Bankrate, Inc.
11760 U.S. Hwy. 1, Ste. 200,
North Palm Beach, FL 33408
Phone: 561-630-2400   **Fax:** 561-625-4540
Web: www.bankrate.com

Bankrate has operations in California, Florida, and New York.

PRODUCTS/OPERATIONS

2006 Sales

	$ mil.	% of total
Online publishing	64.0	80
Print publishing & licensing	15.7	20
Total	**79.7**	**100**

Selected Distribution Agreements
America Online
CNN
Dollar Stretcher
Internet Broadcasting System
MSN
USA Today
Yahoo!

Selected Web Sites
Bankrate.com
Interest.com
FastFind.com
Mortgage-calc.com

COMPETITORS

Bloomberg L.P.
E-LOAN
Forbes
Insure.com
InsWeb
Intuit
Kiplinger
LendingTree
MarketWatch
McGraw-Hill
Morningstar
Motley Fool
PCQuote.com
PNC Financial
Reuters
SmartMoney
TheStreet.com
Value Line

HISTORICAL FINANCIALS

Company Type: Public

Income Statement — FYE: December 31

	REVENUE ($ mil.)	NET INCOME ($ mil.)	NET PROFIT MARGIN	EMPLOYEES
12/06	79.7	10.0	12.5%	163
12/05	49.0	9.7	19.8%	159
12/04	39.2	13.4	34.2%	—
12/03	36.6	12.1	33.1%	—
12/02	26.6	6.7	25.2%	109
Annual Growth	31.6%	10.5%	—	10.6%

2006 Year-End Financials

Debt ratio: —
Return on equity: 9.0%
Cash ($ mil.): 109.9
Current ratio: 20.36
Long-term debt ($ mil.): —
No. of shares (mil.): 18.2
Dividends
Yield: —
Payout: —
Market value ($ mil.): 691.6
R&D as % of sales: —
Advertising as % of sales: —

Stock History — NASDAQ (GS): RATE

	STOCK PRICE ($) FY Close	P/E High/Low		PER SHARE ($) Earnings	Dividends	Book Value
12/06	37.95	93	45	0.56	—	9.34
12/05	29.52	61	21	0.57	—	3.33
12/04	13.85	25	8	0.84	—	2.68
12/03	12.38	25	4	0.79	—	1.65
12/02	3.85	9	1	0.46	—	0.76
Annual Growth	77.2%	—	—	5.0%	—	87.2%

BankUnited Financial

BankUnited Financial is keeping it all together. The financial institution is the holding company for BankUnited, one of Florida's largest banking institutions with some 90 branches. The federal savings bank's deposit options include CDs and checking, NOW, and money market accounts. One- to four-family residential mortgages account for around 85% of BankUnited's loan portfolio. The bank's other loan offerings include commercial and multifamily mortgages and construction and land loans. BankUnited sells some of the mortgages it originates on the secondary market, often retaining the loan servicing functions.

BankUnited Financial competes with larger rivals through its "micro-market" strategy, targeting consumers and small to midsized businesses with banking offices tailored to their specific South Florida communities; the local offices tout the company's decentralized decision-making.

The company plans to open fewer branches in 2008, instead deepening its connection to customers in existing locations and improving operations. CEO Alfred Camner controls 9% of the company.

EXECUTIVES

Chairman and CEO, BankUnited Financial and BankUnited: Alfred R. Camner, age 63, $2,950,000 pay
Vice Chairman and Secretary: Lawrence H. Blum, age 64
President, COO, and Director; President and COO, BankUnited: Ramiro A. Ortiz, age 57, $1,054,937 pay
SEVP and CFO, BankUnited Financial and BankUnited: Humberto L. (Bert) Lopez, age 48
SEVP Corporate Finance: James R. (Jim) Foster, age 61, $424,896 pay (prior to promotion)
SEVP Corporate and Commercial Banking, BankUnited: Abel L. Iglesias, age 44, $492,483 pay (prior to promotion)
SEVP Neighborhood Banking, BankUnited: Carlos R. Fernandez-Guzman, age 51
EVP and General Auditor, BankUnited: Joris M. Jabouin, age 39
EVP Commercial Real Estate, BankUnited: Clay F. Wilson, age 48
EVP Banking Services, BankUnited: Douglas B. Sawyer, age 50
EVP Corporate Real Estate Services, BankUnited: Robert A. Marsden, age 65
EVP Human Resources, BankUnited: Roberta R. Kressel, age 52
EVP Wealth Management: Hunting F. Deutsch, age 55
Auditors: PricewaterhouseCoopers LLP

LOCATIONS

HQ: BankUnited Financial Corporation
255 Alhambra Cir., Coral Gables, FL 33134
Phone: 305-569-2000   **Fax:** 305-569-2057
Web: www.bankunitedfla.com

BankUnited Financial operates 86 branches and two loan production offices in Florida, and another seven loan offices outside the state.

PRODUCTS/OPERATIONS

2007 Sales

	$ mil.	% of total
Interest		
Loans, including fees	876.8	87
Mortgage-backed securities	50.7	5
Investments & other	31.4	3
Noninterest		
Net gain on sale of loans & other assets	9.8	1
Loan servicing & other fees	21.0	2
Other	13.2	1
Total	**1,002.9**	**100**

Selected Subsidiaries and Affiliates

BankUnited, FSB
  Bay Holdings, Inc.
  BU Delaware, Inc.
  BU REIT, Inc.
  CRE Properties, Inc.
  T&D Properties of South Florida, Inc.
BankUnited Financial Services, Incorporated

COMPETITORS

Bank of America
Bank of Florida
BankAtlantic
Citibank
Firstbank Florida
JPMorgan Chase
OptimumBank
Sun American Bancorp
SunTrust
U.S. Bancorp
Wachovia
Washington Mutual

HISTORICAL FINANCIALS

Company Type: Public

Income Statement — FYE: September 30

	ASSETS ($ mil.)	NET INCOME ($ mil.)	INCOME AS % OF ASSETS	EMPLOYEES
9/07	15,046.3	81.4	0.5%	—
9/06	13,570.9	83.9	0.6%	1,350
9/05	10,667.7	27.5	0.3%	1,137
9/04	8,710.4	50.7	0.6%	—
9/03	7,145.1	39.1	0.5%	—
Annual Growth	20.5%	20.1%	—	18.7%

2007 Year-End Financials

Equity as % of assets: 5.4%
Return on assets: 0.6%
Return on equity: 10.4%
Long-term debt ($ mil.): 553.8
No. of shares (mil.): 34.9
Market value ($ mil.): 542.5
Dividends
Yield: 0.1%
Payout: 0.9%
Sales ($ mil.): 1,002.9
R&D as % of sales: —
Advertising as % of sales: —

Stock History — NASDAQ (GS): BKUNA

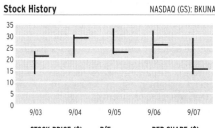

	STOCK PRICE ($) FY Close	P/E High/Low		PER SHARE ($) Earnings	Dividends	Book Value
9/07	15.54	13	6	2.14	0.02	23.26
9/06	26.07	14	9	2.30	0.02	20.84
9/05	22.87	39	26	0.85	0.01	16.93
9/04	29.15	19	13	1.58	—	16.69
9/03	21.20	17	10	1.36	—	15.35
Annual Growth	(7.5%)	—	—	12.0%	41.4%	10.9%

Bare Escentuals

When it comes to keeping its customers looking naturally pretty, Bare Escentuals has a mineral interest. The company, which rolled out its bareMinerals makeup brand in 1976 along with its first retail store, develops, markets, and sells natural cosmetics, skin care, and body care items. Brand names include RareMinerals, i.d. bareMinerals, md formulations, and its namesake line, among others. Formerly STB Beauty, Bare Escentuals sells its products through its more than 30 company-owned US boutiques, about 330 retailers, some 900 spas and salons, infomercials, and several Web sites. Berkshire Partners LLC and JH MDB Investors own a majority stake in the firm, which went public in September 2006.

The cosmetics firm raised $352 million in the 16-million-share initial public offering. The company plans to use the net proceeds to repay a portion of its debt valued at more than $229 million and fund future growth initiatives.

The company peddles products via its primary shopping Web sites: www.bareminerals.com and www.mdformulations.com.

The face of Bare Escentuals and its operations are likely to morph as the company shifts to cater to its customers' changing needs. Customers typically choose its earthy and lightweight foundation as an alternative to liquid or cream makeup, which can be heavy. For several years Bare Escentuals has earned the designation as a top seller at specialty retailers Sephora and Ulta. And its foundation products generated nearly half of the cosmetic company's sales in 2006. Until other product categories drive the retailer and manufacturer's revenue, however, the fate of Bare Escentuals is tied to the trend of women shifting to a sheer, more natural foundation. Also, three customers, Sephora, Ulta, and QVC, accounted for 40% of the firm's sales in 2006.

Bare Escentuals attributes its 57% growth in net sales since 2002 to its marketing and distributing model that consists of an assortment of wholesaling and retailing ventures. At the wholesale level its strategy is to increase sales at specialty retailers, home shopping TV shows (such as QVC), and spas and salons. Boosting the number of company-owned boutiques is a key component of the company's retail strategy, as well as instituting more savvy media spending for infomercials.

The company, which changed its name from STB Beauty to Bare Escentuals in February 2006, is exploring an international expansion and pinpointing Japan, Germany, France, South Korea, and the UK as geographical areas of interest. In 2007 it acquired European cosmetics distributor Cosmeceuticals Ltd. and renamed the company Bare Escentuals UK. Bare Escentuals experienced a slight bump in the road in November 2007, when the president of its wholesale and international sales resigned.

EXECUTIVES

Chairman: Ross M. Jones, age 42
CEO and Director: Leslie A. Blodgett, age 44, $600,000 pay
SVP, CFO, COO, and Secretary: Myles B. McCormick, age 34, $350,000 pay
SVP Direct to Consumer Business: Karen Barner
Chief Marketing Officer: James (Jim) Taschetta
Auditors: Ernst & Young LLP

LOCATIONS

HQ: Bare Escentuals, Inc.
71 Stevenson St., 22nd Fl.,
San Francisco, CA 94105
Phone: 415-489-5000   **Fax:** 877-963-3329
Web: www.bareescentuals.com

2006 Sales

	$ mil.	% of total
North America	377.9	96
Other countries	16.6	4
Total	**394.5**	**100**

PRODUCTS/OPERATIONS

2006 Sales

	$ mil.	% of total
Wholesale	209.5	53
Retail	185.0	47
Total	**394.5**	**100**

2006 Retail Sales

	$ mil.	% of total
Retail		
Infomercial	129.0	33
Boutiques	56.0	14
Wholesale		
Premium wholesale	109.8	28
Home shopping television	49.7	13
Spas and salons	33.4	8
International	16.6	4
Total	**394.5**	**100**

COMPETITORS

Avon	Ideal Shopping Direct
BeautiControl	L'Oréal
Beauty Brands	Mary Kay
BeneFit Cosmetics	Nu Skin
Borlind of Germany, Inc.	OrthoNeutrogena
CA Botana	Procter & Gamble
Canderm Pharma	PureBeauty
Clarins	Quixtar
Clinique Laboratories	QVC
CVS/Caremark	Revlon
DLI Holding	Rite Aid
drugstore.com	Sally Beauty
Elizabeth Arden Inc	Ulta
Estée Lauder Cosmetics	Vertical Branding
The Forever Group	Walgreen
Fresh Inc.	Whole Foods
Guthy-Renker	

HISTORICAL FINANCIALS

Company Type: Public

Income Statement

FYE: Sunday nearest December 31

	REVENUE ($ mil.)	NET INCOME ($ mil.)	NET PROFIT MARGIN	EMPLOYEES
12/06	394.5	50.2	12.7%	863
12/05	259.3	23.9	9.2%	576
12/04	141.8	4.0	2.8%	—
12/03	94.7	11.8	12.5%	—
Annual Growth	**60.9%**	**62.0%**	**—**	**49.8%**

2006 Year-End Financials

Debt ratio: —
Return on equity: —
Cash ($ mil.): 20.9
Current ratio: 2.12
Long-term debt ($ mil.): 321.6
No. of shares (mil.): 89.3
Dividends
  Yield: —
  Payout: —
Market value ($ mil.): 2,775.0
R&D as % of sales: —
Advertising as % of sales: —

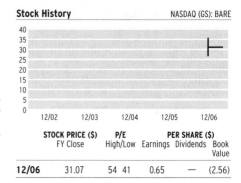

Stock History

NASDAQ (GS): BARE

	STOCK PRICE ($) FY Close	P/E High/Low	PER SHARE ($) Earnings	Dividends	Book Value
12/06	31.07	54 41	0.65	—	(2.56)

Basic Energy Services

Oil and gas producers turn to Basic Energy Services for the fundamentals. The company provides well site services with its fleet of well-servicing rigs (at more than 360, the third-largest in the US behind Key Energy Services and Nabors Industries), fluid service trucks, and related equipment. These services include acidizing, cementing, fluid handling, fracing, well construction, well maintenance, and workover. Basic Energy Services serves producers operating in Louisiana, New Mexico, Oklahoma, and Texas. It is a consolidator in the fragmented well services industry. Investment firm DLJ Merchant Banking Partners III, L.P., controls the company.

Basic Energy Services has pursued a strategy of growth through acquisitions. In 2004 the company acquired underbalanced drilling services company Energy Air Drilling Service, and wireline firm AWS Wireline Services. In 2006 it acquired Globe Well Service and five other firms.

That year it also acquired Chaparral Services and Reddline Services for $20 million. In early 2007 the company agreed to buy two barge-mounted workover rigs and related equipment from Parker Drilling for $26 million.

In 2007 Basic Energy Services acquired pressure pumping equipment operator JetStar Consolidated Holdings for $120 million, Sledge Drilling Holding Corp. for $51 million, and Steve Carter, Inc. and Hughes Services, Inc. for $20 million.

EXECUTIVES

Chairman: Steven A. Webster, age 55
President, CEO, and Director:
  Kenneth V. (Ken) Huseman, age 55, $382,692 pay
SVP, CFO, Treasurer, and Secretary: Alan Krenek, age 51, $227,308 pay
SVP Rig and Truck Operations:
  Charles W. (Charlie) Swift, age 57, $176,154 pay
VP Risk Management: Mark D. Rankin, age 53
VP Equipment and Safety: Dub William Harrison, age 49, $147,692 pay
VP Human Resources: James E. Tyner, age 56, $135,891 pay
VP Corporate Development, Rental and Fishing Tool Operations: T.M. (Roe) Patterson, age 32
Auditors: KPMG LLP

LOCATIONS

HQ: Basic Energy Services, Inc.
400 W. Illinios, Ste. 800, Midland, TX 79701
Phone: 432-620-5500 **Fax:** 432-620-5501
Web: www.basicenergyservices.com

Basic Energy Services operates in Louisiana, New Mexico, Oklahoma, Texas, and in the Rocky Mountains.

PRODUCTS/OPERATIONS

2006 Sales

	$ mil.	% of total
Well servicing	330.7	45
Fluid services	194.7	27
Drilling & completion services	154.4	21
Well site construction services	50.4	7
Total	**730.2**	**100**

COMPETITORS

BJ Services
Halliburton
Key Energy
Nabors Industries
Pride International
Schlumberger
Weatherford International

HISTORICAL FINANCIALS

Company Type: Public

Income Statement				FYE: December 31
	REVENUE ($ mil.)	NET INCOME ($ mil.)	NET PROFIT MARGIN	EMPLOYEES
12/06	730.2	98.8	13.5%	4,000
12/05	459.8	44.8	9.7%	3,280
12/04	311.5	12.9	4.1%	—
12/03	180.9	2.8	1.5%	—
12/02	108.8	(1.3)	—	—
Annual Growth	**61.0%**	**—**	**—**	**22.0%**

2006 Year-End Financials

Debt ratio: 66.1%
Return on equity: 31.0%
Cash ($ mil.): 51.4
Current ratio: 2.34
Long-term debt ($ mil.): 250.7
No. of shares (mil.): 38.3
Dividends
  Yield: —
  Payout: —
Market value ($ mil.): 944.0
R&D as % of sales: —
Advertising as % of sales: —

Stock History

NYSE: BAS

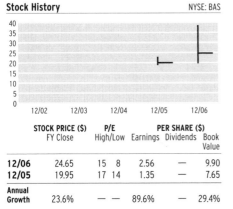

	STOCK PRICE ($) FY Close	P/E High/Low		PER SHARE ($) Earnings	Dividends	Book Value
12/06	24.65	15	8	2.56	—	9.90
12/05	19.95	17	14	1.35	—	7.65
Annual Growth	**23.6%**	**—**	**—**	**89.6%**	**—**	**29.4%**

Bay National

Bay National Corporation is staying afloat in the banking waters. The institution is a holding company for Bay National Bank, which operates two banking locations in Baltimore and Salisbury, Maryland. Targeting small to midsized businesses and individuals (primarily those associated with business customers as well as professionals and high-net-worth individuals), Bay National Bank offers traditional banking products including checking and savings accounts, CDs, and loans. (Commercial loans and real estate construction, combined, account for about 75% of its lending portfolio.) The company partners with other firms to provide its clients with investment advisory, risk management, and employee benefit services.

Bay National Bank's offices are organized in a nontraditional fashion, with customer transactions taking place at bank personnel desks rather than teller windows.

Directors and executives collectively own about 20% of the company.

EXECUTIVES

Chairman, President, and CEO, Bay National and Bay National Bank: Hugh W. Mohler, age 61, $325,000 pay
EVP, CFO, Secretary, and Treasurer; EVP, CFO, Chief Compliance Officer, Secretary, and Treasurer, Bay National Bank: Mark A. Semanie, age 43, $252,000 pay
EVP and Chief Credit Officer, Bay National Bank: Richard J. Oppitz, age 60, $196,000 pay (partial-year salary)
SVP, Corporate Banking, Baltimore, Bay National Bank: Warren F. (Boot) Boutilier
SVP, Corporate Banking, Baltimore, Bay National Bank: Curt H. G. Heinfelden
SVP, Corporate Banking, Baltimore, Bay National Bank: Hugh L. Robinson II
VP, Marketing and Investor Relations, Bay National Corporation and Bay National Bank: Lucy Mohler
Auditors: Stegman & Company

LOCATIONS

HQ: Bay National Corporation
2328 W. Joppa Rd., Lutherville, MD 21093
Phone: 410-494-2580 **Fax:** 410-494-2589
Web: www.baynational.com

PRODUCTS/OPERATIONS

2006 Sales

	$ mil.	% of total
Interest		
Interest & fees on loans	19.1	92
Interest on federal funds sold & other overnight investments	0.6	3
Taxable interest & dividends on investment securities	0.1	1
Noninterest		
Service charges on deposit accounts	0.1	1
Gain on sale of mortgage loans & other income	0.7	3
Total	**20.6**	**100**

COMPETITORS

Bank of America	Harbor Bankshares
BCSB Bankcorp	M&T Bank
Calvin B. Taylor Bankshares	Patapsco Bancorp
	Provident Bankshares
Carrollton Bancorp	SunTrust
First Mariner Bancorp	Wachovia

HISTORICAL FINANCIALS

Company Type: Public

Income Statement				FYE: December 31
	ASSETS ($ mil.)	NET INCOME ($ mil.)	INCOME AS % OF ASSETS	EMPLOYEES
12/06	254.8	2.4	0.9%	57
12/05	210.0	2.7	1.3%	56
12/04	170.8	0.8	0.5%	—
12/03	122.3	0.0	—	—
12/02	84.6	(1.0)	—	—
Annual Growth	**31.7%**	**—**	**—**	**1.8%**

2006 Year-End Financials

Equity as % of assets: 7.4%
Return on assets: 1.0%
Return on equity: 13.7%
Long-term debt ($ mil.): 8.0
No. of shares (mil.): 1.9
Market value ($ mil.): 33.8
Dividends
  Yield: —
  Payout: —
Sales ($ mil.): 20.6
R&D as % of sales: —
Advertising as % of sales: —

Stock History

NASDAQ (GM): BAYN

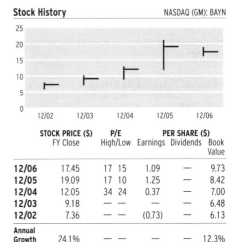

	STOCK PRICE ($) FY Close	P/E High/Low		PER SHARE ($) Earnings	Dividends	Book Value
12/06	17.45	17	15	1.09	—	9.73
12/05	19.09	17	10	1.25	—	8.42
12/04	12.05	34	24	0.37	—	7.00
12/03	9.18	—	—	—	—	6.48
12/02	7.36	—	—	(0.73)	—	6.13
Annual Growth	**24.1%**	**—**	**—**	**—**	**—**	**12.3%**

Beach First National Bancshares

Locals call the area The Grand Strand but it could also be called The Millions Strand. Beach First National Bancshares is the holding company for Beach First National Bank, a community bank serving South Carolina's Myrtle Beach and Hilton Head Island. Targeting commercial customers in the community, the bank's branches provide traditional deposit services, including checking and savings accounts, money markets, IRAs, and CDs. Real estate loans — mostly commercial — make up about 75% of the bank's loan portfolio. The bank also writes business loans and consumer loans. Beach First National Bank was established in 1996.

Executives and directors collectively own more than 30% of Beach First National Bancshares.

EXECUTIVES

Chairman, Beach First National Bancshares and Beach First National Bank: Raymond E. (Ray) Cleary III, age 58
President, CEO, and Director; President and CEO, Beach First National Bank:
Walter E. (Walt) Standish III, age 56, $150,000 pay
EVP and CFO: Gary S. Austin
Assistant Secretary; EVP and Chief Credit Officer, Beach First National Bank:
M. Katharine (Katie) Huntley, age 56, $235,308 pay
EVP and Business Development Officer, Beach First National Bank: Julien E. Springs, age 50, $212,327 pay
VP and Marketing Director, Beach First National Bank:
Barbara W. Marshall
VP and Regional Manager, Hilton Head, Beach First National Bank: Paul Walter
VP, Human Resources, Bearch First National Bank:
Lorie Y. Runion
Auditors: Elliott Davis LLC

LOCATIONS

HQ: Beach First National Bancshares, Inc.
3751 Robert M.Grissom Pkwy., Ste. 100,
Myrtle Beach, SC 29577
Phone: 843-626-2265   **Fax:** 843-916-7818
Web: www.beachfirst.com

PRODUCTS/OPERATIONS

2006 Sales

	$ mil.	% of total
Interest		
Loans, including fees	33.1	82
Investment securities	2.9	7
Other	0.5	1
Noninterest		
Mortgage operations	2.1	5
Service fees on deposit accounts	0.5	1
Other	1.4	4
Total	**40.5**	**100**

COMPETITORS

Bank of America
BB&T
CNB Corp.
First Citizens BancShares
HCSB Financial
RBC Centura Banks
South Financial
Wachovia

HISTORICAL FINANCIALS

Company Type: Public

Income Statement
FYE: December 31

	ASSETS ($ mil.)	NET INCOME ($ mil.)	INCOME AS % OF ASSETS	EMPLOYEES
12/06	520.2	6.2	1.2%	125
12/05	397.4	3.4	0.9%	62
12/04	242.1	1.4	0.6%	—
12/03	165.1	1.0	0.6%	—
12/02	118.4	0.7	0.6%	—
Annual Growth	**44.8%**	**72.5%**	**—**	**101.6%**

2006 Year-End Financials

Equity as % of assets: 8.7%   Dividends
Return on assets: 1.4%   Yield: —
Return on equity: 14.7%   Payout: —
Long-term debt ($ mil.): 17.5   Sales ($ mil.): 40.5
No. of shares (mil.): 4.8   R&D as % of sales: —
Market value ($ mil.): 91.2   Advertising as % of sales: —

Stock History

NASDAQ (GM): BFNB

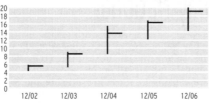

	STOCK PRICE ($) FY Close	P/E High/Low		PER SHARE ($) Earnings	Dividends	Book Value
12/06	19.13	16	11	1.27	—	9.53
12/05	16.33	20	15	0.82	—	12.34
12/04	13.67	33	19	0.46	—	8.11
12/03	8.56	27	16	0.33	—	11.13
12/02	5.53	24	19	0.24	—	10.57
Annual Growth	**36.4%**	**—**	**—**	**51.7%**	**—**	**(2.5%)**

Benjamin Franklin Bancorp

It's all about the Benjamins at Benjamin Franklin Bancorp. The holding company operates through Benjamin Franklin Bank, which has nine branches southwest of Boston in the Massachusetts towns of Middlesex, Norfolk, and Worcester counties. It offers traditional deposit products to individual and small to midsized business customers. Its primary business (accounting for about 70% of its assets) is lending. Residential mortgage loans make up the lion's share — more than 40% — of Benjamin Franklin's total loan portfolio. Commercial mortgage loans account for about 35%. The remainder of its portfolio consists of business, construction, consumer, and home equity lines of credit and loans.

EXECUTIVES

Chairman, Benjamin Franklin Bancorp and Benjamin Franklin Bank: Alfred H. Wahlers, age 73
President, CEO, and Director; President and CEO, Benjamin Franklin Bank: Thomas R. Venables, age 51, $422,000 pay
CFO and Treasurer; EVP and CFO, Benjamin Franklin Bank: Claire S. Bean, age 54, $279,000 pay
SVP Risk Management and Compliance, Benjamin Franklin Bank: Michael J. Piemonte, age 53, $113,400 pay
SVP and Senior Lending Officer, Benjamin Franklin Bank: Rose M. Buckley, age 39, $189,014 pay (prior to title change)
SVP Retail Banking, Benjamin Franklin Bank: Mariane E. Broadhurst, age 50, $150,800 pay
VP Human Resources, Benjamin Franklin Bank: Kathleen P. (Kathy) Sawyer, age 50
Secretary and Director; Clerk, Benjamin Franklin Bank: Anne M. King, age 77
Auditors: Wolf & Company, P.C.

LOCATIONS

HQ: Benjamin Franklin Bancorp, Inc.
58 Main St., Franklin, MA 02038
Phone: 508-528-7000   **Fax:** 508-520-8364
Web: www.benfranklinbank.com

PRODUCTS/OPERATIONS

2006 Sales

	$ mil.	% of total
Interest income		
Loans	37.7	75
Debt securities	5.4	11
Other	1.2	2
ATM servicing fees	3.1	6
Deposit service fees	1.4	3
Loan service fees	0.5	1
Other	1.0	2
Total	**50.3**	**100**

COMPETITORS

Bank of America
Citigroup
Citizens Financial Group
Eastern Bank
JPMorgan Chase
Sovereign Bancorp
Wachovia

HISTORICAL FINANCIALS

Company Type: Public

Income Statement
FYE: December 31

	ASSETS ($ mil.)	NET INCOME ($ mil.)	INCOME AS % OF ASSETS	EMPLOYEES
12/06	913.7	4.7	0.5%	169
12/05	867.1	0.4	0.0%	140
12/04	517.4	1.7	0.3%	133
12/03	458.8	1.7	0.4%	—
12/02	452.2	2.7	0.6%	—
Annual Growth	**19.2%**	**14.9%**	**—**	**12.7%**

2006 Year-End Financials

Equity as % of assets: 12.0%   Dividends
Return on assets: 0.5%   Yield: 1.0%
Return on equity: 4.3%   Payout: 28.3%
Long-term debt ($ mil.): 149.0   Sales ($ mil.): 50.3
No. of shares (mil.): 8.2   R&D as % of sales: —
Market value ($ mil.): 134.5   Advertising as % of sales: —

Stock History

NASDAQ (GM): BFBC

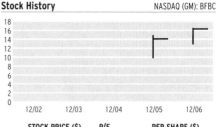

	STOCK PRICE ($) FY Close	P/E High/Low		PER SHARE ($) Earnings	Dividends	Book Value
12/06	16.30	27	22	0.60	0.17	13.26
12/05	14.07	—	—	—	0.06	12.74
Annual Growth	**15.8%**	**—**	**—**	**—**	**183.3%**	**4.1%**

Berkshire Hills Bancorp

Berkshire Hills Bancorp is the holding company for Berkshire Bank, which serves individuals and small businesses through more than 30 branches in western Massachusetts, eastern New York, and southern Vermont. The bank provides an array of retail products, including savings, checking, and money market accounts; CDs; and IRAs. It also offers insurance and investments. Residential mortgages make up more than 35% of the company's loan portfolio, which also includes commercial mortgages (more than 30%), consumer loans (about 20%), and business loans. Berkshire Hills Bancorp also owns Berkshire Municipal Bank, which collects deposits from municipalities and other government entities in New York.

Berkshire Hills Bancorp expanded its presence in western Massachusetts with its 2005 purchase of Woronoco Bancorp. In 2007 it bought Factory Point Bancorp, the holding company for Factory Point National Bank of Manchester Center. The deal gave Berkshire Hills Bancorp its first seven branches in southern Vermont.

The company is eyeing further expansion into neighboring Connecticut.

EXECUTIVES

Chairman: Lawrence A. (Larry) Bossidy, age 73
President, CEO, and Director, Berkshire Hills Bancorp and Berkshire Bank: Michael P. Daly, age 45, $535,000 pay
EVP, CFO, and Treasurer: Kevin P. Riley
EVP, Commercial Banking, and Regional President, Pioneer Valley: Michael J. (Mike) Oleksak, age 48
SVP General Counsel, and Secretary: Gerald A. Denmark
SVP Asset Management and Trust: Thomas W. Barney
SVP and Chief Risk Officer: Shepard D. Rainie
SVP Commercial Lending: Michael J. Ferry
SVP Human Resources: Linda A. Johnston
SVP Retail Banking and Operations, Berkshire Hills Bancorp and Berkshire Bank: Gayle P. Fawcett, age 53
SVP Retail Lending and Marketing: Charles A. Bercury
President, Berkshire Insurance Group: Ross D. Gorman
Auditors: Wolf & Company, P.C.

LOCATIONS

HQ: Berkshire Hills Bancorp, Inc.
24 North St., Pittsfield, MA 01201
Phone: 413-443-5601   **Fax:** 413-443-3587
Web: www.berkshirebank.com

PRODUCTS/OPERATIONS

2006 Sales

	$ mil.	% of total
Interest		
Loans	100.8	76
Securities	16.9	13
Cash & cash equivalents	0.3	—
Noninterest		
Deposit service fees	5.8	4
Insurance commissions & fees	3.8	3
Wealth management fees	3.3	2
Other	2.3	2
Total	**133.2**	**100**

Selected Subsidiaries

Berkshire Bank
  Berkshire Insurance Group, Inc.
  Berkshire Municipal Bank

COMPETITORS

Bank of America
Citizens Financial Group
Hudson City Bancorp
Legacy Bancorp
Pathfinder Bancorp
TD Banknorth

HISTORICAL FINANCIALS

Company Type: Public

Income Statement

FYE: December 31

	ASSETS ($ mil.)	NET INCOME ($ mil.)	INCOME AS % OF ASSETS	EMPLOYEES
12/06	2,149.6	11.3	0.5%	522
12/05	2,035.6	8.2	0.4%	399
12/04	1,310.1	11.5	0.9%	—
12/03	1,218.6	9.0	0.7%	—
12/02	1,045.6	1.8	0.2%	277
Annual Growth	**19.7%**	**58.3%**	**—**	**17.2%**

2006 Year-End Financials

Equity as % of assets: 12.0%
Return on assets: 0.5%
Return on equity: 4.5%
Long-term debt ($ mil.): 360.5
No. of shares (mil.): 8.7
Market value ($ mil.): 291.6
Dividends
  Yield: 1.7%
  Payout: 43.4%
Sales ($ mil.): 133.2
R&D as % of sales: —
Advertising as % of sales: —

Stock History

NASDAQ (GS): BHLB

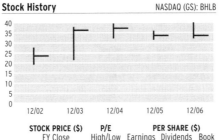

	STOCK PRICE ($) FY Close	P/E High/Low		PER SHARE ($) Earnings	Dividends	Book Value
12/06	33.46	31	25	1.29	0.56	29.63
12/05	33.50	32	29	1.10	—	28.81
12/04	37.15	20	16	2.01	—	22.43
12/03	36.20	24	14	1.57	—	20.87
12/02	23.55	91	65	0.30	—	24.70
Annual Growth	**9.2%**	**—**	**—**	**44.0%**	**—**	**4.7%**

Berry Petroleum

It may be small fruit in the giant petroleum industry, but Berry Petroleum delivers the juice. The company buys properties with heavy crude oil reserves for exploitation and sale to refining companies. Berry Petroleum's core properties are in California's Kern, Los Angeles, and Ventura counties; it has proved reserves of 150.3 million barrels of oil equivalent. The company squeezes the most from its assets by using thermal recovery: Steam is injected into heavy crude oil reserves to reduce oil viscosity and allow it to flow to the surface. Berry Petroleum also owns three gas-fired cogeneration facilities. In 2005 the company acquired 130,000 acres of oil and gas assets in Colorado from J-W Operating Company.

In 2006 Berry Petroleum acquired a 50% stake in some natural gas assets in the Piceance Basin of western Colorado from a private concern for $150 million.

EXECUTIVES

Chairman: Martin H. Young Jr., age 54
President, CEO, and Director: Robert F. Heinemann, age 53, $1,187,500 pay
COO: Michael Duginski, age 41, $467,092 pay
EVP and CFO: Ralph J. Goehring, age 50, $419,846 pay
VP Rocky Mountain/Mid-Continent Production: Daniel G. (Dan) Anderson, age 44, $302,850 pay
VP California Production: George T. (Tim) Crawford, age 46
VP Rocky Mountain/Mid-Continent Exploration: Bruce S. Kelso, age 51, $284,250 pay
VP Human Resources: Walter B. Ayers, age 63
Corporate Secretary: Kenneth A. Olson, age 51
Investor Relations Specialist: Todd A. Crabtree
Treasurer and Assistant Secretary: Steven B. Wilson, age 44
Auditors: PricewaterhouseCoopers LLP

LOCATIONS

HQ: Berry Petroleum Company
5201 Truxtun Ave., Ste. 300, Bakersfield, CA 93309
Phone: 661-616-3900   **Fax:** 661-616-3881
Web: www.bry.com

Berry Petroleum operates primarily in California. It also has oil assets in the Rocky Mountains.

PRODUCTS/OPERATIONS

2006 Sales

	$ mil.	% of total
Oil & gas	430.5	89
Electricity	52.9	11
Other	2.9	—
Total	**486.3**	**100**

COMPETITORS

Aera Energy
Chevron
Petrohawk Energy
Royal Dutch Shell
Royale Energy
Samson Oil
Vulcan Energy

HISTORICAL FINANCIALS

Company Type: Public

Income Statement

FYE: December 31

	REVENUE ($ mil.)	NET INCOME ($ mil.)	NET PROFIT MARGIN	EMPLOYEES
12/06	486.3	107.9	22.2%	243
12/05	406.7	112.4	27.6%	209
12/04	275.0	69.2	25.2%	—
12/03	180.9	32.4	17.9%	—
12/02	132.5	30.0	22.6%	113
Annual Growth	**38.4%**	**37.7%**	**—**	**21.1%**

2006 Year-End Financials

Debt ratio: 99.3%
Return on equity: 28.3%
Cash ($ mil.): 8.4
Current ratio: 0.46
Long-term debt ($ mil.): 424.8
No. of shares (mil.): 42.1
Dividends
  Yield: 1.0%
  Payout: 12.4%
Market value ($ mil.): 1,305.5
R&D as % of sales: —
Advertising as % of sales: —

	STOCK PRICE ($) FY Close	P/E High/Low		Earnings	PER SHARE ($) Dividends	Book Value
12/06	31.01	17	11	2.41	0.30	10.16
12/05	28.60	14	8	2.50	0.30	15.84
12/04	23.85	16	6	1.54	0.26	12.49
12/03	10.13	13	9	0.78	0.22	9.44
12/02	8.52	13	10	0.69	0.20	8.25
Annual Growth	38.1%	—	—	36.7%	10.7%	5.3%

Beverly Hills Bancorp

If Californy is the place you oughta be, load up your cash and deposit it in Beverly . . . Beverly Hills Bancorp, that is. The holding company owns First Bank of Beverly Hills, which conducts wholesale banking operations and has one Southern California retail branch. The bank's focus is on the origination of construction and permanent real estate loans, especially for commercial (more than half of the bank's loan portfolio) and multifamily (about 35%) uses. Most of its borrowers are in California and other Western states. The company conducts mortgage investment operations through investment subsidiary WFC.

Beverly Hills Bancorp sold its Beverly Hills branch location in 2006, in line with the company's focus on increasingly moving toward wholesale banking. It now has a single retail banking office located in Calabasas. The bank also expanded its operations into construction and development lending in 2006. As part of its strategy shift, First Bank of Beverly Hills in 2005 converted from a thrift to a commercial bank. The company moved its headquarters from Oregon to California in 2004; it also changed its name to Beverly Hills Bancorp from Wilshire Financial Services Group that year. Director Howard Amster owns about 8% Beverly Hills Bancorp, and director Robert Kanner owns 6%.

EXECUTIVES

Chairman and CEO; President and CEO, First Bank of Beverly Hills: Larry B. Faigin, age 64, $91,667 pay (prior to title change)
EVP and CFO; EVP and CFO, First Bank of Beverly Hills: Takeo K. Sasaki, age 38, $228,667 pay
EVP and Chief Credit Officer, First Bank of Beverly Hills: Annette J. Vecchio, age 56, $217,000 pay (prior to promotion)
EVP Business Development: Craig W. Kolasinski, age 44, $345,000 pay
EVP and Chief Administrative Officer, First Bank of Beverly Hills: Bryce W. Miller, age 44, $195,000 pay
Secretary: Carol Schardt
Human Resources: Susan Christian
EVP and Chief Lending Officer, Beverly Hills Bancorp and First Bank of Beverly Hills: Eric C. Rosa, age 58
Auditors: Deloitte & Touche LLP

LOCATIONS

HQ: Beverly Hills Bancorp Inc.
23901 Calabasas Rd., Ste. 1050,
Calabasas, CA 91302
Phone: 818-223-8084   **Fax:** 818-223-9531
Web: www.fbbh.com

PRODUCTS/OPERATIONS

2006 Sales

	$ mil.	% of total
Interest		
Loans	67.5	69
Mortgage-backed securities	18.5	19
Other	2.2	2
Gain on sale of branch	8.5	9
Other	1.5	1
Total	**98.2**	**100**

COMPETITORS

Alliance Bancshares (CA)
Bank of America
Bank of the West
California National Bank
UnionBanCal
Washington Mutual
Wells Fargo

HISTORICAL FINANCIALS

Company Type: Public

Income Statement				FYE: December 31
	ASSETS ($ mil.)	NET INCOME ($ mil.)	INCOME AS % OF ASSETS	EMPLOYEES
12/06	1,623.8	14.8	0.9%	47
12/05	1,403.7	15.1	1.1%	52
12/04	1,338.9	25.6	1.9%	—
12/03	975.3	6.9	0.7%	—
12/02	843.0	2.0	0.2%	—
Annual Growth	17.8%	64.9%	—	(9.6%)

2006 Year-End Financials

Equity as % of assets: 9.6%	Dividends
Return on assets: 1.0%	Yield: 6.0%
Return on equity: 9.0%	Payout: 69.4%
Long-term debt ($ mil.): 46.4	Sales ($ mil.): 98.2
No. of shares (mil.): 18.7	R&D as % of sales: —
Market value ($ mil.): 155.2	Advertising as % of sales: —

Stock History   NASDAQ (GS): BHBC

	STOCK PRICE ($) FY Close	P/E High/Low		Earnings	PER SHARE ($) Dividends	Book Value
12/06	8.29	15	11	0.72	0.50	8.30
12/05	10.37	16	13	0.70	0.38	8.15
12/04	10.10	9	7	1.20	0.13	8.05
12/03	6.00	19	9	0.34	—	6.65
12/02	3.30	36	20	0.10	—	5.47
Annual Growth	25.9%	—	—	63.8%	96.1%	11.0%

Bidz.com, Inc.

Bidz.com combines the markdowns of a dollar store, the format of an auction house, and the convenience of the Internet to bring sparkling deals to customers. The company buys closeout merchandise and sells it using a live-auction format, with no reserve prices and $1 opening bids, even on items that might retail for more than $20,000. It mostly sells jewelry, including gold, platinum, and silver items set with diamonds, and other precious and semi-precious stones, but visitors will also find deals on electronics and collectibles such as art and antiques, coins, and sports cards. Chairman and CEO David Zinberg and his sister, VP Marina Zinberg, each own about 15% of the company's stock.

The Internet auctioneer sought to raise funds through an initial public offering filed in March 2006. After reducing the size of the offering to 3 million shares from 6.2 million shares and a tepid reception from investors the company postponed the IPO indefinitely.

Bidz.com purchased more than 25% of its merchandise from jewelry liquidator LA Jewelers, Inc. in 2006, making that company Bidz.com's largest supplier.

EXECUTIVES

Chairman, President, and CEO: David Zinberg, age 49, $482,083 pay
CFO, Secretary, Treasurer, and Director: Lawrence Y. Kong, age 46, $358,958 pay
VP, Development: Anatoli Lau, age 35
VP, Technology: Yuri Mordovskoi, age 44
CTO: Leon Kuperman, age 33
Chief Compliance Officer and Controller: Larry E. Russell, age 55
Auditors: Stonefield Josephson, Inc.

LOCATIONS

HQ: Bidz.com, Inc.
3562 Eastham Dr., Culver City, CA 90232
Phone: 310-280-7373   **Fax:** 310-280-7375
Web: www.bidz.com

2006 Sales

	$ mil.	% of total
US	104.3	79
International	27.5	21
Total	**131.8**	**100**

COMPETITORS

Blue Nile
Costco Wholesale
eBay
Finlay Enterprises
HSN
J. C. Penney
Overstock.com
QVC
Reeds Jewelers
Target
uBid
Walmart.com
Zale

HISTORICAL FINANCIALS

Company Type: Public

Income Statement				FYE: December 31
	REVENUE ($ mil.)	NET INCOME ($ mil.)	NET PROFIT MARGIN	EMPLOYEES
12/06	131.8	5.4	4.1%	198
12/05	90.6	2.6	2.9%	170
12/04	65.3	0.8	1.2%	—
12/03	47.7	(5.8)	—	—
Annual Growth	40.3%	—	—	16.5%

2006 Year-End Financials

Debt ratio: 0.0%
Return on equity: 126.9%
Cash ($ mil.): —
Current ratio: —
Long-term debt ($ mil.): 0.0

Net Income History

NASDAQ (CM): BIDZ

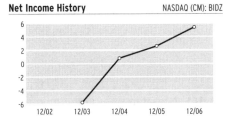

Bill Barrett Corporation

Bill Barrett Corp. (named after a veteran oil industry wildcatter) is hoping for a Rocky Mountain high as it digs down deep for oil and gas. The company focuses its exploration and development activities in the Wind River, Uinta, Powder River, Williston, Denver-Julesburg, Big Horn, and Paradox Basins and the Montana and Utah Overthrusts. Bill Barrett holds more than 1.2 million net undeveloped leasehold acres. In 2006 the oil and gas firm had working interests in 394 drilling locations and had estimated net proved reserves of 428.4 billion cu. ft. of natural gas equivalent.

Bill Barrett was established in 2002 by former managers of Barrett Resources (which was acquired by The Williams Companies in 2001). The company went public in 2004. In 2006 Bill Barrett acquired CH4 Corp. for $82 million.

EXECUTIVES

Chairman and CEO: Fredrick J. (Fred) Barrett, age 46, $650,154 pay
President, COO, and Director: Joseph N. (Joe) Jaggers, age 53, $442,500 pay
SVP, General Counsel, and Corporate Secretary: Francis B. Barron, age 44, $219,254 pay (prior to title change)
SVP, Land: Huntington T. Walker, age 51
SVP, Exploration, Northern Division: Terry R. Barrett, age 47, $291,231 pay
SVP, Exploration, Southern Division: Kurt M. Reinecke, age 48, $267,231 pay
SVP, Geophysics: Wilfred R. (Roy) Roux, age 49
VP, Accounting: David R. Macosko, age 45
VP, Government and Regulatory Affairs: Duane J. Zavadil, age 47
Auditors: Deloitte & Touche LLP

LOCATIONS

HQ: Bill Barrett Corporation
1099 18th St., Ste. 2300, Denver, CO 80202
Phone: 303-293-9100   **Fax:** 303-291-0420
Web: www.billbarrettcorp.com

PRODUCTS/OPERATIONS

2006 Sales

	% of total
Sempra Energy Trading	21
Xcel Energy	10
ONEOK	10
Other customers	59
Total	**100**

2006 Sales

	$ mil.	% of total
Oil & gas production	344.1	92
Other	31.2	8
Total	**375.3**	**100**

COMPETITORS

Abraxas Petroleum
Delta Petroleum
Double Eagle Petroleum

HISTORICAL FINANCIALS

Company Type: Public

Income Statement				FYE: December 31
	REVENUE ($ mil.)	NET INCOME ($ mil.)	NET PROFIT MARGIN	EMPLOYEES
12/06	375.3	62.0	16.5%	216
12/05	288.8	23.8	8.2%	190
12/04	170.0	(5.3)	—	—
12/03	75.4	(4.0)	—	—
12/02	16.1	(5.0)	—	—
Annual Growth	119.7%	—	—	13.7%

2006 Year-End Financials

Debt ratio: 24.9%
Return on equity: 8.9%
Cash ($ mil.): 79.5
Current ratio: 1.16
Long-term debt ($ mil.): 188.0
No. of shares (mil.): 44.1
Dividends
  Yield: —
  Payout: —
Market value ($ mil.): 1,201.1
R&D as % of sales: —
Advertising as % of sales: —

Stock History

NYSE: BBG

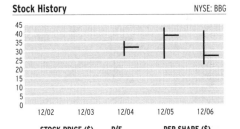

	STOCK PRICE ($) FY Close	P/E High/Low	PER SHARE ($) Earnings	Dividends	Book Value
12/06	27.21	29 16	1.40	—	17.14
12/05	38.61	77 47	0.55	—	14.48
12/04	31.99	— —	(15.40)	—	14.30
Annual Growth	(7.8%)	— —	—	—	9.4%

BioSante Pharmaceuticals

BioSante Pharmaceuticals wants to be the patron saint of hormonal ups and downs. The firm is developing topical hormone therapy gels to deliver supplemental estradiol, progestogen, or testosterone. Lead product Elestrin has received its FDA approval to treat menopausal symptoms in women. The company's other product candidates still in development include gels that treat female sexual dysfunction (LibiGel) and testosterone deficiency in men (Bio-T-Gel). BioSante has licensed to Solvay Pharmaceuticals its Bio-E/P-Gel, a combination of estrogen and progestogen to help menopausal women.

Upon receiving FDA approval for Elestrin (formerly known as Bio-E-Gel) in 2006, BioSante struck an exclusive agreement allowing Bradley Pharmaceuticals to market the product in the US.

BioSante is also working on its BioVant calcium phosphate (CaP) nanoparticle-based technology which it hopes will improve vaccine efficacy and could make vaccines and drug therapies that are only available by injection available by mouth or through inhalation. Its BioAir delivery system is being evaluated to see if it might be used to develop an inhaled form of insulin for diabetics. The company is also working with DynPort to assess the possibility of an anthrax vaccine based on the BioVant technology.

Most of the company's hormone therapy products are licensed from Antares Pharma, Inc.

Director Ross Mangano controls nearly 10% of the company's voting stock.

EXECUTIVES

Chairman: Louis W. Sullivan, age 73
Vice Chairman, President, and CEO: Stephen M. Simes, age 55, $514,800 pay
CFO, Treasurer, and Secretary: Phillip B. Donenberg, age 47, $250,286 pay
VP Corporate Development: Joy Thomas
Auditors: Deloitte & Touche LLP

LOCATIONS

HQ: BioSante Pharmaceuticals, Inc.
111 Barclay Blvd., Lincolnshire, IL 60069
Phone: 847-478-0500   **Fax:** 847-478-9152
Web: www.biosantepharma.com

BioSante Pharmaceuticals has facilities in Georgia and Illinois.

PRODUCTS/OPERATIONS

2006 Sales

	$ mil.	% of total
Licensing revenue	14.1	98
Grant revenue	0.2	2
Other revenue	0.1	—
Total	**14.4**	**100**

Selected Product Candidates

CaP products
  BioAir (inhalable drug delivery system)
  BioOral (oral drug delivery system)
  BioVant (vaccine delivery system)

Hormone therapy products
Elestrin (transdermal estrogen supplement)
Bio-E/P-Gel (transdermal estrogen and progestogen supplement)
Bio-T-Gel (transdermal testosterone supplement for men)
LibiGel (transdermal testosterone supplement for women)
LibiGel-E/T (transdermal estrogen and testosterone supplement for women)

COMPETITORS

Auxilium Pharmaceuticals	Sanofi-Aventis U.S
GlaxoSmithKline	Solvay Pharmaceuticals
Merck	VIVUS
Noven Pharmaceuticals	Watson Pharmaceuticals
Procter & Gamble	Wyeth Pharmaceuticals

HISTORICAL FINANCIALS
Company Type: Public

Income Statement
FYE: December 31

	REVENUE ($ mil.)	NET INCOME ($ mil.)	NET PROFIT MARGIN	EMPLOYEES
12/06	14.4	2.8	19.4%	8
12/05	0.3	(9.6)	—	14
12/04	0.1	(12.0)	—	—
12/03	0.1	(6.0)	—	—
12/02	2.8	(3.8)	—	—
Annual Growth	50.6%	—	—	(42.9%)

2006 Year-End Financials
Debt ratio: —
Return on equity: 22.5%
Cash ($ mil.): 11.4
Current ratio: 5.17
Long-term debt ($ mil.): —

Net Income History
NASDAQ (GM): BPAX

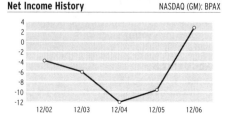

Bitstream Inc.

Bitstream counts on its fonts to keep business flowing. The company develops software that creates and manages typefaces. It has a library of more than 500 fonts and develops technology for delivering typographic capabilities to hardware, software, and Web applications. Bitstream also develops browser software for mobile handsets. Its products include the ThunderHawk browser, as well as text distribution applications (TrueDoc) and font managers (Font Reserve). Subsidiary Pageflex offers publishing software that designs and creates custom business documents based on customer profiles. Bitstream's MyFonts.com subsidiary offers a Web site for locating, testing, and purchasing different fonts.

The company licenses its products to original equipment manufacturers (OEMs) and software and technology vendors. Customers in the US account for about 80% of the company's sales.

EXECUTIVES
Chairman: Charles W. Ying, age 60
President, CEO, General Counsel, and Director: Anna M. Chagnon, age 40, $360,000 pay
VP and CFO: James P. (Jim) Dore, age 48, $210,000 pay
VP and CTO: John S. Collins, age 67, $182,000 pay
VP Engineering: Costas Kitsos, age 46, $225,000 pay
VP Research and Development: Sampo Kaasila, age 46, $210,000 pay
Auditors: PricewaterhouseCoopers LLP

LOCATIONS
HQ: Bitstream Inc.
245 1st St., 17th Fl., Cambridge, MA 02142
Phone: 617-497-6222   **Fax:** 617-868-0784
Web: www.bitstream.com

2006 Sales

	$ mil.	% of total
US	16.9	83
Canada	1.1	5
UK	0.6	3
Japan	0.4	2
Other countries	1.3	7
Total	**20.3**	**100**

PRODUCTS/OPERATIONS

2006 Sales

	$ mil.	% of total
Software licenses	16.9	84
Services	3.4	16
Total	**20.3**	**100**

COMPETITORS
Adobe
Agfa
Bytemobile
Corel
Microsoft
Monotype
Novarra
Objectif Lune
Opera Software
Quark
Xerox

HISTORICAL FINANCIALS
Company Type: Public

Income Statement
FYE: December 31

	REVENUE ($ mil.)	NET INCOME ($ mil.)	NET PROFIT MARGIN	EMPLOYEES
12/06	20.3	3.2	15.8%	67
12/05	15.6	1.0	6.4%	62
12/04	11.6	(0.6)	—	—
12/03	9.7	(1.2)	—	—
12/02	8.5	(1.0)	—	55
Annual Growth	24.3%	—	—	5.1%

2006 Year-End Financials
Debt ratio: —
Return on equity: 39.2%
Cash ($ mil.): 11.0
Current ratio: 3.35
Long-term debt ($ mil.): —
No. of shares (mil.): 9.3
Dividends
Yield: —
Payout: —
Market value ($ mil.): 80.9
R&D as % of sales: —
Advertising as % of sales: —

Stock History
NASDAQ (CM): BITS

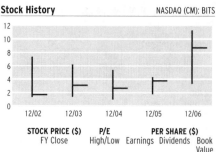

	STOCK PRICE ($) FY Close	P/E High/Low	PER SHARE ($) Earnings	Dividends	Book Value
12/06	8.70	37 11	0.30	—	1.14
12/05	3.76	38 17	0.11	—	0.66
12/04	2.65	— —	(0.07)	—	0.52
12/03	3.07	— —	(0.14)	—	0.58
12/02	1.68	— —	(0.12)	—	0.71
Annual Growth	50.9%	— —	—	—	12.7%

BJ's Restaurants

The Windy City inspires the food and drink at BJ's. BJ's Restaurants owns and operates about 55 restaurants in six western states (mostly in California) under the names BJ's Restaurant & Brewery, BJ's Pizza & Grill, and BJ's Restaurant & Brewhouse. The casual-dining eateries offer Chicago-style pizza, salad, sandwiches, pasta, and the company's own hand-crafted beers. Its dozen Restaurant & Brewery locations, which feature an onsite microbrewery, help supply beer to the rest of the chain. California food service distributor (and BJ's supplier) Jacmar owns more than 15% of the company.

BJ's has been increasing the rate of its expansion the past few years, opening almost a dozen new locations in 2006. The company is focused on making its Restaurant & Brewhouse format its flagship concept and planned to open more than a dozen new units during 2007.

Golden Resorts, a California-based real estate investment firm, owns almost 15% of BJ's.

EXECUTIVES
Co-Chairman: Jeremiah J. (Jerry) Hennessy, age 48, $312,600 pay
Co-Chairman, VP, and Secretary: Paul A. Motenko, age 52, $312,600 pay
President, CEO, and Director: Gerald W. (Jerry) Deitchle, age 55, $495,000 pay
EVP and CFO: Gregory S. (Greg) Levin, age 39, $335,174 pay
EVP and Chief Development Officer: Gregory S. (Greg) Lynds, age 45, $304,704 pay
SVP Brewing Operations: Alexander M. (Alex) Puchner, age 44
SVP Design and Marketing and Chief Design Officer: R. Dean Gerrie, age 55
SVP Restaurant Operations: Lon F. Ledwith, age 49
VP Marketing: Melanie Bruno-Carbone
President, BJ's Restaurants Foundation: Robert (Rob) DeLiema
Chief Human Resources Officer: Thomas F. (Tom) Norton, age 36
Chief Supply Chain Officer: John D. Allegretto, age 43, $268,934 pay
Auditors: Ernst & Young LLP

LOCATIONS

HQ: BJ's Restaurants, Inc.
7755 Center Ave., Ste. 300,
Huntington Beach, CA 92647
Phone: 714-500-2400
Web: www.bjsbrewhouse.com

2006 Locations

	No.
California	35
Texas	8
Arizona	4
Colorado	3
Oregon	3
Nevada	2
Total	**55**

PRODUCTS/OPERATIONS

2006 Locations

	No.
BJ's Restaurant & Brewhouse	36
BJ's Restaurant & Brewery	12
BJ's Pizza & Grill	7
Total	**55**

COMPETITORS

Applebee's	OSI Restaurant Partners
Brinker	Pat & Oscars
California Pizza Kitchen	Pizza Hut
Carlson Restaurants	Rock Bottom Restaurants
Darden	Round Table Pizza
Gordon Biersch	Shakey's
Metromedia	Straw Hat
N.U. Pizza	Uno Restaurants

HISTORICAL FINANCIALS

Company Type: Public

Income Statement				FYE: Tuesday nearest December 31
	REVENUE ($ mil.)	NET INCOME ($ mil.)	NET PROFIT MARGIN	EMPLOYEES
12/06	238.9	9.8	4.1%	5,341
12/05	178.2	8.4	4.7%	5,341
12/04	129.1	6.3	4.9%	—
12/03	103.0	3.6	3.5%	—
12/02	75.7	1.7	2.2%	2,686
Annual Growth	**33.3%**	**55.0%**	**—**	**18.7%**

2006 Year-End Financials

Debt ratio: —
Return on equity: 5.9%
Cash ($ mil.): 84.7
Current ratio: 2.62
Long-term debt ($ mil.): —
No. of shares (mil.): 26.1
Dividends
  Yield: —
  Payout: —
Market value ($ mil.): 526.7
R&D as % of sales: —
Advertising as % of sales: —

Stock History

NASDAQ (GS): BJRI

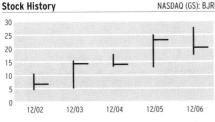

	STOCK PRICE ($) FY Close	P/E High/Low		PER SHARE ($) Earnings	Dividends	Book Value
12/06	20.21	67	43	0.41	—	7.78
12/05	23.07	69	36	0.36	—	5.67
12/04	14.00	59	45	0.30	—	3.98
12/03	14.30	85	29	0.18	—	3.62
12/02	6.68	116	53	0.09	—	3.45
Annual Growth	**31.9%**	**—**	**—**	**46.1%**	**—**	**22.6%**

Blue Nile

Blue Nile helps tech-savvy Marc Antonys woo their Cleopatras. The company, which offers luxury-grade jewelry online at bluenile.com, sells loose diamonds, settings, engagement rings, and other jewelry made of gold, platinum, and silver set with diamonds, pearls, emeralds, rubies, and sapphires. The e-tailer, offering over 1,000 styles of jewelry, also sells men's and women's watches and accessories. Blue Nile also operates Canadian and UK Web sites. CEO Mark Vadon, a discouraged engagement-ring shopper, and Ben Elowitz, formerly of Fatbrain.com, founded the site in 1999 as RockShop.com and, briefly, Internet Diamonds Inc., before adopting the Blue Nile brand name later that year.

Blue Nile features a build-your-own program for choosing engagement rings, earrings, and pendants on its Web site. The program allows customers to shop for and view diamonds based on carat, clarity, color, cut, and price range. Diamond engagement rings account for some 70% of Blue Nile's annual revenue. In August 2007 the company appointed Diane Irvine, CFO since 1999, as its president and Robin Easton, previously with PACCAR, as its CFO.

EXECUTIVES

Chairman and CEO: Mark Vadon, age 37
President and Director: Diane Irvine, age 48
CFO: Robin Easton
SVP: Darrell Cavens, age 34, $200,000 pay
SVP: Dwight Gaston, age 37, $200,000 pay
SVP: Susan Bell, age 49, $210,000 pay
VP, Finance, Controller, and Secretary: Terri K. Maupin, age 45, $148,897 pay
Senior Manager Public Relations: John Baird
Auditors: Deloitte & Touche LLP

LOCATIONS

HQ: Blue Nile, Inc.
705 5th Ave. South, Ste. 900, Seattle, WA 98104
Phone: 206-336-6700   **Fax:** 206-336-6750
Web: www.bluenile.com

PRODUCTS/OPERATIONS

Selected Products

Accessories
  Cuff links
  Desk accessories
  Frames
  Key rings
  Money clips
  Pens
Bracelets
Earrings
Necklaces and pendants
Watches
  Men's
  Women's
Wedding and anniversary rings

Selected Materials

Diamonds
Gemstones
  Emeralds
  Rubies
  Sapphires
Gold
Pearls
Platinum
Silver

COMPETITORS

Amazon.com
Cartier
Christie's
Costco Wholesale
eBay
Fortunoff
Friedman's Inc.
Gucci
H. Stern
Helzberg Diamonds
HSN
Ice.com
Lazare Kaplan
Mondera
Neiman Marcus
Nordstrom
QVC
Reeds Jewelers
Saks Fifth Avenue
Saks Inc.
SAM'S CLUB
Samuels Jewelers
Signet
Sotheby's
Tiffany & Co.
Topaz Group
Union Diamond
Van Cleef & Arpels
Wal-Mart
Zale

HISTORICAL FINANCIALS

Company Type: Public

Income Statement				FYE: December 31
	REVENUE ($ mil.)	NET INCOME ($ mil.)	NET PROFIT MARGIN	EMPLOYEES
12/06	251.6	13.1	5.2%	161
12/05	203.2	13.1	6.4%	146
12/04	169.2	10.0	5.9%	—
12/03	128.9	27.0	20.9%	—
12/02	72.1	1.6	2.2%	—
Annual Growth	**36.7%**	**69.2%**	**—**	**10.3%**

2006 Year-End Financials

Debt ratio: —
Return on equity: 20.3%
Cash ($ mil.): 98.4
Current ratio: 1.56
Long-term debt ($ mil.): —
No. of shares (mil.): 16.0
Dividends
  Yield: —
  Payout: —
Market value ($ mil.): 589.2
R&D as % of sales: —
Advertising as % of sales: —

Stock History

NASDAQ (GS): NILE

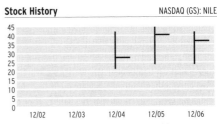

	STOCK PRICE ($) FY Close	P/E High/Low		PER SHARE ($) Earnings	Dividends	Book Value
12/06	36.89	55	32	0.76	—	2.96
12/05	40.31	62	34	0.71	—	4.70
12/04	27.62	74	39	0.56	—	4.72
Annual Growth	**15.6%**	**—**	**—**	**16.5%**	**—**	**(20.8%)**

BNC Bancorp

BNC Bancorp knows the ABCs of the financial world. The firm is the holding company for Bank of North Carolina, which has banking locations and loan offices in central and northeastern portions of the state. The bank offers community-oriented services to local business and retail customers, providing checking, savings, and other deposit accounts. Its loan portfolio is mainly composed of residential and commercial mortgages and business loans. Bank of North Carolina also offers mutual funds, annuities, and other investment products and services. BNC Bancorp acquired SterlingSouth Bank & Trust, a Greensboro banking company.

Company director Lenin Peters owns about 12% of BNC Bancorp; chairman W. Groome Fulton owns 6% and president W. Swope Montgomery 3%; as a group, executives and directors own nearly 30%.

EXECUTIVES

Chairman: W. Groome Fulton Jr., age 68
President, CEO, and Director; President and CEO, Bank of North Carolina: W. Swope Montgomery Jr., age 58, $439,900 pay
EVP, COO, and Director; EVP and COO, Bank of North Carolina: Richard D. Callicutt II, age 47, $323,250 pay
EVP, Secretary, and CFO; EVP and CFO, Bank of North Carolina: David B. Spencer, age 44, $318,250 pay
EVP, Chief Administration Officer, and Director, BNC Bancorp and Bank of North Carolina: Ralph N. Strayhorn III, age 52, $148,570 pay (partial-year salary)
Secretary and Director: Richard F. Wood, age 62
Auditors: Cherry, Bekaert & Holland, LLP

LOCATIONS

HQ: BNC Bancorp
831 Julian Ave., Thomasville, NC 27360
Phone: 336-476-9200   **Fax:** 336-476-5818
Web: www.bankofnc.com

PRODUCTS/OPERATIONS

2006 Sales

	$ mil.	% of total
Interest		
Loans, including fees	50.0	88
State & municipal securities	2.6	5
Other	0.6	1
Noninterest		
Service charges	2.4	4
Mortgage fees	0.6	1
Cash surrender of life insurance	0.6	1
Other	0.2	—
Total	**57.0**	**100**

COMPETITORS

Bank of America
Bank of Oak Ridge
Bank of the Carolinas
BB&T
Carolina Bank
First Bancorp (NC)
First Citizens BancShares
FNB United
NewBridge Bancorp
Piedmont Federal
RBC Centura Banks
Southern Community Financial
Wachovia

HISTORICAL FINANCIALS

Company Type: Public

Income Statement

FYE: December 31

	ASSETS ($ mil.)	NET INCOME ($ mil.)	INCOME AS % OF ASSETS	EMPLOYEES
12/06	951.7	6.2	0.7%	193
12/05	594.5	4.5	0.8%	142
12/04	497.5	3.8	0.8%	—
12/03	372.3	3.4	0.9%	—
12/02	306.6	2.6	0.8%	—
Annual Growth	**32.7%**	**24.3%**	**—**	**35.9%**

2006 Year-End Financials

Equity as % of assets: 7.6%
Return on assets: 0.8%
Return on equity: 11.7%
Long-term debt ($ mil.): 81.7
No. of shares (mil.): 6.1
Market value ($ mil.): 113.3

Dividends
 Yield: 0.8%
 Payout: 13.5%
Sales ($ mil.): 57.0
R&D as % of sales: —
Advertising as % of sales: —

Stock History

NASDAQ (CM): BNCN

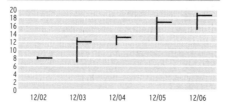

	STOCK PRICE ($) FY Close	P/E High/Low		PER SHARE ($) Earnings	Dividends	Book Value
12/06	18.58	18	15	1.04	0.14	11.89
12/05	16.86	20	14	0.88	0.12	7.58
12/04	13.09	18	15	0.75	0.10	8.34
12/03	12.00	19	11	0.66	1.61	7.59
12/02	7.93	15	14	0.54	—	7.79
Annual Growth	**23.7%**	**—**	**—**	**17.8%**	**(55.7%)**	**11.1%**

Boardwalk Pipeline Partners

Boardwalk Pipeline Partners is in the business of interstate transportation, gathering, and storage of natural gas. The company operates through two subsidiaries — Texas Gas Transmission and Gulf South Pipeline Company — with a combined 13,400 miles of pipeline in 11 states. Texas Gas operates in Arkansas, Illinois, Indiana, Kentucky, Louisiana, Mississippi, Ohio, Tennessee, and Texas. Gulf South operates in Alabama, Florida, Louisiana, Mississippi, and Texas. Customers include local gas distribution companies, local governments, other interstate and intrastate pipeline companies, direct industrial users, and electric power generators. Boardwalk Pipeline Partners is owned by Loews Corporation.

Boardwalk Pipeline Partners has taken over the business formerly held by Loews unit Boardwalk Pipelines, LLC. In the reorganization, Loews retained an 83.5% stake in the new company. The remaining 2% stake belongs to Boardwalk GP, LLC, a Loews subsidiary and the managing general partner in Boardwalk Pipeline Partners.

EXECUTIVES

Chairman, Boardwalk GP, LLC: Arthur L. Rebell, age 66
CEO and Director, Boardwalk GP, LLC: Rolf A. Gafvert, age 53
President and Director, Boardwalk GP, LLC: H. Dean Jones II, age 54
SVP, CFO, and Treasurer: Jamie L. Buskill, age 42
VP, Controller, and Chief Accounting Officer: Steven Barkauskas
VP Tax: James Jones
Investor Relations: Monique Vo
Auditors: Deloitte & Touche LLP

LOCATIONS

HQ: Boardwalk Pipeline Partners, LP
3800 Frederica St., Owensboro, KY 42301
Phone: 270-926-8686   **Fax:** 270-688-5872
Web: www.boardwalkpipelines.com

PRODUCTS/OPERATIONS

2006 Sales

	$ mil.	% of total
Gas transportation	508.2	84
Parking & lending	49.2	8
Gas storage	32.4	5
Other	17.8	3
Total	**607.6**	**100**

COMPETITORS

Columbia Gulf Transmission
El Paso
Energy Future
Florida Gas Transmission
Southwest Gas
Williams Gas Pipeline

HISTORICAL FINANCIALS

Company Type: Public

Income Statement

FYE: December 31

	REVENUE ($ mil.)	NET INCOME ($ mil.)	NET PROFIT MARGIN	EMPLOYEES
12/06	607.6	197.6	32.5%	1,150
12/05	560.5	100.9	18.0%	1,100
12/04	263.6	48.8	18.5%	1,100
12/03	142.9	22.5	15.7%	—
Annual Growth	**62.0%**	**106.3%**	**—**	**2.2%**

2006 Year-End Financials

Debt ratio: 106.2%
Return on equity: 17.5%
Cash ($ mil.): 399.0
Current ratio: 2.40
Long-term debt ($ mil.): 1,350.9
No. of shares (mil.): 75.2

Dividends
 Yield: 4.3%
 Payout: 71.4%
Market value ($ mil.): 2,316.3
R&D as % of sales: —
Advertising as % of sales: —

Stock History

NYSE: BWP

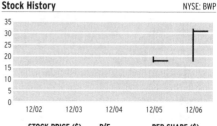

	STOCK PRICE ($) FY Close	P/E High/Low		PER SHARE ($) Earnings	Dividends	Book Value
12/06	30.82	17	10	1.85	1.32	16.93
12/05	17.98	56	50	0.35	—	14.48
Annual Growth	**71.4%**	**—**	**—**	**428.6%**	**—**	**16.9%**

BofI Holding, Inc.

BofI wants you to leave the suckers behind in your bank's long drive-through window line and begin banking online. BofI Holding owns Bank of Internet USA, a nationwide savings bank operated online. The automated Internet-based banking platform allows Bank of Internet to keep customer fees fairly low and offer interest rates that are somewhat higher than average. The bank focuses on deposit products and multi-family real estate lending (some 75% of its loan portfolio, even though they are only offered in selected states). Residential mortgages make up more than 20% of the loan portfolio and are offered throughout the US. Bank of Internet USA targets such groups as students, senior citizens, and RV users.

The Chipman First Family Limited Partnership, managed by director Michael Chipman, owns more than 9% of BofI Holding. BofI chairman Jerry Englert owns more than 7% of the company; director J. Gary Burke and former director Robert Eprile each own more than 5%.

EXECUTIVES

Chairman: Jerry F. Englert, age 66
Vice Chairman: Theodore C. (Ted) Allrich, age 61
President; COO, Bank of Internet USA and Director:
Gary L. Evans, age 58, $221,506 pay
SVP and CFO; VP and CFO, Bank of Internet USA:
Andrew J. Micheletti, age 48, $180,821 pay
VP and CTO, Bank of Internet USA:
Michael J. (Mike) Berengolts, age 35, $137,532 pay
VP Internet Development, Bank of Internet USA:
Barbara Fronek
VP and Chief Loan Officer: Kenneth D. (Kenn) Darling
Multifamily Chief Credit Officer, Bank of Internet USA:
Patrick A. Dunn, age 40, $426,242 pay
(prior to title change)
CEO, B of I Holding, Inc and Bank of Internet USA:
Gregory Garrabrants, age 37

LOCATIONS

HQ: BofI Holding, Inc.
12777 High Bluff Dr., Ste. 100,
San Diego, CA 92130
Phone: 858-350-6200   **Fax:** 858-350-0443
Web: www.bofiholding.com

PRODUCTS/OPERATIONS

2007 Sales

	$ mil.	% of total
Interest		
Loans	29.4	64
Investments	15.2	33
Noninterest		
Prepayment penalty fee income	0.4	1
Mortgage banking income	0.1	—
Gain on sale of securities	0.4	1
Banking service fees & other	0.3	1
Total	**45.8**	**100**

COMPETITORS

Bank of America	First IB
CalFirst	ING DIRECT
Citigroup	interState Net Bank
E*TRADE Bank	NetBank
ebank	WebFinancial
Emigrant Bank	Wells Fargo
FB BanCorp	

HISTORICAL FINANCIALS

Company Type: Public

Income Statement

FYE: June 30

	ASSETS ($ mil.)	NET INCOME ($ mil.)	INCOME AS % OF ASSETS	EMPLOYEES
6/07	947.2	3.3	0.3%	40
6/06	737.8	3.3	0.4%	26
6/05	609.5	2.9	0.5%	26
6/04	405.0	2.2	0.5%	—
6/03	273.5	1.7	0.6%	—
Annual Growth	**36.4%**	**18.0%**	**—**	**24.0%**

2007 Year-End Financials

Equity as % of assets: 7.1%
Return on assets: 0.4%
Return on equity: 5.0%
Long-term debt ($ mil.): 5.2
No. of shares (mil.): 8.3
Market value ($ mil.): 59.9
Dividends
  Yield: —
  Payout: —
Sales ($ mil.): 45.8
R&D as % of sales: —
Advertising as % of sales: —

Stock History

NASDAQ (GM): BOFI

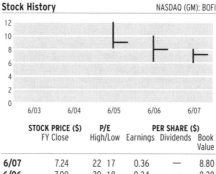

	STOCK PRICE ($) FY Close	P/E High/Low	PER SHARE ($) Earnings	Dividends	Book Value
6/07	7.24	22 17	0.36	—	8.80
6/06	7.99	29 18	0.34	—	8.38
6/05	9.04	30 21	0.40	—	8.27
Annual Growth	**(10.5%)**	**— —**	**(5.1%)**	**—**	**3.1%**

Bois d'Arc Energy

Like its namesake tree, Bois d'Arc Energy has strong roots and a flexible growth strategy. The oil and natural gas exploration and production independent focuses on the Gulf of Mexico shelf. Bois d'Arc Energy concentrates on this region because of its vast area of undiscovered reserves and because major oil companies have moved on to larger projects in the deepwater Gulf of Mexico. The company has proved reserves of 344 billion cu. ft. of natural gas equivalent (80% proved developed and 64% natural gas). Bois d'Arc Energy serves as operator for approximately 98% of its properties. Comstock Resources controls Bois d'Arc Energy.

Between 1997 and the end of 2006, the company's exploration program has yielded 77 successful exploration wells out of a total of 106 drilled, for a success rate of 73%.

EXECUTIVES

Chairman: M. Jay Allison, age 51
CEO, President, and Director: Gary W. Blackie, age 59, $360,000 pay
SVP, CFO, Secretary, and Director: Roland O. Burns, age 47
VP Exploration: William E. Holman
VP Operations: Greg T. Martin, $212,500 pay
Auditors: Ernst & Young LLP

LOCATIONS

HQ: Bois d'Arc Energy, Inc.
600 Travis St., Ste. 5200, Houston, TX 77002
Phone: 713-228-0438   **Fax:** 713-228-1759
Web: www.boisdarcenergy.com

COMPETITORS

Forest Oil
Meridian Resource
Newfield Exploration

HISTORICAL FINANCIALS

Company Type: Public

Income Statement

FYE: December 31

	REVENUE ($ mil.)	NET INCOME ($ mil.)	NET PROFIT MARGIN	EMPLOYEES
12/06	254.7	55.0	21.6%	23
12/05	184.4	(51.7)	—	20
12/04	133.4	51.9	38.9%	13
12/03	76.1	10.1	13.2%	—
12/02	96.7	16.2	16.8%	—
Annual Growth	**38.1%**	**—**	**—**	**15.0%**

2006 Year-End Financials

Debt ratio: 19.4%
Return on equity: 11.8%
Cash ($ mil.): 9.5
Current ratio: 0.82
Long-term debt ($ mil.): 100.0
No. of shares (mil.): 66.4
Dividends
  Yield: —
  Payout: —
Market value ($ mil.): 971.9
R&D as % of sales: —
Advertising as % of sales: —

Stock History

NYSE: BDE

	STOCK PRICE ($) FY Close	P/E High/Low	PER SHARE ($) Earnings	Dividends	Book Value
12/06	14.63	24 16	0.84	—	7.78
12/05	15.86	— —	(0.89)	—	6.53
Annual Growth	**(7.8%)**	**— —**	**—**	**—**	**19.0%**

Bolt Technology

Bolt Technology's action is technology, the kind used to map out oil and gas discoveries. The company provides geophysical equipment to the oil and gas industry. Its marine air guns help produce 3-D seismic maps for oil and gas exploration by firing high-pressure air into the water, producing elastic waves that penetrate deep into the earth. These waves are then used to create a "map" of the subsurface geography. Through its Custom Products subsidiary, Bolt Technology makes miniature industrial clutches and brakes used in airplane video systems, hospital beds, barcode labelers, and banking machines. The company's customers in 2006 included WesternGeco (22% of sales) and CCG-Veritas (15%).

Bolt Technology was established in 1962. In 2004 the company completed development of stage one of its digital Seismic Source Monitoring System, designed to enhance the accuracy of its air gun seismic technology.

In 2006 the company was awarded a contract by BP Exploration (Caspian Sea) Limited for the supply of a portable Annular Port Air Gun source array.

EXECUTIVES

Chairman, President, and CEO: Raymond M. Soto, age 68, $694,400 pay
SVP Finance, CFO, and Director: Joseph Espeso, age 65, $312,000 pay
SVP Marketing, Secretary, and Director:
  Joseph (Joe) Mayerick Jr., age 65, $312,000 pay
Director Human Resources: Jolsen Stetso
President, Real Time: Allen Nance
Auditors: McGladrey & Pullen, LLP

LOCATIONS

HQ: Bolt Technology Corporation
  4 Duke Place, Norwalk, CT 06854
Phone: 203-853-0700   **Fax:** 203-854-9601
Web: www.bolt-technology.com

Bolt Technology operates manufacturing facilities in Connecticut and Texas.

2007 Sales

	$ mil.	% of total
Norway	15.8	31
US	13.9	28
United Arab Emirates	7.8	15
France	3.0	6
China	2.3	4
UK	1.4	3
India	.7	1
Other	5.6	11
Total	**50.5**	**100**

PRODUCTS/OPERATIONS

2007 Sales

	$ mil.	% of total
Geophysical equipment	46.9	93
Industrial products	3.6	7
Total	**50.5**	**100**

Selected Subsidiaries

A-G Geophysical Products, Inc. (underwater electrical connectors and cables, air gun hydrophones, and pressure transducers)
Custom Products Corporation (miniature industrial clutches, brakes, and sub-fractional horsepower electric motors)

COMPETITORS

Allegheny Technologies
CGGVeritas
Dawson Geophysical
ION Geophysical
OYO Geospace

HISTORICAL FINANCIALS

Company Type: Public

Income Statement

FYE: June 30

	REVENUE ($ mil.)	NET INCOME ($ mil.)	NET PROFIT MARGIN	EMPLOYEES
6/07	50.5	10.6	21.0%	113
6/06	32.6	4.8	14.7%	100
6/05	18.8	1.7	9.0%	86
6/04	14.8	0.9	6.1%	—
6/03	10.8	(0.2)	—	—
Annual Growth	**47.1%**	**—**	**—**	**14.6%**

2007 Year-End Financials

Debt ratio: —
Return on equity: 30.7%
Cash ($ mil.): 10.0
Current ratio: 5.28
Long-term debt ($ mil.): —

Net Income History

AMEX: BTJ

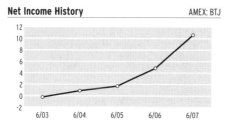

Boots & Coots

Boots & Coots International Well Control scoots to the rescue of oil companies faced with oil and gas well blowouts and fires. Besides being in the "hellfighting" business, the company contains oil and hazardous material spills, restores affected sites, and provides snubbing and noncritical services such as troubleshooting and contingency planning. Post-Gulf War contracts in Iraq, as well as the disposal of noncore operations, helped the company mitigate some of its earlier financial difficulties. Boots & Coots' founders, including Boots Hansen and Coots Mathews, learned their trade working for industry pioneer Red Adair. Oil States International unit Oil States Energy Services owns 15% of the company.

The company participates in a global strategic alliance with Halliburton. Boots & Coots is directly involved in Halliburton's well control projects that require firefighting and risk management expertise. In 2006 the company acquired the hydraulic well control business of Oil States International.

EXECUTIVES

Chairman: Douglas E. (Doug) Swanson, age 68
President, CEO, COO, and Director:
  Jerry L. Winchester, age 47, $268,000 pay
CFO: Gabriel (Gabe) Aldape, age 47
EVP: Dewitt H. Edwards, age 48
EVP: Don B. Cobb, age 50
VP Well Control: Danny Clayton
VP Engineering: John Garner
VP Business Development: Larry Burleson
VP Information Technology and Human Resources:
  Kelly Hebert
General Counsel and Secretary: Brian Keith
Auditors: UHY LLP

LOCATIONS

HQ: Boots & Coots International Well Control, Inc.
  7908 N. Sam Houston Pkwy. West, Ste. 500,
  Houston, TX 77064
Phone: 281-931-8884   **Fax:** 281-931-8392
Web: www.bncg.com

Boots & Coots International Well Control operates through its office in Houston.

2006 Sales

	% of total
US	26
Other countries	74
Total	**100**

PRODUCTS/OPERATIONS

2006 Sales

	$ mil.	% of total
Well intervention	76.6	79
Response	20.4	21
Total	**97.0**	**100**

COMPETITORS

Global Industries
RPC
Superior Energy
Wild Well Control

HISTORICAL FINANCIALS

Company Type: Public

Income Statement

FYE: December 31

	REVENUE ($ mil.)	NET INCOME ($ mil.)	NET PROFIT MARGIN	EMPLOYEES
12/06	97.0	11.2	11.5%	399
12/05	29.5	2.8	9.5%	355
12/04	24.2	(0.3)	—	—
12/03	35.9	7.1	19.8%	—
12/02	14.1	(9.2)	—	46
Annual Growth	**62.0%**	**—**	**—**	**71.6%**

2006 Year-End Financials

Debt ratio: 76.8%
Return on equity: 53.1%
Cash ($ mil.): 5.3
Current ratio: 1.95
Long-term debt ($ mil.): 29.5
No. of shares (mil.): 59.2
Dividends
  Yield: —
  Payout: —
Market value ($ mil.): 132.6
R&D as % of sales: —
Advertising as % of sales: —

Stock History

AMEX: WEL

	STOCK PRICE ($) FY Close	P/E High/Low		PER SHARE ($) Earnings	Dividends	Book Value
12/06	2.24	12	5	0.21	—	0.65
12/05	1.04	27	13	0.06	—	0.13
12/04	0.91	—	—	(0.04)	—	0.04
12/03	1.26	39	2	0.26	—	0.01
12/02	0.64	—	—	(1.12)	—	(0.20)
Annual Growth	**36.8%**	**—**	**—**	**—**	**—**	**—**

Boston Private Financial Holdings

Boston Private — isn't that David Kelley's new TV series? Not exactly: The company is the parent of regional banks and financial companies serving primarily well-to-do and institutional clients on both coasts. Its subsidiaries' services and products include deposit accounts, brokerage, and investment management. Boston Private Bank & Trust operates a handful of New England branch locations; Borel Private Bank & Trust has three Northern California offices. The company serves Southern California through First State Bank of California (FSB). Commercial loans account for 43% of its loan portfolio. Boston Private also offers construction, residential construction, and home equity loans, as well as other types.

The company acquired First State Bank of California (FSB) in 2004 (it later bought Encino State Bank and merged it into FSB's operations).

In 2005 Boston Private moved into the fast-growing Florida market with the acquisition of Gibraltar Financial, which owns five Gibraltar Bank locations (primarily serving businesses and wealthy individuals). The next year it acquired the newly formed Anchor Holdings, consisting of the investment companies Anchor Capital and Anchor Russell.

In 2007 it acquired Charter Financial for nearly $71 million. Charter Financial is the private bank holding company for Washington state bank Charter Bank. That year it made another private bank acquisition when it bought 70% of Davidson Capital Management. The acquisition will allow Boston Private to reach well-to-do Philadelphia Main Line customers.

EXECUTIVES

Chairman and CEO: Timothy L. Vaill, age 65, $620,000 pay
Vice Chair and President: Walter M. Pressey, age 62, $450,000 pay (prior to title change)
Vice Chair and President, Western Region: Jonathan H. (JP) Parker, age 61, $648,000 pay
CFO: David Kaye, age 43
Head, Wealth Advisory: Joseph H. (Jay) Cromarty, age 50, $710,000 pay
EVP, General Counsel, and Secretary: Margaret W. (Megan) Chambers, age 46
EVP and Corporate Development Manager: Kathryn A. (Katie) Kearney
SVP, Human Resources, Boston Private Bank & Trust: Pilar Pueyo
VP, Investor Relations: Erica E. Smith
Controller and Treasurer: William H. Morton
Auditors: KPMG LLP

LOCATIONS

HQ: Boston Private Financial Holdings, Inc.
10 Post Office Sq., Boston, MA 02109
Phone: 617-912-1900   **Fax:** 617-912-4550
Web: www.bostonprivate.com

PRODUCTS/OPERATIONS

2006 Sales

	$ mil.	% of total
Interest		
Loans	272.8	58
Securities	19.3	4
Other	7.9	2
Noninterest		
Investment management & trust fees	137.7	29
Wealth advisory fees	20.8	4
Other	12.9	3
Total	**471.4**	**100**

Selected Subsidiaries and Affiliate Partners

Anchor Capital Holdings
Bingham, Osborn & Scarborough, LLC (49.7%; fee only wealth management)
Borel Private Bank & Trust Company (San Mateo, California)
Boston Private Bank & Trust Company
Boston Private Value Investors, Inc. (investment management; Concord, New Hampshire)
Coldstream Capital Management, Inc. (wealth management; Bellevue, Washington)
Dalton, Greiner, Hartman, Maher & Co., LLC (investment management; New York City)
First Private Bank & Trust
First State Bank of California (Los Angeles)
Gibraltar Private Bank & Trust Company
KLS Professional Advisors Group, LLC (investment management; New York City)
RINET Company, LLC (financial planning; Boston)
Sand Hill Advisors, Inc. (investment management; Palo Alto, California)
Westfield Capital Management, LLC (investment advising; Boston)

COMPETITORS

Bank of America
Brown Brothers Harriman
Central Bancorp
Century Bancorp (MA)
Citigroup
Citizens Financial Group
FMR
Merrill Lynch
Morgan Stanley
Sovereign Bancorp
TD Banknorth

HISTORICAL FINANCIALS

Company Type: Public

Income Statement

FYE: December 31

	ASSETS ($ mil.)	NET INCOME ($ mil.)	INCOME AS % OF ASSETS	EMPLOYEES
12/06	5,763.5	54.4	0.9%	1,031
12/05	5,134.1	46.3	0.9%	892
12/04	3,270.3	33.6	1.0%	—
12/03	2,196.3	21.8	1.0%	—
12/02	1,820.7	23.7	1.3%	391
Annual Growth	**33.4%**	**23.1%**	**—**	**27.4%**

2006 Year-End Financials

Equity as % of assets: 11.0%
Return on assets: 1.0%
Return on equity: 9.3%
Long-term debt ($ mil.): 836.9
No. of shares (mil.): 36.6
Market value ($ mil.): 1,032.2
Dividends
Yield: 1.1%
Payout: 22.4%
Sales ($ mil.): 471.4
R&D as % of sales: —
Advertising as % of sales: —

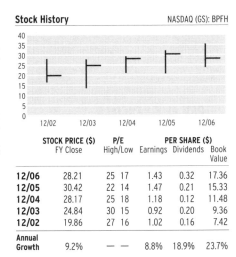

Stock History

NASDAQ (GS): BPFH

	STOCK PRICE ($) FY Close	P/E High/Low		Earnings	PER SHARE ($) Dividends	Book Value
12/06	28.21	25	17	1.43	0.32	17.36
12/05	30.42	22	14	1.47	0.21	15.33
12/04	28.17	25	18	1.18	0.12	11.48
12/03	24.84	30	15	0.92	0.20	9.36
12/02	19.86	27	16	1.02	0.16	7.42
Annual Growth	**9.2%**	**—**	**—**	**8.8%**	**18.9%**	**23.7%**

BreitBurn Energy Partners

Oil and gas futures burn brightly for BreitBurn Energy Partners, one of California's largest independent exploration and production companies. With its assets concentrated in Southern California (Los Angeles Basin) and Wyoming (Big Horn and Wind River Basins), the company has proved reserves of 30.7 million barrels of oil equivalent. BreitBurn Energy Partners' predecessor was founded in 1998 by Randall Breitenbach and Halbert Washburn. Breitenbach and Washburn serve as co-CEOs of BreitBurn Energy Partners' general partner, BreitBurn GP LLC. Canada's Provident Energy Trust acquired 92% of the predecessor company in 2004. It retained about 70% of BreitBurn Energy Partners following its 2006 IPO.

BreitBurn Energy Partners is pursuing a strategy of acquiring long-lived assets with relatively low-risk exploitation and development opportunities. It also hopes to use its association with Provident Energy Trust to secure attractive acquisition opportunities.

In 2007 the company agreed to acquire Quicksilver Resources for $750 million.

EXECUTIVES

Chairman: Randall J. (Randy) Findlay, age 58
Co-CEO and Director: Randall H. (Randy) Breitenbach, age 47
Co-CEO and Director: Halbert S. (Hal) Washburn, age 47
COO: Mark L. Pease, age 49
CFO: James G. Jackson, age 43
EVP and General Counsel: Gregory C. Brown, age 57
VP Operations: Chris E. Williamson, age 50
Treasurer: Bruce D. McFarland, age 51
Controller: Lawrence C. Smith, age 54
Auditors: PricewaterhouseCoopers LLP

LOCATIONS

HQ: BreitBurn Energy Partners L.P.
515 S. Flower St., Ste. 4800, Los Angeles, CA 90071
Phone: 213-225-5900   **Fax:** 213-225-5916
Web: www.breitburn.com

COMPETITORS

Aera Energy
Berry Petroleum
Bill Barrett
Chevron
Windsor Energy Resources

HISTORICAL FINANCIALS

Company Type: Public

Income Statement

FYE: December 31

	REVENUE ($ mil.)	NET INCOME ($ mil.)	NET PROFIT MARGIN	EMPLOYEES
12/06	138.0	49.9	36.2%	150
12/05	101.9	39.0	38.3%	146
12/04	41.2	3.3	8.0%	—
12/03	42.2	14.6	34.6%	—
Annual Growth	48.4%	50.6%	—	2.7%

2006 Year-End Financials

Debt ratio: 0.9%
Return on equity: 23.9%
Cash ($ mil.): 4.1
Current ratio: 1.56
Long-term debt ($ mil.): 1.6
No. of shares (mil.): 22.0

Dividends
Yield: —
Payout: —
Market value ($ mil.): 529.6
R&D as % of sales: —
Advertising as % of sales: —

Stock History

NASDAQ (GM): BBEP

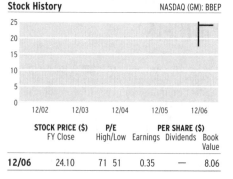

	STOCK PRICE ($) FY Close	P/E High/Low		PER SHARE ($) Earnings	Dividends	Book Value
12/06	24.10	71	51	0.35	—	8.06

Bridge Capital Holdings

Bridge Capital Holdings wants to help its business clients get from here to there. It was formed in 2004 to be the holding company for Bridge Bank. A relative neophyte itself, the bank opened in 2001 to serve small, midsized, and emerging technology businesses primarily in California's Silicon Valley. It operates regional offices in Palo Alto and San Jose; Small Business Administration (SBA) loan production facilities in Fresno, San Ramon, and Santa Clara; and has SBA representatives in Bakersfield and San Diego. Bridge Bank formed a holding company to give it more flexibility to engage in a wider range of financial activities and to acquire other financial firms.

Chairman Allan Kramer, an investment adviser for a partnership dealing with public, private, and angel investments, owns more than 4% of Bridge Capital Holdings; directors and executive officers, as a group, own 20%.

EXECUTIVES

Chairman, Bridge Capital Holdings and Bridge Bank: Allan C. Kramer, age 70
President, CEO, and Director, Bridge Capital Holdings and Bridge Bank: Daniel P. (Dan) Myers, age 46, $573,750 pay
EVP, CFO, and Chief Administrative Officer, Bridge Capital Holdings and Bridge Bank: Thomas A. (Tom) Sa, age 45, $331,250 pay (prior to promotion)
EVP and Secretary; EVP and CTO, Bridge Bank: Kenneth B. (Ken) Silveira, age 62, $289,000 pay
EVP and COO, Bridge Bank: Timothy W. (Tim) Boothe, age 40, $326,250 pay (prior to promotion)
EVP and President, Palo Alto Office, Bridge Bank: Kenneth D. (Ken) Brenner
Director; EVP, Bridge Bank; President, Specialty Markets: Robert P. (Bob) Gionfriddo, age 61, $325,000 pay
Auditors: Vavrinek, Trine, Day & Co., LLP

LOCATIONS

HQ: Bridge Capital Holdings
55 Almaden Blvd., San Jose, CA 95113
Phone: 408-423-8500 **Fax:** 408-423-8520
Web: www.bridgebank.com

PRODUCTS/OPERATIONS

2006 Sales

	$ mil.	% of total
Interest		
Loans	48.3	85
Federal funds sold	4.0	7
Securities & other	0.7	1
Noninterest		
Gain on sale of SBA loans	1.3	2
Service charges & other	2.5	5
Total	**56.8**	**100**

COMPETITORS

Bank of America
Bank of the West
Comerica
Heritage Commerce
SVB Financial
Technology Credit Union
Wells Fargo

HISTORICAL FINANCIALS

Company Type: Public

Income Statement

FYE: December 31

	ASSETS ($ mil.)	NET INCOME ($ mil.)	INCOME AS % OF ASSETS	EMPLOYEES
12/06	722.0	8.6	1.2%	134
12/05	536.5	5.7	1.1%	103
12/04	402.0	3.0	0.7%	—
Annual Growth	34.0%	69.3%	—	30.1%

2006 Year-End Financials

Equity as % of assets: 6.8%
Return on assets: 1.4%
Return on equity: 19.4%
Long-term debt ($ mil.): 17.5
No. of shares (mil.): 6.3
Market value ($ mil.): 129.2

Dividends
Yield: —
Payout: —
Sales ($ mil.): 56.8
R&D as % of sales: —
Advertising as % of sales: —

Stock History

NASDAQ (GM): BBNK

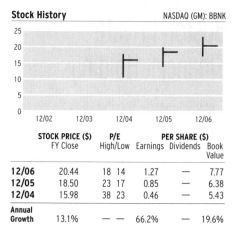

	STOCK PRICE ($) FY Close	P/E High/Low		PER SHARE ($) Earnings	Dividends	Book Value
12/06	20.44	18	14	1.27	—	7.77
12/05	18.50	23	17	0.85	—	6.38
12/04	15.98	38	23	0.46	—	5.43
Annual Growth	13.1%	—	—	66.2%	—	19.6%

Bronco Drilling

Bronco Drilling is game to compete in that wild ride called oil and gas drilling, where the chances of getting bucked off are as likely as the chance of making a buck. The contract land driller owns a fleet of 65 land drilling rigs, of which 51 are in use. Bronco Drilling plans to refurbish its inventoried rigs and make them operational by the end of 2006. Many of its rigs, ranging from 500 to 2,000 horsepower, can drill to depths between 15,000 and 25,000 feet. The company, which serves natural gas production firms across the US, has 67 trucks to transport its rigs. In 2008 Allis-Chalmers Energy agreed to buy Bronco Drilling for $437.8 million.

Bronco Drilling is upgrading its inventoried rigs to enable them to reach the depths required to explore for deep natural gas reserves. The company's most powerful rigs can also drill horizontal wells, an increasingly productive and popular form of natural gas exploration in the US and Canada.

Bronco Drilling began operations in 2001 with the purchase of a 650-horsepower rig, and has grown through the acquisition of additional rigs.

EXECUTIVES

Chairman and CEO: D. Frank Harrison, age 59, $741,346 pay
President: Mark Dubberstein
CFO, Secretary, and Treasurer: Zachary M. Graves, age 31, $404,231 pay
SVP, Rig Operations: Larry Bartlett, age 53, $361,642 pay
VP, Corporate Finance: Matt Porter
Investor Relations: Bob Jarvis
Chief Accounting Officer: Steven R. Starke
General Counsel and Assistant Secretary: David C. Treadwell
Controller: Rebecca D. Smith
Auditors: Grant Thornton LLP

LOCATIONS

HQ: Bronco Drilling Company, Inc.
16217 N. May Ave., Edmond, OK 73013
Phone: 405-242-4444   **Fax:** 405-285-0478
Web: broncodrill.com

Bronco Drilling operates in Colorado, Kansas, North Dakota, Oklahoma, and Texas.

PRODUCTS/OPERATIONS

2006 Sales

	% of total
Chesapeake Energy Corporation	7
Comstock Oil & Gas	5
Other customers	88
Total	**100**

COMPETITORS

Ensign Energy Services
Helmerich & Payne
Nabors Industries
Patterson-UTI Energy
Pioneer Drilling
Pride International
Union Drilling
Unit Corporation

HISTORICAL FINANCIALS

Company Type: Public

Income Statement

FYE: December 31

	REVENUE ($ mil.)	NET INCOME ($ mil.)	NET PROFIT MARGIN	EMPLOYEES
12/06	285.8	59.8	20.9%	2,050
12/05	77.9	5.1	6.5%	1,400
12/04	21.9	(2.8)	—	360
12/03	12.5	(1.5)	—	2050
12/02	3.1	(1.9)	—	—
Annual Growth	**209.9%**	**—**	**—**	**0.0%**

2006 Year-End Financials

Debt ratio: 18.9%
Return on equity: 20.6%
Cash ($ mil.): 10.6
Current ratio: 2.05
Long-term debt ($ mil.): 64.1
No. of shares (mil.): 24.9
Dividends
  Yield: —
  Payout: —
Market value ($ mil.): 428.7
R&D as % of sales: —
Advertising as % of sales: —

Stock History

NASDAQ (CM): BRNC

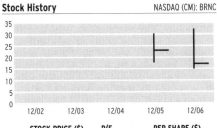

	STOCK PRICE ($) FY Close	P/E High/Low		Earnings	PER SHARE ($) Dividends	Book Value
12/06	17.19	13	6	2.43	—	13.63
12/05	23.01	97	58	0.31	—	10.33
Annual Growth	**(25.3%)**	**—**	**—**	**683.9%**	**—**	**31.9%**

Brooke Corporation

Here comes the death of the (independent) insurance salesman: Brooke Corporation offers financial services and insurance policies, mainly property/casualty insurance, through its network of some 700 franchise locations in about 40 states. The company believes its franchise system (which includes selling insurance through local owners) is more effective than regular independent agent models. Brooke also provides consulting, lending, and brokerage services through subsidiaries such as Brooke Credit Corporation and CJD and Associates. Brooke Holdings, which is controlled by brothers Robert Orr and Leland Orr (Brooke Corporation chairman and CFO, respectively), owns about 57% of Brooke Corporation.

In 2006 Brooke Franchise acquired the property and casualty retail customer accounts from InsWeb Insurance Services. It also acquired a savings banks called Generations Bank, which was renamed Brooke Savings Bank. The bank locations offer standard banking services to referrals from company insurance agents.

Brooke Corporation in 2007 spun off its Brooke Credit Corporation into a merger with Oakmont Acquisitions Corporation. Brooke Corporation will retain a controlling interest in the new organization.

EXECUTIVES

Chairman: Robert D. Orr, age 53, $380,000 pay
Vice Chairman, CFO, and Assistant Secretary:
Leland G. Orr, age 44, $210,000 pay
President, CEO, and Director: Keith Bouchey
VP and Treasurer: Anita K. Lowry, age 51
Senior Counsel: Carl Baranowski
National VP, Operations, Brooke Franchise:
Dane Devlin
Senior Credit Manager, Brooke Credit: Wayne Kindrick
Communications and Public Relations:
Stephanie Felder
Director, Brooke Franchise: Chad S. Maxwell, age 32
Auditors: Summers, Spencer & Callison, CPAs,
Chartered

LOCATIONS

HQ: Brooke Corporation
10950 Grandview Dr., Ste. 600,
Overland Park, KS 66210
Phone: 913-661-0123   **Fax:** 913-451-3183
Web: www.brookecorp.com

PRODUCTS/OPERATIONS

2006 Sales

	$ mil.	% of total
Insurance commissions	102.0	57
Initial franchise fees	34.9	19
Interest income	19.7	11
Consulting fees	9.9	5
Gains on sale of businesses	3.1	2
Other	10.1	6
Total	**179.7**	**100**

COMPETITORS

AIG	Marsh & McLennan
Allstate	Nationwide
Aon	NovaStar Financial
Arthur Gallagher	State Farm
DCAP Group	

HISTORICAL FINANCIALS

Company Type: Public

Income Statement

FYE: December 31

	REVENUE ($ mil.)	NET INCOME ($ mil.)	NET PROFIT MARGIN	EMPLOYEES
12/06	179.7	10.7	6.0%	572
12/05	145.4	9.7	6.7%	647
12/04	101.9	6.7	6.6%	—
12/03	66.0	4.2	6.4%	—
12/02	40.4	1.5	3.7%	—
Annual Growth	**45.2%**	**63.4%**	**—**	**(11.6%)**

2006 Year-End Financials

Debt ratio: 102.4%
Return on equity: 22.8%
Cash ($ mil.): 91.7
Current ratio: 1.45
Long-term debt ($ mil.): 55.8
No. of shares (mil.): 12.6
Dividends
  Yield: 6.1%
  Payout: 92.1%
Market value ($ mil.): 144.4
R&D as % of sales: —
Advertising as % of sales: —

Stock History

NASDAQ (GM): BXXX

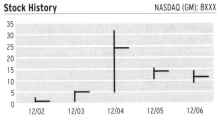

	STOCK PRICE ($) FY Close	P/E High/Low		Earnings	PER SHARE ($) Dividends	Book Value
12/06	11.50	18	12	0.76	0.70	4.50
12/05	14.05	18	13	0.86	0.32	3.33
12/04	24.16	48	8	0.65	—	0.78
12/03	5.05	13	3	0.40	—	1.24
12/02	1.08	19	7	0.13	—	3.98
Annual Growth	**80.6%**	**—**	**—**	**55.5%**	**118.8%**	**3.1%**

Brookline Bancorp

Brookline Bancorp owns Brookline Bank, a community-oriented financial institution with about 15 branches in the Boston area. The banks offer checking, savings, NOW, and money market accounts, as well as IRAs and CDs. In 2003 the bank started offering indirect auto loans originated by car dealerships; they now account for the largest portion of its loan portfolio (nearly 30%). Multifamily residential and commercial mortgages each account for about 20%. The company bought another Boston-area banking company, Mystic Financial, the parent of Medford Co-Operative Bank, in early 2005. Institutional investors hold more than a third of Brookline Bancorp's stock.

EXECUTIVES

Chairman, President, and CEO, Brookline Bancorp and Brookline Bank: Richard P. Chapman Jr., age 72, $530,000 pay
EVP and Director; President and Senior Loan Officer, Brookline Bank: Charles H. Peck, age 66, $235,000 pay

SVP and CFO, Brookline Bancorp; EVP and CFO, Brookline Bank: Paul R. Bechet, age 64, $215,000 pay
SVP, Commercial Lending: William R. MacKenzie
SVP, Indirect Auto Lending, Brookline Bank: David J. Pallin, age 67, $155,000 pay
Secretary and Director: George C. Caner Jr., age 81
President and CEO, Eastern Funding: Michael J. Fanger, age 49, $195,750 pay
Auditors: KPMG LLP

LOCATIONS

HQ: Brookline Bancorp, Inc.
   160 Washington St., Brookline, MA 02447
Phone: 617-730-3500   **Fax:** 617-730-3552
Web: www.brooklinebank.com

PRODUCTS/OPERATIONS

2006 Sales

	$ mil.	% of total
Interest		
Loans	110.7	81
Debt securities	15.0	11
Short-term investments	5.3	4
Other securities	1.6	1
Noninterest	3.9	3
Total	**136.5**	**100**

COMPETITORS

Bank of America	Citizens Financial Group
Boston Private	Eastern Bank
Capital Crossing	Sovereign Bancorp
Central Bancorp	TD Banknorth
Century Bancorp (MA)	Wainwright Bank

HISTORICAL FINANCIALS

Company Type: Public

Income Statement — FYE: December 31

	ASSETS ($ mil.)	NET INCOME ($ mil.)	INCOME AS % OF ASSETS	EMPLOYEES
12/06	2,373.0	20.8	0.9%	248
12/05	2,214.7	22.0	1.0%	202
12/04	1,694.5	17.8	1.1%	—
12/03	1,524.0	14.5	1.0%	—
12/02	1,423.4	21.9	1.5%	126
Annual Growth	**13.6%**	**(1.3%)**	**—**	**18.4%**

2006 Year-End Financials

Equity as % of assets: 24.6%
Return on assets: 0.9%
Return on equity: 3.5%
Long-term debt ($ mil.): 481.0
No. of shares (mil.): 61.6
Market value ($ mil.): 811.1
Dividends
   Yield: 5.6%
   Payout: 217.6%
Sales ($ mil.): 136.5
R&D as % of sales: —
Advertising as % of sales: —

Stock History

NASDAQ (GS): BRKL

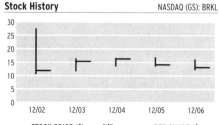

	STOCK PRICE ($) FY Close	P/E High/Low	Earnings	Dividends	Book Value
12/06	13.17	47 37	0.34	0.74	9.46
12/05	14.17	46 38	0.36	0.74	9.78
12/04	16.32	53 44	0.31	0.65	9.89
12/03	15.34	65 48	0.25	0.54	10.31
12/02	11.90	72 28	0.38	0.49	10.80
Annual Growth	**2.6%**	**— —**	**(2.7%)**	**10.9%**	**(3.2%)**

Brooklyn Federal Bancorp

Brooklyn Federal Bancorp won't sell you a bridge, but it might loan you money to build one yourself. It's the holding company for Brooklyn Federal Savings Bank, which has been operating since 1887. The bank provides traditional savings and loan services to area individuals and businesses. The bank focuses on real estate lending; commercial mortgages make up more than 35% of a loan portfolio that also includes single-family home mortgages (nearly 30%) and multifamily residential loans (nearly 25%). As one might expect, the thrift operates in the New York City area, with two branches in Brooklyn and two on Long Island. Mutual holding company BFS Bancorp owns 70% of Brooklyn Federal Bancorp.

In an effort to increase its interest earnings, Brooklyn Federal Bancorp has been writing more commercial mortgages and construction loans. Those loans represented about a quarter of the company's loan book in 2001 but were up to nearly 45% by 2006.

The bank is exploring locations for opening new branch offices.

EXECUTIVES

Chairman: John A. Loconsolo, age 86
CEO and Vice Chairman: Angelo J. Di Lorenzo, age 65, $378,000 pay
President and COO: Richard A. Kielty, age 57, $189,000 pay
CFO: Ralph Walther, $122,000 pay
SVP and Loan Servicing Officer: Marilyn Alberici, $125,000 pay
VP and Chief Lending Officer: Marc Leno, age 47, $168,000 pay
VP and Residential Mortgage Officer: Daniel Bennett
VP and Retail Banking Officer: Salvatore Gargaro
VP and Retail Banking Administrator: Rosemary Demeo
Auditors: Beard Miller Company LLP

LOCATIONS

HQ: Brooklyn Federal Bancorp, Inc.
   81 Court St., Brooklyn, NY 11201
Phone: 718-855-8500   **Fax:** 718-858-5174
Web: www.brooklynbank.com

PRODUCTS/OPERATIONS

2007 Sales

	$ mil.	% of total
Interest		
First mortgage & other loans	23.5	76
Mortgage-backed securities	3.4	11
Other securities & interest-earning assets	0.8	3
Non-interest		
Banking fees & service charges	2.3	7
Net gain on sale of loans held for sale	0.3	1
Other	0.6	2
Total	**30.9**	**100**

COMPETITORS

Apple Bank	JPMorgan Chase
Astoria Financial	New York Community
Bank of America	Bancorp
Berkshire Bancorp	Oneida Financial
Bridge Bancorp	Pathfinder Bancorp
Citibank	Ridgewood Savings Bank
Dime	Smithtown Bancorp
Emigrant Bank	State Bancorp
First of Long Island	

HISTORICAL FINANCIALS

Company Type: Public

Income Statement — FYE: September 30

	ASSETS ($ mil.)	NET INCOME ($ mil.)	INCOME AS % OF ASSETS	EMPLOYEES
9/07	390.4	3.8	1.0%	94
9/06	408.0	4.6	1.1%	—
9/05	340.9	3.8	1.1%	59
Annual Growth	**7.0%**	**0.0%**	**—**	**26.2%**

2007 Year-End Financials

Equity as % of assets: 21.8%
Return on assets: 1.0%
Return on equity: 4.6%
Long-term debt ($ mil.): 1.9
No. of shares (mil.): 13.3
Market value ($ mil.): 183.0
Dividends
   Yield: 0.7%
   Payout: 34.5%
Sales ($ mil.): 30.9
R&D as % of sales: —
Advertising as % of sales: —

Stock History

NASDAQ (GM): BFSB

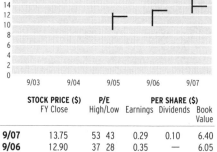

	STOCK PRICE ($) FY Close	P/E High/Low	Earnings	Dividends	Book Value
9/07	13.75	53 43	0.29	0.10	6.40
9/06	12.90	37 28	0.35	—	6.05
9/05	11.69	82 61	0.15	—	5.69
Annual Growth	**8.5%**	**— —**	**39.0%**	**—**	**6.1%**

Brooks Automation

Brooks Automation supplies a steady stream of production tools and factory automation products for chip makers and suppliers of chip-making equipment. The company makes tool automation products, such as vacuum robots and cluster assemblies used by semiconductor manufacturers. Brooks' wafer handling systems include vacuum cassette elevator loadlocks, transfer robots, and thermal conditioning modules and aligners. The company also makes vacuum equipment for makers of flat-panel displays and data storage devices. Customers include Lam Research, Novellus Systems, and Samsung Electronics. Brooks derives some two-thirds of its sales from customers in North America.

Brooks has sold its Brooks Software division to rival Applied Materials for $125 million in cash. Brooks Software provided one-eighth of Brooks Automation's sales. The company sees the sale as a way to focus on its core semiconductor-related hardware businesses.

The Antitrust Division of the US Department of Justice requested more information from Applied and Brooks on the software transaction, temporarily delaying the closing of the deal.

Brooks has grown by acquiring smaller businesses that expand its product lines and geographical reach; purchases have included makers of factory automation software and precision air flow control systems. The company crowned this buying spree — and became the dominant force in its market niche — with the 2002 purchase of archrival PRI Automation.

The Securities and Exchange Commission has initiated an informal inquiry into company practices on the timing and purchasing of stock-option grants. Brooks warned investors not to rely on audited financial results from fiscal 1999 through fiscal 2005, restating those results to more accurately reflect the financial impact of option grants. The company joined a host of other publicly held firms in cleaning up corporate policies on when executives and board members may date and exercise their stock options.

When directors Roger Emerick and Amin Khoury voluntarily resigned from the board in 2006, soon after the SEC's move, they made a point of renouncing their stock options and restricted stock awards, vested and unvested, to avoid any appearance of impropriety. Both had served on the board for more than a decade, prior to Brooks Automation's 1995 IPO.

Retired co-founder Robert Therrien was indicted for federal income tax evasion in mid-2007. The SEC also brought civil charges against him for alleged violations of federal securities laws. Brooks said it was cooperating with both federal prosecutors and the SEC in the case, which is not expected to result in any charges against the company.

Therrien stepped down as CEO in 2004 and retired as chairman in 2006. Former directors Emerick and Khoury were on the board's compensation committee that awarded stock-option grants to Therrien during his tenure at the company.

Mazama Capital Management owns about 12% of Brooks Automation. T. Rowe Price holds around 8% of the company. Nierenberg Investment Management has an equity stake of nearly 6%.

HISTORY

Norman Brooks founded Brooks Associates in 1978 to develop semiconductor automation equipment. Its vacuum transfer innovations set new standards for the industry. After the firm was sold to the Aeronca Electronics unit of Fleet Aerospace (now Magellan Aerospace) in 1985, Brooks served as its VP and general manager. In 1989 Brooks, chip testing equipment executive Robert Therrien, and several members of the Brooks management team repurchased the operation. As CEO of the new Brooks Automation, Therrien moved the company away from batch processing toward one-at-a-time wafer handling technology.

Brooks went public in 1995. In 1996 it bought Canadian equipment control products maker Techware Systems. In 1998 the company acquired factory automation software company FASTech Integration and won a software contract from Toshiba. Norman Brooks died in 1998.

In 2000 Brooks acquired automation software companies AutoSimulations and Auto-Soft from Daifuku America. The company continued its acquisition strategy in 2001 when it bought Progressive Technologies (precision air flow and pressure control systems), General Precision Inc. (fab mini-environments), and Switzerland-based Tec-Sem (photolithography tool buffers and batch transfer systems).

Also in 2001 Brooks announced plans to acquire rival PRI Automation in a deal initially valued at $380 million. (By the time the deal closed in 2002, Brooks' heightened stock price meant that the deal was worth more than $530 million.) In mid-2002 the company completed its purchase of PRI and changed its name to Brooks-PRI Automation. Also that year it bought Germany-based Hermos Informatik from Hermos Group for about $40 million.

Early in 2003 the company changed its name back to Brooks Automation. The next year COO Edward Grady succeeded Therrien as CEO; Therrien remained chairman.

In mid-2005 Brooks sold the assets of its Specialty Equipment and Life Sciences division, formerly Intelligent Automation Systems (IAS). Later that year Brooks acquired vacuum systems maker Helix Technology in a stock-swap transaction valued at $454 million. With the purchase, the former shareholders of Helix owned about 39% of Brooks.

Co-founder Robert Therrien stepped down as chairman and left the board in early 2006. Joseph Martin, a long-time director of the company and the former vice chairman of Fairchild Semiconductor, succeeded Therrien as chairman.

In mid-2006 Brooks acquired Synetics Solutions from Yaskawa Electric and formed a 50/50 joint venture in Japan with Yaskawa, called Yaskawa Brooks Automation (YBA).

In early 2007 Brooks sold its Brooks Software division to Applied Materials for $125 million in cash.

Also in 2007 CEO Edward Grady set plans to retire. The company tapped director Robert Lepofsky — who is older than Grady — to succeed him. Lepofsky had served on the Brooks board since October 2005, when the company acquired Helix Technology, where he once was the chairman and CEO.

EXECUTIVES

Chairman: Joseph R. (Joe) Martin, age 60
CEO and Director: Robert J. (Bob) Lepofsky, age 63
President and COO, Enterprise Software Group: Joseph M. (Joe) Bellini, age 47
EVP and CFO: Martin S. Headley, age 50
SVP, General Counsel, and Secretary: Thomas S. (Tom) Grilk, age 60, $469,402 pay
SVP and Corporate Controller: Richard C. (Rich) Small, age 50
President, Automation Systems Group: Michael W. Pippins, age 47
President, Global Customer Operations Group: Ralf Wuellner
Director, Investor Relations: Michael W. (Mike) McCarthy
Auditors: PricewaterhouseCoopers LLP

LOCATIONS

HQ: Brooks Automation, Inc.
15 Elizabeth Dr., Chelmsford, MA 01824
Phone: 978-262-2400 **Fax:** 978-262-2500
Web: www.brooks.com

Brooks Automation has operations in Canada, China, France, Germany, India, Israel, Japan, Malaysia, Singapore, South Korea, Taiwan, the UK, and the US.

2007 Sales

	$ mil.	% of total
North America	496.3	67
Asia/Pacific	148.1	20
Europe	98.9	13
Total	**743.3**	**100**

PRODUCTS/OPERATIONS

2007 Sales

	$ mil.	% of total
Automation Systems	462.8	62
Critical Components	156.1	21
Global Customer Support	124.4	17
Total	**743.3**	**100**

2007 Sales

	$ mil.	% of total
Products	613.5	83
Services	129.8	17
Total	**743.3**	**100**

Selected Products

Equipment Automation
  Aligners
  Cassette elevator load locks
  Equipment front end modules (EFEMs)
  Indexers
  Minienvironments
  Transfer robots
  Wafer handling systems
Factory Automation Hardware
  Front opening unified pods (FOUPs)
  Load ports
  Reticle handling and storage
  Sorters and indexers
  Standard mechanical interfaces (SMIFs)
  Wafer inspection

COMPETITORS

Amtech Systems	INFICON
Applied Materials	Kawasaki Heavy Industries
Asyst Technologies	Micro Component
Cohu	Technology
Daifuku	MKS Instruments
Daikin	Rorze
Electroglas	Sanmina-SCI
Entegris	Sumitomo Heavy
Flextronics	Industries
Fortrend Engineering	TDK
Hon Hai	

HISTORICAL FINANCIALS

Company Type: Public

Income Statement

FYE: September 30

	REVENUE ($ mil.)	NET INCOME ($ mil.)	NET PROFIT MARGIN	EMPLOYEES
9/07	743.3	151.5	20.4%	2,200
9/06	692.9	25.9	3.7%	2,400
9/05	463.8	(11.6)	—	1,800
9/04	539.8	17.7	3.3%	—
9/03	343.6	(185.8)	—	—
Annual Growth	**21.3%**	**—**	**—**	**10.6%**

2007 Year-End Financials

Debt ratio: —
Return on equity: 18.3%
Cash ($ mil.): 248.3
Current ratio: 3.36
Long-term debt ($ mil.): —
No. of shares (mil.): 70.4

Dividends
  Yield: —
  Payout: —
Market value ($ mil.): 1,002.8
R&D as % of sales: —
Advertising as % of sales: —

Stock History

NASDAQ (GS): BRKS

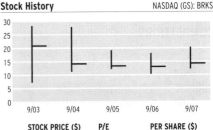

	STOCK PRICE ($) FY Close	P/E High/Low		PER SHARE ($) Earnings	Dividends	Book Value
9/07	14.24	10	6	2.04	—	12.21
9/06	13.05	50	29	0.36	—	10.59
9/05	13.33	—	—	(0.26)	—	4.16
9/04	14.15	67	28	0.41	—	7.00
9/03	20.90	—	—	(5.05)	—	3.67
Annual Growth	**(9.1%)**			**—**	**—**	**35.1%**

Bucyrus International

Bucyrus International caters to those who mine their own business. The company (formerly Bucyrus-Erie Co.) provides replacement parts and services (almost 65% of sales) to the surface mining industry. Bucyrus also makes large excavation machinery used for surface mining. Its products, which include walking draglines, electric mining shovels, and blast-hole drills, are used for mining coal, gold, iron ore, and other minerals. Bucyrus' customers are primarily large companies and quasi-governmental agencies operating in South America and Australia, Canada, China, India, South Africa, and the US.

EXECUTIVES

Chairman: Theodore C. Rogers, age 73
President, CEO, and Director: Timothy W. Sullivan, age 53, $609,504 pay
COO: Kenneth W. Krueger, age 50, $320,004 pay
CFO, Controller, and Secretary: Craig R. Mackus, age 54, $274,848 pay
EVP Global Markets and Strategic Support: William S. Tate, age 58
Chief Accounting Officer: Mark J. Knapp
Treasurer: John F. Bosbous, age 54, $161,700 pay
Director, Marketing: Kent Henschen
Auditors: Deloitte & Touche LLP

LOCATIONS

HQ: Bucyrus International, Inc.
1100 Milwaukee Ave., South Milwaukee, WI 53172
Phone: 414-768-4000   **Fax:** 414-768-4474
Web: www.bucyrus.com

2006 Sales

	$ mil.	% of total
North America		
US	379.8	51
Canada	50.2	7
Australia	118.9	16
Chile	96.3	13
Africa	36.5	5
Other regions	56.3	8
Total	**738.0**	**100**

PRODUCTS/OPERATIONS

2006 Sales

	$ mil.	% of total
Parts & services	482.3	65
Machines	255.7	35
Total	**738.0**	**100**

COMPETITORS

Atlas Copco
Baker Hughes
Caterpillar
Charles Machine
CNH
Harnischfeger Corporation
Joy Global
Joy Mining
Komatsu
Sandvik
Terex

HISTORICAL FINANCIALS

Company Type: Public

Income Statement

FYE: December 31

	REVENUE ($ mil.)	NET INCOME ($ mil.)	NET PROFIT MARGIN	EMPLOYEES
12/06	738.0	70.3	9.5%	2,400
12/05	575.0	53.6	9.3%	2,125
12/04	454.2	6.1	1.3%	—
12/03	337.7	(3.6)	—	—
12/02	289.6	(10.8)	—	—
Annual Growth	**26.3%**	**—**	**—**	**12.9%**

2006 Year-End Financials

Debt ratio: 27.8%
Return on equity: 27.2%
Cash ($ mil.): 9.6
Current ratio: 2.21
Long-term debt ($ mil.): 82.3
No. of shares (mil.): 31.6
Dividends
    Yield: 0.5%
    Payout: 10.8%
Market value ($ mil.): 1,634.4
R&D as % of sales: —
Advertising as % of sales: —

Stock History

NASDAQ (GS): BUCY

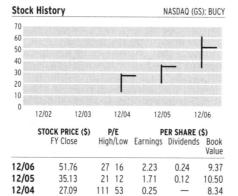

	STOCK PRICE ($) FY Close	P/E High/Low		PER SHARE ($) Earnings	Dividends	Book Value
12/06	51.76	27	16	2.23	0.24	9.37
12/05	35.13	21	12	1.71	0.12	10.50
12/04	27.09	111	53	0.25	—	8.34
Annual Growth	**38.2%**	**—**	**—**	**198.7%**	**100.0%**	**6.0%**

Buffalo Wild Wings

Hot sauce fuels the flight of this restaurateur. Buffalo Wild Wings (BWW) operates a chain of about 430 Buffalo Wild Wings Grill & Bar quick-casual dining spots in more than 35 states that specialize in Buffalo-style chicken wings. The eateries offer more than a dozen dipping sauces to go with their spicy wings, as well as a complement of other items such as chicken tenders and legs. BWW's menu also offers appetizers, burgers, tacos, salads, and desserts, along with beer, wine, and other beverages. The company owns and operates about 140 of the restaurants, while the rest are operated by franchisees.

The company has been expanding rapidly since its 2003 IPO, opening almost 60 new locations in 2006. It planned to continue that pace during 2007. BWW's expansion plans call for franchised locations to account for about two-thirds of its new locations; the company is aiming to reach 1,000 locations by 2013.

Jim Disbrow and Scott Lowery opened the first Buffalo Wild Wings restaurant on the campus of Ohio State University in Columbus in 1982. (Legend has it that they started the eatery because they craved the style of chicken wings they had eaten in Buffalo, New York.) Originally called Buffalo Wild Wings & Weck (a reference to the Kimmelweck brand rolls used for sandwiches),

the chain became known as BW3 for short. Rapid expansion and financial mismanagement pushed Buffalo Wild Wings to the brink of bankruptcy by the mid-1990s. Sally Smith became CEO in 1996 and helped retool the chain's branding strategy to appeal more to families and non-students.

Chairman Kenneth Dahlberg owns about 10% of BWW.

EXECUTIVES

Chairman: Kenneth H. Dahlberg, age 89
President, CEO, and Director: Sally J. Smith, age 49
EVP, CFO, and Treasurer: Mary J. Twinem, age 46
EVP and General Counsel: James M. Schmidt, age 47
SVP Development and Franchising: Lee Sanders, age 54
SVP Information Systems: Craig W. Donoghue, age 45
SVP Operations: Judith A. (Judy) Shoulak, age 47
SVP Marketing and Brand Development: Kathleen M. (Kathy) Benning, age 44
SVP Human Resources: Linda G. Traylor, age 55
Auditors: KPMG LLP

LOCATIONS

HQ: Buffalo Wild Wings, Inc.
1600 Utica Ave. South, Ste. 700, Minneapolis, MN 55416
Phone: 952-593-9943   **Fax:** 952-593-9787
Web: www.buffalowildwings.com

2006 Locations

	No.
Ohio	81
Texas	45
Indiana	30
Illinois	27
Michigan	26
Minnesota	19
Florida	14
Kentucky	14
Virginia	14
Missouri	13
Colorado	11
North Carolina	11
Wisconsin	11
Arizona	10
Nevada	9
Tennessee	9
Alabama	8
Georgia	7
Kansas	7
Nebraska	7
New York	7
Iowa	6
Louisiana	6
Mississippi	5
Oklahoma	5
Other states	24
Total	**429**

PRODUCTS/OPERATIONS

2006 Sales

	$ mil.	% of total
Restaurants	247.2	89
Franchising	31.0	11
Total	**278.2**	**100**

2006 Locations

	No.
Franchised	290
Company-owned	139
Total	**429**

COMPETITORS

Applebee's	Hooters
Brinker	Houlihan's
Carlson Restaurants	Metromedia
Damon's	O'Charley's
Darden	Romacorp
Dave & Buster's	Wing Zone
Family Sports Concepts	Wingstop
Fox & Hound Restaurant	Zaxby's

HISTORICAL FINANCIALS

Company Type: Public

Income Statement

FYE: Last Sunday in December

	REVENUE ($ mil.)	NET INCOME ($ mil.)	NET PROFIT MARGIN	EMPLOYEES
12/06	278.2	16.3	5.9%	7,482
12/05	209.7	8.9	4.2%	6,125
12/04	171.1	7.2	4.2%	—
12/03	126.5	3.6	2.8%	—
12/02	96.1	3.1	3.2%	—
Annual Growth	30.4%	51.4%	—	22.2%

2006 Year-End Financials

Debt ratio: 5.2%
Return on equity: 15.3%
Cash ($ mil.): 64.6
Current ratio: 2.91
Long-term debt ($ mil.): 6.0
No. of shares (mil.): 8.8

Dividends
  Yield: —
  Payout: —
Market value ($ mil.): 234.0
R&D as % of sales: —
Advertising as % of sales: —

Stock History

NASDAQ (GS): BWLD

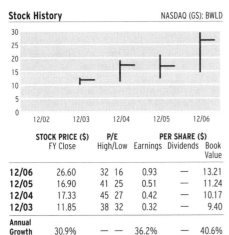

	STOCK PRICE ($) FY Close	P/E High/Low	PER SHARE ($) Earnings	Dividends	Book Value
12/06	26.60	32 16	0.93	—	13.21
12/05	16.90	41 25	0.51	—	11.24
12/04	17.33	45 27	0.42	—	10.17
12/03	11.85	38 32	0.32	—	9.40
Annual Growth	30.9%	— —	36.2%	—	40.6%

Build-A-Bear Workshop

The Build-A-Bear Workshop covers the "bear" necessities and much more. Located mainly in malls, the stores allow kids to design their own teddy bears and other stuffed animals complete with clothing (formal wear to western wear), shoes (including Skechers), and a barrage of accessories (eyewear, cell phones, and the like). Customers can also build bears online. Other offerings include the in-store Build-A-Party, online features such as e-cards, and bear fashions that match outfits sold at Tween Brands clothing stores. The company, founded by CEO Maxine Clark in 1997, operates 275-plus stores in Canada, the UK, and the US, as well as franchised stores in other countries. Clark owns about 17% of the company.

Exclusive franchise agreements with UK-based Amsbra Limited saw the opening of the first Build-A-Bear Workshop in the UK in 2003, with other overseas stores following in Australia, Denmark, Japan, and South Korea. In 2006 the company's UK subsidiary, Build-A-Bear Workshop UK Holdings, acquired The Bear Factory, a U.K.-based stuffed animal retailer, for about $41 million. The transaction included the acquisition of Amsbra, its franchisee in the UK. In all, the company operates more than 30 franchised stores overseas.

In 2005 the company opened its biggest store (22,000 square feet) to date at Fifth Avenue and 46th Street in Manhattan. In 2006 the first Build-A-Bear Workshop At The Zoo opened at the Saint Louis Zoo. The company also operates stores in five Major League Baseball ballparks. The company is exploring these types of non-traditional retail venues and planned a new store at the St. Louis Science Center in 2007.

Build-A-Bear planned to open about 40 new stores in North America in 2007, as well as a dozen new stores in the UK and France. Franchisees planned to open about 25 stores internationally in 2007.

A deal inked with toy maker Hasbro includes a specialty-sized line of stuffed animals, clothing, and accessories. Build-A-Bear has also introduced a line of dolls called Friends 2B Made that have their own range of clothing and accessories. The company also plans to add the Build-A-Dino concept to certain locations. In addition, Build-A-Bear has entered a deal with Retail Entertainment Concepts (in which it owns a 25% stake) to open a new concept store called Ridemakerz, focused on boys and cars.

The company opened a new warehouse in Groveport, Ohio, near Columbus, in 2006. The new 350,000-square-foot facility serves as Build-A-Bear's primary distribution center for North America. (Previously, the company used three distribution centers operated by third-party providers.)

The company has hired Lehman Brothers to explore strategic business alternatives for the company. Directors Barney Ebsworth, Frank Vest, James Gould, and William Reisler collectively control about 60% of the company.

EXECUTIVES

Chairman and Chief Executive Bear: Maxine K. Clark, age 58, $556,731 pay
President and Chief Operating Bear: Robert (Scott) Seay, age 44
Chief Financial Bear, Treasurer, and Secretary: Tina Klocke, age 47, $245,192 pay
Chief Marketing Bear: Teresa Kroll, age 52, $235,192 pay
Chief Information Bear: Dave Finnegan
Chief Workshop Bear: Paul Bundonis, age 45
Director, Investor Relations: Molly R. Salky, age 50
Director, Public Relations: Jill Saunders
Managing Director, Bear and Human Resources: Darlene Elder
General Counsel Bearister: T. William (Bill) Alvey III, age 37
Managing Director, Business Bearvelopment: David Armstrong
Managing Director, Bear Marketing: Nancy Schwartz
Managing Director, Beartroller: Mark Shurtleff
Auditors: KPMG LLP

LOCATIONS

HQ: Build-A-Bear Workshop, Inc.
  1954 Innerbelt Business Center Dr.,
  St. Louis, MO 63114
Phone: 314-423-8000   **Fax:** 314-423-8188
Web: www.buildabear.com

2006 Franchised Locations

	No.
Japan	7
Australia	6
Denmark	5
Taiwan	3
Other	13
Total	**34**

2006 US Locations

	No.
California	23
Texas	16
Florida	12
New Jersey	12
New York	12
Ohio	10
Massachusetts	9
Pennsylvania	8
Georgia	7
Illinois	7
North Carolina	7
Colorado	6
Indiana	6
Missouri	6
Tennessee	6
Virginia	6
Connecticut	5
Arizona	4
Maryland	4
Michigan	4
Washington	4
Arkansas	3
Iowa	3
Kentucky	3
Louisiana	3
Nevada	3
Oregon	3
South Carolina	3
Utah	3
Wisconsin	3
Other states	19
Total	**220**

PRODUCTS/OPERATIONS

Selected Products

Clothing
  Athletic uniforms (MLB, NBA, NHL)
  Casual sportswear
  Costumes
  Dress up
  Hibernities (sleepwear)
  Outerwear
  T-shirts
  UndiBears (underwear)
Accessories
  Backpacks
  Bear Care products
  Camping equipment
  Cell phones
  Comfy Stuff Fur-niture
  Glasses and sunglasses
  Handbags
  Hats
  Paw Wear (shoes and sandals)
  SKECHERS shoes (licensed)
  Slippers
  Socks
  Sports equipment
  Totes

COMPETITORS

Amazon.com	Kmart
Bear Wagner	Mattel
Boyds Collection	North American Bear
CNN	Russ Berrie
Enesco	Sears
Gambro AB	Target
Gund	Toys "R" Us
Hallmark	Ty
Hamleys	Vermont Teddy Bear
Hasbro	Wal-Mart

HISTORICAL FINANCIALS

Company Type: Public

Income Statement

FYE: Saturday nearest December 31

	REVENUE ($ mil.)	NET INCOME ($ mil.)	NET PROFIT MARGIN	EMPLOYEES
12/06	437.1	29.5	6.7%	6,900
12/05	361.8	27.3	7.5%	6,350
12/04	301.7	20.0	6.6%	—
12/03	213.7	8.0	3.7%	—
12/02	169.1	5.9	3.5%	—
Annual Growth	26.8%	49.5%	—	8.7%

2006 Year-End Financials

Debt ratio: —
Return on equity: 20.0%
Cash ($ mil.): 53.1
Current ratio: 1.29
Long-term debt ($ mil.): —
No. of shares (mil.): 20.5

Dividends
  Yield: —
  Payout: —
Market value ($ mil.): 575.5
R&D as % of sales: —
Advertising as % of sales: —

Stock History

NYSE: BBW

	STOCK PRICE ($) FY Close	P/E High/Low		PER SHARE ($) Earnings	Dividends	Book Value
12/06	28.02	23	14	1.44	—	8.00
12/05	29.64	27	14	1.35	—	6.48
12/04	35.15	33	22	1.07	—	4.88
Annual Growth	(10.7%)	—	—	16.0%	—	28.0%

Cal Dive International

Cal Dive International may or may not be California dreaming, but its waking hours are spent beneath the waters of the Gulf of Mexico. The subsea contractor operates a fleet of 24 surface and saturation diving support vessels and 11 construction barges. It installs and maintains offshore platforms, pipelines, and production systems on the Outer Continental Shelf of the Gulf of Mexico, as well as in offshore markets in the Middle East, Southeast Asia, and Trinidad. Following its 2006 IPO, the formerly wholly owned subsidiary of Helix Energy Solutions is 73%-owned by that company. In 2007 Cal Dive acquired Horizon Offshore in a $650 million deal.

Cal Dive also provides shallow water diving services and performs salvage operations on abandoned fields.

The subsea contractor has a proven track record of executing acquisitions that complement its fleet and enhance its service capabilities, especially in the Gulf of Mexico. In 2005 it added 13 vessels, including acquiring the diving and shallow water pipelay assets of Acergy that operate in the waters of the Gulf of Mexico and Trinidad.

EXECUTIVES

Chairman: Owen E. Kratz, age 53
President, CEO, and Director: Quinn J. Hébert, age 44, $250,000 pay
EVP and COO: Scott T. Naughton, age 53, $190,000 pay
EVP, CFO, and Treasurer: G. Kregg Lunsford, age 39, $224,000 pay
VP, General Counsel, and Secretary: Lisa Manget Buchanan, age 48, $151,560 pay (partial-year salary)
Auditors: Ernst & Young LLP

LOCATIONS

HQ: Cal Dive International, Inc.
  400 N. Sam Houston Pkwy East, Ste. 1000,
  Houston, TX 77060
Phone: 281-618-0400   **Fax:** 281-618-0501
Web: www.caldive.com

2006 Sales

	$ mil.	% of total
US	439.5	86
Other countries	70.4	14
Total	**509.9**	**100**

PRODUCTS/OPERATIONS

2006 Sales

	% of total
Chevron	16
Other customers	84
Total	**100**

COMPETITORS

Acergy
Global Industries
Halliburton
McDermott
Oceaneering International
Parker Drilling
Pride International
Saipem
Subsea 7
Technip
TETRA Technologies
Tidewater Inc.

HISTORICAL FINANCIALS

Company Type: Public

Income Statement

FYE: December 31

	REVENUE ($ mil.)	NET INCOME ($ mil.)	NET PROFIT MARGIN	EMPLOYEES
12/06	509.9	119.4	23.4%	1,300
12/05	224.3	37.7	16.8%	—
12/04	125.8	7.7	6.1%	—
12/03	135.5	10.8	8.0%	—
Annual Growth	55.5%	122.8%	—	—

2006 Year-End Financials

Debt ratio: 134.4%
Return on equity: 71.2%
Cash ($ mil.): 22.7
Current ratio: 2.87
Long-term debt ($ mil.): 212.0
No. of shares (mil.): 84.3

Dividends
  Yield: —
  Payout: —
Market value ($ mil.): 1,057.9
R&D as % of sales: —
Advertising as % of sales: —

Stock History

NYSE: DVR

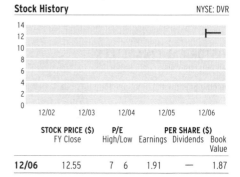

	STOCK PRICE ($) FY Close	P/E High/Low		PER SHARE ($) Earnings	Dividends	Book Value
12/06	12.55	7	6	1.91	—	1.87

Cal-Maine Foods

What comes first, the chicken or the egg? For Cal-Maine Foods, it's definitely the egg and some 24 million laying hens help settle the question. The company is one of the largest fresh egg producers in the US. Cal-Maine sells its eggs to supermarkets across the US. It also produces specialty eggs which it sells under the EggLand's Best and Farmhouse labels. The company has operations in Arkansas, Georgia, Kansas, Kentucky, Louisiana, Mississippi, New Mexico, North Carolina, Ohio, Oklahoma, South Carolina, Tennessee, Texas, and Utah and include breeding facilities, hatcheries, feed mills, shell-egg production and pullet-growing sites, and processing, packing, and wholesaling operations.

The company controls all aspects of the business, from hatching the chicks, making the feed they eat, housing the hens, and distributing their eggs. Most of the eggs Cal-Maine sells are produced at its own facilities; the rest are produced by contractors who use Cal-Maine flocks and feed. Its strategy is to grow by acquisitions. The company says it has completed 13 acquisitions since 1989.

In 2006 the company formed a 50-50 joint venture (Green Forest Foods) with Pier 44 Properties to lease and operate Green Forest Egg's production assets, which included about 1 million laying hens at facilities located in Arkansas. The next year, Cal-Maine bought out Pier 44's interest in Green Forest. The purchase price was not disclosed. Cal-Maine completed yet another acquisition in 2007 — the shell-egg division of George's Inc., for which it paid $11 million in cash.

Founder, chairman, and CEO Fred Adams Jr. and his immediate family control the company.

HISTORY

One can argue about the chicken or the egg, but Fred Adams Jr. came first at Cal-Maine. A former salesman with pet food giant Ralston Purina (now Nestlé Purina PetCare), Adams founded a poultry and egg business in Mendenhall, Mississippi, in 1957. He focused exclusively on egg sales in 1960 and merged his company in 1969 with Maine Egg Farms and Dairy Fresh Foods in California to form Cal-Maine Foods.

Cal-Maine cracked new markets through internal growth and the acquisition of rival egg firms. The company acquired Egg City (Arkansas, 1989), Sunny Fresh Foods (Arkansas, 1990), Sunnyside Eggs (North Carolina, 1991), Wayne Detling Farms (Ohio,1994), A&G Farms (Kentucky, 1995), and Sunbest Farms (Arkansas, 1996). After going public in 1996, Cal-Maine bought two Georgia firms: Southern Empire Egg Farm (1997) and J&S Farms (1998).

In 1998 the company sold off its egg products division, which provided food makers with egg whites and yolks and accounted for 4% of total sales. In 1999 Cal-Maine bought two egg producers and processors: Kentucky-based Hudson Brothers and Texas-based Smith Farms. Declining supplies in the cyclical egg market and increasing demand in late 2000 raised the company out of the loss column for the first time in 18 months.

In late 2001 Cal-Maine's board of directors voted to explore the possibility of the company becoming privately held but abandoned the idea because of a sagging egg market. Industry-wide overproduction helped to drive down egg prices, pecking away at the company's profits in 2002.

In 2003 Cal-Maine's board of directors voted to take the company private. However, as demand for eggs shot up, so did Cal-Maine stock prices, and shareholders were unconvinced such a move would benefit them. Faced with shareholder lawsuits, in November of that year the board voted to terminate the proposal to take the company private.

After years of oversupply and weak prices, starting in 2003 the entire egg industry enjoyed a boost from the popular protein-heavy Atkins diet. Cal-Maine's sales jumped as people chose hard-boiled eggs as snacks. However, by 2004 its popularity had peaked, leaving the market (and Cal-Maine) with an egg glut and plunging sales. In 2005 the company acquired egg supplier Hillandale Farms.

EXECUTIVES

Chairman and CEO: Fred R. Adams Jr., age 75, $405,640 pay
Vice Chairman: Richard K. Looper, age 80, $217,861 pay
President, COO, and Director:
 Adolphus B. (Dolph) Baker, age 50, $303,498 pay
VP, CFO, and Director: Timothy A. Dawson, age 53
VP and Controller: Charles F. Collins, age 63
VP Operations and Production: Jack B. Self, age 74, $207,931 pay
VP Feed Mill Division: Joe M. Wyatt, age 68
VP Sales, Eastern Operations: Ken Paramore
VP Sales: Charles J. (Jeff) Hardin
Director Human Resources: Alan Holland
General Counsel: James Neeld III
Auditors: Ernst & Young LLP

LOCATIONS

HQ: Cal-Maine Foods, Inc.
 3320 Woodrow Wilson Ave., Jackson, MS 39209
Phone: 601-948-6813   **Fax:** 601-969-0905
Web: www.calmainefoods.com

PRODUCTS/OPERATIONS

Selected Affiliates and Subsidiaries

American Egg Products, Inc. (44%)
Benton County Foods, LLC (90%)
Cal-Maine Farms, Inc.
CMF of Kansas, LLC (99%)
Delta Egg Farm LLC (50%)
Hillandale, LLC
South Texas Protein, LLC (22%)
Specialty Eggs LLC (50%)
Texas Egg Products, LLC (37%)
Texas Egg, LLC (43%)

Selected Brands

Cal-Maine
Egg-Land's Best (vegetarian fed, licensed)
Farmhouse (from uncaged birds)
Rio Grande
Sunups

COMPETITORS

Cooper Farms
Crystal Farms
Egg Innovations
Golden Oval Eggs
Hi Point Industries
Hickman's Family Farms
Ise America
Michael Foods Egg Products
Michael Foods, Inc.
Moark
Rose Acre Farms
Sunny Fresh Foods

HISTORICAL FINANCIALS

Company Type: Public

Income Statement

FYE: Saturday nearest May 31

	REVENUE ($ mil.)	NET INCOME ($ mil.)	NET PROFIT MARGIN	EMPLOYEES
5/07	598.1	36.7	6.1%	1,600
5/06	477.6	(1.0)	—	—
5/05	375.3	(10.4)	—	1,400
5/04	572.3	66.4	11.6%	—
5/03	387.5	12.2	3.1%	—
Annual Growth	11.5%	31.7%	—	6.9%

2007 Year-End Financials

Debt ratio: 70.2%
Return on equity: 26.6%
Cash ($ mil.): 54.5
Current ratio: 2.06
Long-term debt ($ mil.): 109.3
No. of shares (mil.): 21.2

Dividends
 Yield: 0.4%
 Payout: 3.2%
Market value ($ mil.): 285.3
R&D as % of sales: —
Advertising as % of sales: —

Stock History

NASDAQ (GM): CALM

	STOCK PRICE ($) FY Close	P/E High/Low		PER SHARE ($) Earnings	Dividends	Book Value
5/07	13.46	9	4	1.55	0.05	7.35
5/06	7.19	—	—	(0.04)	0.05	3.41
5/05	6.76	—	—	(0.43)	0.03	3.47
5/04	13.80	8	1	2.73	0.03	3.99
5/03	2.62	5	3	0.51	0.03	6.24
Annual Growth	50.6%	—	—	32.0%	13.6%	4.2%

Capella Education

Capella Education gets students ready to wear a graduation cap and gown. The fast-growing company operates Capella University, an online university that offers undergraduate and graduate degree programs in business, organization and management, education, psychology, human services, and information technology. Nearly 18,000 students are enrolled in the school, which employs about 900 faculty members (some 85% of which are part-time employees). Students seeking doctoral degrees account for more than 40% of enrollment. Some 70% of revenues stem from federal student financial aid programs.

EXECUTIVES

Chairman and CEO; Chancellor, Capella University:
 Stephen G. (Steve) Shank, age 63, $410,385 pay
Vice Chairman, External University Initiatives and President Emeritus, Capella University:
 Michael J. (Mike) Offerman, age 59, $272,923 pay
President and COO; Director, Capella University:
 Kenneth (Ken) Sobaski, age 51, $567,229 pay
SVP and CFO: Lois M. Martin, age 45, $277,923 pay
SVP Marketing: Reed A. Watson, age 48
VP and CIO: Scott M. Henkel, age 52, $227,600 pay
VP Government Affairs, General Counsel, and Secretary: Gregory W. (Greg) Thom, age 50
VP Human Resources: Elizabeth M. (Betsy) Rausch, age 55
Dean, School of Human Services: Christopher Cassirer
Provost, Capella University: Karen Viechnicki
Dean, Harold Abel School of Psychology: Garvey House
Dean, School of Business and School of Technology, Capella University: Kurt Linberg
Dean, School of Education, Capella University: Harry McLenighan
Dean, School of Undergraduate Studies: Feranda Williamson
Director Public Relations: Irene Silber
Director Investor Relations: Heide Erickson
Auditors: Ernst & Young LLP

LOCATIONS

HQ: Capella Education Company
 225 S. 6th St., 9th Fl., Minneapolis, MN 55402
Phone: 612-339-8650   **Fax:** 612-977-5060
Web: www.capellauniversity.edu

PRODUCTS/OPERATIONS

Selected Schools and Colleges

Harold Abel School of Psychology
School of Business and Technology
School of Education
School of Human Services

Degree Plans

Bachelor's
Master's
MBA
PhD and PsyD

Areas of Study

Business
Counseling
Criminal Justice
Health Care Administration
Higher Education
Human Resources & Training
Human Services
Information Technology
Instructional Design for Online Learning
K-12 Education
Non-Profit Management
Project Management
Psychology
Social & Community Services

COMPETITORS

Apollo Group
Cardean Learning Group
The College Network
Corinthian Colleges
DeVry
eCollege.com
Jones Knowledge
Kaplan
Laureate Education
Strayer Education
VCampus

HISTORICAL FINANCIALS

Company Type: Public

Income Statement

FYE: December 31

	REVENUE ($ mil.)	NET INCOME ($ mil.)	NET PROFIT MARGIN	EMPLOYEES
12/06	179.9	13.4	7.4%	904
12/05	149.2	10.3	6.9%	—
12/04	117.7	18.8	16.0%	—
12/03	81.8	4.4	5.4%	—
12/02	35.0	(5.7)	—	380
Annual Growth	50.6%	—	—	24.2%

2006 Year-End Financials

Debt ratio: 0.0%
Return on equity: 26.9%
Cash ($ mil.): 87.7
Current ratio: 3.20
Long-term debt ($ mil.): 0.0
No. of shares (mil.): 16.0

Dividends
  Yield: —
  Payout: —
Market value ($ mil.): 388.0
R&D as % of sales: —
Advertising as % of sales: —

Stock History

NASDAQ (GM): CPLA

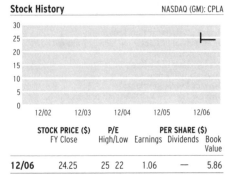

	STOCK PRICE ($) FY Close	P/E High/Low	Earnings	Dividends	Book Value
12/06	24.25	25 22	1.06	—	5.86

Capital Bank

Capital Bank Corporation is the holding company for Capital Bank, which capitalizes on the hot Research Triangle area it serves. Founded in 1997, the bank has more than 25 offices in central and western North Carolina. It provides a range of consumer and commercial banking services, including savings, checking, and money market accounts, as well as CDs, IRAs, and credit cards. Commercial loans, made primarily to small and midsized businesses, make up nearly 60% of the bank's loan portfolio; construction loans are around 25%. The bank also issues mortgages, home equity lines, and consumer loans. Capital Bank Corporation bought 1st State Bancorp in 2006.

EXECUTIVES

Chairman: Oscar A. Keller III, age 63
President, CEO, and Director; President and CEO, Capital Bank: B. Grant Yarber, age 42, $450,000 pay
CFO: Michael Moore, age 50
EVP and Chief Credit Officer, Capital Bank Corporation and Capital Bank: Mark Redmond, age 39, $142,077 pay
EVP and Regional President: Fairfax C. Reynolds, age 54
EVP and Chief Banking Officer, Capital Bank: David Morgan, age 47
SVP North Wake Community: Todd Warrick
SVP and Asheville City Executive: Al Davis
SVP and Support Services Executive, Capital Bank: Jennifer Benefield
SVP Marketing, Training, and Development, Capital Bank: Willard Ross
SVP and Chief Accounting Officer: Lyn Hittle, age 54
Chief Sales and Marketing Officer: Andrew J. (Andy) Shene
Operations Executive: Robert W. Malburg Jr.
Director Human Resources: Teresa White
Auditors: Grant Thornton LLP

LOCATIONS

HQ: Capital Bank Corporation
  333 Fayetteville, Ste. 700, Raleigh, NC 27601
Phone: 919-645-6400   **Fax:** 919-645-6435
Web: www.capitalbank-nc.com

Capital Bank has branches in Alamance, Buncombe, Catawba, Chatham, Granville, Guilford, Lee, and Wake counties.

PRODUCTS/OPERATIONS

2006 Sales

	$ mil.	% of total
Interest		
Loans & loan fees	76.2	79
Investment securities	9.0	9
Federal funds & other	1.7	2
Noninterest		
Service charges & other fees	3.9	4
Mortgage fees & revenues	2.1	2
Other fees & income	3.4	4
Total	**96.3**	**100**

COMPETITORS

Bank of America
BB&T
First Capital Bank
First Citizens BancShares
RBC Centura Banks
SunTrust
Wachovia

HISTORICAL FINANCIALS

Company Type: Public

Income Statement

FYE: December 31

	ASSETS ($ mil.)	NET INCOME ($ mil.)	INCOME AS % OF ASSETS	EMPLOYEES
12/06	1,422.4	12.3	0.9%	332
12/05	960.9	6.7	0.7%	295
12/04	882.3	5.3	0.6%	—
12/03	857.7	1.0	0.1%	—
12/02	841.0	4.3	0.5%	242
Annual Growth	14.0%	30.0%	—	8.2%

2006 Year-End Financials

Equity as % of assets: 11.4%
Return on assets: 1.0%
Return on equity: 10.0%
Long-term debt ($ mil.): 156.9
No. of shares (mil.): 11.4
Market value ($ mil.): 197.5

Dividends
  Yield: 1.0%
  Payout: 17.0%
Sales ($ mil.): 96.3
R&D as % of sales: —
Advertising as % of sales: —

Stock History

NASDAQ (GS): CBKN

	STOCK PRICE ($) FY Close	P/E High/Low	Earnings	Dividends	Book Value
12/06	17.33	17 14	1.06	0.18	14.19
12/05	15.35	20 15	0.97	0.24	7.11
12/04	18.36	25 20	0.77	0.16	11.76
12/03	15.48	113 86	0.15	0.25	11.15
12/02	12.94	22 14	0.76	0.15	11.44
Annual Growth	7.6%	— —	8.7%	4.7%	5.5%

Capital Corp of the West

Capital Corp of the West counts on County Bank for its capital. The holding company owns County Bank, which serves California's San Joaquin Valley through more than 40 offices. Serving individuals and small to midsized businesses, the bank offers standard retail products such as savings, checking, and money market accounts, as well as individual retirement accounts and CDs. Its portfolio is mainly made up of real estate mortgages (about 45% of its loan book) and business loans (about 25%), but the bank also writes consumer and construction loans.

Capital Corp of the West sold its asset management unit, Regency Investment Advisors, to that company's president in 2004. Three years later, Capital Corp of the West branched into the factoring business by acquiring Bay View Funding, which has five business development offices nationwide. Also in 2007 the company acquired about a dozen branches in California from National Bank of Arizona.

1867 Western Financial Corporation, the holding company for Bank of Stockton, owns more than 11% of Capital Corp of the West.

EXECUTIVES

Chairman: Jerry E. Callister, age 64
President, CEO, and Director; CEO, County Bank: Thomas T. (Tom) Hawker, age 64, $375,056 pay
EVP, CFO, and Treasurer: David A. Heaberlin, age 57, $109,297 pay (partial-year salary)
EVP and General Counsel: Richard de la Pena, age 56
EVP and Chief Administrative Officer, Capital Corp of the West and County Bank: Katherine Wohlford, age 50, $125,980 pay
President and COO, County Bank: Ed J. Rocha, age 54, $275,009 pay
EVP and Chief Credit Officer, County Bank: John J. Incandela, age 46, $199,381 pay
Corporate Secretary: Denise Butler
Auditors: KPMG LLP

LOCATIONS

HQ: Capital Corp of the West
550 W. Main, Merced, CA 95340
Phone: 209-725-2269   **Fax:** 209-725-4550
Web: www.ccow.com

Capital Corp of the West has operations in the California communities of Atwater, Ceres, Clovis, Dos Palos, Fresno, Hilmar, Livingston, Los Banos, Madera, Mariposa, Merced, Modesto, Newman, Riverbank, Sacramento, San Francisco, San Jose, Sonora, Stockton, and Turlock.

PRODUCTS/OPERATIONS

2006 Sales

	$ mil.	% of total
Interest		
Loans	100.5	75
Securities & other	21.7	16
Service charges on deposits	6.1	5
Other	6.0	4
Total	**134.3**	**100**

COMPETITORS

BancWest
Bank of America
Central Valley Community Bancorp
Pacific State Bancorp
Sierra Bancorp
TriCo Bancshares
UnionBanCal
United Security Bancshares
Washington Mutual
Wells Fargo
Westamerica

HISTORICAL FINANCIALS

Company Type: Public

Income Statement   FYE: December 31

	ASSETS ($ mil.)	NET INCOME ($ mil.)	INCOME AS % OF ASSETS	EMPLOYEES
12/06	1,961.5	22.7	1.2%	421
12/05	1,756.8	21.0	1.2%	370
12/04	1,447.8	12.3	0.8%	—
12/03	1,234.5	13.6	1.1%	—
12/02	1,034.2	10.4	1.0%	286
Annual Growth	**17.4%**	**21.5%**	**—**	**10.1%**

2006 Year-End Financials

Equity as % of assets: 7.5%
Return on assets: 1.2%
Return on equity: 16.8%
Long-term debt ($ mil.): 183.7
No. of shares (mil.): 10.8
Market value ($ mil.): 345.8
Dividends
  Yield: 0.9%
  Payout: 14.0%
Sales ($ mil.): 134.3
R&D as % of sales: —
Advertising as % of sales: —

Stock History   NASDAQ (GS): CCOW

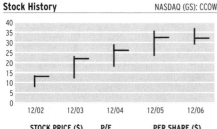

	STOCK PRICE ($) FY Close	P/E High/Low	Earnings	PER SHARE ($) Dividends	Book Value
12/06	32.09	18 14	2.07	0.29	13.69
12/05	32.45	18 12	1.94	0.15	11.56
12/04	26.11	25 16	1.14	0.06	17.86
12/03	21.96	18 10	1.30	0.58	15.81
12/02	13.08	14 8	0.97	0.58	14.49
Annual Growth	**25.2%**	**— —**	**20.9%**	**(15.9%)**	**(1.4%)**

Capital Southwest

Capital Southwest is one of a handful of publicly traded private equity firms in the US. The company owns significant stakes in nearly 20 companies, many of them in Texas, as well as small stakes in about a dozen public companies. The firm offers early-stage, mezzanine, and recapitalization financing, as well as funding for management buyouts to companies involved in a variety of industries. Its 12 largest holdings, including Alamo Group, Hologic, Palm Harbor Homes, and RectorSeal, account for nearly 90% of the value of the company's investment portfolio.

Chairman William Thomas owns more than 15% of the company's stock.

EXECUTIVES

Chairman: William R. Thomas, age 78, $260,417 pay
President, CEO, and Director: Gary L. Martin, age 61
CFO and Controller: Tracy L. Morris
SVP: William M. Ashbaugh, age 52, $266,250 pay
VP: Jeffrey G. Peterson, age 33
Secretary and Treasurer: Susan K. Hodgson, age 45
Investment Associate: William R. Thomas III, age 35
Auditors: Grant Thornton LLP

LOCATIONS

HQ: Capital Southwest Corporation
12900 Preston Rd., Ste. 700, Dallas, TX 75230
Phone: 972-233-8242   **Fax:** 972-233-7362
Web: www.capitalsouthwest.com

PRODUCTS/OPERATIONS

Selected Holdings

Alamo Group, Inc. (29%, mowing, excavation, and street-sweeping equipment)
All Components, Inc. (57%, electronic contract manufacturing)
Alltel Corporation (less than 1%)
AT&T Corp. (less than 1%)
Balco, Inc. (89%, specialty architectural products)
Boxx Technologies, Inc. (15%, workstations for computer graphics imaging and design)
CMI Holding Company, Inc. (19%; devices to relieve congestive heart failure)
Cenveo (less than 1%)
Comcast Corporation (less than 1%)
Dennis Tool Company (67%, diamond compacts used in oil field drill bits)
Discovery Holding Corporation (less than 1%)
Extreme International, Inc. (53%, radio and television commercial and corporate video production)
FMC Corporation (less than 1%)
FMC Technologies, Inc. (less than 1%)
Heeling, Inc. (43%, skate shoes)
Hologic, Inc. (less than 1%)
Kimberly-Clark Corporation (less than 1%)
Liberty Global, Inc. (less than 1%)
Liberty Media Corporation (less than 1%)
Lifemark Group (100%, cemeteries, mortuaries, and mausoleums in Northern California)
Media Recovery, Inc. (87%, computer and automation supplies)
Pallet One, Inc. (10%, wood pallet manufacturing)
Palm Harbor Homes, Inc. (35%, new home construction)
PETsMART Inc. (less than 1%)
Pharmafab, Inc. (68%, branded and generic drugs)
The Rectorseal Corporation (100%, specialty chemicals)
Sprint Nextel Corporation (less than 1%)
Texas Capital Bancshares, Inc. (2%, regional bank)
Via Holdings, Inc. (29%, office seating)
Wellogix, Inc. (20%, software for the oil and gas industry)
The Whitmore Manufacturing Company (80%)

COMPETITORS

American Capital Strategies
Brantley Capital
Gladstone Capital
MACC Private Equities
MCG Capital

HISTORICAL FINANCIALS

Company Type: Public

Income Statement   FYE: March 31

	REVENUE ($ mil.)	NET INCOME ($ mil.)	NET PROFIT MARGIN	EMPLOYEES
3/07	169.6	166.9	98.4%	7
3/06	98.6	96.2	97.6%	7
3/05	22.7	14.2	62.6%	—
3/04	4.7	85.5	1,819.1%	—
3/03	5.4	(41.7)	—	—
Annual Growth	**136.7%**	**—**	**—**	**0.0%**

2007 Year-End Financials

Debt ratio: —
Return on equity: 29.7%
Cash ($ mil.): 38.8
Current ratio: —
Long-term debt ($ mil.): —
No. of shares (mil.): 3.9
Dividends
  Yield: 0.4%
  Payout: —
Market value ($ mil.): 597.2
R&D as % of sales: —
Advertising as % of sales: —

Stock History   NASDAQ (GM): CSWC

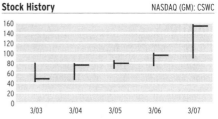

	STOCK PRICE ($) FY Close	P/E High/Low	Earnings	PER SHARE ($) Dividends	Book Value
3/07	153.67	— —	—	0.60	186.75
3/06	95.50	— —	—	0.40	102.74
3/05	79.10	— —	—	0.20	78.44
3/04	75.47	— —	—	0.60	75.35
3/03	48.15	— —	—	0.60	53.92
Annual Growth	**33.7%**	**— —**	**—**	**0.0%**	**36.4%**

CapitalSouth Bancorp

CapitalSouth Bancorp (formerly Financial Investors of the South) is the holding company for CapitalSouth Bank (formerly Bank of Alabama), which serves metropolitan areas in northern and central Alabama and northern Florida. From about 10 branch locations, the commercial bank offers standard retail products and services, including checking and savings accounts, money market accounts, and CDs. The company focuses on real estate lending: Mortgages account for more than 40% of its loan portfolio. Other loans include construction, commercial, and consumer loans. Targeting the Hispanic community, CapitalSouth Bank operates some offices under the name Banco Hispano that are fully staffed with bilingual personnel.

CapitalSouth Bank's target market areas are Birmingham, Huntsville, and Montgomery, Alabama; and Jacksonville, Florida. It also has a loan production office in Atlanta, Georgia. Additionally, CapitalSouth Bank sells insurance through its CapitalSouth Insurance (CS Agency) division.

In 2006 CapitalSouth Bank merged banking subsidiary Capital Bank into its primary CapitalSouth Bank subsidiary.

The company bought Jacksonville, Florida-based bank holding company Monticello Bancshares in 2007.

EXECUTIVES

Chairman and CEO, CapitalSouth and CapitalSouth Bank: W. Dan Puckett, age 62
President and Director: W. Flake Oakley IV, age 53
SVP, Secretary, and CFO, CapitalSouth and CapitalSouth Bank: Carol W. Marsh, age 44, $152,500 pay
City President, Birmingham, CapitalSouth Bank: William D. (Wil) Puckett II, age 37
President and COO, CapitalSouth Bank: John E. Bentley, age 47
City President, Huntsville, CapitalSouth Bank: Richard T. Perdue, age 52, $154,749 pay
SVP and Jacksonville City President, CapitalSouth Bank: Fred Coble, age 46, $156,437 pay
Chief Credit Officer: Daniel W. Gibson
Auditors: KPMG LLP

LOCATIONS

HQ: CapitalSouth Bancorp
2340 Woodcrest Place, Ste. 200,
Birmingham, AL 35209
Phone: 205-870-1939   **Fax:** 205-879-3885
Web: www.capitalsouthbank.com

CapitalSouth Bancorp subsidiary Capital Bank has five branches in Birmingham, Alabama, two in Montgomery, and one in Huntsville. It also has a branch in Jacksonville, Florida.

PRODUCTS/OPERATIONS

2006 Sales

	$ mil.	% of total
Interest		
Interest & fees on loans	28.1	82
Securities	2.6	8
Other	0.3	1
Noninterest		
Service charges on deposits	1.1	3
Gain on sale of nonmarketable equity securities	1.0	3
Other	1.3	3
Total	**34.4**	**100**

COMPETITORS

Alabama National BanCorp	National City
BancorpSouth	Regions Financial
Bank of America	SunTrust
Colonial BancGroup	Wachovia
Compass Bancshares	Washington Mutual
EverBank Financial	

HISTORICAL FINANCIALS

Company Type: Public

Income Statement				FYE: December 31
	ASSETS ($ mil.)	NET INCOME ($ mil.)	INCOME AS % OF ASSETS	EMPLOYEES
12/06	482.0	2.9	0.6%	124
12/05	423.5	2.6	0.6%	124
12/04	337.7	1.9	0.6%	—
12/03	293.3	1.5	0.5%	—
Annual Growth	18.0%	24.7%	—	0.0%

2006 Year-End Financials

Equity as % of assets: 8.6%	Dividends
Return on assets: 0.6%	Yield: 0.9%
Return on equity: 7.4%	Payout: 18.6%
Long-term debt ($ mil.): 13.7	Sales ($ mil.): 34.4
No. of shares (mil.): 3.0	R&D as % of sales: —
Market value ($ mil.): 56.5	Advertising as % of sales: —

Stock History   NASDAQ (GM): CAPB

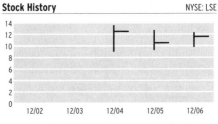

	STOCK PRICE ($) FY Close	P/E High/Low		PER SHARE ($) Earnings	Dividends	Book Value
12/06	19.00	24	19	0.97	0.18	13.89
12/05	18.31	17	16	1.12	0.10	12.92
Annual Growth	3.8%	—	—	(13.4%)	80.0%	7.5%

CapLease, Inc.

CapLease Funding (formerly Capital Lease Funding) has an interest in business properties. The commercial mortgage lender finances and owns net-leased properties, including double-net, triple-net, and bond leases. The company focuses on financing and investing diversely within the capital structure. These practices include equity, debt, and mezzanine investments and the holding of the assets for the medium to long term. CapLease Funding's origination network encompasses more than 200 brokerages operating throughout the US. It also buys and sells commercial properties inhabited by investment-grade tenants. The firm's loans are funded through lines of credit provided by Bank of America and Wachovia Bank.

Founded in 1995, CapLease Funding has financed about $3 billion in credit tenant lease (CTL) loans covering in excess of 500 properties. CTL loans are generally considered only cost-effective for long-term leases; however, CapLease Funding has patented a short-term, 10-year CTL program designed to offer borrowers greater flexibility in obtaining CTL financing.

In addition to structuring, underwriting, and funding CTL loans, CapLease Funding also partners with developers of net leased properties and offers advisory services to individual borrowers, corporations, and net leased property investors.

In 2004 Aon Corporation, the REIT's largest tenant, accounted for more than 15% of revenues.

EXECUTIVES

Chairman and CEO: Paul H. McDowell, age 46
President and Director: William R. (Bill) Pollert, age 59
EVP Program Development: Edwin J. Glickman, age 68
SVP, CFO, and Treasurer: Shawn P. Seale, age 41
SVP and Chief Accounting Officer: John E. Warch, age 49
SVP and Chief Investment Officer: Robert C. Blanz, age 47
SVP Investments: Michael J. Heneghan, age 46
SVP Marketing and Sales: Christopher Crovatto

VP, General Counsel, and Secretary: Paul C. Hughes, age 37
Office Manager: Mary Kay Downey
Auditors: McGladrey & Pullen, LLP

LOCATIONS

HQ: CapLease, Inc.
1065 Avenue of the Americas, 19th Fl.,
New York, NY 10018
Phone: 212-217-6300   **Fax:** 212-217-6301
Web: www.caplease.com

PRODUCTS/OPERATIONS

2006 Sales

	$ mil.	% of total
Rental revenue	78.7	63
Interest income	32.5	26
Property expense recoveries	8.8	7
Gain on sale of mortgage loans & securities	2.9	2
Other	1.9	2
Total	**124.8**	**100**

COMPETITORS

AMAC
BRT Realty
Dynex Capital
Gramercy
iStar Financial Inc
Lexington Realty Trust
Redwood Trust
Transcontinental Realty
U.S. Bancorp

HISTORICAL FINANCIALS

Company Type: Public

Income Statement				FYE: December 31
	REVENUE ($ mil.)	NET INCOME ($ mil.)	NET PROFIT MARGIN	EMPLOYEES
12/06	124.8	7.3	5.8%	21
12/05	73.1	5.1	7.0%	21
12/04	21.0	1.4	6.7%	—
12/03	19.1	6.6	34.6%	—
12/02	18.5	0.8	4.3%	—
Annual Growth	61.2%	73.8%	—	0.0%

2006 Year-End Financials

Debt ratio: 400.1%	Dividends
Return on equity: 2.9%	Yield: 6.9%
Cash ($ mil.): 4.4	Payout: 571.4%
Current ratio: —	Market value ($ mil.): 395.5
Long-term debt ($ mil.): 1,096.3	R&D as % of sales: —
No. of shares (mil.): 34.1	Advertising as % of sales: —

Stock History   NYSE: LSE

	STOCK PRICE ($) FY Close	P/E High/Low		PER SHARE ($) Earnings	Dividends	Book Value
12/06	11.60	87	71	0.14	0.80	9.02
12/05	10.53	79	59	0.16	0.74	9.69
12/04	12.50	225	152	0.06	0.25	9.21
Annual Growth	(3.7%)	—	—	52.8%	78.9%	(1.0%)

Caraco Pharmaceutical

Caraco Pharmaceutical Laboratories develops generic and private label prescription and OTC drugs. Caraco currently sells about 20 generics, including high blood pressure therapy metoprolol tartrate, diabetes treatment metformin hydrochloride, and seizure and panic disorder treatment clonazepam (sold by Roche as Klonopin). Indian drugmaker Sun Pharmaceutical Industries owns two-thirds of the company and licenses the US marketing rights to Caraco for the drugs it sells. The company's top customers include wholesalers McKesson, AmerisourceBergen, and Cardinal Health.

Sales made to these three clients collectively account for nearly 60% of total revenue. Caraco also has a sales contract with the Veterans Administration to buy metformin hydrochloride.

EXECUTIVES

Chairman: Dilip S. Shanghvi, age 51
CEO and Director: Daniel H. Movens, age 49, $499,150 pay
SVP Technical: Robert Kurkiewicz, age 56, $177,962 pay
SVP Business Strategies: Gurpartap Singh, age 38
Director, Commercial: Jayesh Shah
Director, Manufacturing: Kaushikkumar Gandhi
Director, Marketing: Derrick Mann
Director, Technical: Daniel Barone
Investor Relations: Michael Marcotte
Director, Business Development: David Risk
Manager, Investor Relations: Aaron Miles
Interim CFO: Mukul Rathi, age 35
Auditors: Rehmann Robson

LOCATIONS

HQ: Caraco Pharmaceutical Laboratories, Ltd.
1150 Elijah McCoy Dr., Detroit, MI 48202
Phone: 313-871-8400   **Fax:** 313-871-8314
Web: www.caraco.com

PRODUCTS/OPERATIONS

2007 Sales

	$ mil.	% of total
Opiate agonist/analgesic	31.2	27
Antidiabetic	30.1	26
Antihypertensive drug/beta blocker	19.8	17
Antidepressant	14.1	12
Anticonvulsant	4.3	4
Antianxiety drug	4.0	3
Antipsychotic	3.5	3
Skeletal muscle relaxant	2.9	2
Nonsteroidal antiinflammatory agent	2.9	2
Cardiac	2.4	2
Vascular & migraine headache suppressant	1.0	1
Other	0.8	1
Total	**117.0**	**100**

Selected Products

Carbamazepine (Tegretol, epilepsy)
Clonazepam (Klonopin, seizures and panic disorder)
Flurbiprofen (Ansaid, arthritis)
Metformin hydrochloride (Glucophage, diabetes)
Metoprolol tartrate (Lopressor, hypertension)
Oxaprozin (Daypro, arthritis)
Paromomycin sulfate (Humatin, antibiotic)
Salsalate (Disalcid, decongestant)

COMPETITORS

Acura Pharmaceuticals
Barr Pharmaceuticals
Hi-Tech Pharmacal
Impax Laboratories
Mylan Labs
Par Pharmaceutical
SkyePharma
Watson Pharmaceuticals
Xechem

HISTORICAL FINANCIALS
Company Type: Public

Income Statement
FYE: March 31

	REVENUE ($ mil.)	NET INCOME ($ mil.)	NET PROFIT MARGIN	EMPLOYEES
3/07	117.0	26.9	23.0%	718
3/06	82.8	(10.4)	—	272
3/05*	17.3	(4.3)	—	—
12/04	60.3	(0.2)	—	—
12/03	45.5	11.2	24.6%	—
Annual Growth	**26.6%**	**24.5%**	**—**	**164.0%**

*Fiscal year change

2007 Year-End Financials

Debt ratio: —
Return on equity: 1,028.7%
Cash ($ mil.): 33.9
Current ratio: 4.95
Long-term debt ($ mil.): —
No. of shares (mil.): 28.1
Dividends
  Yield: —
  Payout: —
Market value ($ mil.): 342.3
R&D as % of sales: —
Advertising as % of sales: —

Stock History
AMEX: CPD

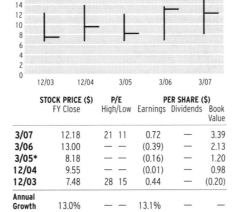

	STOCK PRICE ($) FY Close	P/E High	P/E Low	Earnings	Dividends	Book Value
3/07	12.18	21	11	0.72	—	3.39
3/06	13.00	—	—	(0.39)	—	2.13
3/05*	8.18	—	—	(0.16)	—	1.20
12/04	9.55	—	—	(0.01)	—	0.98
12/03	7.48	28	15	0.44	—	(0.20)
Annual Growth	**13.0%**	**—**	**—**	**13.1%**	**—**	**—**

*Fiscal year change

Cardiac Science

Cardiac Science Corporation wants to grab hold of your heart. The company makes cardiovascular monitoring and therapeutic equipment, including automated external defibrillators and stress test systems that analyze the heart's performance under stress. Cardiac Science also offers monitoring systems for extended surveillance, ECG management systems, and telemetry devices for evaluation of the heart during rehabilitation exercise. In addition, Cardiac Science sells accessories such as lead wires and electrodes and provides product repair and technical support services. The firm uses a direct sales force in the US and distributors abroad.

The company was formed in 2005 following the merging of Quinton Cardiology Systems with Cardiac Science, Inc., a provider of automated external defibrillators.

EXECUTIVES

Chairman: Raymond W. Cohen, age 47
Vice Chairman: Ruediger Naumann-Etienne, age 60
President, CEO, and Director: John R. Hinson, age 44, $338,173 pay
SVP, CFO, and Secretary: Michael K. (Mike) Matysik, age 47, $243,985 pay
SVP Sales, Marketing, and Service: Allan R. Criss, age 47
VP and Corporate Controller: Daphne Taylor
VP Engineering: Brian R. Lee, age 51
VP Finance and Administration: Tim Way
VP Operations: Feroze D. Motafram, age 52
VP Cardiology Sales, North America: Darryl R. Lustig, age 51, $237,977 pay
President Sales, Public Access Defibrillation: Alfred E. Ford Jr.
Auditors: KPMG LLP

LOCATIONS

HQ: Cardiac Science Corporation
3303 Monte Villa Pkwy., Bothell, WA 98021
Phone: 425-402-2000   **Fax:** 425-402-2001
Web: www.cardiacscience.com

PRODUCTS/OPERATIONS

2006 Sales

	$ mil.	% of total
Cardiac monitoring	71.0	46
Defibrillation	67.4	43
Service	17.0	11
Total	**155.4**	**100**

Selected Products

Eclipse Premier (electrocardiograph)
Holter monitoring systems
Powerheart AEDs
Pyramis (data management system)
Q-Stress (stress test systems)
Q-Tel RMS (telemetry devices)

COMPETITORS

GE Healthcare
Medtronic
Midmark Corporation
Philips Electronics
Siemens Medical
Spacelabs Healthcare
Welch Allyn
ZOLL

HISTORICAL FINANCIALS
Company Type: Public

Income Statement
FYE: December 31

	REVENUE ($ mil.)	NET INCOME ($ mil.)	NET PROFIT MARGIN	EMPLOYEES
12/06	155.4	0.1	0.1%	556
12/05	106.7	(1.2)	—	511
12/04	89.6	15.1	16.8%	661
Annual Growth	**31.7%**	**(91.9%)**	**—**	**(8.3%)**

2006 Year-End Financials

Debt ratio: —
Return on equity: 0.0%
Cash ($ mil.): 10.4
Current ratio: 1.95
Long-term debt ($ mil.): —
No. of shares (mil.): 22.6
Dividends
  Yield: —
  Payout: —
Market value ($ mil.): 182.4
R&D as % of sales: —
Advertising as % of sales: —

	STOCK PRICE ($) FY Close	P/E High/Low	PER SHARE ($) Earnings	Dividends	Book Value
12/06	8.07	— —	—	—	9.54
12/05	9.05	— —	(0.08)	—	9.47
Annual Growth	(10.8%)	— —	—	—	0.8%

Cardinal Financial

Cardinal Financial can help you keep out of the red. The holding company owns Cardinal Bank, which was founded in 1997 to provide a local alternative in the rapidly consolidating Virginia banking industry. The bank operates more than 20 branches in the Northern Virginia suburbs of Washington, DC. It offers commercial and retail checking, savings, and money market accounts; IRAs; and CDs. Commercial loans and mortgages make up nearly half of Cardinal Financial's loan portfolio, which also includes residential real estate, construction, home equity, and consumer loans. Subsidiary Cardinal Wealth Services provides brokerage and investment services in alliance with Raymond James Financial.

Other units include George Mason Mortgage, which originates residential mortgages for sale into the secondary market through nearly ten branches in Northern Virginia, and investment manager Wilson/Bennett Capital Management, which focuses on value-oriented investing and large-cap stocks. In 2006 Cardinal Bank acquired the trust business of FBR National Trust from Friedman, Billings, Ramsey Group.

EXECUTIVES

Chairman and CEO: Bernard H. Clineburg, age 58, $596,638 pay
Vice Chairman: John H. Rust Jr., age 59
President; SEVP, Cardinal Bank: Kendal E. Carson, age 50
EVP and COO, Cardinal Financial and Cardinal Bank: Kim C. Liddell, age 45, $151,912 pay (partial-year salary)
EVP and CFO: Mark A. Wendel, age 48
EVP and Chief Compliance Officer: Eleanor D. Schmidt, age 44
SVP, Controller, and Secretary: Jennifer L. Deacon
SVP, Marketing Manager: Paulette P. Cross
Chairman and CEO, George Mason Mortgage: D. Gene Merrill, age 61
Chief Credit Officer; President, Cardinal Bank: Christopher W. Bergstrom, age 47, $265,195 pay
President, George Mason Mortgage: H. Ed Dean, age 37
President and CEO, Cardinal Wealth Services: Rex W. Wagner
President, Cardinal Bank, Washington: Kathleen Walsh (Kate) Carr, age 61
Regional President, Cardinal Bank: F. Kevin Reynolds, age 47, $265,546 pay
EVP, Real Estate Lending, Cardinal Bank: Dennis M. Griffith, age 57, $264,985 pay
Auditors: KPMG LLP

LOCATIONS

HQ: Cardinal Financial Corporation
8270 Greensboro Dr., Ste. 500, McLean, VA 22102
Phone: 703-584-3400   **Fax:** 703-584-3410
Web: www.cardinalbank.com

PRODUCTS/OPERATIONS

2006 Sales

	$ mil.	% of total
Interest		
Loans receivable	51.9	48
Loans held for sale	19.3	18
Investment securities	14.6	13
Other	1.6	1
Noninterest		
Net gain on sales of loans	10.1	9
Investment fee income	3.3	3
Management fee income	2.2	2
Loan service charges	2.2	2
Other	3.9	4
Total	**109.1**	**100**

COMPETITORS

Access National
Bank of America
BB&T
Chevy Chase Bank
Millennium Bankshares
SunTrust
United Bankshares
Virginia Commerce Bancorp
Wachovia

HISTORICAL FINANCIALS

Company Type: Public

Income Statement
FYE: December 31

	ASSETS ($ mil.)	NET INCOME ($ mil.)	INCOME AS % OF ASSETS	EMPLOYEES
12/06	1,638.4	7.4	0.5%	406
12/05	1,452.3	9.9	0.7%	406
12/04	1,211.6	3.5	0.3%	—
12/03	636.3	6.2	1.0%	—
12/02	486.3	(0.5)	—	136
Annual Growth	35.5%	—	—	31.4%

2006 Year-End Financials

Equity as % of assets: 9.5%
Return on assets: 0.5%
Return on equity: 4.9%
Long-term debt ($ mil.): 244.0
No. of shares (mil.): 24.5
Market value ($ mil.): 250.7
Dividends
Yield: 0.4%
Payout: 13.3%
Sales ($ mil.): 109.1
R&D as % of sales: —
Advertising as % of sales: —

Stock History
NASDAQ (GS): CFNL

	STOCK PRICE ($) FY Close	P/E High/Low	PER SHARE ($) Earnings	Dividends	Book Value
12/06	10.25	46 32	0.30	0.04	6.37
12/05	11.00	27 18	0.44	0.01	6.07
12/04	11.14	60 43	0.19	—	5.15
12/03	8.27	16 8	0.54	—	5.22
12/02	4.35	— —	(0.13)	—	4.05
Annual Growth	23.9%	— —	—	300.0%	12.0%

Carolina Bank

You'll have to ask James Taylor if he's going to Carolina Bank Holdings in his mind. The firm owns Carolina Bank, which targets individuals and small to midsized businesses for customers. The community-oriented financial institution offers such standard services as checking and savings accounts, money market and individual retirement accounts, CDs, ATM and debit cards, and online banking and bill payment. Its lending activities typically consist of commercial real estate loans, residential mortgages, construction and land development loans, and business loans.

In 2007 Carolina Bank introduced a new division called Carolina Bank Wholesale Mortgage (CBWM). Specializing in products sold in the secondary market, CBWM offers Fannie Mae/Freddie Mac, FHA/VA, Jumbo, and other prime loan types to select customers (brokers, community banks, and credit unions) in North Carolina, South Carolina, Virginia, and other southeastern states.

Executive officers and directors collectively own more than 15% of Carolina Bank Holdings.

EXECUTIVES

Chairman: John D. (Jay) Cornet, age 60
Vice Chairman: Gary N. Brown, age 62
President, CEO, and Director; President and CEO, Carolina Bank: Robert T. Braswell, age 54, $315,633 pay
Treasurer and Secretary; EVP, CFO, and Secretary, Carolina Bank: T. Allen Liles, age 54, $175,254 pay
EVP and Senior Loan Officer, Carolina Bank: Gunnar N. R. Fromen, age 58, $173,051 pay
EVP and Chief Credit Officer, Carolina Bank: Daniel D. Hornfeck, age 39, $126,179 pay
SVP and Market Executive, Burlington, Carolina Bank: W. Keith Strickland
SVP and Market Executive, High Point, Carolina Bank: Chip Harris
SVP and Retail Banking Manager, Carolina Bank: F. Virginia Grimes
SVP and Market Executive, Asheboro, Carolina Bank: W. McDuffy (Duffy) Johnson
SVP and Commercial Loan Officer, Carolina Bank: Paul L. Kennedy
Human Resources and Accounting Officer, Carolina Bank: Angela J. Nowlin
Auditors: Cherry, Bekaert & Holland, LLP

LOCATIONS

HQ: Carolina Bank Holdings Inc.
528 College Rd., Greensboro, NC 27410
Phone: 336-288-1898   **Fax:** 336-286-5553
Web: www.carolinabank.com

PRODUCTS/OPERATIONS

2006 Sales

	$ mil.	% of total
Interest		
Loans	23.2	81
Securities	3.2	11
Other	0.4	1
Noninterest		
Service charges	0.7	3
Mortgage banking income	0.4	1
Other	0.7	3
Total	**28.6**	**100**

COMPETITORS

AF Financial
BB&T
First Citizens BancShares
FNB United
RBC Centura Banks
Wachovia

HISTORICAL FINANCIALS

Company Type: Public

Income Statement

FYE: December 31

	ASSETS ($ mil.)	NET INCOME ($ mil.)	INCOME AS % OF ASSETS	EMPLOYEES
12/06	411.6	2.8	0.7%	72
12/05	365.2	2.0	0.5%	59
12/04	311.5	1.6	0.5%	—
12/03	226.9	1.1	0.5%	—
12/02	189.9	0.6	0.3%	—
Annual Growth	21.3%	47.0%	—	22.0%

2006 Year-End Financials

Equity as % of assets: 6.3%
Return on assets: 0.7%
Return on equity: 11.5%
Long-term debt ($ mil.): 10.3
No. of shares (mil.): 2.7
Market value ($ mil.): 29.8

Dividends
Yield: —
Payout: —
Sales ($ mil.): 28.6
R&D as % of sales: —
Advertising as % of sales: —

Stock History

NASDAQ (CM): CLBH

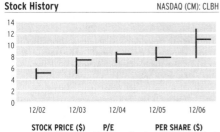

	STOCK PRICE ($) FY Close	P/E High/Low	Earnings	PER SHARE ($) Dividends	Book Value
12/06	10.94	15 9	0.83	—	9.52
12/05	7.82	16 12	0.61	—	8.38
12/04	8.39	18 14	0.49	1.27	9.38
12/03	7.38	22 14	0.35	—	10.44
12/02	5.09	18 13	0.32	—	9.93
Annual Growth	21.1%	— —	26.9%	—	(1.0%)

Carrizo Oil & Gas

Carrizo Oil & Gas sees its future in 3-D. An independent exploration and production company that drills in proven onshore fields along the Gulf Coast of Texas and Louisiana, Carrizo aggressively acquires 3-D seismic data and arranges land lease options in conjunction with conducting seismic surveys. As part of a new strategy, the company is exploiting deeper, over-pressured targets, which generally require higher cost. Carrizo has additional properties in North Texas, the Rockies, Alabama, Arkansas, Kentucky, New Mexico, and in the UK North Sea. Its total proved reserves stand at 210.0 billion cu. ft. of natural gas equivalent. Chairman Steven Webster owns about 10% of Carrizo.

The company has reported an exploratory drilling success rate in the onshore Gulf Coast area of 84%, and a 100% drilling success rate in the Barnett Shale area.

EXECUTIVES

Chairman: Steven A. Webster, age 55
President, CEO, and Director: S. P. Johnson IV, age 52, $643,958 pay
VP, CFO, Secretary, and Treasurer: Paul F. Boling, age 54, $328,639 pay
VP Business Development: Andrew R. Agosto
VP Exploration: Gregory E. Evans, age 58, $337,770 pay
VP Operations: J. Bradley (Brad) Fisher, age 47, $461,907 pay
VP and Director Investor Relations: B. Allen Connell
VP Land: Richard H. Smith, age 49, $103,356 pay (partial-year salary)
Human Resources: Deborah (Debbie) Soho
Auditors: Pannell Kerr Forster of Texas, P.C.

LOCATIONS

HQ: Carrizo Oil & Gas, Inc.
1000 Louisiana St., Ste. 1500, Houston, TX 77002
Phone: 713-328-1000 **Fax:** 713-328-1035
Web: www.carrizo.cc

PRODUCTS/OPERATIONS

2006 Sales

	% of total
Chevron	11
Reichman Petroleum	10
Other customers	79
Total	**100**

COMPETITORS

Abraxas Petroleum
Adams Resources
BP
Brigham Exploration
Chesapeake Energy
Chevron
Clayton Williams Energy
Comstock Resources
Exxon Mobil
Forest Oil
Newfield Exploration
Pioneer Natural Resources
Samson
Shell Oil
TOTAL

HISTORICAL FINANCIALS

Company Type: Public

Income Statement

FYE: December 31

	REVENUE ($ mil.)	NET INCOME ($ mil.)	NET PROFIT MARGIN	EMPLOYEES
12/06	82.9	18.3	22.1%	68
12/05	78.2	10.6	13.6%	50
12/04	52.4	11.1	21.2%	—
12/03	38.5	7.9	20.5%	—
12/02	26.8	4.8	17.9%	36
Annual Growth	32.6%	39.7%	—	17.2%

2006 Year-End Financials

Debt ratio: 88.2%
Return on equity: 10.0%
Cash ($ mil.): 11.1
Current ratio: 0.71
Long-term debt ($ mil.): 187.3
No. of shares (mil.): 26.0

Dividends
Yield: —
Payout: —
Market value ($ mil.): 754.0
R&D as % of sales: —
Advertising as % of sales: —

Stock History

NASDAQ (GS): CRZO

	STOCK PRICE ($) FY Close	P/E High/Low	Earnings	PER SHARE ($) Dividends	Book Value
12/06	29.02	48 30	0.71	—	8.17
12/05	24.70	72 23	0.44	—	6.41
12/04	11.30	24 13	0.49	—	5.46
12/03	7.20	18 10	0.43	—	5.21
12/02	5.27	24 13	0.26	—	4.71
Annual Growth	53.2%	— —	28.5%	—	14.7%

CAS Medical Systems

CAS Medical Systems makes blood pressure measurement devices, vital signs monitors, apnea monitors, and neonatal supplies. Major brands include the MAXNIBP blood pressure technology, the CAS 750 vital signs monitor, and the AMI and 511 cardio-respiratory monitoring system. Subsidiary Statcorp makes blood pressure cuffs, pressure infuser cuffs, and blood filter products. The company sells its products in Europe, North America, Latin America, and the Pacific Rim to hospitals and other health care professionals. Customer Medtronic accounts for more than 10% of sales.

EXECUTIVES

Chairman: Louis P. (Lou) Scheps, age 75
President and CEO: Andrew E. Kersey, age 46, $210,000 pay (prior to title change)
CFO and Secretary: Jeffery A. Baird, age 53, $190,000 pay
Auditors: UHY LLP

LOCATIONS

HQ: CAS Medical Systems, Inc.
44 E. Industrial Rd., Branford, CT 06405
Phone: 203-488-6056 **Fax:** 203-488-9438
Web: www.casmed.com

2006 Sales

	$ mil.	% of total
US	27.5	78
International	7.7	22
Total	**35.2**	**100**

COMPETITORS

CardioDynamics
Criticare
Philips Electronics
Somanetics
VSM MedTech

HISTORICAL FINANCIALS

Company Type: Public

Income Statement

FYE: December 31

	REVENUE ($ mil.)	NET INCOME ($ mil.)	NET PROFIT MARGIN	EMPLOYEES
12/06	35.2	1.8	5.1%	152
12/05	26.9	1.8	6.7%	143
12/04	19.9	1.2	6.0%	—
12/03	16.9	0.7	4.1%	—
12/02	15.0	(0.3)	—	—
Annual Growth	23.8%	—	—	6.3%

2006 Year-End Financials

Debt ratio: 30.2%
Return on equity: 16.6%
Cash ($ mil.): 1.3
Current ratio: 2.82
Long-term debt ($ mil.): 3.8
No. of shares (mil.): 10.6

Dividends
  Yield: —
  Payout: —
Market value ($ mil.): 84.7
R&D as % of sales: —
Advertising as % of sales: —

Stock History

NASDAQ (GM): CASM

	STOCK PRICE ($) FY Close	P/E High/Low		PER SHARE ($) Earnings	Dividends	Book Value
12/06	8.00	107	37	0.14	—	1.19
12/05	8.65	61	40	0.15	—	0.92
12/04	2.25	27	11	0.11	—	0.73
12/03	1.40	21	5	0.07	—	0.64
12/02	0.34	—	—	(0.03)	—	0.57
Annual Growth	120.2%	—	—	—	—	20.4%

Cascade Bancorp

Forget the dirty dishes. Cascade Bancorp wants to provide sparkling customer service. It's the holding company for Bank of the Cascades, which operates about 35 branches in central, northwestern, and southern Oregon, as well as the Boise, Idaho area through its Farmers and Merchants State Bank division. Targeting individuals and small to midsized businesses, the banks offer traditional retail banking services and trust and investment services. More than two-thirds of the company's loan portfolio is composed of construction, residential mortgage, and commercial real estate loans; business loans make up about 30%.

In 2006 Cascade Bancorp acquired Idaho-based F&M Holding Company, parent of Farmers & Merchants State Bank, which operates about a dozen branches in and around Boise. The acquisition provided a strategic expansion opportunity for Cascade, which is adding northwest growth markets to its franchise.

David Bolger, who owned F&M Holding, is now the largest stakeholder in Cascade Bancorp, with a more than 20% stake.

EXECUTIVES

Chairman: Gary L. Hoffman, age 66
Vice Chairman: Jerol E. Andres, age 63
President, CEO, and Director; CEO, Bank of the Cascades: Patricia L. Moss, age 53, $323,841 pay
EVP and COO; President and COO, Bank of the Cascades: Michael J. (Mike) Delvin, age 58, $220,250 pay
EVP, CFO, and Secretary, Cascade Bancorp and Bank of The Cascades: Gregory D. Newton, age 55, $187,000 pay
EVP, Human Resources: Peggy L. Biss, age 49, $275,400 pay
EVP, Mortgage Division, Bank of the Cascades: Frank I. Wheeler, age 59
President, Farmers & Merchants State Bank: Michael M. (Mike) Mooney, age 56, $126,667 pay
EVP and Chief Credit Officer, Bank of the Cascades: Frank R. Weis, age 56, $171,360 pay
Auditors: Symonds, Evans & Company, P.C.

LOCATIONS

HQ: Cascade Bancorp
  1100 NW Wall St., Bend, OR 97701
Phone: 541-385-6205   **Fax:** 541-382-8780
Web: www.botc.com

PRODUCTS/OPERATIONS

2006 Sales

	$ mil.	% of total
Interest income		
Interest & fees on loans	132.5	85
Securities	5.2	3
Other	0.9	1
Noninterest income		
Service charges on deposits	8.0	5
Card and merchant fees	3.4	2
Mortgage banking income	3.0	2
Other	3.8	2
Total	**156.8**	**100**

COMPETITORS

Bank of America
Banner Corp
Columbia Bancorp (OR)
FHLB Seattle
Sterling Financial (WA)
Umpqua Holdings
U.S. Bancorp
Washington Federal
Washington Mutual
Wells Fargo
West Coast Bancorp
Zions Bank

HISTORICAL FINANCIALS

Company Type: Public

Income Statement

FYE: December 31

	ASSETS ($ mil.)	NET INCOME ($ mil.)	INCOME AS % OF ASSETS	EMPLOYEES
12/06	2,249.3	35.7	1.6%	573
12/05	1,269.7	22.4	1.8%	336
12/04	1,004.8	16.0	1.6%	—
12/03	734.7	13.9	1.9%	—
12/02	578.4	11.7	2.0%	238
Annual Growth	40.4%	32.2%	—	24.6%

2006 Year-End Financials

Equity as % of assets: 11.6%
Return on assets: 2.0%
Return on equity: 19.5%
Long-term debt ($ mil.): 239.9
No. of shares (mil.): 28.3
Market value ($ mil.): 879.1

Dividends
  Yield: 0.9%
  Payout: 21.6%
Sales ($ mil.): 156.8
R&D as % of sales: —
Advertising as % of sales: —

Stock History

NASDAQ (CM): CACB

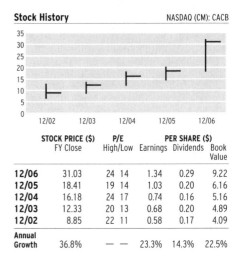

	STOCK PRICE ($) FY Close	P/E High/Low		PER SHARE ($) Earnings	Dividends	Book Value
12/06	31.03	24	14	1.34	0.29	9.22
12/05	18.41	19	14	1.03	0.20	6.16
12/04	16.18	24	17	0.74	0.16	5.16
12/03	12.33	20	13	0.68	0.20	4.89
12/02	8.85	22	11	0.58	0.17	4.09
Annual Growth	36.8%	—	—	23.3%	14.3%	22.5%

Cash America

If cash is king, then Cash America International is king of pawns. Ruling over a kingdom of nearly 500 locations in 22 states, it's one of the largest providers of secured, non-recourse loans (known as pawn loans) in the nation. It operates through Cash America Pawn and SuperPawn shops; customers collateralize high-interest loans with jewelry, electronics, and other items. If the loans aren't repaid, the firm sells the collateral in its stores. Cash America also offers cash advances, check cashing, and money orders and transfers through stores operating as Cashland Financial Services and Cash America Payday Advance. Check cashing services are offered through about 140 owned and franchised Mr. Payroll stores.

The company continues to expand through the acquisition of established pawnshops and cash advance facilities within Cash America's current geographic scope. After selling its UK retail operations in 2004, the company made a return visit in 2007 with plans to offer cash advances there through an online platform.

Cash America expanded its horizons in 2006 with the purchase of the Chicago-based Check Giant, a company that makes short-term advances via the Internet using the name CashNetUSA.

But Cash America isn't built on selling pawned merchandise alone. The firm charges up to 300% on the loans it makes. About a third of the loans are not redeemed and the collateral is sold.

HISTORY

When Jack Daugherty was a student, he hocked his guitar to finance dates. In 1970, after quitting school, he opened a pawnshop that was so successful he used the proceeds to invest in oil. When oil took a downturn, he returned to the pawn business, incorporating Cash America in 1984; it went public in 1987.

Cash America bought UK-based Harvey & Thompson Ltd. in 1992; two years later, the company acquired Sweden's Svensk Pantbelåning. Operational problems, including a failed retail venture, caused a brief downturn in 1995, but Cash America refocused on its core business and recovered in 1996. As part of a low-cost expansion program, the next year the firm introduced a Cash America franchise plan to independent pawnshop owners. Over the next two years, Cash America expanded further in Texas and Utah. In 1998 Mr. Payroll rolled out automated check-cashing machines that identified customers by their facial features; it formed an alliance with Crestar to supplement the bank's Virginia supermarket branches with the machines. Also that year the company launched its Rent-A-Tire subsidiary in Texas.

In 1999 Cash America expanded its automated check cashing business, participating in InnoVentry, a joint venture with Wells Fargo (the venture ceased operations in 2001). In 2000 Cash America got lots of publicity (presumably unwanted) when its nine-story headquarters in downtown Fort Worth was slammed by a tornado; the building was later renovated. In an attempt to focus on lending activities, subsidiary Rent-A-Tire was sold off in 2002. The following year Cash America doubled its cash advance operations with the purchase of Cashland Financial Services. With a desire to concentrate on US operations, Cash America sold off its operations in Sweden and UK in 2004, while at the same time expanding its presence in Southern California with the purchase of UrgentMoney and GoldX.

EXECUTIVES

Chairman: Jack R. Daugherty, age 59
President, CEO, and Director: Daniel R. (Dan) Feehan, age 56, $650,544 pay
EVP and CFO: Thomas A. Bessant Jr., age 48, $323,001 pay
EVP, General Counsel, and Secretary: J. Curtis Linscott
EVP Administration: Robert D. Brockman, age 52
EVP Business Development: Michael D. Gaston, age 62, $283,579 pay
EVP Business Development: James H. Kauffman, age 62, $364,965 pay
President, Retail Lending Services:
Jerry A. Wackerhagen, age 51
President, Internet Lending Services: Albert Goldstein
President, Shared Services: John A. McDorman, age 60
Auditors: PricewaterhouseCoopers LLP

LOCATIONS

HQ: Cash America International, Inc.
1600 W. 7th St., Fort Worth, TX 76102
Phone: 817-335-1100   **Fax:** 817-570-1225
Web: www.cashamerica.com

2006 Pawn Shop Locations

	No.
Texas	194
Florida	67
Nevada	25
Tennessee	21
Louisiana	20
Georgia	17
Missouri	16
Oklahoma	15
Indiana	13
Illinois	12
Arizona	11
Kentucky	10
North Carolina	10
Alabama	9
Utah	7
Ohio	6
South Carolina	6
Alaska	5
Colorado	5
Washington	5
California	1
Total	**475**

PRODUCTS/OPERATIONS

2006 Sales

	$ mil.	% of total
Sale of merchandise	335.5	48
Cash advance fees	195.1	28
Finance & service charges	149.5	22
Check cashing royalties & fees	13.1	2
Total	**693.2**	**100**

COMPETITORS

Ace Cash Express
Advance America
Cash Converters
DGSE Companies
Dollar Financial
EZCORP
First Cash Financial Services
Winmark
World Acceptance
Xponential

HISTORICAL FINANCIALS

Company Type: Public

Income Statement

FYE: December 31

	ASSETS ($ mil.)	NET INCOME ($ mil.)	INCOME AS % OF ASSETS	EMPLOYEES
12/06	776.2	60.9	7.8%	5,152
12/05	598.7	45.0	7.5%	4,565
12/04	555.2	56.8	10.2%	—
12/03	489.5	30.0	6.1%	—
12/02	376.5	19.3	5.1%	3,096
Annual Growth	19.8%	33.3%	—	13.6%

2006 Year-End Financials

Equity as % of assets: 56.8%
Return on assets: 8.9%
Return on equity: 14.9%
Long-term debt ($ mil.): 203.0
No. of shares (mil.): 29.7
Market value ($ mil.): 1,391.5
Dividends
Yield: 0.2%
Payout: 5.0%
Sales ($ mil.): 693.2
R&D as % of sales: —
Advertising as % of sales: —

Stock History

NYSE: CSH

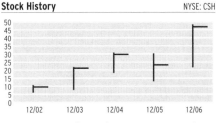

	STOCK PRICE ($) FY Close	P/E High/Low		PER SHARE ($) Earnings	Dividends	Book Value
12/06	46.90	24	11	2.00	0.10	14.85
12/05	23.19	20	9	1.49	0.10	12.76
12/04	29.73	16	10	1.92	0.35	11.40
12/03	21.18	19	7	1.13	0.07	9.81
12/02	9.52	13	8	0.78	0.05	7.92
Annual Growth	49.0%	—	—	26.5%	18.9%	17.0%

Cathay General Bancorp

Cathay General Bancorp (previously known as plain ol' Cathay Bancorp) is the holding company for Cathay Bank, which caters to Chinese and Vietnamese individuals and businesses from branches in California (the lion's share), New York, Massachusetts, Washington State, and Texas. It also has branches in Hong Kong, Shanghai, and Taipei. Real estate subsidiary Cathay Investment has an office in Taiwan. The bank focuses on Vietnamese and Chinese low- to middle-income customers. Services include retail banking (deposits and loans) and online stock trading and mutual funds through Cathay Wealth Management. Commercial mortgages account for slightly more than half of the bank's portfolio; business loans comprise nearly a quarter.

After acquiring rival GBC Bancorp in 2003, Cathay General sought to acquire New York-based Great Eastern Bank, a privately held bank with five branches. It ended up in a bidding war with UCBH Holdings over the prize, but in 2006 Great Eastern voted in favor of Cathay General, calling its bid a "superior proposal." The deal closed in 2005.

The bank did not rest on its laurels. In 2006 it bought a 20% stake in First Sino Bank of Shanghai for around $52.2 million. The deal gave it the right to name two directors. The company also bought New Asia Bancorp for $23.5 million and United Heritage Bank for $9.4 million, which gave Cathay Bank its first office in New Jersey.

EXECUTIVES

Chairman, President, and CEO, Cathay General Bancorp and Cathay Bank: Dunson K. Cheng, age 61, $1,782,000 pay
Executive Vice Chairman and COO, Cathay General Bancorp and Cathay Bank: Peter Wu, age 58, $818,625 pay
Vice Chairman Emeritus, Cathay General Bancorp and Cathay Bank: George T.M. Ching, age 89
Vice Chairman Emeritus, Cathay General Bancorp and Cathay Bank: Wilbur K. Woo, age 88
EVP, CFO, and Treasurer, Cathay General Bancorp; EVP and CFO, Cathay Bank: Heng W. Chen, age 54, $501,800 pay
EVP and Director; SEVP and Chief Lending Officer, Cathay Bank: Anthony M. Tang, age 53, $532,730 pay
EVP and Chief Credit Officer, Cathay Bank: Kim R. Bingham, age 50
EVP Branch Administration, Cathay Bank: Irwin Wong, age 58, $410,134 pay
SVP and General Counsel, Cathay General Bancorp and Cathay Bank: Perry P. Oei, age 44
SVP and Director Human Resources, Cathay Bank: Jennifer Laforcarde
Secretary and Director, Cathay General Bancorp and Cathay Bank: Michael M. Y. Chang, age 69
Auditors: KPMG LLP

LOCATIONS

HQ: Cathay General Bancorp
777 N. Broadway, Los Angeles, CA 90012
Phone: 626-582-7380   **Fax:** 213-625-1368
Web: www.cathaybank.com

PRODUCTS/OPERATIONS

2006 Sales

	$ mil.	% of total
Interest & dividends		
Loans	419.5	82
Securities	68.8	13
Other	3.2	1
Noninterest		
Letters of credit commissions	5.4	1
Service fees on deposits	4.8	1
Other	11.3	2
Total	**513.0**	**100**

COMPETITORS

Bank of America
Citibank
East West Bancorp
Hanmi Financial
Nara Bancorp
UCBH Holdings
U.S. Bancorp
Washington Mutual
Wells Fargo
Wilshire Bancorp

HISTORICAL FINANCIALS

Company Type: Public

Income Statement

FYE: December 31

	ASSETS ($ mil.)	NET INCOME ($ mil.)	INCOME AS % OF ASSETS	EMPLOYEES
12/06	8,026.5	117.6	1.5%	1,051
12/05	6,397.5	104.1	1.6%	900
12/04	6,098.0	86.8	1.4%	—
12/03	5,541.9	55.6	1.0%	—
12/02	2,754.0	48.7	1.8%	5
Annual Growth	**30.7%**	**24.7%**	**—**	**280.8%**

2006 Year-End Financials

Equity as % of assets: 11.7%
Return on assets: 1.6%
Return on equity: 13.7%
Long-term debt ($ mil.): 134.1
No. of shares (mil.): 51.9
Market value ($ mil.): 1,792.1

Dividends
Yield: 1.0%
Payout: 15.9%
Sales ($ mil.): 513.0
R&D as % of sales: —
Advertising as % of sales: —

Stock History

NASDAQ (GS): CATY

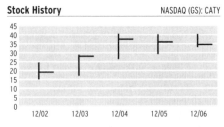

	STOCK PRICE ($) FY Close	P/E High/Low	PER SHARE ($) Earnings	PER SHARE ($) Dividends	PER SHARE ($) Book Value
12/06	34.51	18 15	2.27	0.36	18.16
12/05	35.94	19 14	2.05	0.27	15.41
12/04	37.50	23 16	1.72	0.21	14.12
12/03	28.00	20 12	1.42	0.28	24.97
12/02	19.00	18 11	1.35	0.20	16.00
Annual Growth	**16.1%**	**— —**	**13.9%**	**15.8%**	**3.2%**

Cbeyond, Inc.

Cbeyond isn't looking past the 25 million small businesses in the US to find customers for its broadband services. The facilities-based Voice over Internet Protocol (VoIP) carrier, formerly known as Cbeyond Communications, provides local and long-distance services and broadband Internet access over its own private IP network. The company hopes to side-step stiff competition from incumbent carriers by focusing on the traditionally underserved small-business market.

Cbeyond offers services in the Atlanta, Dallas, Denver, Chicago, Houston, and Los Angeles metro areas and plans to expand services to additional markets. In 2006 the company began offering mobile voice and data services as a mobile virtual network operator (MVNO). The service operates as CbeyondMobile.

Investors in Cbeyond include Madison Dearborn Partners (22%), Battery Ventures (13%), and VantagePoint Ventures Partners (13%). Cisco Systems, which supplies the company's VoIP technology, owns 7%.

EXECUTIVES

Chairman, President, and CEO: James F. (Jim) Geiger, age 48, $449,505 pay
COO: Richard J. Batelaan, age 41, $233,822 pay
EVP and CFO: J. Robert (Bob) Fugate, age 46, $319,000 pay
EVP Sales and Service: Robert R. (Bob) Morrice, age 58, $296,746 pay
CTO: Christopher C. (Chris) Gatch, age 34, $233,822 pay
VP and CIO: Joseph A. (Joe) Oesterling, age 39, $233,822 pay
VP and Chief Marketing Officer: Brooks A. Robinson, age 35, $233,822 pay
VP Finance and Treasurer: Kurt J. Abkemeier, age 37
VP Human Resources: Joan L. Tolliver
VP Sales: Cleveland A. Lewis
Chief Accounting Officer: Henry C. Lyon, age 42, $233,822 pay
Auditors: Ernst & Young LLP

LOCATIONS

HQ: Cbeyond, Inc.
320 Interstate North Pkwy. SE, Ste. 300, Atlanta, GA 30339
Phone: 678-424-2400   **Fax:** 678-424-2500
Web: www.cbeyond.net

2006 Sales

	% of total
Atlanta	30
Denver	27
Dallas	24
Houston	12
Chicago	6
Los Angeles	1
Total	**100**

PRODUCTS/OPERATIONS

2006 Sales

	% of total
Customer revenue	97
Terminating access revenue	3
Total	**100**

Selected Services

Broadband Internet access
Calling cards
Conference calling
E-mail
Local voice access
Long-distance voice
Toll-Free
Virtual private network (VPN)
Voicemail
Web hosting

COMPETITORS

8x8
AT&T
BellSouth
Birch Telecom
Cablevision Systems
Comcast
Covad Communications Group
Cox Communications
Deltathree
DSL.net
ICG Communications
ITC^DeltaCom
McLeodUSA
NuVox
Qwest
Time Warner Cable
Time Warner Telecom
Verizon
Vonage
XO Holdings

HISTORICAL FINANCIALS

Company Type: Public

Income Statement

FYE: December 31

	REVENUE ($ mil.)	NET INCOME ($ mil.)	NET PROFIT MARGIN	EMPLOYEES
12/06	213.9	7.8	3.6%	905
12/05	159.1	3.7	2.3%	707
12/04	113.3	(11.5)	—	586
12/03	65.5	(29.5)	—	—
12/02	21.0	(47.2)	—	380
Annual Growth	**78.6%**	**—**	**—**	**24.2%**

2006 Year-End Financials

Debt ratio: —
Return on equity: 9.4%
Cash ($ mil.): 44.1
Current ratio: 1.30
Long-term debt ($ mil.): —
No. of shares (mil.): 27.4

Dividends
Yield: —
Payout: —
Market value ($ mil.): 838.7
R&D as % of sales: —
Advertising as % of sales: —

Stock History

NASDAQ (GM): CBEY

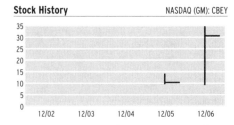

	STOCK PRICE ($) FY Close	P/E High/Low	PER SHARE ($) Earnings	PER SHARE ($) Dividends	PER SHARE ($) Book Value
12/06	30.59	128 35	0.27	—	3.32
12/05	10.30	— —	(1.16)	—	2.80
Annual Growth	**197.0%**	**— —**	**—**	**—**	**18.8%**

CECO Environmental

CECO Environmental wants to clear the air. Through its subsidiaries, CECO Environmental makes industrial ventilation and pollution control systems, including air filters to remove airborne solid and liquid pollutants. The company serves customers in the automotive, chemical, electronics, pharmaceutical, and textile industries, among others. Customers have included General Motors, Honda, and Procter & Gamble. CECO Enviromental also provides custom metal fabrication services, making components for its own ventilation systems. CEO Phillip DeZwirek and his family control CECO Environmental.

In 2007 the company acquired Effox, Inc., which designs and makes dampers and expansion joints for use in flue gas and process air handling systems.

EXECUTIVES

Chairman and CEO: Phillip DeZwirek, age 69, $340,000 pay
President and Director; President and CEO, CECO Group, Inc.: Richard J. Blum, age 60, $297,500 pay
SVP Sales and Marketing and Assistant Secretary; President, Kirk & Blum: David D. Blum, age 49, $222,500 pay
VP Finance and Administration and CFO: Dennis W. Blazer, age 57, $190,000 pay
VP Sales: Mike Meyer
President, CECO Filters: Mary Keenan
President and General Manager, KBD/Technic: Gerry A. Lanham
President and General Manager, CECOAire: Dale P. Arvin
President and General Manager, New Busch Co., Inc.: William W. Frank
Secretary and Director: Jason L. DeZwirek, age 36
Auditors: Battelle & Battelle LLP

LOCATIONS

HQ: CECO Environmental Corp.
3120 Forrer St., Cincinnati, OH 45209
Phone: 513-458-2600   **Fax:** 513-458-2647
Web: www.cecoenviro.com

CECO Environmental maintains facilities in Illinois, Mississippi, North Carolina, Ohio, Pennsylvania, and Tennessee, as well as in Canada and India.

PRODUCTS/OPERATIONS

Selected Subsidiaries
CECO Group, Inc.
  CECO Abatement Systems, Inc.
  CECOaire, Inc.
  CECO Filters, Inc.
  H.M. White, Inc.
  kbd/Technic, Inc.
  The Kirk & Blum Manufacturing Company
    CECO Filters India Pvt. Ltd. (India)
    New Busch Co., Inc.

COMPETITORS

Clyde Bergemann EEC
Pall
United Air Specialists

HISTORICAL FINANCIALS
Company Type: Public

Income Statement

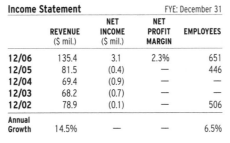

	REVENUE ($ mil.)	NET INCOME ($ mil.)	NET PROFIT MARGIN	EMPLOYEES
12/06	135.4	3.1	2.3%	651
12/05	81.5	(0.4)	—	446
12/04	69.4	(0.9)	—	—
12/03	68.2	(0.7)	—	—
12/02	78.9	(0.1)	—	506
Annual Growth	14.5%	—	—	6.5%

FYE: December 31

2006 Year-End Financials

Debt ratio: 99.7%
Return on equity: 28.6%
Cash ($ mil.): 0.4
Current ratio: 1.50
Long-term debt ($ mil.): 14.9
No. of shares (mil.): 11.5
Dividends
  Yield: —
  Payout: —
Market value ($ mil.): 103.0
R&D as % of sales: —
Advertising as % of sales: —

Stock History

NASDAQ (GM): CECE

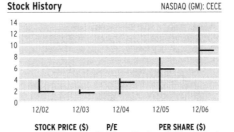

	STOCK PRICE ($) FY Close	P/E High/Low	Earnings	Dividends	Book Value
12/06	8.97	54 23	0.24	—	1.30
12/05	5.74	— —	(0.04)	—	0.68
12/04	3.44	— —	(0.09)	—	0.73
12/03	1.65	— —	(0.07)	—	0.80
12/02	1.85	— —	(0.01)	—	0.98
Annual Growth	48.4%	— —	—	—	7.3%

Cedar Fair

Cedar Fair wants to take you for the ride of your life. The firm owns and manages 11 amusement parks, six outdoor water parks, one indoor water park, and six hotels. Properties include Knott's Berry Farm in California, Michigan's Adventure, and Valleyfair in Minnesota. Knott's Berry Farm operates year-round, while other parks are open daily from May through Labor Day, and mainly on weekends only in September and October. The firm's Cedar Point park in Ohio boasts the Top Thrill Dragster, which is one of the world's tallest and fastest roller coasters at 420 feet with a top speed of 120 mph. Cedar Fair bought Paramount Parks from CBS Corp. in 2006. The parks together draw more than 19 million visitors a year.

Despite the overall downturn in the tourism market, Cedar Fair has been able to maintain a respectable share price, largely because its parks are the only ones in several markets. As a result the company is investing about $80 million to expand and upgrade.

To expand its Ohio market, Cedar Fair bought the Six Flags Worlds of Adventure park near Cleveland. It paid rival Six Flags $145 million for the location and renamed the park Geauga Lake, which became exclusively a water park attraction.

The addition of Paramount Parks, which cost the firm $1.24 billion to buy, gave Cedar Fair another five parks in the US and Canada and an additional 13 million visitors a year.

EXECUTIVES

Chairman, President, and CEO:
  Richard L. (Dick) Kinzel, age 66, $2,292,693 pay
COO: Jacob T. (Jack) Falfas, age 55, $941,731 pay
SVP Marketing and Sales, West Coast: Carolyn Kehler, age 59
Corporate VP Finance and CFO: Peter J. Crage, age 45, $599,424 pay
Corporate VP Planning and Design: Robert A. Decker, age 45
Corporate VP Marketing and Advertising:
  Lee Ann Alexakos, age 51
Regional VP: H. Philip Bender, age 50, $388,394 pay
Regional VP: Larry L. MacKenzie, age 51
VP and Corporate Controller: Brian C. Witherow, age 40
VP Administration: Craig J. Freeman, age 53
VP and General Manager, Cedar Point:
  H. John Hildebrandt, age 57, $348,954 pay
VP and General Manager, Knott's Berry Farm:
  Marty Keithley, age 54
Auditors: Deloitte & Touche LLP

LOCATIONS

HQ: Cedar Fair, L.P.
  1 Cedar Point Dr., Sandusky, OH 44870
Phone: 419-626-0830   **Fax:** 419-627-2260
Web: www.cedarfair.com

PRODUCTS/OPERATIONS

2006 Sales

	$ mil.	% of total
Admissions	459.5	55
Food, merchandise & games	306.9	37
Accommodations & other	65.0	8
Total	**831.4**	**100**

Selected Operations
Carowinds (Charlotte, NC)
Cedar Point (Sandusky, OH)
  Breakers Express (limited-service hotel)
  Camper Village (RV park)
  Castaway Bay (indoor water park)
  Cedar Point Marina
  Hotel Breakers
  Sandcastle Suites Hotel
  Soak City (water park)
Dorney Park & Wildwater Kingdom (South Whitehall Township, PA)
Geauga Lake & Wildwater Kingdom (Aurora, OH)
  Geauga Lake Campgrounds
  Geauga Lake Hotel
Great America (Santa Clara, CA)
Kings Dominion (Doswell, VA)
Kings Island (Cinncinati, OH)
Knott's Berry Farm (Buena Park, CA)
  Knott's Berry Farm Hotel
  Knott's California Marketplace (dining & shopping area)
  Knott's Soak City-Orange County (water park)
  Knott's Soak City — Palm Springs (water park, CA)
  Knott's Soak City — San Diego (water park)
Michigan's Adventure (Muskegon, MI)
Valleyfair (Shakopee, MN)
Wonderland (Toronto)
Worlds of Fun (Kansas City, MO)
  Oceans of Fun (water park)
  Worlds of Fun Village (cottages, cabins, and RV park)

COMPETITORS

Adventureland	LEGO
Busch Entertainment	Six Flags
Disney Parks & Resorts	Universal Parks
Herschend Entertainment	Zoological Society of San
Hershey Entertainment	Diego

HISTORICAL FINANCIALS

Company Type: Public

Income Statement

FYE: December 31

	REVENUE ($ mil.)	NET INCOME ($ mil.)	NET PROFIT MARGIN	EMPLOYEES
12/06	831.4	87.5	10.5%	31,850
12/05	568.7	160.9	28.3%	16,200
12/04	542.0	78.3	14.4%	—
12/03	510.0	85.9	16.8%	—
12/02	502.9	71.4	14.2%	15,300
Annual Growth	13.4%	5.2%	—	20.1%

2006 Year-End Financials

Debt ratio: 428.5%
Return on equity: 20.7%
Cash ($ mil.): 30.2
Current ratio: 0.66
Long-term debt ($ mil.): 1,759.7
No. of shares (mil.): 54.1

Dividends
  Yield: 6.7%
  Payout: 117.6%
Market value ($ mil.): 1,504.8
R&D as % of sales: —
Advertising as % of sales: —

Stock History

NYSE: FUN

	STOCK PRICE ($) FY Close	P/E High/Low		PER SHARE ($) Earnings	Dividends	Book Value
12/06	27.82	19	15	1.59	1.87	7.59
12/05	28.54	12	9	2.93	1.83	8.07
12/04	32.90	24	19	1.47	1.79	6.93
12/03	30.75	19	14	1.67	1.74	6.10
12/02	23.60	18	14	1.39	1.65	6.04
Annual Growth	4.2%	—	—	3.4%	3.2%	5.9%

Celgene Corporation

A terror from the past has provided hope in the present. Celgene's flagship product Thalomid, a form of the infamous thalidomide, treats multiple myeloma (bone marrow cancer), as well as a type of leprosy; thalidomide was a sedative and morning sickness therapy used in Europe in the late 1950s until it was linked to birth defects and pulled from the market. Revlimid, which won FDA approval in late 2005, treats a malignant blood disease called MDS; it received approval for treating multiple myeloma the following year. The company develops drugs primarily to treat inflammatory diseases and cancer. Subsidiary Celgene Cellular Therapeutics researches stem cell therapies and provides placental stem cell banking.

Celgene sells Alkeran, another multiple myeloma treatment, through a supply and dis-

tribution agreement with GlaxoSmithKline. It has licensed its internally developed Focalin, a relative of ADHD drug Ritalin, to Novartis.

Celgene's top customers are drug distributors Cardinal Health (which accounts for nearly 20% of sales), McKesson (16% of sales), and AmerisourceBergen (12%).

In late 2007 Celgene announced plans to acquire Pharmion for $2.9 billion. The two companies are already familiar with each other: Pharmion has held the right to market Thalomid in Europe, and Celgene already owns 6% of Pharmion.

EXECUTIVES

Chairman and CEO: Sol J. Barer, age 61
President, COO, and Director: Robert J. (Bob) Hugin, age 52
EVP, Pharmaceutical Research and Development; Chief Scientific Officer: David I. (Dave) Stirling
SVP and CFO: David W. Gryska, age 50
SVP, Sales and Marketing: Francis Brown
SVP, Regulatory Affairs, Pharmacovigilance, and Project Management: Graham Burton
SVP, Research and Development; SVP, Celgro: George W. J. Matcham
VP, Human Resources: Mary Weger
VP, Medical Affairs and Chief Medical Officer: Jerome B. (Jerry) Zeldis
VP, Corporate Communications: Brian P. Gill
President, International: Aart Brouwer, age 67
President, Celgene Research: Thomas O. (Tom) Daniel
Director, Treasury and Risk Management: Catherine B. Elflein
Secretary: Robert C. Butler
Auditors: KPMG LLP

LOCATIONS

HQ: Celgene Corporation
  86 Morris Ave., Summit, NJ 07901
Phone: 908-673-9000   **Fax:** 908-673-9001
Web: www.celgene.com

2006 Sales

	$ mil.	% of total
US	845.4	94
Europe	43.0	5
Other regions	10.5	1
Total	**898.9**	**100**

PRODUCTS/OPERATIONS

2006 Sales

	$ mil.	% of total
Products		
THALOMID	433.0	48
REVLIMID	320.6	36
ALKERAN	50.3	
FOCALIN	7.3	6
Other	0.4	—
Royalties	69.1	8
Collaborations & other	18.2	2
Total	**898.9**	**100**

Selected Products

Approved
  ALKERAN (multiple myeloma and ovarian cancer, licensed from GlaxoSmithKline)
  FOCALIN (attention deficit hyperactivity disorder, marketed by Novartis)
  LIFEBANK USA (stem cell banking kit)
  THALOMID (complications from leprosy, multiple myeloma)
  REVLIMID (multiple myeloma, myelodysplastic syndromes)
In Development
  CC-4047 (multiple myeloma, myelofibrosis, and solid tumors)
  CC-8490 (brain cancer)
  CC-10004 (chronic inflammatory diseases)
  CC-11006 (blood cancers)

COMPETITORS

Amgen	MGI PHARMA
AstraZeneca	Millennium
Biogen Idec	Novartis
Bristol-Myers Squibb	Pfizer
Cell Therapeutics	Roche
Eli Lilly	Sanofi-Aventis
EntreMed	Shire
Genentech	SuperGen
Johnson & Johnson	Vertex
Merck	

HISTORICAL FINANCIALS

Company Type: Public

Income Statement

FYE: December 31

	REVENUE ($ mil.)	NET INCOME ($ mil.)	NET PROFIT MARGIN	EMPLOYEES
12/06	898.9	69.0	7.7%	1,287
12/05	536.9	63.7	11.9%	944
12/04	377.5	52.8	14.0%	—
12/03	271.5	13.5	5.0%	—
12/02	135.8	(100.0)	—	560
Annual Growth	60.4%	—	—	23.1%

2006 Year-End Financials

Debt ratio: 21.4%
Return on equity: 5.3%
Cash ($ mil.): 1,982.2
Current ratio: 9.64
Long-term debt ($ mil.): 422.5
No. of shares (mil.): 376.0

Dividends
  Yield: —
  Payout: —
Market value ($ mil.): 21,633.3
R&D as % of sales: —
Advertising as % of sales: —

Stock History

NASDAQ (GS): CELG

	STOCK PRICE ($) FY Close	P/E High/Low		PER SHARE ($) Earnings	Dividends	Book Value
12/06	57.53	334	175	0.18	—	5.26
12/05	32.40	182	69	0.18	—	1.86
12/04	13.26	105	60	0.16	—	2.89
12/03	11.22	306	126	0.04	—	3.81
12/02	5.37	—	—	(0.32)	—	3.44
Annual Growth	80.9%	—	—	—	—	11.2%

Center Financial

Center Financial wants to be in the middle of your finances. Center Financial Corporation is the holding company for Center Bank, which has about 15 branches in Southern California, as well as in Chicago and Seattle. It also operates nearly ten additional loan production offices scattered across the US mainland and Hawaii in areas heavily concentrated with Korean-American businesses and individuals, Center Financial's target market. The bank focuses on commercial lending, including Small Business Administration loans and short-term trade finance for importers/exporters. It is buying First

Intercontinental Bank, which serves the Atlanta area's Asian community through four branches.

Commercial real estate loans comprise the largest portion of Center Financial's loan portfolio (more than 65%), followed by commercial operating loans (nearly 20%). The bank also offers auto loans and credit cards.

In 2004 Center Financial acquired its first full-service branch outside of California when it bought the Korea Exchange Bank's Chicago office. The company also expanded its loan production office network in 2004, adding branches in Atlanta, Dallas, Honolulu, and Houston. It opened a location in the Seattle area the following year.

Fund manager FMR owns nearly 10% of Center Financial.

EXECUTIVES

President, CEO and Director: Jae Whan (J. W.) Yoo, age 58
EVP, General Counsel, Corporate Secretary and Chief Risk Officer: Lisa Kim Pai
EVP and CFO: Lonny Robinson, age 50
SVP and Chief Lending Officer: Susanna H. Rivera
SVP and Chief Credit officer: Jason K. Kim
VP and Branch Manager, UniBank Seattle: Jai Hee Han
Auditors: Grant Thornton LLP

LOCATIONS

HQ: Center Financial Corporation
  3435 Wilshire Blvd., Ste. 700,
  Los Angeles, CA 90010
Phone: 213-251-2222   **Fax:** 213-386-6774
Web: www.centerbank.com

Center Financial has bank branches in Artesia, Buena Park, Colton, Gardena, Garden Grove, Irvine, Los Angeles (6), Northridge, San Diego, and Torrance, California, as well as Chicago and Seattle. It has loan production offices in Atlanta, Dallas, Denver, Honolulu, Houston, Las Vegas, Phoenix, Seattle, and Washington, DC.

PRODUCTS/OPERATIONS

2006 Sales

	$ mil.	% of total
Interest		
Loans, including fees	114.3	78
Investment securities	8.1	5
Other	2.4	2
Noninterest		
Customer service fees	8.2	6
Trade finance transactions	3.4	2
Gain on sale of loans	3.3	2
Other	7.4	5
Total	**147.1**	**100**

COMPETITORS

Bank of America
City National
First Republic (CA)
Hanmi Financial
Nara Bancorp
Washington Mutual
Wells Fargo
Wilshire Bancorp

HISTORICAL FINANCIALS
Company Type: Public

Income Statement   FYE: December 31

	ASSETS ($ mil.)	NET INCOME ($ mil.)	INCOME AS % OF ASSETS	EMPLOYEES
12/06	1,843.3	26.2	1.4%	344
12/05	1,661.0	24.6	1.5%	327
12/04	1,338.1	14.2	1.1%	—
12/03	1,027.4	11.6	1.1%	—
12/02	818.6	9.4	1.1%	—
Annual Growth	**22.5%**	**29.2%**	**—**	**5.2%**

2006 Year-End Financials

Equity as % of assets: 7.6%
Return on assets: 1.5%
Return on equity: 20.7%
Long-term debt ($ mil.): 248.1
No. of shares (mil.): 16.6
Market value ($ mil.): 398.7
Dividends
  Yield: 0.7%
  Payout: 10.2%
Sales ($ mil.): 147.1
R&D as % of sales: —
Advertising as % of sales: —

Stock History   NASDAQ (GS): CLFC

	STOCK PRICE ($) FY Close	P/E High/Low	PER SHARE ($) Earnings	Dividends	Book Value
12/06	23.97	17 14	1.57	0.16	8.46
12/05	25.16	18 16	1.48	0.04	6.86
12/04	20.02	25 15	0.86	—	5.57
12/03	13.63	20 8	0.72	—	4.88
12/02	6.18	20 7	0.61	—	9.16
Annual Growth	**40.3%**	**— —**	**26.7%**	**300.0%**	**(2.0%)**

Centerline Holding

Centerline Holding Company helps keep the multifamily housing finance market liquid. Through subsidiaries, the firm (formerly CharterMac) invests in tax-exempt multifamily mortgage bonds issued by state and municipal governments to finance the construction or rehabilitation of multifamily housing, particularly properties meeting low-income housing tax credit requirements. The company's Centerline Capital subsidiary (formerly CharterMac Capital) has raised more than $8 billion in capital from institutional and retail investors by sponsoring real estate investment funds that are also used to finance multifamily properties.

In 2006 the company acquired ARCap Investors, which sponsors funds of high-yield collateralized mortgage-backed securities.

In addition, Centerline has subsidiaries that originate and underwrite loans for multifamily housing on behalf of Fannie Mae, Freddie Mac, the Federal Housing Association (FHA), and other entities.

EXECUTIVES

Chairman and Trustee: Stephen M. Ross, age 66
Trustee; President and CEO, Centerline Capital Group: Marc D. Schnitzer, age 46, $1,021,323 pay (prior to title change)
CFO: Robert L. (Rob) Levy, age 41
SVP: Matthew J. Stern
Executive Managing Director and CIO, Centerline Capital Group: Donald J. (Don) Meyer, age 56
Executive Managing Director and Co-Head Commercial Real Estate Group, Centerline Capital Group: Daryl J. Carter, age 51
HR Director; Managing Director, Centerline Captial Group: Katherine B. (Kelly) Schnur, age 42
Head of Asset Management Group; Senior Managing Director, Centerline Capital Group: Christopher J. Crouch, age 56
General Counsel; Senior Managing Director, Centerline Capital Group: John D'Amico
Auditors: Deloitte & Touche LLP

LOCATIONS

HQ: Centerline Holding Company
  625 Madison Ave., New York, NY 10022
Phone: 212-317-5700   **Fax:** 212-751-3550
Web: www.centerline.com

PRODUCTS/OPERATIONS

2006 Sales

	$ mil.	% of total
Interest		
Mortgage revenue bonds	156.5	40
Other	34.2	9
Fee income	84.2	22
Revenues of consolidated partnerships	83.7	22
Other	28.7	7
Total	**387.3**	**100**

COMPETITORS

Arbor Commercial
Fannie Mae
Freddie Mac
Fremont Investment & Loan
Long Beach Mortgage
MuniMae
PB Capital
WFMC

HISTORICAL FINANCIALS
Company Type: Public

Income Statement   FYE: December 31

	ASSETS ($ mil.)	NET INCOME ($ mil.)	INCOME AS % OF ASSETS	EMPLOYEES
12/06	9,688.5	41.3	0.4%	500
12/05	6,978.8	59.0	0.8%	400
12/04	5,757.4	65.4	1.1%	—
12/03	2,583.3	66.6	2.6%	—
12/02	1,852.9	60.8	3.3%	220
Annual Growth	**51.2%**	**(9.2%)**	**—**	**22.8%**

2006 Year-End Financials

Equity as % of assets: 7.7%
Return on assets: 0.5%
Return on equity: 5.2%
Long-term debt ($ mil.): 5,094.5
No. of shares (mil.): 51.3
Market value ($ mil.): 1,102.3
Dividends
  Yield: —
  Payout: —
Sales ($ mil.): 387.3
R&D as % of sales: —
Advertising as % of sales: —

	STOCK PRICE ($) FY Close	P/E High/Low		PER SHARE ($) Earnings	Dividends	Book Value
12/06	21.47	37	27	0.62	—	18.51
12/05	21.18	25	19	0.98	1.65	20.18
12/04	24.44	21	15	1.19	1.57	17.57
12/03	21.13	17	13	1.31	1.37	18.27
12/02	17.37	14	11	1.31	1.26	18.31
Annual Growth	5.4%	—	—	(17.1%)	9.4%	0.3%

CenterState Banks

CenterState Banks of Florida is a multibank holding company serving Central Florida from some 35 branch locations. It owns CenterState Bank of Florida, CenterState Bank West Florida, CenterState Bank Central Florida, and Valrico State Bank. The banks offer standard retail products and services including checking and savings accounts, money market accounts, and CDs. They focus on real estate lending, with commercial mortgages accounting for more than 40% of the firm's total loan portfolio, while residential mortgages account for nearly 30%. The banks also sell mutual funds, annuities, and other investment products. CenterState Banks bought Valrico Bancorp in 2007.

CenterState Banks sold CenterState Bank Mid Florida to Atlantic Southern Financial Group in 2007; it had acquired CenterState Bank Mid Florida, a community bank with three locations, the previous year.

Also in 2006 CenterState Banks of Florida merged its First National Bank of Polk County subsidiary into CenterState Bank of Florida.

EXECUTIVES

Chairman, President, and CEO; Chairman, CenterState Bank Central Florida, CenterState Bank West Florida, and CenterState Bank Mid Florida:
Ernest S. (Ernie) Pinner, age 59, $350,000 pay
EVP; President and CEO, Centerstate Bank of Florida:
John Corbett
SVP, CFO, and Corporate Secretary: James J. Antal, age 55, $193,500 pay
SVP, COO, and Treasurer; Chairman, CenterState Bank of Florida; President, C.S. Processing:
George H. Carefoot, age 63, $189,522 pay
President and CEO, CenterState Bank Central Florida:
Thomas E. White, age 52, $217,215 pay
President and CEO, CenterState Bank West Florida and CenterState Bank Mid Florida: Timothy A. Pierson
COO, CenterState Bank of Florida: Jennifer Ison

LOCATIONS

HQ: CenterState Banks of Florida, Inc.
1101 1st St. South, Ste. 202,
Winter Haven, FL 33880
Phone: 863-293-2600   **Fax:** 863-291-3994
Web: www.csflbanks.com

PRODUCTS/OPERATIONS

2006 Sales

	$ mil.	% of total
Interest		
Loans	46.5	71
Investment securities	9.7	15
Other	3.0	5
Noninterest		
Service charges on deposit accounts	3.4	5
Other	2.7	4
Total	**65.3**	**100**

COMPETITORS

Bank of America
BankAtlantic
Colonial BancGroup
South Financial
SunTrust
Wachovia

HISTORICAL FINANCIALS
Company Type: Public

Income Statement
FYE: December 31

	ASSETS ($ mil.)	NET INCOME ($ mil.)	INCOME AS % OF ASSETS	EMPLOYEES
12/06	1,077.1	8.5	0.8%	320
12/05	871.5	6.3	0.7%	275
12/04	753.8	4.4	0.6%	—
12/03	608.9	2.6	0.4%	—
12/02	494.8	2.4	0.5%	233
Annual Growth	21.5%	37.2%	—	8.3%

2006 Year-End Financials

Equity as % of assets: 10.9%
Return on assets: 0.9%
Return on equity: 7.9%
Long-term debt ($ mil.): 10.0
No. of shares (mil.): 11.1
Market value ($ mil.): 232.6
Dividends
  Yield: 0.7%
  Payout: 18.7%
Sales ($ mil.): 65.3
R&D as % of sales: —
Advertising as % of sales: —

Stock History
NASDAQ (GM): CSFL

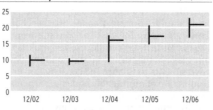

	STOCK PRICE ($) FY Close	P/E High/Low		PER SHARE ($) Earnings	Dividends	Book Value
12/06	20.90	30	23	0.75	0.14	10.54
12/05	17.25	31	23	0.65	0.13	18.52
12/04	16.00	30	16	0.57	0.12	14.17
12/03	9.50	26	22	0.38	0.11	12.45
12/02	9.83	27	20	0.41	0.10	11.87
Annual Growth	20.8%	—	—	16.3%	8.8%	(2.9%)

Central European Distribution

Central European Distribution Corporation (CEDC) helped Poland toast its post-Communist economy in 1991 when co-founders William O. Carey and Jeffrey Peterson introduced Foster's lager to the country. CEDC imports and distributes more than 700 brands of beer, spirits, and wines in Poland through more than 39,000 outlets. CEDC offers spirits made by Bacardi and Diageo. Other brands include Beck's Pilsner, Corona, Jim Beam, and E&J Gallo wines. Also a vodka distiller, the company's flagship products include Bols, Soplica, and Royal Vodka. The company owns two distilleries and operates 16 distribution centers throughout the country and offers next-day order delivery.

CEDC plans to grow through the addition of regional offices and brands throughout Poland. To that end, the purchase of vodka maker Bols, Poland's third largest distiller, from Rémy Cointreau in 2005 not only added the distillery but brought exclusive import deals covering Rémy Martin, Piper-Heidsieck, Cointreau, and Metaxa.

CEDC also owns a majority stake in Polmos Bialystok, Poland's second largest vodka distiller and producer of the Absolwent and Zubrowka brands. Fitting in with its growth strategy, the company owns Delikates, an alcohol distributor serving central Poland. CEDC added the rights to popular Polish rum brand Rum Senorita, and acquired another Polish distributor (Classic) in 2006.

Chairman and CEO William V. Carey owns about 10% of CEDC.

EXECUTIVES

Chairman, President, and CEO: William V. Carey, age 42, $587,500 pay
VP and COO: Evangelos Evangelou, age 39, $332,812 pay
VP and CFO: Christopher (Chris) Biedermann, age 39, $245,606 pay
VP, Secretary, and Director Investor Relations: James Archbold, age 46, $170,000 pay
VP and Export Director: Richard S. Roberts, age 58, $104,166 pay
Auditors: PricewaterhouseCoopers Sp. z o.o.

LOCATIONS

HQ: Central European Distribution Corporation
2 Bala Plaza, Ste. 300, Bala Cynwyd, PA 19004
Phone: 610-660-7817   **Fax:** 610-667-3308
Web: www.cedc.com.pl

COMPETITORS

Carlsberg
Diageo
Heineken
InBev
Nestlé
Pernod Ricard
Rémy Cointreau
SABMiller
Suntory Ltd.

HISTORICAL FINANCIALS

Company Type: Public

Income Statement

FYE: December 31

	REVENUE ($ mil.)	NET INCOME ($ mil.)	NET PROFIT MARGIN	EMPLOYEES
12/06	944.1	55.5	5.9%	3,015
12/05	749.4	20.3	2.7%	2,917
12/04	580.7	21.8	3.8%	—
12/03	429.1	15.1	3.5%	—
12/02	294.0	8.3	2.8%	1,480
Annual Growth	33.9%	60.8%	—	19.5%

2006 Year-End Financials

Debt ratio: 75.7%
Return on equity: 12.4%
Cash ($ mil.): 159.4
Current ratio: 1.57
Long-term debt ($ mil.): 394.6
No. of shares (mil.): 38.4

Dividends
 Yield: —
 Payout: —
Market value ($ mil.): 1,141.8
R&D as % of sales: —
Advertising as % of sales: —

Stock History

NASDAQ (GS): CEDC

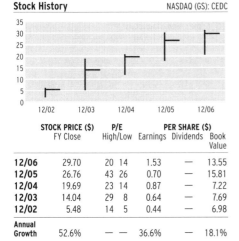

	STOCK PRICE ($) FY Close	P/E High/Low		PER SHARE ($) Earnings	Dividends	Book Value
12/06	29.70	20	14	1.53	—	13.55
12/05	26.76	43	26	0.70	—	15.81
12/04	19.69	23	14	0.87	—	7.22
12/03	14.04	29	8	0.64	—	7.69
12/02	5.48	14	5	0.44	—	6.98
Annual Growth	52.6%	—	—	36.6%	—	18.1%

Central Jersey Bancorp

Central Jersey Bancorp (formerly Monmouth Community Bancorp) is keeping the Garden State funded. The institution is the holding company for Central Jersey Bank, created by the merger of Monmouth Community Bank and Allaire Community Bank in 2005. Central Jersey Bank has about 15 branches in Monmouth and Ocean counties; they offer standard deposit products such as checking and savings accounts, CDs, and IRAs, as well as ancillary offerings like debit cards, wire transfers, and safe deposit boxes. Lending activities mainly consist of commercial real estate loans (some two-thirds of all loans), business and industrial loans, home equity loans, and second mortgages.

The bank has announced plans to open new branches in existing market areas.

John Brockriede, a bank director since early 2005, owns 5% of Central Jersey Bancorp; collectively, bank executive officers and directors own a 28% stake.

EXECUTIVES

Chairman: George S. Callas, age 74
President, CEO, and Director; President and CEO, Central Jersey Bank: James S. Vaccaro, age 50, $257,500 pay
SEVP, COO, Secretary, and Director; SEVP, COO, and Secretary, Central Jersey Bank: Robert S. Vuono, age 57, $165,855 pay
EVP and Chief Lending Officer, Central Jersey Bancorp and Central Jersey Bank: Richard O. Lindsey, age 65, $147,500 pay
EVP Commercial Lending, Central Jersey Bank: Kevin W. Hunt, $113,816 pay
EVP, CFO, Treasurer, and Assistant Secretary, Central Jersey Bancorp and Central Jersey Bank: Anthony Giordano III, age 41, $117,500 pay
EVP and Senior Lending Officer: Robert E. Wallace, age 59
EVP and Commercial Lending Officer: Thomas J. Garrity, age 47
SVP Human Resources, Central Jersey Bank: Gail Corrigan
Auditors: KPMG LLP

LOCATIONS

HQ: Central Jersey Bancorp
 627 2nd Ave., Long Branch, NJ 07740
Phone: 732-571-1300   **Fax:** 732-571-1037
Web: www.mcbna.com

PRODUCTS/OPERATIONS

2006 Sales

	$ mil.	% of total
Interest		
Interest & fees on loans	23.2	74
Interest on securities available-for-sale	4.5	14
Interest on securities held-to-maturity	1.0	3
Interest on federal funds sold & due from banks	0.8	3
Noninterest		
Service charges on deposit accounts	1.4	5
Income on bank owned life insurance	0.1	—
Gain on the sale of loans held-for-sale	0.2	1
Total	31.2	100

COMPETITORS

Amboy Bancorp
Bank of New York Mellon
Brunswick Bancorp
Commerce Bancorp
Magyar Bancorp
OceanFirst Financial
Peapack-Gladstone Financial
PNC Financial
Sovereign Bancorp
Sun Bancorp (NJ)
Wachovia

HISTORICAL FINANCIALS

Company Type: Public

Income Statement

FYE: December 31

	ASSETS ($ mil.)	NET INCOME ($ mil.)	INCOME AS % OF ASSETS	EMPLOYEES
12/06	516.3	2.5	0.5%	147
12/05	514.6	2.6	0.5%	152
12/04	254.1	1.2	0.5%	—
12/03	222.6	0.5	0.2%	—
12/02	179.5	0.8	0.4%	—
Annual Growth	30.2%	33.0%	—	(3.3%)

2006 Year-End Financials

Equity as % of assets: 12.7%
Return on assets: 0.5%
Return on equity: 3.9%
Long-term debt ($ mil.): 22.3
No. of shares (mil.): 8.3
Market value ($ mil.): 65.3

Dividends
 Yield: —
 Payout: —
Sales ($ mil.): 31.2
R&D as % of sales: —
Advertising as % of sales: —

Stock History

NASDAQ (GM): CJBK

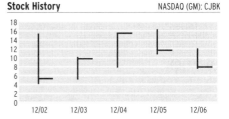

	STOCK PRICE ($) FY Close	P/E High/Low		PER SHARE ($) Earnings	Dividends	Book Value
12/06	7.91	45	29	0.27	—	7.94
12/05	11.63	58	39	0.28	—	7.89
12/04	15.44	55	28	0.28	—	8.52
12/03	9.77	88	46	0.11	—	9.61
12/02	5.30	63	18	0.24	—	10.11
Annual Growth	10.5%	—	—	3.0%	—	(5.9%)

Central Pacific Financial

When in the Central Pacific, do as the islanders do! This might include doing business with Central Pacific Financial, the holding company for Central Pacific Bank. The bank operates nearly 40 branch locations throughout the Hawaiian Islands. Targeting individuals and local businesses, the bank provides such standard retail banking products as checking and savings accounts, money market accounts, and CDs. Commercial real estate loans make up about a third of the bank's loan portfolio, which also includes residential mortgages (more than 20%) and business, construction, and consumer loans. The company has real estate loan production offices in California, Hawaii, and Washington.

Its Datatronix Financial Services subsidiary, which offered data-processing support to financial institutions in California and Hawaii, ceased operations in 2006. In 2005 the company acquired Hawaii HomeLoans, which it renamed Central Pacific HomeLoans. The addition of Central Pacific HomeLoans expanded Central Pacific Financial's mortgage offerings, making it one of the largest mortgage writers in the state. Central Pacific Bank also provides business cash management services, equipment leasing, and trust and investment services.

EXECUTIVES

Chairman, Central Pacific Financial and Central Pacific Bank: Ronald K. Migita, age 65
Vice Chairman, President, and CEO, Central Pacific Financial and Central Pacific Bank: Clinton L. (Clint) Arnoldus, age 60, $630,000 pay
Vice Chairman and CFO, Central Pacific Financial and Central Pacific Bank: Dean K. Hirata, age 50, $243,700 pay (prior to promotion)
Vice Chairman of Central Pacific Bank and CEO of Central Pacific HomeLoans: Blenn A. Fujimoto, age 49, $220,700 pay (prior to promotion)
EVP and Chief Credit Officer: Curtis W. Chinn, age 51
EVP Operations and Services, Central Pacific Financial and Central Pacific Bank: Denis K. Isono, age 55, $200,600 pay

SVP and Corporate Secretary: Glenn K.C. Ching
VP and Public Relations and Communications Manager:
Ann Takiguchi Marcos
Auditors: KPMG LLP

LOCATIONS

HQ: Central Pacific Financial Corp.
220 S. King St., Honolulu, HI 96813
Phone: 808-544-0500   **Fax:** 808-531-2875
Web: www.cpbi.com

Central Pacific Financial operates branches on the
islands of Hawaii (2), Kauai (1), Maui (3), and Oahu (31).
The company also has four loan production offices in
California and two in Washington.

PRODUCTS/OPERATIONS

2006 Sales

	% of total
Interest & fees on loans	77
Securities	11
Service charges on deposit accounts	4
Gain on sales of loans	1
Income from fiduciary activities	1
Other	6
Total	**100**

COMPETITORS

American Savings Bank	Mitsubishi UFJ Financial
BancWest	Group
Bank of Hawaii	Territorial Savings
First Hawaiian Bank	Washington Mutual
Hawaiian Electric	Wells Fargo
Industries	

HISTORICAL FINANCIALS

Company Type: Public

Income Statement				FYE: December 31
	ASSETS ($ mil.)	NET INCOME ($ mil.)	INCOME AS % OF ASSETS	EMPLOYEES
12/06	5,487.2	79.2	1.4%	1,008
12/05	5,239.1	72.5	1.4%	904
12/04	4,651.9	37.4	0.8%	—
12/03	2,170.3	33.9	1.6%	—
12/02	2,028.2	33.3	1.6%	506
Annual Growth	28.3%	24.2%	—	18.8%

2006 Year-End Financials

Equity as % of assets: 13.5%
Return on assets: 1.5%
Return on equity: 11.2%
Long-term debt ($ mil.): 740.2
No. of shares (mil.): 30.7
Market value ($ mil.): 1,190.3
Dividends
 Yield: 2.3%
 Payout: 34.2%
Sales ($ mil.): 365.0
R&D as % of sales: —
Advertising as % of sales: —

Stock History

NYSE: CPF

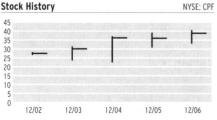

	STOCK PRICE ($) FY Close	P/E High/Low		PER SHARE ($) Earnings	Dividends	Book Value
12/06	38.76	16	13	2.57	0.88	24.04
12/05	35.92	16	13	2.38	0.73	22.22
12/04	36.17	20	12	1.87	0.64	20.09
12/03	30.04	15	12	2.07	0.64	12.11
12/02	27.45	14	13	2.04	—	10.86
Annual Growth	9.0%	—	—	5.9%	11.2%	22.0%

Central Valley Community Bancorp

Central Valley Community Bancorp wants to
be at the very core of your banking activities. It's
the holding company for Central Valley Community Bank (formerly Clovis Community
Bank), which offers individual and business customers traditional banking services in and
around the California counties of Fresno,
Madera, and Sacramento. Deposit services include checking, savings, and money market accounts; IRAs; and CDs. The bank offers credit
card services and originates a variety of loans, including residential mortgage, business, personal,
and agricultural loans.

Director Louis McMurray owns approximately
11% of the company's outstanding shares, chairman Daniel Cunningham and director Steven
McDonald each own about 7%.

EXECUTIVES

**President, CEO, and Director, Central Valley
Community Bancorp and Central Valley Community
Bank:** Daniel J. Doyle, age 60, $280,000 pay
SVP and CFO: David A. (Dave) Kinross, age 42,
$100,000 pay (partial-year salary)
**SVP, Commercial and Business Banking, Central Valley
Community Bank:** Gary Quisenberry, age 55,
$159,250 pay
**SVP and Credit Administrator, Central Valley
Community Bancorp; SVP and Chief Credit Officer,
Central Valley Community Bank:**
Thomas L. (Tom) Sommer, age 59, $145,616 pay
SVP, Financial Institutions Department:
Donald J. Robinson
SVP: Lydia Shaw
Corporate Secretary: Cathy Ponte
**Director, Marketing and Communications, Central
Valley Community Bank:** Debbie Cohen
Auditors: Perry-Smith LLP

LOCATIONS

HQ: Central Valley Community Bancorp
600 Pollasky Ave., Clovis, CA 93612
Phone: 559-298-1775   **Fax:** 559-221-4376
Web: www.cvcb.com

PRODUCTS/OPERATIONS

2006 Sales

	$ mil.	% of total
Interest		
Interest & fees on loans	25.5	71
Interest on federal funds sold	1.2	3
Interest & dividends on investment securities:		
Taxable	3.2	9
Exempt from federal income taxes	1.0	3
Noninterest		
Service charges	2.5	7
Loan placement fees	0.4	1
Appreciation in cash surrender value of bank owned life insurance	0.3	1
Gain from bank owned life insurance	0.6	2
Net realized gains on sales & calls of investment securities	0.1	—
Federal Home Loan Bank stock dividends	0.1	—
Gain on sale & disposal of equipment	0.2	—
Other income	1.0	3
Total	**36.1**	**100**

COMPETITORS

American River Bankshares	TriCo Bancshares
Bank of America	UnionBanCal
Capital Corp of the West	United Security Bancshares
Comerica	Washington Mutual
RCB Corp.	Wells Fargo
Sierra Bancorp	

HISTORICAL FINANCIALS

Company Type: Public

Income Statement				FYE: December 31
	ASSETS ($ mil.)	NET INCOME ($ mil.)	INCOME AS % OF ASSETS	EMPLOYEES
12/06	500.1	6.9	1.4%	162
12/05	483.7	6.0	1.2%	284
12/04	368.1	3.7	1.0%	—
12/03	327.9	3.4	1.0%	—
12/02	283.0	2.8	1.0%	—
Annual Growth	15.3%	25.3%	—	(43.0%)

2006 Year-End Financials

Equity as % of assets: 10.0%
Return on assets: 1.4%
Return on equity: 15.1%
Long-term debt ($ mil.): —
No. of shares (mil.): 6.0
Market value ($ mil.): 89.1
Dividends
 Yield: —
 Payout: —
Sales ($ mil.): 36.1
R&D as % of sales: —
Advertising as % of sales: —

Stock History

NASDAQ (CM): CVCY

	STOCK PRICE ($) FY Close	P/E High/Low		PER SHARE ($) Earnings	Dividends	Book Value
12/06	14.75	18	13	1.07	—	8.24
12/05	15.00	17	12	0.94	—	7.05
12/04	11.69	24	16	0.63	0.05	11.26
12/03	11.38	50	12	0.60	0.05	10.28
12/02	7.47	15	10	0.51	0.03	9.36
Annual Growth	18.5%	—	—	20.4%	29.1%	(3.1%)

Century Casinos

In the 19th century, people rushed to Cripple
Creek, Colorado, seeking their fortune in gold.
Today, thanks to Century Casinos, they can do
basically the same thing. Its Womacks Casino
and Hotel in Cripple Creek offers some 550 slot
machines and video devices, as well as a handful
of gaming tables. Century Casinos also owns the
Century Casino and Hotel, in Central City, Colorado. Outside the US the company owns the
Caledon Hotel, Spa & Casino near Cape Town,
South Africa; the Century Casino and Hotel in
Edmonton, Canada; and the Casino Millennium
in the Marriott hotel in Prague, Czech Republic.
It is also the casino concessionaire for cruise
lines Oceania and ResidenSea.

Century Casinos has been making small acquisitions to expand its portfolio and centralize

ownership of some properties. In 2007 the firm acquired a 33% ownership interest in Casinos Poland, which owns seven casinos and one slot arcade in Poland. The following year it acquired the remaining 35% of Century Casino and Hotel that it didn't already own in 2008.

The company also owns 60% of, and provides technical casino services to, Century Casino Newcastle, in Newcastle, South Africa.

Century Casinos' investors include chairman and co-CEO Erwin Haitzmann (13%) and founder Thomas Graf (18%).

EXECUTIVES

Chairman and Co-CEO: Erwin Haitzmann, age 53
Vice Chairman, President, and Co-CEO:
  Peter Hoetzinger, age 44, $588,831 pay
SVP, Secretary, and Treasurer: Larry J. Hannappel,
  age 54, $195,650 pay
Chief Accounting Officer: Ray Sienko, age 49,
  $125,609 pay
Managing Director, Century Casinos Africa:
  Rossouw Lubbe
**General Manager, Century Casino, Central City,
  Colorado:** Mickey Rosenbaum
**General Manager, Womacks Casino, Cripple Creek,
  Colorado:** Sam Cocharo
General Manager, Century Casino, Alberta, Canada:
  Geoff Smith
**General Manager, Century Casino Millennium, Prague,
  Czech Republic:** Michael Grill
**General Manager, Century Casino, Newcastle, South
  Africa:** John McGregor
Investor Relations and Communications Manager:
  Ulrike Pichler
Auditors: Grant Thornton LLP

LOCATIONS

HQ: Century Casinos, Inc.
  1263 Lake Plaza Dr., Ste. A,
  Colorado Springs, CO 80906
Phone: 719-527-8300   **Fax:** 719-527-8301
Web: www.cnty.com

PRODUCTS/OPERATIONS

2006 Sales

	$ mil.	% of total
Casino	54.5	88
Hotel, food & beverage	6.1	10
Other	1.2	2
Promotional	(5.5)	—
Total	**56.3**	**100**

COMPETITORS

Global Casinos
Isle of Capri Casinos
Nevada Gold & Casinos
Riviera Holdings
Trans World Corporation

HISTORICAL FINANCIALS

Company Type: Public

Income Statement

FYE: December 31

	REVENUE ($ mil.)	NET INCOME ($ mil.)	NET PROFIT MARGIN	EMPLOYEES
12/06	56.3	7.6	13.5%	1,000
12/05	37.4	4.5	12.0%	517
12/04	35.8	4.7	13.1%	—
12/03	31.4	3.3	10.5%	—
12/02	29.3	3.1	10.6%	550
Annual Growth	**17.7%**	**25.1%**	**—**	**16.1%**

2006 Year-End Financials

Debt ratio: 55.8%
Return on equity: 7.9%
Cash ($ mil.): 37.3
Current ratio: 1.14
Long-term debt ($ mil.): 56.0
No. of shares (mil.): 23.0
Dividends
  Yield: —
  Payout: —
Market value ($ mil.): 256.7
R&D as % of sales: —
Advertising as % of sales: —

Stock History

NASDAQ (CM): CNTY

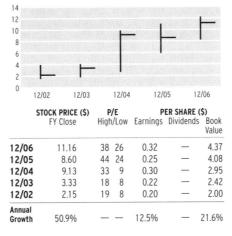

	STOCK PRICE ($) FY Close	P/E High/Low		PER SHARE ($) Earnings	Dividends	Book Value
12/06	11.16	38	26	0.32	—	4.37
12/05	8.60	44	24	0.25	—	4.08
12/04	9.13	33	9	0.30	—	2.95
12/03	3.33	18	8	0.22	—	2.42
12/02	2.15	19	8	0.20	—	2.00
Annual Growth	**50.9%**	**—**	**—**	**12.5%**	**—**	**21.6%**

Ceradyne, Inc.

A bull in a china shop wouldn't stand a chance against Ceradyne's ceramics. The company's advanced technical ceramics products combine hardness with light weight and the ability to withstand high temperatures, resist corrosion, and insulate against electricity. Some uses of Ceradyne's materials include armor for military helicopters, missile nose cones, body armor for soldiers, diesel engine components, ceramic industrial products, and orthodontic brackets. The company sells to contractors and OEMs. The US government and other government agencies represent nearly three-quarters of sales.

With the conflicts in Afghanistan and Iraq, Ceradyne has been booking hundreds of millions of dollars in orders for body armor from the US Army and US Marine Corps. It also has received orders for vehicle armor from the US military.

In mid-2006 Ceradyne exercised its more recent diversification strategy with the purchase of an 86,000-sq.-ft. industrial facility in Quebec and a boron carbide/aluminum product line known as Boral. The company paid AAR Corp. approximately $14 million for the facility, equipment, product line, and inventory, officially marking its entrance into the universe of manufacturing and marketing structural neutron-absorbing materials.

Ceradyne moved further into that market in 2007 by acquiring EaglePicher Boron for nearly $70 million in cash. The former EaglePicher unit makes the B10 boron isotope, used for both nuclear waste containment and nuclear power plant neutron radiation control, and the B11 isotope, used as a dopant in semiconductor manufacturing processes. EP Boron also produces complementary chemical isotopes used in the normal operation and control of nuclear power plants. EP Boron will function as a wholly owned subsidiary of Ceradyne.

The company has also acquired Minco, a manufacturer of fused-silica powders and a supplier to Ceradyne's Thermo Materials division. Ceradyne paid about $27.5 million in cash. Minco's powders are used in Ceradyne's fused-silica ceramic crucibles, which are employed in manufacturing photovoltaic solar cells made from polycrystalline silicon (polysilicon). Fused-silica powders are greatly in demand at Ceradyne's new crucible factory in Tianjin, China.

Ceradyne acquired raw materials supplier ESK Ceramics and injection moldings firm Quest Technology in 2004.

Co-founder and chairman Joel Moskowitz owns 8% of the company.

EXECUTIVES

Chairman, President, and CEO: Joel P. Moskowitz,
  age 67, $1,181,355 pay
CFO and Corporate Secretary:
  Jerrold J. (Jerry) Pellizzon, age 53, $582,414 pay
VP; President, Thermo Materials: Bruce R. Lockhart,
  age 44
**VP; President, North American Operations and
  Assistant Corporate Secretary:** David P. Reed, age 52,
  $639,796 pay
VP; President, Semicon Associates: Jeff Waldal, age 42
VP, Armor Operations: Marc A. King, age 60
VP Nuclear and Semiconductor Business Units:
  Michael A. Kraft, age 44, $464,245 pay
Chief Technology Officer: Thomas Juengling
VP: Matthew Karmel, age 56
VP, Operations: Kenneth R. Morris, age 53
President, Minco: Tom Cole
Auditors: PricewaterhouseCoopers LLP

LOCATIONS

HQ: Ceradyne, Inc.
  3169 Red Hill Ave., Costa Mesa, CA 92626
Phone: 714-549-0421   **Fax:** 714-549-5787
Web: www.ceradyne.com

Ceradyne operates facilities in Canada, China, France, Germany, and the US.

2006 Sales

	% of total
US	84
Other countries	16
Total	**100**

PRODUCTS/OPERATIONS

2006 Sales

	$ mil.	% of total
Advanced Ceramics	528.7	75
ESK Ceramics	148.1	21
Thermo Materials	15.0	2
Semicon Associates	9.1	1
Ceradyne Canada	2.4	1
Adjustments	(40.4)	—
Total	**662.9**	**100**

2006 Sales by Market

	% of total
Defense	76
Industrial	17
Automotive & diesel	5
Commercial	2
Total	**100**

Selected Applications

Defense
  Military aircraft and vehicle armor
  Missile radomes
  Personnel (body) armor

Industrial
  Fused silica ceramic crucibles
  Industrial wear components
  Photovoltaic (solar cell) manufacturing
  Precision ceramics
  Samarium cobalt permanent magnets
  Semiconductor equipment components
Commercial
  Orthodontic brackets
Automotive
  Ceramic armor for armored civilian vehicles
  Diesel truck engine components

COMPETITORS

Align Technology
Alloy Steel
American Technical Ceramics
Arotech
BAE Systems Land and Armaments
Cookson Group
CoorsTek
Dyson Group
GE
GEA Group
H.C. Starck
Hitachi
Kennametal
Kyocera
Morgan Crucible
NGK INSULATORS
NP Aerospace
Point Blank Solutions
Refractron
Rockwood Holdings
Saint-Gobain

HISTORICAL FINANCIALS

Company Type: Public

Income Statement

FYE: December 31

	REVENUE ($ mil.)	NET INCOME ($ mil.)	NET PROFIT MARGIN	EMPLOYEES
12/06	662.9	128.4	19.4%	2,205
12/05	368.3	46.8	12.7%	1,835
12/04	215.6	27.6	12.8%	—
12/03	101.5	11.2	11.0%	—
12/02	61.2	2.7	4.4%	435
Annual Growth	81.4%	162.6%	—	50.0%

2006 Year-End Financials

Debt ratio: 29.8%
Return on equity: 39.1%
Cash ($ mil.): 204.1
Current ratio: 5.75
Long-term debt ($ mil.): 121.0
No. of shares (mil.): 27.1

Dividends
  Yield: —
  Payout: —
Market value ($ mil.): 1,532.2
R&D as % of sales: —
Advertising as % of sales: —

Stock History

NASDAQ (GS): CRDN

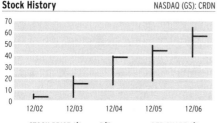

	STOCK PRICE ($) FY Close	P/E High/Low		PER SHARE ($) Earnings	Dividends	Book Value
12/06	56.50	14	8	4.69	—	14.99
12/05	43.80	26	10	1.86	—	9.35
12/04	38.14	35	13	1.12	—	5.52
12/03	15.14	42	7	0.51	—	8.17
12/02	3.47	41	15	0.14	—	5.06
Annual Growth	100.9%	—	—	140.6%	—	31.2%

Chart Industries

They're just chillin' at Chart Industries. The company (which was acquired by First Reserve in 2005 for $460 million) designs equipment for low-temperature uses, including cryogenic systems that can operate at temperatures near absolute zero. Chart's vessels are used to process, liquefy, store, and transport gases and are marketed to petrochemical and natural gas processors, producers of industrial gas, and satellite testing companies. The company also performs engineered bulk gas installations, and makes specialty liquid nitrogen end-use equipment used in the hydrocarbon processing and industrial gas industries. First Reserve owns about 48% of Chart Industries.

To streamline operations, Chart Industries reorganized its subsidiaries into three business segments: Distribution & Storage, Biomedical, and Energy & Chemicals.

Chart Industries' products are sold worldwide; the US accounts for three-quarters of sales.

In 2006 the company acquired Cooler Service Company of Tulsa, Oklahoma, for nearly $16 million, net of cash. Cooler Service makes custom air-cooled heat exchangers for hydrocarbon, petrochemical, and industrial gas processing and power generation. The firm became part of the Energy & Chemicals segment.

Capital Research and Management owns nearly 9% of Chart Industries.

HISTORY

In 1986 Arthur Holmes teamed up with his brother Charles to purchase ALTEC International, a struggling maker of brazed aluminum heat exchangers that dated to 1949. The brothers turned ALTEC around and used it to acquire undervalued companies. From 1986 to 1991, they purchased storage and transportation equipment for liquefied gases and high-pressure cryogenic equipment, including Greenville Tube Corporation (stainless steel tubing, 1987); Process Engineering, Inc. (cryogenic tanks, 1990); and Process Systems International (cold boxes, 1991). The Holmes brothers finally established a public holding company in 1992, and named it Chart Industries (for CHarles and ARThur).

The company ran into trouble over the next few years trying to make its acquisitions profitable. Chart restructured its most troubled unit, Process Engineering, Inc., in 1994. It bought cryogenic vacuum pumps maker CVI to build systems for NASA. In 1995 the company began supplying vacuum equipment for the Laser Interferometer Gravitational-Wave Observatory project, a research program that searches for cosmic gravitational waves.

In 1997 Chart bought Cryenco Sciences, which makes cryogenic road trailers. The next year the company acquired the Industrial Heat Exchanger division of UK-based IMI Marston (IMI sold the Marston aerospace business in 1999). In a move intended to increase foreign sales, Chart in 1999 bought MVE Holding, a cryogenic storage and transportation company with facilities in the US and Europe, for $240 million in cash. The company also expanded its cryogenic equipment repair services across the US with the purchase of Northcoast Cryogenics.

Chart signed an agreement in 2000 to build and maintain a new liquid natural gas fueling station for Waste Management. The new refueling

station will be the world's largest, capable of refueling 120 trucks per four hours. In March 2002 the company announced it would place surcharges on its bulk storage tanks to offset the tariffs set by the US government on imported steel products, which would increase manufacturing costs.

In 2003 the NYSE suspended trading of the company's shares after the company fell below continued listing standards and fell into bankruptcy protection. Later that year, Chart Industries came out of bankruptcy protection with a new board membership and senior management. Chairman Arthur Holmes also resigned his post in 2003, but continued as a board member until 2005.

Chart Industries filed for another IPO in 2006, applying to list on the Big Board once more. The company had to settle for a Nasdaq listing, but completed its IPO in mid-2006.

EXECUTIVES

Chairman, President, and CEO: Samuel F. Thomas, age 55
EVP, CFO, and Treasurer: Michael F. Biehl, age 51, $235,000 pay
VP, General Counsel, and Secretary: Matthew J. Klaben, age 37, $171,977 pay
VP, Human Resources: Mark H. Ludwig
Chief Accounting Officer, Controller, and Assistant Treasurer: James H. Hoppel Jr., age 43, $153,000 pay
Chairman and Managing Director, Chart Ferox: Hans Lonsain, age 52
President, Energy and Chemicals Group: John T. Romain
President, Distribution and Storage Group: Thomas M. (Tom) Carey
President, Chart Asia: Eric M. Rottier
President, Biomedical Group: Steven T. (Steve) Shaw
Auditors: Ernst & Young LLP

LOCATIONS

HQ: Chart Industries, Inc.
  1 Infinity Corporate Centre Dr., Ste. 300, Garfield Heights, OH 44125
Phone: 440-753-1490 **Fax:** 440-753-1491
Web: www.chart-ind.com

Chart Industries has operations in Australia, China, the Czech Republic, Germany, the UK, and the US.

2006 Sales

	$ mil.	% of total
US	403.6	75
Czech Republic	73.6	14
Other countries	60.3	11
Total	537.5	100

PRODUCTS/OPERATIONS

2006 Sales

	$ mil.	% of total
Distribution & storage	268.3	50
Energy & chemicals	190.7	35
Biomedical	78.5	15
Total	537.5	100

Selected Products

Cold boxes (reduce the temperature of gas mixtures to liquefy and separate them)
Cryogenic components (pumps, valves, vacuum-jacketed piping systems, and specialty components)
Cryogenic storage tanks (tanks, trailers, intermodal containers, and railcars)
Heat exchangers (facilitate cooling and liquefaction of air or hydrocarbons)
Space simulation systems (satellite and spacecraft testing)
Thermal vacuum systems (aerospace and research applications)

COMPETITORS

Air Products	L'Air Liquide
Chicago Bridge & Iron	The Linde Group
Cobham	Matrix Service
Covidien	Nordon et Compagnie
Flowserve	QualMark
Graham Corporation	Reliance Steel
Harsco	Senior plc
Ingersoll-Rand	Sumitomo Metal Industries
Kobe Steel	Technip

HISTORICAL FINANCIALS

Company Type: Public

Income Statement				FYE: December 31
	REVENUE ($ mil.)	NET INCOME ($ mil.)	NET PROFIT MARGIN	EMPLOYEES
12/06	537.5	26.9	5.0%	2,703
12/05	403.1	8.4	2.1%	2,271
12/04	305.6	22.6	7.4%	1,770
12/03	265.6	(7.0)	—	1,524
12/02	296.3	(130.8)	—	2,022
Annual Growth	16.1%	—	—	7.5%

2006 Year-End Financials

Debt ratio: 132.0%	Dividends
Return on equity: 16.0%	Yield: —
Cash ($ mil.): 20.9	Payout: —
Current ratio: 1.66	Market value ($ mil.): 414.8
Long-term debt ($ mil.): 290.0	R&D as % of sales: —
No. of shares (mil.): 25.6	Advertising as % of sales: —

Stock History

NASDAQ (GS): GTLS

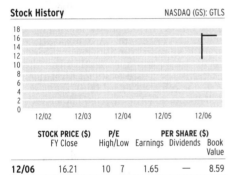

	STOCK PRICE ($) FY Close	P/E High/Low		PER SHARE ($) Earnings	Dividends	Book Value
12/06	16.21	10	7	1.65	—	8.59

Cherokee, Inc.

Cherokee has a license to make money. The company licenses its trademarks, which include Cherokee, Sideout, and Carole Little, to retailers and wholesalers of apparel, footwear, and accessories. The key premises behind Cherokee's business are that large retailers can source merchandise more efficiently than individual brand owners and that licensed brands can sell better for retailers than private labels. In addition to licensing its own brands, Cherokee helps other brand owners gain licensing contracts. Target, the company's largest customer, accounts for more than 40% of Cherokee's royalty revenue; other licensees include TJX, Zellers (in Canada), and Tesco (in Europe).

Royalties ordinarily account for all of Cherokee's sales. In fiscal 2007, however, the company recorded about 45% of its revenue from the sale of a contract involving the licensing of the Mossimo brand. Cherokee sought to buy Mossimo in 2006, but the company dropped its bid after rival Iconix Brand Group agreed to pay Cherokee about $33 million for its share of Mossimo's royalty from its license to Target. (Cherokee had helped establish Mossimo's deal with Target.)

Although it was unsuccessful in its effort to buy Mossimo, Cherokee has indicated that it will continue to consider acquisitions. Licensing its trademarks in markets outside the US is another key to the company's growth strategy. In 2007 the company signed a licensing agreement with Comercial Mexicana, a leading retailer in Mexico, for use of the Cherokee brand on clothing, apparel, and accessories.

At the same time, Cherokee is considering other ways to increase shareholder value. It announced in December 2007 that it had hired a financial adviser to help evaluate options that could include a sale of the company.

Cherokee chairman and CEO Robert Margolis has a 12% stake in the company.

EXECUTIVES

Chairman and CEO: Robert Margolis, age 59
President, Operations: Howard Siegel, age 52
CFO: Russell J. Riopelle, age 43
EVP Brand Development: Sandi Stuart, age 55
SVP: Larry Sass, age 45
SVP Brand Development: Anthony Damiani
VP Marketing: Mark Nawrocki, age 39
Corporate Secretary: Carol Gratzke, age 57
Global Brand Director: Jessica Cramer
Brand Director, Mexico and Central and South America: Lourdes Mestre
Auditors: Moss Adams, LLP

LOCATIONS

HQ: Cherokee, Inc.
6835 Valjean Ave., Van Nuys, CA 91406
Phone: 818-908-9868   **Fax:** 818-908-9191
Web: www.cherokeegroup.com

2007 Sales

	$ mil.	% of total
North America	62.1	81
Europe	14.4	19
Other regions	0.1	—
Total	**76.6**	**100**

PRODUCTS/OPERATIONS

2007 Sales

	$ mil.	% of total
Royalties	43.6	57
Sale of Mossimo finder's fee contract	33.0	43
Total	**76.6**	**100**

Selected Trademarks

All That Jazz
Carole Little
Cherokee
Chorus Line
CLII
Molly Malloy
Saint Tropez-West
Sideout
Sideout Sport

COMPETITORS

The Gap	Martha Stewart Living
Iconix Brand Group	NIKE
Levi Strauss	Quiksilver
Liz Claiborne	VF

HISTORICAL FINANCIALS

Company Type: Public

Income Statement				FYE: January 31
	REVENUE ($ mil.)	NET INCOME ($ mil.)	NET PROFIT MARGIN	EMPLOYEES
1/07	76.6	34.8	45.4%	18
1/06	42.7	18.3	42.9%	17
1/05	38.9	17.2	44.2%	16
1/04	36.3	14.2	39.1%	—
1/03	33.1	13.0	39.3%	17
Annual Growth	23.3%	27.9%	—	1.4%

2007 Year-End Financials

Debt ratio: —	Dividends
Return on equity: 117.7%	Yield: 5.8%
Cash ($ mil.): 44.6	Payout: 64.9%
Current ratio: 2.06	Market value ($ mil.): 393.7
Long-term debt ($ mil.): —	R&D as % of sales: —
No. of shares (mil.): 8.9	Advertising as % of sales: —

Stock History

NASDAQ (GS): CHKE

	STOCK PRICE ($) FY Close	P/E High/Low		PER SHARE ($) Earnings	Dividends	Book Value
1/07	44.17	12	9	3.93	2.55	4.06
1/06	39.49	19	15	2.07	2.15	2.62
1/05	33.39	19	10	1.97	1.72	2.54
1/04	20.23	14	9	1.68	0.38	3.16
1/03	15.15	15	8	1.54	—	1.43
Annual Growth	30.7%	—	—	26.4%	88.6%	29.8%

Chipotle Mexican Grill

This company is spicing up the restaurant business. Chipotle Mexican Grill operates a chain of more than 580 quick-casual Mexican eateries in almost 30 states. Customers can build a 1-1/4 pound burrito or taco from a lineup that includes chicken, steak, barbecue, or free-range pork, as well as beans, rice, guacamole, and various other veggies and salsas. The company maintains that with extras its menu offers more than 65,000 choices. Chipotle also serves chips and salsa, beer, and margaritas. Many of the eateries can be found in urban retail areas; nearly all of the restaurants are company-owned.

Chipotle distinguishes itself from its competitors by offering "food with integrity" — that is, it uses animal products that are naturally raised and antibiotic free. It also uses only fresh vegetables and beans (organic whenever possible) and made-on-site sauces. In addition Chipotle has no "corporate" look to its restaurants, preferring to design and build individual outlets that suit their space.

CEO Steve Ells, who trained at the Culinary Institute of America, was working in the kitchen of San Francisco's Stars restaurant when he decided to switch from gourmet food to burritos.

His father loaned him the money to open his first store, and later invested $2 million in the growing operation. Chipotle had expanded to 14 locations when McDonald's acquired the business in 1998. After funding Chipotle's rapid expansion, the Golden Arches spun off a 35% stake in the business through an IPO in 2006 and later divested its remaining shares.

EXECUTIVES

Chairman and CEO: M. Steven (Steve) Ells, age 43, $870,602 pay
President, COO, and Director: Montgomery F. (Monty) Moran, age 41
CFO and Chief Development Officer: John R. (Jack) Hartung, age 50, $544,187 pay
Chief Administrative Officer: Robert D. (Bob) Wilner, age 53, $431,817 pay
Executive Director, Human Resources: Ann Dowell
Director, IT: Joel Chrisman
Director, Marketing: Jim Adams
Director, Operations: Lisa Crosby
Director, Public Relations: Chris Arnold
Director, Purchasing: Ann Daniels
Investor Relations: Brian Prenoveau
Investor Relations: Thomas (Tom) Ryan
Auditors: Ernst & Young LLP

LOCATIONS

HQ: Chipotle Mexican Grill, Inc.
1543 Wazee St., Ste. 200, Denver, CO 80202
Phone: 303-595-4000   **Fax:** 303-595-4014
Web: www.chipotle.com

2006 Locations

	No.
California	79
Ohio	71
Texas	65
Colorado	61
Illinois	49
Minnesota	39
Virginia	25
Arizona	24
Florida	23
Maryland	23
New York	17
Kansas	15
Georgia	11
Missouri	11
Indiana	10
Wisconsin	9
Washington	8
Nebraska	7
Michigan	6
Oregon	6
Washington, DC	6
Kentucky	5
Nevada	5
New Jersey	2
North Carolina	2
Massachusetts	1
Pennsylvania	1
Total	**581**

COMPETITORS

ABP Corporation	Panda Restaurant Group
Arby's	Panera Bread
Del Taco	Qdoba
Einstein Noah Restaurant Group	Quiznos
El Pollo Loco	Red Robin
Fresh Enterprises	Rubio's Restaurants
Moe's Southwest Grill	Subway
Noodles & Company	Taco Bell
	Taco Del Mar

HISTORICAL FINANCIALS

Company Type: Public

Income Statement

FYE: December 31

	REVENUE ($ mil.)	NET INCOME ($ mil.)	NET PROFIT MARGIN	EMPLOYEES
12/06	822.9	41.4	5.0%	15,000
12/05	627.7	37.7	6.0%	13,000
12/04	470.7	6.1	1.3%	—
12/03	315.5	(7.7)	—	—
12/02	204.6	(17.3)	—	—
Annual Growth	**41.6%**	—	—	**15.4%**

2006 Year-End Financials

Debt ratio: —
Return on equity: 10.6%
Cash ($ mil.): 153.6
Current ratio: 2.92
Long-term debt ($ mil.): —
No. of shares (mil.): 14.2
Dividends
  Yield: —
  Payout: —
Market value ($ mil.): 810.7
R&D as % of sales: —
Advertising as % of sales: —

Stock History

NYSE: CMG

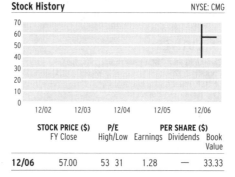

	STOCK PRICE ($) FY Close	P/E High/Low	PER SHARE ($) Earnings	Dividends	Book Value
12/06	57.00	53 31	1.28	—	33.33

Ciena Corporation

Ciena doesn't limit itself to just one color of the spectrum. The company makes transport and switching equipment that increases the capacity of long-distance fiber-optic networks by transmitting multiple light signals simultaneously over the same circuit. It also sells transport systems for metro and enterprise wide-area networks, as well as broadband access products that enable communications companies to deliver Internet protocol (IP) services, such as Voice over IP (VoIP), IP video, and DSL. Ciena serves telecom service providers, cable companies, large enterprises, and government entities.

Converged Ethernet infrastructure — including optical switches and transport systems for edge, metro, and core deployments, as well as edge devices that allow telecom service providers to transition from older technologies such as ATM and frame relay to Ethernet and IP/MPLS networks — account for more than 80% of Ciena's sales. Its Ethernet access unit provides Broadband Loop Carrier (BLC) systems and integrated broadband upgrade systems for legacy Digital Loop Carriers. Its global network services include network design, installation, and maintenance services, as well as consulting and vendor management.

Ciena makes about 70% of its sales in the US, but the company has seen international sales grow steadily as a percentage of revenue in recent years. Ciena counts telecommunications

carriers AT&T and Sprint Nextel among its major customers.

Early in 2008 the company agreed to purchase Ethernet specialist World Wide Packets for about $290 million in cash and stock.

HISTORY

David Huber founded CIENA in 1992 after General Instrument (now part of Motorola) shut the optical research lab he managed. He licensed technology from the company and began looking for funding. Two years later he had the backing of Sevin Rosen Funds and lined up an experienced manager, Patrick Nettles, to head the company. In 1995 CIENA (a name that Nettles thought up while taking a shower) won its first customer — Sprint. Sales to Sprint accounted for all of CIENA's revenues the next year.

CIENA went public in 1997, and that year it developed a second-generation product, MultiWave Sentry, which interfaces with more communications equipment and requires fewer transmission terminals. CIENA also diversified into short-distance optical transport with MultiWave Firefly. Huber took his stock profits (a reported $300 million) in 1997 and left over disagreements with Nettles concerning the company's research strategy.

In 1998 CIENA bought ATI Telecom International, an optical networking systems installer. Severe price pressure, brought on by several new competitors, led to a drop in profits that year. Telecom equipment maker Tellabs agreed to acquire CIENA in 1998, but the deal fell through after CIENA lost several key contracts. The next year CIENA spent over $1 billion on fiber-optic equipment makers Omnia and Lightera. The related charges caused losses for fiscal 1999. In 2000 the company signed up GTE (bought by Bell Atlantic to form Verizon Communications) spinoff Genuity as a customer.

The company bought another fiber optic equipment maker, privately held Cyras Systems, in a stock deal valued at about $1.1 billion the next year. Also in 2001, chief operating officer Gary Smith was appointed CEO; Patrick Nettles remained chairman. In 2002 CIENA acquired ONI Systems in a stock deal valued at about $400 million. CIENA bought smaller rivals ONI Systems, WaveSmith, and Akara in 2003 to gain ground in the market for optical equipment used to build metropolitan area networks and acquired Catena Networks and Internet Photonics in 2004. Later that year, the company changed the formatting of its name from CIENA to Ciena.

EXECUTIVES

Chairman: Patrick H. Nettles, age 64, $300,000 pay
President, CEO, and Director: Gary B. Smith, age 47, $812,500 pay
SVP and COO: Arthur D. Smith, age 41, $426,563 pay
SVP and CFO: James E. (Jim) Moylan Jr., age 56
SVP Products and Technology and CTO: Stephen B. Alexander, age 48, $426,563 pay
SVP, General Counsel, and Secretary: Russell B. Stevenson Jr., age 66
SVP and Chief Development Officer: Jesús León, age 60
SVP Corporate Development: James Frodsham, age 38
SVP Strategic Planning: Thomas (Tom) Mock
SVP Worldwide Sales: Michael G. (Mike) Aquino, age 51, $487,410 pay
VP, Controller, and Treasurer: Andrew C. Petrik, age 44
VP and General Manager, Europe, Middle East, and Africa: Francois Locoh-Donou
VP and Managing Director, Ciena Government Solutions: David L. (Dave) Peed
VP Worldwide Services and Support: Christopher Smith

Chief Communications Officer: Suzanne DuLong
VP Global Human Resources: Lynn Moore
Press Relations: Nicole Anderson
Investor Relations: Jessica Towns
Auditors: PricewaterhouseCoopers LLP

LOCATIONS

HQ: Ciena Corporation
1201 Winterson Rd., Linthicum, MD 21090
Phone: 410-865-8500 **Fax:** 410-694-5750
Web: www.ciena.com

2007 Sales

	$ mil.	% of total
US	553.6	71
Other countries	226.2	29
Total	**779.8**	**100**

PRODUCTS/OPERATIONS

2007 Sales

	$ mil.	% of total
Products	695.3	89
Services	84.5	11
Total	**779.8**	**100**

2007 Sales

	$ mil.	% of total
Converged Ethernet infrastructure	645.2	83
Global network services	84.5	11
Ethernet access	50.1	6
Total	**779.8**	**100**

Selected Products

Converged Ethernet infrastructure
  Packet internetworking (CN 5000, DN 7000)
  Transport and switching (CN 4200, CoreDirector, CoreStream)
Global network services
  Deployment services
  Maintenance and support
  Network analysis, design, and planning
  Network optimization
  Project management
Ethernet Access (CNX-5)
Network and service management tools (ON-Center)

COMPETITORS

ADC Telecommunications	NEC
ADVA	Nokia Siemens Networks
Alcatel-Lucent	Nortel Networks
Cisco Systems	Redback Networks
Ericsson	Sycamore Networks
Fujitsu	Tellabs
Hitachi	UTStarcom
Huawei Technologies	ZTE
MRV Communications	

HISTORICAL FINANCIALS

Company Type: Public

Income Statement

FYE: October 31

	REVENUE ($ mil.)	NET INCOME ($ mil.)	NET PROFIT MARGIN	EMPLOYEES
10/07	779.8	82.8	10.6%	1,797
10/06	564.1	0.6	0.1%	1,485
10/05	427.3	(435.7)	—	1,497
10/04	298.7	(789.5)	—	—
10/03	283.1	(386.5)	—	—
Annual Growth	**28.8%**	**—**	**—**	**9.6%**

2007 Year-End Financials

Debt ratio: 94.1%
Return on equity: 10.3%
Cash ($ mil.): 1,718.2
Current ratio: 2.70
Long-term debt ($ mil.): 800.0
No. of shares (mil.): 86.8
Dividends
  Yield: —
  Payout: —
Market value ($ mil.): 4,152.0
R&D as % of sales: —
Advertising as % of sales: —

Stock History

NASDAQ (GS): CIEN

	STOCK PRICE ($) FY Close	P/E High/Low		PER SHARE ($) Earnings	Dividends	Book Value
10/07	47.86	57	25	0.87	—	9.80
10/06	23.51	2,989	233	0.01	—	8.88
10/05	2.37	—	—	(5.32)	—	1.27
10/04	2.47	—	—	(10.57)	—	2.02
10/03	6.41	—	—	(6.09)	—	2.81
Annual Growth	**65.3%**			**—**	**—**	**36.6%**

Citi Trends

Citi Trends hopes to transport its customers to Trend City as quickly as possible. The urban fashion apparel and accessory chain operates about 320 stores in 20 US states focusing primarily on the African-American market. Its brand-name and private-label offerings — which include hip-hop jeans and oversized T-shirts; men's, women's, and children's clothing; shoes; housewares; and accessories — are sold at 20%-60% less than department and specialty stores' regular prices. Founded in 1946 as Allied Department Stores, the company was acquired by Hampshire Equity Partners and was renamed Citi Trends in 1999. The fast-growing company went public in 2005. Hampshire Equity Partners owns about 46% of Citi Trends.

The chain opened about 40 new stores last year — including its first in Indiana and Missouri — and plans to open as many as 48 new stores in the coming year.

Citi Trends purchased a new distribution center in South Carolina in late 2005, expecting the 286,500-sq.-ft. property to be large enough to support an additional 250 to 300 stores; allowing room for future company expansion.

EXECUTIVES

Chairman and CEO: R. Edward (Ed) Anderson, age 57, $357,471 pay
President and Chief Merchandising Officer: George A. Bellino, age 60, $257,408 pay
SVP Store Operations: James A. Dunn, age 50, $174,763 pay
SVP and CFO: Bruce D. Smith, age 48
SVP Human Resources: Ivy D. Council, age 50
Interim Principal Financial and Accounting Officer and Director of Financial Reporting: Christopher Bergen, age 34, $89,423 pay
Auditors: KPMG LLP

LOCATIONS

HQ: Citi Trends, Inc.
102 Fahm St., Savannah, GA 31401
Phone: 912-236-1561 **Fax:** 912-443-3674
Web: www.cititrends.com

2007 Stores

	No.
Georgia	50
South Carolina	33
North Carolina	32
Texas	25
Florida	23
Louisiana	23
Alabama	21
Mississippi	20
Virginia	15
Tennessee	11
Ohio	7
Arkansas	6
Indiana	4
Maryland	4
Kentucky	2
Missouri	1
Total	**277**

PRODUCTS/OPERATIONS

2007 Sales

	% of total
Women's	36
Children's	26
Men's	22
Accessories	14
Home decor	2
Total	**100**

COMPETITORS

Burlington Coat Factory	Kmart
Dollar General	Rainbow Apparel
DOTS	Ross Stores
Family Dollar Stores	TJX Companies
Finish Line	Wal-Mart

HISTORICAL FINANCIALS

Company Type: Public

Income Statement

FYE: Saturday nearest January 31

	REVENUE ($ mil.)	NET INCOME ($ mil.)	NET PROFIT MARGIN	EMPLOYEES
1/07	381.9	21.4	5.6%	3,000
1/06	289.8	14.2	4.9%	2,800
1/05	203.4	7.3	3.6%	—
1/04	157.2	5.9	3.8%	—
1/03	124.9	5.0	4.0%	—
Annual Growth	**32.2%**	**43.8%**	**—**	**7.1%**

2007 Year-End Financials

Debt ratio: 2.5%
Return on equity: 21.2%
Cash ($ mil.): 77.7
Current ratio: 2.27
Long-term debt ($ mil.): 3.0
No. of shares (mil.): 13.8
Dividends
  Yield: —
  Payout: —
Market value ($ mil.): 544.1
R&D as % of sales: —
Advertising as % of sales: —

Stock History

NASDAQ (GS): CTRN

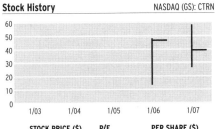

	STOCK PRICE ($) FY Close	P/E High/Low		PER SHARE ($) Earnings	Dividends	Book Value
1/07	39.41	38	18	1.51	—	8.56
1/06	46.71	44	13	1.08	—	6.44
Annual Growth	**(15.6%)**	**—**	**—**	**39.8%**	**—**	**33.0%**

Citizens South Banking Corporation

Never mind the region, Citizens South Banking Corporation is more concerned with interest rising again. The institution is the holding company for Citizens South Bank, which provides banking products and services from more than a dozen full-service locations in the central Piedmont area of North Carolina. Deposit products include checking, savings, and money market accounts; CDs; and IRAs. The company writes real estate loans (about 80% of its loan portfolio), consumer loans, and business loans. The bank's subsidiary, Citizens South Financial Services (dba Citizens South Investment Services), sells uninsured financial products.

Citizens South Banking Corporation has worked to broaden its offerings since its initial public offering in 1998. It lowered the number of one- to four-family residential mortgages from about two-thirds of its loan portfolio in 2000 to about 15% in 2006, while increasing the number of nonresidential real estate loans.

Executive officers and directors (including chairman David Hoyle, also a North Carolina state senator) collectively own nearly 20% of the company.

EXECUTIVES

Chairman: David W. Hoyle, age 68
Vice Chairman: Ben R. Rudisill II, age 63
President, CEO, and Director, Citizens South Banking Corporation; President and CEO, Citizens South Bank: Kim S. Price, age 51, $235,000 pay
EVP, CFO, and Treasurer, Citizens South Banking Corporation and Citizens South Bank: Gary F. Hoskins, age 44, $112,508 pay
EVP, Chief Administrative Officer, and Secretary, Citizens South Banking Corporation and Citizens South Bank: Paul L. Teem Jr., age 59, $111,632 pay
EVP, Citizens South Bank: Daniel M. Boyd IV, age 45, $124,928 pay
EVP, Citizens South Bank: Vance B. (Burt) Brinson Jr., age 60, $135,020 pay
EVP, Citizens South Bank: Dennis O. Livingston, age 52
EVP and Director; EVP, Citizens South Bank: David C. McGuirt, age 65
SVP and Chief Credit Officer, Citizens South Bank: Michael R. Maguire, age 49, $110,272 pay
SVP, Citizens South Bank: Kimberly G. Cooke, age 38
VP Human Resources, Citizens South Bank: Betty B. Gaddis
Auditors: Cherry, Bekaert & Holland, LLP

LOCATIONS

HQ: Citizens South Banking Corporation
519 S. New Hope Rd., Gastonia, NC 28054
Phone: 704-868-5200   **Fax:** 704-868-5226
Web: www.citizenssouth.com

PRODUCTS/OPERATIONS

2006 Sales

	$ mil.	% of total
Interest		
Loans	37.5	76
Investment securities	2.8	6
Mortgage-backed & related securities	2.6	5
Noninterest		
Fee income on deposit accounts	2.9	6
Fee income on mortgage banking & lending activities	1.3	3
Increase in value of bank-owned life insurance	0.8	2
Other	1.2	2
Total	**49.1**	**100**

COMPETITORS

American Community Bancshares
Bank of America
BB&T
Carolina Trust Bank
Clover Community Bankshares
Coddle Creek Financial
First Charter
First Citizens BancShares
First Trust Bank
NewBridge Bancorp
Peoples Bancorp (NC)
RBC Centura Banks
Uwharrie Capital
Wachovia

HISTORICAL FINANCIALS

Company Type: Public

Income Statement

	ASSETS ($ mil.)	NET INCOME ($ mil.)	INCOME AS % OF ASSETS	EMPLOYEES
				FYE: December 31
12/06	743.4	5.4	0.7%	151
12/05	701.1	3.3	0.5%	160
12/04	509.0	3.0	0.6%	—
12/03	495.8	3.4	0.7%	—
12/02	492.6	4.5	0.9%	114
Annual Growth	**10.8%**	**4.7%**	**—**	**7.3%**

2006 Year-End Financials

Equity as % of assets: 11.6%
Return on assets: 0.7%
Return on equity: 6.3%
Long-term debt ($ mil.): 78.9
No. of shares (mil.): 8.1
Market value ($ mil.): 105.0
Dividends
Yield: 2.3%
Payout: 43.3%
Sales ($ mil.): 49.1
R&D as % of sales: —
Advertising as % of sales: —

Stock History

NASDAQ (GM): CSBC

	STOCK PRICE ($) FY Close	P/E High/Low		PER SHARE ($) Earnings	Dividends	Book Value
12/06	12.94	21	18	0.67	0.29	10.60
12/05	11.95	32	25	0.45	0.14	10.16
12/04	14.27	38	33	0.38	0.19	7.99
12/03	13.95	39	26	0.39	0.24	9.67
12/02	10.20	20	19	0.51	0.05	10.63
Annual Growth	**6.1%**	**—**	**—**	**7.1%**	**55.2%**	**(0.1%)**

CKX, Inc.

CKX is ready to sing *Viva Las Vegas*, but any singing will be critiqued by Simon of *American Idol* fame. The company controls 85% of Elvis Presley Enterprises, which manages the King's estate and licenses his likeness, songs, and name, as well as operating tours of Graceland. The company also owns 19 Entertainment, the firm responsible for the *American Idol* TV show, and has a "long-term agreement" with *Idol* creator Simon Fuller. Additionally, CKX has a stake in the name, image, likeness, and intellectual property of Muhammad Ali. Entertainment impresario Robert Sillerman owns 35% of CKX. Sillerman and Fuller have made a $1.33 billion offer to take the company private with other members of CKX management.

CKX subsidiary Morra, Brezner, Steinberg & Tenenbaum Entertainment (MBST), a talent agency, represents several big name stars.

MBST manages comedic actors like Robin Williams and Billy Crystal and produces films and TV programs. In 2006 CKX paid $50 million in cash for an 80% stake in Muhammad Ali Enterprises. CKX purchased 19 Entertainment and sealed a deal with its founder and face man, Simon Fuller, for about $156 million in cash and stock in 2005.

The company (formerly Sports Entertainment Enterprises) once owned All-American SportPark but now hums a different tune. The firm changed its name from Sports Entertainment Enterprises to CKX; CK stands for "content is king" while X is Sillerman's trademark. Sillerman founded radio station operator SFX Broadcasting (he later sold the company) and its concert promoting subsidiary SFX Entertainment (now part of Clear Channel Communications).

EXECUTIVES

Chairman and CEO: Robert F. X. Sillerman, age 56
President: Michael G. Ferrel, age 48
SEVP, COO, and Director: Mitchell J. Slater, age 44
SEVP, Director Legal and Governmental Affairs, and Board Member: Howard J. Tytel, age 58
EVP, CFO, Treasurer, and Director: Thomas P. Benson, age 42
EVP, Chief Corporate Development Officer, and Secretary: Kraig G. Fox
Director; CEO, 19 Entertainment: Simon Fuller, age 44
CEO, Elvis Presley Enterprises: Jack Soden, age 58
Auditors: Deloitte & Touche LLC

LOCATIONS

HQ: CKX, Inc.
650 Madison Ave., New York, NY 10022
Phone: 212-838-3100   **Fax:** 212-872-1473
Web: ir.ckx.com

PRODUCTS/OPERATIONS

2007 Sales

	$ mil.	% of total
19 Entertainment	193.0	72
Presley business		
Graceland operations	40.9	15
Royalties & licensing	21.9	8
Ali business	6.2	2
MBST	4.9	2
Total	**266.8**	**100**

COMPETITORS

Brillstein-Grey
CAA
The Endeavor Agency
The Firm
Gersh Agency
Herschend Entertainment
IMG
Sony/ATV
United Talent
Warning Management Services
William Morris

HISTORICAL FINANCIALS

Company Type: Public

Income Statement

FYE: December 31

	REVENUE ($ mil.)	NET INCOME ($ mil.)	NET PROFIT MARGIN	EMPLOYEES
12/07	266.8	12.1	4.6%	—
12/06	219.7	14.7	6.7%	95
12/05	166.6	10.3	6.2%	67
12/04	0.0	(0.1)	—	487
12/03	0.0	(0.1)	—	546
Annual Growth	26.5%	—	—	(44.2%)

2007 Year-End Financials

Debt ratio: 38.4%
Return on equity: 4.5%
Cash ($ mil.): 57.1
Current ratio: 1.80
Long-term debt ($ mil.): 102.4
No. of shares (mil.): 95.4
Dividends
　Yield: —
　Payout: —
Market value ($ mil.): 1,104.4
R&D as % of sales: —
Advertising as % of sales: —

Stock History

NASDAQ (GS): CKXE

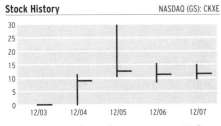

	STOCK PRICE ($) FY Close	P/E High/Low		PER SHARE ($) Earnings	Dividends	Book Value
12/07	11.58	135	88	0.11	—	3.04
12/06	11.32	191	106	0.08	—	3.94
12/05	12.54	—	—	(0.35)	—	3.57
12/04	9.00	—	—	(0.03)	—	0.00
12/03	0.05	—	—	(0.02)	—	0.00
Annual Growth	290.1%	—	—	—	—	(7.7%)

Cleco Corporation

Down in the Louisiana bayous, Cleco comes alive with the click of a light-switch. The holding company's utility unit, Cleco Power, generates, transmits, and distributes electricity to 268,000 residential and business customers in 104 communities in Louisiana. Cleco Power has a generating capacity of more than 1,350 MW from its interests in fossil-fueled power plants. It also purchases power from other utilities and energy marketers, and it sells some excess power to wholesale customers. Subsidiary Cleco Midstream Resources develops merchant power plants and offers energy management services.

In 2005 the company estimated costs for repairing damage caused by Hurricane Katrina to be up to $125 million.

Cleco has sold its engineering and construction assets and has exited the energy trading business. The company is also selling some non-core independent power production assets, and it has sold its natural gas transportation and oil and gas production assets.

In 2005 Cleco's indirect subsidiary Perryville Energy Partners, L.L.C. sold its 718-megawatt plant to Entergy Louisiana, Inc. for roughly $162 million.

In 2006 Cleco Power began constructing an additional 600-MW power plant at its Rodemacher facility.

EXECUTIVES

Chairman: J. Patrick Garrett, age 63
President, CEO and Director:
　Michael H. (Mike) Madison, age 58, $422,116 pay
SVP and CFO: Kathleen F. Nolen, age 46, $220,615 pay
SVP Corporate Services: George W. Bausewine, age 52
SVP, Employee and Corporate Services, Cleco and Cleco Power: Catherine C. Powell, age 49
SVP Governmental Affairs and Chief Diversity Officer: Jeffrey W. Hall, age 56
SVP and COO Cleco Midstream Resources:
　Samuel H. (Sam) Charlton III, age 61, $227,000 pay
SVP, General Counsel and Director of Regulatory Compliance: Wade A. Hoefling, age 52
VP and Chief Accounting Officer: R. Russell Davis, age 49
VP Regulated Generation Development:
　William G. (Bill) Fontenot, age 44, $210,008 pay
President and COO Cleco Power: Dilek Samil, age 51, $304,078 pay
Manager, Corporate and Strategic Communications: Susan Broussard
Investor Relations Contact: Mike Burns
Auditors: PricewaterhouseCoopers LLP

LOCATIONS

HQ: Cleco Corporation
　2030 Donahue Ferry Rd., Pineville, LA 71360
Phone: 318-484-7400　　**Fax:** 318-484-7488
Web: www.cleco.com

Cleco provides electricity to customers in 104 communities in central and southeastern Louisiana. The company has nonregulated operations in Louisiana and Texas.

PRODUCTS/OPERATIONS

2006 Sales

	$ mil.	% of total
Fuel cost recovery	617.3	62
Electric operations	342.1	34
Electric customer credits	4.7	1
Intercompany revenue	2.0	—
Other	30.1	3
Total	**996.2**	**100**

Selected Subsidiaries

Cleco Midstream Resources LLC
　Acadia Power Holding LLC (power generation)
　Cleco Evangeline LLC (power generation)
　Cleco Generation Services LLC (power plant services)
Cleco Power LLC (formerly Cleco Utility Group, regulated utility operations)

COMPETITORS

AEP	Entergy
Aquila	ONEOK
Atmos Energy	PG&E
CenterPoint Energy	Southern Company
Duke Energy	Xcel Energy

HISTORICAL FINANCIALS

Company Type: Public

Income Statement

FYE: December 31

	REVENUE ($ mil.)	NET INCOME ($ mil.)	NET PROFIT MARGIN	EMPLOYEES
12/06	996.2	64.8	6.5%	2,067
12/05	914.0	59.1	6.5%	1,158
12/04	59.1	12.5	21.2%	1,165
12/03	876.2	(34.9)	—	1,203
12/02	724.1	71.9	9.9%	1,214
Annual Growth	8.3%	(2.6%)	—	14.2%

2006 Year-End Financials

Debt ratio: —
Return on equity: —
Cash ($ mil.): 144.9
Current ratio: 1.11
Long-term debt ($ mil.): 519.3
No. of shares (mil.): 59.9
Dividends
　Yield: 3.6%
　Payout: —
Market value ($ mil.): 1,511.7
R&D as % of sales: —
Advertising as % of sales: —

Stock History

NYSE: CNL

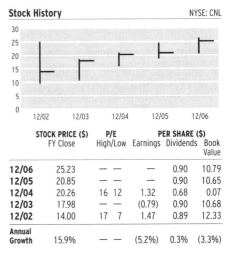

	STOCK PRICE ($) FY Close	P/E High/Low		PER SHARE ($) Earnings	Dividends	Book Value
12/06	25.23	—	—	—	0.90	10.79
12/05	20.85	—	—	—	0.90	10.65
12/04	20.26	16	12	1.32	0.68	0.07
12/03	17.98	—	—	(0.79)	0.90	10.68
12/02	14.00	17	7	1.47	0.89	12.33
Annual Growth	15.9%	—	—	(5.2%)	0.3%	(3.3%)

Coeur d'Alene Mines

Coeur d'Alene Mines gets to the heart of the matter when it comes to precious metals. A leading primary silver producer, the company holds interests in silver and gold properties in North America, South America, Africa, and Australia. It produces about 13 million ounces of silver and 115,000 ounces of gold annually. Coeur d'Alene has proved and probable reserves of about 215 million ounces of silver and 1.5 million ounces of gold. Coeur d'Alene produces most of its revenue from the Rochester mine in Nevada and the Cerro Bayo mine in Chile. In 2007 it bought Australian miner Bolnisi Gold and the Canadian Palmarejo in a deal valued at $1.1 billion.

Sales of silver account for about two-thirds of the company's revenue. Most of the its minerals are sold to bullion-trading banks and to smelters.

Besides its primary operations in the US and Chile, Coeur d'Alene has interests in exploration-stage properties in Argentina, Bolivia, Chile, Tanzania, and the US. The company moved to expand its holdings in Australia in 2005. The following year, Coeur d'Alene sold its Coeur Silver Valley subsidiary (and its Galena mine) to U.S. Silver Corporation for $15 million.

The move came as the company began to look to redirect its attention to lower-cost and longer-life silver properties.

The combination with Bolnisi and Palmarejo created the world's largest primary silver producer. Those two companies are already linked in that Bolnsi owns almost three-quarters of Palmarejo, whose biggest asset is the Palmarejo silver and gold project in the state of Chihuahua, Mexico.

EXECUTIVES

Chairman, President, and CEO: Dennis E. Wheeler, age 64, $980,569 pay
EVP, CFO, and Treasurer: James A. Sabala, age 53, $397,375 pay
SVP and Chief Administrative Officer: Gary W. Banbury, age 54
SVP Exploration: Donald J. Birak, age 53, $322,461 pay
SVP North American Operations: Harry Cougher, age 64
SVP Project Development: Alan L. Wilder, age 58, $324,940 pay
SVP Corporate Development: Mitchell J. Krebs, age 36, $327,024 pay
VP, General Counsel, and Corporate Secretary: Kelli C. Kast, age 41
VP Finance: Sergio Ducoing
VP Human Resources: Larry A. Nelson
VP, Controller, and Chief Accounting Officer: Thomas T. (Tom) Angelos, age 50
Treasurer: Carolyn S. Turner, age 38
Director Investor Relations: Tony Ebersole
President, South American Operations: James K. Duff, age 62
Auditors: KPMG LLP

LOCATIONS

HQ: Coeur d'Alene Mines Corporation
400 Coeur d'Alene Mines Bldg., 505 Front Ave., Coeur d'Alene, ID 83816
Phone: 208-667-3511   **Fax:** 208-667-2213
Web: www.coeur.com

Coeur d'Alene has properties in Argentina, Australia, Bolivia, Chile, Tanzania, and the US (Alaska and Nevada).

2006 Sales

	$ mil.	% of total
US	102.4	47
Chile	50.3	23
Argentina	34.7	16
Australia	29.2	14
Total	**216.6**	**100**

PRODUCTS/OPERATIONS

2006 Sales

	$ mil.	% of total
Rochester	102.4	47
Cerro Bayo	50.3	23
Martha	34.7	16
Broken Hill	23.8	11
Endeavor	5.4	3
Total	**216.6**	**100**

2006 Sales

	$ mil.	% of total
Silver	147.8	68
Gold	68.8	32
Total	**216.6**	**100**

Selected Properties

Cerro Bayo (gold and silver, Chile)
Kensington (gold, Alaska)
Martha (silver, Argentina)
Palmarejo (gold and silver, Mexico)
Rochester (gold and silver, Nevada)

COMPETITORS

Agnico-Eagle
Barrick Gold
BHP Billiton
Hecla Mining
Kinross Gold
Meridian Gold
Newmont Mining
Peñoles
Vale Inco

HISTORICAL FINANCIALS

Company Type: Public

Income Statement

FYE: December 31

	REVENUE ($ mil.)	NET INCOME ($ mil.)	NET PROFIT MARGIN	EMPLOYEES
12/06	216.6	88.5	40.9%	931
12/05	172.3	10.6	6.2%	1,206
12/04	133.4	(16.9)	—	—
12/03	110.5	(66.2)	—	—
12/02	94.5	(81.2)	—	767
Annual Growth	**23.0%**	**—**	**—**	**5.0%**

2006 Year-End Financials

Debt ratio: 31.0%
Return on equity: 19.2%
Cash ($ mil.): 341.0
Current ratio: 7.55
Long-term debt ($ mil.): 180.0
No. of shares (mil.): 278.0
Dividends
  Yield: —
  Payout: —
Market value ($ mil.): 1,376.1
R&D as % of sales: —
Advertising as % of sales: —

Stock History

NYSE: CDE

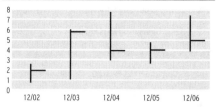

	STOCK PRICE ($) FY Close	P/E High	P/E Low	PER SHARE ($) Earnings	PER SHARE ($) Dividends	PER SHARE ($) Book Value
12/06	4.95	25	13	0.30	—	2.09
12/05	4.00	117	68	0.04	—	1.23
12/04	3.93	—	—	(0.08)	—	1.22
12/03	5.78	—	—	(0.39)	—	0.93
12/02	1.92	—	—	(1.04)	—	0.40
Annual Growth	**26.7%**	**—**	**—**	**—**	**—**	**51.3%**

Coffee Holding Co.

Coffee Holding Co. has brewed up the idea of selling a wide spectrum of raw and roasted Arabica coffee beans to wholesalers like Green Mountain Roasters as well as private-label coffees to foodservice suppliers such as Nash Finch. Coffee Holding imports its beans from Indonesia, Mexico, and South America through several dealers. In addition to producing private-label coffees for stores, the company also sells name brands including IL CLASSICO and S&W. Its Cafe Caribe espresso coffee targets the Hispanic market. The company has expanded its offerings through partnerships. CEO Andrew Gordon, son of company founder Sterling Gordon, and the Gordon family own about 60% of the company.

The company produces some 422 different private-label coffees for both food wholesalers and food retailers. It also offers specialty instant coffees, and instant cappuccinos and hot chocolates, as well as a line of tea products.

Green Mountain accounted for 25% of the company's sales in 2007; Sav-A-Lot accounted for 13%.

EXECUTIVES

President, CEO, CFO, Treasurer, and Director: Andrew Gordon, age 44, $321,422 pay
EVP Operations, Secretary, and Director: David Gordon, age 42, $274,631 pay
Director Specialty Coffee: Karen Gordon
Auditors: Lazar Levine & Felix LLP

LOCATIONS

HQ: Coffee Holding Co., Inc.
4401 1st Ave., Ste. 1507, Brooklyn, NY 11232
Phone: 718-832-0800   **Fax:** 718-832-0892
Web: www.coffeeholding.com

PRODUCTS/OPERATIONS

Selected Brands

Café Caribe
Café Supremo
Don Manuel
Fifth Avenue
IL CLASSICO
S&W
Via Roma

COMPETITORS

Caribou Coffee
The Coffee Bean
Community Coffee
Diedrich Coffee
Farmer Bros.
Folger
It's A Grind
Kraft Foods
Kroger
Nestlé
Nestlé USA
Peet's
Procter & Gamble
Rowland Coffee Roasters
S&D Coffee
Sara Lee Food & Beverage
Segafredo
Starbucks
Tully's Coffee

HISTORICAL FINANCIALS

Company Type: Public

Income Statement

FYE: October 31

	REVENUE ($ mil.)	NET INCOME ($ mil.)	NET PROFIT MARGIN	EMPLOYEES
10/06	51.2	0.7	1.4%	79
10/05	41.5	1.2	2.9%	74
10/04	28.0	0.9	3.2%	—
10/03	20.2	0.6	3.0%	—
10/02	17.4	0.8	4.6%	33
Annual Growth	**31.0%**	**(3.3%)**	**—**	**24.4%**

2006 Year-End Financials

Debt ratio: —
Return on equity: 6.4%
Cash ($ mil.): 5.4
Current ratio: 2.13
Long-term debt ($ mil.): —
No. of shares (mil.): 5.5
Dividends
  Yield: —
  Payout: —
Market value ($ mil.): 21.6
R&D as % of sales: —
Advertising as % of sales: —

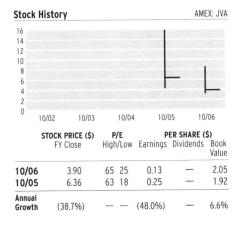

	STOCK PRICE ($) FY Close	P/E High/Low	PER SHARE ($) Earnings	Dividends	Book Value
10/06	3.90	65 25	0.13	—	2.05
10/05	6.36	63 18	0.25	—	1.92
Annual Growth	(38.7%)	— —	(48.0%)	—	6.6%

Coinstar, Inc.

Coinstar takes the contents of your penny jar and turns it into real money. The company owns and operates more than 13,500 coin-counting machines in the US, Canada, and the UK, and some 300,000 entertainment services (skill-crane, bulk vending, and kiddie ride) machines across the US and Mexico. Coinstar operates more than 14,000 point-of-sale terminals and around 400 stand-alone e-payment kiosks in the US and the UK. The coin-counting units are located mainly in supermarkets (such as Kroger and SUPERVALU); the entertainment services machines can be found in more than 33,000 retail locations including Wal-Mart and Kmart stores. Coinstar also offers prepaid services cards, money transfers, and gift cards.

Coinstar's machines charge transaction fees (of which retail partners receive a portion) and transmit information to the company daily, reducing downtime by alerting field service staff when collection or maintenance is necessary. In 2005 consumers processed more than $2.6 billion worth of coins through the company's coin-counting machines.

Coinstar has transitioned from a one-product company — offering just coin-counting services — to a business with a variety of products and services through several key acquisitions. Its most recent service allows customers to change their coins for retailer gift cards or eCertificates, a move that will cheer anyone who has ever stood in line behind someone counting out exact change. Partners include Eddie Bauer and Amazon in the US and British greeting card chain Clinton Cards.

In a move designed to provide greater access to drugstore customers, Coinstar bought Chicago-based CellCards of Illinois in 2004. CellCards offers a set of prepaid products, including wireless, long-distance, and MasterCard cards, in addition to bill payment capabilities for public services such as utilities. Later that year Coinstar acquired ACMI Holdings and its two subsidiaries, American Coin Merchandising and Wellspring Capital Management, for $235 million in cash. ACMI Holdings, operating as SugarLoaf Creations, owns and operates coin-operated amusement vending equipment such as plush toy "grabbers," kiddie rides, and video games.

In 2005 Coinstar acquired Mundo Communications Network (dba El Toro Prepaid), adding retail accounts and additional pay-as-you-go products to its e-payment services. Later that year it acquired Amusement Factory, an amusement vending machine company based in California with machines in some 14,000 stores across the country.

Its acquisition of a nearly 50% interest in McDonald's Corporation subsidiary Redbox Automated Retail and a stake in Video Vending New York (dba DVDXpress) gave it a toehold into the self-service DVD rental business.

Continuing its investment streak, Coinstar bought Travelex Holdings' Travelex Money Transfer business for $27 million in cash (presumably not in change). Travelex Money Transfer operates in nearly 140 countries.

It also agreed to buy GroupEx Financial Corporation, a money transfer service that operates between the US and Latin America.

EXECUTIVES

Chairman: Keith D. Grinstein, age 47
CEO and Director: David W. (Dave) Cole, age 60, $400,014 pay
CFO: Brian V. Turner, age 47, $350,168 pay
SVP and General Manager, Worldwide Coin: Alexander C. (Alex) Camara, age 42
SVP Sales: James C. (Jim) Blakely, age 51, $247,572 pay
SVP; General Manager, Entertainment Services: Michael J. Skinner, age 53
SVP Operations: John P. Reilly, age 42
SVP; General Manager, E-Payment Services: Stephen J. (Steve) Verleye, age 48, $226,044 pay
VP, General Counsel, and Corporate Secretary: Donald R. (Don) Rench, age 40
VP Human Resources: Denise Rubin
VP Marketing: Gretchen J. Marks, age 46
Chief Accounting Officer and Controller: Richard C. (Rich) Deck, age 37
Director Public Relations: Marci Maule
Auditors: KPMG LLP

LOCATIONS

HQ: Coinstar, Inc.
  1800 114th Ave. SE, Bellevue, WA 98004
Phone: 425-943-8000   **Fax:** 425-637-0045
Web: www.coinstar.com

2006 Sales

	$ mil.	% of total
North America	500.4	94
International	34.0	6
Total	**534.4**	**100**

PRODUCTS/OPERATIONS

Select Subsidiaries

ACMI Asia Inc.
Adventure Vending Inc.
Coinstar Entertainment Services, Inc.
Bellword GmbH (Germany)
CellCards LLC
Coin-Op Factory Inc.
Coinstar E-Payment Services Inc.
Coinstar International, Inc.
Coinstar Money Transfer Limited (UK)
El Toro Prepaid Inc.
Entertainment Vending Management, LLC
Folz Vending, Inc.
Sesame Holdings, Inc.
Southwest Entertainment Vending Inc.
Sugarloaf Amusement Vending, S. de R.L. de C.V. (Mexico)
Telepay S.A. (Spain)
Travelex Money Transfer LLC

COMPETITORS

Cash Systems
Cash Technologies
Cummins-American
Dollar Financial
Global Payment Technologies
Safeway

HISTORICAL FINANCIALS

Company Type: Public

Income Statement

	REVENUE ($ mil.)	NET INCOME ($ mil.)	NET PROFIT MARGIN	EMPLOYEES
12/06	534.4	18.6	3.5%	1,900
12/05	459.7	22.3	4.9%	2,000
12/04	307.1	20.4	6.6%	—
12/03	176.1	19.6	11.1%	—
12/02	155.7	58.5	37.6%	557
Annual Growth	36.1%	(24.9%)	—	35.9%

FYE: December 31

2006 Year-End Financials

Debt ratio: 59.9%
Return on equity: 6.0%
Cash ($ mil.): 178.2
Current ratio: 1.37
Long-term debt ($ mil.): 192.4
No. of shares (mil.): 27.8
Dividends
  Yield: —
  Payout: —
Market value ($ mil.): 850.3
R&D as % of sales: —
Advertising as % of sales: —

Stock History   NASDAQ (GS): CSTR

	STOCK PRICE ($) FY Close	P/E High/Low	PER SHARE ($) Earnings	Dividends	Book Value
12/06	30.57	52 33	0.66	—	11.55
12/05	22.83	32 20	0.86	—	10.59
12/04	26.83	30 16	0.93	—	8.96
12/03	18.11	29 13	0.90	—	5.38
12/02	22.65	14 8	2.58	—	4.82
Annual Growth	7.8%	— —	(28.9%)	—	24.4%

Comarco, Inc.

Comarco helps keep the wireless world working. The company, operating through its subsidiary, Comarco Wireless Technologies, provides wireless network monitoring products to telecommunications carriers and equipment vendors. Its testing equipment and billing system software help operators of cellular and PCS networks optimize their systems and monitor quality. Comarco also installs and maintains emergency call boxes. The company's other products include a line of battery chargers, under the ChargeSource brand name, that charge nearly all cellular phones, laptop computers, and handheld devices.

Comarco in 2006 sold its 18% interest in SwissQual, a Switzerland-based wireless test and measurement company, to a subsidiary of UK telecom equipment manufacturer Spirent Communications. SwissQual is continuing to distribute Comarco's Seven.Five testing equipment in European markets.

EXECUTIVES

President, CEO, and Director: Thomas A. Franza, age 64, $652,916 pay
SVP and General Manager, Wireless Test Solutions: Mark Chapman, age 45
Corporate Secretary and VP Administration: Peggy L. Vessell, age 62
VP and CFO: Daniel R. Lutz, age 42, $331,930 pay
VP and CTO, Comarco Wireless Technologies: Thomas W. Lanni, age 54
VP Call Box Systems, Comarco Wireless Technologies: Sebastian E. Gutierrez, age 45
VP Supply Chain Management, Comarco Wireless Technologies: John McMunn, age 57, $280,000 pay
VP Corporate Quality: Bahram Nazardad, age 51
VP Comarco Wireless Technologies, Inc.: Fredrik L. Torstensson, age 37
Auditors: BDO Seidman, LLP

LOCATIONS

HQ: Comarco, Inc.
25541 Commercentre Dr., Lake Forest, CA 92630
Phone: 949-599-7400   **Fax:** 949-599-1415
Web: www.comarco.com

2007 Sales

	$ mil.	% of total
Americas		
North America	38.6	81
Others	2.2	5
Europe	6.3	13
Asia/Pacific	.7	1
Total	**47.8**	**100**

PRODUCTS/OPERATIONS

2007 Sales

	$ mil.	% of total
Products	42.7	89
Services	5.1	11
Total	**47.8**	**100**

Selected Subsidiaries

Comarco Wireless International, Inc. (formerly known as Comarco Wireless Europe, Inc.)
Comarco Wireless Technologies, Inc.

COMPETITORS

Agilent Technologies	Ericsson
Andrew Corporation	Fellowes
Arrow Resources	Hubbell
Ascom Holding	Mobility Electronics
Belkin	Spirent

HISTORICAL FINANCIALS

Company Type: Public

Income Statement

FYE: January 31

	REVENUE ($ mil.)	NET INCOME ($ mil.)	NET PROFIT MARGIN	EMPLOYEES
1/07	47.8	1.8	3.8%	120
1/06	46.9	6.3	13.4%	142
1/05	29.2	(10.1)	—	—
1/04	34.3	(1.3)	—	—
1/03	36.8	(10.6)	—	143
Annual Growth	**6.8%**	**—**	**—**	**(4.3%)**

2007 Year-End Financials

Debt ratio: —	Dividends
Return on equity: 4.9%	Yield: —
Cash ($ mil.): 27.3	Payout: —
Current ratio: 4.21	Market value ($ mil.): 56.4
Long-term debt ($ mil.): —	R&D as % of sales: —
No. of shares (mil.): 7.4	Advertising as % of sales: —

Stock History   NASDAQ (GM): CMRO

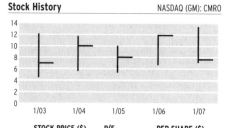

	STOCK PRICE ($) FY Close	P/E High/Low		PER SHARE ($) Earnings	Dividends	Book Value
1/07	7.65	55	30	0.24	—	5.15
1/06	11.85	14	8	0.85	—	4.86
1/05	8.02	—	—	(1.37)	—	4.01
1/04	10.01	—	—	(0.17)	—	5.24
1/03	6.97	—	—	(1.51)	—	5.31
Annual Growth	**2.4%**	**—**	**—**	**—**	**—**	**(0.7%)**

Commercial Vehicle Group

CB radio lingo might have gone the way of mood rings, but Commercial Vehicle Group (CVG) is still a trucker's good buddy. The company makes components for the cabs of heavy-duty trucks that help keep drivers comfortable and safe. Products include seats and suspension seat systems, interior trim (instrument panels, door panels, headliners), mirrors, wiper systems, and controls. The company's customers include heavy-duty truck manufacturers such as Navistar's International Truck (22% of sales), PACCAR (17%), and Daimler AG's Daimler Trucks North America subsidiary (formerly Freightliner, 13%). Besides truck manufacturers, CVG sells its products to the fleet maintenance aftermarket and to manufacturers of construction equipment and buses.

Expansion through key acquisitions is the name of the game for CVG.

In 2005 CVG paid $107.5 million for the assets of Mayflower Vehicle Systems North American Commercial Vehicle Operations, a maker of truck cab frames and assemblies, sleeper boxes, and other components. (The Mayflower Vehicle Systems unit posted revenue of about $207 million in 2004.) CVG also purchased Monona Corporation and its Monona Wire Corporation subsidiary for $55 million, adding eight manufacturing facilities in the US (in Illinois, Iowa, and Wisconsin) and Mexico. Monona makes electronic wire harnesses and instrument panel assemblies and

assembles cabs for Caterpillar, Oshkosh Truck, Deere, and other construction equipment companies. That year it also purchased plastic molded parts maker Cabarrus Plastics.

The addition of Mayflower's operations contributed significantly to CVG's 2005 revenue. In fact cab structures surpassed seating systems as the company's top-earning product segment.

In late 2006 CVG bought commercial truck and bus seat manufacturer C.I.E.B. Kahovec spol. of the Czech Republic. The move gives CVG a foothold in the European market upon which it hopes to build in the future.

The following year CVG bought PEKM Kabeltechnik from the Prettl Group for $21 million. PEKM Kabeltechnik is a maker of electronic wiring harnesses for commercial trucks. PEKM Kabeltechnik has operations in the Czech Republic and Ukraine. Later in 2007 CVG bought the injection molding and heavy-gauge thermoforming fabrication division of Gage Industries.

EXECUTIVES

Chairman: Scott D. Rued, age 50
President, CEO, and Director: Mervin Dunn, age 53, $600,000 pay
EVP, Business Development: Kevin Frailey
VP, Finance and CFO: Chad M. Utrup, $305,000 pay
VP, Human Resources: James F. Williams, age 60, $230,000 pay
VP, Mergers and Acquisitions: James A. Lindsey, age 49
VP, Purchasing: Chris Mapes
VP and General Manager, Interior Systems Division: Ken Bush
VP and General Manager, Engineered Vehicle Structures Division: Patrick (Pat) Miller
VP and General Manager, CVG Electrical/Mechanical Division: Bill Haushalter
President, CVG Americas; President, Mayflower Vehicle Systems: Gerald L. (Jerry) Armstrong, age 45, $320,000 pay
President, CVG International: William Gordon Boyd, age 59, $504,066 pay
President, CVG, Europe and Asia: Donald P. Lorraine, age 51, $573,285 pay
Director, Investor Relations and Corporate Communications: John M. Hyre
Auditors: Deloitte & Touche LLP

LOCATIONS

HQ: Commercial Vehicle Group, Inc.
6530 W. Campus Way, New Albany, OH 43054
Phone: 614-289-5360   **Fax:** 614-289-5367
Web: www.cvgrp.com

Commercial Vehicle Group operates manufacturing facilities in Australia, Belgium, China, the Czech Republic, Mexico, the UK, and the US.

2006 Sales

	$ mil.	% of total
North America	800.1	87
Other regions	118.7	13
Total	**918.8**	**100**

PRODUCTS/OPERATIONS

2006 Sales

	$ mil.	% of total
Cab structures, sleeper boxes, body panels & structural components	317.7	35
Seats & seating systems	266.4	29
Trim systems & components	158.7	17
Mirrors, wipers & controls	72.6	8
Electronic wire harnesses & panel assemblies	103.4	11
Total	**918.8**	**100**

2006 Sales by Customer

	% of total
International	22
PACCAR	17
Freightliner	13
Volvo/Mack	13
Caterpillar	8
Komatsu	2
Deer & Co.	2
Oshkosh Truck	2
Other	21
Total	**100**

2006 Sales by End-User Market

	% of total
Heavy truck OEM	60
Construction	18
Aftermarket & OEM service	10
Military	3
Bus	2
Agriculture	1
Other	6
Total	**100**

COMPETITORS

Accuride	Ogihara
Consolidated Metco	Stoneridge
Defiance Metal Products	Tomkins
Delphi	Trico Products
Findlay Industries	Trim Masters
Johnson Electric	Valeo
LEONI	Yazaki
Magna International	

HISTORICAL FINANCIALS

Company Type: Public

Income Statement

FYE: December 31

	REVENUE ($ mil.)	NET INCOME ($ mil.)	NET PROFIT MARGIN	EMPLOYEES
12/06	918.8	58.0	6.3%	5,790
12/05	754.5	49.4	6.5%	5,339
12/04	380.4	17.5	4.6%	—
12/03	287.6	4.0	1.4%	—
12/02	298.7	(45.5)	—	—
Annual Growth	**32.4%**	**—**	**—**	**8.4%**

2006 Year-End Financials

Debt ratio: 60.4%
Return on equity: 24.8%
Cash ($ mil.): 19.8
Current ratio: 2.04
Long-term debt ($ mil.): 160.0
No. of shares (mil.): 21.4

Dividends
  Yield: —
  Payout: —
Market value ($ mil.): 465.8
R&D as % of sales: —
Advertising as % of sales: —

Stock History

NASDAQ (GS): CVGI

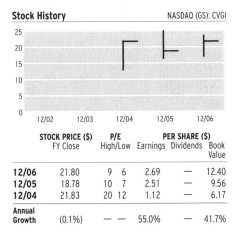

	STOCK PRICE ($) FY Close	P/E High/Low		PER SHARE ($) Earnings	Dividends	Book Value
12/06	21.80	9	6	2.69	—	12.40
12/05	18.78	10	7	2.51	—	9.56
12/04	21.83	20	12	1.12	—	6.17
Annual Growth	**(0.1%)**	**—**	**—**	**55.0%**	**—**	**41.7%**

Commonwealth Bankshares

Commonwealth Bankshares is the holding company for the Bank of the Commonwealth, which has about 10 branches in the Hampton Roads area of southeastern Virginia. The commercial bank attracts deposits from individuals and small to midsized businesses in the communities of Chesapeake, Norfolk, Portsmouth, and Virginia Beach by offering checking and savings accounts, IRAs, and CDs. In addition, it has subsidiaries that offer residential mortgages, brokerage and investment services, and insurance. Commercial mortgages represent nearly half of the company's loan portfolio; construction and development loans are more than a quarter. The bank also originates business and consumer loans.

EXECUTIVES

Chairman, President, and CEO, Commonwealth Bankshares and Bank of the Commonwealth: Edward J. Woodard Jr., age 65, $428,300 pay
EVP, CFO, and Secretary, Commonwealth Bankshares and Bank of the Commonwealth: Cynthia A. Sabol, age 45, $193,815 pay
EVP and Chief Lending Officer, Bank of the Commonwealth: Simon Hounslow, age 43, $176,462 pay
EVP and Commercial Loan Officer, Bank of the Commonwealth: Stephen G. Fields, age 44, $156,538 pay
SVP and Chief Information Officer, Bank of the Commonwealth: Deborah B. Coon
SVP and Senior Trust Officer, Bank of the Commonwealth: Richard Early
SVP and Commercial Loan Officer, Bank of the Commonwealth: Robert L. White
VP and Human Resources Officer, Bank of the Commonwealth: Linda W. Greenough
Accounting Officer, Bank of the Commonwealth: Pamela L. Perkins
Auditors: PKF Witt Mares, PLC

LOCATIONS

HQ: Commonwealth Bankshares, Inc.
  403 Boush St., Norfolk, VA 23510
Phone: 757-446-6900   **Fax:** 757-446-6929
Web: www.bankofthecommonwealth.com

PRODUCTS/OPERATIONS

2006 Sales

	$ mil.	% of total
Interest		
Loans, including fees	52.0	89
Other	0.9	2
Noninterest		
Mortgage brokerage income	1.6	3
Service charges on deposit accounts	1.1	2
Title insurance	0.9	2
Investment services	0.7	1
Other	0.8	1
Total	**58.0**	**100**

COMPETITORS

Bank of America	Monarch Financial
BB&T	RBC Centura Banks
Hampton Roads Bankshares	SunTrust
Heritage Bankshares	Wachovia

HISTORICAL FINANCIALS

Company Type: Public

Income Statement

FYE: December 31

	ASSETS ($ mil.)	NET INCOME ($ mil.)	INCOME AS % OF ASSETS	EMPLOYEES
12/06	715.2	10.1	1.4%	184
12/05	549.5	6.6	1.2%	142
12/04	374.1	3.1	0.8%	—
12/03	318.3	2.5	0.8%	—
12/02	256.5	1.7	0.7%	84
Annual Growth	**29.2%**	**56.1%**	**—**	**21.7%**

2006 Year-End Financials

Equity as % of assets: 14.4%
Return on assets: 1.6%
Return on equity: 12.2%
Long-term debt ($ mil.): 26.0
No. of shares (mil.): 6.8
Market value ($ mil.): 171.1

Dividends
  Yield: 0.8%
  Payout: 12.9%
Sales ($ mil.): 58.0
R&D as % of sales: —
Advertising as % of sales: —

Stock History

NASDAQ (GM): CWBS

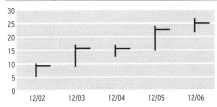

	STOCK PRICE ($) FY Close	P/E High/Low		PER SHARE ($) Earnings	Dividends	Book Value
12/06	25.00	17	14	1.55	0.20	15.08
12/05	22.65	17	11	1.36	0.17	15.40
12/04	15.58	17	13	0.96	0.08	12.40
12/03	15.70	20	11	0.85	0.13	10.16
12/02	9.28	14	7	0.73	—	8.97
Annual Growth	**28.1%**	**—**	**—**	**20.7%**	**15.4%**	**13.9%**

Community Bancorp

Las Vegas = Lost Wages? Not if Community Bank of Nevada has something to say about it. The subsidiary of holding company Community Bancorp (not to be confused with the similarly named firm in Vermont) operates about 15 branches in and around Sin City. The company also owns Community Bank of Arizona (formerly Cactus Commerce Bank), which operates in the Phoenix metro area. The banks offer such deposit products as checking and savings accounts, NOW and money market accounts, CDs, and IRAs. Community Bancorp has played a part in Las Vegas' rapid growth by lending to area businesses; the loan portfolio is strongly dominated by construction loans and commercial mortgages.

Community Bancorp is looking to boost its quotient of commercial and industrial loans, including Small Business Administration (SBA) loans. It operates loan production offices in Las Vegas, Phoenix, and San Diego. The company has grown through acquisitions (including its purchase of rival Valley Bancorp in 2006); it plans to continue its acquisitive strategy, as well as to open new branches in its existing markets.

EXECUTIVES

Chairman, President, and CEO; CEO, Community Bank of Nevada; Interim CEO, Community Bank of Arizona: Edward M. (Ed) Jamison, age 59
EVP, COO, and Director; President and CEO, Community Bank of Nevada: Lawrence K. Scott, age 47
EVP and CFO, Community Bank of Nevada: Cathy Robinson, age 47, $320,000 pay
EVP and COO, Community Bank of Nevada: Bruce Ford, age 42, $348,827 pay (prior to promotion)
EVP and CFO: Patrick Hartman, age 58
EVP and Chief Credit Administration Officer, Community Bank of Nevada: Don F. Bigger, age 55, $212,017 pay
SVP and Chief Accounting Officer: Jeff Chase
EVP and Corporate Relations Officer, Community Bank of Nevada: Barry L. Hulin, age 61
EVP, Chief Credit Officer, and Director, Community Bank of Arizona: Jim Nelson, age 51
VP and Marketing Director: Blake Boyer
President, Community Bank of Arizona: Stephen R. Curley
Auditors: McGladrey & Pullen, LLP

LOCATIONS

HQ: Community Bancorp
 400 S. 4th St., Ste. 215, Las Vegas, NV 89101
Phone: 702-878-0700   **Fax:** 702-947-3502
Web: www.communitybanknv.com

PRODUCTS/OPERATIONS

2006 Sales

	$ mil.	% of total
Interest		
Loans	79.7	89
Securities	6.9	8
Service charges	1.9	2
Other	0.6	1
Total	**89.1**	**100**

COMPETITORS

Bank of America
BOK Financial
Citibank
Nevada State Bank
Silver State Bancorp
U.S. Bancorp
Washington Mutual
Wells Fargo
Western Alliance
Zions Bancorporation

HISTORICAL FINANCIALS

Company Type: Public

Income Statement

FYE: December 31

	ASSETS ($ mil.)	NET INCOME ($ mil.)	INCOME AS % OF ASSETS	EMPLOYEES
12/06	1,570.4	15.6	1.0%	244
12/05	892.7	10.1	1.1%	166
12/04	574.0	5.4	0.9%	—
12/03	463.4	5.2	1.1%	—
12/02	400.6	4.7	1.2%	—
Annual Growth	**40.7%**	**35.0%**	**—**	**47.0%**

2006 Year-End Financials

Equity as % of assets: 13.9%
Return on assets: 1.3%
Return on equity: 9.6%
Long-term debt ($ mil.): 143.4
No. of shares (mil.): 10.4
Market value ($ mil.): 313.6
Dividends
 Yield: —
 Payout: —
Sales ($ mil.): 89.1
R&D as % of sales: —
Advertising as % of sales: —

Stock History

NASDAQ (GM): CBON

	STOCK PRICE ($) FY Close	P/E High/Low	PER SHARE ($) Earnings	Dividends	Book Value
12/06	30.19	18 15	1.92	—	21.07
12/05	31.61	24 16	1.42	—	14.48
12/04	30.60	30 25	1.10	—	11.49
Annual Growth	**(0.7%)**	**— —**	**32.1%**	**—**	**35.4%**

Community Capital Bancshares

Community Capital Bancshares has taken hometown to heart. In 1999 the company opened Albany Bank & Trust, a community bank serving southwestern Georgia through three branches. It then made its first acquisition in 2003, buying First Bank of Dothan, which is now AB&T National Bank and operates two branches in Alabama. The banks offer standard deposit products and services including checking and savings accounts, money market accounts, CDs, and IRAs. The company mainly uses these deposits to fund residential and commercial construction loans and mortgages, as well as business and consumer loans. Real estate loans comprise about 80% of its loan book.

EXECUTIVES

Chairman: Charles M. Jones III, age 57, $24,450 pay
President, CEO, and Director, Community Capital Bancshares and Albany Bank & Trust: John H. Monk Jr., age 56
Director; President and CEO, Albany Bank &Trust National Bank: Keith G. Beckham, age 46
Chief Credit Officer, Albany Bank & Trust: Paul E. Joiner Jr., $139,541 pay (prior to promotion)
CFO, Community Capital and Albany Bank & Trust; VP, AB&T National Bank: David J. Baranko, age 51, $108,164 pay
EVP and Senior Lending Officer, Albany Bank & Trust: David C. Guillebeau, age 45, $127,755 pay
Director, Human Resources, Albany Bank & Trust: Misty Bruce
General Auditor, Albany Bank & Trust: Stan W. Edmonds
Auditors: Mauldin & Jenkins, LLC

LOCATIONS

HQ: Community Capital Bancshares, Inc.
 2815 Meredyth Dr., Albany, GA 31707
Phone: 229-446-2265   **Fax:** 229-446-7030
Web: www.albanybankandtrust.com

PRODUCTS/OPERATIONS

2006 Sales

	$ mil.	% of total
Interest		
Loans	20.9	81
Securities	1.9	7
Other	0.3	1
Noninterest		
Service charges on deposit accounts	1.2	5
Other	1.6	6
Total	**25.9**	**100**

COMPETITORS

Ameris
Bank of America
Colony Bankcorp
Regions Financial
Southwest Georgia Financial
SunTrust
Synovus

HISTORICAL FINANCIALS

Company Type: Public

Income Statement

FYE: December 31

	ASSETS ($ mil.)	NET INCOME ($ mil.)	INCOME AS % OF ASSETS	EMPLOYEES
12/06	296.9	0.4	0.1%	84
12/05	309.5	0.1	0.0%	81
12/04	195.3	0.9	0.5%	—
12/03	158.7	0.6	0.4%	—
12/02	109.2	0.6	0.5%	39
Annual Growth	**28.4%**	**(9.6%)**	**—**	**21.1%**

2006 Year-End Financials

Equity as % of assets: 9.0%
Return on assets: 0.1%
Return on equity: 1.5%
Long-term debt ($ mil.): 31.1
No. of shares (mil.): 3.0
Market value ($ mil.): 37.9
Dividends
 Yield: 0.6%
 Payout: 57.1%
Sales ($ mil.): 25.9
R&D as % of sales: —
Advertising as % of sales: —

Stock History

NASDAQ (CM): ALBY

	STOCK PRICE ($) FY Close	P/E High/Low	PER SHARE ($) Earnings	Dividends	Book Value
12/06	12.53	96 70	0.14	0.08	8.85
12/05	10.90	340 253	0.04	0.08	8.54
12/04	11.62	38 26	0.38	0.06	8.77
12/03	12.00	38 26	0.39	0.04	7.64
12/02	11.10	29 17	0.38	—	6.81
Annual Growth	**3.1%**	**— —**	**(22.1%)**	**26.0%**	**6.8%**

CommVault Systems

CommVault Systems doesn't want your data locked away in an inaccessible vault. The company provides software that customers use to manage and store enterprise data. CommVault's products are used for tasks such as data migration, backup, archiving, data replication, and disaster recovery. Its customers come from industries such as manufacturing, financial services, health care, and transportation, as well as from the public sector. CommVault's strategic partners include systems integrators and professional services firms, distributors and resellers, and technology providers.

The company was founded as an independent segment of Bell Laboratories in 1988; senior management (backed in part by funding from Sprout Group) purchased the company's assets from Lucent Technologies in 1996.

EXECUTIVES

Chairman, President, and CEO:
N. Robert (Bob) Hammer, age 65, $599,712 pay
EVP, COO, and Director: Alan G. (Al) Bunte, age 54, $387,546 pay
VP and CFO: Louis F. (Lou) Miceli, age 57, $380,631 pay
VP, General Counsel, and Secretary:
Warren H. Mondschein
VP Europe, Middle East, and Africa: Steven Rose, age 48
VP Human Resources: William (Bill) Beattie
VP Marketing and Business Development:
David (Dave) West, age 41, $284,154 pay
VP Operations: Allen Shoemaker
VP Product Development: Anand Prahlad, age 38
VP Sales, Americas: Ron Miiller, age 39, $397,512 pay
VP Sales Operations: Brian D. McAteer
Auditors: Ernst & Young LLP

LOCATIONS

HQ: CommVault Systems, Inc.
2 Crescent Place, Oceanport, NJ 07757
Phone: 732-870-4000   **Fax:** 732-870-4525
Web: www.commvault.com

2007 Sales

	$ mil.	% of total
US	105.1	70
Other countries	46.0	30
Total	**151.1**	**100**

PRODUCTS/OPERATIONS

2007 Sales

	$ mil.	% of total
Software	83.9	56
Services	67.2	44
Total	**151.1**	**100**

Selected Products

QiNetix Suite
Data Classification
DataArchiver
DataMigrator
Galaxy Backup & Recovery Data
QNet (data managing and reporting)
QuickRecovery
StorageManager

COMPETITORS

CA, Inc.	Hewlett-Packard
Double-Take Software	IBM Software
EMC	Symantec

HISTORICAL FINANCIALS

Company Type: Public

Income Statement

FYE: March 31

	REVENUE ($ mil.)	NET INCOME ($ mil.)	NET PROFIT MARGIN	EMPLOYEES
3/07	151.1	64.3	42.6%	727
3/06	109.5	10.8	9.9%	—
3/05	82.6	0.5	0.6%	—
3/04	61.2	(11.7)	—	—
3/03	44.4	(16.4)	—	325
Annual Growth	**35.8%**	—	—	**22.3%**

2007 Year-End Financials

Debt ratio: —	Dividends
Return on equity: —	Yield: —
Cash ($ mil.): 65.0	Payout: —
Current ratio: 1.53	Market value ($ mil.): 679.9
Long-term debt ($ mil.): —	R&D as % of sales: —
No. of shares (mil.): 42.0	Advertising as % of sales: —

Stock History

NASDAQ (GM): CVLT

	STOCK PRICE ($) FY Close	P/E High/Low	Earnings	Dividends	Book Value
3/07	16.20	— —	(1.35)	—	1.87

Comstock Resources

Comstock Resources' stock in trade is producing natural gas and oil. The midsized independent oil and gas company has proved reserves of 851 billion cu. ft. of natural gas equivalent (77% in the form of natural gas) on its properties in four major areas — East Texas and North Louisiana, Mississippi, South Texas, Southeast Texas, and the Gulf of Mexico. Comstock Resources operates 392 of the 752 producing wells in which it holds an interest. The company has grown by exploiting its existing reserves and through acquisitions. Comstock Resources owns a controlling interest in Bois d'Arc Energy, a publicly held company which conducts exploration and production operations in the Gulf of Mexico.

In 2004 Comstock Resources acquired producing properties from Ovation Energy for $62 million.

In 2005 the company acquired assets from EnSight Energy Partners for $192.5 million. It acquired additional oil and gas properties in 2006 for $67.2 million.

EXECUTIVES

Chairman, President, and CEO: M. Jay Allison, age 51, $2,825,000 pay
COO: Mack D. Good, age 56, $550,000 pay
SVP, CFO, Secretary, Treasurer, and Director:
Roland O. Burns, age 47, $1,090,000 pay

VP Accounting and Controller: Daniel K. Presley, age 46, $310,000 pay
VP Marketing: Stephen P. Neukom, age 57, $320,000 pay
VP Land and General Counsel: D. Dale Gillette, age 61
VP Financial Reporting: Richard D. Singer, age 52
Auditors: Ernst & Young LLP

LOCATIONS

HQ: Comstock Resources, Inc.
5300 Town and Country Blvd., Ste. 500,
Frisco, TX 75034
Phone: 972-668-8800   **Fax:** 972-668-8812
Web: www.comstockresources.com

2006 Reserves

	% of total
Offshore (Bois d'Arc Energy)	40
East Texas & North Louisiana	30
South Texas	19
Mississippi	5
Other regions	6
Total	**100**

PRODUCTS/OPERATIONS

2006 Sales

	% of total
Shell Oil	42
National Energy & Trading LP	13
Other customers	45
Total	**100**

COMPETITORS

Abraxas Petroleum
Anadarko Petroleum
Apache
ATP Oil & Gas
BP
Brigham Exploration
Carrizo Oil & Gas
Chevron
Devon Energy
Exxon Mobil
Forest Oil
Meridian Resource
Pioneer Natural Resources
Shell Oil
Stone Energy
TOTAL

HISTORICAL FINANCIALS

Company Type: Public

Income Statement

FYE: December 31

	REVENUE ($ mil.)	NET INCOME ($ mil.)	NET PROFIT MARGIN	EMPLOYEES
12/06	511.9	70.7	13.8%	130
12/05	303.3	60.5	19.9%	89
12/04	261.6	46.9	17.9%	—
12/03	235.1	53.9	22.9%	—
12/02	142.1	11.5	8.1%	62
Annual Growth	**37.8%**	**57.5%**	—	**20.3%**

2006 Year-End Financials

Debt ratio: 66.7%	Dividends
Return on equity: 11.2%	Yield: —
Cash ($ mil.): 10.7	Payout: —
Current ratio: 0.65	Market value ($ mil.): 1,378.9
Long-term debt ($ mil.): 455.0	R&D as % of sales: —
No. of shares (mil.): 44.4	Advertising as % of sales: —

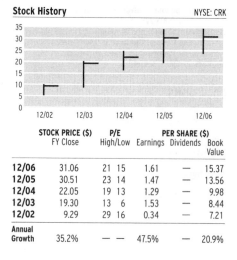

	STOCK PRICE ($)	P/E		PER SHARE ($)		
	FY Close	High/Low	Earnings	Dividends	Book Value
12/06	31.06	21 15	1.61	—	15.37
12/05	30.51	23 14	1.47	—	13.56
12/04	22.05	19 13	1.29	—	9.98
12/03	19.30	13 6	1.53	—	8.44
12/02	9.29	29 16	0.34	—	7.21
Annual Growth	35.2%	— —	47.5%	—	20.9%

COMSYS IT Partners

In need of a technical whiz? COMSYS IT Partners supplies temporary information technology (IT) personnel from more than 45 offices in the US, as well as from facilities in Canada and the UK. The company also helps companies recruit and hire permanent IT professionals and provides ad hoc project teams that develop and implement applications either on- or offsite. COMSYS IT Partners employs about 5,000 IT professionals and serves customers in the finance, health care, pharmaceutical, telecom, manufacturing, and transportation industries, as well as government entities. Wachovia Investors owns 39% of the company, which was formed when COMSYS Holding merged with publicly traded Venturi Partners in 2004.

COMSYS IT Partners also provides vendor management services (VMS) under the vWorx brand name. The product utilizes Web software to better manage the expenditures associated with the clients' contracted services. The vWorx service is part of an effort by COMSYS IT Partners to market business process outsourcing (BPO) services along with its core staffing offerings. That initiative gathered momentum in December 2007 when the company acquired T. Williams Consulting (TWC), a provider of recruitment process outsourcing (RPO) and HR consulting services.

The TWC deal capped a series of acquisitions by COMSYS IT Partners in 2007. The company expanded its geographic reach and diversified its staffing and services offerings by buying Argus Connection (IT staffing and consulting), Plum Rhino Consulting (finance and accounting staffing), and Praeos Technologies (business intelligence and business analytics sectors).

EXECUTIVES

CEO and Director: Larry L. Enterline, age 54, $526,390 pay
EVP and COO: Michael H. (Mike) Barker, age 52, $342,720 pay

SVP, General Counsel, and Secretary: Ken R. Bramlett Jr., age 47, $257,625 pay
SVP Corporate Development: David L. Kerr, age 54, $284,600 pay
SVP Managed Solutions: Albert S. (Kip) Wright IV
SVP Sales: Jerry Jewell
SVP Customer Service: Brian Westphal
SVP and Chief Accounting Officer: Amy Bobbitt
VP Marketing and Sales: Ralph Kirkland
VP Human Resources: Terry V. Bell
VP Technical Services: Andrew F. (Andy) Adams
Marketing Communications Manager: Erin Tanji
Auditors: Ernst & Young LLP

LOCATIONS

HQ: COMSYS IT Partners, Inc.
4400 Post Oak Pkwy., Ste. 1800, Houston, TX 77027
Phone: 713-386-1400   **Fax:** 713-961-0719
Web: www.comsys.com

PRODUCTS/OPERATIONS

COMPETITORS

Ablest	Kelly Services
Adecco	Kforce
Aerotek	Manpower
Ajilon Consulting	MPS
Analysts International	Pomeroy IT
Butler International	RCM Technologies
CDI	Robert Half
ClearPoint Business Resources	Spherion
COMFORCE	StarTek
Computer Task Group	TEKsystems
Hewitt Associates	Watson Wyatt
Judge Group	Westaff

HISTORICAL FINANCIALS
Company Type: Public

Income Statement
FYE: Sunday nearest December 31

	REVENUE ($ mil.)	NET INCOME ($ mil.)	NET PROFIT MARGIN	EMPLOYEES
12/06	736.6	21.0	2.9%	4,297
12/05	661.7	2.2	0.3%	5,661
12/04	437.0	(55.2)	—	
Annual Growth	29.8%	—	—	(24.1%)

2006 Year-End Financials
Debt ratio: 98.7%
Return on equity: 25.3%
Cash ($ mil.): 1.6
Current ratio: 1.07
Long-term debt ($ mil.): 93.5
No. of shares (mil.): 19.3
Dividends
  Yield: —
  Payout: —
Market value ($ mil.): 389.6
R&D as % of sales: —
Advertising as % of sales: —

Stock History
NASDAQ (GM): CITP

	STOCK PRICE ($)	P/E		PER SHARE ($)		
	FY Close	High/Low	Earnings	Dividends	Book Value
12/06	20.21	20 9	1.10	—	4.92
12/05	11.05	151 66	0.14	—	3.79
12/04	10.00	— —	(14.20)	—	2.32
Annual Growth	42.2%	— —	—	—	45.5%

Concho Resources

Concho Resources explores and develops properties, located primarily in the Permian Basin region of eastern New Mexico and the western area of Texas, for the production of oil and gas. It also owns properties in North Dakota and Arkansas. More than half of the company's 467 billion cu. ft. in proven reserves is made up of crude oil while the rest consists of natural gas. Concho Resources gets two-thirds of its sales from crude oil. Customers include such energy marketers as Navajo Refining Company (53% of sales) and DCP Midstream (18%). The company has over 80 producing wells in operation. Chase Oil owns 48% of the company.

EXECUTIVES

Chairman and CEO: Timothy A. Leach, age 47, $333,333 pay
President, COO, and Director: Steven L. Beal, age 48, $333,333 pay
VP, General Counsel, and Secretary: David W. Copeland, age 50, $233,333 pay
VP, CFO, and Treasurer: Curt F. Kamradt, age 44, $233,333 pay
VP Exploration and Land: David M. Thomas III, age 52, $233,333 pay
VP Engineering and Operations: E. Joseph Wright, age 47, $233,333 pay
Auditors: Grant Thornton LLP

LOCATIONS

HQ: Concho Resources Inc.
550 W. Texas Ave., Ste. 1300, Midland, TX 79701
Phone: 432-683-7443   **Fax:** 432-683-7441

PRODUCTS/OPERATIONS

2006 Sales

	$ mil.	% of total
Oil	131.8	67
Natural gas	66.5	33
Total	**198.3**	**100**

COMPETITORS

Chevron	Exxon Mobil
ConocoPhillips	Marathon Petroleum

HISTORICAL FINANCIALS
Company Type: Public

Income Statement
FYE: December 31

	REVENUE ($ mil.)	NET INCOME ($ mil.)	NET PROFIT MARGIN	EMPLOYEES
12/06	198.3	19.7	9.9%	80
12/05	54.9	2.0	3.6%	—
12/04	3.6	(2.7)	—	—
Annual Growth	642.2%	—	—	—

2006 Year-End Financials
Debt ratio: 86.1%
Return on equity: 5.8%
Cash ($ mil.): 7.1
Current ratio: 0.90
Long-term debt ($ mil.): 495.1

Net Income History

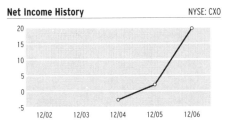

Concur Technologies

Having trouble keeping track of "entertainment" expenses from that "business" trip to Las Vegas? Concur Technologies offers corporate expense management software that enables businesses to automate and streamline the process for submitting and approving employee expense reports. Concur's software features Web-based modules for tracking, submitting, and processing reports for travel and entertainment costs, as well as applications to track employee requests for vendor payments. Concur licenses its software directly to companies and offers its applications by subscription through application service providers.

In 2006 Concur acquired corporate travel software company Outtask.

EXECUTIVES

Chairman and CEO: S. Steven (Steve) Singh, age 46, $375,833 pay
President and COO: Rajeev Singh, age 39, $334,833 pay
CFO: John F. Adair, age 53
CTO, EVP Worldwide Marketing, and Director: Michael W. Hilton, age 43, $261,133 pay
EVP Sales and Business Development: Michael L. Eberhard, $369,816 pay
EVP Research and Development: Tom DePasquale
SVP Information Services: Michael Bowden, $267,187 pay
Chief Legal Officer and Corporate Secretary: Kyle R. Sugamele, age 45
Senior Manager Marketing Communications, US: Hubie Sturtevant
Investor Relations Contact: John Torrey
Auditors: Grant Thornton LLP

LOCATIONS

HQ: Concur Technologies, Inc.
 18400 NE Union Hill Rd., Redmond, WA 98052
Phone: 425-702-8808   **Fax:** 425-702-8828
Web: www.concur.com

2006 Sales

	$ mil.	% of total
US	85.3	88
Europe	8.2	8
Other	3.6	4
Total	**97.1**	**100**

PRODUCTS/OPERATIONS

2006 Sales

	$ mil.	% of total
Subscription	80.5	83
Consulting & other	16.6	17
Total	**97.1**	**100**

Selected Services
Consulting
Customer support
Training

Selected Software
Concur Compliance Solution (fraud detection)
Concur Expense (travel and entertainment expense management)
Concur Imaging Service (electronic capture, storage, and archive of receipts and invoices)
Concur Payment (employee request for vendor payment)
Concur Travel Integration (travel procurement and expense management)

COMPETITORS

American Express
Ariba
Bank of America
Compuware
Gelco Information Network
IBM
OneMind Connect
Oracle
SAP
Wells Fargo

HISTORICAL FINANCIALS
Company Type: Public

Income Statement

	REVENUE ($ mil.)	NET INCOME ($ mil.)	NET PROFIT MARGIN	EMPLOYEES
9/06	97.1	34.2	35.2%	575
9/05	71.8	5.4	7.5%	395
9/04	56.5	2.0	3.5%	—
9/03	56.7	1.0	1.8%	—
9/02	45.1	(12.3)	—	338
Annual Growth	**21.1%**	**—**	**—**	**14.2%**

FYE: September 30

2006 Year-End Financials

Debt ratio: 11.5%
Return on equity: 46.2%
Cash ($ mil.): 16.3
Current ratio: 1.25
Long-term debt ($ mil.): 13.5
No. of shares (mil.): 36.1
Dividends
 Yield: —
 Payout: —
Market value ($ mil.): 525.9
R&D as % of sales: —
Advertising as % of sales: —

Stock History

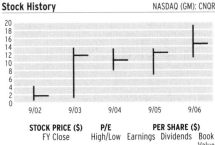

	STOCK PRICE ($) FY Close	P/E High/Low		PER SHARE ($) Earnings	Dividends	Book Value
9/06	14.55	22	13	0.87	—	3.25
9/05	12.37	88	47	0.15	—	0.86
9/04	10.49	221	135	0.06	—	0.91
9/03	11.74	450	45	0.03	—	0.80
9/02	1.73	—	—	(0.46)	—	0.75
Annual Growth	**70.3%**	**—**	**—**	**—**	**—**	**44.1%**

Consumer Portfolio Services

Consumer Portfolio Services (CPS) buys, sells, and services auto loans made to consumers who probably don't have portfolios. In other words, the company lends to subprime borrowers who can't get traditional financing due to poor or limited credit. CPS purchases contracts from more than 8,600 dealers in 48 states, some 90% of which are franchised new car dealers. The remaining are independent used car dealers, and more than 85% of the contracts CPS acquires finance used vehicles. Investment firm Levine Leichtman Capital Partners owns more than a quarter of the company, which has operations in California, Florida, Illinois, and Virginia.

EXECUTIVES

Chairman, President, and CEO: Charles E. Bradley Jr., age 47
SVP and CFO: Jeffrey P. (Jeff) Fritz, age 47, $437,000 pay
SVP and Chief Investment Officer: Robert E. Riedl, age 43
SVP Servicing: Christopher (Chris) Terry, age 39
SVP Collections: Nicholas P. Brockman, age 62
SVP Originations: Curtis K. Powell, age 50
SVP, General Counsel, and Secretary: Mark A. Creatura, age 46
VP Human Resources: Missy Hennessey
Auditors: McGladrey & Pullen, LLP

LOCATIONS

HQ: Consumer Portfolio Services, Inc.
 16355 Laguna Canyon Rd., Irvine, CA 92618
Phone: 949-753-6800   **Fax:** 949-753-6805
Web: www.consumerportfolio.com

PRODUCTS/OPERATIONS

2006 Sales

	$ mil.	% of total
Interest income	263.6	95
Servicing fees	2.9	1
Other income	12.4	4
Total	**278.9**	**100**

COMPETITORS

The Aegis Consumer Funding Group, Inc.
AmeriCredit
Credit Acceptance
Daimler
First Investors Financial Services
FirstCity Financial
Ford Motor Credit
GMAC
Nissan
Toyota Motor Credit
Triad Financial
Union Acceptance Company
United PanAm Financial

HISTORICAL FINANCIALS

Company Type: Public

Income Statement

FYE: December 31

	ASSETS ($ mil.)	NET INCOME ($ mil.)	INCOME AS % OF ASSETS	EMPLOYEES
12/06	1,728.3	39.6	2.3%	789
12/05	1,155.1	3.4	0.3%	749
12/04	766.6	(15.9)	—	—
12/03	492.5	0.4	0.1%	—
12/02	285.5	20.4	7.1%	643
Annual Growth	56.9%	18.0%	—	5.2%

2006 Year-End Financials

Equity as % of assets: 6.5%
Return on assets: 2.7%
Return on equity: 42.8%
Long-term debt ($ mil.): 1,585.9
No. of shares (mil.): 21.6
Market value ($ mil.): 140.5
Dividends
  Yield: —
  Payout: —
Sales ($ mil.): 278.9
R&D as % of sales: —
Advertising as % of sales: —

Stock History

NASDAQ (GM): CPSS

	STOCK PRICE ($) FY Close	P/E High/Low	PER SHARE ($) Earnings	Dividends	Book Value
12/06	6.51	5 3	1.64	—	5.17
12/05	5.75	46 25	0.14	—	3.37
12/04	4.87	— —	(0.75)	—	3.24
12/03	3.72	209 75	0.02	—	3.99
12/02	2.09	4 1	0.97	—	4.08
Annual Growth	32.8%	— —	14.0%	—	6.1%

Continucare Corporation

Continucare keeps on caring for South and Central Florida's Medicare recipients. The company provides primary care medical services through a network of 20 centers in Broward, Miami-Dade, and Hillsborough counties. It also provides practice management services to about 15 independent doctors' practices affiliated with Humana. A majority of the patients who seek care at Continucare clinics and practices are members of Medicare Advantage health plans; virtually all of the company's revenue comes from managed care contracts with HMOs operated by Humana, Vista Healthplan of South Florida, and Wellcare.

Continucare provides medical services to about 40,000 patients, most of them through capitated arrangements in which participating health plans pay a set monthly fee (usually a percentage of premiums) for each member. Humana accounts for a majority of revenue.

Continucare also serves participants in Medicaid health plans, though to a much lesser extent than its Medicare customer base.

The company plans to grow by increasing its patient volume at its existing clinics and by expanding its physician practice management services. In 2006 it acquired Miami Dade Health Centers, which operated five primary care medical centers catering to Medicare and Medicaid HMO members. Director Philip Frost owns nearly 45% of Continucare.

EXECUTIVES

Chairman, President, and CEO:
  Richard C. Pfenniger Jr., age 51, $478,327 pay
Vice Chairman: Luis Cruz, age 46
EVP Operations: Gemma Rosello, age 51, $272,827 pay
EVP: Jose M. Garcia
SVP Finance, CFO, Treasurer, and Secretary:
  Fernando L. Fernandez, age 46, $263,769 pay
SVP Center Operations: Sadita Bustamante
SVP Marketing and Business Development:
  Luis H. Izquierdo, age 52, $264,062 pay
VP Support Services: Holly Lopez
Chief Medical Officer, Miami-Dade County:
  Alfredo Ginory
Chief Medical Officer, Broward: Jorge Luna
Chief Medical Officer, Tampa Bay Area: Mark Stern
Regional Medical Director: Martha Irabien
Auditors: Ernst & Young LLP

LOCATIONS

HQ: Continucare Corporation
  7200 Corporate Center Dr., Ste. 600,
  Miami, FL 33126
Phone: 305-500-2000   **Fax:** 305-500-2080
Web: www.continucare.com

Continucare operates in central and southern Florida.

PRODUCTS/OPERATIONS

2007 Sales

	$ mil.	% of total
Medical services	216.9	100
Management fees & other	0.2	—
Total	**217.1**	**100**

COMPETITORS

Baptist Health South Florida
HCA
MetCare
Mount Sinai Medical Center of Florida
North Broward Hospital District
Public Health Trust
South Broward Hospital District
Tenet Healthcare

HISTORICAL FINANCIALS

Company Type: Public

Income Statement

FYE: June 30

	REVENUE ($ mil.)	NET INCOME ($ mil.)	NET PROFIT MARGIN	EMPLOYEES
6/07	217.1	6.3	2.9%	563
6/06	133.0	5.3	4.0%	—
6/05	112.2	15.9	14.2%	255
6/04	101.8	4.7	4.6%	—
6/03	101.4	0.1	0.1%	—
Annual Growth	21.0%	181.7%	—	48.6%

2007 Year-End Financials

Debt ratio: 0.2%
Return on equity: 8.9%
Cash ($ mil.): 7.3
Current ratio: 3.58
Long-term debt ($ mil.): 0.2
No. of shares (mil.): 70.1
Dividends
  Yield: —
  Payout: —
Market value ($ mil.): 216.7
R&D as % of sales: —
Advertising as % of sales: —

Stock History

AMEX: CNU

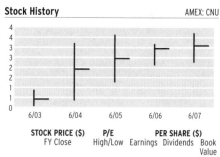

	STOCK PRICE ($) FY Close	P/E High/Low	PER SHARE ($) Earnings	Dividends	Book Value
6/07	3.09	37 23	0.10	—	1.48
6/06	2.95	32 22	0.10	—	0.53
6/05	2.45	12 4	0.31	—	0.61
6/04	1.92	35 4	0.09	—	0.33
6/03	0.42	— —	—	—	0.05
Annual Growth	64.7%	— —	3.6%	—	133.7%

Cooperative Bankshares

The word of the day is always "cooperation" at Cooperative Bankshares. The holding company for Cooperative Bank operates some 20 branches throughout eastern and southern Carolina. Targeting individuals and small to mid-sized businesses, the bank provides checking and savings accounts, CDs, and IRAs. Investment products and services such as discount securities brokerage, annuities, and mutual funds are available through a third-party provider. Residential mortgages account for about 48% of Cooperative Bankshares' loan portfolio, which includes commercial real estate, construction, business, and consumer loans. Cooperative Bankshares also owns Lumina Mortgage, which has offices in North Carolina.

Cooperative bought South Carolina bank Bank of Jefferson, allowing it to move into that state.

CEO Frederick Willetts owns more than 17% of the company; bank investor Jeffrey Gendell, through Tontine Financial Partners, owns nearly 9%.

EXECUTIVES

Chairman, President, and CEO, Cooperative Bankshares and Cooperative Bank; President, Lumina Mortgage: Frederick Willetts III, age 56, $295,000 pay
EVP and COO: O. C. (Buddy) Burrell Jr., age 58, $191,750 pay
SVP and CFO: Todd L. Sammons, age 43, $146,025 pay
SVP, Mortgage Lending: Dickson B. Bridger, age 47, $146,025 pay
VP, Retail Banking Operations, Cooperative Bank: Sandra B. Carr
VP, Business Banking, Cooperative Bank: George B. Church
VP, Human Resources, Cooperative Bank: Dare C. Rhodes
VP, Information Services, Cooperative Bank: Raymond A. Martin
VP, Marketing and Corporate Secretary, Cooperative Bank: Linda B. Garland
Auditors: Dixon Hughes PLLC

LOCATIONS

HQ: Cooperative Bankshares, Inc.
201 Market St., Wilmington, NC 28401
Phone: 910-343-0181 **Fax:** 910-251-1652
Web: www.coop-bank.com

PRODUCTS/OPERATIONS

2006 Sales

	$ mil.	% of total
Interest		
Loans	53.8	87
Securities & other	2.7	5
Noninterest		
Deposit-related fees	2.1	3
Gain on sale of loans	1.8	3
Service charges & fees on loans	0.6	1
Other	0.6	1
Total	**61.6**	**100**

COMPETITORS

Bank of America
BB&T
ECB Bancorp
First Bancorp (NC)
First Charter
First Citizens BancShares
First Community Bancshares
First Financial Holdings
First South Bancorp (NC)
RBC Centura Banks
Regions Financial
South Financial
SunTrust
Waccamaw Bankshares
Wachovia

HISTORICAL FINANCIALS

Company Type: Public

Income Statement

FYE: December 31

	ASSETS ($ mil.)	NET INCOME ($ mil.)	INCOME AS % OF ASSETS	EMPLOYEES
12/06	860.1	7.6	0.9%	220
12/05	746.3	5.5	0.7%	208
12/04	550.1	4.7	0.9%	—
12/03	502.3	5.4	1.1%	—
12/02	504.2	4.9	1.0%	129
Annual Growth	**14.3%**	**11.6%**	**—**	**14.3%**

2006 Year-End Financials

Equity as % of assets: 6.7%
Return on assets: 0.9%
Return on equity: 14.0%
Long-term debt ($ mil.): 108.5
No. of shares (mil.): 6.5
Market value ($ mil.): 116.5
Dividends
Yield: 0.9%
Payout: 14.8%
Sales ($ mil.): 61.6
R&D as % of sales: —
Advertising as % of sales: —

Stock History

NASDAQ (GM): COOP

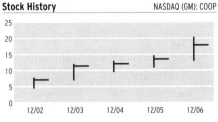

	STOCK PRICE ($) FY Close	P/E High/Low		PER SHARE ($) Earnings	Dividends	Book Value
12/06	17.89	18	11	1.15	0.17	8.85
12/05	13.57	17	13	0.84	0.10	11.87
12/04	12.10	27	20	0.48	0.05	16.40
12/03	11.39	14	9	0.83	0.09	15.14
12/02	7.08	10	6	0.77	0.07	13.56
Annual Growth	**26.1%**	**—**	**—**	**10.5%**	**24.8%**	**(10.1%)**

Copano Energy

Copano Energy hopes its business goes down the tubes. The natural gas pipeline and processing company operates and maintains a network of natural gas gathering and intrastate pipelines (totaling more than 5,000 miles) in Texas' Gulf Coast region and in Oklahoma. This includes 144 miles of pipelines owned by Webb/Duval Gatherers, an unconsolidated general partnership 62.5%-owned by Copano Energy. The company also provides natural gas processing operations through its Houston Central Processing plant and Sheridan NGL pipeline. Copano Energy went public in late 2004. Chairman and CEO John Eckel holds an 11% stake in the company.

The company acquired Tulsa-based ScissorTail Energy, LLC for $500 million in 2005. ScissorTail's assets include 3,200 miles of gas gathering pipelines and three processing plants. Copano agreed to acquire Cimmarron Gathering for $95 million in 2007. Cimmarron operates 3,800 miles of pipelines, the great majority of which is held for future development.

EXECUTIVES

Chairman and CEO: John R. Eckel Jr., age 55, $349,000 pay
President and COO: R. Bruce Northcutt, age 47, $244,000 pay
EVP; President and COO, Copano Energy/Rocky Mountains: John A. Raber
SVP and CFO: Matthew J. (Matt) Assiff, age 40, $200,000 pay
SVP Transportation and Supply, Texas Gulf Coast: Brian D. Eckhart, age 51
SVP Corporate Development: Ronald W. Bopp, age 60, $224,000 pay
SVP, General Counsel, and Secretary: Douglas L. Lawing, age 46
VP and Controller: Lari Paradee, age 44
VP Government and Regulatory Affairs: Kathryn S. De Young, age 46
VP Finance: Carl A. Luna, age 37
VP and CIO: Stephen J. Uthoff
Auditors: Deloitte & Touche LLP

LOCATIONS

HQ: Copano Energy, L.L.C.
2727 Allen Pkwy., Ste. 1200, Houston, TX 77019
Phone: 713-621-9547 **Fax:** 713-621-9545
Web: www.copanoenergy.com

Copano Energy operates pipelines and processing plants located in the Gulf Coast region of Texas, and in Oklahoma.

PRODUCTS/OPERATIONS

2006 Sales

	$ mil.	% of total
Natural gas	448.1	52
Natural gas liquids	369.9	43
Transportation, compression & processing fees	16.2	2
Other	26.1	3
Total	**860.3**	**100**

Selected Operations

Texas Gulf Coast Pipelines
Texas Gulf Coast Processing
Houston Central Processing plant
Sheridan NGL pipeline

COMPETITORS

CenterPoint Energy
Crosstex Energy, Inc.
Southwestern Energy

HISTORICAL FINANCIALS

Company Type: Public

Income Statement

FYE: December 31

	REVENUE ($ mil.)	NET INCOME ($ mil.)	NET PROFIT MARGIN	EMPLOYEES
12/06	860.3	65.1	7.6%	225
12/05	747.7	30.4	4.1%	206
12/04	437.7	(0.9)	—	—
12/03	384.6	(4.7)	—	80
12/02	224.9	(1.6)	—	—
Annual Growth	**39.9%**	**—**	**—**	**41.2%**

2006 Year-End Financials

Debt ratio: 54.0%
Return on equity: 17.3%
Cash ($ mil.): 53.5
Current ratio: 1.17
Long-term debt ($ mil.): 255.0
No. of shares (mil.): 17.6
Dividends
Yield: 4.3%
Payout: 73.7%
Market value ($ mil.): 524.3
R&D as % of sales: —
Advertising as % of sales: —

Stock History

NASDAQ (GS): CPNO

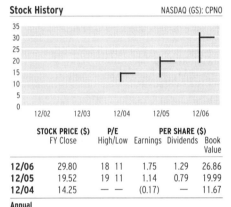

	STOCK PRICE ($) FY Close	P/E High/Low		PER SHARE ($) Earnings	Dividends	Book Value
12/06	29.80	18	11	1.75	1.29	26.86
12/05	19.52	19	11	1.14	0.79	19.99
12/04	14.25	—	—	(0.17)	—	11.67
Annual Growth	**44.6%**	**—**	**—**	**—**	**63.3%**	**51.7%**

The Corporate Executive Board

Don't fear the competition; learn from them. So says The Corporate Executive Board Company (CEB), a provider of business research and analysis services to more than 3,700 companies worldwide. Its 40-plus program areas cover "best practices" in such areas as finance, human resources, information technology, operations, and sales and marketing. Unlike consulting firms, which engage with one client at a time, CEB operates on a membership-based business model. Members subscribe to one or more of the company's programs and participate in the research and analysis, thus sharing expertise with others. Besides reports on best practices, CEB offers seminars, customized research briefs, and decision-support tools.

The company's plans for growth rely on adding more clients to its network, persuading existing clients to subscribe to more research programs, and expanding its list of program areas. It has added more than 10 programs since 2005. In mid-2007, CEB acquired ITtoolbox, an online professional networking provider, for $59 million. The buyout gives CEB access to more than 1 million of ITtoolbox's users in the IT and professional community.

CEB was spun off in 1999 from The Advisory Board Company, which offers similar research and analysis services for clients in the health care industry. A noncompete agreement that prevented CEB from seeking health care clients and kept The Advisory Board from operating outside that industry expired in January 2007; subsequently, the companies agreed to collaborate on selected projects and to continue not competing in core businesses.

EXECUTIVES

Chairman and CEO: Thomas L. Monahan III, age 40
CFO: Timothy R. (Tim) Yost, age 36
CIO: Jonathan N. Dyke
General Manager: Peter Freire
Chief Administrative Officer: Pete Buer
Chief Human Resources Officer: Melody L. Jones, age 45
Chief Research Officer: Derek C. M. van Bever, age 49
Controller, Treasurer, and Secretary: James Edgemond
Executive Director, Operations and Procurement: Mikel Durham
Executive Director, Research: Michael P. (Mike) Kostoff
Investor Relations: Lisa Herold
Media and Public Relations: Christina Borg
Auditors: Ernst & Young LLP

LOCATIONS

HQ: The Corporate Executive Board Company
2000 Pennsylvania Ave. NW, Ste. 6000, Washington, DC 20006
Phone: 202-777-5000 **Fax:** 202-777-5100
Web: www.executiveboard.com

PRODUCTS/OPERATIONS

Selected Practice Areas

Communications
Financial services
General management
Human resources
Information technology
Legal and compliance
Operations and procurement
Sales and marketing
Strategy and research and development

COMPETITORS

Accenture
BearingPoint
Booz Allen
Boston Consulting
Conference Board
McKinsey & Company

HISTORICAL FINANCIALS

Company Type: Public

Income Statement

FYE: December 31

	REVENUE ($ mil.)	NET INCOME ($ mil.)	NET PROFIT MARGIN	EMPLOYEES
12/06	460.6	79.2	17.2%	2,279
12/05	362.2	75.1	20.7%	1,865
12/04	280.7	53.7	19.1%	—
12/03	210.2	35.7	17.0%	—
12/02	162.4	29.6	18.2%	997
Annual Growth	29.8%	27.9%	—	23.0%

2006 Year-End Financials

Debt ratio: —
Return on equity: 22.5%
Cash ($ mil.): 290.9
Current ratio: 1.20
Long-term debt ($ mil.): —
No. of shares (mil.): 38.9
Dividends
Yield: 1.4%
Payout: 61.9%
Market value ($ mil.): 3,415.7
R&D as % of sales: —
Advertising as % of sales: —

Stock History

NASDAQ (GS): EXBD

	STOCK PRICE ($) FY Close	P/E High/Low		PER SHARE ($) Earnings	Dividends	Book Value
12/06	87.70	58	42	1.94	1.20	8.16
12/05	89.70	50	34	1.83	0.20	9.76
12/04	66.94	52	33	1.34	0.22	8.41
12/03	46.67	56	30	0.93	—	6.49
12/02	31.92	51	30	0.79	—	5.74
Annual Growth	28.7%	—	—	25.2%	133.5%	9.2%

Corus Bankshares

Money is at the heart of the matter for Corus Bankshares, the holding company for Corus Bank, which operates about a dozen branches in the Chicago metropolitan area. The bank offers traditional retail banking services for consumers and businesses. Its primary emphasis is on commercial real estate loans, especially condominium construction, which make up around 94% of its loan portfolio. In Chicago and Milwaukee, the bank provides clearing, depository, and credit services to nearly 500 check cashing businesses. Chairman Joseph Glickman and his family together own 42% of the company.

Corus Bank lends nationwide, helping to diversify its commercial real estate-heavy loan portfolio. In fact, about 80% of its loan commitments are secured by properties outside its home state of Illinois, in Atlanta, Chicago, Phoenix, Las Vegas, New York City, and Washington, DC, as well as in Florida and California.

EXECUTIVES

Chairman: Joseph C. Glickman, age 91
President, CEO, and Director: Robert J. Glickman, age 60, $1,000,000 pay
EVP, CFO, Secretary, and Treasurer: Timothy H. (Tim) Taylor, age 41, $681,000 pay
EVP Commercial Lending: Michael G. Stein, age 46, $275,000 pay
EVP Retail Banking: Randy P. Curtis, age 48, $570,000 pay
SVP and Chief Accounting Officer: Michael E. Dulberg, age 41
SVP Commercial Lending: Terence W. Keenan, age 61, $355,587 pay
SVP Commercial Lending: Timothy J. Stodder, $200,000 pay
SVP Finance: Richard J. Koretz, age 43, $395,000 pay
SVP Operations: Michael W. Jump, age 61
VP Human Resources: Jennifer Haughey
Auditors: Ernst & Young LLP

LOCATIONS

HQ: Corus Bankshares, Inc.
3959 N. Lincoln Ave., Chicago, IL 60613
Phone: 800-555-5710 **Fax:** 773-832-3460
Web: www.corusbank.com

PRODUCTS/OPERATIONS

2006 Sales

	$ mil.	% of total
Interest		
Interest & fees on loans	500.9	66
Securities	221.9	29
Federal funds sold	18.3	3
Noninterest		
Service charges on deposit accounts	11.0	1
Securities gains	6.1	1
Other	2.2	—
Total	**760.4**	**100**

COMPETITORS

ABN AMRO
Bank of America
Citigroup
Citizens Republic Bancorp
Fifth Third
First Midwest Bancorp
Harris Bankcorp
LaSalle Bank
MB Financial
National City
Wells Fargo
Wintrust Financial

HISTORICAL FINANCIALS

Company Type: Public

Income Statement

FYE: December 31

	ASSETS ($ mil.)	NET INCOME ($ mil.)	INCOME AS % OF ASSETS	EMPLOYEES
12/06	10,057.8	189.4	1.9%	534
12/05	8,458.7	137.2	1.6%	519
12/04	5,017.8	97.9	2.0%	—
12/03	3,643.8	58.4	1.6%	—
12/02	2,617.1	49.3	1.9%	475
Annual Growth	40.0%	40.0%	—	3.0%

2006 Year-End Financials

Equity as % of assets: 8.4%
Return on assets: 2.0%
Return on equity: 24.7%
Long-term debt ($ mil.): 423.5
No. of shares (mil.): 56.2
Market value ($ mil.): 1,297.6
Dividends
Yield: 3.9%
Payout: 27.4%
Sales ($ mil.): 760.4
R&D as % of sales: —
Advertising as % of sales: —

Stock History

NASDAQ (GS): CORS

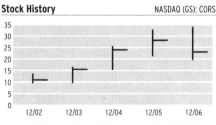

	STOCK PRICE ($) FY Close	P/E High/Low		PER SHARE ($) Earnings	Dividends	Book Value
12/06	23.07	10	6	3.28	0.90	15.01
12/05	28.14	14	9	2.38	0.70	24.70
12/04	24.00	15	9	1.70	0.63	21.57
12/03	15.51	16	10	1.02	0.41	19.48
12/02	10.91	16	11	0.86	0.16	34.14
Annual Growth	20.6%	—	—	39.7%	54.0%	(18.6%)

Cowlitz Bancorporation

Cowlitz Bancorporation is the holding company for Cowlitz Bank and its Bay Bank division, which serve southwestern Washington and the Seattle and Portland, Oregon, areas through about 10 branches and loan production offices. Targeting small and midsized businesses and retail customers, the banks mainly use deposits to originate commercial mortgages (around 30% of the company's loan portfolio), business loans (34%), and construction, residential mortgage, and consumer loans. The company also originates long-term residential real estate loans through its Bay Mortgage division.

In 2005 Cowlitz Bancorporation acquired AEA Bancshares, the holding company for Seattle's Asia-Europe-Americas (AEA) Bank, which adopted the Bay Bank name after the transaction.

Former chairman Benjamin Namatinia owns more than 15% of the company. Private equity firm Crescent Capital, which owns nearly 10%, has made an unsolicited bid to acquire all of Cowlitz Bancorporation.

EXECUTIVES

Chairman: Phillip S. (Phill) Rowley, age 60
President, CEO, and Director; President and CEO, Cowlitz Bank: Richard J. Fitzpatrick, age 58, $369,075 pay
VP and CFO, Cowlitz Bancorporation; EVP and CFO, Cowlitz Bank: Gerald L. Brickey, age 54
VP and General Auditor: Loree Vandenberg, age 40, $137,264 pay
VP, Administration and Secretary: Lynda Altman, age 42
VP, Administrative Officer, and Secretary; SVP Administration, Cowlitz Bank: Lynda Larrabee, age 44
VP Credit Administrator and Director; EVP and Chief Credit Administrator, Cowlitz Bank: Ernie Ballou, age 58, $238,761 pay
SVP and Commercial Lending Manager, Cowlitz Bank: Terry Minnihan
SVP and Regional Manager, Bay Bank: Al Shott
VP and Branch Manager, Bay Bank: Karen Twietmeyer
VP Information Technology, Cowlitz Bank: Sue Rodgers, age 48
Director; Chairman, Cowlitz Bank: Linda M. Tubbs, age 59
Auditors: Moss Adams, LLP

LOCATIONS

HQ: Cowlitz Bancorporation
927 Commerce Ave., Longview, WA 98632
Phone: 360-423-9800 **Fax:** 360-423-3562
Web: www.cowlitzbancorp.com

Cowlitz Bancorporation has branches and offices in Cowlitz and King counties in Washington; in the Portland, Oregon metropolitan area; and surrounding counties in Washington and northwest Oregon.

PRODUCTS/OPERATIONS

2006 Sales

	% of total
Interest	
Loans, including fees	82
Investment securities	8
Other	1
Noninterest	
Deposit service charges	2
Fiduciary income	1
Other	6
Total	**100**

COMPETITORS

Bank of America	Sterling Financial (WA)
Columbia Banking	Timberland Bancorp
First Mutual Bancshares	Washington Mutual
Heritage Financial	Wells Fargo
Riverview Bancorp	

HISTORICAL FINANCIALS

Company Type: Public

Income Statement
FYE: December 31

	ASSETS ($ mil.)	NET INCOME ($ mil.)	INCOME AS % OF ASSETS	EMPLOYEES
12/06	468.4	4.8	1.0%	135
12/05	370.1	3.0	0.8%	119
12/04	273.3	1.9	0.7%	—
12/03	268.8	0.1	0.0%	—
12/02	345.2	1.5	0.4%	200
Annual Growth	**7.9%**	**33.7%**	**—**	**(9.4%)**

2006 Year-End Financials

Equity as % of assets: 10.8%
Return on assets: 1.1%
Return on equity: 10.0%
Long-term debt ($ mil.): 12.4
No. of shares (mil.): 4.9
Market value ($ mil.): 82.0
Dividends
  Yield: —
  Payout: —
Sales ($ mil.): 34.8
R&D as % of sales: —
Advertising as % of sales: —

Stock History
NASDAQ (GM): CWLZ

	STOCK PRICE ($) FY Close	P/E High/Low	Earnings	Dividends	Book Value
12/06	16.78	19 14	0.93	—	10.37
12/05	14.40	22 16	0.66	—	9.42
12/04	11.14	24 20	0.47	—	8.55
12/03	11.25	400 201	0.03	—	8.16
12/02	7.59	20 13	0.39	—	8.19
Annual Growth	**21.9%**	**— —**	**24.3%**	**—**	**6.1%**

CRA International

Whether you need an expert to help you run your business, testify for you in court, or evaluate the finances of an acquisition candidate, CRA International wants to help. The company's 770-plus consultants offer economic and business counsel from more than 25 offices, mainly in North America but also in Europe, the Middle East, and the Asia/Pacific region. CRA has organized its practices into three main areas: finance (valuation and accounting, insurance, and risk management); litigation and applied economics (competition, intellectual property, trade, and transfer pricing); and business consulting. Clients include companies from a variety of industries, government agencies, and law firms.

CRA International has expanded through a series of acquisitions — more than 10 since 1998 — and the firm intends to continue to look for complementary businesses to buy. In 2006 it bought the assets of Washington, DC-based consulting firm Ballentine Barbera Group, a specialist in transfer pricing services. At the same time, CRA International is working to control operating costs as it expands.

Most of CRA International's revenue comes from continuing engagements and repeat business from existing clients. Work related to antitrust issues and mergers and acquisitions accounts for a quarter of the firm's revenue.

EXECUTIVES

Chairman: Rowland T. (Row) Moriarty, age 60
Chairman Emeritus: Franklin M. (Frank) Fisher, age 72
President, CEO, and Director: James C. Burrows, age 63, $1,650,000 pay
EVP, Chief Corporate Development Officer, and Head of Europe and Middle East: Frederick Baird
EVP and Chief Strategy Officer: Arnold J. (Arnie) Lowenstein, age 53, $1,250,000 pay
EVP and Head of Finance Platform: Paul A. Maleh, age 43, $1,575,000 pay
EVP and Head of Strategy and Business Consulting Platform: Gregory K. Bell, age 46, $2,840,385 pay
EVP and Head of Litigation and Applied Economics Platform: Monica G. Noether, age 53, $930,769 pay
EVP, CFO, and Treasurer: Wayne D. Mackie, age 58
VP and General Counsel: Jonathan D. Yellin
VP and Director, Economic and Policy Analysis: Brian Fisher
VP, Energy and Environment: Dean C. Maschoff
Secretary: Peter M. Rosenblum
Marketing Director: John Michaels
Auditors: KPMG LLP

LOCATIONS

HQ: CRA International, Inc.
200 Clarendon St., Ste. T-33, Boston, MA 02116
Phone: 617-425-3000 **Fax:** 617-425-3132
Web: www.crai.com

2007 Sales

	$ mil.	% of total
US	289.1	73
UK	77.3	20
Australia	14.5	4
Other countries	13.8	3
Total	**394.6**	**100**

PRODUCTS/OPERATIONS

Selected Practice Areas

Finance
  Enterprise risk management
  Financial accounting and valuation
  Financial markets
  Forensic services
  Insurance economics
  Legal business consulting
Litigation and applied economics
  Financial economics
  Global antitrust and competition economics
  Intellectual property
  International arbitration
  International trade
  Labor and employment
  Mergers and acquisitions
  Regulation
  Services to financial institutions
  Transfer pricing
Business consulting
  Auctions and competitive bidding
  Competitive strategy
  Environmental strategy
  Intellectual property and technology management
  Litigation and arbitration support
  Organization and performance improvement
  Public policy and regulatory economics
  Risk management
  Transaction advisory services

COMPETITORS

Accenture	Economics Research
Bain & Company	Exponent
BearingPoint	FTI Consulting
Booz Allen	Huron Consulting
Boston Consulting	LECG
Capgemini	McKinsey & Company
Cornerstone Research	Navigant Consulting
Deloitte Consulting	PA Consulting

HISTORICAL FINANCIALS

Company Type: Public

Income Statement
FYE: Last Saturday in November

	REVENUE ($ mil.)	NET INCOME ($ mil.)	NET PROFIT MARGIN	EMPLOYEES
11/07	394.6	32.6	8.3%	—
11/06	349.9	27.4	7.8%	733
11/05	295.5	24.6	8.3%	906
11/04	216.7	16.3	7.5%	—
11/03	163.5	11.4	7.0%	—
Annual Growth	24.6%	30.0%	—	(19.1%)

2007 Year-End Financials

Debt ratio: 35.8%
Return on equity: 13.0%
Cash ($ mil.): 100.5
Current ratio: 2.52
Long-term debt ($ mil.): 90.0
No. of shares (mil.): 10.8
Dividends
Yield: —
Payout: —
Market value ($ mil.): 506.0
R&D as % of sales: —
Advertising as % of sales: —

Stock History
NASDAQ (GS): CRAI

	STOCK PRICE ($) FY Close	P/E High/Low		Earnings	PER SHARE ($) Dividends	Book Value
11/07	47.01	21	16	2.68	—	23.33
11/06	52.21	24	19	2.24	—	21.70
11/05	45.77	27	19	2.13	—	18.20
11/04	43.18	28	18	1.55	—	12.80
11/03	32.75	31	11	1.16	—	11.60
Annual Growth	9.5%	—	—	23.3%	—	19.1%

Crescent Banking

This crescent gives a whole new meaning to "dough boy." Crescent Banking Company is the holding company of Crescent Bank & Trust, which serves north-central Georgia from about a dozen branches and loan offices. The bank offers standard services such as checking and savings accounts, money market accounts, CDs, and IRAs. The company mainly uses funds from deposits to originate loans secured by real estate in its market area, such as residential and commercial mortgages and construction and land development loans, which account for more than 90% of its loan portfolio. Other offerings include business loans and consumer installment loans.

Crescent Banking Company bought Alpharetta, Georgia-based bank Futurus Financial Services in 2005.

Director Michael Lowe owns more than 20% of Crescent Banking Company. Including his stake, directors and executive officers own more than 40% of the firm.

EXECUTIVES

Chairman: John S. Dean Sr., age 68
President, CEO, and Director, Crescent Banking Company and Crescent Bank & Trust; Secretary, Crescent Mortgage Services: J. Donald Boggus Jr., age 44, $350,000 pay
EVP and CFO, Crescent Banking Company and Crescent Bank & Trust: Leland W. Brantley Jr., age 36, $245,000 pay
EVP and Chief of Lending Administration, Crescent Bank & Trust: A. Bradley Rutledge Sr., age 44, $293,282 pay
EVP and Chief of Lending Production, Crescent Bank & Trust: Anthony N. (Tony) Stancil, age 44, $300,000 pay
EVP and Retail Administrator, Crescent Bank & Trust: Bonnie B. Boling, age 53, $154,894 pay
SVP and County President, Crescent Bank & Trust, Cumming: Dave Denton
SVP and Loan Officer, Crescent Bank & Trust: Lorrie L. Shaw
Banking Officer and Human Resources Manager, Crescent Bank & Trust: Eva Howell
Auditors: Dixon Hughes PLLC

LOCATIONS

HQ: Crescent Banking Company
7 Caring Way, Jasper, GA 30143
Phone: 678-454-2266   **Fax:** 678-454-2282
Web: www.crescentbank.com

PRODUCTS/OPERATIONS

2006 Sales

	$ mil.	% of total
Interest		
Loans, including fees	52.1	88
Federal funds sold	1.8	3
Securities	1.1	2
Other	0.1	—
Noninterest		
Service charges on deposit accounts	1.0	2
Other	3.3	5
Total	59.4	100

COMPETITORS

Bank of America
BB&T
Chestatee Bancshares
GB&T Bancshares
Habersham Bancorp
Regions Financial
Wachovia

HISTORICAL FINANCIALS

Company Type: Public

Income Statement
FYE: December 31

	ASSETS ($ mil.)	NET INCOME ($ mil.)	INCOME AS % OF ASSETS	EMPLOYEES
12/06	779.7	7.3	0.9%	199
12/05	704.1	4.1	0.6%	196
12/04	513.4	(0.8)	—	—
12/03	366.4	17.3	4.7%	—
12/02	559.4	11.5	2.1%	230
Annual Growth	8.7%	(10.7%)	—	(3.6%)

2006 Year-End Financials

Equity as % of assets: 7.9%
Return on assets: 1.0%
Return on equity: 12.5%
Long-term debt ($ mil.): 35.9
No. of shares (mil.): 2.6
Market value ($ mil.): 60.8
Dividends
Yield: 1.1%
Payout: 19.0%
Sales ($ mil.): 59.4
R&D as % of sales: —
Advertising as % of sales: —

Stock History
NASDAQ (CM): CSNT

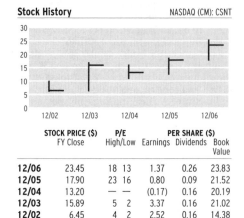

	STOCK PRICE ($) FY Close	P/E High/Low		Earnings	PER SHARE ($) Dividends	Book Value
12/06	23.45	18	13	1.37	0.26	23.83
12/05	17.90	23	16	0.80	0.09	21.52
12/04	13.20	—	—	(0.17)	0.16	20.19
12/03	15.89	5	2	3.37	0.16	21.02
12/02	6.45	4	2	2.52	0.16	14.38
Annual Growth	38.1%	—	—	(14.1%)	12.9%	13.5%

Crescent Financial

This Crescent can help you wrench the most bang from your buck. Crescent Financial is the holding company for Crescent State Bank, which operates branches in the Raleigh, North Carolina area. The community bank offers standard products and services, including checking and savings accounts, NOW and sweep accounts, lines of credit, and cash management services. Commercial mortgages make up about half of its loan portfolio; construction loans make up about 20%. The company also writes industrial loans, home equity loans, and residential mortgages.

Crescent Financial bought Port City Capital Bank, which kept its name, in 2006.

Executive officers and directors collectively own nearly 20% of the company.

EXECUTIVES

Chairman: Bruce I. Howell, age 64
President, CEO, and Director, Crescent Financial and Crescent State Bank: Michael G. Carlton, age 45, $282,218 pay
VP and Secretary; SVP and CFO, Crescent State Bank: Bruce W. Elder, age 44, $167,473 pay
President and CEO, Port City Capital Bank: W. Keith Betts, age 50
EVP and CFO, Port City Capital Bank: Lawrence S. Brobst
EVP and Senior Lending Officer, Port City Capital Bank: John M. Franck
SVP and COO, Crescent State Bank: Ray D. Vaughn, age 54
SVP and Chief Lending Officer, Crescent State Bank: Thomas E. Holder Jr., age 47, $161,165 pay
SVP, Crescent State Bank: James F. Byrd
SVP, Crescent State Bank: Douglas M. Gay
SVP, Crescent State Bank: Jonathan H. Taylor
Auditors: Dixon Hughes PLLC

LOCATIONS

HQ: Crescent Financial Corporation
1005 High House Rd., Cary, NC 27513
Phone: 919-460-7770 **Fax:** 919-460-2512
Web: www.crescentstatebank.com

PRODUCTS/OPERATIONS

2006 Sales

	$ mil.	% of total
Interest		
Loans, including fees	33.1	84
Securities & other	3.6	9
Noninterest		
Fees on deposit accounts	1.3	3
Mortgage loan origination fees	0.6	2
Other	0.7	2
Total	**39.3**	**100**

COMPETITORS

Bank of America
BB&T
Capital Bank
Cardinal State Bank
KS Bancorp
M&F Bancorp
North State Bancorp
RBC Centura Banks
Wachovia
Wake Forest Bancshares

HISTORICAL FINANCIALS

Company Type: Public

Income Statement — FYE: December 31

	ASSETS ($ mil.)	NET INCOME ($ mil.)	INCOME AS % OF ASSETS	EMPLOYEES
12/06	697.9	4.9	0.7%	129
12/05	410.8	3.1	0.8%	99
12/04	331.2	2.3	0.7%	—
12/03	273.7	1.6	0.6%	—
12/02	182.0	1.2	0.7%	—
Annual Growth	**39.9%**	**42.2%**	**—**	**30.3%**

2006 Year-End Financials

Equity as % of assets: 11.9%
Return on assets: 0.9%
Return on equity: 7.9%
Long-term debt ($ mil.): 45.3
No. of shares (mil.): 8.3
Market value ($ mil.): 96.1

Dividends
Yield: —
Payout: —
Sales ($ mil.): 39.3
R&D as % of sales: —
Advertising as % of sales: —

Stock History — NASDAQ (CM): CRFN

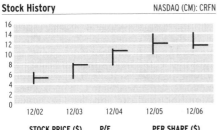

	STOCK PRICE ($) FY Close	P/E High/Low	PER SHARE ($) Earnings	Dividends	Book Value
12/06	11.63	22 17	0.65	—	10.05
12/05	12.02	25 18	0.55	1.70	8.25
12/04	10.58	25 18	0.43	1.51	7.51
12/03	7.79	23 15	0.35	1.23	8.26
12/02	5.20	18 12	0.35	—	8.27
Annual Growth	**22.3%**	**— —**	**16.7%**	**17.6%**	**5.0%**

Crocs, Inc.

Crocs is taking a bite out of the footwear industry. Its trademark colorful slip-on shoes have gained popularity in the watersports arena and in mainstream fashion. The shoes, sold under the Crocs name, are made of proprietary closed-cell resin; Jibbitz are their popular add-ons. They're designed for men, women, and children and feature a rear handle. The firm operates manufacturing facilities in Canada, Mexico, and Italy. Suppliers in China, Italy, Romania, and the US make the rest. It distributes through retailers, including Dillard's, Nordstrom, REI, and The Sports Authority. The company is expanding on both domestic and international fronts and through acquisitions, such as Ocean Minded, LLC, in 2007.

In recent years Crocs has been snapping up add-on firms and looking to innovative technology to pump out the next popular product. Environmentally focused Ocean Minded designs and makes sandals for young sports enthusiasts. The deal, valued at nearly $2 million plus incentives for hitting earnings targets over a three-year period, is expected to give Crocs a boost in its retail and distribution operations, as well as expand its reach overseas. Ocean Minded, which serves surf and skate fans, allows Crocs to gain a foothold in this trendy niche. As part of the agreement, Ocean Minded became a wholly owned subsidiary of Crocs, with Ocean Minded's founder Robert Allison remaining on board.

To extend its reach into the accessories business, the firm acquired family-run Jibbitz LLC, which makes items to decorate Crocs clogs, for about $10 million in late 2006. (Crocs carries some 1,100 Jibbitz designs to help customers personalize their footwear.) Also in the second half of 2006, Crocs bought EXO Italia, maker of ethylene vinyl acetate-based finished products.

To compete in the sports arena, Crocs in early 2007 purchased Fury, which specializes in manufacturing sports-protection items — such as sticks, gloves, pants, and shin and elbow pads — using its Croslite antimicrobial material.

Its licensing efforts, which allow the company to diversify its sources of revenue, haven't been lost either. In fact, it's a growing add-on business for the footwear maker. Crocs expanded its agreements with the NFL and NHL to give it rights to use all NFL and NHL team logos, as well as those for the football league, the Super Bowl, and Pro Bowl. To attract its younger customers, Crocs has been busy inking deals since mid-2006, when it announced an agreement with Disney to make a limited edition line of Crocs footwear named Disney by Crocs. Crocs partnered with Warner Bros. Consumer Products in early 2007 to offer a roster of DC Comics Super Heroes legendary characters, such as Batman, Superman, Wonder Woman, and others. The footwear firm and Marvel Entertainment paired up months later to greatly expand Crocs' superhero portfolio and add punch to its Jibbitz charms sales. The licensing deal, inked in May 2007, makes Captain America, The Incredible Hulk, Spider-Man, and other comic book heroes available to Crocs customers in the US and Canada.

The shoes sell in 11,000 US shops, such as Nordstrom and specialty stores, and in 80 countries. Crocs gets most of its revenue from sales to customers younger than 18 years old and older than 30.

EXECUTIVES

Chairman: Richard L. Sharp, age 61
President, CEO, and Director: Ronald R. (Ron) Snyder, age 51, $1,000,000 pay
COO and EVP: John P. McCarvel, age 51
SVP Finance, CFO, and Treasurer: Russ Hammer, age 51
SVP Retail Division: Peter S. Case, age 47, $331,500 pay
VP Finance: Caryn D. Ellison, $250,000 pay
VP Customer Relations: Lyndon V. (Duke) Hanson III
VP Sales and Marketing: Michael C. Margolis, age 56, $288,500 pay
Auditors: Deloitte & Touche LLP

LOCATIONS

HQ: Crocs, Inc.
6328 Monarch Park Place, Niwot, CO 80503
Phone: 303-848-7000 **Fax:** 303-468-4266
Web: www.crocs.com

2006 Sales

	$ mil.	% of total
US	242.2	69
Asia	54.4	15
Europe	30.3	9
Canada	21.8	6
Mexico	1.5	—
All other	4.6	1
Total	**354.7**	**100**

PRODUCTS/OPERATIONS

2006 Sales

	$ mil.	% of total
Shoes	342.4	96
Other	12.3	4
Total	**354.7**	**100**

COMPETITORS

adidas
Birkenstock Distribution USA
Columbia Sportswear
Deckers Outdoor
L.L. Bean
NIKE
R. Griggs
São Paulo Alpargatas
Skechers U.S.A.
Timberland
Wolverine World Wide

HISTORICAL FINANCIALS

Company Type: Public

Income Statement — FYE: December 31

	REVENUE ($ mil.)	NET INCOME ($ mil.)	NET PROFIT MARGIN	EMPLOYEES
12/06	354.7	64.4	18.2%	2,900
12/05	108.6	17.0	15.7%	1,130
12/04	13.5	(1.5)	—	260
12/03	1.2	(1.2)	—	—
12/02	0.0	(0.4)	—	8
Annual Growth	**—**	**—**	**—**	**336.3%**

2006 Year-End Financials

Debt ratio: 0.1%
Return on equity: 56.7%
Cash ($ mil.): 67.9
Current ratio: 2.70
Long-term debt ($ mil.): 0.1
No. of shares (mil.): 39.9

Dividends
Yield: —
Payout: —
Market value ($ mil.): 862.2
R&D as % of sales: —
Advertising as % of sales: —

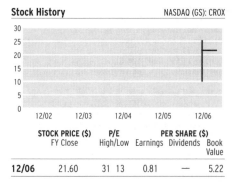

	STOCK PRICE ($)	P/E	PER SHARE ($)		
	FY Close	High/Low	Earnings	Dividends	Book Value
12/06	21.60	31 13	0.81	—	5.22

Cuisine Solutions

Whether you're traveling for pleasure or to serve your country, this company tries to make sure you get a good meal. Cuisine Solutions is a leading supplier of prepared meals for a variety of customers, including travel and transportation providers, the military, retail stores, and foodservice operators. Through its production facilities in the US and France, the company makes fully cooked and frozen meals, including chicken, seafood, and beef items, along with pasta and sauces, and distributes those meals throughout the US and in Europe. The family of chairman Jean-Louis Vilgrain owns about 60% of the company.

With the US deploying more personnel overseas, sales to the military and military suppliers have been a rapidly growing part of Cuisine Solutions' business. Ocean Direct, a leading distributor that serves the US Army, accounts for about 10% of sales. Meanwhile, the company has also seen some growth in its retail food business; warehouse club retailer Costco accounts for 15% of revenue.

In addition to its manufacturing facilities in the US and France, Cuisine Solutions has a 10% stake in a production facility in Chile. In 2007 the company expanded into Spain, hiring famed chef Andoni Luiz Aduriz as a consultant.

HISTORY

Cuisine Solutions began in 1972 as Ile France, which sold baguettes to restaurants in the Washington, DC, area. It was renamed Vie de France, and by 1974 it had bakeries in Boston, Philadelphia, and Washington. Needing money to expand, the company allowed Jean-Louis Vilgrain, of France's Grands Moulins de Paris, to buy a 26% stake in the company; he became chairman and CEO in 1977. In 1979 Vie de France created a chain of cafe/restaurants that were soon franchised. It went public in 1984.

In 1990 Vie de France opened its first *sous vide* plant in Virginia. The next year Stanislas Vilgrain, son of the chairman and head of the *sous vide* operation, was named president and COO. The company's bakeries and restaurants were sold to Vie de France Yamazaki (an unrelated Japanese business) in 1991 and 1994, respectively. In 1994 Vie de France opened a *sous vide* plant in Norway.

The company struggled with high costs and operating losses throughout the mid-1990s. In 1997 Vie de France restructured its sales operation to focus on the banquet industry and beefed up its internal sales team. It also adopted a new name — Cuisine Solutions. In 1998 the company completed its reorganization process and began pursuing international expansion. It acquired a *sous vide* plant in France in 1999.

Its 1998 joint venture with Sanoli Indústria e Comércio de Alimentacão to launch Cuisine Solutions Brazil also enhanced its global presence; however, due to legal difficulties with its partner, the company terminated its activities in Brazil in 2002. Cuisine Solutions also exited its Norway manufacturing operations in 2004 due to a lack of profitability; it transferred its seafood operations to Cuisine Solutions Chile, in which it acquired a minority stake.

EXECUTIVES

Chairman: Jean-Louis Vilgrain, age 73
President, CEO, and Director: Stanislas Vilgrain, age 48
COO: L. Felipe Hasselmann, age 38, $249,104 pay
CFO, Treasurer, and Corporate Secretary:
  Ronald R. Zilkowski, age 50
VP Product Development: Marc Brennet
VP Sales: Gerard J. Bertholon, age 47, $145,000 pay
VP and Controller: Ronnie Lai
Director Military Accounts: Elizabeth Lauer
Manager Marketing: Lillian Liu
Auditors: BDO Seidman, LLP

LOCATIONS

HQ: Cuisine Solutions, Inc.
  85 S. Bragg St., Ste. 600, Alexandria, VA 22312
Phone: 703-270-2900   **Fax:** 703-750-1158
Web: www.cuisinesolutions.com

2007 Sales

	$ mil.	% of total
US	55.9	70
Europe	24.1	30
Other regions	0.3	—
Total	**80.3**	**100**

PRODUCTS/OPERATIONS

2007 Sales

	$ mil.	% of total
Retail	23.7	30
On Board Services	19.4	24
Military	17.6	22
Foodservice	13.7	17
Restaurant chains	5.9	7
Total	**80.3**	**100**

Selected Operations

On Board Services (transportation and tourism meal services)
Retail (in-store meal services and frozen packaged foods)
Military (on-site meal services for military personnel)
Foodservice (catering and event foodservices)
Restaurant chains (foodservice supply for restaurant operators)

COMPETITORS

Armanino Foods of Distinction
ConAgra
Gate Gourmet
Kraft Foods
LSG Sky Chefs
Monterey Gourmet Foods
Overhill Farms
Performance Food
Sanderson Farms
SYSCO
Tyson Foods
U.S. Foodservice

HISTORICAL FINANCIALS

Company Type: Public

Income Statement

FYE: Last Saturday in June

	REVENUE ($ mil.)	NET INCOME ($ mil.)	NET PROFIT MARGIN	EMPLOYEES
6/07	80.3	10.5	13.1%	354
6/06	64.1	3.7	5.8%	302
6/05	46.3	1.7	3.7%	263
6/04	36.7	(1.0)	—	230
6/03	27.8	(4.1)	—	180
Annual Growth	**30.4%**	**—**	**—**	**18.4%**

2007 Year-End Financials

Debt ratio: 22.4%
Return on equity: 55.4%
Cash ($ mil.): 0.6
Current ratio: 1.88
Long-term debt ($ mil.): 5.5
No. of shares (mil.): 16.6
Dividends
  Yield: —
  Payout: —
Market value ($ mil.): 100.6
R&D as % of sales: —
Advertising as % of sales: —

Stock History

AMEX: FZN

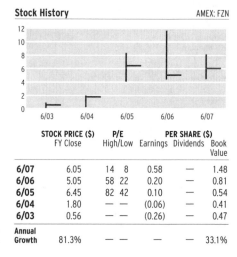

	STOCK PRICE ($)	P/E	PER SHARE ($)		
	FY Close	High/Low	Earnings	Dividends	Book Value
6/07	6.05	14 8	0.58	—	1.48
6/06	5.05	58 22	0.20	—	0.81
6/05	6.45	82 42	0.10	—	0.54
6/04	1.80	— —	(0.06)	—	0.41
6/03	0.56	— —	(0.26)	—	0.47
Annual Growth	**81.3%**	**— —**	**—**	**—**	**33.1%**

Cutera, Inc.

Cutera has a handle on hairy situations and a firm plan for flabby faces. The firm makes lasers for medical and aesthetic use in doctors' offices and spas. Its FDA-approved devices are marketed under the names CoolGlide, Solera, and Xeo and are used for hair removal and treatments to reduce pigmented lesions (age and sun spots), wrinkles, and veins. Its Titan line of products uses deep tissue heating to firm up saggy facial skin. The company markets its products through a direct sales force and a distributor in the US and relies on a small sales group and distributors in about 30 other countries. Director Annette Campbell-White controls about 21% of the company.

Beyond dermatologists and plastic surgeons, Cutera is increasing its sales to gynecologists, primary care physicians, and medically supervised spas. The company is also working to expand its international reach.

EXECUTIVES

President, CEO, and Director: Kevin P. Connors, age 45, $762,233 pay
VP CFO, Finance, and Administration:
Ronald J. Santilli, age 47, $421,878 pay
VP Research and Development and Director:
David A. Gollnick, age 43, $416,110 pay
VP Human Resources: Stacie Rodgers
VP North American Sales: John J. Connors, age 42, $167,980 pay
VP International: Robert J. Shine Jr., age 38, $206,265 pay
Auditors: PricewaterhouseCoopers LLP

LOCATIONS

HQ: Cutera, Inc.
3240 Bayshore Blvd., Brisbane, CA 94005
Phone: 415-657-5500   **Fax:** 415-330-2444
Web: www.cutera.com

2006 Sales

	$ mil.	% of total
US	69.9	70
Asia, excluding Japan	8.4	8
Japan	7.4	7
Europe	7.2	7
Rest of world	7.8	8
Total	**100.7**	**100**

PRODUCTS/OPERATIONS

2006 Sales

	$ mil.	% of total
Products	84.7	84
Product upgrades	6.0	6
Service	5.9	6
Titan refills	4.1	4
Total	**100.7**	**100**

COMPETITORS

Candela Corporation
Cynosure
IRIDEX
Lumenis
Palomar Medical
Syneron
Thermage

HISTORICAL FINANCIALS

Company Type: Public

Income Statement

FYE: December 31

	REVENUE ($ mil.)	NET INCOME ($ mil.)	NET PROFIT MARGIN	EMPLOYEES
12/06	100.7	2.1	2.1%	221
12/05	75.6	13.8	18.3%	195
12/04	52.6	3.8	7.2%	—
12/03	39.1	3.1	7.9%	—
12/02	28.3	0.7	2.5%	—
Annual Growth	**37.3%**	**31.6%**	**—**	**13.3%**

2006 Year-End Financials

Debt ratio: —
Return on equity: 2.0%
Cash ($ mil.): 108.3
Current ratio: 6.77
Long-term debt ($ mil.): —
No. of shares (mil.): 12.9
Dividends
Yield: —
Payout: —
Market value ($ mil.): 349.4
R&D as % of sales: —
Advertising as % of sales: —

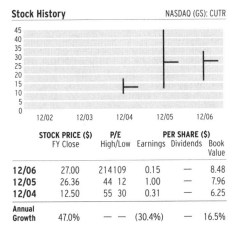

Stock History   NASDAQ (GS): CUTR

	STOCK PRICE ($) FY Close	P/E High/Low	PER SHARE ($) Earnings	Dividends	Book Value
12/06	27.00	214 109	0.15	—	8.48
12/05	26.36	44 12	1.00	—	7.96
12/04	12.50	55 30	0.31	—	6.25
Annual Growth	**47.0%**	**— —**	**(30.4%)**	**—**	**16.5%**

CyberSource Corporation

Cyber security has to start somewhere. CyberSource provides software and services that help ensure that e-commerce and other Internet-based transactions are processed securely. Companies use its software to process credit card payments and electronic checks, as well as to screen for payment fraud. Other applications manage gift certificate programs and verify personal information. The company's software can be integrated with other enterprise applications from vendors such as Microsoft, Oracle, and SAP. In addition to its software, CyberSource offers outsourced payment processing and fraud detection services.

The company processes some 200 million transactions per year for its customers including British Airways, H&R Block, Overstock.com, and Starbucks.

In 2006 the company acquired BidPay.com from First Data. The following year CyberSource purchased Authorize.Net for about $662 million. In late 2007 the company shut down its BidPay subsidiary.

HISTORY

Founded in 1994 by William McKiernan — former president of antivirus specialist McAfee — and John Pettitt, CyberSource was orginially an online retailer that sold software through its software.net Web site. The company operated like a traditional mail-order catalog until 1995, when it began offering "electronic delivery" for several of its titles. The company used its proprietary Electronic Distribution Technology (EDT) to encrypt the digital content for secure transmission.

Several companies, including QUALCOMM, Insignia Systems, and Wall Data (now a part of NetManage), contracted CyberSource's fraud prevention division to conduct their online transactions. In 1996 the company signed an agreement with the US Department of Defense to offer electronic ordering and distribution of software to federal employees for the first time.

In 1997 the company spun off its fraud prevention unit as CyberSource while its retail operation,

renamed software.net, later became Beyond.com. (Beyond.com went public in a high-flying IPO but crashed with the tech bubble implosion. Renamed Beyond Corporation, it filed for Chapter 11 bankruptcy protection in 2002.)

Backed by investors including Microsoft cofounder Paul Allen, GE Capital, and Visa, CyberSource went public in 1999. It used $140 million of its IPO cash to acquire PaylinX, which developed software used to integrate and manage telephone and online payment operations. Many online retailers fizzled away after the dot-com bubble burst in 2000, but thanks to its blue chip client list — anchored by Visa — CyberSource managed to survive.

EXECUTIVES

Chairman and CEO: William S. (Bill) McKiernan, age 51, $318,750 pay
President and COO: Scott R. Cruickshank, age 45
EVP Product Development and CTO: Robert J. Ford, age 58, $285,000 pay
SVP Finance and CFO: Steven D. Pellizzer, age 38, $218,750 pay
SVP Worldwide Sales: Michael A. Walsh, age 39, $215,000 pay
VP Customer Support: Patricia A. (Trish) Martin, age 46
VP Engineering: Jay Martin
VP Marketing: Perry S. Dembner, age 47
VP Product Management: Kirsten Fry-Sanchez, age 48
VP Professional Services: David A. Glaser
VP and General Counsel: David J. Kim, age 40
VP Operations: George Barby, age 52
President BidPay.com: David Hansen, age 49
Director Corporate Communications and Investor Relations: Bruce Frymire
Auditors: Ernst & Young LLP

LOCATIONS

HQ: CyberSource Corporation
1295 Charleston Rd., Mountain View, CA 94043
Phone: 650-965-6000   **Fax:** 650-625-9145
Web: www.cybersource.com

PRODUCTS/OPERATIONS

Transaction Services and Software

Address information standardization and validation
Credit card authorization
Electronic payment
Export control
Fraud prediction and detection
Gift certificate and promotional coupon issuance and redemption
Payment services implementation and integration
Payment systems management (CyberSource Payment Manager)
Reporting systems development and integration
Risk management operation assessment
Sales and use tax calculation

Professional Services

Business process analyses
Capacity planning and security
Commerce infrastructure integration
Custom reporting
Database sizing
Disaster recovery
Finance and administrative process/systems impact
Installation and integration
Maintenance
Sales and customer service process/systems impact
System optimization
Technology selection
Transaction cost analyses

COMPETITORS

Bottomline Technologies	Retail Decisions
Fair Isaac	SAS Institute
First Data	SPSS
IBM	Sterling Commerce
InfoSpace	VeriSign
Microsoft	

HISTORICAL FINANCIALS

Company Type: Public

Income Statement

FYE: December 31

	REVENUE ($ mil.)	NET INCOME ($ mil.)	NET PROFIT MARGIN	EMPLOYEES
12/06	70.3	14.4	20.5%	247
12/05	50.5	9.3	18.4%	185
12/04	36.7	4.5	12.3%	—
12/03	27.5	(5.4)	—	—
12/02	28.0	(12.5)	—	163
Annual Growth	25.9%	—	—	11.0%

2006 Year-End Financials

Debt ratio: —
Return on equity: 21.2%
Cash ($ mil.): 54.9
Current ratio: 8.16
Long-term debt ($ mil.): —
No. of shares (mil.): 34.9
Dividends
Yield: —
Payout: —
Market value ($ mil.): 384.7
R&D as % of sales: —
Advertising as % of sales: —

Stock History

NASDAQ (GM): CYBS

	STOCK PRICE ($) FY Close	P/E High/Low		PER SHARE ($) Earnings	Dividends	Book Value
12/06	11.02	33	16	0.39	—	2.25
12/05	6.60	31	18	0.26	—	1.68
12/04	7.15	78	33	0.12	—	1.42
12/03	5.16	—	—	(0.17)	—	1.33
12/02	2.45	—	—	(0.38)	—	1.51
Annual Growth	45.6%	—	—	—	—	10.6%

Daktronics, Inc.

Daktronics always knows the score. The company designs and manufactures electronic display systems. Its products include scoreboards, game timers, shot clocks, and animation displays for sports facilities; advertising and information displays for businesses; and electronic messaging displays used by transportation departments for motorist alerts. Other applications include airport information, securities trading, and outdoor advertising signs. Daktronics has converted many of its products to LED technology. The company's high-profile installations include two of the biggest scoreboards in the world, for the football stadiums of the Miami Dolphins and the University of Texas Longhorns.

The company has organized into five business units — Commercial, Small Sports Venues, Live Events, Transportation, and International. Each focused business unit is led by a company VP. Daktronics sees the new organizational structure allowing each business unit to draw on corporate resources for its specific market, while also providing flexibility and accountability.

Daktronics' programmable signs display everything from a pitcher's statistics to road conditions to the time and temperature. Its products also tally votes in legislative chambers and tout beer in Times Square. With its 2004 acquisition of UK-based European Timing Systems, Daktronics' signs also keep cricket and rugby scores in the UK. About 90% of the company's sales comes from the US.

Because its products are becoming more affordable, Daktronics is selling more to midsized universities and the minor leagues. The company is also seeing an increase in sales to commercial customers, due in part to Daktronics' increased use of LEDs; the technology has become more popular since the mid-1990s because of its visual clarity and cost efficiency.

In 2006 Daktronics acquired the assets of Hoffend & Sons for about $4 million. Hoffend was a manufacturer of hoist systems for sports and theatrical venues, and functioned as a supplier to Daktronics. The business became the Vortek division of Daktronics Hoist.

The Louisiana Superdome, damaged by Hurricane Katrina, underwent renovation in 2006. The work included new scoreboards and displays from Daktronics, valued at nearly $6 million.

Co-founder Aelred Kurtenbach (chairman) and his brother Frank (VP) together own about 9% of Daktronics.

HISTORY

Daktronics was founded in a garage in 1968 by engineering professors Aelred Kurtenbach and Duane Sander (who later became dean of engineering at South Dakota State University). The company name comes from combining "Dakota" with "electronics." Two years later the company delivered its first product, a voting display system for the Utah legislature. Scoreboards were added to the product line in 1971; commercial displays, in 1973. It introduced computerized controllers in the late 1970s.

The 1980 Winter Olympics in Lake Placid, New York, marked the first time the company provided scoreboards to the Olympic games. During the 1980s Daktronics began installing displays in major-league sports stadiums. In 1988 it bought auto-racing timing equipment maker Chondek. Daktronics continued to advance sign technology during the 1990s, acquiring technology for light-emitting diode (LED) displays. It went public in 1994.

The company supplied five displays and 24 digital clocks to Times Square locations in 1995. Daktronics also provided scoreboards to the 1996 Atlanta Summer Olympics. That year the blue LED, a tiny bulb used with green and red LEDs to produce color on large TV-like screens, was introduced. This allowed the company to add video to its scoreboards. In 1998 Daktronics installed systems in the Indianapolis Motor Speedway, and sports venues in Cleveland, Seattle, and Phoenix.

The company's displays were featured at the 2000 Olympics in Sydney. In 2001 Daktronics bought 80% of Servtrotech (a Canadian electronic display system maker) and Sportslink, Ltd. (a large screen video rental display company). James Morgan became CEO in 2001; Kurtenbach remained chairman.

In July 2003 the company won a contract to provide digital advertising and information displays at the Hubert H. Humphrey Metrodome in Minneapolis. The following year Daktronics expanded its product line and geographic reach with the acquisition of UK-based European Timing Systems (scoreboards and timing systems for cricket, aquatics, and rugby), now known as Daktronics UK.

Also in late 2004 the company acquired the assets of Dodge Electronics, doing business as Dodge Systems, a supplier of audio systems for sports facilities.

Daktronics expanded its manufacturing facilities in 2006, adding 110,000 sq. ft. of space to its main manufacturing facility in Brookings, South Dakota, and leasing a vacant plant in Sioux Falls with 120,000 sq. ft. of manufacturing space.

In early 2007 the company acquired an existing plant in Redwood Falls, Minnesota, from Emerson Electric. Daktronics will use the facility to manufacture its Galaxy line of electronic message displays. Moving Galaxy production to Minnesota freed up manufacturing space at the company's plant in Brookings.

At the same time the company began construction of a new facility in Brookings for office and warehouse space, a $19 million project.

EXECUTIVES

Chairman: Aelred J. (Al) Kurtenbach, age 74, $187,550 pay
President, CEO, and Director: James B. (Jim) Morgan, age 61, $348,369 pay
CFO and Treasurer: William R. (Bill) Retterath, age 47, $199,085 pay
VP Sales and Director: Frank J. Kurtenbach, age 68
VP Commercial and Transportation: Bradley T. (Brad) Wiemann, age 45, $167,618 pay
VP IT: Seth T. Hansen, age 43
VP Live Events: Reece A. Kurtenbach, age 43
VP Human Resources: Carla S. Gatzke, age 45
VP Small Sports Venue: Dan Bierschbach
Support Manager, Marketing and Sales: Mark Steinkamp
Product Manager: Jay deBlonk
Manager, Regional Sales: Kyle Adams
Regional Sales Representative: Corey Williams
Auditors: Ernst & Young LLP

LOCATIONS

HQ: Daktronics, Inc.
331 32nd Ave., Brookings, SD 57006
Phone: 605-697-4000 **Fax:** 605-697-4700
Web: www.daktronics.com

Daktronics has manufacturing facilities in North America, with offices in Canada, China, France, Germany, the United Arab Emirates, the UK, and the US.

2007 Sales

	$ mil.	% of total
US	389.2	90
Other countries	44.0	10
Total	**433.2**	**100**

PRODUCTS/OPERATIONS

Selected Applications and Brands

Business (text-based message displays)
- DataMaster
- DataTime
- DataTrac
- InfoNet
- Galaxy

Sports (indoor and outdoor scoreboards)
- All Sport
- DakStats
- OmniSport

Transportation (traffic direction and motorist information)
- Vanguard

Video (displays combining video, graphics, animation, and text)
- ProAd
- ProStar

COMPETITORS

Advance Display Technologies	Mitsubishi Electric
Advanced Optics Electronics	Opto Tech
Aristocrat Leisure	Panasonic
AutoComm	PolyVision
Colorado Time Systems	Screen Technology
DRI Corp	Sony
LSI Industries	Trans-Lux
	Waytronx

HISTORICAL FINANCIALS

Company Type: Public

Income Statement

FYE: Saturday nearest April 30

	REVENUE ($ mil.)	NET INCOME ($ mil.)	NET PROFIT MARGIN	EMPLOYEES
4/07	433.2	24.4	5.6%	3,200
4/06	309.4	21.0	6.8%	2,100
4/05	230.4	15.7	6.8%	1,630
4/04	209.9	17.7	8.4%	—
4/03	177.8	12.5	7.0%	—
Annual Growth	24.9%	18.2%	—	40.1%

2007 Year-End Financials

Debt ratio: 0.7%
Return on equity: 17.5%
Cash ($ mil.): 2.6
Current ratio: 1.44
Long-term debt ($ mil.): 1.1
No. of shares (mil.): 39.5

Dividends
Yield: 0.3%
Payout: 10.2%
Market value ($ mil.): 945.5
R&D as % of sales: —
Advertising as % of sales: —

Stock History

NASDAQ (GS): DAKT

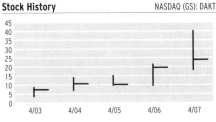

	STOCK PRICE ($) FY Close	P/E High/Low		PER SHARE ($) Earnings	Dividends	Book Value
4/07	23.92	68	31	0.59	0.06	3.89
4/06	19.61	41	18	0.52	0.05	3.22
4/05	10.18	38	25	0.39	—	5.43
4/04	10.61	31	16	0.44	—	4.57
4/03	7.34	27	11	0.32	—	3.52
Annual Growth	34.4%	—	—	16.5%	20.0%	2.5%

Darwin Professional Underwriters

Having liability insurance is an evolutionary imperative at Darwin Professional Underwriters, a specialty insurer providing professional liability coverage to a number of customer groups, including health care facilities, doctors, insurance agents, and technology providers. Its three main product lines are errors and omissions (E&O) liability insurance, medical malpractice insurance, and directors and officers (D&O) liability insurance. It sells policies both on an admitted basis (through Darwin National Assurance) and a surplus lines basis (through Darwin Select) in most parts of the US. The company was founded in 2003 by CEO Stephen Stills and Alleghany Corporation, which owns more than half of the firm.

EXECUTIVES

Chairman, President, and CEO: Stephen J. Sills, age 58, $489,353 pay
SVP, CFO, and Director: John L. (Jack) Sennott Jr., age 41, $257,500 pay
SVP and Chief Underwriting Officer: David J. Newman, age 51, $239,900 pay
SVP and CIO: Robert J. (Bob) Asensio, age 50
SVP and Chief Actuary: Paul C. Martin, age 54
SVP, Underwriting and Distribution: Paul F. Romano, age 47, $257,500 pay
SVP and General Counsel: Mark I. Rosen, age 55, $326,227 pay
Secretary and Director: Christopher K. Dalrymple, age 39
Auditors: KPMG LLP

LOCATIONS

HQ: Darwin Professional Underwriters, Inc.
9 Farm Springs Rd., Farmington, CT 06032
Phone: 860-284-1300   **Fax:** 860-284-1301
Web: www.darwinpro.com

PRODUCTS/OPERATIONS

2006 Sales

	$ mil.	% of total
Net premiums earned	132.4	89
Net investment income	16.4	11
Total	**148.8**	**100**

COMPETITORS

- ACE Limited
- AIG
- Arch Insurance Group
- AXIS Capital Holdings
- Chubb Corp
- CNA Financial
- The Hartford
- HCC Insurance
- Liberty Mutual
- Lloyd's
- Markel
- Navigators
- OneBeacon
- Philadelphia Consolidated
- RSUI Group
- Travelers Companies
- United States Liability Insurance Group
- W. R. Berkley
- XL Capital
- Zurich Financial Services

HISTORICAL FINANCIALS

Company Type: Public

Income Statement

FYE: December 31

	ASSETS ($ mil.)	NET INCOME ($ mil.)	INCOME AS % OF ASSETS	EMPLOYEES
12/06	635.3	16.0	2.5%	116
12/05	447.0	3.7	0.8%	—
12/04	146.1	0.1	0.1%	—
Annual Growth	108.5%	1,164.9%	—	—

2006 Year-End Financials

Equity as % of assets: 34.3%
Return on assets: 3.0%
Return on equity: 7.7%
Long-term debt ($ mil.): —
No. of shares (mil.): 17.0
Market value ($ mil.): 399.8

Dividends
Yield: —
Payout: —
Sales ($ mil.): 148.8
R&D as % of sales: —
Advertising as % of sales: —

Stock History

NYSE: DR

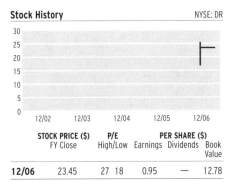

	STOCK PRICE ($) FY Close	P/E High/Low		PER SHARE ($) Earnings	Dividends	Book Value
12/06	23.45	27	18	0.95	—	12.78

Dawson Geophysical

The oil industry can be shaky at times, but Dawson Geophysical always looks for good vibrations. The company, founded in 1952, provides data acquisition and data processing services including the analysis of 2-D, 3-D, and 4-D seismic data to assess potential underground oil and gas deposits. Dawson Geophysical's customers, both major and independent oil and gas operators, use the data in exploration and development activities. The company's 15 3-D seismic data acquisition crews work in the lower 48 states of the US; data processing is performed by geophysicists at the firm's computer center in Midland, Texas.

A rebound in the oil industry has enabled Dawson Geophysical to put more crews back to work, although competition has driven down the prices. The company has expanded the number of data acquisition crews it has working in the field and has upgraded its data processing center. 3-D seismic services account for the majority of the company's total sales. One customer accounted for 49% of the firm's revenues in 2007.

That year Dawson Geophysical took delivery of 18 vibrator energy source units, increasing its total count to 113 units company-wide.

HISTORY

Geophysicist Decker Dawson started the company in 1952 as a sole proprietorship, with one crew. At the time, seismic surveying consisted of setting off dynamite charges and recording tremors on a 24-channel recorder. In the 1950s and 1960s the company upgraded its services as technologies improved.

When the 1973 OPEC oil embargo fueled a major US oil exploration drive, Dawson Geophysical brought on line the nation's first 120-channel land-based system and the country's second 1,000-channel system. Anticipating demand for 3-D seismic data, the firm went public in 1981 to raise capital to develop the technology. In 1988 it became one of the first companies to employ 3-D seismic surveying in West Texas. Demand for Dawson Geophysical's services increased during the 1990s.

In 1995 a work-related vehicle crash killed four Dawson employees and opened the company up to yet-to-be adjudicated lawsuits. The company raised about $21 million in a public stock offering in 1997 to fund expansion and reduce its debt. It bought $6 million worth of new equipment that year.

El Niño storms in 1998 disrupted work and crimped Dawson Geophysical's earnings. Worse, world oil prices softened, suggesting that oil companies would stop drilling. A backlog of orders, however, helped Dawson withstand market conditions for a while, but by early 1999 the firm was operating only one crew. In 1999 the industry as a whole began to rebound, and Dawson put five of its six crews back in operation in 2000.

In 2003 Dawson completed the opening of an office in Oklahoma City in an effort to better serve the US Midcontinent region.

EXECUTIVES

Chairman: L. Decker Dawson, age 87
President, CEO, and Director: Stephen C. Jumper, age 46
EVP, CFO, and Secretary: Christina W. Hagan, age 52, $145,243 pay
EVP: Howell W. Pardue, age 71
EVP and COO: C. Ray Tobias, age 49
VP: K. S. Forsdick, age 56
VP: A. Mark Nelson, age 47
VP: George E. McDonald, age 54
Treasurer: Melody Y. Crowl, age 43
Human Resources: Olga Smoot
Auditors: KPMG LLP

LOCATIONS

HQ: Dawson Geophysical Company
508 W. Wall, Ste. 800, Midland, TX 79701
Phone: 432-684-3000   **Fax:** 432-684-3030
Web: www.dawson3d.com

Dawson Geophysical operates throughout the lower 48 states in the US through offices in Denver; Houston and Midland, Texas; and Oklahoma City.

PRODUCTS/OPERATIONS

Services

Data processing and analysis
Seismic data acquisition services

COMPETITORS

CGGVeritas
ION Geophysical
OYO Geospace
Paradigm Ltd.
Petroleum Geo-Services
Seitel
TGC Industries
TGS-NOPEC
WesternGeco

HISTORICAL FINANCIALS

Company Type: Public

Income Statement

FYE: September 30

	REVENUE ($ mil.)	NET INCOME ($ mil.)	NET PROFIT MARGIN	EMPLOYEES
9/07	257.8	27.2	10.6%	1,345
9/06	168.6	15.9	9.4%	1,023
9/05	116.7	10.0	8.6%	—
9/04	69.3	8.6	12.4%	—
9/03	51.6	(0.9)	—	—
Annual Growth	49.5%	—	—	31.5%

2007 Year-End Financials

Debt ratio: —
Return on equity: 20.3%
Cash ($ mil.): 14.9
Current ratio: 1.96
Long-term debt ($ mil.): —
No. of shares (mil.): 7.7
Dividends
  Yield: —
  Payout: —
Market value ($ mil.): 593.6
R&D as % of sales: —
Advertising as % of sales: —

Stock History

NASDAQ (GM): DWSN

	STOCK PRICE ($) FY Close	P/E High/Low		PER SHARE ($) Earnings	Dividends	Book Value
9/07	77.51	24	8	3.54	—	19.48
9/06	29.70	19	11	2.09	—	15.79
9/05	30.25	22	12	1.48	—	13.62
9/04	20.92	17	4	1.53	—	8.92
9/03	6.89	—	—	(0.16)	—	7.41
Annual Growth	83.1%	—	—	—	—	27.3%

DealerTrack Holdings

DealerTrack Holdings helps car dealers play their cards right in the financing game. The company provides Web-based software that links automotive dealerships with banks, finance companies, credit unions, credit reporting agencies, and other players in the car sales and financing process. Through its software, DealerTrack connects clients to its network of auto dealers, financing sources, and other service and information providers. The company, which generates revenues through subscriptions and transaction-based fees, also offers tools that automate credit application processing, ensure document legal compliance, and execute electronic financing contracts.

In 2005 the company bought the assets of Automotive Lease Guide (a provider of lease residual value data for automobiles), North American Advanced Technology (tools for automating after-market product administration), and Chrome Systems (data collection and enhancement tools for vertical industries).

In May 2007 the company acquired Arkona, a provider of automotive and power sports management products and services.

EXECUTIVES

Chairman, President, and CEO: Mark F. O'Neil, age 48, $495,040 pay
SVP, CFO, and Treasurer: Robert J. Cox III, age 41, $260,000 pay
SVP, General Counsel, and Secretary: Eric D. Jacobs, age 40, $260,000 pay
SVP and Head of Dealer Solutions: Raj Sundaram, age 39
SVP and Head of Network Solutions: David P. Trinder, age 47
SVP, Strategy and Development, DealerTrack, Inc.: Richard McLeer, age 42
VP, Marketing: Alexi Venneri
CEO, Automotive Lease Guide: John A. Blair, age 46, $260,000 pay
SVP and CIO, DealerTrack, Inc.: Charles J. Giglia, age 55
SVP, Customer Development, DealerTrack, Inc.: Rick G. Von Pusch, age 44
VP, Human Resources, DealerTrack, Inc.: Ana M. Herrera, age 50
Auditors: PricewaterhouseCoopers LLP

LOCATIONS

HQ: DealerTrack Holdings, Inc.
1111 Marcus Ave., Ste. M04,
Lake Success, NY 11042
Phone: 516-734-3600   **Fax:** 516-734-3809
Web: www.dealertrack.com

COMPETITORS

ACI Worldwide, Inc.
ADP
Auto Data Network
Microsoft Dynamics
NSB Retail Systems
Reynolds and Reynolds
RouteOne

HISTORICAL FINANCIALS

Company Type: Public

Income Statement

FYE: December 31

	REVENUE ($ mil.)	NET INCOME ($ mil.)	NET PROFIT MARGIN	EMPLOYEES
12/06	173.3	19.3	11.1%	670
12/05	120.2	4.5	3.7%	539
12/04	70.0	11.3	16.1%	499
12/03	38.7	(3.3)	—	—
12/02	11.7	(16.8)	—	—
Annual Growth	96.2%	—	—	15.9%

2006 Year-End Financials

Debt ratio: 1.0%
Return on equity: 8.2%
Cash ($ mil.): 171.2
Current ratio: 6.72
Long-term debt ($ mil.): 3.0
No. of shares (mil.): 39.6
Dividends
  Yield: —
  Payout: —
Market value ($ mil.): 1,164.1
R&D as % of sales: —
Advertising as % of sales: —

Stock History

NASDAQ (GM): TRAK

	STOCK PRICE ($) FY Close	P/E High/Low		PER SHARE ($) Earnings	Dividends	Book Value
12/06	29.42	59	36	0.51	—	7.19
12/05	20.98	177	154	0.12	—	5.28
Annual Growth	40.2%	—	—	325.0%	—	36.2%

Dearborn Bancorp

Frankly, my Dearborn, they do give a damn. Dearborn Bancorp is the holding company for Fidelity Bank (formerly Community Bank of Dearborn). The bank has about 20 branches and lending centers in suburban Detroit and points west, offering checking and savings accounts, money market accounts, and CDs. Lending activities include commercial mortgages (more than half of the company's loan portfolio), as well as residential, business, consumer, and construction loans. Dearborn Bancorp also has a subsidiary that provides auditing and consulting services to other community banks. Community Bank of Dearborn changed its name after its parent company acquired Fidelity Bank in 2007.

EXECUTIVES

Chairman, Dearborn Bancorp and Fidelity Bank: John E. Demmer, age 83
President, CEO, and Director; President and CEO, Fidelity Bank: Michael J. Ross, age 56, $424,039 pay
VP, Treasurer, and Secretary; SVP, CFO, and Secretary, Fidelity Bank: Jeffrey L. Karafa, age 42, $195,885 pay
President, Community Bank Audit Services; VP Internal Audit, Fidelity Bank: Wynn C. Miller
President, Community Bank Mortgage; VP Credit Administration, Fidelity Bank: Daniel P. (Dan) Brophy
Northeast Regional President, Fidelity Bank: Stephen C. Tarczy, age 57, $219,039 pay
Oakland Regional President, Fidelity Bank: John A. Lindsey
Washtenaw Regional President, Fidelity Bank: Walter G. Byers, age 57
SVP and Head of Lending, Fidelity Bank: Warren R. Musson, age 50, $219,039 pay
SVP and Head of Retail, Fidelity Bank: Jeffrey J. Wolber, age 51, $161,808 pay
Human Resources Officer, Fidelity Bank: Elizabeth A. Pizzo
Auditors: BKD, LLP

LOCATIONS

HQ: Dearborn Bancorp, Inc.
1360 Porter St., Dearborn, MI 48124
Phone: 313-565-5700 **Fax:** 313-561-2291
Web: www.fidbank.com

Dearborn Bancorp has offices in the southeastern Michigan communities of Allen Park, Ann Arbor, Auburn Hills, Bingham Farms, Birmingham, Bloomfield Township, Canton, Clinton Township, Dearborn, Dearborn Heights, Plymouth, Saline, Shelby Township, Southfield, and Southgate.

PRODUCTS/OPERATIONS

2006 Sales

	$ mil.	% of total
Interest		
Loans	52.3	95
Other	1.6	3
Noninterest	1.0	2
Total	**54.9**	**100**

Selected Subsidiaries

Fidelity Bank
Community Bank Audit Services, Inc.
Community Bank Insurance Agency, Inc.
Community Bank Mortgage, Inc.

COMPETITORS

Comerica	Huntington Bancshares
Fifth Third	LaSalle Bank
Flagstar Bancorp	National City

HISTORICAL FINANCIALS
Company Type: Public

Income Statement
FYE: December 31

	ASSETS ($ mil.)	NET INCOME ($ mil.)	INCOME AS % OF ASSETS	EMPLOYEES
12/06	855.9	7.8	0.9%	161
12/05	706.5	7.5	1.1%	151
12/04	652.7	5.5	0.8%	—
12/03	446.1	3.5	0.8%	—
12/02	325.1	2.7	0.8%	112
Annual Growth	**27.4%**	**30.4%**	**—**	**9.5%**

2006 Year-End Financials

Equity as % of assets: 16.9%
Return on assets: 1.0%
Return on equity: 6.8%
Long-term debt ($ mil.): 10.0
No. of shares (mil.): 9.0
Market value ($ mil.): 170.5
Dividends
Yield: —
Payout: —
Sales ($ mil.): 54.9
R&D as % of sales: —
Advertising as % of sales: —

Stock History
NASDAQ (GM): DEAR

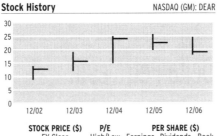

	STOCK PRICE ($) FY Close	P/E High/Low	PER SHARE ($) Earnings	Dividends	Book Value
12/06	19.00	22 16	1.11	—	16.15
12/05	22.45	21 17	1.20	1.77	15.53
12/04	23.99	23 14	1.05	2.51	15.56
12/03	15.58	23 15	0.83	1.64	11.76
12/02	12.70	21 14	0.66	1.64	11.74
Annual Growth	**10.6%**	**— —**	**13.9%**	**2.6%**	**8.3%**

Deckers Outdoor

There's no business like shoe business for Deckers Outdoor. The company makes and markets Teva sports sandals — a cross between a hiking boot and a flip-flop. They're used for walking, hiking, and rafting, among other pursuits. While imitations flood the market, the firm distinguishes Teva from its numerous competitors by avoiding distribution in off-price outlets, creating a stronger brand image for the sandals. Other product lines include Simple (casual footwear) and UGG (sheepskin boots/shoes). Deckers Outdoor's products are made by independent contractors in Asia, Australia, and New Zealand. Chairman Douglas Otto owns about 13% of the company.

Deckers Outdoor sells through independent distributors, catalogs, the Internet, and two company-owned retail outlets.

The company intends to continue its growth by expanding internationally and acquiring or developing new brands. International growth is being supported through additional offices in Europe and Asia for advertising, distribution, marketing, and sales initiatives.

A rise in UGG sales has led to a debate over whether the name is generic or a trademark that could possibly be defended over international boundaries. Australian makers of the sheepskin boots, traditionally called uggs, contend that the name is generic, akin to trying to protect the name "sneaker" as a trademark.

HISTORY

Douglas Otto and his former partner, Karl Lopker, founded Styled Steers in 1973. But the small, obscure maker of leather sandals gained prominence with a line of multicolored rubber sandals. Surfers in Hawaii called them "deckers," and the company soon adopted the name. In 1985 Deckers Outdoor licensed Teva from river guide Mark Thatcher, who invented the Teva strapping system for rafters to ensure sandals remained attached in turbulent waters. Teva sport sandals became a popular form of casual footwear, largely through word of mouth. The company is the exclusive licensee of Teva shoes, the design of which Thatcher has defended repeatedly against would-be copycats.

In 1994 Deckers Outdoor expanded the Teva line to include closed footwear. With the popularity of Teva sandals seemingly on the wane, the next year it diversified, acquiring rival shoe companies Alp Sport Sandals and UGG Holdings and expanding into the women's and children's markets. A glut of sports sandals depressed sales the following year, but with new products and new marketing, Teva sales increased in 1997.

That year, targeting international expansion, the company acquired German distribution rights to Simple shoes from Vision Warenhandels. Also in 1997 Deckers Outdoor sold its interest in Trukke Winter Sports Products to focus on its core lines.

Thatcher settled with Wal-Mart Stores in 1998 after suing the company over patent and copyright infringement. The firm exited the manufacturing business that year and turned production over to suppliers, mainly in China. In mid-1999 Deckers Outdoor renewed its license with Thatcher through 2011. Continuing to divest noncore operations, in 2000 the company sold its 50% interest in Heirlooms, the makers of the Picante line. The company also hired an ex-adidas exec to help increase Teva's global business (26% in 1999).

In 2000 Otto gave up the president in his title to Peter Benjamin, who was charged with rejuvenating and giving each brand more individualized marketing. In 2001 sales slumped nearly 20% due in part to the weak economy and a bankruptcy filing by one of Deckers Outdoor's largest customers, Track n' Trail. In late 2002, Peter Benjamin resigned as president so that he could return to focusing on sales to Asia.

The company purchased Teva's total assets from its inventor and trademarks and patents holder, Mark Thatcher, in November 2002.

In the second half of 2003 the UGG brand enjoyed unusually rapid growth in demand, helping to send Deckers Outdoor's sales up 22% for the year. In 2004 Deckers inked licensing agreements for the manufacture of UGG handbags and outerwear, as well as gloves, hats, and scarves. The same year the company signed a separate licensing deal with RMP Athletic Locker for the manufacture of Teva sportswear.

In April 2005 Angel Martinez, a former Reebok executive, became president and CEO of the company. Doug Otto retains his position as chairman of the board.

EXECUTIVES

Chairman: Douglas B. Otto, age 55
President, CEO, and Director: Angel R. Martinez, age 51, $500,000 pay
COO: Zohar Ziv, age 54, $248,110 pay (partial-year salary)
Chief, Sustainable Initiatives: Patrick C. Devaney, age 52, $200,000 pay
SVP, International Operations: Colin G. Clark, age 44, $225,000 pay
VP, Consumer Direct: John A. Kalinich, age 39
VP, Operations: Janice M. Howell, age 57
President, Teva Brand: Peter K. (Pete) Worley, age 46
President, Ugg and Simple Divisions:
Constance X. (Connie) Rishwain, age 49, $225,000 pay
Human Resources Coordinator: Jennifer Foth
Director, Human Resources: Nate Christensen
Auditors: KPMG LLP

LOCATIONS

HQ: Deckers Outdoor Corporation
495-A S. Fairview Ave., Goleta, CA 93117
Phone: 805-967-7611 **Fax:** 805-967-7862
Web: www.deckers.com

2006 Sales

	$ mil.	% of total
US	266.1	87
Other countries	38.3	13
Total	**304.4**	**100**

PRODUCTS/OPERATIONS

2006 Sales

	$ mil.	% of total
UGG wholesale	182.4	60
Teva wholesale	75.3	25
Consumer direct	35.8	12
Simple wholesale	10.9	3
Total	**304.4**	**100**

COMPETITORS

adidas	NIKE
Birkenstock	Patagonia, Inc.
Columbia Sportswear	Phoenix Footwear
Converse	PUMA
Crocs	Quiksilver
Diesel SpA	R. Griggs
Fila USA	Rocky Brands
Guess?	Skechers U.S.A.
Jimlar	Steven Madden
Kenneth Cole	Timberland
K-Swiss	Vans
L.L. Bean	Wolverine World Wide

HISTORICAL FINANCIALS

Company Type: Public

Income Statement

FYE: December 31

	REVENUE ($ mil.)	NET INCOME ($ mil.)	NET PROFIT MARGIN	EMPLOYEES
12/06	304.4	30.6	10.1%	276
12/05	264.8	31.8	12.0%	225
12/04	214.8	25.5	11.9%	—
12/03	121.1	9.1	7.5%	—
12/02	99.1	(7.3)	—	162
Annual Growth	**32.4%**	**—**	**—**	**14.2%**

2006 Year-End Financials

Debt ratio: —
Return on equity: 15.8%
Cash ($ mil.): 98.9
Current ratio: 4.74
Long-term debt ($ mil.): —
No. of shares (mil.): 12.6
Dividends
  Yield: —
  Payout: —
Market value ($ mil.): 754.7
R&D as % of sales: —
Advertising as % of sales: —

		STOCK PRICE ($) FY Close	P/E High/Low		PER SHARE ($) Earnings	Dividends	Book Value
12/06		59.95	25	12	2.38	—	16.72
12/05		27.62	19	7	2.48	—	14.28
12/04		46.99	23	8	2.10	—	11.57
12/03		20.50	29	4	0.77	—	7.25
12/02		3.34	—	—	(0.75)	—	6.89
Annual Growth		**105.8%**	**—**	**—**	**—**	**—**	**24.8%**

Delta Petroleum

An independent oil and gas exploration and production company, Delta Petroleum has been dealt a good hand in estimated proved reserves. In 2006 it reported reserves of 302.4 billion cu. ft. of natural gas equivalent, 53% of which is in the Rocky Mountains. The company also has assets in the Gulf Coast region and the Columbia River Basin in southeastern Washington. It had oil and gas leasehold properties covering approximately 1.25 million acres. Delta Petroleum operates three major subsidiaries: Castle Texas Exploration Limited Partnership, Delta Exploration Company, Inc., and Piper Petroleum Company. It controls Amber Resources. In 2007 the company agreed to sell a 35% stake to Tracinda Corp. for $684 million.

In 2002 Delta Petroleum acquired the US oil and gas assets of Castle Energy and in 2004 it acquired Alpine Resources' oil assets. The company bought Savant Resources for $85 million in 2005. In 2006 Delta Petroleum acquired Castle Energy.

EXECUTIVES

Chairman and CEO: Roger A. Parker, age 46, $493,000 pay
President, COO, and Director: John R. Wallace, age 48
EVP, General Counsel, and Secretary:
Stanley F. (Ted) Freedman, age 59, $247,000 pay
CFO and Treasurer: Kevin K. Nanke, age 43, $247,000 pay
Auditors: KPMG LLP

LOCATIONS

HQ: Delta Petroleum Corporation
370 17th St., Ste. 4300, Denver, CO 80202
Phone: 303-293-9133 **Fax:** 303-298-8251
Web: www.deltapetro.com

2006 Proved Reserves

	% of total
Rocky Mountains	53
Gulf Coast	37
Offshore California	1
Other regions	9
Total	**100**

PRODUCTS/OPERATIONS

2006 Sales

	$ mil.	% of total
Oil & gas	124.2	69
Contract drilling & trucking fees	57.2	31
Total	**181.4**	**100**

COMPETITORS

BP
Brigham Exploration
Cabot Oil & Gas
Chesapeake Energy
Chevron
Comstock Resources
CREDO Petroleum
Denbury Resources
Devon Energy
El Paso
Exxon Mobil
Forest Oil
Meridian Resource
Noble Energy
Occidental Petroleum
Pioneer Natural Resources
Range Resources
Royal Dutch Shell
Swift Energy

HISTORICAL FINANCIALS

Company Type: Public

Income Statement

FYE: December 31

	REVENUE ($ mil.)	NET INCOME ($ mil.)	NET PROFIT MARGIN	EMPLOYEES
12/06	181.4	0.4	0.2%	122
12/05*	61.8	(0.6)	—	96
6/05	94.7	15.1	15.9%	95
6/04	36.4	5.1	14.0%	—
6/03	25.8	1.3	5.0%	—
Annual Growth	**62.8%**	**(25.5%)**	**—**	**13.3%**

*Fiscal year change

2006 Year-End Financials

Debt ratio: 85.6%
Return on equity: 0.1%
Cash ($ mil.): 18.5
Current ratio: 0.64
Long-term debt ($ mil.): 366.5
No. of shares (mil.): 54.4
Dividends
  Yield: —
  Payout: —
Market value ($ mil.): 1,260.8
R&D as % of sales: —
Advertising as % of sales: —

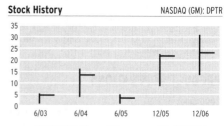

	STOCK PRICE ($) FY Close	P/E High/Low		PER SHARE ($) Earnings	Dividends	Book Value
12/06	23.16	3,068	1,379	0.01	—	7.87
12/05*	21.77	—	—	(0.01)	—	6.70
6/05	3.40	13	3	0.36	—	4.65
6/04	13.45	94	24	0.17	—	4.84
6/03	4.58	100	25	0.05	—	2.06
Annual Growth	**50.0%**	**—**	**—**	**(33.1%)**	**—**	**39.8%**

*Fiscal year change

Deltek, Inc.

Deltek isn't afraid to tackle tough projects. The company provides project management software designed to meet the needs of professional services firms and project-based businesses. Its applications handle expense reporting, human resources administration, materials management, customer management, and sales force automation. Deltek integrates tools from partners such as Cognos and Microsoft with its own software, and it provides consulting and implementation services. Donald and Kenneth deLaski (father and son) co-founded Deltek in 1983. Private equity firm New Mountain Partners owns a 74% stake in the company.

With more than 12,000 customers, Deltek targets a variety of industries, including aerospace, construction, engineering, and information technology. It also serves government agencies.

The company has used acquisitions to expand its offerings in recent years including the purchases of Wind2 Software (October 2005), WST Corporation (March 2006), C/S Solutions (July 2006), and Applied Integration Management Corporation (April 2007).

Prior to its 2007 IPO, Deltek had traded shares publicly (1996 IPO) until being taken private in 2002.

EXECUTIVES

Chairman, President, and CEO: Kevin T. Parker, age 47, $450,000 pay
EVP, CFO, and Treasurer: James C. (Jim) Reagan, age 48, $315,000 pay
EVP and Chief Marketing Officer: William D. (Bill) Clark, age 47
EVP Products and Strategy: Richard P. (Rick) Lowrey, age 47
EVP Product Development: Eric J. Brehm, age 48
EVP Worldwide Sales: Carolyn J. Parent, age 41, $317,708 pay
EVP Global Support: David Hare
EVP Professional Services: Richard M. (Rick) Lowenstein, age 44
SVP and General Counsel: David R. Schwiesow, age 56
SVP Human Resources: Holly C. Kortright, age 40
Director Public Relations: Andrea Carl
Auditors: Deloitte & Touche LLP

LOCATIONS

HQ: Deltek, Inc.
13880 Dulles Corner Ln., Herndon, VA 20171
Phone: 703-734-8606   **Fax:** 703-734-1146
Web: www.deltek.com

PRODUCTS/OPERATIONS

2006 Sales

	$ mil.	% of total
Software license fees	75.0	33
Consulting services	66.6	29
Maintenance & support services	83.2	36
Other	3.5	2
Total	**228.3**	**100**

Selected Products

Deltek Costpoint (ERP software for large organizations)
Deltek Enterprise Project Management Solutions (project management suite)
Deltek GCS Premier (project accounting for federal contractors)
Deltek Vision (Web-based suite automation for professional services firms)

COMPETITORS

Artemis International Solutions
CA, Inc.
Lawson Software
Oracle
Primavera Systems
SAP
Ultimate Software

HISTORICAL FINANCIALS

Company Type: Public

Income Statement

FYE: December 31

	REVENUE ($ mil.)	NET INCOME ($ mil.)	NET PROFIT MARGIN	EMPLOYEES
12/06	228.3	15.3	6.7%	1,041
12/05	153.0	8.7	5.7%	—
12/04	121.2	27.9	23.0%	—
Annual Growth	**37.2%**	**(25.9%)**	**—**	**—**

2006 Year-End Financials

Debt ratio: —
Return on equity: —
Cash ($ mil.): 6.7
Current ratio: 0.72
Long-term debt ($ mil.): 210.4

Net Income History

NASDAQ (GS): PROJ

30
25
20
15
10
5
0
12/02   12/03   12/04   12/05   12/06

Denbury Resources

Denbury Resources has long since capped its oil and gas operations in its native Canada to try its luck in the Deep South. The independent exploration and production company has estimated proved reserves of 174.3 million barrels of oil equivalent and working interests in wells across Louisiana, Mississippi, Texas, and in the Gulf of Mexico. In Mississippi it also owns wells that produce carbon dioxide (CO2), which it uses to force oil out of the ground at nearby abandoned wells. In 2002 Denbury Resources bought Genesis Energy LLC, the general partner of Gulf Coast crude oil marketer Genesis Energy, L.P., and the Gulf Coast properties of Coho Energy.

In 2007 the company agreed to buy a number of oil and gas fields from Anadarko Petroleum for $42 million. It later sold its gas operations located in Louisiana for about $180 million.

EXECUTIVES

Chairman: Ronald G. Greene, age 58
President, CEO, and Director: Gareth Roberts, age 54
SVP, CFO, Secretary, and Treasurer: Phil Rykhoek, age 50
SVP Operations: Robert Cornelius, age 52
SVP Reservoir Engineering: Ronald T. (Tracy) Evans, age 44
VP and Chief Accounting Officer: Mark C. Allen, age 39
VP Land: Ray Dubuisson, age 56
VP Marketing: Dan Cole, age 54
Director Investor Relations: Laurie Burkes
Human Resources: Sandy Sandusky
Auditors: PricewaterhouseCoopers LLP

LOCATIONS

HQ: Denbury Resources Inc.
5100 Tennyson Pkwy., Ste. 1200, Plano, TX 75024
Phone: 972-673-2000   **Fax:** 972-673-2150
Web: www.denbury.com

Denbury Resources operates in Louisiana, Mississippi, Texas, and the Gulf of Mexico.

PRODUCTS/OPERATIONS

2006 Sales

	$ mil.	% of total
Oil, natural gas & related products	716.5	98
CO2 sales and transportation fees	9.4	1
Other	5.6	1
Total	**731.5**	**100**

Selected Subsidiaries

Denbury Gathering & Marketing, Inc.
Denbury Marine, L.L.C.
Genesis Energy, Inc.

COMPETITORS

Abraxas Petroleum	McMoRan Exploration
Apache	Meridian Resource
BP	Murphy Oil
Chevron	Newfield Exploration
Delta Petroleum	Royal Dutch Shell
Exxon Mobil	Swift Energy
Forest Oil	

HISTORICAL FINANCIALS

Company Type: Public

Income Statement

FYE: December 31

	REVENUE ($ mil.)	NET INCOME ($ mil.)	NET PROFIT MARGIN	EMPLOYEES
12/06	731.5	202.5	27.7%	596
12/05	560.4	166.5	29.7%	460
12/04	383.0	82.4	21.5%	—
12/03	333.0	56.5	17.0%	—
12/02	285.1	46.8	16.4%	356
Annual Growth	**26.6%**	**44.2%**	**—**	**13.7%**

2006 Year-End Financials

Debt ratio: 47.1%
Return on equity: 22.0%
Cash ($ mil.): 80.8
Current ratio: 0.91
Long-term debt ($ mil.): 521.0
No. of shares (mil.): 120.1
Dividends
  Yield: —
  Payout: —
Market value ($ mil.): 3,338.6
R&D as % of sales: —
Advertising as % of sales: —

Stock History

NYSE: DNR

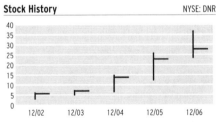

40
35
30
25
20
15
10
5
0
12/02   12/03   12/04   12/05   12/06

	STOCK PRICE ($) FY Close	P/E High/Low		Earnings	PER SHARE ($) Dividends	Book Value
12/06	27.79	22	14	1.64	—	9.21
12/05	22.78	18	9	1.39	—	6.40
12/04	13.73	20	9	0.72	—	9.58
12/03	6.95	14	10	0.51	—	7.77
12/02	5.65	14	7	0.43	—	6.83
Annual Growth	**48.9%**	**—**	**—**	**39.7%**	**—**	**7.7%**

Dialysis Corporation

Dialysis Corporation of America provides inpatient and outpatient dialysis services to patients suffering from chronic kidney failure (also known as end-stage renal disease) and other kidney diseases. The company operates some 30 outpatient dialysis facilities in seven states. In addition, Dialysis Corp. provides management services for kidney dialysis centers and in-home dialysis services. Medicare reimbursements account for about half of the company's sales. Dialysis Corp. acquired its former parent, Medicore, in 2005. The company has absorbed Medicore's disposable medical product operations.

The company is continuing to grow both through the acquisition of existing centers (three in 2006) and the establishment of new centers (also three in 2006). Dialysis Corp. is also acquiring a Georgia facility that it manages.

EXECUTIVES

Chairman: Thomas K. Langbein, age 61
President, CEO, and Director: Stephen W. Everett, age 50, $374,039 pay
VP, CFO, Chief Accounting Officer, and Treasurer: Daniel R. Ouzts, age 60, $127,116 pay
VP Clinical Services: Joanne Zimmerman, $152,210 pay
VP Operations: Thomas P. Carey, age 54, $150,000 pay
Auditors: Moore Stephens, P.C.

LOCATIONS

HQ: Dialysis Corporation of America
1302 Concourse Dr., Ste. 204,
Linthicum, MD 21090
Phone: 410-694-0500 **Fax:** 410-694-0596
Web: www.dialysiscorporation.com

Dialysis Corporation of America has operations in Georgia, Maryland, New Jersey, Ohio, Pennsylvania, South Carolina, and Virginia.

PRODUCTS/OPERATIONS

2006 Sales

	$ mil.	% of total
Medical services	61.1	98
Product sales	0.9	1
Other	0.5	1
Total	**62.5**	**100**

COMPETITORS

Baxter
DaVita
Dialysis Clinic Inc
Fresenius
Fresenius Medical Care
PSS World Medical
Spectrum Laboratories

HISTORICAL FINANCIALS

Company Type: Public

Income Statement				FYE: December 31
	REVENUE ($ mil.)	NET INCOME ($ mil.)	NET PROFIT MARGIN	EMPLOYEES
12/06	62.5	3.0	4.8%	468
12/05	45.4	1.9	4.2%	493
12/04	41.0	2.2	5.4%	—
12/03	30.3	1.1	3.6%	—
12/02	25.6	1.2	4.7%	263
Annual Growth	25.0%	25.7%	—	15.5%

2006 Year-End Financials

Debt ratio: 29.7%
Return on equity: 11.0%
Cash ($ mil.): 3.5
Current ratio: 3.00
Long-term debt ($ mil.): 8.6
No. of shares (mil.): 9.6
Dividends
  Yield: —
  Payout: —
Market value ($ mil.): 121.6
R&D as % of sales: —
Advertising as % of sales: —

Stock History

NASDAQ (GM): DCAI

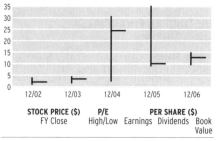

	STOCK PRICE ($) FY Close	P/E High/Low		PER SHARE ($) Earnings	Dividends	Book Value
12/06	12.71	46	30	0.32	—	3.04
12/05	10.03	175	46	0.20	—	2.76
12/04	24.43	122	10	0.25	—	1.57
12/03	3.35	33	13	0.13	—	1.38
12/02	1.99	26	7	0.14	—	2.50
Annual Growth	59.0%	—		23.0%	—	5.0%

Diamond Hill Investment Group

Diamond Hill Investment Group, through flagship subsidiary Diamond Hill Capital Management, oversees approximately $4 million in assets, most of it invested in equities. Serving institutional and high-net-worth individual clients, the company administers several mutual funds and sells them mainly through independent investment advisors, broker-dealers, 401(k) plans, and an office in Columbus, Ohio. It also manages separate accounts and hedge funds. Executives, directors, and employees of Diamond Hill Investment Group own about a quarter of the company.

EXECUTIVES

President, CEO, and Director; Chief Investment Officer, Diamond Hill Capital Management, Inc.: Roderick H. (Ric) Dillon Jr., age 50, $530,000 pay
CFO, Secretary, and Treasurer; President, Diamond Hill Funds: James F. (Jim) Laird Jr., age 50, $285,750 pay
Chairman, Diamond Hill Funds: Thomas E. (Tom) Line
Managing Director, Equities, Diamond Hill Capital Management: Charles S. (Chuck) Bath, age 52
Managing Director, Strategic Income, Diamond Hill Investments: Kent K. Rinker, age 57
Director, Key Accounts: Tamala S. (Tammi) Gourley
Director, Marketing: Patricia L. (Trish) Schindler
Portfolio Manager, Equities; Portfolio Manager, Diamond Hill Small-Mid Cap Fund: Christopher A. (Chris) Welch
Portfolio Manager, Strategic Income: William P. Zox
Portfolio Manager, Equities; Portfolio Manager, Diamond Hill Select Fund: William C. (Bill) Dierker
Coporate Controller and Chief Compliance Officer, Diamond Hills Funds: Gary R. Young
Managing Director, Planning and Operations: Randall J. Demyan
Auditors: Plante & Moran, PLLC

LOCATIONS

HQ: Diamond Hill Investment Group, Inc.
325 John H. McConnell Blvd., Ste. 200,
Columbus, OH 43215
Phone: 614-255-3333 **Fax:** 614-255-3363
Web: www.diamond-hill.com

PRODUCTS/OPERATIONS

2006 Sales

	$ mil.	% of total
Investment advisory	20.2	63
Performance incentive	8.0	25
Mutual fund administration	3.7	12
Total	**31.9**	**100**

COMPETITORS

AllianceBernstein	Franklin Resources
American Century	GAMCO Investors
Calamos Asset Management	Janus Capital
	Legg Mason
Cohen & Steers	MFS
Columbia Management Group	Putnam
	Raymond James Financial
Davis Advisers	Sanders Morris Harris
Duncan-Hurst	T. Rowe Price
Edward Jones	The Vanguard Group
FMR	Waddell & Reed

HISTORICAL FINANCIALS

Company Type: Public

Income Statement				FYE: December 31
	ASSETS ($ mil.)	NET INCOME ($ mil.)	INCOME AS % OF ASSETS	EMPLOYEES
12/06	37.2	8.1	21.8%	32
12/05	12.8	3.7	28.9%	21
12/04	4.0	(0.2)	—	—
12/03	3.3	(1.0)	—	—
12/02	3.9	(2.5)	—	13
Annual Growth	75.7%	—	—	25.3%

2006 Year-End Financials

Equity as % of assets: 55.1%
Return on assets: 32.4%
Return on equity: 51.7%
Long-term debt ($ mil.): —
No. of shares (mil.): 1.8
Market value ($ mil.): 153.9
Dividends
  Yield: —
  Payout: —
Sales ($ mil.): 31.9
R&D as % of sales: —
Advertising as % of sales: —

Stock History

NASDAQ (GM): DHIL

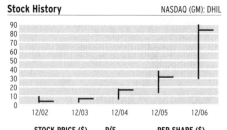

	STOCK PRICE ($) FY Close	P/E High/Low		PER SHARE ($) Earnings	Dividends	Book Value
12/06	83.73	25	8	3.63	—	11.14
12/05	31.30	21	8	1.83	—	6.18
12/04	16.75	—	—	(0.11)	—	2.21
12/03	6.94	—	—	(0.68)	—	2.08
12/02	3.92	—	—	(1.73)	—	2.58
Annual Growth	115.0%	—		—	—	44.1%

Digital River

Digital River helps keep the e-commerce flowing. The company provides technology and services that enable its clients to sell their products on the Web without building an e-commerce platform from the ground up. Using its own proprietary server technology, Digital River offers Web development and hosting, transaction processing, fulfillment, and fraud screening services to more than 40,000 customers operating online retail and distribution businesses. It also provides its customers with Web traffic data that allows them to better market their online presence. Security software client Symantec accounted for 30% of total sales in 2006. Digital River has been growing through a steady stream of acquisitions.

In 2007, Digital River fortified its e-commerce offerings when it acquired Netgiro Systems AB, an online payment services provider based in Sweden. The year before, Digital River bought MindVision, a software provider specializing in installation programs. In 2005, the company snatched up sales channel management software maker Commerce5.

In addition, Digital River's tributaries are branching out internationally. The company bought software distributor element 5 GmbH for $120 million in 2004, expanding its presence in Europe; element 5 changed its name to Digital River GmbH in 2006. Extending its foothold in Europe, the company launched two subsidiaries in Ireland and Luxembourg in mid-2006.

Most of Digital River's business comes from software publishers and online software retailers, but it is trying to build up more business with manufacturers and distributors of physical goods.

Digital River was established in 1994 and began offering online stores for its clients in 1996.

EXECUTIVES

CEO and Director: Joel A. Ronning
CFO: Thomas M. (Tom) Donnelly, age 42
SVP Global Client Development: Don Peterson
VP Investor Relations: Bob Kleiber
Associate Director Public Relations: Gerri Dyrek
Senior Public Relations Specialist: Kristin Mattson
Auditors: Ernst & Young LLP

LOCATIONS

HQ: Digital River, Inc.
9625 W. 76th St., Ste. 150, Eden Prairie, MN 55344
Phone: 952-253-1234 **Fax:** 952-253-8497
Web: www.digitalriver.com

Digital River has offices throughout the US, as well as in Germany, Ireland, Japan, Luxembourg, Taiwan, and the UK.

2006 Sales

	% of total
US	59
Europe	28
Other regions	13
Total	**100**

PRODUCTS/OPERATIONS

Selected Services

Customer service
Digital and physical fulfillment
Fraud detection
Merchandising and marketing
Transaction processing
Web commerce hosting

COMPETITORS

Accenture	GSI Commerce
Amazon.com	IBM
aQuantive	INTERSHOP
Ariba	Microsoft
Art Technology Group	NaviSite
BEA Systems	Oracle
BroadVision	SAP
CyberSource	Sterling Commerce
DoubleClick	USinternetworking
eBay	ValueClick
EDS	Vignette

HISTORICAL FINANCIALS

Company Type: Public

Income Statement

FYE: December 31

	REVENUE ($ mil.)	NET INCOME ($ mil.)	NET PROFIT MARGIN	EMPLOYEES
12/06	307.6	60.8	19.8%	1,086
12/05	220.4	54.3	24.6%	948
12/04	154.1	35.3	22.9%	—
12/03	101.2	17.1	16.9%	—
12/02	77.8	(0.5)	—	481
Annual Growth	**41.0%**	**—**	**—**	**22.6%**

2006 Year-End Financials

Debt ratio: 32.3%
Return on equity: 13.4%
Cash ($ mil.): 625.9
Current ratio: 3.42
Long-term debt ($ mil.): 195.0
No. of shares (mil.): 40.5
Dividends
  Yield: —
  Payout: —
Market value ($ mil.): 2,257.2
R&D as % of sales: —
Advertising as % of sales: —

Stock History

NASDAQ (GS): DRIV

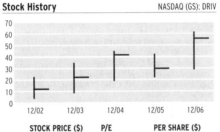

	STOCK PRICE ($) FY Close	P/E High/Low	PER SHARE ($) Earnings	Dividends	Book Value
12/06	55.79	44 21	1.40	—	14.92
12/05	29.74	31 16	1.36	—	8.71
12/04	41.61	46 20	0.96	—	5.73
12/03	22.10	66 17	0.52	—	4.19
12/02	11.95	— —	(0.02)	—	2.08
Annual Growth	**47.0%**	**— —**	**—**	**—**	**63.7%**

Diodes Incorporated

Diodes Incorporated knows how important it is to be discrete in business. The company manufactures discrete semiconductors — fixed-function devices that are much less complex than integrated circuits. Diodes' products are used by makers of consumer electronics, automotive, computing, and telecommunications gear. The company makes hundreds of products (including diodes, transistors, and rectifiers) that vary in voltage, current, and switching speeds. Customers include Delphi, Intel, Nortel Networks, and Samsung Electronics. Lite-On Semiconductor, a company that is part of Taiwan's Lite-On Technology, owns about 23% of Diodes. Lite-On Semiconductor is also Diodes' biggest customer and its biggest supplier.

Diodes draws more than 70% of its sales from customers in Asia, where it has significant manufacturing operations.

The company has expanded its market reach by focusing on higher-margin, proprietary product lines, such as high-density arrays and ultraminiature switching diodes used in mobile applications.

In early 2006 Diodes acquired Anachip, a fabless semiconductor firm in Taiwan, for about $30 million in cash. Anachip develops power management chips, analog integrated circuits used in such products as brushless DC motor fans, LCD monitors and TVs, modems, portable DVD players, and power supplies.

Later that year the company acquired APD Semiconductor, another fabless firm, based in the US with operations in Taiwan. APD develops discrete semiconductors. The purchase price was about $8 million.

Diodes has set plans to transfer its analog wafer probe and final test operations from Taiwan to China by mid-2007. The move will affect about 40 employees in Hsinchu, Taiwan, where product design, research and development, sales, marketing, administration, and support service employees will continue to operate.

Munder Capital Management owns nearly 6% of Diodes.

EXECUTIVES

Chairman: Raymond Soong, age 65
Vice Chairman: C. H. Chen, age 64
President, CEO, and Director: Keh-Shew Lu, age 60, $315,000 pay
CFO, Secretary, and Treasurer: Carl C. Wertz, age 52, $164,000 pay
SVP Operations: Joseph Liu, age 65, $229,000 pay
SVP Sales and Marketing: Mark A. King, age 48, $197,000 pay
SVP Finance: Richard White, age 59
VP Product Development: Francis Tang, age 53
VP Corporate Administration: Edmund (Ed) Tang, age 59
Auditors: Moss Adams, LLP

LOCATIONS

HQ: Diodes Incorporated
3050 E. Hillcrest Dr., Westlake Village, CA 91362
Phone: 805-446-4800 **Fax:** 805-446-4850
Web: www.diodes.com

Diodes has facilities in China, France, Hong Kong, Taiwan, and the US.

2006 Sales

	$ mil.	% of total
Asia/Pacific		
China	118.3	35
Taiwan	96.4	28
US	76.4	22
Other countries	52.2	15
Total	**343.3**	**100**

PRODUCTS/OPERATIONS

Selected Products

Diodes
  Schottky diodes
  Switching diodes
  Zener diodes
High-density arrays
Metal oxide semiconductor field-effect transistors (MOSFETs)
Rectifiers
  Bridge rectifiers
  Schottky rectifiers
  Standard, fast, superfast, and ultrafast recovery rectifiers

Transient voltage suppressors
　Thyristor surge protection devices
　Zener transient-voltage suppressors
Transistors
　Bipolar transistors
　Darlington transistors
　Prebiased transistors

COMPETITORS

APC — MGE
Fairchild Semiconductor
Infineon Technologies
International Rectifier
IXYS
M/A-Com
Microsemi
NXP
ON Semiconductor
ROHM
Siliconix
STMicroelectronics
Toshiba Semiconductor
Vishay Intertechnology
Zetex

HISTORICAL FINANCIALS

Company Type: Public

Income Statement

FYE: December 31

	REVENUE ($ mil.)	NET INCOME ($ mil.)	NET PROFIT MARGIN	EMPLOYEES
12/06	343.3	48.1	14.0%	2,268
12/05	214.8	33.3	15.5%	1,621
12/04	185.7	25.5	13.7%	—
12/03	136.9	10.1	7.4%	—
12/02	115.8	5.8	5.0%	958
Annual Growth	31.2%	69.7%	—	24.0%

2006 Year-End Financials

Debt ratio: 81.1%
Return on equity: 18.5%
Cash ($ mil.): 339.9
Current ratio: 5.74
Long-term debt ($ mil.): 238.6
No. of shares (mil.): 26.0
Dividends
　Yield: —
　Payout: —
Market value ($ mil.): 614.1
R&D as % of sales: —
Advertising as % of sales: —

Stock History

NASDAQ (GS): DIOD

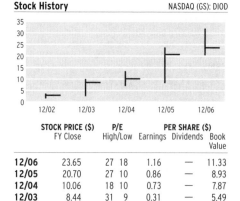

	STOCK PRICE ($) FY Close	P/E High/Low		PER SHARE ($) Earnings	Dividends	Book Value
12/06	23.65	27	18	1.16	—	11.33
12/05	20.70	27	10	0.86	—	8.93
12/04	10.06	18	10	0.73	—	7.87
12/03	8.44	31	9	0.31	—	5.49
12/02	2.85	17	9	0.19	—	7.02
Annual Growth	69.7%	—	—	57.2%	—	12.7%

Directed Electronics

Please step away from the vehicle. Directed Electronics, one of the world's top manufacturers of auto security systems, delivers products with a bite — or sting — intended to keep would-be car thieves at arm's length. Brand names include Viper, Python, and Hornet. Directed Electronics also makes keyless entry and remote start systems for automobiles and offers GPS tracking systems. In addition, the company manufactures car audio equipment, including speakers and amplifiers. Miami-based investment firm Trivest Partners (and affiliates of Trivest) control a nearly 40% stake in Directed Electronics.

Other Directed Electronics offerings include mobile video systems, speakers for home audio systems, and Sirius satellite radio products.

The company sells its products through a variety of channels, including automotive parts retailers, car dealers, electronics chains, and mass merchandisers. Best Buy and Circuit City are major customers. (Best Buy accounts for 24% of sales; Circuit City, 14%.)

EXECUTIVES

Chairman: Troy D. Templeton, age 46
President, CEO, and Director: James E. (Jim) Minarik, age 54, $630,000 pay
EVP and CFO: Kevin P. Duffy, age 32
SVP Engineering and Product Development: Mark E. Rutledge, age 36, $218,504 pay
SVP Sales: Glenn R. Busse, age 44
SVP Finance and Treasurer: Richard J. (Rich) Hirshberg, age 53, $218,500 pay
VP Operations and Information Technology: Michael N. Smith, age 40
VP, Secretary, and General Counsel: KC Bean, age 43
President, Astroflex: Jean Desmarais
President Emeritus and Chief Strategist, Home Audio: Sanford M. Gross
President, Polk Audio: James M. (Jim) Herd
President, Trilogix: Derek Schumann
Manager Corporate Communications: Kennedy Gammage
Auditors: PricewaterhouseCoopers LLP

LOCATIONS

HQ: Directed Electronics, Inc.
　1 Viper Way, Vista, CA 92081
Phone: 760-598-6200　**Fax:** 760-598-6400
Web: www.directed.com

COMPETITORS

Audiovox
Bose
Clarion
Harman International
Kenwood
Phoenix Gold
Pioneer Corporation
Rockford
SANYO
Winner International

HISTORICAL FINANCIALS

Company Type: Public

Income Statement

FYE: December 31

	REVENUE ($ mil.)	NET INCOME ($ mil.)	NET PROFIT MARGIN	EMPLOYEES
12/06	437.8	21.0	4.8%	513
12/05	304.6	(5.1)	—	236
12/04	189.9	14.0	7.4%	235
12/03	131.8	12.5	9.5%	—
12/02	123.7	12.8	10.3%	210
Annual Growth	37.2%	13.2%	—	25.0%

2006 Year-End Financials

Debt ratio: 272.7%
Return on equity: 18.8%
Cash ($ mil.): 9.9
Current ratio: 2.00
Long-term debt ($ mil.): 339.2
No. of shares (mil.): 25.2
Dividends
　Yield: —
　Payout: —
Market value ($ mil.): 288.1
R&D as % of sales: —
Advertising as % of sales: —

Stock History

NASDAQ (GM): DEIX

	STOCK PRICE ($) FY Close	P/E High/Low		PER SHARE ($) Earnings	Dividends	Book Value
12/06	11.45	22	13	0.81	—	4.94
12/05	14.39	—	—	(0.27)	—	4.02
Annual Growth	(20.4%)	—	—	—	—	23.0%

DivX, Inc.

FX from DVDs benefit from DivX. DivX, the technology, is a digital media format. The company DivX first introduced a video compression-decompression (or codec) software library that has been downloaded more than 200 million times. It has built on the success of this technology by distributing the DivX software through its own Web site and through licenses with consumer video hardware original equipment manufacturers (OEMs) including Samsung and Philips. The company also has begun working with video content developers to integrate DivX technology into the creation process. Jordan Greenhall and executives Darrius Thompson, Joe Bezdek, Tay Nguyen, and Gej Vashisht-Rota founded DivX in 2000.

Once known as DivXNetworks, the company began as Project Mayo, a collection of underground video "experts" (replace with "hackers" if desired) who developed the technology to pirate DVD video based on the MPEG-4 video format.

In 2006 the company acquired online community platform developer Corporate Green in a cash-and-stock transaction.

Leading investors in the company include Los Angeles-based Zone Venture Fund (21%), WI Harper Group of San Francisco (9%), and New York-based Insight Holdings (7%). Former CEO Greenhall owns 8%.

EXECUTIVES

CEO and Director: Kevin Hell, age 43
EVP and CFO: Dan L. Halvorson
EVP Corporate Development and Legal: David J. Richter, age 38, $217,563 pay
SVP Sales and Marketing: Pamela Thompson Johnston
VP and Group Business Manager Media Experience and Director: Jérome (Gej) Vashisht-Rota, age 33
VP Investor Relations and Compliance: Karen Fisher
VP Marketing: Mark Viken
VP and Group Business Manager, Media Languages: Patrice Lagrange

CTO: Chris Russell, age 40, $159,039 pay
General Counsel: Johnny Chen
Senior Director Finance and Treasurer: Trevor Renfield
Director Product Development: Tay Nguyen
Director Corporate Communications: Tom Huntington
Brand Director: Joe Bezdek
Auditors: Ernst & Young LLP

LOCATIONS

HQ: DivX, Inc.
   4780 Eastgate Mall, San Diego, CA 92121
Phone: 858-882-0600   **Fax:** 858-882-0601
Web: www.divx.com

PRODUCTS/OPERATIONS

2006 Sales

	% of total
Technology licensing	75
Media & other distribution & services	25
Total	**100**

COMPETITORS

Adobe
Amazon.com
Apple
CinemaNow
ContentGuard
Google
Intertrust Technologies
Microsoft
Movielink
NDS Group
Netflix
News Corp.
RealNetworks
Sony
Yahoo!

HISTORICAL FINANCIALS

Company Type: Public

Income Statement				FYE: December 31
	REVENUE ($ mil.)	NET INCOME ($ mil.)	NET PROFIT MARGIN	EMPLOYEES
12/06	59.3	16.4	27.7%	108
12/05	33.0	2.3	7.0%	—
12/04	16.4	(4.3)	—	—
12/03	7.7	(3.9)	—	—
Annual Growth	**97.5%**	**—**	**—**	**—**

2006 Year-End Financials

Debt ratio: 0.1%
Return on equity: 20.9%
Cash ($ mil.): 148.9
Current ratio: 13.46
Long-term debt ($ mil.): 0.1
No. of shares (mil.): 33.0
Dividends
   Yield: —
   Payout: —
Market value ($ mil.): 762.1
R&D as % of sales: —
Advertising as % of sales: —

Stock History

NASDAQ (GM): DIVX

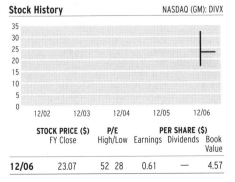

	STOCK PRICE ($) FY Close	P/E High/Low		PER SHARE ($) Earnings	Dividends	Book Value
12/06	23.07	52	28	0.61	—	4.57

Dolby Laboratories

Talk about having a sound business model. Dolby Laboratories is the market leader in developing sound processing and noise reduction systems for use in professional and consumer audio and video equipment. Though it does make some of its own products, Dolby mostly licenses its technology to other manufacturers. The firm has about 1,000 patents and 870 trademarks worldwide. In film, the Dolby Digital format has become the de facto audio standard; its systems equip movie screens around the globe. The company has expanded into digital audio compression. American engineer and physicist Ray Dolby founded the firm in London in 1965 and moved it to San Francisco in 1977. He controls 91% of the company's voting power.

The more than 40-year-old company has managed to remain a technological ruler. Dolby Laboratories is the leading maker of the digital sound technology built into DVD and CD players, surround-sound theater systems, and high-definition TV sets. Its system records the sounds of nearly every movie, professional music performance, and radio and TV broadcast in the world. About 70% of the company's sales come from outside the US. Customer CyberLink Corporation, a licensee that develops DVD software for personal computers, accounts for about 10% of Dolby's revenue.

EXECUTIVES

Chairman: Ray M. Dolby, age 74
President, CEO, and Director:
   N. William (Bill) Jasper, Jr., age 60, $1,212,901 pay
EVP Business Affairs: Martin A. (Marty) Jaffe, age 54, $620,657 pay
EVP and CFO: Kevin J. Yeaman, age 41, $619,733 pay (partial-year salary)
EVP, General Counsel, and Secretary: Mark Anderson, age 49, $523,526 pay
EVP Products and Technology: Tim Partridge, age 45
SVP; Managing Director, UK: David Watts, age 54, $568,395 pay
SVP; General Manager Consumer Division:
   Ramzi Haidamus, age 43
SVP and CTO: Craig Todd
VP Human Resources: Sherie Berger
Auditors: KPMG LLP

LOCATIONS

HQ: Dolby Laboratories, Inc.
   100 Potrero Ave., San Francisco, CA 94103
Phone: 415-558-0200   **Fax:** 415-863-1373
Web: www.dolby.com

2007 Sales

	% of total
US	30
Japan	20
Europe	19
Taiwan	11
China	10
Other regions	10
Total	**100**

PRODUCTS/OPERATIONS

2007 Sales

	$ mil.	% of total
Technology licensing	387.1	80
Product Sales	67.5	14
Production services	27.4	6
Total	**482.0**	**100**

Selected Dolby Technologies

Advanced Audio Coding (AAC, audio compression technology)
Dolby AC-2 (digital audio processing for satellite and digital audio storage)
Dolby Digital (digital sound for film soundtracks and DVDs)
Dolby Digital Surround EX (expanded surround sound for theaters)
Dolby E (eight-channel digital sound systems)
Dolby Headphone (audio processing for headphone applications)
Dolby SR (spectral recording, used in professional audio equipment)
Dolby Surround (four-channel sound for home theaters)

Selected Customers

ABC	Loews Cineplex
AMC Entertainment	NBC
CBS	New Line Cinema
Cinemark USA	Nintendo
CyberLink	Paramount
DreamWorks	Regal Cinemas
Electronic Arts	Walt Disney
HBO	Warner Brothers

COMPETITORS

Ascent Media	RealNetworks
DivX	Sony
DTS	Spatializer
Eastman Kodak	SRS Labs
Microsoft	THOMSON
NEC	THX
QSound Labs	

HISTORICAL FINANCIALS

Company Type: Public

Income Statement				FYE: Last Friday in September
	REVENUE ($ mil.)	NET INCOME ($ mil.)	NET PROFIT MARGIN	EMPLOYEES
9/07	482.0	142.8	29.6%	976
9/06	391.5	89.6	22.9%	864
9/05	328.0	52.3	15.9%	825
9/04	289.0	39.8	13.8%	—
9/03	217.5	31.0	14.3%	—
Annual Growth	**22.0%**	**46.5%**		**8.8%**

2007 Year-End Financials

Debt ratio: 1.2%
Return on equity: 20.5%
Cash ($ mil.): 599.7
Current ratio: 5.12
Long-term debt ($ mil.): 9.7
No. of shares (mil.): 49.4
Dividends
   Yield: —
   Payout: —
Market value ($ mil.): 1,718.5
R&D as % of sales: —
Advertising as % of sales: —

Stock History

NYSE: DLB

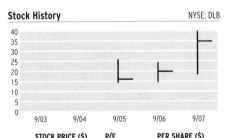

	STOCK PRICE ($) FY Close	P/E High/Low		PER SHARE ($) Earnings	Dividends	Book Value
9/07	34.82	32	15	1.26	—	16.15
9/06	19.85	30	18	0.80	—	15.82
9/05	16.00	51	29	0.50	—	13.92
Annual Growth	**47.5%**	**—**	**—**	**58.7%**	**—**	**7.7%**

Double-Take Software

Double-Take Software helps companies take a second look at their data protection. Formerly called NSI Software, the company provides data replication and storage software designed to help businesses protect and manage data assets. It also offers professional services such as consulting, implementation, support, and training. The company's customers come from fields such as education, financial and legal services, government, health care, manufacturing, retail, and telecommunications. Entities affiliated with private equity firm ABS Capital Partners own about 30% of the company; Double-Take directors Ashoke Goswami and Laura Witt are general partners of ABS.

Double-Take sells to server makers such as Dell and Hewlett-Packard, distributors including Bell Microproducts and Tech Data, and through resellers.

Double-Take expanded internationally with the 2006 acquisition of France-based Sunbelt System Software, a distributor of the company's software throughout Europe and the Middle East. Double-Take generated about 30% of its revenues outside the US in 2006.

EXECUTIVES

Chairman, President, and CEO: Dean F. Goodermote, age 54, $355,000 pay
CFO: S. Craig Huke, age 44, $275,000 pay
CTO: David J. Demlow, age 39, $167,846 pay
VP Engineering: Robert L. (Rob) Beeler, age 41
VP Europe, Middle East, and Africa; President Double-Take EMEA: Jo Murciano
VP Sales and Marketing: Daniel M. (Dan) Jones, age 39, $379,475 pay
VP Professional Services and Support:
  Michael (Mike) Lesh, age 62, $159,808 pay
VP Global Consulting Practices: Gerard (Jerry) Gregory
Systems Engineer: David Paquette
Marketing Manager: Danielle Pryor
Director Business Development: Christian Tate
Auditors: Eisner LLP

LOCATIONS

HQ: Double-Take Software, Inc.
  257 Turnpike Rd., Ste. 210,
  Southborough, MA 01772
Phone: 877-335-5674   **Fax:** 508-229-0866
Web: www.nsisoftware.com

2006 Sales

	$ mil.	% of total
North America	43.1	71
Europe, Middle East & Africa	15.8	26
Asia/Pacific	1.9	3
Total	**60.8**	**100**

PRODUCTS/OPERATIONS

2006 Sales

	$ mil.	% of total
Software licenses	38.4	63
Maintenance & professional services	22.4	37
Total	**60.8**	**100**

COMPETITORS

CA, Inc.
CommVault
DataCore
EMC
FalconStor
Hitachi Data Systems
IBM
Microsoft
Symantec
TimeSpring Software

HISTORICAL FINANCIALS

Company Type: Public

Income Statement

FYE: December 31

	REVENUE ($ mil.)	NET INCOME ($ mil.)	NET PROFIT MARGIN	EMPLOYEES
12/06	60.8	6.8	11.2%	301
12/05	40.7	(3.8)	—	—
12/04	29.8	(8.0)	—	—
12/03	23.9	(8.0)	—	200
Annual Growth	**36.5%**	**—**	**—**	**14.6%**

2006 Year-End Financials

Debt ratio: 0.0%
Return on equity: —
Cash ($ mil.): 55.2
Current ratio: 2.56
Long-term debt ($ mil.): 0.0
No. of shares (mil.): 20.7
Dividends
  Yield: —
  Payout: —
Market value ($ mil.): 267.0
R&D as % of sales: —
Advertising as % of sales: —

Stock History

NASDAQ (GM): DBTK

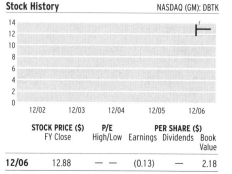

	STOCK PRICE ($) FY Close	P/E High/Low		PER SHARE ($) Earnings	Dividends	Book Value
12/06	12.88	—	—	(0.13)	—	2.18

Dreams, Inc.

How could you lose with Troy Aikman, Emmitt Smith, Randy Moss, and Jerry Rice on your team? Dreams, doing business as Field of Dreams, makes sports memorabilia (jerseys, photographs, plaques, balls); owns and operates some 30 stores; sells sports-related retail franchises; and runs two collectibles shows. It has licensing deals with the NFL, MLB, NHL, NBA, NCAA, NASCAR, and other entities. Its Dream Products (doing business as Mounted Memories) unit oversees the manufacturing and distribution duties, while the Dreams Franchise Corporation unit is in the business of selling retail franchises. Dreams acquired the *Chicago Sun-Times* Show from Sportsnews Productions in September 2007.

For some 15 years, Mounted Memories has worked with George Johnson, whose company sold the *Chicago Sun-Times* Show. The deal allows Dreams to add yet another channel through which to sell its collectibles. The *Chicago Sun-Times* Show is held in March and November each year.

Starting in 2002 the company began operating a few of its own retail outlets. It also sells through several Web sites. Its e-commerce division sells more than 30,000 products, including apparel, auto accessories, autographed memorabilia, DVDs, and other items.

President and director Ross Tannenbaum owns more than 25% of the company's stock. Chairman Sam Battistone, Jeffrey Rosenberg, and Donald Friedman each own about 6%.

EXECUTIVES

Chairman: Sam D. Battistone, age 67
President, CEO, and Director: Ross Tannenbaum, age 45, $363,750 pay
SVP, Strategic Planning and Corporate Secretary: David M. Greene, age 45, $165,000 pay
VP and CFO: Dorothy Doucet-Sillano, age 50
CIO: Mano Sivashanmugam, age 36
Controller: Jaime Adamczyk
President, Retail Division: Kevin Bates, age 39
President, Manufacturing Division: Mitch Adelstein, age 42
Auditors: Friedman, Cohen, Taubman & Company, LLC

LOCATIONS

HQ: Dreams, Inc.
  2 S. University Dr., Ste. 325, Plantation, FL 33324
Phone: 954-377-0002   **Fax:** 954-475-8785
Web: www.fieldofdreams.com

PRODUCTS/OPERATIONS

2007 Sales

	$ mil.	% of total
Retail	39.4	70
Retail	15.0	27
Franchise fees & royalties	1.1	2
Management fees	0.3	1
Other	0.2	—
Total	**56.0**	**100**

COMPETITORS

Academy Sports & Outdoors
Collectors Universe
Creative Producers
Donruss
Sports Authority
United Business Media
Upper Deck

HISTORICAL FINANCIALS

Company Type: Public

Income Statement

FYE: March 31

	REVENUE ($ mil.)	NET INCOME ($ mil.)	NET PROFIT MARGIN	EMPLOYEES
3/07	56.0	1.0	1.8%	255
3/06	42.7	2.5	5.9%	180
3/05	33.0	(0.5)	—	—
3/04	21.8	(0.5)	—	—
3/03	17.8	0.4	2.2%	—
Annual Growth	**33.2%**	**25.7%**	**—**	**41.7%**

2007 Year-End Financials

Debt ratio: 27.6%
Return on equity: 4.9%
Cash ($ mil.): 0.8
Current ratio: 4.28
Long-term debt ($ mil.): 6.7
No. of shares (mil.): 37.0
Dividends
  Yield: —
  Payout: —
Market value ($ mil.): 125.3
R&D as % of sales: —
Advertising as % of sales: —

Stock History

	STOCK PRICE ($)	P/E		PER SHARE ($)		
	FY Close	High/Low	Earnings	Dividends	Book Value	
3/07	3.39	134 18	0.03	—	0.66	
3/06	1.02	10 1	0.12	—	0.09	
3/05	0.30	— —	(0.06)	—	0.18	
3/04	2.10	— —	(0.06)	—	0.18	
3/03	0.90	37 13	0.06	—	0.19	
Annual Growth	39.3%	— —	(15.9%)	—	36.4%	

Dril-Quip, Inc.

Dril-Quip equips the guys with the drills — the oil and gas industry. Its products include drilling and production riser systems, subsea and surface wellheads and production trees, wellhead connectors and diverters, mudline hanger systems, and specialty connectors and pipe. The company, which specializes in deep-water or severe-condition equipment, also provides installation, reconditioning, and tool-rental services. Dril-Quip has major manufacturing plants in Singapore, the UK, and the US. Co-chairmen and co-founders Larry Reimert, Gary Smith, and Mike Walker own 10%, 10%, and 14% of the company, respectively.

The company was established in 1981.

In 2006 Dril-Quip installed its first subsea control system, a "signal on power" multiplex system that controls both a satellite subsea tree and subsea manifold.

EXECUTIVES

Co-Chairman and Co-CEO: Larry E. Reimert, age 60, $541,158 pay
Co-Chairman and Co-CEO: J. Mike Walker, age 64, $541,158 pay
Co-Chairman and Co-CEO: Gary D. Smith, age 64, $541,158 pay
VP Finance and CFO: Jerry M. Brooks, age 56, $253,206 pay
Auditors: BDO Seidman, LLP

LOCATIONS

HQ: Dril-Quip, Inc.
13550 Hempstead Hwy., Houston, TX 77040
Phone: 713-939-7711   **Fax:** 713-939-8063
Web: www.dril-quip.com

Dril-Quip operates manufacturing facilites in Texas, as well as in Singapore and in the UK. It has sales, service, and reconditioning facilities in New Orleans, and in Australia, Brazil, China, Denmark, Egypt, France, the Netherlands, Nigeria, and Norway.

2006 Sales

	$ mil.	% of total
Western Hemisphere	219.0	50
Eastern Hemisphere	165.0	37
Asia/Pacific	58.7	13
Total	**442.7**	**100**

PRODUCTS/OPERATIONS

2006 Sales

	$ mil.	% of total
Products	372.5	84
Services	70.2	16
Total	**442.7**	**100**

Selected Products and Services

Product Group
 Diverters
 Drilling riser systems
 Mudline hanger systems
 Platform production trees
 Platform wellheads
 Production risers
 Specialty connectors
 Subsea production trees
 Subsea wellheads
 Surface wellheads
 Wellhead connectors
 Valves
 Well systems
Service Group
 Field installation
 Reconditioning
 Rental

COMPETITORS

ABB
Aker Kværner
Cameron International
FMC
Global Power Equipment
Grant Prideco
McDermott
W-H Energy Services

HISTORICAL FINANCIALS

Company Type: Public

Income Statement

FYE: December 31

	REVENUE ($ mil.)	NET INCOME ($ mil.)	NET PROFIT MARGIN	EMPLOYEES
12/06	442.7	86.9	19.6%	—
12/05	340.8	32.6	9.6%	1,514
12/04	221.6	12.5	5.6%	—
12/03	219.5	8.9	4.1%	—
12/02	215.8	8.7	4.0%	1,454
Annual Growth	19.7%	77.8%	—	1.4%

2006 Year-End Financials

Debt ratio: 0.6%
Return on equity: 21.8%
Cash ($ mil.): 135.4
Current ratio: 3.95
Long-term debt ($ mil.): 2.9
No. of shares (mil.): 40.4

Dividends
 Yield: —
 Payout: —
Market value ($ mil.): 1,580.4
R&D as % of sales: —
Advertising as % of sales: —

Stock History

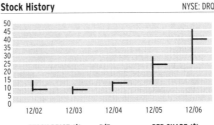

	STOCK PRICE ($)	P/E		PER SHARE ($)		
	FY Close	High/Low	Earnings	Dividends	Book Value	
12/06	39.16	21 11	2.15	—	11.58	
12/05	23.60	108 44	0.26	—	17.10	
12/04	12.13	35 20	0.36	—	12.51	
12/03	8.15	38 22	0.26	—	11.54	
12/02	8.45	55 31	0.25	—	10.72	
Annual Growth	46.7%	— —	71.2%	—	2.0%	

Duff & Phelps

Duff & Phelps provides financial advisory services to public and private corporations, investment firms, law firms, and public accounting firms. The company specializes in offering fairness opinions regarding financial reporting, tax valuations, real estate and other asset valuations, and dispute resolution. It also offers investment banking services to companies undergoing mergers and acquisitions, financial restructurings, private placements of shares, or other transactions. Its Chanin Capital Partners unit, which it acquired in 2006, provides similar services to smaller firms. Duff & Phelps has about 15 US offices, five in Europe, and one in Tokyo.

EXECUTIVES

Chairman and CEO: Noah Gottdiener, age 50
President and Director: Gerard (Gerry) Creagh, age 49
EVP and CFO: Jacob Silverman, age 35
EVP and COO: Brett Marschke, age 44
EVP, General Counsel, and Secretary:
 Edward S. Forman, age 38
Auditors: Grant Thornton LLP

LOCATIONS

HQ: Duff & Phelps Corporation
55 East 52nd. St., Fl. 31, New York, NY 10055
Phone: 212-871-2000
Web: www.duffandphelps.com

PRODUCTS/OPERATIONS

2006 Sales

	$ mil.	% of total
Financial advisory	189.5	73
Investment banking	57.3	22
Reimbursable expenses	12.5	5
Total	**259.3**	**100**

COMPETITORS

Accenture
Bear Stearns
Citigroup Global Markets
Deloitte
Ernst & Young Global
Goldman Sachs
Grant Thornton International
H&R Block
KPMG
Lehman Brothers
Merrill Lynch
Morgan Stanley
PricewaterhouseCoopers
RBC Dain Rauscher
UBS Financial Services

HISTORICAL FINANCIALS

Company Type: Public

Income Statement

FYE: December 31

	REVENUE ($ mil.)	NET INCOME ($ mil.)	NET PROFIT MARGIN	EMPLOYEES
12/06	259.3	10.5	4.0%	870
12/05	78.2	(12.5)	—	—
12/04	30.5	1.8	5.9%	—
Annual Growth	191.6%	141.5%	—	—

2006 Year-End Financials

Debt ratio: 3,775.2%
Return on equity: —
Cash ($ mil.): 59.1
Current ratio: 1.64
Long-term debt ($ mil.): 77.2

Net Income History

```
 15
 10
  5
  0
 -5
-10
-15
    12/02   12/03   12/04   12/05   12/06
```

DXP Enterprises

DXP Enterprises is well-equipped to meet its customers' needs. The company distributes maintenance, repair, and operating (MRO) equipment and products, primarily to the oil and gas, petrochemical, and wood products industries. It also distributes centrifugal pumps, rotary gear pumps, plunger pumps, mixing and metering equipment, and other fluid-handling equipment as well as bearings and power transmission equipment, general mill (cutting tools) and safety supplies, and electrical products (wire conduit). DXP's MRO unit also provides system design, fabrication, and repair services. Chairman, CEO, and president David Little owns about 22% of the company; SVP David Vinson owns about 33%.

DXP's electrical contractor division, which only accounts for about 1% of annual sales, sells a range of electrical products including wire conduit, wiring devices, electrical fittings and boxes, tools, and accessories.

DXP tends to grow by acquiring niche companies that enhance its existing businesses.

In 2005 DXP bolstered its fluid-handling offerings by acquiring Cincinnati-based R.A. Mueller Inc., for $9 million. The purchase added fluid transfer, mixing, and metering product lines, along with customers from Indiana, Kentucky, Ohio, and West Virginia. The following year DXP spent about $10 million to buy the companies Production Pump and Marine Tech, both of which make and service pumps used in petroleum and utilities operations.

Later in 2006, DXP bought Safety International, a maker of safety products. The company than paid more than $5 million for Gulf Coast Torch & Regulator, which distributes welding supplies. It bought Safety Alliance, which provides safety and environmental consulting and training services, as well as safety equipment sales, service, and rental, for $2.5 million.

The following year the company agreed to acquire southeastern US pump supplier Delta Process Equipment for $10 million. Still later in 2007 DXP agreed to purchase Precision Industries, Inc. for about $160 million. Precision Industries is an industrial distribution company with 160 nationwide stocking locations; the company also offers supply chain services. The company continued its growth through acquisition strategy into 2008 when it paid close to $5 million for Rocky Mtn. Supply, which supplies bearings, belts, and industrial and hydraulic hoses.

EXECUTIVES

Chairman, President, and CEO: David R. Little, age 55, $348,000 pay
SVP Finance, CFO, and Secretary: Mac McConnell, age 53, $172,128 pay
SVP Innovative Pumping Solutions: David C. Vinson, age 56, $149,000 pay
SVP Business to Business: J. Michael Wappler, age 54
SVP Sales and Marketing: John J. Jeffery, age 39
SVP Service Centers: Gregory Oliver, age 47
Director Human Resources: Rob Kobler
President and COO, Precision Industries: Chris W. Circo

LOCATIONS

HQ: DXP Enterprises, Inc.
7272 Pinemont, Houston, TX 77040
Phone: 713-996-4700   **Fax:** 713-996-4701
Web: www.dxpe.com

DXP Enterprises' MRO segment operates nearly 40 branch distribution facilities in Louisiana, Montana, New Mexico, Ohio, Oklahoma, Texas, and Wyoming. The Electrical Contractor segment operates from a facility in Tennessee.

PRODUCTS/OPERATIONS

2006 Sales

	$ mil.	% of total
Maintenance, repair & operating (MRO)	277.0	99
Electrical contractor	2.8	1
Total	**279.8**	**100**

Selected Products

Maintenance, Repair, and Operating (MRO) Equipment and Products
Fluid handling equipment
Air-operated diaphragm pumps
Centrifugal pumps
Piston pumps
Plunger pumps
Rotary gear pumps
General mill and safety supplies
Abrasives
Coatings and lubricants
Cutting tools
Eye and face protection products
Fasteners
First aid products
Hand tools
Hazardous material handling products
Instrumentation and respiratory protection products
Janitorial products
Pneumatic tools
Protection products
Tapes and adhesive products
Welding equipment
Hoses
Expansion joints
Hydraulic hoses
Industrial fittings
Stainless steel hoses
Teflon hoses
Power Transmission Equipment
Brakes
Chain drives
Clutches
Conveyors
Flexible coupling drives
Gears
Speed reducers
Sprockets

Electrical Contractor Products
Batteries
Electrical fittings and boxes
Fans and fuses
Heaters
Lamps
Lighting
Lugs
Signaling devices,
Switch gear
Tape
Tools
Wire conduit
Wire nuts
Wiring devices

COMPETITORS

Applied Industrial Technologies
Dillon Supply
DoALL
Graco Inc.
HWC
Industrial Distribution Group
J & L Industrial Supply
MSC Industrial Direct
Production Tool Supply
Roper Industries
R.S. Hughes

HISTORICAL FINANCIALS

Company Type: Public

Income Statement

FYE: December 31

	REVENUE ($ mil.)	NET INCOME ($ mil.)	NET PROFIT MARGIN	EMPLOYEES
12/06	279.8	11.9	4.3%	763
12/05	185.4	5.5	3.0%	519
12/04	160.6	2.8	1.7%	—
12/03	150.7	2.1	1.4%	—
12/02	148.1	(0.1)	—	513
Annual Growth	**17.2%**	**—**	**—**	**10.4%**

2006 Year-End Financials

Debt ratio: 98.5%
Return on equity: 43.1%
Cash ($ mil.): 2.5
Current ratio: 1.90
Long-term debt ($ mil.): 35.2
No. of shares (mil.): 5.3
Dividends
 Yield: —
 Payout: —
Market value ($ mil.): 186.2
R&D as % of sales: —
Advertising as % of sales: —

Stock History

NASDAQ (CM): DXPE

```
 60
 50
 40
 30
 20
 10
  0
    12/02   12/03   12/04   12/05   12/06
```

	STOCK PRICE ($) FY Close	P/E High/Low		PER SHARE ($) Earnings	Dividends	Book Value
12/06	35.04	28	8	2.08	—	6.72
12/05	17.20	28	5	0.94	—	3.88
12/04	4.81	13	7	0.50	—	3.13
12/03	4.09	10	2	0.42	—	2.48
12/02	1.09	—	—	(0.05)	—	1.99
Annual Growth	**138.1%**			**—**	**—**	**35.6%**

Dynamic Materials

Dynamic Materials Corporation (DMC) has an explosive personality when it comes to working with metal. The company (formerly Explosive Fabricators) uses explosives to metallurgically bond, or "clad," metal plates (usually joining a corrosion-resistant alloy and carbon steel). Clad metal is used to make heavy-duty industrial pressure vessels and heat exchangers. The company also produces components using more traditional metalworking techniques such as machining, rolling, and hydraulic expansion. DMC's AMK Welding subsidiary machines and welds parts primarily for the commercial aircraft and aerospace industries.

Geographically, the US accounts for about half of sales. The company has stretched its global sales and marketing efforts to serve Australia, Europe, East Asia, and Latin America. DMC has also fortified its presence in Europe by purchasing Nobelclad Europe.

DMC further bolstered its presence in Europe in 2007 when it bought Germany-based DYNAenergetics, a maker of clad metal plates and assorted explosives-related oil-field products, for about $96.6 million.

EXECUTIVES

Chairman: Dean K. Allen, age 71
President, CEO, and Director: Yvon Pierre Cariou, age 61, $304,500 pay
VP, CFO, and Secretary: Richard A. (Rick) Santa, age 56, $334,675 pay
VP, Marketing and Sales: John G. Banker, age 60, $310,000 pay
Controller: Don Rittenhouse
Director, Human Resources: Elaine Braught
Auditors: Ernst & Young LLP

LOCATIONS

HQ: Dynamic Materials Corporation
    5405 Spine Rd., Boulder, CO 80301
Phone: 303-665-5700   **Fax:** 303-604-1897
Web: www.dynamicmaterials.com

Dynamic Materials Corporation has plants and other assets in Colorado, Connecticut, and Pennsylvania in the US, as well as in France and Sweden.

2006 Sales

	$ mil.	% of total
US	56.4	50
Russia	11.1	10
Canada	10.8	10
France	4.8	4
India	3.8	3
Italy	3.5	3
South Korea	3.1	3
Belgium	2.5	2
Spain	2.5	2
Germany	2.3	2
Netherlands	2.0	2
China	1.0	1
Malaysia	0.3	—
Australia	0.2	—
Other countries	9.2	8
Total	**113.5**	**100**

PRODUCTS/OPERATIONS

2006 Sales

	$ mil.	% of total
Explosive Metalworking	108.4	96
AMK Welding	5.1	4
Total	**113.5**	**100**

COMPETITORS

Alliant Techsystems
AMETEK
Asahi Kasei
Eagle-Picher
HITCO
Japan Steel Works
Kaiser Aluminum

HISTORICAL FINANCIALS

Company Type: Public

Income Statement

FYE: December 31

	REVENUE ($ mil.)	NET INCOME ($ mil.)	NET PROFIT MARGIN	EMPLOYEES
12/06	113.5	20.8	18.3%	210
12/05	79.3	10.4	13.1%	181
12/04	54.2	2.8	5.2%	—
12/03	40.3	(0.7)	—	—
12/02	45.7	0.2	0.4%	234
Annual Growth	**25.5%**	**219.3%**	**—**	**(2.7%)**

2006 Year-End Financials

Debt ratio: 0.7%
Return on equity: 45.0%
Cash ($ mil.): 20.9
Current ratio: 2.52
Long-term debt ($ mil.): 0.4
No. of shares (mil.): 12.0
Dividends
  Yield: 0.5%
  Payout: 8.8%
Market value ($ mil.): 336.7
R&D as % of sales: —
Advertising as % of sales: —

Stock History

NASDAQ (GS): BOOM

	STOCK PRICE ($) FY Close	P/E High/Low	PER SHARE ($) Earnings	Dividends	Book Value
12/06	28.10	25 15	1.70	0.15	4.81
12/05	30.02	38 5	0.86	0.10	2.97
12/04	6.07	33 5	0.26	—	3.77
12/03	1.50	— —	(0.07)	—	3.06
12/02	1.19	138 67	0.01	—	3.07
Annual Growth	**120.4%**	**— —**	**261.1%**	**50.0%**	**11.8%**

Eagle Bancorp

For those nest eggs that need a little help hatching, holding company Eagle Bancorp would recommend its community-oriented EagleBank subsidiary. The bank serves businesses and individuals through about 10 branches in Washington, DC, and its Maryland suburbs. Deposit products include checking, savings, and money market accounts; certificates of deposit; and IRAs. Commercial real estate loans make up more than half of the bank's loan portfolio, which also includes business (more than 20% of the portfolio), consumer, home equity, and construction loans.

EXECUTIVES

Chairman: Leonard L. Abel, age 81
Vice Chairman, President, and Treasurer; Chairman, EagleBank: Ronald D. (Ron) Paul, age 52, $140,000 pay
Director; EVP and COO, EagleBank; President, EagleBank (Washington, DC): Michael T. (Mike) Flynn, age 60, $274,492 pay (prior to promotion)
EVP and COO, EagleBank: Thomas D. Murphy, age 60, $240,137 pay
EVP and CFO, EagleBank: James H. Langmead, age 59
EVP and Chief Lending Officer, EagleBank: Martha Foulon-Tonat, age 52, $222,211 pay
EVP and Chief Administrative Officer, EagleBank: Susan G. Riel, age 58, $222,118 pay
VP Marketing and Advertising Manager, EagleBank: Janette S. Shaw
VP and Business Development Officer: Jackie Starr
VP and Team Leader, Commercial Lending, EagleBank: John A. Beck Jr.
VP and Director, Human Resources: Joanie Heavey
Auditors: Stegman & Company

LOCATIONS

HQ: Eagle Bancorp, Inc.
    7815 Woodmont Ave., Bethesda, MD 20814
Phone: 301-986-1800   **Fax:** 301-986-8529
Web: www.eaglebankmd.com

PRODUCTS/OPERATIONS

2006 Sales

	$ mil.	% of total
Interest		
Loans, including fees	45.8	84
Investment securities, including dividends	3.3	6
Other	1.2	2
Noninterest		
Service charges on deposits	1.4	3
Gain on sale of loans	1.1	2
Other	1.4	3
Total	**54.2**	**100**

COMPETITORS

Bank of America
BB&T
Chevy Chase Bank
Provident Bankshares
SunTrust
Wachovia

HISTORICAL FINANCIALS

Company Type: Public

Income Statement

FYE: December 31

	ASSETS ($ mil.)	NET INCOME ($ mil.)	INCOME AS % OF ASSETS	EMPLOYEES
12/06	773.5	8.0	1.0%	171
12/05	672.3	7.5	1.1%	145
12/04	553.5	5.1	0.9%	—
12/03	443.0	3.2	0.7%	—
12/02	347.8	2.7	0.8%	81
Annual Growth	**22.1%**	**31.2%**	**—**	**20.5%**

2006 Year-End Financials

Equity as % of assets: 9.4%
Return on assets: 1.1%
Return on equity: 11.6%
Long-term debt ($ mil.): 22.0
No. of shares (mil.): 9.5
Market value ($ mil.): 164.9
Dividends
  Yield: 1.3%
  Payout: 28.4%
Sales ($ mil.): 54.2
R&D as % of sales: —
Advertising as % of sales: —

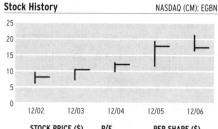

	STOCK PRICE ($) FY Close	P/E High/Low	PER SHARE ($) Earnings	Dividends	Book Value
12/06	17.40	26 20	0.81	0.23	7.69
12/05	17.81	25 15	0.77	0.20	9.04
12/04	12.13	31 24	0.41	—	10.80
12/03	10.46	23 16	0.46	—	9.81
12/02	8.08	19 12	0.51	—	6.91
Annual Growth	21.1%	— —	12.3%	15.0%	2.7%

East West Bancorp

Getting directions to pay a visit to this bank may be tricky. East West Bancorp is the holding company for East West Bank, which operates about 70 branches in and around Los Angeles and the San Francisco Bay area, plus one each in Houston, Beijing, Shanghai, and Hong Kong. The bank offers personal and business loans; checking, savings, and money market accounts; CDs; insurance; and merchant credit card processing services.

The bank caters to the Chinese-American community and provides international banking and trade financing to importers/exporters doing business in the Asia/Pacific region. East West Bank offers multilingual service in English, Cantonese, Mandarin, Vietnamese, and Spanish.

East West Bancorp has been making about one acquisition per year since 1999. In 2007 the company bought Desert Community Bank, which has about 10 branches between Los Angeles and Las Vegas and kept its name following the acquisition. The previous year East West Bancorp bought Los Angeles-area rival Standard Bank; it purchased United National Bank, which had 11 branches in California and Houston, the year before that.

Commercial and industrial real estate loans account for nearly half of the company's loan portfolio, constituting the largest segment of East West's lending. The company also writes multifamily real estate, residential mortgage, construction, business, and consumer loans.

EXECUTIVES

Chairman, President, and CEO, East West Bancorp and East West Bank: Dominic Ng, age 48, $2,190,000 pay
EVP, CFO, and Director; EVP and CFO, East West Bank: Julia S. Gouw, age 47, $458,338 pay
EVP and CIO, East West Bank: Robert L. Dingle Jr., age 55
EVP, General Counsel, and Secretary, East West Bancorp and East West Bank: Douglas P. Krause, age 50, $348,338 pay
EVP and Chief Credit Officer, East West Bank: William J. Lewis, age 66, $347,504 pay
EVP and Chief Strategic Officer, East West Bank: David L. Spigner, age 47

EVP and Director of Commercial Lending, East West Bank: Donald S. Chow, age 56
EVP and Director Corporate Banking, East West Bank: Wellington Chen, age 49, $316,670 pay
EVP and Director of International Trade Banking, East West Bank: Kwok-Yin Cheng, age 54
EVP and Director of Business Banking, East West Bank: Andy Yen, age 49
Auditors: Deloitte & Touche LLP

LOCATIONS

HQ: East West Bancorp, Inc.
135 N. Los Robles Ave., Pasadena, CA 91101
Phone: 626-768-6000   **Fax:** 626-799-3167
Web: www.eastwestbank.com

PRODUCTS/OPERATIONS

2006 Sales

	$ mil.	% of total
Interest		
Loans receivable, including fees	587.8	84
Investment securities available for sale	60.6	9
Other	11.6	2
Noninterest		
Branch fees	11.3	2
Letters of credit fees & commissions	8.7	1
Other	14.4	2
Total	**694.4**	**100**

COMPETITORS

Bank of America	City National
Bank of East Asia	Nara Bancorp
Cathay General Bancorp	UCBH Holdings
Citibank	Washington Mutual

HISTORICAL FINANCIALS

Company Type: Public

Income Statement
FYE: December 31

	ASSETS ($ mil.)	NET INCOME ($ mil.)	INCOME AS % OF ASSETS	EMPLOYEES
12/06	10,823.7	143.4	1.3%	1,312
12/05	8,278.3	108.4	1.3%	1,078
12/04	6,028.9	78.0	1.3%	—
12/03	4,055.4	59.0	1.5%	—
12/02	3,321.5	49.5	1.5%	581
Annual Growth	34.4%	30.5%	—	22.6%

2006 Year-End Financials

Equity as % of assets: 9.4%	Dividends
Return on assets: 1.5%	Yield: 0.6%
Return on equity: 16.4%	Payout: 8.5%
Long-term debt ($ mil.): 195.4	Sales ($ mil.): 694.4
No. of shares (mil.): 61.4	R&D as % of sales: —
Market value ($ mil.): 2,175.9	Advertising as % of sales: —

Stock History
NASDAQ (GS): EWBC

	STOCK PRICE ($) FY Close	P/E High/Low	PER SHARE ($) Earnings	Dividends	Book Value
12/06	35.42	18 15	2.35	0.20	16.59
12/05	36.49	21 16	1.97	0.20	12.95
12/04	41.96	29 16	1.49	0.10	9.80
12/03	26.84	23 12	1.19	0.20	14.82
12/02	18.04	19 12	1.00	0.14	12.65
Annual Growth	18.4%	— —	23.8%	9.3%	7.0%

Eastern Insurance Holdings

Through its operating subsidiaries, Eastern Insurance Holdings sells workers' compensation and some group benefits coverage to companies with fewer than 300 employees. It sells its workers' compensation products mostly in suburban Delaware, Maryland, and Pennsylvania through subsidiaries Eastern Alliance and Allied Eastern; its Eastern Re unit, based in the Cayman Islands, provides workers compensation products through "rent-a-captive" arrangements to self-insured groups. Eastern Life and Heath Insurance Company (formerly known as Educators Mutual) underwrites group benefits, including dental, term life, and disability coverage, for businesses in the mid-Atlantic, southeastern, and midwestern states.

Eastern Re also provides specialty reinsurance for underground storage and non-hazardous waste transportation insurance programs.

Additionally, the company provides claims administration and risk management services for self-insured workers' compensation and property/casualty groups.

The firm converted from a mutual company to a stock company in 2006.

EXECUTIVES

Chairman: Robert M. McAlaine, age 69
CEO and Director: Bruce M. Eckert, age 62
President and COO: Michael L. Boguski, age 43
Treasurer and CFO: Kevin M. Shook, age 38
SVP Marketing: Robert A. (Bob) Gilpin, age 39
VP, Administration and Client Services: Pamela J. Reynolds
VP, Claims: Suzanne M. Emmet, age 44
VP, Finance: Brent L. Shirk
VP, Insurance Services: M. Christine Gimber, age 45
VP and Actuary: Scott A. Humpert
CIO: Harry Talbert
President, IBSi: Alex T. Schneebacher Jr.
VP and Secretary, Educators Mutual Life Insurance and IBSi: Kimberly A. Rankin
Auditors: Beard Miller Company LLP

LOCATIONS

HQ: Eastern Insurance Holdings, Inc.
25 Race Ave., Lancaster, PA 17603
Phone: 717-396-7095   **Fax:** 717-399-3781
Web: www.easterninsuranceholdings.com

COMPETITORS

Aetna
AIG
Assurant
Cincinnati Financial
Erie Insurance Group
GUARD Insurance
Guardian Life
MetLife
Penn National Mutual Casualty
PMA Consultants
Selective Insurance

HISTORICAL FINANCIALS

Company Type: Public

Income Statement

	ASSETS ($ mil.)	NET INCOME ($ mil.)	INCOME AS % OF ASSETS	EMPLOYEES
12/06	368.2	8.3	2.3%	136
12/05	111.2	1.1	1.0%	148
12/04	111.7	1.8	1.6%	—
Annual Growth	81.6%	114.7%	—	(8.1%)

FYE: December 31

2006 Year-End Financials

Equity as % of assets: 47.2%
Return on assets: 3.5%
Return on equity: 7.0%
Long-term debt ($ mil.): 8.0
No. of shares (mil.): 11.4
Market value ($ mil.): 165.3

Dividends
  Yield: —
  Payout: —
Sales ($ mil.): 87.0
R&D as % of sales: —
Advertising as % of sales: —

Stock History

NASDAQ (GM): EIHI

	STOCK PRICE ($) FY Close	P/E High/Low	PER SHARE ($) Earnings	Dividends	Book Value
12/06	14.56	23 18	0.65	—	15.31

Edgewater Technology

Edgewater Technology is on the cutting edge of technology management consulting. Among other things, Edgewater helps businesses improve call center operations, design customized software applications, and build integrated systems. Its managed services division allows clients to outsource management and maintenance of information technology (IT) facilities. The company has expertise in such industries as financial services, health care, insurance, and higher education. It targets middle-market clients and offers specialized services to divisions of large (Global 2000) firms. Its clients include American Express, Merrill, and MIT.

Subsidiary Ranzal & Associates, acquired in 2004, helps companies develop business intelligence systems, based primarily on Hyperion software applications.

In 2006 Edgewater acquired Connecticut-based consulting firm National Decision Systems, which specializes in strategic business process consulting. The acquired company brings expertise in such industry verticals as hospitality consumer goods and financial services; it also adds merger and acquisition consulting and research advisory services to Edgewater's service offering.

Formerly known as StaffMark, the company sold its staffing business units in 2000 to focus on providing IT consulting services.

HISTORY

Edgewater Technology was founded as StaffMark in 1996 when Clete Brewer and his father, Jerry, merged six regional staffing companies (Brewer Personnel Services, founded by Clete Brewer; Prostaff Personnel; Maxwell Companies; Blethen Group; First Choice Staffing; and Human Resources Associates). The company went public in 1996 and embarked on an aggressive acquisition campaign.

In 1997 StaffMark acquired, among others, Structured Logic Co., a leading New York City-based IT recruiting firm. Among its 18 acquisitions in 1998 were clinical trials support company ClinForce, legal services firm Strategic Legal Resources, and IT group Independent Software Services. StaffMark also branched into the UK with the purchase of placement firm Robert Walters. The next year it acquired Edgewater Technology, a Boston-based Internet consulting and system integration firm founded in 1992.

With its debt load growing and its market value sinking, the company decided to put its focus on the Internet and sold its Commercial Services Division (along with the StaffMark name) in 2000. Adopting the Edgewater Technology name, it later spun off staffing firm Robert Walters on the London Stock Exchange and sold its IntelliMark division. Tragedy struck near the close of 2000 when a disgruntled employee at Edgewater Technology's headquarters shot and killed seven of his co-workers. The next year Edgewater sold the rest of its staffing-related businesses, including its ClinForce unit. In 2002 the company laid off 20% of its employees to cut costs following a slowdown in its IT business. In 2003 Edgewater acquired Virginia-based software and systems integration development company Intelix.

EXECUTIVES

Chairman, President, and CEO: Shirley Singleton, age 55, $481,250 pay
COO: David J. Gallo, age 45, $378,625 pay
CFO, Secretary, and Treasurer: Kevin R. Rhodes, age 38, $220,313 pay
EVP, CTO, and Chief Strategy Officer: David Clancey, age 51, $423,500 pay
SVP Strategic Services and Accounts: John Flavin
VP Business Development: Betsy Norris
VP Consulting: Steve Bailey
VP Consulting Services: John Inselman
VP Consulting, Southern Region: William Hall
VP Corporate Communications: Barbara Warren-Sica
VP Delivery Management and Methodology: Eva Vinson
VP Human Resources: Kristin Zaepfel, age 43, $151,731 pay
VP Consulting Services, Northern Operations: Lawrence (Larry) Fortin
VP Operations, Ranzal & Associates: Veda Gagliardi
VP Technology: Joseph Navetta
President, Ranzal & Associates: Robin Ranzal
Auditors: Deloitte & Touche LLP

LOCATIONS

HQ: Edgewater Technology, Inc.
20 Harvard Mill Sq., Wakefield, MA 01880
Phone: 781-246-3343   **Fax:** 781-246-5903
Web: www.edgewater.com

Edgewater Technology operates through offices in Arkansas, Connecticut, New Hampshire, New York, and Virginia. Subsidiary Ranzal & Associates has offices in Florida, Georgia, Massachusetts, Michigan, New York, South Carolina, and Virginia.

PRODUCTS/OPERATIONS

2006 Sales

	% of total
Service	94
Software	2
Other	4
Total	**100**

Selected Services

Application server development and administration
Architecture design and development
Data analysis and visualization
Data integration, analytics, and warehousing
Database design and development
Web and portal development

COMPETITORS

Accenture	Infosys
Answerthink	Keane
Bain & Company	Knightsbridge Solutions
Booz Allen	LogicaCMG
Boston Consulting	Longview Solutions
Cognizant Tech Solutions	McKinsey & Company
Diamond Management & Technology	MicroStrategy
EDS	Oracle
Hewlett-Packard	Perficient
IBM	SAP
IBM Global Services	Sapient
INDUS Corp.	Satyam
Informatica	Tata Consultancy
Inforte	Wipro

HISTORICAL FINANCIALS

Company Type: Public

Income Statement

FYE: December 31

	REVENUE ($ mil.)	NET INCOME ($ mil.)	NET PROFIT MARGIN	EMPLOYEES
12/06	60.1	3.2	5.3%	303
12/05	43.1	1.6	3.7%	282
12/04	25.3	(0.6)	—	205
12/03	25.0	1.0	4.0%	—
12/02	18.7	(23.5)	—	152
Annual Growth	33.9%	—	—	18.8%

2006 Year-End Financials

Debt ratio: 0.9%
Return on equity: 3.9%
Cash ($ mil.): 33.1
Current ratio: 5.38
Long-term debt ($ mil.): 0.8
No. of shares (mil.): 11.5

Dividends
  Yield: —
  Payout: —
Market value ($ mil.): 70.4
R&D as % of sales: —
Advertising as % of sales: —

Stock History

NASDAQ (GM): EDGW

	STOCK PRICE ($) FY Close	P/E High/Low	PER SHARE ($) Earnings	Dividends	Book Value
12/06	6.11	29 19	0.27	—	7.49
12/05	5.90	42 26	0.15	—	7.31
12/04	4.90	— —	(0.05)	—	7.26
12/03	4.92	72 46	0.08	—	7.12
12/02	4.72	— —	(2.03)	—	7.06
Annual Growth	6.7%	—	—	—	1.5%

eHealth, Inc.

eHealth brought e-commerce to the insurance business. Through its eHealthInsurance Services subsidiary, the company sells health insurance online to nearly 400,000 individual, family, and small business members. The company is licensed to sell in all 50 states and Washington, DC, and it has partnerships with some 160 health insurance carriers. It offers more than 7,000 products online — including health, dental, and vision insurance products from the likes of Aetna, Humana, Kaiser Permanente, and Unicare, as well as more than 40 Blue Cross and Blue Shield licensees. The company was founded in 1997.

eHealth is trying to fill a gap in the health insurance brokerage business, left by large brokers who cater to large and mid-sized companies and local agents who sell to individuals and small businesses but offer plans from a limited number of carriers. eHealth's technology platform and nationwide presence allow customers to get online rate quotes and side-by-side plan comparisons from a much wider range of providers. The company's online applications are delivered electronically to insurance carriers' information systems, reducing the time it takes to process and enroll new members.

The company gets most of its revenue (upwards of 90%) from commissions off sales of policies. A much smaller amount comes from advertising sponsorships on its Web site and licensing agreements with agents and carriers who use the company's e-commerce technology. The company launched its online advertising business in 2006.

eHealth is working to build greater brand awareness with consumers and drive more traffic to its Web site. The company has marketing partnerships with financial and online services firms — including Aon, Wells Fargo, and Esurance — to help get potential customers to its site. By making more people aware of the company's offering and by providing more products from an ever-growing network of carriers, the company hopes to grow its membership.

Though the company operates a technology center in China, all its revenues come from the US. It is looking for opportunities, however, to expand its sales into international markets.

Commissions and fees generated from its contracts with Golden Rule Insurance account for about 15% of eHealth's revenue. Its contracts with Blue Cross of California and Unicare (both subsidiaries of WellPoint) bring in 12%.

EXECUTIVES

Chairman, President, and CEO: Gary L. Lauer, age 55, $300,000 pay
EVP Business Operations: Bruce A. Telkamp, age 40
EVP Technology and CTO: Sheldon X. Wang, age 48
SVP and CFO: Stuart M. Huizinga, age 45, $190,000 pay
SVP Sales: Samuel C. (Sam) Gibbs III, age 50
SVP Carrier Relations: Robert S. Hurley, age 48
Auditors: Ernst & Young LLP

LOCATIONS

HQ: eHealth, Inc.
  440 E. Middlefield Rd., Mountain View, CA 94043
Phone: 650-584-2700 **Fax:** 650-961-2153
Web: www.ehealthinsurance.com

eHealth sells insurance in all 50 US states. It has facilities in the US and China.

PRODUCTS/OPERATIONS

2006 Sales

	$ mil.	% of total
Commissions	58.9	96
Sponsorships, licensing & other	2.4	4
Total	**61.3**	**100**

Selected Insurance Carriers

Aetna
Anthem Blue Cross and Blue Shield
Arkansas Blue Cross Blue Shield
Assurant Health
Blue Cross of California
Blue Cross Blue Shield of Texas
CareFirst
CIGNA
ConnectiCare
Coventry Health Care
Golden Rule Insurance
HealthNet
Humana
Kaiser Permanente
Mountain State BlueCross BlueShield
Oxford Health Plans
PacifiCare
Unicare

COMPETITORS

Aflac
Aon
Arthur Gallagher
Bollinger, Inc.
Marsh Inc.
Wells Fargo Insurance Services
Willis Group

HISTORICAL FINANCIALS

Company Type: Public

Income Statement

FYE: December 31

	REVENUE ($ mil.)	NET INCOME ($ mil.)	NET PROFIT MARGIN	EMPLOYEES
12/06	61.3	16.5	26.9%	357
12/05	41.8	(0.4)	—	—
12/04	30.2	(3.3)	—	—
12/03	22.2	(3.2)	—	—
Annual Growth	**40.3%**	—	—	—

2006 Year-End Financials

Debt ratio: —
Return on equity: 187.9%
Cash ($ mil.): 90.5
Current ratio: 10.75
Long-term debt ($ mil.): —
No. of shares (mil.): 21.7
Dividends
  Yield: —
  Payout: —
Market value ($ mil.): 437.4
R&D as % of sales: —
Advertising as % of sales: —

Stock History

NASDAQ (GM): EHTH

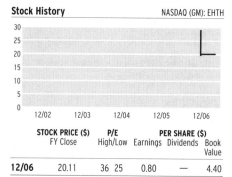

	STOCK PRICE ($) FY Close	P/E High/Low	PER SHARE ($) Earnings	Dividends	Book Value
12/06	20.11	36 25	0.80	—	4.40

Elecsys Corporation

Many companies elect Elecsys to make their electronics. Elecsys is a contract manufacturer of electronic assemblies and displays. Through subsidiary DCI, Inc., the company makes custom electronic assemblies — including printed circuit boards, electronic modules, LCDs, and light-emitting diodes (LEDs) — for OEMs in the aerospace, communications, medical, and other industries. Five customers account for about half of the company's sales. In 2007 Elecsys acquired the assets of Radix International, a supplier of ultra-rugged handheld computers and portable printers. DCI previously manufactured most of Radix's product line on a contract basis.

Acquiring Radix's business will substantially increase the annual sales of Elecsys. Radix posted fiscal 2007 sales of more than $10 million. The acquisition cost Elecsys about $2.2 million, and the company assumed around $1.4 million in liabilities. The transaction includes performance-based compensation over five years, which may total up to $1.75 million.

In 2004 Elecsys acquired subsidiary Network Technologies Group (NTG), which offers remote monitoring systems for the oil and gas pipeline industry.

Elecsys sold its aircraft navigation aids business, which had accounted for most sales, in 2001 to focus on DCI. In 2006 the company sold its former headquarters building for around $1.75 million.

CEO Karl Gemperli owns about 15% of Elecsys, including stock options. Chairman Robert Taylor holds around 7% of the company. Director Stan Gegen has an equity stake of approximately 5%. All officers and directors of the company as a group own nearly 36% of Elecsys.

EXECUTIVES

Chairman: Robert D. Taylor, age 61
President, CEO, and Director; President and CEO, DCI: Karl B. Gemperli, age 44, $158,770 pay
VP, CFO, and Secretary; VP Finance, DCI: Todd A. Daniels, age 40, $110,619 pay
President, NTG: Michael J. (Mike) Reed, age 53
VP Operations, DCI: Michael D. (Mike) Morgan, age 54, $136,225 pay
VP Engineering, DCI: Christopher G. (Chris) Thomas, age 41, $106,227 pay
VP Sales and Marketing, DCI: Phillip A. Schoettlin, age 44
Auditors: McGladrey & Pullen, LLP

LOCATIONS

HQ: Elecsys Corporation
  15301 W. 109th St., Lenexa, KS 66219
Phone: 913-647-0158 **Fax:** 913-647-0132
Web: www.elecsyscorp.com

PRODUCTS/OPERATIONS

2007 Sales

	$ mil.	% of total
Electronic manufacturing services	18.9	95
Remote monitoring solutions	0.9	5
Total	**19.8**	**100**

Selected Products and Services

Electronic Assembly
  Ball grid array
  Surface mount
  Through hole
Electromechanical Assembly and Wiring
  Complete box build
  System integration
Microelectronic Assembly
  Chip on board
  Chip on glass
  Direct die attach
  Pulsed heat TAB attach
  Wire bonding
Mobile Computing
  Handheld computers
  Portable printers
Remote monitoring devices for railroad crossings
  and oil and gas pipelines (ScadaNET)

COMPETITORS

American Innovations
Analogic
Benchmark Electronics
Celestica
Coretec
Flextronics
Jabil
NovAtel
Planar Systems
Sanmina-SCI

HISTORICAL FINANCIALS

Company Type: Public

Income Statement

	REVENUE ($ mil.)	NET INCOME ($ mil.)	NET PROFIT MARGIN	EMPLOYEES
4/07	19.8	1.0	5.1%	129
4/06	14.7	1.7	11.6%	106
4/05	12.3	0.7	5.7%	97
4/04	10.6	0.0	—	80
4/03	11.3	(1.4)	—	114
Annual Growth	15.1%	—	—	3.1%

FYE: April 30

2007 Year-End Financials

Debt ratio: 50.7%
Return on equity: 14.8%
Cash ($ mil.): 0.5
Current ratio: 2.01
Long-term debt ($ mil.): 3.7
No. of shares (mil.): 3.3

Dividends
  Yield: —
  Payout: —
Market value ($ mil.): 18.7
R&D as % of sales: —
Advertising as % of sales: —

Stock History

AMEX: ASY

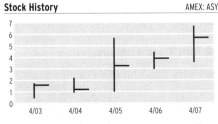

	STOCK PRICE ($) FY Close	P/E High/Low	PER SHARE ($) Earnings	Dividends	Book Value
4/07	5.69	21 12	0.31	—	2.23
4/06	3.90	9 6	0.49	—	1.91
4/05	3.25	24 5	0.23	—	1.40
4/04	1.20	215 97	0.01	—	1.09
4/03	1.58	— —	(0.49)	—	1.08
Annual Growth	37.8%	— —	—	—	20.0%

Emergent BioSolutions

Emergent BioSolutions protects your thorax against anthrax. Emergent BioSolutions develops and produces, for the US government and commercial markets, drugs that treat or protect against infectious diseases and bio-agents. The company supplies BioThrax (the US's only FDA-approved anthrax vaccine) primarily to the departments of Defense and Health and Human Services (HHS). The firm's biodefense unit is also developing a post-exposure treatment for anthrax and a preventive vaccine for botulinum toxin. For commercial markets, Emergent is working on therapies and vaccines for typhoid, Group B strep, and hepatitis B, among other things. Chairman and CEO Fuad El-Hibri controls about 80% of the company.

Nearly all of Emergent's revenue comes from sales of BioThrax to its US government customers. Under its Defense and HHS contracts, it has supplied millions of doses for vaccination of military personnel and to replenish the nation's stockpile of medical treatments for terrorist attacks and other disasters.

The company has benefited from the spike in biodefense spending that followed the attacks of September 11, 2001, and the still unsolved cases of anthrax infection of the same year. In particular, the Project Bioshield law, which took effect in 2004, authorized billions of dollars in additional funds for procurement of countermeasures to bioterror agents.

Emergent's anthrax vaccine, which is based on decades-old technology, has not avoided controversy, though. Courts temporarily halted the military's mandatory vaccination program using BioThrax in 2004, after some soldiers refused to take it and filed suit, citing the drug's serious side effects and a lack of testing on humans. The military has since resumed mandatory vaccinations.

Another blow to Emergent came when HHS awarded a huge contract for 75 million doses of a newer anthrax vaccine to rival VaxGen. HHS cancelled the contract in 2007, however, when VaxGen failed to achieve development milestones on time.

Emergent wants to move beyond its US government customer base by targeting state and local governments (who may want stockpiles for inoculating first responders), as well as foreign governments. It has established marketing operations in Singapore and Germany to target international markets.

And while it depends on biodefense markets for most of its revenue currently, it is trying to balance its drug development efforts between biodefense and commercial candidates. The company has built its commercial vaccine business through several acquisitions, starting with the 2003 purchase of vaccine-developer Antex Biologics. It also bought UK vaccine developer Microscience (renamed Emergent Europe) in 2005 and Germany-based biotech ViVacs in 2006.

Emergent's product development strategy involves acquiring or in-licensing candidates in the clinical development stage (thus bypassing costly and time-consuming discovery and preclinical phases) and seeing them through the clinical regulatory process. It has established collaborations for some of its products, including one with the UK's Health Protection Agency for its botulinum toxin program and another with Sanofi Pasteur on the development of a meningitis B vaccine.

The company's 2006 initial public offering raised funds for clinical trials and the construction of a large-scale production facility in Lansing, Michigan.

EXECUTIVES

CEO and Chairman: Fuad El-Hibri, age 49
COO: Edward J. Arcuri, age 57, $231,923 pay
President and Secretary: Daniel J. Abdun-Nabi, age 53
EVP Manufacturing Operations; President and CEO Emergent Biodefense Operations Lansing Inc: Robert G. Kramer Sr., age 50, $369,371 pay
SVP Corporate Affairs: Kyle W. Keese, age 45
SVP Finance and Administration, CFO, and Treasurer: R. Don Elsey, age 54, $236,519 pay
SVP Corporate Development: Mauro Gibellini
SVP Legal Affairs and General Counsel: Denise Esposito
SVP Medical and Clinical Development: Thomas K. Zink
Chief Scientific Officer and President Emergent Product Development UK Limited: Steven Chatfield, age 50, $225,162 pay
President Product Development: Michael J. Langford
President Emergent Product Deveopment UK: Stephen Lockhart
VP Investor Relations: Robert G. Burrows
Director Communications and Government Affairs, BioPort: Kimberly Brennen (Kim) Root
Auditors: Ernst & Young LLP

LOCATIONS

HQ: Emergent BioSolutions Inc.
  2273 Research Blvd., Ste. 400, Rockville, MD 20850
Phone: 301-795-1800   **Fax:** 301-795-1899
Web: www.emergentbiosolutions.com

Emergent BioSolutions has laboratory and manufacturing facilities in the US and UK.

PRODUCTS/OPERATIONS

2006 Sales

	$ mil.	% of total
Products	148.0	97
Contracts & grants	4.7	3
Total	152.7	100

Selected Product and Product Candidates

Marketed
  BioThrax (preventive anthrax vaccine)
In development
  Biodefense
    Anthrax immune globulin (post-exposure treatment for anthrax infection)
    Botulinum immune globulin (post-exposure treatment for botulinum toxin illness)
    Recombinant bivalent botulinum vaccine (botulinum toxin preventive vaccine)
  Commercial
    Typhoid vaccine
    Hepatitis B vaccine
    Group B streptococcus vaccine

COMPETITORS

Acambis
AVANT Immunotherapeutics
Avecia
bioMérieux
Cangene
DOR BioPharma
Elusys Therapeutics
GlaxoSmithKline
Health Protection Agency
Human Genome Sciences
Merck
Novartis
Sanofi Pasteur
VaxGen
Wyeth

HISTORICAL FINANCIALS

Company Type: Public

Income Statement

	REVENUE ($ mil.)	NET INCOME ($ mil.)	NET PROFIT MARGIN	EMPLOYEES
12/06	152.7	22.8	14.9%	494
12/05	130.7	15.8	12.1%	—
12/04	83.5	11.5	13.8%	—
12/03	55.8	4.5	8.1%	400
Annual Growth	39.9%	71.8%	—	7.3%

FYE: December 31

2006 Year-End Financials

Debt ratio: 22.7%
Return on equity: 23.0%
Cash ($ mil.): 76.4
Current ratio: 2.29
Long-term debt ($ mil.): 31.4
No. of shares (mil.): 27.6

Dividends
  Yield: —
  Payout: —
Market value ($ mil.): 308.0
R&D as % of sales: —
Advertising as % of sales: —

Stock History

NYSE: EBS

	STOCK PRICE ($) FY Close	P/E High/Low	PER SHARE ($) Earnings	Dividends	Book Value
12/06	11.16	14 10	0.93	—	5.02

Empire Resources

When it comes to aluminum, Empire Resources is especially resourceful. The company distributes semifinished aluminum products, including sheet, foil, wire, plate, and coil. Products are sold primarily to manufacturers of appliances, automobiles, packaging, and housing materials. Empire Resources provides a variety of related services, including sourcing of aluminum products, storage and delivery, and handling foreign exchange transactions. Company president and CEO Nathan Kahn and CFO Sandra Kahn, who are husband and wife, own 54% of Empire Resources.

Empire Resources relies on a single supplier, Hulett Aluminium, for more than half of its products. However, Empire Resources has begun to make its own aluminum extrusions. As for customers, Ryerson is the company's largest, accounting for about 15% of sales.

EXECUTIVES

Chairman: William Spier, age 72
President, CEO, and Director: Nathan Kahn, age 52, $900,000 pay
VP, CFO, Secretary, Treasurer, and Director: Sandra R. Kahn, age 49, $325,000 pay
VP Sales and Director: Harvey Wrubel, age 53, $312,300 pay
VP Investor Relations: David Kronfeld
Customer Service Manager: Ginette Raymond
Human Resources: Deborah Waltuch
Auditors: Eisner LLP

LOCATIONS

HQ: Empire Resources, Inc.
1 Parker Plaza, Fort Lee, NJ 07024
Phone: 201-944-2200   **Fax:** 201-944-2226
Web: www.empireresources.com

Empire Resources operates from offices in Maryland and New Jersey and sells its products throughout North America and in Australia, Europe, and New Zealand.

2006 Sales

	$ mil.	% of total
US	348.1	82
Pacific Rim, Canada & Europe	77.9	18
Total	**426.0**	**100**

PRODUCTS/OPERATIONS

Selected Aluminum Products

Circles
Coil/sheet
Foil
Plate
Profiles/extruded products
Treadplate

COMPETITORS

Alcoa
Commercial Metals
Rio Tinto Alcan

HISTORICAL FINANCIALS

Company Type: Public

Income Statement

	REVENUE ($ mil.)	NET INCOME ($ mil.)	NET PROFIT MARGIN	EMPLOYEES
12/06	426.0	8.7	2.0%	65
12/05	358.5	9.5	2.6%	50
12/04	212.6	4.8	2.3%	—
12/03	184.4	3.5	1.9%	—
12/02	158.7	2.4	1.5%	21
Annual Growth	28.0%	38.0%	—	32.6%

FYE: December 31

2006 Year-End Financials

Debt ratio: 7.1%
Return on equity: 31.7%
Cash ($ mil.): 2.3
Current ratio: 1.15
Long-term debt ($ mil.): 2.2
No. of shares (mil.): 9.8

Dividends
  Yield: 3.3%
  Payout: 41.4%
Market value ($ mil.): 107.1
R&D as % of sales: —
Advertising as % of sales: —

Stock History

AMEX: ERS

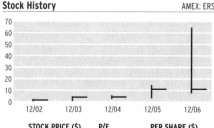

	STOCK PRICE ($) FY Close	P/E High/Low	PER SHARE ($) Earnings	Dividends	Book Value
12/06	10.94	74 9	0.87	0.36	3.13
12/05	10.89	15 4	0.96	0.35	2.48
12/04	4.12	10 6	0.49	0.22	1.87
12/03	3.95	11 3	0.37	0.16	1.59
12/02	1.40	7 3	0.23	—	1.37
Annual Growth	67.2%	— —	39.5%	31.0%	22.9%

Encore Acquisition

"Drill it again, and buy some more oil and gas properties" appear to be operating guidelines for Encore Acquisition, an independent oil and natural gas company engaged in the acquisition, development, and exploitation of reserves in several basins. Operations include drilling in the Williston Basin of Montana and North Dakota, the Permian Basin of Texas and New Mexico, and the Anadarko Basin of Oklahoma. Its proved reserves of 206 million barrels of oil equivalent are primarily from its Cedar Creek Anticline asset (in Montana and North Dakota). Encore Acquisition was formed in 1998 by J.P. Morgan Partners, Warburg Pincus & Co., and Natural Gas Partners.

In 2004 the company acquired Cortez Oil & Gas. In 2005 Encore Acquisition bought oil and gas properties in Oklahoma, Montana, and North Dakota, from some private companies for about $123 million. It also purchased oil and gas properties in the Permian Basin in West Texas and the Anadarko Basin in Oklahoma from Kerr-McGee for $104 million.

In 2007 the company acquired assets in the Elk Basin and Gooseberry oil fields in Wyoming from Anadarko Petroleum for $400 million.

EXECUTIVES

Chairman: I. Jon Brumley, age 68, $800,000 pay
President, CEO, and Director: Jon S. (Jonny) Brumley, age 36, $933,333 pay
SVP and COO: L. Ben Nivens, age 46, $371,250 pay
SVP, CFO, and Treasurer: Robert C. Reeves, age 37, $204,375 pay (prior to title change)
SVP, General Counsel, and Corporate Secretary: Philip D. Devlin, age 62
VP Mid-Continent Region: Thomas H. (Tom) Olle, age 52, $339,583 pay
VP Acquisitions: John W. Arms, age 40
VP Marketing: Andy R. Lowe, age 55
VP Land: Kevin Treadway, age 41
Director Human Resources: Don Lott
Auditors: Ernst & Young LLP

LOCATIONS

HQ: Encore Acquisition Company
777 Main St., Ste. 1400, Fort Worth, TX 76102
Phone: 817-877-9955   **Fax:** 817-877-1655
Web: www.encoreacq.com

Encore Acquisition has operations in Louisiana, Montana, New Mexico, North Dakota, Oklahoma, and Texas.

PRODUCTS/OPERATIONS

2006 Sales

	$ mil.	% of total
Oil	347.0	54
Oil Marketing	147.6	23
Natural Gas	146.3	23
Total	**640.9**	**100**

COMPETITORS

Abraxas Petroleum
Anadarko Petroleum
Apache
BP
Exxon Mobil
Pioneer Natural Resources
Royal Dutch Shell

HISTORICAL FINANCIALS

Company Type: Public

Income Statement

FYE: December 31

	REVENUE ($ mil.)	NET INCOME ($ mil.)	NET PROFIT MARGIN	EMPLOYEES
12/06	640.9	92.4	14.4%	236
12/05	457.3	103.4	22.6%	205
12/04	298.5	82.2	27.5%	—
12/03	220.1	63.6	28.9%	—
12/02	160.7	37.7	23.5%	108
Annual Growth	41.3%	25.1%	—	21.6%

2006 Year-End Financials

Debt ratio: 85.7%
Return on equity: 13.6%
Cash ($ mil.): 18.1
Current ratio: 0.78
Long-term debt ($ mil.): 700.4
No. of shares (mil.): 53.0

Dividends
  Yield: —
  Payout: —
Market value ($ mil.): 1,301.2
R&D as % of sales: —
Advertising as % of sales: —

Stock History

NYSE: EAC

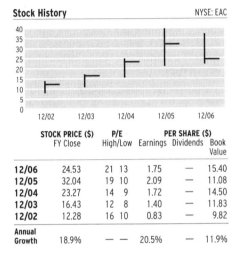

	STOCK PRICE ($) FY Close	P/E High/Low		PER SHARE ($) Earnings	Dividends	Book Value
12/06	24.53	21	13	1.75	—	15.40
12/05	32.04	19	10	2.09	—	11.08
12/04	23.27	14	9	1.72	—	14.50
12/03	16.43	12	8	1.40	—	11.83
12/02	12.28	16	10	0.83	—	9.82
Annual Growth	18.9%	—	—	20.5%	—	11.9%

Ennis, Inc.

Ennis (formerly Ennis Business Forms) is in the forms and fashion business. It makes a variety of custom business forms and promotional products (Post-it Notes, presentation products, advertising specialty items). It also sells printed bank forms, secure and negotiable documents, and apparel. Most of its sales, however, come from custom items. The firm sells throughout the US — to end users and forms distributors and resellers. It operates more than 35 manufacturing plants in 16 states, as well as in Mexico and Canada. Ennis runs a dozen other units, including Adams McClure (retail promotions), Northstar Computer Forms (bank forms), and Alstyle Apparel.

Ennis is continuing to grow through acquisitions. In 2006 it acquired Block Graphics for an undisclosed amount. The Block purchase added envelopes and additional short-run print products like continuous and cut-sheet forms to Ennis' offerings. Previously the company expanded its business forms and labels segment through purchases of Crabar/GBF and Royal Business Forms. Ennis' Alstyle Apparel (promotional apparel) buy helped the firm expand into T-shirt and activewear manufacturing and distribution.

The company continued adding to its business with the acquisitions of B&D Litho and Skyline Business Forms in 2007.

EXECUTIVES

Chairman, President, and CEO: Keith S. Walters, age 57, $713,461 pay
EVP and Treasurer: Michael D. Magill, age 59, $380,769 pay
VP Administration and Director: Ronald M. Graham, age 59, $228,462 pay
VP Apparel Division; President, Alstyle Apparel: Todd Scarborough, age 39, $354,461 pay
VP Finance, CFO, and Secretary: Richard L. Travis Jr., age 51, $236,538 pay
VP Operations: Terry Pennington
Director Human Resources: Richard Maresh
Director Marketing: Steven Osterloh
Auditors: Grant Thornton LLP

LOCATIONS

HQ: Ennis, Inc.
  2441 Presidential Pkwy., Midlothian, TX 76065
Phone: 972-775-9801   **Fax:** 972-775-9820
Web: www.ennis.com

Ennis has manufacturing plants in California, Colorado, Illinois, Iowa, Georgia, Kansas, Michigan, Minnesota, Missouri, Nevada, New Jersey, Ohio, Oregon, Pennsylvania, Tennessee, Texas, Virginia, and Wisconsin. It also has manufacturing facilities in Mexico.

PRODUCTS/OPERATIONS

2007 Sales

	% of total
Print	56
Apparel	44
Total	**100**

Selected Segments and Products

Apparel Solutions
  Activewear
Print Solutions
  Business forms
  Financial solutions
  Other printed business products
  Promotional solutions

COMPETITORS

Avery Dennison	Office Depot
Cenveo	OfficeMax
Delta Apparel	R.R. Donnelley
DELUXEPINPOINT	Russell Corporation
Gildan Activewear	Standard Register
Hanes Companies	Staples
Liberty Enterprises	

HISTORICAL FINANCIALS

Company Type: Public

Income Statement

FYE: Last day of February

	REVENUE ($ mil.)	NET INCOME ($ mil.)	NET PROFIT MARGIN	EMPLOYEES
2/07	584.7	41.6	7.1%	6,383
2/06	559.4	40.5	7.2%	5,950
2/05	365.4	23.0	6.3%	—
2/04	259.4	18.0	6.9%	—
2/03	240.8	15.3	6.4%	2,298
Annual Growth	24.8%	28.4%	—	29.1%

2007 Year-End Financials

Debt ratio: 28.1%
Return on equity: 13.6%
Cash ($ mil.): 3.6
Current ratio: 3.08
Long-term debt ($ mil.): 89.0
No. of shares (mil.): 25.6

Dividends
  Yield: 1.8%
  Payout: 29.0%
Market value ($ mil.): 659.9
R&D as % of sales: —
Advertising as % of sales: —

Stock History

NYSE: EBF

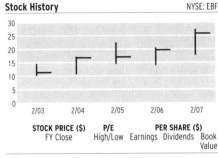

	STOCK PRICE ($) FY Close	P/E High/Low		PER SHARE ($) Earnings	Dividends	Book Value
2/07	25.80	17	11	1.62	0.47	12.37
2/06	19.72	13	9	1.58	0.62	11.67
2/05	17.08	19	12	1.19	0.62	10.69
2/04	16.83	16	10	1.08	0.47	6.75
2/03	11.32	15	11	0.93	0.62	5.93
Annual Growth	22.9%	—	—	14.9%	(6.7%)	20.2%

Entegris, Inc.

Entegris products are integral to making semiconductors and computer disk drives. The company makes more than 10,000 products used to transport and protect semiconductor and disk drive materials during processing. Its semiconductor products include wafer carriers, storage boxes, and chip trays, as well as chemical delivery products, such as pipes, fittings, and valves. Its disk drive offerings include shippers, stamper cases, and transport trays. Top customers for Entegris include AMD, Dainippon Screen Manufacturing, Freescale Semiconductor, IBM, Seagate Technology, Siltronic, and Taiwan Semiconductor Manufacturing. The company has more than 3,000 customers.

Entegris has expanded its offerings with a number of acquisitions, including privately held Electrol Specialties Company, a maker of equipment used in biopharmaceutical production, and the wafer carrier and reticle carrier product lines of Asyst Technologies. It also formed a joint venture called Entegris Precision Technology with Taiwan-based electronics conglomerate Mitac-Synnex Group; the venture was established to make chemical-storage products used in semiconductor manufacturing. In 2005 Entegris acquired Mykrolis in a stock deal valued at approximately $580 million. It also divested two non-core businesses, clean-in-place equipment for life science applications, and tape-and-reel systems used in electronics manufacturing.

Early the following year it sold its gas delivery product line, which is used in semiconductor production equipment, to Celerity.

Through all the ups and downs of the volatile semiconductor market, Entegris has recorded an annual profit for more than three decades running. T. Rowe Price owns about 10% of Entegris. Cooke & Bieler holds nearly 7% of the company. Investor Gerald Catanacci has an equity stake of around 5%.

EXECUTIVES

Chairman: James E. (Jim) Dauwalter, age 55, $1,003,025 pay
President, CEO, and Director: Gideon Argov, age 50, $600,000 pay
EVP and COO: Jean-Marc Pandraud, age 53, $384,766 pay
EVP and Chief Administrative Officer: Bertrand Loy, age 41, $340,625 pay
SVP and Chief Technology and Innovation Officer: John Goodman, age 47
SVP, General Counsel, and Secretary: Peter W. Walcott, age 60, $287,937 pay
SVP, Human Resources: John J. (Joe) Murphy, age 54
SVP, Strategic Planning and Business Development and Principal Accounting Officer: Gregory B. (Greg) Graves, age 46
VP, Corporate Relations: Steve Cantor
Auditors: KPMG LLP

LOCATIONS

HQ: Entegris, Inc.
　3500 Lyman Blvd., Chaska, MN 55318
Phone: 952-556-3131　　**Fax:** 952-556-1880
Web: www.entegris.com

Entegris has facilities in China, France, Germany, Japan, Malaysia, Singapore, South Korea, Taiwan, and the US.

2006 Sales

	$ mil.	% of total
US	195.9	29
Japan	153.3	23
Taiwan	82.7	12
South Korea	56.1	8
Singapore	30.8	4
Germany	25.6	4
Malaysia	25.1	4
Other countries	109.2	16
Total	**678.7**	**100**

PRODUCTS/OPERATIONS

2006 Sales

	$ mil.	% of total
Semiconductor products	531.0	78
Data storage products	44.5	7
Other	103.2	15
Total	**678.7**	**100**

Selected Products

Disk Manufacturing
　Boxes
　Glass master carriers
　Packages
　Process carriers
　Shippers
　Stamper cases
　Substrate packages
　Transport trays
Fluid Handling
　Containers
　Sanitary tubing
　Valves and fittings
Fuel Cell Production
　Components
　Materials
　Subassemblies
Semiconductor Manufacturing
　Test, assembly, and packaging
　　Chip and matrix trays
　　Wafer shippers and carriers
　Wafer handling
　　Pods
　　Reticle carriers
　　Wafer transport and process carriers
　　Work-in-progress boxes

COMPETITORS

3M	Pall
Air Products	Parker Hannifin
Amtech Systems	Peak International
Brooks Automation	Plastic Omnium
Flowserve	Roper Industries
Illinois Tool Works	SAES Getters
L'Air Liquide	Saint-Gobain
Mirae	Shin-Etsu Chemical
MKS Instruments	

HISTORICAL FINANCIALS

Company Type: Public

Income Statement

				FYE: December 31
	REVENUE ($ mil.)	NET INCOME ($ mil.)	NET PROFIT MARGIN	EMPLOYEES
12/06*	678.7	63.5	9.4%	3,000
8/05	367.1	9.4	2.6%	2,750
8/04	346.8	24.8	7.2%	—
8/03	248.8	1.3	0.5%	—
8/02	219.8	2.8	1.3%	1,720
Annual Growth	**32.6%**	**118.2%**	**—**	**14.9%**

*Fiscal year change

2006 Year-End Financials

Debt ratio: 0.3%
Return on equity: 6.2%
Cash ($ mil.): 275.0
Current ratio: 5.29
Long-term debt ($ mil.): 3.0
No. of shares (mil.): 132.8

Dividends
　Yield: —
　Payout: —
Market value ($ mil.): 1,436.6
R&D as % of sales: —
Advertising as % of sales: —

Stock History

NASDAQ (GS): ENTG

	STOCK PRICE ($) FY Close	P/E High/Low	PER SHARE ($) Earnings	Dividends	Book Value
12/06*	10.82	26　18	0.46	—	7.65
8/05	10.34	100　64	0.12	—	7.56
8/04	8.20	49　24	0.32	—	5.07
8/03	14.72	780　213	0.02	—	4.66
8/02	9.03	476　165	0.04	—	4.53
Annual Growth	**4.6%**	**—　—**	**84.2%**	**—**	**14.0%**

*Fiscal year change

Enterprise Financial Services

Enterprise Financial Services wants you to boldly bank where many have banked before. It's the holding company for Enterprise Bank & Trust, which primarily targets closely held businesses and their owners, but also markets to individuals in the St. Louis and Kansas City metropolitan areas. Through more than ten branches the bank offers standard products such as checking, savings, and money market accounts and certificates of deposit. Loans to businesses, including commercial mortgages and operating loans, make up most of the company's lending activities. To a lesser extent, it originates consumer, construction, and residential mortgage loans.

A division of the bank, Enterprise Trust (formerly Enterprise Financial Advisors), provides fee-based trust services, personal financial planning, estate planning, and corporate planning services. Enterprise Business Consulting offers business consulting services such as strategic planning and executive recruiting; Enterprise Wealth Products Group offers life, annuity, disability income, and long-term care insurance, as well as mutual funds.

Enterprise Financial Services acquired a controlling interest in Nashville-based Millennium Brokerage Group in late 2005. The life insurance advisory company, which has more than a dozen offices supporting business in 49 states, operates under its own brand and is now a wholly owned subsidiary of Enterprise Financial.

In 2006 the company acquired Kansas City-based NorthStar Bancshares, which operated five branches in Missouri and Kansas. Enterprise Financial also has designs on expanding to Arizona.

EXECUTIVES

Chairman and EVP; Chairman and CEO, Enterprise Bank & Trust: Peter F. Benoist, age 59, $366,667 pay
Vice Chairman, President, and CEO: Kevin G. Eichner, age 56, $480,000 pay
EVP and CFO: Frank H. Sanfilippo, age 44, $182,493 pay
SVP, Human Resources: Mark Murtha
SVP, Support Center Operations: Joseph (Joe) Feld
VP and Corporate Secretary: Karen Sher
Chairman, Kansas City Region, Enterprise Bank & Trust: Jack L. Sutherland, $368,059 pay
President and Chief Credit Officer, Enterprise Bank & Trust: Stephen P. (Steve) Marsh, age 51, $221,800 pay
President and CEO, Enterprise Trust: Paul L. Vogel
President, Kansas City Region, Enterprise Bank & Trust: Linda Hanson
President, Kansas City North Region, Enterprise Bank & Trust: Angela Wasson-Hunt
President and CEO, Clayco Banc Corporation: Jeffrey (Jeff) Kiefer
Auditors: KPMG LLP

LOCATIONS

HQ: Enterprise Financial Services Corp
　150 N. Meramec Ave., Clayton, MO 63105
Phone: 314-725-5500　　**Fax:** 314-812-4025
Web: www.enterprisebank.com

PRODUCTS/OPERATIONS

2006 Sales

	$ mil.	% of total
Interest		
Loans, including fees	88.4	79
Securities	4.3	4
Other	1.7	2
Noninterest		
Wealth management	13.8	12
Service charges on deposit accounts	2.2	2
Other	0.9	1
Total	**111.3**	**100**

COMPETITORS

Bank of America
Commerce Bancshares
First Clover Leaf Financial
Midwest BankCentre
Pulaski Financial
U.S. Bancorp

HISTORICAL FINANCIALS

Company Type: Public

Income Statement

FYE: December 31

	ASSETS ($ mil.)	NET INCOME ($ mil.)	INCOME AS % OF ASSETS	EMPLOYEES
12/06	1,535.6	15.5	1.0%	329
12/05	1,287.0	11.3	0.9%	261
12/04	1,059.9	8.2	0.8%	—
12/03	907.7	6.9	0.8%	—
12/02	876.8	5.0	0.6%	—
Annual Growth	15.0%	32.7%	—	26.1%

2006 Year-End Financials

Equity as % of assets: 8.7%
Return on assets: 1.1%
Return on equity: 13.7%
Long-term debt ($ mil.): 48.8
No. of shares (mil.): 11.5
Market value ($ mil.): 376.0
Dividends
Yield: 0.6%
Payout: 13.2%
Sales ($ mil.): 111.3
R&D as % of sales: —
Advertising as % of sales: —

Stock History

NASDAQ (GM): EFSC

	STOCK PRICE ($) FY Close	P/E High/Low	PER SHARE ($) Earnings	Dividends	Book Value
12/06	32.58	25 17	1.36	0.18	11.52
12/05	22.68	26 17	1.05	0.14	8.85
12/04	18.50	24 16	0.82	—	7.44
12/03	14.00	20 18	0.70	—	6.80
12/02	12.50	25 17	0.52	—	6.19
Annual Growth	27.1%	— —	27.2%	28.6%	16.8%

Entertainment Distribution

Entertainment Distribution Company (EDC) decided to get into a more entertaining line of work. Once a provider of messaging systems, the firm now manufactures and distributes prerecorded CDs and DVDs for music and movie companies. In 2005 the company, formerly named Glenayre, acquired some CD and DVD manufacturing operations of Universal Music Group (UMG). The acquired business, called Entertainment Distribution Company, became a unit of Glenayre and was the company's only continuing business segment. Glenayre subsequently changed its name to EDC. It has an agreement to make and distribute UMG's CDs and DVDs in North America and central Europe. The State Investment Board of Wisconsin owns nearly 20% of EDC.

UMG accounts for 87% of sales. In 2006 EDC acquired CD replicator Deluxe Global Media Services Blackburn from The Rank Group for $6 million in cash.

The company sold its messaging business to IP Unity for $25 million in cash in early 2007. Its

messaging operations included network hardware and software systems used to enable calling services such as integrated voice, data, fax messaging, and voice-activated dialing. The company marketed the lines to wireless carriers and the regional Bell companies, as well as other equipment manufacturers.

HISTORY

Canadian communications company Glentel founded Glenayre Electronics Manufacturing in 1963 to design electronic equipment. In 1979 the company entered the mobile radio (not cellular) telephone and paging markets and grew as demand increased during the 1980s. Glenayre went public in 1983.

In 1989 Glenayre moved its headquarters from Canada to the US and opened its first international office in Singapore. In 1992 the company was acquired by N-W Group, a public holding company for pipeline and real estate investments. The group changed its name to Glenayre Technologies and sold its pipeline and real estate businesses.

Glenayre's messaging products increased sales by 87% in 1995. Among its introductions were a two-way paging service and technology for providing wireless telephone service to isolated areas. Glenayre stepped up efforts to capture contracts abroad by opening offices in South America and Asia.

The company expanded its telecommunications and paging capabilities in 1997 when it acquired CNET (network management), Wireless Access (two-way paging), and Open Development (telecommunications services). The acquisitions and revamped sales mix caused losses that year.

In 1999, after another year of losses, the company brought in communications industry veteran Eric Doggett as CEO; former chief executive Clarke Bailey became chairman. Doggett streamlined operations, sold Glenayre's microwave communications division, cut its workforce by nearly 30%, and — in 2000 — installed new key executives.

In 2001 the company edged back into the black and exited the wireless messaging business to focus on enhanced services and unified messaging products; it also moved its corporate headquarters to the Atlanta area where a voicemail products division was located.

Prompted by the withering of the one-way paging market and the generally depressed climate of the telecom industry, Glenayre underwent a massive restructuring of its operations throughout 2001, 2002, and 2003. The process resulted in a workforce reduction of three quarters of its employees, salary cuts for some management, and an influx of new management.

Glenayre acquired some CD and DVD manufacturing operations of Universal Music Group in 2005. The company changed its name to Entertainment Distribution Company in 2007.

EXECUTIVES

Chairman: Clarke H. Bailey, age 53, $802,170 pay (prior to title change)
Vice Chairman: Ramon D. Ardizzone, age 69
Chairman, Entertainment Distribution Company, LLC: James (Jim) Caparro, age 55, $750,022 pay (prior to title change)
CTO: Sonny Bettis
Interim CEO, CFO, Treasurer, and Secretary: Jordan M. Copland, age 45, $872,450 pay (partial-year salary)

EVP Corporate Development: Matthew K. Behrent, age 36, $678,553 pay
SVP Business Development and Marketing: Rolf Madson, age 44
SVP Operations: Stan Little
SVP Worldwide Sales: Nigel Waller
VP Customer Service: Scott Murphy
VP Finance: David Hetzler
VP Manufacturing and Information Systems: Bryant Burke
VP Product Management: Mark Yaphe
VP Research and Development: David Simpson
President, Messaging Business: Bruce M. Bales
President, Entertainment Distribution Company, LLC: Thomas Costabile, age 53, $450,008 pay
EVP Business Development, Sales, and Marketing, Entertainment Distribution Company, LLC: John V. Madison, age 57
EVP International Operations, Entertainment Distribution Company, LLC: Roger J. Morgan, age 42, $293,865 pay
Auditors: Ernst & Young LLP

LOCATIONS

HQ: Entertainment Distribution Company, Inc.
825 8th Ave., 23rd Fl., New York, NY 10019
Phone: 212-333-8400
Web: www.edcllc.com

2006 Sales

	$ mil.	% of total
Germany	168.7	48
US	140.3	40
UK	38.9	11
Other regions	0.6	1
Total	**348.5**	**100**

PRODUCTS/OPERATIONS

2006 Sales

	% of total
Products	77
Services	23
Total	**100**

COMPETITORS

Cinram
Entertainment One
Handleman
Navarre
Sony BMG
Source Interlink
Technicolor Inc.

HISTORICAL FINANCIALS

Company Type: Public

Income Statement

FYE: December 31

	REVENUE ($ mil.)	NET INCOME ($ mil.)	NET PROFIT MARGIN	EMPLOYEES
12/06	348.5	4.0	1.1%	2,200
12/05	267.8	8.0	3.0%	2,193
12/04	50.6	4.5	8.9%	—
12/03	58.2	1.6	2.7%	—
12/02	67.4	(7.8)	—	456
Annual Growth	50.8%	—	—	48.2%

2006 Year-End Financials

Debt ratio: 42.7%
Return on equity: 3.7%
Cash ($ mil.): 98.1
Current ratio: 1.55
Long-term debt ($ mil.): 48.2
No. of shares (mil.): 69.3
Dividends
Yield: —
Payout: —
Market value ($ mil.): 177.5
R&D as % of sales: —
Advertising as % of sales: —

	STOCK PRICE ($) FY Close	P/E High/Low		PER SHARE ($) Earnings	Dividends	Book Value
12/06	2.56	100	33	0.06	—	1.63
12/05	3.25	40	16	0.11	—	1.52
12/04	2.18	61	20	0.07	—	1.42
12/03	2.69	174	38	0.02	—	1.36
12/02	1.14	—	—	(0.12)	—	1.34
Annual Growth	22.4%	—	—	—	—	4.9%

Epic Bancorp

It's not *The Grapes of Wrath* or *Splendor in the Grass*, but it is an epic. Epic Bancorp is the holding company for Tamalpais Bank, which has seven branches in northern California's tony Marin County. The bank targets individuals, small to midsized businesses, and high-networth consumers, offering such services as savings and checking accounts, money market accounts, CDs, and online banking. Its lending activities primarily consist of commercial mortgages (more than half of the company's loan portfolio) and mortgages secured by multifamily housing (nearly 30%).

The company also has a loan production office in Santa Rosa that focuses on Small Business Administration (SBA) loans. Financial planning and asset management are provided through subsidiary Tamalpais Wealth Advisors (formerly Epic Wealth Management), which oversees approximately $250 million in assets.

EXECUTIVES

Chairman: Kit M. Cole, age 66, $180,000 pay
Vice Chairman: Carolyn B. Horan, age 75
President, CEO, and Director; Vice Chairman, President, and CEO, Tamalpais Bank: Mark Garwood, age 52
COO, Epic Wealth Management: William D. Osher
CFO, Epic Bancorp and Epic Wealth Management; EVP and CFO, Tamalpais Bank: Michael E. Moulton, age 45, $159,907 pay (prior to title change)
SVP and Senior Operations Officer, Tamalpais Bank: Gunnel H. Bergstrom, age 57
SVP and CIO, Tamalpais Bank: Erwin V. Martinez
SVP and Chief Lending Officer, Tamalpais Bank: Michael Rice
SVP and Director of Retail Banking, Tamalpais Bank: Joseph Durso
SVP and Senior Credit Officer, Tamalpais Bank: Jean Silveira, age 60
SVP and Chief Accounting Officer, Tamalpais Bank: Karry Bryan
Auditors: Vavrinek, Trine, Day & Co., LLP

LOCATIONS

HQ: Epic Bancorp
630 Las Gallinas Ave., San Rafael, CA 94903
Phone: 415-526-6400   **Fax:** 415-526-6414
Web: www.epicbancorp.com

Epic Bancorp's Tamalpais Bank operates branches in the California cities of Corte Madera, Greenbrae, Mill Valley, San Anselmo, San Rafael (2), and Tiburon; the company also has loan production offices in Sacramento and Santa Rosa.

PRODUCTS/OPERATIONS

2006 Sales

	$ mil.	% of total
Interest		
Loans, including fees	33.2	87
Investment securities	1.9	5
Other	0.7	2
Noninterest		
Gain on sale of loans	0.8	2
Loan fees & other	1.4	4
Total	**38.0**	**100**

COMPETITORS

Bank of America
Bank of Marin
First Banks
First Republic (CA)
UnionBanCal
Washington Mutual
Wells Fargo
Westamerica

HISTORICAL FINANCIALS

Company Type: Public

Income Statement

	ASSETS ($ mil.)	NET INCOME ($ mil.)	INCOME AS % OF ASSETS	EMPLOYEES	FYE: December 31
12/06	503.5	3.9	0.8%	75	
12/05	461.8	4.1	0.9%	73	
12/04	425.6	3.5	0.8%	—	
Annual Growth	8.8%	5.6%	—	2.7%	

2006 Year-End Financials

Equity as % of assets: 6.1%
Return on assets: 0.8%
Return on equity: 13.5%
Long-term debt ($ mil.): 13.4
No. of shares (mil.): 4.0
Market value ($ mil.): 53.7
Dividends
  Yield: 1.1%
  Payout: 15.2%
Sales ($ mil.): 38.0
R&D as % of sales: —
Advertising as % of sales: —

	STOCK PRICE ($) FY Close	P/E High/Low		PER SHARE ($) Earnings	Dividends	Book Value
12/06	13.55	16	13	0.99	0.15	7.80
12/05	15.86	17	12	1.01	0.08	7.30
12/04	13.47	19	12	0.88	0.02	6.32
Annual Growth	0.3%	—	—	6.1%	173.9%	11.1%

Epicor Software

Epicor Software hopes the middle of the road proves paved with gold. The company provides enterprise resource planning software for mid-sized businesses. Epicor's software integrates back-office applications for manufacturing, distribution, and accounting with customer relationship management functions, including sales, marketing, and customer support. The company's software also includes collaborative applications that link employees, distributors, and suppliers, encompassing operations such as supply chain management, sourcing, and procurement.

Epicor primarily targets midsized customers with annual sales between $10 million and $1 billion. The company's more than 20,000 clients come from industries such as manufacturing, distribution, financial services, and hospitality.

In late 2005 the company acquired CRS Retail Technology Group for about $123.5 million.

HISTORY

Platinum Holdings was founded in 1984 by Gerald Blackie, former CEO of bankrupt software maker Heritage Computing, and former Heritage programmers Timothy McMullen and Kevin Riegelsberger. They introduced the Platinum line of financial accounting software in 1985. Platinum expanded by signing marketing agreements with Arthur Andersen in 1987 and IBM in 1989. In 1992 the company went public and changed its name to Platinum Software.

Two years later Platinum revealed that it had misstated its earnings by booking some sales before they had closed. The company paid $17 million to settle a class-action lawsuit and reorganized. (Blackie and two other ex-execs were later forced to repay hundreds of thousands of dollars in gains and bonuses.)

George Klaus was recruited as CEO in 1996 after twice turning down Platinum's board. The company quickly expanded into enterprise resource planning applications through acquisitions. The next year it bought customer relationship management software developer Clientele Software and manufacturing and distribution software provider FocusSoft. The moves helped Platinum to a profitable fiscal 1998, its first in six years. In late 1998 it bought larger rival DataWorks, cut 15% of its workforce, and changed its fiscal year to December.

The next year the company settled a trademark lawsuit, filed in 1997, with PLATINUM Technology, and Platinum changed its name to Epicor Software in 1999.

Amid declining sales in 2001 the company restructured, cutting jobs and selling its Impresa and Platinum for Windows product lines.

Epicor boosted its procurement and supply chain management offerings by acquiring certain assets of Clarus in 2002. In 2004 the company purchased Scala Business Solutions for about $45 million, as well as buying the assets of Platsoft and Strongline.

EXECUTIVES

Chairman and CEO: L. George Klaus, age 66, $1,417,576 pay
President and COO: Mark A. Duffell, age 45, $650,723 pay
EVP and CFO: Michael A. Piraino, age 53, $451,592 pay
EVP, Worldwide Sales: Lauri Klaus

SVP and Chief Marketing Officer: John Hiraoka
SVP and General Counsel: John D. Ireland
SVP, Worldwide Support: Daniel (Dan) Whelan, age 40
SVP and General Manager, CRS Retail Systems:
Kathy Frommer
SVP, Worldwide Research and Development:
Paul Farrell
SVP, Worldwide Consulting: Paul Pinto
VP, Information Systems: Rick Parrish
Senior Director, Investor Relations: Damon S. Wright
Director, Public Relations and Analyst Relations:
Lisa A. Preuss
Auditors: McGladrey & Pullen, LLP

LOCATIONS

HQ: Epicor Software Corporation
18200 Von Karman Ave., Ste. 1000,
Irvine, CA 92612
Phone: 949-585-4000   **Fax:** 949-585-4091
Web: www.epicor.com

PRODUCTS/OPERATIONS

2006 Sales

	$ mil.	% of total
Maintenance	150.1	39
Consulting	107.5	28
License fees	99.5	26
Hardware & other	27.0	7
Total	**384.1**	**100**

Selected Software

Enterprise resource management (Epicor Enterprise)

Selected Services

Consulting
Custom software development
Technical support
Training

COMPETITORS

Lawson Software
Microsoft
Oracle
Pivotal
QAD
SAP

HISTORICAL FINANCIALS

Company Type: Public

Income Statement

FYE: December 31

	REVENUE ($ mil.)	NET INCOME ($ mil.)	NET PROFIT MARGIN	EMPLOYEES
12/06	384.1	23.8	6.2%	2,178
12/05	289.4	52.0	18.0%	1,887
12/04	226.2	25.3	11.2%	—
12/03	155.4	9.3	6.0%	—
12/02	143.5	(7.3)	—	799
Annual Growth	27.9%	—	—	28.5%

2006 Year-End Financials

Debt ratio: 47.1%
Return on equity: 12.6%
Cash ($ mil.): 70.2
Current ratio: 1.41
Long-term debt ($ mil.): 98.3
No. of shares (mil.): 58.8
Dividends
  Yield: —
  Payout: —
Market value ($ mil.): 794.5
R&D as % of sales: —
Advertising as % of sales: —

Stock History   NASDAQ (GS): EPIC

	STOCK PRICE ($) FY Close	P/E High/Low	PER SHARE ($) Earnings	Dividends	Book Value
12/06	13.51	35 23	0.42	—	3.55
12/05	14.13	18 11	0.92	—	3.06
12/04	14.09	38 21	0.47	—	1.90
12/03	12.76	76 7	0.18	—	0.64
12/02	1.25	— —	(0.17)	—	0.09
Annual Growth	81.3%	— —	—	—	154.0%

EPIQ Systems

EPIQ Systems wants to make bankruptcy quick and painless. The company provides case and document management software for bankruptcy, class action, mass tort, and other legal proceedings. Its software automates tasks including legal notice and claims management, funds distribution, and government reporting. EPIQ's software line includes products for Chapter 7 liquidations, Chapter 13 individual debt reorganizations, and Chapter 11 reorganizations. The company, which caters primarily to bankruptcy trustees as opposed to debtors and creditors, also offers Chapter 11 case management services. Through subsidiary Poorman-Douglas, EPIQ provides software for class action, mass tort, and bankruptcy case administration.

Because most bankruptcies fall under the Chapter 7 or Chapter 13 models — which together account for 99% of all bankruptcy filings — EPIQ has focused primarily on its products for these types of filings. Looking to cover the bankruptcy spectrum by moving into the Chapter 11 market, EPIQ acquired Chapter 11 case management service provider Bankruptcy Services LLC in 2003.

In 2004 the company expanded beyond the bankruptcy market with its $116 million purchase of Poorman-Douglas, a provider of software and technology-based services for class action, mass tort, and bankruptcy case administration. EPIQ has sold its infrastructure software business, including its DataExpress data file transmission software product line.

In November 2005 EPIQ acquired nMatrix, a provider of case and document management products for electronic discovery and litigation support, for approximately $125 million.

EXECUTIVES

Chairman and CEO: Tom W. Olofson, age 65,
$1,275,000 pay
President, COO, and Director: Christopher E. Olofson,
age 37, $1,275,000 pay
EVP, CFO, and Corporate Secretary:
Elizabeth M. (Betsy) Braham, age 48, $925,000 pay
CEO, Poorman-Douglas: Jeffrey B. Baker, age 53,
$350,000 pay

President, Bankruptcy Services: Ron L. Jacobs, age 50,
$878,000 pay
SVP, Bankruptcy Services: Kathleen S. Gerber
Managing Director, Class Action and Claims Administration: Timothy B. Corcoran, age 39
Managing Director, Corporate Restructuring Solutions:
Lorenzo Mendizabal, age 47
Investor Relations: Mary Ellen Berthold
Auditors: Deloitte & Touche LLP

LOCATIONS

HQ: EPIQ Systems, Inc.
501 Kansas Ave., Kansas City, KS 66105
Phone: 913-621-9500   **Fax:** 913-321-1243
Web: www.epiqsystems.com

EPIQ Systems has offices in California, Florida, Kansas, New York, and Oregon.

PRODUCTS/OPERATIONS

Software and Services

Bankruptcy Services (Chapter 11 case management services and technology)
CasePower (trustee case management software for Chapter 13 filings)
Class action, mass tort, and bankruptcy case administration software (Poorman-Douglas)
CPT (trustee case management software for Chapter 7 filings)
DCI (trustee case management software for Chapter 7 filings)
Eagle Trust (trustee case management software for Chapter 7 filings)
TCMS (trustee case management system for Chapter 7 filings)
TSI (trustee case management software for Chapter 13 filings)

COMPETITORS

Fios
Fiserv
JPMorgan Chase
Kroll Ontrack
LexisNexis
Misys
SunGard
Thomson Elite

HISTORICAL FINANCIALS

Company Type: Public

Income Statement

FYE: December 31

	REVENUE ($ mil.)	NET INCOME ($ mil.)	NET PROFIT MARGIN	EMPLOYEES
12/06	224.2	35.1	15.7%	500
12/05	106.3	(3.8)	—	500
12/04	125.4	9.7	7.7%	—
12/03	67.9	8.7	12.8%	—
12/02	38.3	8.2	21.4%	170
Annual Growth	55.5%	43.8%	—	31.0%

2006 Year-End Financials

Debt ratio: 45.5%
Return on equity: 21.6%
Cash ($ mil.): 5.3
Current ratio: 0.49
Long-term debt ($ mil.): 83.9
No. of shares (mil.): 19.5
Dividends
  Yield: —
  Payout: —
Market value ($ mil.): 220.4
R&D as % of sales: —
Advertising as % of sales: —

NASDAQ (GS): EPIQ

	STOCK PRICE ($) FY Close	P/E High/Low		PER SHARE ($) Earnings	Dividends	Book Value
12/06	11.31	15	9	1.05	—	9.46
12/05	12.36	—	—	(0.14)	—	7.30
12/04	9.76	40	24	0.35	—	7.82
12/03	11.41	48	31	0.32	—	7.27
12/02	10.18	40	22	0.36	—	6.19
Annual Growth	2.7%	—	—	30.7%	—	11.2%

Epoch Holding

Epoch Holding owns Epoch Investments Partners (EIP), which manages investments for retirement plans, mutual fund clients, endowments, foundations, and other high-net-worth clients. EIP has approximately $3.5 billion of assets under management, including some $1 billion added since the beginning of 2006. Formerly known as J Net Enterprises, the company was once one of Nevada's largest gaming-machine operators and even tried its hand at Internet-based e-commerce before acquiring EIP in 2004. Partners and directors of Epoch Holding own a majority of the company.

EXECUTIVES

Chairman: Allan R. Tessler, age 71
CEO and Director: William W. Priest, age 66, $600,000 pay
President and COO: Timothy T. (Tim) Taussig, age 50, $600,000 pay
CFO: Adam Borak, age 40, $404,615 pay
EVP and Head of Client Relations: J. Philip Clark, age 55, $397,500 pay
EVP, Head of U.S. Equities, and Portfolio Manager: David N. Pearl, age 48, $600,000 pay
VP Business Administration and Assistant Compliance Officer: Neeraj Garg
VP Consultant Relations: Robert V. Martin
VP Performance: Jason Root
VP Analyst: Thuy Tran
VP International Trader: Nishu Trivedi
Senior Equity Analyst, Epoch Investment Partners: Chris Wolters
Managing Director, Portfolio Manager, and Senior Analyst: Emily Baker
Managing Director Public Funds Relations: Ronan J. Burke
Auditors: CF & Co., LLP

LOCATIONS

HQ: Epoch Holding Corporation
640 5th Ave., 18th Fl., New York, NY 10019
Phone: 212-303-7200   **Fax:** 212-202-4948
Web: www.eipny.com

COMPETITORS

AllianceBernstein
BlackRock
GAMCO Investors
Goldman Sachs
JPMorgan Asset Management
Morgan Stanley Investment Management
Old Mutual (US)

HISTORICAL FINANCIALS

Company Type: Public

Income Statement

FYE: June 30

	ASSETS ($ mil.)	NET INCOME ($ mil.)	INCOME AS % OF ASSETS	EMPLOYEES
6/07	39.4	7.9	20.1%	43
6/06	13.6	(5.7)	—	—
6/05	13.0	(6.5)	—	28
6/04	17.1	(1.0)	—	28
6/03	20.8	(3.8)	—	23
Annual Growth	17.3%	—	—	16.9%

2007 Year-End Financials

Equity as % of assets: 89.9%
Return on assets: 29.8%
Return on equity: 35.7%
Long-term debt ($ mil.): —
No. of shares (mil.): 19.9
Market value ($ mil.): 266.9
Dividends
Yield: —
Payout: —
Sales ($ mil.): 23.9
R&D as % of sales: —
Advertising as % of sales: —

Stock History

NASDAQ (CM): EPHC

	STOCK PRICE ($) FY Close	P/E High/Low		PER SHARE ($) Earnings	Dividends	Book Value
6/07	13.39	51	11	0.35	—	1.78
6/06	5.08	—	—	(0.31)	—	0.45
6/05	4.30	—	—	(0.36)	—	0.52
6/04	3.00	—	—	(0.15)	—	0.71
6/03	1.08	—	—	(0.45)	—	1.11
Annual Growth	87.6%	—	—	—	—	12.6%

Euronet Worldwide

Euronet Worldwide might soon have the whole world in its net — thanks to its network of ATMs and other electronic financial services. Banks, card issuers, and other institutions pay the firm for managing transactions at nearly 9,000 ATMs and some 300,000 point-of-sale terminals in 100 countries across Africa, Europe, India, and the Middle East. Euronet Worldwide also offers related EFT (electronic funds transfer) services; its software division offers banking products, including ATM management, credit and debit card systems, and wireless banking. It also provides terminals that let mobile phone users recharge their prepaid airtime plans. The company placed an unsolicited bid for rival MoneyGram in late 2007.

Euronet Worldwide management posited that its own strengths (overseas ATM and money transfers) would complement those of MoneyGram (transfers between the US and Mexico). The company's offer of $1.65 billion in stock has been initially declined, but it plans to pursue the bid.

The company has shifted from operating company-owned ATMs to managing outsourced ATMs for banks, selling networks in the early part of the decade. The company has also been making acquisitions in the growing prepaid transactions arena over the past several years. Deals include the acquisition of US and European companies, including its 2007 acquisition of Ria Envia for around $490 million. That year it agreed to acquire Envios de Valores La Nacional Corp., a US-based money transfer firm. About half of La Nacional's business is transferring funds to the Dominican Republic.

It also acquired mobile prepayment processor Brodos SRL, the Romanian subsidiary of Germany's Brodos AG. The company entered China in 2006 with its 75%-owned joint venture with Ray Holdings.

Chairman and CEO Michael Brown owns 7% of the company.

EXECUTIVES

Chairman and CEO: Michael J. (Mike) Brown, age 50
President: Kevin Caponecchi
EVP and CFO: Rick L. Weller, age 49, $304,850 pay
EVP and COO, Prepaid Processing: Miro I. Bergman, age 44, $317,500 pay
EVP and Director: Paul S. Althasen, age 42
EVP, General Counsel, and Secretary: Jeffrey B. (Jeff) Newman, age 52, $422,057 pay
SVP; Managing Director, Asia Pacific EFT Processing: Anthony (Tony) Grandidge
SVP; Managing Director, Western Europe EFT Processing: Roger Heinz, age 43
SVP Human Resources: Karyn C. Zaborny
VP; Managing Director, Software: Cindy Ashcraft
VP Software Solutions: Douglas (Doug) Goodwin
VP, Software Solutions: David (Dave) Morgan
Marketing Communications Manager: Shruthi Dyapaiah
President, Euronet Payments and Remittance (EPR): Patrick Brown
President, PaySpot: Tom Cregan
Auditors: KPMG LLP

LOCATIONS

HQ: Euronet Worldwide, Inc.
4601 College Blvd., Ste. 300, Leawood, KS 66211
Phone: 913-327-4200   **Fax:** 913-327-1921
Web: www.euronetworldwide.com

Euronet operates principal offices in the US in Arkansas, Kansas, and North Carolina, as well as in Australia, Bulgaria, Croatia, the Czech Republic, Egypt, Germany, Greece, New Zealand, Poland, Romania, Russia, Serbia, Slovakia, Spain, Ukraine, and the UK. It operates processing centers in Kansas, as well as in China, Greece Hungary, India, and Serbia.

PRODUCTS/OPERATIONS

2006 Sales

	$ mil.	% of total
Prepaid processing	470.9	75
EFT processing	130.7	21
Software solutions	27.6	4
Total	**629.2**	**100**

Selected Subsidiaries

Bankomat 24/Euronet Sp. z o.o. (Poland)
Call Processing Inc. (US)
Delta Euronet GmbH (Germany)
EFT Services Hellas EPE (Greece)
e-pay Australia Holdings Pty Ltd (Australia)
Euronet Adminisztracios Szolgaltato Kft (Hungary)
Euronet Card Services, S.A. (Greece, formerly
   Instreamline S.A.)
Europlanet a.d. (Federal Republic of Serbia)
EWI Foreign Holdings Limited (Cyprus)
PaySpot Inc. (US)
Transact Elektronische Zahlungssysteme GmbH
   (Germany)

COMPETITORS

American Express
Barclays
EDS
First Data
Global Payments
Hypercom
Magyar Telekom
MasterCard
Orange Business
Telefónica O2 Czech Republic
Telekom Austria
TeliaSonera
TRM

HISTORICAL FINANCIALS

Company Type: Public

Income Statement

FYE: December 31

	REVENUE ($ mil.)	NET INCOME ($ mil.)	NET PROFIT MARGIN	EMPLOYEES
12/06	629.2	46.3	7.4%	1,098
12/05	531.2	27.4	5.2%	926
12/04	381.1	18.4	4.8%	—
12/03	204.4	11.8	5.8%	—
12/02	71.1	(6.5)	—	385
Annual Growth	72.5%	—	—	30.0%

2006 Year-End Financials

Debt ratio: 125.7%
Return on equity: 18.7%
Cash ($ mil.): 401.8
Current ratio: 1.70
Long-term debt ($ mil.): 362.5
No. of shares (mil.): 37.4

Dividends
   Yield: —
   Payout: —
Market value ($ mil.): 1,111.6
R&D as % of sales: —
Advertising as % of sales: —

Stock History

NASDAQ (GS): EEFT

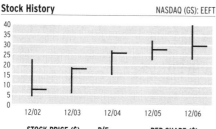

	STOCK PRICE ($) FY Close	P/E High/Low	PER SHARE ($) Earnings	Dividends	Book Value
12/06	29.69	34 20	1.17	—	7.70
12/05	27.80	43 31	0.74	—	5.77
12/04	26.02	49 28	0.55	—	4.28
12/03	18.04	45 15	0.41	—	2.77
12/02	7.51	— —	(0.28)	—	0.26
Annual Growth	41.0%	— —	—	—	133.7%

Evercore Partners

Ever looking to the core of a business to find untapped potential, Evercore Partners provides financial, restructuring, and mergers and acquisitions advisory services to corporate clients. The company also manages private equity investments, including holdings in American Media, publisher of *National Enquirer* and *Star* magazines, Fidelity National Information Services, and advertising and marketing firm Vertis, on behalf of institutional and high-net-worth clients. It also has a venture capital fund. Evercore was launched in 1996 by Roger Altman, who formerly led investment banking and merger advisory practices at Lehman Brothers and The Blackstone Group.

An investment banking "boutique" that does not offer underwriting or banking services, Evercore has been an advisor on several high-profile transactions: In early 2005 it helped the erstwhile SBC Corporation hammer out its bid for AT&T, then advised the new AT&T on its acquisition of BellSouth a year later. It also assisted General Motors on the sale of a majority interest in the carmaker's GMAC unit.

In 2005 Evercore formed Evercore Asset Management, which serves institutional investors and focuses on small- and mid-cap equities. The following year the company also acquired Protego, a boutique investment bank founded by Pedro Aspe, Mexico's former Minister of Finance. In addition to corporate advisory services, Protego specializes in financing municipal infrastructure and energy projects in Mexico.

Evercore hopes to utilize funds from its 2006 IPO to start another private equity fund and to expand in Japan, where it has a joint venture with Mizuho Securities and The Bridgeford Group. Evercore acquired UK investment firm Braveheart Financial Services in a stock-only deal in late 2006.

EXECUTIVES

Co-Chairman and Co-CEO: Roger C. Altman, age 61
Co-Chairman and Senior Managing Director; Chairman and CEO, Protego: Pedro Aspe, age 56
Co-Vice Chairman: Eduardo G. Mestre, age 58
Co-Vice Chairman: Bernard Taylor, age 51
President, Co-CEO, Chief Investment Officer, and Director: Austin M. Beutner, age 47
CEO and Director, Protego Asset Management Business: Sergio Sanchez
CFO: Robert B. Walsh
Senior Managing Director; Vice Chairman, Evercore Capital Partners: John T. Dillon, age 68
Senior Managing Director and Head Marketing, Investment Management Business: Gail S. Landis
Senior Managing Director and General Counsel: Adam B. Frankel, age 39
Senior Managing Director and COO, Investment Management Business: Kathleen G. Reiland, age 42
Senior Managing Director and COO, Corporate Advisory Business: Timothy G. LaLonde
Principal Accounting Officer and Controller: Paul Pensa
Auditors: Deloitte & Touche LLP

LOCATIONS

HQ: Evercore Partners Inc.
   55 E. 52nd St., 43rd Fl., New York, NY 10055
Phone: 212-857-3100   **Fax:** 212-857-3101
Web: www.evercore.com

Evercore Partners has offices in London; Los Angeles; Mexico City; Monterrey, Mexico; New York; and San Francisco.

PRODUCTS/OPERATIONS

2006 Sales

	$ mil.	% of total
Advisory revenue	183.8	85
Investment management revenue	23.3	11
Interest & other	9.4	4
Total	**216.5**	**100**

Selected Investments

American Media, Inc. (publishing)
Continental Energy Services, Inc. (non-utility electric generation)
Davis Petroleum Corp. (oil and gas exploration)
Diagnostic Imaging Group, LLC (diagnostic imaging centers)
Energy Partners, Ltd. (oil and gas exploration)
Fidelity National Information Services, Inc. (data processing)
Michigan Electric Transmission Company, LLC
Resources Connection, Inc. (outsourced staffing services)
Specialty Products & Insulation Co.
Telenet Group Holding N.V. (telecom provider, Belgium)
TestEquity, LLC (testing and diagnostic equipment)
Vertis, Inc. (advertising and marketing)

COMPETITORS

Allen & Company
Apollo Advisors
Blackstone Group
Citigroup Global Markets
Credit Suisse
Gleacher Partners
Goldman Sachs
Greenhill
Lazard
Lehman Brothers
Merrill Lynch
Morgan Stanley
Sequoia Capital
Thomas H. Lee Partners
UBS Investment Bank

HISTORICAL FINANCIALS

Company Type: Public

Income Statement

FYE: December 31

	REVENUE ($ mil.)	NET INCOME ($ mil.)	NET PROFIT MARGIN	EMPLOYEES
12/06	216.5	69.7	32.2%	247
12/05	125.6	63.2	50.3%	120
12/04	86.3	49.8	57.7%	—
12/03	60.1	34.3	57.1%	—
Annual Growth	53.3%	26.7%	—	105.8%

2006 Year-End Financials

Debt ratio: 0.1%
Return on equity: 85.0%
Cash ($ mil.): 153.8
Current ratio: 1.42
Long-term debt ($ mil.): 0.1
No. of shares (mil.): 6.4

Dividends
   Yield: —
   Payout: —
Market value ($ mil.): 234.3
R&D as % of sales: —
Advertising as % of sales: —

Stock History

NYSE: EVR

	STOCK PRICE ($) FY Close	P/E High/Low	PER SHARE ($) Earnings	Dividends	Book Value
12/06	36.85	53 32	0.76	—	17.69

EXCO Resources

EXCO Resources puts extra effort into oil and gas exploration and production operations in Colorado, Ohio, Oklahoma, Pennsylvania, Texas, and West Virginia. The company has proved reserves of 1.2 trillion cu. ft. of natural gas equivalent. EXCO Resources holds stakes in 7,794 gross wells. In 2004 the company bought North Coast Energy for $225.1 million. In 2005 TXOK (a Boone Pickens-controlled affiliate) acquired ONEOK Energy. Following EXCO Resources' 2006 IPO, TXOK became a subsidiary in a move that added 223.3 billion cu. ft. of natural gas equivalent to the company's reserves. That year the company acquired Progress Energy's Winchester Energy natural gas unit for $1.2 billion.

The company's indirect acquisition of ONEOK Energy has strengthened its holdings in East Texas and the Mid-Continent region. In 2005 EXCO Resources sold Addison Energy to NAL Oil and Gas Trust for $442.7 million.

In 2007 the company acquired the Louisiana natural gas fields of Anadarko Petroleum for $1.6 billion in cash. It subsequently bought other Anadarko oil and gas assets in the Mid-Continent and Gulf Coast areas of Oklahoma and Texas for $860 million.

Chairman and CEO Douglas Miller bought EXCO Resources in 2003 and took it private until the IPO three years later.

EXECUTIVES

Chairman and CEO: Douglas H. Miller, age 60, $2,824,945 pay
Vice Chairman, President, and Secretary: Stephen F. Smith, age 66, $240,000 pay
VP, CFO, and Treasurer: J. Douglas Ramsey, age 47
VP and COO: Harold L. Hickey, age 51, $271,000 pay (prior to promotion)
VP, Controller, and Chief Accounting Officer: Mark E. Wilson, age 48
VP: Charles R. Evans, age 54, $496,904 pay (prior to title change)
VP, General Counsel, and Secretary: William L. Boeing, age 52
VP Operations: Michael R. Chambers Sr., age 53
Auditors: KPMG LLP

LOCATIONS

HQ: EXCO Resources, Inc.
12377 Merit Dr., Ste. 1700, Dallas, TX 75251
Phone: 214-368-2084   **Fax:** 214-368-2087
Web: www.excoresources.com

EXCO Resources operates in Colorado, Ohio, Oklahoma, Pennsylvania, Texas, and West Virginia.

PRODUCTS/OPERATIONS

2006 Proved Reserves

	% of total
Natural gas	92
Oil & NGLs	8
Total	**100**

COMPETITORS

Belden & Blake
Cabot Oil & Gas
Petroleum Development

HISTORICAL FINANCIALS

Company Type: Public

Income Statement

FYE: December 31

	REVENUE ($ mil.)	NET INCOME ($ mil.)	NET PROFIT MARGIN	EMPLOYEES
12/06	559.5	138.9	24.8%	471
12/05	34.8	0.9	2.6%	314
12/04	92.8	6.2	6.7%	—
12/03	32.1	5.2	16.2%	132
Annual Growth	**159.3%**	**198.9%**	**—**	**52.8%**

2006 Year-End Financials

Debt ratio: 179.1%
Return on equity: 18.2%
Cash ($ mil.): 114.4
Current ratio: 1.24
Long-term debt ($ mil.): 2,112.6
No. of shares (mil.): 104.2
Dividends
    Yield: —
    Payout: —
Market value ($ mil.): 1,762.7
R&D as % of sales: —
Advertising as % of sales: —

Stock History

NYSE: XCO

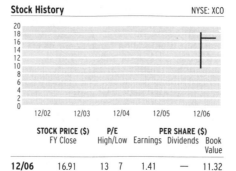

	STOCK PRICE ($) FY Close	P/E High/Low		PER SHARE ($) Earnings	Dividends	Book Value
12/06	16.91	13	7	1.41	—	11.32

ExlService Holdings

Have an extra-large task you'd rather not take on? Outsource it to ExlService Holdings. The company, known as EXL, offers business process outsourcing (BPO), research and analytics, and consulting services, mainly to companies in the banking, financial services, and insurance industries. Its BPO offerings, which generate about 80% of its sales, include claims processing, collections, customer support, and finance and accounting. The company's top customer, UK insurer Norwich Union, accounts for about one-third of its sales. Affiliates of Texas investment firm Oak Hill Capital Partners control a 38% stake in EXL.

EXL markets and sells its services through offices in the US and the UK and operates from facilities in India. Its revenue is split evenly between US and UK customers. Besides Norwich Union, major customers include UK utility Centrica (about 15% of sales) and US-based enterprises such as American Express, Dell Financial Services, IndyMac Bank, and Prudential Financial.

EXL hopes to grow primarily by selling more services to existing customers. In addition, the company wants to add more Global 1,000 companies to its client list.

The company expanded in 2006 by acquiring Inductis, a provider of consulting and data analysis services for companies in the financial services, insurance, and information services industries. Inductis, which posted sales of about $21 million in 2005, continues to operate under its own brand as part of EXL's research and analytics segment.

EXECUTIVES

Chairman: Steven B. Gruber, age 49
Vice Chairman and CEO: Vikram Talwar, age 57, $890,000 pay
President, COO, and Director: Rohit Kapoor, age 42
VP and CFO: Matt Appel, age 51
VP and General Counsel, EXL: Amit Shashank, age 37, $355,523 pay
VP and Business Leader Insurance Operations, EXL India: Lalit Vij, age 40
VP and Business Leader, Business Process Risk Advisory: Narasimha Kini, age 38, $245,000 pay
VP Finance, EXL India: Vinay Mittal, age 42
VP and Business Leader: Vikas Bhalla, age 35
VP Marketing, EXL Service: Alka Misra
VP and Global Head, Human Resources: Amitabh Hajela
VP and Chief Sales and Marketing Officer, EXL: Krishna Nacha
Head, BPO Operations: Pavan Bagai, age 45, $222,961 pay
Head, Investor Relations and Corporate Development Operations: Jarrod Yahes
Auditors: Ernst & Young LLP

LOCATIONS

HQ: ExlService Holdings, Inc.
350 Park Ave., 10th Fl., New York, NY 10022
Phone: 212-277-7100   **Fax:** 212-277-7111
Web: www.exlservice.com

2006 Sales

	$ mil.	% of total
US	61.0	50
UK	60.4	50
Other countries	0.3	—
Total	**121.8**	**100**

PRODUCTS/OPERATIONS

2006 Sales

	$ mil.	% of total
Business process outsourcing	97.8	80
Research & analytics	15.0	12
Advisory	9.0	8
Total	**121.8**	**100**

COMPETITORS

Accenture
Affiliated Computer Services
Capita
EDS
IBM Global Services
Infosys
Liberata
Tata Consultancy
Wipro
WNS (Holdings)
Xchanging

HISTORICAL FINANCIALS

Company Type: Public

Income Statement

FYE: December 31

	REVENUE ($ mil.)	NET INCOME ($ mil.)	NET PROFIT MARGIN	EMPLOYEES
12/06	121.8	14.1	11.6%	8,200
12/05	73.9	7.1	9.6%	—
12/04	60.5	5.4	8.9%	—
12/03	27.8	(0.5)	—	2,626
Annual Growth	**63.6%**	**—**	**—**	**46.2%**

2006 Year-End Financials

Debt ratio: 0.2%
Return on equity: 17.8%
Cash ($ mil.): 86.5
Current ratio: 3.26
Long-term debt ($ mil.): 0.2
No. of shares (mil.): 28.3

Dividends
  Yield: —
  Payout: —
Market value ($ mil.): 594.6
R&D as % of sales: —
Advertising as % of sales: —

Stock History

NASDAQ (GS): EXLS

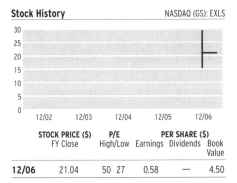

	STOCK PRICE ($) FY Close	P/E High/Low	PER SHARE ($) Earnings	Dividends	Book Value
12/06	21.04	50 27	0.58	—	4.50

F5 Networks

F5 Networks wants to help your network take a load off. The company's products include application delivery controllers and software that are used to manage and route network traffic. Companies including Microsoft and The Motley Fool use F5's products for tasks such as load balancing, availability assurance, and security assessment. Its customers come from a variety of industries, including telecommunication, financial services, manufacturing, and e-commerce. The company also offers services such as network monitoring, performance analysis, and training.

F5 sells primarily though distributors, systems integrators, and resellers, but it also maintains a direct sales force. Distributing giants Avnet Technology Solutions and Ingram Micro together accounted for about a quarter of the company's sales in fiscal 2007.

F5 purchased storage virtualization specialist Acopia Networks for $210 million in 2007. The company acquired rival Swan Labs, a supplier of wide area network optimization and application acceleration tools, for $43 million in cash in 2005. In 2004 F5 acquired MagniFire WebSystems as part of a push to expand its application security product line.

F5's offerings can be incorporated into a variety of enterprise software and systems, including databases, CRM software, ERP applications, and Web services.

EXECUTIVES

President, CEO, and Director: John McAdam, age 56, $884,861 pay
SVP and CFO: Andy Reinland, age 43
SVP and Chief Accounting Officer: John Rodriguez, age 47
SVP Business Operations: Edward J. Eames, age 49, $435,666 pay
SVP Marketing and Business Development: Dan Matte, age 41, $310,297 pay

SVP Product Development and CTO: Karl D. Triebes, age 40, $492,550 pay
SVP and General Counsel: Jeffrey A. (Jeff) Christianson, age 50
VP of Product Management and Marketing: Erik Giesa
VP North American Sales: Mark Anderson, age 45
Auditors: PricewaterhouseCoopers LLP

LOCATIONS

HQ: F5 Networks, Inc.
  401 Elliott Ave. West, Seattle, WA 98119
Phone: 206-272-5555   **Fax:** 206-272-5556
Web: www.f5.com

2007 Sales

	$ mil.	% of total
Americas	307.1	58
Europe, Middle East & Africa	92.7	18
Asia/Pacific		
Japan	64.3	12
Other countries	61.6	12
Total	**525.7**	**100**

PRODUCTS/OPERATIONS

2007 Sales

	$ mil.	% of total
Products	392.9	75
Services	132.8	25
Total	**525.7**	**100**

Selected Products

Application delivery controllers (BIG-IP)
Application security management applications (ASM)
File virtualization (ARX)
Management console (Enterprise Manager)
SSL/VPN access appliances (FirePass)
WAN optimization (WANJet)
Web application performance (WebAccelerator)

Selected Services

Installation
Network management
Performance analysis
Technical support
Training

COMPETITORS

Brocade Communications
Check Point Software
Cisco Systems
Citrix Systems
EMC
Foundry Networks
Juniper Networks
NetApp
Nokia
Nortel Networks
Packeteer
Radware
Riverbed Technology
SonicWALL
Symantec

HISTORICAL FINANCIALS

Company Type: Public

Income Statement

FYE: September 30

	REVENUE ($ mil.)	NET INCOME ($ mil.)	NET PROFIT MARGIN	EMPLOYEES
9/07	525.7	77.0	14.6%	1,582
9/06	394.0	66.0	16.8%	1,068
9/05	281.4	46.9	16.7%	—
9/04	171.2	33.0	19.3%	—
9/03	115.9	4.1	3.5%	—
Annual Growth	**45.9%**	**108.2%**	**—**	**48.1%**

2007 Year-End Financials

Debt ratio: —
Return on equity: 11.1%
Cash ($ mil.): 258.5
Current ratio: 2.52
Long-term debt ($ mil.): —
No. of shares (mil.): 84.4

Dividends
  Yield: —
  Payout: —
Market value ($ mil.): 3,138.1
R&D as % of sales: —
Advertising as % of sales: —

Stock History

NASDAQ (GS): FFIV

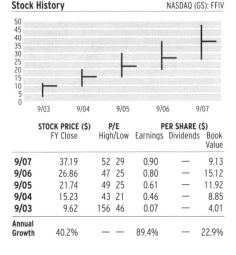

	STOCK PRICE ($) FY Close	P/E High/Low	PER SHARE ($) Earnings	Dividends	Book Value
9/07	37.19	52 29	0.90	—	9.13
9/06	26.86	47 25	0.80	—	15.12
9/05	21.74	49 25	0.61	—	11.92
9/04	15.23	43 21	0.46	—	8.85
9/03	9.62	156 46	0.07	—	4.01
Annual Growth	**40.2%**	**— —**	**89.4%**	**—**	**22.9%**

FactSet Research Systems

Analysts, portfolio managers, and investment bankers know FactSet Research Systems has the scoop. The company offers financial information from more than 200 databases focusing on areas such as broker research data, financial information, and newswires. FactSet complements its databases with a variety of software for use in downloading and manipulating the data. Among the company's applications are tools for presentations, data warehousing, economic analysis, portfolio analysis, and report writing. Revenues are derived from month-to-month subscriptions to services, databases, and financial applications. About 75% of revenue comes from investment managers; investment banking clients account for the rest.

In 2006 the company expanded with the purchase of europrospectus.com, which it subsequently rebranded as FactSet Global Filings Limited, a provider of equity, fixed income, and derivatives prospectuses.

FactSet in 2007 released its ExcelConnect offering, which enables data and analytics to be compatible with Microsoft Excel. Also that year the company enhanced its wireless capabilities, giving users access to market, company, and portfolio information via PDAs and other wireless devices.

Vice chairman Charles Snyder owns about 6% of FactSet.

HISTORY

Howard Wille and Charles Snyder founded FactSet in 1978. Both had previously worked for Wall Street investment firm Faulkner Dawkins & Sullivan (acquired by Shearson Hayden Stone in 1977). The company spent the

1980s building its client base and developing software that allowed clients to manipulate data on their own PCs.

FactSet opened an office in London in 1993 and one in Tokyo the next year. In 1994 the company added Morgan Stanley Capital International and EDGAR SEC filings to its database offerings. It added World Bank subsidiary International Finance Corp. in 1995 and the Russell U.S. Equity Profile report and Toyo Keizai, a Japanese company database, the next year. FactSet went public in 1996. Market Guide's information on US firms and ADRs (American depositary receipts) as well as the economic and financial databases of DRI/McGraw-Hill were added in 1997.

Snyder retired in 1999 but remained vice chairman. The following year Wille retired and Philip Hadley became chairman and CEO. The company made its first acquisition in 2000 when it bought Innovative Systems Techniques (Insyte), a maker of database management and decision support systems.

The company then began acquiring several content businesses. Its 2003 purchase of Mergerstat gave the company a database of global merger and acquisition and related information. In 2004 the company purchased JCF Group, a provider of broker estimates and other financial data to institutional investors, and CallStreet, a provider of quarterly earnings call transcripts to the investment community. The following year the company purchased TrueCourse, a provider of corporate competitive intelligence.

FactSet continued its acquisition spree with the 2005 purchase of Derivative Solutions (DSI), which offers fixed income analytics, portfolio management, and risk management services to financial institutions, and the 2006 purchase of AlphaMetrics, which provides institutional clients with software for capturing, measuring, and ranking financial information.

EXECUTIVES

Chairman and CEO: Philip A. Hadley, age 45, $799,615 pay
Vice Chairman: Charles J. Snyder, age 65
President, COO, and Director: Michael F. DiChristina, age 45, $799,615 pay
SVP, CFO, and Treasurer: Peter G. Walsh, age 41, $569,615 pay
SVP and CTO: Jeff Young
SVP and Chief Content Officer: Townsend Thomas, age 43, $349,615 pay
SVP and Director International Operations: Scott L. Beyer
SVP and Director Investment Banking and Brokerage Services: Kieran M. Kennedy, age 42
SVP and Director U.S. Investment Management Services: Michael D. Frankenfield, age 42, $629,038 pay
SVP and Director Software Engineering: Mark J. Hale
SVP and Director Analytical Products: Christopher (Chris) Ellis
SVP and Director Leadership Development: Laura C. Ruhe
SVP and Director Development Research and Market Data: Goran Skoko
CEO, Derivative Solutions: Douglas Wheeler
Auditors: PricewaterhouseCoopers LLP

LOCATIONS

HQ: FactSet Research Systems Inc.
  601 Merritt 7, Norwalk, CT 06851
Phone: 203-810-1000   **Fax:** 203-810-1001
Web: www.factset.com

2007 Sales

	$ mil.	% of total
US	335.3	71
UK	67.0	14
Other countries	73.5	15
Total	**475.8**	**100**

PRODUCTS/OPERATIONS

Selected Applications

Company Analysis
Data Warehousing
Economic Analysis
Fixed Income Analysis
Pitchbook Building
Portfolio Analysis
Quantitative Analysis
Real-time Market Data

COMPETITORS

Bloomberg L.P.
Data Transmission Network
Dow Jones
Hoover's, Inc.
IDD Information Services
INVESTools
LexisNexis
McGraw-Hill
MSCI
OneSource
Pearson
Reuters
Thomson Corporation
Track Data

HISTORICAL FINANCIALS

Company Type: Public

Income Statement

FYE: August 31

	REVENUE ($ mil.)	NET INCOME ($ mil.)	NET PROFIT MARGIN	EMPLOYEES
8/07	475.8	109.6	23.0%	1,653
8/06	387.4	82.9	21.4%	1,431
8/05	312.6	71.8	23.0%	1,226
8/04	251.9	58.0	23.0%	—
8/03	222.3	51.4	23.1%	—
Annual Growth	21.0%	20.8%	—	16.1%

2007 Year-End Financials

Debt ratio: —
Return on equity: 28.5%
Cash ($ mil.): 186.2
Current ratio: 2.78
Long-term debt ($ mil.): —
No. of shares (mil.): 48.3
Dividends
  Yield: 0.6%
  Payout: 16.8%
Market value ($ mil.): 2,897.5
R&D as % of sales: —
Advertising as % of sales: —

Stock History

NYSE: FDS

	STOCK PRICE ($) FY Close	P/E High/Low	PER SHARE ($) Earnings	PER SHARE ($) Dividends	PER SHARE ($) Book Value
8/07	59.93	33 20	2.14	0.36	8.47
8/06	44.10	29 19	1.64	0.22	7.34
8/05	35.00	28 19	1.43	0.20	5.55
8/04	29.69	31 20	1.15	0.17	5.28
8/03	32.37	33 15	0.99	0.15	6.31
Annual Growth	16.6%	— —	21.3%	24.5%	7.6%

FARO Technologies

FARO Technologies is putting the Arm on companies around the world — and they like it. With the touch of its mechanical arm, FARO's Control Station measuring system can facilitate reverse engineering of an undocumented part or a competitor's product. The FARO Arm is a portable, jointed device that simulates the human arm's movement and works with FARO's CAM2 3-D measurement software to take measurements, perform reverse engineering, and inspect parts by comparing them to digital designs. Aerospace, automotive, consumer goods, and heavy equipment companies such as Boeing, Caterpillar, General Motors, and Siemens use FARO Arm units in their factories. The company has more than 6,000 customers worldwide.

Customers located outside the Americas account for more than half of sales. The company has grown internationally by opening sales offices in Asia and Europe.

FARO has expanded its product lines through internal development, as well as the 2002 acquisition of SpatialMetrix, a maker of laser trackers and metrology software.

FMR (Fidelity Investments) owns nearly 15% of FARO Technologies. Downtown Associates holds nearly 10% of the company. Co-founder and chairman Simon Raab has an equity stake of nearly 9%. Franklin Advisors owns about 8%. Lazard Asset Management holds nearly 6%. Principled Asset Management and Sovereign Asset Management count FARO equity stakes of around 5% among their assets.

EXECUTIVES

President, CEO, and Director: Jay W. Freeland, age 37, $484,962 pay
SVP and CFO: Keith S. Bair, age 51, $137,595 pay
SVP Engineering and CTO: Jim West, age 54
SVP Human Resources: John E. Townsley
SVP and Managing Director, Asia Pacific: Stephen C. Garwood
VP and CTO: Allen S. Sajedi, age 47
Director, Sales and Marketing: David Morse, age 33
Managing Director of FARO Europe: Siegfried K. Buss, age 41
Software Product Development Manager: Ken Steffey
Global Public Relations Officer: Darin Sahler
Auditors: Grant Thornton LLP

LOCATIONS

HQ: FARO Technologies, Inc.
  125 Technology Park, Lake Mary, FL 32746
Phone: 407-333-9911   **Fax:** 407-333-4181
Web: www.faro.com

FARO Technologies has manufacturing facilities in Germany, Singapore, Switzerland, and the US, with sales and support offices around the world.

2006 Sales

	$ mil.	% of total
Americas	62.9	41
Europe/Africa	60.9	40
Asia/Pacific	28.6	19
Total	**152.4**	**100**

PRODUCTS/OPERATIONS

Products

3-D measurement system (Control Station; includes
FAROarm articulated arm, SoftCheck Tool custom
software, and a touch-screen computer)
Laser tracker (portable 3-D measurement device)
Measurement and statistical process control software
(CAM2)
Automotive design (CAM2 Automotive)
Computer-assisted design (CAM2 CAD Analyzer)
Measurement (CAM2 Measure)
Process control and measurement (CAM2 SPC
Process)

COMPETITORS

ANSYS
Autodesk
Braintech
Cimatron
Dassault
Delcam
Hexagon AB
Leica Geosystems
Parametric Technology
Perceptron
Renishaw
Veri-Tek

HISTORICAL FINANCIALS

Company Type: Public

Income Statement
FYE: December 31

	REVENUE ($ mil.)	NET INCOME ($ mil.)	NET PROFIT MARGIN	EMPLOYEES
12/06	152.4	8.2	5.4%	641
12/05	125.6	8.2	6.5%	657
12/04	97.0	14.9	15.4%	—
12/03	71.8	8.3	11.6%	—
12/02	46.3	(2.0)	—	291
Annual Growth	34.7%	—	—	21.8%

2006 Year-End Financials

Debt ratio: 0.1%
Return on equity: 7.8%
Cash ($ mil.): 31.5
Current ratio: 3.54
Long-term debt ($ mil.): 0.1
No. of shares (mil.): 14.5
Dividends
  Yield: —
  Payout: —
Market value ($ mil.): 347.7
R&D as % of sales: —
Advertising as % of sales: —

Stock History
NASDAQ (GM): FARO

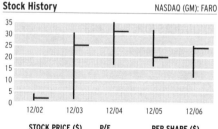

	STOCK PRICE ($) FY Close	P/E High/Low		Earnings	PER SHARE ($) Dividends	Book Value
12/06	24.04	44	21	0.56	—	7.68
12/05	20.00	56	29	0.57	—	6.92
12/04	31.18	33	16	1.06	—	6.38
12/03	24.98	47	3	0.64	—	5.11
12/02	1.89	—	—	(0.17)	—	2.81
Annual Growth	88.9%	—	—	—	—	28.6%

Federal Trust Corporation

This company would prefer it if you *did* make a federal case of things. Federal Trust Corporation is the holding company for Federal Trust Bank, which serves central Florida and the state's Atlantic coast through about ten branches. The bank provides traditional retail offerings including personal and business checking accounts, savings accounts, CDs, and online banking. Residential mortgage loans make up more than 55% of the company's loan portfolio; other offerings include construction and land development loans, commercial mortgages, and to a lesser extent, business and consumer loans.

The company formed a mortgage banking unit, Federal Trust Mortgage, which began operations at the beginning of 2006. The subsidiary now handles most of the company's residential lending business and buys and sells residential mortgages in the secondary market.

EXECUTIVES

Chairman: Robert G. Cox, age 66
CEO and Director; Chairman, CEO and President, Federal Trust Bank: Dennis T. Ward, age 56
President, Federal Trust Mortgage Company: Thomas Spatola
EVP and CFO, Federal Trust and Federal Trust Bank: Gregory E. Smith, $160,750 pay
EVP and Senior Loan Officer, Federal Trust Bank: Mark E. McRae
SVP, Branch Administration, Federal Trust Bank: Jennifer B. Brodnax, $100,000 pay
SVP and Chief Credit Officer, Federal Trust Bank: Lindsay Sandham
VP and Sales Manager, Federal Trust Bank: Winifred Chatman
Corporate Secretary: Marcia Zdanys
Auditors: Hacker, Johnson & Smith PA

LOCATIONS

HQ: Federal Trust Corporation
312 W. 1st St., Sanford, FL 32771
Phone: 407-323-1833   **Fax:** 407-645-1501
Web: www.federaltrust.com

Federal Trust has branches in Casselberry, Deltona, Eustis, Lake Mary, New Smyrna Beach, Orange City, Port Orange, Sanford, and Winter Park, Florida.

PRODUCTS/OPERATIONS

2006 Sales

	$ mil.	% of total
Interest		
Loans	39.9	87
Securities	3.3	7
Other	0.7	1
Noninterest		
Service charges & fees	0.5	1
Other	1.7	4
Total	**46.1**	**100**

COMPETITORS

Bank of America
Colonial BancGroup
Regions Financial
SunTrust
TrustCo Bank Corp NY
Wachovia
Washington Mutual

HISTORICAL FINANCIALS

Company Type: Public

Income Statement
FYE: December 31

	ASSETS ($ mil.)	NET INCOME ($ mil.)	INCOME AS % OF ASSETS	EMPLOYEES
12/06	723.0	3.4	0.5%	100
12/05	735.4	4.4	0.6%	87
12/04	603.1	3.1	0.5%	—
12/03	468.2	2.8	0.6%	—
12/02	368.0	2.1	0.6%	—
Annual Growth	18.4%	12.8%	—	14.9%

2006 Year-End Financials

Equity as % of assets: 7.6%
Return on assets: 0.5%
Return on equity: 6.9%
Long-term debt ($ mil.): 9.1
No. of shares (mil.): 9.4
Market value ($ mil.): 94.8
Dividends
  Yield: 1.8%
  Payout: 48.6%
Sales ($ mil.): 46.1
R&D as % of sales: —
Advertising as % of sales: —

Stock History
AMEX: FDT

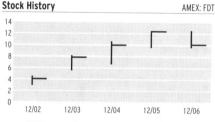

	STOCK PRICE ($) FY Close	P/E High/Low		Earnings	PER SHARE ($) Dividends	Book Value
12/06	10.10	34	26	0.37	0.18	5.82
12/05	12.38	23	18	0.53	0.13	5.32
12/04	10.00	25	16	0.42	0.07	4.89
12/03	7.84	20	14	0.41	0.03	3.97
12/02	4.05	13	9	0.33	—	3.80
Annual Growth	25.7%	—	—	2.9%	81.7%	11.2%

The Female Health Company

Move over, Trojan Man! Here comes The Female Health Company, maker of condoms for women. The polyurethane female condom is the only female contraceptive that is FDA-approved for preventing both pregnancy and sexually transmitted diseases. The firm's condoms are marketed in the US (under the FC Female Condom name), as well as Brazil and Venezuela and Asian and European countries such as China, India, Japan, and the UK. Outside the US, many of its products bear the Femidom name. Female Health also provides low-cost female condoms in Africa through an agreement with the Joint United Nations Programme on HIV/AIDS (UNAIDS). It sponsors the Female Health Foundation, which provides women with health education.

The company's second generation female condom, called FC2, is made of a nitrile polymer, which allows for a faster, cheaper manufacturing process. The FC2 has been approved by the European Union and is under review by the World Health Organization and the U.S. Food and Drug

Administration. However, Female Health has not yet had any sales of the new product. The primary difference between the FC condom and the FC2 condom is that the FC condom can be cleaned and reused.

Director Stephen Dearhold owns some 17% of the company's stock, and his fellow director Richard Wenninger owns about 13%.

EXECUTIVES

Chairman, CEO, and Acting President: O. B. Parrish, age 73, $110,833 pay (prior to title change)
Senior Strategic Adviser and Director: Mary Ann Leeper, age 66, $204,167 pay (prior to title change)
VP and CFO: Donna Felch, age 59, $133,252 pay (partial-year salary)
VP, Finance: Robert R. Zic, age 43
VP and General Manager, The Female Health Company (UK): Michael (Mike) Pope, age 49, $168,811 pay
VP, Sales: Jack Weissman, age 59
Secretary and Director: William R. Garguilo Jr., age 78
Controller: Janet Lee
Auditors: McGladrey & Pullen, LLP

LOCATIONS

HQ: The Female Health Company
515 N. State St., Ste. 2225, Chicago, IL 60610
Phone: 312-595-9123   **Fax:** 312-595-9122
Web: www.femalehealth.com

Female Health manufactures the FC at a manufacturing facility in London. The FC2 is manufactured in Malaysia.

Female condoms are sold commercially in the US, as well as in Australia, Brazil, Canada, Denmark, France, Germany, Holland, Italy, Japan, Mexico, Spain, Suriname, Switzerland, Turkey, the UK, and Venezuela.

2007 Sales

	$ mil.	% of total
Zimbabwe	4.1	22
South Africa	3.8	20
US	2.5	13
France	1.2	6
Zambia	0.9	5
Other	6.8	4
Total	**19.3**	**100**

PRODUCTS/OPERATIONS

Female Condom Brand Names

FC Female Condom
FC2 Female Condom
The Female Condom
Femidom
Femy
Reality

COMPETITORS

Ansell
Bayer Schering Pharma
G & D Enterprises
Instead, Inc.
Johnson & Johnson
Meiji Seika
SSL International
Watson Pharmaceuticals

HISTORICAL FINANCIALS

Company Type: Public

Income Statement

FYE: September 30

	REVENUE ($ mil.)	NET INCOME ($ mil.)	NET PROFIT MARGIN	EMPLOYEES
9/07	19.3	1.7	8.8%	166
9/06	14.8	0.3	2.0%	—
9/05	11.2	(1.4)	—	—
9/04	8.8	(2.0)	—	—
9/03	9.1	(2.4)	—	—
Annual Growth	**20.7%**	**—**	**—**	**—**

2007 Year-End Financials

Debt ratio: —
Return on equity: 27.8%
Cash ($ mil.): 0.9
Current ratio: 3.97
Long-term debt ($ mil.): —
No. of shares (mil.): 26.4
Dividends
  Yield: —
  Payout: —
Market value ($ mil.): 62.1
R&D as % of sales: —
Advertising as % of sales: —

Stock History

AMEX: FHC

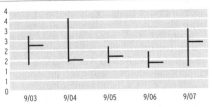

	STOCK PRICE ($) FY Close	P/E High/Low	PER SHARE ($) Earnings	Dividends	Book Value
9/07	2.35	50 19	0.06	—	0.28
9/06	1.33	185 110	0.01	—	0.20
9/05	1.66	— —	(0.07)	—	0.14
9/04	1.50	— —	(0.11)	—	0.09
9/03	2.25	— —	(0.13)	—	0.03
Annual Growth	**1.1%**	**— —**	**—**	**—**	**83.1%**

First Advantage

I screen, you screen, we all screen with First Advantage. Created after The First American Corporation acquired US SEARCH.com and merged it with its Screening Technology (FAST) Division, First Advantage provides such risk management services as employment background screening, occupational health (especially drug testing), tenant screening (credit history, eviction actions, and rental payment history), and motor vehicle reports. Its First Advantage Investigative Services subsidiary provides investigative services for detecting insurance fraud. Individual locater services are also available. First American owns about 80% of First Advantage.

First Advantage has an apparent shopping habit too. The company has scooped up more than 25 service providers in the last few years, expanding its global reach and beefing up its litigation support and employment-screening services. First American's Credit Information Group (CIG) was acquired in 2005, which included that company's mortgage, automotive, consumer, and subprime credit businesses. In exchange, First American's ownership of First Advantage increased from 67% to 80%.

The company also acquired Quest Research, a leading employment-screening-services provider in India and East Asia. In addition to its customers at home, the subsidiary provides outsourced services for other screening companies in the US and Europe. Now dubbed First Advantage Quest Research, the company has offices in India, Asia, and Australia. The company's Asian coverage expanded in 2006 when First Advantage bought Tokyo-based Brooke Consulting and Sydney-based Refsure Worldwide.

Further adding to its investigative capabilities, First Advantage acquired majority ownership of PrideRock, a company that digitizes and transmits fingerprints to law enforcement agencies for employee-background checks. Other acquisitions include ITax, a provider of tax credit services, and Data Recovery Services, which provides restored digital data for attorneys and companies. In late 2006 First Advantage acquired EvidentData, a computer forensics and electronic discovery consulting firm.

Credit reporter Experian owns about 6% of the company.

EXECUTIVES

Chairman: Parker S. Kennedy, age 59
President, CEO, and Director: Anand K. Nallathambi, age 46
EVP Operations: Akshaya Mehta, age 47, $310,000 pay
EVP and CFO: John Lamson, age 56, $275,000 pay
EVP Operations, Strategic Growth Initiatives: Todd L. Mavis, age 44
EVP Operations, Transportation Services Division: Debbie Klarfeld
SVP and Chief Marketing Officer: Rick Mansfield, age 43
SVP Corporate Development and Group President, Investigative and Litigation Support Services Segment: Andrew Macdonald, age 44
VP and General Counsel: Julie A. Waters, age 41
VP Human Resources: Anita Tefft
Group President, Employment Services Segment: Bart K. Valdez, age 45
Group President, Multifamily Services Segment: Evan Barnett, age 59, $349,250 pay
Group President, Dealer Services Segment: Howard L. Tischler, age 53
President, Tax Consulting Services Division: Beth Henricks, age 47
President, Transportation Services Division: Billie Lee
Auditors: PricewaterhouseCoopers LLP

LOCATIONS

HQ: First Advantage Corporation
100 Carillon Pkwy., St. Petersburg, FL 33716
Phone: 727-214-3411   **Fax:** 727-214-3410
Web: www.fadv.com

First Advantage has more than 42 US offices in Arizona, California, Colorado, Delaware, Florida, Maryland, New York, and Wisconsin, as well as an office in Canada and a service center in India.

PRODUCTS/OPERATIONS

2006 Sales by Services

	% of total
Employer	25
Lender	23
Data	19
Dealer (auto)	16
Multifamily	9
Investigative & litigation support	8
Total	**100**

COMPETITORS

ADP Screening and Selection
ChoicePoint
Deloitte
Ernst & Young Global
eScreen
Guardsmark
KPMG
Kroll
LabCorp
PricewaterhouseCoopers
USIS

HISTORICAL FINANCIALS
Company Type: Public

Income Statement
FYE: December 31

	REVENUE ($ mil.)	NET INCOME ($ mil.)	NET PROFIT MARGIN	EMPLOYEES
12/06	817.6	66.2	8.1%	4,400
12/05	643.8	58.4	9.1%	3,800
12/04	266.5	9.9	3.7%	—
12/03	166.5	2.8	1.7%	—
Annual Growth	70.0%	187.0%	—	15.8%

2006 Year-End Financials
Debt ratio: 26.6%
Return on equity: 10.5%
Cash ($ mil.): 31.9
Current ratio: 1.45
Long-term debt ($ mil.): 179.5
No. of shares (mil.): 10.5

Dividends
Yield: —
Payout: —
Market value ($ mil.): 240.0
R&D as % of sales: —
Advertising as % of sales: —

Stock History
NASDAQ (GS): FADV

	STOCK PRICE ($) FY Close	P/E High/Low	Earnings	PER SHARE ($) Dividends	Book Value
12/06	22.96	25 16	1.14	—	64.58
12/05	26.71	29 17	1.09	—	59.52
12/04	20.40	51 30	0.45	—	39.91
12/03	19.12	286 100	0.14	—	45.90
Annual Growth	6.3%	— —	101.2%	—	12.1%

First Bancshares

Hoping to be first in the hearts of its customers, The First Bancshares is the holding company for The First, A National Banking Association, a community bank with nearly 10 branches in southern Mississippi. Customers are offered such standard deposit services as checking, savings, NOW, money market, and individual retirement accounts. The bank also offers commercial customers loans for working capital, business expansion, equipment, and machinery. Consumer loan products include auto, home, education, and equity lines of credit. Commercial and residential mortgages and construction loans make up the bulk (more than three-quarters) of the bank's total loan portfolio.

In 2006 The First Bancshares bought smaller south Mississippi rival First National Bank of Wiggins, which operates from a single banking office in Wiggins.

Chairman and CEO David Johnson owns more than 5% of The First Bancshares.

EXECUTIVES
Chairman and CEO, The First Bancshares and The First: David E. Johnson, age 53, $158,104 pay
President and Director; President, Picayune Branch and Southern Region: M. Ray (Hoppy) Cole Jr., age 45, $141,247 pay
EVP and CFO, The First Bancshares and The First: DeeDee Lowery, age 40, $100,700 pay
VP, Human Resources: Marsie H. White
President, Laurel Branch, The First: Luther C. Holcomb
President, Bay St. Louis Branch, The First: Charles E. (Dusty) Rhodes
President, Pascagoula Branch, The First: Ellen Cole
President, Wiggins Branch, The First: Benny Bell
EVP and COO, The First Bancsshares and The First: David O. Thoms Jr., age 62, $77,666 pay
EVP and Chief Credit Officer, The First: John M. Shappley
EVP and Mortgage Department Manager, The First: Canda Smith Olmi
VP and Director of Marketing, The First: Lee Wade
Auditors: T.E. Lott & Company

LOCATIONS
HQ: The First Bancshares, Inc.
6480 US Hwy. 98 West, Hattiesburg, MS 39402
Phone: 601-268-8998 **Fax:** 601-268-8904
Web: www.thefirstbank.com

The First Bancshares operates in Mississippi's Forrest, Jackson, Jones, Lamar, and Pearl River counties.

COMPETITORS
BancorpSouth
Hancock Holding
Peoples Financial
Renasant
Trustmark

HISTORICAL FINANCIALS
Company Type: Public

Income Statement
FYE: December 31

	ASSETS ($ mil.)	NET INCOME ($ mil.)	INCOME AS % OF ASSETS	EMPLOYEES
12/06	417.8	3.3	0.8%	168
12/05	294.4	1.9	0.6%	—
12/04	212.4	1.2	0.6%	—
12/03	164.9	1.0	0.6%	—
12/02	157.4	0.9	0.6%	—
Annual Growth	27.6%	38.4%	—	—

2006 Year-End Financials
Equity as % of assets: 7.7%
Return on assets: 0.9%
Return on equity: 13.0%
Long-term debt ($ mil.): 32.2
No. of shares (mil.): 2.9
Market value ($ mil.): 86.5

Dividends
Yield: 0.5%
Payout: 12.6%
Sales ($ mil.): 26.0
R&D as % of sales: —
Advertising as % of sales: —

Stock History
NASDAQ (CM): FBMS

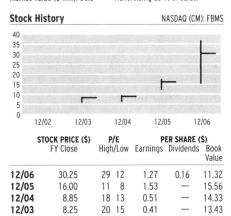

	STOCK PRICE ($) FY Close	P/E High/Low	Earnings	PER SHARE ($) Dividends	Book Value
12/06	30.25	29 12	1.27	0.16	11.32
12/05	16.00	11 8	1.53	—	15.56
12/04	8.85	18 13	0.51	—	14.33
12/03	8.25	20 15	0.41	—	13.43
Annual Growth	54.2%	— —	37.0%	—	(3.0%)

First Community Bancorp

First Community Bancorp wants to be *numero uno* in Southern California. It is the holding company for Pacific Western Bank, which operates about 65 branches in Los Angeles, Orange, Riverside, San Bernardino, and San Diego counties. Mortgages make up nearly 60% of the bank's loan portfolio; construction and business loans each weigh in at around 20% of the portfolio. (The bank does make a small number of consumer and other loans.) The bank's asset-lending and factoring operations (First Community Financial) are active in Arizona, California, and Texas.

First Community Bancorp has grown by feverishly buying community banks throughout Southern California. The company has acquired more than a dozen other banks since 2000, including Community Bancorp, First American Bank, and Foothill Independent Bank. Acquisitions are typically merged into Pacific Western Bank's operations.

It bought Business Finance Capital Corporation, a California financing company, in 2007.

EXECUTIVES
Chairman: John M. Eggemeyer III, age 61
CEO and Director; Chairman and CEO, Pacific Western Bank: Matthew P. Wagner, age 50, $491,667 pay
President; President and Director, Pacific Western Bank: Michael J. (Mike) Perdue, age 52
EVP and CFO; EVP and Director, Pacific Western Bank: Victor R. Santoro, age 58, $341,667 pay
EVP and Chief Credit Officer, First Community Bancorp and Pacific Western Bank: Robert G. Dyck, age 50
EVP, General Counsel, and Secretary, First Community Bancorp and Pacific Western Bank; Director, Pacific Western Bank: Jared M. Wolff, age 38, $251,667 pay
EVP Human Resources, First Community Bancorp and Pacific Western Bank: Michael L. Thompson, age 61, $162,500 pay
EVP; Manager Operations and Systems First Community Bancorp and Pacific Western Bank: Mark Christian, age 43
EVP; EVP and CFO, Pacific Western Bank: Lynn M. Hopkins, age 39
Auditors: KPMG LLP

LOCATIONS
HQ: First Community Bancorp
401 W. A St., San Diego, CA 92101
Phone: 619-233-5588 **Fax:** 619-235-1268
Web: www.firstcommunitybancorp.com

PRODUCTS/OPERATIONS

2006 Sales

	% of total
Interest	
Loans	91
Securities & other	3
Service charges on deposit accounts	3
Other commissions & fees	2
Other	1
Total	**100**

COMPETITORS

Bank of America
California Bank & Trust
California National Bank
Downey Financial
Rabobank America
San Diego County
  Credit Union
UnionBanCal
U.S. Bancorp
Washington Mutual
Wells Fargo

HISTORICAL FINANCIALS

Company Type: Public

Income Statement

	ASSETS ($ mil.)	NET INCOME ($ mil.)	INCOME AS % OF ASSETS	EMPLOYEES
12/06	5,553.3	76.0	1.4%	1,010
12/05	3,226.4	50.4	1.6%	681
12/04	3,046.9	36.4	1.2%	—
12/03	2,422.3	32.1	1.3%	—
12/02	2,115.9	16.9	0.8%	—
Annual Growth	27.3%	45.6%	—	48.3%

2006 Year-End Financials

Equity as % of assets: 21.0%
Return on assets: 1.7%
Return on equity: 9.1%
Long-term debt ($ mil.): 648.2
No. of shares (mil.): 29.6
Market value ($ mil.): 1,549.1
Dividends
  Yield: 2.3%
  Payout: 37.7%
Sales ($ mil.): 320.4
R&D as % of sales: —
Advertising as % of sales: —

Stock History

NASDAQ (GS): FCBP

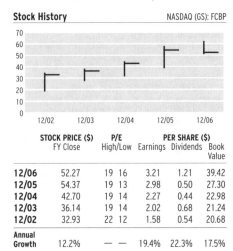

	STOCK PRICE ($) FY Close	P/E High/Low		PER SHARE ($) Earnings	Dividends	Book Value
12/06	52.27	19	16	3.21	1.21	39.42
12/05	54.37	19	13	2.98	0.50	27.30
12/04	42.70	19	14	2.27	0.44	22.98
12/03	36.14	19	14	2.02	0.68	21.24
12/02	32.93	22	12	1.58	0.54	20.68
Annual Growth	12.2%	—	—	19.4%	22.3%	17.5%

First Community Bank

Although not the first community bank in America, First Community Bank Corporation is the holding company for First Community Bank of America, which has about 10 branches in the Sunshine State's Tampa Bay area. The thrift concentrates on real estate lending, with commercial mortgages and residential mortgages representing the bulk of its activities. It also makes business and consumer installment loans. Chairman Robert M. Menke owns about 35% of First Community Bank Corporation of America; company officers and directors collectively own nearly 51%.

EXECUTIVES

Chairman: Robert M. Menke, age 73
President, CEO, and Director; CEO and Director, First Community Bank: Kenneth P. Cherven, age 47, $312,562 pay
EVP and COO: Sue A. Gilman, age 52
CFO: Stan B. McClelland, age 55
Regional President, Charlotte County, First Community Bank: Michael J. Bullerdick, age 53, $154,404 pay
Regional President, Hillsborough County, First Community Bank: Siede T. (Sie) Kamide, age 50, $119,100 pay
Regional President, Pinellas County, First Community Bank: Scott C. Boyle, age 52, $230,671 pay
Regional President, Pasco County, First Community Bank: Ralph W. Cumbee, age 50
EVP and Senior Credit Officer, First Community Bank: Thomas P. Croom
EVP, First Community Bank: Clifton E. Tufts, age 45, $180,901 pay
VP, Human Resources, First Community Bank: Patricia TC Daerda
Auditors: Hacker, Johnson & Smith PA

LOCATIONS

HQ: First Community Bank Corporation of America
  9001 Belcher Rd., Pinellas Park, FL 33782
Phone: 727-520-0987   **Fax:** 727-471-0010
Web: www.efirstcommbank.com

PRODUCTS/OPERATIONS

2006 Sales

	$ mil.	% of total
Interest income		
Loans	23.7	91
Securities	0.6	2
Other interest earning assets	0.2	1
Noninterest income		
Service charges on deposit accounts	0.7	3
Other service charges & fees	0.2	1
Income from bank owned life insurance	0.1	0
Gain on sale of loans held for sale	0.2	1
Other	0.3	1
Total	**26.0**	**100**

COMPETITORS

Bank of America
BankAtlantic
Colonial BancGroup
F.N.B. (PA)
South Financial
SunTrust
Wachovia
Whitney Holding

HISTORICAL FINANCIALS

Company Type: Public

Income Statement

FYE: December 31

	ASSETS ($ mil.)	NET INCOME ($ mil.)	INCOME AS % OF ASSETS	EMPLOYEES
12/06	390.9	3.7	0.9%	110
12/05	324.8	2.9	0.9%	74
12/04	241.8	2.0	0.8%	—
12/03	180.4	1.5	0.8%	—
12/02	147.3	0.8	0.5%	49
Annual Growth	27.6%	46.6%	—	22.4%

2006 Year-End Financials

Equity as % of assets: 8.6%
Return on assets: 1.0%
Return on equity: 11.8%
Long-term debt ($ mil.): 6.3
No. of shares (mil.): 3.8
Market value ($ mil.): 69.1
Dividends
  Yield: —
  Payout: —
Sales ($ mil.): 26.0
R&D as % of sales: —
Advertising as % of sales: —

Stock History

NASDAQ (CM): FCFL

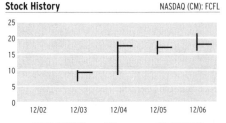

	STOCK PRICE ($) FY Close	P/E High/Low		PER SHARE ($) Earnings	Dividends	Book Value
12/06	17.99	25	19	0.85	—	8.77
12/05	17.04	25	20	0.74	1.30	7.68
12/04	17.54	35	16	0.53	—	11.17
12/03	9.25	20	14	0.48	—	10.12
Annual Growth	24.8%	—	—	21.0%	—	(4.7%)

First Community Corporation

Putting first things first, First Community is the holding company for First Community Bank, which serves individuals and smaller businesses in central South Carolina's Lexington, Richland, and Newberry counties. Through about a dozen offices, the bank offers such products and services as checking and savings accounts, money market accounts, CDs, IRAs, credit cards, insurance, and investment services. Commercial mortgages make up about 50% of First Community Bank's loan portfolio, which also includes residential mortgages and business, consumer, and construction loans. The company bought DutchFork Bancshares in 2004 and DeKalb Bankshares (parent of The Bank of Camden) in 2006.

EXECUTIVES

Chairman, First Community Corporation and First Community Bank: James C. (Jim) Leventis, age 69
Vice Chairman; Vice Chairman and EVP, First Community Bank: J. Thomas (Tommy) Johnson, age 59, $179,697 pay
President, CEO, and Director, First Community Corporation and First Community Bank: Michael C. (Mike) Crapps, age 48, $213,245 pay
SVP and CFO: Joseph G. Sawyer, age 56, $125,500 pay
SVP and Chief Credit Officer: David K. Proctor, age 50, $115,042 pay
SVP and Group Executive: J. Ted Nissen, age 45, $116,050 pay
SVP and Director Marketing: Robin D. Brown
Auditors: Elliott Davis LLC

LOCATIONS

HQ: First Community Corporation
5455 Sunset Blvd., Lexington, SC 29072
Phone: 803-951-2265   **Fax:** 803-951-1722
Web: www.firstcommunitysc.com

PRODUCTS/OPERATIONS

2006 Sales

	$ mil.	% of total
Interest		
Loans	18.6	59
Investment securities	7.9	25
Other	0.7	2
Deposit service charge	2.4	8
Mortgage origination fees	.5	1
Other	1.6	5
Total	**31.7**	**100**

COMPETITORS

Bank of America
BB&T
First Citizens Bancorporation
Regions Financial
Security Federal
South Financial
Synovus
Wachovia

HISTORICAL FINANCIALS

Company Type: Public

Income Statement

FYE: December 31

	ASSETS ($ mil.)	NET INCOME ($ mil.)	INCOME AS % OF ASSETS	EMPLOYEES
12/06	548.1	3.5	0.6%	137
12/05	467.5	3.1	0.7%	123
12/04	455.7	2.2	0.5%	—
12/03	215.0	1.8	0.8%	—
12/02	195.2	1.5	0.8%	—
Annual Growth	**29.4%**	**23.6%**	**—**	**11.4%**

2006 Year-End Financials

Equity as % of assets: 11.5%
Return on assets: 0.7%
Return on equity: 6.1%
Long-term debt ($ mil.): 15.6
No. of shares (mil.): 3.3
Market value ($ mil.): 54.6
Dividends
Yield: 1.4%
Payout: 20.9%
Sales ($ mil.): 31.7
R&D as % of sales: —
Advertising as % of sales: —

Stock History

NASDAQ (CM): FCCO

	STOCK PRICE ($) FY Close	P/E High/Low		PER SHARE ($) Earnings	Dividends	Book Value
12/06	16.72	18	15	1.10	0.23	19.36
12/05	18.50	22	16	1.04	0.20	17.82
12/04	19.97	22	17	1.09	0.10	18.09
12/03	21.75	21	13	1.08	0.19	12.21
12/02	13.30	18	13	0.90	0.08	11.61
Annual Growth	**5.9%**	**—**	**—**	**5.1%**	**30.2%**	**13.6%**

First Marblehead Corporation

With a Harvard education costing six figures, that government student loan just isn't going to cut it anymore. Enter First Marblehead. The company creates programs and provides services for lenders who offer private (not secured by the government) student loans. First Marblehead provides marketing, servicing, processing, securitization, and guarantee services. The company bought the loan processing services business of The Education Resources Institute (TERI) in 1991, more than doubling its size. Houston Rockets owner Leslie Alexander owns more than a quarter of the company; while insurance heavy William Berkley (of W. R. Berkley) owns about 20% independently and through Interlaken Investment Partners.

Goldman Sachs plans to acquire a 17% stake in First Marblehead for $260.5 million. It will hold less than 10% of the voting shares but will have the right to name a director. Former chairman and CEO Daniel Maxwell Meyers controls more than 11% of First Marblehead, while vice chairman Stephen Anbinder owns nearly 6%.

EXECUTIVES

Chairman and General Counsel: Peter B. Tarr, age 56, $2,381,317 pay (partial-year salary)
Vice Chairman: Stephen E. Anbinder, age 70, $1,222,298 pay
President, CEO, COO, and Director: Jack L. Kopnisky, $2,257,215 pay (prior to title change)
SEVP and CFO: John A. Hupalo, age 48, $1,170,833 pay (prior to promotion)
EVP and Chief Administration Officer: Anne P. Bowen, age 56, $841,666 pay
EVP and CIO: Richard E. (Dick) Ross
EVP Business Development: Sandra M. (Sandy) Stark
EVP Client Services; President, First Marblehead Education Resources: Andrew J. (Andy) Hawley, age 44
EVP and Chief Risk Officer: William Baumer
EVP and Chief Marketing Officer: Greg D. Johnson
EVP Product Strategy: Stein I. Skaane
SVP, Treasurer, and Chief Accounting Officer: Kenneth Klipper, age 47
Auditors: KPMG LLP

LOCATIONS

HQ: The First Marblehead Corporation
The Prudential Tower, 800 Boylston St., 34th Fl., Boston, MA 02199
Phone: 617-638-2000   **Fax:** 617-638-2100
Web: www.firstmarblehead.com

PRODUCTS/OPERATIONS

2007 Sales

	$ mil.	% of total
Structural advisory fees	502.7	57
Residuals	212.3	24
Processing fees from TERI	134.8	15
Administrative & other	30.9	4
Total	**880.7**	**100**

COMPETITORS

Access Group
American Student Assistance
Bank of America
Campus Door
Citigroup
Educational Funding of The South
KeyCorp
Sallie Mae
Sallie Mae Servicing
Student Loan Xpress
Wells Fargo

HISTORICAL FINANCIALS

Company Type: Public

Income Statement

FYE: June 30

	ASSETS ($ mil.)	NET INCOME ($ mil.)	INCOME AS % OF ASSETS	EMPLOYEES
6/07	1,214.5	371.3	30.6%	1,042
6/06	770.3	236.0	30.6%	932
6/05	558.2	159.7	28.6%	842
6/04	360.1	75.3	20.9%	—
6/03	87.1	31.5	36.2%	—
Annual Growth	**93.2%**	**85.3%**	**—**	**11.2%**

2007 Year-End Financials

Equity as % of assets: 69.4%
Return on assets: 37.4%
Return on equity: 52.3%
Long-term debt ($ mil.): 9.3
No. of shares (mil.): 93.3
Market value ($ mil.): 3,606.7
Dividends
Yield: 1.5%
Payout: 14.8%
Sales ($ mil.): 880.7
R&D as % of sales: —
Advertising as % of sales: —

Stock History

NYSE: FMD

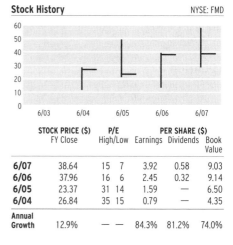

	STOCK PRICE ($) FY Close	P/E High/Low		PER SHARE ($) Earnings	Dividends	Book Value
6/07	38.64	15	7	3.92	0.58	9.03
6/06	37.96	16	6	2.45	0.32	9.14
6/05	23.37	31	14	1.59	—	6.50
6/04	26.84	35	15	0.79	—	4.35
Annual Growth	**12.9%**	**—**	**—**	**84.3%**	**81.2%**	**74.0%**

First National Bancshares

The first thing you should know about First National Bancshares is that it is the holding company for First National Bank of the South, also known as First National Bank of Spartanburg. The bank serves the South Carolina communities of Spartanburg, Charleston, Columbia, and Greenville from more than a half-dozen branches and several loan production offices. The bank opened for business in 2000 and the holding company began trading on Nasdaq in 2005. First National Bancshares also operates a trust company, as well as small business lending division First National Business Capital. The company acquired fellow South Carolina bank

Carolina National Corporation and its four-branch Carolina National Bank in 2008.

The bank has also launched a wholesale mortgage lending unit. Commercial real estate loans represent the largest portion of the company's lending portfolio (about 60%), followed by residential mortgages (nearly 30%).

EXECUTIVES

Chairman Emeritus and Director: Norman F. Pulliam, age 64
President, CEO, and Director; President and CEO, First National Bank of the South: Jerry L. Calvert, age 58, $260,000 pay
EVP and CFO, First National Bancshares and First National Bank of the South: Kitty B. Payne, age 36, $135,769 pay
EVP, Chief Lending Officer, and Community Reinvestment Act Officer, First National Bank of the South: David H. Zabriskie, age 45, $145,961 pay
EVP and Retail Banking Manager, First National Bank of the South: Robert W. (Bob) Murdoch Jr., age 62, $120,769 pay
SVP Commercial Banking and Business Development, First National Bank of the South: Louie W. Blanton
SVP and Director of Wholesale Mortgage, First National Bank of the South: John Higdon
SVP and Commercial Banking Officer, Spartanburg, First National Bank of the South:
Sidney H. (Sid) Walker
SVP Retail Sales and Service Manager, First National Bank of the South: Kent S. Dill
VP and Human Resource Manager, First National Bank of the South: Van Clark
Market President, Charleston, First National Bank of the South: Rudy Gill
Auditors: Elliott Davis LLC

LOCATIONS

HQ: First National Bancshares, Inc.
215 N. Pine St., Spartanburg, SC 29302
Phone: 864-948-9001   **Fax:** 864-948-0001
Web: www.firstnational-online.com

PRODUCTS/OPERATIONS

2006 Sales

	$ mil.	% of total
Interest		
Loans	26.2	84
Securities	2.4	8
Federal funds sold & other	0.3	1
Noninterest		
Service charges & fees on deposit accounts	1.1	3
Gain on sale of guaranteed		
portion of SBA loans	0.3	1
Loan service charges & fees	0.2	1
Mortgage loan fees from correspondent bank	0.2	1
Other	0.2	1
Total	**30.9**	**100**

COMPETITORS

Bank of America
Bank of South Carolina
BB&T
First Citizens Bancorporation
South Financial
SunTrust
Synovus
Wachovia

HISTORICAL FINANCIALS

Company Type: Public

Income Statement

	ASSETS ($ mil.)	NET INCOME ($ mil.)	INCOME AS % OF ASSETS	EMPLOYEES
12/06	465.4	4.1	0.9%	102
12/05	328.7	2.8	0.9%	77
12/04	236.3	1.8	0.8%	—
12/03	180.6	0.9	0.5%	—
12/02	139.2	0.6	0.4%	—
Annual Growth	**35.2%**	**61.7%**	**—**	**32.5%**

FYE: December 31

2006 Year-End Financials

Equity as % of assets: 5.8%
Return on assets: 1.0%
Return on equity: 16.7%
Long-term debt ($ mil.): 13.4
No. of shares (mil.): 3.7
Market value ($ mil.): 55.3
Dividends
  Yield: —
  Payout: —
Sales ($ mil.): 30.9
R&D as % of sales: —
Advertising as % of sales: —

Stock History

NASDAQ (GM): FNSC

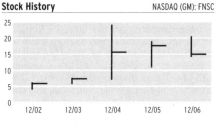

	STOCK PRICE ($) FY Close	P/E High/Low		PER SHARE ($) Earnings	Dividends	Book Value
12/06	14.95	22	15	0.94	—	7.29
12/05	17.60	26	15	0.73	—	7.04
12/04	15.58	49	15	0.49	—	7.72
12/03	7.35	28	22	0.26	—	6.78
12/02	5.88	34	23	0.18	—	9.60
Annual Growth	**26.3%**	**—**	**—**	**51.2%**	**—**	**(6.6%)**

First National Lincoln

First National Lincoln is the holding company for The First, a regional bank serving coastal Maine from about 15 branches. Tracing its roots to 1852, the bank offers traditional retail products and services, including checking and savings accounts, CDs, IRAs, and loans. Residential mortgages make up about half of the company's loan portfolio; business loans account for nearly 30%. Bank division First Advisors offers private banking and investment management services. First National Lincoln acquired competitor FNB Bankshares and its First National Bank of Bar Harbor subsidiary in early 2005.

First National Bank was subsequently merged into First National Lincoln subsidiary The First National Bank of Damariscotta, which was renamed The First.

EXECUTIVES

Chairman, First National Lincoln and The First: Robert B. Gregory, age 53
President, CEO, and Director, First National Lincoln and The First: Daniel R. Daigneault, age 54, $324,900 pay
EVP, COO, and Director; EVP and COO, The First: Tony C. McKim, age 39, $181,944 pay
EVP and Clerk; EVP Banking Services and Senior Loan Officer, The First: Charles A. Wootton, age 50, $157,035 pay
EVP, CFO, and Treasurer, First National Lincoln and The First: F. Stephen Ward, age 53, $167,865 pay
SVP Human Resources, Compliance, and CRA Officer: Susan A. Norton, age 46
SVP Retail Services: Richard M. Elder, age 41
SVP and Senior Business Relationship Officer, The First: Jeffrey C. Dalrymple, age 51
SVP Operations, The First: Ronald J. Wrobel, age 47, $108,300 pay
Human Resources Officer, The First: Denise C. Griffin
Auditors: Berry, Dunn, McNeil & Parker

LOCATIONS

HQ: First National Lincoln Corporation
223 Main St., Damariscotta, ME 04543
Phone: 207-563-3195   **Fax:** 207-563-6853
Web: www.the1st.com

PRODUCTS/OPERATIONS

2006 Sales

	$ mil.	% of total
Interest		
Loans, including fees	54.6	73
Investments & other	9.6	13
Noninterest		
Service charges on deposit accounts	2.8	4
Fiduciary & investment management income	1.9	3
Other	5.6	7
Total	**74.5**	**100**

COMPETITORS

Camden National
KeyCorp
Northeast Bancorp
TD Banknorth

HISTORICAL FINANCIALS

Company Type: Public

Income Statement

	ASSETS ($ mil.)	NET INCOME ($ mil.)	INCOME AS % OF ASSETS	EMPLOYEES
12/06	1,104.9	12.3	1.1%	212
12/05	1,042.2	12.8	1.2%	216
12/04	634.2	8.5	1.3%	—
12/03	568.8	7.4	1.3%	—
12/02	494.1	6.5	1.3%	134
Annual Growth	**22.3%**	**17.3%**	**—**	**12.2%**

FYE: December 31

2006 Year-End Financials

Equity as % of assets: 9.7%
Return on assets: 1.1%
Return on equity: 11.7%
Long-term debt ($ mil.): 179.9
No. of shares (mil.): 9.8
Market value ($ mil.): 163.4
Dividends
  Yield: 3.5%
  Payout: 47.2%
Sales ($ mil.): 74.5
R&D as % of sales: —
Advertising as % of sales: —

Stock History

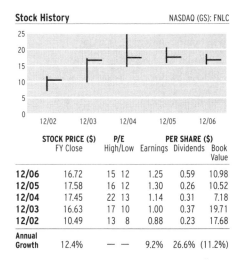

NASDAQ (GS): FNLC

	STOCK PRICE ($) FY Close	P/E High/Low		PER SHARE ($) Earnings	Dividends	Book Value
12/06	16.72	15	12	1.25	0.59	10.98
12/05	17.58	16	12	1.30	0.26	10.52
12/04	17.45	22	13	1.14	0.31	7.18
12/03	16.63	17	10	1.00	0.37	19.71
12/02	10.49	13	8	0.88	0.23	17.68
Annual Growth	12.4%	—	—	9.2%	26.6%	(11.2%)

First Niagara Financial

A lot of water and a few barrels have gone over Niagara Falls since First Niagara Bank was founded. Tracing its roots to 1870, the flagship subsidiary of acquisitive First Niagara Financial Group operates more than 115 offices in western and central New York, offering deposit and loan products, brokerage services, insurance, investments, and asset management. Residential mortgages comprise more than 40% of the company's loan portfolio; commercial real estate loans are more than 30%. The company's First Niagara Commercial Bank subsidiary accepts municipal deposits. First Niagara Financial is buying Great Lakes Bancorp, the parent of Greater Buffalo Savings Bank.

First Niagara Financial has more than doubled in size with a recent acquisition spree; it had fewer than 50 branches operating under its banner at the end of 2003. That year, First Niagara Financial acquired Finger Lakes Bancorp. It bought Troy Financial in 2004 and Hudson River Bancorp the following year.

Also in 2005 First Niagara Financial acquired employee benefits administration and consulting firm Burke Group, and its First Niagara Risk Management subsidiary acquired and absorbed Hatch Leonard Naples, one of the region's largest insurance agencies in 2005. It bought another Buffalo-area insurance agency, Gernold Agency, in 2006. The company has acquired six insurance agencies since entering the business in 1999.

EXECUTIVES

Chairman: G. Thomas Bowers, age 62
President, CEO, and Director: John R. Koelmel, age 54, $772,583 pay (prior to promotion)
CFO: Michael W. Harrington
EVP and Chief Lending Officer: G. Gary Berner, age 58, $698,908 pay
EVP and Chief Administrative Officer; EVP, Human Resources and Administration, First Niagara Bank: Kathleen P. Monti, age 55, $265,384 pay
EVP, Consumer Banking and Central New York Regional Executive: David J. Nasca, age 46, $246,574 pay
Interim EVP, Consumer Banking: Frank J. Polino, age 44

SVP, Corporate Development: Daniel A. Dintino Jr., age 41, $177,251 pay
VP, Marketing and Public Relations: Charles D. Clark
Assistant VP and Investor Relations Contact: Christopher J. Thome
Corporate Secretary: Robert N. Murphy
Auditors: KPMG LLP

LOCATIONS

HQ: First Niagara Financial Group, Inc.
6950 S. Transit Rd., Lockport, NY 14095
Phone: 716-625-7500   **Fax:** 716-625-8405
Web: www.fnfg.com

PRODUCTS/OPERATIONS

2006 Sales

	$ mil.	% of total
Interest		
Loans & leases	360.0	69
Securities available for sale	52.0	10
Money market & other investments	3.8	1
Noninterest		
Risk management services	44.1	8
Banking services	38.7	7
Other	28.4	5
Total	**527.0**	**100**

COMPETITORS

Alliance Financial	KeyCorp
Citigroup	M&T Bank
Citizens Financial Group	NBT Bancorp
Community Bank System	Tompkins Financial
HSBC USA	TrustCo Bank Corp NY
JPMorgan Chase	

HISTORICAL FINANCIALS

Company Type: Public

Income Statement

FYE: December 31

	ASSETS ($ mil.)	NET INCOME ($ mil.)	INCOME AS % OF ASSETS	EMPLOYEES
12/06	7,945.5	91.9	1.2%	1,922
12/05	8,064.8	92.9	1.2%	1,984
12/04	5,078.4	51.8	1.0%	—
12/03	3,589.5	36.1	1.0%	—
12/02	2,934.8	30.8	1.0%	945
Annual Growth	28.3%	31.4%	—	19.4%

2006 Year-End Financials

Equity as % of assets: 17.5%	Dividends
Return on assets: 1.1%	Yield: 3.1%
Return on equity: 6.7%	Payout: 54.1%
Long-term debt ($ mil.): 447.3	Sales ($ mil.): 527.0
No. of shares (mil.): 110.7	R&D as % of sales: —
Market value ($ mil.): 1,645.3	Advertising as % of sales: —

Stock History

NASDAQ (GS): FNFG

	STOCK PRICE ($) FY Close	P/E High/Low		PER SHARE ($) Earnings	Dividends	Book Value
12/06	14.86	18	16	0.85	0.46	12.53
12/05	14.47	18	14	0.84	0.38	12.18
12/04	13.95	24	18	0.65	0.23	11.25
12/03	14.97	31	19	0.53	0.22	10.29
12/02	10.10	26	13	0.47	—	10.98
Annual Growth	10.1%	—	—	16.0%	27.9%	3.4%

First Regional Bancorp

Wholesale banking company First Regional Bancorp caters to Southern California businesses through First Regional Bank. With about 10 locations, the bank mainly offers real estate loans (accounting for the majority of its portfolio), as well as commercial and construction loans. It specializes in equipment finance and midsized residential and commercial projects. Because of the bank's business focus, it has fewer customer deposit accounts than its competitors, but accounts typically have high balances. First Regional Bancorp also offers merchant credit card clearing and trust services, as well as administrative services for self-directed retirement plans. Chairman Jack Sweeney owns nearly 30% of the company.

EXECUTIVES

Chairman: Jack A. Sweeney, age 77, $1,224,535 pay
Vice Chairman: Lawrence J. Sherman, age 83
President, CEO, and Director, First Regional Bancorp and First Regional Bank: H. Anthony Gartshore, age 63, $744,097 pay
CFO, First Regional Bancorp and First Regional Bank: Elizabeth Thompson, age 46, $139,601 pay
Secretary and Director; EVP, COO, and Secretary, First Regional Bank: Thomas E. McCullough, age 54, $571,096 pay
General Counsel; EVP, General Counsel, and Director, First Regional Bank: Steven J. Sweeney, age 42, $216,409 pay
President, Trust Administration Services: James Wagner
EVP, Trust Administration Services: Paul Maxwell
Auditors: Deloitte & Touche LLP

LOCATIONS

HQ: First Regional Bancorp
1801 Century Park East, Ste. 800,
Los Angeles, CA 90067
Phone: 310-552-1776   **Fax:** 310-552-1772
Web: www.firstregional.com

First Regional Bancorp primarily serves the businesses of California's Los Angeles, Orange, and Ventura counties, with operations in Agoura Hills, Carlsbad, Encino, Glendale, Hollywood, Irvine, Los Angeles. Santa Monica, Torrance, and Westlake Village.

PRODUCTS/OPERATIONS

2006 Sales

	$ mil.	% of total
Interest		
Loans, including fees	160.7	94
Other	1.0	1
Customer service fees	7.0	4
Other	1.4	1
Total	**170.1**	**100**

COMPETITORS

Alliance Bancshares (CA)
American Business Bank
California National Bank
Citigroup
City National
Comerica
East West Bancorp
First Republic (CA)
UnionBanCal
U.S. Bancorp
Wells Fargo

HISTORICAL FINANCIALS

Company Type: Public

Income Statement

FYE: December 31

	ASSETS ($ mil.)	NET INCOME ($ mil.)	INCOME AS % OF ASSETS	EMPLOYEES
12/06	2,074.6	38.3	1.8%	264
12/05	1,811.7	26.5	1.5%	224
12/04	1,306.1	11.1	0.8%	—
12/03	775.3	4.6	0.6%	—
12/02	467.3	3.0	0.6%	132
Annual Growth	45.2%	89.0%	—	18.9%

2006 Year-End Financials

Equity as % of assets: 7.1%
Return on assets: 2.0%
Return on equity: 30.3%
Long-term debt ($ mil.): 93.1
No. of shares (mil.): 12.3
Market value ($ mil.): 418.7

Dividends
  Yield: —
  Payout: —
Sales ($ mil.): 170.1
R&D as % of sales: —
Advertising as % of sales: —

Stock History

NASDAQ (GM): FRGB

	STOCK PRICE ($) FY Close	P/E High/Low		Earnings	PER SHARE ($) Dividends	Book Value
12/06	34.09	12	8	2.95	—	11.97
12/05	22.52	15	9	2.06	—	25.99
12/04	18.00	20	10	0.95	—	19.40
12/03	9.77	19	8	0.53	—	12.28
12/02	5.21	14	9	0.38	—	10.57
Annual Growth	59.9%	—	—	66.9%	—	3.2%

First Security Group

Pardon me boy, as Glenn Miller would say, but if you've got your fare and a trifle to spare, you might want to turn to First Security Group. The holding company for FSGBank operates about 40 branches in eastern and middle Tennessee (including Chattanooga) and northern Georgia; in addition to the FSGBank brand, the company also operates certain locations under the Catoosa Community Bank, Dalton Whitfield Bank, Jackson Bank & Trust, and Primer Banco Seguro names. The bank offers standard deposit and lending services, including checking and savings accounts and CDs. Real estate mortgages make up more than half of First Security's loan portfolio, which also includes construction, business, and consumer loans.

First Security Group also has two leasing subsidiaries (J&S Leasing and Kenesaw Leasing) and a wealth management division, which offers financial planning, trust management, and other services. Its Primer Banco Seguro branches target northern Georgia's Latino community. The company went public in 2004, using funds from its IPO to help fuel its growth strategies, which include acquiring other banks and *de novo* branching in its target markets, which currently include the I-40 and I-75 corridors in Tennessee and Georgia.

EXECUTIVES

Chairman and CEO, First Security Group and FSGBank: Rodger B. Holley, age 59
President and COO, First Security Group and FSGBank and Director:
Lloyd L. (Monty) Montgomery III, age 52
EVP, CFO, and Secretary, First Security Group and FSGBank: William L. (Chip) Lusk Jr., age 38, $199,180 pay
VP, Controller, and Principal Accounting Officer:
John R. Haddock, age 28
Regional President, Chattanooga, FSGBank:
R. Ryan Murphy III
Regional President, Dalton Whitfield Bank:
J. Alan Wells
Regional President, Sweetwater, Tennessee, FSGBank:
Cary Davis
Auditors: Joseph Decosimo and Company, LLP

LOCATIONS

HQ: First Security Group, Inc.
  531 Broad St., Chattanooga, TN 37402
Phone: 423-266-2000   **Fax:** 423-267-3383
Web: www.fsgbank.com

First Security Group operates in Tennessee's Bradley, Hamilton, Jackson, Jefferson, Knox, Loudon, McMinn, Monroe, Putnam, and Union counties, and in Georgia's Catoosa and Whitfield counties.

PRODUCTS/OPERATIONS

2006 Sales

	$ mil.	% of total
Interest income		
Loans	68.0	79
Securities & other	7.1	8
Service charges on deposit accounts	4.8	6
Other	6.0	7
Total	**85.9**	**100**

COMPETITORS

Bank of America
BB&T
Cornerstone Bancshares
First Horizon
Green Bankshares
Jefferson Bancshares
Regions Financial
SunTrust
Tennessee Commerce Bancorp
Wachovia

HISTORICAL FINANCIALS

Company Type: Public

Income Statement

FYE: December 31

	ASSETS ($ mil.)	NET INCOME ($ mil.)	INCOME AS % OF ASSETS	EMPLOYEES
12/06	1,129.8	11.1	1.0%	376
12/05	1,040.7	9.6	0.9%	366
12/04	766.7	4.3	0.6%	—
12/03	644.8	2.5	0.4%	—
Annual Growth	20.6%	43.7%	—	18.8%

2006 Year-End Financials

Equity as % of assets: 12.8%
Return on assets: 1.0%
Return on equity: 7.8%
Long-term debt ($ mil.): 24.8
No. of shares (mil.): 17.8
Market value ($ mil.): 204.8

Dividends
  Yield: 1.1%
  Payout: 20.6%
Sales ($ mil.): 85.9
R&D as % of sales: —
Advertising as % of sales: —

Stock History

NASDAQ (GS): FSGI

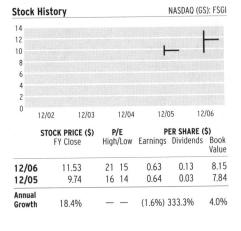

	STOCK PRICE ($) FY Close	P/E High/Low		Earnings	PER SHARE ($) Dividends	Book Value
12/06	11.53	21	15	0.63	0.13	8.15
12/05	9.74	16	14	0.64	0.03	7.84
Annual Growth	18.4%	—	—	(1.6%)	333.3%	4.0%

First Solar

Ready to go solar? Maybe you should first get into film. First Solar makes solar-power modules with a thin-film semiconductor technology that doesn't use silicon. A worldwide shortage of polycrystalline silicon is holding back some producers of silicon-based solar cells, which can't get enough raw material to meet demand. First Solar uses a sheet of glass as a substrate, coated with a film of cadmium telluride, for its products. Nearly all of the company's sales of solar modules are to five customers in Germany. The estate of John Walton (of the Wal-Mart Waltons, who died in a 2005 plane crash) owns 54% of First Solar.

First Solar touts its solar modules as cheaper to make than polysilicon-based solar modules, which currently dominate the world market. First Solar produces its solar modules at a plant in Ohio, while building a second factory in Germany. The company has also begun construction on a third manufacturing facility in Malaysia.

In 2006 First Solar completed the expansion of its Ohio plant, a move that tripled production capacity there. The German plant will more than double that increased capacity when it comes online, and the Malaysian facility will add another 100 MW of capacity. That means in the year and a half from the middle of 2006 to the end of 2008, the company will have increased capacity from 25 MW to 275 MW. All this increased production has enabled the company to boost sales tenfold from 2004 to 2006.

In late 2007 the company signed a long-term module supply agreement with a subsidiary of Babcock & Brown and with Ecostream Switzerland GmbH, a subsidiary of Econcern BV. The agreement is estimated to be worth about $1 billion over four years, from 2008 to 2012. To handle the increased volume of production as a result, First Solar's board authorized the construction of a fourth manufacturing plant in Malaysia. The new plant's four production lines will bring to 16 the number of production lines the company has in Malaysia.

EXECUTIVES

Chairman and CEO: Michael J. Ahearn, age 50
President and Director: Bruce Sohn, age 46
COO: George A. (Chip) Hambro, age 43
CFO: Jens Meyerhoff, age 42
EVP and General Counsel: John T. Gaffney, age 47
EVP: Kenneth M. Schultz, age 44
VP and General Counsel: Paul Kacir, age 41
Auditors: PricewaterhouseCoopers LLP

LOCATIONS

HQ: First Solar, Inc.
4050 E. Cotton Center Blvd., Bldg. 6, Ste. 68,
Phoenix, AZ 85040
Phone: 602-414-9300   **Fax:** 602-414-9400
Web: www.firstsolar.com

First Solar has operations in Germany and the US.

2006 Sales

	$ mil.	% of total
Germany	128.3	95
Other countries	6.7	5
Total	**135.0**	**100**

COMPETITORS

Ascent Solar
BP Solar
Energy Conversion
Evergreen Solar
Kaneka
Kyocera Solar
Mitsubishi Heavy Industries
Q-Cells
Renewable Energy
SANYO
SCHOTT Solar
Sharp Corporation
SolarWorld
SunPower
Suntech Power

HISTORICAL FINANCIALS

Company Type: Public

Income Statement

FYE: December 31

	REVENUE ($ mil.)	NET INCOME ($ mil.)	NET PROFIT MARGIN	EMPLOYEES
12/06	135.0	4.0	3.0%	723
12/05	48.1	(6.5)	—	—
12/04	13.5	(16.8)	—	—
12/03	3.2	(28.0)	—	—
Annual Growth	248.1%	—	—	—

2006 Year-End Financials

Debt ratio: 14.8%
Return on equity: 1.9%
Cash ($ mil.): 308.4
Current ratio: 7.46
Long-term debt ($ mil.): 61.0
No. of shares (mil.): 72.3
Dividends
  Yield: —
  Payout: —
Market value ($ mil.): 2,158.4
R&D as % of sales: —
Advertising as % of sales: —

Stock History

NASDAQ (GM): FSLR

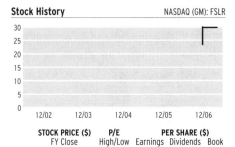

	STOCK PRICE ($) FY Close	P/E High/Low	Earnings	PER SHARE ($) Dividends	Book Value
12/06	29.84	429 336	0.07	—	5.69

First State Bancorporation

First State has cornered the Four Corners market. The bank is the holding company for First Community Bank, which operates about 50 branches in New Mexico, Colorado, Arizona, and Utah. Founded in 1922, First State provides retail banking services such as checking and savings accounts, money market accounts, and CDs, as well as credit cards. Lending activities focus on residential real estate and construction, together accounting for about 70% of the bank's loan portfolio. The bank expanded in New Mexico and entered Arizona with its 2006 acquisition of Access Anytime Bancorp; it also purchased New Mexico Financial Corporation, which operates several branches through subsidiary Ranchers Bank.

In 2007 it acquired Front Range Capital Corp., parent of Heritage Bank, in a $72 million cash deal. Heritage has 13 branches in Colorado.

First State intends to continue growing in its current markets, focusing on the Denver; Albuquerque and Santa Fe, New Mexico; Colorado Springs; and Salt Lake City metro areas.

EXECUTIVES

Chairman: Leonard J. DeLayo Jr., age 58
President and CEO: Michael R. Stanford, age 54, $507,055 pay
EVP, COO, Treasurer, and Director; President and COO, First Community Bank: H. Patrick Dee, age 52, $363,000 pay
EVP, Secretary, and Corporate Counsel: Marshall G. Martin, age 68, $162,000 pay
EVP Branch Administration: James E. Warden, age 49, $165,000 pay
EVP Human Resources; EVP, First Community Bank: Theresa A. Gabel, age 57, $170,000 pay
SVP and Chief Credit Officer: Pamela Smith
SVP, CFO, and Chief Accounting Officer; SVP and CFO, First Community Bank: Christopher C. Spencer, age 49, $211,000 pay
President, Mortgage Lending Division: John Jackson
Auditors: KPMG LLP

LOCATIONS

HQ: First State Bancorporation
7900 Jefferson NE, Albuquerque, NM 87109
Phone: 505-241-7500   **Fax:** 505-241-7572
Web: www.fsbnm.com

PRODUCTS/OPERATIONS

2006 Sales

	$ mil.	% of total
Interest income		
Interest & fees on loans	161.6	80
Securities	19.2	10
Other	1.0	1
Noninterest income		
Service charges on deposit accounts	7.6	4
Gain on sale of mortgage loans	4.9	2
Credit and debit card transaction fees	3.0	1
Other	4.2	2
Total	**201.5**	**100**

COMPETITORS

Bank of America
Bank of the West
BOK Financial
Capitol Bancorp
Compass Bancshares
Wells Fargo

HISTORICAL FINANCIALS

Company Type: Public

Income Statement

FYE: December 31

	ASSETS ($ mil.)	NET INCOME ($ mil.)	INCOME AS % OF ASSETS	EMPLOYEES
12/06	2,801.6	22.8	0.8%	864
12/05	2,157.6	21.4	1.0%	663
12/04	1,815.5	15.2	0.8%	—
12/03	1,646.7	14.9	0.9%	—
12/02	1,386.9	10.0	0.7%	418
Annual Growth	19.2%	22.9%	—	19.9%

2006 Year-End Financials

Equity as % of assets: 10.9%
Return on assets: 0.9%
Return on equity: 9.8%
Long-term debt ($ mil.): 57.7
No. of shares (mil.): 20.8
Market value ($ mil.): 514.2
Dividends
  Yield: 1.3%
  Payout: 25.4%
Sales ($ mil.): 201.5
R&D as % of sales: —
Advertising as % of sales: —

Stock History

NASDAQ (GS): FSNM

	STOCK PRICE ($) FY Close	P/E High/Low	Earnings	PER SHARE ($) Dividends	Book Value
12/06	24.75	22 18	1.26	0.32	14.67
12/05	23.99	19 12	1.36	0.25	10.41
12/04	18.38	20 15	0.99	0.17	9.42
12/03	17.38	19 11	0.98	0.22	17.41
12/02	12.40	17 11	0.83	0.19	16.03
Annual Growth	18.9%	— —	11.0%	13.9%	(2.2%)

First State Financial

The Sunshine State certainly wasn't the first state, but First State Financial is the holding company for First State Bank, which serves west-central Florida's Sarasota and Pinellas counties through about a half-dozen branch locations. The bank offers such standard deposit services as checking and savings accounts, money market and retirement accounts, and certificates of deposit. Commercial real estate lending (at more than 50%) dominates First State Financial's loan portfolio, which also includes business loans, residential mortgages, and construction loans.

First State Financial has experienced organic growth in its existing markets; it is also looking to grow through acquisition. Directors Thomas Wright, Marshall Reynolds, and Daniel Harrington each own more than 5% of First State Financial's stock; they are also three of the four company directors who have seats on the board of Pittsburgh-based Portec Rail Products.

EXECUTIVES

Chairman: Neal W. Scaggs, age 71
President, CEO, and Director: John E. (Jed) Wilkinson, age 59
President, Pinellas County Division, First State Bank: David E. (Dave) Ruppel, age 53
President, Sarasota Division, First State Bank: Paul D. Thatcher
EVP and Senior Credit Officer, First State Bank: Lester P. Snyder, age 42
SVP and CFO, First State Financial and First State Bank: Dennis Grinsteiner, age 62, $125,306 pay
Corporate Secretary: Marion DeLay

LOCATIONS

HQ: First State Financial Corporation
22 S. Links Ave., Sarasota, FL 34236
Phone: 941-929-9000 **Fax:** 941-951-6189
Web: www.firststatefl.com

First State Financial has operations in the Florida cities of Clearwater, St. Petersburg, Sarasota, and Seminole.

PRODUCTS/OPERATIONS

2006 Sales

	$ mil.	% of total
Interest		
Loans	29.8	87
Securities & other	1.6	4
Mortgage banking fees	1.3	4
Service charges & fees	1.5	5
Total	**34.2**	**100**

COMPETITORS

Bank of America
BB&T
RBC Centura Banks
SunTrust
Superior Bancorp
Wachovia
Whitney Holding

HISTORICAL FINANCIALS

Company Type: Public

Income Statement

FYE: December 31

	ASSETS ($ mil.)	NET INCOME ($ mil.)	INCOME AS % OF ASSETS	EMPLOYEES
12/06	453.5	5.3	1.2%	109
12/05	372.7	3.8	1.0%	93
12/04	274.0	2.1	0.8%	—
12/03	212.3	0.8	0.4%	—
12/02	153.5	0.4	0.3%	—
Annual Growth	**31.1%**	**90.8%**	**—**	**17.2%**

2006 Year-End Financials

Equity as % of assets: 10.7%
Return on assets: 1.3%
Return on equity: 11.4%
Long-term debt ($ mil.): —
No. of shares (mil.): 5.9
Market value ($ mil.): 99.3
Dividends
Yield: 1.7%
Payout: 32.2%
Sales ($ mil.): 34.2
R&D as % of sales: —
Advertising as % of sales: —

Stock History

NASDAQ (GM): FSTF

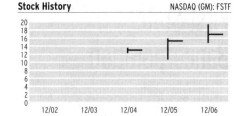

	STOCK PRICE ($) FY Close	P/E High/Low		PER SHARE ($) Earnings	Dividends	Book Value
12/06	16.90	21	17	0.90	0.29	8.26
12/05	15.27	24	17	0.65	0.20	7.59
12/04	13.02	23	21	0.59	—	7.20
Annual Growth	**13.9%**	**—**	**—**	**23.5%**	**45.0%**	**7.1%**

FirstFed Financial

Southern Californians are on a first come, FirstFed basis. FirstFed Financial is the savings and loan holding company for First Federal Bank of California. Founded in 1929, First Federal serves consumers and businesses through some 30 branches and six lending offices. The bank uses funds from deposits mainly to finance single-family residential real estate mortgages, which account for about 75% of FirstFed's total loans, and mortgages for multifamily units, which comprise another 21%. It also writes business loans. Subsidiary Oceanside Insurance Agency sells annuities. The company received regulatory approval to commence trust operations in 2004.

Buoyed by Southern California's robust housing market, FirstFed had been able to maintain a squeaky clean loan portfolio; it made no provisions for bad loans from 1998 through 2003 (it recorded a $3 million provision for loan losses in 2004), and nonperforming assets account for a miniscule 0.07% of its balance sheet. That all changed drastically in 2005; that year the company made a $19.8 million provision for loan losses; nonperforming assets fell to 0.05%.

Things worsened as interest rates rose and homebuyers defaulted on their loans, and in 2006 FirstFed's nonperforming assets more than tripled.

Investment management companies own around one-third of FirstFed.

EXECUTIVES

President, COO, and Director: James P. Giraldin, age 54, $751,700 pay
EVP and Chief Credit Officer: David W. Anderson, age 37, $251,505 pay
EVP and CFO: Douglas J. Goddard, age 53, $294,216 pay
EVP and President, Retail Banking: Shannon Millard, age 43, $530,000 pay (prior to title change)
EVP, Community Banking: Brad McCoy, age 36, $442,236 pay
SVP, General Counsel, and Corporate Secretary: Ann E. Lederer
SVP and Controller: Brenda J. Battey
Chairman and CEO, FirstFed Financial and First Federal Bank of California: Babette E. Heimbuch, age 58, $975,560 pay

SVP, Loan Service, First Federal Bank of California: Carol Baxter
SVP, Marketing, First Federal Bank of California: Evon G. Rosen
SVP, Human Resources, First Federal Bank of California: Caroline Galbraith
Auditors: Grant Thornton LLP

LOCATIONS

HQ: FirstFed Financial Corp.
401 Wilshire Blvd., Santa Monica, CA 90401
Phone: 310-319-6000 **Fax:** 310-319-2100
Web: www.firstfedca.com

PRODUCTS/OPERATIONS

2006 Sales

	$ mil.	% of total
Interest		
Loans	682.7	94
Interest & dividends on investments	27.0	4
Interest on mortgage-backed securities	2.9	—
Noninterest		
Loan servicing & other fees	9.2	1
Gain on sale of loans	6.2	1
Other	0.9	—
Total	**728.9**	**100**

COMPETITORS

Bank of America
City National
UnionBanCal
Washington Mutual
Wells Fargo

HISTORICAL FINANCIALS

Company Type: Public

Income Statement

FYE: December 31

	ASSETS ($ mil.)	NET INCOME ($ mil.)	INCOME AS % OF ASSETS	EMPLOYEES
12/06	9,295.6	129.1	1.4%	603
12/05	10,457.0	91.7	0.9%	—
12/04	7,469.0	65.8	0.9%	—
12/03	4,825.0	64.5	1.3%	—
12/02	4,253.7	55.2	1.3%	497
Annual Growth	**21.6%**	**23.7%**	**—**	**5.0%**

2006 Year-End Financials

Equity as % of assets: 7.6%
Return on assets: 1.3%
Return on equity: 20.2%
Long-term debt ($ mil.): 100.0
No. of shares (mil.): 16.6
Market value ($ mil.): 1,114.9
Dividends
Yield: —
Payout: —
Sales ($ mil.): 728.9
R&D as % of sales: —
Advertising as % of sales: —

Stock History

NYSE: FED

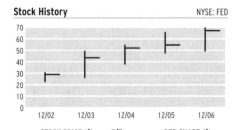

	STOCK PRICE ($) FY Close	P/E High/Low		PER SHARE ($) Earnings	Dividends	Book Value
12/06	66.97	9	6	7.65	—	42.33
12/05	54.52	12	9	5.43	—	34.46
12/04	51.87	14	10	3.85	—	28.94
12/03	43.50	13	7	3.70	—	25.61
12/02	28.95	10	7	3.15	—	21.95
Annual Growth	**23.3%**	**—**	**—**	**24.8%**	**—**	**17.8%**

Flotek Industries

Flotek Industries works to keep oil and gas flowing. The company gets half of its sales from chemicals used in the cementing and stimulation of oil and gas wells. (Cementing holds well casings in place; stimulation opens up cracks in the earth to allow for the easier flow of oil.) Flotek also makes the equipment used in cementing and stimulation, as well as Petrovalve downhole pump valves (used to pump off the liquids in gas wells) and Turbeco casing centralizers (used to center pipe). The company markets its products throughout the US and is expanding into international markets.

Flotek's been working on a bit of an acquisitions spree the past few years. In 2005 the company acquired the oilfield shale-shaker screen manufacturing assets of Phoenix E&P Technology, and it acquired downhole tool company Spindle Sales and Services.

The following year the company acquired the drilling tool assets of Can-Ok Field Services and Stabilizer Technology to further expand its equipment sale, rental, and service operations. It also bought Total Well Solutions and Teal Supply Co. (dba Triumph Drilling Tools), two more drilling equipment providers, at the beginning of 2007. The next year brought another acquisition when Flotek agreed to buy Teledrift for $95 million. The acquired company makes wireless tools for survey and measurement while drilling.

EXECUTIVES

Chairman, President, and CEO: Jerry D. Dumas Sr., age 71, $408,631 pay
SVP, CESI Chemicals: Richard L. (Rick) Johnson II
SVP, Petrovalve: Oscar H. Rivas
VP and CFO: Lisa G. Meier, age 34, $225,278 pay
VP: Roger K. Padgham
VP, Equipment Specialties: Kevin Edgley
VP, Material Translogistics: Michael C. Gillespie
VP, Turbeco: Terry A. Lowrey
President, Artificial Lift: Paul Deutch
President, Flotek Technology and Engineering: Robert Wittman
Auditors: UHY LLP

LOCATIONS

HQ: Flotek Industries Inc.
   7030 Empire Central Dr., Houston, TX 77040
Phone: 713-849-9911   **Fax:** 713-896-4511
Web: www.flotekind.com

Flotek has manufacturing facilities in the US and the Netherlands and sells its products in Asia, the Middle East, and North and South America.

PRODUCTS/OPERATIONS

2006 Sales

	$ mil.	% of total
Chemicals & Logistics	50.5	50
Drilling Products	36.8	37
Artificial Lifts	13.3	13
Total	100.6	100

Selected Products

Specialty Chemicals
   Acidizing, cementing, and fracturing chemicals for oil
      and gas wells

Equipment Manufacturing
   Acid pump vehicles
   Bulk material handling facilities contracting
   Cement mixing units
   Hydraulic fracturing blenders
   Nitrogen equipment units

Downhole Equipment
   Downhole pumps valves
   Rigid centralizers

COMPETITORS

Baker Hughes
BJ Services
CARBO Ceramics
Champion Technologies
FMC Technologies

Lubrizol
Nalco Energy Services
Natural Gas Services
Schlumberger

HISTORICAL FINANCIALS

Company Type: Public

Income Statement

FYE: December 31

	REVENUE ($ mil.)	NET INCOME ($ mil.)	NET PROFIT MARGIN	EMPLOYEES
12/06	100.6	11.4	11.3%	253
12/05	52.9	7.7	14.6%	157
12/04	21.9	2.2	10.0%	—
12/03	14.8	(7.4)	—	—
12/02	13.3	(5.5)	—	—
Annual Growth	65.8%	—	—	61.1%

2006 Year-End Financials

Debt ratio: 15.3%
Return on equity: 25.7%
Cash ($ mil.): 0.5
Current ratio: 1.84
Long-term debt ($ mil.): 8.2
No. of shares (mil.): 8.8

Dividends
   Yield: —
   Payout: —
Market value ($ mil.): 123.8
R&D as % of sales: —
Advertising as % of sales: —

Stock History

AMEX: FTK

	STOCK PRICE ($) FY Close	P/E High/Low	Earnings	Dividends	Book Value
12/06	14.02	25 11	0.61	—	6.06
12/05	9.32	24 14	0.47	—	4.23
Annual Growth	50.4%	— —	29.8%	—	43.2%

FNB United Corp.

Some central North Carolinians stand firmly united in their choice to do business with FNB United. The bank holding company owns First National Bank and Trust, which has about 45 banking offices. (In some markets, the bank operates as Catawba Valley Bank, First Gaston Bank, or Northwestern Bank.) Retail services and products include checking, savings, NOW, and money market accounts; CDs; IRAs; and credit cards. The bank concentrates on real estate and business lending: commercial mortgages, residential mortgages, and business loans each account for about 25% of the loan portfolio, which also includes construction and consumer loans.

Subsidiary Dover Mortgage Company originates mortgage loans for sale into the secondary market; the company has about 10 loan production offices in its home state. FNB United has grown through acquisition, including United Financial (2005) and Integrity Financial (2006). The charters of the banks acquired in those acquisitions have been merged into First National Bank and Trust's.

EXECUTIVES

Chairman and President; Chairman and President, First National Bank and Trust: Michael C. Miller, age 56, $390,328 pay
Vice Chairman: Eugene B. McLaurin II, age 49
CFO; VP, Treasurer, and EVP, CommunityONE Bank: Mark A. Severson, age 53
Chief Banking Officer: R. Mark Hensley
Chief Human Resources Officer: Deborah B. Auman
Chief Wealth Management Officer: Timothy C. Britt
Chief Credit Officer: William S. Bruton
Chief Lending Officer: Eddie M. Causey
Chief Risk Officer: Dean S. Tingey
VP and Director; EVP and SVP, First National Bank: R. Larry Campbell, age 62, $174,139 pay
President, Dover Mortgage: Harvey W. Goldberg
Auditors: Dixon Hughes PLLC

LOCATIONS

HQ: FNB United Corp.
   150 South Fayetteville St., Asheboro, NC 27203
Phone: 336-626-8300   **Fax:** 336-625-2452
Web: www.myyesbank.com

FNB United has operations in North Carolina's Alamance, Alexander, Ashe, Catawba, Chatham, Gaston, Guilford, Iredell, Montgomery, Moore, Orange, Randolph, Richmond, Rowan, Scotland, Watauga and Wilkes counties.

PRODUCTS/OPERATIONS

2006 Sales

	$ mil.	% of total
Interest income		
Interest & fees on loans	92.6	75
Securities & other	10.8	9
Service charges on deposits	8.2	7
Mortgage loan sales	4.8	4
Cardholder & merchant services	1.9	1
Trust & investment services	1.5	1
Other noninterest	3.3	3
Total	123.1	100

COMPETITORS

Bank of Granite
BB&T
BNC Bancorp
Capital Bank
Capitol Bancorp
Carolina Bank
First Bancorp (NC)
First Citizens BancShares
First Merchants
NewBridge Bancorp
RBC Centura Banks
Regions Financial
Southern Community Financial
Wachovia
Yadkin Valley Financial Corporation

HISTORICAL FINANCIALS

Company Type: Public

Income Statement

FYE: December 31

	ASSETS ($ mil.)	NET INCOME ($ mil.)	INCOME AS % OF ASSETS	EMPLOYEES
12/06	1,814.9	12.2	0.7%	584
12/05	1,102.1	9.9	0.9%	350
12/04	862.9	6.6	0.8%	—
12/03	773.2	8.4	1.1%	—
12/02	754.4	8.2	1.1%	260
Annual Growth	24.5%	10.4%	—	22.4%

2006 Year-End Financials

Equity as % of assets: 11.4%
Return on assets: 0.8%
Return on equity: 7.9%
Long-term debt ($ mil.): 78.0
No. of shares (mil.): 11.3
Market value ($ mil.): 207.1
Dividends
　Yield: 3.4%
　Payout: 49.6%
Sales ($ mil.): 123.1
R&D as % of sales: —
Advertising as % of sales: —

Stock History

NASDAQ (GS): FNBN

	STOCK PRICE ($) FY Close	P/E High/Low		PER SHARE ($) Earnings	Dividends	Book Value
12/06	18.34	17	14	1.25	0.62	18.39
12/05	19.00	13	10	1.69	0.47	16.06
12/04	19.14	20	14	1.13	0.45	14.65
12/03	21.18	22	13	1.43	0.59	14.32
12/02	19.39	13	9	1.58	0.58	13.49
Annual Growth	(1.4%)	—	—	(5.7%)	1.7%	8.0%

Force Protection

Force Protection's vehicles protect military forces from blast forces. The company makes armored land vehicles designed to protect troops from landmines, bombs, and hostile fire. Force Protection's products include the 22-ton Buffalo, which is designed for mine-clearing operations, and the Cougar, a lighter-weight vehicle with similar armoring that can be used for route clearance support, urban patrol, and other activities. The Cheetah is the smallest of the company's offerings. It is used for reconnaissance and other urban operations. The US Marine Corps accounts for about 59% of Force Protection's sales; the US Army accounts for about 14%. About 10% of sales are to friendly foreign governments.

The US military plans to start replacing its fleet of Humvees between 2009 and 2011 under its Joint Light Tactical Vehicle (JLTV) program. Force Protection plans to bid for the contract by throwing the Cheetah's hat into the JLTV ring. Competition for the JLTV contract — about 200,000 vehicles worth — is anticipated to be quite intense.

The Pentagon has decided the next generation JLTV will be the MRAP — or mine-resistant, ambush-protected vehicle. Several companies have been tapped to deliver MRAPs, as the US military's needs are too great to be filled by a lone contractor. For its share, Force Protection formed the joint venture Force Dynamics with partner General Dynamics Land Systems to deliver MRAPs to the US military.

In 2007 Force Protection began investing in the expansion of its South Carolina production facility. In 2006 Force Protection delivered 300 vehicles which are now all fielded in battle. By the end of 2007 Force Protection, through its joint venture with General Dynamics, was delivering nearly 350 MRAP vehicles per month.

Late in 2007 the US Marine Corp. cut the number of MRAPs it planned to order by about 40%, citing improved security in Iraq.

EXECUTIVES

CEO and Director: Gordon McGilton, age 63, $445,576 pay
President and Director: Michael Moody, age 61
COO: Raymond W. Pollard, age 64, $169,677 pay (partial-year salary)
CFO and Treasurer: Michael S. Durski
SVP Vehicle Operations: Mark V. Edwards, age 45, $144,070 pay
VP Integrated Logistics Support: Murray Hammick, $115,000 pay
VP Marketing and Government Relations: Michael Aldrich, $160,000 pay
VP Program Management; Secretary, Force Dynamics: Damon Walsh
VP Engineering: Mike Gilbert, $160,000 pay
President, Force Protection Industries, Inc.: Ted M. McQuinn, $159,919 pay
Co-General Counsel: Lenna Ruth Macdonald, age 41
Co-General Counsel: Denise D. Speaks
Auditors: Jaspers + Hall, PC

LOCATIONS

HQ: Force Protection, Inc.
　9801 Hwy. 78, Bldg. 1, Ladson, SC 29456
Phone: 843-740-7015 　 **Fax:** 843-740-1973
Web: www.forceprotectioninc.com

COMPETITORS

AM General
BAE Systems Land and Armaments
General Dynamics Land Systems
International Truck and Engine
Krauss-Maffei Wegmann
Oshkosh Truck
Textron

HISTORICAL FINANCIALS

Company Type: Public

Income Statement

FYE: December 31

	REVENUE ($ mil.)	NET INCOME ($ mil.)	NET PROFIT MARGIN	EMPLOYEES
12/06	196.0	18.2	9.3%	658
12/05	49.7	(14.4)	—	—
12/04	10.3	(10.3)	—	—
12/03	6.3	(5.3)	—	—
12/02	2.6	(5.4)	—	—
Annual Growth	194.7%	—	—	—

2006 Year-End Financials

Debt ratio: —
Return on equity: 17.2%
Cash ($ mil.): 156.3
Current ratio: 4.66
Long-term debt ($ mil.): —
No. of shares (mil.): 66.8
Dividends
　Yield: —
　Payout: —
Market value ($ mil.): 1,162.3
R&D as % of sales: —
Advertising as % of sales: —

Stock History

NASDAQ (CM): FRPT

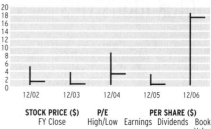

	STOCK PRICE ($) FY Close	P/E High/Low		PER SHARE ($) Earnings	Dividends	Book Value
12/06	17.41	51	2	0.36	—	3.26
12/05	0.78	—	—	(0.51)	—	(0.18)
12/04	3.34	—	—	(0.29)	—	0.01
12/03	0.84	—	—	(0.36)	—	(0.00)
12/02	1.44	—	—	(1.08)	—	0.01
Annual Growth	86.5%	—	—	—	—	313.3%

FormFactor, Inc.

Good evening, and welcome to FormFactor! On tonight's show, our contestants will dive off a high platform, retrieve a silicon wafer at the bottom of the water tank, and then run tests on the semiconductors! Using an interconnect technology it calls MicroSpring, FormFactor makes wafer probe cards that test semiconductor circuits (especially memory chips) while they are still part of semiconductor wafers — before the wafers are cut into individual chips. FormFactor touts the process for its cost-effectiveness, since it allows testing of many chips at once across a range of scales and temperatures. The company has also licensed MicroSpring technology for other applications in chip packaging.

The company's top customers include Elpida (about 23% of sales), Intel (nearly 13%), and Powerchip Semiconductor (12%).

While the company posted positive results in 2007, with healthy growth in sales and profits, orders weakened late in the year and profitability slipped in the fourth quarter, with business conditions continuing to deteriorate in early 2008. FormFactor responded with a cost reduction plan, including a reduction in workforce of about 14%.

In 2006 FormFactor joined the Semiconductor Test Consortium, formed to develop a common test platform for semiconductors.

FormFactor has been involved in patent litigation against rival Phicom Corp. in South Korea since early 2004. The long-running litigation is in the discovery process. The Korean Patent Court upheld FormFactor's Korean patent in mid-2006. The Seoul Central District Court denied the company's request for a preliminary injunction in early 2007.

FMR (Fidelity Investments) owns about 13% of FormFactor. Franklin Resources holds nearly 8% of the company. CEO Igor Khandros has an equity stake of nearly 6%.

EXECUTIVES

Chairperson: James A. (Jim) Prestridge, age 75
CEO and Director: Igor Y. Khandros, age 52, $436,835 pay
President and Director: Mario Ruscev

CFO: Ronald C. (Ron) Foster, age 57, $285,962 pay
SVP Operations: Richard M. Freeman, age 57
SVP Development and CTO:
 Benjamin N. (Ben) Eldridge, $265,050 pay
SVP, General Counsel, and Secretary:
 Stuart L. Merkadeau, age 46, $259,896 pay
SVP Strategic Initiatives; Chairman, FormFactor K.K.:
 Yoshikazu Hatsukano
SVP Marketing and Global Applications, Product
 Business Group: Jorge L. Titinger, age 46
SVP New Business Development: Peter B. Mathews,
 age 44
VP Marketing: Stefan Zschiegner
VP Worldwide Sales: Roger Hitchcock
VP Human Resources: Hank Feir
Auditors: PricewaterhouseCoopers LLP

LOCATIONS

HQ: FormFactor, Inc.
 7005 Southfront Rd., Livermore, CA 94551
Phone: 925-290-4000   Fax: 925-290-4010
Web: www.formfactor.com

FormFactor has offices in Germany, Italy, Japan, South
Korea, Taiwan, and the US.

2006 Sales

	$ mil.	% of total
Asia/Pacific		
Japan	110.8	30
Other countries	123.4	33
North America	109.0	30
Europe	26.0	7
Total	**369.2**	**100**

PRODUCTS/OPERATIONS

Selected Products

MicroSpring interconnects (T1, T2 type contacts;
 BladeRunner contacts)
Probe cards
Probe heads (PH50, PH75, PH100, PH150 models)

COMPETITORS

Advantest
ASE Test
Cadence Design
Cascade Microtech
Electroglas
Everett Charles Technologies
Interconnect Devices
LogicVision
LTX
Mentor Graphics
Mitsubishi Materials
PDF Solutions
Synopsys, Inc.
Teradyne
Tokyo Electron

HISTORICAL FINANCIALS

Company Type: Public

Income Statement

	REVENUE ($ mil.)	NET INCOME ($ mil.)	NET PROFIT MARGIN	EMPLOYEES
				FYE: Last Saturday in December
12/06	369.2	57.2	15.5%	936
12/05	237.5	30.2	12.7%	653
12/04	177.8	25.2	14.2%	485
12/03	98.3	7.5	7.6%	341
12/02	78.7	10.4	13.2%	289
Annual Growth	47.2%	53.1%	—	34.2%

2006 Year-End Financials

Debt ratio: —
Return on equity: 12.3%
Cash ($ mil.): 492.4
Current ratio: 7.87
Long-term debt ($ mil.): —
No. of shares (mil.): 46.9
Dividends
 Yield: —
 Payout: —
Market value ($ mil.): 1,745.6
R&D as % of sales: —
Advertising as % of sales: —

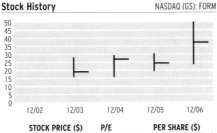

	STOCK PRICE ($) FY Close	P/E High/Low	PER SHARE ($) Earnings	Dividends	Book Value
12/06	37.25	41 20	1.21	—	13.10
12/05	24.43	41 27	0.73	—	7.90
12/04	26.86	46 25	0.63	—	6.82
12/03	19.00	146 85	0.19	—	5.84
Annual Growth	25.2%	— —	36.4%	—	—

FPB Bancorp

FPB Bancorp is for the birds. The *snow* birds, that is. It's the holding company for First Peoples Bank, which targets retired winter visitors, as well as year-round residents and small to mid-sized businesses primarily in the Florida counties of St. Lucie and Martin. The five-branch bank operates in Fort Pierce, Palm City, Port St. Lucie, Stuart, and Vero Beach, offering such standard deposit products as checking, savings, and money market accounts. Business loans and commercial real estate loans together account for more than three-quarters of the bank's loan portfolio, which is rounded out by construction, consumer, and residential real estate loans.

EXECUTIVES

Chairman, FPB Bancorp and First Peoples Bank:
 Gary A. Berger, age 57
Vice Chairman, FPB Bancorp and First Peoples Bank:
 Paul A. Zinter, age 52
President, CEO, and Director, FPB Bancorp and First
 Peoples Bank: David W. Skiles, age 59, $182,165 pay
EVP and COO; EVP, COO, Security Officer,
 Compliance Officer, and Information Systems
 Technology Officer, First Peoples Bank: Marge Riley,
 age 58, $140,658 pay
SVP and CFO, FPB Bancorp and First Peoples Bank:
 Nancy E. Aumack, age 58, $123,425 pay
SVP and Senior Lending Officer, FPB Bancorp and
 First Peoples Bank: Stephen J. Krumfolz, age 55
SVP, Deposit Operations, FPB Bancorp and First
 Peoples Bank: Melissa M. Favorite, age 37
SVP; SVP, Residential Living: Thomas Eby, age 57
Director and Secretary, FPB Bancorp and First Peoples
 Bank: Ann L. Decker, age 55
Auditors: Hacker, Johnson & Smith PA

LOCATIONS

HQ: FPB Bancorp, Inc.
 1301 SE Port St. Lucie Blvd.,
 Port St. Lucie, FL 34952
Phone: 772-398-1388   Fax: 772-398-1399
Web: www.1stpeoplesbank.com

COMPETITORS

Alabama National BancCorp
Bank of America
National City
Riverside Financial Group
Seacoast Banking
SunTrust
Wachovia

HISTORICAL FINANCIALS

Company Type: Public

Income Statement

	ASSETS ($ mil.)	NET INCOME ($ mil.)	INCOME AS % OF ASSETS	EMPLOYEES
				FYE: December 31
12/06	153.4	0.6	0.4%	71
12/05	127.3	0.8	0.6%	56
12/04	94.6	0.1	0.1%	—
12/03	70.1	0.2	0.3%	—
12/02	58.8	0.1	0.2%	—
Annual Growth	27.1%	56.5%	—	26.8%

2006 Year-End Financials

Equity as % of assets: 13.7%
Return on assets: 0.4%
Return on equity: 2.9%
Long-term debt ($ mil.): —
No. of shares (mil.): 1.9
Market value ($ mil.): 31.8
Dividends
 Yield: —
 Payout: —
Sales ($ mil.): 11.4
R&D as % of sales: —
Advertising as % of sales: —

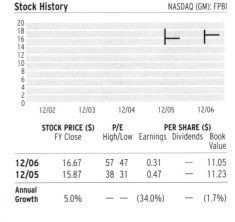

	STOCK PRICE ($) FY Close	P/E High/Low	PER SHARE ($) Earnings	Dividends	Book Value
12/06	16.67	57 47	0.31	—	11.05
12/05	15.87	38 31	0.47	—	11.23
Annual Growth	5.0%	— —	(34.0%)	—	(1.7%)

Franklin Bank

A bubble in the housing market doesn't rankle Franklin Bank Corp. The company is the parent of Franklin Bank, a thrift with about 40 branches in the Austin, Tyler, and Kingsland areas of central and east Texas. In addition to these locations, the company has more than 35 offices in some 20 states from which it originates residential mortgages and residential construction loans. It also purchases mortgages on the secondary market and provides financing to small and midsized mortgage banking companies.

Franklin was founded in 2001 by executives of the former Bank United Corp. The institution is acquiring the First National Bank of Bryan.

Franklin is eyeing growth by opening branches or buying banks in east Texas, as evidenced by its acquisition of Equity Bank, an institution with offices in Mount Vernon and Winnsboro, Texas. In 2003 Franklin bought northeast Texas' Jacksonville Bancorp; its Jacksonville Savings Bank subsidiary retained its name following the transaction.

EXECUTIVES

Chairman: Lewis S. Ranieri, age 60
President, CEO, and Director; Chairman, President, and CEO, Franklin Bank: Anthony J. Nocella, age 65, $672,917 pay
EVP, CFO, and Treasurer; CFO, Franklin Bank: Russell McCann, age 50, $333,431 pay
VP and Secretary: Diane Tregre
President, Access Lending, Franklin Bank: David Fleig
President, Elgin Bank; Market Manager, Bastrop County: Jeff Carter
EVP and Chief Credit Officer, Franklin Bank: Max Epperson, age 64
President and COO, Franklin Bank: Andy Black, age 54
EVP and Managing Director, Administration, Franklin Bank: Glenn Mealey, age 44, $402,328 pay
EVP and Managing Director, Commercial Lending, Franklin Bank: Michael Davitt, age 57, $390,981 pay
EVP and Managing Director, Mortgage Banking, Franklin Bank: Daniel E. Cooper, age 49, $315,464 pay
EVP and CIO, Franklin Bank: Jan Scofield-Robbins, age 51
Investor Relations: Kris Dillon
Auditors: Deloitte & Touche LLP

LOCATIONS

HQ: Franklin Bank Corp.
9800 Richmond Ave., Ste. 680, Houston, TX 77042
Phone: 713-339-8900   **Fax:** 713-343-8122
Web: www.bankfranklin.com

PRODUCTS/OPERATIONS

2006 Sales

	% of total
Interest	
Loans	88
Mortgage-backed securities	5
Cash equivalents & short-term investments	4
Noninterest	3
Total	**100**

COMPETITORS

Bank of America
Colonial BancGroup
Compass Bancshares
Cullen/Frost Bankers
First State Bank Central Texas
Henderson Citizens Bancshares
Lone Star Bank
PlainsCapital
Southside Bancshares
Temple-Inland
Washington Mutual
Wells Fargo

HISTORICAL FINANCIALS

Company Type: Public

Income Statement

		FYE: December 31		
	ASSETS ($ mil.)	NET INCOME ($ mil.)	INCOME AS % OF ASSETS	EMPLOYEES
12/06	5,537.4	19.4	0.4%	627
12/05	4,471.3	26.3	0.6%	710
12/04	3,479.7	23.1	0.7%	—
12/03	2,251.3	3.2	0.1%	—
12/02	365.7	(0.7)	—	—
Annual Growth	**97.3%**	**—**	**—**	**(11.7%)**

2006 Year-End Financials

Equity as % of assets: 6.3%
Return on assets: 0.4%
Return on equity: 5.7%
Long-term debt ($ mil.): 108.1
No. of shares (mil.): 23.6
Market value ($ mil.): 484.9

Dividends
  Yield: —
  Payout: —
Sales ($ mil.): 308.2
R&D as % of sales: —
Advertising as % of sales: —

Stock History

NASDAQ (GS): FBTX

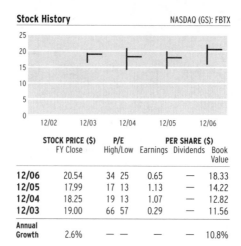

	STOCK PRICE ($) FY Close	P/E High/Low		Earnings	PER SHARE ($) Dividends	Book Value
12/06	20.54	34	25	0.65	—	18.33
12/05	17.99	17	13	1.13	—	14.22
12/04	18.25	19	13	1.07	—	12.82
12/03	19.00	66	57	0.29	—	11.56
Annual Growth	**2.6%**	**—**	**—**	**—**	**—**	**10.8%**

Frontier Financial

Frontier Financial serves the part of the western frontier that includes Washington and Oregon. Its Frontier Bank subsidiary operates about 50 offices that offer standard retail products, including savings, checking, and money market accounts and certificates of deposit. Funds gathered are largely used to originate real estate construction and land development loans (more than 45% of the company's portfolio) and commercial mortgages (more than 30%). Lending activities also include residential mortgage, business, agriculture, and consumer loans. Other offerings include asset management, life insurance, annuities, and trust services.

Frontier Financial expanded into Oregon with its 2007 acquisition of Bank of Salem, which also owned two other branches operating as Bank of Portland and Bank of Tigard. A deal to buy Washington Banking Company is pending.

EXECUTIVES

Chairman, Frontier Financial, Frontier Bank, and FFP: Robert J. (Bob) Dickson, age 73
President, CEO, and Director; CEO, Frontier Bank; EVP, FFP: John J. Dickson, age 46, $619,783 pay
EVP and Chief Risk Officer: Ellen Sas
EVP and Chief Credit Officer: Robert W. (Rob) Robinson
Director; President, FFP: Michael J. Clementz, age 63, $353,456 pay (prior to title change)
President and Chief Banking Officer, Frontier Bank: Lyle E. Ryan, $375,496 pay
President, Real Estate Division, Frontier Bank: James W. (Jim) Ries, $351,375 pay
CFO, Frontier Financial and FFP: Carol E. Wheeler, age 50, $224,197 pay
EVP and COO, Frontier Bank: R. James Mathison
EVP, Operations and Human Resources, Frontier Bank: Connie L. Pachek, $288,188 pay
EVP and Cashier, Frontier Bank: Ross S. Maynard
Secretary and Treasurer, Frontier Financial and FFP: James F. (Jim) Felicetty, age 63
Auditors: Moss Adams, LLP

LOCATIONS

HQ: Frontier Financial Corporation
332 SW Everett Mall Way, Everett, WA 98204
Phone: 425-514-0700   **Fax:** 425-514-0718
Web: www.frontierbank.com

PRODUCTS/OPERATIONS

2006 Sales

	$ mil.	% of total
Interest		
Loans, including fees	244.5	92
Investment securities	4.2	2
Federal funds sold	1.4	—
Noninterest		
Service charges	4.2	2
Sale of loans	1.5	—
Other	10.0	4
Total	**265.8**	**100**

COMPETITORS

Bank of America
Cascade Financial
CityBank
Columbia Banking
Horizon Financial
KeyCorp
U.S. Bancorp
Washington Mutual
Wells Fargo

HISTORICAL FINANCIALS

Company Type: Public

Income Statement

			FYE: December 31	
	ASSETS ($ mil.)	NET INCOME ($ mil.)	INCOME AS % OF ASSETS	EMPLOYEES
12/06	3,238.5	68.9	2.1%	721
12/05	2,637.0	51.6	2.0%	663
12/04	2,243.4	43.0	1.9%	—
12/03	2,075.4	39.6	1.9%	—
12/02	1,943.7	36.0	1.9%	558
Annual Growth	**13.6%**	**17.6%**	**—**	**6.6%**

2006 Year-End Financials

Equity as % of assets: 12.2%
Return on assets: 2.3%
Return on equity: 19.9%
Long-term debt ($ mil.): 5.2
No. of shares (mil.): 45.4
Market value ($ mil.): 1,325.6

Dividends
  Yield: 1.7%
  Payout: 32.9%
Sales ($ mil.): 265.8
R&D as % of sales: —
Advertising as % of sales: —

Stock History

NASDAQ (GS): FTBK

	STOCK PRICE ($) FY Close	P/E High/Low		Earnings	PER SHARE ($) Dividends	Book Value
12/06	29.23	21	13	1.52	0.50	8.72
12/05	21.33	19	13	1.21	0.40	10.41
12/04	17.16	18	14	1.02	0.25	13.56
12/03	14.76	16	11	0.94	0.31	11.83
12/02	11.37	16	13	0.83	0.27	10.57
Annual Growth	**26.6%**	**—**	**—**	**16.3%**	**16.7%**	**(4.7%)**

FTI Consulting

When someone has been cooking the books, FTI Consulting has a recipe for recovery. The company is one of the leading providers of forensic accounting and litigation support services in the US. Its experts offer investigative services to companies confronted with problems such as fraud in order to assist them in their legal defense or pursuit of recoveries. FTI also provides consulting services related to corporate finance and restructuring, such as advice on mergers and acquisitions and performance improvement. Other consulting service areas include economics, strategic and financial communications, and technology. FTI's main clients are large business enterprises and major law firms.

FTI has diversified its service offerings and expanded its geographic reach through a number of acquisitions of niche-market firms. It entered the strategic and financial communications field in 2006 when it bought London-based Financial Dynamics for $260 million. (The acquired business changed its name to FD in 2007.)

Outside the US, where the company has offices in about 30 cities, FTI and its subsidiaries maintain facilities in the Asia/Pacific region, Africa, Europe, Latin America, and the Middle East. US-based clients account for the vast majority of the company's sales, however.

EXECUTIVES

Chairman: Dennis J. Shaughnessy, age 60
President, CEO, and Director: Jack B. Dunn IV, age 56
EVP and COO: Dominic (Dom) DiNapoli, age 51
EVP and CFO: Jorge A. Celaya, age 41
EVP and Chief Legal and Risk Management Officer:
John A. MacColl, age 58
EVP and Chief Development Officer:
David G. Bannister, age 51
SVP and General Counsel: Eric Miller
SVP, Controller, and Chief Accounting Officer:
Catherine Freeman, age 51
VP Treasurer: Ronald Reno
Group CEO, Financial Dynamics: Charles Watson
President and CEO, Financial Dynamics US:
Declan Kelly
Director Human Resources: Liz Behrmann
Associate General Counsel and Secretary:
Joanne F. Catanese
Auditors: KPMG LLP

LOCATIONS

HQ: FTI Consulting, Inc.
500 E. Pratt St., Ste. 1400, Baltimore, MD 21202
Phone: 410-951-4800   **Fax:** 410-224-8378
Web: www.fticonsulting.com

PRODUCTS/OPERATIONS

2006 Sales

	$ mil.	% of total
Corporate Finance/Restructuring	212.6	30
Forensic/Litigation	193.3	27
Economic	144.1	20
Technology	117.2	17
Strategic & Financial Communications	40.7	6
Total	**707.9**	**100**

Selected Services and Operating Units

Corporate Finance
    Creditor and Lender Services
    FTI Capital Advisors, LLC
    FTI Palladium Partners (Interim Management)
    Equity Sponsor Services
    Transaction Advisory Services

Economic Consulting
    FTI Helios
    Lexecon
    Network Industries Strategies
Forensic and Litigation Consulting
    Dispute Advisory Services
    Investigations and Forensic Accounting
    Trial Services
    Construction Solutions
    Healthcare
    Intellectual Property
    Insurance
Strategic Communications
    FD
Technology
    Application Solutions
    Technology Consulting
    Technology Services

COMPETITORS

Accenture	EDS
Bain & Company	Ernst & Young Global
BearingPoint	Huron Consulting
Booz Allen	IBM
Boston Consulting	KPMG
Cornerstone Research	LECG
CRA International	McKinsey & Company
Deloitte	Navigant Consulting
Deloitte Consulting	PA Consulting
Economics Research	PricewaterhouseCoopers
Associates	

HISTORICAL FINANCIALS

Company Type: Public

Income Statement

FYE: December 31

	REVENUE ($ mil.)	NET INCOME ($ mil.)	NET PROFIT MARGIN	EMPLOYEES
12/06	707.9	42.0	5.9%	2,079
12/05	539.5	56.4	10.5%	1,338
12/04	427.0	42.9	10.0%	—
12/03	375.7	59.5	15.8%	—
12/02	224.1	37.2	16.6%	769
Annual Growth	**33.3%**	**3.1%**	**—**	**28.2%**

2006 Year-End Financials

Debt ratio: 100.0%
Return on equity: 8.2%
Cash ($ mil.): 91.9
Current ratio: 1.65
Long-term debt ($ mil.): 565.3
No. of shares (mil.): 41.9
Dividends
    Yield: —
    Payout: —
Market value ($ mil.): 1,168.3
R&D as % of sales: —
Advertising as % of sales: —

Stock History

NYSE: FCN

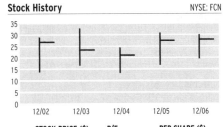

	STOCK PRICE ($) FY Close	P/E High	Low	PER SHARE ($) Earnings	Dividends	Book Value
12/06	27.89	29	19	1.04	—	13.49
12/05	27.44	23	13	1.35	—	11.65
12/04	21.07	24	13	1.01	—	11.68
12/03	23.37	23	12	1.41	—	10.77
12/02	26.77	26	13	1.09	—	11.16
Annual Growth	**1.0%**	**—**	**—**	**(1.2%)**	**—**	**4.8%**

Fuel Tech

Thanks in part to the Clean Air Act, Fuel Tech (formerly Fuel-Tech N.V.) is batting in the clean-up position. Through its Fuel Tech subsidiary, the company sells NOxOUT, equipped with a retrofittable system, for the reduction of nitrogen oxide in boilers, incinerators, furnaces, and other combustion sources. The air pollution control company also makes Fuel Chem to reduce slag formation and corrosion in boilers and furnaces. The company has discontinued marketing its ACUITIV software, which allowed the viewing of complex data in virtual reality. Fuel Tech owns about 6% of Clean Diesel Technologies. Chairman Ralph Bailey owns almost 20% of Fuel Tech.

In November 2005 Fuel Tech won a $6 million contract to install NOxOUT on two 600-megawatt boilers at China Power Investment's Kanshan power plant in the Jiangsu province of China.

EXECUTIVES

Chairman: Ralph E. Bailey, age 84
Deputy Chairman; CEO, Atlantis Components:
Douglas G. Bailey, age 57
President, CEO, and Director: John F. Norris Jr., age 58
SVP, CFO, and Treasurer: Vincent J. (Vince) Arnone, age 44
SVP Advanced Technology and Regulatory Affairs:
Vincent M. Albanese, age 59, $281,138 pay
SVP International Business Development and Project Execution: Michael P. (Mike) Maley, age 50
SVP Sales and Marketing: Stephen P. Brady, age 51
VP, Corporate Secretary, General Counsel, and Director:
Charles W. Grinnell, age 71
VP Business Development and Marketing:
Kevin R. Dougherty, age 46
VP Corporate Development: Nolan R. Schwartz, age 55, $289,800 pay
VP Investor Relations and Corporate Communications:
Tracy H. Krumme, age 40
Auditors: Grant Thornton LLP

LOCATIONS

HQ: Fuel Tech, Inc.
512 Kingsland Dr., Batavia, IL 60510
Phone: 630-845-4500   **Fax:** 630-845-4501
Web: www.fueltechnv.com

Fuel Tech has facilities in Canada, Germany, Italy, Jamaica, the Netherlands, the Netherlands Antilles, and the US.

2006 Sales

	$ mil.	% of total
US	57.6	77
Other countries	17.5	23
Total	**75.1**	**100**

PRODUCTS/OPERATIONS

2006 Sales

	$ mil.	% of total
Nitrogen oxide reduction	46.4	62
Fuel treatment chemical	28.7	38
Total	**75.1**	**100**

COMPETITORS

ALSTOM
Babcock & Wilcox
BASF Catalysts
Clyde Bergemann EEC
Foster Wheeler
Peerless Mfg.
United Air Specialists

HISTORICAL FINANCIALS

Company Type: Public

Income Statement				FYE: December 31
	REVENUE ($ mil.)	NET INCOME ($ mil.)	NET PROFIT MARGIN	EMPLOYEES
12/06	75.1	6.8	9.1%	137
12/05	52.9	7.6	14.4%	104
12/04	30.8	1.6	5.2%	—
12/03	35.7	1.1	3.1%	—
12/02	32.6	3.1	9.5%	84
Annual Growth	23.2%	21.7%	—	13.0%

2006 Year-End Financials

Debt ratio: —
Return on equity: 17.7%
Cash ($ mil.): 32.4
Current ratio: 3.21
Long-term debt ($ mil.): —
No. of shares (mil.): 22.1
Dividends
  Yield: —
  Payout: —
Market value ($ mil.): 544.2
R&D as % of sales: —
Advertising as % of sales: —

Stock History

NASDAQ (GM): FTEK

	STOCK PRICE ($) FY Close	P/E High/Low		PER SHARE ($) Earnings	Dividends	Book Value
12/06	24.64	98	29	0.28	—	2.16
12/05	9.07	31	14	0.33	—	1.43
12/04	4.67	80	49	0.07	—	0.97
12/03	3.55	124	58	0.05	—	0.89
12/02	4.19	52	20	0.14	—	0.86
Annual Growth	55.7%	—	—	18.9%	—	26.0%

G-III Apparel

G-III Apparel Group has the leather part of Stevie Nicks' leather and lace wrapped up. It's best known for making leather jackets under the names G-III, Marvin Richards, Black Rivet, Winlet, Siena Studio, La Nouvelle Renaissance, and other labels, as well as under licensed names. It also makes leather and other pants, skirts, and sportswear. Nearly two-thirds of its sales are generated from licensed apparel it makes for the NFL, NBA, NHL, and MLB teams, as well as for Jones New York, Nine West, and Kenneth Cole. Its customers include department stores, such as Federated, and mass merchants the likes of Wal-Mart. Father and son team Aron and Morris Goldfarb own some 23% of G-III Apparel.

Having been big in licensing for a decade, the company has inked several deals that maintain its strategy and mix of licensed and non-licensed products. G-III bought Jessica Howard Ltd. in May 2007 to extend its reach into dresses and add the Jessica Howard and Eliza J. brand names to its portfolio. Acquiring Industrial Cotton the same month brought expanded junior denim products. The purchases also gave G-III a foothold in new retail outlets, with the brands

selling in Dillard's, Nordstrom, Sears, Kohl's, and Coldwater Creek, among others.

G-III Apparel also acquired two outerwear businesses in 2005 that brought with them the Marvin Richards and Winlit labels. The acquisitions also gave G-III Apparel licenses with Calvin Klein for men's and women's outerwear, St. John Knits for women's outerwear, men and women's outerwear under the Guess? brand name, as well as Ellen Tracy and BCBG by Max Azria.

Wanting to add more Calvins to its drawers, G-III partnered with Calvin Klein, again, in early 2006 and late 2007 when it agreed to make and distribute women's dresses in the US, Canada, and Mexico under the Calvin Klein label and sportswear under the Calvin Klein Performance label for the same markets. A deal that G-III inked with Christian Casey (owner of Sean John) was modified in early 2008. While Casey will continue to make men's and women's items under the Sean John label, the company's license to make junior women's sportswear reverted back to Casey.

G-III does most of its business in the US, with 99% of its business generated within the country's borders.

EXECUTIVES

Chairman and CEO: Morris Goldfarb, age 56, $1,327,160 pay
Vice Chairman; President, Marvin Richards Division: Sammy Aaron, age 47
President: Jeanette Nostra, age 55, $582,212 pay
COO and Secretary: Wayne S. Miller, age 49
CFO and Treasurer: Neal S. Nackman, age 47
VP, Women's Sales Division of G-III Leather Fashions: Deborah Gaertner, age 52, $325,000 pay
Auditors: Ernst & Young LLP

LOCATIONS

HQ: G-III Apparel Group, Ltd.
  512 7th Ave., New York, NY 10018
Phone: 212-403-0500   **Fax:** 212-403-0551
Web: www.g-iii.com

2007 Sales

	% of total
US	99
Non-US	1
Total	**100**

PRODUCTS/OPERATIONS

2007 Sales

	$ mil.	% of total
Licensed	268.9	63
Non-licensed	158.1	37
Total	**427.0**	**100**

Selected Licenses

Calvin Klein
Cole Haan
Ellen Tracy
IZOD
Jones New York
Kenneth Cole Productions
Major League Baseball
National Basketball Association
National Football League
National Hockey League
Nine West
Sean John
Tommy Hilfiger

COMPETITORS

Amerex Group
Armani
Burlington Coat Factory
Columbia Sportswear
The Gap
L.L. Bean
NIKE
North Face
Wilsons The Leather Experts

HISTORICAL FINANCIALS

Company Type: Public

Income Statement				FYE: January 31
	REVENUE ($ mil.)	NET INCOME ($ mil.)	NET PROFIT MARGIN	EMPLOYEES
1/07	427.0	13.2	3.1%	510
1/06	324.1	7.1	2.2%	510
1/05	214.3	0.7	0.3%	—
1/04	224.1	8.4	3.7%	—
1/03	202.6	0.4	0.2%	302
Annual Growth	20.5%	139.7%	—	14.0%

2007 Year-End Financials

Debt ratio: 11.4%
Return on equity: 13.4%
Cash ($ mil.): 12.0
Current ratio: 2.85
Long-term debt ($ mil.): 13.1
No. of shares (mil.): 14.2
Dividends
  Yield: —
  Payout: —
Market value ($ mil.): 307.3
R&D as % of sales: —
Advertising as % of sales: —

Stock History

NASDAQ (GM): GIII

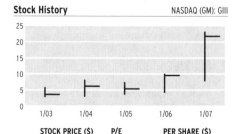

	STOCK PRICE ($) FY Close	P/E High/Low		PER SHARE ($) Earnings	Dividends	Book Value
1/07	21.70	24	8	0.94	—	8.17
1/06	9.53	17	7	0.58	—	6.65
1/05	5.37	121	63	0.06	—	9.20
1/04	6.15	11	4	0.76	—	9.19
1/03	3.59	170	90	0.03	—	8.11
Annual Growth	56.8%	—	—	136.6%	—	0.2%

Gaiam, Inc.

If you're into living a healthy sustainable lifestyle, Gaiam is your kind of company. The name Gaiam (pronounced "guy-um") is a combination of Gaia (the Earth goddess) and "I am." The company's more than 10,000 products (7,000 are proprietary items) include environmentally friendly paraphernalia divided into five categories: Sustainable Economy, Healthy Living, Alternative Healthcare, Personal Development, and Ecological Lifestyles. Top sellers include solar panels, yoga and pilates DVDs, and natural cleaners. Gaiam markets through catalogs, its Web sites, and other retailers (including Costco and Target). CEO Jirka Rysavy, founder of Corporate Express, started Gaiam in 1988; he owns about 34% of the company.

In 2005 Gaiam purchased substantially all of the assets of GoodTimes Entertainment, a creator and distributor of entertainment programming, for approximately $40 million. GoodTimes Entertainment's library consists of about 2,000 titles, including wellness franchises such as The Firm and Tae Bo, children's classics, and numerous theatrical releases. The acquisition raised Gaiam's market share in the fitness/wellness media category to over 40%.

Furthering its penetration of the subscription-based media market, in 2006 the company acquired a 63% stake in Cinema Circle for $6.9 million. Cinema Circle owns Spiritual Cinema Circle, which caters to "spiritual" moviegoers with its subscription-based DVD film club.

EXECUTIVES

Chairman and CEO: Jirka Rysavy, age 53, $296,712 pay
President and Director; CEO, North American Operations: Lynn Powers, age 57, $396,712 pay
CFO and Treasurer: Vilia Valentine, age 47
VP, Operations: Mark Lipien, age 43
VP, Corporate Development and Secretary: John Jackson, age 49
President, New Media: Rob Sussman
President, Worldwide Distribution: Jane Pemberton
Human Resources and Benefits Manager: Jackie Abraham
Auditors: Ehrhardt Keefe Steiner & Hottman PC

LOCATIONS

HQ: Gaiam, Inc.
360 Interlocken Blvd., Broomfield, CO 80021
Phone: 303-222-3600   **Fax:** 303-222-3700
Web: www.gaiam.com

2006 Sales

	$ mil.	% of total
US	206.6	94
International	12.9	6
Total	**219.5**	**100**

PRODUCTS/OPERATIONS

2006 Sales

	$ mil.	% of total
Direct to consumer	125.7	57
Business to business	93.8	43
Total	**219.5**	**100**

Selected Products

Aromatherapy
Back and neck care products
Bedding and bath items
Books
Candles and incense
CDs
Children's clothing
Children's fitness products and information
DVDs
Energy-efficient light bulbs
Energy systems
Exercise equipment
Fitness clothing
Gardening and composting products
Health programs
Herbs and supplements
Magnets
Massage and bodywork products
Meals and snack products
Meditation and spirituality products
Organic cleaning products
Organic cotton bedding
Pest-control products
Pet-care products
Pet food
Pilates information and accessories
Solar panels
Toys
Vitamins and minerals
Water filters and other water-quality products
Wellness information
Yoga information and accessories

COMPETITORS

Alticor	Lands' End
Body Shop	Nature's Sunshine
Coldwater Creek	NIKE
Forever Living	Reebok
GNC	Seventh Generation
Goldhil Home Media	Shaklee
Hain Celestial	Triumph Apparel
Home Depot	Unicity
Intimate Brands	Williams-Sonoma

HISTORICAL FINANCIALS

Company Type: Public

Income Statement

FYE: December 31

	REVENUE ($ mil.)	NET INCOME ($ mil.)	NET PROFIT MARGIN	EMPLOYEES
12/06	219.5	5.6	2.6%	363
12/05	142.5	1.3	0.9%	367
12/04	96.7	(4.6)	—	267
12/03	102.0	(1.0)	—	285
12/02	111.4	5.4	4.8%	241
Annual Growth	**18.5%**	**0.9%**	**—**	**10.8%**

2006 Year-End Financials

Debt ratio: —
Return on equity: 3.4%
Cash ($ mil.): 104.9
Current ratio: 6.25
Long-term debt ($ mil.): —
No. of shares (mil.): 21.7
Dividends
  Yield: —
  Payout: —
Market value ($ mil.): 297.5
R&D as % of sales: —
Advertising as % of sales: —

Stock History

NASDAQ (GM): GAIA

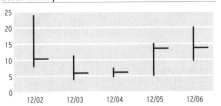

	STOCK PRICE ($) FY Close	P/E High/Low	PER SHARE ($) Earnings	Dividends	Book Value
12/06	13.68	87 43	0.23	—	10.05
12/05	13.51	186 65	0.08	—	7.15
12/04	6.15	— —	(0.32)	—	7.05
12/03	5.95	— —	(0.07)	—	7.55
12/02	10.37	63 21	0.38	—	7.59
Annual Growth	**7.2%**	**— —**	**(11.8%)**	**—**	**7.3%**

GAINSCO, INC.

Although at times it might be more appropriate, you wouldn't call an insurance company LOSSCO, would you? GAINSCO's subsidiaries General Agents Insurance Company of America and MGA Insurance sell personal nonstandard auto insurance in over 40 states. Restructuring its operations, GAINSCO exited all of its commercial lines of business, including auto, garage, liability, property, and specialty lines such as lawyers and educators insurance. The company does much of its business in Florida but has laid the groundwork for sales growth in Arizona, California, Nevada, New Mexico, South Carolina,

and Texas. GAINSCO executives and directors collectively own 70% of the company.

Chairman Robert Stallings controls 23% of GAINSCO; EVP James Reis controls 11%, and director John Goff controls 34% through Goff Moore Strategic Partners.

EXECUTIVES

Chairman: Robert W. Stallings, age 57, $546,719 pay
Vice Chairman: Joel C. Puckett, age 63
President, CEO, and Director: Glenn W. Anderson, age 54, $772,229 pay
EVP and Chief Risk Management Officer: James R. Reis, age 49, $317,159 pay
SVP, Corporate Affairs and Human Resources: Richard M. Buxton, age 58, $205,000 pay
SVP, CFO, and Chief Accounting Officer: Daniel J. Coots, age 55
SVP and Chief Investment Officer: Terence J. Lynch
President, Southwest Region: Brian L. Kirkham
President, Southeast Region: Michael S. Johnston, age 45, $248,000 pay
President, South Central Region: E. Wade Chance
General Counsel and Secretary: John S. Daniels, age 58
Director, Information Technology: Phillip J. West
Auditors: KPMG LLP

LOCATIONS

HQ: GAINSCO, INC.
3333 Lee Pkwy., Ste. 1200, Dallas, TX 75219
Phone: 972-629-4301   **Fax:** 972-629-4302
Web: www.gainsco.com

PRODUCTS/OPERATIONS

2006 Sales

	$ mil.	% of total
Net premiums earned	186.8	90
Agency revenues	12.4	6
Net investment income	7.0	4
Other	0.3	—
Total	**206.5**	**100**

Selected Subsidiaries

DLT Insurance Adjusters, Inc.
GAINSCO Service Corp.
General Agents Insurance Company of America, Inc.
Lalande Financial Group, Inc.
National Specialty Lines, Inc.

COMPETITORS

Allstate
Farmers Group
GEICO
Progressive Corporation
State Farm

HISTORICAL FINANCIALS

Company Type: Public

Income Statement

FYE: December 31

	ASSETS ($ mil.)	NET INCOME ($ mil.)	INCOME AS % OF ASSETS	EMPLOYEES
12/06	289.3	11.4	3.9%	391
12/05	212.2	8.9	4.2%	295
12/04	164.6	5.5	3.3%	—
12/03	185.7	3.4	1.8%	—
12/02	214.4	(8.8)	—	—
Annual Growth	**7.8%**	**—**	**—**	**32.5%**

2006 Year-End Financials

Equity as % of assets: 29.3%
Return on assets: 4.5%
Return on equity: 16.1%
Long-term debt ($ mil.): 45.0
No. of shares (mil.): 24.9
Market value ($ mil.): 198.2
Dividends
  Yield: —
  Payout: —
Sales ($ mil.): 206.5
R&D as % of sales: —
Advertising as % of sales: —

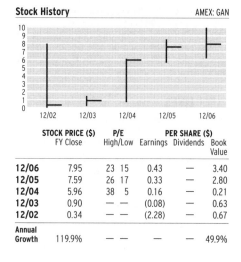

	STOCK PRICE ($) FY Close	P/E High/Low		PER SHARE ($) Earnings	Dividends	Book Value
12/06	7.95	23	15	0.43	—	3.40
12/05	7.59	26	17	0.33	—	2.80
12/04	5.96	38	5	0.16	—	0.21
12/03	0.90	—	—	(0.08)	—	0.63
12/02	0.34	—	—	(2.28)	—	0.67
Annual Growth	119.9%	—	—	—	—	49.9%

Gaming Partners International

This company doesn't care if gamblers win or crap out, as long as they do it using its products. Gaming Partners International is a leading manufacturer of casino gaming products, including dealing shoes, dice, gaming chips, playing cards, and roulette wheels. It also supplies table furniture and layouts for blackjack, poker, baccarat, craps, and other casino games. With manufacturing facilities in the US, Mexico, and France, the company markets its products under the brands Bourgogne et Grasset, Bud Jones, and Paulson to casino operators around the world. Director Elisabeth Carretté owns 49% of Gaming Partners International.

The company continues to look to foreign markets for growth as legalized gambling spreads into more countries. It has been particularly focused on growing its presence in Asia, which now accounts for 45% of sales. Meanwhile, it has placed particular emphasis on its line of gaming chips embedded with radio frequency ID (RFID) technology that allows casinos to ensure the validity of chips in play and discourages counterfeiting.

HISTORY

Paul Endy Sr. distributed cards to legal gaming establishments in California in the 1940s and 1950s. His son, Paul Jr., struck out on his own in 1963 when he bought a bankrupt dice factory in Las Vegas. Over time the company's offerings expanded, and Paul-Son (the name originally differentiated Paul Jr.'s business from his father's) became the big fish in its small market. The business received a big boost when New Jersey legalized gambling (other states soon followed suit), and when Native Americans entered the business to boost tribal income and employment. Paul-Son was able to solidify its hold on the market. Paul Jr.'s son Eric, an audiologist by training, joined the company in 1983.

Paul-Son went public in 1994, but took a beating the next year when gambling operations that

bought equipment from the company on credit folded. With DeBartolo Entertainment the company formed Brand One Marketing in 1997 to market Paul-Son collectible and commemorative chips and playing cards. It bought out DeBartolo's share in 1998. Founder Paul Endy Jr. died the following year, and his son Eric took over the business.

In 2000 Paul-Son won major accounts to provide playing cards to Harrah's Louisiana casino and gambling chips to Trump Casinos-Atlantic City. The following year the company filed a letter of intent to acquire US competitor Bud Jones Co. and its French parent Bourgogne et Grasset (B&G), manufacturers and suppliers of gaming equipment. When the deadline passed, Paul-Son demanded a $1 million termination fee. Arbitration had begun before both companies agreed to reenter talks.

In 2002 Paul-Son and B&G reached a definitive agreement to combine the companies whereby B&G and Bud Jones became wholly owned subsidiaries of Paul-Son. As a result of the combination, Endy stepped down as chairman and CEO and became EVP. B&G director Francois Carretté became chairman, and Gerard Charlier assumed the roles of president and CEO. The following year Paul-Son merged Bud Jones with Paul-Son Gaming Supplies, consolidating the two gaming supply manufacturing units into a single facility.

In 2004 Paul-Son changed its name to Gaming Partners International Corporation to reflect the significant changes the company had undergone since merging with B&G.

EXECUTIVES

President, CEO, and Director: Gérard P. Charlier, age 68, $244,325 pay
CFO: David W. Grimes, age 48, $4,308 pay (partial-year salary)
Chief Legal and Gaming Compliance Officer: Laura McAllister Cox, age 47, $207,692 pay
Corporate Secretary: Gay A. Nordfelt, age 57
Manager Human Resources: Jennifer Jones
Auditors: Deloitte & Touche LLP

LOCATIONS

HQ: Gaming Partners International Corporation
1700 Industrial Rd., Las Vegas, NV 89102
Phone: 702-384-2425   **Fax:** 702-384-1965
Web: www.gpigaming.com

2006 Sales

	$ mil.	% of total
Asia	33.6	45
US	29.3	40
Europe	6.7	9
Other regions	4.3	6
Total	**73.9**	**100**

PRODUCTS/OPERATIONS

2006 Sales

	$ mil.	% of total
Casino chips	53.6	72
Table layouts	5.1	7
Playing cards	4.2	6
Gaming furniture	2.9	4
Dice	2.5	4
Table accessories & other	5.6	7
Total	**73.9**	**100**

COMPETITORS

CHIPCO International	Midwest Game Supply
elixir	Shuffle Master
Jarden	USPCC
Lucky Gaming	

HISTORICAL FINANCIALS

Company Type: Public

Income Statement

	REVENUE ($ mil.)	NET INCOME ($ mil.)	NET PROFIT MARGIN	EMPLOYEES	FYE: December 31
12/06	73.9	5.1	6.9%	760	
12/05	57.1	4.3	7.5%	870	
12/04	44.6	2.6	5.8%	—	
12/03	36.2	1.2	3.3%	—	
12/02	21.9	(2.2)	—	480	
Annual Growth	35.5%	—	—	12.2%	

2006 Year-End Financials

Debt ratio: 8.4%	Dividends
Return on equity: 17.4%	Yield: 0.7%
Cash ($ mil.): 11.6	Payout: 21.0%
Current ratio: 2.29	Market value ($ mil.): 145.6
Long-term debt ($ mil.): 2.8	R&D as % of sales: —
No. of shares (mil.): 8.1	Advertising as % of sales: —

	STOCK PRICE ($) FY Close	P/E High/Low		PER SHARE ($) Earnings	Dividends	Book Value
12/06	17.99	42	14	0.62	0.13	4.03
12/05	11.18	48	19	0.53	0.10	3.29
12/04	20.63	76	13	0.34	—	2.80
12/03	5.75	39	20	0.16	—	2.34
12/02	4.24	—	—	(0.42)	—	2.05
Annual Growth	43.5%	—	—	—	30.0%	18.5%

Gateway Financial

Gateway Financial Holdings wants to be the portal to all things financial in northeastern North Carolina and Virginia's Tidewater region. Subsidiary Gateway Bank & Trust is a full-service bank with some 20 branches offering products including checking and savings accounts, CDs, IRAs, and merchant services. It primarily uses funds from deposits to write real estate loans: Construction loans, commercial mortgages, and commercial loans account for more than 70% of its loan portfolio. It also offers business, consumer, and home equity loans. Subsidiaries Gateway Insurance Services and Gateway Investment Services offer insurance and investment products and services.

Already growing in Virginia as evidenced by the acquisition of C.D. West & Company insurance agency and the purchase of The Bank of Richmond, Gateway Financial plans to expand its operations in the Raleigh, North Carolina area. It expects to open about five branches in the region by 2008.

EXECUTIVES

Chairman, President, and CEO; Chairman and CEO, Gateway Bank & Trust: Daniel B. (Ben) Berry, age 51, $425,000 pay
President and COO: David R. Twiddy, age 48, $250,000 pay
SEVP and Chief Administrative Officer, Gateway Bank & Trust: Donna C. Kitchen
SEVP and CFO: Theodore L. (Teddy) Salter
SEVP and Chief Credit Officer, Gateway Bank & Trust: J. Frank Horne
SEVP and Chief Commercial Banking Officer, Virginia; Market President, Virginia Region, Gateway Bank: Steven C. Layden
President and CEO, Gateway Insurance Services, Inc.: Brian J. Hellenga
President, Gateway Financial Mortgage, Inc.: Kevin Pack
Auditors: Dixon Hughes PLLC

LOCATIONS

HQ: Gateway Financial Holdings, Inc.
1580 Laskin Rd., Virginia Beach, VA 23451
Phone: 757-422-4055   **Fax:** 757-422-4056
Web: www.trustgateway.com

PRODUCTS/OPERATIONS

2006 Sales

	% of total
Interest	
Interest & fees on loans	80
Investment securities available for sale:	
Taxable	6
Other interest & dividends	1
Noninterest	
Service charges on deposit accounts	4
Mortgage operations	2
Insurance operations	3
Brokerage operations	1
Gain on sale of securities	1
Income from bank-owned life insurance	1
Other service charges & fees	1
Total	**100**

COMPETITORS

BB&T	Optimal Group
Commonwealth	Provident Bankshares
Bankshares	RBC Centura Banks
First Citizens BancShares	Shore Financial
Hampton Roads	SuffolkFirst Bank
Bankshares	SunTrust
Heritage Bankshares	TowneBank
Monarch Financial	Wachovia
Old Point Financial	

HISTORICAL FINANCIALS

Company Type: Public

Income Statement

	ASSETS ($ mil.)	NET INCOME ($ mil.)	INCOME AS % OF ASSETS	EMPLOYEES
				FYE: December 31
12/06	1,207.5	5.3	0.4%	327
12/05	882.4	3.9	0.4%	245
12/04	535.7	2.0	0.4%	—
12/03	314.8	1.2	0.4%	—
12/02	231.1	0.6	0.3%	—
Annual Growth	51.2%	72.4%	—	33.5%

2006 Year-End Financials

Equity as % of assets: 9.1%	Dividends
Return on assets: 0.5%	Yield: 1.3%
Return on equity: 5.1%	Payout: 40.4%
Long-term debt ($ mil.): 152.4	Sales ($ mil.): 84.6
No. of shares (mil.): 11.0	R&D as % of sales: —
Market value ($ mil.): 157.3	Advertising as % of sales: —

Stock History

NASDAQ (GM): GBTS

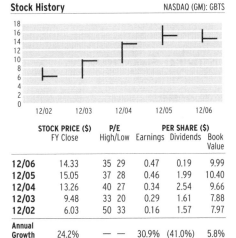

	STOCK PRICE ($) FY Close	P/E High/Low		PER SHARE ($) Earnings	Dividends	Book Value
12/06	14.33	35	29	0.47	0.19	9.99
12/05	15.05	37	28	0.46	1.99	10.40
12/04	13.26	40	27	0.34	2.54	9.66
12/03	9.48	33	20	0.29	1.61	7.88
12/02	6.03	50	33	0.16	1.57	7.97
Annual Growth	24.2%	—	—	30.9%	(41.0%)	5.8%

GB&T Bancshares

Could GB&T stand for Grab 'em, Bag 'em, and Tag 'em? Ever-acquisitive GB&T Bancshares is the multibank holding company for Gainesville Bank & Trust (and its Bank of Athens, Lumpkin County Bank, and Southern Heritage Bank divisions), United Bank & Trust, Community Trust Bank, HomeTown Bank of Villa Rica, First National Bank of the South, First National Bank of Gwinnett, and Mountain State Bank. The community banks serve individuals and businesses through about 30 branches near Atlanta. Loans secured by real estate, including residential and commercial mortgages and construction loans, make up approximately 90% of the company's loan portfolio.

GB&T Bancshares acquired Lumpkin County Bank and Southern Heritage Bank in 2004. The following year it acquired hometown competitor FNBG Bancshares and its First National Bank of Gwinnett subsidiary.

Eager to keep growing, GB&T Bancshares in 2006 bought Georgia's Mountain Bancshares, parent of Mountain State Bank, which has branches in Georgia's Dawson and Forsyth counties, among the fastest-growing counties in the state and the nation.

The acquisitive will now be the acquired: SunTrust Banks is buying GB&T Bancshares in a transaction valued at $153.7 million.

EXECUTIVES

Chairman: Philip A. Wilheit, age 63
Vice Chairman: Samuel L. (Sam) Oliver, age 65
President and CEO, Community Trust Bank: Randall K. (Randy) Taylor
President, CEO, and Director; CEO, Gainesville Bank & Trust: Richard A. Hunt Jr., age 63, $492,900 pay
President and CEO, United Bank & Trust: David T. Sawyer
President and COO, Gainesville Bank & Trust: J. Michael (Mike) Whitmire

EVP and CFO, GB&T Bancshares and Gainesville Bank & Trust: Gregory L. Hamby, age 53, $253,918 pay
EVP and Chief Credit Officer: Sid J. Sims
EVP Corporate Lending, Gainesville Bank & Trust: John B. Stump
SVP Marketing, Gainesville Bank & Trust: W. Michael Banks
Secretary and Director: Alan A. Wayne, age 65
President and CEO, HomeTown Bank of Villa Rica: James I. Owens
President and CEO, First National Bank of the South: Chatfield S. Daniel
President and CEO, First National Bank of Gwinnett: Paul Jones
President and CEO, Mountain State Bank: Spencer Strickland
Auditors: Mauldin & Jenkins, LLC

LOCATIONS

HQ: GB&T Bancshares, Inc.
500 Jesse Jewell Pkwy. SE, Gainesville, GA 30501
Phone: 770-532-1212   **Fax:** 770-531-7368
Web: www.gbtbancshares.com

PRODUCTS/OPERATIONS

2006 Sales

	$ mil.	% of total
Interest		
Loans, including fees	116.6	85
Securities	9.0	7
Other	0.9	—
Noninterest		
Service charges on deposit accounts	6.3	5
Mortgage origination fees	2.7	2
Other	1.6	1
Total	**137.1**	**100**

COMPETITORS

Bank of America
BB&T
Colonial BancGroup
Crescent Banking
Fidelity Southern
Habersham Bancorp
Regions Financial
SunTrust
Wachovia

HISTORICAL FINANCIALS

Company Type: Public

Income Statement

	ASSETS ($ mil.)	NET INCOME ($ mil.)	INCOME AS % OF ASSETS	EMPLOYEES
				FYE: December 31
12/06	1,900.4	9.5	0.5%	505
12/05	1,584.1	12.0	0.8%	452
12/04	1,274.1	9.8	0.8%	—
12/03	944.3	7.7	0.8%	—
12/02	742.0	6.5	0.9%	312
Annual Growth	26.5%	10.0%	—	12.8%

2006 Year-End Financials

Equity as % of assets: 12.3%	Dividends
Return on assets: 0.5%	Yield: 1.6%
Return on equity: 4.4%	Payout: 51.5%
Long-term debt ($ mil.): 127.3	Sales ($ mil.): 137.1
No. of shares (mil.): 14.1	R&D as % of sales: —
Market value ($ mil.): 313.3	Advertising as % of sales: —

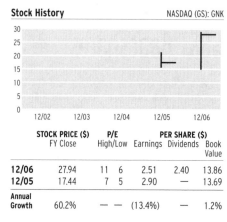
	STOCK PRICE ($) FY Close	P/E High/Low		PER SHARE ($) Earnings	Dividends	Book Value
12/06	22.17	34	30	0.68	0.35	16.51
12/05	21.41	27	20	0.93	0.33	15.54
12/04	24.12	26	17	1.04	0.15	14.84
12/03	18.90	20	13	1.03	0.28	14.25
12/02	14.39	14	10	1.06	0.27	11.35
Annual Growth	11.4%	—	—	(10.5%)	6.7%	9.8%

Genco Shipping and Trading

Marine transportation company Genco Shipping & Trading transports dry cargo in a wet environment. The company maintains a fleet of more than 25 oceangoing dry bulk carriers, which it charters mainly on long-term contracts to shippers of bulk commodities and marine transportation companies. Its fleet has an overall capacity of about 1.9 million deadweight tons (DWT). Genco Shipping's vessels transport cargo such as coal, grain, iron ore, and steel products. Customers include shippers such as BHP Billiton and Cargill and shipping lines such as Lauritzen Bulkers and NYK.

Genco Shipping, which bought its first 15 vessels in 2004 and 2005 from a subsidiary of China National Cereals Oil and Foodstuffs Corp. (COFCO), plans to continue to expand its fleet through acquisitions, and in 2006 and 2007 the company agreed to invest about $1.5 billion in a series of vessel purchases. Once all the deals are done, the company will own more than 30 vessels with an overall carrying capacity of some 2.7 million DWT.

Fleet Acquisition, an entity controlled by investment firm Oaktree Capital Management, owns an 18% stake in Genco Shipping. Company chairman Peter Georgiopoulos, who is also the chairman and CEO of crude oil transporter General Maritime, owns 14%.

EXECUTIVES

Chairman: Peter C. Georgiopoulos, age 46
President: Robert Gerald Buchanan, age 58, $450,000 pay (partial-year salary)
CFO, Principal Accounting Officer, Secretary, and Treasurer: John C. Wobensmith, age 37, $675,000 pay (partial-year salary)
Auditors: Deloitte & Touche LLP

LOCATIONS

HQ: Genco Shipping & Trading Limited
 299 Park Ave., 20th Fl., New York, NY 10171
Phone: 646-443-8550 **Fax:** 646-443-8551
Web: gencoshipping.com

COMPETITORS

A.P. Møller - Mærsk
DryShips Inc.
Eagle Bulk Shipping
Excel Maritime Carriers
Hanjin Shipping
Kawasaki Kisen
Mitsui O.S.K. Lines
Overseas Shipholding Group
Pacific Basin Shipping

HISTORICAL FINANCIALS

Company Type: Public

Income Statement				FYE: December 31
	REVENUE ($ mil.)	NET INCOME ($ mil.)	NET PROFIT MARGIN	EMPLOYEES
12/06	133.2	63.5	47.7%	475
12/05	116.9	54.5	46.6%	408
12/04	1.9	0.9	47.4%	140
Annual Growth	737.3%	740.0%	—	84.2%

2006 Year-End Financials

Debt ratio: 59.0%
Return on equity: 18.1%
Cash ($ mil.): 73.6
Current ratio: 5.81
Long-term debt ($ mil.): 208.4
No. of shares (mil.): 25.5
Dividends
 Yield: 8.6%
 Payout: 95.6%
Market value ($ mil.): 712.6
R&D as % of sales: —
Advertising as % of sales: —

	STOCK PRICE ($) FY Close	P/E High/Low		PER SHARE ($) Earnings	Dividends	Book Value
12/06	27.94	11	6	2.51	2.40	13.86
12/05	17.44	7	5	2.90	—	13.69
Annual Growth	60.2%	—	—	(13.4%)	—	1.2%

Genesee & Wyoming

Genesee & Wyoming once relied on the salt of the earth — hauling salt on a 14-mile railroad for one customer. Now the company owns stakes in about 50 short-line and regional freight railroads that operate over a total of some 10,500 miles of track. The company is North America's #2 operator of short-line railroads, behind RailAmerica. Freight transported by Genesee & Wyoming railroads includes coal, coke, and ores; lumber and forest products; and pulp and paper products. Outside the US, the company has operations in Australia, Bolivia, and Canada. Chairman Mortimer Fuller, great-grandson of founder Edward L. Fuller, controls a 40% voting stake in Genesee & Wyoming.

The company hopes to continue to grow by acquiring railroads, not only in the US but also in other markets. In June 2006 Genesee & Wyoming bought out joint venture partner Wesfarmers to take full ownership of the companies'

South Australia operations. At the same time, the companies sold their railroad business in Western Australia.

Genesee & Wyoming expanded significantly in 2005 by buying 14 short-line railroads from Rail Management Corp. for $243 million in cash and $1.7 million in assumed debt. The 14 railroads operate over a total of more than 900 miles of track, mainly in the southeastern US. Genesee & Wyoming added three more railroads in the southeastern US in 2006, gaining more than 40 miles of track in Alabama, Georgia, and Virginia.

In 2007 the company moved to liquidate its railroad business in Mexico, Ferrocarriles Chiapas-Mayab, which suffered extensive infrastructure damage from Hurricane Stan in 2005. Later in the year, it announced it was acquiring Maryland Midland Railway for about $29 million. The deal will give Genesee & Wyoming an additional 63 miles of track and 10 locomotives.

Besides its railroad operations, Genesee & Wyoming provides freight car switching and related services for industrial companies that own railroad facilities.

EXECUTIVES

Chairman: Mortimer B. Fuller III, age 64
Vice Chairman: Charles N. Marshall, age 64, $537,000 pay
President, CEO, and Director: John C. Hellmann, age 36
COO: James W. Benz, age 58, $395,000 pay
CFO: Timothy J. Gallagher, age 44
EVP, Corporate Development: Mark W. Hastings
EVP, Government and Industry Affairs: Robert Grossman, age 63
SVP, Administration and Human Resources: Shayne L. Magdoff
VP, Accounting and Controller: Gerald A. Sattora
VP, Corporate Development and Treasurer: Matthew O. Walsh
General Counsel and Secretary: Allison M. Fergus, age 33
Chief Human Resources Officer: Matthew C. Bush
Director, Corporate Communications: Michael E. Williams
Auditors: PricewaterhouseCoopers LLP

LOCATIONS

HQ: Genesee & Wyoming Inc.
 66 Field Point Rd., Greenwich, CT 06830
Phone: 203-629-3722 **Fax:** 203-661-4106
Web: www.gwrr.com

PRODUCTS/OPERATIONS

2006 Sales

	$ mil.	% of total
Freight		
Pulp & Paper	69.5	14
Coal, Coke & Ores	59.4	12
Metals	36.7	8
Minerals & Stone	36.2	8
Lumber & Forest Products	34.9	7
Farm & Food Products	30.0	6
Chemicals-Plastics	24.9	5
Petroleum Products	22.7	5
Autos & Auto Parts	7.0	1
Intermodal	1.7	—
Other	12.9	3
Nonfreight		
Railcar switching	65.7	14
Car hire and rental	22.5	5
Fuel sales to third parties	13.8	3
Demurrage and storage	12.4	3
Car repair services	5.8	1
Other	22.7	5
Total	**478.9**	**100**

COMPETITORS

Arkansas Best	FedEx
Burlington Northern	Heartland Express
Santa Fe	J.B. Hunt
Canadian National Railway	Kansas City Southern
Canadian Pacific Railway	Landstar System
Celadon	Norfolk Southern
Central Freight Lines	OmniTRAX
Conrail	RailAmerica
CSX	Union Pacific

HISTORICAL FINANCIALS

Company Type: Public

Income Statement

FYE: December 31

	REVENUE ($ mil.)	NET INCOME ($ mil.)	NET PROFIT MARGIN	EMPLOYEES
12/06	478.9	134.0	28.0%	2,677
12/05	385.4	50.1	13.0%	3,513
12/04	303.8	37.6	12.4%	3,093
12/03	244.8	28.7	11.7%	2,889
12/02	209.5	25.6	12.2%	2,829
Annual Growth	23.0%	51.3%	—	(1.4%)

2006 Year-End Financials

Debt ratio: 46.4%
Return on equity: 29.2%
Cash ($ mil.): 240.2
Current ratio: 1.68
Long-term debt ($ mil.): 241.3
No. of shares (mil.): 37.6

Dividends
 Yield: —
 Payout: —
Market value ($ mil.): 987.5
R&D as % of sales: —
Advertising as % of sales: —

Stock History

NYSE: GWR

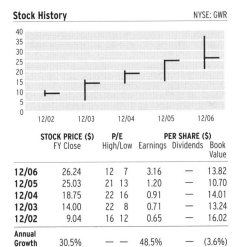

	STOCK PRICE ($) FY Close	P/E High/Low		PER SHARE ($) Earnings	Dividends	Book Value
12/06	26.24	12	7	3.16	—	13.82
12/05	25.03	21	13	1.20	—	10.70
12/04	18.75	22	16	0.91	—	14.01
12/03	14.00	22	8	0.71	—	13.24
12/02	9.04	16	12	0.65	—	16.02
Annual Growth	30.5%	—	—	48.5%	—	(3.6%)

GeoEye, Inc.

Look up and say "cheese." GeoEye, formerly known as ORBIMAGE Holdings, provides satellite-collected Earth imagery and geospatial information for commercial and government organizations. It operates three high-resolution imaging satellites (IKONOS, OrbView-2, and OrbView-3) that collect detailed land, sea, and atmospheric images, which the company processes and distributes. The company's imagery and information is used for a variety of applications, including mapping, environmental monitoring, urban planning, resource management, homeland defense, national security, and emergency preparedness. GeoEye also offers advanced image processing and production software.

In early 2006 ORBIMAGE acquired top competitor Space Imaging in a deal valued at $58.5 million. The combined company then began operating as GeoEye. A year later it purchased M.J. Harden Associates, a digital aerial imagery specialist, from General Electric.

The US government is GeoEye's largest customer — specifically the National Geospatial-Intelligence Agency (NGA). GeoEye produces and transmits up to 50,000 images each month through its satellite operations and image processing centers.

ORBIMAGE got its start in 1993; originally an operating division of Orbital Sciences, it was spun off as a separate company in 1997. The company underwent restructuring under Chapter 11 bankruptcy protection due to expenses related to legal disputes with Orbital Sciences over license agreements with the former parent. The company settled its differences with Orbital Sciences and emerged from bankruptcy late in 2003.

EXECUTIVES

Chairman: James A. Abrahamson, age 74
President, CEO, and Director: Matthew M. O'Connell, age 54, $1,307,465 pay
COO: William Schuster, age 56, $284,938 pay
EVP and CFO: Henry Dubois, age 45
SVP, General Counsel, and Secretary: William L. Warren, age 41, $204,930 pay
VP National Security and Intelligence Programs: Gary G. Adkins, age 56
VP, Finance and Corporate Controller: Tony A. Anzilotti, age 45
VP International Sales: Paolo E. Colombi, age 58
VP Corporate Communications: Mark E. Brender, age 57
VP Product Engineering: Ray Helmering, age 69
VP Engineering: Lee Demitry, age 54, $221,883 pay
VP North American Sales: Thornton W. (Bill) Wilt Jr., age 61
VP Human Resources: Angela Galyean, age 44
Auditors: BDO Seidman, LLP

LOCATIONS

HQ: GeoEye, Inc.
 21700 Atlantic Blvd., Dulles, VA 20166
Phone: 703-480-7500 **Fax:** 703-450-9570
Web: www.geoeye.com

GeoEye, formerly ORBIMAGE Holdings, operates facilities in Alaska, Oklahoma, West Virginia, and Sweden.

2006 Sales

	% of total
US	54
Other	46
Total	**100**

COMPETITORS

DigitalGlobe
Orbital Sciences
Trimble Navigation

HISTORICAL FINANCIALS

Company Type: Public

Income Statement

FYE: December 31

	REVENUE ($ mil.)	NET INCOME ($ mil.)	NET PROFIT MARGIN	EMPLOYEES
12/06	151.2	23.4	15.5%	318
12/05	40.7	(24.3)	—	295
12/04	31.0	(24.7)	—	133
Annual Growth	120.8%	—	—	54.6%

2006 Year-End Financials

Debt ratio: 150.9%
Return on equity: 15.6%
Cash ($ mil.): 199.7
Current ratio: 2.38
Long-term debt ($ mil.): 246.1
No. of shares (mil.): 17.5

Dividends
 Yield: —
 Payout: —
Market value ($ mil.): 338.1
R&D as % of sales: —
Advertising as % of sales: —

Stock History

NASDAQ (GM): GEOY

	STOCK PRICE ($) FY Close	P/E High/Low		PER SHARE ($) Earnings	Dividends	Book Value
12/06	19.35	19	14	1.08	—	9.33
12/05	10.95	—	—	(1.50)	—	7.85
12/04	18.50	—	—	(3.80)	—	8.66
Annual Growth	2.3%	—	—	—	—	3.8%

GeoMet, Inc.

Hoping that high oil prices will drive its geometric financial growth, GeoMet is engaged in the exploration and production of natural gas from coalbed methane properties in the Cahaba Basin in Alabama and the Appalachian Basin in West Virginia and Virginia. The methane gas explorer is developing 77,000 acres in the Gurnee field in the Cahaba Basin and in the Pond Creek field in the Appalachian Basin. GeoMet also controls 203,000 net acres of coalbed methane assets in British Columbia, Colorado, Louisiana, and West Virginia. In 2006 the company reported 325.7 billion cu. ft. of estimated proved reserves. Director Howard Keenan, general partner of Yorktown Energy Partners, owns nearly 42% of GeoMet.

GeoMet was founded in 1985 as a consulting company to the coalbed methane industry. It became an operator and developer of coalbed methane properties in 1993. In addition to accelerating drilling projects in its core areas, the company is also seeking out opportunistic acquisitions of coal bed methane producing properties.

EXECUTIVES

Chairman, President, and CEO: J. Darby Seré, age 60, $345,000 pay
EVP and CFO: William C. Rankin, age 58, $270,000 pay
SVP, Exploration and Director: Philip G. Malone, age 59, $214,500 pay
SVP, Operations: Brett S. Camp, age 49, $214,500 pay
VP, Chief Accounting Officer, and Controller: Tony Oviedo
Auditors: Deloitte & Touche LLP

LOCATIONS

HQ: GeoMet, Inc.
 909 Fannin, Ste. 1850, Houston, TX 77010
Phone: 713-659-3855 **Fax:** 713-571-6394
Web: www.geometinc.com

PRODUCTS/OPERATIONS

2006 Sales

	$ mil.	% of total
Gas sales	44.9	77
Gas marketing	13.0	23
Operating fees & other	0.2	—
Total	**58.1**	**100**

COMPETITORS

Belden & Blake	Quest Resource
CNX Gas	Sharpe Resources
Galaxy Energy	St. Mary Land &
Peabody Energy	Exploration

HISTORICAL FINANCIALS

Company Type: Public

Income Statement

FYE: December 31

	REVENUE ($ mil.)	NET INCOME ($ mil.)	NET PROFIT MARGIN	EMPLOYEES
12/06	58.1	17.3	29.8%	77
12/05	42.0	(1.6)	—	63
12/04	21.5	3.8	17.7%	—
12/03	12.0	2.5	20.8%	—
Annual Growth	**69.2%**	**90.6%**	**—**	**22.2%**

2006 Year-End Financials

Debt ratio: 29.0%
Return on equity: 11.3%
Cash ($ mil.): 5.7
Current ratio: 0.91
Long-term debt ($ mil.): 60.8
No. of shares (mil.): 38.7
Dividends
　Yield: —
　Payout: —
Market value ($ mil.): 402.3
R&D as % of sales: —
Advertising as % of sales: —

Stock History

NASDAQ (GM): GMET

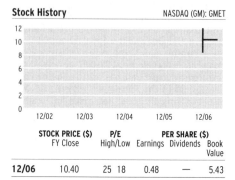

	STOCK PRICE ($) FY Close	P/E High/Low	PER SHARE ($) Earnings	Dividends	Book Value
12/06	10.40	25 18	0.48	—	5.43

GeoPharma, Inc.

GeoPharma makes a world of health care products, from generic antibiotics to weight loss aids and nutritionals. Its main business — contract manufacturing of nutritional supplements — is done through subsidiary Innovative Health Products. Another subsidiary, Libi Labs, focuses on private-label nutraceutical and cosmeceutical manufacturing. GeoPharma also develops some of its own products, including dietary supplements through Breakthrough Engineered Nutrition (also known as DelMar Labs) and generic drugs through Belcher Pharmaceuticals. Its marketed diet products include appetite suppressants DEX-L10 and Cortiloss, which are distributed through mass retailers, drug stores, and health food stores.

GeoPharma's Go2PBM unit offers pharmacy benefit management services to health insurers. However, all of Go2PBM's revenues came from a contract with a managed care plan called CarePlus Health, a relationship that the two companies terminated in 2007.

GeoPharma's Belcher Pharmaceuticals subsidiary has been trying to break into the generic drugmaking business, with several compounds in development or awaiting FDA approval. Among other things, it has patented a stabilizing technology to be used with Levothyroxine, a thyroid drug that Abbott Labs sells under the brand name Synthroid. Belcher is developing versions of stabilized Levothyroxine for both human and veterinary use. Additionally, the company has won marketing approval for Mucotrol, a treatment for oral lesions associated with cancer treatments. Mucotrol, which works by coating the inside of the mouth, is approved as a medical device, rather than a drug. It is marketed in the US by Cura Pharmaceuticals.

GeoPharma has expanded its drug development and its branded nutritional businesses through a number of acquisitions. In 2005 it bought Consolidated Pharmaceutical Group, a developer of generic antibiotics, and created American Antibiotics to oversee the newly acquired operations; it owns a 51% stake in American Antibiotics.

The company acquired Dynamic Health Products, a distributor of sports nutrition products and dietary supplements, in 2007. Dynamic Health Products is led by two members of the Taneja family, the family that also helms GeoPharma. Health care entrepreneur Jugal Taneja is the principal shareholder and chairman of both firms; his sons, Mihir Taneja and Mandeep Taneja, are the CEOs of GeoPharma and Dynamic Health Products, respectively.

Before the ink on the Dynamic Health Products deal had dried, GeoPharma announced another acquisition, purchasing drug delivery company EZ-Med Technologies; EZ-Med develops chewables that make bitter drugs more palatable, as well as a line of veterinary nutritional supplements.

EXECUTIVES

Chairman: Jugal K. Taneja, age 64
CEO, Secretary, and Director: Mihir K. Taneja, age 33, $266,425 pay
President and Director: Kotha S. Sekharam, age 53, $214,076 pay
VP, CFO, and Director: Carol Dore-Falcone, age 43, $201,053 pay
General Counsel and Director: Mandeep K. Taneja, age 34
Auditors: Brimmer, Burek & Keelan LLP

LOCATIONS

HQ: GeoPharma, Inc.
　6950 Bryan Dairy Rd., Largo, FL 33777
Phone: 727-544-8866　　**Fax:** 727-544-4386
Web: www.onlineihp.com

PRODUCTS/OPERATIONS

2007 Sales

	$ mil.	% of total
Manufacturing	27.3	46
PBM	20.1	34
Distribution	12.1	20
Pharmaceuticals	0.3	—
Total	**59.8**	**100**

Selected Subsidiaries

Belcher Pharmaceuticals, Inc.
Breakthrough Engineered Nutrition, Inc.
Dynamic Health Products, Inc.
Go2PBM Services, Inc.
IHP Marketing, Inc.
Libi Labs, Inc.

COMPETITORS

AOL
Bactolac Pharmaceutical
BJ's Wholesale Club
Carrington Labs
Costco Wholesale
CVS/Caremark
Enzymatic Therapy, Inc.
Express Scripts
Jenny Craig
Leiner Health Products
NAI
Nature's Sunshine
NBTY
Nexgen
Nutraceutical
NutriSystem
Reliv'
Shaklee
Unicity
USANA Health Sciences
Walgreen
Yahoo!

HISTORICAL FINANCIALS

Company Type: Public

Income Statement

FYE: March 31

	REVENUE ($ mil.)	NET INCOME ($ mil.)	NET PROFIT MARGIN	EMPLOYEES
3/07	59.8	2.5	4.2%	180
3/06	49.7	1.8	3.6%	150
3/05	28.2	(0.9)	—	103
3/04	23.0	1.1	4.8%	83
3/03	14.7	1.1	7.5%	68
Annual Growth	**42.0%**	**22.8%**	**—**	**27.6%**

2007 Year-End Financials

Debt ratio: 12.5%
Return on equity: 10.8%
Cash ($ mil.): 0.7
Current ratio: 1.76
Long-term debt ($ mil.): 3.1
No. of shares (mil.): 10.2
Dividends
　Yield: —
　Payout: —
Market value ($ mil.): 45.0
R&D as % of sales: —
Advertising as % of sales: —

Stock History

NASDAQ (CM): GORX

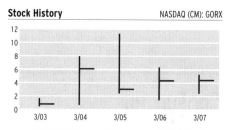

	STOCK PRICE ($) FY Close	P/E High/Low	PER SHARE ($) Earnings	Dividends	Book Value
3/07	4.40	27 13	0.19	—	2.42
3/06	4.34	45 11	0.14	—	2.13
3/05	3.05	—　—	(0.17)	—	1.71
3/04	6.10	72　7	0.11	—	2.18
3/03	0.81	11　4	0.15	1.10	0.59
Annual Growth	**52.7%**	**—　—**	**6.1%**	**—**	**42.1%**

GFI Group

A financial matchmaker, GFI Group makes sure the party of the first part gets together with the party of the second part. The company is an inter-dealer brokerage that acts as an intermediary for institutional clients such as banks, brokers, insurance companies, hedge funds, and utilities. The firm trades primarily in derivatives, which tend to be less liquid and thus harder to trade than other assets, and also offers data and analytical tools for market analysis. Its FENIC software is used for the foreign exchange derivatives market as well as credit, freight, and energy. Jersey Partners, which is controlled by chairman and CEO Michael Gooch, owns about 44% of GFI.

GFI made headlines in August 2005 when it acquired leading oil products broker Starsupply Petroleum LLC. GFI embarked on a joint venture with London-based shipbroker A.C.M. Shipping in 2002.

EXECUTIVES

Chairman and CEO: Michael Gooch, age 48, $1,100,000 pay
President and Director: Colin Heffron, age 44, $1,510,000 pay
COO: Ronald (Ron) Levi, age 45, $1,297,166 pay (prior to promotion)
CFO: James A. Peers, age 56, $710,000 pay
EVP, Corporate Development: J. Christopher Giancarlo, age 47
Senior Managing Director and Head of E-Commerce: Jurgen Breuer, age 41, $952,159 pay
Senior Managing Director and Head of Credit Product Brokerage, North America: Donald P. (Don) Fewer, age 43
General Counsel and Corporate Secretary: Scott Pintoff, age 36
Global Human Resources Director: Sheena Griffiths, age 40
Public Relations Manager: Alan Bright
Investor Relations Manager: Chris Ann Casaburri
Auditors: Deloitte & Touche LLP

LOCATIONS

HQ: GFI Group Inc.
100 Wall St., New York, NY 10005
Phone: 212-968-4100   **Fax:** 212-968-4124
Web: www.gfigroup.com

GFI has offices in New York City; Sugarland, Texas; and Englewood, NJ; it also has offices in Hong Kong, London, Paris, Singapore, Sydney, and Tokyo.

2006 Sales

	% of total
North America	46
Europe	45
Asia-Pacific	9
Total	**100**

PRODUCTS/OPERATIONS

2006 Sales

	$ mil.	% of total
Brokerage		
Agency commissions	557.9	75
Principal transactions	151.2	20
Analytics and market data	18.7	3
Interest	9.1	1
Contracts & other	10.3	1
Total	**747.2**	**100**

COMPETITORS

BGC Partner
Cantor Fitzgerald
eSpeed
ICAP
Interactive Brokers
Susquehanna International
VIEL

HISTORICAL FINANCIALS

Company Type: Public

Income Statement

FYE: December 31

	REVENUE ($ mil.)	NET INCOME ($ mil.)	NET PROFIT MARGIN	EMPLOYEES
12/06	747.2	61.1	8.2%	1,438
12/05	533.6	48.1	9.0%	1,151
12/04	385.0	23.1	6.0%	—
12/03	265.8	14.5	5.5%	—
12/02	275.2	12.3	4.5%	—
Annual Growth	**28.4%**	**49.3%**	**—**	**24.9%**

2006 Year-End Financials

Debt ratio: 27.3%
Return on equity: 21.5%
Cash ($ mil.): 189.5
Current ratio: —
Long-term debt ($ mil.): 90.3
No. of shares (mil.): 28.7
Dividends
  Yield: —
  Payout: —
Market value ($ mil.): 1,786.8
R&D as % of sales: —
Advertising as % of sales: —

Stock History

NASDAQ (GS): GFIG

	STOCK PRICE ($) FY Close	P/E High/Low		PER SHARE ($) Earnings	Dividends	Book Value
12/06	62.26	32	21	2.09	—	11.52
12/05	47.43	30	13	1.74	—	8.54
Annual Growth	**31.3%**	**—**	**—**	**20.1%**	**—**	**34.9%**

Glacier Bancorp

Glacier Bancorp serves Big Sky Country. The company owns more than a dozen community banks, including Glacier Bank, Western Security Bank, Big Sky Western Bank, Citizens State Bank, and 1st Bank. Together they serve individuals, small to midsized businesses, not-for-profits, and public entities in Montana, Idaho, Utah, Washington, and Wyoming through nearly 90 branches. Investment services are offered through Raymond James Financial. Glacier Bancorp's lending activities consist mostly of commercial real estate loans (about 30% of the banks' portfolio) and business loans (more than 25%).

The company's strategy is to grow its business through selective acquisitions. To that end, it bought First National Bank of Morgan located in Morgan County, Utah, and Montana-based bank holding company Citizens Development in 2006. Glacier Bancorp purchased North Side State Bank in 2007, then merged it into 1st Bank, Glacier's Evanston, Wyoming-based banking subsidiary.

EXECUTIVES

Chairman, Glacier Bancorp and Glacier Bank: Everit A. Sliter, age 68
President, CEO, and Director: Michael J. (Mick) Blodnick, age 54, $498,438 pay
EVP and Chief Administrative Officer: Don Chery
SVP and CFO: Ronald J. (Ron) Copher, age 50
SVP, Information Technology: Mark D. MacMillan
SVP, Credit Administration: Barry L. Johnston
SVP, Human Resources: Robin S. Roush
SVP, Operations: Marcia L. Johnson
VP and Controller: Donald B. McCarthy
Director; Chairman, First Security Bank of Missoula: Allen J. Fetscher, age 61
President and CEO, First Security Bank of Missoula: William L. Bouchee, age 64, $108,060 pay
Director; President, CEO, and Director, Mountain West Bank: Jon W. Hippler, age 62, $328,508 pay
Chairman, Glacier Bank of Whitefish: Michael J. Gwiazdon
Chairman, Mountain West Bank: Charles R. Nipp
Chairman, Western Security Bank: Ruben R. Day
Auditors: BKD, LLP

LOCATIONS

HQ: Glacier Bancorp, Inc.
49 Commons Loop, Kalispell, MT 59901
Phone: 406-751-4200   **Fax:** 406-751-4729
Web: www.glacierbancorp.com

PRODUCTS/OPERATIONS

2006 Sales

	$ mil.	% of total
Interest income		
Commercial loans	119.2	39
Real estate loans	52.2	17
Consumer & other loans	40.3	13
Securities & other	41.6	14
Noninterest income		
Service charges & fees	37.1	12
Gain on sale of loans	10.8	4
Other	4.0	1
Total	**305.2**	**100**

COMPETITORS

BancWest
Eagle Bancorp
First Citizens Banc Corp
First Interstate
Sterling Financial (WA)
U.S. Bancorp
Wells Fargo

HISTORICAL FINANCIALS

Company Type: Public

Income Statement

FYE: December 31

	ASSETS ($ mil.)	NET INCOME ($ mil.)	INCOME AS % OF ASSETS	EMPLOYEES
12/06	4,467.7	61.1	1.4%	1,356
12/05	3,706.3	52.4	1.4%	1,125
12/04	3,010.7	44.6	1.5%	935
12/03	2,739.6	38.0	1.4%	885
12/02	2,281.3	32.4	1.4%	809
Annual Growth	**18.3%**	**17.2%**	**—**	**13.8%**

2006 Year-End Financials

Equity as % of assets: 10.2%
Return on assets: 1.5%
Return on equity: 15.5%
Long-term debt ($ mil.): 283.8
No. of shares (mil.): 52.3
Market value ($ mil.): 1,278.3
Dividends
  Yield: 1.8%
  Payout: 35.5%
Sales ($ mil.): 305.2
R&D as % of sales: —
Advertising as % of sales: —

Stock History

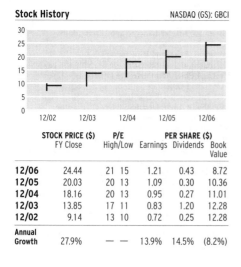

	STOCK PRICE ($) FY Close	P/E High/Low		PER SHARE ($) Earnings	Dividends	Book Value
12/06	24.44	21	15	1.21	0.43	8.72
12/05	20.03	20	13	1.09	0.30	10.36
12/04	18.16	20	13	0.95	0.27	11.01
12/03	13.85	17	11	0.83	1.20	12.28
12/02	9.14	13	10	0.72	0.25	12.28
Annual Growth	27.9%	—	—	13.9%	14.5%	(8.2%)

GlobalSCAPE, Inc.

GlobalSCAPE is pretty cute, for a software company. With packages like CuteFTP and CuteSITE Builder, GlobalSCAPE provides content management, file management, and Web site development tools for businesses and individuals. GlobalSCAPE's software can be downloaded from its Web site, and the company sells CD-ROM versions in Fry's and other retail stores. Its CuteFTP and CuteFTP Pro products, which enable file transfers via the Internet and other networks, account for about 70% of sales. Formed in 1996 as the Internet subsidiary of ATSI Communications, GlobalSCAPE became independent in 2002, when investors Thomas Brown and David Mann (who collectively own 70% of the company) acquired a controlling interest.

EXECUTIVES

Chairman: Thomas W. Brown, age 64
President, CEO, and Director: Charles R. (Randy) Poole, age 64
VP, CFO, and Treasurer: Kelly E. Simmons, age 52
VP and CTO: Gregory Hoffer, age 35
VP Operations: Timothy J. (Tim) Barton, age 42
VP Sales: Jeffrey Gehring, age 51
VP Investor Relations and Business Operations: K. Earl Posey, age 64
VP Professional Services: Doug Conyers
VP Marketing: Ellen Ohlenbusch
Chief Scientist: Tsachi (Chuck) Shavit, age 50
Auditors: PMB Helin Donovan, LLP

LOCATIONS

HQ: GlobalSCAPE, Inc.
6000 Northwest Pkwy., Ste. 100,
San Antonio, TX 78249
Phone: 210-308-8267   **Fax:** 210-308-8297
Web: www.globalscape.com

PRODUCTS/OPERATIONS

2006 Sales

	$ mil.	% of total
Software	9.4	85
Services	1.6	15
Total	**11.0**	**100**

Selected Software

CuteFTP (file transfer protocol software)
CuteFTP Pro (FTP for information technology professionals)
CuteHTML (text-based HTML editor for creating Web pages)
CuteMAP (image-mapping tool for creating Web site navigation grpahics)
CuteSITE Builder (Web site development application)
CuteZIP (file compression program for file transfer and storage)
Enhanced File Transfer Server
PureCMS (Web content management)
Secure FTP Server
SnapEdit (Web site creation and publishing software)
Web Survey (program for conducting surveys on the Web)

COMPETITORS

Avivo
CrownPeak Technology
Ektron
FileNet
IBM Software
Interwoven
Ipswitch
iUpload
MarketTools
Microsoft
Open Text
RealNetworks
Vignette

HISTORICAL FINANCIALS

Company Type: Public

Income Statement

	REVENUE ($ mil.)	NET INCOME ($ mil.)	NET PROFIT MARGIN	EMPLOYEES
12/06	11.0	2.0	18.2%	56
12/05	6.7	1.5	22.4%	41
12/04	4.9	0.2	4.1%	39
12/03	4.8	(0.6)	—	35
12/02	5.3	(0.6)	—	37
Annual Growth	20.0%	—	—	10.9%

FYE: December 31

2006 Year-End Financials

Debt ratio: 32.1%
Return on equity: 34.8%
Cash ($ mil.): 4.6
Current ratio: 1.75
Long-term debt ($ mil.): 3.1
No. of shares (mil.): 16.5
Dividends
  Yield: —
  Payout: —
Market value ($ mil.): 48.0
R&D as % of sales: —
Advertising as % of sales: —

Stock History

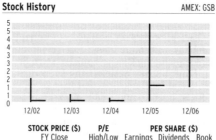

	STOCK PRICE ($) FY Close	P/E High/Low		PER SHARE ($) Earnings	Dividends	Book Value
12/06	2.91	31	9	0.12	—	0.58
12/05	1.11	54	2	0.09	—	0.14
12/04	0.16	30	11	0.01	—	0.03
12/03	0.16	—	—	(0.05)	—	0.02
12/02	0.15	—	—	(0.05)	—	0.07
Annual Growth	109.9%	—	—	—	—	70.8%

Globalstar, Inc.

Is the success of another mobile phone network written in the stars? Globalstar hopes so. The satellite communications company bets on simplicity with a "bent pipe" design: Because its earthbound gateways connect to terrestrial phone networks, the system avoids complex in-orbit switching and satellite-to-satellite transmissions envisioned for other networks. It serves up voice and data using digital CDMA (code division multiple access) technology developed by Globalstar co-founder QUALCOMM. The firm's satellites bounce calls from special mobile phones back to ground-based gateways connected to traditional phone networks. Private equity firm Thermo Capital Partners owns 63% of Globalstar; QUALCOMM owns 7%.

In 2007 Globalstar made public the problems facing its aging satellites, including a reduced availability of two-way voice and data communications as well as reduced call duration. Facing the possibility of completely losing two-way voice and data service, the company has accelerated its launch of spare satellites and continues to seek solutions to the problem.

Globalstar has predicted that unless it finds a solution, and if the problems continue and worsen, all the company's satellites launched between 1998 and 2000 will cease to support two-way communications, severely impacting the company's services. It has also offered pricing incentives to prevent a massive exodus of customers frustrated by service, and non-service, woes. Globalstar has discovered that while the competition to provide telephone service in the world's most remote regions is sparse, so are the customers.

The company, which relies on such traditional cellular partners as Vodafone and China Mobile (Hong Kong) to provide retail service, acts as a wholesale supplier of network capacity.

HISTORY

Ford Aerospace, a subsidiary of Ford Motor Company, had the concept of developing mobile communications for automobiles in 1986, but the idea was soon abandoned. In 1990 Ford Aerospace was acquired by Loral Corp. and the satellite manufacturing unit, based in Palo Alto, California, was renamed Space Systems/Loral (SS/Loral).

A year later Loral and QUALCOMM announced Globalstar, an $850 million, 48-satellite system designed to compete with Motorola's Iridium project (which shut down in 2000 but reemerged as Iridium Satellite, snatched from bankruptcy by a defense contract).

Incorporated in 1994, the venture went public the next year as Globalstar Telecommunications (a holding company and general partner of operating unit Globalstar, L.P.). Loral and Lockheed Martin merged in 1996, giving Lockheed Martin a 20% stake in Globalstar. Loral's space and communications interests, including Globalstar, transferred to Loral Space & Communications.

In early 1998 Globalstar launched its first four satellites; days later, QUALCOMM chairman Irwin Jacobs placed a call to Globalstar CEO Bernard Schwartz. The San Diego-to-New York phone call validated the use of QUALCOMM's code division multiple access (CDMA) technology. Three more launches of four satellites each quickly followed. However, a rocket malfunction on another launch cost the company 12 satellites.

Globalstar began 1999 with two successful launches of four satellites each, and completed the launch of the satellite constellation in 2000. That year it commenced commercial operations in several countries. The company raised hackles among doubters, however, when it drew down a $250 million bank line of credit, then immediately defaulted — leaving such partners as QUALCOMM and Lockheed Martin (who had guaranteed the loan) to repay.

In 2001 Globalstar suspended payments on its debt to conserve cash for operations. Schwartz stepped down as chairman and CEO that year, and Inmarsat veteran Olof Lundberg took over.

The company cut its workforce by more than 70% in order to maintain enough cash to continue operations, and in 2001 it began negotiating with creditors on a restructuring plan. In 2002 Globalstar, L.P. filed for Chapter 11 bankruptcy protection under the shadow of $3.3 billion in debt.

The next year Thermo Capital agreed to pay $43 million for a controlling stake in the company (with the remaining equity distributed among creditors) and Globalstar came out of bankruptcy in 2004 with no debt and about 100,000 subscribers. That same year Jay Monroe was elected chairman; he became CEO in 2005.

EXECUTIVES

Chairman and CEO: James (Jay) Monroe III, age 52
Interim SVP Strategic Initiatives and Space Operations; President, Global Operations: Anthony J. (Tony) Navarra, age 59
SVP Engineering and Ground Operations: Robert D. (Bob) Miller, age 43
SVP, International Sales, Marketing and Customer Care; General Manager, Globalstar Canada: Steven F. Bell, age 42
SVP Sales and Marketing: Dennis C. Allen, age 56
VP and CFO: Fuad Ahmad, age 37
VP Engineering and Product Development: Paul A. Monte, age 48
VP Legal and Regulatory Affairs: William F. (Bill) Adler, age 61
Secretary and Director: Richard S. Roberts, age 61
Media Contact: Dean Hirasawa
Human Resources Specialist: Carla Filipe
Auditors: Crowe Chizek and Company LLP

LOCATIONS

HQ: Globalstar, Inc.
461 S. Milpitas Blvd., Milpitas, CA 95035
Phone: 408-933-4000   **Fax:** 408-933-4100
Web: www.globalstar.com

2006 Sales

	% of total
Service	
US	34
Canada	24
Europe	4
Central & South America	3
Others	2
Subscriber equipment	
US	17
Canada	6
Europe	4
Central & South America	3
Others	3
Total	**100**

PRODUCTS/OPERATIONS

2006 Sales

	% of total
Service revenue	
Mobile voice & data	52
Fixed voice & data	6
Satellite data modems	1
Asset tracking & monitoring	1
Independent gateway operators	6
Other	1
Subscriber equipment sales	
Mobile equipment	17
Fixed equipment	5
Data equipment	1
Accessories/misc.	10
Total	**100**

Selected Partners

AXONN, LLC
Guardian Mobility Corporation
QUALCOMM
Space Systems/Loral, Inc.
Spatial Data, Inc.
WaveCall Communications, Inc.

COMPETITORS

ICO Global Communications
Inmarsat
Iridium Satellite
Mobile Satellite Ventures
Optus

HISTORICAL FINANCIALS

Company Type: Public

Income Statement

FYE: December 31

	REVENUE ($ mil.)	NET INCOME ($ mil.)	NET PROFIT MARGIN	EMPLOYEES
12/06	136.7	23.6	17.3%	349
12/05	127.2	18.7	14.7%	—
12/04	84.4	0.4	0.5%	—
12/03	60.2	(266.4)	—	—
12/02	0.0	(55.2)	—	148
Annual Growth	—	—	—	23.9%

2006 Year-End Financials

Debt ratio: 0.2%
Return on equity: 14.2%
Cash ($ mil.): 43.7
Current ratio: 1.95
Long-term debt ($ mil.): 0.4
No. of shares (mil.): 72.5
Dividends
  Yield: —
  Payout: —
Market value ($ mil.): 1,009.1
R&D as % of sales: —
Advertising as % of sales: —

Stock History

NASDAQ (GM): GSAT

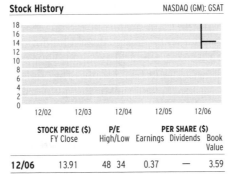

	STOCK PRICE ($) FY Close	P/E High/Low	PER SHARE ($) Earnings	Dividends	Book Value
12/06	13.91	48 34	0.37	—	3.59

GMX Resources

The natural resources in productive, hydrocarbon-rich geological basins are the target for GMX Resources. The Oklahoma-based independent oil and natural gas company explores on more than 19,244 combined net acres located in the Sabine Uplift in Texas and Louisiana, and the Tatum basin in New Mexico. With 96 net producing wells, in 2006 GMX Resources reported proved reserves of 258.4 billion cu. ft. of natural gas equivalent. It has a large inventory of drilling and recompletion projects with an estimated 181.9 billion cu. ft. of natural gas equivalent of proved undeveloped reserves. Ken L. Kenworthy Jr. and Ken L. Kenworthy Sr. each own about 6% of the company.

President and petroleum geologist Ken Kenworthy Jr. and his father Ken L. Kenworthy Sr. founded GMX Resources in 1998. The company is pursuing a strategy of developing its proved undeveloped properties in East Texas.

EXECUTIVES

President, CEO, and Director: Ken L. Kenworthy Jr., age 50, $225,000 pay
VP Gas Marketing: Keith Leffel, age 58
VP Land Department: Gary D. Jackson, age 57, $44,333 pay
CFO, Secretary, and Treasurer: James (Jim) Merrill, age 39
Land Manager: Kyle Kenworthy
Operations Manager: Rick Hart Jr., age 51
Land Division Order Analyst: Debra Barker
Data Base Analyst: Bill Welch
Production Analyst: Diane Newman
Reservoir Engineer: Tim Benton
Drilling and Completions: Charles Pope
Staff Accountant: Ken Kenworthy III
Office Manager and Administrator, Public Relations and Payroll: Amber Croisant
Auditors: KPMG LLP

LOCATIONS

HQ: GMX Resources Inc.
9400 N. Broadway, Ste. 600,
Oklahoma City, OK 73114
Phone: 405-600-0711   **Fax:** 405-600-0600
Web: www.gmxresources.com

2006 Net Acreage

	% of total
East Texas/Louisiana	99
Southeast New Mexico	1
Total	**100**

PRODUCTS/OPERATIONS

2006 Proved Reserves

	% of total
Natural gas	94
Crude oil	6
Total	**100**

COMPETITORS

BP
Cabot Oil & Gas
Chevron
Devon Energy
Exxon Mobil
Frontier Oil
Royal Dutch Shell
Southwestern Energy

HISTORICAL FINANCIALS

Company Type: Public

Income Statement

FYE: December 31

	REVENUE ($ mil.)	NET INCOME ($ mil.)	NET PROFIT MARGIN	EMPLOYEES
12/06	32.0	9.0	28.1%	99
12/05	19.2	7.2	37.5%	16
12/04	7.8	1.4	17.9%	11
12/03	5.4	0.5	9.3%	8
12/02	6.0	(0.4)	—	16
Annual Growth	52.0%	—	—	57.7%

2006 Year-End Financials

Debt ratio: 31.6%
Return on equity: 9.3%
Cash ($ mil.): 6.1
Current ratio: 0.47
Long-term debt ($ mil.): 41.6
No. of shares (mil.): 11.2

Dividends
  Yield: —
  Payout: —
Market value ($ mil.): 399.1
R&D as % of sales: —
Advertising as % of sales: —

Stock History

NASDAQ (GM): GMXR

	STOCK PRICE ($) FY Close	P/E High/Low	PER SHARE ($) Earnings	Dividends	Book Value
12/06	35.50	79 39	0.64	—	11.70
12/05	36.00	54 8	0.79	—	6.14
12/04	6.97	44 13	0.19	—	4.02
12/03	4.01	56 8	0.08	—	3.44
12/02	1.92	— —	(0.07)	—	3.30
Annual Growth	107.4%	— —	—	—	37.2%

Golden Star Resources

Gold gets top billing at Golden Star Resources. The company's main assets are in southern Ghana, in West Africa's Ashanti gold belt, and include the Bogoso, Prestea, and Wassa properties. Overall, the company has proved and probable reserves of about 4 million ounces of gold. In addition, the company has interests in gold exploration projects elsewhere in Africa (Congo, Cote d'Ivoire, Mali, Sierra Leone) and South America (Chile, Peru, Suriname). In 2005 Golden Star expanded in Africa by acquiring St. Jude Resources for $118 million. Golden Star owned a controlling stake in EURO Ressources, until late 2006 when it sold most of its stake in the company.

EXECUTIVES

Chairman: Ian A. MacGregor, age 72
Interim President and Interim CEO:
  Thomas G. (Tom) Mair, age 51
Interim CFO and Interim Compliance Officer:
  Roger Palmer, age 57
VP Wassa: Richard Q. Gray, age 48
VP Corporate Development and Investor Relations:
  Bruce Higson-Smith, age 46, $201,000 pay
General Manager Bogosa/Prestea: Colin J. S. Belshaw, age 52, $113,000 pay
VP Exploration: Douglas A. (Doug) Jones, age 51, $177,000 pay
VP Sustainability: Mark Thorpe
VP Technical Services: Peter Bourke
VP Ghana: Daniel M. A. Owiredu, age 39
VP Human Resources and Administration: Ted Strickler
Treasurer and Interim Corporate Secretary:
  Bryant Veazey
Auditors: PricewaterhouseCoopers LLP

LOCATIONS

HQ: Golden Star Resources Ltd.
  10901 W. Toller Dr., Ste. 300, Littleton, CO 80127
Phone: 303-830-9000   **Fax:** 303-830-9094
Web: www.gsr.com

COMPETITORS

AngloGold Ashanti
Barrick Gold
IAMGOLD
Newmont Mining

HISTORICAL FINANCIALS

Company Type: Public

Income Statement

FYE: December 31

	REVENUE ($ mil.)	NET INCOME ($ mil.)	NET PROFIT MARGIN	EMPLOYEES
12/06	128.7	57.9	45.0%	1,800
12/05	95.5	(13.5)	—	1,500
12/04	65.0	2.6	4.0%	1,150
12/03	64.4	13.4	20.8%	1,000
12/02	38.8	6.8	17.5%	1,084
Annual Growth	35.0%	70.8%	—	13.5%

2006 Year-End Financials

Debt ratio: 17.7%
Return on equity: 14.5%
Cash ($ mil.): 34.8
Current ratio: 1.31
Long-term debt ($ mil.): 71.4
No. of shares (mil.): 207.9

Dividends
  Yield: —
  Payout: —
Market value ($ mil.): 613.3
R&D as % of sales: —
Advertising as % of sales: —

Stock History

AMEX: GSS

	STOCK PRICE ($) FY Close	P/E High/Low	PER SHARE ($) Earnings	Dividends	Book Value
12/06	2.95	14 8	0.28	—	1.95
12/05	2.64	— —	(0.09)	—	1.90
12/04	4.01	373 170	0.02	—	1.53
12/03	6.97	79 13	0.11	—	1.49
12/02	1.87	23 8	0.09	—	0.47
Annual Growth	12.1%	— —	32.8%	—	42.6%

Goodrich Petroleum

From deep in the mystic Miocene sands and the good rich rocks of ancient Mother Earth, Goodrich Petroleum brings forth oil and gas. The independent exploration and production company delves into formations dating to the Miocene and Frio Age in southern Louisiana, where it has most of its proved reserves. The company also operates in the Cotton Valley trend in Texas and Louisiana, and it leases acreage in Michigan. Goodrich Petroleum owns interests in 139 active oil and gas wells and has estimated proved reserves of 206.2 billion cu. ft. of natural gas equivalent. Chairman Patrick Malloy owns 19% of the company; director Josiah Austin, 20%.

In a strategic move to boost its reserves and production, Goodrich Petroleum has launched a development drilling program in the Cotton Valley trend of East Texas and Northwest Louisiana.

In 2007 the company acquired drilling and development rights in 16,800 gross acres in the Angelina River play in Nacogdoches and Angelina counties in Texas, boosting its gross acreage in that area to 68,675 acres.

EXECUTIVES

Chairman: Patrick E. Malloy III, age 64
Vice Chairman and CEO: Walter G. (Gil) Goodrich, age 48, $330,000 pay
President, COO and Director: Robert C. Turnham Jr., age 49, $275,000 pay
EVP and CFO: David R. Looney, age 50, $168,173 pay
EVP: Mark E. Ferchau, age 53, $250,000 pay
VP Geology: Andrew W. Bagot
VP Geophysics: Kenneth A. Jeffers
VP Land: James G. Marston III
VP and Controller: Jan L. Schott, age 37
Auditors: KPMG LLP

LOCATIONS

HQ: Goodrich Petroleum Corporation
  808 Travis St., Ste. 1320, Houston, TX 77002
Phone: 713-780-9494   **Fax:** 713-780-9254
Web: www.goodrichpetroleum.com

Goodrich Petroleum has holdings in Louisiana, Michigan, and Texas.

PRODUCTS/OPERATIONS

2006 Sales

	% of total
Louis Dreyfus Corporation	35
Shell Trading	15
Other customers	50
Total	**100**

COMPETITORS

Abraxas Petroleum
Anadarko Petroleum
Barnwell Industries
Black Hills
Cabot Oil & Gas
Dorchester Minerals
Petrohawk Energy
Pioneer Natural Resources
Range Resources

HISTORICAL FINANCIALS

Company Type: Public

Income Statement

	REVENUE ($ mil.)	NET INCOME ($ mil.)	NET PROFIT MARGIN	EMPLOYEES
12/06	116.2	1.6	1.4%	84
12/05	68.3	(17.5)	—	64
12/04	47.3	18.5	39.1%	52
12/03	32.7	3.7	11.3%	37
12/02	19.1	0.2	1.0%	37
Annual Growth	57.1%	68.2%	—	22.7%

2006 Year-End Financials

Debt ratio: 99.3%
Return on equity: 0.8%
Cash ($ mil.): 19.8
Current ratio: 0.65
Long-term debt ($ mil.): 201.5
No. of shares (mil.): 28.2
Dividends
  Yield: —
  Payout: —
Market value ($ mil.): 1,020.9
R&D as % of sales: —
Advertising as % of sales: —

Stock History

NYSE: GDP

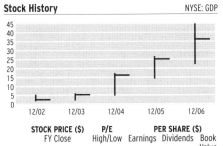

	STOCK PRICE ($) FY Close	P/E High/Low		Earnings	PER SHARE ($) Dividends	Book Value
12/06	36.18	—	—	(0.24)	—	7.27
12/05	25.15	—	—	(0.78)	—	7.32
12/04	16.21	—	—	(0.88)	—	3.17
12/03	5.23	38	16	0.15	—	2.60
12/02	2.50	—	—	(0.03)	—	2.61
Annual Growth	95.0%	—	—	—	—	29.1%

Graham Corporation

You're not crackers if you know that Graham Corporation takes the biscuit when it comes to helping companies make beer, soap, and other products. The company makes vacuum systems, pumps, compressors, and heat exchangers designed to create vacuums, condense steam, or produce heat. Graham sells its equipment to manufacturers in the petroleum, plastics, chemicals, food processing, and other industries, where its gear is used in processes ranging from power generation to brewing beer and making soap. The company sells its products directly and through independent sales representatives worldwide.

Graham Corporation has seen demand for its products increase in recent years across the globe, largely due to oil and gas and other energy industries. In US and Western European markets an emphasis on fuel sources other than crude oil has led to the creation of new facilities utilizing products similar to the company's pumps, condensers, vacuums, and heat transfer products. Additionally, increased demand for consumer products in emerging markets has also led to a rise in manufacturing facilities. Graham has been attempting to address those markets

through geographic expansion as well as increasing its production capacity.

Graham Corporation was founded in 1983 as the successor company to Graham Manufacturing Co., Inc., which was incorporated in 1936 under the leadership of Harold Graham.

EXECUTIVES

Chairman: Jerald D. Bidlack, age 72
President, CEO, and Director: James R. Lines, age 46, $249,764 pay
VP Finance and Administration, and CFO: J. Ronald Hansen, age 61, $252,222 pay
VP Operations: Alan E. Smith, age 41
Corporate Secretary and Director: Cornelius S. Van Rees, age 79
Auditors: Deloitte & Touche LLP

LOCATIONS

HQ: Graham Corporation
  20 Florence Ave., Batavia, NY 14020
Phone: 585-343-2216   **Fax:** 585-343-1177
Web: www.graham-mfg.com

2007 Sales

	$ mil.	% of total
US	33.0	50
Middle East	15.2	23
Asia	11.1	17
Canada	2.8	4
Australia & New Zealand	1.6	3
Mexico	0.6	1
South America	0.6	1
Western Europe	0.6	1
Africa	0.1	—
Other	0.2	—
Total	**65.8**	**100**

PRODUCTS/OPERATIONS

2007 Sales

	$ mil.	% of total
Heat transfer equipment	28.3	43
Vacuum equipment	26.7	41
Other	10.8	16
Total	**65.8**	**100**

Selected Products

Helical coil exchangers
Liquid ring vacuum pumps and compressors
Plate and frame exchangers
Steam jet ejector vacuum systems
Surface condensers

COMPETITORS

Amsted	IDEX
Connell	Ingersoll-Rand
Cooper Industries	Parker Hannifin HPD
Dover Corporation	Pfeiffer Vacuum
Haskel	Weatherford International

HISTORICAL FINANCIALS

Company Type: Public

Income Statement

FYE: March 31

	REVENUE ($ mil.)	NET INCOME ($ mil.)	NET PROFIT MARGIN	EMPLOYEES
3/07	65.8	5.8	8.8%	265
3/06	55.2	3.6	6.5%	250
3/05	41.3	(2.9)	—	243
3/04	43.3	(1.1)	—	—
3/03	49.4	0.1	0.2%	—
Annual Growth	7.4%	176.0%	—	4.4%

2007 Year-End Financials

Debt ratio: 0.2%
Return on equity: 20.1%
Cash ($ mil.): 15.1
Current ratio: 2.21
Long-term debt ($ mil.): 0.1
No. of shares (mil.): 3.9
Dividends
  Yield: 0.6%
  Payout: 6.8%
Market value ($ mil.): 51.2
R&D as % of sales: —
Advertising as % of sales: —

Stock History

AMEX: GHM

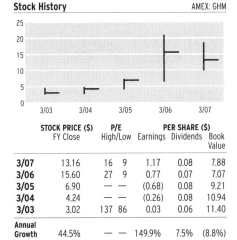

	STOCK PRICE ($) FY Close	P/E High/Low		Earnings	PER SHARE ($) Dividends	Book Value
3/07	13.16	16	9	1.17	0.08	7.88
3/06	15.60	27	9	0.77	0.07	7.07
3/05	6.90	—	—	(0.68)	0.08	9.21
3/04	4.24	—	—	(0.26)	0.08	10.94
3/03	3.02	137	86	0.03	0.06	11.40
Annual Growth	44.5%	—	—	149.9%	7.5%	(8.8%)

Green Bankshares

Green Bankshares (formerly Greene County Bancshares) is the holding company for GreenBank (the erstwhile Greene County Bank), which operates nearly 50 branches in eastern and central Tennessee and across the North Carolina border. The bank focuses on real estate lending, with commercial mortgages making up approximately 60% of its loan portfolio and residential mortgages adding almost another 20%. Its deposit products include checking and savings accounts and CDs. In 2007 the company bought Civitas BancGroup and its Cumberland Bank subsidiary, which added about a dozen branches in the Nashville area.

GreenBank subsidiary Superior Financial Services operates eight consumer finance facilities in the bank's market area. Through other units, the bank operates a subprime auto lending office and a title agency location. Another unit, President's Trust, offers trust and money management services.

Green Bankshares plans to continue to grow by acquiring other companies or bank branches located within a 300-mile radius of its home base of Greene County, Tennessee.

EXECUTIVES

Chairman and CEO, Greene County Bancshares and Greene County Bank: R. Stan Puckett, age 51, $117,810 pay
President, COO, and Director, Greene County Bancshares and Greene County Bank: Kenneth R. (Kent) Vaught, age 42, $65,450 pay
EVP and CFO: James E. Adams, age 62, $200,000 pay
President, GCB Acceptance: Jeff Smith
Regional President, Sumner, Rutherford and Lawrence Counties and Director: Ronald E. (Ed) Mayberry, age 53, $174,900 pay
President, Superior Financial Services: David L. Raulerson

SVP and CIO, Greene County Bancshares and Greene County Bank: William C. (Bill) Adams, age 50
SVP and Chief Credit Officer, Greene County Bank: Stephen L. (Steve) Droke, age 57, $182,000 pay
SVP and Regional Executive, Cocke County, TN, Greene County, TN, and Madison County, NC: Allen R. Jones
SVP and Retail Banking Manager, Greene County Bank: G. Frank Snyder, age 47
SVP and Division Manager, GCB Mortgage; President, Fairway Title: Cathy Neubert
SVP and Chief Human Resources Officer, Greene County Bank: Steve D. Ottinger, age 57
Auditors: Dixon Hughes PLLC

LOCATIONS

HQ: Green Bankshares, Inc
100 N. Main St., Greeneville, TN 37743
Phone: 423-639-5111   **Fax:** 423-787-1235
Web: www.mybankconnection.com

PRODUCTS/OPERATIONS

2006 Sales

	$ mil.	% of total
Interest		
Loans, including fees	114.5	83
Taxable securities	2.3	2
Other	0.6	—
Noninterest		
Service charges & fees	15.0	11
Mortgage banking	1.1	1
Other	4.6	3
Total	**138.1**	**100**

Selected Subsidiaries

Greene County Bank
  Fairway Title Company
  GCB Acceptance Corporation
  Superior Financial Services, Inc.

Selected Banking Divisions

American Fidelity Bank
Bank of Athens
Bank of Bulls Gap
Bank of Lawrence County
Bank of Niota
Clacksville Community Bank
Cocke County Bank
Community Bank of Loudon County
Community Trust Bank
First Bristol Bank
First Independent Bank
Greene County Bank
Hamblen County Bank
Hawkins County Bank
Middle Tennessee Bank & Trust
President's Trust
Rutherford Bank and Trust
Sullivan County Bank
Washington County Bank

COMPETITORS

Bank of America	RBC Centura Banks
BB&T	Regions Financial
First Horizon	SunTrust

HISTORICAL FINANCIALS

Company Type: Public

Income Statement

FYE: December 31

	ASSETS ($ mil.)	NET INCOME ($ mil.)	INCOME AS % OF ASSETS	EMPLOYEES
12/06	1,772.7	21.3	1.2%	609
12/05	1,620.0	14.2	0.9%	561
12/04	1,233.4	12.0	1.0%	474
12/03	1,108.5	10.2	0.9%	451
12/02	899.4	9.8	1.1%	386
Annual Growth	**18.5%**	**21.4%**	**—**	**12.1%**

2006 Year-End Financials

Equity as % of assets: 10.4%	Dividends
Return on assets: 1.3%	Yield: 1.6%
Return on equity: 12.1%	Payout: 29.9%
Long-term debt ($ mil.): 13.4	Sales ($ mil.): 138.1
No. of shares (mil.): —	R&D as % of sales: —
Market value ($ mil.): —	Advertising as % of sales: —

Stock History

NASDAQ (GS): GCBS

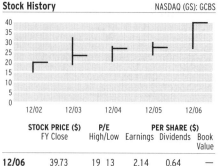

	STOCK PRICE ($) FY Close	P/E High/Low		PER SHARE ($) Earnings	Dividends	Book Value
12/06	39.73	19	13	2.14	0.64	—
12/05	27.36	17	14	1.71	—	—
12/04	26.80	18	13	1.55	—	—
12/03	23.28	22	13	1.47	—	—
12/02	19.75	14	10	1.43	—	—
Annual Growth	**19.1%**	**—**	**—**	**10.6%**	**—**	**—**

Green Mountain Coffee Roasters

Green Mountain Coffee Roasters' business amounts to more than a hill of beans. The company offers about 180 varieties of coffee, cocoa, and tea, which it sells to wholesale customers including supermarkets, convenience stores, resorts, and office-delivery services. Among its customers are ExxonMobil's convenience stores nationwide and McDonald's restaurants in New England and the Albany, New York area. Green Mountain's coffee is also sold under the Newman's Own Organics brand, as well as its namesake Green Mountain Coffee label. The company also sells the Keuring single-cup brewing systems for office and home use.

Supermarket and convenience store sales account for about 40% of the company's coffee sales. Green Mountain's flagship customers, such as Ben & Jerry's Homemade, Wild Oats Markets, Nestlé Waters North America, and Sodexho, have improved the company's visibility and aided its expansion across the US from its roots on the East Coast.

The purchase of Keurig has proven to be a smart move for Green Mountain. Sales for the company's Keurig segment in 2007 increased more than 78% when compared to 2006.

Chairman and CEO Robert Stiller owns about 32% of Green Mountain.

HISTORY

In 1981 Robert Stiller had his first cup of Green Mountain coffee at a small Vermont coffee shop. He was so impressed, he bought the one-store company (using proceeds from the sale of E-Z Wider, the marijuana-rolling-paper-business he co-founded in 1971). Stiller sought a wider market, and in 1984 he began generating word-of-mouth business by donating coffee to charities and civic groups and placing mail-order ads. By 1985 Green Mountain Coffee had four stores and was turning a profit.

Using direct-mail sales as a vanguard, Green Mountain continued its efforts to build a multi-channel distribution network. It was successful: Supermarkets began selling Green Mountain coffees, and institutions such as the Harvard Club began serving them. The company added retail locations in the late 1980s and early 1990s and went public in 1993. It had 12 stores by 1994, but earnings suffered as Green Mountain's expansion outpaced its sales growth.

The company began selling its products online in 1995, and Business Express Airlines began serving Green Mountain coffee on its flights in the US and Canada. Delta Air Lines' shuttle service followed suit the next year. Green Mountain signed a five-year agreement with Mobil Oil (later, ExxonMobil) in 1997 to provide coffee at its On The Run convenience stores.

Green Mountain inked a deal in 1998 with American Skiing Company to supply its nine US ski resorts, including Vermont's Killington and Sugarbush resorts. Also that year it expanded its organic coffee line, revamped its Web site, and began closing or selling its retail operations to concentrate on its wholesale business; all stores were closed by August 1999. Also in 1999 Green Mountain partnered with Keurig to offer one-cup brewing varieties of its coffees.

In 2000 the company agreed to supply coffee to more than 900 (up from nearly 500) ExxonMobil corporately owned convenience stores; as part of the deal, Green Mountain also became the recommended coffee to about 13,000 ExxonMobil dealer and franchise store locations. In mid-2001 Green Mountain purchased the Frontier Organic Coffee brand from Frontier Natural Products Co-op for about $2.4 million.

Green Mountain began selling coffee under the Newman's Own name in 2003. That same year, the company signed an agreement with Hain Celestial Group to sell a line of teas.

In 2004 the company expanded its Vermont manufacturing and distribution facility with a 52,000-sq.-ft. warehouse and packaging plant. The added space boosted Green Mountain annual production capacity from 17 million pounds of coffee to 50 million pounds. Also in 2004, the company announced plans to sell Heifer Hope Blend, an organic coffee that generates income for Heifer Project International. The organization provides support and training for coffee farmers in Guatemala.

Green Mountain has pinned its growth hopes to the trend of "single-cup" brewers. The company had been a minority owner of single-cup brewing-system manufacturer Keurig since 2002. In 2006 Green Mountain acquired the remaining 65% of Keurig that it did not already own for $104 million.

That year it also announced that in conjunction with International Paper, it created an environmentally friendly coffee cup made of corn, natural paper, and water, which, unlike traditional paper cups, will breakdown into organic matter after use. Green Mountain plans to use the new cup in all of its US outlets.

EXECUTIVES

Chairman: Robert P. (Bob) Stiller, age 64, $627,175 pay
COO: Richard Scott McCreary, age 48, $358,844 pay
VP, CFO, Secretary, and Treasurer:
Frances G. (Fran) Rathke, age 47, $311,897 pay
VP and CIO: James K. (Jim) Prevo, age 54
VP Corporate Social Responsibility:
Michael (Mike) Dupee, age 39
VP Development; Chairman, Keurig:
Stephen J. (Steve) Sabol, age 46
VP Environmental Affairs: Paul Comey, age 57
VP Human Resources and Organizational Development:
Kathryn S. (Kathy) Brooks, age 52, $196,226 pay
VP Sales: James E. (Jim) Travis, age 44, $293,838 pay
VP Marketing: Thomas J. (T.J.) Whalen, age 36
VP Supply Chain Operations:
Jonathan C. (Jon) Wettstein, age 59
Investor Services Coordinator: Maureen Martin
President, Keurig: Nicholas (Nick) Lazaris, age 57
President, CEO, and Director:
Lawrence J. (Larry) Blanford, age 54
Auditors: PricewaterhouseCoopers LLP

LOCATIONS

HQ: Green Mountain Coffee Roasters, Inc.
33 Coffee Ln., Waterbury, VT 05676
Phone: 802-244-5621   **Fax:** 802-244-5436
Web: www.greenmountaincoffee.com

PRODUCTS/OPERATIONS

2007 Sales

	% of total
Green Mountain coffee	64
Keurig	36
Total	**100**

2007 Green Mountain Coffee Shipped

	% of total
Office coffee service	27
Supermarkets	24
Convenience stores	21
Foodservice	20
Consumer direct	4
Resellers	4
Total	**100**

COMPETITORS

Bucks County Nut and Coffee	Kraft Foods
Cafe Britt Coffee	Mars, Incorporated
Caribou Coffee	Nestlé
The Coffee Bean	Peet's
Community Coffee	Procter & Gamble
Diedrich Coffee	Republic of Tea
Dunkin	Sara Lee
Farmer Bros.	Starbucks
Fireside Coffee	Tully's Coffee
Hawaii Coffee	Van Houtte

HISTORICAL FINANCIALS

Company Type: Public

Income Statement				FYE: Last Saturday in September
	REVENUE ($ mil.)	NET INCOME ($ mil.)	NET PROFIT MARGIN	EMPLOYEES
9/07	341.6	12.8	3.7%	995
9/06	225.3	8.4	3.7%	849
9/05	161.5	9.0	5.6%	676
9/04	137.4	7.8	5.7%	608
9/03	116.7	6.3	5.4%	573
Annual Growth	**30.8%**	**19.4%**	**—**	**14.8%**

2007 Year-End Financials

Debt ratio: 90.9%
Return on equity: 14.7%
Cash ($ mil.): 3.2
Current ratio: 1.54
Long-term debt ($ mil.): 90.1
No. of shares (mil.): 23.5
Dividends
  Yield: —
  Payout: —
Market value ($ mil.): 781.3
R&D as % of sales: —
Advertising as % of sales: —

Stock History

NASDAQ (GS): GMCR

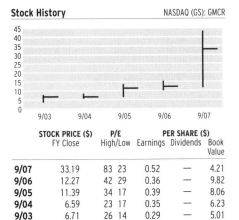

	STOCK PRICE ($) FY Close	P/E High/Low		PER SHARE ($) Earnings	Dividends	Book Value
9/07	33.19	83	23	0.52	—	4.21
9/06	12.27	42	29	0.36	—	9.82
9/05	11.39	34	17	0.39	—	8.06
9/04	6.59	23	17	0.35	—	6.23
9/03	6.71	26	14	0.29	—	5.01
Annual Growth	**49.1%**	**—**	**—**	**15.7%**	**—**	**(4.3%)**

Greenfield Online

Greenfield Online harvests marketing data using the Internet. The company provides survey research services, gathering demographic data over the Web from its panel of more than 1 million people. It performs surveys to track brand awareness and test new advertising campaigns for its clients, as well as to measure consumer interest in new products and services. Its Ciao subsidiary provides comparison shopping services featuring consumer products such as computers, electronics, and vehicles, primarily to the European market. Greenfield Online's clients mostly include consulting and market research firms such as Taylor Nelson Sofres and GfK, and its Ciao subsidiary also counts eBay and Google as major clients.

In 2005 the company greatly expanded its European footprint and panel offerings with the purchases of Rapidata.net, Zing Wireless, and Ciao. At the end of that year, Greenfield Online announced its plans to "rightsize" the company which included closing offices in San Francisco, and Durham, as well as reducing its head count in its Encino office. In all, the company cut almost 40 positions from its rolls in 2006.

Founded as a unit of Greenfield Consulting in 1994, Greenfield Online was spun off in 1999 and went public in 2004; Greenfield Consulting was later acquired by The Kantar Group, the marketing services division of advertising conglomerate WPP.

EXECUTIVES

Chairman: Joel R. Mesznik, age 63
President, CEO, and Director: Albert Angrisani, age 57
EVP, CFO, and Treasurer: Robert E. (Bob) Bies, age 48
EVP Business Optimization: Hugh O. Davis, age 34
EVP Global Internet Survey Solutions: Keith Price, age 34

SVP Asia: Andrew C. (Andy) Ellis, age 34
SVP and Managing Director, Europe; Managing Director, Ciao: Nicolas Metzke, age 40
VP Sales, Comparison Shopping, Ciao:
Stephan Muzikant
VP Investor Relations: Cynthia C. Brockhoff
VP Technology and Operations, Comparison Shopping, Ciao: Daniel Keller
VP Corporate Development, Secretary, and General Counsel: Jonathan A. Flatow, age 45
Auditors: PricewaterhouseCoopers LLP

LOCATIONS

HQ: Greenfield Online, Inc.
21 River Rd., Wilton, CT 06897
Phone: 203-834-8585   **Fax:** 203-834-8686
Web: www.greenfield.com

2006 Sales

	$ mil.	% of total
US	60.3	60
Germany	20.5	21
UK	12.4	12
Other countries	7.1	7
Total	**100.3**	**100**

PRODUCTS/OPERATIONS

2006 Sales

	$ mil.	% of total
Internet survey solutions	80.5	80
Comparison shopping	19.8	20
Total	**100.3**	**100**

COMPETITORS

Edison Media Research
Gallup
Harris Interactive
International Demographics
Ipsos
Kantar Group
Lightspeed Research
Luth Research
Maritz Research
MyPoints.com
NPD
Opinion Research
SPSS
Survey Sampling
Synovate
Walker Information
Zogby

HISTORICAL FINANCIALS

Company Type: Public

Income Statement				FYE: December 31
	REVENUE ($ mil.)	NET INCOME ($ mil.)	NET PROFIT MARGIN	EMPLOYEES
12/06	100.3	8.4	8.4%	675
12/05	89.2	(66.0)	—	584
12/04	44.4	5.7	12.8%	281
12/03	25.9	1.6	6.2%	190
12/02	14.9	(2.4)	—	—
Annual Growth	**61.1%**	**—**	**—**	**52.6%**

2006 Year-End Financials

Debt ratio: 0.0%
Return on equity: 5.9%
Cash ($ mil.): 37.0
Current ratio: 2.51
Long-term debt ($ mil.): 0.0
No. of shares (mil.): 25.5
Dividends
  Yield: —
  Payout: —
Market value ($ mil.): 364.5
R&D as % of sales: —
Advertising as % of sales: —

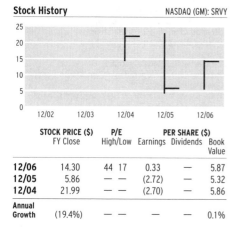

	STOCK PRICE ($) FY Close	P/E High/Low		Earnings	PER SHARE ($) Dividends	Book Value
12/06	14.30	44	17	0.33	—	5.87
12/05	5.86	—	—	(2.72)	—	5.32
12/04	21.99	—	—	(2.70)	—	5.86
Annual Growth	(19.4%)	—	—	—	—	0.1%

Greenhill & Co

It's no secret what the favorite color is around the offices of Greenhill & Co. The investment bank specializes in mergers and acquisitions, corporate restructurings, and merchant banking for clients worldwide. Merchant banking activities are conducted through the firm's Greenhill Capital Partners unit, which makes private equity investments typically in the $10 million to $75 million range. Greenhill was founded in 1996 by former Morgan Stanley president Robert Greenhill. It left the ever-shrinking ranks of independent, privately owned investment banks in 2004 when it completed its first public stock offering.

Expanding its North American presence, Greenhill opened an office in Toronto in 2006. The company closed its first buyout fund in Europe late the following year.

In 2005 the company closed its second private equity fund, which raised some $875 million. The firm used the proceeds to invest in mid-market companies in the energy, telecommunications, and financial services sectors. Portfolio companies from Greenhill's first fund include Global Signal, Everlast Energy, and Heartland Payment Systems.

CEO Bob Greenhill and his family own about 20% of the company.

EXECUTIVES

Chairman: Robert F. (Bob) Greenhill, age 71, $600,000 pay
Vice Chairman: Lord James Blyth of Rowington, age 67
Co-CEO and Director: Scott L. Bok, age 48, $600,000 pay
Co-CEO and Director: Simon A. Borrows, age 48, $621,961 pay
CFO: John D. Liu, age 39, $600,000 pay
Chairman, Greenhill Capital Partners: Robert H. (Bob) Niehaus, age 51, $600,000 pay
Managing Director, General Counsel, and Secretary: Ulrika Ekman, age 44
Managing Director, Finance, Regulation, and Operations and Chief Compliance Officer: Harold (Hal) Rodriguez Jr., age 51
Controller: Jodi Goetz
Director of Information Technology: John Shaffer
Manager of Human Resources: Julie Kaeli
Auditors: Ernst & Young LLP

LOCATIONS

HQ: Greenhill & Co, Inc.
300 Park Ave., 23rd Fl., New York, NY 10022
Phone: 212-389-1500   **Fax:** 212-389-1700
Web: www.greenhill-co.com

2006 Sales

	$ mil.	% of total
US	182.5	63
Europe	108.1	37
Total	**290.6**	**100**

PRODUCTS/OPERATIONS

2006 Sales

	$ mil.	% of total
Financial advisory services	209.8	72
Merchant banking fund management & other	77.6	27
Interest income	3.2	1
Total	**290.6**	**100**

COMPETITORS

Blackstone Group	Lazard
Citigroup Global Markets	Lehman Brothers
Cohen & Steers	Merrill Lynch
Collins Stewart (US)	Morgan Joseph
Credit Suisse (USA)	Morgan Stanley
Goldman Sachs	Robert W. Baird & Co.
Houlihan Lokey	Stephens
Jefferies Group	Thomas Weisel Partners
JPMorgan Chase	UBS Investment Bank

HISTORICAL FINANCIALS

Company Type: Public

Income Statement

FYE: December 31

	REVENUE ($ mil.)	NET INCOME ($ mil.)	NET PROFIT MARGIN	EMPLOYEES
12/06	290.6	75.7	26.0%	201
12/05	221.1	55.5	25.1%	151
12/04	151.9	38.3	25.2%	—
12/03	126.7	45.4	35.8%	—
12/02	112.6	57.8	51.3%	—
Annual Growth	26.7%	7.0%	—	33.1%

2006 Year-End Financials

Debt ratio: 12.5%
Return on equity: 56.0%
Cash ($ mil.): 62.4
Current ratio: —
Long-term debt ($ mil.): 19.5
No. of shares (mil.): 28.5

Dividends
  Yield: 0.9%
  Payout: 27.5%
Market value ($ mil.): 2,100.9
R&D as % of sales: —
Advertising as % of sales: —

Stock History

NYSE: GHL

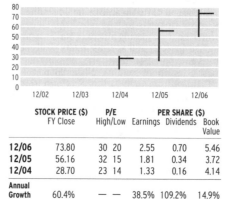

	STOCK PRICE ($) FY Close	P/E High/Low		Earnings	PER SHARE ($) Dividends	Book Value
12/06	73.80	30	20	2.55	0.70	5.46
12/05	56.16	32	15	1.81	0.34	3.72
12/04	28.70	23	14	1.33	0.16	4.14
Annual Growth	60.4%	—	—	38.5%	109.2%	14.9%

Grey Wolf

Grey Wolf makes its living hunting down on-shore oil and gas drilling contracts. The company performs onshore contract drilling, primarily for natural gas, using a US-based fleet of 118 marketed rigs that can reach depths of up to 40,000 ft. Grey Wolf's operations are focused on six regions: Mid-Continent; South Texas; the Gulf Coast (Texas and Louisiana); Ark-La-Tex (northeastern Texas, northern Louisiana, and southern Arkansas); southern Mississippi and Alabama; and the Rocky Mountains. The company provides rigs, related equipment, and field personnel to customers on a turnkey, footage, or day-work basis.

Grey Wolf, which has survived difficult market conditions for the deep-drilling segment of the industry by selling off noncore assets and cutting personnel and wages, is slowly recovering. It has closed its operations in Venezuela to focus more on the producing regions of the US. Buoyed by rising oil prices, the company has moved into a new drilling market, the Rocky Mountains. It has also expanded its West Texas operations by increasing the number of rigs in this region. Through more investment in turnkey operations (drilling contracts that pay on completion of the well), Grey Wolf hopes to stabilize revenue growth.

In 2004 the company acquired New Patriot Drilling for $51 million.

HISTORY

Grey Wolf began as an oil and gas exploration and production company, DI Industries, in 1980. In 1985 DI formed subsidiary Drillers, Inc., which specialized in oil and gas contract drilling, because of a sharp increase in demand for drilling rigs. The next year the price of oil collapsed, along with the US market for drilling rigs. DI turned to opportunities in Central and South America and began conducting drilling operations in Argentina, El Salvador, Guatemala, Mexico, and Venezuela.

Increased competition, slack demand, and heavy debt caused the company to struggle in the 1990s, racking up a string of unprofitable years. In 1995 founding CEO Max Dillard resigned. The next year DI embarked on a total overhaul that included selling its oil and gas producing properties and shutting in all its foreign operations (except Venezuela). The company also exited noncore US markets.

Buoyed by surging rig demand in 1996, DI also began aggressively expanding, adding about 100 drilling rigs in its targeted markets. In 1997 the company purchased Grey Wolf Drilling Company, a leading drilling contractor in the Texas and Louisiana Gulf Coast area with 18 rigs, and adopted the corporate name as its own.

In 1998 Grey Wolf bought Murco Drilling Corporation, a Louisiana-based company with 10 rigs operating in the Ark-La-Tex and Mississippi/Alabama markets. Low oil prices suppressed demand for land rigs in 1998, and Grey Wolf cut personnel and sold more noncore assets. It also suspended its drilling activities in Venezuela, the last of its international operations (and subsequently exited the business in 2001).

Lifted by rising oil prices, the company moved into a new drilling market, the Rocky Mountains, through a two-year contract with Burlington Resources. Later that year, Grey Wolf began operations in West Texas and Southeast New Mexico.

EXECUTIVES

Chairman, President, and CEO:
Thomas P. (Tom) Richards, age 63, $575,000 pay
Vice Chairman: William R. Ziegler, age 64
EVP and COO: David J. Crowley, age 48
EVP, CFO, and Secretary: David W. Wehlmann, age 48, $312,000 pay
SVP Operations: Edward S. Jacob III, age 54, $255,000 pay
SVP Human Resources: Robert J. Proffit, age 51, $185,000 pay
VP and Controller: Kent D. Cauley, age 36, $150,000 pay
VP and Treasurer: Donald J. Guedry Jr., age 50
VP Arkansas, Louisiana, Texas Division:
Forrest M. Conley Jr.
VP Gulf Coast Division: Dale Love
VP Rocky Mountain Division: Ray Smith
Auditors: KPMG LLP

LOCATIONS

HQ: Grey Wolf, Inc.
10370 Richmond Ave., Ste. 600, Houston, TX 77042
Phone: 713-435-6100   **Fax:** 713-435-6170
Web: www.gwdrilling.com

Grey Wolf operates in Alabama, Arkansas, Louisiana, Mississippi, Texas, and in the Rocky Mountains.

PRODUCTS/OPERATIONS

2006 Sales

	$ mil.	% of total
Daywork operations	736.8	78
Turnkey operations	208.7	22
Total	**945.5**	**100**

Contract Services

Daywork (drill rigs, related equipment, and personnel only, on a fixed per-day rate)
Footage (fixed amount of payment for each foot drilled)
Turnkey (drill rig, related equipment, personnel, and engineering services, on a fixed price rate)

COMPETITORS

Baker Hughes
Diamond Offshore
ENSCO
Helmerich & Payne
Nabors Industries
Noble
Parker Drilling
Patterson-UTI Energy
Pioneer Drilling
Precision Drilling
Pride International
Schlumberger
Transocean Inc.
Unit Corporation

HISTORICAL FINANCIALS

Company Type: Public

Income Statement

FYE: December 31

	REVENUE ($ mil.)	NET INCOME ($ mil.)	NET PROFIT MARGIN	EMPLOYEES
12/06	945.5	219.9	23.3%	3,400
12/05	697.0	120.6	17.3%	3,200
12/04	424.6	8.1	1.9%	—
12/03	286.0	(30.2)	—	—
12/02	250.3	(21.5)	—	1,750
Annual Growth	**39.4%**	**—**	**—**	**18.1%**

2006 Year-End Financials

Debt ratio: 51.5%	Dividends
Return on equity: 48.7%	Yield: —
Cash ($ mil.): 230.6	Payout: —
Current ratio: 3.07	Market value ($ mil.): 1,275.5
Long-term debt ($ mil.): 275.0	R&D as % of sales: —
No. of shares (mil.): 185.9	Advertising as % of sales: —

Stock History

AMEX: GW

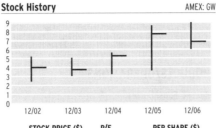

	STOCK PRICE ($) FY Close	P/E High/Low		PER SHARE ($) Earnings	Dividends	Book Value
12/06	6.86	9	6	0.98	—	2.87
12/05	7.73	16	7	0.54	—	1.92
12/04	5.27	140	83	0.04	—	1.25
12/03	3.74	—	—	(0.17)	—	1.08
12/02	3.99	—	—	(0.12)	—	1.24
Annual Growth	**14.5%**	**—**	**—**	**—**	**—**	**23.2%**

GSI Commerce

GSI Commerce offers e-commerce packages organized across three categories: technology, logistics and customer care, and marketing. It creates and operates Web sites for about 60 retailers and consumer goods manufacturers in addition to its own fogdog.com sporting goods retail operation. The company offers Web site design and hosting services as well as merchandising for such clients as palmOne, Polo Ralph Lauren, Reebok, and Sport Chalet. GSI also offers outsourced order fulfillment, customer service, and Web analytics services. In addition to retailers and manufacturers, the company serves media outlets such as HBO, Nickelodeon, and PBS, as well as professional sports teams.

GSI's growth strategy remains simple: As a client's e-commerce business grows, so does its own. Its plan is to continue to enhance its online platform offerings while also seeking out new partners.

In 2008 the company agreed to buy e-Dialog, a provider of e-mail marketing services for companies in the US and Europe, for $157 million. If the deal is completed, e-Dialog will operate under its own brand as a unit of GSI.

The proposed e-Dialog purchase comes on the heels of two acquisitions by GSI in 2007. The company bought Accretive Commerce, a provider of customer service, order management, and shipment fulfillment for e-commerce companies, for about $98 million, and it paid about $8 million for Zendor.com, a UK-based online retail company. Also in 2007, GSI Commerce added a blog and an RSS syndication feature to its e-commerce services.

GSI founder and CEO Michael Rubin owns nearly 16% of the company. QVC and SOFTBANK own 20% and 18%, respectively.

EXECUTIVES

Chairman, President, and CEO: Michael G. Rubin, age 34, $449,500 pay
EVP Global Operations: Robert (Bob) Wuesthoff, age 49, $350,000 pay
EVP Merchandising: Robert W. (Bob) Liewald, age 58
EVP and CIO: Stephen J. Gold, age 47, $354,000 pay
EVP, Secretary, and General Counsel: Arthur H. Miller, age 53
EVP Sales; President and COO, GSI Commerce West: Damon Mintzer, age 41, $379,800 pay
EVP Partner Services: Steven C. Davis, age 36
EVP Partner Strategy and Marketing: Fiona P. Dias, age 42
EVP Business Management: J. Scott (Scott) Hardy
SVP and CFO: Michael R. Conn, age 36, $304,018 pay
SVP Human Resources: James (Jim) Flanagan, age 43
Director Corporate Communications: Greg Ryan
Auditors: Deloitte & Touche LLP

LOCATIONS

HQ: GSI Commerce, Inc.
935 1st Ave., King of Prussia, PA 19406
Phone: 610-491-7000
Web: www.gsicommerce.com

PRODUCTS/OPERATIONS

2006 Sales

		$ mil.	% of total
Products			
	Sporting goods	314.7	52
	Other	146.5	24
E-commerce services		148.3	24
Total		**609.5**	**100**

COMPETITORS

Accenture	IBM
Acxiom	Innotrac
Akqa Inc.	INTERSHOP
Amazon.com	Menlo Worldwide
aQuantive	Microsoft
Ariba	NaviSite
Art Technology Group	Oracle
Avenue ARazorfish	PFSweb
BEA Systems	SAP
Blast Radius	Sitel
BroadVision	StarTek
Convergys	Sterling Commerce
Coremetrics	UPS
CyberSource	UPS Supply Chain
DHL Global Mail	Solutions
Digital River	USinternetworking
Digitas	ValueVision Media
EDS	Vignette
Experian	West Corporation
Grey Group	

HISTORICAL FINANCIALS

Company Type: Public

Income Statement

FYE: December 31

	REVENUE ($ mil.)	NET INCOME ($ mil.)	NET PROFIT MARGIN	EMPLOYEES
12/06	609.5	53.7	8.8%	2,521
12/05	440.4	2.7	0.6%	1,729
12/04	335.1	(0.3)	—	—
12/03	241.9	(12.1)	—	—
12/02	172.6	(33.8)	—	731
Annual Growth	**37.1%**	**—**	**—**	**36.3%**

2006 Year-End Financials

Debt ratio: 30.9%	Dividends
Return on equity: 28.2%	Yield: —
Cash ($ mil.): 184.5	Payout: —
Current ratio: 1.77	Market value ($ mil.): 860.2
Long-term debt ($ mil.): 70.4	R&D as % of sales: —
No. of shares (mil.): 45.9	Advertising as % of sales: —

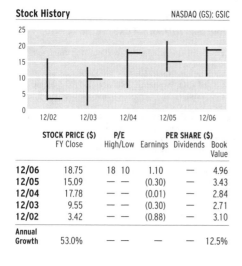

Stock History

	STOCK PRICE ($) FY Close	P/E High/Low		PER SHARE ($) Earnings	Dividends	Book Value
12/06	18.75	18	10	1.10	—	4.96
12/05	15.09	—	—	(0.30)	—	3.43
12/04	17.78	—	—	(0.01)	—	2.84
12/03	9.55	—	—	(0.30)	—	2.71
12/02	3.42	—	—	(0.88)	—	3.10
Annual Growth	53.0%	—	—	—	—	12.5%

Gulf Island Fabrication

Through its subsidiaries, holding company Gulf Island Fabrication makes islands in the stream — the Gulf Stream, that is. Its subsidiaries make offshore drilling and production platforms for use mainly in the Gulf of Mexico. Products include jackets and deck sections of fixed production platforms, hull and deck sections of floating production platforms, piles, subsea templates, wellhead protectors, and various production, compressor, and utility modules. Gulf Island also produces and repairs pressure vessels and refurbishes existing platforms. Chevron accounted for some 42% of Gulf Island's sales in 2006.

Gulf Island has more than 250 acres devoted to fabrication activities, a large assembly capacity allowing it to work on both shallow water units and complex deepwater structures. Its property has a water frontage along the Houma Navigational Canal, only 30 miles from the central Gulf of Mexico. In 2006 the company acquired Technip subsidiary Gulf Marine Fabricators for $40 million.

EXECUTIVES

Chairman, President, and CEO: Kerry J. Chauvin, age 59, $405,000 pay
EVP Marketing: Murphy A. Bourke, age 62, $198,000 pay
EVP Operations: Kirk J. Meche, age 44, $205,000 pay
President and CEO, Dolphin Services:
William (Bill) Fromenthal
President and CEO, Gulf Island L.L.C.:
William G. Blanchard, age 48, $141,102 pay
President and CEO, Southport LLC: Jacques C. Olivier
VP Finance, CFO, and Treasurer: Robin A. Seibert, age 50
President, G. M. Fabricators, L. P.: Johannes Ikdal
Manager, Human Resources: Herb Ledet
Coordinator Investor Relations:
Deborah Kern-Knoblock
Auditors: Ernst & Young LLP

LOCATIONS

HQ: Gulf Island Fabrication, Inc.
583 Thompson Rd., Houma, LA 70363
Phone: 985-872-2100   **Fax:** 985-872-2129
Web: www.gulfisland.com

2006 Sales

	$ mil.	% of total
US	290.8	93
Other countries	21.4	7
Total	**312.2**	**100**

PRODUCTS/OPERATIONS

Selected Subsidiaries

Dolphin Services, Inc. (offshore construction, fabrication, inshore construction, steel sales, and sand blasting and coating)
G.M. Fabricators (offshore construction and fabrication)
Gulf Island, LLC (offshore construction)
Southport, Inc. (fabrication of living quarters for offshore platforms)

COMPETITORS

Acergy
Global Industries
Hyundai Heavy Industries
J. Ray McDermott
Kiewit Offshore
NATCO
Oceaneering International
Technip
Tidewater Inc.

HISTORICAL FINANCIALS

Company Type: Public

Income Statement

FYE: December 31

	REVENUE ($ mil.)	NET INCOME ($ mil.)	NET PROFIT MARGIN	EMPLOYEES
12/06	312.2	21.3	6.8%	1,800
12/05	188.5	13.0	6.9%	1,150
12/04	173.9	12.0	6.9%	—
12/03	203.7	15.8	7.8%	—
12/02	142.9	5.6	3.9%	975
Annual Growth	21.6%	39.7%	—	16.6%

2006 Year-End Financials

Debt ratio: —
Return on equity: 12.6%
Cash ($ mil.): 10.3
Current ratio: 2.36
Long-term debt ($ mil.): —
No. of shares (mil.): 14.1
Dividends
Yield: 0.8%
Payout: 19.6%
Market value ($ mil.): 520.9
R&D as % of sales: —
Advertising as % of sales: —

Stock History

	STOCK PRICE ($) FY Close	P/E High/Low		PER SHARE ($) Earnings	Dividends	Book Value
12/06	36.90	26	11	1.53	0.30	14.22
12/05	24.31	29	17	1.05	0.22	11.26
12/04	21.83	26	16	0.99	0.15	10.42
12/03	17.03	14	11	1.33	—	9.46
12/02	16.25	41	18	0.47	—	8.09
Annual Growth	22.8%	—	—	34.3%	41.4%	15.2%

GulfMark Offshore

GulfMark Offshore makes its mark on the high seas. The company offers support services for the construction, positioning, and operation of offshore oil and natural gas rigs and platforms. It owns, manages, or charters 59 vessels located primarily in the North Sea (33 vessels), Southeast Asia (12), and offshore Brazil (4). Marine services include anchor handling; cargo, supply, and crew transportation; towing; and emergency services. Some of its ships conduct seismic data gathering and provide diving support. GulfMark Offshore serves both oil majors and smaller independents. Lehman Brothers owns 9.6% of the company.

The company operates on a smaller scale in some of the world's other offshore oil patches, including India, the Gulf of Mexico, and West/South Africa.

EXECUTIVES

Chairman: David J. Butters, age 66
President, CEO, and Director: Bruce A. Streeter, age 58
EVP Finance, CFO, Secretary, and Treasurer:
Edward A. (Ed) Guthrie, age 62, $564,000 pay
EVP Finance, CFO, Secretary, and Treasurer:
John E. (Gene) Leech, age 54, $552,250 pay
VP North Sea Operations; Managing Director, Gulf Offshore North Sea: David D. E. Kenwright
VP Marketing: Thomas J. (Tom) Collins
VP Investor Relations: Russell Bay
Auditors: UHY LLP

LOCATIONS

HQ: GulfMark Offshore, Inc.
10111 Richmond Ave., Ste. 340, Houston, TX 77042
Phone: 713-963-9522   **Fax:** 713-963-9796
Web: www.gulfmark.com

GulfMark Offshore operates in the North Sea, off the coasts of Brazil, India, and Mexico, and in Southeast Asia, South and West Africa, and in the Mediterranean.

2006 Sales

	$ mil.	% of total
North Sea	199.4	79
Southeast Asia	27.4	11
Americas	24.1	10
Total	**250.9**	**100**

PRODUCTS/OPERATIONS

Selected Subsidiaries

Gulf Marine (Servicos Maritimos) do Brasil Limitada (Brazil)
GulfMark Norge AS (Norway)
GulfMark North Sea Ltd. (UK)
GulfMark Rederia (Norway)
Gulf Marine Far East PTE, Ltd. (Singapore)
Gulf Offshore Marine International, S. de R.L. (Panama)
GM Offshore, Inc.
Gulf Offshore Guernsey, Ltd. (UK)
Gulf Offshore N.S. Ltd. (UK)
S.E.A. Personnel Services Limited (UK)
Sea Truck (UK) Ltd.
Semaring Logistics (M) Sdn. Bhd.(Malaysia)

COMPETITORS

Acergy
Global Industries
SEACOR
Tidewater Inc.
Trico Marine

HISTORICAL FINANCIALS

Company Type: Public

Income Statement				FYE: December 31
	REVENUE ($ mil.)	NET INCOME ($ mil.)	NET PROFIT MARGIN	EMPLOYEES
12/06	250.9	89.7	35.8%	1,243
12/05	204.0	38.4	18.8%	1,212
12/04	139.3	(4.6)	—	1,085
12/03	129.9	0.5	0.4%	1,175
12/02	133.9	24.0	17.9%	1,126
Annual Growth	17.0%	39.0%	—	2.5%

2006 Year-End Financials

Debt ratio: 29.5%
Return on equity: 20.8%
Cash ($ mil.): 82.8
Current ratio: 3.75
Long-term debt ($ mil.): 160.0
No. of shares (mil.): 22.7

Dividends
  Yield: —
  Payout: —
Market value ($ mil.): 848.5
R&D as % of sales: —
Advertising as % of sales: —

Stock History

NYSE: GLF

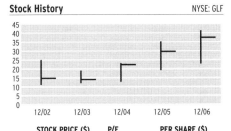

	STOCK PRICE ($) FY Close	P/E High/Low		PER SHARE ($) Earnings Dividends		Book Value
12/06	37.41	10	5	4.28	—	23.87
12/05	29.62	19	11	1.86	—	15.71
12/04	22.27	—	—	(0.23)	—	15.70
12/03	14.00	621	413	0.03	—	14.60
12/02	14.75	20	9	1.22	—	12.80
Annual Growth	26.2%	—	—	36.9%	—	16.9%

Gulfport Energy

Gulfport Energy puts most of its eggs into just a couple of baskets. The exploration and production company sells 100% of its oil to Shell and 96% of its gas to Chevron. It operates off the Gulf Coast of Louisiana, with a heavy concentration on two fields: West Cote Blanche Bay and Hackberry Fields. Gulfport operates about 90 producing wells and has proved reserves of nearly 25 million barrels of oil equivalent. The company emerged from the ashes of WRT Energy, which filed for bankruptcy in 1996 amid allegations of fraud. Gulfport emerged from Chapter 11 bankruptcy protection in 1997.

EXECUTIVES

Chairman: Mike Liddell, age 53, $239,716 pay
CEO and Director: James D. (Jim) Palm, age 62, $224,000 pay
VP, CFO, and Secretary: Michael G. (Mike) Moore, $310,875 pay
Director Investor Relations: John Kilgallon
Auditors: Grant Thornton LLP

LOCATIONS

HQ: Gulfport Energy Corporation
14313 N. May Ave., Ste. 100,
Oklahoma City, OK 73134
Phone: 405-848-8807   **Fax:** 405-848-8816
Web: www.gulfportenergy.com

COMPETITORS

Abraxas Petroleum
Apache
Exxon Mobil

HISTORICAL FINANCIALS

Company Type: Public

Income Statement				FYE: December 31
	REVENUE ($ mil.)	NET INCOME ($ mil.)	NET PROFIT MARGIN	EMPLOYEES
12/06	60.4	27.8	46.0%	151
12/05	27.6	10.9	39.5%	63
12/04	23.2	4.3	18.5%	40
12/03	15.9	0.6	3.8%	25
12/02	12.1	0.4	3.3%	14
Annual Growth	49.5%	188.7%	—	81.2%

2006 Year-End Financials

Debt ratio: 29.8%
Return on equity: 26.7%
Cash ($ mil.): 6.6
Current ratio: 0.76
Long-term debt ($ mil.): 36.9
No. of shares (mil.): 35.1

Dividends
  Yield: —
  Payout: —
Market value ($ mil.): 477.0
R&D as % of sales: —
Advertising as % of sales: —

Stock History

NASDAQ (GS): GPOR

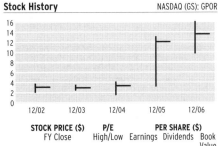

	STOCK PRICE ($) FY Close	P/E High/Low		PER SHARE ($) Earnings Dividends		Book Value
12/06	13.59	20	12	0.82	—	3.53
12/05	12.05	38	10	0.34	—	2.62
12/04	3.30	14	6	0.28	—	1.53
12/03	2.90	—	—	(0.02)	—	3.27
12/02	3.05	—	—	(0.06)	—	3.29
Annual Growth	45.3%	—	—	—	—	1.8%

Hallmark Financial Services

Personal or commercial, on the ground or in the air, Hallmark Financial sells insurance to cover risks both general and exceptional. Its Hallmark General Agency unit provides general commercial property/casualty insurance while its Texas General Agency sells specialty property/casualty coverage to businesses that don't fit into standard coverage. Its Aerospace unit provides general and specialty aviation insurance to both commercial and private pilots and small airports. Hallmark's Phoenix unit writes

higher-risk non-standard personal auto insurance to folks in the southwestern and northwestern US. Chairman Mark Schwarz owns 70% of the company, primarily through his investment firm, Newcastle Partners.

Hallmark Financial has built itself up through acquisitions including Texas General Agency (2006), Aerospace Holdings (2006), and Phoenix Indemnity (2003).

Through a contract with Old American County Mutual Fire Insurance, the company offers non-standard personal auto insurance in Texas.

EXECUTIVES

Chairman: Mark E. Schwarz, age 47
President and CEO: Mark J. Morrison, age 47
EVP Commercial Lines and COO; President, HGA Operating Unit: Kevin T. Kasitz, age 44
EVP Personal Lines; President, Phoenix Operating Unit: Brookland F. Davis, age 43
SVP and Chief Accounting Officer: Jeffrey R. Passmore, age 39
CIO: Gregory P. Birdsall
Chief Actuary: Richard N. Gibson
President, Aerospace Operating Unit: Curtis R. Donnell, age 68
President, TGA Operating Unit: Donald E. Meyer, age 51
Auditors: KPMG LLP

LOCATIONS

HQ: Hallmark Financial Services, Inc.
777 Main St., Ste. 1000, Fort Worth, TX 76102
Phone: 817-348-1600   **Fax:** 817-348-1815
Web: www.hallmarkgrp.com

PRODUCTS/OPERATIONS

2006 Sales

	$ mil.	% of total
Premiums		
Standard commercial	70.0	34
Specialty commercial	39.6	20
Personal	42.3	21
Commission & fees	35.3	17
Investment income	10.4	5
Finance charges	4.0	2
Processing & service fees	2.3	1
Realized gains (losses)	(1.5)	—
Other	0.3	—
Total	**202.7**	**100**

Selected Subsidiaries

Aerospace Special Risk, Inc.
Allrisk Insurance Agency, Inc.
American Hallmark Agencies, Inc.
American Hallmark General Agency, Inc. (d/b/a Phoenix General Agency)
American Hallmark Insurance Company of Texas
Effective Claims Management, Inc.
Gulf States Insurance Company
Hallmark Claims Service, Inc (d/b/a Phoenix General Agency)
Hallmark Finance Corporation
Hallmark General Agency, Inc.
Hallmark Underwriters, Inc.
Pan American Acceptance Corporation
Phoenix Indemnity Insurance Company
Texas General Agency, Inc.
TGA Special Risk, Inc.

COMPETITORS

AIG
Allstate
GEICO
GMAC Insurance
The Hartford
Penn-America

Progressive Corporation
Safeco
Safeway Insurance
State Farm
Travelers Companies
Zurich American

HISTORICAL FINANCIALS

Company Type: Public

Income Statement

FYE: December 31

	ASSETS ($ mil.)	NET INCOME ($ mil.)	INCOME AS % OF ASSETS	EMPLOYEES
12/06	416.0	9.2	2.2%	347
12/05	208.9	9.2	4.4%	165
12/04	82.5	5.8	7.0%	179
12/03	83.8	8.7	10.4%	186
12/02	82.8	(1.7)	—	203
Annual Growth	49.7%	—	—	14.3%

2006 Year-End Financials

Equity as % of assets: 36.2%
Return on assets: 2.9%
Return on equity: 7.8%
Long-term debt ($ mil.): 35.8
No. of shares (mil.): 20.8
Market value ($ mil.): 205.8

Dividends
  Yield: —
  Payout: —
Sales ($ mil.): 202.7
R&D as % of sales: —
Advertising as % of sales: —

Stock History

NASDAQ (GM): HALL

	STOCK PRICE ($) FY Close	P/E High/Low		PER SHARE ($) Earnings	Dividends	Book Value
12/06	9.91	19	16	0.53	—	7.26
12/05	8.16	12	7	0.78	—	0.98
12/04	7.20	9	3	0.96	—	0.90
12/03	4.74	3	1	2.76	—	0.75
12/02	4.20	—	—	(0.90)	—	0.77
Annual Growth	23.9%	—	—	—	—	75.1%

H&E Equipment Services

Whether you're a he or a she, if you have a project that requires heavy lifting, H&E Equipment Services can help. The company sells and rents new and used equipment for construction, earthmoving, and material handling. H&E Equipment also offers parts and services such as planned maintenance, mobile service, repair, fleet management, and crane remanufacturing. The company markets its products and services throughout the US and represents lift, crane, and truck manufacturing companies such as JLG, Bobcat, and Komatsu. Private equity firm Bruckmann, Rosser, Sherrill & Co. and its members own nearly 40% of the company.

H&E Equipment was formed in 2002 through the merger of Head & Engquist (a subsidiary of Gulf Wide Industries) and ICM Equipment Company. Before their merger, the regional, integrated equipment service companies Head & Engquist (founded in 1961) and ICM Equipment Company (established in 1971) were operating in contiguous geographic markets.

H&E Equipment has expanded its business through the $60 million acquisition of Eagle High Reach Equipment (now named H&E California Holding), which rents heavy equipment to industrial and construction firms in southern California. The acquisition was funded out of the proceeds from H&E's 2006 IPO.

The following year the company acquired mid-Atlantic construction equipment distributor J.W. Burress for about $98 million. Burress shareholders could receive up to an additional $15 million over three years if Burress continues to sell, rent, and repair Hitachi equipment. Hitachi-related revenues represent more than one-quarter of the distributor's annual sales.

EXECUTIVES

Chairman: Gary W. Bagley, age 60
President, CEO, and Director: John M. Engquist, age 53, $1,283,750 pay
CFO and Secretary: Leslie S. Magee, age 38, $450,800 pay
EVP and General Manager: Bradley W. Barber, age 34, $524,458 pay
VP, Cranes and Earthmoving: William W. Fox, age 63, $334,465 pay
VP Fleet Management: Dale W. Roesener, age 50
VP, Lift Trucks: Kenneth R. Sharp Jr., age 60
VP, Product Support: John D. Jones, age 49, $363,462 pay
Auditors: BDO Seidman, LLP

LOCATIONS

HQ: H&E Equipment Services, Inc.
  11100 Mead Rd., Ste. 200, Baton Rouge, LA 70816
Phone: 225-298-5200   **Fax:** 225-298-5377
Web: www.he-equipment.com

H&E Equipment operates nearly 50 facilities in Alabama, Arizona, Arkansas, California, Colorado, Florida, Georgia, Idaho, Louisiana, Mississippi, Montana, New Mexico, Nevada, North Carolina, Oklahoma, Texas, Tennessee, and Utah.

PRODUCTS/OPERATIONS

2006 Sales

	$ mil.	% of total
Equipment rentals	251.4	31
New equipment sales	241.3	30
Used equipment sales	133.9	17
Parts sales	82.1	10
Services	53.7	7
Other	42.0	5
Total	**804.4**	**100**

Selected Products

Aerial lifts
Backhoes
Boom trucks
Compactors/rollers
Compressors
Concrete equipment and tools
Cranes
Demolition tools
Dozers
Dump trucks
Excavators
Forklifts
Generators
Haul trucks
Heaters
Hoists/gantries
Industrial-personnel vehicles
Lighting
Material lifts
Motor graders
Pavers
Pumps
Rammers

Screeners
Sewer equipment
Skid loaders
Sweepers/scrubbers
Trailers
Water transporters (trailers, trucks, and wagons)
Welders
Wheel loaders

COMPETITORS

AMECO
Atlas Lift Truck Rentals
Hertz
NES Rentals
Park Corporation

RSC Holdings Inc.
Sunbelt Rentals
United Rentals
Western Power

HISTORICAL FINANCIALS

Company Type: Public

Income Statement

FYE: December 31

	REVENUE ($ mil.)	NET INCOME ($ mil.)	NET PROFIT MARGIN	EMPLOYEES
12/06	804.4	32.7	4.1%	1,677
12/05	600.2	28.2	4.7%	1,448
12/04	478.2	(13.7)	—	1,318
12/03	414.0	(46.0)	—	1,293
12/02	351.7	(13.1)	—	—
Annual Growth	23.0%	—	—	9.1%

2006 Year-End Financials

Debt ratio: 109.0%
Return on equity: 28.4%
Cash ($ mil.): 9.3
Current ratio: 0.99
Long-term debt ($ mil.): 256.8
No. of shares (mil.): 38.2

Dividends
  Yield: —
  Payout: —
Market value ($ mil.): 946.0
R&D as % of sales: —
Advertising as % of sales: —

Stock History

NASDAQ (GS): HEES

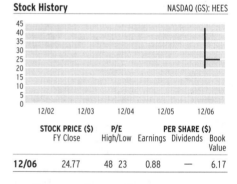

	STOCK PRICE ($) FY Close	P/E High/Low		PER SHARE ($) Earnings	Dividends	Book Value
12/06	24.77	48	23	0.88	—	6.17

Hanmi Financial

No hand-me-down operation, Hanmi Financial is headquartered in a penthouse suite along Los Angeles' Wilshire Boulevard. It's the holding company for Hanmi Bank, which serves California's Korean-American communities in Los Angeles, Orange, San Diego, San Francisco, and Santa Clara counties. Through more than 20 branches, the bank offers retail and small-business banking, with an emphasis on the latter. Commercial and industrial loans, including Small Business Administration and international loans, account for some 60% of Hanmi Financial's loan portfolio. Commercial real estate loans account for more than 30%.

Hanmi Financial bought rival Pacific Union Bank in 2004. The following year Hanmi Bank expanded beyond California by opening loan production offices in Annandale, Virginia, and Chicago to go with an existing office in Seattle. It now has loan offices in California, Colorado, Georgia, Illinois, Texas, Virginia, and Washington.

EXECUTIVES

Chairman: Joon Hyung Lee, age 63
Interim CEO and Chief Credit Officer:
  Chung Hoon Youk, age 54
EVP and CFO: Eung-Rae (Brian) Cho, age 47
SVP and Regional Executive Officer:
  Suki H. Murayama, age 54, $196,198 pay
SVP and Manager, Capital Markets Group:
  Dong Wook Kim
SVP and Chief Lending Officer: Hassan Bouayad
SVP, Hanmi Bank: Eunice U. Lim, age 50, $159,278 pay
  (prior to title change)
SVP and Deputy Chief Credit Officer:
  Haekyong (Jane) Kim
Chief Planning and Marketing Officer: J. Han Park
Chief of Banking Services: Steve Choe
Chief of Operations: Greg Kim
Human Resources Manager: Miung Kim
Investor Relations: Stephanie Yoon
Auditors: KPMG LLP

LOCATIONS

HQ: Hanmi Financial Corporation
  3660 Wilshire Blvd., Penthouse Ste. A,
  Los Angeles, CA 90010
Phone: 213-382-2200   **Fax:** 213-384-0990
Web: www.hanmifinancial.com

PRODUCTS/OPERATIONS

2006 Sales

	$ mil.	% of total
Interest		
Loans, including fees	239.1	81
Investments & other	21.1	7
Noninterest		
Service charges on deposit accounts	17.1	6
Other service charges & fees	9.0	3
Other	9.5	3
Total	**295.8**	**100**

COMPETITORS

Bank of America
Cathay General Bancorp
Center Financial
East West Bancorp
Nara Bancorp
UCBH Holdings
Washington Mutual
Wells Fargo
Wilshire Bancorp

HISTORICAL FINANCIALS

Company Type: Public

Income Statement				FYE: December 31
	ASSETS ($ mil.)	NET INCOME ($ mil.)	INCOME AS % OF ASSETS	EMPLOYEES
12/06	3,725.2	65.7	1.8%	589
12/05	3,414.3	58.2	1.7%	552
12/04	3,104.2	36.7	1.2%	—
12/03	1,785.8	19.2	1.1%	—
12/02	1,456.3	17.0	1.2%	356
Annual Growth	**26.5%**	**40.2%**	**—**	**13.4%**

2006 Year-End Financials

Equity as % of assets: 13.1%	Dividends
Return on assets: 1.8%	Yield: 1.1%
Return on equity: 14.4%	Payout: 18.0%
Long-term debt ($ mil.): 82.4	Sales ($ mil.): 295.8
No. of shares (mil.): 49.1	R&D as % of sales: —
Market value ($ mil.): 1,105.7	Advertising as % of sales: —

Stock History   NASDAQ (GS): HAFC

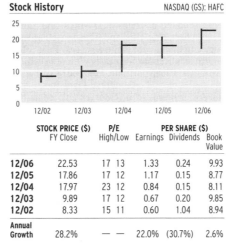

	STOCK PRICE ($) FY Close	P/E High/Low		PER SHARE ($) Earnings	Dividends	Book Value
12/06	22.53	17	13	1.33	0.24	9.93
12/05	17.86	17	12	1.17	0.15	8.77
12/04	17.97	23	12	0.84	0.15	8.11
12/03	9.89	17	12	0.67	0.20	9.85
12/02	8.33	15	11	0.60	1.04	8.94
Annual Growth	**28.2%**	**—**	**—**	**22.0%**	**(30.7%)**	**2.6%**

Hansen Natural

No matter the weather, Hansen Natural always has the energy to reach for the blue sky. The company has expanded its stable of "alternative" sodas, juices, and teas to include a wide variety of energy drinks, such as the popular Monster brand. Other products made by Hansen include fruit juice, smoothies, iced tea, and dry juice mixes — most of which are sold under the Hansen's brand name. The company sells its products to grocery chains, wholesale clubs, and distributors, mainly in the US and Canada. Chairman and CEO Rodney Sacks and vice chairman Hilton Schlosberg each own approximately 20% of Hansen.

The $18 billion "alternative" beverage industry has grown increasingly crowded with bottled water and juices from beverage giants Coca-Cola and PepsiCo. Hansen's product line includes "functional" drinks made by adding Echinacea, ginseng, guarana, and other supplements to food and drinks.

Hansen produces numerous lines of energy drinks (most with a mixture of caffeine, sugar, and vitamins), and the segment now pulls in some 86% of the company's sales. Hansen's Lost Energy is a joint marketing initiative with surf board designer Lost International. Its Rumba Energy Juice is an all-juice product designed to replace both morning coffee and juice. In 2006 the company struck a distribution deal with Anheuser-Busch for its energy drinks. It also has an agreement with Cadbury Bebidas for the distribution of its Monster energy drinks in Mexico. In order to concentrate on its liquid offerings, Hansen discontinued its line of nutrition bars and cereals.

In addition to the US and Canada, select Hansen's products are available in Mexico, Central and South America, the Caribbean, Japan, Korea, and Saudi Arabia.

EXECUTIVES

Chairman and CEO: Rodney C. Sacks, age 57, $400,000 pay
Vice Chairman, COO, CFO, President, and Secretary: Hilton H. Schlosberg, age 54, $400,000 pay
VP, Finance: Thomas J. Kelly, age 52, $200,000 pay
Assistant Secretary and Director: Benjamin M. Polk, age 56
Director, Human Resources: Linda Lopez
President, Monster Beverage Division: Mark J. Hall, age 51, $450,000 pay
Auditors: Deloitte & Touche LLP

LOCATIONS

HQ: Hansen Natural Corporation
  1010 Railroad St., Corona, CA 92882
Phone: 951-739-6200   **Fax:** 951-739-6220
Web: www.hansens.com

2006 Sales by Distribution Channel

	% of total
Full-service distributors	69
Club stores, drug chains & mass merchandisers	14
Retail grocery & specialty chains & wholesalers	12
Health food distributors	2
Other channels	3
Total	**100**

PRODUCTS/OPERATIONS

2006 Sales

	$ mil.	% of total
Energy drinks	519.0	86
Non-carbonated beverages	60.2	10
Carbonated beverages	26.6	4
Total	**605.8**	**100**

Selected Brands and Products

Bottled Water
  Hansen's (foodservice only)
Energy Drinks
  Ace Energy
  Energade
  Energy Formula
  Energy Island Blast Smoothie
  Java Monster
  Joker Mad Energy
  Lost Energy
  Monster Energy
  Rumba Energy
  Unbound Energy
Dry Juice Mixes
  Fizzit
Juices
  Apple
  Apple Grape
  Apple Strawberry
  Grape
  Juice Slam
  Junior Juice
  Organic Apple
  Pomegranate
  Smoothie
  White Grape
  Dry Juice Mixes
  Fizzi
Soda
  Blue Sky
  Hansen's Natural and Diet
  Hansen's Natural Green Tea
  Hansen's Signature
Tea
  Iced Green
  Lychee Black
  Peach Tree
  Pomegranate Green

COMPETITORS

Cadbury Schweppes	Naked Juice
Chiquita Brands	National Beverage
Clearly Canadian	National Grape Cooperative
Coca-Cola	Nestlé
Coca-Cola North America	Nestlé Waters
Cool Mountain Beverages	Ocean Spray
Cott	Odwalla
Cranberries Limited	PepsiCo
Del Monte Foods	Red Bull
Dole Food	Reed's
Energy Brands	Smucker
Ferolito, Vultaggio	Snapple
Fuze Beverage	South Beach Beverage
Gatorade	Sunny Delight
Global Beverage	Tree Top
Goya	Tropicana
Hobarama	Unilever
Impulse Energy USA	Veryfine
IZZE	Welch's
Jones Soda	Wet Planet Beverages
Mott's	XELR8

HISTORICAL FINANCIALS

Company Type: Public

Income Statement

FYE: December 31

	REVENUE ($ mil.)	NET INCOME ($ mil.)	NET PROFIT MARGIN	EMPLOYEES
12/06	605.8	97.9	16.2%	748
12/05	348.9	62.8	18.0%	363
12/04	180.3	20.4	11.3%	—
12/03	110.3	5.9	5.3%	—
12/02	92.1	3.0	3.3%	111
Annual Growth	60.1%	139.0%	—	61.1%

2006 Year-End Financials

Debt ratio: 0.0%	Dividends
Return on equity: 55.8%	Yield: —
Cash ($ mil.): 136.8	Payout: —
Current ratio: 4.38	Market value ($ mil.): 3,033.2
Long-term debt ($ mil.): 0.0	R&D as % of sales: —
No. of shares (mil.): 90.1	Advertising as % of sales: —

Stock History

NASDAQ (GS): HANS

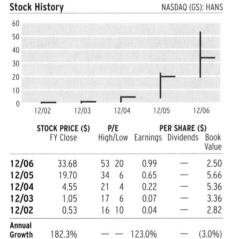

	STOCK PRICE ($) FY Close	P/E High/Low		PER SHARE ($) Earnings	Dividends	Book Value
12/06	33.68	53	20	0.99	—	2.50
12/05	19.70	34	6	0.65	—	5.66
12/04	4.55	21	4	0.22	—	5.36
12/03	1.05	17	6	0.07	—	3.36
12/02	0.53	16	10	0.04	—	2.82
Annual Growth	182.3%	—	—	123.0%	—	(3.0%)

Hawthorn Bancshares

Hawthorn Bancshares keeps a hawkeye on its money — and its clients' money. The holding company for Hawthorn Bank operates more than 20 branches in Missouri. The bank offers such deposit products as checking, savings, and money market accounts, CDs, and IRAs, as well as lending, trust, and brokerage services. Real estate mortgages account for nearly 60% of Hawthorn Bancshares' loan portfolio, followed by real estate construction and commercial loans (more than 15% each) and, to a lesser extent, consumer loans. The company in 2007 consolidated four bank charters under the Hawthorn Bank charter and changed the holding company's name from Exchange National Bancshares.

As part of the change (which consolidated the company's former subsidiaries Exchange National Bank, Osage Valley Bank, and Bank 10 under the Hawthorn Bank banner), the company relocated its headquarters to the Kansas City metro area.

Former chairman, president, and CEO Donald Campbell owns more than 5% of the company; activist investor Jeffrey Gendell owns 7%.

EXECUTIVES

Chairman and CEO: James E. Smith, age 61, $359,513 pay
President and Director: David T. Turner, age 49, $244,365 pay
SVP and Secretary: Kathleen L. Bruegenhemke, age 40
Treasurer; SVP and Controller, Exchange National Bank: Richard G. Rose, age 54, $110,913 pay
Auditors: KPMG LLP

LOCATIONS

HQ: Hawthorn Bancshares, Inc.
    300 SW Longview Blvd., Lee's Summit, MO 64081
Phone: 816-347-8100   **Fax:** 816-268-6318
Web: www.exchangebancshares.com

PRODUCTS/OPERATIONS

2006 Sales

	$ mil.	% of total
Interest		
Loans, including fees	62.6	78
Securities	7.6	10
Other	1.7	2
Noninterest		
Service charges on deposit accounts	5.7	7
Trust department income	0.8	1
Other	1.6	2
Total	**80.0**	**100**

COMPETITORS

Bank of America
Central Bancompany
Commerce Bancshares
First Bancshares (MO)
National City
Pulaski Financial
UMB Financial
U.S. Bancorp
Wells Fargo

HISTORICAL FINANCIALS

Company Type: Public

Income Statement

FYE: December 31

	ASSETS ($ mil.)	NET INCOME ($ mil.)	INCOME AS % OF ASSETS	EMPLOYEES
12/06	1,142.7	10.9	1.0%	389
12/05	1,126.5	9.9	0.9%	377
12/04	923.9	8.3	0.9%	292
12/03	875.6	9.0	1.0%	280
12/02	794.4	8.1	1.0%	268
Annual Growth	9.5%	7.7%	—	9.8%

2006 Year-End Financials

Equity as % of assets: 9.2%	Dividends
Return on assets: 1.0%	Yield: —
Return on equity: 10.8%	Payout: —
Long-term debt ($ mil.): 98.6	Sales ($ mil.): 80.0
No. of shares (mil.): 4.2	R&D as % of sales: —
Market value ($ mil.): 131.4	Advertising as % of sales: —

Stock History

NASDAQ (GM): HWBK

	STOCK PRICE ($) FY Close	P/E High/Low		PER SHARE ($) Earnings	Dividends	Book Value
12/06	31.50	13	11	2.59	—	25.17
12/05	29.51	13	11	2.36	—	23.20
12/04	28.87	19	14	1.98	—	22.01
12/03	36.20	20	10	2.15	—	21.05
12/02	22.31	41	30	0.57	—	29.81
Annual Growth	9.0%	—	—	46.0%	—	(4.1%)

Health Grades

Health Grades (which does business as HealthGrades) takes the health care industry to school. The company offers report cards on hospitals, physicians, nursing homes, home health agencies, hospice programs, and other health care providers. It sells the quality and patient safety information to a number of constituencies, including consumers, health plans, employers, and liability insurance companies. Hospitals themselves represent its biggest customer base, however; providers can license HealthGrades' ratings and trademarks (its Distinguished Hospital Award, for instance) to use in their marketing campaigns. They also come to the company for quality improvement consulting.

HealthGrades' database has ratings and profiles on the US's more than 5,000 hospitals, as well as some 700,000 doctors and thousands of nursing homes and other health care providers.

Consumers can access certain basic information about these providers online for free but have to pay a fee for more in-depth profiles. For employers and insurers, the company offers a wide array of information products (under the umbrella brand Health Management Suite). In addition to quality reports, HealthGrades offers medical cost calculators and disease management tools that an employer, for instance, could license and provide to its employees to help them make cost-effective health care decisions.

Doctors aren't left out of the HealthGrades' business model either. The company's Internet Patient Acquisition program lets doctors create online profiles that consumers can look at free of charge. In 2006 HealthGrades signed a multiyear deal with Tenet Healthcare to use the program to promote Tenet-affiliated physicians.

HealthGrades has alliances with J.D. Power and Associates (for that company's customer satisfaction know-how) and 3M Health Information Systems (for its rating software and coding expertise).

EXECUTIVES

Chairman, President, and CEO: Kerry R. Hicks, age 47, $390,542 pay
Vice Chairman: J.D. Kleinke, age 45
EVP: Steve Wood, age 63
EVP: David G. Hicks, age 48, $240,407 pay
EVP: Sarah P. Loughran, age 42, $246,212 pay
SVP, CFO, Secretary, and Treasurer: Allen Dodge, age 39, $190,340 pay
SVP Internet Patient Acquisition: Tod Baker
SVP Medical Affairs and Chief Medical Officer: Samantha Collier
SVP Provider Sales: Kirk Schreck
VP Internet Advertising: Allen Silkin
Director, Human Resources: Carloyne Petty
Auditors: Grant Thornton LLP

LOCATIONS

HQ: Health Grades, Inc.
500 Golden Ridge Rd., Golden, CO 80401
Phone: 303-716-0041 **Fax:** 303-716-1298
Web: www.healthgrades.com

PRODUCTS/OPERATIONS

2006 Sales

	$ mil.	% of total
Provider Services	20.1	72
Internet Business Group	5.1	18
Strategic Health Solutions	2.6	10
Total	**27.8**	**100**

Selected Products and Services

Provider Services
  Hospital marketing programs
    America's 50 Best Hospitals
    Distinguished Hospital Program for Patient Safety
    Strategic Quality Initiative
    Strategic Quality Partnership
  Quality improvement services
    Quality Assessment
    Quality Assessment and Implementation
    Quality Report for Hospital Professionals
Internet Business Group
  Healthcare Quality Reports for Consumers
  Internet Patient Acquisition program (marketing tools for physicians)
Strategic Health Solutions (for employers, benefit consultants, payors, and others)
  Decision Points (health care decision-making tools)
  Healthcare Quality Guides
  Health Management Suite (customized sets of quality data)
  Medical Cost Calculator

COMPETITORS

CareScience
GE Healthcare
Premier, Inc.
Solucient
WebMD Health

HISTORICAL FINANCIALS

Company Type: Public

Income Statement				FYE: December 31
	REVENUE ($ mil.)	NET INCOME ($ mil.)	NET PROFIT MARGIN	EMPLOYEES
12/06	27.8	3.2	11.5%	123
12/05	20.8	4.1	19.7%	106
12/04	14.5	1.8	12.4%	67
12/03	8.8	(1.3)	—	56
12/02	5.3	(1.6)	—	48
Annual Growth	51.3%	—	—	26.5%

2006 Year-End Financials

Debt ratio: 0.0%
Return on equity: 29.4%
Cash ($ mil.): 16.0
Current ratio: 1.38
Long-term debt ($ mil.): 0.0
No. of shares (mil.): 28.5
Dividends
  Yield: —
  Payout: —
Market value ($ mil.): 127.8
R&D as % of sales: —
Advertising as % of sales: —

Stock History

NASDAQ (CM): HGRD

	STOCK PRICE ($) FY Close	P/E High/Low	PER SHARE ($) Earnings	Dividends	Book Value
12/06	4.49	78 33	0.09	—	0.43
12/05	6.32	54 23	0.12	—	0.34
12/04	2.90	65 11	0.05	—	0.14
12/03	0.60	— —	(0.05)	—	0.06
12/02	0.03	— —	(0.05)	—	0.13
Annual Growth	249.8%	— —	—	—	33.8%

HealthStream, Inc.

HealthStream replenishes the well of knowledge for medical workers. The company offers Internet-based educational and training content for health care professionals. Courses train employees on new equipment, introduce new pharmaceuticals, provide continuing education credits, and disseminate regulatory information. The company's flagship Internet-based product, the Healthstream Learning Center, has nearly 1.5 million subscribers. HealthStream generates sales from subscription fees based on the number of users and type of content provided. Its clients include health care organizations, pharmaceutical companies, and medical device firms. CEO Robert Frist owns 26% of HealthStream.

It added research products when it acquired Data Management & Research, Inc., in 2005. DMR provides surveys, data analyses, and other research measurement products for patients, doctors, and others in the health care community.

In 2007 the company acquired The Jackson Organization, Research Consultants, Inc. TJO also offers patient and hospital surveys and research analysis tools.

EXECUTIVES

Chairman, President, and CEO: Robert A. Frist Jr., age 39, $137,508 pay
EVP and Interim CFO: Arthur E. Newman, age 57
SVP: J. Edward (Eddie) Pearson
VP Sales: Greg Horne
Director Information Technology: Steve Moore
Human Resources: Meredith Hawn
Auditors: Ernst & Young LLP

LOCATIONS

HQ: HealthStream, Inc.
209 10th Ave. South, Ste. 450, Nashville, TN 37203
Phone: 615-301-3100 **Fax:** 615-301-3200
Web: www.healthstream.com

HealthStream has operations in Dallas, Denver, Laurel, Maryland, and Nashville, Tennessee.

PRODUCTS/OPERATIONS

2006 Sales

	$ mil.	% of total
Healthcare organizations & professionals	25.4	80
Pharmaceutical & medical device companies	6.4	20
Total	**31.8**	**100**

COMPETITORS

A.D.A.M.
AMA
EBSCO
Medsite
Saba Software
SumTotal

HISTORICAL FINANCIALS

Company Type: Public

Income Statement				FYE: December 31
	REVENUE ($ mil.)	NET INCOME ($ mil.)	NET PROFIT MARGIN	EMPLOYEES
12/06	31.8	2.5	7.9%	160
12/05	27.4	1.9	6.9%	160
12/04	20.1	(1.0)	—	146
12/03	18.2	(3.4)	—	143
12/02	15.8	(16.6)	—	175
Annual Growth	19.1%	—	—	(2.2%)

2006 Year-End Financials

Debt ratio: 0.4%
Return on equity: 9.0%
Cash ($ mil.): 12.7
Current ratio: 2.01
Long-term debt ($ mil.): 0.1
No. of shares (mil.): 21.9
Dividends
  Yield: —
  Payout: —
Market value ($ mil.): 86.6
R&D as % of sales: —
Advertising as % of sales: —

Stock History

NASDAQ (GM): HSTM

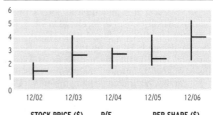

	STOCK PRICE ($) FY Close	P/E High/Low	PER SHARE ($) Earnings	Dividends	Book Value
12/06	3.95	47 21	0.11	—	1.35
12/05	2.33	45 21	0.09	—	1.20
12/04	2.68	— —	(0.05)	—	1.05
12/03	2.60	— —	(0.17)	—	1.10
12/02	1.41	— —	(0.82)	—	1.27
Annual Growth	29.4%	— —	—	—	1.5%

Healthways, Inc.

Healthways (formerly American Healthways) paves the way for disease management. The company provides care management, as well as wellness programs, for health plans, hospitals, and self-insured employers nationwide. Its services help plan members with diabetes, respiratory diseases, cancer, and other chronic and serious diseases to coordinate their health care, keep up with treatment plans, and maintain healthy behaviors. The company also has screening and prevention programs to find people who are at risk for various diseases and to promote healthy living. And through a partnership with Medco Health, it helps users manage their prescription drugs.

In 2006 the firm acquired preventive health services provider AXIA Health Management for more than $450 million. The acquisition added a host of wellness services, such as fitness and nutrition programs, to Healthways' service offering. Among them are an online smoking cessation support group called QuitNet and the SilverSneakers fitness program for seniors.

Healthways provides services to some 2.5 million people in all 50 states, Puerto Rico, and Guam. Health insurer CIGNA, its largest customer, accounts for more than 20% of revenue.

Healthways set up shop overseas in 2007, with a contract to provide disease management and wellness services to members of German health insurer Deutsche Angestellten Krankenkasse.

In 2006 the company announced plans to acquire disease management company LifeMasters Supported Selfcare, but the agreement was later terminated. Healthways inked the deal to acquire AXIA shortly thereafter.

HISTORY

In 1981 Thomas Cigarran and Henry Herr (alumni of a company that's now part of HCA) joined with venture capitalist Martin Koldyke to found American Healthcorp to buy hospitals. The company diversified, entering the diabetes market in 1984 and arthritis care in 1987.

With profitability lagging, the company sold its hospitals to focus on niche care. In the same spirit, it de-emphasized arthritis care in 1990. The company went public in 1991.

After a brief foray into obesity treatment, the company in 1994 invested in AmSurg, a manager of ambulatory surgery centers. (AmSurg was spun off in 1997.)

By the late 1990s the company increasingly targeted HMOs. It signed its first contract with Principal Health Care (1996, ended in 1998 after Coventry Health Care bought the HMO). Contracts with such HMOs as John Deere Health Care and Health Options of Blue Cross & Blue Shield of Florida followed in 1998.

To standardize income, the company in 1998 converted its contracts from shared savings arrangements (in which the company's earnings were based on the payers' savings) to fee-based arrangements. In 1999 American Healthcorp began offering a cardiac health management program to its hospital and HMO clients; that year it changed its name to American Healthways to reflect its expanded product line.

American Healthways in 2000 signed a deal with Agilent Technologies to offer that company's home heart monitoring systems to its patients. It also launched MYHEALTHWAYS, a Web-based application, which offers disease-prevention plans to health plan members.

In 2001 American Healthways launched Comprehensive Care Enhancement Programs, under which all health plan members are screened and provided with any needed health care programs.

In 2003 the company acquired Company StatusOne Health Systems in order to expand its health management service offerings for high-risk populations. American Healthways changed its name to Healthways in early 2006.

EXECUTIVES

Chairman: Thomas G. Cigarran, age 66, $250,000 pay
President, CEO, and Director: Ben R. Leedle Jr., age 46, $916,800 pay
EVP, CFO, and Secretary: Mary A. Chaput, age 57
EVP and COO: James E. Pope, age 54
EVP and Chief Strategy Officer: Robert E. Stone, age 61, $460,680 pay
EVP: Mary D. Hunter, age 62
EVP: Matthew E. Kelliher, age 52, $460,680 pay
EVP and CIO: Robert L. Chaput, age 57
SVP, Chief Accounting Officer, and Corporate Controller: Alfred Lumsdaine, age 42
SVP and Chief Communications Officer: Nicholas E. Dantona
SVP, Outcomes Improvement and Chief Medical Officer: Dexter Shurney
SVP Human Resources: Christopher Cigarran
SVP Marketing: Carol Murdock
Director, Center for Health Research: Brenda Motheral, age 38
Auditors: Ernst & Young LLP

LOCATIONS

HQ: Healthways, Inc.
3841 Green Hills Village Dr., Nashville, TN 37215
Phone: 615-665-1122   **Fax:** 615-665-7697
Web: www.healthways.com

COMPETITORS

APS Healthcare
AvMed Health Plans
CareGuide
Express Scripts
I-trax
Matria Healthcare
OptumHealth
SHPS

HISTORICAL FINANCIALS

Company Type: Public

Income Statement

FYE: August 31

	REVENUE ($ mil.)	NET INCOME ($ mil.)	NET PROFIT MARGIN	EMPLOYEES
8/07	615.6	45.1	7.3%	3,800
8/06	412.3	37.2	9.0%	2,855
8/05	312.5	33.1	10.6%	2,231
8/04	245.4	26.1	10.6%	1,875
8/03	165.5	18.5	11.2%	1,511
Annual Growth	38.9%	25.0%	—	25.9%

2007 Year-End Financials

Debt ratio: 81.9%
Return on equity: 14.1%
Cash ($ mil.): 47.7
Current ratio: 1.08
Long-term debt ($ mil.): 297.1
No. of shares (mil.): 35.6
Dividends
  Yield: —
  Payout: —
Market value ($ mil.): 1,773.2
R&D as % of sales: —
Advertising as % of sales: —

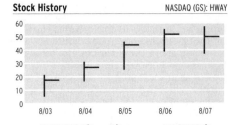

	STOCK PRICE ($) FY Close	P/E High/Low		PER SHARE ($) Earnings	Dividends	Book Value
8/07	49.80	47	31	1.22	—	10.19
8/06	51.62	54	38	1.02	—	7.94
8/05	43.70	49	28	0.93	—	6.12
8/04	27.00	41	23	0.75	—	4.71
8/03	17.54	37	10	0.56	—	7.12
Annual Growth	29.8%	—	—	21.5%	—	9.4%

Hecla Mining

Not all that glitters at Hecla Mining is gold — in fact, most of it is silver. Hecla explores for and mines gold, silver, lead, and zinc. It produces about 6 million ounces of silver and 175,000 ounces of gold annually; silver accounts for more than half of the company's sales. Hecla operates mines in the US (Alaska and Idaho), Mexico, and Venezuela. The company's Greens Creek mine in Alaska is a joint venture managed by Kennecott Greens Creek Mining in which Kennecott Minerals controls the majority stake. Hecla is focusing its exploration and development efforts on its properties in Venezuela.

EXECUTIVES

CEO, President, and Director: Phillips S. Baker Jr., age 47, $581,338 pay
SVP, Operations: Ronald W. Clayton, age 48, $280,675 pay
SVP, General Counsel and Secretary: Philip C. Wolf, age 59, $283,029 pay
VP and CFO: Lewis E. Walde, age 40, $236,425 pay
VP; President, Minera Hecla Venezolana: Michael H. Callahan, age 43, $308,905 pay
VP, Investor and Public Relations: Vicki J. Veltkamp, age 50
VP, Exploration: Dean W. A. McDonald, age 50
VP Corporate Development: Don Poirier
Director, Human Resources: George Lytle
Auditors: BDO Seidman, LLP

LOCATIONS

HQ: Hecla Mining Company
6500 N. Mineral Dr., Ste. 200,
Coeur d'Alene, ID 83815
Phone: 208-769-4100   **Fax:** 208-769-7612
Web: www.hecla-mining.com

2006 Sales

	$ mil.	% of total
Canada	94.3	43
Japan	47.0	23
Venezuela	28.4	13
South Korea	22.7	10
UK	13.4	6
Mexico	4.8	2
China	4.0	2
US	2.8	1
Total	**217.4**	**100**

PRODUCTS/OPERATIONS

2006 Sales

	$ mil.	% of total
La Camorra	94.8	44
Greens Creek	69.2	32
Lucky Friday	52.4	24
San Sebastian	1.0	—
Total	**217.4**	**100**

Selected Properties

La Camorra mine (gold, Venezuela)
Greens Creek mine (30%, silver, Alaska)
Lucky Friday mine (silver and lead, Idaho)
San Sabastian mine (silver, Mexico)

COMPETITORS

Agnico-Eagle
Apex Silver Mines
Barrick Gold
Canyon Resources
Coeur d'Alene Mines
Newmont Mining
Pan American Silver
Peñoles
Vale do Rio Doce

HISTORICAL FINANCIALS

Company Type: Public

Income Statement

FYE: December 31

	REVENUE ($ mil.)	NET INCOME ($ mil.)	NET PROFIT MARGIN	EMPLOYEES
12/06	217.4	69.1	31.8%	1,163
12/05	110.2	(25.4)	—	1,191
12/04	130.8	(6.1)	—	1,417
12/03	116.3	(6.0)	—	1,074
12/02	105.7	8.6	8.1%	720
Annual Growth	**19.8%**	**68.4%**	**—**	**12.7%**

2006 Year-End Financials

Debt ratio: —
Return on equity: 35.8%
Cash ($ mil.): 101.3
Current ratio: 3.16
Long-term debt ($ mil.): —
No. of shares (mil.): 119.8

Dividends
  Yield: —
  Payout: —
Market value ($ mil.): 917.4
R&D as % of sales: —
Advertising as % of sales: —

Stock History

NYSE: HL

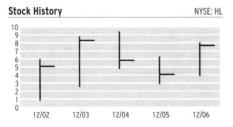

	STOCK PRICE ($) FY Close	P/E High/Low	PER SHARE ($) Earnings	Dividends	Book Value
12/06	7.66	14 7	0.57	—	1.88
12/05	4.06	— —	(0.22)	—	1.36
12/04	5.83	— —	(0.15)	—	1.43
12/03	8.29	— —	(0.16)	—	1.48
12/02	5.06	— —	(0.18)	—	0.83
Annual Growth	**10.9%**	**— —**	**—**	**—**	**22.4%**

Heelys, Inc.

Heelys can't touch Elvis as The King of Rock 'n' Roll but the company has made a name for itself with those who walk and roll. The firm's flagship product, HEELYS-wheeled footwear, includes a replaceable wheel in the heel that enables the user to transition to skating. Among its other products are helmets and other protective gear, as well as more wheels. Founded in 2000, Heelys has been on a roll since and sells its product line at retailers and department stores such as Dick's Sporting Goods, Nordstrom, and Zappos.com. The company also has independent distributors in Japan, South Korea, and Southeast Asia. Heelys generates about 95% of its net sales from its HEELYS-wheeled footwear.

Heelys is searching for a new CEO following the resignation in February 2008 of Michael Staffaroni. Staffaroni, who served as chief executive since 2001, was succeeded on an interim basis by Ralph Parks, formerly president and CEO of FootAction USA.

In 2007 Heelys is looking to diversify its products portfolio by expanding into apparel, backpacks, and non-wheeled footwear. The footwear firm rolled out its Gamer by Heelys collection for the 2007 holiday shopping season.

Heelys filed with the Securities and Exchange Commission to raise as much as $115 million through an initial public offering, which priced at $21 a share when it went public in December 2006. The company plans to use IPO funds to pay off debt, develop new products, improve infrastructure, and increase staff. Gary Martin, president and CEO of Capital Southwest Corporation, was appointed non-executive chairman in August 2007.

EXECUTIVES

Chairman: Gary L. Martin, age 61
Interim CEO and Director: Ralph T. Parks, age 62
SVP and Director: Patrick F. Hamner, age 50
SVP Global Sales: Charles D. Beery, age 55, $364,704 pay
SVP Marketing: Donald K. (Don) Carroll
VP, Finance, CFO, Secretary, and Treasurer: Michael W. Hessong, age 41
VP International: John W. O'Neil
VP Marketing: James S. (Jim) Peliotes, age 40
VP, Design and Development: Robert W. (Bob) Byrne, age 43
Director, Research and Development, and Director: Roger R. Adams, age 52
Auditors: Deloitte & Touche LLP

LOCATIONS

HQ: Heelys, Inc.
  3200 Belmeade Dr., Ste. 100, Carrollton, TX 75006
Phone: 214-390-1831   **Fax:** 214-390-1661
Web: www.heelys.com

COMPETITORS

adidas
NIKE
Reebok

HISTORICAL FINANCIALS

Company Type: Public

Income Statement

FYE: December 31

	REVENUE ($ mil.)	NET INCOME ($ mil.)	NET PROFIT MARGIN	EMPLOYEES
12/06	188.2	29.2	15.5%	41
12/05	44.0	4.3	9.8%	—
12/04	21.3	0.8	3.8%	—
12/03	22.2	1.1	5.0%	—
Annual Growth	**103.9%**	**198.3%**	**—**	**—**

2006 Year-End Financials

Debt ratio: —
Return on equity: 56.9%
Cash ($ mil.): 54.2
Current ratio: 8.36
Long-term debt ($ mil.): —
No. of shares (mil.): 27.0

Dividends
  Yield: —
  Payout: —
Market value ($ mil.): 868.3
R&D as % of sales: —
Advertising as % of sales: —

Stock History

NASDAQ (GM): HLYS

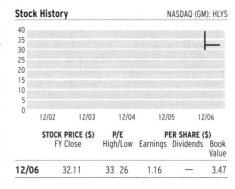

	STOCK PRICE ($) FY Close	P/E High/Low	PER SHARE ($) Earnings	Dividends	Book Value
12/06	32.11	33 26	1.16	—	3.47

HEICO Corporation

Here's a HEICO haiku: HEICO companies/ Providing for jet engines/ In flight or on land. Through the subsidiaries that make up the company's Flight Support Group, HEICO manufactures parts for jet engines that can be substituted for original parts. Products include combustion chambers and compressor blades. Flight Support operations, which include repair and overhaul services, account for more than 75% of HEICO's sales. Subsidiaries in HEICO's Electronic Technologies Group make a variety of electro-optical, electronic, and microwave products, primarily for defense applications.

HEICO has benefited by diversifying its product line. Customers outside the commercial aviation industry, such as electronics, industrial, medical, and telecommunications companies, account for a significant portion of the company's sales.

In 2006 HEICO's Flight Support Group acquired Arger Enterprises, a subsidiary of Melrose PLC. Arger makes and distributes aircraft parts, mainly for the commercial aviation market. Also in 2006, HEICO bought a controlling stake in Prime Air Parts, which deals in spare parts for aircraft.

The following year HEICO's Electronic Technologies Group acquired EMD Technologies, a maker of high voltage energy generators used in medical, industrial imaging, and baggage scanning systems. Details of the transaction were not disclosed.

A few years of careful acquisitions complimented by organic growth contributed to record sales and profits for HEICO in fiscal 2007. The company's Flight Support Group led the charge with a 38% increase in sales; Electronic Technologies was no slouch with an 8% increase.

Chairman and CEO Laurans Mendelson and his family own about 23% of HEICO; Florida investor Herbert Wertheim owns about 11%. Lufthansa holds a 20% stake in HEICO Aerospace (the umbrella company for the company's Flight Support Group).

HISTORY

Founded in 1957 as Heinicke Instruments to make laboratory products, the company moved into jet engine parts in 1974 with the acquisition of Jet Avion. The company changed its name to HEICO (a shortened version of its previous name) in 1985. After a faulty combustion chamber erupted in flames that year, the FAA ordered all combustion chambers on US jets to be inspected and, if necessary, replaced. HEICO's sales skyrocketed, but descended back to earth after airlines found they had overstocked.

By the early 1990s defense cutbacks and declining aircraft orders reduced business, and HEICO began to diversify. In 1991 it formed MediTek to acquire medical imaging facilities but then sold the company to U.S. Diagnostic for $24 million five years later. Lufthansa Technik AG, the service subsidiary of Deutsche Lufthansa, paid HEICO $26 million for a 20% stake in HEICO's flight support operations in 1997.

HEICO acquired jet engine parts companies McClain International and Rogers-Dierks in 1998. The next year the company added Radiant Power (back-up power supplies and battery packs for aerospace applications), Turbine Kinetics and AeroKinetics (replacement parts for aircraft engines), Santa Barbara Infrared (infrared and ground support equipment), and Thermal Structures (insulation products).

HEICO sold its Trilectron Industries ground support equipment subsidiary to Illinois Tool Works in 2000 in a deal worth about $64 million. The following year the company formed a joint venture with AMR (parent of American Airlines) to accelerate development of FAA-approved replacement parts. Also in 2001, HEICO bought Inertial Airline Services, Avitech Engineering Corp., and Aviation Facilities, Inc. In 2003 HEICO acquired Niacc Technology, an aircraft component repair and overhaul company.

The company added to its aerospace electronics operations with the acquisition of Connectronics, a maker of high-voltage wire and interconnection devices, in 2004.

In November 2005 HEICO moved to expand its flight support business by buying a 51% stake in Seal Dynamics, a designer and distributor of hydraulic, pneumatic, mechanical, and electromechanical components for the commercial, regional, and general aviation markets.

EXECUTIVES

Chairman, President, and CEO: Laurans A. Mendelson, age 69, $1,571,460 pay
EVP and CFO: Thomas S. Irwin, age 61, $817,918 pay
EVP and Director; President and CEO, HEICO Aerospace: Eric A. Mendelson, age 42, $817,918 pay
EVP, General Counsel, President and CEO, HEICO Electronics Technologies, and Director: Victor H. Mendelson, age 40, $817,918 pay
EVP, HEICO Aerospace: James L. Reum, age 76
Auditors: Deloitte & Touche LLP

LOCATIONS

HQ: HEICO Corporation
3000 Taft St., Hollywood, FL 33021
Phone: 954-987-4000 **Fax:** 954-987-8228
Web: www.heico.com

2007 Sales

	$ mil.	% of total
US	365.6	72
Other countries	142.3	28
Total	**507.9**	**100**

PRODUCTS/OPERATIONS

2007 Sales

	$ mil.	% of total
Flight Support Group	383.9	76
Electronic Technologies Group	124.0	24
Total	**507.9**	**100**

Selected Subsidiaries and Affiliates

Flight Support
HEICO Aerospace Holdings Corp. (HEICO Aerospace, 80%)
Aircraft Technology, Inc.
Aviation Facilities, Inc.
Future Aviation, Inc.
HEICO Aerospace Corporation
HEICO Aerospace Parts Corp.
Jet Avion Corporation
Jetseal, Inc.
LPI Industries Corporation
McClain International, Inc.
Niacc-Avitech Technologies Inc.
Northwings Accessories Corporation
Rogers-Dierks, Inc.
Thermal Structures, Inc.
Turbine Kinetics, Inc.
Electronic Technologies
HEICO Electronic Technologies Corp.
Analog Modules, Inc.
Connectronics Corporation
Leader Tech, Inc.
Lumina Power, Inc.
Radiant Power Corp.
Santa Barbara Infrared, Inc.
Sierra Microwave Technology, LLC

COMPETITORS

AAR
Barnes Group
BBA Aviation
CIC International
DeCrane
Doncasters
GE Aviation
Goodrich Corporation
Kellstrom Aerospace
Ladish Co.
Pratt & Whitney
Rolls-Royce
SIFCO
TIMCO Aviation
Triumph Group
United Technologies
Wyman-Gordon

HISTORICAL FINANCIALS

Company Type: Public

Income Statement

FYE: October 31

	REVENUE ($ mil.)	NET INCOME ($ mil.)	NET PROFIT MARGIN	EMPLOYEES
10/07	507.9	39.0	7.7%	2,185
10/06	392.2	31.9	8.1%	1,843
10/05	269.6	22.8	8.5%	1,556
10/04	215.7	20.6	9.6%	1,263
10/03	176.4	12.2	6.9%	1,011
Annual Growth	**30.3%**	**33.7%**	**—**	**21.2%**

2007 Year-End Financials

Debt ratio: 14.5%	Dividends
Return on equity: 11.3%	Yield: 0.1%
Cash ($ mil.): 4.9	Payout: 2.8%
Current ratio: 2.49	Market value ($ mil.): 573.7
Long-term debt ($ mil.): 53.8	R&D as % of sales: —
No. of shares (mil.): 10.5	Advertising as % of sales: —

Stock History

NYSE: HEI

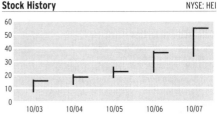

	STOCK PRICE ($) FY Close	P/E High/Low		PER SHARE ($) Earnings	Dividends	Book Value
10/07	54.44	38	23	1.45	0.04	35.26
10/06	36.28	31	18	1.20	0.08	30.77
10/05	22.17	29	21	0.87	0.05	27.19
10/04	18.10	25	16	0.80	0.05	24.99
10/03	15.30	31	15	0.50	0.05	22.86
Annual Growth	**37.3%**	**—**	**—**	**30.5%**	**(5.4%)**	**11.4%**

Hercules Technology Growth Capital

Hercules Technology Growth Capital (HTGC) performs its feats of strength with money. The closed-end investment firm offers financing vehicles to companies in the technology and life sciences sectors. HTCG provides primarily private companies (as well as some public ones) with such products as mezzanine loans, senior secured loans, and select private equity investments. Loans typically range from $1 million to $25 million. HTGC's portfolio includes around 70 companies representing more than $280 million in committed capital. Portfolio companies include IKANO Communications, Occam Networks, and Talisma. Co-founder and CEO Manuel Henriquez owns about 5% of HTGC.

EXECUTIVES

Chairman and CEO: Manuel A. Henriquez, age 41
CFO: David M. Lund, age 53
CTO: Shane A. Stettenbenz
Senior Managing Director and Group Head of Technology: Samir (Sam) Bhaumik, age 43
Senior Managing Director and Group Head of Life Science: Parag I. Shah
Managing Director, Life Sciences: Kathleen (Kathy) Conte
Managing Director, Technology: Mark S. Denomme
Managing Director, Technology: Kevin L. Grossman
Managing Director, Technology: Roy Y. Liu
Managing Director, Business Development: Gregory (Greg) Roth
Managing Director, Technology: Kimberly Davis King
Managing Director, Technology: Jason Sanders
Chief Legal Officer: H. Scott Harvey
Controller: Jessica Baron
Auditors: Ernst & Young LLP

LOCATIONS

HQ: Hercules Technology Growth Capital, Inc.
400 Hamilton Ave., Ste. 310, Palo Alto, CA 94301
Phone: 650-289-3060   **Fax:** 650-473-9194
Web: www.herculestech.com

Hercules Technology Growth Capital is headquartered in Silicon Valley; it also operates offices in Boston; Boulder, Colorado; Chicago; Columbus, Ohio; and Los Angeles.

PRODUCTS/OPERATIONS

2006 Sales

	$ mil.	% of total
Interest	26.3	89
Fees	3.2	11
Total	**29.5**	**100**

2006 Portfolio By Business Segment

	% of total
Biopharmaceuticals	41
Software	14
Electronics & computer hardware	11
Consumer & business products	8
Communications & networking	7
Medical devices & equipment	7
Semiconductors	5
Internet consumer & business services	4
Energy	3
Total	**100**

COMPETITORS

Accel Partners
Astellas Venture Management
August Capital
Bay Partners
De Novo Ventures
Draper Fisher Jurvetson
Enterprise Partners
Francisco Partners
The Gores Group
IVP
Kleiner Perkins
Mayfield Fund
Menlo Ventures
Norwest Venture Partners
Scale Venture Partners
Sequoia Capital
Sutter Hill Ventures
Trinity Ventures

HISTORICAL FINANCIALS

Company Type: Public

Income Statement				FYE: December 31
	REVENUE ($ mil.)	NET INCOME ($ mil.)	NET PROFIT MARGIN	EMPLOYEES
12/06	29.5	11.4	38.6%	26
12/05	10.7	2.1	19.6%	19
12/04	0.2	(2.0)	—	11
Annual Growth	1,114.5%	—	—	53.7%

2006 Year-End Financials

Debt ratio: 16.1%
Return on equity: 6.2%
Cash ($ mil.): 16.4
Current ratio: —
Long-term debt ($ mil.): 41.0
No. of shares (mil.): 23.0
Dividends
  Yield: 8.4%
  Payout: 142.9%
Market value ($ mil.): 327.6
R&D as % of sales: —
Advertising as % of sales: —

Stock History			NASDAQ (GM): HTGC

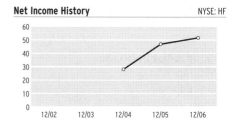

| 12/02 | 12/03 | 12/04 | 12/05 | 12/06 |

	STOCK PRICE ($) FY Close	P/E High/Low	PER SHARE ($) Earnings	Dividends	Book Value
12/06	14.25	17 13	0.84	1.20	11.11
12/05	11.99	48 32	0.30	0.03	11.67
Annual Growth	18.8%	— —	180.0%	3,900.0%	(4.8%)

HFF, Inc.

HFF (also known as Holliday Fenoglio Fowler) is keeping it real as one of the US's largest companies providing capital markets services related to commercial real estate. With nearly 20 offices across the country, HFF helps clients find lenders for their commercial mortgage needs, select joint venture capital partners, and find buyers for their commercial properties. The firm was once owned by Australia-based Lend Lease, however, an investor group composed of HFF associates bought the company in 2003. Three years later the company filed to go public as HFF Inc.

HFF plans to grow by opening additional offices in key US markets; it is also eyeing operations in foreign markets. Affiliate HFF Securities was formed in 2004. The Los Angeles-based investment banking firm offers advisory services, including real estate, financial, valuation, legal, and tax expertise; it also provides private equity fundraising and institutional marketing services for public and private real estate companies.

EXECUTIVES

CEO and Director: John H. Pelusi Jr., age 52, $1,990,073 pay
COO: Nancy O. Goodson, age 49, $275,000 pay
CFO: Gregory R. Conley, age 46
Executive Managing Director, Los Angeles: Scott F. McMullin
Executive Managing Director, Miami: Manuel De Zárraga
Senior Managing Director, New York City: Whitney H. (Whit) Wilcox
Executive Managing Director, Washington, D.C.: Stephen C. Conley
Managing Director, Miami: Patrick Poggi
Auditors: Ernst & Young LLP

LOCATIONS

HQ: HFF, Inc.
One Oxford Centre, 301 Grant St., Ste. 600, Pittsburgh, PA 15219
Phone: 412-281-8714   **Fax:** 412-281-2792
Web: www.hfflp.com

HFF has operations in Atlanta; Boston; Chicago; Dallas; Florham Park, New Jersey; Hartford, Connecticut; Houston; Indianapolis; Los Angeles; Miami; New York; Orange County, California; Pittsburgh; Portland, Oregon; San Diego; San Francisco; Washington, DC; and Westport, Connecticut.

PRODUCTS/OPERATIONS

2006 Sales

	$ mil.	% of total
Capital markets services	225.2	98
Other	4.5	2
Total	**229.7**	**100**

COMPETITORS

Allied Capital	Fremont General
Arbor Commercial	Irwin Financial
Boston Capital	Jones Lang LaSalle
Capmark	Legg Mason
CB Richard Ellis	NorthMarq Capital
Cushman & Wakefield	Ocwen Financial
Eastdil Secured	Trammell Crow Company

HISTORICAL FINANCIALS

Company Type: Public

Income Statement				FYE: December 31
	ASSETS ($ mil.)	NET INCOME ($ mil.)	INCOME AS % OF ASSETS	EMPLOYEES
12/06	154.3	51.5	33.4%	400
12/05	89.9	46.8	52.1%	355
12/04	56.1	28.1	50.1%	312
Annual Growth	65.8%	35.4%	—	13.2%

2006 Year-End Financials

Equity as % of assets: —
Return on assets: 42.2%
Return on equity: 655.3%
Long-term debt ($ mil.): 0.1
Sales ($ mil.): 229.7

Net Income History		NYSE: HF

| 12/02 | 12/03 | 12/04 | 12/05 | 12/06 |

Hiland Partners

Hiland Partners is looking for the higher ground of increased profits. The company, which went public in 2005, is a combination of Hiland Partners LLC and Continental Gas, a former subsidiary of Continental Resources. Hiland provides natural gas gathering and processing services to customers in the Mid-Continent and Rocky Mountain regions of the US through 13 gas gathering systems with 1,844 miles of pipeline, five natural gas processing plants, three natural gas treating facilities, and three NGL fractionation plants. It also provides air compression and water injection services for oil and gas recovery operations in North Dakota. Chairman Harold Hamm owns 57.8% of the company.

In 2006 Hiland Partners acquired more than 550 miles of natural gas gathering pipelines and other assets from Enogex Gas Gathering for $93 million.

EXECUTIVES

Chairman, Hiland Partners GP, LLC: Harold G. Hamm, age 62

President, CEO, and Director, Hiland Partners GP, LLC: Joseph L. Griffin, age 46

VP Finance, CFO, Secretary, and Director, Hiland Partners GP, LLC: Ken Maples, age 45

VP Business Development, Hiland Partners GP, LLC: Ron Hill, age 57

VP Operations and Engineering, Hiland Partners GP, LLC: Robert W. Shain, age 57

Auditors: Grant Thornton LLP

LOCATIONS

HQ: Hiland Partners, LP
205 W. Maple, Ste. 1100, Enid, OK 73701
Phone: 580-242-6040   **Fax:** 580-548-5188
Web: www.hilandpartners.com

Hiland Partners operates primarily in the Mid-Continent and Rocky Mountain regions of the US through its office in Enid, Oklahoma.

PRODUCTS/OPERATIONS

2006 Sales

	$ mil.	% of total
Midstream operations		
Third parties	210.7	96
Affiliates	4.2	2
Compression services	4.8	2
Total	**219.7**	**100**

COMPETITORS

Atlas America
Belden & Blake
DCP Midstream Partners
Enogex
Equitrans

HISTORICAL FINANCIALS

Company Type: Public

Income Statement				FYE: December 31
	REVENUE ($ mil.)	NET INCOME ($ mil.)	NET PROFIT MARGIN	EMPLOYEES
12/06	219.7	14.7	6.7%	95
12/05	166.6	10.3	6.2%	67
12/04	98.3	4.9	5.0%	51
12/03	10.6	3.4	32.3%	42
12/02	5.7	1.5	26.5%	—
Annual Growth	**149.2%**	**76.9%**	**—**	**31.3%**

2006 Year-End Financials

Debt ratio: 87.8%
Return on equity: 9.6%
Cash ($ mil.): 15.1
Current ratio: 1.54
Long-term debt ($ mil.): 147.4
No. of shares (mil.): 5.2
Dividends
Yield: 4.8%
Payout: 194.9%
Market value ($ mil.): 282.6
R&D as % of sales: —
Advertising as % of sales: —

Stock History				NASDAQ (GS): HLND

	STOCK PRICE ($) FY Close	P/E High/Low		PER SHARE ($) Earnings	Dividends	Book Value
12/06	54.70	42	27	1.36	2.65	32.47
12/05	36.81	35	21	1.32	1.20	31.80
Annual Growth	**48.6%**			**3.0%**	**120.8%**	**2.1%**

HireRight, Inc.

It would be just plain silly to hire wrong. HireRight provides Web-based pre-employment screening services for human resources and security professionals. The company helps businesses perform background verification, drug screening, and skills and behavioral assessment for prospective new hires. Serving about 1,400 customers, HireRight's main product offering includes its Extended Workforce Screening Solution suite of software applications. Major shareholders include private equity fund NCP-1, L.P (formerly known as Mellon Ventures — 29%), Doll Capital Management (23%), and affiliates of The St. Paul Travelers Companies (21%). HireRight was founded in 1995.

The company's chief subsidiary, HireRight Estonia AS, is based in Tallinn, Estonia. HireRight offers its products and services to more than 200 countries around the globe. Proceeds from its 2007 IPO will be used to expand its international presence as well as to augment its sales and marketing efforts. It also plans to use the money to invest in other technologies, products, and services related to the background verification sector.

Chairman, president, and CEO Eric Boden has an almost 11% ownership stake in the company.

EXECUTIVES

Chairman, President, and CEO: Eric J. Boden, age 58, $273,077 pay

CFO and Secretary: Jeffrey A. (Jeff) Wahba, age 50, $170,077 pay

VP Engineering: Stefano Malnati, age 44, $206,923 pay

VP Marketing and Business Development: David M. Nachman, age 40, $219,885 pay

VP Operations: Lisa A. Gallagher, age 44

VP Worldwide Sales: Glen E. Schrank, age 50, $187,612 pay

VP Information Technology and Information Security: Alexander F. (Alex) Munro, age 40

VP Human Resources: Barbara M. Nieto, age 42

VP Product Management: Robert J. (Rob) Pickell

Auditors: Deloitte & Touche LLP

LOCATIONS

HQ: HireRight, Inc.
5151 California Ave., Irvine, CA 92617
Phone: 949-428-5800   **Fax:** 949-428-5801
Web: www.hireright.com

COMPETITORS

ChoicePoint
First Advantage
Know It All Background Research
Kroll
Verifications, Inc.

HISTORICAL FINANCIALS

Company Type: Public

Income Statement				FYE: December 31
	REVENUE ($ mil.)	NET INCOME ($ mil.)	NET PROFIT MARGIN	EMPLOYEES
12/06	58.1	10.9	18.8%	390
12/05	43.0	0.0	—	367
12/04	31.8	(0.3)	—	—
12/03	21.1	(1.7)	—	175
Annual Growth	**40.2%**	**—**		**30.6%**

2006 Year-End Financials

Debt ratio: —
Return on equity: —
Cash ($ mil.): 8.4
Current ratio: 2.38
Long-term debt ($ mil.): —

Net Income History   NASDAQ (GM): HIRE

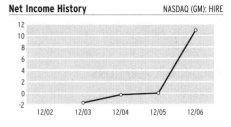

Hittite Microwave

And lo, the Hittites did rise up out of their land, and they sacked Babylon. Actually, these Hittites rise up out of the Commonwealth of Massachusetts, and they're out to sell semiconductors. Hittite Microwave designs and develops microwave, millimeter-wave, and radio-frequency (RF) chips for aerospace, broadband, cellular, and military applications. In addition to amplifiers, frequency multipliers, mixers, modulators, switches, and other components, the company provides custom RF integrated circuits (ICs). Boeing and Motorola are among Hittite's more than 2,700 customers. Chairman emeritus and founder Yalcin Ayasli controls 47% of Hittite Microwave.

Hittite Microwave is a fabless semiconductor company, which means that it contracts out the production of its chips to other companies, known as silicon foundries. Hittite's principal foundry contractors are Atmel, Global Communication Semiconductors (GCS), IBM Microelectronics, M/A-Com, Taiwan Semiconductor, TriQuint Semiconductor, United Monolithic Semiconductors (UMS), and WIN Semiconductors. Hittite also competes with some of those companies with its microwave and RF ICs.

The company has agreed to license the Velocium line of monolithic microwave ICs and related intellectual property from Northrop Grumman Space Technology. Hittite will assume customer contracts from Northrop Grumman under the deal and will become the worldwide supplier for the Velocium devices. The giant military contractor will serve as a foundry contractor to Hittite in fabricating the products.

In 2005 Hittite acquired the assets of Q-DOT, a government R&D contractor, from Simtek for $2.2 million in cash.

Hittite does a lot of its own semiconductor assembly and testing at its facilities in Massachusetts. In 2005 the company established its first remote design center, in Istanbul, Turkey.

EXECUTIVES

Chairman Emeritus: Yalcin Ayasli, age 61

Chairman, President, and CEO: Stephen G. Daly, age 41, $300,000 pay

CTO: Michael J. Koechlin, age 47, $232,500 pay

VP, Operations: Brian J. Jablonski, age 47, $187,692 pay

VP, CFO, and Treasurer: William W. Boecke, age 55, $231,692 pay

VP, Sales and Marketing: Norman G. Hildreth Jr., age 44, $231,154 pay

VP Engineering: Michael Olson

Auditors: PricewaterhouseCoopers LLP

LOCATIONS

HQ: Hittite Microwave Corporation
20 Alpha Rd., Chelmsford, MA 01824
Phone: 978-250-3343   **Fax:** 978-250-3373
Web: www.hittite.com

Hittite Microwave has facilities in Canada, China, Germany, South Korea, Sweden, Turkey, the UK, and the US.

2006 Sales

	$ mil.	% of total
US	59.4	46
Other countries	70.9	54
Total	**130.3**	**100**

PRODUCTS/OPERATIONS

Selected Products

Amplifiers
Attenuators
Frequency dividers and detectors
Frequency multipliers
Mixers and converters
Modulators
Oscillators
Sensors
Switches

COMPETITORS

Advanced Control
  Components
ANADIGICS
Analog Devices
Avago Technologies
Endwave
Eudyna Devices
L-3 Communications
Linear Technology
M/A-Com
Merrimac Industries
NEC Electronics
Peregrine Semi
Powerwave Technologies
RF Micro Devices
RF Monolithics
SiRF Technology
Skyworks
TriQuint
WJ Communications

HISTORICAL FINANCIALS

Company Type: Public

Income Statement

FYE: December 31

	REVENUE ($ mil.)	NET INCOME ($ mil.)	NET PROFIT MARGIN	EMPLOYEES
12/06	130.3	42.7	32.8%	267
12/05	80.7	21.1	26.1%	220
12/04	61.7	13.4	21.7%	186
12/03	42.0	7.2	17.1%	—
Annual Growth	**45.8%**	**81.0%**	**—**	**19.8%**

2006 Year-End Financials

Debt ratio: —
Return on equity: 35.7%
Cash ($ mil.): 122.6
Current ratio: 10.10
Long-term debt ($ mil.): —
No. of shares (mil.): 30.7
Dividends
  Yield: —
  Payout: —
Market value ($ mil.): 992.5
R&D as % of sales: —
Advertising as % of sales: —

Stock History

NASDAQ (GS): HITT

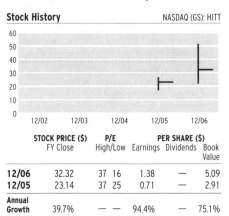

	STOCK PRICE ($) FY Close	P/E High/Low		PER SHARE ($) Earnings	Dividends	Book Value
12/06	32.32	37	16	1.38	—	5.09
12/05	23.14	37	25	0.71	—	2.91
Annual Growth	**39.7%**	**—**	**—**	**94.4%**	**—**	**75.1%**

Hollywood Media

This company helps gets people to the theatre and the local multiplex. Hollywood Media Corp. is a leading provider of live theater tickets, including Broadway and off-Broadway productions, as well as performances in London's West End district through Broadway.com, Theatre.com, and its 1-800-BROADWAY phone service. Its Theatre Direct International subsidiary provides wholesale tickets to groups and travel agents. In addition, Hollywood Media Corp. operates Hollywood.com, which offers movie reviews, trailers, and showtimes, and it owns a 26% stake in MovieTickets.com.

While live theatre ticket sales now account for more than 80% of the company's business, its core business historically has been movie information. Its consumer-oriented Hollywood.com site generates revenue primarily through advertising (which accounts for nearly 10% of sales).

The company sold its Source Business (which provided movie and events showtimes information and data, and consisted of CinemaSource, EventSource, and ExhibitorAds) to West World Media in 2007 for some $23 million. Source Business founder Brett West owns West World. As part of the deal, West World will share its movie showtimes and events data with Hollywood Media. In return, Hollywood Media will provide movie and entertainment-related content to West World.

The company sold its Baseline StudioSystems unit, which provides a database of information on the movie and television industry, to The New York Times Company for $35 million in 2006.

In addition to these operations, Hollywood Media has a small but growing intellectual property division that owns or controls the rights to certain characters and concepts by such authors as Tom Clancy, Mickey Spillane, and Isaac Asimov. It develops those properties into books (through 51%-owned Tekno Books), movies and TV shows, software, and other merchandise. The company also owns and operates the cable television networks Hollywood.com Television and Broadway.com Television.

Founders (and husband and wife) Mitchell Rubenstein and Laurie Silvers together own nearly 5% of the company.

HISTORY

Sci-Fi Channel founders Mitchell Rubenstein and Laurie Silvers founded Big Entertainment in 1993 after selling the Sci-Fi Channel to USA Networks (now part of The NBC Television Network) the previous year. They took Big Entertainment public in 1993, and by 1994 the company had published its first comic books under the Tekno-Comix imprint and opened seven retail outlets in Florida and Virginia. It also established Tekno Books, a publishing and book packaging division.

Big Entertainment formed NetCo Partners in 1995 (a joint venture with C.P. Group) to publish and license new characters, including those from Tom Clancy's NetForce. The company was not making money, however, and it stopped printing comics in 1997 and opened more entertainment stores and mall kiosks. Big Entertainment also signed an agreement with Magic Johnson's June Bug Enterprises that year to make a line of children's books and cartoon characters.

Hurting financially, the company closed 21 kiosks in 1998 and opened its bige.com Web site. Soon, online sales were bringing in $20,000 a day. The next year the company bought Hollywood.com from newspaper publisher Times Mirror (now part of Tribune) for $31 million and CinemaSource for $6.5 million. The company later changed its name to Hollywood.com. Expanding into Latin America, it also launched a version of its Hollywood.com site for Brazil (and launched versions for Mexico, Argentina, and China the following year).

Broadcaster CBS took a 30% stake in exchange for promotion and branding rights in 2000. Later that year the company teamed with movie theater companies AMC Entertainment, National Amusements, and Famous Players (later acquired by Cineplex Galaxy) to create MovieTickets.com, a joint venture to sell movie tickets via the Web (Hoyts Cinemas and Marcus Theatres later joined the venture), and launched the now defunct sister site MusicSite.com. It also acquired BroadwayTheater.com and Theater Direct International, and launched Broadway.com, its live theater information Web site. In late 2000 the company changed its name to Hollywood Media Corp.

The company continued to fortify its subscription-based data content services in 2002. It merged its Baseline and Fountain Media Services' FilmTracker, a move that would bulk up Baseline's offerings. Later that year it announced the launch of two new digital cable television channels: "Totally Hollywood TV" and "Totally Broadway TV." Also in 2002 Viacom exchanged its 30% stake in Hollywood Media for $49 million in advertising inventory.

The following year the company reorganized its operations around a few key business divisions, including Data Syndication (Source Business), Internet, Broadway ticketing, and intellectual properties. It later added its Cable TV segment, which comprises Hollywood.com Television and Broadway.com Television, two Video On Demand channels that offer interactive entertainment information.

In 2007 the company sold its Source Business back to its founder for $23 million.

EXECUTIVES

Chairman and CEO: Mitchell (Mitch) Rubenstein, age 53, $510,800 pay
Vice Chairman, President, and Secretary: Laurie S. Silvers, age 55, $459,450 pay
EVP, Broadway Ticketing: Jerome Kane
Chief Accounting Officer: Scott A. Gomez, age 31, $192,500 pay
VP: Steven Marder
VP, Operations, CinemaSource, EventSource, and ExhibitorAds: James Devin
President, Showtix: Patricia Daily
President, Broadway Ticketing: Matt Kupchin
President and COO, Hollywood.com: Kevin Davis
Auditors: Kaufman, Rossin & Co.

LOCATIONS

HQ: Hollywood Media Corp.
2255 Glades Rd., Ste. 221 A., Boca Raton, FL 33431
Phone: 561-998-8000   **Fax:** 561-998-2974
Web: www.hollywood.com

Hollywood Media Corp. has operations in Connecticut, Florida, New York, and Wisconsin. It has international offices in the UK.

PRODUCTS/OPERATIONS

2006 Sales

	$ mil.	% of total
Broadway ticketing	98.1	85
Internet ad sales	9.9	8
Data business	6.5	6
Intellectual properties	1.2	1
Cable TV	0.2	—
Total	**115.9**	**100**

Selected Operations

Broadway ticketing
  1-800-BROADWAY
  Broadway.com
  Theatre Direct International
  Theatre.com

Internet holdings
  Hollywood.com
  MovieTickets.com (26%)

Intellectual properties
  Tekno Books (51%, book development and licensing)
  NetCo Partners (50%, licensing and development)

Television
  Broadway.com Television (cable TV channel)
  Hollywood.com Television (cable TV channel)

COMPETITORS

Amazon.com	StubHub
E! Entertainment	TicketCity.com
Television	Ticketmaster
Fandango	Tickets.com
Nielsen Business Media	TicketWeb
Reed Business Information	Tribune Media Services
Shubert Organization	

HISTORICAL FINANCIALS

Company Type: Public

Income Statement

FYE: December 31

	REVENUE ($ mil.)	NET INCOME ($ mil.)	NET PROFIT MARGIN	EMPLOYEES
12/06	115.9	9.5	8.2%	230
12/05	95.6	(8.9)	—	271
12/04	73.0	(11.6)	—	271
12/03	64.9	(7.4)	—	202
12/02	58.2	(81.6)	—	218
Annual Growth	**18.8%**	**—**	**—**	**1.3%**

2006 Year-End Financials

Debt ratio: 2.6%	Dividends
Return on equity: 19.4%	Yield: —
Cash ($ mil.): 27.5	Payout: —
Current ratio: 1.39	Market value ($ mil.): 141.2
Long-term debt ($ mil.): 1.5	R&D as % of sales: —
No. of shares (mil.): 33.6	Advertising as % of sales: —

Stock History

NASDAQ (GM): HOLL

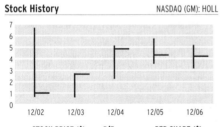

	STOCK PRICE ($) FY Close	P/E High/Low		PER SHARE ($) Earnings	Dividends	Book Value
12/06	4.20	18	11	0.29	—	1.66
12/05	4.31	—	—	(0.28)	—	1.30
12/04	4.85	—	—	(0.42)	—	1.49
12/03	2.66	—	—	(0.36)	—	1.57
12/02	1.00	—	—	(3.18)	—	2.04
Annual Growth	**43.2%**	**—**	**—**	**—**	**—**	**(5.0%)**

Hologic, Inc.

With its mammography and breast biopsy systems, Hologic puts the squeeze on women to help save their lives. Its mammography products include film-based and digital systems, as well as the workstations and computer-aided detection systems that interpret the images. Additional products include X-ray and ultrasound bone densitometers, which detect and monitor osteoporosis, and breast biopsy collection systems (branded ATEC) sold by its Suros division. With its 2007 merger with women's health firm Cytyc, Hologic gained several other product lines, including tests to screen for cervical cancer. The company markets its products to hospitals, and clinical labs worldwide through distributors and a direct sales force.

Hologic paid more than $6 billion for the larger Cytyc, which, like Hologic, was headquartered in the Boston area. The two companies had been discussing a tie-up off and on since 2004 and create a force to be reckoned with in the women's health sector, with expected annual revenues of $1.7 billion.

Hologic hopes it can take advantage of cross-selling opportunities that arise from combining the two companies' complementary product lines. Cytyc adds products in the areas of cervical cancer screening, prenatal diagnostics, and breast cancer treatment to Hologic's existing portfolio of breast health and osteoporosis products.

Cytyc marketed its ThinPrep cervical cancer screening system as a better alternative to the conventional Pap smear. It also made surgical systems to treat excessive menstrual bleeding and radiation therapy products for breast and brain cancer, as well as a preterm birth diagnostic called the FullTerm Fetal Fibronectin Test.

In early 2008 Hologic agreed to sell the marketing rights for Gestiva, an investigational drug for preventing preterm births that it had gained in the Cytyc merger, to K-V Pharmaceutical.

Both Cytyc and Hologic had already been in expansion mode prior to the merger, adding product lines in complementary areas through a number of smaller acquisitions. One such Hologic acquisition in 2007, of California-based BioLucent, added the MammoPad breast cushion, a pad designed to alleviate the discomfort of getting a mammogram.

In addition to its women's health products, Hologic manufactures and sells photoconductor materials used in electrophotographic devices and small fluoroscopic imaging systems used by orthopedic surgeons on extremities such as hands, feet, and knees. The company is also the US distributor of Esaote's MRI systems designed for use on extremities.

HISTORY

In 1981 S. David Ellenbogen and Jay Stein founded Diagnostic Technology (DTI) and developed a digital angiography product. A Squibb subsidiary bought DTI in 1982, and in 1985 Ellenbogen and Stein founded Hologic.

The firm shipped its first bone scanner in 1987 and went public in 1990. Increased global focus on women's health fueled Hologic's growth in 1994. That year it penetrated the Latin American and Japanese markets, and Medicare patients started receiving reimbursement for bone density examinations. Also in 1994 Hologic partnered with Serex to develop a test to monitor biochemical indicators of bone loss (Ostex International joined the effort in 1996).

Targeting private practices requiring less-expensive equipment, Hologic bought Walker Magnetic Group's ultrasound bone analyzer business and that of European rival Sophia Medical Systems in 1995. That year it purchased FluoroScan Imaging Systems, a maker of X-ray equipment.

In 1998 the company introduced its Sahara Clinical Bone Sonometer in the US. In 1999 Hologic acquired Direct Radiography, another X-ray equipment maker. That year Fleet Business Credit, which had an agreement with Hologic through which it purchased bone densitometers and then leased them to physicians, pulled out of the partnership; sales sank, and Hologic filed a lawsuit against Fleet to recoup losses. Also in 1999 Hologic sold its Medical Data Management division to focus on core operations.

In 2000 the company bought the US operations of medical imaging company Trex Medical Corporation. This acquisition added the Lorad-brand line of mammography and breast biopsy systems, to Hologic's operations. The acquisition was costly, and, to recover, Hologic implemented a restructuring plan in 2001 that led to a reduction of the workforce, a reduction of operating expenses, and phasing out unprofitable units. The company closed its conventional X-ray equipment manufacturing facility in Littleton, Massachusetts and relocated some of the product lines and personnel to Bedford, Massachusetts.

With a renewed appetite for growth, in 2005 Hologic resumed its acquisition strategy, starting with the purchase of Fischer Imaging's SenoScan digital mammography and MammoTest stereotactic breast biopsy systems for $32 million. The following year it acquired R2 Technology for $220 million to gain that company's computer-aided detection (CAD) technology. Also in 2006 it acquired breast biopsy and tissue excision device producer Suros Surgical Systems for $240 million.

EXECUTIVES

Chairman: Patrick J. Sullivan, age 56
Chairman Emeritus and CTO: Jay A. Stein, age 65, $417,914 pay
CEO: John W. (Jack) Cumming, age 62, $1,261,348 pay
President and COO: Robert A. Cascella, age 53, $867,580 pay
EVP Finance and Administration, CFO, Treasurer, Secretary, and Director: Glenn P. Muir, age 48, $730,033 pay
SVP Business Development: Thomas Umbel
SVP International Sales: Mark A. Duerst
SVP Sales and Strategic Accounts: John R. Pekarsky, age 54, $521,756 pay
SVP and Chief Accounting Officer: Robert H. Lavallee
SVP; President, GYN Surgical Products: Tony Kingsley
SVP Human Resources: David J. Brady
VP Information Systems and CIO: David M. Rudzinsky
VP and General Counsel: Andrew Stone
VP Financial Planning and Analysis: Stephen J. Furlong
VP; President, Suros Surgical: James Pearson
President, Cytyc Diagnostic Products: Howard Doran
Director Investor Relations: Frances Crecco
Director Corporate Communications: Sue Hetzler
Auditors: Ernst & Young LLP

LOCATIONS

HQ: Hologic, Inc.
35 Crosby Dr., Bedford, MA 01730
Phone: 781-999-7300 **Fax:** 781-280-0669
Web: www.hologic.com

2007 Sales

	% of total
US	75
Europe	15
Asia	5
Other regions	5
Total	**100**

PRODUCTS/OPERATIONS

2007 Sales

	$ mil.	% of total
Mammography/breast care	588.9	80
Osteoporosis assessment	64.5	9
Other	85.0	11
Total	**738.4**	**100**

Selected Products

ATEC (Automated Tissue Excision and Collection, breast biopsy system)
FullTerm Fetal Fibronectin Test (preterm birth risk assessment)
InSight fluoroscan imaging system (mini c-arm X-ray imaging devices)
Lorad Affinity (mammography system)
Lorad M-IV (mammography system)
MammoPad (mammography breast cushion)
MammoSite (breast cancer radiation therapy system)
NovaSure (treatment system for menorrhagia)
QDR series bone densitometer
Sahara Bone Sonometer (ultrasound-based densitometer)
StereoLoc (stereotactic breast biopsy systems)
ThinPrep System (cervical cancer screening)

Selected Subsidiaries

AEG Elektrofotografie GmbH (Germany)
BioLucent, LLC
Cytyc Corporation
R2 Technology, Inc.
Suros Surgical Systems, Inc.

COMPETITORS

Agfa	Johnson & Johnson
BD	Microsulis
Boston Scientific	MonoGen
C. R. Bard	North American Scientific
Carestream Health	Philips Electronics
Cedara Software	QIAGEN
Clarient	Sectra
FUJIFILM	SenoRx
GE Healthcare	Siemens Medical
GE OEC Medical Systems	TomoTherapy
iCAD	Toshiba
Intact Medical Corporation	Varian Medical Systems

HISTORICAL FINANCIALS

Company Type: Public

Income Statement

FYE: Last Saturday in September

	REVENUE ($ mil.)	NET INCOME ($ mil.)	NET PROFIT MARGIN	EMPLOYEES
9/07	738.4	94.6	12.8%	3,580
9/06	462.7	27.4	5.9%	1,617
9/05	287.7	28.3	9.8%	870
9/04	228.7	12.2	5.3%	761
9/03	204.0	2.9	1.4%	722
Annual Growth	**37.9%**	**139.0%**	**—**	**49.2%**

2007 Year-End Financials

Debt ratio: 1.1%	Dividends
Return on equity: 13.4%	Yield: —
Cash ($ mil.): 100.4	Payout: —
Current ratio: 2.23	Market value ($ mil.): 3,357.6
Long-term debt ($ mil.): 9.2	R&D as % of sales: —
No. of shares (mil.): 55.0	Advertising as % of sales: —

Stock History

NASDAQ (GS): HOLX

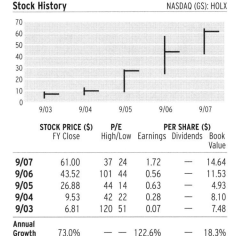

	STOCK PRICE ($) FY Close	P/E High/Low		PER SHARE ($) Earnings	Dividends	Book Value
9/07	61.00	37	24	1.72	—	14.64
9/06	43.52	101	44	0.56	—	11.53
9/05	26.88	44	14	0.63	—	4.93
9/04	9.53	42	22	0.28	—	8.10
9/03	6.81	120	51	0.07	—	7.48
Annual Growth	**73.0%**	**—**	**—**	**122.6%**	**—**	**18.3%**

Home BancShares

At this Home, you don't have to stash your cash under the mattress. Instead, you can choose from five bank subsidiaries in Arkansas and Florida. Home BancShares serves businesses and individuals in central and north central Arkansas through Bank of Mountain View, Community Bank, First State Bank, and Twin City Bank. It serves the Florida Keys and southwestern Florida through Marine Bank. With a combined network of some 50 branches, the banks offer checking, savings, and NOW and money market accounts, and CDs. The banks focus on commercial real estate and development loans, which make up more than 60% of a lending portfolio that also includes residential mortgage, business, and other loans.

Non-bank subsidiaries provide bank customers with trust and title services and insurance products. Home BancShares made several acquisitions in 2005, including the purchase of a 20% stake in White River Bancshares, parent company for Signature Bank of Arkansas. The company has grown through the addition of *de novo* branches, and continues to look for potential acquisitions in its geographical markets. The bank holding company went public via an IPO in 2006.

Chairman John Allison and his family own about 15% of the company. Vice chairman Richard Ashley controls 6%, and company co-founder Robert "Bunny" Adcock (now an Arkansas banking official) owns 5%.

EXECUTIVES

Chairman and CEO; Chairman, First State Bank:
John W. Allison, age 60
Vice Chairman: Richard H. Ashley, age 51
President, COO, and Director: Ron W. Strother, age 58, $300,000 pay
CFO and Treasurer: Randy E. Mayor, age 41, $267,250 pay

CEO, Bank of Mountain View:
M. L. Mickey Waddington, age 63
President and CEO, Twin City Bank: Robert F. Birch Jr., age 56, $256,500 pay
President and CEO, Community Bank:
Tracey M. French, age 45
President and CEO, Marine Bank:
Robert Hunter Padgett, age 48
Secretary and Director; President and CEO, First State Bank: C. Randall Sims, age 52, $290,000 pay
Director, Financial Reporting and Investor Relations: Brian Davis, age 41
Auditors: BKD, LLP

LOCATIONS

HQ: Home BancShares, Inc.
719 Harkrider, Conway, AR 72032
Phone: 501-328-4770 **Fax:** 501-329-9139
Web: www.homebancshares.com

Home BancShares has operations in the Arkansas communities of Beebe, Cabot, Conway, Greenbrier, Jacksonville, Little Rock, Lonoke, Maumelle, Mayflower, Mountain View, North Little Rock, Searcy, Sherwood, Vilonia, and Ward; and in the Florida communities of Islamorada, Key Largo, Key West, Marathon, Marco Island, Port Charlotte, Punta Gorda, and Summerland Key.

PRODUCTS/OPERATIONS

2006 Sales

	% of total
Interest	
Loans	70
Securities & other	16
Service charges on deposit accounts	7
Other service charges & fees	3
Mortgage banking	1
Other	3
Total	**100**

COMPETITORS

Bank of America
Bank of Florida
Bank of the Ozarks
BB&T
First Federal Bancshares of Arkansas
First State Financial
Regions Financial
Simmons First
TIB Financial
U.S. Bancorp

HISTORICAL FINANCIALS

Company Type: Public

Income Statement

FYE: December 31

	ASSETS ($ mil.)	NET INCOME ($ mil.)	INCOME AS % OF ASSETS	EMPLOYEES
12/06	2,190.6	15.9	0.7%	562
12/05	1,911.5	11.4	0.6%	544
12/04	805.2	9.2	1.1%	—
Annual Growth	**64.9%**	**31.5%**	**—**	**3.3%**

2006 Year-End Financials

Equity as % of assets: 10.6%	Dividends
Return on assets: 0.8%	Yield: 0.2%
Return on equity: 8.0%	Payout: 5.0%
Long-term debt ($ mil.): 44.7	Sales ($ mil.): 143.3
No. of shares (mil.): 17.2	R&D as % of sales: —
Market value ($ mil.): 413.6	Advertising as % of sales: —

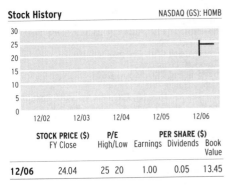

	STOCK PRICE ($) FY Close	P/E High/Low	PER SHARE ($) Earnings	Dividends	Book Value
12/06	24.04	25 20	1.00	0.05	13.45

Home Solutions of America

Home Solutions of America can't solve the problems of hurricanes and flooding in coastal areas, but the company *can* do something about the aftermath. It provides specialty interior services through a number of subsidiaries. Home Solutions Restoration of Louisiana and PW Stephens provide recovery services (debris removal, dehumidification); the latter firm, along with Fiber Seal Systems, also provides such restoration services as air decontamination and removal of mold and asbestos. The company's rebuilding and remodeling operations include kitchen cabinet and counter construction and installation performed by subsidiaries Southern Exposure, SouthernStone Cabinets, and Cornerstone Building and Remodeling.

The company has agreements for manufacture and installation of cabinets and countertops with such clients as Centex and The Home Depot in selected markets. Home Solutions of America, as part of its growth-by-acquisition strategy, is aggressively seeking out and acquiring complementary specialty residential services businesses. In 2005, it acquired the assets of Florida Environmental Remediation Services. The purchase of the restoration company expanded Home Solutions of America's presence in Florida and opens markets in Louisiana and Mississippi. The next year the company acquired Fireline Restoration, a home recovery and restoration provider, for $11.5 million. Fireline Restoration also operates in Florida, Louisiana, and Mississippi.

EXECUTIVES

Chairman and CEO: Frank J. Fradella, age 51, $962,500 pay
President and COO: Rick J. O'Brien, age 40, $500,000 pay
EVP and Director; President Restoration and Construction Services and Fireline Restoration: Brian Marshall, age 43
SVP and CFO: Jeffrey M. Mattich, $367,000 pay
VP; President, Southern Exposure Holdings, Southern Exposure Unlimited of Florida, and S.E. Tops of Florida: Dale W. Mars, age 57, $200,000 pay
Auditors: Corbin & Company, LLP

LOCATIONS

HQ: Home Solutions of America, Inc.
    1500 Dragon St., Ste. B, Dallas, TX 75207
Phone: 214-623-8446   **Fax:** 214-333-9435
Web: www.hsoacorp.com

PRODUCTS/OPERATIONS

2006 Sales

	$ mil.	% of total
Restoration & recovery services	88.7	70
Interior services	38.5	30
Total	**127.2**	**100**

Selected Subsidiaries

Cornerstone Marble & Granite, Inc.
Fiber-Seal Systems, L.P.
Fireline Restoration, Inc.
FSS Holdings Corp.
Home Solutions Restoration of Louisiana, Inc.
P.W. Stephens, Inc.
S.E. Tops of Florida, Inc.
Southern Exposure Holdings, Inc.
Southern Exposure Unlimited of Florida, Inc.
SouthernStone Cabinets, Inc. (50%)

COMPETITORS

The BMS Enterprises
InStar Services
Masco
PDG Environmental
ServiceMaster
Servpro Industries
WaterMasters Restoration

HISTORICAL FINANCIALS

Company Type: Public

Income Statement   FYE: December 31

	REVENUE ($ mil.)	NET INCOME ($ mil.)	NET PROFIT MARGIN	EMPLOYEES
12/06	127.2	17.9	14.1%	458
12/05	68.1	7.2	10.6%	483
12/04	31.1	2.6	8.4%	186
12/03	14.0	(0.7)	—	195
12/02	2.6	(0.5)	—	166
Annual Growth	**164.5%**	**—**	**—**	**28.9%**

2006 Year-End Financials

Debt ratio: 17.0%
Return on equity: 16.3%
Cash ($ mil.): 8.7
Current ratio: 1.93
Long-term debt ($ mil.): 24.5
No. of shares (mil.): 47.3

Dividends
  Yield: —
  Payout: —
Market value ($ mil.): 277.2
R&D as % of sales: —
Advertising as % of sales: —

Stock History   NASDAQ (GM): HSOA

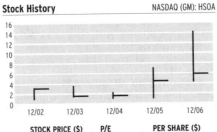

	STOCK PRICE ($) FY Close	P/E High/Low	PER SHARE ($) Earnings	Dividends	Book Value
12/06	5.86	33 10	0.43	—	3.04
12/05	4.48	28 4	0.25	—	2.13
12/04	1.57	22 11	0.10	—	1.26
12/03	1.52	— —	(0.06)	—	1.04
12/02	3.10	— —	(0.05)	—	0.42
Annual Growth	**17.3%**	**— —**	**—**	**—**	**63.8%**

Horizon Financial

Horizon Financial is the holding company for Horizon Bank, which serves Skagit, Snohomish, Pierce, and Whatcom counties along Puget Sound in northwestern Washington. Founded in 1922, the bank offers traditional products and services through about 25 branches and loan centers. Funds from deposits, such as CDs and checking, savings, and money market accounts, are primarily used to originate loans secured by real estate. Commercial mortgages make up about 25% of the bank's loan portfolio; construction and land development loans are almost 40%. Horizon Bank also issues home equity, business, commercial construction, and consumer loans.

EXECUTIVES

Chairman: V. Lawrence (Laury) Evans, age 60, $307,558 pay
President, CEO, and Director; CEO, Horizon Bank: Richard P. (Rich) Jacobson, age 44, $173,424 pay
EVP and Director; President and COO, Horizon Bank: Dennis C. Joines, age 57, $259,842 pay
SVP; Controller, Horizon Bank: Kelli J. Holz, age 38
EVP, Commercial Banking, Horizon Bank: Steve L. Hoekstra, age 56, $168,722 pay
SVP and Mortgage Loan Operations Manager, Horizon Bank: Tammy D. Barnett, age 41
SVP and Operations Manager, Horizon Bank: A. R. (Gus) Ayala, age 55
SVP and Senior Commercial Real Estate Lending Executive, Horizon Bank: Frank Jeretzky, age 58
SVP and Retail Sales Manager, Horizon Bank: Jane L. VanVoorst, age 54
SVP, Horizon Bank: David E. McCrea, age 43
VP and Human Resources Manager, Horizon Bank: Christine Anderson
Auditors: Moss Adams, LLP

LOCATIONS

HQ: Horizon Financial Corp.
    1500 Cornwall Ave., Bellingham, WA 98225
Phone: 360-733-3050   **Fax:** 360-733-7019
Web: www.horizonbank.com

PRODUCTS/OPERATIONS

2007 Sales

	$ mil.	% of total
Interest Income		
Interest on loans	88.6	90
Investments & mortgage-backed securities		
Taxable interest	3.5	4
Nontaxable interest income	0.3	—
Dividends	0.2	—
Noninterest Income		
Service fees	3.3	3
Net gain on sales of loans	0.8	1
Other	1.7	2
Total	**98.4**	**100**

COMPETITORS

Bank of America
Banner Corp
Cascade Financial
CityBank
First Mutual Bancshares
Frontier Financial
KeyCorp
U.S. Bancorp
Washington Banking
Washington Federal
Washington Mutual
Wells Fargo

HISTORICAL FINANCIALS

Company Type: Public

Income Statement

FYE: March 31

	ASSETS ($ mil.)	NET INCOME ($ mil.)	INCOME AS % OF ASSETS	EMPLOYEES
3/07	1,270.3	19.0	1.5%	288
3/06	1,116.7	15.7	1.4%	276
3/05	997.6	13.1	1.3%	—
3/04	858.9	12.9	1.5%	—
Annual Growth	13.9%	13.8%	—	4.3%

2007 Year-End Financials

Equity as % of assets: 9.8%
Return on assets: 1.6%
Return on equity: 16.0%
Long-term debt ($ mil.): 159.0
No. of shares (mil.): 12.3
Market value ($ mil.): 270.6
Dividends
  Yield: 1.6%
  Payout: 23.5%
Sales ($ mil.): 98.4
R&D as % of sales: —
Advertising as % of sales: —

Stock History

NASDAQ (GS): HRZB

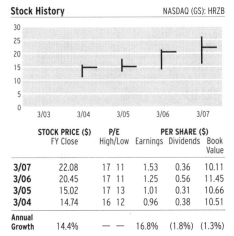

	STOCK PRICE ($) FY Close	P/E High/Low		PER SHARE ($) Earnings	Dividends	Book Value
3/07	22.08	17	11	1.53	0.36	10.11
3/06	20.45	17	11	1.25	0.56	11.45
3/05	15.02	17	13	1.01	0.31	10.66
3/04	14.74	16	12	0.96	0.38	10.51
Annual Growth	14.4%	—	—	16.8%	(1.8%)	(1.3%)

Hornbeck Offshore Services

At the beck and call of oil companies, Hornbeck Offshore Services provides marine transportation of oil field equipment and supplies and petroleum products. The company operates offshore supply vessels (OSVs) that support offshore oil and gas drilling and production in the deepwater regions of the Gulf of Mexico. The company's fleet of about 25 OSVs transports cargo such as pipe and drilling mud, as well as rig crew members. In addition, Hornbeck Offshore operates oceangoing tug and tank barge units that transport crude and refined petroleum products in the northeastern US and in Puerto Rico. Its fleet includes about a dozen tugs and 20 barges.

The company's OSVs, which were built beginning in 1997, were designed specifically to take advantage of the trend toward deepwater exploration in the Gulf of Mexico. Operations in US waters account for most of Hornbeck's sales, but the company also undertakes work in international offshore oil production areas.

Hornbeck plans to grow by expanding both its OSV fleet and its tug and tank barge fleet. Along these lines, in mid-2007 it agreed to acquire 20 offshore supply vessels from Nabors Industries for

about $186 million. In addition, the company hopes to sell more services to existing customers, particularly to integrated oil and gas companies that can use OSVs in their exploration and production operations, and tug and tank barge units in their refining and marketing operations.

The William Herbert Hunt Trust Estate, based in Dallas, owns 8% of Hornbeck.

EXECUTIVES

Chairman, President, CEO, and Secretary: Todd M. Hornbeck, age 38, $450,000 pay
EVP and COO: Carl G. Annessa, age 50, $290,000 pay
EVP and CFO: James O. Harp Jr., age 46, $270,000 pay
SVP and General Counsel: Samuel A. Giberga, age 45, $225,000 pay
VP and CIO: John S. Cook, age 37, $200,000 pay
Corporate Controller: Timothy P. McCarthy, age 38, $232,800 pay
Manager, Business Development, Offshore Supply Vessels: Cleve E. Ammons
Manager, Sales, Tugs and Tank Barges: Paul Cooke
Director, Quality, Health, Safety, and Environment: Andrew Bruzdzinski
Treasurer: Mark Myrtue
Auditors: Ernst & Young LLP

LOCATIONS

HQ: Hornbeck Offshore Services, Inc.
103 Northpark Blvd., Ste. 300, Covington, LA 70433
Phone: 985-727-2000   **Fax:** 985-727-2006
Web: www.hornbeckoffshore.com

PRODUCTS/OPERATIONS

2006 Sales

	$ mil.	% of total
Offshore supply vessels		
US	141.3	51
Other countries	25.0	9
Tugs & tank barges		
US	100.3	37
Other countries	7.9	3
Total	**274.5**	**100**

COMPETITORS

Apex Oil
Chemoil
Colonial Pipeline
Crowley Maritime
GulfMark Offshore
K-Sea Transportation
Overseas Shipholding Group
Plantation Pipe Line
SEACOR
Siem Offshore
Tidewater Inc.
Trico Marine
U.S. Shipping

HISTORICAL FINANCIALS

Company Type: Public

Income Statement

FYE: December 31

	REVENUE ($ mil.)	NET INCOME ($ mil.)	NET PROFIT MARGIN	EMPLOYEES
12/06	274.5	75.7	27.6%	742
12/05	182.6	37.4	20.5%	657
12/04	132.3	(2.5)	—	601
12/03	110.8	11.2	10.1%	556
12/02	92.6	11.6	12.5%	446
Annual Growth	31.2%	59.8%	—	13.6%

2006 Year-End Financials

Debt ratio: 120.8%
Return on equity: 17.1%
Cash ($ mil.): 474.3
Current ratio: 13.97
Long-term debt ($ mil.): 549.5
No. of shares (mil.): 25.6
Dividends
  Yield: —
  Payout: —
Market value ($ mil.): 912.5
R&D as % of sales: —
Advertising as % of sales: —

Stock History

NYSE: HOS

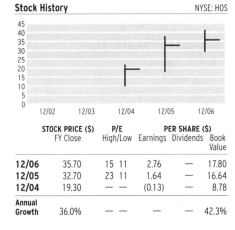

	STOCK PRICE ($) FY Close	P/E High/Low		PER SHARE ($) Earnings	Dividends	Book Value
12/06	35.70	15	11	2.76	—	17.80
12/05	32.70	23	11	1.64	—	16.64
12/04	19.30	—	—	(0.13)	—	8.78
Annual Growth	36.0%	—	—	—	—	42.3%

Houston Wire & Cable

Houston Wire & Cable may have a Texas name, but it can keep customers wired from Seattle to Tampa. The company distributes specialty wire and cable products such as cable terminators, fiber-optic cables, and bare copper and building wire, as well as voice, data, and premise wire. It also provides cable management services (a custom program designed for wire and cable requirements) and an asset-management program (for the development and management of inventory). Houston Wire & Cable, which is 38%-owned by investment firm Code Hennessy & Simmons, operates 11 regional distribution centers and sells primarily to electrical distributors.

Code Hennessy & Simmons acquired the company in 1997 and owned a 76% stake prior to Houston Wire & Cable's 2006 IPO. Code Hennessy & Simmons further reduced its stake through a 2007 share offering.

Founded in 1975, Houston Wire & Cable annually sells more than 20,000 products made by leading manufacturers of electrical wire and cable. The company serves approximately 2,700 customers a year.

EXECUTIVES

Chairman: Scott L. Thompson, age 47
President, CEO, and Director: Charles A. Sorrentino, age 62, $383,173 pay
CFO, Treasurer, and Secretary: Nicol G. (Nic) Graham, age 54, $167,000 pay
VP and Controller: Eric W. Davis, age 45
VP, Logistics: Christopher R. McLeod, age 44
VP, Marketing and Merchandising: James L. Pokluda III, age 41
VP, National Business Development: Eric S. Blankenship, age 54
Director, Human Resources: Carol M. Sims, age 46
Director, Information Services: Marilyn J. McMahon, age 58
Marketing Coordinator: Jennifer Missey
Coordinator, Investor Relations: Hope Novosad
Auditors: Ernst & Young LLP

LOCATIONS

HQ: Houston Wire & Cable Company
10201 North Loop East, Houston, TX 77029
Phone: 713-609-2100 **Fax:** 713-609-2101
Web: www.houwire.com

Houston Wire & Cable has distribution centers in California, Florida, Georgia, Illinois, Louisiana, North Carolina, Pennsylvania, Texas, and Washington.

PRODUCTS/OPERATIONS

Selected Products

Armored cable
Bare copper and building wire
Cable terminators
Fiber-optic cables
Flexible and portable cord
Lead and high-temperature cable
Medium-voltage power cable
Mining cable
Outside plant communication cable
Voice, data, and premise wire

COMPETITORS

Accu-Tech
DXP Enterprises
Electro-Wire
Elliott Electric Supply
Graybar Electric
Stuart C. Irby
WESCO International
Wholesale Electric

HISTORICAL FINANCIALS

Company Type: Public

Income Statement

FYE: December 31

	REVENUE ($ mil.)	NET INCOME ($ mil.)	NET PROFIT MARGIN	EMPLOYEES
12/06	323.5	30.7	9.5%	293
12/05	214.0	12.5	5.8%	—
12/04	172.7	4.8	2.8%	—
12/03	149.1	0.2	0.1%	—
Annual Growth	29.5%	435.4%	—	—

2006 Year-End Financials

Debt ratio: 14.8%
Return on equity: 74.5%
Cash ($ mil.): —
Current ratio: 4.76
Long-term debt ($ mil.): 12.1
No. of shares (mil.): 20.9
Dividends
  Yield: —
  Payout: —
Market value ($ mil.): 436.1
R&D as % of sales: —
Advertising as % of sales: —

Stock History

NASDAQ (GM): HWCC

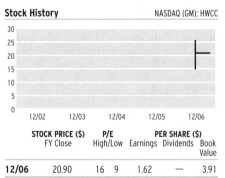

	STOCK PRICE ($) FY Close	P/E High/Low		PER SHARE ($) Earnings	Dividends	Book Value
12/06	20.90	16	9	1.62	—	3.91

Hungarian Telephone and Cable

Hungarian Telephone and Cable (HTCC) has stretched across the Atlantic to provide fixed-line local phone service in three regions of Hungary. Created in 1992 on the heels of the privatization of Hungarian telecom monopoly Magyar Telekom, HTCC consolidated its operations under one subsidiary, Hungarotel Tavkozlesi. It maintains about 228,000 access lines and offers Internet and long-distance services, as well as Voice over Internet Protocol (VoIP). The company acquired alternative telecom carrier PanTel, which provides voice and data services to businesses throughout Hungary and into other European countries, and purchased Invitel in 2007. Denmark's TDC owns about 68% of HTCC.

Invitel is Hungary's second largest fixed-line telecommunications service provider. Its acquisition creates a telecommunications company with greater market share and make it a more formidable competitor for the privatized Magyar Telekom.

In 2007 HTCC purchased the Hungarian business of alternative telecom operator Tele2 in a €4 million deal. Tele2 Hungary resells fixed-line services with nearly half a million customers.

TDC gained its controlling interest in the company by purchasing shares held by Ashmore Investment Management, which previously acquired the roughly 19% stake held by US-based Citizens Communications. Hungary's Postabank sold its 20% stake to institutional investors.

EXECUTIVES

Chairman: Jesper Theill Eriksen, age 39
Vice Chairman: Carsten D. Revsbech, age 38
President and CEO: Martin Lea, age 49
CFO: Robert Bowker, age 40
General Counsel and Secretary: Peter T. Noone, age 44, $236,061 pay
Chief Commercial Officer: Tamas Vagany, age 32, $129,373 pay (partial-year salary)
Head Corporate Business Development: Alex Wurtz, age 56, $96,300 pay
Auditors: KPMG Hungaria Kft.

LOCATIONS

HQ: Hungarian Telephone and Cable Corp.
1201 Third Ave., Ste. 3400, Seattle, WA 98101
Phone: 206-654-0204 **Fax:** 206-652-2911
Web: www.htcc.hu

Hungarian Telephone and Cable Corp. operates in more than 260 Hungarian municipalities in areas bordering Austria, Romania, Slovakia, and Slovenia. PanTel's network covers all of Hungary and extends into Austria, Bulgaria, Croatia, the Czech Republic, Romania, Serbia, Slovakia, Slovenia, and Ukraine.

PRODUCTS/OPERATIONS

2006 Sales

	$ mil.	% of total
Telephone services	106.3	55
Network services	68.5	35
Other	18.9	10
Total	**193.7**	**100**

Selected Services

Audio text services
Data transmission
Internet access
Internet service provider (Globonet)

Local exchange access
Long-distance (domestic and international)
Toll-free calling
Voice mail
Voice over Internet Protocol (VoIP)

COMPETITORS

BT
Deutsche Telekom AG
Magyar Telekom
Swisscom
Tele2
TeliaSonera
T-Mobile International
Vodafone

HISTORICAL FINANCIALS

Company Type: Public

Income Statement

FYE: December 31

	REVENUE ($ mil.)	NET INCOME ($ mil.)	NET PROFIT MARGIN	EMPLOYEES
12/06	193.7	21.1	10.9%	700
12/05	110.2	2.9	2.6%	700
12/04	60.3	16.2	26.9%	900
12/03	59.6	12.5	21.0%	600
12/02	52.2	27.3	52.3%	603
Annual Growth	38.8%	(6.2%)	—	3.8%

2006 Year-End Financials

Debt ratio: 133.1%
Return on equity: 26.7%
Cash ($ mil.): 31.8
Current ratio: 0.66
Long-term debt ($ mil.): 115.8
No. of shares (mil.): 12.8
Dividends
  Yield: —
  Payout: —
Market value ($ mil.): 193.5
R&D as % of sales: —
Advertising as % of sales: —

Stock History

AMEX: HTC

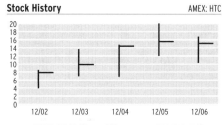

	STOCK PRICE ($) FY Close	P/E High/Low		PER SHARE ($) Earnings	Dividends	Book Value
12/06	15.10	12	8	1.34	—	6.79
12/05	15.55	99	61	0.20	—	5.54
12/04	14.40	12	6	1.25	—	6.43
12/03	9.86	14	7	0.97	—	3.79
12/02	7.87	4	2	2.17	—	2.47
Annual Growth	17.7%	—	—	(11.4%)	—	28.8%

Huron Consulting

Huron Consulting Group dredges through financial statements when businesses fail to stay afloat. The firm provides a variety of financial consulting services to corporate clients that are in financial distress or involved in other legal and regulatory disputes. Its consultants offer forensic accounting and economic analysis expertise and often serve as expert witnesses. Huron Consulting also provides a range of operations consulting services to help keep companies out of dire financial straits. The business was started in 2002 by a group of former Arthur

Andersen partners, including Huron Consulting chairman, president, and CEO Gary Holdren.

Since its founding, Huron Consulting has nearly quadrupled the number of consultants it employs, partly through acquisitions but largely via organic growth. The company has benefited from increased scrutiny of accounting practices by the SEC, a lawsuit-happy populace in the US, Sarbanes-Oxley legislation, and an upswing in mergers and acquisitions.

Huron Consulting's own M&A activity in 2007 has included the purchases of Wellspring Partners, a management consulting firm specializing in hospitals and health systems, for $65 million; Callaway Partners, which specializes in finance- and accounting-related services, for $60 million; and project management and turnaround specialist Glass & Associates, for $30 million. Also in 2007 Huron Consulting opened an office in Tokyo, its first outside the US.

Holdren owns about 6% of Huron Consulting.

EXECUTIVES

Chairman, President, and CEO: Gary E. Holdren, age 56, $1,575,000 pay
Vice Chairman: George E. Massaro, age 59
COO and Quality Officer: Daniel P. (Dan) Broadhurst, age 48
VP, CFO, and Treasurer: Gary L. Burge, age 53, $540,000 pay
VP, General Counsel and Corporate Secretary: Natalia Delgado, age 53
VP, Human Resources: Mary M. Sawall, age 51, $500,000 pay
VP, Corporate Consulting Practice: Stanley N. Logan
Corporate Communications: Jennifer Frost Hennagir
Auditors: PricewaterhouseCoopers LLP

LOCATIONS

HQ: Huron Consulting Group Inc.
550 W. Van Buren St., Chicago, IL 60607
Phone: 312-583-8700　　**Fax:** 312-583-8701
Web: www.huronconsultinggroup.com

Huron Consulting Group has offices in Boston; Charlotte, North Carolina; Chicago; Houston; Los Angeles; New York City; San Francisco; and Washington, DC.

PRODUCTS/OPERATIONS

2006 Sales

	$ mil.	% of total
Operational consulting	150.1	47
Financial consulting	138.5	43
Reimbursable expenses	33.3	10
Total	**321.9**	**100**

Selected Practice Areas and Services

Operational consulting
　Health care
　Higher education
　Legal business consulting
　Performance improvement
　Shareholder returns
　Strategic sourcing
Financial consulting
　Corporate advisory services
　Disputes and investigations
　Economic consulting
　Interim management and focused consulting
　Valuation

COMPETITORS

Accenture
Bain & Company
BearingPoint
Booz Allen
Boston Consulting
CRA International
Deloitte
Ernst & Young Global
FTI Consulting
KPMG
LECG
McKinsey & Company
Navigant Consulting
PricewaterhouseCoopers

HISTORICAL FINANCIALS

Company Type: Public

Income Statement

FYE: December 31

	REVENUE ($ mil.)	NET INCOME ($ mil.)	NET PROFIT MARGIN	EMPLOYEES
12/06	321.9	26.7	8.3%	1,035
12/05	226.0	17.8	7.9%	773
12/04	173.9	10.9	6.3%	612
12/03	110.3	(1.1)	—	—
Annual Growth	42.9%	—	—	30.0%

2006 Year-End Financials

Debt ratio: 0.9%
Return on equity: 27.8%
Cash ($ mil.): 16.6
Current ratio: 1.51
Long-term debt ($ mil.): 1.0
No. of shares (mil.): 18.1
Dividends
　Yield: —
　Payout: —
Market value ($ mil.): 819.4
R&D as % of sales: —
Advertising as % of sales: —

Stock History

NASDAQ (GS): HURN

	STOCK PRICE ($) FY Close	P/E High/Low		PER SHARE ($) Earnings	Dividends	Book Value
12/06	45.34	30	15	1.54	—	6.45
12/05	23.99	28	18	1.05	—	4.38
12/04	22.20	34	25	0.72	—	3.01
Annual Growth	42.9%	—	—	46.2%	—	46.4%

ICF International

Consultant ICF International (formerly ICF Consulting) sees opportunity in government spending. The firm advises government entities and businesses on issues related to defense and homeland security, energy, the environment, and social programs. It groups its consulting and information technology services into three main categories: advice, implementation, and evaluation and improvement. ICF International gets about 90% of its revenue from federal, state, and local government agencies in the US; a contract with the State of Louisiana related to the resettlement of people displaced by hurricanes accounts for some 35%. Entities related to investment firm CM Equity Partners own about 55% of ICF International.

The firm won the contract for the Louisiana resettlement program, known as The Road Home, in June 2006. Under the contract, which could be worth as much as $756 million over three years,

ICF International and its subcontractors are processing applications for housing assistance. The company has set up a dozen facilities in Louisiana and Texas, hired about 2,000 people, and implemented a public education campaign.

Fueled in part by its 2006 IPO, ICF International has been growing via acquisitions. In 2007 it bought Advanced Performance Consulting Group, Energy and Environmental Analysis, and Simat, Helliesen & Eichner, (SH&E), a consulting firm that specializes in the international air transportation industry. ICF International paid about $51 million for SH&E, which was expected to have revenues of about $36 million in 2007.

In 2008 ICF International agreed to pay $50 million for Jones & Stokes Associates, a consulting firm that focuses on environmental planning and natural resource management services. Jones & Stokes is expected to have sales of about $72 million in 2008.

The former ICF Consulting changed its name to ICF International in April 2006 in order to reflect its expanded geographic presence. Outside the US, the firm has offices in London, Moscow, New Delhi, Rio de Janeiro, and Toronto. Besides gaining more clients outside the US, ICF International hopes to grow by selling more services to existing clients and by moving into markets related to education, social and criminal justice, and veterans' affairs programs.

EXECUTIVES

Chairman, President, and CEO: Sudhakar Kesavan, age 51
EVP and COO: John Wasson, age 44
EVP, IFC Caliber: Gerald (Jerry) Croan, age 56
EVP, Technology and Management Solutions: Ellen Glover, age 51
EVP, Business and Corporate Development: Donald Zimmerman
EVP, Corporate Secretary, and General Counsel: Judith B. Kassel
SVP, CFO, and Secretary: Alan Stewart, age 51
SVP, Energy and Resources: Philip Mihlmester
SVP, Environment, Transportation, and Regulation: Sergio Ostria
SVP, Homeland and National Security: Michael Byrne
SVP, Social Programs and Strategic Communications: Isabel Reiff
SVP, Human Resources: M. Miriam Wardak, age 40
SVP; President, Simat, Helliesen & Eichner: David Treitel
President, EEA: Joel Bluestein
President and CEO, Advanced Performance Consulting Group: Kimberly (Kymm) McCabe
Auditors: Grant Thornton LLP

LOCATIONS

HQ: ICF International, Inc.
9300 Lee Hwy., Fairfax, VA 22031
Phone: 703-934-3000　　**Fax:** 703-934-3740
Web: www.icfi.com

PRODUCTS/OPERATIONS

2006 Sales by Client

	% of total
US federal government	49
State & local government	40
Commercial & international	11
Total	**100**

2006 Sales by Market

	% of total
Health, human services & social programs	53
Homeland security & defense	18
Environment & infrastructure	17
Energy	12
Total	**100**

Selected Services

Economic, policy, and regulatory analysis
Human capital strategies
Information technology
Management consulting
Market assessment
Program management
Regulatory support
Scientific and risk assessment
Strategic communications
Training and education

COMPETITORS

BearingPoint	Navigant Consulting
Booz Allen	Northrop Grumman
CRA International	PA Consulting
L-3 Communications	SAIC
Lockheed Martin	SRA International

HISTORICAL FINANCIALS

Company Type: Public

Income Statement

FYE: December 31

	REVENUE ($ mil.)	NET INCOME ($ mil.)	NET PROFIT MARGIN	EMPLOYEES
12/06	331.3	11.9	3.6%	2,000
12/05	177.2	2.0	1.1%	—
12/04	139.5	3.0	2.2%	—
12/03	145.8	2.4	1.6%	1,000
Annual Growth	31.5%	70.5%	—	26.0%

2006 Year-End Financials

Debt ratio: —
Return on equity: 14.3%
Cash ($ mil.): 3.0
Current ratio: 1.23
Long-term debt ($ mil.): —
No. of shares (mil.): 13.9
Dividends
  Yield: —
  Payout: —
Market value ($ mil.): 201.5
R&D as % of sales: —
Advertising as % of sales: —

Stock History

NASDAQ (GM): ICFI

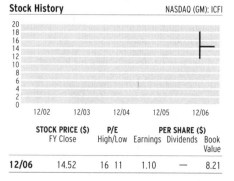

	STOCK PRICE ($) FY Close	P/E High/Low	PER SHARE ($) Earnings	Dividends	Book Value
12/06	14.52	16 11	1.10	—	8.21

ICU Medical

ICU Medical sees the future of infection prevention. The company's devices protect health care workers and patients from the spread of diseases such as HIV and hepatitis. ICU Medical's primary products are intravenous (IV) connection devices (including CLAVE needleless connectors) that reduce the risk of needle sticks and disconnections. The firm also makes custom IV sets, many of which use CLAVE connectors and other ICU products, for third parties. Additionally, ICU Medical makes critical care equipment, including angiography kits and heart monitors, through a manufacturing agreement with Hos-

pira. CEO George Lopez and his family own more than a quarter of ICU Medical.

Hospira is the company's biggest client, contributing more than 75% of sales.

In 2005 the company purchased Hospira's Salt Lake City manufacturing plant, which produces catheters, angiography kits, and cardiac monitors. Hospira has a twenty-year agreement with ICU Medical to buy all products made at the Salt Lake City plant. Through another agreement with Hospira, ICU Medical makes and co-promotes custom IV systems under the name SetSource.

The deals with Hospira have allowed the company to diversify its product line beyond its primary CLAVE products, which account for about 35% of sales. ICU Medical has also introduced some new products, including IV sets for diabetes and oncology.

EXECUTIVES

Chairman, President, and CEO: George A. Lopez, age 59, $1,050,000 pay
CFO, Secretary, and Treasurer:
  Francis J. (Frank) O'Brien, age 64, $420,000 pay
VP Marketing: Alison D. Burcar, age 34, $180,000 pay
VP Sales: Richard A. (Richie) Costello, age 43, $317,500 pay
VP International Sales: Greg Pratt
VP Operations: Steven C. (Steve) Riggs, age 48, $274,000 pay
Director, Human Resources: James J. (Jim) Reitz
Controller: Scott E. Lamb, age 45
Manager, Hospital Sales, Central Region: Randy Clark
Manager, Hospital Sales, Western Region: Joe Vienneau
Manager, Hospital Sales, Eastern Region: Paul Curtin
Auditors: McGladrey & Pullen, LLP

LOCATIONS

HQ: ICU Medical, Inc.
  951 Calle Amanecer, San Clemente, CA 92673
Phone: 949-366-2183   **Fax:** 949-366-8368
Web: www.icumed.com

PRODUCTS/OPERATIONS

Selected Products

CLAVE (needleless IV connector)
CLC2000 (connector preventing the backflow of blood)
Io2 Valve (one- or two-way drug delivery system)
Lopez Valve (valve permitting intermittent injections without disconnection)
Orbit 90 (diabetes set)
TEGO Connector (connector for use in hemodialysis)

COMPETITORS

Alaris Medical	Cardinal Health
B. Braun Melsungen	Covidien
Baxter	Edwards Lifesciences
BD	Hospira
Boston Scientific	Merit Medical Systems

HISTORICAL FINANCIALS

Company Type: Public

Income Statement

FYE: December 31

	REVENUE ($ mil.)	NET INCOME ($ mil.)	NET PROFIT MARGIN	EMPLOYEES
12/06	201.6	25.7	12.7%	1,819
12/05	157.5	20.3	12.9%	1,373
12/04	75.6	5.0	6.6%	—
12/03	107.3	22.3	20.8%	—
12/02	87.8	19.7	22.4%	773
Annual Growth	23.1%	6.9%	—	23.9%

2006 Year-End Financials

Debt ratio: —
Return on equity: 12.4%
Cash ($ mil.): 116.9
Current ratio: 10.77
Long-term debt ($ mil.): —
No. of shares (mil.): 14.6
Dividends
  Yield: —
  Payout: —
Market value ($ mil.): 595.4
R&D as % of sales: —
Advertising as % of sales: —

Stock History

NASDAQ (GS): ICUI

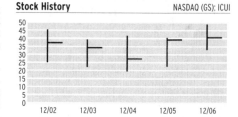

	STOCK PRICE ($) FY Close	P/E High/Low	PER SHARE ($) Earnings	Dividends	Book Value
12/06	40.68	30 20	1.64	—	15.36
12/05	39.21	30 17	1.35	—	13.38
12/04	27.34	125 61	0.33	—	11.52
12/03	34.29	26 15	1.48	—	11.39
12/02	37.30	35 20	1.28	2.50	10.45
Annual Growth	2.2%	— —	6.4%	—	10.1%

Illumina, Inc.

Illumina elucidates the human genome. The firm makes instruments used by life sciences and pharmaceutical researchers to test and analyze genes. With its Oligator technology, Illumina makes short pieces of DNA and with partner Invitrogen markets the products to researchers. Illumina also sells systems (based on its proprietary BeadArray technology) that facilitate large-scale testing of genetic variation and function in groups of people. The tests allow medical researchers to determine what genetic combinations are associated with various diseases, enabling faster diagnosis, better drugs, and individualized treatment. Customers include pharma and biotech companies, research centers, and academic institutions.

In 2007 Illumina acquired fellow genomics firm Solexa, adding expertise in DNA sequencing, small RNA analysis, and gene expression analysis technologies. The previous year it acquired privately held CyVera, which gave Illumina entry into the in vitro and molecular diagnostics markets.

Illumina inked a deal with deCODE genetics in 2006 to develop gene-based diagnostic tests.

The company was a leading participant in the International HapMap Project, a successor to the Human Genome Project that mapped genetic variations in an effort to improve understanding of the relationships between genetics and disease. Illumina received a $9.1 million grant from the National Institutes of Health for its work on the project, which was completed in 2005.

EXECUTIVES

Chairman: William H. (Bill) Rastetter, age 60
President, CEO, and Director: Jay T. Flatley, age 55, $573,467 pay
SVP, COO, and Director; General Manager, Microarray Business: John R. Stuelpnagel, age 50, $357,928 pay
SVP and General Counsel: Christian G. Cabou, age 59
SVP, CFO, and Acting General Manager Sequencing: Christian O. Henry, age 39, $156,531 pay (partial-year salary)
SVP Corporate and Market Development: Arthur E. Holden, age 55
SVP Commercial Operations: Tristan B. Orpin, age 41, $222,942 pay
VP and CIO: Scott D. Kahn, age 47
VP Engineering: Robert C. Kain, age 47
VP Manufacturing: David C. Douglas, age 53
VP Worldwide Sales: Matthew L. (Matt) Posard
VP and Chief Scientist: David Bentley
VP Human Resources: Kevin Harley, age 48
VP Marketing: Omead Ostadan, age 34
Public Relations Manager: Maurissa Bornstein
Senior Director Investor Relations: Peter J. Fromen
Auditors: Ernst & Young LLP

LOCATIONS

HQ: Illumina, Inc.
9885 Towne Centre Dr., San Diego, CA 92121
Phone: 858-202-4500   **Fax:** 858-202-4545
Web: www.illumina.com

2006 Sales

	% of total
US	56
Europe	30
Asia	8
Other regions	6
Total	**100**

PRODUCTS/OPERATIONS

2006 Sales

	$ mil.	% of total
Products	155.8	84
Services & other	27.5	15
Research	1.3	1
Total	**184.6**	**100**

COMPETITORS

454 Life Sciences
Affymetrix
Agilent Technologies
Applied Biosystems
Beckman Coulter
Caliper Life Sciences
GE Healthcare Bio-Sciences
Helicos
Luminex
Monogram Biosciences
Perlegen
Roche Diagnostics
Sequenom
Third Wave Technologies
Vermillion

HISTORICAL FINANCIALS

Company Type: Public

Income Statement

FYE: December 31

	REVENUE ($ mil.)	NET INCOME ($ mil.)	NET PROFIT MARGIN	EMPLOYEES
12/06	184.6	40.0	21.7%	596
12/05	73.5	(20.9)	—	375
12/04	50.6	(6.2)	—	—
12/03	28.0	(27.1)	—	—
12/02	10.0	(40.3)	—	233
Annual Growth	**107.3%**	**—**	**—**	**26.5%**

Debt ratio: —
Return on equity: 25.0%
Cash ($ mil.): 130.8
Current ratio: 5.74
Long-term debt ($ mil.): —
No. of shares (mil.): 46.9

Dividends
  Yield: —
  Payout: —
Market value ($ mil.): 1,842.0
R&D as % of sales: —
Advertising as % of sales: —

Stock History

NASDAQ (GM): ILMN

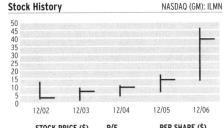

	STOCK PRICE ($) FY Close	P/E High/Low		Earnings	PER SHARE ($) Dividends	Book Value
12/06	39.31	56	17	0.82	—	5.28
12/05	14.10	—	—	(0.52)	—	1.76
12/04	9.48	—	—	(0.17)	—	1.90
12/03	7.01	—	—	(0.85)	—	1.44
12/02	3.12	—	—	(1.31)	—	2.21
Annual Growth	**88.4%**	**—**	**—**	**—**	**—**	**24.4%**

ImClone Systems

ImClone Systems hopes to put all the drama behind it and just get on with the business of making drugs. The biotech firm is focused on developing monoclonal antibody therapies for cancer. Its only approved product is Erbitux, a treatment for colorectal cancer, as well as head and neck cancers; the drug is co-promoted with Bristol-Myers Squibb (which holds a 17% stake in ImClone) in North America and with Merck KGaA elsewhere. ImClone Systems is developing Erbitux as a possible treatment for other kinds of cancer; the company is also working on additional cancer-fighting antibody therapies.

The success of Erbitux was threatened in 2006, when a federal court ruled that scientists from an Israeli research group were the real holders of a key patent underlying Erbitux. ImClone had been licensing the patent from Sanofi-Aventis.

The Israeli plaintiffs in the patent dispute were from Yeda Research and Development, part of the Weizmann Institute of Science. After months of uncertainty, in late 2007 ImClone and Sanofi-Aventis settled with Yeda, each agreeing to pay the research institute $60 million. ImClone also agreed to pay Yeda a small royalty on worldwide Erbitux sales and continues to pay Sanofi-Aventis royalties on sales of the drug outside the US. The disputed patent-covered technology involving the combination of an antibody like Erbitux with chemotherapy to slow tumor growth.

Patent litigation was not the only blow Erbitux suffered in 2006: rival biotech Amgen also won FDA approval that year for a similar (and cheaper) drug to treat colorectal cancer. Earlier in the year, to avoid a costly competitive struggle, the company had put itself on the auction block; but after months without an adequate acquisition offer, ImClone decided to remain independent.

Billionaire investor Carl Icahn, who owns about 14% of the company, won election to the board of directors in 2006, along with several associates, and began immediately agitating for change. Critical of the company's leadership, Icahn called for an overhaul of the board and the resignation of its chairman David Kies. Kies resigned in October 2006, and Icahn was appointed in his stead.

Icahn also headed up the search for a new chief executive, after forcing out interim CEO Joseph Fischer. The company named John Johnson (a former Johnson & Johnson executive) to the post in 2007; Johnson is the company's fifth chief executives since founder Sam Waksal, convicted of illegal insider trading in a scandal involving lifestyle guru Martha Stewart, resigned in 2002.

With Erbitux its only product on the market, expanding the drug's approved uses has been a top priority for ImClone. The firm won approval in 2006 to use the drug to treat head and neck cancer. It might also be a viable treatment for lung cancer.

ImClone doesn't want to be a one-drug wonder, however. The company's R&D pipeline is filled with potential antibody therapies that slow tumor growth by targeting tumor cell growth factors and inhibiting angiogenesis (the formation of new blood vessels). To focus on its core development programs, ImClone has halted its small molecule and vaccine research programs and terminated a partnership with UCB to co-develop CDP-791, an investigational anti-cancer antibody.

EXECUTIVES

Chairman: Carl C. Icahn, age 71
CEO and Director: John H. Johnson, age 49
SVP and Chief Medical Officer: Eric K. Rowinsky, age 51
SVP Biopharmaceutical Operations: Richard P. Crowley, age 51
SVP Commercial Operations: Michael P. Bailey, age 42
VP Engineering and Facilities: Gary Paulter
VP Field Operations: Douglas E. Swan, age 55
VP Medical Affairs: Dvorit Samid
VP Project Management: Margaret Dalesandro, age 60
VP Regulatory Affairs (Clinical and CMC): Cheryl Anderson
VP Regulatory CMC and Operations: Elizabeth Yamashita
VP Human Resources: David Schloss
VP and Interim General Counsel: Gregory T. Mayes
Auditors: KPMG LLP

LOCATIONS

HQ: ImClone Systems Incorporated
180 Varick St., New York, NY 10014
Phone: 212-645-1405   **Fax:** 212-645-2054
Web: www.imclone.com

ImClone Systems has facilities in New Jersey and New York.

PRODUCTS/OPERATIONS

2006 Sales

	% of total
Royalties	43
License fees & milestones	34
Manufacturing	13
Collaborative agreements	10
Total	**100**

Selected Products

Approved
  ERBITUX (colorectal, head and neck cancers)
In Development
  ERBITUX (pancreatic and lung cancers)
  IMC-A12 (advanced solid tumors)
  IMC-11F8 (advanced solid tumors)
  IMC-1121B (advanced solid tumors)

COMPETITORS

Amgen	Micromet
AstraZeneca	Novartis
EntreMed	OSI Pharmaceuticals
Genentech	Pfizer
Genzyme Oncology	Seattle Genetics
GlaxoSmithKline	Wyeth
Medarex	YM BioSciences
Merck KGaA	

HISTORICAL FINANCIALS

Company Type: Public

Income Statement

FYE: December 31

	REVENUE ($ mil.)	NET INCOME ($ mil.)	NET PROFIT MARGIN	EMPLOYEES
12/06	677.8	370.7	54.7%	993
12/05	383.7	86.5	22.5%	991
12/04	388.7	113.7	29.3%	—
12/03	80.8	(112.5)	—	—
12/02	60.0	(157.9)	—	—
Annual Growth	83.3%	—	—	0.2%

2006 Year-End Financials

Debt ratio: 79.0%	Dividends
Return on equity: 73.3%	Yield: —
Cash ($ mil.): 1,044.2	Payout: —
Current ratio: 5.32	Market value ($ mil.): 2,288.2
Long-term debt ($ mil.): 600.0	R&D as % of sales: —
No. of shares (mil.): 85.5	Advertising as % of sales: —

Stock History

NASDAQ (GS): IMCL

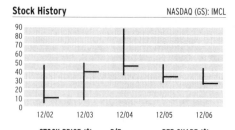

	STOCK PRICE ($) FY Close	P/E High/Low		PER SHARE ($) Earnings	Dividends	Book Value
12/06	26.76	10	6	4.11	—	8.88
12/05	34.24	47	28	1.01	—	3.00
12/04	46.08	66	27	1.33	—	2.15
12/03	39.66	—	—	(1.52)	—	(3.60)
12/02	10.62	—	—	(2.15)	—	(2.52)
Annual Growth	26.0%	—	—	—	—	—

Independence Holding

Independence Holding would like to hold your insurance policy. Through subsidiaries (including Madison National Life Insurance and Standard Security Life Insurance Company of New York), it sells and reinsures health, life, and annuity products and services, such as group disability and term life, and credit life. The company also supplies medical stop-loss insurance (which allows employers to limit their exposure to high health insurance claims.) In addition, the company provides reinsurance and point-of-service coverage to the managed care market. Geneve Holdings, controlled by Independence Holding chairman Ed Netter, owns 55% of the company.

The firm's growth strategy involves buying up blocks of insurance policies and sometimes the

companies that issued them. In 2006 it acquired Insurers Administrative Corporation, which came with a suitcase full of third-party administered Consumer Driven Health Plans (CDHPs). That same year it also acquired a marketing organization, including its key staff and a $50 million block of small group major medical business. The deals nearly doubled Independence Holding's own block of fully-insured medical businesses. Independence Holding owns 48% of (and exerts managerial control over) American Independence, which specializes in employer medical stop-loss and managed care insurance. The company does business throughout the US, the Virgin Islands, and Puerto Rico.

EXECUTIVES

Chairman: Edward (Ed) Netter, age 74
Vice Chairman: Steven B. Lapin, age 61
President and CEO: Roy T. K. Thung, age 63
Co-COO; Chief Legal Officer; Secretary; Chief Administrative Officer, Standard Security; COO, AMIC and Independence American Insurance: David T. Kettig, age 48
Co-COO and SVP: Scott M. Wood, age 42
SVP and CFO: Teresa A. Herbert, age 45, $328,453 pay
SVP and Chief Strategic Development Officer: Jeffrey Smedsrud, age 48
SVP Life and Annuities: Larry R. Graber, age 57
Chief Health Actuary and SVP: Bernon R. Erickson Jr., age 46
VP and Controller: Colleen P. Maggi
VP General Counsel and Secretary: Adam C. Vanderwoort, age 32
Auditors: KPMG LLP

LOCATIONS

HQ: Independence Holding Company
96 Cummings Point Rd., Stamford, CT 06902
Phone: 203-358-8000 **Fax:** 203-348-3103
Web: www.independenceholding.com

PRODUCTS/OPERATIONS

2006 Sales

	$ mil.	% of total
Premiums earned		
Health	236.8	65
Life & annuity	43.5	12
Net investment income	48.5	13
Fee income	32.5	9
Net realized & unrealized gains	0.6	—
Equity income on AMIC	0.7	—
Other income	2.1	1
Total	**364.7**	**100**

2006 Sales by Segment

	$ mil.	% of total
Medical stop-loss	161.0	44
Fully insured health	62.7	17
Individual life, annuities, & other	61.6	17
Group disability, life, annuities & DBL	54.2	15
Credit life & disability	22.4	6
Net realized & unrealized gains	0.6	—
Corporate	2.2	1
Total	**364.7**	**100**

Selected Subsidiaries and Affiliates

Madison National Life Insurance Company, Inc.
  Credico Insurance Services, Inc.
  IC West
  Madison Investors Corporation
Standard Security Life Insurance Company of New York
  IHC Health Holding Corp
    Group LInk, Inc.
    Health Plan Administrators, Inc.
    IHC Health Solutions
    Insurers Administrative Corporation
    Interlock Corporation
  Majestic Underwriters, LLC
  On-Line Brokerage, Inc.

COMPETITORS

BEST LIFE	The Hartford
CIGNA	Liberty Mutual
CNA Financial	MetLife
Great-West Life & Annuity	Prudential

HISTORICAL FINANCIALS

Company Type: Public

Income Statement

FYE: December 31

	ASSETS ($ mil.)	NET INCOME ($ mil.)	INCOME AS % OF ASSETS	EMPLOYEES
12/06	1,259.7	14.1	1.1%	652
12/05	1,150.9	17.3	1.5%	264
12/04	968.5	22.9	2.4%	—
12/03	898.3	18.6	2.1%	—
12/02	744.1	15.8	2.1%	172
Annual Growth	14.1%	(2.8%)	—	39.5%

2006 Year-End Financials

Equity as % of assets: 18.3%	Dividends
Return on assets: 1.2%	Yield: 0.2%
Return on equity: 6.6%	Payout: 5.4%
Long-term debt ($ mil.): 53.2	Sales ($ mil.): 364.7
No. of shares (mil.): 15.2	R&D as % of sales: —
Market value ($ mil.): 331.3	Advertising as % of sales: —

Stock History

NYSE: IHC

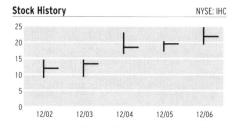

	STOCK PRICE ($) FY Close	P/E High/Low		PER SHARE ($) Earnings	Dividends	Book Value
12/06	21.83	26	21	0.93	0.05	15.23
12/05	19.55	17	14	1.21	0.05	14.06
12/04	18.45	14	10	1.60	—	13.39
12/03	13.33	11	7	1.31	—	21.87
12/02	11.93	13	8	1.10	—	19.84
Annual Growth	16.3%	—	—	(4.1%)	0.0%	(6.4%)

InfoSonics Corporation

InfoSonics answers the call for phone fulfillment. The company distributes wireless handsets and accessories from manufacturers such as Motorola, Nokia, and Samsung. It supplies retailers, wireless carriers, and distributors in the Americas from distribution centers in San Diego and Miami. InfoSonics' services include programming, software loading, and light assembly. Its logistics business includes outsourced supply-chain services such as inventory management and customized packaging. CEO Joseph Ram owns almost a third of the company.

The majority of InfoSonics' sales are in South and Central America. Customers in Argentina, the company's largest market, accounted for almost 60% of revenues in 2006.

In 2004 InfoSonics discontinued its retail operations to focus on its core distribution business. Subsidiary Axcess Mobile had operated the retail segment, which consisted of 10 San Diego-area mall kiosks.

EXECUTIVES

Chairman and CEO: Joseph Ram, age 44, $425,000 pay
EVP and Director: Abraham Rosler, age 46, $195,000 pay
CFO: Jeffrey A. (Jeff) Klausner, age 34, $225,000 pay
President, Latin America: John G. Althoff
VP, Sales and Marketing, North America: Joseph C. (Joe) Murgo, age 38, $154,231 pay
VP, North America: Timmy D. Monico
VP, Finance and Operations: Josh Haims
Commercial Director, Latin America: Christian Camacho
Auditors: Singer Lewak Greenbaum & Goldstein LLP

LOCATIONS

HQ: InfoSonics Corporation
4350 Executive Drive, Ste. 100,
San Diego, CA 92121
Phone: 858-373-1600   **Fax:** 858-373-1505
Web: www.infosonics.com

2006 Sales

	$ mil.	% of total
South America	148.6	62
Central America	80.8	33
North America	11.5	5
Total	**240.9**	**100**

COMPETITORS

Aftermarket Technology
Brightpoint Inc.
Brightstar Corp.
CLST
SED International
TESSCO
UPS Logistics Technologies

HISTORICAL FINANCIALS

Company Type: Public

Income Statement

FYE: December 31

	REVENUE ($ mil.)	NET INCOME ($ mil.)	NET PROFIT MARGIN	EMPLOYEES
12/06	240.9	2.5	1.0%	52
12/05	145.8	2.7	1.9%	28
12/04	73.4	0.0	—	—
12/03	65.1	1.1	1.7%	—
12/02	46.7	0.4	0.9%	—
Annual Growth	**50.7%**	**58.1%**	**—**	**85.7%**

2006 Year-End Financials

Debt ratio: —
Return on equity: 8.9%
Cash ($ mil.): 30.2
Current ratio: 1.81
Long-term debt ($ mil.): —
No. of shares (mil.): 14.2
Dividends
  Yield: —
  Payout: —
Market value ($ mil.): 69.6
R&D as % of sales: —
Advertising as % of sales: —

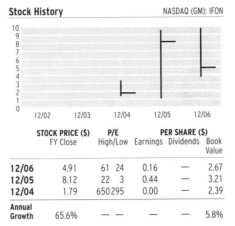

Stock History

NASDAQ (GM): IFON

	STOCK PRICE ($) FY Close	P/E High/Low		PER SHARE ($) Earnings	Dividends	Book Value
12/06	4.91	61	24	0.16	—	2.67
12/05	8.12	22	3	0.44	—	3.21
12/04	1.79	650	295	0.00	—	2.39
Annual Growth	**65.6%**	**—**	**—**	**—**	**—**	**5.8%**

InnerWorkings, Inc.

Printing procurement company Inner-Workings has inserted itself into the process by which corporate customers get print jobs done. The company's proprietary software, PPM4, matches customers' jobs with printing companies' equipment and capacity. The InnerWorkings system submits a job to multiple printers, who then bid for the business. More than 5,000 suppliers participate in the company's network. InnerWorkings' customers include companies in the advertising, consumer products, publishing, and retail industries. Entities controlled by the families of two of InnerWorkings' founders own about 25% of the company, which was formed in 2001.

Most of InnerWorkings' business comes from enterprise customers, for whom the company handles print jobs on a recurring basis. InnerWorkings also takes work from customers on a transactional basis, one order at a time. The company hopes to grow by converting transactional customers to enterprise customers.

Geographic expansion is another key to InnerWorkings's strategy. The company wants to attract more business from outside its home state of Illinois, where about a third of its clients are located (down from two-thirds in 2005). Toward that end, the company is looking to expand its sales force in markets such as Atlanta, Boston, Dallas, Los Angeles, and Minneapolis.

InnerWorkings also is expanding via acquisitions of complementary print management and fulfillment companies. In 2007 the company agreed to buy promotional products distributor Corporate Edge. Earlier in the year the company acquired Philadelphia-based Brown+Partners, which had sales of $17 million in 2006, and gained a presence in Southern California by buying Spectrum Printing Systems, which had sales of about $13 million in 2006. InnerWorkings obtained operations in California, Hawaii, and Nevada in October 2006 by buying Applied Graphics, which posted sales of about $29 million in 2005. Fuel for the deals came from Innerworkings' August 2006 IPO and a January 2007 follow-on offering.

In conjunction with InnerWorkings' May 2006 IPO filing, founders Richard Heise and Eric Lefkofsky left the company's board, but they retain interests through investment vehicles InCorp and Orange Media, as does Lefkofsky's wife, Elizabeth Kramer Lefkofsky.

Affiliates of venture capital firm New Enterprise Associates, represented on InnerWorkings' board by Peter Barris, own 17% of the company.

EXECUTIVES

Chairman: John R. Walter, age 60
President, CEO, and Director: Steven E. (Steve) Zuccarini, age 50, $300,000 pay
COO: Eric D. Belcher, age 38, $339,597 pay
CFO and Secretary: Nicholas J. (Nick) Galassi, age 34, $215,720 pay
Chief Marketing Officer: Mark D. Desky, age 39
CTO: Neil P. Graver, age 36, $104,195 pay (partial-year salary)
EVP Sales: Kevin Harrell, age 44
CIO: Brian Secord
SVP Technology and E-Commerce: Jan Sevcik
SVP Sales Operations/Supply Chain Management: Jonathan Shean
SVP Operations/Solution Delivery: Janet Viane
SVP Enterprise Sales: John Calzaretta
SVP Transactional Sales: Robert Maus
Auditors: Ernst & Young LLP

LOCATIONS

HQ: InnerWorkings, Inc.
600 W. Chicago Ave., Ste. 850, Chicago, IL 60610
Phone: 312-642-3700   **Fax:** 312-642-3704
Web: www.iwprint.com

PRODUCTS/OPERATIONS

2006 Sales

	% of total
Enterprise clients	70
Transactional clients	30
Total	**100**

COMPETITORS

Cirqit
Newline
Quad/Graphics
Quebecor World
R.R. Donnelley
Workflow Management

HISTORICAL FINANCIALS

Company Type: Public

Income Statement

FYE: December 31

	REVENUE ($ mil.)	NET INCOME ($ mil.)	NET PROFIT MARGIN	EMPLOYEES
12/06	160.5	8.3	5.2%	153
12/05	76.9	4.6	6.0%	154
12/04	38.9	1.8	4.6%	85
12/03	16.2	0.7	4.3%	43
Annual Growth	**114.8%**	**128.0%**	**—**	**52.7%**

2006 Year-End Financials

Debt ratio: 0.3%
Return on equity: 20.1%
Cash ($ mil.): 30.6
Current ratio: 2.81
Long-term debt ($ mil.): 0.2
No. of shares (mil.): 44.0
Dividends
  Yield: —
  Payout: —
Market value ($ mil.): 702.5
R&D as % of sales: —
Advertising as % of sales: —

	20 18 16 14 12 10 8 6 4 2 0				
	12/02	12/03	12/04	12/05	12/06

	STOCK PRICE ($) FY Close	P/E High/Low		PER SHARE ($) Earnings	Dividends	Book Value
12/06	15.96	88	47	0.21	—	1.85

Integra LifeSciences

Integra LifeSciences still works in the skin trade, but has become more cerebral. The firm develops biomaterials for regenerating human tissue. In addition, Integra has branched into neuroscience, providing instruments, implants, and monitors for neurosurgery. Implantable collagen matrix technology provides a structure for the regrowth of patients' own tissues. Its extremity reconstruction products include the Dermal Regeneration Template, which replaces skin and reduces the need for conventional grafts. Other lines include infection control, dental surgery, and wound care. Integra LifeSciences sells products directly and through distributors. Chairman Richard Caruso owns about a quarter of the company.

Integra LifeSciences reorganized its European operations in 2005, in an effort to expand its sales, marketing, and distribution activities on the continent. In 2006 the company acquired the Radionics division of Tyco Healthcare (now Covidien) for $80 million. The purchase is expected to further expand Integra LifeSciences' international business.

Later in the same year, Integra LifeSciences acquired Miltex, a provider of surgical and dental hand instruments, for $101 million, and Kinetikos Medical, a manufacturer of orthopedic implants for the extremities.

In 2007 Integra kept up its acquisition activity with the proposed purchase of California-based orthobiologics company IsoTis.

President and CEO Stuart Essig owns 5% of the business.

EXECUTIVES

Chairman: Richard E. Caruso, age 63
President, CEO, and Director: Stuart M. Essig, age 45, $450,000 pay
President Extremity Reconstruction: Robert D. Paltridge, age 49, $258,500 pay
President Medical Instrument Selling: Bob Perrett
EVP and COO: Gerard S. Carlozzi, age 51, $350,000 pay
EVP, Acting CFO, Chief Administrative Officer, and Secretary: John B. Henneman III, age 45, $400,000 pay

SVP Global Marketing: Deborah A. Leonetti, age 51
SVP Global Operations: James A. Oti
SVP Manufacturing Operations: Donald R. Nociolo, age 44
SVP Regulatory, Quality Assurance, and Clinical Affairs: Judith E. O'Grady, age 56
SVP and General Counsel: Richard D. Gorelick
SVP Human Resources: Wilma J. Davis
VP and CIO: Randy Gottlieb
VP and Treasurer: Leigh DeFilippis
VP Clinical Affairs and Chief Scientific Officer: Simon J. Archibald
VP Corporate Development and Investor Relations: John Bostjancic
Auditors: PricewaterhouseCoopers LLP

LOCATIONS

HQ: Integra LifeSciences Holdings Corporation
311 Enterprise Dr., Plainsboro, NJ 08536
Phone: 609-275-0500   **Fax:** 609-275-5363
Web: www.integra-ls.com

Integra LifeSciences has facilities in France, Germany, Puerto Rico, the UK, and the US.

2006 Sales

	$ mil.	% of total
US	317.5	76
Europe	77.1	18
Asia/Pacific	12.3	3
Other countries	12.4	3
Total	**419.3**	**100**

PRODUCTS/OPERATIONS

2006 Sales

	$ mil.	% of total
Medical/surgical equipment	252.9	60
Neurosurgical & orthopedic implants	166.4	40
Total	**419.3**	**100**

COMPETITORS

B. Braun Medical (UK)
Cardinal Health
Codman & Shurtleff
Genzyme Biosurgery
Johnson & Johnson
LifeCell
Medtronic
Organogenesis
Smith & Nephew
Stryker
Synthes
Wright Medical Group

HISTORICAL FINANCIALS

Company Type: Public

Income Statement				FYE: December 31
	REVENUE ($ mil.)	NET INCOME ($ mil.)	NET PROFIT MARGIN	EMPLOYEES
12/06	419.3	29.4	7.0%	2,150
12/05	277.9	37.2	13.4%	1,180
12/04	229.8	17.2	7.5%	—
12/03	185.6	26.9	14.5%	—
12/02	117.8	35.3	30.0%	760
Annual Growth	**37.4%**	**(4.5%)**	**—**	**29.7%**

2006 Year-End Financials

Debt ratio: 0.2%
Return on equity: 10.0%
Cash ($ mil.): 22.7
Current ratio: 0.81
Long-term debt ($ mil.): 0.5
No. of shares (mil.): 27.3
Dividends
Yield: —
Payout: —
Market value ($ mil.): 1,163.4
R&D as % of sales: —
Advertising as % of sales: —

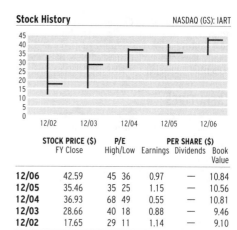

	45 40 35 30 25 20 15 10 5 0				
	12/02	12/03	12/04	12/05	12/06

	STOCK PRICE ($) FY Close	P/E High/Low		PER SHARE ($) Earnings	Dividends	Book Value
12/06	42.59	45	36	0.97	—	10.84
12/05	35.46	35	25	1.15	—	10.56
12/04	36.93	68	49	0.55	—	10.81
12/03	28.66	40	18	0.88	—	9.46
12/02	17.65	29	11	1.14	—	9.10
Annual Growth	**24.6%**	**—**	**—**	**(4.0%)**	**—**	**4.5%**

Intercontinental-Exchange

If there was money to be made in ice futures, IntercontinentalExchange (ICE) would probably trade that as well. The company is a leading on-line marketplace for global commodity trading, primarily of electricity, natural gas, crude oil, refined petroleum products, precious metals, and weather and emission credits. It also owns the ICE Futures, a leading European energy futures and options platform. ICE's 10x Group unit provides real-time market data reports, and the company's eConfirm platform provides electronic trade confirmations. In 2007 the company acquired the New York Board of Trade for $1 billion, and agreed to buy an 8% stake in India's National Commodity & Derivatives Exchange.

ICE also offers real-time OTC clearing and credit and risk management services.

ICE was formed by a group of top financial and energy firms in 2000. The company is based in Atlanta, and has regional offices in Calgary, Chicago, Houston, New York, and Singapore.

In 2007 ICE agreed to buy ChemConnect, Inc.'s US natural gas liquids (NGLs) and chemicals trading business. It also agreed to buy the Winnipeg Commodity Exchange for C$40 million.

EXECUTIVES

Chairman and CEO: Jeffrey C. Sprecher, age 53, $725,000 pay
Vice Chairman: Richard V. Spencer, age 54
President and COO: Charles A. (Chuck) Vice, age 44, $500,000 pay
SVP and CFO: Scott A. Hill
SVP and CTO: Edwin D. Marcial, age 40, $365,000 pay
SVP and Chief Strategic Officer: David S. Goone, age 47, $460,000 pay
SVP, General Counsel, and Secretary: Jonathan H. Short, age 42
VP, Investor Relations and Corporate Communications: Kelly L. Loeffler
President and COO, ICE Futures: David J. Peniket, age 42
President and COO, NYBOT: Thomas W. Farley, age 33
President and COO, ICE Clear US: Thomas Hammond
Auditors: Ernst & Young LLP

LOCATIONS

HQ: IntercontinentalExchange, Inc.
2100 RiverEdge Pkwy., Ste. 500, Atlanta, GA 30328
Phone: 770-857-4700   **Fax:** 770-951-1307
Web: www.theice.com

PRODUCTS/OPERATIONS

2006 Sales

	$ mil.	% of total
OTC	168.8	54
Futures	127.0	40
Market data fees	18.0	6
Total	**313.8**	**100**

Founding Partners

BP p.l.c.
Deutsche Bank AG
The Goldman Sachs Group, Inc.
Morgan Stanley Dean Witter & Co.
Royal Dutch Shell plc
Société Générale
TOTAL S.A.

COMPETITORS

APX
Bloomberg L.P.
CHOICE! Energy
Enporion
ICAP
NYMEX Holdings
Prebon Yamane
Reuters
Unitil

HISTORICAL FINANCIALS

Company Type: Public

Income Statement
FYE: December 31

	REVENUE ($ mil.)	NET INCOME ($ mil.)	NET PROFIT MARGIN	EMPLOYEES
12/06	313.8	143.3	45.7%	226
12/05	155.9	40.4	25.9%	203
12/04	108.4	22.0	20.3%	—
12/03	93.8	13.4	14.3%	—
12/02	125.5	34.7	27.6%	204
Annual Growth	25.7%	42.6%	—	2.6%

2006 Year-End Financials

Debt ratio: —
Return on equity: 41.7%
Cash ($ mil.): 297.8
Current ratio: 9.00
Long-term debt ($ mil.): —
No. of shares (mil.): 58.1
Dividends
 Yield: —
 Payout: —
Market value ($ mil.): 6,271.7
R&D as % of sales: —
Advertising as % of sales: —

Stock History
NYSE: ICE

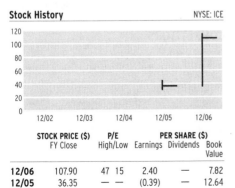

	STOCK PRICE ($) FY Close	P/E High/Low	PER SHARE ($) Earnings	Dividends	Book Value
12/06	107.90	47 15	2.40	—	7.82
12/05	36.35	— —	(0.39)	—	12.64
Annual Growth	196.8%	— —	—	—	(38.2%)

InterDigital, Inc.

InterDigital is more than just interested in digital telecommunications. The company develops and licenses circuitry designs, software, and other technology using CDMA and TDMA (code- and time-division multiple access) wireless telecommunications standards. InterDigital is also developing semiconductors and software to enable voice and data transmissions in mobile phones and portable computing devices.

The company's top customers include NEC and Sharp. It also licenses to Siemens and Sony Ericsson, and to many other makers of chips, software, and telecom equipment.

In mid-2007 the company shortened its name from InterDigital Communications Corporation to InterDigital, Inc. The change was made in connection with a reorganization that will see the company change from a pure R&D and licensing venture to one selling application-specific integrated circuits (ASICs) and making strategic investments, in addition to wireless communications research and technology licensing.

A legal dispute between InterDigital and Nokia over the amount of royalties the Finnish company owed was resolved in InterDigital's favor in late 2005, when a US District Court judge upheld an international tribunal's verdict ordering Nokia to pay additional royalties to InterDigital. In 2006 Nokia agreed to pay $253 million in one lump sum to InterDigital, and the companies agreed to end their litigation against each other. Nokia and InterDigital immediately terminated their original license agreement and began negotiating a new pact.

Those talks apparently came to naught, as InterDigital in 2007 filed a complaint against Nokia with the US International Trade Commission, alleging that Nokia's handsets infringe on patents held by InterDigital.

LG Electronics signed a five-year patent licensing agreement with InterDigital in early 2006. The pact calls for the Korean manufacturer of consumer electronics and home appliances to pay InterDigital a total of $285 million in the first three years of the agreement.

Even more checks should be coming from the Korean peninsula: An international arbitration tribunal has awarded InterDigital $134 million in past royalties, plus interest, from Samsung Electronics. The amount of royalties is tied to the company's patent licensing agreement with Nokia.

Unable to reach a patent licensing agreement with Samsung Electronics, InterDigital filed a complaint against the giant Korean manufacturer with the US International Trade Commission in 2007. It also filed a lawsuit, in US District Court in Delaware, alleging patent infringement by Samsung's Blackjack mobile phone and other models.

The $134 million award against Samsung was upheld by the US District Court for the Southern District of New York in late 2007.

The company expanded its technology portfolio by acquiring the assets of Tantivy Communications, a designer of CDMA-based and other wireless gear, in 2003 for $11.5 million.

Heartland Advisors owns 7% of InterDigital.

EXECUTIVES

Chairman: Harry G. Campagna, age 68
President, CEO, and Director: William J. Merritt, age 48, $617,223 pay
CFO: Scott McQuilkin
EVP Intellectual Property and Chief Legal Officer; President, Patent Licensing: Lawrence F. Shay, age 48
EVP Standards: Brian G. Kiernan, age 60
EVP Business Development and Product Management: Mark A. Lemmo, age 49
EVP Programs and Customer Support: William C. Miller, age 52
EVP Engineering: Jim Nolan
Senior Communications and Investor Relations Officer: Janet M. Point
Chief Scientist and Director: D. Ridgley Bolgiano, age 74
Chief Intellectual Property and Licensing Officer: Bruce G. Bernstein, age 41
Senior Human Resources Officer: Gary D. Isaacs
Deputy General Counsel: Steven W. Sprecher
Auditors: PricewaterhouseCoopers LLP

LOCATIONS

HQ: InterDigital, Inc.
781 3rd Ave., King of Prussia, PA 19406
Phone: 610-878-7800   **Fax:** 610-992-9432
Web: www.interdigital.com

InterDigital has offices in Canada and the US.

2006 Sales

	% of total
Europe	58
Asia	39
US	3
Total	**100**

COMPETITORS

Alcatel-Lucent
Broadcom
Conexant Systems
Freescale Semiconductor
IBM Microelectronics
Infineon Technologies
Intel Corporation
LSI Corp.
Marvell Technology
Nokia
NXP
QUALCOMM
STMicroelectronics
Texas Instruments
Xora

HISTORICAL FINANCIALS

Company Type: Public

Income Statement
FYE: December 31

	REVENUE ($ mil.)	NET INCOME ($ mil.)	NET PROFIT MARGIN	EMPLOYEES
12/06	480.5	225.2	46.9%	343
12/05	163.1	54.7	33.5%	315
12/04	103.7	0.2	0.2%	—
12/03	114.6	34.5	30.1%	—
12/02	87.9	2.5	2.8%	312
Annual Growth	52.9%	208.1%	—	2.4%

2006 Year-End Financials

Debt ratio: 0.4%
Return on equity: 100.1%
Cash ($ mil.): 264.0
Current ratio: 3.74
Long-term debt ($ mil.): 1.2
No. of shares (mil.): 51.3
Dividends
 Yield: —
 Payout: —
Market value ($ mil.): 1,722.7
R&D as % of sales: —
Advertising as % of sales: —

Stock History

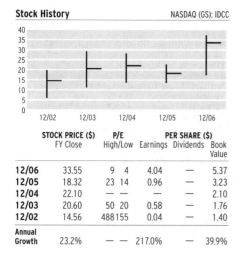

	STOCK PRICE ($) FY Close	P/E High/Low		PER SHARE ($) Earnings	Dividends	Book Value
12/06	33.55	9	4	4.04	—	5.37
12/05	18.32	23	14	0.96	—	3.23
12/04	22.10	—	—	—	—	2.10
12/03	20.60	50	20	0.58	—	1.76
12/02	14.56	488	155	0.04	—	1.40
Annual Growth	23.2%	—	—	217.0%	—	39.9%

International Bancshares

International Bancshares is leading post-NAFTA banking in South Texas. Its International Bank of Commerce and Commerce Bank serve residents and businesses of Texas, Oklahoma, and northern Mexico through some 230 offices. The bulk of the company's portfolio is made up of business loans, including funding for northern Mexico's *maquiladoras*, US-owned plants in Mexico that temporarily import materials for assembly and then re-export to the US. About 30% of the company's deposits come from south of the border. Founder Tony Sanchez, who lost the 2002 race for Texas governor, and his family own around 19% of International Bancshares.

The bank moved northward into Oklahoma with its purchase of Local Financial in 2004. In 2007 it acquired Southwest First Community, Inc., deepening its position in southern Texas.

In addition to commercial and international banking services, International Bancshares provides retail deposit services, insurance and investment products, and mortgages and consumer loans. Subsidiary Gulfstar Group performs merchant and investment banking services.

With most of its stock owned by Hispanic shareholders, International Bancshares is one of the largest minority-owned banks in the nation.

EXECUTIVES

Chairman and President; President and CEO, International Bank of Commerce, Laredo: Dennis E. Nixon, age 64, $754,177 pay
VP and Director; President and CEO, International Bank of Commerce, McAllen: R. David Guerra, age 54, $312,673 pay
Treasurer and Director; SEVP, CFO, and COO, International Bank of Commerce, Laredo: Imelda Navarro, age 49, $246,548 pay
EVP, International Bank of Commerce, Laredo: Edward J. Farias
EVP and Director of International Business Development, International Bank of Commerce, Laredo: Guillermo R. Garcia
EVP and Cashier, International Bank of Commerce, Laredo: Dalia F. Martinez

EVP, International Department, International Bank of Commerce, Laredo: Gerald Schwebel
EVP, Sales and Marketing, International Bank of Commerce, Laredo: J. Jorge Verduzco
Secretary: Marisa V. Santos
Investor Relations Officer: Eliza Gonzalez
Auditors: McGladrey & Pullen, LLP

LOCATIONS

HQ: International Bancshares Corporation
1200 San Bernardo Ave., Laredo, TX 78042
Phone: 956-722-7611   **Fax:** 956-726-6637
Web: www.iboc.com

PRODUCTS/OPERATIONS

2006 Sales

	% of total
Interest	
Loans, including fees	51
Investment securities & other	27
Noninterest	
Service charges on deposit accounts	11
Other service charges, commissions & fees	6
Other investments	2
Other	3
Total	**100**

COMPETITORS

Banamex	Financiero Santander
Bank of America	JPMorgan Chase
BBVA Bancomer	Texas Regional Bancshares
Citigroup	Wells Fargo
Cullen/Frost Bankers	

HISTORICAL FINANCIALS

Company Type: Public

Income Statement

				FYE: December 31
	ASSETS ($ mil.)	NET INCOME ($ mil.)	INCOME AS % OF ASSETS	EMPLOYEES
12/06	10,911.5	117.0	1.1%	3,427
12/05	10,391.8	140.8	1.4%	3,265
12/04	9,918.0	119.0	1.2%	—
12/03	6,578.3	122.1	1.9%	—
12/02	6,495.6	100.6	1.5%	1,937
Annual Growth	13.8%	3.8%	—	15.3%

2006 Year-End Financials

Equity as % of assets: 7.7%
Return on assets: 1.1%
Return on equity: 14.3%
Long-term debt ($ mil.): 2,306.5
No. of shares (mil.): 62.9
Market value ($ mil.): 1,607.1
Dividends
Yield: 2.3%
Payout: 34.9%
Sales ($ mil.): 787.0
R&D as % of sales: —
Advertising as % of sales: —

Stock History

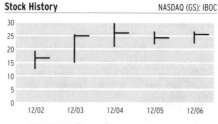

	STOCK PRICE ($) FY Close	P/E High/Low		PER SHARE ($) Earnings	Dividends	Book Value
12/06	25.55	16	14	1.66	0.58	13.38
12/05	24.26	13	11	1.98	0.26	12.44
12/04	26.04	17	12	1.71	—	14.82
12/03	24.94	14	8	1.80	0.45	14.92
12/02	16.69	13	9	1.43	0.29	17.51
Annual Growth	11.2%	—	—	3.8%	18.9%	(6.5%)

Intervest Bancshares

Intervest Bancshares is the holding company for Intervest National Bank, the rather grandly named bank that operates one branch in New York City and six other branches in Pinellas County, Florida. Most of the company's lending activities are real estate-related: Commercial mortgages make up more than half of its loan portfolio, while multifamily residential mortgages account for more than 40%. Some of its lending is carried out by subsidiary Intervest Mortgage Corporation, which primarily originates mortgages for apartment buildings and commercial properties in New York City. Chairman and CEO Lowell Dansker and his sister Helene Bergman control Intervest Bancshares.

EXECUTIVES

Chairman and CEO: Lowell S. Dansker, age 56, $777,317 pay (prior to title change)
CFO and Chief Accouting Officer; SVP, CFO, and Secretary, Intervest National Bank: John J. Arvonio, age 44, $174,375 pay
VP and CFO, Intervest Mortgage: John H. Hoffmann, age 55
President and Director, Intervest National Bank: Raymond C. Sullivan, age 60
President and Director, Florida Division, Intervest National Bank: Keith A. Olsen, age 53, $205,712 pay
VP, Secretary, and Director, Intervest Bancshares and Intervest Mortgage; VP and Director, Intervest National Bank; Administrator, Intervest Statutory Trust: Stephen A. Helman, age 67
Auditors: Hacker, Johnson & Smith PA

LOCATIONS

HQ: Intervest Bancshares Corporation
1 Rockefeller Plaza, Ste. 400, New York, NY 10020
Phone: 212-218-2800   **Fax:** 212-218-8390
Web: www.intervestnatbank.com

PRODUCTS/OPERATIONS

2006 Sales

	$ mil.	% of total
Interest		
Loans receivable	112.4	83
Securities	14.7	11
Other	1.6	1
Noninterest		
Early repayment of mortgages	4.9	4
Mortgage lending activities	1.4	1
Service fees & other	0.5	—
Total	**135.5**	**100**

COMPETITORS

Bank of America
BB&T
Citigroup
Regions Financial
SunTrust
Wachovia

HISTORICAL FINANCIALS

Company Type: Public

Income Statement

FYE: December 31

	ASSETS ($ mil.)	NET INCOME ($ mil.)	INCOME AS % OF ASSETS	EMPLOYEES
12/06	1,971.8	23.5	1.2%	72
12/05	1,706.4	18.2	1.1%	69
12/04	1,316.8	11.4	0.9%	—
12/03	910.6	9.1	1.0%	—
12/02	686.0	6.9	1.0%	57
Annual Growth	30.2%	35.8%	—	6.0%

2006 Year-End Financials

Equity as % of assets: 8.6%
Return on assets: 1.3%
Return on equity: 15.3%
Long-term debt ($ mil.): 163.4
No. of shares (mil.): 8.0
Market value ($ mil.): 274.8

Dividends
Yield: —
Payout: —
Sales ($ mil.): 135.5
R&D as % of sales: —
Advertising as % of sales: —

Stock History

NASDAQ (GS): IBCA

	STOCK PRICE ($) FY Close	P/E High/Low		PER SHARE ($) Earnings	Dividends	Book Value
12/06	34.41	17	8	2.82	—	21.29
12/05	24.75	11	7	2.47	—	18.31
12/04	19.74	12	8	1.71	—	15.30
12/03	14.65	10	7	1.53	—	13.45
12/02	10.80	8	5	1.37	—	12.22
Annual Growth	33.6%	—	—	19.8%	—	14.9%

Intevac, Inc.

Intevac's sputtering doesn't stem from a speech impediment. The company's Equipment division manufactures sputtering systems that deposit alloy films onto hard-disk drives; the films magnetize the drives and thus enable them to record information. The Equipment division also makes sputterers used to make flat-panel displays. Intevac's Imaging division develops sensitive electro-optical devices used in high-performance digital cameras and military targeting equipment. Leading customers include Hitachi Global Storage Technologies and Seagate. Intevac was spun out of the old Varian Associates (later split into Varian, Varian Medical, and Varian Semiconductor) in a 1991 leveraged buyout.

In 2006 the company opened a manufacturing facility in Singapore to expand production capacity and to provide greater support for customers in Asia, which account for around 90% of sales.

In early 2007 Intevac acquired the assets of DeltaNu, a developer of Raman spectrometers, instruments used in forensics, industrial metrology, medical diagnostics, and scientific research. A spinoff from the University of Wyoming,

DeltaNu became a wholly owned subsidiary of Intevac and part of the Imaging division. The company paid $2 million to acquire DeltaNu, with payments of $2 million due in 2008 and 2009, for a total of $6 million.

Later that year Intevac acquired Creative Display Systems (CDS), a developer of high-performance microdisplays for near-eye and portable applications in commercial and military markets. The CDS products will complement those of Intevac Imaging in night vision systems and miniature Raman instruments.

The company is developing an etching system for the semiconductor production equipment market, an application in a new but technically similar area.

Intevac's Equipment division (more than 95% of sales) provides services such as applications support, installation, training, and repair services, as well as spare parts and consumables, for its sputtering systems. The company's Imaging business includes its Photonics division, which collaborates with research firms including Stanford University and The Charles Stark Draper Laboratory to perform research for the US government, as well as its Commercial Imaging division, formed in 2002 to develop products based on its photonics technology for commercial markets, including night vision and long-range video cameras for security applications. The company suspended its development of photodiodes for high-speed fiber-optic systems due to weakness in the telecommunications market at the time; the product has been repositioned for applications in target identification and other military uses.

T. Rowe Price holds nearly 10% of the company. Cross Link Capital has an equity stake of nearly 7%. Redemco owns about 6% of Intevac. Chairman Norman Pond holds around 4%.

EXECUTIVES

Chairman: Norman H. Pond, age 68, $136,166 pay
President, CEO, and Director: Kevin Fairbairn, age 53, $379,026 pay
COO: Luke Marusiak, age 44, $215,078 pay
EVP Finance and CFO: Jeff Andreson, age 45
VP New Product Development: Christopher Lane, age 39
VP Business Development: Ralph Kerns, age 59, $197,029 pay
VP Engineering: Patrick (Pat) Leahey, age 44
VP Engineering: Dave Kelly, age 44
VP Manufacturing: Timothy E. Justyn, age 44
VP Chief Technical Officer: Michael Barnes, age 47, $219,245 pay
Chief Technology Officer: Verle W. Aebi, age 52, $199,106 pay
Director, Human Resources: Kimberly Burk, age 41
Auditors: Grant Thornton LLP

LOCATIONS

HQ: Intevac, Inc.
3560 Bassett St., Santa Clara, CA 95054
Phone: 408-986-9888   **Fax:** 408-727-5739
Web: www.intevac.com

Intevac has operations in China, Japan, Malaysia, Singapore, South Korea, and the US.

2006 Sales

	$ mil.	% of total
Asia	233.2	90
US	26.5	10
Europe	0.2	—
Total	**259.9**	**100**

PRODUCTS/OPERATIONS

2006 Sales

	$ mil.	% of total
Equipment	248.5	96
Imaging	11.4	4
Total	**259.9**	**100**

2006 Sales

	$ mil.	% of total
Systems & components	250.2	96
Technology development	9.7	4
Total	**259.9**	**100**

Selected Products

Equipment
Disk lubrication equipment
Disk sputtering equipment (MDP-250 series)
Flat-panel display sputtering systems (D-Star series)
Commercial Imaging
Laser-illuminated viewing and ranging (LIVAR) systems
Low-cost, low-light-level cameras (NightVista)
Negative-electron-affinity (NEA) electron sources

COMPETITORS

Ahura
Applied Materials
Aviza Technology
CIC International
CMC Electronics
DRS Technologies
e2v
FLIR
Halma
Hamamatsu Corp.
HORIBA
ITT Corp.
Lam Research
Mitsui
Northrop Grumman
Oerlikon
Raytheon
Roper Industries
Smiths Detection
Sumitomo Heavy Industries
Texas Instruments
Thales
Tokyo Electron
ULVAC

HISTORICAL FINANCIALS

Company Type: Public

Income Statement

FYE: December 31

	REVENUE ($ mil.)	NET INCOME ($ mil.)	NET PROFIT MARGIN	EMPLOYEES
12/06	259.9	46.7	18.0%	540
12/05	137.2	16.1	11.7%	362
12/04	69.6	(4.3)	—	—
12/03	36.3	(12.3)	—	—
12/02	33.8	8.8	26.0%	136
Annual Growth	66.5%	51.8%	—	41.2%

2006 Year-End Financials

Debt ratio: —
Return on equity: 40.2%
Cash ($ mil.): 95.0
Current ratio: 2.95
Long-term debt ($ mil.): —
No. of shares (mil.): 21.2

Dividends
Yield: —
Payout: —
Market value ($ mil.): 549.8
R&D as % of sales: —
Advertising as % of sales: —

Intuitive Surgical

Stock History   NASDAQ (GM): IVAC

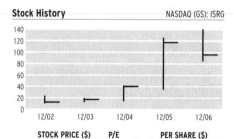

	STOCK PRICE ($) FY Close	P/E High/Low		PER SHARE ($) Earnings	Dividends	Book Value
12/06	25.95	15	6	2.13	—	6.81
12/05	13.20	20	9	0.76	—	4.25
12/04	7.56	—	—	(0.22)	—	3.44
12/03	14.10	—	—	(0.95)	—	1.82
12/02	3.99	8	3	0.66	—	0.87
Annual Growth	59.7%	—	—	34.0%	—	67.3%

Intuitive Surgical

Intuitive Surgical is haptic to meet you. Employing haptics (the science of computer-aided touch sensitivity), the firm has developed the da Vinci Surgical System of software, hardware, and optics to allow doctors to perform robotically aided surgery from a remote console. The company also makes EndoWrist surgical instruments for use with its system. The da Vinci system faithfully reproduces the doctor's hand movements in real time, with surgery performed by tiny electromechanical arms and instruments inserted in the patient's body through small openings. Intuitive sells its products in Asia, Australia, Europe, and North America through both a direct sales force and independent distributors.

Intuitive Surgical is focusing its marketing efforts within specialties including general, cardiothoracic, urologic, and gynecologic surgery. (Prostate-removal surgeries are its most common application.) The company has grown as the FDA approves more uses for the da Vinci system, and as it gains wider acceptance within the medical community.

The company also plans to develop strategic alliances with medical device businesses. It currently has alliances with Medtronic, Olympus Corporation, and Ethicon Endo-Surgery.

EXECUTIVES

Chairman and CEO: Lonnie M. Smith, age 62, $427,500 pay
President and COO: Gary S. Guthart, age 41, $343,750 pay
EVP, Worldwide Sales and Marketing: Jerome J. (Jerry) McNamara, age 49, $258,750 pay
SVP and CFO: Marshall L. Mohr, age 51, $287,500 pay
SVP, Marketing: Richard M. Epstein
SVP and General Counsel: Mark Meltzer
VP, Business Development and Strategic Planning: Aleks Cukic
VP, Customer Service: Colin Morales
VP, Engineering: Sal Brogna
VP, Finance and Treasurer: Benjamin B. (Ben) Gong, $204,000 pay
VP, Human Resources: Heather Hand
VP, Intellectual Property and Licensing: Frank D. Nguyen
Auditors: Ernst & Young LLP

LOCATIONS

HQ: Intuitive Surgical, Inc.
    950 Kifer Rd., Sunnyvale, CA 94086
Phone: 408-523-2100   **Fax:** 408-523-1390
Web: www.intuitivesurgical.com

2006 Sales

	% of total
US	83
Other countries	17
Total	**100**

PRODUCTS/OPERATIONS

2006 Sales

	$ mil.	% of total
Products		
Systems	205.9	55
Instruments & accessories	111.7	30
Services & training	55.1	15
Total	**372.7**	**100**

Selected Products

AESOP Endoscope Positioner
da Vinci Surgical System (surgeon's console, patient-side cart, and InSite 3-D visualization system)
EndoWrist surgical instruments

COMPETITORS

Boston Scientific	Maquet
C. R. Bard	Medtronic
Hitachi	MicroDexterity
Integrated Surgical	Prosurgics
Systems	Terumo Medical
Johnson & Johnson	Toshiba

HISTORICAL FINANCIALS

Company Type: Public

Income Statement   FYE: December 31

	REVENUE ($ mil.)	NET INCOME ($ mil.)	NET PROFIT MARGIN	EMPLOYEES
12/06	372.7	72.0	19.3%	563
12/05	227.3	94.1	41.4%	419
12/04	138.8	23.5	16.9%	—
12/03	91.7	(9.6)	—	—
12/02	72.0	(18.4)	—	290
Annual Growth	50.8%	—	—	18.0%

2006 Year-End Financials

Debt ratio: —
Return on equity: 13.9%
Cash ($ mil.): 239.7
Current ratio: 4.64
Long-term debt ($ mil.): —
No. of shares (mil.): 37.1
Dividends
  Yield: —
  Payout: —
Market value ($ mil.): 3,557.2
R&D as % of sales: —
Advertising as % of sales: —

Stock History   NASDAQ (GS): ISRG

	STOCK PRICE ($) FY Close	P/E High/Low		PER SHARE ($) Earnings	Dividends	Book Value
12/06	95.90	74	45	1.89	—	15.90
12/05	117.27	50	14	2.51	—	12.23
12/04	40.02	61	23	0.67	—	9.20
12/03	17.09	—	—	(0.41)	—	8.44
12/02	12.32	—	—	(1.02)	—	1.73
Annual Growth	67.0%	—	—	—	—	74.0%

inVentiv Health

To sell a new drug, it may be time to get inVentiv. inVentiv Health provides commercial, clinical, and communications services for customers in the life sciences and pharmaceutical industries. The company's commercial services unit provides outsourced sales and marketing services, market research, data collection and management, recruitment, and training. The clinical services unit provides clinical staffing, clinical research and statistical analysis, and executive placement. Serving clients such as Bayer Corporation, Bristol-Myers Squibb, and Noven Pharmaceuticals, inVentiv Health has been growing via a constant stream of acquisitions.

In late 2005 inVentiv purchased health care communications agency inChord Communications for $185 million. The acquisition spurred a restructuring, and in 2006 inVentiv reorganized into three segments: commercial services, clinical services, and communications. The Commercial Services segment (its most lucrative, representing about 47% of sales) includes Health Products Research and Total Data Solutions; the Clinical Services segment consists of Smith Hanley, MedFocus, and HHI Statistical Services.

To expand its communications business, inVentive agreed in 2007 to acquire public relations firm Chamberlain Communications Group, for $13 million, and advertising agency Ignite Health, for $20 million. It also bought brand identity and consulting firm Addison Whitney, pharmaceutical software provider Innovative Health Strategies (for $75 million), and health care public relations agency Chandler Chicco (for $65 million) later that same year.

The deals follow a string of acquisitions by inVentiv in 2006, when the company moved to beef up all three of its business segments. Additional purchases included marketing communications firms Adheris and Jeffrey Simbrow Associates, as well as Synergos, a provider of clinical trial management services. inVentiv expanded its commercial services operations in 2006 by acquiring two training companies, American Speakers Education Research Training (ASERT) and DialogCoach, along with online events producer Maxwell Group, which operates under the MedConference business.

EXECUTIVES

Chairman Emeritus: Daniel M. Snyder, age 42
Chairman and CEO: Eran Broshy, age 48
CEO, Smith Hanley Holding Company: Thomas A. (Tom) Hanley Jr.
COO; President and CEO, inVentiv Commercial Services: Terrell G. (Terry) Herring, age 43
CFO: David Bassin
EVP and Managing Director, GSW Worldwide, Newtown: Mark Frank
EVP, Resource Management, inVentiv Commercial: Tristen Herrstrom
SVP, Ventiv Sales and Marketing Teams: Tom Sottile
Media Contact: Felicia Vonella
Senior Director, Human Resources, inVentiv Commercial: Maureen Stellmach
President, inVentiv Clinical: Michael L. Hlinak
President and CEO, GSW Worldwide: Phil Deschamps
President and COO, Ventiv Pharma Analytics, inVentiv Commercial: Leonard J. Vicciardo
President and COO, Ventiv Pharma Services, inVentiv Commercial: Bill Shearer
President, inVentiv Selling Solutions: Paul Mignon
Auditors: Deloitte & Touche LLP

LOCATIONS

HQ: inVentiv Health, Inc.
Vantage Ct. North, 200 Cottontail Ln.,
Somerset, NJ 08873
Phone: 732-537-4800 **Fax:** 732-537-4912
Web: www.ventiv.com

PRODUCTS/OPERATIONS

2006 Sales

	$ mil.	% of total
inVentiv Commercial	359.4	47
inVentiv Communications	257.0	34
inVentiv Clinical	149.8	19
Total	**766.2**	**100**

Selected Services

Commercial Services
Data collection and management
Drug sample compliance
Medical science liaisons/Clinical educator teams
Planning, analytics, market research
Recruitment
Clinical Services
Clinical research and statistical analysis
Clinical staffing
Executive placement
Communications Services
Advertising
Contract marketing
Interactive medical education
Patient adherence services

COMPETITORS

Access Worldwide
ATC Healthcare
Brand Pharm
Cross Country Healthcare
Heidrick & Struggles
IMS Health
InteliStaf Healthcare
Kforce
Korn/Ferry
Medical Staffing Network
Ogilvy Healthworld
PAREXEL
PDI
Quintiles Transnational
Reynolds and Reynolds
Topin
Verispan

HISTORICAL FINANCIALS

Company Type: Public

Income Statement   FYE: December 31

	REVENUE ($ mil.)	NET INCOME ($ mil.)	NET PROFIT MARGIN	EMPLOYEES
12/06	766.2	51.2	6.7%	5,200
12/05	556.3	43.9	7.9%	4,200
12/04	352.2	31.1	8.8%	—
12/03	224.4	5.8	2.6%	—
12/02	215.4	7.9	3.7%	1,800
Annual Growth	**37.3%**	**59.6%**	**—**	**30.4%**

2006 Year-End Financials

Debt ratio: 51.5%
Return on equity: 16.7%
Cash ($ mil.): 79.9
Current ratio: 1.43
Long-term debt ($ mil.): 184.7
No. of shares (mil.): 30.0
Dividends
  Yield: —
  Payout: —
Market value ($ mil.): 1,059.6
R&D as % of sales: —
Advertising as % of sales: —

Stock History   NASDAQ (GS): VTIV

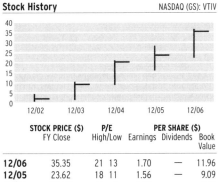

	STOCK PRICE ($) FY Close	P/E High/Low		PER SHARE ($) Earnings	Dividends	Book Value
12/06	35.35	21	13	1.70	—	11.96
12/05	23.62	18	11	1.56	—	9.09
12/04	20.32	17	7	1.22	—	6.71
12/03	9.15	42	7	0.24	—	4.66
12/02	2.03	12	3	0.35	—	4.20
Annual Growth	**104.3%**	**—**	**—**	**48.5%**	**—**	**29.9%**

Investment Technology Group

As its name implies, Investment Technology Group (ITG) combines technology with investing. The company provides automated equity trading products and services related to order management and execution management; it serves institutional investors and brokers throughout the trading process, from analysis before the trade to post-trading evaluation. Core products include its Portfolio System for Institutional Trading (POSIT) crossing system, which lets institutional clients confidentially trade shares and stock portfolios among themselves; ITG Algorithms; and Transaction Cost Analysis. The company is active in the US, Australia, Canada, Asia, and Europe.

ITG has filled in gaps in its service offerings primarily through acquisitions, including the 2006 buys of Macgregor (stock trade management technologies development) and Plexus Group (trading consulting services). Additions to ITG's product mix include crossing opportunity scanner BLOCKalert, launched in 2006 through a joint venture with Merrill Lynch; broker-neutral trading system Radical; and the Channel ITG order management system. ITG has been focusing on overseas growth, as well. Canada and Europe are among its primary target areas.

Jefferies Group spun off ITG in 1999.

EXECUTIVES

Chairman: Maureen O'Hara, age 53
President, CEO and Director: Robert C. (Bob) Gasser, age 43
Managing Director and CFO: Howard C. Naphtali, age 53, $1,356,715 pay
Managing Director, General Counsel, and Secretary: P. Mats Goebels, age 40
Managing Director and Co-Head, Sales and Trading: Christopher J. Heckman, age 46, $1,259,731 pay
Managing Director and Co-Head, Sales and Trading: Anthony J. (Tony) Huck, age 43, $1,259,731 pay
Managing Director, Direct Market Access Services: Andrew Larkin, age 44

Managing Director and Global Head, Product Management: James M. Wright, age 46
Managing Director, Software Development, Technology and Trading Services Support, and Information Security: David L. Meitz, age 43
Managing Director, Marketing, Communications, and Investor Relations: Maureen Murphy
Managing Director; CEO, ITG Solutions Network: Ian Domowitz, age 55, $1,289,731 pay
Managing Director and Global Head, Human Resources: Peter Goldstein
Public Relations: Liz Sendewicz
Auditors: KPMG LLP

LOCATIONS

HQ: Investment Technology Group, Inc.
380 Madison Ave., New York, NY 10017
Phone: 212-588-4000 **Fax:** 212-444-6295
Web: www.itginc.com

Investment Technology Group has domestic offices in Boston; Culver City, California; New York; Rye Brook, New York. Its international offices are located in Dublin, Ireland; Herzelya Pituach, Israel; Hong Kong; London; Madrid; Melbourne; Sydney; Tokyo; and Toronto.

2006 Sales

	$ mil.	% of total
US	476.0	79
International	123.5	21
Total	**599.5**	**100**

PRODUCTS/OPERATIONS

2006 Sales

	$ mil.	% of total
Commissions	494.7	83
Recurring revenue	73.7	12
Other	31.1	5
Total	**599.5**	**100**

Selected Subsidiaries

AlterNet Securities, Inc.
Block Alert LLC (BLOCKalert, 50%)
The Macgregor Group, Inc.
Plexus Plan Sponsor Group, Inc.

COMPETITORS

Gelber Group
GSEC
Liquidnet
Nasdaq Stock Market
NexTrade
NYSE Euronext
TRADEBOOK

HISTORICAL FINANCIALS

Company Type: Public

Income Statement   FYE: December 31

	REVENUE ($ mil.)	NET INCOME ($ mil.)	NET PROFIT MARGIN	EMPLOYEES
12/06	599.5	97.9	16.3%	1,060
12/05	408.2	67.7	16.6%	714
12/04	334.5	41.0	12.3%	—
12/03	334.0	42.0	12.6%	—
12/02	387.6	73.8	19.0%	635
Annual Growth	**11.5%**	**7.3%**	**—**	**13.7%**

2006 Year-End Financials

Debt ratio: 26.5%
Return on equity: 18.3%
Cash ($ mil.): 334.9
Current ratio: —
Long-term debt ($ mil.): 160.9
No. of shares (mil.): 43.8
Dividends
  Yield: —
  Payout: —
Market value ($ mil.): 1,878.6
R&D as % of sales: —
Advertising as % of sales: —

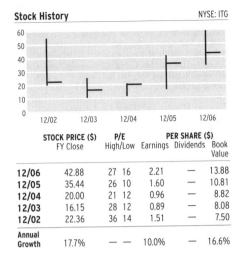

Stock History

NYSE: ITG

	STOCK PRICE ($) FY Close	P/E High/Low		PER SHARE ($) Earnings	Dividends	Book Value
12/06	42.88	27	16	2.21	—	13.88
12/05	35.44	26	10	1.60	—	10.81
12/04	20.00	21	12	0.96	—	8.82
12/03	16.15	28	12	0.89	—	8.08
12/02	22.36	36	14	1.51	—	7.50
Annual Growth	17.7%	—	—	10.0%	—	16.6%

INX Inc.

INX (formerly known as I-Sector) knows the IT sector. The company primarily offers Cisco-based IT infrastructure services and related hardware and software to customers in the educational, governmental, and private sectors. Its InterNetwork Experts division provides infrastructure services including network design and integration, as well as management and security audits. INX sold its Valerent unit — an outsourcer of IT staff for infrastructure management functions such as help desk support and network management — in 2006. Founder, chairman, and CEO James Long owns about 25% of INX.

INX has divested non-core operations to better focus on its Cisco-related offerings. In addition to the Valerent sale, in 2006 it sold its Stratasoft subsidiary, which offered computer telephony integration software. The previous year it acquired Albuquerque, New Mexico-based Network Architects, a provider of services for Internet Protocol (IP) telephony and network infrastructure services, primarily for Cisco products.

EXECUTIVES

Chairman and CEO: James H. Long, age 49, $114,750 pay
President and COO: Mark T. Hilz, age 48
VP and CFO: Brian L. Fontana, age 49
VP Business Development; VP NetSurant: David DeYoung
VP Federal: David Peoples
VP Operations: Paul Klotz, age 45, $198,438 pay (prior to merger)
Controller and Chief Accounting Officer: Larry I. Lawhorn, age 54, $140,727 pay (partial-year salary)
Secretary: Joseph E. Horzepa
Treasurer: Timothy Grothues, age 56
Auditors: Grant Thornton LLP

LOCATIONS

HQ: INX Inc.
6401 Southwest Fwy., Houston, TX 77074
Phone: 713-795-2000 **Fax:** 713-795-2001
Web: www.inxi.com

INX Inc. has branch office operations in Albuquerque, New Mexico; Austin, Texas; Boise, Idaho; Dallas; El Paso, Texas; Eugene, Oregon; Houston, Texas; Los Angeles; Metairie, Louisiana; Portland, Oregon; San Antonio; Seattle; and Washington, DC.

PRODUCTS/OPERATIONS

2006 Sales

	% of total
Products	87
Services	13
Total	**100**

Selected Services

Applications and systems development and integration
Customer relationship management (CRM) systems
Customer service and support applications
Data center design
Enterprise application integration
Information technology (IT) consulting
Network and systems security
Network design and implementation
Network management
Web and network consulting and development

COMPETITORS

AT&T
Avaya
Computer Sciences Corp.
EDS
eOn
Genesys Telecommunications
HP Technology Solutions Group
IBM Global Services
Nortel Networks
Perot Systems
Unisys

HISTORICAL FINANCIALS

Company Type: Public

Income Statement

FYE: December 31

	REVENUE ($ mil.)	NET INCOME ($ mil.)	NET PROFIT MARGIN	EMPLOYEES
12/06	156.0	1.2	0.8%	287
12/05	107.3	(7.9)	—	225
12/04	93.1	1.5	1.6%	—
12/03	62.2	(1.8)	—	—
12/02	42.0	(0.4)	—	146
Annual Growth	38.8%	—	—	18.4%

2006 Year-End Financials

Debt ratio: —
Return on equity: 5.9%
Cash ($ mil.): 1.8
Current ratio: 1.19
Long-term debt ($ mil.): —
No. of shares (mil.): 6.6

Dividends
Yield: —
Payout: —
Market value ($ mil.): 51.9
R&D as % of sales: —
Advertising as % of sales: —

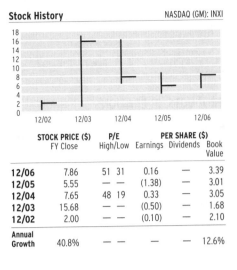

Stock History

NASDAQ (GM): INXI

	STOCK PRICE ($) FY Close	P/E High/Low		PER SHARE ($) Earnings	Dividends	Book Value
12/06	7.86	51	31	0.16	—	3.39
12/05	5.55	—	—	(1.38)	—	3.01
12/04	7.65	48	19	0.33	—	3.05
12/03	15.68	—	—	(0.50)	—	1.68
12/02	2.00	—	—	(0.10)	—	2.10
Annual Growth	40.8%	—	—	—	—	12.6%

ION Geophysical

There's a whole lotta shakin' goin' on at ION Geophysical (formerly Input/Output). The seismic data-acquisition imaging and software systems company helps worldwide petroleum exploration contractors identify and measure subsurface geological structures that could contain oil and gas. ION Geophysical's data acquisition products are capable of processing 3-D, 4-D, and multi-component 3-C seismic data. Its systems include modules for land, marine, and transition areas (such as swamps, shoreline, marsh, and jungle). In 2007 the company changed its name to reflect its expanding range of technological services and programs.

ION Geophysical also makes other products such as geophysical software, helicopter transportable enclosures, seismic sensors, specialty cables and connectors, and radio telemetry systems. Its marine positioning systems enable the company to map the geography of the ocean's floor. The company has sold its Applied MEMS subsidiary to Swiss MEMS (micro-electro mechanical systems) firm Colibrys.

ION Geophysical is turning to new technologies to help boost the demand for its seismic services. While 3-D seismic data acquisition has become a more common offering provided by oil and gas service companies, the company plans to further enhance the quality of survey results in an effort to better compete against other providers. It has acquired AXIS Geophysics, a specialized seismic data processing firm, and has combined it with its Green Mountain Geophysics subsidiary. ION Geophysical has also acquired seismic data software provider Concept Systems for about $36 million, as well as GX Technology for about $130 million.

HISTORY

ION Geophysical was founded in 1968 as Input/Output (I/O) by petroleum industry retiree Aubry Tilley, who pioneered a system for capturing shock waves that was used with existing seismic systems. Tilley sold I/O in 1980 to Walter Kidde & Co., which sold it to Triton Industries in 1986. After a six-year, $25 million research and development project, the company launched its I/O System for land-based seismic data acquisition in 1988.

I/O went public in 1991. The company bought the Exploration Products Group of Western Geophysical (the seismic exploration business of Western Atlas) in 1995. In 1997 I/O bought Green Mountain Geophysics (seismic software), but increased competition and costs related to the Western Geophysical purchase dampened the company's profits that year.

In 1998 I/O acquired CompuSeis (land seismic data-acquisition systems) and DigiCourse (marine positioning equipment). The company's sales and profits plummeted under pressures of an extended industry downturn in 1999 and 2000. I/O's 1999 sales dipped 51% below the previous year's record, and its stock fell to an all-time low. Several executives left the company. James Lapeyre, who had become a company shareholder when DigiCourse was acquired, was named chairman.

After losing money in 2000, sales picked up in 2001 and the company returned to profitability. A decrease in demand for seismic services put the company back in the red in 2002. Also that year, in an effort to boost its technology, I/O acquired AXIS Geophysics and combined it with its Green Mountain Geophysics subsidiary. In 2004 I/O continued to build up its seismic technology services by acquiring Scotland-based Concept Systems for $36 million. It also completed its acquisition of GX Technology for about $130 million. Later that year, I/O sold its Applied MEMS subsidiary to private Swiss firm Colibrys.

EXECUTIVES

Chairman: James M. (Jay) Lapeyre Jr., age 54
President, CEO, and Director: Robert P. (Bob) Peebler, age 59, $482,154 pay (prior to title change)
EVP and CFO: R. Brian Hanson, age 42, $160,962 pay
EVP and COO, I/O Solutions Division: James R. (Jim) Hollis, age 45
SVP Corporate Marketing: Christopher M. (Chris) Friedemann, age 42, $219,231 pay (prior to title change)
SVP General Counsel and Corporate Secretary: David L. Roland, age 45, $205,769 pay (prior to title change)
VP Human Resources: Laura D. Guthrie
VP, Corporate Controller, and Chief Accounting Officer: Michael L. Morrison, age 36
Director Corporate Marketing and Communications: Kelly Kline
Auditors: Ernst & Young LLP

LOCATIONS

HQ: ION Geophysical Corporation
2105 CityWest Blvd., 4th Fl., Houston, TX 77042
Phone: 281-933-3339 **Fax:** 281-879-3626
Web: www.i-o.com

ION Geophysical has four primary facilities in the US. It operates international manufacturing facilities in the Netherlands, the United Arab Emirates, and the UK.

2006 Sales

	$ mil.	% of total
North America	162.3	32
Europe	119.4	24
Asia/Pacific	86.2	17
Middle East	51.8	10
Commonwealth of Independent States	37.3	8
Latin America	15.3	3
Africa & other regions	31.3	6
Total	**503.6**	**100**

PRODUCTS/OPERATIONS

2006 Sales

	$ mil.	% of total
Land imaging	205.8	41
Seismic imaging	146.7	29
Marine imaging	127.9	25
Data management	23.2	5
Total	**503.6**	**100**

Selected Products and Services

Land Imaging Systems Products
  Accessories
    Cables and connectors
    Helicopter transportable enclosures
  Applications software (geophysical software)
  Central electronics units
  Geophones (seismic sensors and acoustical receivers)
  Radio telemetry systems
  Recording systems
  Remote ground equipment
    Multiple remote and line taps
  Reservoir products
  Transition systems
Seismic Imaging Solutions Products and Services
  Processing and imaging for marine environments
  Processing and imaging for land environments (for marsh, jungle, mountainous areas)
  Vibrators
Marine Imaging Systems Products
  Airguns
  Hydrophones (seismic sensors devices)
  Marine energy sources
  Marine positioning systems (DigiCOURSE)
    Acoustical devices
    Compasses
    Velocimeters
  Ocean bottom systems
  Peripherals
  Seismic and data telemetry quality control systems
  Shipboard recording electronics
  Software (Green Mountain Geophysics)
  Streamer systems
    Electronic modules and cabling
Data Management Solutions Products and Services
  Marine imaging systems
  Seabed imaging systems

COMPETITORS

Bolt Technology
CGGVeritas
Dawson Geophysical
OYO Geospace
Schlumberger
TGC Industries
TGS-NOPEC
WesternGeco

HISTORICAL FINANCIALS

Company Type: Public

Income Statement

FYE: December 31

	REVENUE ($ mil.)	NET INCOME ($ mil.)	NET PROFIT MARGIN	EMPLOYEES
12/06	503.6	29.3	5.8%	1,015
12/05	362.7	18.8	5.2%	804
12/04	247.3	(3.0)	—	—
12/03	150.0	(23.1)	—	—
12/02	118.6	(119.9)	—	704
Annual Growth	**43.5%**	**—**	**—**	**9.6%**

2006 Year-End Financials

Debt ratio: 19.2%
Return on equity: 8.4%
Cash ($ mil.): 18.1
Current ratio: 1.97
Long-term debt ($ mil.): 71.0
No. of shares (mil.): 80.1
Dividends
  Yield: —
  Payout: —
Market value ($ mil.): 1,092.1
R&D as % of sales: —
Advertising as % of sales: —

Stock History

NYSE: IO

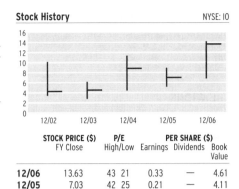

	STOCK PRICE ($) FY Close	P/E High/Low		PER SHARE ($) Earnings	Dividends	Book Value
12/06	13.63	43	21	0.33	—	4.61
12/05	7.03	42	25	0.21	—	4.11
12/04	8.84	—	—	(0.05)	—	4.00
12/03	4.51	—	—	(0.45)	—	2.60
12/02	4.25	—	—	(2.37)	—	2.96
Annual Growth	**33.8%**	**—**	**—**	**—**	**—**	**11.7%**

IPG Photonics

IPG Photonics has its name in lights. The company makes fiber-optic signal amplifiers, fiber lasers, laser diodes, and pump lasers, which are primarily used in materials processing. Its fiber lasers also have applications in medicine and in telecommunications networks to enable voice and data transmission over optical lines, among other uses. IPG has shipped more than 21,000 units to hundreds of customers around the world. The company's customers include BAE SYSTEMS, Mitsubishi Heavy Industries, and Nippon Steel. The Gapontsev family (including CEO Valentin Gapontsev) owns about half of IPG Photonics.

IPG Photonics raised about $100 million in private equity funding, with its investors including Apax Partners, Merrill Lynch, TA Associates, and Winston Partners. The company filed for an IPO in late 2000 and withdrew the registration statement six months later. It filed for another IPO in the summer of 2006 and completed the offering in late 2006.

The company plans to use proceeds of its public offering to repurchase warrants, pay off debts, and for general corporate purposes, including working capital, expansion of manufacturing facilities, purchases of equipment, and expansion of applications development and services.

IPG Photonics has acquired its Chinese distributor, HM Laser, and established a subsidiary, IPG China, with an office in Beijing.

TA Associates owns 9% of IPG Photonics.

EXECUTIVES

Chairman and CEO: Valentin P. Gapontsev, age 69, $987,527 pay
VP and CFO: Timothy P. V. Mammen, age 38, $342,500 pay
VP Operations: Dennis P. Leonard Jr.
VP, Treasurer, and Controller: Paolo Sinni
VP, General Counsel, and Secretary: Angelo P. Lopresti, age 44, $401,815 pay
VP Research and Development: Denis Gapontsev, $321,729 pay
VP Telecommunications Products: George H. BuAbbud
VP Components: Alexander (Alex) Ovtchinnikov, age 45

Director; Managing Director, IPG Laser:
Eugene Shcherbakov, age 61, $395,450 pay
Director; Managing Director, NTO IRE-Polus:
Igor Samartsev, age 45
Director Human Resources: Coral Barry
Auditors: Deloitte & Touche LLP

LOCATIONS

HQ: IPG Photonics Corporation
50 Old Webster Rd., Oxford, MA 01540
Phone: 508-373-1100 **Fax:** 508-373-1103
Web: www.ipgphotonics.com

IPG Photonics has manufacturing operations in
Germany, India, Italy, Russia, and the US, with sales
offices in China, India, Japan, South Korea, the UK, and
the US.

2006 Sales

	$ mil.	% of total
Asia & Australia	48.8	34
Europe	48.5	34
Americas	45.9	32
Total	**143.2**	**100**

PRODUCTS/OPERATIONS

2006 Sales

	$ mil.	% of total
Materials processing	102.3	71
Communications	15.2	11
Advanced applications	14.5	10
Medical	11.2	8
Total	**143.2**	**100**

Selected Products

Broadband light sources
Continuous wave lasers
Diode laser systems
Erbium amplifiers
Fiber amplifiers
Fiber lasers
Fiber-coupled laser diodes
Praseodymium amplifiers
Pulsed fiber lasers
Raman pump lasers and amplifiers
Thulium lasers
Ytterbium lasers

COMPETITORS

Avanex
Bookham
Coherent, Inc.
EMCORE
Excel Technology
FANUC
GSI
JDS Uniphase
Mitsubishi Materials
Newport
Presstek
Rofin-Sinar Technologies
Scientific-Atlanta
Swatch
TRUMPF

HISTORICAL FINANCIALS

Company Type: Public

Income Statement

FYE: December 31

	REVENUE ($ mil.)	NET INCOME ($ mil.)	NET PROFIT MARGIN	EMPLOYEES
12/06	143.2	29.2	20.4%	1,040
12/05	96.4	7.4	7.7%	900
12/04	60.7	2.0	3.3%	—
12/03	33.7	(28.2)	—	—
Annual Growth	62.0%	—	—	15.6%

2006 Year-End Financials

Debt ratio: 19.0%	Dividends
Return on equity: 54.5%	Yield: —
Cash ($ mil.): 75.7	Payout: —
Current ratio: 3.84	Market value ($ mil.): 1,029.6
Long-term debt ($ mil.): 30.1	R&D as % of sales: —
No. of shares (mil.): 42.9	Advertising as % of sales: —

Stock History

NASDAQ (GM): IPGP

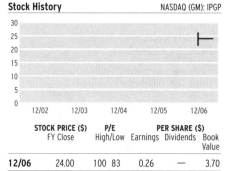

	STOCK PRICE ($) FY Close	P/E High/Low	PER SHARE ($) Earnings	Dividends	Book Value
12/06	24.00	100 83	0.26	—	3.70

---

iRobot Corporation

If you're a Jetsons fan, you'll likely appreciate
iRobot. The company makes robots for all sorts
of applications, from government and military to
toys and appliances. Its Roomba FloorVac and
Scooba are the first of their kind to automatically
clean floors. iRobot also makes the PackBot,
which performs battlefield reconnaissance and
bomb disposal for the US Army, as well as a limited number of the R-Gator, another unmanned
ground vehicle model, alongside Deere & Company. The firm has offices in California, Massachusetts, Virginia, and Hong Kong and sells
through thousands of retail outlets globally. iRobot was founded in 1990 by robot engineers who
performed research at the Massachusetts Institute of Technology.

With its foothold in the robotic appliances
niche, iRobot in 2006 introduced several products including the Roomba for Pets, Roomba
Discovery for Pets, and the Dirt Dog Workshop
Robot, which is designed to keep work spaces
free of sawdust, small nails, and debris.

It's banking, however, on sales of its newer
Scooba (5800 series), introduced in late 2006, to
pay for development costs for the brand. The
5800 debuted at a lower price point than its $399
original 5900 series.

Gregory White, president of the company's
Home Robots division, announced in September
2006 that he would retire in 2007 to become an
educator. iRobot plans to fill the position with
an executive with experience taking similar
products to a global level.

EXECUTIVES

Chairman: Helen Greiner, age 39, $282,749 pay
CEO and Director: Colin Angle, age 41, $281,731 pay
President, Government and Industrial Robots:
Joseph W. (Joe) Dyer, age 61, $277,600 pay
President and General Manager, Home Robots:
Sandra B. Lawrence, age 51
SVP, CFO, and Treasurer: Geoffrey P. (Geoff) Clear,
age 58, $248,461 pay
SVP, Research and Development: Indrajit Purkayastha
SVP, Secretary, and General Counsel:
Glen D. Weinstein, age 36

VP, Financial Controls and Analysis: Alison Dean,
age 42
VP, Information Technology and CIO: Jay Leader
CTO and Director: Rodney A. Brooks, age 53
Corporate Communications: Nancy Dussault
Auditors: PricewaterhouseCoopers LLP

LOCATIONS

HQ: iRobot Corporation
63 South Ave., Burlington, MA 01803
Phone: 781-345-0200 **Fax:** 781-345-0201
Web: www.irobot.com

PRODUCTS/OPERATIONS

2006 Sales

	$ mil.	% of total
Consumer	112.5	60
Government & Industrial	76.5	40
Total	**189.0**	**100**

COMPETITORS

Allen-Vanguard Corporation
AM General
BAE SYSTEMS
BISSELL
Electrolux
GE Consumer & Industrial
General Dynamics
LG Electronics
Lockheed Martin
QinetiQ
REMOTEC UK
Samsung Electronics

HISTORICAL FINANCIALS

Company Type: Public

Income Statement

FYE: December 31

	REVENUE ($ mil.)	NET INCOME ($ mil.)	NET PROFIT MARGIN	EMPLOYEES
12/06	189.0	3.6	1.9%	371
12/05	142.0	2.6	1.8%	276
12/04	95.0	0.2	0.2%	214
12/03	54.3	(7.4)	—	—
12/02	14.8	(10.8)	—	—
Annual Growth	89.0%	—	—	31.7%

2006 Year-End Financials

Debt ratio: —	Dividends
Return on equity: 3.9%	Yield: —
Cash ($ mil.): 70.4	Payout: —
Current ratio: 3.09	Market value ($ mil.): 429.7
Long-term debt ($ mil.): —	R&D as % of sales: —
No. of shares (mil.): 23.8	Advertising as % of sales: —

Stock History

NASDAQ (GM): IRBT

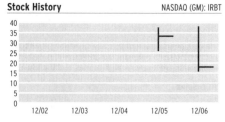

	STOCK PRICE ($) FY Close	P/E High/Low	PER SHARE ($) Earnings	Dividends	Book Value
12/06	18.06	271 115	0.14	—	3.99
12/05	33.33	339 239	0.11	—	3.74
Annual Growth	(45.8%)	— —	27.3%	—	6.7%

ITC Holdings

ITC Holdings owns and operates 2,700 miles of power transmission lines in southeastern Michigan (including Detroit and Ann Arbor). ITC was created in 2003 to acquire International Transmission Company. The independent business transmits electricity from generation facilities to the distribution utilities that serve 4.9 million customers in 13 counties. It monitors the grid from its Michigan Electric Power Coordination Center. ITC is a member of the Midwest ISO, a regional transmission organization. Kohlberg Kravis Roberts (KKR) purchased the company from utility holding company DTE Energy in 2003 and took it public in 2005.

The company's "Thumb Loop Rebuild Project" is replacing the aged wooden utility poles with steel towers that support the electric transmission lines in Tuscola County, Michigan.

In 2006 ITC acquired Michigan Electric Transmission Co. LLC for $865 million. The next year it acquired Alliant Energy subsidiary Interstate Power and Light Company's transmission assets in Illinois, Iowa, and Minnesota for $783 million.

EXECUTIVES

President, CEO, Treasurer, and Director:
Joseph L. Welch, age 58, $1,382,109 pay
EVP and COO: Jon E. Jipping, age 41
EVP and Chief Business Officer: Linda H. Blair, age 37
SVP Finance and CFO: Edward M. Rahill, age 53, $425,294 pay
VP, General Counsel, and Secretary: Daniel J. Oginsky, age 33
VP Major Contracts and Special Projects:
Joseph R. Dudak, age 60
VP Information Technology and Facilities and CIO:
Denis DesRosiers
VP and Controller: Joseph E. Fennell
VP Operations: Elizabeth Howell
President, ITC Great Plains: Carl A. Huslig
Corporate Secretary and Senior Attorney:
Wendy A. McIntyre
Media Contact: Lisa Roseland-Aragon
Auditors: Deloitte & Touche LLP

LOCATIONS

HQ: ITC Holdings Corp.
39500 Orchard Hill Place, Ste. 200, Novi, MI 48375
Phone: 248-374-7100   **Fax:** 248-374-7140
Web: www.itc-holdings.com

PRODUCTS/OPERATIONS

2006 Sales

	$ mil.	% of total
Network	206.5	92
Scheduling, control, & dispatch	8.3	4
Point-to-point	7.0	3
Other	1.8	1
Total	**223.6**	**100**

COMPETITORS

Detroit Edison
Midland Cogeneration Venture
Wolverine Power Supply

HISTORICAL FINANCIALS
Company Type: Public

Income Statement   FYE: December 31

	REVENUE ($ mil.)	NET INCOME ($ mil.)	NET PROFIT MARGIN	EMPLOYEES
12/06	223.6	33.2	14.8%	223
12/05	205.3	34.7	16.9%	137
12/04	126.4	2.6	2.1%	—
Annual Growth	**33.0%**	**257.3%**	**—**	**62.8%**

2006 Year-End Financials

Debt ratio: 237.2%
Return on equity: 8.3%
Cash ($ mil.): 18.0
Current ratio: 1.10
Long-term debt ($ mil.): 1,262.3
No. of shares (mil.): 42.4

Dividends
  Yield: 2.7%
  Payout: 117.4%
Market value ($ mil.): 1,691.6
R&D as % of sales: —
Advertising as % of sales: —

Stock History   NYSE: ITC

	STOCK PRICE ($) FY Close	P/E High/Low	Earnings	Dividends	Book Value
12/06	39.90	45 27	0.92	1.08	12.55
12/05	28.09	29 25	1.06	0.53	7.92
Annual Growth	**42.0%**	**— —**	**(13.2%)**	**103.8%**	**58.4%**

I-trax, Inc.

With I-Trax around, employees can leave a meeting, check their mail, and then stop off for a wellness check-up and never leave their building. I-trax provides health management services to nearly 100 employers, including manufacturers and financial institutions. The company operates some 200 on-site employer-sponsored health care facilities, including primary care, pharmacy, occupational health services, and corporate health services. The company also offers online wellness and disease management services designed to boost worker productivity and lower health care costs by keeping workers healthy.

Founded in 2000, the company has grown through the acquisition of WellComm Group (2002), and the much larger on-site health care service provider CHD Meridian Healthcare (2004) for about $80 million. I-trax plans to expand its on-site operations and other health and productivity services.

EXECUTIVES

Chairman: Frank A. Martin, age 56, $330,000 pay
Vice Chairman: Haywood D. Cochrane Jr., age 58
CEO and Director: R. Dixon Thayer, age 55, $358,000 pay
President, Chief Medical Officer, and Director:
Raymond J. (Ray) Fabius, age 53

SVP Sales and Business Development: Clay Elder
SVP Sales and Account Development, CHD Meridian Healthcare: Peter M. Hotz
SVP and CFO: Bradley Wear
SVP On-Site Operations: Susan Siegel
VP Information Technology Operations: April Lannom
VP General Counsel, and Secretary: Yuri Rozenfeld, age 38, $221,000 pay
Auditors: McGladrey & Pullen, LLP

LOCATIONS

HQ: I-trax, Inc.
4 Hillman Dr., Ste. 130, Chadds Ford, PA 19317
Phone: 610-459-2405   **Fax:** 610-459-4705
Web: www.i-trax.com

I-trax and its CHD Meridian subsidiary have offices and facilities in Nebraska, Nevada, New York, Pennsylvania, and Tennessee.

PRODUCTS/OPERATIONS

Selected Subsidiaries

CHD Meridian Healthcare LLC
I-trax Health Management Solutions, Inc.
I-trax Health Management Solutions, LLC

COMPETITORS

Caremark Pharmacy Services
Concentra
Express Scripts
Healthways, Inc.
Matria Healthcare
SHPS

HISTORICAL FINANCIALS
Company Type: Public

Income Statement   FYE: December 31

	REVENUE ($ mil.)	NET INCOME ($ mil.)	NET PROFIT MARGIN	EMPLOYEES
12/06	124.6	1.8	1.4%	1,905
12/05	115.9	(14.1)	—	1,722
12/04	76.4	(3.9)	—	—
12/03	4.2	(8.1)	—	—
12/02	3.9	(9.4)	—	—
Annual Growth	**137.7%**	**—**	**—**	**10.6%**

2006 Year-End Financials

Debt ratio: 14.0%
Return on equity: 2.8%
Cash ($ mil.): 6.6
Current ratio: 1.12
Long-term debt ($ mil.): 9.2
No. of shares (mil.): 36.6

Dividends
  Yield: —
  Payout: —
Market value ($ mil.): 113.5
R&D as % of sales: —
Advertising as % of sales: —

Stock History   AMEX: DMX

	STOCK PRICE ($) FY Close	P/E High/Low	Earnings	Dividends	Book Value
12/06	3.10	196 100	0.02	—	1.79
12/05	2.05	— —	(0.54)	—	1.89
12/04	1.89	— —	(0.96)	—	2.74
12/03	4.49	— —	(0.74)	—	0.60
12/02	2.75	— —	(1.04)	—	0.90
Annual Growth	**3.0%**	**— —**	**—**	**—**	**18.9%**

Itron, Inc.

Itron aims to make meter reading a desk job. The company is a global supplier of wireless data acquisition and communication products for electric, gas, and water utilities. Itron makes radio- and telephone-based automatic meter reading (AMR) systems, handheld meter reading computers, and meter data acquisition and analysis software. Its systems are installed at more than 2,000 utilities worldwide — many using more than one Itron product. The company also provides consulting, project management, and outsourcing services. Customers include BC Hydro, Old Dominion Electric Cooperative, Ford, Electrabel, and Progress Energy (16% of sales).

Itron continues to grow by acquisitions, acquiring eight companies since the end of 2001, including its acquisition of Schlumberger Electricity Metering (which became the company's Electricity Metering business) in mid-2004. Purchases during 2006 included Flow Metrix, a manufacturer of leak detection systems for underground pipelines, and Quantum Consulting, an energy consulting firm.

The company has acquired Luxembourg-based Actaris Metering Systems for €800 million in cash, plus the assumption of about €445 million in debt, valuing the transaction at about $1.7 billion. Actaris was profitable on 2006 sales of around $1 billion. A former division of Schlumberger that went through an LBO in 2001, Actaris primarily operates in Europe, offering AMR equipment and related services. It has operations in Africa, Asia/Pacific, Australia, and South America.

Itron targets the electric utility, water and public power, and natural gas markets. Customers in the US and Canada account for most of sales.

BlackRock owns more than 9% of Itron. AXA Financial holds nearly 6% of the company, as does Earnest Partners. Invesco has an equity stake of about 5%.

HISTORY

Itron was formed by a group of engineers in 1977 with financial backing from utility Washington Water Power (now Avista). In 1992 Itron acquired EnScan, a maker of mobile automatic meter reading (AMR) systems. The company went public in 1993. During 1994 and 1995 it installed the largest AMR system in the world for the Public Service Company of Colorado (now New Century Energies).

Itron in 1996 won a major contract from Pittsburgh-based Duquesne Light Co. Itron acquired Utility Translation Services (commercial and industrial AMR systems) that year and Design Concepts (outage detection, quality monitoring, and AMR systems that communicate over telephone lines) in 1997. Also that year Itron and UK Data Collections Services (meter reading services) formed joint venture STAR Data Services to provide meter reading and billing services.

Restructuring charges related to cost-cutting efforts contributed to a loss in 1998. The next year Itron won an 11-year pact to provide meter reading services for Southern California Edison's 350,000 customers — a deal worth at least $20 million. During mid-1999 new CEO Michael Chesser led another restructuring — including layoffs and factory closures. Charges led to a loss for the year.

In 2000 Itron spun off part of its manufacturing operations as contract manufacturer Servatron. That year COO LeRoy Nosbaum replaced Chesser as CEO, and was later named chairman.

In 2002 Itron bolstered its energy consulting and software business through the acquisition of several privately held companies: LineSoft (consulting and software for utility transmission and distribution systems) for about $42 million; Regional Economic Research (energy consulting and software) for $14 million; and eMobile Data Corporation (wireless utility workforce management software) for about $6 million. The following year Itron acquired Silicon Energy (enterprise energy management software) for about $71 million.

In 2004 Itron acquired the Electricity Metering business unit of Schlumberger for nearly $250 million.

A major restructuring that year — including the replacement of top executives, the layoff of 15% of its workforce, and the spinoff of its manufacturing operations as Servatron — repositioned Itron to take advantage of new technologies and industry deregulation.

In 2004 Itron reorganized its market segments from five business units to two main segments: hardware and software. Within the hardware segment, the business is broken down into two lines of business, meter data collection and electricity metering.

In 2006 the company expanded into South America's biggest market with the acquisition of ELO Sistemas e Tecnologia, a Brazilian firm that had been distributing Itron products since late 2004 and manufacturing Itron's CENTRON meters since mid-2005. ELO Tecnologia has offices and a manufacturing assembly facility in Campinas and São Paulo, Brazil, and in Chile, employing about 80 people. Itron paid about $2 million in cash for the Brazilian firm.

EXECUTIVES

Chairman and CEO: LeRoy D. Nosbaum, age 60, $650,000 pay
SVP and CFO: Steven M. (Steve) Helmbrecht, age 44, $300,000 pay
SVP, Hardware Solutions: Malcolm Unsworth, age 57, $300,000 pay
SVP, Software Solutions: Philip C. Mezey, age 47, $300,000 pay
SVP and General Counsel: John W. Holleran, age 52
VP, Competitive Resources: Jared P. Serff, age 39, $205,000 pay
VP, Product Marketing: Russell E. (Russ) Vanos
VP, Information Technology and CIO: Chuck McAtee
VP, Investor Relations and Corporate Communications: Deloris Duquette
VP and General Manager, International Market Group: Douglas L. (Doug) Staker, age 47
Auditors: Ernst & Young LLP

LOCATIONS

HQ: Itron, Inc.
2111 N. Molter Rd., Liberty Lake, WA 99019
Phone: 509-924-9900 **Fax:** 509-891-3355
Web: www.itron.com

Itron has facilities in California, Massachusetts, Minnesota, North Carolina, South Carolina, and Washington, and sales offices in Australia, Brazil, Canada, France, Mexico, the Netherlands, Qatar, Taiwan, and the US.

2006 Sales

	$ mil.	% of total
North America	602.9	94
Other regions	41.1	6
Total	**644.0**	**100**

PRODUCTS/OPERATIONS

2006 Sales

	$ mil.	% of total
Hardware Solutions		
Electricity metering	325.0	51
Meter data collection	260.4	40
Software Solutions	58.6	9
Total	**644.0**	**100**

2006 Sales

	$ mil.	% of total
Sales	594.0	92
Service	50.0	8
Total	**644.0**	**100**

Selected Products

Automatic meter reading (AMR) systems and products
    Meter modules (utility meter attachments that transmit data to remote receivers)
    Mobile AMR (transportable systems for mounting on vehicles)
    Network AMR (utility-automated meter readers)
    Off-site meter reading units (remote reading of radio-equipped meters)
    Telephone-based technology (programmable modules for data collection over telephone lines)
Commercial and industrial meters
Forecasting, research, and analysis software
Handheld systems and products (electronic meter reading — EMR — handheld systems)
Surveying software
Workforce automation software (Service-Link)

Services

Engineering consulting
Forecasting services
Installation
Outsourcing
Project management
System design and installation
Training

COMPETITORS

ABB	Honeywell International
Accenture	IBM
Badger Meter	Invensys
Bentley Systems	Landis & Gyr
Capgemini	LogicaCMG
Comverge	Pointer Telocation
ConneXt	Power Measurement
Echelon Corporation	PowerSecure International
Electric & Gas Technology	Roper Industries
eMeter	SAP
E-MON	Schneider Electric
Equitrac	Siemens AG
ESCO Technologies	Ventyx
GE	

HISTORICAL FINANCIALS

Company Type: Public

Income Statement				FYE: December 31
	REVENUE ($ mil.)	NET INCOME ($ mil.)	NET PROFIT MARGIN	EMPLOYEES
12/06	644.0	33.8	5.2%	2,400
12/05	552.7	33.1	6.0%	2,000
12/04	399.2	(5.3)	—	—
12/03	317.0	10.5	3.3%	—
12/02	284.8	8.7	3.1%	1,434
Annual Growth	22.6%	40.4%	—	13.7%

2006 Year-End Financials

Debt ratio: 122.2%
Return on equity: 9.5%
Cash ($ mil.): 396.0
Current ratio: 5.76
Long-term debt ($ mil.): 477.9
No. of shares (mil.): 25.7

Dividends
Yield: —
Payout: —
Market value ($ mil.): 1,331.0
R&D as % of sales: —
Advertising as % of sales: —

Stock History

NASDAQ (GS): ITRI

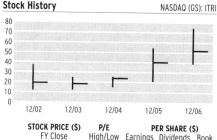

	STOCK PRICE ($) FY Close	P/E High/Low		PER SHARE ($) Earnings	Dividends	Book Value
12/06	51.84	58	31	1.28	—	15.23
12/05	40.04	41	16	1.33	—	12.77
12/04	23.91	—	—	(0.25)	—	8.65
12/03	18.36	50	27	0.48	—	8.62
12/02	19.17	89	31	0.41	—	8.00
Annual Growth	28.2%	—	—	32.9%	—	17.4%

j2 Global Communications

Checked your messages? Customers of j2 Global Communications can retrieve e-mail, faxes, and voicemail from a single phone line. Customers receive a private phone number that can handle unlimited incoming messages. The company, formerly known as JFAX.COM, operates primarily under the eFax, JFAX, and jConnect brands and claims more than 11 million phone numbers for customers located in 37 countries worldwide, including major US cities and international business centers such as Frankfurt, London, and Tokyo. The company counts more than 900,000 paid subscribers with the balance of phone lines going to advertising-supported free subscribers.

The company operates a global network based on both traditional phone infrastructure and Internet Protocol (IP) technology. The network is leased from telecom carriers and from colocation providers in the US and around the globe.

In 2007 j2 Global acquired Irish messaging services firm YAC (as in "you're always connected). The company specializes in hosted messaging and communications services such as inbound call management, fax to e-mail, virtual numbers, audio conferencing, and personal numbers. j2 Global also bought the RapidFax business of Easylink Services International.

Chairman Richard Ressler owns about 5% of the company.

EXECUTIVES

Chairman: Richard S. Ressler, age 49
Co-President and COO: Nehemia (Hemi) Zucker, age 51
Co-President: R. Scott Turicchi, age 44
CFO: Kathleen M. (Kathy) Griggs, age 53
EVP Corporate Strategy: Zohar Loshitzer, age 49

HISTORY

What do rap music, East Berlin, and the dot-com crowds have in common? The answer is Jaye Muller. Born in the former East Germany, Muller moved to Paris at 17 to pursue a rap music career. During a 1994 UK concert tour, he became frustrated at missing too many faxes and phone messages. Conveniently enough, Muller had attended tech school and invented a virtual fax machine. He moved to New York to work on music, but it was the siren song of a universal inbox that haunted him. Finding software programmers in Australia to help develop a system, he launched the company in 1995 as JFAX Communications.

JFAX began offering voice and fax messages via e-mail in 1996 in Atlanta, London, and New York. The service soon caught on, and by the end of the year the company had phone numbers available in 15 cities. Muller snagged professional talent, hiring Motorola's Hemi Zucker as COO.

In 1997 the company introduced its outbound faxing service, and Muller brought in big investors, including Richard Ressler, who left his job at IT firm MAI Systems to become CEO. Shifting coasts, JFAX left New York for Los Angeles. The company penned a deal with QUALCOMM to offer JFAX through its Eudora e-mail client, and closed out the year serving 45 cities.

JFAX came of age in 1998 when it embarked on a three-year marketing agreement with America Online, which promoted JFAX as its exclusive unified messaging service, while e-mail provider Critical Path, Internet portal Yahoo!, and ISP Prodigy became strategic partners. Anxious to get back to his music, at least part time, Muller hired former AT&T executive Gary Hickox as president.

The company went public in 1999 and changed its name to JFAX.COM, and it launched free service in hopes of attracting customers that would upgrade to fee-based plans.

In 2000 JFAX.COM acquired Internet-based messaging provider SureTalk.Com for $9 million. SureTalk's Steven Hamerslag became president (Hickox left the company) and CEO (Ressler became chairman). Later the company changed its name again, this time to j2 Global Communications, and expanded by purchasing rival message services provider eFax.com. When Hamerslag resigned at year's end, the board replaced him with a management team made up of the company's top executives.

The next year j2 Global was granted a US patent for its core technology. Also in 2001 the company announced a planned expansion of its network into Argentina, Chile, Colombia, and Mexico.

Expansion has remained a big part of j2 Global Communications' scheme. The company increased its customer base with the acquisitions of rival messaging services providers SureTalk.com and eFax.com in 2002, and in 2004 it acquired British Columbia-based outsourced e-mail and messaging services provider The Electric Mail Company. That year the company also acquired the unified communications assets, branded Onebox, from Call Sciences. Its expansion plans in Europe got a boost with the company's acquisition in 2005 of UK-based messaging services provider Puma United Communications.

VP, General Counsel, and Secretary:
Jeffrey D. (Jeff) Adelman, age 41
VP Engineering and Network Operations: Doug Chey
VP Finance: Nik Hallberg
VP Human Resources: Patty Brunton
VP Marketing Services and Support: Ken Ford
VP Network Operations: John Bell
VP Product Development: Ken Truesdale
VP Sales: Thomas (Tom) Dolan
VP Global Web Marketing: Mike Pugh
Auditors: Singer Lewak Greenbaum & Goldstein LLP

LOCATIONS

HQ: j2 Global Communications, Inc.
6922 Hollywood Blvd., Ste. 500,
Hollywood, CA 90028
Phone: 323-860-9200   **Fax:** 323-464-1446
Web: www.j2global.com

PRODUCTS/OPERATIONS

2006 Sales

	% of total
Free service telephone numbers	92
Paying telephone numbers	8
Total	**100**

Selected Products

eFax Broadcast (high-volume faxing service)
eFax Corporate (similar to eFax Plus and jConnect Premier but focused on enterprise users)
eFax Plus (unique phone number allows subscribers to receive inbound fax messages in their e-mail inbox and to send documents to any fax number directly from the subscriber's desktop)
eFaxFree (free,advertising-supported service similar to eFax Plus)
jBlast (high-volume faxing service)
jConnect Free (free,advertising-supported service similar to jConnect Premier)
jConnect Premier (unique phone number allows subscribers to receive inbound fax and voicemail messages in their e-mail inbox and to send documents to any fax number directly from the subscriber's desktop)
M4 Internet (outsourced service allows the subscriber to create and execute e-mail campaigns from their desktop)
Messenger Plus (desktop software program allows subscribers to view faxes and listen to voicemail messages received through j2 Global Communications' services)
Onebox (unified communications services suite)
PaperMaster Pro (application allows subscribers to automate the organization, archiving, and retrieving of digital versions of documents and other file types)

COMPETITORS

Active Voice	Deltathree
Auriga Laboratories	EasyLink
CallWave	Notify Technology
Captaris	PPOL
CommTouch Software	Premiere Global Services
Critical Path	

HISTORICAL FINANCIALS

Company Type: Public

Income Statement

FYE: December 31

	REVENUE ($ mil.)	NET INCOME ($ mil.)	NET PROFIT MARGIN	EMPLOYEES
12/06	181.1	53.1	29.3%	341
12/05	143.9	51.3	35.6%	288
12/04	106.3	31.6	29.7%	—
12/03	71.6	35.8	50.0%	—
12/02	48.2	14.3	29.7%	156
Annual Growth	39.2%	38.8%	—	21.6%

2006 Year-End Financials

Debt ratio: —
Return on equity: 23.2%
Cash ($ mil.): 179.1
Current ratio: 5.96
Long-term debt ($ mil.): —
No. of shares (mil.): 49.3
Dividends
  Yield: —
  Payout: —
Market value ($ mil.): 1,343.9
R&D as % of sales: —
Advertising as % of sales: —

Stock History

NASDAQ (GS): JCOM

	STOCK PRICE ($) FY Close	P/E High	P/E Low	PER SHARE ($) Earnings	PER SHARE ($) Dividends	PER SHARE ($) Book Value
12/06	27.25	31	19	1.04	—	5.17
12/05	21.37	24	15	1.00	—	8.23
12/04	17.25	29	15	0.63	—	5.93
12/03	12.40	34	6	0.71	—	4.46
12/02	4.76	24	3	0.30	—	5.13
Annual Growth	54.7%	—	—	36.5%	—	0.2%

Jacksonville Bancorp

Need to stow some greenbacks in Jax? You might check out Jacksonville Bancorp, the holding company for The Jacksonville Bank, which has about five branches in Jacksonville, Florida. The community bank offers consumers and commercial customers standard deposit products, including checking and savings accounts, money market accounts, CDs, and IRAs. The bank's lending is focused on commercial real estate loans, which make up some 60% of its loan portfolio; residential real estate loans add another 20%. The bank also offers business, construction, and consumer loans. Bank subsidiary Fountain Financial is an insurance agency. Jacksonville Bancorp is unrelated to the Illinois corporation of the same name.

In early 2008 the company announced plans to expand via its purchase of privately held Heritage Bancshares, the parent of Heritage Bank of North Florida, which has two branches in the Jacksonville area.

EXECUTIVES

Chairman: Donald E. Roller, age 68
President, CEO, and Director; President and CEO, The Jacksonville Bank: Gilbert J. Pomar III, age 46, $245,000 pay
EVP and CFO, Jacksonville Bancorp and The Jacksonville Bank: Valerie A. Kendall, age 53, $170,000 pay
EVP and Senior Loan Officer, The Jacksonville Bank: Scott M. Hall, age 42, $190,000 pay
SVP and Operations Manager, The Jacksonville Bank: Donna M. Donovan
Downtown Jacksonville Headquarters Manager, The Jacksonville Bank: John Hulsey
Mandarin Branch Manager, The Jacksonville Bank: Kimberly M. Delong
Queen's Harbour Branch Office Manager, The Jacksonville Bank: Lou Vaccaro

LOCATIONS

HQ: Jacksonville Bancorp, Inc.
  100 N. Laura St., Ste. 1000, Jacksonville, FL 32202
Phone: 904-421-3040   **Fax:** 904-421-3050
Web: www.jaxbank.com

PRODUCTS/OPERATIONS

2006 Sales

	$ mil.	% of total
Interest		
Loans, including fees	20.6	89
Securities & other	1.4	6
Service charges on deposit accounts	0.6	3
Other	0.5	2
Total	**23.1**	**100**

COMPETITORS

Alabama National BanCorp
Atlantic BancGroup
Bank of America
Compass Bancshares
Regions Financial
Southeastern Banking
SunTrust
Wachovia

HISTORICAL FINANCIALS

Company Type: Public

Income Statement

FYE: December 31

	ASSETS ($ mil.)	NET INCOME ($ mil.)	INCOME AS % OF ASSETS	EMPLOYEES
12/06	325.6	2.5	0.8%	57
12/05	273.0	2.2	0.8%	120
12/04	223.7	1.3	0.6%	—
12/03	176.9	1.0	0.6%	—
12/02	130.8	0.6	0.5%	28
Annual Growth	25.6%	42.9%	—	19.4%

2006 Year-End Financials

Equity as % of assets: 7.1%
Return on assets: 0.8%
Return on equity: 11.6%
Long-term debt ($ mil.): 7.0
No. of shares (mil.): 1.7
Market value ($ mil.): 57.6
Dividends
  Yield: —
  Payout: —
Sales ($ mil.): 23.1
R&D as % of sales: —
Advertising as % of sales: —

Stock History

NASDAQ (GM): JAXB

	STOCK PRICE ($) FY Close	P/E High	P/E Low	PER SHARE ($) Earnings	PER SHARE ($) Dividends	PER SHARE ($) Book Value
12/06	33.10	28	20	1.39	—	13.29
12/05	33.15	28	21	1.21	—	11.58
12/04	26.95	35	20	0.79	—	10.42
12/03	16.40	26	18	0.67	—	9.14
12/02	11.93	28	20	0.44	—	8.57
Annual Growth	29.1%	—	—	33.3%	—	11.6%

Jones Soda

There's nothing average about Jones Soda. The company bottles and distributes brightly colored beverages with wacky flavors like Twisted Lime and Fufu Berry. Seasonal offerings include Turkey and Gravy for Thanksgiving and Chocolate Fudge for Valentine's Day. It also regularly discontinues flavors and adds new ones. Jones, which distributes its drinks through retailers, including Barnes & Noble cafés, Panera Bread Company, and Starbucks, also customizes its beverage labels with photos submitted by customers. The company sells a line of noncarbonated beverages (Jones Naturals), with added ginseng, zinc, and other ingredients, and citrus-flavored energy drinks under the Jones Energy and WhoopAss labels.

The company's practice of retiring flavors is designed to keep its line of sodas at about 12 flavors. In addition to carbonated and energy drinks, Jones also offers organic tea and juice drinks.

Jones licenses its name, and sells its syrups, to grocer Kroger for a line of Jones Frozen Soda Pops. It also has a licensing agreement with Big Sky Brands for a line of Jones Soda Flavor Booster hard candy.

The company's additional products include lip balm in its soda flavors, apparel, and accessories. The company, which started out pushing its sodas from coolers placed in skate parks and tattoo parlors, fuels its alternative image by sponsoring extreme sport athletes (such as BMX, skate boarding, and surfing); as well as inviting fans to submit flavor suggestions, quotes, and photos for new company labels.

The company acquired vitamin drink mix 24C in 2006 from mindful Inc. and used the drink formula to create a vitamin-enhanced bottled water (Jones 24C).

Its products are available in the US and Canada and are distributed through a network of independent distributors. In 2006 the company announced that it would begin selling its soda in Kmart stores, boosting its presence in the US. The next year it added Wal-Mart to its roster of retail customers. Other large retailers carrying Jones Soda include Safeway, Cost Plus World Market, Maggie Moo's, and Kroger.

In 2007 Jones switched to sweetening its sodas (with the exception of its energy drink) with pure cane sugar rather than high fructose corn syrup, which is used almost exclusively by the carbonated beverage industry. Some scientists argue that unprocessed cane sugar is more healthful than the corn syrup derivative. This move targets consumers who want a more "natural" alternative. Domino Foods, which is owned by Florida Crystals, is Jones' main corn-sugar supplier.

Peter van Stolk stepped down as chairman and CEO at the end of 2007. (He remained as a member of the board.) Scott Bedbury was named interim chairman and Steve Jones, a former CMO of Coca-Cola and CEO of Minute Maid, was tapped as CEO. Van Stolk owns about 8% of Jones Soda.

Vardon Capital Management, L.L.C. owns just over 8% of the company, while Wellington Management Company, LLP, owns just under 7%.

EXECUTIVES

Interim Chairman: Scott Bedbury, age 49
Interim CEO and Director: Stephen C. (Steve) Jones, age 51
Director: Peter M. van Stolk, age 43, $173,150 pay
COO: Joth Ricci, age 39
CFO and Secretary: Hassan N. Natha, age 48, $111,042 pay
SEVP Sales and Marketing: Peter J. Burns, age 46
EVP Sales: Lars P. Nilsen, age 45, $137,627 pay
VP Operations: Eric Chastain
Controller: Melody Morgan
Brand Manager: Mike Spear
Customer Service Manager: Laura Blazyk
Human Resources Manager: Nancy Bucher
Auditors: KPMG LLP

LOCATIONS

HQ: Jones Soda Co.
234 9th Ave. North, Seattle, WA 98109
Phone: 206-624-3357   **Fax:** 206-624-6857
Web: www.jonessoda.com

2006 Sales

	% of total
US	87
Canada	13
Total	**100**

PRODUCTS/OPERATIONS

Selected Brands

Jones Energy
  Big Jones
  Lemon Lime
  Mixed Berry
  Orange
  WhoopAss
Jones Organics
  Berry Green Tea
  Cherry White Tea
  Mandarin Green Tea
  Peach Red Tea
  Strawberry White Tea
  Tropical Red Tea
Jones Naturals
  Bada Bing!
  Bananaberry
  Berry White
  Bohemian Raspberry
  Dave
  D'Peach Mode
  Limes with Orange
  Strawberry Manilow
Jones Soda
  Mid calorie (reduced sugar, carbohydrates, and calories)
    Blueberry
    Tangerine
    Twisted Lime
    Watermelon
  Premium
    Berry Lemonade
    Blue Bubblegum
    Cherry
    Cream Soda
    Crushed Melon
    Fufu Berry
    Green Apple
    Lemon Drop
    MF Grape
    Orange & Cream
    Root Beer
    Strawberry Lime
    Vanilla Cola
  Sugar free
    Black Cherry
    Cream Soda
    Ginger Ale
    Green Apple
    Pink Grapefruit
    Root Beer
    Watermelon

COMPETITORS

Big Red
Cadbury Schweppes
Coca-Cola
Cool Mountain Beverages
Ferolito, Vultaggio
Fuze Beverage
Hansen Natural
Impulse Energy USA
IZZE
Mott's
Naked Juice
National Beverage
National Grape Cooperative
New Attitude Beverage Corporation
Ocean Spray
Odwalla
Old Orchard
PepsiCo
Polar Beverages
Red Bull
Reed's
Snapple
South Beach Beverage
Sunny Delight
Tropicana
Welch's
Wet Planet Beverages

HISTORICAL FINANCIALS

Company Type: Public

Income Statement

FYE: December 31

	REVENUE ($ mil.)	NET INCOME ($ mil.)	NET PROFIT MARGIN	EMPLOYEES
12/06	39.7	4.6	11.6%	67
12/05	34.2	1.3	3.8%	52
12/04	27.5	1.3	4.7%	51
12/03	20.1	0.3	1.5%	38
12/02	18.6	(1.2)	—	34
Annual Growth	**20.9%**	—	—	**18.5%**

2006 Year-End Financials

Debt ratio: 0.0%
Return on equity: 18.9%
Cash ($ mil.): 30.2
Current ratio: 7.96
Long-term debt ($ mil.): 0.0
No. of shares (mil.): 25.6
Dividends
  Yield: —
  Payout: —
Market value ($ mil.): 315.3
R&D as % of sales: —
Advertising as % of sales: —

Stock History

NASDAQ (CM): JSDA

	STOCK PRICE ($) FY Close	P/E High/Low		PER SHARE ($) Earnings	Dividends	Book Value
12/06	12.30	68	27	0.19	—	1.65
12/05	5.40	133	55	0.06	—	0.29
12/04	3.45	73	33	0.06	—	0.21
12/03	2.09	127	12	0.02	—	0.12
12/02	0.23	—	—	(0.06)	—	0.09
Annual Growth	**170.4%**	—	—	—	—	**106.4%**

Jupitermedia Corporation

Owner of Internet.com, Jupitermedia isn't the homepage for the entire Web, but it does put lots of information within reach of your mouse. Targeting IT, business, and creative professionals, the company's media unit publishes industry news and information on more than 150 Web sites in its online network of information channels, and sends out nearly 150 e-newsletters. Jupitermedia provides online images through JupiterImages, which sells subscriptions to its image libraries. The company is primarily focused on its rapidly growing digital asset collections, and had been expanding through acquisitions. Chairman and CEO Alan Meckler owns 35% of Jupitermedia.

Previously named INT Media Group, the company became Jupitermedia after purchasing assets from Jupiter Media Metrix in 2002. The company discontinued JupiterEvents (conferences and trade shows) in 2005 and sold off its JupiterResearch division in 2006.

Jupitermedia had entered talks to be acquired by Getty Images, but the discussions were terminated in 2007.

The company's JupiterImages unit offers more than 7 million images online through brands such as Ablestock.com, Animations.com, Clipart.com, Comstock Images, Creatas Images, Liquid Library, PictureQuest, PhotoObjects.net, Photos.com, and Thinkstock Images.

The company's media division operates five online networks: DevX.com, designed for developers; Internet.com and EarthWeb.com for IT and business professionals; Mediabistro for media professionals; and Graphics.com for creative professionals.

EXECUTIVES

Chairman and CEO: Alan M. Meckler, age 61, $315,000 pay
President, COO, and Director: Christopher S. Cardell, age 47
CFO: Donald J. O'Neill, age 34
SVP and General Manager, Image Operations and Marketing, Jupiterimages: Edward Grossman
SVP and General Counsel: Mitchell S. (Mitch) Eisenberg
SVP and General Manager, JupiterOnlineMedia: Bruce Morris
VP and CTO: Mark Labbe
VP Business Development and Licensing: David M. Arganbright
VP Creative Business Affairs: Maria Kessler
VP Sales, North America, Jupiterimages: Rick Thompson
VP and Editor-in-Chief, JupiterWeb: Augustine Venditto
VP Marketing and Public Relations: Michael DeMilt
VP Human Resources: Michelle Burnham
CEO, Mediabistro.com: Laurel Touby
Auditors: Deloitte & Touche LLP

LOCATIONS

HQ: Jupitermedia Corporation
23 Old Kings Hwy. South, Darien, CT 06820
Phone: 203-662-2800   **Fax:** 203-655-4686
Web: www.jupitermedia.com

Jupitermedia Corporation has offices in Australia, Canada, France, Germany, Spain, the UK, and the US.

PRODUCTS/OPERATIONS

2006 Sales

	$ mil.	% of total
Online images	106.6	78
Online media	30.9	22
Total	**137.5**	**100**

Selected Products and Operations

JupiterImages (digital images for graphics professionals)
  AbleStock.com
  Animations.com
  BananaStock
  Clipart.com
  Comstock Images
  Creatas Images
  Goodshoot.com
  IFA Bilderteam
  Liquid Library
  Photos.com
  PhotoObjects.net
  PictureArts
  PictureQuest
  Thinkstock Footage
  Thinkstock Images
Media division
  DevX.com (content for developers)
  EarthWeb.com (content for IT professionals)
  Graphics.com (news and resources for creative
    professionals)
  Internet.com (content for IT and Internet
    professionals)
  Mediabistro.com (resource for media professionals)

COMPETITORS

CMP Media
CNET Networks
Corbis
Forrester Research
Gartner
Getty Images
International Data Group
TechTarget
Ziff Davis Media

HISTORICAL FINANCIALS

Company Type: Public

Income Statement   FYE: December 31

	REVENUE ($ mil.)	NET INCOME ($ mil.)	NET PROFIT MARGIN	EMPLOYEES
12/06	137.5	13.1	9.5%	678
12/05	124.6	78.4	62.9%	639
12/04	71.9	15.7	21.8%	—
12/03	47.0	1.4	3.0%	—
12/02	40.7	(0.5)	—	265
Annual Growth	**35.6%**	**—**	**—**	**26.5%**

2006 Year-End Financials

Debt ratio: 21.7%
Return on equity: 6.0%
Cash ($ mil.): 8.9
Current ratio: 0.77
Long-term debt ($ mil.): 49.9
No. of shares (mil.): 35.6
Dividends
  Yield: —
  Payout: —
Market value ($ mil.): 282.3
R&D as % of sales: —
Advertising as % of sales: —

Stock History   NASDAQ (GS): JUPM

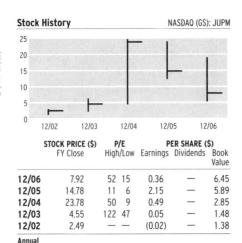

	STOCK PRICE ($) FY Close	P/E High/Low	PER SHARE ($) Earnings	Dividends	Book Value
12/06	7.92	52 15	0.36	—	6.45
12/05	14.78	11 6	2.15	—	5.89
12/04	23.78	50 9	0.49	—	2.85
12/03	4.55	122 47	0.05	—	1.48
12/02	2.49	— —	(0.02)	—	1.38
Annual Growth	**33.5%**	**—** **—**	**—**	**—**	**47.1%**

K12 Inc.

K12 isn't a missing element from the periodic table, but it could help struggling kids learn the periodic table. The "virtual public school" company offers online educational programs for children in kindergarten through 12th grade (K-12). Products include full-time online public schools (in about a dozen states), course material and product sales directly to parents, and individualized supplemental programs offered through traditional public schools. K12's programs are targeted at kids who underperform in public school, aren't safe in public school, or can't attend public school because of travel issues, disabilities, or because they are athletes or performers. CEO Ron Packard founded the company in 2000.

K12 plans to use its IPO proceeds for general corporate purposes and paying down its $6.5 million debt.

The company started out just offering programs for children in kindergarten through second grade. It has gradually expanded and will offer 11th and 12th grade programs in the 2007-2008 school year. K12 had about 27,000 students at the end of August 2007.

EXECUTIVES

Chairman: Andrew H. Tisch, age 57
CEO and Director: Ronald J. (Ron) Packard, age 43
COO and CFO: John F. Baule, age 43
EVP School Services: Bruce J. Davis, age 42
SVP, General Counsel, and Secretary: Howard D. Polsky, age 55
SVP Public Affairs: Bryan W. Flood, age 41
SVP Human Resources: Nancy Hauge, age 53
SVP School Development: Peter G. Stewart, age 38
SVP Product Development: Maria A. Szalay, age 41
SVP Systems and Technology: Ray Williams, age 45
Chief Marketing Officer: Celia Stokes, age 43
Chief Learning Officer: Bror V. H. Saxberg, age 47
Auditors: BDO Seidman, LLP

LOCATIONS

HQ: K12 Inc.
  2300 Corporate Park Dr., Herndon, VA 20171
Phone: 703-483-7000   **Fax:** 703-483-7330
Web: www.k12.com

2006-2007 School Year States

Arizona
Arkansas
California
Colorado
Florida
Idaho
Illinois
Minnesota
Ohio
Pennsylvania
Texas
Washington
Wisconsin

COMPETITORS

Apollo Group
Houghton Mifflin Harcourt
Kaplan
McGraw-Hill
Pearson
Riverdeep

HISTORICAL FINANCIALS

Company Type: Public

Income Statement   FYE: June 30

	REVENUE ($ mil.)	NET INCOME ($ mil.)	NET PROFIT MARGIN	EMPLOYEES
6/07	140.6	3.9	2.8%	636
6/06	116.9	1.4	1.2%	558
6/05	85.3	(3.5)	—	—
6/04	71.4	(7.4)	—	—
Annual Growth	**25.3%**	**—**	**—**	**14.0%**

2007 Year-End Financials

Debt ratio: (2.1%)
Return on equity: —
Cash ($ mil.): 1.7
Current ratio: 1.36
Long-term debt ($ mil.): 4.2

Net Income History   NYSE Arca: LRN

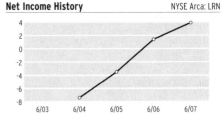

Kadant Inc.

Seeking to hear the "Ka-ching" of increased profits, Kadant makes recycling equipment that turns wastepaper into white and brown grades of recycled paper. The company's main products are stock-preparation equipment, including pulping and trash removal systems; cleaning, screening, and de-inking systems; accessories to clean the rolls of paper-making equipment and to cut and remove sheets of paper; and equipment that recycles water from pulp slurry and processes reusable fiber. Formerly a subsidiary, Kadant was spun off from Thermo Electron (now Thermo Fisher Scientific) in 2001.

Kadant made fiber-based composite building products (from paper-making byproducts, reclaimed plastic, and other materials), including decks and fencing. In 2005, however, it sold the assets of its Kadant Composites business to LDI Composites for around $11 million in cash and the assumption of liabilities. LDI Composites is an affiliate of Liberty Diversified Industries.

Citing a weak European market and needing to save money, Kadant cut 136 jobs near the end of 2004. The jobs were based at the company's unit in France. In 2005 the company expanded significantly through its $102 million acquisition of The Johnson Corporation, which supplies the paper industry worldwide with steam and condensate systems, components, controls, and related services.

The next year, the company's Kadant Black Clawson subsidiary, which manufactures fiberline process equipment and equipment for paper recycling, chemical pulping, and paper machine approach flow systems, received a $7 million contract from Zhejiang Jingxing Paper (China) to create a system that will recover usable fiber from recycled corrugated containers to produce linerboard for packaging applications.

In 2006 the company acquired the assets of Jining Huayi Light Industry Machinery for around $20 million in cash. The Chinese company makes stock-preparation equipment.

The PNC Financial Services Group owns 9% of Kadant. Dimensional Fund Advisors and Wachovia each hold nearly 9% of the company. Wellington Management has an equity stake of about 5%, as does CEO William Rainville.

EXECUTIVES

Chairman, President, and CEO: William A. Rainville, age 65, $1,932,000 pay
EVP and COO: Edward J. Sindoni, age 62, $535,000 pay
EVP and CFO: Thomas M. O'Brien, age 55, $562,000 pay
EVP: Jonathan W. Painter, age 48, $435,000 pay
VP, General Counsel, and Secretary: Sandra L. Lambert, age 51
VP, Finance and Chief Accounting Officer:
Michael J. McKenney, age 45
VP: Edwin D. Healy, age 69, $390,000 pay
VP: Eric T. Langevin, age 44
VP, Marketing: Wesley A. Martz
Treasurer: Daniel J. Walsh
Auditors: Ernst & Young LLP

LOCATIONS

HQ: Kadant Inc.
1 Technology Park Dr., Westford, MA 01886
Phone: 978-776-2000   **Fax:** 978-635-1593
Web: www.kadant.com

Kadant has operations in Brazil, Canada, China, France, Mexico, the Netherlands, Sweden, the UK, and the US.

2006 Sales

	$ mil.	% of total
US	210.5	57
France	61.2	17
Other countries	95.5	26
Adjustments	(25.6)	—
Total	**341.6**	**100**

PRODUCTS/OPERATIONS

2006 Sales

	$ mil.	% of total
Pulp & papermaking	327.5	96
Fiber-based products & casting products	14.1	4
Total	**341.6**	**100**

Selected Subsidiaries

ArcLine Products, Inc.
Kadant Black Clawson, Inc.
Kadant Fibergen Inc.
Kadant International Holdings Inc.
Kadant Johnson Inc.
Kadant Web Systems Inc.

COMPETITORS

Ahlstrom	Lorentzen & Wettre
Albany International	Louisiana-Pacific
Andritz AG	Metso
AstenJohnson	Parsons & Whittemore
Barco	Sandusky Intl.
Columbus McKinnon	Tamfelt Corp.
Deublin	Voith
GLV	

HISTORICAL FINANCIALS
Company Type: Public

Income Statement			FYE: Saturday after December 31
	REVENUE ($ mil.)	NET INCOME ($ mil.)	NET PROFIT MARGIN	EMPLOYEES
12/06	341.6	17.1	5.0%	2,000
12/05	243.7	6.9	2.8%	1,400
12/04	195.0	0.6	0.3%	—
12/03	203.5	11.8	5.8%	—
12/02	185.7	(26.8)	—	1,060
Annual Growth	**16.5%**	**—**	**—**	**17.2%**

2006 Year-End Financials

Debt ratio: 18.8%	Dividends
Return on equity: 7.7%	Yield: —
Cash ($ mil.): 39.6	Payout: —
Current ratio: 1.92	Market value ($ mil.): 341.0
Long-term debt ($ mil.): 44.7	R&D as % of sales: —
No. of shares (mil.): 14.0	Advertising as % of sales: —

Stock History
NYSE: KAI

	STOCK PRICE ($) FY Close	P/E High/Low	PER SHARE ($) Earnings	Dividends	Book Value
12/06	24.38	23 15	1.21	—	17.01
12/05	18.50	47 34	0.49	—	15.32
12/04	20.50	470 354	0.05	—	15.27
12/03	20.85	26 16	0.85	—	15.02
12/02	15.26	— —	(2.04)	—	13.38
Annual Growth	**12.4%**	**— —**	**—**	**—**	**6.2%**

Kendle International

When it comes to research and development, few can hold a candle to Kendle International. The company provides contract research and development services for biotechnology and pharmaceutical companies. Its services, which facilitate Phase I through Phase IV clinical trials, include patient recruitment, clinical monitoring, statistical analysis, and consulting on regulatory issues. Additionally, Kendle's TrialWare software helps customers manage research and clinical trial data. The company's largest therapeutic areas are oncology and central nervous system disorders. Kendle's top client is drug bigwig Pfizer.

As one of the company's primary sources of sales, Pfizer became part of Kendle's Strategic Partners operating unit when it reorganized to focus on customer groups rather than operations. The other operating units are the Americas, Europe, Regulatory Affairs, and Late Phase, which provides services related to Phase III and IV trials and the commercialization of approved drugs.

As part of an effort to build its clinical development business, the company in 2006 acquired Latin America CRO International Clinical Research Limited and the Phase II-IV clinical services business of Charles River Laboratories.

Candace Kendle (CEO) and her husband, Christopher Bergen (president), founded the company and own about 15%.

EXECUTIVES

Chairman and CEO: Candace Kendle, age 61, $394,748 pay
President, COO, and Director:
Christopher C. (Chris) Bergen, age 56, $337,266 pay
SVP, CFO, and Treasurer: Karl (Buzz) Brenkert III, age 59, $228,276 pay
SVP Global Clinical Development: Martha R. Feller, age 58
VP and CIO: Gary M. Wedig
VP and Chief Marketing Officer:
Simon S. Higginbotham, age 46, $241,219 pay
VP Regulatory Affairs and Quality: Melanie A. Bruno
VP Strategic Development and Corporate Treasurer:
Anthony L. (Tony) Forcellini, age 49
VP Global Clinical Development, North America:
Ubavka M. DeNoble
VP Human Resources: Karen Crone
VP Medical Affairs: Thomas B. Smith
VP Global Clinical Safety and Pharmacovigilance:
Ken Hintze
VP Global Sales: Mary Briggs
Director Corporate Communications: Lori Dorer
Investor Relations: Patty Frank
Auditors: Deloitte & Touche LLP

LOCATIONS

HQ: Kendle International Inc.
1200 Carew Tower, 441 Vine St.,
Cincinnati, OH 45202
Phone: 513-381-5550   **Fax:** 513-381-5870
Web: www.kendle.com

With operations in some 60 countries, Kendle International has offices in Africa, Asia, Australia, Central America, Europe, and North America.

2006 Service Sales

	% of total
US	55
Other countries	45
Total	**100**

PRODUCTS/OPERATIONS

2006 Sales

	$ mil.	% of total
Services	283.5	76
Reimbursements	90.4	24
Total	**373.9**	**100**

COMPETITORS

Charles River Laboratories
Covance
ICON
MDS
PAREXEL
Perceptive Informatics
Pharmaceutical Product Development
Quintiles Transnational

HISTORICAL FINANCIALS

Company Type: Public

Income Statement

FYE: December 31

	REVENUE ($ mil.)	NET INCOME ($ mil.)	NET PROFIT MARGIN	EMPLOYEES
12/06	373.9	8.5	2.3%	3,050
12/05	250.6	10.7	4.3%	1,900
12/04	215.9	3.6	1.7%	—
12/03	209.7	(1.7)	—	—
12/02	214.0	(54.8)	—	1,650
Annual Growth	15.0%	—	—	16.6%

2006 Year-End Financials

Debt ratio: 141.2%
Return on equity: 6.5%
Cash ($ mil.): 22.3
Current ratio: 1.51
Long-term debt ($ mil.): 197.9
No. of shares (mil.): 14.4

Dividends
  Yield: —
  Payout: —
Market value ($ mil.): 454.3
R&D as % of sales: —
Advertising as % of sales: —

Stock History

NASDAQ (GS): KNDL

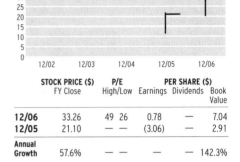

	STOCK PRICE ($) FY Close	P/E High/Low		PER SHARE ($) Earnings	Dividends	Book Value
12/06	31.45	71	37	0.58	—	9.70
12/05	25.74	39	10	0.76	—	8.70
12/04	8.80	38	19	0.27	—	7.76
12/03	6.34	—	—	(0.13)	—	7.37
12/02	8.80	—	—	(4.30)	—	7.35
Annual Growth	37.5%	—	—	—	—	7.2%

Kenexa Corporation

Kenexa wants to streamline your HR processes. The company markets Web-based applications that automate human resources activities, such as recruitment, skills testing, and tracking of employee development. Kenexa also offers outsourcing options to clients, taking over part or all of the recruitment and hiring process. In addition, the company conducts employee surveys for its customers. Kenexa sells its services and software products mostly on a subscription basis to about 3,000 large and medium-sized corporations. The company was founded in 1987.

Kenexa hopes to expand into markets in Europe, the Middle East, and the Asia/Pacific region. (In 2006, only 10% of the company's sales came from outside the US.) To help achieve these goals, the company acquired Psychometric Services, a London-based diagnostic test provider, in late 2006 for $7.6 million.

Also in 2006 Kenexa bought recruiting software providers BrassRing and Webhire, consultant Knowledge Workers, and survey firm Gantz Wiley Research. The acquisitions were fueled in part by the proceeds of an IPO launched in mid-2005.

EXECUTIVES

Chairman and CEO: Nooruddin S. (Rudy) Karsan Sr., age 49, $500,000 pay
CFO: Donald F. (Don) Volk, age 57, $300,000 pay
EVP: Bill L. Erickson, age 57
VP Business Development: Archie L. Jones Jr., age 35, $180,000 pay
VP Employment Branding: Tim Geisert
President, COO, and Director: Troy A. Kanter, age 39, $400,000 pay
President, Kenexa Government Solutions: William Sebra
CTO: Ramarao V. Velpuri, age 43
Chief Marketing Officer: Sarah M. Teten, age 33, $180,000 pay
Chief People Officer: Phillip (Phil) Stewart
Auditors: BDO Seidman, LLP

LOCATIONS

HQ: Kenexa Corporation
  650 E. Swedesford Rd., 2nd Fl., Wayne, PA 19087
Phone: 610-971-9171   **Fax:** 610-971-9181
Web: www.kenexa.com

Kenexa Corporation has offices in England, India, Malaysia, and the US.

2006 Sales

	% of total
US	90
Europe, Middle East & Africa	6
Canada	3
Asia Pacific & other	1
Total	**100**

PRODUCTS/OPERATIONS

2006 Sales

	$ mil.	% of total
Subscription	90.5	81
Other	21.6	19
Total	**112.1**	**100**

COMPETITORS

Authoria
Gallup
iCIMS
Integrated Performance Systems
ISGN
Lawson Software
Oracle
Peopleclick
Pilat Technologies International
PreVisor
SAP
SHL Group
Spring Group
Taleo
Vurv
Workstream

HISTORICAL FINANCIALS

Company Type: Public

Income Statement

FYE: December 31

	REVENUE ($ mil.)	NET INCOME ($ mil.)	NET PROFIT MARGIN	EMPLOYEES
12/06	112.1	15.9	14.2%	1,220
12/05	65.6	6.1	9.3%	693
12/04	46.3	(4.1)	—	—
12/03	34.0	(12.2)	—	—
Annual Growth	48.8%	—	—	76.0%

2006 Year-End Financials

Debt ratio: 30.8%
Return on equity: 16.1%
Cash ($ mil.): 42.5
Current ratio: 1.16
Long-term debt ($ mil.): 45.3
No. of shares (mil.): 20.9

Dividends
  Yield: —
  Payout: —
Market value ($ mil.): 695.1
R&D as % of sales: —
Advertising as % of sales: —

Stock History

NASDAQ (GM): KNXA

	STOCK PRICE ($) FY Close	P/E High/Low		PER SHARE ($) Earnings	Dividends	Book Value
12/06	33.26	49	26	0.78	—	7.04
12/05	21.10	—	—	(3.06)	—	2.91
Annual Growth	57.6%	—	—	—	—	142.3%

The Knot, Inc.

Here comes the bride, surfing online. The Knot is a leading online publisher serving the wedding market sector with content and services through TheKnot.com. The site offers advice and information on topics from engagement to honeymoon, as well as wedding planning tools (budget planner, gown finder), chat rooms, a directory of local resources, and an online gift store. The company's WeddingChannel.com offers online registry services. Other sites include TheNest.com and PartySpot.com. The firm also licenses its content to Web portal MSN and cable operator Comcast. In addition to online content, The Knot publishes *The Knot Wedding Magazine*, more than a dozen regional magazines, and books on lifestyle topics.

Looking to expand its reach into new lifestyle segments, The Knot launched TheNest.com in 2004 to offer content and services for newlyweds. The following year it acquired GreatBoyfriends, operator of dating sites GreatBoyfriends.com and GreatGirlfriends.com.

Exploring a natural growth of its brand, the company acquired the publishing business and related assets of OAM Solutions, the publisher of *Lilaguides*, local information guides for new parents, for $2.1 million in 2006. The Knot continued its expansion later that year with the purchase of competitor WeddingChannel.com for about $60 million in cash and more than 1 million shares of stock. The Knot bought the company for its Web-based bridal registry services, and to be more attractive to advertisers.

Comcast and retailer Federated Department Stores each own more than 15% of the company, while Time Warner has a 5% stake.

EXECUTIVES

Chairman and CEO: David Liu, age 43, $378,709 pay
COO, Assistant Secretary, and Director:
 Sandra (Sandy) Stiles, age 57, $339,220 pay
President and Chief Marketing Officer: Janet Scardino
CFO, Treasurer, and Secretary: Richard Szefc, age 59,
 $378,333 pay
CTO: Armando Cardenas-Nolazco, age 45, $213,928 pay
SVP and Group Publishing Director: Denise Favorule
VP Business Integration: Rob Fassino
Editor-in-Chief: Carley Roney, age 38
Executive Editor: Rosie Amodio
Director Online Art: Lori Richmond
Weddings Editor: Christa Vagnozzi
Editorial Production Coordinator: Melissa Mariola
Auditors: Ernst & Young LLP

LOCATIONS

HQ: The Knot, Inc.
 462 Broadway, 6th Fl., New York, NY 10013
Phone: 212-219-8555   **Fax:** 212-219-1929
Web: www.theknot.com

PRODUCTS/OPERATIONS

2006 Sales

	$ mil.	% of total
Sponsorships & advertising	36.6	50
Merchandising	15.0	4
Registry	3.0	21
Publishing & other	18.1	25
Total	**72.7**	**100**

COMPETITORS

About Inc.
AOL
Condé Nast
Fairchild Publications
iVillage
Martha Stewart Living
Meredith Corporation
WE: Women's Entertainment
Yahoo!

HISTORICAL FINANCIALS

Company Type: Public

Income Statement
FYE: December 31

	REVENUE ($ mil.)	NET INCOME ($ mil.)	NET PROFIT MARGIN	EMPLOYEES
12/06	72.7	23.4	32.2%	367
12/05	51.4	4.0	7.8%	260
12/04	41.4	1.3	3.1%	—
12/03	36.7	1.1	3.0%	—
12/02	29.5	(5.1)	—	—
Annual Growth	**25.3%**	**—**	**—**	**41.2%**

2006 Year-End Financials

Debt ratio: 0.0%
Return on equity: 22.7%
Cash ($ mil.): 80.6
Current ratio: 5.61
Long-term debt ($ mil.): 0.1
No. of shares (mil.): 31.1
Dividends
 Yield: —
 Payout: —
Market value ($ mil.): 816.8
R&D as % of sales: —
Advertising as % of sales: —

Stock History
NASDAQ (GM): KNOT

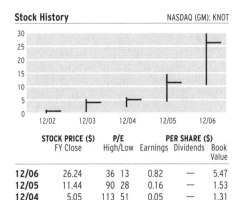

	STOCK PRICE ($) FY Close	P/E High/Low	PER SHARE ($) Earnings	Dividends	Book Value
12/06	26.24	36 13	0.82	—	5.47
12/05	11.44	90 28	0.16	—	1.53
12/04	5.05	113 51	0.05	—	1.31
12/03	4.00	100 14	0.05	—	1.26
12/02	0.81	— —	(0.28)	—	0.87
Annual Growth	**138.6%**	**— —**	**—**	**—**	**58.3%**

Kowabunga, Inc.

Is your company result #2,359 on a search list? Kowabunga is only too enthused to help. The company (formerly Think Partnership) has subsidiary operations in three principal service segments: advertising, direct, and network. The advertising segment offers traditional online and off-line ad agency services. The direct segment primarily provides lead generation and search engine optimization products and services, while its consumer offerings (also part of the direct segment) include online dating and an online real estate school that provides the happy couple with a rewarding future. Kowabunga's network services include Web design and applications support, as well as Internet marketing networks.

Aligning itself with its most notable affiliated marketing brand name, Think Partnership changed its name to Kowabunga in early 2008.

In terms of a growth strategy, the company is making a dent into the lucrative Asia Pacific Web market. In early 2007, it launched its new Web site — available in Chinese as well as English — showcasing its array of products and services.

The company in 2006 introduced "My Affiliate Program," a service for creating, automating, managing, and optimizing affiliate relationships. In 2005 the company acquired affiliate marketing services provider PrimaryAds, expanding its efforts to capitalize on the booming search engine market.

EXECUTIVES

Chairman: M. Alex White
President, CEO, Secretary, and Director:
 Scott P. Mitchell, age 35
COO: Stan Antonuk, age 39
CFO and Treasurer: Jody Brown, age 35
SVP Corporate Communications and Investor Relations: Xavier Hermosillo, age 54
VP Finance: Kate Dennison
VP Finance: Tara Morgan
VP Marketing: Rachel Honoway
VP Strategic Partnerships: Tobias Teeter

President, Think Direct: R. Brady Whittingham, age 37
President, Think International: Jim Banks
President, Think Network: Ken Harlan
General Counsel: Vaughn W. Duff
CTO: John Linden, age 29
Chief Revenue Officer: Stephen E. Lerch, age 52
Auditors: Blackman Kallick Bartelstein, LLP

LOCATIONS

HQ: Kowabunga, Inc.
 15550 Lightwave Dr., Clearwater, FL 33760
Phone: 727-324-0046   **Fax:** 727-324-0063
Web: www.kowabunga.com

PRODUCTS/OPERATIONS

2006 Sales

	$ mil.	% of total
Advertising	25.3	35
Direct	17.7	24
Network	16.7	23
Consumer	12.9	18
Adjustments	(0.7)	—
Total	**71.9**	**100**

Selected Subsidiaries

Advertising
 MarketSmart Advertising, Inc. (off-line advertising agency)
 Web Diversity Ltd. (search management and optimization services)
Direct
 Cherish, Inc. (online dating services)
 Personals Plus, Inc.
 Vintacom Florida, Inc.
 iLead Media, Inc. (lead generation services)
 Morex Marketing, LLC (lead generation services)
 Real Estate School Online, Inc.
Network
 KowaBunga! Marketing, Inc. (Internet marketing software)
 Litmus Media (Click fraud protected advertising distribution technologies)
 Ozona Online Network, Inc. (Web design and related services)
 PrimaryAds Inc. (cost-per-ad affiliate marketing network)

COMPETITORS

Advertising.com
Commission Junction
InfoSpace
LinkShare
Overstock.com
ValueClick

HISTORICAL FINANCIALS

Company Type: Public

Income Statement
FYE: December 31

	REVENUE ($ mil.)	NET INCOME ($ mil.)	NET PROFIT MARGIN	EMPLOYEES
12/06	71.9	0.6	0.8%	254
12/05	40.4	0.0	—	287
12/04	17.6	1.8	10.2%	—
12/03	7.1	0.3	4.2%	—
12/02	4.1	(2.5)	—	—
Annual Growth	**104.6%**	**—**	**—**	**(11.5%)**

2006 Year-End Financials

Debt ratio: —
Return on equity: 0.9%
Cash ($ mil.): 4.2
Current ratio: 1.54
Long-term debt ($ mil.): —
No. of shares (mil.): 64.2
Dividends
 Yield: —
 Payout: —
Market value ($ mil.): 207.5
R&D as % of sales: —
Advertising as % of sales: —

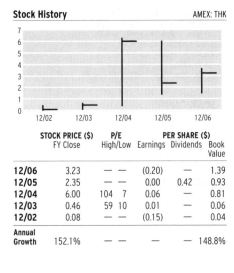

Stock History

Stock History — AMEX: THK

	STOCK PRICE ($) FY Close	P/E High/Low		PER SHARE ($) Earnings	Dividends	Book Value
12/06	3.23	—	—	(0.20)	—	1.39
12/05	2.35	—	—	0.00	0.42	0.93
12/04	6.00	104	7	0.06	—	0.81
12/03	0.46	59	10	0.01	—	0.06
12/02	0.08	—	—	(0.15)	—	0.04
Annual Growth	152.1%	—	—	—	—	148.8%

Kreisler Manufacturing

Your Chrysler might have a hemi under the hood, but this Kreisler focuses on bigger engines. Kreisler Manufacturing, through subsidiary Kreisler Industrial, makes precision metal components for commercial and military aircraft engines and industrial gas turbines. Tube assemblies — used to transfer fuel for combustion, hydraulic fluid for thrust reversers, and oil for lubrication — account for most of the company's sales. A second subsidiary, Kreisler Polska, supplies machined components to Kreisler Industrial from a manufacturing plant in Krakow, Poland. Chairman Wallace Kelly controls a 38% stake in Kreisler Manufacturing.

Three industrial customers and the US government account for more than 80% of Kreisler Manufacturing's sales. The company has benefited from increased demand for the engines used to power two US military aircraft: the F/A-22 Raptor and the F-35 Joint Strike Fighter (officially named the Lightning II).

EXECUTIVES

Chairman: Wallace N. Kelly, age 67
Co-President, CEO, and Director; Co-President and CEO, Kreisler Industrial; President, Kreisler Polska: Michael D. Stern, age 41, $193,423 pay
Co-President, CFO, Secretary, Treasurer, and VP, Kreisler Polska: Edward A. Stern, age 46, $193,423 pay
Human Resources Manager: Lisa Sibrel
Auditors: Rothstein, Kass & Company, P.C.

LOCATIONS

HQ: Kreisler Manufacturing Corporation
180 Van Riper Ave., Elmwood Park, NJ 07407
Phone: 201-791-0700 **Fax:** 201-791-8015
Web: www.kreisler-ind.com

PRODUCTS/OPERATIONS

2007 Sales

	$ mil.	% of total
Military	10.9	46
Commercial	10.3	43
Industrial Gas Turbine	2.7	11
Total	**23.9**	**100**

COMPETITORS

Argo-Tech
Ducommun
Héroux-Devtek
Magellan Aerospace
Pacific Aerospace
Triumph Group

HISTORICAL FINANCIALS

Company Type: Public

Income Statement
FYE: June 30

	REVENUE ($ mil.)	NET INCOME ($ mil.)	NET PROFIT MARGIN	EMPLOYEES
6/07	23.9	2.0	8.4%	201
6/06	19.7	1.2	6.1%	155
6/05	14.4	0.2	1.4%	124
6/04	12.3	(0.7)	—	—
6/03	12.5	(0.7)	—	—
Annual Growth	17.6%	—	—	27.3%

2007 Year-End Financials

Debt ratio: 2.0%
Return on equity: 16.8%
Cash ($ mil.): 5.6
Current ratio: 5.66
Long-term debt ($ mil.): 0.3
No. of shares (mil.): 1.9

Dividends
 Yield: —
 Payout: —
Market value ($ mil.): 29.0
R&D as % of sales: —
Advertising as % of sales: —

Stock History
NASDAQ (CM): KRSL

	STOCK PRICE ($) FY Close	P/E High/Low		PER SHARE ($) Earnings	Dividends	Book Value
6/07	15.52	27	9	1.04	—	7.03
6/06	13.37	26	8	0.63	—	5.86
6/05	5.30	81	46	0.10	—	5.23
6/04	7.20	—	—	(0.37)	—	5.23
6/03	4.80	—	—	(0.36)	—	5.61
Annual Growth	34.1%	—	—	—	—	5.8%

K-Sea Transportation

If you're transporting refined petroleum products, it's OK to go by K-Sea. K-Sea Tranportation operates a fleet of more than 70 tank barges and about 60 tugboats to propel them. Overall, the company's fleet has a carrying capacity of more than 4.2 million barrels. K-Sea serves major oil companies, refiners, and oil traders, primarily along the east and west coasts of the US. About 80% of its business comes from one-year or longer contracts; major customers include BP, Chevron, ConocoPhillips, Exxon Mobil, and Rio Energy. Investment funds managed by Jefferies Capital Partners, an affiliate of Jefferies Group, own a controlling stake in K-Sea.

Over the years the company has increased its fleet both by contracting to have new vessels built and by acquisitions, and it hopes to continue to pursue both strategies. K-Sea expanded its western operations in August 2007 when it acquired Seattle-based Sirius Maritime and Hawaii-based Smith Maritime for $205 million. The deal increased the carrying capacity of K-Sea's fleet by more than 20%.

While expanding its fleet, K-Sea hopes to maintain a mix of business tilted in favor of long-term contracts, or time charters, rather than voyage-by-voyage charters. Time charters tend to provide a more stable revenue stream.

Nearly all of K-Sea's vessels operate under the Jones Act, which restricts marine shipping between US ports to vessels built in the US and owned and operated by US companies.

EXECUTIVES

Chairman: James J. Dowling, age 61
President, CEO, and Director: Timothy J. Casey, age 46, $239,038 pay
CFO: John J. Nicola, age 53, $180,192 pay
VP Administration and Secretary: Richard P. Falcinelli, age 46, $180,192 pay
VP Business Development: Carl Eklof Jr.
VP Corporate Development: Charles Kauffman, age 56
VP Operations: Thomas M. Sullivan, age 48, $180,192 pay
VP Sales and Marketing: Gregory Haslinsky, age 44, $134,808 pay
Controller: Terrence Gill
Director Human Resources: Dennis Luba
Director Safety and Compliance: Richard Heym
Auditors: PricewaterhouseCoopers LLP

LOCATIONS

HQ: K-Sea Transportation Partners L.P.
1 Tower Center Blvd., 17th Fl.,
East Brunswick, NJ 10303
Phone: 732-339-6100 **Fax:** 732-339-6140
Web: www.k-sea.com

PRODUCTS/OPERATIONS

2007 Sales

	$ mil.	% of total
Voyage	216.9	96
Bareboat charter & other	9.7	4
Total	**226.6**	**100**

COMPETITORS

Apex Oil
Chemoil
Colonial Pipeline
Crowley Maritime
Hornbeck Offshore
Overseas Shipholding Group
Plantation Pipe Line
U.S. Shipping

HISTORICAL FINANCIALS

Company Type: Public

Income Statement
FYE: June 30

	REVENUE ($ mil.)	NET INCOME ($ mil.)	NET PROFIT MARGIN	EMPLOYEES
6/07	226.6	15.8	7.0%	925
6/06	182.8	5.9	3.2%	690
6/05	121.4	8.1	6.7%	490
6/04	95.8	21.2	22.1%	—
Annual Growth	33.2%	(9.3%)	—	37.4%

210

2007 Year-End Financials

Debt ratio: 154.0%
Return on equity: 10.0%
Cash ($ mil.): 0.9
Current ratio: 0.72
Long-term debt ($ mil.): 235.0
No. of shares (mil.): 6.8

Dividends
  Yield: 5.5%
  Payout: 167.7%
Market value ($ mil.): 321.5
R&D as % of sales: —
Advertising as % of sales: —

Stock History

NYSE: KSP

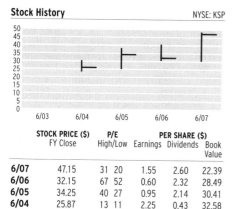

	STOCK PRICE ($) FY Close	P/E High/Low		PER SHARE ($) Earnings	Dividends	Book Value
6/07	47.15	31	20	1.55	2.60	22.39
6/06	32.15	67	52	0.60	2.32	28.49
6/05	34.25	40	27	0.95	2.14	30.41
6/04	25.87	13	11	2.25	0.43	32.58
Annual Growth	**22.2%**	—	—	**(11.7%)**	**82.2%**	**(11.8%)**

KSW, Inc.

KSW may have a need to vent on occasion, but the company still knows how to keep its cool. The company installs heating, ventilating, and air conditioning systems through its operating subsidiary, KSW Mechanical Services, Inc. Operating in the New York metropolitan area, the company does not generally bid on projects less than $3 million. Customers include Bovis Lend Lease, which accounts for about 40% of KSW's total revenues, Newmark Construction Services (18%), Glenwood Management (10%), and Shanska USA Building (10%). Chairman, president, CEO, and secretary Floyd Warkol owns 15% of KSW.

EXECUTIVES

Chairman, President, CEO, and Secretary:
 Floyd Warkol, age 59, $500,000 pay
CFO: Richard W. Lucas, age 40, $155,000 pay
General Counsel and Director of Investor Relations:
 James F. Oliviero, age 60, $210,000 pay
Director, Human Resources: Rudy Bisnauth
COO, KSW Mechanical: Vincent Terraferma, age 56,
 $255,000 pay
Auditors: J.H. Cohn LLP

LOCATIONS

HQ: KSW, Inc.
 37-16 23rd St., Long Island City, NY 11101
Phone: 718-361-6500   **Fax:** 718-784-1943

COMPETITORS

Carrier
Colonial Commercial
Fedders
Ice Cap
Johnson Controls
Lennox
Nordyne
Trane Inc.

HISTORICAL FINANCIALS

Company Type: Public

Income Statement

FYE: December 31

	REVENUE ($ mil.)	NET INCOME ($ mil.)	NET PROFIT MARGIN	EMPLOYEES
12/06	77.1	2.8	3.6%	45
12/05	53.4	2.7	5.1%	43
12/04	26.3	(1.3)	—	31
12/03	35.0	0.8	2.3%	45
12/02	46.5	(2.3)	—	45
Annual Growth	**13.5%**	—		**0.0%**

2006 Year-End Financials

Debt ratio: —
Return on equity: 24.7%
Cash ($ mil.): 14.8
Current ratio: 1.55
Long-term debt ($ mil.): —
No. of shares (mil.): 5.8

Dividends
  Yield: 0.8%
  Payout: 13.0%
Market value ($ mil.): 40.6
R&D as % of sales: —
Advertising as % of sales: —

Stock History

AMEX: KSW

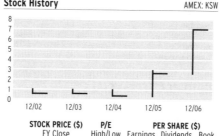

	STOCK PRICE ($) FY Close	P/E High/Low		PER SHARE ($) Earnings	Dividends	Book Value
12/06	7.05	15	6	0.46	0.06	2.28
12/05	2.67	6	1	0.48	—	1.74
12/04	0.39	—	—	(0.23)	—	1.24
12/03	0.59	7	4	0.14	—	1.47
12/02	0.56	—	—	(0.39)	—	1.31
Annual Growth	**88.4%**	—	—	—	—	**14.9%**

LaBranche & Co

LaBranche & Co specializes in being a specialist. The company regulates trading in the common stock of more than 550 NYSE firms, including Dow Jones components AT&T, Exxon Mobil, Merck, and 3M. One of the oldest and largest specialists, LaBranche & Co matches buyers and sellers and compensates for demand imbalances by buying or selling stocks for its own account. The company also has a unit that focuses on options, futures, and exchange-traded funds (ETFs), as well as others that focus on foreign markets. It sold its AMEX specialist operations, which made markets for some 85 stocks, to Cohen Specialists in 2007. Privately held Horizon Asset Management owns nearly a quarter of LaBranche & Co.

Subsidiary LaBranche Financial Services performs brokerage and clearing services for institutional clients. The great-grandfather of chairman and CEO Michael LaBranche (owner of more than 5% of the firm) founded LaBranche & Co in 1924.

EXECUTIVES

Chairman, President, and CEO:
 George M. L. (Michael) LaBranche IV, age 52,
 $1,900,000 pay
EVP and Director; CEO, LaBranche & Co. LLC:
 Alfred O. Hayward Jr., age 60, $1,350,000 pay
COO: William J. Burke III, age 53, $780,000 pay
SVP and CFO: Jeffrey A. McCutcheon, age 43
General Counsel and Corporate Secretary:
 Stephen H. Gray, age 37, $535,000 pay
CEO, LaBranche Financial Services:
 L. Thomas Patterson
**Group Director, Corporate Relations and Business
 Development:** John Longobardi
Auditors: KPMG LLP

LOCATIONS

HQ: LaBranche & Co Inc.
 1 Exchange Plaza, 25th Fl., New York, NY 10006
Phone: 212-425-1144   **Fax:** 212-344-1469
Web: www.labranche.com

PRODUCTS/OPERATIONS

2006 Sales

	$ mil.	% of total
Net gain on corporate equities, not readily marketable	238.6	35
Principal transactions	180.9	27
Stock borrow interest	158.1	24
Commissions	69.8	10
Interest & other	26.6	4
Total	**674.0**	**100**

2006 Sales by Segment

	% of total
Specialist	64
Execution	8
Other	28
Total	**100**

COMPETITORS

Bank of America
Bear Wagner
GSEC
Knight Capital
Madoff Securities
Susquehanna International Group, LLP
Van der Moolen

HISTORICAL FINANCIALS

Company Type: Public

Income Statement

FYE: December 31

	REVENUE ($ mil.)	NET INCOME ($ mil.)	NET PROFIT MARGIN	EMPLOYEES
12/06	674.0	136.8	20.3%	429
12/05	340.2	37.5	11.0%	525
12/04	319.0	(43.8)	—	—
12/03	306.0	(179.4)	—	—
12/02	452.8	87.2	19.3%	595
Annual Growth	**10.5%**	**11.9%**	—	**(7.9%)**

2006 Year-End Financials

Debt ratio: 53.3%
Return on equity: 17.0%
Cash ($ mil.): 599.8
Current ratio: —
Long-term debt ($ mil.): 466.2
No. of shares (mil.): 60.7

Dividends
  Yield: —
  Payout: —
Market value ($ mil.): 597.0
R&D as % of sales: —
Advertising as % of sales: —

Stock History

NYSE: LAB

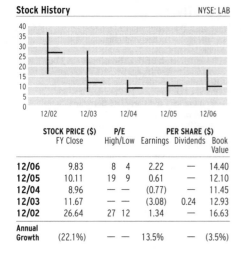

	STOCK PRICE ($) FY Close	P/E High/Low		PER SHARE ($) Earnings	Dividends	Book Value
12/06	9.83	8	4	2.22	—	14.40
12/05	10.11	19	9	0.61	—	12.10
12/04	8.96	—	—	(0.77)	—	11.45
12/03	11.67	—	—	(3.08)	0.24	12.93
12/02	26.64	27	12	1.34	—	16.63
Annual Growth	(22.1%)	—	—	13.5%	—	(3.5%)

Ladish Co.

Ladish got its start in 1905 when Herman Ladish bought a 1,500-pound steam hammer. Today the company designs and manufactures high-strength forged and cast metal components for aerospace and industrial markets. Jet engine parts, missile components, landing gear, helicopter rotors, and other aerospace products generate more than 80% of the company's sales; general industrial components account for the rest. Aerospace industry giants Rolls-Royce, United Technologies, and General Electric together account for 50% of Ladish's sales. Investment firms Provident Investment Counsel, Tygh Capital Management, Luther King Capital Management, and Lazard Asset Management each control about 5% of Ladish.

Ladish is familiar with export markets — about half of its sales come from outside the US (the UK accounts for half of all foreign sales). The company made its first step into manufacturing products overseas by buying Polish industrial forging company HSW-Zaklad Kuznia Matrycowa (ZKM) for $11.3 million in November 2005. Ladish bolstered its ability to produce precision machined aerospace components with the 2006 purchase of Valley Machining of LaCrosse, Wisconsin.

EXECUTIVES

Chairman, President, and CEO: Kerry L. Woody, age 55, $387,813 pay
VP, Engineering: Gene E. Bunge, age 61
VP, Human Resources: Lawrence C. Hammond, age 59, $169,271 pay
VP, Law, Finance, and Secretary: Wayne E. Larsen, age 52, $252,733 pay
VP, Materials Management: David L. Provan, age 57
VP, Quality and Metallurgy: George Groppi, age 58
President, Ladish Forging: Gary J. Vroman, age 47, $185,294 pay
President, Pacific Cast Technologies, Inc.: Randy B. Turner, age 57, $201,000 pay
President and Managing Director, Zaklad Kuznia Matrycowa: Jozef Burdzy, age 55
President, Stowe Machine: John Delaney, age 57
President, Valley Machining: Robert C. Miller, age 56
Auditors: KPMG LLP

LOCATIONS

HQ: Ladish Co., Inc.
5481 S. Packard Ave., Cudahy, WI 53110
Phone: 414-747-2611   **Fax:** 414-747-2963
Web: www.ladishco.com

Ladish has manufacturing plants in the US (Connecticut, Oregon, and Wisconsin) and in Poland.

PRODUCTS/OPERATIONS

2006 Sales

	$ mil.	% of total
Jet engine components	231	62
Aerospace components	69	19
General industrial components	69	19
Total	**369**	**100**

COMPETITORS

Barnes Group
Citation Corporation
Goodrich Corporation
HEICO
Precision Castparts
Titanium Metals
Triumph Group
Wyman-Gordon

HISTORICAL FINANCIALS

Company Type: Public

Income Statement

FYE: December 31

	REVENUE ($ mil.)	NET INCOME ($ mil.)	NET PROFIT MARGIN	EMPLOYEES
12/06	369.3	28.5	7.7%	1,200
12/05	266.8	13.7	5.1%	1,950
12/04	208.7	3.8	1.8%	—
12/03	179.9	0.0	—	—
12/02	188.5	1.6	0.8%	1,074
Annual Growth	18.3%	105.4%	—	2.8%

2006 Year-End Financials

Debt ratio: 30.1%
Return on equity: 21.1%
Cash ($ mil.): 3.4
Current ratio: 3.06
Long-term debt ($ mil.): 46.0
No. of shares (mil.): 14.5
Dividends
  Yield: —
  Payout: —
Market value ($ mil.): 537.8
R&D as % of sales: —
Advertising as % of sales: —

Stock History

NASDAQ (GM): LDSH

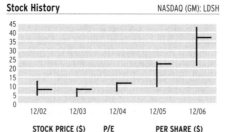

	STOCK PRICE ($) FY Close	P/E High/Low		PER SHARE ($) Earnings	Dividends	Book Value
12/06	37.08	21	11	2.00	—	10.53
12/05	22.35	24	10	0.98	—	8.38
12/04	11.60	42	26	0.28	—	8.96
12/03	8.12	—	—	—	—	8.96
12/02	8.06	104	42	0.12	—	9.09
Annual Growth	46.5%	—	—	102.1%	—	3.7%

Lakes Entertainment

Even though Lakes Entertainment doesn't own a casino, it still keeps its eye on the slots. The company develops and manages Indian-owned casino properties. Lakes Entertainment has agreements with five tribes for new casino development projects in Michigan, California, and Oklahoma. It is also developing a non-Indian casino in Mississippi and new casino table games. In addition, Lakes Entertainment owns some 60% of WPT Enterprises, a producer of gaming-themed TV programming and a gaming Web site. The company ended their relationship with the Kickapoo Tribe of Texas, which involved the management of the tribe's Lucky Eagle Casino, in 2005. Chairman and CEO Lyle Berman owns about 21% of Lakes Entertainment.

WPT Enterprises is the creator of the *World Poker Tour*, a TV show based on a series of poker tournaments that airs on the Travel Channel.

EXECUTIVES

Chairman and CEO: Lyle Berman, age 65, $707,200 pay
President, CFO, Secretary, Treasurer, and Director: Timothy J. Cope, age 55, $497,200 pay
VP Development: Richard Bienapfl, $270,000 pay
VP Human Resources: Christine (Chris) Moon
VP Food and Beverage: Mark Sicilia, $280,000 pay
Investor Relations: Janice Saeugling
Auditors: Piercy Bowler Taylor & Kern

LOCATIONS

HQ: Lakes Entertainment, Inc.
130 Cheshire Ln., Ste. 101, Minnetonka, MN 55305
Phone: 952-449-9092   **Fax:** 952-449-9353
Web: www.lakesgaming.com

COMPETITORS

Bravo Company
Choctaw Resort Development Enterprise
Colville Tribal Enterprise Corporation
Gordon Gaming

HISTORICAL FINANCIALS

Company Type: Public

Income Statement

FYE: Sunday nearest December 31

	REVENUE ($ mil.)	NET INCOME ($ mil.)	NET PROFIT MARGIN	EMPLOYEES
12/06	81.6	19.8	24.3%	50
12/05	23.4	(11.9)	—	—
12/04	17.6	(4.0)	—	—
12/03	4.3	(4.0)	—	—
12/02	1.5	(11.5)	—	30
Annual Growth	171.6%	—	—	13.6%

2006 Year-End Financials

Debt ratio: 51.0%
Return on equity: 10.3%
Cash ($ mil.): 82.4
Current ratio: 3.00
Long-term debt ($ mil.): 104.5
No. of shares (mil.): 22.9
Dividends
  Yield: —
  Payout: —
Market value ($ mil.): 247.6
R&D as % of sales: —
Advertising as % of sales: —

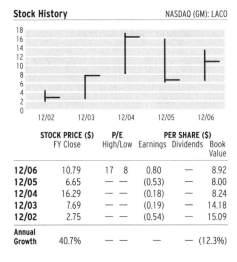

	STOCK PRICE ($) FY Close	P/E High/Low	PER SHARE ($) Earnings	Dividends	Book Value
12/06	10.79	17 8	0.80	—	8.92
12/05	6.65	— —	(0.53)	—	8.00
12/04	16.29	— —	(0.18)	—	8.24
12/03	7.69	— —	(0.19)	—	14.18
12/02	2.75	— —	(0.54)	—	15.09
Annual Growth	40.7%	— —	—	—	(12.3%)

Layne Christensen

Layne Christensen cuts its way through the upper crust. The company provides drilling and construction services primarily related to water, wastewater treatment, and mineral exploration. The company serves such clients as public and private water utilities, industrial companies, mining firms, and heavy civil construction firms. It has operations throughout the Americas, as well as in Africa, Australia, and Europe. Layne Christensen's Water and Wastewater Infrastructure segment accounts for about two-thirds of the company’s sales. Mineral exploration work accounts for most of the remainder. The group has also entered the energy field, producing coalbed methane.

The 2005 purchase of Reynolds gave Layne Christensen new water and wastewater treatment capabilities. The company used the acquisition as impetus to combine its water resources and geoconstruction operations under one new segment, Water and Wastewater Infrastructure, which includes water system development; well and pump rehabilitation; water and wastewater treatment plant construction; sewer rehabilitation; and environmental assessment drilling.

Additional acquisitions have further bolstered the water and wastewater group; in 2007 the company acquired SolmeteX, whose products remove toxins from water, for $13.5 million in cash.

Layne Christensen's Mineral Exploration division provides aboveground and underground drilling services, mainly for mining companies' exploration and development activities. Its services include core drilling, diamond, reverse circulation, dual tube, hammer, and rotary airblast methods.

The company launched its Energy unit in 2002 and is focused on developing unconventional gas, including coalbed methane. Layne Christensen sees the unit as having great growth potential, given increased demand for cleaner-burning fuels. The company has working interests in developed and undeveloped Cherokee Basin properties in Kansas and Oklahoma.

Activist investor Warren Lichtenstein controls about 5% of Layne Christensen through Steel Partners; the hedge fund had owned more than 9% of Layne Christensen, but cut its stake in 2006. Earlier that year, Steel Partners and the company had a go-round regarding the size of the board and how many seats Steel Partners should have on it; after a settlement was reached, Lichtenstein left the board but appointed another Steel Partners affiliate to take the place.

HISTORY

Layne Christensen was formed in 1882 as Layne Inc., a water well drilling equipment maker, by Mahlon Layne, a Kansas homesteader who had experimented with drilling techniques on his own land. During the early 20th century, Layne & Sons drilled water wells for individuals and small cities throughout Kansas. After WWII the company became a regional player. Reflecting its expansion into western states, Layne Inc. changed its name to Layne-Western in the 1960s.

In 1968 the company was acquired by Marley Holdings. Under new management, Layne-Western became an acquisition vehicle. Its most significant purchase in the 1970s was Singer, a major well-drilling and pump-repair business with operations across the western US. In 1991 Layne-Western began providing drilling services for mineral exploration in Mexico.

The next year Marley spun off the company as Layne, Inc. It expanded internationally, opening offices in Mexico and Thailand in 1995 and operating in Argentina, Bolivia, Canada, Chile, and Peru. Also that year Layne acquired Christensen Boyles, a top provider of drilling services for mining concerns. The firm changed its name to Layne Christensen in 1996.

Continuing its acquisition strategy, in 1997 the company acquired Stanley Mining Services, a top Australian and African mining concern, and in 1998 bought two African drilling firms, Drillinti Africa and Afridrill. A year later it acquired Italian pump manufacturer Tecniwell and two Louisiana-based oil and gas service companies, Vibration Technologies and Toledo Oil and Gas Services.

The company created Layne Financial in 2000 to provide funding options for water supply and treatment system upgrade and development. In 2001 Layne Christensen sold manufacturing unit Christensen Products to Swedish industrial equipment maker Atlas Copco. Also that year Layne Water Development and Storage was created to provide risk-management and financial services for water resources and development companies.

In 2002 the group restructured its operations along its primary product lines. To enhance its position in the coalbed methane industry, Layne Christensen acquired oil and gas engineering and geological firm Mohajir Engineering in 2003.

The company sold two of its energy segment subsidiaries in 2004 — Toledo Oil and Gas Services and Layne Christensen Canada Limited. That year Layne Christensen strengthened its water resources presence on the West Coast by acquiring Beylik Drilling and Pump Service, a water drilling company in California, for about $14.7 million.

In 2005 the company purchased privately held Reynolds, a designer and builder of water and wastewater treatment plants, for $60 million and 2.2 million shares of stock. The deal added waste treatment and sewer rehabilitation capabilities to Layne Christensen's offerings.

EXECUTIVES

Chairman: David A. B. Brown, age 63
President, CEO, and Director: Andrew B. Schmitt, age 58, $628,900 pay
EVP and Director: Jeffrey J. (Jeff) Reynolds, age 40, $224,397 pay (prior to promotion)
SVP and Division President, Water Resources: Gregory F. (Greg) Aluce, age 51
SVP and Division President, Mineral Exploration: Eric R. Despain, age 58, $267,220 pay
SVP, General Counsel, and Secretary: Steven F. Crooke, age 50, $258,411 pay
VP, Finance, and Treasurer: Jerry W. Fanska, age 58, $290,463 pay
VP, Human Resources: John Wright
Division President, Geoconstruction: Pier L. Iovino, age 60
Manager, Information Technology: Glenn Johnson
Analyst, Information Technology/Human Resources: Lindsey A. Rupp
Auditors: Deloitte & Touche LLP

LOCATIONS

HQ: Layne Christensen Company
1900 Shawnee Mission Pkwy.,
Mission Woods, KS 66205
Phone: 913-362-0510   **Fax:** 913-362-0133
Web: www.laynechristensen.com

Layne Christensen has about 90 offices, operating in most regions of the US and in Africa, Australia, Canada, Italy, and Mexico. It also works through foreign affiliates in Mexico and South America.

2007 Sales

	$ mil.	% of total
US	596.0	82
Australia/Africa	78.6	11
Mexico	32.8	5
Other	15.4	2
Total	**722.8**	**100**

PRODUCTS/OPERATIONS

2007 Sales

	$ mil.	% of total
Water & Wastewater Infrastructure	531.9	74
Mineral Exploration	148.9	20
Energy	27.1	4
Other	14.9	2
Total	**722.8**	**100**

COMPETITORS

Baker Hughes
Barnwell Industries
Black & Veatch
GeoTek Engineering & Testing Services
Insituform Technologies
Major Drilling Group
Parsons Corporation
STS Consultants
Water Development Corporation

HISTORICAL FINANCIALS

Company Type: Public

Income Statement

FYE: January 31

	REVENUE ($ mil.)	NET INCOME ($ mil.)	NET PROFIT MARGIN	EMPLOYEES
1/07	722.8	26.3	3.6%	3,919
1/06	463.0	14.7	3.2%	3,551
1/05	343.5	9.8	2.9%	—
1/04	272.0	2.7	1.0%	—
1/03	269.9	(13.5)	—	2,414
Annual Growth	27.9%	—	—	12.9%

2007 Year-End Financials

Debt ratio: 73.9%
Return on equity: 14.0%
Cash ($ mil.): 21.3
Current ratio: 1.43
Long-term debt ($ mil.): 151.6
No. of shares (mil.): 15.5

Dividends
  Yield: —
  Payout: —
Market value ($ mil.): 543.6
R&D as % of sales: —
Advertising as % of sales: —

Stock History

NASDAQ (GS): LAYN

	STOCK PRICE ($) FY Close	P/E High/Low		PER SHARE ($) Earnings	Dividends	Book Value
1/07	35.03	22	15	1.68	—	13.21
1/06	30.15	29	14	1.05	—	11.27
1/05	18.50	27	17	0.75	—	8.30
1/04	12.51	63	33	0.21	—	7.47
1/03	8.55	—	—	(1.11)	—	7.03
Annual Growth	42.3%	—	—	—	—	17.1%

LCA-Vision Inc.

LCA-Vision thinks its services are a sight better than glasses. The company provides laser vision correction procedures at more than 60 LasikPlus free-standing facilities. LCA-Vision's facilities treat nearsightedness, farsightedness, and astigmatism primarily using laser-in-situkeratomileusis (LASIK), which reshapes the cornea with a computer-guided excimer laser. Additionally, the company's centers offer photorefractive keratectomy (PRK) and other corrective procedures. LCA-Vision operates through centers located in major cities across more than 30 states.

The company supplies the equipment, facilities, staff, and support services to run the centers, and contracts with independent ophthalmologists to perform eye exams and surgeries. It uses excimer lasers made by Bausch & Lomb, Advanced Medical Optics, and Alcon.

LCA-Vision's strategy for growth is to offset the high-cost of laser vision correction with customer financing plans and arrangements with managed care organizations, as well as to open new laser vision correction centers. It opened 20 new facilities in 2005 and 2006.

EXECUTIVES

Non-Executive Chairman: E. Anthony (Tony) Woods, age 67
CEO and Director: Steven C. Straus, age 52
Principal Financial Officer: Alan H. Buckey, age 46, $285,000 pay
SVP Human Resources: Stephen M. Jones
VP Investor Relations: Patricia Forsythe
Director Human Resources: Karen Leisring
Director Management Information Systems: Mark Good
Chief Marketing Officer: James H. Brenner
Auditors: Ernst & Young LLP

LOCATIONS

HQ: LCA-Vision Inc.
  7840 Montgomery Rd., Cincinnati, OH 45236
Phone: 513-792-9292   **Fax:** 513-792-5620
Web: www.lca-vision.com

LCA-Vision operates centers in 32 states and Washington, DC.

PRODUCTS/OPERATIONS

Selected Subsidiaries

Lasik Insurance Company Ltd.
LCA-Vision (Canada) Inc.
The Baltimore Laser Sight Center, Ltd.
The Toronto Laservision Centre (1992) Inc. (Canada)

COMPETITORS

AmSurg
NovaMed
OptiCare
TLC Vision

HISTORICAL FINANCIALS

Company Type: Public

Income Statement

FYE: December 31

	REVENUE ($ mil.)	NET INCOME ($ mil.)	NET PROFIT MARGIN	EMPLOYEES
12/06	238.9	28.4	11.9%	700
12/05	192.4	31.6	16.4%	574
12/04	127.1	32.0	25.2%	—
12/03	81.4	7.3	9.0%	—
12/02	61.8	(3.8)	—	233
Annual Growth	40.2%	—	—	31.7%

2006 Year-End Financials

Debt ratio: 2.2%
Return on equity: 22.4%
Cash ($ mil.): 98.1
Current ratio: 3.38
Long-term debt ($ mil.): 2.4
No. of shares (mil.): 19.8

Dividends
  Yield: 1.6%
  Payout: 40.3%
Market value ($ mil.): 681.1
R&D as % of sales: —
Advertising as % of sales: —

Stock History

NASDAQ (GS): LCAV

	STOCK PRICE ($) FY Close	P/E High/Low		PER SHARE ($) Earnings	Dividends	Book Value
12/06	34.36	43	22	1.34	0.54	5.51
12/05	47.51	35	15	1.47	0.36	6.94
12/04	23.39	16	8	1.54	0.05	5.53
12/03	14.11	34	3	0.44	—	5.94
12/02	1.52	—	—	(0.23)	—	2.99
Annual Growth	118.0%	—	—	—	228.6%	16.5%

LECG Corporation

You ask, "Can I get a witness?" and LECG answers, "Yes!" The firm provides expert testimony and consulting services to a wide range of corporate clients and government agencies on issues such as competition and antitrust, intellectual property, labor and employment, and property insurance claims. In addition, LECG offers in-depth studies and advisory services. Clients typically come from industries such as energy, financial services, health care and pharmaceuticals, and telecommunications and have included Dow Chemical and New England Power. LECG operates primarily in the US; the firm also has offices elsewhere in the Americas and in Europe and the Asia/Pacific region.

Acquisitions — more than 10 since 2003 — have been a key component of LECG's growth strategy. In 2007 the company acquired Secura Group, a consulting firm targeting the financial services and compliance markets that is expected to add overseas bank customers to LECG's client list. LECG in 2006 bought the assets of BMB Mack Barclay, an expert services firm specializing in economic and accounting issues.

Vice Chairman and co-founder David Teece, a professor in the business school of the University of California, Berkeley, owns about 7% of LECG.

EXECUTIVES

Chairman: Garrett F. Bouton, age 62
Vice Chairman: David J. Teece, age 58
CEO and Director: Michael J. Jeffery, age 59
EVP, CFO, and Assistant Secretary: Steven R. Fife, age 47
EVP and Managing Director, Chicago: Craig Elson
VP, Chief Legal Officer, and Secretary: Marvin A. Tenenbaum, age 55
VP, General Counsel, and Assistant Secretary: Carol Kerr, age 42
Chief Accounting Officer: Gary S. Yellin, age 55
Director of Administration: Tina M. Bussone, age 34
Director Client Services (Los Angeles): Bryan Vitner
Director of Investor Relations: Erin Glenn
Senior Managing Director, Intellectual Property Practice; Office Director, Washington, DC: Robert N. Yerman
Senior Managing Director, National Forensic Accounting (Chicago): John Salomon
Head of Global Financial and Accounting Securities Group: Richard Boulton
Director Marketing and Communications: Maggie T. Watkins
Auditors: Deloitte & Touche LLP

LOCATIONS

HQ: LECG Corporation
  2000 Powell St., Ste. 600, Emeryville, CA 94608
Phone: 510-985-6700   **Fax:** 510-653-9898
Web: www.lecg.com

2006 Sales

	$ mil.	% of total
US	303.7	86
Other countries	50.2	14
Total	353.9	100

PRODUCTS/OPERATIONS

Selected Practice Areas

Antitrust and competition
Bankruptcy
Claims services
Electronic discovery
Energy
Entertainment, sports, and media
Environment and insurance claims
Finance and damages
Forensic accounting
Health care
Intellectual property
International arbitration
Labor and employment
Life sciences
Mergers and acquisitions
Petroleum and chemicals
Property insurance claims
Public policy
Securities
Stock options backdating
Strategy and performance improvement
Telecommunications
Transfer pricing
Transportation

COMPETITORS

Accenture	Deloitte Consulting
Bain & Company	Economics Research
BearingPoint	Associates
Booz Allen	FTI Consulting
Boston Consulting	Huron Consulting
Capgemini	McKinsey & Company
Cornerstone Research	Navigant Consulting
CRA International	PA Consulting

HISTORICAL FINANCIALS

Company Type: Public

Income Statement

FYE: December 31

	REVENUE ($ mil.)	NET INCOME ($ mil.)	NET PROFIT MARGIN	EMPLOYEES
12/06	353.9	21.5	6.1%	1,196
12/05	286.7	22.4	7.8%	1,151
12/04	216.6	17.1	7.9%	—
12/03	165.6	26.7	16.1%	—
12/02	133.7	(12.1)	—	—
Annual Growth	27.6%	—	—	3.9%

2006 Year-End Financials

Debt ratio: —
Return on equity: 10.1%
Cash ($ mil.): 26.5
Current ratio: 2.21
Long-term debt ($ mil.): —
No. of shares (mil.): 24.9
Dividends
  Yield: —
  Payout: —
Market value ($ mil.): 460.3
R&D as % of sales: —
Advertising as % of sales: —

Stock History

NASDAQ (GS): XPRT

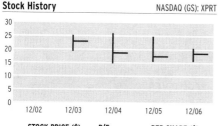

	STOCK PRICE ($) FY Close	P/E High/Low	Earnings	Dividends	Book Value
12/06	18.48	24 19	0.85	—	9.28
12/05	17.38	27 17	0.91	—	8.05
12/04	18.65	35 21	0.73	—	6.77
12/03	22.89	21 17	1.17	—	5.72
Annual Growth	(6.9%)	— —	—	—	—

LHC Group

LHC operates care facilities and provides home health care services to rural markets in the southern US. The company's more than 100 home nursing agencies provide care to Medicare beneficiaries with such services as private duty nursing, physical therapy, and medically oriented social services, while its six hospices provide palliative care for terminal patients. Its four acute-care hospitals are based inside host hospitals and serve patients who no longer need intensive care, but still require complex care in a hospital setting. The company also owns or manages several outpatient rehabilitation clinics and provides rehabilitation services to third parties. Chairman and CEO Keith Myers owns 24% of the company.

Regulatory changes have made it less attractive to operate acute-care hospitals within host hospitals, prompting the company to shift away from such facility-based services. Instead the company sees its future lying with acquisitions of additional home health care businesses in new geographic markets.

To that end, in mid-2006 LHC acquired the Kentucky and Florida-based operations of Lifeline Home Health Care. The company then agreed to sell its ownership in a Georgia medical center. To expand its reach in Tennessee, in 2007 LHC agreed to purchase Extendicare of West Tennessee, which has four home health agencies.

EXECUTIVES

Chairman and CEO: Keith G. Myers, age 48, $393,483 pay
President, COO, and Director: John L. Indest, age 55, $341,993 pay
SVP and CFO: Peter J. (Pete) Roman, age 57
SVP Acquisitions and Market Development: Daryl J. Doise, age 50, $242,157 pay
SVP General Counsel: Richard A. MacMillan, age 56
SVP Operations: Donald D. Stelly, age 39
VP Government Affairs: Harold Taylor
VP and Chief Administrative Officer: Marcus Macip
Director, Clinical Operations, Facilities Based Division: Margaret Blansett
Director, Education and Clinical Program Development: Heidi Landry
Director, Information Systems: Morris Sanford
Director, Investor Relations: Eric C. Elliott
Manager, Human Resources: Lolanda Butler Brown
Manager, Marketing: Blaine Williams
Auditors: Ernst & Young LLP

LOCATIONS

HQ: LHC Group, Inc.
  420 W. Pinhook Rd., Ste. A, Lafayette, LA 70503
Phone: 337-233-1307   **Fax:** 337-235-8037
Web: www.lhcgroup.com

LHC Group has facilities located in Alabama, Arkansas, Florida, Kentucky, Louisiana, Mississippi, Texas, and West Virginia.

PRODUCTS/OPERATIONS

2006 Sales

	$ mil.	% of total
Home-based services	164.7	77
Facility-based services	50.6	23
Total	**215.3**	**100**

COMPETITORS

Almost Family
Amedisys
American HomePatient
Girling Health Care
Guardian Home Care Holdings
Health First
Kindred Healthcare
Personal-Touch Home Care

HISTORICAL FINANCIALS

Company Type: Public

Income Statement

FYE: December 31

	REVENUE ($ mil.)	NET INCOME ($ mil.)	NET PROFIT MARGIN	EMPLOYEES
12/06	215.3	20.6	9.6%	3,959
12/05	162.6	10.1	6.2%	3,415
12/04	123.0	9.3	7.6%	—
12/03	72.4	2.8	3.9%	—
12/02	53.8	2.8	5.2%	—
Annual Growth	41.4%	64.7%	—	15.9%

2006 Year-End Financials

Debt ratio: 2.6%
Return on equity: 20.6%
Cash ($ mil.): 26.9
Current ratio: 4.17
Long-term debt ($ mil.): 3.2
No. of shares (mil.): 17.7
Dividends
  Yield: —
  Payout: —
Market value ($ mil.): 505.5
R&D as % of sales: —
Advertising as % of sales: —

Stock History

NASDAQ (GM): LHCG

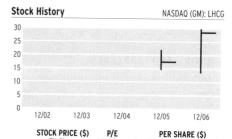

	STOCK PRICE ($) FY Close	P/E High/Low	Earnings	Dividends	Book Value
12/06	28.51	23 11	1.27	—	6.87
12/05	17.43	37 25	0.59	—	4.74
Annual Growth	63.6%	— —	115.3%	—	45.1%

Life Partners Holdings

Life Partners Holdings, parent company of Life Partners, Inc. (LPI), makes its bucks by helping its customers make a buck. The company offers individual consumers viatical and life settlements; the former helps terminally ill patients (such as those living with AIDS and cancer) sell their life insurance policies for immediate cash, while the latter involves LPI purchasing policies from wealthy seniors (defined as a person 65 years of age or older with a life expectancy of 15 years or less). Life Partners makes its money from fees earned by facilitating viatical and life settlements; broker referrals account for about 90% of its business. Chairman and CEO Brian Pardo owns more than 50% of the company.

The company uses Sterling Trust, a subsidiary of United Western Bancorp, as an independent escrow agent to close its transactions.

Life Partners has been stepping up marketing efforts to institutional investors, which the company sees as key to its future growth. Since 2006 it has served as advisor and purchasing agent for a group of closed-end investment funds based in the Bahamas.

EXECUTIVES

Chairman, President, and CEO; CEO, Life Partners, Inc.: Brian D. Pardo, age 64, $450,000 pay
CFO and Treasurer: Nina Piper
Secretary, General Counsel, and Director; President, Life Partners, Inc.: R. Scott Peden, age 43, $166,002 pay
COO and CIO, Life Partners, Inc.: Mark Embry, age 51, $157,415 pay
VP Administration, Life Partners, Inc.: Deborah Carr
VP Policy Administration, Life Partners, Inc.: Kurt D. Carr

LOCATIONS

HQ: Life Partners Holdings, Inc.
204 Woodhew, Waco, TX 76712
Phone: 254-751-7797   **Fax:** 254-751-1025
Web: www.lphi.net

COMPETITORS

Coventry First
Life Equity
Living Benefits

HISTORICAL FINANCIALS

Company Type: Public

Income Statement

FYE: February 28

	ASSETS ($ mil.)	NET INCOME ($ mil.)	INCOME AS % OF ASSETS	EMPLOYEES
2/07	16.6	3.6	21.7%	37
2/06	12.0	1.1	9.2%	37
2/05	10.3	2.7	26.2%	—
2/04	9.0	2.5	27.8%	—
2/03	6.8	1.9	27.9%	—
Annual Growth	25.0%	17.3%	—	0.0%

2007 Year-End Financials

Equity as % of assets: 46.4%
Return on assets: 25.2%
Return on equity: 55.6%
Long-term debt ($ mil.): 0.3
No. of shares (mil.): 9.6
Market value ($ mil.): 77.5
Dividends
  Yield: 2.6%
  Payout: 67.7%
Sales ($ mil.): 29.8
R&D as % of sales: —
Advertising as % of sales: —

Stock History

NASDAQ (GM): LPHI

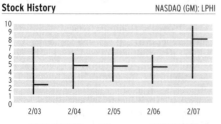

	STOCK PRICE ($) FY Close	P/E High/Low		PER SHARE ($) Earnings	Dividends	Book Value
2/07	8.06	31	10	0.31	0.21	0.80
2/06	4.60	62	21	0.10	0.12	0.54
2/05	4.70	31	13	0.22	0.16	0.65
2/04	4.77	30	9	0.21	0.11	0.51
2/03	2.36	44	8	0.16	0.09	0.40
Annual Growth	35.9%	—	—	18.0%	23.6%	18.9%

LIFE TIME FITNESS

LIFE TIME FITNESS wants to help you keep your New Year's resolutions. The company operates some 60 exercise and recreation centers in 13 states, including Illinois, Indiana, Michigan, Texas, and Virginia.

LIFE TIME FITNESS' facilities offer swimming pools, basketball and racquet courts, child care centers, spas, dining services, and climbing walls, in addition to some 400 pieces of exercise equipment. Membership dues range from about $50 to $60 per month for individuals and from $90 to $130 per month for couples and families. The company's members can access the facilities 24 hours a day, seven days a week.

EXECUTIVES

Chairman and CEO: Bahram Akradi, age 45, $870,000 pay
President and COO: Michael J. Gerend, age 42, $280,000 pay
EVP and CFO: Michael R. (Mike) Robinson, age 47, $280,000 pay
EVP Corporate Development, Secretary, and General Counsel: Eric J. Buss, age 40, $230,000 pay
EVP Real Estate and Development: Mark L. Zaebst, age 47, $261,365 pay
SVP Operations: Mike Brown, age 49
SVP Life Time University: Jeff Zwiefel
SVP Human Resources: Steve Lundeen
VP Marketing: David Campbell
VP Business-to-Business: Guy Gunderson
Auditors: Deloitte & Touche

LOCATIONS

HQ: LIFE TIME FITNESS, Inc.
6442 City West Pkwy., Eden Prairie, MN 55344
Phone: 952-947-0000   **Fax:** 952-947-9137
Web: www.lifetimefitness.com

PRODUCTS/OPERATIONS

2006 Sales

	$ mil.	% of total
Membership dues	339.6	66
In-center revenue (trainers, sales of products, rentals)	138.3	27
Enrollment fees	22.4	4
Other	11.6	3
Total	**511.9**	**100**

COMPETITORS

24 Hour Fitness
Bally Total Fitness
Gold's Gym
LA Fitness
The Sports Club

Town Sports International
Wellbridge
World Gym
YMCA

HISTORICAL FINANCIALS

Company Type: Public

Income Statement

FYE: December 31

	REVENUE ($ mil.)	NET INCOME ($ mil.)	NET PROFIT MARGIN	EMPLOYEES
12/06	511.9	50.6	9.9%	12,350
12/05	390.1	41.2	10.6%	9,500
12/04	312.0	28.9	9.3%	8,400
12/03	256.9	20.6	8.0%	—
12/02	195.2	7.4	3.8%	—
Annual Growth	27.3%	61.7%	—	21.3%

2006 Year-End Financials

Debt ratio: 95.4%
Return on equity: 14.4%
Cash ($ mil.): 6.9
Current ratio: 0.28
Long-term debt ($ mil.): 374.3
No. of shares (mil.): 36.8
Dividends
  Yield: —
  Payout: —
Market value ($ mil.): 1,786.0
R&D as % of sales: —
Advertising as % of sales: —

Stock History

NYSE: LTM

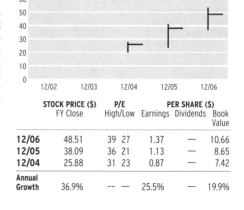

	STOCK PRICE ($) FY Close	P/E High/Low		PER SHARE ($) Earnings	Dividends	Book Value
12/06	48.51	39	27	1.37	—	10.66
12/05	38.09	36	21	1.13	—	8.65
12/04	25.88	31	23	0.87	—	7.42
Annual Growth	36.9%	—	—	25.5%	—	19.9%

LifeCell Corporation

LifeCell puts new life into the tissue graft market. The company makes skin graft materials processed from cadaver skin. Its products, which have been used in more than 900,000 procedures, include AlloDerm, used in reconstructive plastic, dental, and burn surgeries; Cymetra, an injectable form of AlloDerm; and Repliform, used in urologic and gynecological procedures. The company also makes graft products for orthopedic applications. These products are sold in the US and abroad through a direct sales force and distributors that include Boston Scientific, Wright Medical, and Stryker.

LifeCell found itself pulling some of its products off the market in late 2005. Some AlloDerm, Repliform, and GraftJacket products were voluntarily recalled after it was discovered that Biomedical Tissue Services (BTS), a tissue recovery organization used by LifeCell, had not followed FDA guidelines for donor consent and screening. (BTS was accused of stealing body parts from cadavers.) LifeCell relies on some 50 tissue recovery organizations; it no longer uses BTS as a supplier.

The company is researching new applications for its products and plans in 2007 to launch animal-based XenoDerm, a version of AlloDerm made from pig skin.

EXECUTIVES

Chairman, President, and CEO: Paul G. Thomas, age 51, $784,592 pay
SVP Commercial Operations: Lisa N. Colleran, age 49, $378,479 pay
SVP Development and Regulatory Affairs: Bruce S. Lamb, age 51, $268,887 pay (partial-year salary)
VP Finance and Administration and CFO: Steven T. Sobieski, age 50, $336,748 pay
Auditors: PricewaterhouseCoopers LLP

LOCATIONS

HQ: LifeCell Corporation
1 Millennium Way, Branchburg, NJ 08876
Phone: 908-947-1100   **Fax:** 908-947-1200
Web: www.lifecell.com

PRODUCTS/OPERATIONS

2006 Sales

	% of total
Reconstructive	87
Orthopedic	7
Urogynecology	6
Total	**100**

Selected Products

AlloCraft DBM (bone void filler for orthopedic markets, distributed by Stryker)
AlloDerm (skin graft tissue for the reconstructive plastic, burn and dental markets)
Cymetra (skin graft tissue for the reconstructive plastic and dermatology markets)
GraftJacket (skin graft tissue for orthopedic markets, distributed by Wright Medical)
Repliform (skin graft tissue for the urogynecology markets)

COMPETITORS

BioMimetic	Osteotech
C. R. Bard	Regeneration Technologies
Cook Incorporated	Synthes
Forticell Bioscience	Tissue Science Labs
Integra LifeSciences	Tutogen Medical
Johnson & Johnson	W.L. Gore
Mentor Corporation	Wright Medical Group
Organogenesis	

HISTORICAL FINANCIALS

Company Type: Public

Income Statement

FYE: December 31

	REVENUE ($ mil.)	NET INCOME ($ mil.)	NET PROFIT MARGIN	EMPLOYEES
12/06	141.7	20.5	14.5%	335
12/05	94.4	12.0	12.7%	269
12/04	61.1	7.2	11.8%	—
12/03	40.3	18.7	46.4%	—
12/02	34.4	1.4	4.1%	168
Annual Growth	**42.5%**	**95.6%**	**—**	**18.8%**

2006 Year-End Financials

Debt ratio: —
Return on equity: 18.5%
Cash ($ mil.): 71.0
Current ratio: 4.40
Long-term debt ($ mil.): —
No. of shares (mil.): 33.8
Dividends
Yield: —
Payout: —
Market value ($ mil.): 815.5
R&D as % of sales: —
Advertising as % of sales: —

Stock History

NASDAQ (GS): LIFC

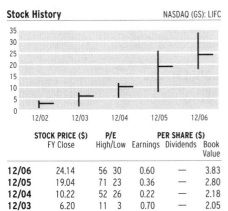

	STOCK PRICE ($) FY Close	P/E High/Low		PER SHARE ($) Earnings	Dividends	Book Value
12/06	24.14	56	30	0.60	—	3.83
12/05	19.04	71	23	0.36	—	2.80
12/04	10.22	52	26	0.22	—	2.18
12/03	6.20	11	3	0.70	—	2.05
12/02	3.01	66	21	0.06	—	0.84
Annual Growth	**68.3%**			**77.8%**	**—**	**46.3%**

Lifetime Brands

Take-out meals and frozen dinners? Not in this lifetime. Lifetime Brands designs and distributes cutlery, cutting boards, bakeware, and kitchen widgets under the Baker's Advantage, Cuisinart, Farberware, Gemco, Hoffritz, Kamenstein, Hoan, and Roshco names, among others. The company also offers items under licensed brands and sells its varied lines in the US and Europe through high-end retailers, supermarkets, and discount stores. The firm operates more than 80 Farberware and Pfaltzgraff outlet stores in 25 states. Founder Milton Cohen and his family own 25% of the firm; his late partners' descendants, CEO Jeffrey Siegel and SVP Craig Phillips, own 22%.

The majority of Lifetime's products are sourced from some 450 suppliers, primarily located in China. To keep its products from going stale, the company developed or redesigned some 3,000 products in 2006 and had made plans to do the same with about 3,600 additional items in 2007.

Lifetime Brands has been busy developing its tabletop segment, allowing its customers to set a full table and the company to boast a complete dinnerware portfolio. Tabletop products represented some 27% of Lifetime Brands' revenue in 2006 and was established primarily through its purchase of Salton and The Pfaltzgraff Co. in 2005. Lifetime Brands also purchased flatware maker Syratech in 2006. Syratech brought with it new product categories, such as picture frames and photo albums. It added to its flatware and sterling silver giftware offerings in 2007 when it bought Lenox Group's Gorham, Kirk Stieff, Whiting, and Durgin brands.

The manufacturer is also targeting Mexico as an area for growth. In 2007 Lifetime Brands acquired a 30% stake in Ekco, which is Mexico's largest housewares maker, for some $23 million. The deal allows Lifetime Brands to expand into Mexico and other Latin American markets.

Those acquisitions are just the latest in a slew of purchases over the past several years that have fueled Lifetime Brands' growth. In addition, the company has been aggressive in licensing brand names, such as DBK-Daniel Boulud Kitchen, Farberware, Joseph Abboud, and Sabatier.

Lifetime Brands tried but failed to acquire the WearEver cookware and bakeware unit of Global Home Products at auction in August 2006.

As the company's largest customer, Wal-Mart (including its Sam's Club warehouse chain) accounts for some 17% of annual sales.

EXECUTIVES

Chairman, President, and CEO: Jeffrey (Jeff) Siegel, age 64, $1,826,869 pay
Vice Chairman and COO: Ronald Shiftan, age 62, $612,054 pay
President, Excel Tabletop Division: Steven Lizak
President, Direct-To-Consumer Division: Bill Margulis
EVP and President, Sales: Evan Miller, age 42, $737,821 pay
EVP; President, Cutlery and Cutting Boards, Bakeware, and At-Home Entertaining Divisions: Robert (Bob) Reichenbach, age 57, $525,000 pay
EVP and Group President, Flatware and Home Decor Divisions: Alan R. Kanter, age 54, $1,735,529 pay

SVP, Finance, Treasurer, and CFO: Laurence Winoker, age 51
SVP and General Manager, Roscho, Casa Moda, and Hoffritz Divisions: Gary Latzman
SVP, Product Development: Bill Lazaroff
SVP, Distribution, Secretary, and Director: Craig Phillips, age 57
SVP and Chief Marketing Officer, Cutlery and Cutting Boards Division: Howard Ammerman
VP; President, Kitchenware Division: Larry Sklute, age 62, $450,040 pay
VP, Product Development: Fred Botterbusch
VP, Human Resources: Mindy Ross
Investor Relations: Harriet Fried
Auditors: Ernst & Young LLP

LOCATIONS

HQ: Lifetime Brands, Inc.
1000 Stewart Ave., Garden City, NY 11530
Phone: 516-683-6000   **Fax:** 516-683-6116
Web: www.lifetimebrands.com

PRODUCTS/OPERATIONS

2006 Sales

	$ mil.	% of total
Wholesale	374.1	82
Direct-to-consumer	83.3	18
Total	**457.4**	**100**

2006 Wholesale Sales

	$ mil.	% of total
Food preparation	239.2	64
Tabletop	100.2	27
Home decor	32.3	9
Other, bath hardware & accessories	2.4	1
Total	**374.1**	**100**

Selected Products

Bakeware
Barbecue accessories
Barware
Cutlery
Cutting boards
Home Furnishings
Kitchenware

COMPETITORS

Anchor Hocking
ARC International
Barbeques Galore
Guy Degrenne
Newell Rubbermaid
Pampered Chef
Tupperware
Wilton Products
WKI Holding

HISTORICAL FINANCIALS

Company Type: Public

Income Statement

FYE: December 31

	REVENUE ($ mil.)	NET INCOME ($ mil.)	NET PROFIT MARGIN	EMPLOYEES
12/06	457.4	15.5	3.4%	1,199
12/05	307.9	14.1	4.6%	1,686
12/04	189.5	8.5	4.5%	—
12/03	160.4	8.4	5.2%	—
12/02	131.2	2.2	1.7%	657
Annual Growth	**36.6%**	**62.9%**	**—**	**16.2%**

2006 Year-End Financials

Debt ratio: 49.5%
Return on equity: 10.3%
Cash ($ mil.): 0.2
Current ratio: 2.58
Long-term debt ($ mil.): 80.0
No. of shares (mil.): 13.3
Dividends
Yield: 1.5%
Payout: 21.9%
Market value ($ mil.): 218.2
R&D as % of sales: —
Advertising as % of sales: —

Stock History

NASDAQ (GS): LCUT

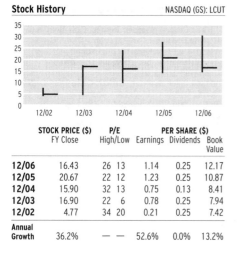

	STOCK PRICE ($) FY Close	P/E High/Low		PER SHARE ($) Earnings	Dividends	Book Value
12/06	16.43	26	13	1.14	0.25	12.17
12/05	20.67	22	12	1.23	0.25	10.87
12/04	15.90	32	13	0.75	0.13	8.41
12/03	16.90	22	6	0.78	0.25	7.94
12/02	4.77	34	20	0.21	0.25	7.42
Annual Growth	36.2%	—	—	52.6%	0.0%	13.2%

Lifeway Foods

Kefir is not milk with a pedigree, but it *is* cultured, and it's the lifeblood of Lifeway Foods. In addition to the yogurt-like dairy beverage called kefir, the company's products include Farmer's Cheese, Sweet Kiss (a sweetened cheese spread), and Soy-Treat, a soy-based kefir. A drinkable yogurt product is aimed at the Hispanic market with the brand name La Fruta. A longtime staple in the dairy cases of health-food stores, Lifeway has seen its distribution area grow as a result of increased production capacity and distribution help from minority shareholder French food giant Groupe Danone.

Lifeway's products are widely available in Illinois (mainly in the Chicago area) and the Philadelphia area. The company's products achieved main-stream status in 2005, having been introduced at Costco, Target, and Wal-Mart stores. Internationally, the company's products are distributed in Canada (Ontario and Quebec provinces).

Lifeway acquired Philadelphia-based cream cheese company Ilya's Farms in 2004. While keeping the Ilya's Farms brand, Lifeway has used its production facilities and distribution center to better penetrate markets in the eastern US. In 2006 it bought kefir maker Helios for approximately $4 million in cash and stock. While no employees lost their jobs, production at Helios' Minnesota plant was transferred to Lifeway's Illinois site.

Groupe Danone owns about 20% of Lifeway.

EXECUTIVES

Chairman: Ludmila Smolyansky, age 58
President, CEO, and Director: Julie Smolyansky, age 31, $139,769 pay
CFO, Chief Accounting Officer, and Controller: Edward P. (Ed) Smolyansky, $123,846 pay
VP Operations and Secretary: Valeriy (Val) Nikolenko, age 61, $106,625 pay
Auditors: Plante & Moran, PLLC

LOCATIONS

HQ: Lifeway Foods, Inc.
6431 W. Oakton St., Morton Grove, IL 60053
Phone: 847-967-1010   **Fax:** 847-967-6558
Web: lifeway.net

PRODUCTS/OPERATIONS

Selected Products
Basics Plus (enhanced kefir beverage)
Golden Zesta (vegetable-based seasoning)
Kefir (cultured milk beverage)
Kefir Starter (powdered mix)
Krestyanski Tworog (kefir-based cheese spread)
La Fruta (yogurt beverage)
Lifeway Farmer Cheese
SoyTreat (soy-based kefir beverage)
Sweet Kiss (sweetened Farmer Cheese spread)
Tuscan (yogurt beverage)

COMPETITORS

8th Continent
Dean Foods
Galaxy Nutritional Foods
General Mills
Hain Celestial
Kraft Foods
Odwalla
Organic Valley
Stonyfield Farm
Tofutti Brands
Vitasoy International
WhiteWave

HISTORICAL FINANCIALS
Company Type: Public

Income Statement			FYE: December 31	
	REVENUE ($ mil.)	NET INCOME ($ mil.)	NET PROFIT MARGIN	EMPLOYEES
12/06	27.7	2.9	10.5%	120
12/05	20.1	2.5	12.4%	86
12/04	16.3	2.0	12.3%	—
12/03	14.9	2.2	14.8%	—
12/02	12.2	1.5	12.3%	50
Annual Growth	22.8%	17.9%	—	24.5%

2006 Year-End Financials
Debt ratio: 24.2%
Return on equity: 13.3%
Cash ($ mil.): 10.0
Current ratio: 5.50
Long-term debt ($ mil.): 5.8
No. of shares (mil.): 16.9
Dividends
  Yield: —
  Payout: —
Market value ($ mil.): 157.9
R&D as % of sales: —
Advertising as % of sales: —

Stock History

NASDAQ (GM): LWAY

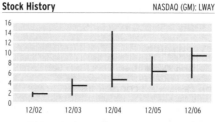

	STOCK PRICE ($) FY Close	P/E High/Low		PER SHARE ($) Earnings	Dividends	Book Value
12/06	9.35	64	30	0.17	—	1.41
12/05	6.22	30	12	0.30	—	2.37
12/04	4.57	118	27	0.12	—	2.12
12/03	3.38	36	12	0.13	—	1.87
12/02	1.76	22	14	0.09	—	2.86
Annual Growth	51.8%	—	—	17.2%	—	(16.3%)

Limco-Piedmont Inc.

Limco-Piedmont wants to keep planes out of limbo while waiting for repairs. The company (formerly Limco-Airepair) performs aircraft component maintenance, repairs, and overhaul services for commercial and military planes as well as air cargo carriers. Most of its work is on heat transfer parts. Limco-Piedmont also makes heat transfer equipment used in airplanes and offers inventory management and parts procurement for airlines. Parts services account for about a quarter of the company's business. Major customers include the US government, KLM Royal Dutch Airlines, Lufthansa, and Bell Helicopter. The company, a subsidiary of Israeli aircraft parts maker TAT Technologies, went public in July 2007.

Limco-Piedmont plans to use IPO proceeds to pay down debt and acquire new businesses. Its last purchase was the 2005 acquisition of Piedmont, which expanded the company's repair and maintenance services from just heat transfer components to auxiliary power units, propellers, pneumatic ducting, and landing gear. It also added the parts services offerings.

EXECUTIVES

Chairman: Giora Inbar
CEO and Director: Shaul Menachem, age 60, $603,742 pay
CFO: Shabtai Moshiashvili, age 34, $80,711 pay (partial-year salary)
President, Piedmont Aviation Component Services: Ehud Netivi
President, Limco Airepair Inc.: Bob Koch
Auditors: Tullius Taylor Sartain & Sartain LLP

LOCATIONS

HQ: Limco-Piedmont Inc.
5304 S. Lawton Ave., Tulsa, OK 74107
Phone: 918-445-4300
Web: www.limcopiedmont.com

2006 Sales	$ mil.	% of total
North America	43.0	73
Europe	12.4	21
Asia	1.6	3
Israel and other	2.0	3
Total	**59.0**	**100**

PRODUCTS/OPERATIONS

2006 Sales	$ mil.	% of total
Maintenance, repair & overhaul services	43.8	74
Parts services	15.2	26
Total	**59.0**	**100**

COMPETITORS

AAR
AMETEK
Chromalloy Gas Turbine Corporation
DAE
Hamilton Sundstrand
Hawker Pacific
Honeywell Aerospace

HISTORICAL FINANCIALS

Company Type: Public

Income Statement

FYE: December 31

	REVENUE ($ mil.)	NET INCOME ($ mil.)	NET PROFIT MARGIN	EMPLOYEES
12/06	59.0	4.3	7.3%	283
12/05	31.7	1.9	6.0%	—
12/04	14.1	1.0	7.1%	—
Annual Growth	104.6%	107.4%	—	—

2006 Year-End Financials

Debt ratio: 23.4%
Return on equity: 28.8%
Cash ($ mil.): 4.3

Current ratio: 1.69
Long-term debt ($ mil.): 4.0

Net Income History

NASDAQ (GM): LIMC

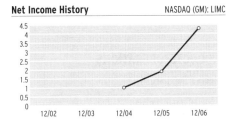

Lindsay Corporation

Drought conditions can sometimes be a blessing for Lindsay Corporation. The company is a leading maker of center-pivot and lateral-move irrigation systems for the agriculture industry. Lindsay sells its Zimmatic irrigation systems through a worldwide network of dealers to farmers in more than 90 countries. Its electrically powered irrigation systems are designed to use both water and labor more efficiently than do traditional "flood" or "surface" irrigation systems. Lindsay also offers replacement parts for its irrigation products. The company's infrastructure division makes movable barriers for traffic management and crash cushions for improved roadway safety.

Strong agricultural commodity prices, lower interest rates, and the Environmental Quality Incentives Program (EQIP) have increased demand for the company's irrigation equipment.

Lindsay Corporation aimed to enter a new market segment in 2006 when it acquired Barrier Systems Inc. of California for $35 million in cash. Barrier Systems is a maker of specialty roadway barriers and crash cushion products used to increase highway safety and reduce traffic congestion.

Later in 2006 Lindsay complimented its new infrastructure segment with the purchase of Italy's Snoline, S.P.A., a maker of road marking and other roadway safety equipment.

In 2007 Lindsay further augmented its infrastructure division with the purchase of certain assets of Traffic Maintenance Attenuators, Inc. and Albert W. Unrath, Inc. (or U-Mad). U-Mad designs truck- and trailer-mounted crash attenuators that improve motorist safety and protect workers in roadway work zones.

Early in 2008 Lindsay grew its irrigation division with the acquisition of Watertronics, Inc., a maker of water pumping stations and controls that are used in the golf, landscaping, and municipal markets.

HISTORY

Lindsay Manufacturing was founded in 1955 as a farm equipment repair firm. In 1969 the company introduced its first Zimmatic-brand center-pivot irrigation system. Diversified agricultural firm DEKALB bought Lindsay in 1974. Gary Parker was appointed Lindsay's CEO in 1984, and in 1988 DEKALB spun off the company.

Lindsay's export revenues grew to a peak of $48 million (44% of total revenues) in 1992. The company began losing market share in Saudi Arabia (its major non-US market) when the Saudi government put an end to farm subsidies in 1994. That year investment firm Bass Management Trust, led by Perry, Sid, and Lee Bass, bought an initial 7% stake in the firm. In 1995 exports slumped to only 10% of total revenues.

Bass Management Trust increased its stake in Lindsay to about 18% in 1997, then upped it to 27% the following year. With the Asian financial crisis hurting foreign sales and US farmers unable to afford equipment outlays, Lindsay's revenues dropped 25% in fiscal 1999. That year Bass Management Trust decreased its stake in the company to 15%.

Parker retired in 2000. He was replaced by Richard Parod, who had been the VP of Toro Corporation's Irrigation Division. Also that year Lindsay acquired Colorado-based irrigation systems maker Oasis Enterprises.

In 2001 Lindsay acquired a facility in La Chappelle d'Aligne, France, in order to establish a European location for the manufacture of its irrigation products. As part of its continuing global expansion, Lindsay established Lindsay Africa to promote local manufacturing, inventory, and support for the long term in 2002.

In 2003 the company introduced its Growth Smart Micro Climate Station, which enables farmers to monitor precise evapotranspiration readings and graphic modeling to predict potentially damaging situations in the fields. In 2006 the company changed its name from Lindsay Manufacturing to Lindsay Corporation.

EXECUTIVES

Chairman: Michael N. Christodolou, age 46
President, CEO, and Director: Richard W. (Rick) Parod, age 54, $4,330,556 pay
SVP Finance, CFO, Treasurer, and Secretary: David B. Downing, age 52, $355,366 pay
VP Domestic Sales: Robert S. Snoozy, age 61, $258,918 pay
VP Research and Development: Charles H. Meis, age 61
VP and CIO: Douglas A. Taylor, age 44
VP Manufacturing: Matthew T. Cahill, age 45, $242,129 pay
VP Engineering: Jochen Pfrenger, age 41
VP Marketing: Dirk A. Lenie, age 53, $256,544 pay
VP Market Services: Gary E. Kaplan, age 46
VP Human Resources: Randy S. Hester, age 44
VP International Irrigation: Samir A. Haidar, age 56
VP Corporate Development: Mark A. Roth, age 33
Auditors: KPMG LLP

LOCATIONS

HQ: Lindsay Corporation
    2707 N. 108th St., Ste. 102, Omaha, NE 68164
Phone: 402-428-2131   **Fax:** 402-428-7232
Web: www.lindsaymanufacturing.com

2007 Sales

	$ mil.	% of total
US	192.5	68
Europe, Africa, Australia & Middle East	57.4	20
Mexico & Latin America	19.4	7
Other regions	12.6	5
Total	**281.9**	**100**

PRODUCTS/OPERATIONS

2007 Sales

	$ mil.	% of total
Irrigation	216.5	77
Infrastructure	65.4	23
Total	**281.9**	**100**

Selected Products

Irrigation
    Center-pivot irrigation systems
    Chemical injection systems
    Irrigation controls
    Lateral-move irrigation systems
    Remote monitoring and control systems
Infrastructure
    Crash cushions
    Movable barriers
    Specialty barriers

COMPETITORS

AK Steel
Habasit Holding USA
Irrideco International
Quanex Corporation
Toro
Valmont Industries

HISTORICAL FINANCIALS

Company Type: Public

Income Statement

FYE: August 31

	REVENUE ($ mil.)	NET INCOME ($ mil.)	NET PROFIT MARGIN	EMPLOYEES
8/07	281.9	15.6	5.5%	899
8/06	226.0	11.7	5.2%	763
8/05	177.3	4.8	2.7%	645
8/04	196.7	9.3	4.7%	—
8/03	163.4	12.9	7.9%	—
Annual Growth	14.6%	4.9%	—	18.1%

2007 Year-End Financials

Debt ratio: 22.5%
Return on equity: 11.9%
Cash ($ mil.): 48.6
Current ratio: 2.91
Long-term debt ($ mil.): 31.8
No. of shares (mil.): 17.7

Dividends
    Yield: 0.7%
    Payout: 19.8%
Market value ($ mil.): 719.2
R&D as % of sales: —
Advertising as % of sales: —

Stock History

NYSE: LNN

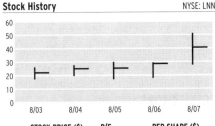

	STOCK PRICE ($) FY Close	P/E High/Low		PER SHARE ($) Earnings	Dividends	Book Value
8/07	40.53	39	21	1.31	0.26	7.95
8/06	28.52	29	18	1.00	0.25	6.87
8/05	25.30	72	43	0.41	0.17	9.49
8/04	24.96	35	26	0.78	0.16	9.53
8/03	22.10	24	16	1.08	0.16	8.89
Annual Growth	16.4%	—	—	4.9%	12.9%	(2.8%)

Linn Energy

It's a Linn-Linn situation. CEO Michael Linn's namesake company Linn Energy has successfully drilled for natural gas in the Appalachian Basin. The natural gas exploration and production company has made 17 property acquisitions between 2003 and 2007 in California, New York, Oklahoma, Pennsylvania, Texas, Virginia, and West Virginia. The company has proved reserves of 454.1 billion cu. ft. of natural gas equivalent. Linn Energy has focused on shallow drilling (2,500 to 5,500 feet). In 2007 the company acquired Dominion Resource's mid-continental exploration and production assets for $2.05 billion. Quantum Energy Partners controls 17.6% of Linn Energy; CEO Linn, 7.3%.

Linn Energy has pursued a strategy of buying mature properties and extending the life of these natural gas fields by workovers and improved field operations, including the use of additional production equipment and drilling activities.

In 2007 the company agreed to buy Lamamco Drilling's mid-continental oil and gas properties for $552 million.

EXECUTIVES

Chairman and CEO: Michael C. (Mike) Linn, age 55
President and COO: Mark E. Ellis, age 51
EVP and CFO: Kolja Rockov, age 36
SVP and Secretary: Roland P. (Chip) Keddie, age 54
SVP and Chief Accounting Officer: Lisa D. Anderson, age 45
SVP, Eastern Operations: Thomas A. (Tom) Lopus, age 48
SVP, Western Operations: Arden L. Walker Jr., age 47
SVP, General Counsel, and Corporate Secretary: Charlene A. Ripley, age 43
VP Gathering and Marketing, Penn West Pipeline: Curtis L. Tipton, age 47
VP Investor Relations: Clay P. Jeansonne
Auditors: KPMG LLP

LOCATIONS

HQ: Linn Energy, LLC
J P Morgan Chase Tower, 600 Travis, Ste. 7000, Houston, TX 77002
Phone: 281-605-4100   **Fax:** 281-605-4104
Web: www.linnenergy.com

PRODUCTS/OPERATIONS

2006 Sales

	$ mil.	% of total
Gain on oil & gas derivatives	103.3	54
Natural gas & oil	80.4	42
Natural gas marketing	5.6	3
Other	1.8	1
Total	**191.1**	**100**

COMPETITORS

Belden & Blake
Cabot Oil & Gas
Equitable Resources
Petroleum Development
Range Resources

HISTORICAL FINANCIALS

Company Type: Public

Income Statement

FYE: December 31

	REVENUE ($ mil.)	NET INCOME ($ mil.)	NET PROFIT MARGIN	EMPLOYEES
12/06	191.1	79.2	41.4%	220
12/05	49.7	(56.3)	—	130
12/04	21.9	(4.0)	—	—
12/03	3.3	(1.3)	—	—
Annual Growth	**286.9%**	**—**	**—**	**69.2%**

2006 Year-End Financials

Debt ratio: 97.2%
Return on equity: 39.2%
Cash ($ mil.): 44.4
Current ratio: 3.87
Long-term debt ($ mil.): 438.2
No. of shares (mil.): 33.6
Dividends
  Yield: 3.6%
  Payout: 44.1%
Market value ($ mil.): 1,074.1
R&D as % of sales: —
Advertising as % of sales: —

Stock History

NASDAQ (GS): LINE

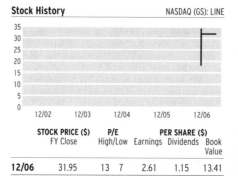

	STOCK PRICE ($) FY Close	P/E High/Low	PER SHARE ($) Earnings	PER SHARE ($) Dividends	PER SHARE ($) Book Value
12/06	31.95	13 7	2.61	1.15	13.41

LivePerson, Inc.

LivePerson wants to inject some life into your customer service operations. The company provides online, hosted software applications that enable retailers and other companies selling goods online to communicate with customers. LivePerson's Timpani software enables communications through multiple channels, including text-based chat, e-mail, and customer self-service tools. Clients install an icon on their Web sites that, when clicked, opens a dialogue window with customer service representatives. As part of its services, LivePerson also maintains transcripts of customer interactions and offers the option of conducting user exit surveys.

LivePerson provides its services via the application service provider (ASP) model, hosting all of the required software on its servers. In addition to its click-to-chat services, the company also offers tools to manage online sales as well as FAQ, e-mail, and document management services.

The company's clients come from fields such as retail, computer software and hardware, telecommunications, and financial services; customers have included Microsoft, Neiman Marcus, and EarthLink. In 2006 the company acquired Proficient Systems, a provider of hosted proactive chat applications.

EXECUTIVES

Chairman and CEO: Robert P. LoCascio, age 38, $275,000 pay
President, CFO, and Director: Timothy E. (Tim) Bixby, age 42
EVP Marketing: Kevin Kohn
EVP and General Manager, Tel Aviv: Eli Campo
SVP Product Marketing: Jackson L. (Jack) Wilson Jr., age 59
SVP Sales: Jim Dicso
General Manager, SMB: Philippe Lang
Co-CTO: Tal Goldberg
Co-CTO: Eyal Halahmi
Auditors: BDO Seidman, LLP

LOCATIONS

HQ: LivePerson, Inc.
462 7th Ave., 3rd Fl., New York, NY 10018
Phone: 212-609-4200   **Fax:** 212-609-4201
Web: www.liveperson.com

PRODUCTS/OPERATIONS

Selected Software

Timpani suite
  Timpani Contact Center
  Timpani Sales and Marketing
  Timpani SB Chat (for small businesses)
  Timpani SB Contact Center (for small businesses)

COMPETITORS

eGain Communications
Kana
Oracle
RightNow Technologies

HISTORICAL FINANCIALS

Company Type: Public

Income Statement

FYE: December 31

	REVENUE ($ mil.)	NET INCOME ($ mil.)	NET PROFIT MARGIN	EMPLOYEES
12/06	33.5	2.2	6.6%	178
12/05	22.3	2.5	11.2%	111
12/04	17.4	2.1	12.1%	—
12/03	12.0	(0.8)	—	—
12/02	8.2	(6.8)	—	64
Annual Growth	**42.2%**	**—**	**—**	**29.1%**

2006 Year-End Financials

Debt ratio: —
Return on equity: 8.5%
Cash ($ mil.): 21.7
Current ratio: 3.38
Long-term debt ($ mil.): —
No. of shares (mil.): 41.1
Dividends
  Yield: —
  Payout: —
Market value ($ mil.): 214.8
R&D as % of sales: —
Advertising as % of sales: —

Stock History

NASDAQ (CM): LPSN

	STOCK PRICE ($) FY Close	P/E High/Low	PER SHARE ($) Earnings	PER SHARE ($) Dividends	PER SHARE ($) Book Value
12/06	5.23	157 74	0.05	—	0.84
12/05	5.61	95 37	0.06	—	0.45
12/04	3.15	125 37	0.05	—	0.36
12/03	5.00	— —	(0.02)	—	0.25
12/02	0.94	— —	(0.20)	—	0.23
Annual Growth	**53.6%**	**— —**	**—**	**—**	**38.0%**

LKQ Corporation

Ever wonder what happens to a car once the insurance company declares it "totaled"? Enter LKQ. A nationwide recycler of damaged cars, LKQ buys wrecked cars at auction and distributes the reusable parts to collision repair and mechanical repair shops. LKQ buys popular models such as the Honda Accord, Toyota Camry, and Ford Explorer, from which it salvages reusable parts including engines, front-end assemblies, doors, and fenders. The company sells mechanical parts that can't be reused as-is to parts reconditioners; items such as fluids, batteries, and tires are sold to other recyclers. LKQ operates from more than 100 facilities throughout the US.

LKQ expanded in December 2005 by buying A-Reliable Auto Parts, an operator of three parts recycling facilities in the Chicago area, and Fit-Rite Body Parts, an operator of seven replacement parts warehouses in the northeastern US. In February 2006 the company acquired Transwheel, a refurbisher and distributor of aluminum alloy wheels. Later that year LKQ bought an aftermarket business, operating under the name Global Automotive Parts, with warehouses in California, Oregon, and Washington. LKQ also acquired three parts recycling facilities in Michigan around the same time.

In 2007 LKQ again expanded its network of automotive recycling centers with the purchase of Pintendre Autos, Inc. of Canada. Pintendre has annual sales of about $29 million.

Later in 2007 LKQ acquired fellow aftermarket parts concern Keystone Automotive for about $811 million. The combined company can provide a more comprehensive assortment of reusable replacement parts while enhancing customer service with a larger network of distribution centers. Keystone is now a subsidiary of LKQ.

Because insurance companies and extended warranty providers influence decisions about which replacement parts are used, LKQ leverages its national distribution system to build relationships with those companies, some of which maintain networks of repair facilities.

Chairman Donald Flynn owns about 7% of LKQ; SVP Leonard Damron owns a 6% stake.

EXECUTIVES

Chairman: Donald F. Flynn, age 67
President, CEO, and Director: Joseph M. Holsten, age 55, $1,250,000 pay
EVP and CFO: Mark T. Spears, age 50, $690,000 pay
SVP, Southeast Region: Leonard A. Damron, age 56, $390,000 pay
SVP, Development, Associate General Counsel, and Assistant Secretary: Walter P. Hanley, age 41, $330,022 pay
VP, Finance and Controller: Frank P. Erlain, age 52
VP, General Counsel, and Secretary: Victor M. Casini, age 45
VP, Midwest Region: H. Bradley Willen, age 48, $330,000 pay
VP, Insurance Services and Aftermarket Operations: Robert L. Wagman, age 43
VP, West and Central Regions and Core Operations: Steven H. Jones, age 48, $375,000 pay
Director; President and CEO, Keystone Automotive Industries: Richard L. (Rick) Keister, age 61
Auditors: Deloitte & Touche LLP

LOCATIONS

HQ: LKQ Corporation
120 N. LaSalle St., Ste. 3300, Chicago, IL 60602
Phone: 312-621-1950   **Fax:** 312-621-1969
Web: www.lkqcorp.com

COMPETITORS

ArvinMeritor	Schnitzer Steel
Delphi	Valeo
Federal-Mogul	VDO Automotive

HISTORICAL FINANCIALS

Company Type: Public

Income Statement

FYE: December 31

	REVENUE ($ mil.)	NET INCOME ($ mil.)	NET PROFIT MARGIN	EMPLOYEES
12/06	789.4	44.4	5.6%	4,270
12/05	547.4	30.9	5.6%	3,370
12/04	424.8	20.6	4.8%	—
12/03	328.0	14.6	4.5%	—
12/02	287.1	(38.9)	—	—
Annual Growth	28.8%	—	—	26.7%

2006 Year-End Financials

Debt ratio: 22.9%
Return on equity: 12.0%
Cash ($ mil.): 4.0
Current ratio: 2.99
Long-term debt ($ mil.): 92.0
No. of shares (mil.): 53.3

Dividends
  Yield: —
  Payout: —
Market value ($ mil.): 1,225.4
R&D as % of sales: —
Advertising as % of sales: —

Stock History

NASDAQ (GS): LKQX

	STOCK PRICE ($) FY Close	P/E High/Low	PER SHARE ($) Earnings	Dividends	Book Value
12/06	22.99	64 44	0.40	—	7.53
12/05	17.31	57 26	0.31	—	6.64
12/04	10.03	45 29	0.23	—	9.90
12/03	8.98	46 35	0.20	—	8.93
Annual Growth	36.8%	— —	—	—	2.3%

LMI Aerospace

It don't mean a thing if it ain't got a wing. LMI Aerospace makes key airplane structures, including door frames, cockpit window-frame assemblies, wing leading-edge skins, flap slats, fuselage skins, and interior components. The company fabricates, machines, finishes, and integrates more than 30,000 aluminum and specialty alloy components for commercial, corporate, and military aircraft. LMI's Tempco unit offers machining services to companies in the medical and semiconductor technology industries as well as for aircraft manufacturers. Major customers include Boeing, Gulfstream, Bombardier, Sikorsky, and Spirit AeroSystems. CEO Ronald Saks owns about 22% of the company.

In February 2006 LMI diversified by acquiring consulting firm Technical Change Associates (TCA), which specializes in lean manufacturing, facility layout and business planning. The Ogden, Utah-based company had contracted with LMI since 1993; it will continue to operate as a stand-alone entity.

The following year LMI acquired D3 Technologies, Inc., a provider of engineering and design services to commercial and military aircraft, for $65 million. D3 customers have included Boeing, Airbus North America, Vought, and Spirit AeroSystems.

EXECUTIVES

Chairman: Joseph Burstein, age 79
President, CEO, and Director: Ronald S. (Ron) Saks, age 63, $270,600 pay
CFO and Secretary: Lawrence E. (Ed) Dickinson, age 47, $186,242 pay
VP, Operations, Central Region: Robert T. (Bob) Grah, age 52, $198,736 pay
VP, Regional Manager: Duane E. Hahn, age 51
CIO and Director of Supplier Management and Procurement: Michael J. (Mike) Biffignani, age 47, $175,275 pay
Director, Military Market Sector: Ted Kretschmar
Director, Human Resources: Cindy Maness
Director, Quality Assurance: Bruce Grimes
President and CEO, D3 Technologies: Ryan P. Bogan
Auditors: BDO Seidman, LLP

LOCATIONS

HQ: LMI Aerospace, Inc.
411 Fountain Lakes Blvd., St. Charles, MO 63301
Phone: 636-946-6525   **Fax:** 636-949-1576
Web: www.lmiaerospace.com

LMI Aerospace has facilities in California, Georgia, Kansas, Missouri, Oklahoma, Texas, and Washington, as well as in Mexico.

PRODUCTS/OPERATIONS

Selected Products

Cockpit window-frame assemblies
Door-assembly structural details
Fuselage skins and supports
Interior component details
Landing-light lens assemblies
Leading-edge wing slats, flaps, and lens assemblies
Passenger and cargo door frames and supports
Structural sheet metal and extruded components
Thrust reversers and engine nacelles/cowlings
Wing panels and floor beams
Wing skins

COMPETITORS

AAR
Avcorp Industries
BE Aerospace
Breeze-Eastern
CPI Aerostructures
DeCrane
Ducommun
Goodrich Corporation
HEICO
Magellan Aerospace
Synchronous Aerospace

HISTORICAL FINANCIALS

Company Type: Public

Income Statement

FYE: December 31

	REVENUE ($ mil.)	NET INCOME ($ mil.)	NET PROFIT MARGIN	EMPLOYEES
12/06	123.0	10.7	8.7%	916
12/05	101.1	5.2	5.1%	673
12/04	85.9	0.4	0.5%	—
12/03	75.9	(4.0)	—	—
12/02	81.3	(8.3)	—	884
Annual Growth	10.9%	—	--	0.9%

2006 Year-End Financials

Debt ratio: 0.6%
Return on equity: 16.4%
Cash ($ mil.): 26.6
Current ratio: 5.65
Long-term debt ($ mil.): 0.6
No. of shares (mil.): 11.2

Dividends
  Yield: —
  Payout: —
Market value ($ mil.): 173.2
R&D as % of sales: —
Advertising as % of sales: —

Stock History

NASDAQ (GM): LMIA

	STOCK PRICE ($) FY Close	P/E High/Low	PER SHARE ($) Earnings	Dividends	Book Value
12/06	15.48	24 12	1.01	—	8.09
12/05	14.16	26 7	0.61	—	4.76
12/04	5.41	167 20	0.05	—	4.17
12/03	1.99	— —	(0.49)	—	4.13
12/02	2.16	— —	(1.03)	—	4.61
Annual Growth	63.6%	— —	—	—	15.1%

Logility, Inc.

Logility brings logic and agility to the task of managing global supply chains. The company's Voyager software helps large corporations manage relationships with raw materials suppliers, distributors, partners, and customers. Compatible with a variety of enterprise resource planning software, including offerings from IBM and SSA Global Technologies, Logility's products address specific supply chain needs, such as boosting inventory in response to promotions, or collaborating online with partners and suppliers. Customers have included Haverty's Furniture, Mercury Marine, and Pfizer. The company sells its products both directly and through American Software, which owns an 88% stake in Logility.

Looking to expand its international business, the company acquired Demand Management (also known as Demand Solutions) in 2004 for $9.5 million in cash. Demand Management's value-added reseller network extended to more than 70 countries around the world.

HISTORY

Logility was originally the Supply Chain Planning division of American Software. James Edenfield and Thomas Newberry started American Computer Systems in 1970 after leaving top jobs at a software development company. They developed a sales forecasting program for textile maker West Point-Pepperell (now West Point-Stevens), modified it for sale to other textile producers, and then adapted and sold the software to companies outside the textile industry. In 1978 American Computer Systems merged with American Software & Computer (founded 1971) and adopted the name American Software.

In 1997 American Software formed Logility and combined it with another subsidiary, Distribution Sciences, an operation that became Logility's transportation management and planning unit. Logility went public that year. Later it introduced a software suite designed for the pharmaceutical industry. In 1998 Logility expanded its reach through distribution agreements with vendors in Mexico and Brazil.

Logility, staking a claim online, introduced a suite of Web-based business-to-business software products and application hosting services in 1999.

In 2004 Logility formed a business alliance with Adjoined Consulting, which provides management and technology consulting services.

EXECUTIVES

Chairman: James C. Edenfield, age 72
President, CEO, and Director:
  J. Michael (Mike) Edenfield, age 49, $765,000 pay
CFO: Vincent C. (Vince) Klinges, age 44, $212,000 pay
EVP Worldwide Sales and Marketing: H. Allan Dow, age 43, $465,686 pay
VP Customer Service: Donald L. Thomas, age 60, $224,201 pay
VP Marketing: Karin L. Bursa
VP Research and Development: Mark A. Balte
VP Professional Services: Leonard G. Sherwinski
Controller and Principal Accounting Officer:
  Herman Moncrief, age 33
Investor Relations: Pat McManus
Media Relations: Michelle Duke
Auditors: KPMG LLP

LOCATIONS

HQ: Logility, Inc.
  470 E. Paces Ferry Rd. NE, Atlanta, GA 30305
Phone: 404-261-9777   **Fax:** 404-264-5206
Web: www.logility.com

2007 Sales

	% of total
US	85
Other countries	15
Total	**100**

PRODUCTS/OPERATIONS

2007 Sales

	$ mil.	% of total
Maintenance	20.7	47
License fees	16.3	37
Services & other	6.8	16
Total	**43.8**	**100**

COMPETITORS

i2 Technologies
JDA Software
Oracle
RedPrairie
SAP

HISTORICAL FINANCIALS

Company Type: Public

Income Statement

FYE: April 30

	REVENUE ($ mil.)	NET INCOME ($ mil.)	NET PROFIT MARGIN	EMPLOYEES
4/07	43.8	6.0	13.7%	137
4/06	37.3	8.0	21.4%	139
4/05	24.9	(0.6)	—	141
4/04	22.8	1.7	7.5%	—
4/03	24.8	2.3	9.3%	—
Annual Growth	15.3%	27.1%	—	(1.4%)

2007 Year-End Financials

Debt ratio: —
Return on equity: 16.2%
Cash ($ mil.): 32.3
Current ratio: 2.66
Long-term debt ($ mil.): —
No. of shares (mil.): 12.9

Dividends
  Yield: —
  Payout: —
Market value ($ mil.): 127.2
R&D as % of sales: —
Advertising as % of sales: —

Stock History

NASDAQ (GM): LGTY

	STOCK PRICE ($) FY Close	P/E High/Low	PER SHARE ($) Earnings	Dividends	Book Value
4/07	9.85	26 14	0.45	—	3.13
4/06	9.70	21 7	0.60	—	2.63
4/05	4.30	— —	(0.05)	—	2.39
4/04	4.94	47 25	0.13	—	2.46
4/03	3.30	24 11	0.17	—	2.34
Annual Growth	31.4%	— —	27.6%	—	7.5%

LoJack Corporation

LoJack's signature product helps police recover stolen vehicles — a chilling thought for those driving hot cars. When a car equipped with a LoJack transmitter is stolen, its radio signal is activated and tracked by police. LoJack rents tracking computers to law enforcement agencies, then markets transponders to dealers and operators in some 25 states and the District of Columbia. The company also markets products for cargo tracking and recovery. LoJack provides installation and maintenance of its units, which are manufactured by third parties. The company markets its products internationally in more than 25 countries. Canada-based subsidiary Boomerang Tracking uses cellular technology to track stolen vehicles.

LoJack believes that its radio-frequency (RF) technology and Boomerang's cellular technology are superior to Global Positioning System (GPS)-based tracking systems, which cannot detect objects in buildings or containers. However, LoJack is researching ways to combine RF, cellular, and GPS technologies in a new product that would allow for increased geographic coverage.

EXECUTIVES

Chairman and CEO: Richard T. Riley, age 51
President, COO, and Director:
Ronald V. (Ron) Waters III, age 55
EVP, General Counsel, and Clerk: Thomas A. Wooters, age 66, $249,212 pay
EVP and CTO: William R. Duvall, age 55, $265,077 pay
SVP and CFO: Michael Umana, age 44, $203,000 pay
SVP; General Manager, International: Thomas M. Camp, age 43
SVP; General Manager, U.S. Automotive:
Kevin M. Mullins, age 52, $221,173 pay
Director Human Resources: Mark Bornemann
Director Corporate Communications: Paul McMahon
Auditors: Deloitte & Touche LLP

LOCATIONS

HQ: LoJack Corporation
200 Lowder Brook Dr., Ste. 1000,
Westwood, MA 02090
Phone: 781-251-4700   **Fax:** 781-251-4649
Web: www.lojack.com

2006 Sales

	$ mil.	% of total
Domestic	147.0	69
International	46.4	22
Boomerang	19.9	9
Total	**213.3**	**100**

COMPETITORS

Audiovox	Remote Dynamics
Directed Electronics	STRATTEC
Ituran	Winner International
OnStar	

HISTORICAL FINANCIALS

Company Type: Public

Income Statement

FYE: December 31

	REVENUE ($ mil.)	NET INCOME ($ mil.)	NET PROFIT MARGIN	EMPLOYEES
12/06	213.3	16.5	7.7%	913
12/05	190.7	18.4	9.6%	890
12/04	145.7	10.4	7.1%	—
12/03	125.8	7.6	6.0%	—
12/02	116.4	1.8	1.5%	688
Annual Growth	**16.3%**	**74.0%**	**—**	**7.3%**

2006 Year-End Financials

Debt ratio: 8.4%
Return on equity: 15.4%
Cash ($ mil.): 46.5
Current ratio: 2.22
Long-term debt ($ mil.): 9.2
No. of shares (mil.): 18.6
Dividends
  Yield: —
  Payout: —
Market value ($ mil.): 317.3
R&D as % of sales: —
Advertising as % of sales: —

Stock History

NASDAQ (GS): LOJN

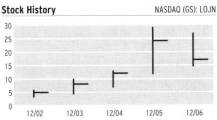

	STOCK PRICE ($) FY Close	P/E High/Low		Earnings	PER SHARE ($) Dividends	Book Value
12/06	17.08	31	17	0.86	—	5.92
12/05	24.13	30	12	0.96	—	5.49
12/04	12.09	20	11	0.64	—	3.71
12/03	8.06	19	9	0.51	—	1.95
12/02	4.94	47	28	0.12	—	1.38
Annual Growth	**36.4%**		**—**	**63.6%**	**—**	**43.9%**

LoopNet, Inc.

Feeling out of the loop when it comes to commercial real estate? LoopNet provides information services to the commercial real estate market through its namesake Web site, LoopNet.com, an online marketplace that includes approximately 515,000 property listings. The company offers a free basic membership, as well as a subscription-based premium membership. LoopNet has about 2.2 million registered members. The company also offers LoopLink, which helps real estate brokers integrate LoopNet listings into their own Web sites; BizBuySell, an online marketplace for operating businesses that are for sale; and commercial real estate network Cityfeet.com.

In 2007 LoopNet acquired online firm Cityfeet.com. The deal, worth about $15 million, adds Cityfeet.com's online distribution network for commercial property listings to LoopNet's business. The Cityfeet Network distributes listings to more than 100 partners, including the Web sites of the *New York Times*, the *Boston Globe*, and the *Los Angeles Times*.

EXECUTIVES

Chairman and CEO: Richard J. (Rich) Boyle Jr., $261,750 pay
President and COO: Thomas Byrne, $209,000 pay
SVP Finance and Administration, CFO, and Secretary:
Brent Stumme, age 45, $209,000 pay
SVP Information Technology and CTO:
Wayne Warthen, age 43, $205,200 pay
SVP Business and Product Development and Chief Product Officer: Jason Greenman, age 39, $209,000 pay
Public Relations: Cary Brazeman
Auditors: Ernst & Young LLP

LOCATIONS

HQ: LoopNet, Inc.
185 Berry St., Ste. 4000, San Francisco, CA 94107
Phone: 415-243-4200   **Fax:** 415-764-1622
Web: www.loopnet.com

PRODUCTS/OPERATIONS

Selected Offerings

BizBuySell (businesses for sale listings)
Cityfeet (online commercial real estate network)
LoopLink (listing integration service)
LoopLender (financing service)
LoopNet.com (commercial real estate listings)

COMPETITORS

CoStar Group	PropertyInfo
Fidelity National Financial	Stewart Transaction
First American	Solutions
First American RES	

HISTORICAL FINANCIALS

Company Type: Public

Income Statement

FYE: December 31

	REVENUE ($ mil.)	NET INCOME ($ mil.)	NET PROFIT MARGIN	EMPLOYEES
12/06	48.4	15.5	32.0%	198
12/05	31.0	18.9	61.0%	138
12/04	17.0	3.7	21.8%	—
12/03	10.5	1.7	16.2%	—
Annual Growth	**66.4%**	**108.9%**	**—**	**43.5%**

2006 Year-End Financials

Debt ratio: —
Return on equity: 39.4%
Cash ($ mil.): 89.0
Current ratio: 9.03
Long-term debt ($ mil.): —
No. of shares (mil.): 37.9
Dividends
  Yield: —
  Payout: —
Market value ($ mil.): 567.7
R&D as % of sales: —
Advertising as % of sales: —

Stock History

NASDAQ (GM): LOOP

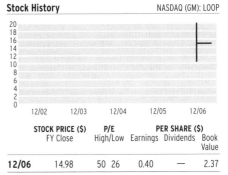

	STOCK PRICE ($) FY Close	P/E High/Low		Earnings	PER SHARE ($) Dividends	Book Value
12/06	14.98	50	26	0.40	—	2.37

LOUD Technologies

LOUD Technologies helps musicians bring their music to the masses. Best known for its multichannel mixing consoles, which allow engineers to combine some 100 sound channels, the company also manufactures amplifiers, monitor speakers, and digital mixing consoles. In addition to studio recording, LOUD Technologies' equipment is used in CD and CD-ROM authoring, live sound reinforcement, and video postproduction. It also owns loudspeaker manufacturer Eastern Acoustic Works (EAW).

LOUD Technologies' products are sold through thousands of retail outlets and a network of installed sound contractors in the US, as well as through distributors worldwide. It acquired Martin Audio Ltd in April 2007.

A UK-based company, Martin Audio is expected to boost LOUD's international distribution as well as its share of the global audio industry.

LOUD Technologies has been branching out from its traditional line of products through a series of acquisitions. In recent years it bought St. Louis Music, a manufacturer and distributor of branded musical instruments and professional audio products.

Investment firm Sun Capital owns some 74% of LOUD Technologies.

HISTORY

In 1970, 20-year-old Greg Mackie and childhood friend Martin Schneider co-founded Technical Audio Products Co. (TAPCO) to make public address systems. Within a few years TAPCO's sales grew to the multimillions; both men left the company in 1978. That year Mackie started AudioControl, a maker of consumer audio equalizers and analyzers.

Mackie left AudioControl in 1985 and three years later started Mackie Designs by turning out compact mixers from his three-bedroom condo in Edmonds, Washington. Mackie debuted its 8-Bus mixer consoles for multitrack recording and live sound in 1993 and its SR Series (sound reinforcement) of audio mixers in 1995. That year the company went public.

Mackie began selling power amplifiers in 1996, and the next year started making powered monitor speakers, which combine signal processing, power amplifiers, and speakers in a single cabinet. The company later unveiled its digital 8-Bus console system in 1998, developed with Apogee Electronics, and added a 56-channel console to its SR Series mixer line.

After acquiring Italy's Radio Cine Forniture (loudspeakers, now Mackie Italy) in 1998, the company established its Mackie Industrial division in 1999 to make sound systems for installation by professional contractors. When profits dipped the company trimmed its Woodinville, Washington, workforce in mid-1999. CEO Roy Wemyss resigned shortly thereafter.

In 2000 the company acquired Eastern Acoustic Works, a Massachusetts-based manufacturer of professional loudspeaker systems used in sports arenas and concert halls. It also bought Canadian software developer Acuma Labs and launched its first line of hard disc recorder products. The next year it bought Sydec, a Belgian manufacturer of digital audio products.

In February 2003 the company announced its voluntary Nasdaq delisting and began trading on the OTC Bulletin Board. Also that month Sun Capital Partners, a Boca Raton-based private investment firm, acquired about 75% of the company. In September Mackie Designs announced the company was changing its name to LOUD Technologies to eliminate confusion around the company name Mackie and the Mackie brand. In December the company sold its Italian operations, Mackie Designs S.p.A., and also formed the EAW commercial systems group in order to consolidate all of its commercial audio products.

In 2005 LOUD acquired St. Louis Music, a manufacturer and distributor of branded musical instruments and professional audio products.

EXECUTIVES

Chairman, President, and CEO:
 James T. (Jamie) Engen, age 44
CFO: Gerald Ng, age 46
SVP Engineering: Gary M. Reilly, age 54
SVP, Entertainment and Artist Relations:
 Edward (Ted) Kornblum, age 40
SVP Operations: Shawn C. Powers, age 49, $165,000 pay
SVP, Sales: Stanley J. Morgan, age 57
SVP, Domestic Sales: Michael MacDonald
VP, Finance and Accounting: Glenn Walcott
VP, Independent Dealers: Scott Schumer
VP, Key Accounts: Alex Nelson
VP, National Accounts: Dan Gallagher
VP, EAW: Jeffrey Cox
VP, Assistant Secretary, and Director:
 Mark E. Kuchenrither, age 46
Director, Customer Fulfillment: Carolyn Hommer
Director, Operations: Jim Shaw
Director, International Sales: David (Dave) Christensen
Director, Product Development: Mike Newman
Director, US Installed Sound Market: Kurt Metzler
Manager, Public Relations: Kyle Ritland
Auditors: KPMG LLP

LOCATIONS

HQ: LOUD Technologies Inc.
 16220 Wood-Red Rd. NE, Woodinville, WA 98072
Phone: 425-892-6500   **Fax:** 425-487-4337
Web: www.loud-technologies.com

2006 Sales

	$ mil.	% of total
US	141.7	66
Europe	25.9	12
Rest of the world	47.4	22
Total	**215.0**	**100**

PRODUCTS/OPERATIONS

Selected Brands

EAW (high-end sound reinforcement)
EAW Commercial (commercial and industrial audio)
Mackie (entry-level retail products)
SIA (measurement, system alignment, and analysis tools)
TAPCO (entry-level retail products)

COMPETITORS

Avid Technology
Bose
Crown Audio
Eminence Speaker
Euphonix
Fender Musical Instruments
Harman International
Line 6
Meyer Sound
Peavey Electronics
Philips North America
QSC Audio
Shure
TEAC
Yamaha

HISTORICAL FINANCIALS

Company Type: Public

Income Statement

FYE: December 31

	REVENUE ($ mil.)	NET INCOME ($ mil.)	NET PROFIT MARGIN	EMPLOYEES
12/06	215.0	0.6	0.3%	658
12/05	204.3	3.8	1.9%	704
12/04	123.3	(2.3)	—	408
12/03	130.8	(21.8)	—	468
12/02	188.0	(37.9)	—	1,036
Annual Growth	**3.4%**	**—**	**—**	**(10.7%)**

2006 Year-End Financials

Debt ratio: 393.1%
Return on equity: 6.2%
Cash ($ mil.): 0.3
Current ratio: 1.50
Long-term debt ($ mil.): 40.1
No. of shares (mil.): 4.6
Dividends
 Yield: —
 Payout: —
Market value ($ mil.): 68.9
R&D as % of sales: —
Advertising as % of sales: —

Stock History

NASDAQ (CM): LTEC

	STOCK PRICE ($) FY Close	P/E High/Low	PER SHARE ($) Earnings	Dividends	Book Value
12/06	15.05	152 89	0.13	—	2.23
12/05	16.00	24 12	0.76	—	1.99
12/04	10.00	— —	(0.50)	—	0.15
12/03	10.10	— —	(5.55)	—	0.04
12/02	6.90	— —	(15.20)	—	1.37
Annual Growth	**21.5%**	**— —**	**—**	**—**	**12.9%**

Lufkin Industries

Lufkin Industries is all geared up to help pump oil. Through its Oil Field division the company manufactures and services pumping units, automation equipment, and foundry castings. It also provides computer control equipment and analytical services used to maximize well efficiency. Through its Power Transmission unit, Lufkin manufactures and services gearboxes used in large-scale industrial applications. It has expanded its product offerings through the acquisition of Basin Technical Services. Lufkin has strengthened its presence in Canada through the acquisition of D&R Oilfield Services. In 2008 the company announced that it would exit its truck trailer manufacturing business.

EXECUTIVES

Chairman and CEO: Douglas V. Smith, age 65, $1,150,000 pay
President and Director: John F. (Jay) Glick, age 55, $383,308 pay
EVP: Larry M. Hoes, age 61, $554,039 pay
VP, CFO, and Treasurer: Robert D. Leslie, age 62, $383,846 pay
VP, General Counsel, and Secretary: Paul G. Perez, age 62, $365,846 pay
VP and General Manager Trailer Division:
 Scott H. Semlinger, age 54
VP and General Manager Power Transmission Division:
 Terry L. Orr, age 62
VP and General Manager Oil Field Division:
 Mark E. Crews, age 51
Auditors: Deloitte & Touche LLP

LOCATIONS

HQ: Lufkin Industries, Inc.
 601 S. Raguet, Lufkin, TX 75904
Phone: 936-634-2211   **Fax:** 936-637-5272
Web: www.lufkin.com

Lufkin Industries operates manufacturing facilities in Lufkin, Texas, as well as in Argentina, Canada, and France.

2006 Sales

	$ mil.	% of total
North America		
US	428.2	71
Canada	40.1	10
Latin America	60.1	7
Europe	32.8	5
Other regions	44.3	7
Total	**605.5**	**100**

PRODUCTS/OPERATIONS

2006 Sales

	$ mil.	% of total
Oil field	401.2	66
Power transmission	124.9	21
Trailer	79.4	13
Total	**605.5**	**100**

COMPETITORS

CE Franklin
Citation Corporation
Fontaine Trailer
Great Dane
INTERMET
Twin Disc
Utility Trailer
Wabash National
Weatherford International
Wells Cargo

HISTORICAL FINANCIALS

Company Type: Public

Income Statement

FYE: December 31

	REVENUE ($ mil.)	NET INCOME ($ mil.)	NET PROFIT MARGIN	EMPLOYEES
12/06	605.5	73.0	12.1%	3,000
12/05	492.2	44.5	9.0%	2,700
12/04	356.3	14.4	4.0%	—
12/03	262.3	9.7	3.7%	—
12/02	228.7	8.5	3.7%	1,800
Annual Growth	27.6%	71.2%	—	13.6%

2006 Year-End Financials

Debt ratio: —
Return on equity: 24.8%
Cash ($ mil.): 57.8
Current ratio: 3.96
Long-term debt ($ mil.): —
No. of shares (mil.): 15.3

Dividends
  Yield: 1.1%
  Payout: 12.8%
Market value ($ mil.): 890.0
R&D as % of sales: —
Advertising as % of sales: —

Stock History

NASDAQ (GS): LUFK

	STOCK PRICE ($) FY Close	P/E High	P/E Low	PER SHARE ($) Earnings	Dividends	Book Value
12/06	58.08	15	9	4.83	0.62	21.42
12/05	49.87	19	6	3.03	0.38	17.26
12/04	19.82	20	13	1.03	0.27	29.89
12/03	14.38	20	13	0.73	0.36	28.56
12/02	11.73	24	17	0.63	0.27	27.41
Annual Growth	49.2%	—	—	66.4%	23.1%	(6.0%)

Mac-Gray Corporation

No change for laundry or copies? Mac-Gray operates debit card- and coin-operated washers and dryers in about 58,000 apartment buildings, dorms, and other housing complexes in more than 40 states and the District of Columbia. It also supplies card- and coin-operated copiers for college and public libraries, as well as MicroFridge units (combo refrigerator, freezer, and microwave) for academic, military, and other housing facilities. In addition, Mac-Gray distributes equipment to laundromats, hotels, hospitals, and restaurants. Laundry facilities account for the majority of the company's earnings. Chairman and CEO Stewart MacDonald and his family own about 35% of the firm, which was founded in 1927.

Mac-Gray has grown in recent years through several acquisitions. The company expanded its portfolio in 2005 by purchasing the laundry facilities management business of Web Service Company in more than a dozen western and southern states. Web Service Company retained ownership of its operations in California, Hawaii, and Nevada. The transaction, at a cost of about $110 million, included contracts, related equipment, service fleets, and other assets. It repeated the act in early 2006 — buying the assets of Massachusetts-based multi-housing laundry provider Lundermac for about $11.5 million — and again in 2007 with its purchase of 50-year-old Hof Service Company for some $43 million. Buying Hof, with operations that are highly concentrated in Maryland (Baltimore), Virginia, and Washington, DC, assures profitability for Mac-Gray in those markets.

In late 2006 Mac-Gray turned down a merger offer from its #1 rival, Coinmach.

EXECUTIVES

Chairman and CEO: Stewart Gray MacDonald Jr., age 57, $565,000 pay
EVP, CFO, and Treasurer: Michael J. Shea, age 57, $401,600 pay
EVP Sales: Neil F. MacLellan III, age 47, $347,200 pay
EVP Operations: Philip Emma, age 51
CIO and CTO: Robert J. (Bob) Tuttle, age 54, $227,600 pay
VP, General Counsel, and Secretary: Linda A. Serafini, age 55, $172,327 pay (partial-year salary)
VP and General Manager, Hof Laundry Systems: Daryle Bobb
Auditors: PricewaterhouseCoopers LLP

LOCATIONS

HQ: Mac-Gray Corporation
404 Wyman St., Ste. 400, Waltham, MA 02451
Phone: 781-487-7600   **Fax:** 781-487-7601
Web: www.mac-gray.com

PRODUCTS/OPERATIONS

2006 Sales

	$ mil.	% of total
Laundry facilities management	229.7	82
MicroFridge sales and rental	30.4	11
Laundry equipment sales	16.7	6
Reprographics facilities management	2.5	1
Total	**279.3**	**100**

COMPETITORS

Absocold
Coinmach
DRYCLEAN USA
GE
Kinko's
SANYO
SpinCycle
Wal-Mart

HISTORICAL FINANCIALS

Company Type: Public

Income Statement

FYE: December 31

	REVENUE ($ mil.)	NET INCOME ($ mil.)	NET PROFIT MARGIN	EMPLOYEES
12/06	279.3	0.9	0.3%	737
12/05	260.6	12.1	4.6%	743
12/04	182.7	5.3	2.9%	—
12/03	149.7	4.1	2.7%	—
12/02	150.4	2.9	1.9%	475
Annual Growth	16.7%	(25.4%)	—	11.6%

2006 Year-End Financials

Debt ratio: 191.9%
Return on equity: 1.0%
Cash ($ mil.): 12.0
Current ratio: 1.05
Long-term debt ($ mil.): 175.8
No. of shares (mil.): 13.1

Dividends
  Yield: —
  Payout: —
Market value ($ mil.): 155.9
R&D as % of sales: —
Advertising as % of sales: —

Stock History

NYSE: TUC

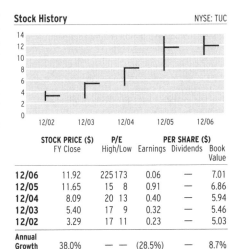

	STOCK PRICE ($) FY Close	P/E High	P/E Low	PER SHARE ($) Earnings	Dividends	Book Value
12/06	11.92	225	173	0.06	—	7.01
12/05	11.65	15	8	0.91	—	6.86
12/04	8.09	20	13	0.40	—	5.94
12/03	5.40	17	9	0.32	—	5.46
12/02	3.29	17	11	0.23	—	5.03
Annual Growth	38.0%	—	—	(28.5%)	—	8.7%

M & F Worldwide

M & F Worldwide sticks to it. Its Mafco Worldwide flavorings company is one of the world's largest makers of licorice extract, primarily for candy and as a tobacco additive (Altria alone accounts for more than 35% of Mafco's sales). Its primary flavoring brand is Magnasweet, but the company also sells Right Dress, a gardening mulch that is a byproduct of processing licorice root. M & F Worldwide has expanded into the security printing business through its acquisition of Clarke American Checks from Honeywell. Chairman Ron Perelman controls about 37% of the company through his MacAndrews & Forbes Holdings (formerly Mafco Holdings).

Management at M & F Worldwide is acutely aware that a large chunk of its sales comes from the tobacco industry. As a result, the company is looking for broader uses of Magnasweet flavoring in the food, pharmaceutical, and cosmetic industries. The company ensures a steady supply of licorice root by purchasing it from numerous countries around the world. Most of its supplies originate in Afghanistan, Azerbaijan, China, Iraq, Kazakhstan, Pakistan, Tajikistan, Turkey, Turkmenistan, and Uzbekistan.

The company upped the balance of its checkprinting business in 2007 when it acquired competitor John H. Harland Company for $1.7 billion, which it combined with its Clarke American operations. M & F has three other business lines: Mafco Worldwide (licorice); Harland Financial Solutions (core-processing, retail, and lending solutions software); and Scantron (data collection, testing, and assessment products).

Barry F. Schwartz was named as permanent CEO of the company in 2008.

HISTORY

In 2001 M & F purchased Panavision, a leading maker of camera systems used to film movies and television shows. Perelman was a majority owner of Panavision prior to its purchase by M & F. To settle litigation surrounding the purchase, in 2002 M & F sold its 83% stake in Panavision back to Perelman.

EXECUTIVES

Chairman: Ronald O. (Ron) Perelman, age 64
CEO, General Counsel, and Director: Barry F. Schwartz, age 58
EVP and CFO: Paul G. Savas, age 44
SVP Corporate Communications: Christine M. Taylor
VP, Treasurer, and Controller: Alison M. Horowitz
Director; President and CEO, Mafco Worldwide:
  Stephen G. Taub, age 55, $965,000 pay
Director; President and CEO, Harland Clarke Corp.:
  Charles T. (Chuck) Dawson, age 57
Auditors: Ernst & Young LLP

LOCATIONS

HQ: M & F Worldwide Corp.
  35 E. 62nd St., New York, NY 10021
Phone: 212-572-8600   **Fax:** 212-572-8650
Web: www.mandfworldwide.com

PRODUCTS/OPERATIONS

2006 Sales

	$ mil.	% of total
Financial institution check services	523	72
Direct-to-consumer check services	101	14
Licorice products	98	14
Total	**722**	**100**

Selected Subsidiaries

Domestic
  B(2)Direct, Inc.
  Checks in the Mail, Inc.
  Clarke American Checks, Inc.
  Clarke American Corp.
  Concord Pacific Corporation (50%)
  Core Skills Inc.
  EVD Holdings Inc.
  Flavors Holdings, Inc.
  Jensen Kelly Corporation
  Mafco Shanghai Corporation
  Mafco Worldwide Corporation
  PCT International Holdings, Inc.
  Pneumo Abex, LLC

Foreign
  EVD Holdings S.A.S. (France)
  Extraits Vegetaux Et Derives, S.A. (France)
  Mafco Weihai Green Industry of Science and
    Technology Co. Ltd. (40%, China)
  Wei Feng Enterprises Co. Ltd. (50%, British Virgin
    Islands)
  Xianyang Concord Natural Products Co. Ltd. (50%,
    China)
  Zhangjiagang Free Trade Zone MAFCO Liantai Biotech
    Co., Ltd. (50%, China)

COMPETITORS

Adams Extract & Spice	International Flavors
Ajinomoto	McCormick & Company
American Banknote	R. Torre
CSM	Safeguard
Danisco A/S	Scotts Miracle-Gro
Deluxe Corporation	Sensient
DELUXEPINPOINT	Standard Register
Ennis	Stirling Foods
Entner-Stuart	Wrigley

HISTORICAL FINANCIALS

Company Type: Public

Income Statement

	REVENUE ($ mil.)	NET INCOME ($ mil.)	NET PROFIT MARGIN	EMPLOYEES
FYE: December 31				
12/06	722.0	36.2	5.0%	3,462
12/05	121.4	24.0	19.8%	207
12/04	93.4	25.2	27.0%	—
12/03	95.7	23.2	24.2%	—
12/02	96.9	24.1	24.9%	268
Annual Growth	**65.2%**	**10.7%**	**—**	**89.6%**

2006 Year-End Financials

Debt ratio: 157.1%
Return on equity: 9.4%
Cash ($ mil.): 93.4
Current ratio: 1.69
Long-term debt ($ mil.): 645.0
No. of shares (mil.): 20.2

Dividends
  Yield: —
  Payout: —
Market value ($ mil.): 511.1
R&D as % of sales: —
Advertising as % of sales: —

Stock History

NYSE: MFW

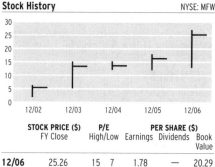

	STOCK PRICE ($) FY Close	P/E High/Low		PER SHARE ($) Earnings	Dividends	Book Value
12/06	25.26	15	7	1.78	—	20.29
12/05	16.32	15	10	1.21	—	18.69
12/04	13.62	12	10	1.26	—	17.81
12/03	13.36	12	4	1.21	—	16.57
12/02	5.40	6	2	0.96	—	15.13
Annual Growth	**47.1%**	**—**	**—**	**16.7%**	**—**	**7.6%**

Mariner Energy

Despite its name, oil and gas exploration and production company Mariner Energy is not all at sea. True, the independent explores in both the deep and shallow waters of the Gulf of Mexico, where it has the bulk of its proved reserves. But the landlocked Permian Basin of West Texas is also an area of focus. The company has estimated proved reserves of 715.5 billion cu. ft. of natural gas equivalent. Mariner Energy was owned by an Enron affiliate before the bankrupt Enron sold the company to Carlyle/Riverstone in 2004. Carlyle/Riverstone sold its controlling stake in Mariner Energy to institutional buyers in 2005 to pay down the oil company's debt. In 2006 the company acquired Forest Oil's Gulf of Mexico assets.

An early entrant in the Gulf of Mexico's growing deepwater exploration business, Mariner Energy has discovered seven new fields there since 1992. The company first filed to go public as Marine Energy, LLC, in 2000 but withdrew the offer in 2002.

In 2006 it sold its 20% stake in a Gulf of Mexico project to the project's operator (Petrobras America Inc.) for about $32 million.

In 2007 the company acquired additional Spraberry interests in the Permian Basin for $122.5 million and StatoilHydro's Gulf of Mexico shelf assets for $243 million.

EXECUTIVES

Chairman, President, and CEO: Scott D. Josey, age 49, $1,475,000 pay
COO: Dalton F. Polasek Jr., age 55, $825,000 pay
SVP, CFO, and Treasurer: John H. Karnes, age 45, $400,000 pay
SVP, General Counsel, and Secretary:
  Teresa G. Bushman, age 57
SVP and Chief Exploration Officer:
  Michiel C. (Mike) van den Bold, age 43, $640,000 pay

SVP Shelf and Onshore: Judd A. Hansen, age 51, $626,140 pay
SVP Corporate Development: Jesus G. Melendrez, age 48
SVP Deepwater: Cory L. Loegering, age 51
VP Reservoir Engineering: Richard A. Molohon, age 52
Human Resources: Emily McClung
Auditors: Deloitte & Touche LLP

LOCATIONS

HQ: Mariner Energy, Inc.
  2000 W. Sam Houston Pkwy. South,
  1 BriarLake Plaza, Ste. 2000,
  Houston, TX 77042
Phone: 713-954-5500
Web: www.mariner-energy.com

Mariner Energy explores for and produces oil and gas in the Gulf of Mexico and West Texas.

PRODUCTS/OPERATIONS

2006 Estimated Proved Reserves

	% of total
Natural gas	60
Crude oil, condensate & NGLs	40
Total	**100**

COMPETITORS

Abraxas Petroleum
BP
Brigham Exploration
Chesapeake Energy
Chevron
Devon Energy
Exxon Mobil
Pioneer Natural Resources
Range Resources
Royal Dutch Shell

HISTORICAL FINANCIALS

Company Type: Public

Income Statement

	REVENUE ($ mil.)	NET INCOME ($ mil.)	NET PROFIT MARGIN	EMPLOYEES
FYE: December 31				
12/06	659.5	121.5	18.4%	217
12/05	199.7	40.5	20.3%	196
12/04	214.2	68.4	31.9%	53
12/03	142.5	38.2	26.8%	—
12/02	158.2	30.0	19.0%	43
Annual Growth	**42.9%**	**41.9%**	**—**	**49.9%**

2006 Year-End Financials

Debt ratio: 50.2%
Return on equity: 16.0%
Cash ($ mil.): 64.1
Current ratio: 1.29
Long-term debt ($ mil.): 654.0
No. of shares (mil.): 86.4

Dividends
  Yield: —
  Payout: —
Market value ($ mil.): 1,693.0
R&D as % of sales: —
Advertising as % of sales: —

Stock History

NYSE: ME

	STOCK PRICE ($) FY Close	P/E High/Low		PER SHARE ($) Earnings	Dividends	Book Value
12/06	19.60	14	9	1.58	—	15.08

MarkWest Energy Partners

MarkWest Energy Partners marks its territory as the energy markets of America. A spinoff from oil and gas company MarkWest Hydrocarbon, MarkWest Energy Partners was created in 2002 to hold the natural gas gathering and processing assets of its parent. MarkWest Energy Partners has natural gas and natural gas liquids pipelines, storage terminals, and gathering and processing pipelines and fractionation plants in the Appalachian Basin, Michigan, and the Southwest. MarkWest Hydrocarbon retains a 17% stake in the partnership and controls its general partner. However, in 2007 the company agreed to acquire MarkWest Hydrocarbon.

MarkWest Energy Partners has implemented a growth strategy associated with the expansion of its current pipeline system. The company has acquired Pinnacle Natural Gas, the owner of three natural gas pipelines in Texas. It has also acquired Hobbs Lateral pipeline, a connector to the Northern Natural Gas interstate pipeline and power generation stations in New Mexico, from Energy Spectrum.

MarkWest Energy Partners has expanded its gathering system capabilities through the acquisition of American Central East Texas Gas' gathering system and natural gas processing operations for about $240 million. The company also acquired the Javelina gas processing and fractionation facility in South Texas for $156 million.

EXECUTIVES

Chairman, MarkWest Energy GP, L.L.C (General Partner): John M. Fox, age 66
President, CEO, and Director, MarkWest Energy GP, L.L.C (General Partner): Frank M. Semple, age 55, $428,462 pay
SVP and CFO, MarkWest Energy GP, L.L.C (General Partner): Nancy K. Buese, age 37
SVP and COO, MarkWest Energy GP, L.L.C (General Partner): John C. Mollenkopf, age 45
SVP and Chief Commercial Officer, MarkWest Energy GP, L.L.C (General Partner): Randy S. Nickerson, age 45
SVP Corporate Services, MarkWest Energy GP, L.L.C (General Partner): David L. Young, age 47, $253,462 pay
VP Finance, Treasurer, and Assistant Secretary, MarkWest Energy GP, L.L.C (General Partner): Andrew L. (Andy) Schroeder, age 48
VP Risk and Compliance, MarkWest Energy GP, L.L.C (General Partner): Richard A. Ostberg, age 41
SVP, General Counsel, and Secretary, MarkWest Energy GP, L.L.C (General Partner): C. Corwin Bromley, age 49
NGL Marketer: Diana H. Finley
Auditors: Deloitte & Touche LLP

LOCATIONS

HQ: MarkWest Energy Partners, L.P.
1515 Arapahoe St., Tower 2, Ste. 700, Denver, CO 80202
Phone: 303-290-8700   **Fax:** 303-290-8769
Web: www.markwest.com

MarkWest operates pipelines and facilities in Michigan, as well as in the Appalachian, Southwest, and Gulf Coast regions of the US.

2006 Sales

	% of total
Southwest	
Oklahoma	37
East Texas	21
Other	15
Appalachia	13
Gulf Coast	12
Michigan	2
Total	**100**

PRODUCTS/OPERATIONS

2006 Sales

	% of total
Unaffiliated parties	86
Affiliates	13
Derivative gain	1
Total	**100**

COMPETITORS

DCP Midstream Partners
Dynegy
Enterprise Products
Kinder Morgan Energy Partners
Williams Companies

HISTORICAL FINANCIALS

Company Type: Public

Income Statement			FYE: December 31
	REVENUE ($ mil.)	NET INCOME ($ mil.)	NET PROFIT MARGIN	EMPLOYEES
---	---	---	---	---
12/06	629.9	70.1	11.1%	0
12/05	499.1	2.4	0.5%	0
12/04	301.3	10.0	3.3%	0
12/03	117.5	5.8	4.9%	0
12/02	70.3	21.8	31.0%	0
Annual Growth	**73.0%**	**33.9%**	**—**	**—**

2006 Year-End Financials

Debt ratio: 116.7%
Return on equity: 18.5%
Cash ($ mil.): 38.6
Current ratio: 1.03
Long-term debt ($ mil.): 528.2
No. of shares (mil.): 31.2
Dividends
Yield: 6.0%
Payout: 73.4%
Market value ($ mil.): 929.5
R&D as % of sales: —
Advertising as % of sales: —

Stock History

AMEX: MWE

	STOCK PRICE ($) FY Close	P/E High/Low		PER SHARE ($) Earnings	Dividends	Book Value
12/06	29.83	12	8	2.44	1.79	14.52
12/05	23.22	2,675	2,100	0.01	1.60	27.75
12/04	24.31	37	26	0.65	1.10	31.55
12/03	20.35	43	24	0.48	0.61	16.27
12/02	11.65	5	4	2.41	—	25.20
Annual Growth	**26.5%**	**—**	**—**	**0.3%**	**43.2%**	**(12.9%)**

Martin Midstream Partners

Martin Midstream Partners moves petroleum products. The company gets most of its sales from the distribution of liquefied petroleum gases (LPGs). Martin Midstream buys the LPGs from natural gas processors and oil refiners and sells them to propane retailers and industrial customers. Martin Midstream also manufactures fertilizer and provides marine transportation and storage of liquid hydrocarbons. The company, which operates primarily in the Gulf Coast region of the US, has acquired the bulk of Tesoro's Marine Services assets. In 2007 the company agreed to buy Woodlawn Pipeline Company for about $33 million. Martin Resource Management controls a about a 39% stake in Martin Midstream and owns its general partner.

The limited partnership was formed in 2002 by privately held Martin Resource Management. The parent company has operated an LPG distribution business since the 1950s. It moved into marine transportation operations in the late 1980s, and into fertilizer and terminalling businesses in the early 1990s.

In 2005 Martin Midstream acquired A & A Fertilizer for $6 million and CF Martin Sulphur, L.P. for $18.1 million. It acquired two tugs and asphalt and marine terminals in 2006.

EXECUTIVES

President, CEO, and Director: Ruben S. Martin III, age 56, $118,434 pay
EVP and COO: Donald R. (Don) Neumeyer, age 60, $91,401 pay
EVP and CFO: Robert D. Bondurant, age 49, $87,492 pay
EVP, Chief Administrative Officer, and Controller: Wesley M. Skelton, age 60, $81,910 pay
EVP and Director; General Manager, Marine Operations: Scott D. Martin, age 42
VP, General Counsel, and Secretary: Chris Booth, age 39
General Manager, CF Martin Sulphur: Dick Wilkinson
Marketing Distribution Manager, CF Martin Sulphur: Darla Martin
President, Natural Gas Gathering, Processing, and LPG Distribution: Bob Dun
Auditors: KPMG LLP

LOCATIONS

HQ: Martin Midstream Partners L.P.
4200 Stone Rd., Kilgore, TX 75662
Phone: 903-983-6200   **Fax:** 903-983-6262
Web: www.martinmidstream.com

Martin Midstream Partners operates LPG facilities in Louisiana, Mississippi, and Texas. It also owns fertilizer plants in Arizona, Illinois, Texas, and Utah, and marine facilities across the Gulf Coast.

PRODUCTS/OPERATIONS

2006 Sales

	$ mil.	% of total
Natural gas services	389.7	68
Sulfur	61.3	11
Marine transportation	47.8	8
Fertilizer	41.3	7
Terminalling & storage	36.3	6
Total	**576.4**	**100**

COMPETITORS

George Warren	TEPPCO Partners
Penn Octane	Williams Companies
SandRidge Energy	

HISTORICAL FINANCIALS

Company Type: Public

Income Statement

FYE: December 31

	REVENUE ($ mil.)	NET INCOME ($ mil.)	NET PROFIT MARGIN	EMPLOYEES
12/06	576.4	22.2	3.9%	0
12/05	438.4	13.9	3.2%	—
12/04	294.1	12.3	4.2%	—
12/03	192.7	12.0	6.2%	—
12/02	149.9	6.2	4.1%	—
Annual Growth	40.0%	37.6%	—	—

2006 Year-End Financials

Debt ratio: 88.8%
Return on equity: 15.1%
Cash ($ mil.): 3.7
Current ratio: 1.26
Long-term debt ($ mil.): 176.2
No. of shares (mil.): 10.6
Dividends
Yield: 7.3%
Payout: 144.4%
Market value ($ mil.): 352.5
R&D as % of sales: —
Advertising as % of sales: —

Stock History

NASDAQ (GS): MMLP

	STOCK PRICE ($) FY Close	P/E High/Low	PER SHARE ($) Earnings	Dividends	Book Value
12/06	33.24	21 17	1.69	2.44	18.72
12/05	29.70	22 18	1.58	2.19	16.39
12/04	29.93	21 16	1.45	1.58	17.89
12/03	30.53	19 11	1.64	1.81	15.82
12/02	17.75	47 41	0.40	—	16.24
Annual Growth	17.0%	— —	43.4%	10.5%	3.6%

Masimo Corporation

Masimo is counting on the pulse oximetry monitoring market not being saturated. The company's Signal Extraction Technology (SET) noninvasively monitors arterial blood-oxygen saturation levels and pulse rates in patients. Masimo's product range offers pulse oximeters in both hand-held and stand-alone (bedside) form. Recent developments include carbon monoxide (CO) monitoring features, as well. The company licenses SET-based products to more than 35 medical equipment companies, including Cardinal Health, Medtronic, Welch Allyn, and Zoll Medical. Product benefits include provision of real-time information and elimination of signal interference, such as patient movements.

Masimo intends to use the proceeds from its 2007 IPO on capital expenses and to develop additional products. Some of the funds may also go towards acquisitions.

CEO Joe Kiani holds 11% of Masimo's stock.

EXECUTIVES

Chairman and CEO: Joe E. Kiani, age 42
EVP and CFO: Mark P. de Raad, age 47
EVP Engineering and CTO: Ammar Al-Ali, age 43
EVP Operations and CIO: Yongsam Lee, age 42
EVP Business Development, Secretary, and General Counsel: Christopher (Chris) Kilpatrick, age 50
EVP Engineering: Anand Sampath, age 40
EVP Human Resources: Dave Jennings
President, Worldwide OEM Business: Mohamed Elmandjra, age 43
President, Masimo Americas: Rick Fishel, age 49
President, Masimo Europe: Olivier Berthon, age 40
Media Relations: Tom McCall
Auditors: Grant Thornton LLP

LOCATIONS

HQ: Masimo Corporation
40 Parker, Irvine, CA 92618
Phone: 949-297-7000 **Fax:** 949-297-7001
Web: www.masimo.com

PRODUCTS/OPERATIONS

2006 Sales

	$ mil.	% of total
Products	155.1	69
Royalty & license fees	69.2	31
Total	224.3	100

Selected Products

IntelliVue
RadLink
RadNet
Rainbow SET oximeters (Radical and Rad series, provides CO monitoring)
SET oximeter sensors
SET oximeters (Radical and Rad series)
VueLink

COMPETITORS

Covidien
Criticare
GE Healthcare
Philips Medical Systems
Spacelabs Healthcare

HISTORICAL FINANCIALS

Company Type: Public

Income Statement

FYE: December 31

	REVENUE ($ mil.)	NET INCOME ($ mil.)	NET PROFIT MARGIN	EMPLOYEES
12/06	224.3	181.8	81.1%	1,224
12/05	107.9	33.4	31.0%	—
12/04	69.4	(3.8)	—	—
Annual Growth	79.8%	—	—	—

2006 Year-End Financials

Debt ratio: (43.1%)
Return on equity: —
Cash ($ mil.): 55.4
Current ratio: 1.35
Long-term debt ($ mil.): 13.5

Net Income History

NASDAQ (GM): MASI

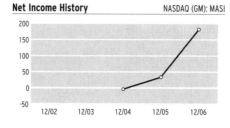

MedAssets, Inc.

MedAssets helps hospitals widen their profit margins — or at least not lose quite as much. The company's Spend Management segment operates a group purchasing organization that negotiates prices for hospitals and health systems which then get better deals on medical supplies and devices. Its Revenue Cycle Management segment provides software and consulting services that help track and analyze a hospital's revenue stream. Such services aim to increase collections and reduce account balances. It counts more than 125 health systems as customers, including Christiana Care, Banner Health, and Fletcher Allen.

MedAssets went public in 2007 and plans to use the proceeds to pay down debt from earlier acquisitions. Though acquisitions helped the company expand, no additional purchases are planned in the near future.

Through his holdings in Galen Associates, vice chairman Bruce Wesson controls 16% of the company. Director John Rutherford controls nearly 13% through Parthenon Capital.

EXECUTIVES

Chairman, President, and CEO: John A. Bardis, age 51
Vice Chairman: Terry Mulligan, age 62
Vice Chairman: Bruce F. (Toby) Wesson, age 64
COO, Chief Customer Officer, and Director: Rand A. Ballard, age 52
EVP Strategy and Mergers and Acquisitions: Howard W. Deichen
EVP and Chief Legal and Administrative Officer: Jonathan H. Glenn, age 56
SVP and and Chief Accounting Officer: Scott E. Gressett, age 37
SVP, Human Resources: Lynn Howard
SVP and CFO: L. Neil Hunn, age 35
Corporate SVP, Marketing and Marketing Communications: Gary Johnson
Chief Medical Officer: Nicholas J. (Nick) Sears
Chief Information and Technology Officer: Randy Sparkman
Auditors: BDO Seidman, LLP

LOCATIONS

HQ: MedAssets, Inc.
100 N. Point Center East, Ste. 200, Alpharetta, GA 30022
Phone: 678-323-2500 **Fax:** 678-323-2501
Web: www.medassets.com

PRODUCTS/OPERATIONS

2006 Sales

	$ mil.	% of total
Spend Management	97.4	67
Revenue Cycle Management	48.8	33
Total	146.2	100

COMPETITORS

Broadlane
CareMedic
Eclipsys
HealthTrust
McKesson
MEDITECH
Novation
Premier, Inc.
Siemens Medical
SSI Group
Stockamp & Associates

HISTORICAL FINANCIALS
Company Type: Public

Income Statement
FYE: December 31

	REVENUE ($ mil.)	NET INCOME ($ mil.)	NET PROFIT MARGIN	EMPLOYEES
12/06	146.2	8.6	5.9%	1,100
12/05	98.6	16.5	16.7%	—
12/04	75.4	2.1	2.8%	—
Annual Growth	39.2%	102.4%	—	—

2006 Year-End Financials
Debt ratio: (106.3%)
Return on equity: —
Cash ($ mil.): 23.5
Current ratio: 0.85
Long-term debt ($ mil.): 177.8

Net Income History
NASDAQ (GM): MDAS

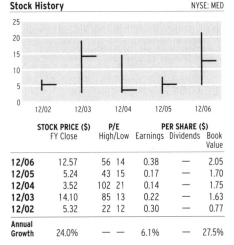

Medifast, Inc.

Medifast is helping people slim down and shape up. The company develops, manufactures, and markets health and diet products under its Medifast brand name. The products, which are manufactured by Medifast subsidiary Jason Pharmaceuticals, include meal replacement shakes, protein bars, and a variety of other food and drink items, as well as disease management products for diabetics. Medifast sells its wares online and through doctor's offices; in addition, its Take Shape for Life subsidiary distributes the products through a direct marketing and sales network of independent distributors it calls Health Coaches.

In addition to its weight control and disease management products, Medifast also operates a chain of Hi-Energy and Medifast Weight Control centers across the US.

Chairman Bradley MacDonald owns 6% of the company.

EXECUTIVES
Chairman: Bradley T. (Brad) MacDonald, age 59
CEO: Michael S. McDevitt, age 29
President and COO: Margaret MacDonald
EVP and Director; CEO, Take Shape for Life: Leo V. Willliams III, $125,000 pay
SVP Sales: Rick Logsdail
SVP Medifast Weight Control Centers: Joseph J. DiBartolomeo, age 50
Corporate VP of Infrastructure and Development: Richard Law
VP Corporate Communications: Jamie Elwood
VP Finance: Brendan Connors
Director Research and Development: Lisa M. Davis
Auditors: Bagell, Josephs, Levine & Company, LLC

LOCATIONS
HQ: Medifast, Inc.
11445 Cronhill Dr., Owings Mills, MD 21117
Phone: 410-581-8042   **Fax:** 410-581-8070
Web: www.medifast.net

COMPETITORS

Beverly Hills Weight Loss
eDiets.com
Herbalife Ltd.
Jenny Craig
PacificHealth
Pure Weight Loss
Slim-Fast
Weight Watchers

HISTORICAL FINANCIALS
Company Type: Public

Income Statement
FYE: December 31

	REVENUE ($ mil.)	NET INCOME ($ mil.)	NET PROFIT MARGIN	EMPLOYEES
12/06	74.1	5.2	7.0%	265
12/05	40.1	2.4	6.0%	164
12/04	27.3	1.8	6.6%	—
12/03	25.4	2.4	9.4%	—
12/02	12.3	2.6	21.1%	55
Annual Growth	56.7%	18.9%	—	48.2%

2006 Year-End Financials
Debt ratio: 12.6%
Return on equity: 21.0%
Cash ($ mil.): 2.6
Current ratio: 2.83
Long-term debt ($ mil.): 3.5
No. of shares (mil.): 13.6
Dividends
Yield: —
Payout: —
Market value ($ mil.): 171.5
R&D as % of sales: —
Advertising as % of sales: —

Stock History
NYSE: MED

	STOCK PRICE ($) FY Close	P/E High/Low		Earnings	PER SHARE ($) Dividends	Book Value
12/06	12.57	56	14	0.38	—	2.05
12/05	5.24	43	15	0.17	—	1.70
12/04	3.52	102	21	0.14	—	1.75
12/03	14.10	85	13	0.22	—	1.63
12/02	5.32	22	12	0.30	—	0.77
Annual Growth	24.0%	—	—	6.1%	—	27.5%

Mellanox Technologies

InfiniBand rocks, thinks Mellanox. Mellanox Technologies, a fabless semiconductor company, designs chips around the InfiniBand data exchange standard, which regulates the way network components such as servers and data storage systems communicate with each other. InfiniBand, which has drawn the support of corporate titans including Dell and Sun Microsystems, is intended to replace the older Ethernet and Fibre Channel networking standards. Mellanox sells its adapters and switches to scores of customers in the server, communications, and data storage markets.

Leading customers include Voltaire (about 18% of sales), Cisco Systems (14%), Hewlett-Packard (12%), and SilverStorm Technologies (11%).

The company has developed a host channel adapter, the ConnectX IB, that combines InfiniBand with 10-Gigabit Ethernet capabilities. While InfiniBand is considered technically superior to Ethernet, it has yet to gain widespread implementation in enterprise networks. Mellanox will make the technology available in both stand-alone chips and in adapters.

Mellanox Technologies will use proceeds from its 2007 IPO to fund product development, the leading expenditure for fabless semiconductor companies, and for working capital, sales and marketing activities, capital expenditures, and potential acquisitions.

As a fabless firm, Mellanox contracts out its manufacturing. Taiwan Semiconductor Manufacturing Co. (TSMC) makes the chips designed by the company. Advanced Semiconductor Engineering (ASE) assembles, packages, and tests its chips. Flextronics International manufactures and tests its adapter cards.

The company has grown rapidly and turned profitable in 2005. It has an accumulated deficit of about $69 million.

Four-fifths of Mellanox's full-time employees are based in Israel.

The company raised more than $89 million in private equity funding. Its investors include Bessemer Venture Partners, Dell, IBM, Intel Capital, Sequoia Capital (which owns about 9% of Mellanox), Sun Micro, U.S. Venture Partners (also around 9%), and Vitesse Semiconductor.

CEO Eyal Waldman owns about 12% of Mellanox Technologies. Officers and directors as a group hold nearly 37% of the company.

EXECUTIVES
Chairman, President, and CEO: Eyal Waldman, age 46, $225,000 pay
CFO: Michael Gray, age 50, $211,730 pay
VP, Architecture: Michael Kagan, age 49, $136,228 pay
VP, Engineering: Roni Ashuri, age 46
VP, Operations and Engineering: Shai Cohen, $128,076 pay
VP, Systems Solutions: Yuval Leader
VP, Worldwide Sales: David (Dave) Sheffler, age 51, $213,730 pay
VP, Product Marketing: Thad Omura, age 32, $187,768 pay
Director of Human Resources: Lee-Ann Stewart
Auditors: PricewaterhouseCoopers LLP

LOCATIONS
HQ: Mellanox Technologies, Ltd.
2900 Stender Way, Santa Clara, CA 95054
Phone: 408-970-3400   **Fax:** 408-970-3403
Web: www.mellanox.com

Mellanox Technologies has facilities in Israel and the US.

2006 Sales
	$ mil.	% of total
North America	28.7	59
Israel	10.0	21
Europe	5.4	11
Asia	4.4	9
Total	**48.5**	**100**

PRODUCTS/OPERATIONS

2006 Sales
	$ mil.	% of total
Cards	26.4	54
Semiconductors	19.4	40
Switches	1.2	3
Options & other	1.5	3
Total	**48.5**	**100**

Selected Products

InfiniBridge integrated circuits
  Host channel adapters
  Switches
  Target channel adapters
InfiniHost integrated circuits and cards
  Host channel adapters with integrated physical layer serializer/deserializer interfaces
InfiniScale integrated circuits
  Scalable switches with integrated physical layer serializer/deserializer interfaces

COMPETITORS

Applied Micro Circuits	Myricom
Broadcom	NEC
Emulex	NetEffect
Fujitsu	NetLogic Microsystems
IBM Microelectronics	PMC-Sierra
Intel Corporation	QLogic
LSI Corp.	TranSwitch
Marvell Technology	Tundra Semiconductor
Mindspeed	

HISTORICAL FINANCIALS

Company Type: Public

Income Statement			FYE: December 31	
	REVENUE ($ mil.)	NET INCOME ($ mil.)	NET PROFIT MARGIN	EMPLOYEES
12/06	48.5	7.3	15.1%	180
12/05	42.1	3.2	7.6%	—
12/04	20.3	(8.9)	—	—
12/03	10.2	(15.6)	—	—
Annual Growth	68.2%	—	—	—

2006 Year-End Financials
Debt ratio: —
Return on equity: —
Cash ($ mil.): 21.3
Current ratio: 3.04
Long-term debt ($ mil.): 0.5

Net Income History   NASDAQ (GM): MLNX

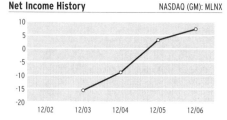

MEMSIC, Inc.

It's all in the name. MEMSIC makes micro-electromechanical systems (MEMS), integrated circuit (IC) products that allow a single chip to process signals from several sources. The company's specialized circuits are used as accelerometers (used to measure tilt and other motion) and sensors in automotive and consumer-electronics applications. The company partners with such companies as Sensata Technologies. Its customers include Autoliv and Mitsubishi Electric. MEMSIC has operations in China, buying land in Wuxi in 2003 and opening a factory for MEMS fabrication in 2004.

MEMSIC plans to use proceeds from its 2007 IPO for expanding its manufacturing facility and for general corporate purposes.

The company contracts out some production to TSMC in Taiwan and Nantong-Fujitsu Microelectronics in China. It employs a CMOS process in manufacturing its devices, one of the most commonly used manufacturing technologies in semiconductor fabrication.

Accelerometers have traditionally been used in automotive airbags, sensing when the airbags should inflate. More recent applications include the remote controls on Nintendo's Wii game console and Apple's iPhone (to sense when the phone is tilted from one side to another).

MEMSIC was backed by Still River Fund (which owns about 12% of the company), InveStar Semiconductor Development Fund (nearly 11%), Celtic House Venture Partners (nearly 13%), and Elufar Limited, among others.

President and CEO Yang Zhao owns about 7% of MEMSIC.

EXECUTIVES

Chairman: Paul M. Zavracky, age 59
President, CEO, and Director: Yang Zhao, age 44
CFO: Shang Hsiao, age 46
VP, Operations and General Manager: Feiming Huang, age 41
VP, Technology: Albert M. Leung
VP, Marketing and Business Development: Patrick (Pat) Chiumiento, age 57
VP, Finance: Patricia Niu, age 40
VP, Engineering: Gary O'Brien, age 43
VP, Sales and Marketing: Xin Liu
Media Relations: Kerri Giard
Auditors: Ernst & Young LLP

LOCATIONS

HQ: MEMSIC, Inc.
  One Tech Dr., Ste. 325, Andover, MA 01810
Phone: 978-738-0900   **Fax:** 978-738-0196
Web: www.memsic.com

MEMSIC has operations in China and the US.

2006 Sales

	$ mil.	% of total
Asia/Pacific		
Japan	3.3	25
Other countries	6.6	50
North America	2.5	19
Europe & other regions	0.7	6
Total	**13.1**	**100**

PRODUCTS/OPERATIONS

2006 Sales

	$ mil.	% of total
Mobile phone	5.1	39
Consumer	4.2	32
Automotive	2.8	21
Industrial & other	1.0	8
Total	**13.1**	**100**

COMPETITORS

Analog Devices
Apogee Technology
Axsys
CST
Freescale Semiconductor
Honeywell International
Measurement Specialties
MEMSCAP
Optek Technology
Sensata
STMicroelectronics
Ziptronix

HISTORICAL FINANCIALS

Company Type: Public

Income Statement			FYE: December 31	
	REVENUE ($ mil.)	NET INCOME ($ mil.)	NET PROFIT MARGIN	EMPLOYEES
12/06	13.1	0.5	3.8%	219
12/05	9.1	0.1	1.1%	162
12/04	6.9	1.6	23.2%	100
Annual Growth	37.8%	(44.1%)	—	48.0%

2006 Year-End Financials
Debt ratio: 0.0%
Return on equity: —
Cash ($ mil.): 7.1
Current ratio: 6.38
Long-term debt ($ mil.): 0.0

Net Income History   NASDAQ (GM): MEMS

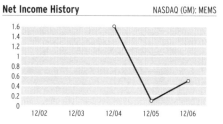

Mercantile Bank

Mercantile Bank Corporation is the holding company for Mercantile Bank of Michigan (formerly Mercantile Bank of West Michigan), which operates nearly 10 branches in and around Grand Rapids, and in the college towns of Ann Arbor and East Lansing. (The latter were community bank's first foray outside the western part of Michigan, prompting the name change in 2005.) The bank targets local consumers and businesses, offering standard retail banking services such as checking and savings accounts, NOW and money market accounts, and CDs. Loans for real estate secured by non-residential properties make up almost half of the company's loan portfolio; business loans are more than a quarter.

Mercantile Bank also offers financial planning and brokerage services via an agreement with Raymond James Financial.

Subsidiary Mercantile Bank Mortgage originates home loans while another unit, Mercantile Insurance Center sells insurance products. Mercantile Bank dissolved its Mercantile BIDCO subsidiary, which provided specialized commercial financing, in 2005.

EXECUTIVES

Chairman, President, and CEO; Chairman and CEO, Mercantile Bank of Michigan: Michael H. Price, age 50, $402,000 pay
EVP and COO; President and COO, Mercantile Bank of Michigan: Robert B. Kaminski Jr., age 45, $250,000 pay
SVP, CFO, and Treasurer; SVP and CFO, Mercantile Bank: Charles E. (Chuck) Christmas, age 41, $210,000 pay
VP and Branch Manager: Cheri L. Stanton

SVP and CIO, Mercantile Bank: John Schulte
SVP, Business Development and Marketing Officer,
 Mercantile Bank: Deborah A. (Deb) Rogers
SVP and Human Resources Director, Mercantile Bank:
 Lonna Wiersma
SVP and Manager, Mercantile BIDCO:
 Craig A. Woodman
Auditors: BDO Seidman, LLP

LOCATIONS

HQ: Mercantile Bank Corporation
 310 Leonard St. NW, Grand Rapids, MI 49504
Phone: 616-406-3000
Web: www.mercbank.com

PRODUCTS/OPERATIONS

2006 Sales

	$ mil.	% of total
Interest		
Loans & leases, including fees	127.4	89
Securities	9.3	7
Other	0.5	—
Noninterest		
Service charges on accounts	1.4	1
Increase in cash surrender value		
of bank-owned life insurance policies	1.2	1
Other	2.7	2
Total	**142.5**	**100**

COMPETITORS

Chemical Financial	Independent Bank (MI)
Comerica	LaSalle Bank
Fifth Third	Macatawa Bank
Flagstar Bancorp	National City
Huntington Bancshares	

HISTORICAL FINANCIALS

Company Type: Public

Income Statement — FYE: December 31

	ASSETS ($ mil.)	NET INCOME ($ mil.)	INCOME AS % OF ASSETS	EMPLOYEES
12/06	2,067.3	19.9	1.0%	325
12/05	1,838.2	17.9	1.0%	304
12/04	1,536.1	13.7	0.9%	—
12/03	1,202.8	10.0	0.8%	—
12/02	921.9	7.8	0.8%	134
Annual Growth	**22.4%**	**26.4%**	**—**	**24.8%**

2006 Year-End Financials

Equity as % of assets: 8.3%
Return on assets: 1.0%
Return on equity: 12.2%
Long-term debt ($ mil.): 36.3
No. of shares (mil.): 8.0
Market value ($ mil.): 288.0
Dividends
 Yield: 1.3%
 Payout: 20.6%
Sales ($ mil.): 142.5
R&D as % of sales: —
Advertising as % of sales: —

Stock History — NASDAQ (GS): MBWM

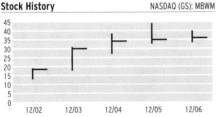

	STOCK PRICE ($) FY Close	P/E High/Low		PER SHARE ($) Earnings	Dividends	Book Value
12/06	35.90	17	14	2.33	0.48	21.43
12/05	34.92	21	16	2.10	0.29	20.44
12/04	34.12	24	17	1.62	0.23	19.69
12/03	30.03	22	13	1.39	1.95	19.13
12/02	18.53	16	11	1.16	0.82	14.77
Annual Growth	**18.0%**	**—**	**—**	**19.0%**	**(12.5%)**	**9.8%**

Mercer Insurance

Dating back to 1844, Mercer Insurance Group offers a range of property/casualty insurance policies through subsidiaries such as Mercer Mutual Insurance, Mercer Insurance Company of New Jersey, and Franklin Insurance. The company focuses on commercial coverage for small to midsized businesses and personal homeowners (the majority of personal lines) and automobile insurance. Mercer Insurance Group markets its products in six states — Arizona, California, Nevada, New Jersey, Pennsylvania, and Oregon. The company further expanded its reach through the 2005 acquisition of California-based Financial Pacific Insurance.

Financial Pacific provides specialty commercial coverage in four western states. The company holds licenses to write coverage in 22 states, and is seeking opportunities to expand.

The acquisition of Financial Pacific quadrupled the company's business in California — in 2006 more than 50% of the company's premiums were written in California.

Director H. Thomas Davis Jr. owns 6% of Mercer Insurance Group; directors and executive officers collectively control 13% of the company.

EXECUTIVES

Chairman: Richard G. Van Noy, age 65
President, CEO, and Director: Andrew R. Speaker, age 44, $571,150 pay
SVP Finance and CFO: David B. Merclean, age 56, $321,077 pay
SVP, Chief Underwriting Officer, and Secretary:
 Paul D. Ehrhardt, age 49, $367,355 pay
SVP; President, Financial Pacific Insurance Company:
 Robert T. Kingsley, age 40
SVP and CIO: Paul R. Cockery, age 56
Director: H. Thomas Davis Jr., age 58, $174,026 pay
Treasurer: Gordon A. Coleman, age 48, $136,118 pay
Human Resources: Debbie Johnstone
Auditors: KPMG LLP

LOCATIONS

HQ: Mercer Insurance Group, Inc.
 10 N. Hwy. 31, Pennington, NJ 08534
Phone: 609-737-0426   **Fax:** 609-737-8719
Web: www.franklininsurance.com

PRODUCTS/OPERATIONS

2006 Sales

	$ mil.	% of total
Commercial lines premiums	115.1	77
Personal lines permiums	22.6	15
Het investment income	10.1	7
Realized investment gains	0.1	—
Other	2.0	1
Total	**149.9**	**100**

COMPETITORS

ACE Limited	The Hartford
AIG	Liberty Mutual
Allstate	MetLife
American Financial	Progressive Corporation
Chubb Corp	Prudential
CNA Financial	Safeco
Farmers Group	State Farm
GEICO	Travelers Companies

HISTORICAL FINANCIALS

Company Type: Public

Income Statement — FYE: December 31

	ASSETS ($ mil.)	NET INCOME ($ mil.)	INCOME AS % OF ASSETS	EMPLOYEES
12/06	507.0	10.6	2.1%	214
12/05	446.7	7.0	1.6%	193
12/04	180.4	3.3	1.8%	—
12/03	175.9	0.6	0.3%	—
12/02	105.8	2.2	2.1%	86
Annual Growth	**48.0%**	**48.2%**	**—**	**25.6%**

2006 Year-End Financials

Equity as % of assets: 22.8%
Return on assets: 2.2%
Return on equity: 9.7%
Long-term debt ($ mil.): 18.5
No. of shares (mil.): 6.6
Market value ($ mil.): 133.0
Dividends
 Yield: 0.7%
 Payout: 8.8%
Sales ($ mil.): 149.9
R&D as % of sales: —
Advertising as % of sales: —

Stock History — NASDAQ (GM): MIGP

	STOCK PRICE ($) FY Close	P/E High/Low		PER SHARE ($) Earnings	Dividends	Book Value
12/06	20.21	16	9	1.71	0.15	17.60
12/05	15.00	13	11	1.14	—	16.00
12/04	13.43	28	22	0.51	—	15.30
12/03	12.55	—	—	—	—	15.65
Annual Growth	**17.2%**	**—**	**—**	**83.1%**	**—**	**4.0%**

Mesa Laboratories

Mesa Laboratories is reaching a plateau in the field of measurements. The company makes niche-market electronic measurement, testing, and recording instruments for medical, food processing, electronics, and aerospace applications. Mesa's products include sensors that record temperature, humidity, and pressure levels; flowmeters for water treatment, polymerization, and chemical processing applications; and sonic concentration analyzers. The company also makes kidney hemodialysis treatment products, including metering equipment and machines that clean dialyzers (or filters) for reuse.

In 2006 Mesa Labs acquired Raven Biological Laboratories for nearly $7 million in cash and stock. Raven Labs manufactures biological indicators and provides sterilization validation services. Raven's products are used by dental offices and hospitals, and by manufacturers of medical devices and pharmaceuticals, for quality control testing in sterilization processes. Mesa Labs paid $3.5 million in cash and exchanged 223,243 shares of common stock to acquire Raven Labs.

Mesa Labs provides repair, recalibration, and certification services. Nearly three-quarters of sales are to customers located in the US.

CEO Luke Schmieder owns about 11% of Mesa Laboratories. FMR (Fidelity Investments) holds nearly 8% of the company. Director Robert Dwyer has an equity stake of around 6%.

EXECUTIVES

Chairman, CEO, and Treasurer: Luke R. Schmieder, age 63, $206,147 pay
President and COO: John J. Sullivan, age 53, $224,005 pay
VP Finance, CFO, Chief Accounting Officer, and Secretary: Steven W. Peterson, age 49, $154,475 pay
VP Sales and Marketing: Glenn Adriance
Auditors: Ehrhardt Keefe Steiner & Hottman PC

LOCATIONS

HQ: Mesa Laboratories, Inc.
12100 W. 6th Ave., Lakewood, CO 80228
Phone: 303-987-8000   **Fax:** 303-987-8989
Web: www.mesalabs.com

Mesa Laboratories has facilities in Colorado and Nebraska.

2007 Sales

	$ mil.	% of total
US	12.7	74
Other countries	4.5	26
Total	**17.2**	**100**

PRODUCTS/OPERATIONS

2007 Sales

	$ mil.	% of total
Product sales	13.9	81
Parts & service	3.3	19
Total	**17.2**	**100**

Selected Products

Biological and chemical indicators (Raven Biological Laboratories)

Electronic thermal sensors
 DATATRACE
 DATATRACE Micropack Tracers
 ELOGG
 Flatpack Tracers
 FRB Tracers

Hemodialysis products (Automata)
 Database management software (Reuse Data Management System)
 Dialyzer reprocessors (ECHO MM-1000)
 Meters (Western Meters)

Sonic fluid measurement products (NuSonics)
 Sonic concentration analyzers
 Sonic flowmeters

COMPETITORS

3M Health Care
Badger Meter
Cantel Medical
Danaher
Ellab
Emerson Electric
Euro Tech
GE
K-Tron
Mikron Infrared
Minntech
Rockwell Medical
Siemens Corp
Siemens Water Technologies
STERIS
Teledyne Isco
Thermo Fisher Scientific

HISTORICAL FINANCIALS

Company Type: Public

Income Statement

FYE: March 31

	REVENUE ($ mil.)	NET INCOME ($ mil.)	NET PROFIT MARGIN	EMPLOYEES
3/07	17.2	4.0	23.3%	100
3/06	11.6	2.8	24.1%	52
3/05	10.0	2.3	23.0%	47
3/04	9.1	2.1	23.1%	—
3/03	9.1	2.1	23.1%	—
Annual Growth	**17.3%**	**17.5%**	**—**	**45.9%**

2007 Year-End Financials

Debt ratio: —
Return on equity: 22.4%
Cash ($ mil.): 3.3
Current ratio: 7.37
Long-term debt ($ mil.): —
No. of shares (mil.): 3.2
Dividends
 Yield: 2.1%
 Payout: 32.8%
Market value ($ mil.): 60.4
R&D as % of sales: —
Advertising as % of sales: —

Stock History

NASDAQ (GM): MLAB

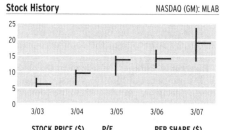

	STOCK PRICE ($) FY Close	P/E High/Low		PER SHARE ($) Earnings	Dividends	Book Value
3/07	19.00	19	11	1.22	0.40	6.52
3/06	14.11	18	12	0.92	0.51	5.07
3/05	13.75	20	12	0.74	0.42	5.06
3/04	9.55	15	9	0.68	0.25	5.01
3/03	6.15	12	8	0.64	—	4.68
Annual Growth	**32.6%**	**—**	**—**	**17.5%**	**17.0%**	**8.7%**

Metalico, Inc.

No, dude, it's not a heavy metal band, but Metalico *is* into metal — specifically, scrap metal recycling and lead fabrication. The company collects ferrous and nonferrous metal at six facilities in western New York and recycles it into usable scrap. Recycled ferrous metal (iron and steel) is sold mainly to steelmakers, particularly to operators of electric arc furnace minimills. Metalico's nonferrous scrap includes aluminum, which is sold to makers of aluminum products; the company operates its own secondary aluminum smelter. Metalico engages in lead fabrication at five US facilities. Its lead products include sheet (for roofing) and shot (for reloading).

In 2006 Metalico agreed to buy Niles Iron & Metal Company, a leading northeastern Ohio-based scrap metal recycling business, but the deal fell through.

EXECUTIVES

Chairman, President, and CEO: Carlos E. Agüero, age 53, $400,572 pay
EVP and Director: Michael J. Drury, age 50, $280,340 pay
EVP, General Counsel, and Secretary: Arnold S. Graber, age 53, $258,450 pay

SVP and CFO: Eric W. Finlayson, age 48, $182,120 pay
VP and Corporate Controller: Kevin R. Whalen, age 43
VP, Business Development: David J. DelBianco, age 45
VP, Operations: Warren Jennings, age 49, $230,000 pay
Auditors: McGladrey & Pullen, LLP

LOCATIONS

HQ: Metalico, Inc.
186 North Ave. East, Cranford, NJ 07016
Phone: 908-497-9610   **Fax:** 908-497-1097
Web: www.metalico.com

PRODUCTS/OPERATIONS

2006 Sales

	$ mil.	% of total
Scrap metal recycling		
Nonferrous metals	85.6	41
Ferrous metals	43.5	21
Lead fabrication	78.6	38
Total	**207.7**	**100**

COMPETITORS

David J. Joseph
Doe Run
Joseph Behr and Sons
Metal Management
OmniSource
Philip Services
Sanders Lead

HISTORICAL FINANCIALS

Company Type: Public

Income Statement

FYE: December 31

	REVENUE ($ mil.)	NET INCOME ($ mil.)	NET PROFIT MARGIN	EMPLOYEES
12/06	207.7	10.3	5.0%	391
12/05	164.3	5.6	3.4%	457
12/04	115.4	6.7	5.8%	—
12/03	61.3	2.0	3.3%	—
12/02	59.3	2.8	4.7%	—
Annual Growth	**36.8%**	**38.5%**	**—**	**(14.4%)**

2006 Year-End Financials

Debt ratio: 33.1%
Return on equity: 37.1%
Cash ($ mil.): 1.5
Current ratio: 2.08
Long-term debt ($ mil.): 13.1
No. of shares (mil.): 11.8
Dividends
 Yield: —
 Payout: —
Market value ($ mil.): 59.4
R&D as % of sales: —
Advertising as % of sales: —

Stock History

AMEX: MEA

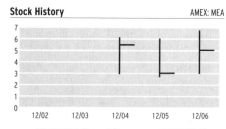

	STOCK PRICE ($) FY Close	P/E High/Low		PER SHARE ($) Earnings	Dividends	Book Value
12/06	5.05	17	8	0.40	—	6.27
12/05	3.03	26	12	0.23	—	6.90
12/04	5.50	21	10	0.29	—	5.71
Annual Growth	**(4.2%)**	**—**	**—**	**17.4%**	**—**	**4.8%**

MetroCorp Bancshares

MetroCorp Bancshares takes a cosmopolitan approach to banking. The holding company's MetroBank subsidiary targets the large — and growing — ethnic populations of the Houston and Dallas metropolitan areas, while its Metro United Bank (formerly First United Bank, acquired in 2005) similarly serves the San Diego and Los Angeles areas.

Through about 15 branches, the banks focus on Hispanic- and Asian-owned businesses. Commercial mortgages make up almost half of the company's loan portfolio; business loans, including SBA loans, are more than 40%. The banks also offer import-export finance services and loans guaranteed by the government of Taiwan. They provide a full range of consumer banking services, as well.

MetroCorp Bancshares opened an office in China, and bought a branch in Irvine, California from Omni Bank in 2006. It is also opening new branches in loan production offices within its existing market areas.

EXECUTIVES

Chairman, MetroCorp Bancshares and MetroBank: Don J. Wang, age 62
Executive Vice Chairman, President, and CEO; Vice Chairman and CEO, MetroBank; Chairman, Metro United Bank: George M. Lee, age 58, $274,041 pay
EVP; Vice Chairman and CEO, Metro United Bank: Mitchell W. Kitayama, age 50, $180,000 pay
EVP and CFO, MetroCorp Bancshares and MetroBank: David C. Choi, age 49, $169,375 pay
EVP, Secretary, and Director; President and Director, MetroBank; Director, Metro United Bank: David Tai, age 55, $198,758 pay
SVP, Information Systems, MetroCorp Bancshares and MetroBank: Andy Hou
SVP, Operations, MetroCorp Bancshares and MetroBank: Regina J. Tunchez
Chief Loan Administrative and Human Resources Officer: Michelle Phung
President, First United: Andrew C. Yip
EVP and Chief Credit Officer, MetroBank: Terrance J. (Terry) Tangen, age 59, $173,344 pay
Auditors: PricewaterhouseCoopers LLP

LOCATIONS

HQ: MetroCorp Bancshares, Inc.
9600 Bellaire Blvd., Ste. 252, Houston, TX 77036
Phone: 713-776-3876   **Fax:** 713-414-3575
Web: www.metrobank-na.com

PRODUCTS/OPERATIONS

2006 Sales

	$ mil.	% of total
Interest		
Loans	73.1	77
Taxable securities	8.6	9
Other	5.0	5
Noninterest		
Service fees	5.6	6
Loan-related fees	1.6	2
Other	0.7	1
Total	**94.6**	**100**

COMPETITORS

Bank of America	Prosperity Bancshares
Citibank	Wells Fargo
Cullen/Frost Bankers	Wilshire Bancorp
JPMorgan Chase	Zions Bancorporation

HISTORICAL FINANCIALS

Company Type: Public

Income Statement

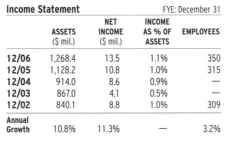

FYE: December 31

	ASSETS ($ mil.)	NET INCOME ($ mil.)	INCOME AS % OF ASSETS	EMPLOYEES
12/06	1,268.4	13.5	1.1%	350
12/05	1,128.2	10.8	1.0%	315
12/04	914.0	8.6	0.9%	—
12/03	867.0	4.1	0.5%	—
12/02	840.1	8.8	1.0%	309
Annual Growth	**10.8%**	**11.3%**	**—**	**3.2%**

2006 Year-End Financials

Equity as % of assets: 8.4%
Return on assets: 1.1%
Return on equity: 13.6%
Long-term debt ($ mil.): 62.4
No. of shares (mil.): 10.9
Market value ($ mil.): 230.3
Dividends
Yield: 0.8%
Payout: 13.1%
Sales ($ mil.): 94.6
R&D as % of sales: —
Advertising as % of sales: —

Stock History

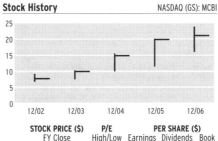

NASDAQ (GS): MCBI

	STOCK PRICE ($) FY Close	P/E High/Low		Earnings	Dividends	Book Value
12/06	21.04	19	13	1.22	0.16	9.68
12/05	19.83	20	12	0.99	0.16	12.75
12/04	14.84	19	13	0.79	0.04	11.93
12/03	9.95	27	20	0.38	—	10.95
12/02	7.73	11	9	0.82	—	10.59
Annual Growth	**28.4%**	**—**	**—**	**10.4%**	**100.0%**	**(2.2%)**

The Middleby Corporation

The Middleby Corporation certainly can stand the heat — its commercial and institutional food-service equipment can be found in kitchens in more than 100 countries. Middleby makes equipment for use in such operations as restaurants, retail outlets, and hotels. The company manufactures conveyor cooking equipment (Middleby Marshall, Blodgett, and CTX); heavy-duty gas equipment like ranges, broilers, and fryers (Pitco Frialator, Nu-Vu, and Southbend); and light- and medium-duty electric cooking equipment like toasters and convection ovens (Toastmaster).

The Middleby Corporation's strategy for growth centers on acquiring cooking-focused companies with patented technologies and which also hold No. 1 or No. 2 positions in their respective markets.

In 2005 Middleby acquired Nu-Vu Food Service for about $12 million. It also purchased Alkar Holdings, Inc., a maker of batch and conveyor ovens and packaging equipment under the brands Alkar and RapidPak for about $27 million.

The following year Middleby acquired Danish specialty convection oven maker Houno A/S for an undisclosed amount.

In 2007 Middleby bought Jade Products Company from Maytag. Jade is a maker of high-end commercial cooking equipment. Although terms of the deal were not disclosed, Jade earns about $20 million in annual sales.

Later that year Middleby expanded by acquiring Carter-Hoffman, a maker of heated cabinets and rethermalizing equipment, from Carrier Corporation for $16 million. The company also bought the assets of Georgia-based MP Equipment Company, a maker of food processing equipment. MP Equipment's products include breading, mixing, slicing, and battering equipment. The acquisition of MP Equipment will complement Middleby's Alkar and Rapidpak brands of cooking, chilling, and packaging products.

Also in 2007 the company acquired the assets of Wells/Bloomfield (electric cooking products and coffee and tea equipment) from Carrier Commercial Refrigeration for $29 million in cash. Wells/Bloomfield (aka Bloomfield Industries) has annual sales of about $50 million.

Middleby kept the acquisitions feeding frenzy going later in 2007 with its purchase of New Star Holdings International for about $188 million in cash. New Star Holdings makes food-service equipment for the fast-casual and bakery cafe markets under brand names including Lang, Star, and Holman.

Chairman, president, and CEO Selim Bassoul owns about 11% of Middleby; CFO Timothy Fitzgerald owns nearly 2%.

EXECUTIVES

Chairman, President, and CEO; President and CEO, Middleby Marshall, Inc.: Selim A. Bassoul, age 50, $770,000 pay
VP and CFO; CFO, Middleby Marshall: Timothy J. Fitzgerald, age 37, $250,000 pay
VP, Supply Chain and Special Projects: Nazih Ibrahim, age 53, $150,000 pay
VP, Operating Division and Division General Manager: Mark A. Sieron, age 58, $161,035 pay
President, Alkar and RapidPak Divisions: Magdy Albert
President, Jade Range: Ray Williams
President, Worldwide: Lyall D. Newby
President, Pitco Frialator: David Brewer
Treasurer: Martin M. Lindsay, age 42
Investor and Public Relations: Darcy Bretz
Director, Human Resources: Terrie Solar
Auditors: Deloitte & Touche LLP

LOCATIONS

HQ: The Middleby Corporation
1400 Toastmaster Dr., Elgin, IL 60120
Phone: 847-741-3300   **Fax:** 847-741-0015
Web: www.middleby.com

2006 Sales

	$ mil.	% of total
US & Canada	326.0	81
Europe & Middle East	34.8	9
Asia	25.8	6
Latin America	16.5	4
Total	**403.1**	**100**

PRODUCTS/OPERATIONS

2006 Sales

	$ mil.	% of total
Commercial foodservice		
Core cooking equipment	245.6	56
Conveyor oven equipment	64.1	15
International specialty equipment	10.2	2
Counterline cooking equipment	9.3	2
International distribution	56.5	13
Industrial foodservice	55.1	12
Adjustments	(37.7)	—
Total	**403.1**	**100**

Selected Brands

Alkar (batch and conveyor ovens)
Blodgett (ovens, ranges)
MagiKitch'n (charbroilers)
Middleby Marshall (conveyor ovenss)
Nu-Vu (baking ovens)
Pitco Frialator (fryers)
RapidPak (packaging equipment)
Southbend (charbroilers, griddles, ovens, ranges)
Toastmaster (convection ovens, conveyer ovens, toasters)
Wells/Bloomfield (electric cooking products, coffee and tea equipment)

COMPETITORS

Ali SpA
Carrier Commercial Refrigeration
Dover Corporation
Electrolux
Enodis
Ingersoll-Rand
United Technologies
Vulcan-Hart

HISTORICAL FINANCIALS

Company Type: Public

Income Statement				FYE: Saturday nearest December 31

	REVENUE ($ mil.)	NET INCOME ($ mil.)	NET PROFIT MARGIN	EMPLOYEES
12/06	403.1	42.4	10.5%	1,282
12/05	316.7	32.2	10.2%	1,258
12/04	271.1	23.6	8.7%	—
12/03	242.2	18.7	7.7%	—
12/02	229.1	6.1	2.7%	1,042
Annual Growth	**15.2%**	**62.4%**	**—**	**5.3%**

2006 Year-End Financials

Debt ratio: 65.6%
Return on equity: 56.9%
Cash ($ mil.): 3.5
Current ratio: 1.11
Long-term debt ($ mil.): 66.0
No. of shares (mil.): 8.0
Dividends
  Yield: —
  Payout: —
Market value ($ mil.): 416.2
R&D as % of sales: —
Advertising as % of sales: —

Stock History

NASDAQ (GS): MIDD

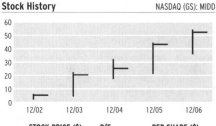

	STOCK PRICE ($) FY Close	P/E High/Low		PER SHARE ($) Earnings	Dividends	Book Value
12/06	52.33	21	14	2.57	—	12.65
12/05	43.25	22	11	1.99	—	6.14
12/04	25.36	27	15	1.19	0.20	0.96
12/03	20.48	22	5	1.00	0.13	6.74
12/02	5.28	17	8	0.34	—	4.94
Annual Growth	**77.4%**	**—**	**—**	**65.8%**	**53.8%**	**26.5%**

MidSouth Bancorp

If you want to bank in the Deep South, try MidSouth. MidSouth Bancorp is the holding company for MidSouth Bank, which operates more than 30 branches in southern Louisiana and East Texas. Targeting individuals and local business customers, the banks offer such standard retail services as checking and savings accounts, savings bonds, investment accounts, and credit card services. They also provide real estate mortgages (nearly 40% of its loan portfolio) and commercial (more than 30%), consumer, construction, and short-term business loans. MidSouth also offers lease-financing loans for business equipment.

The company expanded into Texas with its 2004 purchase of Beaumont-based Lamar Bancshares. It is changing the name of its Lamar Bank branches to MidSouth TX to emphasize the MidSouth brand.

EXECUTIVES

Chairman, MidSouth Bancorp and MidSouth LA: Will G. Charbonnet Sr., age 59
Vice Chairman: J. B. Hargroder, age 76
President, CEO, and Director, MidSouth Bancorp and MidSouth LA: C. R. (Rusty) Cloutier, age 60, $237,700 pay
EVP and CFO, MidSouth Bancorp and MidSouth Banks: J. Eustis Corrigan Jr., age 42, $85,038 pay (partial-year salary)
EVP; SVP and Senior Loan Officer, MidSouth LA: Donald R. (Donnie) Landry, age 50, $147,777 pay
SVP and Chief Marketing Officer: Alexander Calicchia
SVP and Controller: Teri S. Stelly, age 47
Secretary, Treasurer, and Director; SEVP and COO, MidSouth LA: Karen L. Hail, age 53, $179,995 pay
Chairman, Lamar Bank; Director: Joseph V. (Joe) Tortorice Jr., age 56
President, MidSouth Bank Texas: Ron D. Reed
SVP and CIO, MidSouth LA: Jennifer S. Fontenot, age 52, $114,460 pay
SVP and Retail Executive Manager, MidSouth Bank: A. Dwight Utz, age 52, $93,348 pay
Human Resources Director: Sarah Hubal
Investor Relations: Sally D. Gary
Auditors: Porter Keadle Moore, LLP

LOCATIONS

HQ: MidSouth Bancorp, Inc.
  102 Versailles Blvd., Lafayette, LA 70501
Phone: 337-237-8343   **Fax:** 337-267-4434
Web: www.midsouthbank.com

PRODUCTS/OPERATIONS

2006 Sales

	$ mil.	% of total
Interest		
Loans	41.1	66
Securities	8.0	12
Federal funds sold	1.1	2
Noninterest		
Deposit service charges	8.8	14
Other	3.6	6
Total	**62.6**	**100**

COMPETITORS

American Bancorp
Bank of America
Capital One
Encore Bancshares
Franklin Bank
Hancock Holding

Henderson Citizens Bancshares
IBERIABANK
Regions Financial
Teche Holding
Wachovia
Whitney Holding

HISTORICAL FINANCIALS

Company Type: Public

Income Statement				FYE: December 31

	ASSETS ($ mil.)	NET INCOME ($ mil.)	INCOME AS % OF ASSETS	EMPLOYEES
12/06	805.0	8.2	1.0%	371
12/05	698.8	7.3	1.0%	337
12/04	610.1	7.0	1.1%	—
12/03	432.7	6.3	1.5%	—
12/02	382.7	4.4	1.1%	212
Annual Growth	**20.4%**	**16.8%**	**—**	**15.0%**

2006 Year-End Financials

Equity as % of assets: 7.4%
Return on assets: 1.1%
Return on equity: 14.5%
Long-term debt ($ mil.): 15.5
No. of shares (mil.): 6.2
Market value ($ mil.): 185.1
Dividends
  Yield: 0.7%
  Payout: 15.3%
Sales ($ mil.): 62.6
R&D as % of sales: —
Advertising as % of sales: —

Stock History

AMEX: MSL

	STOCK PRICE ($) FY Close	P/E High/Low		PER SHARE ($) Earnings	Dividends	Book Value
12/06	29.68	25	16	1.24	0.19	9.58
12/05	20.56	24	15	1.10	0.22	10.74
12/04	18.70	18	14	1.13	0.14	10.90
12/03	17.45	17	8	1.06	1.34	10.08
12/02	8.72	16	7	0.76	0.13	9.35
Annual Growth	**35.8%**	**—**	**—**	**13.0%**	**10.0%**	**0.6%**

Miller Industries

If you're unfortunate enough to be involved in a car accident or to be marooned by mechanical failure, your next ride might come in a vehicle made by Miller Industries. The company makes bodies for light- and heavy-duty wreckers, along with car carriers and multi-vehicle trailers, at plants in the US and Europe. Its multi-vehicle trailers can carry as many as eight vehicles. Miller Industries' US brand names include Century, Challenger, Champion, Chevron, Eagle, Holmes, Vulcan, and Titan. The company's European brands are Jige (France) and Boniface (UK). Miller and rival Jerr-Dan dominate the US market for wrecker bodies.

In order to reduce expenses and focus on core operations, Miller Industries has exited the towing services business and is winding down the operations of its distribution business. The company's products are sold through independent distributors, 65% of which sell Miller Industries products exclusively.

Miller Industries' adjustments to its business mix paid off. Profits in 2005 were three times those of 2004. In 2006 the company invested some of those profits with the expansion and modernization of its Chattanooga, Tennessee plant by adding 50,000 sq. ft. of floor space and several equipment upgrades.

Founder, chairman, and co-CEO William Miller owns about 14% of the company.

HISTORY

Headed by William Miller, the Miller Group (which owned Challenger Wrecker and Holmes International) acquired the wrecking operations of Century Holdings in 1990 and formed the basis for Miller Industries. However, Miller Industries wasn't officially created until 1994, when the Miller Group placed all its wrecking and towing businesses under that moniker. The company went public in 1995.

With an established base in tow-truck manufacturing, Miller Industries began to expand vertically in 1996. The company created a financial services unit that year to provide loans to towing-service and distribution companies. It started acquiring towing-equipment distributors of its own at that time. Also in 1996 the company moved overseas with the acquisition of European tow-truck makers S.A. Jige Lohr Wreckers (France) and Boniface Engineering Limited (UK).

In early 1997 Miller Industries made a massive push into towing-service companies, creating RoadOne with the intention of becoming a nationwide entity. The company acquired 29 towing-service companies in fiscal 1997, 47 in 1998, and 35 in 1999. Then its pace slowed — Miller Industries acquired only a handful of towing-service businesses in 2000.

Miller proposed a 1-for-5 stock split to shareholders in 2001 in hopes of avoiding being delisted from the New York Stock Exchange. The company managed to keep its shares trading on the NYSE by trimming costs, which it accomplished by moving to exit the distribution and towing services businesses, beginning in 2002. By the end of 2004 Miller had disposed of the assets of RoadOne and nearly all of its distribution operations.

EXECUTIVES

Chairman and Co-CEO: William G. (Bill) Miller, age 60, $180,007 pay
President, Co-CEO, and Director: Jeffrey I. (Jeff) Badgley, age 55, $351,803 pay
EVP, Secretary, and General Counsel: Frank Madonia, age 57, $244,302 pay
EVP and CFO; President, Financial Services Group: J. Vincent Mish, age 55, $231,802 pay
Director, Human Resources: Bill Bakely
Auditors: Joseph Decosimo and Company, LLP

LOCATIONS

HQ: Miller Industries, Inc.
8503 Hilltop Dr., Ooltewah, TN 37363
Phone: 423-238-4171   **Fax:** 423-238-5371
Web: www.millerind.com

Miller Industries has manufacturing facilities in France, the UK, and the US (Pennsylvania and Tennessee).

2006 Sales

	$ mil.	% of total
North America	333.3	81
Other regions	76.1	19
Total	**409.4**	**100**

PRODUCTS/OPERATIONS

Selected Products

Boniface (heavy-duty wreckers for the European market)
Century (wreckers, car carriers)
Challenger (wreckers, car carriers)
Champion (car carriers)
Chevron (wreckers, car carriers, towing and recovery equipment)
Eagle (light-duty wreckers)
Holmes (mid-priced wreckers and car carriers)
Jige (light- and heavy-duty wreckers and car carriers for the European market)
Vulcan (wreckers, car carriers, towing and recovery equipment)

COMPETITORS

Daimler Trucks North America
Jerr-Dan
Mitsubishi Fuso
Peterbilt

HISTORICAL FINANCIALS

Company Type: Public

Income Statement

	REVENUE ($ mil.)	NET INCOME ($ mil.)	NET PROFIT MARGIN	EMPLOYEES
12/06	409.4	45.3	11.1%	1,000
12/05	351.9	18.6	5.3%	900
12/04	236.3	5.5	2.3%	—
12/03	206.0	(14.1)	—	—
12/02	203.1	(45.7)	—	1,000
Annual Growth	**19.2%**	**—**	**—**	**0.0%**

FYE: December 31

2006 Year-End Financials

Debt ratio: 9.3%	Dividends
Return on equity: 50.9%	Yield: —
Cash ($ mil.): 8.2	Payout: —
Current ratio: 2.04	Market value ($ mil.): 276.2
Long-term debt ($ mil.): 10.5	R&D as % of sales: —
No. of shares (mil.): 11.5	Advertising as % of sales: —

Stock History

NYSE: MLR

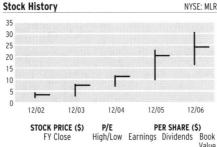

	STOCK PRICE ($) FY Close	P/E High/Low		PER SHARE ($) Earnings	Dividends	Book Value
12/06	24.00	8	4	3.91	—	9.85
12/05	20.29	14	6	1.62	—	5.73
12/04	11.30	23	14	0.50	—	4.18
12/03	7.51	—	—	(1.52)	—	3.00
12/02	3.41	—	—	(4.89)	—	4.25
Annual Growth	**62.9%**	**—**	**—**	**—**	**—**	**23.4%**

Mitcham Industries

Here's a shocker. Mitcham Industries has few rivals that can match 'em when it comes to sales and leasing of seismic equipment to the global seismic industry. The company's seismic equipment offerings include channel boxes, geophones, earth vibrators, various cables, and other peripheral equipment. Through short-term leasing (three to nine months) from Mitcham Industries, oil and gas companies can improve their chances of drilling a productive well and reduce equipment costs. Most of Mitcham Industries' leases are located in North America.

Mitcham Industries' seismic surveys, used to identify and define potential reservoirs of oil and gas, involve generating an acoustic wave into the earth using compressed air, explosives, or vibrators. Geophones then capture the reflected energy, and channel boxes convert the signals from analog to digital data, which is later interpreted.

In an effort to anticipate the need for seismic surveys and create new business, Mitcham Industries formed Drilling Services Inc. (DSI) in 2002. Mitcham sold the newly formed subsidiary in 2003 to WBW Enterprises of Texas in an effort to focus on its core operating units. The company acquired Seamap International, a provider of products and services to the seismic, hydrographic, and offshore industries, in 2005.

Although the company's business has traditionally been concentrated in North America, its leasing activities have been on the rise in Latin America. Mitcham Industries also operates in Asia and Europe, and it has an exclusive marketing agreement with Compagnie Générale de Géophysique's Sercel unit, one of the top seismic equipment makers. The company has expanded its operations to Southeast Asia by acquiring Seismic Asia Pacific, an oceanographic, seismic, and hydrographic equipment provider based in Brisbane, Australia.

HISTORY

Mitcham Industries was founded in 1987 by geophysical industry veteran Billy Mitcham Jr., a former Halliburton employee. The firm's strategy included growing and diversifying its lease pool of seismic equipment, expanding its international presence, and developing alliances with major seismic equipment manufacturers. In 1994 the company entered into an agreement with leading equipment maker Input/Output (I/O): Mitcham Industries bought I/O equipment, and, in turn, I/O referred rental inquiries.

The company went public in 1995. The next year Mitcham Industries penned another agreement with Sercel (a subsidiary of France's Compagnie Générale de Géophysique, S.A.) and became the manufacturer's exclusive worldwide leasing agent. Because Sercel was a major player in Canada, the deal immediately pumped up Mitcham Industries' sales in that country.

After the oil industry downturn in 1998, the company decided it only had room for one major marketing partner: In 1999 it terminated the agreement with I/O and renewed its deal with Sercel. Mitcham Industries launched a stock buyback in 2000.

A year later, the company settled a 1998 lawsuit brought by shareholders (who claimed that Mitcham had made misleading statements about its finances) for about $2.7 million.

In 2002 Mitcham formed subsidiary Drilling Services (DSI) to provide front-end services (permitting, surveying, shot hole drilling, and other activities) for its customers. It later sold the operating assets of DSI to WBW Enterprises and returned it focus to its core operating units.

In 2003 the company moved in to the Southeast Asia market by acquiring Australian-based Seismic Asia Pacific, an equipment supplier to Southeast Asia. In 2004 the company separated the roles of its chairman, president, and CEO positions. Billy Mitcham stepped down as chairman, retaining his roles as president and CEO for the company. Director Peter Blum replaced Mitcham as chairman.

To complement its marine rental and sales business, in 2005 Mitcham purchased Seamap International Holdings and its three subsidiaries in Texas, the UK, and Singapore for $6.5 million. The units produce proprietary products for the seismic, hydrographic, and offshore industries.

EXECUTIVES

Non-Executive Chairman: Peter H. Blum, age 51
President, CEO, and Director: Billy F. Mitcham Jr., age 60, $355,240 pay
EVP Finance, CFO, and Director: Robert P. (Rob) Capps, age 54
VP Business Development: Paul (Guy) Rogers, age 58, $163,527 pay
VP Marine Systems: Guy Malden, age 56, $160,018 pay
Manager Vibes and Drills: Tim Holden
Accounting: Cheryl Wilson
Information Technology and Web Site: Craig Middleton
Sales: Pascal Hythier
Sales: Howard White
Used Equipment Sales: Jim Croix

LOCATIONS

HQ: Mitcham Industries, Inc.
8141 SH 75 South, Huntsville, TX 77342
Phone: 936-291-2277   **Fax:** 936-295-1922
Web: www.mitchamindustries.com

Mitcham Industries has operations in the US, Canada, Singapore, and the UK, and representatives in Argentina, Hungary, and the Netherlands.

2007 Sales

	$ mil.	% of total
North America		
US	11.6	24
Canada	8.3	17
Asia/Australia	9.7	20
UK/Europe	9.3	19
Eurasia	5.0	10
South America	3.1	6
Other	1.9	4
Total	**48.9**	**100**

PRODUCTS/OPERATIONS

2007 Sales

	$ mil.	% of total
Equipment leasing	24.9	51
Equipment sales		
Seamap equipment sales	11.2	23
Lease pool equipment sales	4.3	9
Other equipment sales	8.5	17
Total	**48.9**	**100**

Selected Products

Boats	Radio systems
Buoys	Refraction systems
CDP cables	Seismographs
CDP systems	Shooting systems
Drills	Streamers
Energy sources	Tape trasports
Geophones	Telemetry systems
GPR	Telemetry cables
Heli Bags	Test equipment
Hydrophones	Vehicles
MarshPhones	Vibrators
Plotters	Vibrator electronics

COMPETITORS

Ashtead Group
Baker Hughes
CGGVeritas
Dawson Geophysical
Halliburton
ION Geophysical
OYO Geospace
Petroleum Geo-Services
Schlumberger
Seitel

HISTORICAL FINANCIALS

Company Type: Public

Income Statement

FYE: January 31

	REVENUE ($ mil.)	NET INCOME ($ mil.)	NET PROFIT MARGIN	EMPLOYEES
1/07	48.9	9.3	19.0%	131
1/06	34.6	10.9	31.5%	111
1/05	26.4	2.1	8.0%	—
1/04	22.4	(6.3)	—	—
1/03	19.1	(10.1)	—	138
Annual Growth	**26.5%**	**—**	**—**	**(1.3%)**

2007 Year-End Financials

Debt ratio: 2.5%
Return on equity: 17.4%
Cash ($ mil.): 12.6
Current ratio: 1.61
Long-term debt ($ mil.): 1.5
No. of shares (mil.): 9.7
Dividends
  Yield: —
  Payout: —
Market value ($ mil.): 130.6
R&D as % of sales: —
Advertising as % of sales: —

Stock History

NASDAQ (GM): MIND

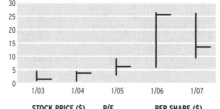

	STOCK PRICE ($) FY Close	P/E High/Low		PER SHARE ($) Earnings	Dividends	Book Value
1/07	13.49	28	10	0.93	—	6.15
1/06	25.54	24	5	1.10	—	5.02
1/05	6.18	39	13	0.23	—	3.42
1/04	3.73	—	—	(0.72)	—	3.50
1/03	1.44	—	—	(1.15)	—	3.85
Annual Growth	**74.9%**	**—**	**—**	**—**	**—**	**12.4%**

Mobile Mini

Mobile Mini knows that storing stuff is no small job. The company manufactures, leases, and sells portable storage containers and mobile offices. Mobile Mini also leases both steel and wood office units in various sizes. Major retailers and construction companies are Mobile Mini's primary customers. Other customers include the US military, municipal governments, and industrial users. Storage units are both manufactured and refurbished (using old oceangoing containers) by Mobile Mini. The company has a leasing fleet of more than 149,000 portable storage units and offices. Mobile Mini's leasing fleet accounts for 90% of total sales.

In 2005 Mobile Mini acquired some of the business of A-One Storage LLC for $7 million. The following year the company bought three companies of the Royal Wolf Group from Triton CSA International B.V. for about $50 million.

EXECUTIVES

Chairman, President, CEO, and Director: Steven G. Bunger, age 45, $410,963 pay
EVP, CFO, General Counsel, Secretary, Treasurer, and Director: Lawrence Trachtenberg, age 50, $293,548 pay
SVP and Chief Accounting Officer: Deborah K. Keeley, age 42, $172,018 pay
Director, Risk Management (HR): Katherine Gallaway
Auditors: Ernst & Young LLP

LOCATIONS

HQ: Mobile Mini, Inc.
7420 S. Kyrene Rd., Ste. 101, Tempe, AZ 85283
Phone: 480-894-6311   **Fax:** 480-894-6433
Web: www.mobilemini.com

Mobile Mini makes storage containers at its plant in Arizona.

2006 Sales

	$ mil.	% of total
US	257.5	94
Other countries	15.9	6
Total	**273.4**	**100**

PRODUCTS/OPERATIONS

2006 Leasing Customers

	% of total
Construction	40
Consumer service & retail business	36
Consumers	7
Industrial & commercial	7
Institutions, government agencies & others	10
Total	**100**

2006 Sales

	$ mil.	% of total
Leasing	245.1	91
Sales	26.8	8
Other	1.5	1
Total	**273.4**	**100**

Selected Products

Mobile offices
Portable storage products
  Manufactured storage units
  Records storage units
  Refurbished storage units

COMPETITORS

AMERCO	Mobile Services Group
GE	Modtech
McGrath RentCorp	Public Storage
Miller Building Systems	Williams Scotsman

HISTORICAL FINANCIALS
Company Type: Public

Income Statement				FYE: December 31
	REVENUE ($ mil.)	NET INCOME ($ mil.)	NET PROFIT MARGIN	EMPLOYEES
12/06	273.4	42.8	15.7%	1,943
12/05	207.2	34.0	16.4%	1,650
12/04	168.3	20.7	12.3%	—
12/03	146.6	5.9	4.0%	—
12/02	133.1	18.2	13.7%	1,420
Annual Growth	19.7%	23.8%	—	8.2%

2006 Year-End Financials

Debt ratio: 68.3%
Return on equity: 12.1%
Cash ($ mil.): 1.4
Current ratio: 1.10
Long-term debt ($ mil.): 302.0
No. of shares (mil.): 35.9

Dividends
 Yield: —
 Payout: —
Market value ($ mil.): 967.1
R&D as % of sales: —
Advertising as % of sales: —

Stock History
NASDAQ (GS): MINI

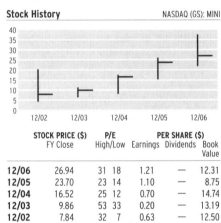

	STOCK PRICE ($) FY Close	P/E High/Low		PER SHARE ($) Earnings	Dividends	Book Value
12/06	26.94	31	18	1.21	—	12.31
12/05	23.70	23	14	1.10	—	8.75
12/04	16.52	25	12	0.70	—	14.74
12/03	9.86	53	33	0.20	—	13.19
12/02	7.84	32	7	0.63	—	12.50
Annual Growth	36.2%	—	—	17.7%	—	(0.4%)

Morningstar, Inc.

Morningstar offers a smorgasbord of financial information to individual, professional, and institutional investors. Its Morningstar.com features content for individual investors on portfolio planning, mutual funds, and stocks. Its *Morningstar Mutual Funds* is a reference publication featuring one-page reports on some 1,600 mutual funds. Other publications include monthly stock newsletter *Morningstar StockInvestor* and monthly fund newsletter *Morningstar FundInvestor*. Its software includes Morningstar Advisor Workstation, a Web-based investment planning system for financial advisors, and Morningstar Direct for institutional investment research professionals. Chairman and CEO Joe Mansueto owns 70% of Morningstar.

The company's Morningstar Style Box, which provides a visual summary of a mutual fund's underlying investment style, and Morningstar Ratings, which rates past performance based on risk- and cost-adjusted returns, have become fixtures on the investment landscape.

Morningstar's key product for institutional clients is Licensed Data, a set of investment data spanning eight core databases, available through electronic data feeds. The company also has an investment consulting practice for institutions that provides asset allocation and fund research.

Morningstar has announced plans to purchase financial information provider Hemscott from Ipreo for about $52 million. The deal is part of Morningstar's strategy to expand outside the US.

HISTORY

Joseph Mansueto founded Morningstar in 1984, using a line borrowed from Thoreau's *Walden* ("The sun is but a morning star"). Armed with an MBA and experience culled from a stint as a securities analyst for Harris Associates, Mansueto published *Mutual Fund Sourcebook,* a tome outlining performance histories and other information on 400 stock mutual funds. The boom in mutual funds during the early 1980s spurred interest in Morningstar's product and prompted the company to add a second publication, *Morningstar Mutual Funds,* two years later.

The company's 1994 acquisition of MarketBase helped the firm add stock information to its coverage. A 5% staff cut in 1996 and the cessation of some of its publications helped reverse Morningstar's sagging fortunes. It took to cyberspace the following year when it launched Morningstar.Net (now Morningstar.com). That year the company partnered with Japanese digital dynamo SOFTBANK to create Morningstar Japan and present financial information to investors in that country.

Don Phillips, who had joined Morningstar as its first analyst in 1986, was appointed CEO in 1998. The company began offering a subscription-based premium service feature for its Web site to offer users expanded financial coverage. In 1999 Morningstar extended its reach, partnering with FPG Research to offer financial information to residents of Australia and New Zealand. Later that year SOFTBANK invested $91 million in Morningstar.

In 2000 the company established MorningstarAdvisor.com, relaunched its flagship site with additional information and tools, and opened offices in Hong Kong, South Korea, and the UK. Founder and chairman Joe Mansueto also assumed the role of CEO in 2000 and made Phillips a managing director of the company.

The following year the company launched its Web site in Germany, Italy, the Netherlands, Spain, and the UK. Morningstar added Australian financial publisher Aspect Huntley to its stable in 2006.

In 2007 the company acquired Standard & Poor's fund data business.

EXECUTIVES

Chairman and CEO: Joseph (Joe) Mansueto, age 50, $100,000 pay
COO: Tao Huang, age 44, $1,015,000 pay
CFO: Scott Cooley, age 38
VP Research and New Product Development: John Rekenthaler, age 46
Managing Director, Strategic Relationships and Business Development: Timothy K. (Tim) Armour, age 58

Chief of Securities Research: Haywood Kelly
General Counsel and Corporate Secretary: Richard E. Robbins, age 44
Director; Managing Director, Corporate Strategy, Research, and Communications: Don Phillips, age 45
Director Business Development: Kishore Gangwani
Director Corporate Communications: Margaret Kirch Cohen
Director Mutual Fund Research; Editor, *Morningstar FundInvestor*: Russel Kinnel
Director Research: Paul D. Kaplan
Director Stock Analysis: Patrick Dorsey
Director Mergers and Acquisitions: Dan Piscatelli
President and Chief Investment Officer, Ibbotson Associates: Peng Chen
President, Morningstar Investment Services: Kunal Kapoor
President, Advisor Business: Chris Boruff, age 41
President, Data Services Business: Elizabeth (Liz) Kirscher, age 42
President, Individual Business: Catherine Gillis Odelbo, age 44, $620,000 pay
President, International Business: Bevin Desmond, age 40
President, Morningstar Associates: Patrick Reinkemeyer, age 41, $1,045,000 pay
Auditors: Ernst & Young LLP

LOCATIONS

HQ: Morningstar, Inc.
 225 W. Wacker Dr., Chicago, IL 60606
Phone: 312-696-6000   **Fax:** 312-696-6001
Web: www.morningstar.com

Morningstar has operations in 16 countries in Asia, Europe, and North America.

PRODUCTS/OPERATIONS

2006 Sales

	$ mil.	% of total
Institutional	146.1	45
Advisor	94.7	30
Individual	80.7	25
Adjustments	(6.3)	—
Total	**315.2**	**100**

Selected Products and Services

MorningstarAdvisor.com (market analysis, stock and fund information, portfolio tools, and investment research for advisors)
Morningstar Advisor Workstation (Web-based investment planning software)
Morningstar FundInvestor (monthly mutual fund newsletter)
Morningstar Licensed Data (electronic investment data feeds)
Morningstar Mutual Funds (semimonthly information on 1,600 mutual funds)
Morningstar Principia (CD-ROM-based investment planning software)
Morningstar StockInvestor (monthly stock newsletter)
Morningstar.com (market analysis, stock and fund information, portfolio tools, and investment research for individuals)

COMPETITORS

Bankrate
Bloomberg L.P.
Dow Jones
Financial Engines
Intuit
Ipreo
MarketWatch
McGraw-Hill
Motley Fool
PCQuote.com
Reuters
TheStreet.com
Thomson Corporation
Value Line
WisdomTree Investments

HISTORICAL FINANCIALS
Company Type: Public

Income Statement
FYE: December 31

	REVENUE ($ mil.)	NET INCOME ($ mil.)	NET PROFIT MARGIN	EMPLOYEES
12/06	315.2	51.8	16.4%	1,440
12/05	227.1	31.1	13.7%	1,130
12/04	179.7	8.8	4.9%	1,000
12/03	139.5	(11.9)	—	—
12/02	109.6	0.4	0.4%	—
Annual Growth	30.2%	237.3%	—	20.0%

2006 Year-End Financials

Debt ratio: —	Dividends
Return on equity: 23.4%	Yield: —
Cash ($ mil.): 163.8	Payout: —
Current ratio: 1.42	Market value ($ mil.): 1,902.4
Long-term debt ($ mil.): —	R&D as % of sales: —
No. of shares (mil.): 42.2	Advertising as % of sales: —

Stock History
NASDAQ (GS): MORN

	STOCK PRICE ($) FY Close	P/E High/Low		PER SHARE ($) Earnings	Dividends	Book Value
12/06	45.05	43	30	1.11	—	6.38
12/05	34.64	53	26	0.70	—	4.31
Annual Growth	30.1%	—	—	58.6%	—	48.0%

MSCI Inc.

You ask your asset manager how your portfolio is doing, but who does he ask? Probably MSCI. The company, formerly Morgan Stanley Capital International, creates equity, fixed income, and hedge fund indices, and offers risk management and portfolio analysis tools used by 24 of the 25 largest asset management firms. Products include MSCI World and EAFE indices, which watch global funds, and BarraOne, which provides Web-based risk analysis. Its MSCI Global Islamic Indices product incorporates allowances for Sharia or Islamic law. Financial services powerhouse Morgan Stanley owns 83% of the company and controls 94% of its votes.

The company filed an IPO in 2007; proceeds from the public offering are being used to pay debt MSCI owed to Morgan Stanley.

MSCI bought risk analysis expert Barra in 2004 as fund managers began to spend more on data. The combined company, which uses a subscription model to sell its products, is able to offer a more well-rounded package of tools to its clients.

Looking to the Muslim world for growth, the company opened an office in Dubai and launched its Islamic Indices in summer 2007.

EXECUTIVES
President, CEO, and Director: Henry A. Fernandez, age 49
COO: David C. Brierwood, age 46
CFO: Michael K. Neborak, age 50
Head of Client Coverage: C.D. Baer Pettit, age 42
Head of Strategy and Business Development: Gary Retelny, age 49
Principal Accounting Officer: Allen P. Heery
Auditors: Deloitte & Touche LLP

LOCATIONS
HQ: MSCI Inc.
88 Pine St., New York, NY 10005
Phone: 212-804-3990   **Fax:** 212-785-9639
Web: www.mscibarra.com

2006 Sales

	$ mil.	% of total
Americas		
US	149.6	48
Other	8.8	3
Europe, Middle East, and Africa		
UK	40.4	13
Other	66.0	21
Asia & Australia		
Japan	27.4	9
Other	18.5	6
Total	**310.7**	**100**

PRODUCTS/OPERATIONS

2006 Sales

	$ mil.	% of total
Equity indices	156.8	50
Equity portfolio analytics	110.0	35
Multi-asset class portfolio analytics	16.9	5
Other	27.0	10
Total	**310.7**	**100**

COMPETITORS
Algorithmics
Deutsche Börse
Dow Jones
FactSet
FTSE Group
Nomura Securities
Northwestern Mutual
RiskMetrics
S&P

HISTORICAL FINANCIALS
Company Type: Public

Income Statement
FYE: November 30

	REVENUE ($ mil.)	NET INCOME ($ mil.)	NET PROFIT MARGIN	EMPLOYEES
11/06	310.7	77.7	25.0%	705
11/05	278.5	51.9	18.6%	—
11/04	178.4	17.8	10.0%	—
Annual Growth	32.0%	108.9%	—	—

2006 Year-End Financials

Debt ratio: 0.0%	Current ratio: 2.09
Return on equity: 9.9%	Long-term debt ($ mil.): 0.0
Cash ($ mil.): 24.4	

Net Income History
NYSE: MXB

Multi-Color Corporation

Multi-Color wants consumers to read its labels. The company produces printed labels for goods such as fabric softeners, food products, and health and beauty aids at about 10 locations in the US. Heat transfer, resealable, shrink wrap, and pressure sensitive are among the label types the company prints and affixes to glass and plastic containers. Multi-Color also offers gravure printing and injection in-mold labels. The company serves more than 650 clients in North and South America. Procter & Gamble accounts for nearly a third of sales, with Miller Lite Brewing representing 17%. In early 2005 Multi-Color acquired NorthStar Print Group (label printing business) from Journal Communications.

Its largest acquisition to date, the $27 million in cash purchase of The NorthStar Print Group (NSPG) bolstered the company's product portfolio and client roster. As a result, cut-and-stack label technology (the ability for labels to be pasted to containers during the labeling process) and the ability to introduce promotional products such as scratch-off coupons, shelf tags, and static clings are now offered by Multi-Color.

The company's Decorating Solutions division (in-mold labels production and heat transfer labels) is by far its most lucrative, representing more than 85% of the company's total sales each year. Its Packaging Services segment accounts for the remaining percentage and provides promotional packaging design services. In mid-2007, Multi-Color sold its Packaging Services division to NFI Industries for $19.2 million, in order to focus on its core label business.

EXECUTIVES
Chairman: Lorrence T. Kellar, age 69
President, CEO, and Director: Francis D. (Frank) Gerace, age 54, $801,482 pay
SVP, Finance, CFO, and Secretary: Dawn H. Bertsche, age 50, $430,797 pay
VP, Controller, and Chief Accounting Officer: James H. Reynolds, age 41, $205,734 pay
VP, Human Resources: Lesha K. Spahr
VP, Operations, Decorating Solutions: Jack Mackert
VP, Operations Controller, Decorating Solutions: Steven T. Walker
VP, Sales and Marketing, Decorating Solutions Division: Mark J. Tangry
President, Decorating Solutions: Donald E. Kneir, age 43, $464,173 pay
Corporate Treasurer: Mary T. Fetch
Director, Marketing: Dirk Edwards
Auditors: Grant Thornton LLP

LOCATIONS
HQ: Multi-Color Corporation
50 E-Business Way, Sharonville, OH 45241
Phone: 513-381-1480   **Fax:** 513-381-2813
Web: www.multicolorcorp.com

PRODUCTS/OPERATIONS

2007 Sales

	$ mil.	% of total
Decorating solutions	192.6	87
Packaging services	30.4	13
Adjustments	(0.6)	—
Total	**222.4**	**100**

Selected Products and Services

Labels
- Heat transfer
- In-mold
- Neck bands
- Peel-away
- Pressure sensitive
- Resealable
- Shrink sleeve

Packaging
- Design
- Kit assembly
- Shipping
- Shrink wrapping

Pre-press

COMPETITORS

Convergent Label Technology
Fort Dearborn
Gibraltar Packaging
H. S. Crocker
Jordan Industries
Outlook Group
Schawk
YORK Label

HISTORICAL FINANCIALS

Company Type: Public

Income Statement				FYE: Sunday nearest March 31
	REVENUE ($ mil.)	NET INCOME ($ mil.)	NET PROFIT MARGIN	EMPLOYEES
3/07	222.4	11.0	4.9%	829
3/06	205.3	9.6	4.7%	1,066
3/05	139.5	8.0	5.7%	—
3/04	127.0	6.5	5.1%	—
3/03	99.6	6.3	6.3%	—
Annual Growth	22.2%	15.0%	—	(22.2%)

2007 Year-End Financials

Debt ratio: —
Return on equity: 18.7%
Cash ($ mil.): 5.8
Current ratio: 1.50
Long-term debt ($ mil.): —
No. of shares (mil.): 6.7

Dividends
Yield: 0.6%
Payout: 12.0%
Market value ($ mil.): 156.7
R&D as % of sales: —
Advertising as % of sales: —

Stock History

NASDAQ (GM): LABL

	STOCK PRICE ($) FY Close	P/E High/Low		PER SHARE ($) Earnings	Dividends	Book Value
3/07	23.43	23	16	1.08	0.13	9.63
3/06	20.03	21	13	0.95	0.10	8.06
3/05	13.03	17	11	0.81	0.03	6.66
3/04	12.63	23	11	0.66	—	5.36
3/03	7.12	12	8	0.66	—	6.39
Annual Growth	34.7%	—	—	13.1%	108.2%	10.8%

MVC Capital

MVC Capital has had a bit of a facelift. Formed as meVC Draper Fisher Jurvetson Fund I in 1999 during the explosion of venture capital investing and the Internet boom, the fund's aim was to let individual investors in on the VC action. Unfortunately, most of its investments failed. In 2000, the firm became a closed-end investment fund registered as a business development company (BDC). After some $120 million in losses, shareholders voted in a new management team and in 2003 hired former Kohlberg Kravis Roberts general partner Michael Tokarz to turn things around. MVC has broadened its focus beyond tech company buyouts to include investments in small to mid-market companies from various industries.

The company's loan or equity investments generally range from $3 million to $25 million. Targets generally have sales of $200 million or less and come from such industries as consumer products, distribution, financial services, information technology, and manufacturing. MVC Capital holds investments in companies in Asia, Europe, and the US.

EXECUTIVES

Chairman and Portfolio Manager: Michael T. Tokarz, age 58
Managing Director: Bruce W. Shewmaker, age 61, $150,000 pay
CFO: Peter F. Seidenberg, age 38
VP and Secretary: Jaclyn Lauren (Jackie) Shapiro, age 28, $175,000 pay
Chief Compliance Officer: Scott Schuenke, age 27
Auditors: Ernst & Young LLP

LOCATIONS

HQ: MVC Capital, Inc.
287 Bowman Ave., Purchase, NY 10577
Phone: 914-701-0310   **Fax:** 914-701-0315
Web: www.mvccapital.com

PRODUCTS/OPERATIONS

2006 Sales

	% of total
Interest & dividends	
Non-control/non-affiliated investments	38
Control investments	21
Affiliate investments	16
Fees	
Control investments	12
Non-control/non-affiliated investments	6
Affiliate investments	3
Other	4
Total	**100**

Selected Portfolio Companies

Amersham Corporation (machined components manufacturing)
BP Clothing LLC (women's clothing line Baby Phat)
Dakota Growers Pasta Company (dry pasta manufacturing)
Impact Confections, Inc. (candy manufacturing and distribution)
JDC Lighting, LLC (commercial lighting distribution)

Marine Exhibition Corporation (owner and operator of Miami Seaquarium)
Octagon Credit Investors, LLC (asset management)
Ohio Medical Corporation (suction and oxygen therapy products)
Phoenix Coal Corporation (coal mining)
PreVisor (pre-employment assessments)
SGDA mbH (landfill remediation, Germany)
SP Industries, Inc. (laboratory equipment manufacturing)
Storage Canada, LLC (doing business as Dino's Storage, self-storage facilities)
Timberland Machines & Irrigation (landscape and irrigation products distribution)
Turf Products, LLC (distribution of turf-maintenance equipment, irrigation systems, and related products)
Vestal Manufacturing Enterprises (iron and steel components manufacturing)
Vitality Foodservice, Inc. (juice and dispensers for the foodservice industry)

COMPETITORS

Allied Capital
Gladstone Capital
Harris & Harris
MCG Capital
Warburg Pincus

HISTORICAL FINANCIALS

Company Type: Public

Income Statement				FYE: October 31
	REVENUE ($ mil.)	NET INCOME ($ mil.)	NET PROFIT MARGIN	EMPLOYEES
10/07	93.9	65.7	70.0%	0
10/06	18.5	47.3	255.7%	13
10/05	12.2	26.3	215.6%	—
10/04	4.0	11.6	290.0%	—
10/03	2.9	(55.5)	—	—
Annual Growth	138.5%	—	—	—

2007 Year-End Financials

Debt ratio: 21.7%
Return on equity: 21.7%
Cash ($ mil.): 84.8
Current ratio: —
Long-term debt ($ mil.): 80.0
No. of shares (mil.): 20.2

Dividends
Yield: 3.2%
Payout: 18.5%
Market value ($ mil.): 345.1
R&D as % of sales: —
Advertising as % of sales: —

Stock History

NYSE: MVC

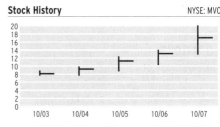

	STOCK PRICE ($) FY Close	P/E High/Low		PER SHARE ($) Earnings	Dividends	Book Value
10/07	17.06	7	4	2.92	0.54	18.25
10/06	13.08	6	4	2.48	0.48	12.41
10/05	11.25	8	6	1.45	0.24	10.41
10/04	9.24	11	9	0.91	—	9.40
10/03	8.10	—	—	(3.42)	—	8.48
Annual Growth	20.5%	—	—	—	50.0%	21.1%

Nara Bancorp

Nara Bancorp is the holding company for Nara Bank, which serves consumers and small to mid-sized minority-owned businesses through nearly 20 branches in Korean districts in California and the New York metropolitan area. It also has loan production offices in the Atlanta, Chicago, Dallas, Denver, Seattle, and Washington, DC areas. Real estate and construction loans make up more than 60% of the company's loan portfolio; the bank also provides commercial loans (about a third of all loans), including Small Business Administration (SBA) loans and equipment lease financing.

In 2005 Nara Bancorp restated its 2002 earnings after its auditor discovered it had improperly accounted for a $600,000 reimbursement to former president and CEO Benjamin Hong for country club dues and auto expenses. The company's CFO was demoted, and a board member was later forced to resign over the incident. Hong's successor, Ho Yang, resigned the following year for unrelated reasons. Min Kim, who replaced Yang, became the company's third CEO in two years.

EXECUTIVES

Chairman, Nara Bancorp and Nara Bank:
Chong-Moon Lee, age 78
President, CEO, and Director: Min J. Kim, age 47, $287,027 pay
EVP and CFO, Nara Bancorp and Nara Bank:
Alvin D. (Al) Kang, age 60, $157,603 pay
EVP and Chief Credit Officer: Bonita I. (Bonnie) Lee, age 42, $266,354 pay
EVP and Human Resources Manager: Elizabeth Wong
SVP and COO: Myung H. Hyun
SVP, Director of Legal Affairs, and Secretary:
Michel Urich
SVP and Controller: Christine Yoon Oh, age 38, $202,188 pay
SVP and Director of Information Technology:
Mona Chui
SVP and SBA Manager: Young K. Oh
SVP and Internal Auditor: Jim Graham
SVP and Eastern Region Manager: Kyu S. Kim
SVP and Chief Risk Officer: Jasna Penich
Secretary: Lisa Pai
Auditors: Crowe Chizek and Company LLP

LOCATIONS

HQ: Nara Bancorp, Inc.
3731 Wilshire Blvd., Ste. 1000,
Los Angeles, CA 90010
Phone: 213-639-1700   **Fax:** 213-235-3033
Web: www.narabank.com

PRODUCTS/OPERATIONS

2006 Sales

	$ mil.	% of total
Interest		
Loans, including fees	144.4	82
Securities	8.4	5
Federal funds sold & other	3.0	2
Noninterest		
Service charges on deposit accounts	6.1	3
Net gains on sales of SBA loans	4.8	3
International service fees	2.7	2
Other income & fees	5.7	3
Total	**175.1**	**100**

COMPETITORS

Bank of America	Hanmi Financial
Broadway Financial	Saehan Bancorp
Center Financial	U.S. Bancorp
East West Bancorp	Wilshire Bancorp

HISTORICAL FINANCIALS

Company Type: Public

Income Statement				FYE: December 31
	ASSETS ($ mil.)	NET INCOME ($ mil.)	INCOME AS % OF ASSETS	EMPLOYEES
12/06	2,047.0	33.8	1.7%	408
12/05	1,775.8	26.9	1.5%	376
12/04	1,507.7	19.8	1.3%	—
12/03	1,260.0	14.3	1.1%	—
12/02	979.3	15.5	1.6%	291
Annual Growth	**20.2%**	**21.5%**	**—**	**8.8%**

2006 Year-End Financials

Equity as % of assets: 9.1%
Return on assets: 1.8%
Return on equity: 20.3%
Long-term debt ($ mil.): 39.3
No. of shares (mil.): 26.1
Market value ($ mil.): 546.2
Dividends
  Yield: 0.5%
  Payout: 8.6%
Sales ($ mil.): 175.1
R&D as % of sales: —
Advertising as % of sales: —

Stock History

NASDAQ (GS): NARA

	STOCK PRICE ($) FY Close	P/E High/Low		PER SHARE ($) Earnings	Dividends	Book Value
12/06	20.92	17	12	1.28	0.11	7.15
12/05	17.78	21	12	1.07	0.11	5.77
12/04	21.27	28	16	0.80	0.08	4.34
12/03	13.80	23	8	0.62	0.10	7.35
12/02	5.16	9	6	0.68	0.08	6.11
Annual Growth	**41.9%**	**—**	**—**	**17.1%**	**8.3%**	**4.0%**

NATCO Group

Looking to oil flow for its cash flow, NATCO Group provides the oil and gas industry with wellhead equipment, systems, and services. NATCO's products include dehydration and desalting units; heaters to prevent solids from forming in gas; gas conditioning equipment; water filtration systems; and production equipment control systems. The company's products are used in oil and gas fields throughout the world, but the US and Canada account for 80% of sales. In 2005 NATCO reorganized its operations into three segments: automation and controls, gas technologies, and oil and water technologies. In 2008 the company agreed to acquire measurement firm Linco-Electromatic for $23 million.

Although the NATCO Group was only formed in 1988, through its several subsidiaries it traces its history of designing, manufacturing, and marketing production equipment and systems to the 1920s.

EXECUTIVES

Chairman and CEO: John U. Clarke, age 55, $846,000 pay
President, COO, and Director: Patrick M. McCarthy, age 62
EVP: C. Frank Smith, age 56, $361,981 pay
EVP Integrated Engineered Solutions:
Robert A. Curcio, age 50, $393,907 pay
EVP Automation & Controls: David R. Volz Jr., age 52
SVP and CFO: Bradley P. Farnsworth, age 54
SVP, Secretary, and General Counsel: Katherine P. Ellis, age 47
SVP Global Ventures: Joseph H. Wilson, age 53
SVP Global Execution: Knut Eriksen, age 57
SVP Human Resources and Administration:
J. Scott Thompson
Auditors: KPMG LLP

LOCATIONS

HQ: NATCO Group Inc.
2950 North Loop West, 7th Fl., Houston, TX 77092
Phone: 713-683-9292   **Fax:** 713-683-6768
Web: www.natcogroup.com

NATCO Group operates through seven manufacturing facilities and more than 50 sales and service offices in Canada, the US, and the UK.

2006 Sales

	$ mil.	% of total
US	362.0	70
UK	73.6	14
Canada	54.3	10
Other countries	29.1	6
Total	**519.0**	**100**

PRODUCTS/OPERATIONS

2006 Sales

	$ mil.	% of total
Oil & water technologies	370.1	71
Automation & controls	86.2	17
Gas technologies	62.7	12
Total	**519.0**	**100**

Selected Products and Services

Carbon dioxide field operations (process to remove CO_2 from oil and gas streams)
Equipment refurbishment
Gas conditioning equipment (removes contaminants and impurities from oil and gas)
Gas Processing Equipment (used for gas and oil extraction)
Heaters (used to reduce the viscosity of oil to increase production)
Oil dehydration equipment (used to remove water from oil)
Parts, service, and training
Separators (used to separate gas, oil, and water)
Water treatment equipment (used to remove contaminants from water)

COMPETITORS

Aker Kværner
Baker Hughes
Exterran
Gulf Island Fabrication
Siemens Water Technologies
UOP
Weatherford International

HISTORICAL FINANCIALS

Company Type: Public

Income Statement
FYE: December 31

	REVENUE ($ mil.)	NET INCOME ($ mil.)	NET PROFIT MARGIN	EMPLOYEES
12/06	519.0	38.0	7.3%	2,304
12/05	400.5	14.2	3.5%	1,802
12/04	321.5	0.6	0.2%	—
12/03	281.5	0.1	0.0%	—
12/02	289.5	3.9	1.3%	1,700
Annual Growth	15.7%	76.7%	—	7.9%

2006 Year-End Financials

Debt ratio: —
Return on equity: 25.8%
Cash ($ mil.): 35.2
Current ratio: 1.61
Long-term debt ($ mil.): —
No. of shares (mil.): 17.4

Dividends
Yield: —
Payout: —
Market value ($ mil.): 553.4
R&D as % of sales: —
Advertising as % of sales: —

Stock History
NYSE: NTG

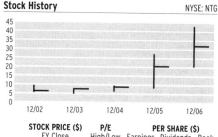

	STOCK PRICE ($) FY Close	P/E High/Low		PER SHARE ($) Earnings	Dividends	Book Value
12/06	31.88	22	10	1.97	—	9.95
12/05	20.46	35	11	0.77	—	7.22
12/04	8.80	—	—	(0.06)	—	6.05
12/03	7.59	—	—	(0.06)	—	5.83
12/02	6.28	38	24	0.24	—	5.81
Annual Growth	50.1%	—	—	69.3%	—	14.4%

National Presto Industries

Sure, the heat is on at National Presto Industries, but it's thermostatically controlled to provide even cooking on nonstick surfaces. Under the Presto brand, the company makes and distributes small appliances and housewares, including pressure cookers, fry pans, deep fryers, griddles, coffeemakers, can openers, electric knives, and pizza ovens. Besides appliances, National Presto Industries operates a defense business that generates as much revenue as its namesake appliances. Also contributing to its bottom line is the firm's Absorbent Products unit, which makes diapers and incontinence items. The company sells through US retailers, primarily mass merchants.

National Presto's defense and absorbent products units are the result of acquisitions, as the company adopts a new strategy for growth. Defense Products, which makes electronic assembly components for the US defense industry, was created through the purchases of AMTEC Corporation and Spectra Technologies. (The firm added to its Defense Products segment in 2006 with the acquisition of ammunition manufacturer Amron

LLC.) Absorbent Products, which makes and markets private-label diapers, was formed when the company acquired Presto Absorbent Products and NCN Hygienic Products. These purchases have allowed Presto to diversify its products portfolio outside the appliances realm.

The company, which manufactured its own products in the US until 2002, now purchases nearly all its products from third-party manufacturers in Asia. Wal-Mart represents some 15% of National Presto's housewares sales. Chairman emeritus Melvin Cohen and his daughter, chairman, president, and CEO Maryjo, together own about 35% of National Presto Industries.

EXECUTIVES

Chairman, President, and CEO: Maryjo Cohen, age 55, $299,000 pay
VP Engineering: Lawrence J. (Larry) Tienor, age 59, $146,500 pay
VP Manufacturing and Purchasing: Neil L. Brown, age 63, $124,400 pay
VP Sales: Donald E. Hoeschen, age 60, $194,870 pay
Secretary and General Counsel: Ian Keyes, age 35
Advertising Manager: Steve Kjaarsgard
Human Resources Manager: Darcy Holman
Auditors: BDO Seidman, LLP

LOCATIONS

HQ: National Presto Industries, Inc.
3925 N. Hastings Way, Eau Claire, WI 54703
Phone: 715-839-2121   **Fax:** 715-839-2122
Web: www.gopresto.com

PRODUCTS/OPERATIONS

2006 Sales

	$ mil.	% of total
Defense products	126.8	42
Housewares/small appliances	124.5	41
Absorbent products	53.4	17
Total	**304.7**	**100**

Selected Products

Housewares/Small Appliances
Can openers
Deep fryers
Electric knife sharpeners
Electric knives
Electric tea kettles
Fry pans, griddles, and multipurpose cookers
Pizza ovens
Pressure cookers and canners
Slicer/shredders
Timers

Defense Products
Precision mechanical and electro-mechanical assemblies
Load, assemble, and pack operations on ordnance-related products

Absorbent Products
Adult incontinent products
Private-label diapers
Puppy pads

COMPETITORS

Applica
Cardinal Supply Chain Medical
GE Consumer & Industrial
Global-Tech Appliances
Hamilton Beach
Johnson & Johnson
Kimberly-Clark
Lockheed Martin
Procter & Gamble
Salton
SEB

HISTORICAL FINANCIALS

Company Type: Public

Income Statement
FYE: December 31

	REVENUE ($ mil.)	NET INCOME ($ mil.)	NET PROFIT MARGIN	EMPLOYEES
12/06	304.7	28.0	9.2%	988
12/05	184.6	16.4	8.9%	552
12/04	159.0	15.4	9.7%	—
12/03	133.8	15.5	11.6%	—
12/02	133.7	8.7	6.5%	301
Annual Growth	22.9%	33.9%	—	34.6%

2006 Year-End Financials

Debt ratio: —
Return on equity: 10.2%
Cash ($ mil.): 143.6
Current ratio: 4.33
Long-term debt ($ mil.): —
No. of shares (mil.): 6.8

Dividends
Yield: 3.5%
Payout: 51.8%
Market value ($ mil.): 409.1
R&D as % of sales: —
Advertising as % of sales: —

Stock History
NYSE: NPK

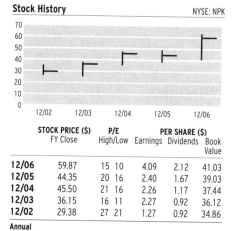

	STOCK PRICE ($) FY Close	P/E High/Low		PER SHARE ($) Earnings	Dividends	Book Value
12/06	59.87	15	10	4.09	2.12	41.03
12/05	44.35	20	16	2.40	1.67	39.03
12/04	45.50	21	16	2.26	1.17	37.44
12/03	36.15	16	11	2.27	0.92	36.12
12/02	29.38	27	21	1.27	0.92	34.86
Annual Growth	19.5%	—	—	34.0%	23.2%	4.2%

Natural Gas Services

The pressure is on to enhance oil and gas well production. Natural Gas Services Group (NGS) manufactures and leases natural gas compressors used to boost oil and gas well production levels. The company also provides flare tip burners, ignition systems, and components used to combust waste gases before entering the atmosphere. NGS leases compressors to third parties in Colorado, Kansas, Louisiana, Michigan, New Mexico, Oklahoma, Texas, and Wyoming. In early 2007 some 974 units of its fleet of 1,111 compressors were rented out to clients. Its main customer, XTO Energy, accounted for 54% of sales in 2006.

Founded in 1998, the company, which has grown through a number of acquisitions, purchased private compressor manufacturer Screw Compression Systems in 2005 for about $15 million in stock.

EXECUTIVES

Chairman, President, and CEO: Stephen C. Taylor, age 54
SVP and Director; President, Screw Compression Systems: Paul D. Hensley, age 55, $180,361 pay
VP Accounting and Treasurer: Earl R. Wait, age 64
VP Technical Services: James R. Hazlett, age 52, $141,750 pay (partial-year salary)
Investor Relations: Jim Drewitz

LOCATIONS

HQ: Natural Gas Services Group, Inc.
2911 S. Country Rd. 1260, Midland, TX 79706
Phone: 432-563-3974   **Fax:** 432-563-4139
Web: www.ngsgi.com

Natural Gas Services operates in Michigan, New Mexico, Oklahoma, and Texas.

PRODUCTS/OPERATIONS

2006 Sales

	$ mil.	% of total
Sales	38.2	61
Rental	23.5	37
Service & maintenance	1.0	2
Total	**62.7**	**100**

COMPETITORS

Baker Hughes	Flotek
BJ Services	Miller Petroleum
CARBO Ceramics	Oilgear
Compressor Systems	Weatherford International
Exterran	

HISTORICAL FINANCIALS

Company Type: Public

Income Statement

FYE: December 31

	REVENUE ($ mil.)	NET INCOME ($ mil.)	NET PROFIT MARGIN	EMPLOYEES
12/06	62.7	7.6	12.1%	266
12/05	49.3	4.4	8.9%	236
12/04	16.0	3.4	21.3%	—
12/03	12.8	1.3	10.2%	—
12/02	10.3	0.8	7.8%	69
Annual Growth	57.1%	75.6%	—	40.1%

2006 Year-End Financials

Debt ratio: 13.8%
Return on equity: 10.3%
Cash ($ mil.): 29.4
Current ratio: 5.19
Long-term debt ($ mil.): 13.9
No. of shares (mil.): 12.0
Dividends
  Yield: —
  Payout: —
Market value ($ mil.): 167.4
R&D as % of sales: —
Advertising as % of sales: —

Stock History

AMEX: NGS

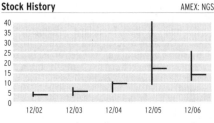

	STOCK PRICE ($) FY Close	P/E High/Low	PER SHARE ($) Earnings	Dividends	Book Value
12/06	13.90	38 17	0.66	—	8.40
12/05	16.96	77 17	0.52	—	5.06
12/04	9.43	20 10	0.52	—	3.38
12/03	5.55	32 16	0.23	—	2.87
12/02	3.88	31 20	0.16	—	2.68
Annual Growth	37.6%	— —	42.5%	—	33.1%

Netflix, Inc.

In a blend of technologies from multiple eras, Netflix steers couch potatoes away from the video store and straight to the mailbox. Its Web site (Netflix.com) offers DVD rentals (70,000-plus titles) to more than 6.3 million subscribers for a monthly fee. The movies are delivered to customers the old-fashioned way: through the US Postal Service. Netflix does not charge late fees or have due dates, and the company's service employs user ratings to predict individual preferences and make movie recommendations. Netflix has more than 40 distribution centers in major US cities. Director Jay Hoag and his Technology Crossover Ventures owns about 20% of the company and CEO Reed Hastings owns about 10%.

In early 2007 Netflix began offering a feature that allows customers to watch selected movies and content instantly via their personal computer. The service is part of the company's greater emphasis on electronic delivery of content.

Building on this service, Netflix and LG Electronics announced plans in early 2008 to sell an LG-branded device that will show movies downloaded through Netflix on TV screens.

In reaction to news that Amazon.com might be entering the US online DVD rental arena (Amazon has already launched its rental service in the UK) and to stay competitive with Blockbuster's online rental offering, the company has cut its monthly fee and has also postponed its UK expansion plans. However, in 2006 Netflix filed suit against Blockbuster, maintaining its online rental service violates Netflix's patent on such a rental system. Blockbuster has countersued, claiming Netflix's patent is unenforceable and was questionably obtained. The two resolved the issue in 2007 in a confidential settlement.

In addition, Netflix had some legal problems of its own. A class-action suit was filed against the firm by customers objecting to its practice known as "throttling," which means that Netflix delays shipments of DVDs to customers who rent the most movies and return them quickly. Users who rented fewer films each month (the company's more profitable customers since Netflix pays for shipping) typically receive their movies quicker. The firm settled the case by offering a free month to 5.5 million current and former subscribers and paying millions in legal fees to the attorneys who originally filed the complaint.

Netflix has also begun to leverage its subscriber base by allowing companies to place ads in Netflix e-mails and on its red mailing envelopes.

EXECUTIVES

Chairman, President, and CEO: Reed Hastings, age 46, $500,000 pay
CFO and Secretary: Barry McCarthy Jr., age 53, $500,000 pay
Chief Content Officer: Ted Sarandos
Chief Marketing Officer: Leslie J. Kilgore, age 41, $650,000 pay
Chief Product Officer: Neil Hunt
Chief Talent Officer: Patricia J. (Patty) McCord
General Counsel: David Hyman
VP IT Development and Interim COO: Andy Rendich
VP Advertising Sales: Peggy Fry
VP Corporate Communications: Ken Ross
VP and Head, Original Content: Bahman Naraghi
Director of Content Acquisition: Cindy Holland
Director of Investor Relations: Deborah Crawford
Director User Interface Engineering: Bill Scott
Auditors: KPMG LLP

LOCATIONS

HQ: Netflix, Inc.
100 Winchester Cir., Los Gatos, CA 95032
Phone: 408-540-3700
Web: www.netflix.com

COMPETITORS

Amazon.com
Apple
Best Buy
Blockbuster
Buy.com
CinemaNow
Columbia House
Comcast
Cox Communications
DIRECTV
Dish Network Corporation
Hastings Entertainment
HBO
Kroger
Movie Gallery
Redbox
Showtime Networks
Starz Entertainment
Target
Time Warner Cable
Wal-Mart

HISTORICAL FINANCIALS

Company Type: Public

Income Statement

FYE: December 31

	REVENUE ($ mil.)	NET INCOME ($ mil.)	NET PROFIT MARGIN	EMPLOYEES
12/06	996.7	49.1	4.9%	1,300
12/05	682.2	42.0	6.2%	985
12/04	506.2	21.6	4.3%	—
12/03	272.2	6.5	2.4%	—
12/02	152.8	(22.0)	—	495
Annual Growth	59.8%	—	—	27.3%

2006 Year-End Financials

Debt ratio: —
Return on equity: 15.3%
Cash ($ mil.): 400.4
Current ratio: 2.21
Long-term debt ($ mil.): —
No. of shares (mil.): 68.6
Dividends
  Yield: —
  Payout: —
Market value ($ mil.): 1,774.3
R&D as % of sales: —
Advertising as % of sales: —

Stock History

NASDAQ (GS): NFLX

	STOCK PRICE ($) FY Close	P/E High/Low	PER SHARE ($) Earnings	Dividends	Book Value
12/06	25.86	47 26	0.71	—	6.04
12/05	27.06	47 14	0.64	—	4.13
12/04	12.33	121 28	0.33	—	2.96
12/03	27.34	305 53	0.10	—	2.22
12/02	5.51	— —	(0.78)	—	3.98
Annual Growth	47.2%	— —	—	—	11.0%

NETGEAR, Inc.

NETGEAR keeps consumers and small businesses wired (and wireless). The company designs a range of networking equipment — hubs, routers, switches, servers, and interfaces — for connecting PCs in home and small business settings to each other and the Internet. NETGEAR sells through distributors, including Ingram Micro (one-quarter of sales) and Tech Data (17%); to retailers such as Circuit City and Best Buy; and directly through its online store. The company uses third-party manufacturing services contractors in China and Taiwan to produce its equipment.

NETGEAR has expanded its international sales presence in recent years, looking to emerging markets such as China and India for growth. The company generates more than half of sales from international markets.

In an effort to expand its multimedia portfolio, NETGEAR acquired home entertainment and control software developer SkipJam in 2006. The following year it acquired Infrant Technologies, a developer of network attached storage (NAS) devices, for $60 million in cash.

Originally spun off from communications equipment giant Nortel Networks in 2000, NETGEAR bought out Nortel's remaining stake in 2002.

EXECUTIVES

Chairman and CEO: Patrick C.S. Lo, age 50, $664,615 pay
CFO: Christine M. Gorjanc, age 50
CTO: Mark G. Merrill, age 52, $273,717 pay
CIO: Thomas (Tom) Holt
SVP Worldwide Sales and Support: David S. Soares, age 40
SVP Engineering: Charles T. (Chuck) Olson, age 51, $286,455 pay
SVP Operations: Michael F. Falcon, age 50, $300,019 pay
VP Product Marketing: Vivek Pathela
VP Engineering, Multimedia Products: Michael Spilo
VP Legal and Corporate Development, General Counsel, and Corporate Secretary: Albert Y. Liu, age 34
Director Corporate Marketing: Doug Hagan
Auditors: PricewaterhouseCoopers LLP

LOCATIONS

HQ: NETGEAR, Inc.
4500 Great American Pkwy., Santa Clara, CA 95054
Phone: 408-907-8000   **Fax:** 408-907-8097
Web: www.netgear.com

2006 Sales

	$ mil.	% of total
US	220.5	38
Europe, Middle East & Africa		
UK	151.0	26
Germany	55.1	10
Other countries	92.1	16
Other regions	54.9	10
Total	**573.6**	**100**

PRODUCTS/OPERATIONS

Selected Products

Broadband access
    Gateways (routers with integrated modems, wireless)
    IP telephony
    Routers
Ethernet networking
    Adapters
    Bridges
    Network interface cards (NICs)
    Peripheral servers
    Switches
    VPN firewalls
Network connectivity
    Media adapters
    Network-attached storage (NAS)
    Powerline adapters and bridges
    Wi-fi phones
    Wireless access points
    Wireless NICs and adapters

COMPETITORS

2Wire	Hewlett-Packard
3Com	Linksys
Allied Telesis	NetApp
ARRIS	Nortel Networks
Belkin	Scientific-Atlanta
Buffalo Technology	SonicWALL
Cisco Systems	Thomson Corporation
Dell	WatchGuard Technologies
D-Link	

HISTORICAL FINANCIALS

Company Type: Public

Income Statement

FYE: December 31

	REVENUE ($ mil.)	NET INCOME ($ mil.)	NET PROFIT MARGIN	EMPLOYEES
12/06	573.6	41.1	7.2%	388
12/05	449.6	33.6	7.5%	307
12/04	383.1	23.5	6.1%	—
12/03	299.3	13.1	4.4%	—
12/02	237.3	8.1	3.4%	—
Annual Growth	**24.7%**	**50.1%**	**—**	**26.4%**

2006 Year-End Financials

Debt ratio: —
Return on equity: 15.5%
Cash ($ mil.): 197.5
Current ratio: 2.96
Long-term debt ($ mil.): —
No. of shares (mil.): 34.0

Dividends
    Yield: —
    Payout: —
Market value ($ mil.): 891.5
R&D as % of sales: —
Advertising as % of sales: —

Stock History

NASDAQ (GS): NTGR

	STOCK PRICE ($) FY Close	P/E High/Low		PER SHARE ($) Earnings	Dividends	Book Value
12/06	26.25	24	14	1.19	—	8.67
12/05	19.25	26	13	0.99	—	7.16
12/04	18.16	28	12	0.72	—	5.89
12/03	15.99	43	26	0.49	—	4.72
Annual Growth	**18.0%**			**—**	**—**	**—**

NetLogic Microsystems

NetLogic Microsystems' chips logically address the content of the Internet. The company designs and sells packet processors and content-addressable memory (CAM) chips, which are used in routers and other devices to optimize speed and search capabilities over the Internet. NetLogic's customers include networking giants Cisco (61% of sales, including Cisco's contract manufacturers), Alcatel-Lucent, Huawei Technologies, and Juniper Networks. The fabless semiconductor company was founded by former CEO Norman Godinho (who owns about 15% of the company) and CTO Varad Srinivasan. NetLogic gets more than half of its sales outside the US.

The company has acquired Aeluros, a developer of 10-gigabit Ethernet interface technologies and semiconductors, for $57 million in cash. The firm's products will expand NetLogic's portfolio in knowledge-based processors, especially in the area of low-power, multi-gigabit interface technology. Knowledge-based processors are chips used in processing packets in computer networks; they are said to operate faster and more securely than comparable processors.

NetLogic reserved 115,000 shares of its common stock in exchange for unvested employee stock options of Aeluros, subject to continued employment vesting requirements. The company may pay out in 2009 an additional $20 million in cash, depending on performance milestones.

In 2006 NetLogic acquired the network search engine products of Cypress Semiconductor for approximately $50 million in common stock, plus up to $20 million in cash and stock depending on revenue milestones. NetLogic acquired the assets and intellectual property of Cypress Semi's Ayama 10000/20000 and NSE70000 network search engine device families, as well as the Sahasra 50000 algorithmic search engine family. The purchase advanced NetLogic's development of lower-cost Layer 7 applications acceleration and security processing for networking systems, among other benefits.

The company's semiconductors are principally produced by Taiwan Semiconductor Manufacturing and United Microelectronics, two of the world's biggest contract manufacturers of chips, known as silicon foundries.

NetLogic was backed by investors including Sevin Rosen Funds.

Gilder, Gagnon, Howe & Co. owns about 8% of NetLogic Microsystems.

EXECUTIVES

Chairman: Leonard C. (Len) Perham, age 63
President, CEO, and Director: Ronald (Ron) Jankov, age 48, $285,000 pay
SVP, Worldwide Business Operations: Ibrahim (Abe) Korgav, age 58, $207,000 pay
SVP, Worldwide Sales: Marcia Zander, age 44, $351,998 pay
VP and CFO: Michael T. (Mike) Tate, age 42
VP, Product Development and CTO: Varadarajan (Varad) Srinivasan, age 56, $212,000 pay
VP, Corporate Development: Niall Bartlett
VP, Engineering: Dimitrios Dimitrelis, age 49
VP, Worldwide Manufacturing: Mozafar (Mo) Maghsoudnia
VP Marketing: Chris O'Reilly
Senior Director Legal Affairs, IP Management, and Secretary: Roland Cortes, age 42
Corporate Controller: Shigeyuki Hamamatsu, age 34, $173,188 pay
Auditors: PricewaterhouseCoopers LLP

LOCATIONS

HQ: NetLogic Microsystems, Inc.
    1875 Charleston Rd., Mountain View, CA 94043
Phone: 650-961-6676   **Fax:** 650-961-1092
Web: www.netlogicmicro.com

NetLogic Microsystems has offices in India and the US.

2006 Sales

	$ mil.	% of total
US	46.2	48
Asia/Pacific		
Malaysia	31.6	33
Other countries	11.8	12
Europe & other regions	7.2	7
Total	**96.8**	**100**

PRODUCTS/OPERATIONS

Selected Products

Classification and forwarding processors
Network search engines
Software development kits
Ternary content-addressable memory (TCAM) search
  accelerators

COMPETITORS

Broadcom
EZchip
hi/fn
Integrated Device Technology
LSI Corp.
Mellanox
NetEffect
Renesas
TranSwitch
Vitesse Semiconductor

HISTORICAL FINANCIALS

Company Type: Public

Income Statement

FYE: December 31

	REVENUE ($ mil.)	NET INCOME ($ mil.)	NET PROFIT MARGIN	EMPLOYEES
12/06	96.8	0.6	0.6%	170
12/05	81.8	16.4	20.0%	—
12/04	47.8	(12.0)	—	—
12/03	13.5	(32.0)	—	—
12/02	2.9	(19.9)	—	—
Annual Growth	**140.4%**	**—**	**—**	**—**

2006 Year-End Financials

Debt ratio: —
Return on equity: 0.6%
Cash ($ mil.): 89.9
Current ratio: 8.00
Long-term debt ($ mil.): —
No. of shares (mil.): 20.4

Dividends
  Yield: —
  Payout: —
Market value ($ mil.): 443.3
R&D as % of sales: —
Advertising as % of sales: —

Stock History

NASDAQ (GM): NETL

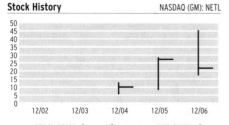

	STOCK PRICE ($) FY Close	P/E High/Low	PER SHARE ($) Earnings	Dividends	Book Value
12/06	21.69	1,501 585	0.03	—	6.97
12/05	27.24	32 10	0.87	—	3.80
12/04	10.00	— —	(1.17)	—	2.74
Annual Growth	**47.3%**	**— —**	**—**	**—**	**59.6%**

NeuroMetrix, Inc.

NeuroMetrix lets doctors keep tabs on your nerves. The company makes medical devices that are used to detect, diagnose, and monitor neurological conditions affecting the peripheral nerves and spine. The company's noninvasive NC-stat System allows physicians to distinguish between pain caused by nerve root compression and pain caused by less serious factors. By making it usable by primary care physicians, the company hopes to reduce the need to send patients on to specialists for such diagnoses, thereby keeping care closer and costs down. The systems are used in nearly 5,000 doctor's offices, clinics, and other health care facilities. NeuroMetrix maintains an active research and development department.

The NC-stat system costs far less than the traditional needle electromyography equipment used by neurologists, and with no needles used, the NC-stat system is more comfortable for patients.

NeuroMetrix struck an exclusive license to market EyeTel Imaging's DigiScope system to physicians' offices in 2006. A year later, it issued $9.9 million worth of stock to acquire the company outright. The deal included the exclusive licensing agreement with Johns Hopkins University where the DigiScope technology was developed. NeuroMetrix intends to expand its marketing of the system into vision care centers supervised by optometrists.

EXECUTIVES

Chairman, President, and CEO: Shai N. Gozani, age 43,
  $375,000 pay
COO: Gary L. Gregory, age 44, $367,367 pay
CFO and Secretary: W. Bradford (Brad) Smith, age 51,
  $326,534 pay
SVP Engineering: Michael Williams, age 50,
  $207,054 pay
SVP Information Technology: Guy Daniello, age 62,
  $199,501 pay
VP Manufacturing: Charles Fendrock
VP Research: Xuan Kong
VP Quality Assurance and Regulatory Affairs:
  Rainer Maas
Chief Medical Officer: James M. Strickland
Medical Director: Eugene A. Lesser
Auditors: PricewaterhouseCoopers LLP

LOCATIONS

HQ: NeuroMetrix, Inc.
    62 4th Ave., Waltham, MA 02451
Phone: 781-890-9989   **Fax:** 781-890-1556
Web: www.neurometrix.com

PRODUCTS/OPERATIONS

2006 Sales

	% of total
Biosensor	86
Diagnostic devices	14
Total	**100**

COMPETITORS

Bio-logic
Cardinal Health
Carl Zeiss Meditec
Medtronic
Optos
Oxford Instruments

HISTORICAL FINANCIALS

Company Type: Public

Income Statement

FYE: December 31

	REVENUE ($ mil.)	NET INCOME ($ mil.)	NET PROFIT MARGIN	EMPLOYEES
12/06	55.3	4.3	7.8%	123
12/05	34.3	0.9	2.6%	100
12/04	17.9	(4.3)	—	—
12/03	9.2	(3.7)	—	—
12/02	4.2	(4.8)	—	—
Annual Growth	**90.5%**	**—**	**—**	**23.0%**

2006 Year-End Financials

Debt ratio: —
Return on equity: 10.8%
Cash ($ mil.): 40.3
Current ratio: 4.85
Long-term debt ($ mil.): —
No. of shares (mil.): 12.6

Dividends
  Yield: —
  Payout: —
Market value ($ mil.): 187.9
R&D as % of sales: —
Advertising as % of sales: —

Stock History

NASDAQ (GM): NURO

	STOCK PRICE ($) FY Close	P/E High/Low	PER SHARE ($) Earnings	Dividends	Book Value
12/06	14.91	125 40	0.33	—	3.44
12/05	27.28	535 122	0.07	—	2.93
12/04	11.75	— —	(2.35)	—	2.83
Annual Growth	**12.6%**	**— —**	**—**	**—**	**10.3%**

NeuStar, Inc.

NeuStar shines on the provision of third-party interoperability services used in telecommunications and Internet networks. NeuStar manages the registry of North American area codes and telephone numbers and the database used by carriers (including Verizon, Sprint, AT&T, and AT&T Mobility) to route phone calls. The company also operates an Internet Registry supporting domain addresses. NeuStar is a leading provider of OSS (Operations Support Systems) clearinghouse services that provide ordering, service provisioning, billing, and customer service functions for telecom carriers and other companies. Investment firm Warburg Pincus owns 10% of the company; AXA Financial owns 8%.

NeuStar is the contracted North American Numbering Plan Administrator, the National Pooling Administrator, the administrator of local number portability for communications carriers in North America, and the lone industry registry for US Common Short Codes.

NeuStar is expanding operations through acquisitions. In 2006 the company bought UltraDNS, a Reston, Virginia-based provider of

DNS and directory services, in a cash deal valued at $61.8 million. It additionally purchased Followap, a mobile instant messaging solutions provider, for $139 million. NeuStar acquired secretariat services provider Foretec Seminars later that year and Webmetrics, a provider of Web and network performance testing services, in 2007.

EXECUTIVES

Chairman and CEO: Jeffrey E. (Jeff) Ganek, age 55, $662,500 pay
President and COO: Lisa A. Hook, age 50
SVP and CFO: Jeffrey A. (Jeff) Babka, age 54, $668,077 pay
SVP and CTO: Mark D. Foster, age 49, $544,327 pay
SVP, General Counsel, and Secretary: Martin Lowen, age 43
SVP and Managing Director International: A. Reza Jafari, age 62
SVP Corporate Development and Marketing: John Spirtos, age 42
SVP External Affairs: Gerald (Jerry) Kovach
SVP Human Resources: Douglas Arnold
SVP Sales and Business Development: Raymond A. (Ray) Saulino
SVP Marketing: Steve Johnson
SVP Ultra Services: Ben Petro
VP IP Services: Michael Misheff
Director Finance and Investor Relations: Brandon Pugh
Auditors: Ernst & Young LLP

LOCATIONS

HQ: NeuStar, Inc.
46000 Center Oak Plaza, Sterling, VA 20166
Phone: 571-434-5400   **Fax:** 571-434-5401
Web: www.neustar.biz

PRODUCTS/OPERATIONS

2006 Sales

	% of total
Addressing	31
Interoperability	17
Infrastructure and other	52
Total	**100**

Selected Services

Advanced services
  Convergence directory services (ENUM)
  Identity management services (Liberty Alliance)
Internet registry services
  .biz
  .cn
  .us
Telephony services
  Local number portability administration
  North American Numbering Plan Administration (NANPA)
  OSS (Operations Support Systems) services

COMPETITORS

Accenture
Amdocs
Billing Services Group
BSG Clearing Solutions
CGI Group
EDS
Evolving Systems
Hewlett-Packard
IBM
ICANN
NetCracker Technology
Oracle
Perot Systems
Register.com
Syniverse
Tucows
VeriSign
XIUS-bcgi

HISTORICAL FINANCIALS

Company Type: Public

Income Statement

	REVENUE ($ mil.)	NET INCOME ($ mil.)	NET PROFIT MARGIN	EMPLOYEES
FYE: December 31				
12/06	333.0	73.9	22.2%	822
12/05	242.5	55.4	22.8%	502
12/04	165.0	45.4	27.5%	—
12/03	111.7	24.0	21.5%	—
Annual Growth	**43.9%**	**45.5%**	**—**	**63.7%**

2006 Year-End Financials

Debt ratio: 1.1%	Dividends
Return on equity: 28.0%	Yield: —
Cash ($ mil.): 58.3	Payout: —
Current ratio: 1.66	Market value ($ mil.): 2,412.0
Long-term debt ($ mil.): 3.9	R&D as % of sales: —
No. of shares (mil.): 74.4	Advertising as % of sales: —

Stock History

NYSE: NSR

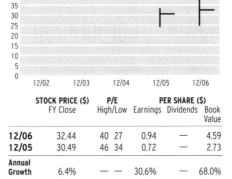

	STOCK PRICE ($) FY Close	P/E High/Low	PER SHARE ($) Earnings	Dividends	Book Value
12/06	32.44	40 27	0.94	—	4.59
12/05	30.49	46 34	0.72	—	2.73
Annual Growth	**6.4%**	**— —**	**30.6%**	**—**	**68.0%**

Neutral Tandem

Neutral Tandem helps telecom providers stay in sync with customers. The company provides third-party interconnection services to competitive carriers via tandem switches, which allow wireline, wireless, and broadband phone providers to exchange traffic between networks without direct connections. Neutral Tandem's services are offered in more than 45 US metropolitan markets as an alternative to using switches provided by the incumbent local exchange carrier (ILEC). The company's customers include Sprint Nextel, Comcast Cable, and AT&T. Doll Capital Management and New Enterprise Associates own 32% and 30% of the company, respectively.

As increasing competition in the industry creates a demand for tandem switching, the company is expanding its services into new markets.

Wireless carriers account for about 50% of the company's revenue and wireline carriers account for about 30%; cable companies and non-carriers account for the rest.

EXECUTIVES

Chairman: James P. Hynes, age 59, $83,077 pay
President, CEO, and Director: Rian J. Wren, age 50, $321,154 pay
EVP and CFO: Robert M. (Rob) Junkroski, age 43, $310,469 pay

EVP and COO: Surendra Saboo, age 48, $201,443 pay
SVP Sales: David Lopez, age 43, $245,912 pay
Auditors: Deloitte & Touche LLP

LOCATIONS

HQ: Neutral Tandem, Inc.
1 S. Wacker Dr., Ste. 200, Chicago, IL 60606
Phone: 312-384-8000   **Fax:** 312-346-3276
Web: www.neutraltandem.com

COMPETITORS

AT&T
New Global Telecom
Qwest
Verizon

HISTORICAL FINANCIALS

Company Type: Public

Income Statement

	REVENUE ($ mil.)	NET INCOME ($ mil.)	NET PROFIT MARGIN	EMPLOYEES
FYE: December 31				
12/06	52.9	5.5	10.4%	122
12/05	28.0	0.2	0.7%	110
12/04	3.4	(5.2)	—	—
12/03	0.0	(0.7)	—	—
Annual Growth	**—**	**—**	**—**	**10.9%**

2006 Year-End Financials

Debt ratio: 1,192.6%	Current ratio: 2.37
Return on equity: —	Long-term debt ($ mil.): 7.6
Cash ($ mil.): 20.1	

Net Income History

NASDAQ (GM): TNDM

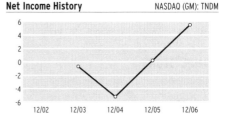

New Century Bancorp

New Century Bancorp was formed in 2003 as the holding company for the aptly named New Century Bank (opened in 2000) and New Century Bank South (formerly New Century Bank of Fayetteville). The banks operate through a handful of branches in central North Carolina's Cumberland, Harnett, Johnston, and Sampson counties. Targeting individuals and small to mid-sized businesses, they offer such services as checking and savings accounts, CDs, IRAs, and loans. The company's loan book includes commercial mortgages, commercial loans, and residential mortgages and construction loans.

With an eye towards expanding out of the city of Fayetteville, the New Century Bancorp subsidiary changed its name from New Century Bank of Fayetteville to New Century Bank South in early 2006. It announced plans to merge New Century Bank South into New Century Bank the following year.

EXECUTIVES

Chairman: C. Lee (Bozie) Tart Jr., age 72
Vice Chairman: Oscar N. Harris, age 66
President, CEO, and Director, New Century Bancorp;
President, New Century Bank South and New Century
Bank: William L. (Bill) Hedgepeth II, age 44
EVP, CFO, and COO; EVP and CFO, New Century
Bank and New Century Bank South: Lisa F. Campbell,
age 39, $120,000 pay
EVP; Chief Banking Officer, New Century Bank and
New Century Bank South: Kevin S. Bunn, age 45
EVP and Chief Operations Officer, New Century Bank
and New Century Bank South: Joan I. Patterson,
age 59
EVP and Chief Credit Officer, New Century Bancorp,
New Century Bank, and New Century Bank South:
J. Daniel Fisher, age 58
SVP, New Century Bank South: John McFadyen
Auditors: Dixon Hughes PLLC

LOCATIONS

HQ: New Century Bancorp, Inc.
700 W. Cumberland St., Dunn, NC 28334
Phone: 910-892-7080   **Fax:** 910-892-9225
Web: www.newcenturybanknc.com

PRODUCTS/OPERATIONS

2006 Sales

	$ mil.	% of total
Interest		
Loans	31.3	80
Investments	2.5	6
Federal funds sold & interest-earning deposits	2.0	5
Noninterest		
Service fees & charges	1.4	4
Fees from presold mortgages	0.7	2
Commissions from SBA loans	0.4	1
Other	0.8	2
Total	**39.1**	**100**

COMPETITORS

Bank of America
BB&T
Capital Bank
Crescent Financial
First Citizens BancShares
First South Bancorp (NC)
Four Oaks Fincorp
KS Bancorp
North State Bancorp
RBC Centura Banks
Southern BancShares
Waccamaw Bankshares
Wachovia
Wake Forest Bancshares

HISTORICAL FINANCIALS

Company Type: Public

Income Statement				FYE: December 31
	ASSETS ($ mil.)	NET INCOME ($ mil.)	INCOME AS % OF ASSETS	EMPLOYEES
12/06	553.0	4.0	0.7%	156
12/05	436.4	3.6	0.8%	92
12/04	328.3	2.1	0.6%	—
12/03	191.8	0.9	0.5%	57
12/02	126.4	0.9	0.7%	—
Annual Growth	**44.6%**	**45.2%**	**—**	**39.9%**

2006 Year-End Financials

Equity as % of assets: 10.4%
Return on assets: 0.8%
Return on equity: 8.8%
Long-term debt ($ mil.): 12.4
No. of shares (mil.): 6.5
Market value ($ mil.): 110.5

Dividends
Yield: —
Payout: —
Sales ($ mil.): 39.1
R&D as % of sales: —
Advertising as % of sales: —

Stock History

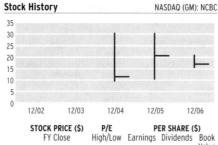

NASDAQ (GM): NCBC

	STOCK PRICE ($) FY Close	P/E High/Low		PER SHARE ($) Earnings	Dividends	Book Value
12/06	16.99	32	24	0.65	—	8.83
12/05	20.63	46	16	0.66	—	7.77
12/04	11.39	77	24	0.39	1.17	10.47
Annual Growth	**22.1%**	**—**	**—**	**29.1%**	**—**	**(8.2%)**

Newport Corporation

Newport helps all sorts of customers take a measured approach. The company makes lasers, precision components, and automated assembly, measurement, and test equipment used in the aerospace, fiber-optic communications, health care, and semiconductor manufacturing industries, and by researchers. Industrial and scientific components, including lenses and other devices for vibration and motion control, account for more than half of sales. Newport also offers automated systems used to make fiber-optic components and photonics. Customers include KLA-Tencor and Applied Materials.

Customers in the US account for about half of sales.

Newport is continuing to grow through new product introductions, primarily in the life sciences and photonics research markets. Sales to the life and health sciences market grew in 2003, while sales to the semiconductor capital equipment and other end markets continued to languish. In 2004 Newport acquired the optical technologies business of Thermo Electron (including laser and optical gear maker Spectra-Physics) for approximately $275 million, in a deal that expanded Newport's capabilities in the photonics, biophotonics, and nanotechnology markets.

Newport sold off its industrial metrology systems unit in 2002. The company has also restructured — including rounds of layoffs and facility closures — in response to continued weakness in the fiber-optic communications and semiconductor equipment markets in the early years of the 21st century. Newport has announced additional restructuring plans, including the elimination of duplicate product lines and support positions, related to the integration of Spectra-Physics.

In late 2005 Newport sold its robotic systems business, which made robotic arms for semiconductor equipment and accounted for less than 5% of sales. It retained certain patents related to robotics technology. What remains of what was the company's Advanced Packaging and Automated Systems division has been folded into the Photonics and Precision Technologies division.

Private Capital Management owns nearly 13% of Newport Corp. Dimensional Fund Advisors holds about 8% of the company. Investor Joseph L. Harrosh has an equity stake of around 6%, while Michael W. Cook Asset Management owns nearly 6%.

EXECUTIVES

President, CEO, and Director: Robert J. Phillippy,
age 47, $308,988 pay
SVP, CFO, and Treasurer: Charles F. Cargile, age 42,
$308,769 pay
SVP, General Counsel, and Secretary: Jeffrey B. Coyne,
age 40, $242,316 pay
VP and General Manager, Photonics and Precision
Technologies Division: Alain Danielo, age 59,
$370,264 pay
VP and General Manager, Lasers Division:
Bruce B. Craig, age 52
VP, Operational Excellence: Donald Mills, age 54
VP, Worldwide Sales and Service: Gary J. Spiegel,
age 56, $261,920 pay
VP, Strategic Marketing and Business Development:
Leif A. Alexandersson, age 51
Director, Marketing: David V. Rossi
Auditors: Ernst & Young LLP

LOCATIONS

HQ: Newport Corporation
1791 Deere Ave., Irvine, CA 92606
Phone: 949-863-3144   **Fax:** 949-253-1680
Web: www.newport.com

Newport has manufacturing facilities in France, the UK, and the US. It has sales offices in Austria, Canada, China, France, Germany, Ireland, Italy, Japan, Jordan, the Netherlands, Taiwan, the UK, and the US.

2006 Sales

	$ mil.	% of total
US	238.4	52
Europe	100.0	22
Asia/Pacific	91.3	20
Other regions	25.0	6
Total	**454.7**	**100**

PRODUCTS/OPERATIONS

2006 Sales

	$ mil.	% of total
Photonics & precision technologies	262.1	58
Lasers	190.8	42
Intellectual property licensing	1.8	—
Total	**454.7**	**100**

2006 Sales by Market

	$ mil.	% of total
Scientific research, aerospace & defense/security	156.5	34
Microelectronics	146.0	32
Life & health sciences	75.1	17
Other	77.1	17
Total	**454.7**	**100**

COMPETITORS

Adept Technology	IPG Photonics
Agilent Technologies	JDS Uniphase
Allied Motion Technologies	Keithley Instruments
Anritsu	Kinetic Systems
Bookham	Melles Griot
Carl Zeiss	Nikon
Coherent, Inc.	Palomar Technologies
Corning	Parker Hannifin
CVI Laser	Renishaw
Danaher	Roper Industries
ESEC	Speedline Technologies
Excel Technology	Thermo Fisher Scientific
EXFO	TRUMPF
II-VI	Zygo
ILX Lightwave	

HISTORICAL FINANCIALS

Company Type: Public

Income Statement

FYE: December 31

	REVENUE ($ mil.)	NET INCOME ($ mil.)	NET PROFIT MARGIN	EMPLOYEES
12/06	454.7	37.4	8.2%	1,950
12/05	403.7	11.6	2.9%	1,870
12/04	285.8	(81.4)	—	—
12/03	134.8	(13.2)	—	—
12/02	164.0	(100.6)	—	1,088
Annual Growth	29.0%	—	—	15.7%

2006 Year-End Financials

Debt ratio: 12.0%
Return on equity: 9.2%
Cash ($ mil.): 85.4
Current ratio: 3.17
Long-term debt ($ mil.): 52.0
No. of shares (mil.): 41.5
Dividends
  Yield: —
  Payout: —
Market value ($ mil.): 868.5
R&D as % of sales: —
Advertising as % of sales: —

Stock History

NASDAQ (GM): NEWP

	STOCK PRICE ($) FY Close	P/E High/Low		PER SHARE ($) Earnings	Dividends	Book Value
12/06	20.95	26	15	0.89	—	10.49
12/05	13.54	61	45	0.27	—	9.41
12/04	14.10	—	—	(1.99)	—	9.66
12/03	16.62	—	—	(0.34)	—	11.23
12/02	12.56	—	—	(2.65)	—	11.58
Annual Growth	13.6%	—	—	—	—	(2.4%)

Nexity Financial

You'll encounter *virtually* no lines while banking with Nexity. Nexity Financial is the holding company for Nexity Bank, which provides correspondent banking services (including outsourced services and loan participations) to smaller community banks in the southeastern US. It also offers online retail banking services to more than 17,000 consumers and commercial customers primarily in the US. Construction loans make up nearly half of Nexity Bank's loan portfolio, which also includes significant quantities of real estate mortgages and business loans. Nexity Financial has correspondent banking offices in Alabama, Florida, Georgia, North Carolina, South Carolina, and Texas.

The company also offers home equity loans to consumers via its Internet channel. In 2006, Nexity Financial launched Nexity Investments, which offers portfolio management services.

EXECUTIVES

Chairman and CEO: Greg L. Lee, age 47, $327,500 pay
President and Director: David E. Long, age 45, $235,000 pay
EVP, CFO, and Director: John J. Moran, age 45, $235,000 pay

EVP and Senior Lending Officer, Nexity Financial and Nexity Bank: Kenneth T. Vassey, age 47, $327,866 pay
EVP Operations, Nexity Financial and Nexity Bank: Cindy W. Russo, age 48, $160,000 pay
President and Managing Director, Nexity Capital Management: John A. Pandtle
Auditors: Mauldin & Jenkins, LLC

LOCATIONS

HQ: Nexity Financial Corporation
  3500 Blue Lake Dr., Ste. 330,
  Birmingham, AL 35243
Phone: 205-298-6391   **Fax:** 205-298-6395
Web: www.nexitybank.com

PRODUCTS/OPERATIONS

2006 Sales

	$ mil.	% of total
Interest		
Loans	45.4	76
Securities & other	12.3	21
Brokerage & investment services	0.8	1
Other	1.1	2
Total	**59.6**	**100**

COMPETITORS

Bankers Bank
Bankrate
Capital One
CUNA Mutual
E*TRADE Bank
Fiserv
Goldleaf Financial Solutions, Inc
ING DIRECT
NetBank
Online Resources
PrimeVest

HISTORICAL FINANCIALS

Company Type: Public

Income Statement

FYE: December 31

	ASSETS ($ mil.)	NET INCOME ($ mil.)	INCOME AS % OF ASSETS	EMPLOYEES
12/06	891.0	6.1	0.7%	94
12/05	784.5	4.5	0.6%	88
12/04	610.8	5.4	0.9%	—
12/03	522.7	4.7	0.9%	—
Annual Growth	19.5%	50.2%	—	6.8%

2006 Year-End Financials

Equity as % of assets: 7.3%
Return on assets: 0.7%
Return on equity: 9.5%
Long-term debt ($ mil.): 122.4
No. of shares (mil.): 8.4
Market value ($ mil.): 100.8
Dividends
  Yield: —
  Payout: —
Sales ($ mil.): 59.6
R&D as % of sales: —
Advertising as % of sales: —

Stock History

NASDAQ (GM): NXTY

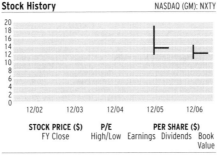

	STOCK PRICE ($) FY Close	P/E High/Low		PER SHARE ($) Earnings	Dividends	Book Value
12/06	12.04	21	16	0.67	—	7.78
12/05	13.40	33	21	0.57	—	7.26
Annual Growth	(10.1%)	—	—	17.5%	—	7.1%

NGAS Resources

In gas we trust could be the new motto for NGAS Resources (formerly Daugherty Resources). The former gold and gas exploration company now primarily searches for and produces natural gas (and some oil) in the Appalachian and Illinois basins through subsidiary Daugherty Petroleum. NGAS Resources has proved reserves of 98.2 billion cu. ft. of natural gas and 453,000 barrels of oil. In 2004 the company began to operate Duke Energy's Stone Mountain natural gas gathering system. It acquired this system in 2006. The company also owns Sentra Corporation, a Kentucky public utility. NGAS Resources' inactive mining assets are in Alaska.

The natural resources company is looking to sell or involve a third party in developing its gold and silver mining properties. It stopped active exploratory work on these properties in 1996.

EXECUTIVES

Chairman, President, and CEO: William S. Daugherty, age 52, $687,000 pay
CFO: Michael P. Windisch, age 33, $343,000 pay
VP Engineering and Secretary; President, Daugherty Petroleum: D. Michael Wallen, age 52, $612,000 pay
VP Acquisitions and Legal Affairs; CEO, Daugherty Petroleum: William G. (Bill) Barr III, age 57, $617,000 pay
VP Land: John R. (Rick) Bender
VP Sales: Michael Hughes
Managing Director Integrated Corporate Relations: Kathleen Heaney
Director Human Resources: Darlene Davis
Auditors: Hall, Kistler & Company LLP

LOCATIONS

HQ: NGAS Resources, Inc.
  120 Prosperous Place, Ste. 201,
  Lexington, KY 40509
Phone: 859-263-3948   **Fax:** 859-263-4228
Web: www.ngas.com

NGAS Resources has oil and gas operations in the Appalachian and Illinois basins (primarily in Kentucky and Tennessee), and has development-stage gold and silver mining sites on the Aleutian Islands near Alaska.

PRODUCTS/OPERATIONS

2006 Sales

	$ mil.	% of total
Contract drilling	50.1	63
Oil & gas production	24.2	30
Gas transmission & compression	5.5	7
Total	**79.8**	**100**

COMPETITORS

Atmos Energy
Belden & Blake
Cabot Oil & Gas
Delta Natural Gas
Miller Petroleum
Penn Virginia
Petroleum Development
Range Resources
Vulcan Energy

HISTORICAL FINANCIALS

Company Type: Public

Income Statement

FYE: December 31

	REVENUE ($ mil.)	NET INCOME ($ mil.)	NET PROFIT MARGIN	EMPLOYEES
12/06	79.8	2.0	2.5%	106
12/05	62.2	0.9	1.4%	84
12/04	48.0	1.6	3.3%	—
12/03	27.4	3.8	13.9%	—
12/02	8.4	0.6	7.1%	23
Annual Growth	75.6%	35.1%	—	46.5%

2006 Year-End Financials

Debt ratio: 87.6%
Return on equity: 2.7%
Cash ($ mil.): 14.4
Current ratio: 0.97
Long-term debt ($ mil.): 66.9
No. of shares (mil.): 21.8

Dividends
Yield: —
Payout: —
Market value ($ mil.): 138.9
R&D as % of sales: —
Advertising as % of sales: —

Stock History

NASDAQ (GS): NGAS

	STOCK PRICE ($) FY Close	P/E High/Low		PER SHARE ($) Earnings	Dividends	Book Value
12/06	6.38	137	71	0.09	—	3.51
12/05	10.49	317	83	0.05	—	3.38
12/04	4.57	70	37	0.10	—	2.64
12/03	5.22	20	3	0.34	—	2.45
12/02	1.02	13	5	0.11	—	1.15
Annual Growth	58.1%	—	—	(4.9%)	—	32.2%

North American Galvanizing

North American Galvanizing & Coatings (formerly Kinark Corporation) is glad that rust never sleeps. The company's North American Galvanizing (NAG) subsidiary hot-dip galvanizes fabricated structural steel components to provide protection against corrosion. NAG galvanizes its iron and steel products by submerging them in molten zinc. Typical galvanizing customers come from the petrochemical, irrigation, and energy and utilities industries. The company has sold its chemical storage and distribution subsidiary, Lake River Corp., and its warehouse storage business, North American Warehousing, to concentrate solely on its hot-dip galvanizing operations. Director and chairman Joseph Morrow owns about 22% of the company.

The company's galvanizing operations accounts for all of company sales. It galvanizes about 400,000,000 pounds of steel products for roughly 1,700 customers annually. NAG also operates a galvanizing facility to make large wireless and electric transmission poles. The galvanizing of tubular steel structures for customers in the communications and utility industries has helped improve overall sales.

NAG has introduced INFRASHIELD SM coating, a special polymer coating system used over hot-dip galvanized products.

In 2005 NAG acquired Gregory Industries' hot-dip galvanizing plant located in Canton, Ohio.

EXECUTIVES

Chairman: Joseph J. (Joe) Morrow, age 67
President, CEO, and Director: Ronald J. Evans, age 57, $255,000 pay
VP, CFO, Treasurer, and Secretary: Beth B. Hood, age 43, $165,000 pay
VP Region I: Gordon Briggs
VP Region II: Craig N. Schaal
Director Sales and Marketing: Brad Blacketer
Manager Human Resources: Judy Johnson
Senior Engineer: Kevin Halstead
Purchasing Manager: Earl Williams Jr.
Controller and Assistant Secretary: Rick Page
Auditors: Deloitte & Touche LLP

LOCATIONS

HQ: North American Galvanizing & Coatings, Inc.
5314 S. Yale Ave., Ste. 1000, Tulsa, OK 74135
Phone: 918-488-9420   **Fax:** 918-488-8172
Web: www.nagalv.com

North American Galvanizing & Coatings has galvanizing plants in Colorado, Kentucky, Missouri, Ohio, Oklahoma, Tennessee, and Texas.

COMPETITORS

AZZ
Dofasco
MNP
Northern Technologies
Olympic Steel
Severstal North America
Steel Technologies

HISTORICAL FINANCIALS

Company Type: Public

Income Statement

FYE: December 31

	REVENUE ($ mil.)	NET INCOME ($ mil.)	NET PROFIT MARGIN	EMPLOYEES
12/06	74.1	4.5	6.1%	368
12/05	47.9	0.6	1.3%	361
12/04	35.8	0.4	1.1%	—
12/03	33.2	(1.0)	—	—
12/02	38.2	1.1	2.9%	364
Annual Growth	18.0%	42.2%	—	0.3%

2006 Year-End Financials

Debt ratio: 17.4%
Return on equity: 20.1%
Cash ($ mil.): 2.0
Current ratio: 1.66
Long-term debt ($ mil.): 4.4
No. of shares (mil.): 8.1

Dividends
Yield: —
Payout: —
Market value ($ mil.): 28.4
R&D as % of sales: —
Advertising as % of sales: —

Stock History

NASDAQ (GM): NGA

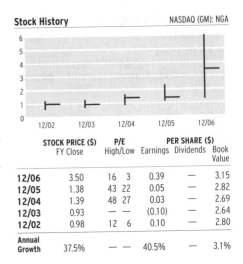

	STOCK PRICE ($) FY Close	P/E High/Low		PER SHARE ($) Earnings	Dividends	Book Value
12/06	3.50	16	3	0.39	—	3.15
12/05	1.38	43	22	0.05	—	2.82
12/04	1.39	48	27	0.03	—	2.69
12/03	0.93	—	—	(0.10)	—	2.64
12/02	0.98	12	6	0.10	—	2.80
Annual Growth	37.5%	—	—	40.5%	—	3.1%

NovaMed, Inc.

NovaMed believes that the eyes are the windows to the pocketbook. As more Americans seek convenient fixes for eye problems, the company has cashed in by acquiring and managing ambulatory surgical centers across the US. Of its more than 30 centers, the majority perform ophthalmologic surgeries exclusively, including cataract and refractive eye surgery and laser vision correction (LASIK and other procedures). The other centers offer health care services in areas such as orthopedics, pain management, and plastic surgery or are multi-specialty centers. Additionally, the company operates optical labs and a marketing services and products division, as well as an optical products purchasing organization.

Most of NovaMed's centers are owned jointly with the physicians who work in them, with NovaMed owning a majority interest. A handful of the centers are wholly owned by the company. Historically, NovaMed focused only on eye-care services, but it has been expanding its offerings in other medical specialties. It plans to grow through acquiring new ambulatory surgery centers and expanding the types of services its new and existing centers provide. In 2006, it acquired ten centers, including two in new markets (Ohio and Arkansas). The company has ended its physician practice management services operations and closed some less profitable facilities. In 2006 it closed one center in Kansas City, Missouri, but continues to operate others in that market. Director Scott Kirk owns about 6% of the company.

EXECUTIVES

Chairman, President, and CEO: Thomas S. Hall, age 47
EVP and CFO: Scott T. Macomber, age 53, $368,022 pay
SVP Corporate Development: Robert C. Goettling
SVP and General Counsel: John W. Lawrence Jr.
SVP Business Development: William J. Kennedy
SVP Corporate Development: Thomas J. Chirillo
VP Optical Services Group: Frank L. Soppa
VP Marketing Services Group; President Patient Education Concepts: Robert D. Watson
VP and Corporate Controller: John P. Hart
Human Resources: Lani Kennedy
Auditors: BDO Seidman, LLP

LOCATIONS

HQ: NovaMed, Inc.
    980 N. Michigan Ave., Ste. 1620, Chicago, IL 60611
Phone: 312-664-4100   **Fax:** 312-664-4250
Web: www.novamed.com

NovaMed owns ambulatory surgery centers in Arkansas, California, Colorado, Florida, Georgia, Illinois, Indiana, Kansas, Louisiana, Michigan, Missouri, Nebraska, New Hampshire, Ohio, Tennessee, Texas, Virginia, and Wisconsin.

PRODUCTS/OPERATIONS

2006 Sales

	$ mil.	% of total
Surgical facilities	85.3	79
Products & other	23.1	21
Total	**108.4**	**100**

COMPETITORS

AmSurg
HCA
LCA
Symbion
TLC Vision
United Surgical Partners

HISTORICAL FINANCIALS

Company Type: Public

Income Statement

FYE: December 31

	REVENUE ($ mil.)	NET INCOME ($ mil.)	NET PROFIT MARGIN	EMPLOYEES
12/06	108.4	5.7	5.3%	666
12/05	81.2	5.6	6.9%	568
12/04	64.6	4.5	7.0%	—
12/03	55.5	3.5	6.3%	—
12/02	53.8	0.2	0.4%	414
Annual Growth	**19.1%**	**131.1%**	**—**	**12.6%**

2006 Year-End Financials

Debt ratio: 89.9%
Return on equity: 9.0%
Cash ($ mil.): 2.7
Current ratio: 1.71
Long-term debt ($ mil.): 61.2
No. of shares (mil.): 23.8

Dividends
  Yield: —
  Payout: —
Market value ($ mil.): 180.3
R&D as % of sales: —
Advertising as % of sales: —

Stock History

NASDAQ (GS): NOVA

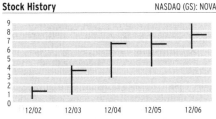

	STOCK PRICE ($) FY Close	P/E High/Low	Earnings	PER SHARE ($) Dividends	Book Value
12/06	7.57	38 26	0.23	—	2.86
12/05	6.53	34 18	0.23	—	2.50
12/04	6.58	35 15	0.19	—	2.55
12/03	3.60	26 6	0.16	—	2.36
12/02	1.30	175 52	0.01	—	2.17
Annual Growth	**55.3%**	**— —**	**119.0%**	**—**	**7.2%**

Novatel Wireless

You *can* take it with you. Novatel Wireless designs wireless modems that let users access the Internet from anywhere. The company offers a series of wireless PC card modems (Merlin), embedded wireless modules for OEMs (Expedite), and desktop wireless gateway consoles (Ovation). Its MobiLink software, bundled with modems and embedded modules, connects mobile devices with wireless WANs. Novatel also offers activation, provisioning, and integration services. Customers include manufacturers, telecom service providers, and wireless service providers.

The company outsources its manufacturing to LG Innotek and Inventec Appliances. Novatel has a distribution and fulfillment deal with Mobiltron for its business in Europe, the Middle East, and Africa. Novatel generated almost 40% of its revenues from international customers in 2006.

EXECUTIVES

Chairman: Peter V. Leparulo, age 48
President: George B. (Brad) Weinert, age 48
SVP and CFO: Kenneth G. (Ken) Leddon
SVP and CTO: Slim S. Souissi, age 41, $312,622 pay
SVP Worldwide Sales and Marketing: Robert M. Hadley, age 44, $432,133 pay
SVP Business Affairs and General Counsel:
  Catherine F. Ratcliffe, age 49, $312,622 pay
SVP Operations: Christopher (Chris) Ross, age 53
VP Communications and Investor Relations:
  Julie Cunningham
VP Sales, Americas and APAC:
  Thomas Wayne Harleman Jr.
VP Product Management: Jon Driscoll
Auditors: KPMG LLP

LOCATIONS

HQ: Novatel Wireless, Inc.
    9645 Scranton Rd., Ste. 205, San Diego, CA 92121
Phone: 858-812-3400   **Fax:** 858-812-3402
Web: www.novatelwireless.com

PRODUCTS/OPERATIONS

Selected Products

3G multimedia application consoles (Ovation)
Embedded modems (Expedite)
PC card modems (Merlin)

COMPETITORS

3Com
Huawei Technologies
Intel Corporation
Kyocera Wireless
Linksys
Motorola, Inc.
Nokia
Option NV
Palm, Inc.
RIM
Sierra Wireless
Socket Communications
Sony Ericsson Mobile
USRobotics
Wavecom

HISTORICAL FINANCIALS

Company Type: Public

Income Statement

FYE: December 31

	REVENUE ($ mil.)	NET INCOME ($ mil.)	NET PROFIT MARGIN	EMPLOYEES
12/06	218.0	0.4	0.2%	235
12/05	161.7	11.1	6.9%	172
12/04	103.7	13.8	13.3%	—
12/03	33.8	(11.6)	—	—
12/02	28.9	(28.3)	—	92
Annual Growth	**65.7%**	**—**	**—**	**26.4%**

2006 Year-End Financials

Debt ratio: —
Return on equity: 0.3%
Cash ($ mil.): 82.7
Current ratio: 2.88
Long-term debt ($ mil.): —
No. of shares (mil.): 29.7

Dividends
  Yield: —
  Payout: —
Market value ($ mil.): 287.6
R&D as % of sales: —
Advertising as % of sales: —

Stock History

NASDAQ (GM): NVTL

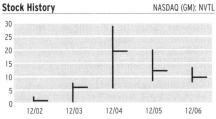

	STOCK PRICE ($) FY Close	P/E High/Low	Earnings	PER SHARE ($) Dividends	Book Value
12/06	9.67	1,318 806	0.01	—	4.51
12/05	12.11	53 23	0.37	—	4.13
12/04	19.41	60 12	0.48	—	3.45
12/03	5.99	— —	(2.14)	—	0.71
12/02	0.97	— —	(10.47)	—	0.93
Annual Growth	**77.7%**	**— —**	**—**	**—**	**48.4%**

Nu Horizons Electronics

Nu Horizons Electronics sees new components on the horizon. The company distributes active components (microprocessors, memory chips, diodes, transistors) from manufacturers such as Intersil, Microsemi, ON Semiconductor, STMicroelectronics, Vitesse Semiconductor, and Xilinx. Subsidiary NIC Components is the exclusive North American distributor of passive components (capacitors and resistors) made by Japan's Nippon Industries. Nu Horizons also offers supply chain management services, such as warehousing, inventory control, purchasing, and transportation, through its Titan Supply Chain Services subsidiary.

About 75% of the company's sales are to customers in the Americas, but Nu Horizons is expanding overseas. Its customers include a wide variety of manufacturers of consumer, medical, industrial, and military electronics.

Nu Horizons and its Titan Logistics subsidiary have received subpoenas from the Securities and Exchange Commission for materials related to the companies' business relationship with

Vitesse Semiconductor. Nu Horizons is cooperating with the SEC inquiry. Vitesse is under investigation by the SEC and the US Department of Justice over the chip company's alleged backdating of stock options and other matters.

Nu Horizons' other subsidiaries include components exporter Nu Horizons International and European distributors Nu Horizons Eurotech and NIC Eurotech.

Dimensional Fund Advisors and Royce & Associates each own about 8% of Nu Horizons Electronics. Wasatch Advisors holds around 7% of the company. Including stock options, CEO Arthur Nadata has an equity stake of more than 6%. COO Richard Schuster owns about 6%, also including options. Babson Capital holds around 6%.

HISTORY

Industry veterans Irving Lubman, Arthur Nadata, and Richard Schuster left a small electronic components distribution company to found Nu Horizons and NIC Components in 1982. Nu Horizons went public the following year. In 1986 it formed an export subsidiary.

Initially, Nu Horizons derived most of its sales from makers of military equipment, and marketing efforts were focused on the East Coast. However, by 1993 military contractors represented just 7% of sales. In 1994 Nu Horizons bought San Jose, California-based Merit Electronics, which became its West Coast operation.

The company continued to broaden its product line. It signed a franchise agreement with Cirrus Logic in 1995, and initiated distribution of Sun Microsystems' components in 1996. Also that year Lubman stepped down as CEO and was replaced by Nadata; Lubman remained chairman. The company formed a UK subsidiary in 1998. Nu Horizons added design engineering services to its portfolio the next year.

In 2000 Nu Horizons signed a distribution agreement with Hitachi and introduced a development tool for the VoIP market. The next year, the company sold its Nu Visions Manufacturing subsidiary (contract design and assembly of circuit boards and related devices) to Golden Gate Capital for about $30 million.

In 2002 Nu Horizons continued to expand its offerings through distribution agreements with California Eastern Laboratories (itself a distributor of NEC products) and networking chip specialist Intersil. Lubman retired as chairman and COO in June 2004; Nadata and Schuster assumed his responsibilities.

In 2005 Nu Horizons opened an office in Mumbai (formerly Bombay), its fourth office in India. Later that year, the company signed a global distribution agreement with IBM Microelectronics, carrying IBM's PowerPC microprocessors, digital video chips, and static random-access memories (SRAMs).

In 2006 the company formed a new division, Nu Horizons Express, specializing in sales and support for lower-volume customers.

Also that year the company acquired a UK distributor, DT Electronics, for about $5.5 million in cash, expanding its European presence. The shareholders of DT Electronics may receive an additional £849,426 to £2.55 million (up to around $5 million) over three years, depending on earnings milestones.

EXECUTIVES

Chairman and CEO: Arthur Nadata, age 61, $539,000 pay
President, COO, Secretary, and Director; President, NIC Components: Richard S. (Rich) Schuster, age 58, $539,000 pay
SVP Global Operations: Steve Mussmacher
SVP Marketing: Rita Megling
SVP Sales, Americas: Kent Smith
VP Finance, CFO, and Treasurer and Director: Kurt Freudenberg, age 49
VP Human Resources and Training Development: Elaine Givner
VP Information Technology: Burt Silverman
VP Global Customer Business Unit: Teresa Shatsoff
VP Global Engineering: Athar Zafar
VP OEM System Sales: Dan Romanelli
VP, Strategic Accounts: Gregg Scott
VP Sales, EMS Americas: Tom Dow
VP Sales, Europe: Phil Gee
VP Strategic Accounts: Dave Nebbia
President, Distribution Division: Dave Bowers
President, Nu Horizons Electronics Asia Pte Ltd.: Wendell Boyd
Auditors: Ernst & Young LLP

LOCATIONS

HQ: Nu Horizons Electronics Corp.
70 Maxess Rd., Melville, NY 11747
Phone: 631-396-5000 **Fax:** 631-396-5050
Web: www.nuhorizons.com

Nu Horizons Electronics has offices in Australia, Canada, China, Germany, Hong Kong, India, Malaysia, Mexico, Singapore, South Korea, Taiwan, Thailand, the UK, and the US.

2007 Sales

	$ mil.	% of total
Americas	554.8	75
Asia/Pacific	148.2	20
Europe	34.5	5
Total	**737.5**	**100**

PRODUCTS/OPERATIONS

Selected Products Distributed

Capacitors
Digital and linear integrated circuits
Diodes
Fiber-optic components
Memory chips
Microprocessors
Microwave components
Networking chipsets
Optocouplers
Radio-frequency components
Relays
Resistors
Transistors

COMPETITORS

All American Semiconductor
Arrow Electronics
Avnet
Bell Microproducts
Digi-Key
Future Electronics
Jaco Electronics
MAST Distributors
N.F. Smith
Premier Farnell
Richardson Electronics
Taitron Components
TTI Inc.
WPG Holdings
Yosun

HISTORICAL FINANCIALS

Company Type: Public

Income Statement

FYE: February 28

	REVENUE ($ mil.)	NET INCOME ($ mil.)	NET PROFIT MARGIN	EMPLOYEES
2/07	737.5	7.7	1.0%	748
2/06	561.3	4.9	0.9%	659
2/05	467.9	3.1	0.7%	—
2/04	345.9	(0.9)	—	—
2/03	302.1	(2.5)	—	483
Annual Growth	**25.0%**	**—**	**—**	**11.6%**

2007 Year-End Financials

Debt ratio: 20.3%
Return on equity: 5.4%
Cash ($ mil.): 4.8
Current ratio: 3.04
Long-term debt ($ mil.): 30.0
No. of shares (mil.): 18.2
Dividends
  Yield: —
  Payout: —
Market value ($ mil.): 179.4
R&D as % of sales: —
Advertising as % of sales: —

Stock History

NASDAQ (GM): NUHC

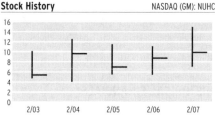

	STOCK PRICE ($) FY Close	P/E High/Low	PER SHARE ($) Earnings	Dividends	Book Value
2/07	9.88	36 18	0.41	—	8.14
2/06	8.73	39 20	0.28	—	7.78
2/05	6.97	67 33	0.17	—	7.57
2/04	9.61	— —	(0.05)	—	7.38
2/03	5.39	— —	(0.14)	—	7.44
Annual Growth	**16.4%**	**— —**	**—**	**—**	**2.3%**

Numerex Corp.

Numerex believes in secure connections. The company operates primarily through two divisions, Uplink and Airdesk Mobile. Uplink provides wireless security messaging products and services. Used in commercial and residential systems, Uplink systems transmit alarms over a dedicated cellular data link to monitoring stations. Airdesk Mobile provides vehicle location and recovery products and distributes wireless radios. Numerex's noncore operations include video-conferencing products, network monitoring hardware and software (Digilog), and wireline data communication technology (DCX).

Numerex acquired Orbit One Communications in 2007. Orbit provides satellite phones and GPS tracking equipment to government agencies and emergency service providers.

EXECUTIVES

Chairman and CEO: Stratton J. Nicolaides, age 53, $275,000 pay
EVP and CFO: Alan B. Catherall, age 53, $200,000 pay
EVP and COO: Michael A. Marett, age 52, $225,000 pay

SVP Corporate Development: Louis Fienberg
SVP Marketing: Chuck Horne
SVP Sales: Michael W. Lang
General Counsel, Secretary, and Director:
 Andrew J. Ryan, age 48
Auditors: Grant Thornton LLP

LOCATIONS

HQ: Numerex Corp.
 1600 Parkwood Cir., Ste. 500, Atlanta, GA 30339
Phone: 770-693-5950   **Fax:** 770-693-5951
Web: www.nmrx.com

PRODUCTS/OPERATIONS

2006 Sales

	$ mil.	% of total
Products	34.5	65
Services	18.3	35
Total	**52.8**	**100**

2006 Sales

	$ mil.	% of total
Wireless data communications	46.3	88
Digital multimedia, networking & wireline security	6.5	12
Total	**52.8**	**100**

COMPETITORS

GE Security	Remote Dynamics
Honeywell ACS	Siemens AG
LoJack	TANDBERG
NAVTEQ	Telular
OnStar	XATA
Polycom	

HISTORICAL FINANCIALS

Company Type: Public

Income Statement
FYE: December 31

	REVENUE ($ mil.)	NET INCOME ($ mil.)	NET PROFIT MARGIN	EMPLOYEES
12/06	52.8	4.1	7.8%	110
12/05	30.0	0.6	2.0%	98
12/04	23.0	(2.1)	—	—
12/03	20.2	(1.4)	—	—
12/02	24.5	(7.4)	—	79
Annual Growth	**21.2%**	**—**	**—**	**8.6%**

2006 Year-End Financials

Debt ratio: 31.6%
Return on equity: 11.9%
Cash ($ mil.): 20.4
Current ratio: 3.18
Long-term debt ($ mil.): 13.1
No. of shares (mil.): 13.3
Dividends
 Yield: —
 Payout: —
Market value ($ mil.): 124.9
R&D as % of sales: —
Advertising as % of sales: —

Stock History
NASDAQ (GM): NMRX

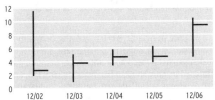

	STOCK PRICE ($) FY Close	P/E High/Low		PER SHARE ($) Earnings	Dividends	Book Value
12/06	9.42	32	15	0.32	—	3.12
12/05	4.73	124	80	0.05	—	2.38
12/04	4.70	—	—	(0.19)	—	2.18
12/03	3.80	—	—	(0.13)	—	2.35
12/02	2.69	—	—	(0.71)	—	2.42
Annual Growth	**36.8%**	**—**	**—**	**—**	**—**	**6.6%**

NutriSystem, Inc.

NutriSystem can help you trim your waistline online. Visitors to the nutrisystem.com Web site can order from the company's more than 130 portion-controlled, shelf-stable foods and supplements, as well as look into individualized calorie plans, one-on-one counseling, behavior modification, and exercise education and maintenance plans. Customers order monthly food packages typically containing 28 breakfasts, lunches, dinners, and desserts, supplemented with fruit and vegetables. NutriSystem owns about 120 Slim and Tone women's fitness centers and also sells its products through a partnership with television-marketer QVC, where it airs 90-minute infomercials.

The company is looking to expand and scale its business for growth. NutriSystem hired former AOL International chairman and CEO Joe Redling in August 2007 as its president and COO. Michael Hagan continued as chairman and CEO of NutriSystem. The weight management firm added Redling to its top ranks based on his expertise in multi-billion-dollar paid subscription businesses, international expansion, and worldwide brand and marketing management.

In December 2007 NutriSystem launched a new diet plan called NutriSystem Advanced, which replaces its core NutriSystem Nourish program. The NutriSystem Advanced meal plan features new ingredient blends including Omega-3 fatty acids and more soluble fibers.

In its first non-US venture, the company expanded its meal plan system into Canada in 2008 and set up a new subsidiary, NutriSystem Canada. The products will be packaged differently than those sold in the US and the company plans to eventually add meals that better reflect Canadian eating habits. NutriSystem also has plans to expand into Europe.

EXECUTIVES

Chairman and CEO: Michael J. Hagan, age 44
President and COO: Joseph M. (Joe) Redling
CFO: David D. Clark, age 43
EVP Program Development and Chief Marketing Officer: Thomas F. (Tom) Connerty, age 44, $620,050 pay
SVP Operations and CIO: Bruce Blair, age 50, $366,923 pay
SVP eCommerce: Chris Terrill
VP Program and Product Development: Jay Satz
VP Human Resources: Carol F. Krause
Director Advertising and Marketing: Shannon Crossin
Auditors: KPMG LLP

LOCATIONS

HQ: NutriSystem, Inc.
 300 Welsh Rd., Bldg. 1, Ste. 100,
 Horsham, PA 19044
Phone: 215-706-5300   **Fax:** 215-706-5388
Web: www.nutrisystem.com

PRODUCTS/OPERATIONS

Selected Food Programs

Men's Program
Men's Silver Program
Women's Diabetic Program
Women's Program
Women's Silver Program
Vegetarian

COMPETITORS

Atkins Nutritionals	PowerBar
Bally Total Fitness	Pure Weight Loss
Beverly Hills Weight Loss	Schiff Nutrition
eDiets.com	Slim-Fast
HMG	Weight Watchers
Jenny Craig	

HISTORICAL FINANCIALS

Company Type: Public

Income Statement
FYE: December 31

	REVENUE ($ mil.)	NET INCOME ($ mil.)	NET PROFIT MARGIN	EMPLOYEES
12/06	568.2	85.1	15.0%	680
12/05	212.5	21.0	9.9%	589
12/04	38.0	1.0	2.6%	—
12/03	22.6	0.8	3.5%	—
12/02	27.6	2.4	8.7%	—
Annual Growth	**113.0%**	**144.0%**	**—**	**15.4%**

2006 Year-End Financials

Debt ratio: —
Return on equity: 75.9%
Cash ($ mil.): 82.3
Current ratio: 3.59
Long-term debt ($ mil.): —
No. of shares (mil.): 35.9
Dividends
 Yield: —
 Payout: —
Market value ($ mil.): 2,274.4
R&D as % of sales: —
Advertising as % of sales: —

Stock History
NASDAQ (GS): NTRI

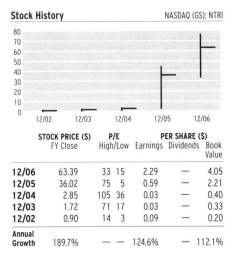

	STOCK PRICE ($) FY Close	P/E High/Low		PER SHARE ($) Earnings	Dividends	Book Value
12/06	63.39	33	15	2.29	—	4.05
12/05	36.02	75	5	0.59	—	2.21
12/04	2.85	105	36	0.03	—	0.40
12/03	1.72	71	17	0.03	—	0.33
12/02	0.90	14	3	0.09	—	0.20
Annual Growth	**189.7%**	**—**	**—**	**124.6%**	**—**	**112.1%**

NYMEX Holdings

What US exchange was formed in 1872 as the Butter and Cheese Exchange? NYMEX Holdings' subsidiary, the New York Mercantile Exchange. From meager dairy roots, it is the world's largest forum for trading energy futures, and the third largest futures exchange in the US. Trading is conducted through two divisions: NYMEX handles the crude oil, gasoline, heating oil, natural gas, platinum, and palladium markets, while COMEX serves as the marketplace for gold, silver, copper, and aluminum futures and options contracts. NYMEX ClearPort clears off-exchange trades and sells market data. The Chicago Mercantile Exchange started facilitating after-hours trading of NYMEX energy, platinum, and palladium futures in late 2006.

NYMEX Holdings went public in 2006, with funds raised to be used for capital expenditures; some $10 million will be paid to owners of COMEX division membership to satisfy the terms of its 1994 merger agreement.

In February 2006 NYMEX's board voted to offer side-by-side open outcry and electronic trading of its benchmark, physically settled energy futures contracts. Side-by-side trading launched during the second quarter of 2006.

In advance of the 2006 IPO, NYMEX sold a 10% stake to private equity firm General Atlantic.

EXECUTIVES

Chairman: Richard Schaeffer, age 54, $650,000 pay (prior to promotion)
Vice Chairman: Thomas Gordon, age 46
President, CEO, and Director: James E. Newsome, age 47, $1,400,000 pay (prior to promotion)
CFO: Kenneth D. (Ken) Shifrin, age 50
EVP and CIO: Samuel H. Gaer, age 40, $960,000 pay
SVP Clearing Services: Sean Keating, age 41
SVP Corporate Development and Strategic Planning: Christopher Rodriguez
SVP New Product Development: Benjamin Chesir
SVP Corporate Governance and Strategic Initiatives: Richard D. Kerschner, age 40
SVP, COMEX: William Purpura
SVP Technology: Ian Wall, age 38
SVP External Affairs: Madeline J. Boyd, age 54
SVP Marketing: Joseph Raia, age 51
SVP Research: Robert A. Levin, age 51
Chief Regulatory Officer: Thomas F. LaSala, age 45
Treasurer and Director: Frank Siciliano, age 59
General Counsel, Chief Administrative Officer, and Secretary: Christopher K. Bowen, age 46, $714,083 pay
Director Corporate Communications and Media Affairs: Anu Ahluwalia
Auditors: KPMG LLP

LOCATIONS

HQ: NYMEX Holdings, Inc.
1 North End Ave., World Financial Center, New York, NY 10282
Phone: 212-299-2000   **Fax:** 212-301-4623
Web: www.nymex.com

PRODUCTS/OPERATIONS

2006 Sales

	$ mil.	% of total
Clearing & transaction fees	419.7	84
Market data fees	63.7	13
Other	13.9	3
Total	**497.3**	**100**

COMPETITORS

AMEX	ICE Futures
CBOE	IntercontinentalExchange
CME	LCH.Clearnet
DTCC	NYSE Euronext
Euronext	Options Clearing

HISTORICAL FINANCIALS

Company Type: Public

Income Statement

	REVENUE ($ mil.)	NET INCOME ($ mil.)	NET PROFIT MARGIN	EMPLOYEES
12/06	497.3	154.8	31.1%	500
12/05	346.6	71.1	20.5%	—
12/04	241.3	27.4	11.4%	—
12/03	188.1	8.9	4.7%	481
12/02	189.2	12.3	6.5%	489
Annual Growth	**27.3%**	**88.4%**	**—**	**0.6%**

2006 Year-End Financials

Debt ratio: 10.4%
Return on equity: 35.0%
Cash ($ mil.): 3,068.6
Current ratio: 1.18
Long-term debt ($ mil.): 80.3
No. of shares (mil.): 89.7

Dividends
  Yield: —
  Payout: —
Market value ($ mil.): 11,121.0
R&D as % of sales: —
Advertising as % of sales: —

Stock History

NYSE: NMX

	STOCK PRICE ($) FY Close	P/E High/Low	PER SHARE ($) Earnings	Dividends	Book Value
12/06	124.01	66 50	2.31	—	8.64

Occam Networks

Occam Networks keeps it simple. The company — named for a 14th-century monk who asserted that the best explanation is the least complex — makes telecom transmission equipment that lets carriers offer traditional and IP (Internet protocol) services over a single, converged network. Its Broadband Loop Carrier (BLC) platform transmits voice signals and packet-based data over the "last mile" of phone networks. Occam also sells cabinets to house the BLC system. The company sells directly to carriers and through resellers. Venture capital firm U.S. Venture Partners owns about 18% of Occam Networks.

EXECUTIVES

Chairman: Steven M. (Steve) Krausz
President, CEO, and Director: Robert L. (Bob) Howard-Anderson, age 50, $353,433 pay
CFO and Secretary: Christopher B. (Chris) Farrell, age 34
CTO: Mark Rumer, age 42, $157,995 pay
VP, Engineering: David C. (Dave) Mason, age 52, $177,569 pay
VP, Operations: Gregory R. (Greg) Dion, age 53, $156,543 pay
VP, Sales and Marketing: Russell J. (Russ) Sharer, age 47, $186,843 pay
VP, Sales: Nathan Harrell
VP, Business Development: Clive Hallatt
VP, Sales, Western Region: Scott Remillard
VP, Sales, Eastern Region: Mark Johnson
Auditors: Singer Lewak Greenbaum & Goldstein LLP

LOCATIONS

HQ: Occam Networks, Inc.
6868 Cortona Dr., Santa Barbara, CA 93117
Phone: 805-692-2900   **Fax:** 805-692-2999
Web: www.occamnetworks.com

COMPETITORS

Actelis	Entrisphere
ADC Telecommunications	Extreme Networks
ADTRAN	Hatteras Networks
Alcatel-Lucent	Nortel Networks
ANDA Networks	Overture Networks
Calix	Tellabs
Ceterus	Zhone Technologies
Cisco Systems	

HISTORICAL FINANCIALS

Company Type: Public

Income Statement

FYE: December 31

	REVENUE ($ mil.)	NET INCOME ($ mil.)	NET PROFIT MARGIN	EMPLOYEES
12/06	68.2	1.2	1.8%	126
12/05	39.2	(7.4)	—	—
12/04	17.3	(15.0)	—	—
12/03	8.0	(20.4)	—	—
12/02	2.4	(32.8)	—	—
Annual Growth	**130.9%**	**—**	**—**	**—**

2006 Year-End Financials

Debt ratio: —
Return on equity: 5.0%
Cash ($ mil.): 63.6
Current ratio: 4.37
Long-term debt ($ mil.): —
No. of shares (mil.): 19.7

Dividends
  Yield: —
  Payout: —
Market value ($ mil.): 325.3
R&D as % of sales: —
Advertising as % of sales: —

Stock History

NASDAQ (GM): OCNW

	STOCK PRICE ($) FY Close	P/E High/Low	PER SHARE ($) Earnings	Dividends	Book Value
12/06	16.50	— —	(0.24)	—	3.46
12/05	11.60	— —	(1.37)	—	(2.85)
12/04	3.60	— —	(2.80)	—	(0.05)
12/03	3.88	— —	(4.40)	—	(0.00)
12/02	2.80	— —	(15.20)	—	0.05
Annual Growth	**55.8%**	**— —**	**—**	**—**	**185.7%**

Old Line Bancshares

Old Line Bancshares is the holding company for Old Line Bank, serving consumers, businesses, and high-net-worth individuals in the Old Line State (Maryland) and in the Washington, DC, area. From about a half-dozen banking locations in Maryland's Prince George and Charles counties, the bank offers standard retail products, including checking and savings accounts, CDs, NOW accounts, and credit and debit cards. The company uses funds from deposits to write business and consumer loans; commercial real estate loans make up more than 45% of the bank's loan portfolio. Old Line Bank also offers luxury boat financing. Old Line Bancshares owns a 50% interest in real estate firm Pointer Ridge Office Investment.

Old Line Bank has plans to open at least three additional branch offices by 2008; while some of these are to be located in the company's current market area, at least one will be located in a county that hasn't previously had its own branch bank.

EXECUTIVES

Chairman, Old Line Bancshares and Old Line Bank: Craig E. Clark, age 64
Vice Chairman, Old Line Bancshares and Old Line Bank: Frank Lucente Jr., age 65
President, CEO, and Director; President and CEO, Old Line Bank: James W. Cornelsen, age 52, $205,000 pay
EVP; EVP and Chief Lending Officer, Old Line Bank: Joseph E. Burnett, age 61, $142,000 pay (prior to promotion)
EVP, CFO, and Secretary; EVP, CFO, Chief Credit Officer, and Secretary, Old Line Bank: Christine M. Rush, age 51, $135,500 pay
SVP, Branch Operations, Old Line Bank: Jeffrey Franklin, age 41
SVP, Old Line Bank: Sandi F. Burnett, age 49
SVP and Treasurer, Old Line Bank: Erin G. Lyddane, age 33
SVP, Old Line Bank: William J. Bush
VP and Branch Manager, Old Line Bank: Cynthia (Cindy) Walsh
Auditors: Rowles & Company, LLP

LOCATIONS

HQ: Old Line Bancshares, Inc.
1525 Pointer Ridge Place, Bowie, MD 20716
Phone: 301-430-2500   **Fax:** 301-932-5458
Web: www.oldlinebank.com

Old Line Bancshares has branches in Accokeek, Clinton, and Waldorf (2), Maryland.

PRODUCTS/OPERATIONS

2006 Sales

	$ mil.	% of total
Interest		
Loans, including fees	9.1	75
Securities	0.6	5
Federal funds sold	1.3	11
Other	0.1	1
Noninterest		
Service charges on deposit accounts	0.3	2
Marine division broker origination fees	0.4	3
Earnings on bank-owned life insurance	0.1	1
Other fees & commissions	0.2	2
Total	**12.1**	**100**

COMPETITORS

Bank of America	M&T Bank
BB&T	PNC Financial
First Mariner Bancorp	Tri-County Financial

HISTORICAL FINANCIALS

Company Type: Public

Income Statement			FYE: December 31
	ASSETS ($ mil.)	NET INCOME ($ mil.)	INCOME AS % OF ASSETS	EMPLOYEES
12/06	218.1	1.6	0.7%	56
12/05	169.0	1.1	0.7%	49
12/04	113.6	0.8	0.7%	—
12/03	89.5	0.5	0.6%	—
12/02	72.2	0.3	0.4%	—
Annual Growth	**31.8%**	**52.0%**	**—**	**14.3%**

Stock History

NASDAQ (CM): OLBK

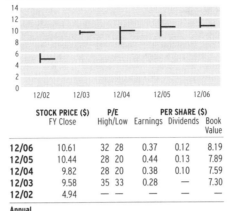

	STOCK PRICE ($) FY Close	P/E High/Low	PER SHARE ($) Earnings	Dividends	Book Value
12/06	10.61	32 28	0.37	0.12	8.19
12/05	10.44	28 20	0.44	0.13	7.89
12/04	9.82	28 20	0.38	0.10	7.59
12/03	9.58	35 33	0.28	—	7.30
12/02	4.94	— —	—	—	—
Annual Growth	**21.1%**	**— —**	**9.7%**	**9.5%**	**3.9%**

OMNI Energy Services

In the transition-zone oil fields along the US Gulf Coast, OMNI Energy Services is omnipresent. OMNI provides oilfield seismic drilling and surveying services for geophysical companies, primarily in environmentally sensitive areas such as the shallow waters off the Louisiana and Texas coasts. The company also provides permitting services and leases oil field equipment to geophysical companies. OMNI has acquired Trussco, a provider of dockside and offshore oil field waste management and environmental cleaning services, for about $10 million. In 2005 it was hired to help clean up the New Orleans Arena and Superdome in the aftermath of Hurricane Katrina. Director Dennis Sciotto owns about 33% of the company.

In an effort to expand its operations, OMNI Energy Services has divided its business into three separate divisions. The Environmental Services division has been formed to hold OMNI's permitting and environmental investigation services. The company's seismic surveying and geophysical analysis operations have been combined to form the Geophysical Support Services division. In 2005 it sold its Aviation Transportation Services division (helicopters and spare parts) to Rotorcraft Leasing for $11 million. That year it acquired oilfield gear lessor Preheat for more than $16 million.

In 2006 the company acquired Rig Tools, a leading Gulf Coast provider of oilfield equipment and specialized oilfield and environmental services. In 2007 it acquired exploration services providers Charles Holston and Cypress Consulting Services, Inc., and certain assets (including a salt water disposal well, related permits, and well-site equipment) from Bailey Operating Inc. It also agreed to buy B.E.G. Liquid Mud Services Corp for $11.8 million.

EXECUTIVES

Chairman, President, and CEO: James C. Eckert, age 58, $200,000 pay
COO: Brian J. Recatto, age 43
EVP: G. Darcy Klug, age 56, $227,692 pay
SVP and CFO: Ronald D. (Ron) Mogel, age 55
VP, Sales and Marketing: Robert H. (Bobby) Rhyne Jr., age 53
VP, Seismic Drilling Operations: John A. Harris, age 49, $125,000 pay
VP, Trussco Operations: Nolan C. Vice Jr., age 49, $111,538 pay
VP, Rig Tools Operations: James V. King, age 70
VP, Human Resources: Lisa Simmons
Secretary: Staci L. Marcelissen
Auditors: Pannell Kerr Forster of Texas, P.C.

LOCATIONS

HQ: OMNI Energy Services Corp.
4500 NE Evangeline Thruway, Carencro, LA 70520
Phone: 337-896-6664   **Fax:** 337-896-6655
Web: www.omnienergy.com

PRODUCTS/OPERATIONS

2006 Sales

	$ mil.	% of total
Drilling	50.6	51
Environmental	27.0	27
Equipment leasing	16.2	17
Other	5.2	5
Total	**99.0**	**100**

Selected Services

Environmental cleaning services
Oil field waste management
Seismic drilling
Seismic surveying
Specialized equipment rental

Selected Equipment

Airboat drilling units
Aluminum marsh ATVs
Highland drilling units
Pontoon Boats
Pullboats
Skid-mounted drilling units
Steel marsh ATVs
Swamp ATVs
Water buggies

COMPETITORS

CGGVeritas	Schlumberger
Clean Harbors	Seitel
Halliburton	Transocean Inc.
Oceaneering International	Trico Marine
Petroleum Geo-Services	

HISTORICAL FINANCIALS

Company Type: Public

Income Statement			FYE: December 31
	REVENUE ($ mil.)	NET INCOME ($ mil.)	NET PROFIT MARGIN	EMPLOYEES
12/06	99.0	21.8	22.0%	600
12/05	43.3	(4.3)	—	258
12/04	51.6	(14.3)	—	—
12/03	37.1	3.5	9.4%	—
12/02	27.8	1.2	4.3%	185
Annual Growth	**37.4%**	**106.5%**	**—**	**34.2%**

2006 Year-End Financials

Debt ratio: 86.4%	**Dividends**
Return on equity: 88.5%	Yield: —
Cash ($ mil.): 13.7	Payout: —
Current ratio: 1.48	Market value ($ mil.): 170.9
Long-term debt ($ mil.): 32.9	R&D as % of sales: —
No. of shares (mil.): 17.5	Advertising as % of sales: —

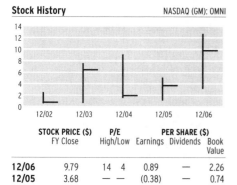

	STOCK PRICE ($) FY Close	P/E High/Low		PER SHARE ($) Earnings	Dividends	Book Value
12/06	9.79	14	4	0.89	—	2.26
12/05	3.68	—	—	(0.38)	—	0.74
12/04	1.94	—	—	(1.35)	—	0.42
12/03	6.45	24	2	0.31	—	2.65
12/02	0.76	30	9	0.08	—	2.17
Annual Growth	89.4%	—	—	82.6%	—	1.0%

Omni Financial Services

Omni Financial Services doesn't try to be everything to everyone. Rather, the holding company for Omni National Bank focuses on commercial lending, such as loans for community redevelopment, small businesses, and residential construction, in addition to asset-based lending and equipment leasing. Commercial mortgages and community redevelopment loans account for around 35% and 25% of the company's loan portfolio, respectively. Also serving local consumers, the bank has about 10 branches and loan production offices, mainly in North Carolina and Georgia, but also in Chicago and Tampa. Chairman and CEO Stephen Klein owns more than 30% of Omni Financial Services; EVP Jeffrey Levine holds more than 10%.

The company has loan offices in Alabama, North Carolina, Pennsylvania, and Texas. It is eyeing other markets for its community redevelopment lending, including Baltimore, Boston, Houston, San Antonio, and Washington, DC.

In 2005 Omni Financial acquired the troubled Georgia Community Bank, which gave the company entry into that state. Omni Financial hopes to use some of the proceeds from its 2006 IPO to purchase other banks or financial services concerns.

In 2007 it bought First Bank Lubbock Bancshares, Inc., its first banking office in Texas.

EXECUTIVES

Chairman and CEO: Stephen M. Klein, age 53, $345,833 pay
President, COO, and Director: Irwin M. Berman, age 46, $221,639 pay
EVP and CFO: Constance Perrine, age 46, $133,077 pay
EVP and Chief Credit Officer: Eugene F. Lawson III, age 57
EVP and Chief Lending Officer: Charles M. Barnwell, age 49, $185,000 pay

LOCATIONS

HQ: Omni Financial Services, Inc.
6 Concourse Pkwy., Ste. 2300, Atlanta, GA 30328
Phone: 770-396-0000   **Fax:** 770-350-1300
Web: www.onb.com

PRODUCTS/OPERATIONS

2006 Sales

	$ mil.	% of total
Interest		
Loans, including fees	44.0	83
Investment securities & other	6.1	12
Gain on sale of loans	1.6	3
Service charges on deposit accounts	0.7	1
Other	0.6	1
Total	**53.0**	**100**

COMPETITORS

Bank of America
BB&T
Fidelity Southern
First Citizens BancShares
RBC Centura Banks
Regions Financial
SunTrust
Synovus
Wachovia

HISTORICAL FINANCIALS

Company Type: Public

Income Statement
FYE: December 31

	ASSETS ($ mil.)	NET INCOME ($ mil.)	INCOME AS % OF ASSETS	EMPLOYEES
12/06	702.8	9.3	1.3%	186
12/05	477.0	4.9	1.0%	—
12/04	317.7	3.6	1.1%	—
Annual Growth	48.7%	60.7%	—	—

2006 Year-End Financials

Equity as % of assets: 10.3%	Dividends
Return on assets: 1.6%	Yield: 0.4%
Return on equity: 18.3%	Payout: 3.7%
Long-term debt ($ mil.): 28.3	Sales ($ mil.): 53.0
No. of shares (mil.): 11.3	R&D as % of sales: —
Market value ($ mil.): 118.1	Advertising as % of sales: —

Stock History
NASDAQ (GM): OFSI

	STOCK PRICE ($) FY Close	P/E High/Low		PER SHARE ($) Earnings	Dividends	Book Value
12/06	10.42	10	9	1.09	0.04	6.38

Omrix Biopharmaceuticals

Omrix Biopharmaceuticals helps keep the operating room from becoming a bloody mess. The company develops biosurgical sealants derived from human plasma to control bleeding during surgical procedures. Ethicon markets the products under the name Evicel in the US and Quixil in the EU and elsewhere. More than 65% of the company's revenues come from its immunotherapy products, including those which treat smallpox vaccine complications (VIG) and the reinfection of transplanted livers with Hepatitis B (HBIG). Immunotherapies make up a large portion of the company's international sales. Founder and CEO Robert Taub owns 24% of Omrix. MPM Bioventures owns an additional 22% of the company.

Omrix's immunotherapy roster also includes a treatment for primary immune deficiencies in adults. Products in development include WNIG to treat West Nile Virus. Omrix is working with the National Institutes of Health on therapeutics to treat avian flu, as well.

The company's biosealants use naturally occurring proteins that create a clot that can adhere to tissue. Omrix and Ethicon are also developing a hemostat device that will work with the sealant in cases of severe bleeding. Other products in development include a thrombin stand-alone to be used in neurosurgery applications.

EXECUTIVES

Chairman: Fredric D. Price, age 62
President, CEO, and Director: Robert Taub, age 59, $450,000 pay
EVP and COO: Nissim Mashiach, age 47
EVP and CFO: Ana I. Stancic, age 50
VP, Secretary, and Director: Philippe Romagnoli, age 59
VP and General Counsel: Nanci Prado, age 37
VP, Business Development: Harold Safferstein, age 42

LOCATIONS

HQ: Omrix Biopharmaceuticals, Inc.
630 5th Ave., 22nd Fl., New York, NY 10111
Phone: 212-887-6500   **Fax:** 212-887-6550
Web: www.omrix.com

2006 Sales

	$ mil.	% of total
Biosurgical products		
Products	13.4	21
Development	5.7	9
Passive immunotherapy products		
Products	43.3	68
Grants	1.2	2
Other	0.2	—
Total	**63.8**	**100**

COMPETITORS

Baxter
CryoLife
CSL Behring
Haemacure
King Pharmaceuticals
ThermoGenesis
ZymoGenetics

HISTORICAL FINANCIALS

Company Type: Public

Income Statement

FYE: December 31

	REVENUE ($ mil.)	NET INCOME ($ mil.)	NET PROFIT MARGIN	EMPLOYEES
12/06	63.8	23.1	36.2%	—
12/05	27.5	(27.7)	—	—
12/04	20.0	(6.6)	—	—
12/03	14.9	(6.6)	—	—
12/02	12.2	(5.5)	—	—
Annual Growth	51.2%	—	—	—

2006 Year-End Financials

Debt ratio: 0.4%
Return on equity: 51.0%
Cash ($ mil.): 81.1
Current ratio: 7.02
Long-term debt ($ mil.): 0.4

Net Income History

NASDAQ (GM): OMRI

On Assignment

Attention, scientists: Tired of unreliable assistants? Try On Assignment. The specialist staffing agency places scientists and other professionals, from lab assistants to nurses, for some 4,800 clients in need of temporary help. The company has two divisions: Healthcare Staffing (nurse travel, clinical lab, health care financial, and diagnostic and imaging staffing services) and Lab Support (scientists and technicians for the pharmaceutical, biotechnology, chemical, food and beverage, and environmental industries). Established in 1985, On Assignment operates from about 85 offices in Belgium, the Netherlands, the UK, and the US. In early 2007, it acquired Oxford Global Resources for $200 million.

Oxford Global Resources offers information technology (IT) and engineering staffing services across a variety of sectors. The deal broadens On Assignment's product offerings as the company enters the IT staffing market.

The company also entered the physician staffing sector when it acquired VISTA Staffing Solutions for about $41 million in cash in 2007. VISTA is headquartered in Salt Lake City and works with a pool of about 1,300 physicians specializing in 30 different medical practices.

On Assignment's most lucrative segment remains its Healthcare Staffing operations, representing nearly 60% of total sales each year. About 95% of the company's revenue derives from the US market.

HISTORY

Chemists Bruce Culver and Raf Dahlquist concocted the company in 1985. Lab Support (its original name) got off to a good start, but the founders were scientists, not business strategists; by 1989 the company was losing steam. The firm's venture investors took over, installing new management under Tom Buelter, who had developed Kelly Services' home care division. He refocused operations to temporary scientific services and turned the company around. It went public in 1992 as On Assignment.

In 1994 On Assignment bought 1st Choice Personnel and Sklar Resource Group, which specialized in temporary placement of financial professionals. The next year it started its Advanced Science Professionals unit to place temps in highly skilled scientific positions. With the 1996 purchase of Minneapolis-based EnviroStaff, On Assignment also began providing temporary workers in environmental fields. On Assignment crossed the border and started operations in Canada in 1997. In 1999 it established Clinical Lab Staff as its fourth division. Also by 1999 the company had opened the first three of several planned European offices in the UK.

In 2001 Buelter relinquished the CEO position to Joe Peterson (Buelter resigned as chairman early the following year). Also in 2002 the company acquired Health Personnel Options Corporation, a provider of temporary travel nurses and other health care professionals. The end of 2003 saw the appointment of Peter Dameris as the president and CEO of On Assignment.

EXECUTIVES

Chairman: Jeremy M. Jones, age 65
President, CEO, and Director: Peter T. Dameris, age 47, $500,000 pay
SVP Finance and CFO: James L. Brill, age 55
SVP Shared Services and CIO: Michael C. Payne, age 47, $216,000 pay
VP Finance and Corporate Controller: Kristi Wolff, $147,608 pay
President, Lab Support: Emmett B. McGrath, age 45, $250,000 pay
President, VISTA Staffing Solutions: Mark S. Brouse, age 51
President, Oxford Global Resources: Michael J. McGowan, age 54
Auditors: Deloitte & Touche LLP

LOCATIONS

HQ: On Assignment, Inc.
26651 W. Agoura Rd., Calabasas, CA 91302
Phone: 818-878-7900   **Fax:** 818-878-7930
Web: www.onassignment.com

2006 Sales

	$ mil.	% of total
US	269.6	94
Other countries	18.0	6
Total	287.6	100

PRODUCTS/OPERATIONS

2006 Sales

	$ mil.	% of total
Health care staffing	170.1	60
Lab support	117.5	40
Total	287.6	100

COMPETITORS

Adecco
AMN Healthcare
ATC Healthcare
CHG Healthcare
Cross Country Healthcare
The Everhart Group
IBM
Kelly Services
Kforce
Manpower
Medical Staffing Network
MPS
Professional Staff
RehabCare
Robert Half

HISTORICAL FINANCIALS

Company Type: Public

Income Statement

FYE: December 31

	REVENUE ($ mil.)	NET INCOME ($ mil.)	NET PROFIT MARGIN	EMPLOYEES
12/06	287.6	11.0	3.8%	13,760
12/05	237.9	(0.1)	—	12,140
12/04	193.6	(42.4)	—	—
12/03	209.6	(81.8)	—	—
12/02	250.3	12.3	4.9%	16,450
Annual Growth	3.5%	(2.8%)	—	(4.4%)

2006 Year-End Financials

Debt ratio: —
Return on equity: 9.1%
Cash ($ mil.): 110.2
Current ratio: 7.64
Long-term debt ($ mil.): —
No. of shares (mil.): 34.1
Dividends
  Yield: —
  Payout: —
Market value ($ mil.): 400.2
R&D as % of sales: —
Advertising as % of sales: —

Stock History

NASDAQ (GM): ASGN

	STOCK PRICE ($) FY Close	P/E High/Low		PER SHARE ($)		
				Earnings	Dividends	Book Value
12/06	11.75	35	21	0.39	—	4.87
12/05	10.91	—	—	—	—	2.96
12/04	5.19	—	—	(1.68)	—	2.95
12/03	5.21	—	—	(3.22)	—	4.60
12/02	8.52	53	12	0.48	—	7.21
Annual Growth	8.4%	—	—	(5.1%)	—	(9.3%)

Oneida Financial

You don't need to be a part of the Iroquois Confederacy to bank with Oneida Financial. The firm is the holding company for Oneida Savings Bank, which operates more than a dozen branches in upstate New York. Founded in 1866, the bank offers savings, checking, NOW, and money market accounts, as well as IRAs and CDs. It specializes in real estate lending, and writes home equity, auto, student, business, and consumer loans as well. Oneida Savings owns insurance agency and investment manager Bailey & Haskell Associates. The company's Bank of Chittenango unit accepts municipal deposits. Oneida Financial MHC, a mutual holding company, owns about 55% of Oneida Financial Corp.

Since 2001 the company has acquired four insurance agencies (which were subsequently merged into Bailey & Haskell), including Parsons, Cote & Company, which it bought in 2006. Oneida Financial has also bought Benefit Consulting Group, a firm that provides employee benefits consulting and retirement plan administration services in central and western New York State.

In 2007 the company acquired Vernon Bank Corporation, the holding company for The National Bank of Vernon, which added three branches to Oneida Savings Bank's network.

EXECUTIVES

Chairman: Richard B. Myers, age 69
President, CEO, and Director; President, CEO, and Trust Officer, Oneida Savings Bank; Chairman, Bailey & Haskell Associates: Michael R. Kallet, age 55, $262,400 pay
EVP, CFO, and Secretary; EVP, CFO, Secretary, and Trust Officer, Oneida Savings Bank; Treasurer and Secretary, Bailey & Haskell Associates: Eric E. Stickels, age 44, $151,600 pay
EVP; EVP, Chief Credit Officer, Oneida Savings Bank: Thomas H. Dixon, age 51, $151,600 pay
SVP, Business Banking Services, Oneida Savings Bank: James L. Lacy
SVP, Trust and Investment Services, Oneida Savings Bank: Charles R. Stevens
Assistant VP and Human Resources Director, Oneida Savings Bank: Joanne W. Mobriant
CEO, Bailey & Haskell Associates: John W. Bailey
Director; President, Bailey & Haskell Associates: John E. Haskell, age 62
Chief Marketing Officer, Bailey & Haskell Associates: William J. Fahy Jr.

LOCATIONS

HQ: Oneida Financial Corp.
182 Main St., Oneida, NY 13421
Phone: 315-363-2000 **Fax:** 315-366-3709
Web: www.oneidabank.com

Oneida Financial has branches in Bridgeport, Camden, Canastota, Chittenango, Cazenovia, Hamilton, and Oneida, New York.

PRODUCTS/OPERATIONS

2006 Sales

	$ mil.	% of total
Interest		
Loans, including fees	16.2	41
Investment securities	5.9	15
Other	0.2	—
Noninterest		
Commissions earned from the sale of financial products	12.7	33
Service charges on deposit accounts	2.4	6
Other	1.8	5
Total	**39.2**	**100**

COMPETITORS

Alliance Financial
Bank of America
Brooklyn Federal Bancorp
Community Bank System
First Niagara Financial
HSBC USA
JPMorgan Chase
KeyCorp
M&T Bank
Rome Bancorp

HISTORICAL FINANCIALS

Company Type: Public

Income Statement

FYE: December 31

	ASSETS ($ mil.)	NET INCOME ($ mil.)	INCOME AS % OF ASSETS	EMPLOYEES
12/06	442.9	4.2	0.9%	287
12/05	436.8	3.9	0.9%	249
12/04	422.6	3.3	0.8%	—
12/03	428.2	3.1	0.7%	—
12/02	416.7	3.2	0.8%	135
Annual Growth	**1.5%**	**7.0%**	**—**	**20.7%**

2006 Year-End Financials

Equity as % of assets: 13.2%
Return on assets: 1.0%
Return on equity: 7.5%
Long-term debt ($ mil.): 62.8
No. of shares (mil.): 7.8
Market value ($ mil.): 91.9
Dividends
  Yield: 3.8%
  Payout: 83.3%
Sales ($ mil.): 39.2
R&D as % of sales: —
Advertising as % of sales: —

Stock History

NASDAQ (CM): ONFC

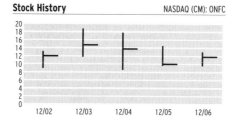

	STOCK PRICE ($) FY Close	P/E High/Low		PER SHARE ($) Earnings	Dividends	Book Value
12/06	11.81	24	18	0.54	0.45	7.51
12/05	10.00	29	20	0.50	0.41	6.97
12/04	13.75	41	20	0.43	0.38	7.03
12/03	14.74	68	44	0.27	0.37	9.98
12/02	12.00	30	21	0.43	0.17	9.49
Annual Growth	**(0.4%)**	**—**	**—**	**5.9%**	**27.6%**	**(5.7%)**

Online Resources

Financial institutions looking for a Web commerce presence can take Online Resources' systems to the bank. The company enables banks and credit unions to offer their account holders online and mobile access to such financial services as remote banking, funds transfer, and electronic bill payment. It also runs a program for credit card issuers that allows cardholders to access accounts, view transactions, and set up payments. E-commerce payment acquirers and large online billers can use the company's CertnFunds to expedite online payments. Founded in 1989, Online Resources serves some 2,600 banks, credit unions, card issuers, and billers across the US.

In 2006 the company bought electronic bill payment and presentment firm Princeton eCom. The deal comes after the company acquired Incurrent Solutions, which provides services related to online credit card use, and Integrated Data Systems (IDS), a private firm that develops and implements software applications for primarily credit unions, in 2005.

EXECUTIVES

Chairman and CEO: Matthew P. Lawlor, age 60, $399,120 pay
President and COO: Raymond T. (Ray) Crosier, age 52, $318,836 pay
EVP, CFO, and Secretary: Catherine A. (Cathy) Graham, age 46, $289,055 pay
EVP and General Manager, Integrated Banking Services: Ronald J. (Ron) Bergamesca
EVP and General Manager, Banking CSP Payments: Stephanie S. Chaufournier
EVP and General Manager, eCommerce Services: Robert R. Craig
SVP Banking Technology Services and CTO: Paul A. Franko
Managing Director, Corporate Communications: Beth Halloran
Human Resources Director: Sherry Mullin
Auditors: KPMG LLP

LOCATIONS

HQ: Online Resources Corporation
4795 Meadow Wood Ln., Ste. 300, Chantilly, VA 20151
Phone: 703-653-3100 **Fax:** 703-653-3105
Web: www.orcc.com

Online Resources operates facilities in Pleasanton and Woodland Hills, California; Newark, Parsippany, and Princeton, New Jersey; and Chantilly and McLean, Virginia.

PRODUCTS/OPERATIONS

2006 Sales

	$ mil.	% of total
Payment services	65.5	71
Account presentation services	8.0	9
Relationship management services	8.0	9
Professional services & other	10.2	11
Total	**91.7**	**100**

COMPETITORS

724 Solutions
BroadVision
Corillian
CUNA Mutual
Digital Insight
EDS
First Data
Fiserv
FundsXpress
Intuit
Jack Henry
Metavante
Microsoft
Open Solutions
Payment Data Systems
Q-UP Systems
S1 Corp.
Sybase
U.S. Central
Yahoo!

HISTORICAL FINANCIALS

Company Type: Public

Income Statement

FYE: December 31

	REVENUE ($ mil.)	NET INCOME ($ mil.)	NET PROFIT MARGIN	EMPLOYEES
12/06	91.7	0.3	0.3%	600
12/05	60.5	22.7	37.5%	421
12/04	42.3	4.0	9.5%	—
12/03	38.4	2.8	7.3%	—
12/02	32.3	(0.4)	—	296
Annual Growth	**29.8%**	**—**	**—**	**19.3%**

2006 Year-End Financials

Debt ratio: 82.3%
Return on equity: 0.3%
Cash ($ mil.): 36.1
Current ratio: 3.50
Long-term debt ($ mil.): 85.0
No. of shares (mil.): 25.8

Dividends
 Yield: —
 Payout: —
Market value ($ mil.): 263.3
R&D as % of sales: —
Advertising as % of sales: —

Stock History

NASDAQ (GS): ORCC

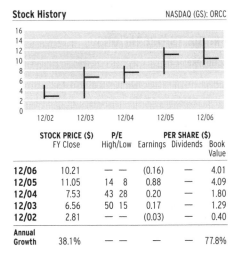

	STOCK PRICE ($) FY Close	P/E High/Low		PER SHARE ($) Earnings	Dividends	Book Value
12/06	10.21	—	—	(0.16)	—	4.01
12/05	11.05	14	8	0.88	—	4.09
12/04	7.53	43	28	0.20	—	1.80
12/03	6.56	50	15	0.17	—	1.29
12/02	2.81	—	—	(0.03)	—	0.40
Annual Growth	38.1%	—	—	—	—	77.8%

Oplink Communications

Oplink Communications puts a shine on network connections. The company makes fiber-optic components that increase the capacity of communications networks. Oplink's dense wavelength division multiplexers transmit several light signals simultaneously over a single glass fiber. Other products amplify the optical signals, monitor wavelength performance, and direct signals along the way to their destinations. Telecom equipment makers, including Nortel, ADVA, and Huawei, incorporate Oplink's components into gear used to build networks, both interoffice and international. Customers in North America account for more than half of sales. Oplink has acquired Optical Communication Products (OCP).

Oplink swapped around $84 million in cash and 857,258 shares of its common stock for Furukawa Electric's 66 million shares of OCP common stock. The company offered to acquire the remainder of OCP's stock for $1.50 a share in cash. Rival Furukawa owned about 58% of OCP. The deal valued OCP at approximately $171 million.

When OCP's board dug in its heels over terms of Oplink's offer, Oplink sweetened the deal, agreeing to pay $1.65 a share, cash on the barrelhead. The transaction closed in late 2007, with OCP becoming a wholly owned subsidiary of Oplink.

Oplink, which has many customers in common with OCP, sees the acquisition as a strategic fit for the company. OCP makes active optical components and subsystems, while Oplink specializes in passive components and subsystems, generally making their product portfolios complementary.

In addition to supplying optical components of its own design, Oplink provides photonic foundry services on a contract basis, making custom optical subsystems and full systems for customers.

FMR (Fidelity Investments) owns about 9% of Oplink Communications. Investors Chao-Jung and Chen Hwa Chang hold nearly 7% of the company. Kopp Investment Advisors owns nearly 6%. Investors Hui Chuan and H. S. Liu have an equity stake of 5% in Oplink.

EXECUTIVES

Chairman: Leonard J. LeBlanc, age 66
President, CEO, and Director: Joseph Y. Liu, age 56, $150,000 pay
CFO: Shirley Yin, age 40
VP Sales: River Gong, age 44, $135,000 pay
VP Operations: Yanfeng Yang, age 43
VP Technology: Jin Hong
VP Business Development, General Counsel, and Secretary: Thomas P. Keegan, age 53
General Manager, China/Macau: Chi-Min (James) Cheng, age 61, $117,500 pay
Auditors: Burr, Pilger & Mayer LLP

LOCATIONS

HQ: Oplink Communications, Inc.
 46335 Landing Pkwy., Fremont, CA 94538
Phone: 510-933-7200　　　**Fax:** 510-933-7300
Web: www.oplink.com

Oplink Communications has manufacturing facilities in China and the US, with sales offices around the world.

2007 Sales

	$ mil.	% of total
North America		
US	50.8	47
Canada	8.6	8
Asia/Pacific	28.3	26
Europe	19.8	19
Total	**107.5**	**100**

PRODUCTS/OPERATIONS

2007 Sales

	% of total
Bandwidth management products	55
Bandwidth creation products	45
Total	**100**

Selected Products

Multiplexing equipment
 Chromatic dispersion compensators
 Dense wavelength division multiplexers (DWDM)
 Dispersion Slope Compensators
 DWDM interleavers
 Noise reduction filters
 Wavelength lockers

Amplification
 Gain flattening filters
 Isolators
 Integrated hybrid components
 Polarization beam combiners
 Tap couplers
 Variable optical attenuators
 WDM pump/signal combiners

Switching equipment
 Add/drop multiplexers
 Circulators
 Optical switches

COMPETITORS

Alliance Fiber Optic	Gemfire
Avago Technologies	Hitachi Cable
Avanex	JDS Uniphase
AXSUN Technologies	MRV Communications
Bookham	New Focus
Ciena	Opnext
Clearfield	Optium
Covega	Santec
DiCon Fiberoptics	Santur
Finisar	Sumitomo Electric
Fujitsu	WaveSplitter
Furukawa Electric	

HISTORICAL FINANCIALS

Company Type: Public

Income Statement

FYE: Sunday nearest June 30

	REVENUE ($ mil.)	NET INCOME ($ mil.)	NET PROFIT MARGIN	EMPLOYEES
6/07	107.5	13.2	12.3%	2,039
6/06	54.8	1.9	3.5%	2,067
6/05	34.4	(2.7)	—	1,546
6/04	34.3	(6.4)	—	975
6/03	22.6	(36.8)	—	676
Annual Growth	47.7%	—	—	31.8%

2007 Year-End Financials

Debt ratio: —
Return on equity: 5.3%
Cash ($ mil.): 184.9
Current ratio: 9.57
Long-term debt ($ mil.): —
No. of shares (mil.): 23.2

Dividends
 Yield: —
 Payout: —
Market value ($ mil.): 347.5
R&D as % of sales: —
Advertising as % of sales: —

Stock History

NASDAQ (GM): OPLK

	STOCK PRICE ($) FY Close	P/E High/Low		PER SHARE ($) Earnings	Dividends	Book Value
6/07	15.00	39	24	0.57	—	11.64
6/06	18.31	228	146	0.09	—	10.55
6/05	11.55	—	—	(0.14)	—	—
6/04	13.44	—	—	(0.28)	—	—
6/03	12.46	—	—	(1.61)	—	—
Annual Growth	4.7%	—	—	—	—	10.3%

Opnext, Inc.

Stay tuned, light-speed communication is coming Opnext. The company makes optoelectronic components used to assemble fiber-optic data and voice communications networks. These laser diode modules, transmitter/receiver devices, and transceivers are incorporated by other equipment makers into larger multiplexing and digital cross-connect systems used in data communications and telecommunications. Customers include Alcatel-Lucent (20% of sales), Cisco Systems (38%), and NEC. Opnext was formerly the fiber-optic components unit of Hitachi's telecom and data infrastructure group.

The company plans to use proceeds from its IPO for working capital and other general corporate purposes, including product development, capital expenditures, and possible acquisitions.

Opnext also counts venture firm Clarity Partners (which owns about 23% of the company) and Marubeni among its investors. Those two firms put $321 million into Opnext in 2001.

Opnext has four business units: optical devices, optical modules, optical subsystems, and pluggable modules.

Hitachi owns about 44% of the company.

EXECUTIVES

Chairman: Naoya Takahashi, age 58
Co-Chairman: David Lee, age 57
President, CEO, and Director: Harry L. Bosco, age 62, $400,000 pay
COO: Gilles Bouchard, age 47
EVP; President, OpNext Japan: Kei Oki, age 59
EVP Business Development and Product Portfolio Management: Michael C. Chan, age 53, $325,000 pay
SVP and CFO: Robert J. Nobile, age 47, $250,000 pay
SVP Global Sales and Marketing:
  Chi-Ho (Christopher) Lin, age 44, $275,000 pay
SVP Module and Device Business Units:
  Tadayuki Kanno
VP Operations and CIO: Larry Dooling
VP Business Management and Secretary:
  Tammy L. Wedemeyer, age 38, $165,000 pay
Media Contact: Rebecca B. Andersen
Auditors: Ernst & Young LLP

LOCATIONS

HQ: Opnext, Inc.
  1 Christopher Way, Eatontown, NJ 07724
Phone: 732-544-3400   **Fax:** 732-544-3540
Web: www.opnext.com

Opnext has operations in China, Germany, Japan, and the US.

2007 Sales

	$ mil.	% of total
US	123.0	55
Europe	58.2	26
Asia/Pacific		
Japan	30.2	14
Other countries	11.5	5
Total	**222.9**	**100**

PRODUCTS/OPERATIONS

Selected Products

Communications laser diodes
Industrial infrared LEDs
Laser diode modules
Photodiode modules
Pluggable transceivers
Receivers
Transceivers
Transmitters
Transponders

COMPETITORS

Avago Technologies	Infinera
Avanex	Intel Corporation
AXSUN Technologies	JDS Uniphase
Bookham	Mitsubishi Electric
CyOptics	MRV Communications
EMCORE	NeoPhotonics
Finisar	Optical Communication
Fujitsu	Optium
Harmonic	Sumitomo Electric
Hitachi Cable	WaveSplitter

HISTORICAL FINANCIALS

Company Type: Public

Income Statement

FYE: March 30

	REVENUE ($ mil.)	NET INCOME ($ mil.)	NET PROFIT MARGIN	EMPLOYEES
3/07	222.9	2.4	1.1%	407
3/06	151.7	(30.5)	—	—
3/05	138.4	(32.7)	—	—
3/04	79.4	(80.5)	—	—
Annual Growth	**41.1%**	**—**	**—**	**—**

2007 Year-End Financials

Debt ratio: 4.0%
Return on equity: 1.2%
Cash ($ mil.): 199.8
Current ratio: 5.38
Long-term debt ($ mil.): 11.9
No. of shares (mil.): 64.5
Dividends
  Yield: —
  Payout: —
Market value ($ mil.): 954.7
R&D as % of sales: —
Advertising as % of sales: —

Stock History

NASDAQ (GM): OPXT

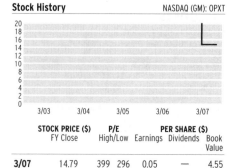

	STOCK PRICE ($) FY Close	P/E High/Low	PER SHARE ($) Earnings	Dividends	Book Value
3/07	14.79	399 296	0.05	—	4.55

Optelecom-NKF, Inc.

Optelecom-NKF chooses to make light of video. The company's Communications Products Division makes optical fiber-based data transmission and signal compression equipment and fiber-optic modems. Its products are used in a number of niche applications, including highway traffic monitoring, air traffic control video monitor displays, security surveillance, and manufacturing process and control applications. Optelecom-NKF's Electro-optics Technology unit makes optical fiber coils used in military rotation-sensing instruments; its customers include defense contractors such as Boeing.

In 2005 Optelecom acquired fiber optics equipment maker NKF Electronics, formerly a subsidiary of Draka Holding, for $26 million; it subsequently changed its name to reflect the addition of NKF's product line.

EXECUTIVES

Chairman, President, and CEO: Edmund D. Ludwig, age 67, $277,000 pay
CFO: Steven T. Tamburo, age 37, $59,022 pay (partial-year salary)
EVP US Federal Systems/Business Development and Director: James (Jim) Armstrong, age 51
EVP, COO, and Director: Thomas (Tom) Overwijn, age 45
VP Manufacturing: Greg Hall
VP Engineering: Coen Hooghiemstra
VP Sales and Marketing: Roland Hooghiemstra
VP Sales and Marketing, Central and South America: Mark Cabrelli
Head Corporate Information Technology: Tony Gaeta
Marketing Communications: Betsy Lanning
Manager Human Resources: Diane Mortazavi
Investor Relations: Rick Alpert
Auditors: Grant Thornton LLP

LOCATIONS

HQ: Optelecom-NKF, Inc.
  12920 Cloverleaf Center Dr.,
  Germantown, MD 20874
Phone: 301-444-2200   **Fax:** 301-444-2299
Web: www.optelecom.com

2006 Sales

	$ mil.	% of total
The Netherlands	16.8	42
US	15.4	39
UK	2.8	7
Spain	2.3	6
Other regions	2.2	6
Total	**39.5**	**100**

PRODUCTS/OPERATIONS

2006 Sales

	$ mil.	% of total
Communications Products Division	38.5	97
Electro Optics Technology Unit	1.0	3
Total	**39.5**	**100**

Selected Products

Communications Products Division
  Closed circuit television and broadcast video audio and data transmission equipment
  Compressed digital video products digitization and compression equipment
  Fiber-optic modems
  High-resolution RGB transmission equipment
  Uncompressed digital video transmission equipment
Electro Optics Technology Unit
  Interferometric Fiber Optic Gyro (IFOG) coils

COMPETITORS

3Com	Harmonic
ADC Telecommunications	JDS Uniphase
Alcatel-Lucent	Nortel Networks
ARRIS	Siemens AG
Cisco Systems	Tellabs

HISTORICAL FINANCIALS

Company Type: Public

Income Statement

FYE: December 31

	REVENUE ($ mil.)	NET INCOME ($ mil.)	NET PROFIT MARGIN	EMPLOYEES
12/06	39.5	1.5	3.8%	177
12/05	33.9	2.7	8.0%	151
12/04	19.4	1.6	8.2%	—
12/03	17.1	3.5	20.5%	—
12/02	14.9	1.6	10.7%	61
Annual Growth	**27.6%**	**(1.6%)**	**—**	**30.5%**

2006 Year-End Financials

Debt ratio: 86.3%
Return on equity: 10.1%
Cash ($ mil.): 3.6
Current ratio: 1.95
Long-term debt ($ mil.): 15.5
No. of shares (mil.): 3.5
Dividends
  Yield: —
  Payout: —
Market value ($ mil.): 36.7
R&D as % of sales: —
Advertising as % of sales: —

Stock History

NASDAQ (CM): OPTC

	STOCK PRICE ($) FY Close	P/E High/Low	PER SHARE ($) Earnings	Dividends	Book Value
12/06	10.49	67 18	0.44	—	5.13
12/05	13.40	20 10	0.80	—	3.56
12/04	9.26	31 16	0.49	—	3.12
12/03	9.09	14 4	1.11	—	2.56
12/02	4.64	12 4	0.56	—	1.28
Annual Growth	**22.6%**	**— —**	**(5.9%)**	**—**	**41.6%**

optionsXpress Holdings

In a hurry to do some options trading? optionsXpress is an online brokerage that provides a customized interface for trading options, stocks, and other products. optionsXpress also offers Xecute, an automated trading product, and StrategyScan, which helps clients identify possible trading strategies for a particular stock. optionsXpress has more than 200,000 customer accounts, with options trades representing about 75% of all trading activity. The company has been licensed in Australia, Canada, Singapore, and the European Union.

The company, which was founded in 2000 and went public in early 2005, launched subsidiary brokersXpress to extend its services to brokers and institutional investors. It also launched a futures platform in 2005.

The company suffered a setback in 2006 when partner INVESTools, an educational investment firm, said it would no longer direct business to optionsXpress but was buying its own trading firm.

Chairman James Gray controls more than 20% of the stock of optionsXpress.

EXECUTIVES

Chairman, optionsXpress Holdings and optionsXpress: James A. Gray, age 41
Vice Chairman; CEO, optionsXpress: Ned W. Bennett, age 64
President, CEO and Director: David A. Fisher, age 38
CEO, brokersXpress: Barry Metzger
CFO: Adam J. DeWitt, age 34, $353,750 pay
Chief Marketing Officer: Paul E. Eppen, age 44
Chief Administrative Officer; CFO, optionsXpress and brokersXpress: Thomas E. Stern, age 61, $350,000 pay
Chief Compliance Officer, optionsXpress Holdings and optionsXpress: Benjamin Morof, age 38, $410,833 pay
Auditors: Ernst & Young LLP

LOCATIONS

HQ: optionsXpress Holdings, Inc.
39 S. LaSalle St., Ste. 220, Chicago, IL 60603
Phone: 312-630-3300   **Fax:** 312-629-5256
Web: www.optionsxpress.com

PRODUCTS/OPERATIONS

2006 Sales

	$ mil.	% of total
Commissions	123.3	65
Other brokerage-related income	33.8	18
Interest income	30.8	16
Other	0.5	1
Total	**188.4**	**100**

COMPETITORS

Alaron
America First Associates
Charles Schwab
Citigroup
E*TRADE Financial
FMR
Interactive Brokers
Merrill Lynch
Scottrade
TD Ameritrade
TradeStation

HISTORICAL FINANCIALS

Company Type: Public

Income Statement

FYE: December 31

	REVENUE ($ mil.)	NET INCOME ($ mil.)	NET PROFIT MARGIN	EMPLOYEES
12/06	188.4	71.7	38.1%	214
12/05	129.0	48.7	37.8%	159
12/04	93.1	31.2	33.5%	—
12/03	48.2	16.4	34.0%	—
12/02	17.3	4.4	25.4%	—
Annual Growth	**81.7%**	**100.9%**	**—**	**34.6%**

2006 Year-End Financials

Debt ratio: —
Return on equity: 47.9%
Cash ($ mil.): 514.1
Current ratio: —
Long-term debt ($ mil.): —
No. of shares (mil.): 62.4
Dividends
 Yield: 0.9%
 Payout: 17.4%
Market value ($ mil.): 1,415.5
R&D as % of sales: —
Advertising as % of sales: —

Stock History

NASDAQ (GS): OXPS

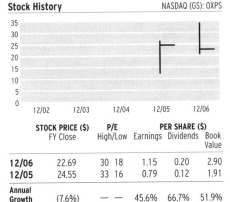

	STOCK PRICE ($) FY Close	P/E High/Low		PER SHARE ($) Earnings	Dividends	Book Value
12/06	22.69	30	18	1.15	0.20	2.90
12/05	24.55	33	16	0.79	0.12	1.91
Annual Growth	**(7.6%)**	**—**	**—**	**45.6%**	**66.7%**	**51.9%**

Orion Energy Systems

Orion Energy Systems wants customers to see the light . . . the high intensity fluorescent (HIF) light, that is. Orion designs, manufactures, and installs energy management systems that include HIF lighting, intelligent lighting controls, and its Apollo Light Pipe product, which collects and focuses daylight without consuming electricity. The firm estimates its products can help cut customers' lighting-related electricity costs by up to 50% and reduce related carbon dioxide emissions. Since Orion's inception in 1996 it has installed lighting in nearly 2,000 North American commercial and industrial facilities. Clients include such companies as GE, Kraft, and OfficeMax.

Orion also sells its products wholesale to electrical contractors and resellers.

A group of more than a dozen directors and current and former officers together own about 30% of the company's stock. Other noteworthy investors include one of Orion's biggest clients, General Electric, which owns about 7%.

EXECUTIVES

Chairman: Thomas A. (Tom) Quadracci, age 59
President, CEO, and Director: Neal R. Verfuerth, age 48
CFO and Treasurer: Daniel J. Waibel, age 47
EVP and Director: Michael J. Potts, age 43
SVP Business Development: John H. Scribante, age 42

VP, General Counsel, and Secretary: Eric von Estorff
VP Operations: Patricia A. Verfuerth, age 48
VP Strategic Initiatives: Erik G. Birkerts, age 40
Auditors: Grant Thornton LLP

LOCATIONS

HQ: Orion Energy Systems, Inc.
1204 Pilgrim Rd., Plymouth, WI 53073
Phone: 920-892-9340   **Fax:** 920-892-9350
Web: www.oriones.com

COMPETITORS

Acuity Brands
Comverge
Cooper Industries
EnerNOC
Graybar Electric
Honeywell International
Johnson Controls
W.W. Grainger

HISTORICAL FINANCIALS

Company Type: Public

Income Statement

FYE: March 31

	REVENUE ($ mil.)	NET INCOME ($ mil.)	NET PROFIT MARGIN	EMPLOYEES
3/07	48.2	0.9	1.9%	180
3/06	33.3	(1.6)	—	—
3/05	21.8	(1.3)	—	—
Annual Growth	**48.7%**	**—**	**—**	**—**

2007 Year-End Financials

Debt ratio: 312.2%
Return on equity: 41.8%
Cash ($ mil.): 0.3
Current ratio: 2.65
Long-term debt ($ mil.): 10.6

Net Income History

NASDAQ (GM): OESX

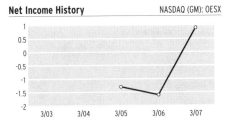

OSG America

Marine transportation company OSG America specializes in hauling refined petroleum products between US ports. Its fleet of more than 15 vessels, consisting of product carriers and tug-barge units, has an overall carrying capacity of about 5 million barrels. The company's clientele is made up primarily of major integrated oil companies and independent refiners; key clients have included Chevron, Sunoco, and Marathon Oil. OSG America was formed as a spinoff of marine transportation company Overseas Shipholding Group (OSG), which retained a controlling interest in OSG America after its November 2007 IPO.

OSG America's market is protected from direct foreign competition by the Merchant Marine Act of 1920. More commonly known as the Jones Act, the law requires that vessels transporting cargo between US ports be built in the US, registered under the US flag, manned by US crews, and owned and operated by US-organized companies.

Along with its own vessels, OSG America has a minority stake in Alaska Tanker, which carries crude oil from Alaska to the continental US.

EXECUTIVES

Chairman: Morten Arntzen, age 52
President, CEO, and Director: Jonathan P. Whitworth, age 40
CFO and Director: Myles R. Itkin, age 59
General Counsel and Secretary: James I. Edelson
Head of Worldwide Human Resources: Robert R. Mozdean
Auditors: Ernst & Young LLP

LOCATIONS

HQ: OSG America L.P.
Two Harbour Place, 302 Knights Run Ave., Ste. 1200, Tampa, FL 33602
Phone: 813-209-0600   **Fax:** 813-221-2769
Web: www.osgamerica.com

COMPETITORS

Colonial Pipeline
Crowley Maritime
Hornbeck Offshore
knight inc

K-Sea Transportation
Plantation Pipe Line
U.S. Shipping

HISTORICAL FINANCIALS

Company Type: Public

Income Statement

	REVENUE ($ mil.)	NET INCOME ($ mil.)	NET PROFIT MARGIN	EMPLOYEES
				FYE: December 31
12/06	88.9	7.7	8.7%	0
12/05	49.8	2.0	4.0%	0
12/04	31.8	1.9	6.0%	—
Annual Growth	67.2%	101.3%	—	—

2006 Year-End Financials

Debt ratio: —
Return on equity: —
Cash ($ mil.): 0.3
Current ratio: 0.83
Long-term debt ($ mil.): 82.0

Net Income History

NYSE: OSP

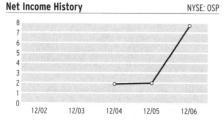

	12/02	12/03	12/04	12/05	12/06

PAB Bankshares

This Park Avenue Bank is not just for the well-heeled. Holding company PAB Bankshares owns Park Avenue Bank, which serves markets in south Georgia and Florida through more than a dozen branches; the company also has loan production offices in north Georgia and in Florida. Catering to consumers and small to midsized businesses, the bank offers traditional services as well as investment advisory and brokerage services through a third-party provider. Construction and commercial real estate loans each make up more than 30% of the company's loan portfolio, which also includes residential mortgage, agricultural, business, and personal loans. Chairman James L. Dewar, Jr. and family own around 15% of PAB Bankshares.

EXECUTIVES

Chairman: James L. Dewar Jr., age 64
President, CEO, and Director: M. Burke Welsh Jr., age 60, $375,750 pay
EVP and Director Operations: R. Wesley Fuller, age 46, $241,075 pay
EVP, CFO, and Treasurer: Donald J. (Jay) Torbert Jr., age 34, $241,750 pay
EVP and Chief Credit Officer, PAB Bankshares and The Park Avenue Bank: William L. (Bill) Kane, age 56, $28,464 pay (partial-year salary)
EVP and Regional President, South Georgia and Florida Markets, PAB Bankshares and The Park Avenue Bank: David H. Gould Jr., age 59, $23,221 pay (partial-year salary)
EVP and Chief Credit Officer: George D. Henderson, age 55
SVP and Commercial Lender, The Park Avenue Bank: Paul Trautman
SVP Human Resources: Brenda Vickery
VP Marketing: Randy Cox
Corporate Secretary: Denise G. McKenzie
Investor Relations: Maryellen Dampier
Auditors: Mauldin & Jenkins, LLC

LOCATIONS

HQ: PAB Bankshares, Inc.
3250 N. Valdosta Rd., Valdosta, GA 31602
Phone: 229-241-2775   **Fax:** 229-241-2774
Web: www.pabbankshares.com

PAB Bankshares operates in the Georgia counties of Appling, Bulloch, Clarke, Cobb, Cook, Decatur, Forsyth, Grady, Gwinnett, Hall, Henry, Jeff Davis, Lowndes, and Oconee. In Florida, the company has operations in Duval, Marion, and St. Johns counties.

PRODUCTS/OPERATIONS

2006 Sales

	$ mil	% of total
Interest		
Loans	67.4	81
Investment securities	8.6	10
Other	1.6	2
Noninterest		
Service charges on deposit accounts	3.9	5
Other fees	1.3	1
Securities transactions & other	0.7	1
Total	**83.5**	**100**

COMPETITORS

Ameris
Bank of America
BB&T
Colonial BancGroup
Colony Bankcorp
First Charter
First Southern
GB&T Bancshares
Habersham Bancorp
Henry County Bancshares

RBC Centura Banks
Regions Financial
Security Bank
Southeastern Banking
Southwest Georgia Financial
SunTrust
United Community Banks
VyStar Credit Union

HISTORICAL FINANCIALS

Company Type: Public

Income Statement

	ASSETS ($ mil.)	NET INCOME ($ mil.)	INCOME AS % OF ASSETS	EMPLOYEES
				FYE: December 31
12/06	1,120.8	13.7	1.2%	330
12/05	1,017.3	12.4	1.2%	314
12/04	869.0	8.5	1.0%	—
12/03	730.7	7.1	1.0%	—
12/02	747.9	6.3	0.8%	325
Annual Growth	10.6%	21.4%	—	0.4%

2006 Year-End Financials

Equity as % of assets: 8.5%
Return on assets: 1.3%
Return on equity: 15.0%
Long-term debt ($ mil.): 10.3
No. of shares (mil.): 9.5
Market value ($ mil.): 202.6
Dividends
  Yield: 2.5%
  Payout: 38.3%
Sales ($ mil.): 83.5
R&D as % of sales: —
Advertising as % of sales: —

Stock History

NASDAQ (GS): PABK

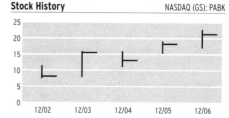

	12/02	12/03	12/04	12/05	12/06

	STOCK PRICE ($) FY Close	P/E High/Low		PER SHARE ($) Earnings	Dividends	Book Value
12/06	21.32	16	12	1.41	0.54	10.03
12/05	18.25	15	12	1.28	0.13	9.19
12/04	13.11	18	13	0.88	—	8.53
12/03	15.54	21	11	0.74	—	8.02
12/02	8.10	17	11	0.67	—	7.56
Annual Growth	27.4%	—	—	20.4%	315.4%	7.3%

Pacific Capital Bancorp

The central coast of California is home to the California Missions, Big Sur, The Channel Islands, and Pacific Capital Bancorp, the holding company for Pacific Capital Bank. The bank, which operates in various markets as First Bank of San Luis Obispo, First National Bank of Central California, Pacific Capital Bank, Santa Barbara Bank & Trust, San Benito Bank, and South Valley National Bank, serves consumers and small businesses in the region through about 50 branches. In addition to community banking services, Pacific Capital also offers investment advice and refund anticipation loan/tax refund transfer services.

Residential mortgages are about 25% of the company's loan portfolio; nonresidential real estate loans are about 20%. Other loans include business, consumer, and construction loans.

The company in 2007 sold its commercial equipment leasing business to Leaf Financial, a unit of Resource America.

In 2004 Pacific Capital acquired Pacific Crest Capital and merged that company's subsidiary, Pacific Crest Bank, into Pacific Capital Bank, expanding Pacific Capital's branch network with the addition of locations in Encino, Beverly Hills, and San Diego. In 2005 it acquired First Bancshares, the holding company for First Bank of San Luis Obispo. Since the acquisitions, Pacific Capital has a presence in every county along California's Central Coast.

EXECUTIVES

Chairman, Pacific Capital Bancorp and Pacific Capital Bank: Edward E. Birch, age 68
Vice Chairman, Pacific Capital Bancorp and Pacific Capital Bank; Chairman, First National Bank of Central California: D. Vernon Horton, age 67
Vice Chairman, Pacific Capital Bancorp and Pacific Capital Bank; President, First National Bank of Central California: Clayton C. Larson, age 60, $453,077 pay

President, CEO, and Director, Pacific Capital Bancorp and Pacific Capital Bank: William S. Thomas Jr., age 63, $535,961 pay
EVP, Chief Administrative Officer, and General Counsel: Frederick W. (Fred) Clough, age 63, $326,154 pay
EVP, Wealth Management Services: George Leis, age 46, $417,692 pay
EVP, SBA and Income Producing Property Lending: Gary Wehrle, age 64
SVP and Chief Credit Officer: Chuck Tulloh
SVP and Director, Human Resources: Sherrell Reefer, age 55
SVP, Investor Relations and Corporate Communications: Deborah L. Whiteley
SVP and Corporate Secretary: Carol M. Zepke
Interim CFO and Chief Risk Officer: Brad Cowie
Auditors: Ernst & Young LLP

LOCATIONS

HQ: Pacific Capital Bancorp
1021 Anacapa St., Santa Barbara, CA 93101
Phone: 805-564-6405   **Fax:** 805-882-3888
Web: www.pcbancorp.com

Pacific Capital Bancorp has operations in the California counties of Los Angeles, Monterey, San Benito, San Diego, San Luis Obispo, Santa Barbara, Santa Clara, Santa Cruz, and Ventura.

PRODUCTS/OPERATIONS

2006 Sales

	$ mil.	% of total
Interest		
Loans	508.3	70
Securities & other	56.2	8
Noninterest		
Refund transfer fees	44.9	6
Net gain on sale of tax refund loans	43.2	6
Trust & investment advisory fees	20.3	3
Other service charges, commissions & fees	26.2	4
Service charges on deposit accounts	16.5	2
Other	10.9	1
Total	**726.5**	**100**

COMPETITORS

Bank of America
Bank of the West
First Republic (CA)
Harrington West Financial
Rabobank America
Washington Mutual
Wells Fargo
Wescom Credit Union

HISTORICAL FINANCIALS

Company Type: Public

Income Statement				FYE: December 31
	ASSETS ($ mil.)	NET INCOME ($ mil.)	INCOME AS % OF ASSETS	EMPLOYEES
12/06	7,494.8	94.5	1.3%	1,622
12/05	6,876.2	99.3	1.4%	1,505
12/04	6,024.8	87.9	1.5%	—
12/03	4,859.6	75.7	1.6%	—
12/02	4,219.2	74.8	1.8%	1,225
Annual Growth	15.4%	6.0%	—	7.3%

2006 Year-End Financials

Equity as % of assets: 8.2%
Return on assets: 1.3%
Return on equity: 16.3%
Long-term debt ($ mil.): 1,401.2
No. of shares (mil.): 46.9
Market value ($ mil.): 1,574.2
Dividends
Yield: 2.6%
Payout: 43.8%
Sales ($ mil.): 726.5
R&D as % of sales: —
Advertising as % of sales: —

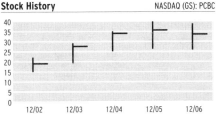

	STOCK PRICE ($) FY Close	P/E High/Low		PER SHARE ($)		
				Earnings	Dividends	Book Value
12/06	33.58	19	13	2.01	0.88	13.17
12/05	35.61	18	12	2.14	0.58	11.69
12/04	33.99	18	13	1.92	0.34	10.05
12/03	27.61	18	12	1.64	0.47	11.75
12/02	19.09	14	10	1.61	—	10.74
Annual Growth	15.2%	—	—	5.7%	23.3%	5.2%

Pacific Continental

Pacific Continental Corporation is the holding company for Pacific Continental Bank, which has about a dozen locations in the Eugene and Portland, Oregon areas and two more in the Seattle area. The bank attracts deposits from consumers, local businesses, professional service providers, and not-for-profits by offering such retail products as checking and money market accounts, IRAs, and CDs. Its lending activities consist mainly of real estate loans (more than three-quarters of its loan portfolio). Pacific Continental Bank also has a consumer finance division and is a preferred Small Business Administration (SBA) lender.

To commercial clients, the bank also offers credit card transaction processing and credit cards for businesses.

In 2005 Pacific Continental Corporation acquired NWB Financial Corporation, the holding company for Seattle-area Northwest Business Bank, which was merged into Pacific Continental Bank.

EXECUTIVES

Chairman: Robert A. Ballin, age 65
CEO and Director: Hal M. Brown, age 53, $334,290 pay (prior to title change)
President and COO, Pacific Continental Corporation and Pacific Continental Bank: Roger S. Busse, age 51, $211,629 pay (prior to promotion)
EVP and CFO, Pacific Continental Corporation and Pacific Continental Bank: Michael A. (Mick) Reynolds, age 55, $162,139 pay
EVP and Chief Credit Officer: Casey R. Hogan, age 48
EVP and CIO: Patricia K. (Pat) Haxby, age 56
EVP and Director, Portland/Vancouver Operations: Daniel J. (Dan) Hempy, age 47, $230,104 pay
EVP and Director, Lane County Operations: Mitchell J. (Mitch) Hagstrom, age 50, $165,784 pay
EVP and Director, Seattle Operations: Basant Singh, age 50
EVP and Director, Commercial Real Estate Markets: Charlotte A. Boxer, age 56
SVP and Human Resources Director, SPHR: Carol A. Batchelor, age 45
SVP and Senior Credit Administrator: Damon Rose
VP and General Counsel: Barbara R. Shields
Auditors: Moss Adams, LLP

LOCATIONS

HQ: Pacific Continental Corporation
111 W. 7th Ave., Eugene, OR 97401
Phone: 541-686-8685   **Fax:** 541-344-2843
Web: www.therightbank.com

Pacific Continental has banking branches in Beaverton, Eugene, Junction City, Portland, Springfield, and Tualatin, Oregon; and Bellevue, Seattle, and Vancouver, Washington.

PRODUCTS/OPERATIONS

2006 Sales

	$ mil.	% of total
Interest		
Loans	60.3	91
Investment securities & other	1.7	3
Noninterest		
Service charges on deposit accounts	1.3	2
Other fees, principally bankcard processing	1.5	2
Other	1.6	2
Total	**66.4**	**100**

COMPETITORS

Bank of America
Cowlitz Bancorporation
KeyCorp
Umpqua Holdings
U.S. Bancorp
Washington Federal
Washington Mutual
Wells Fargo

HISTORICAL FINANCIALS

Company Type: Public

Income Statement				FYE: December 31
	ASSETS ($ mil.)	NET INCOME ($ mil.)	INCOME AS % OF ASSETS	EMPLOYEES
12/06	885.3	12.6	1.4%	257
12/05	791.8	9.6	1.2%	229
12/04	516.6	7.9	1.5%	—
12/03	425.8	6.8	1.6%	—
12/02	379.9	3.5	0.9%	156
Annual Growth	23.6%	37.7%	—	13.3%

2006 Year-End Financials

Equity as % of assets: 10.8%
Return on assets: 1.5%
Return on equity: 14.2%
Long-term debt ($ mil.): 8.3
No. of shares (mil.): 10.6
Market value ($ mil.): 188.3
Dividends
Yield: 1.6%
Payout: 27.1%
Sales ($ mil.): 66.4
R&D as % of sales: —
Advertising as % of sales: —

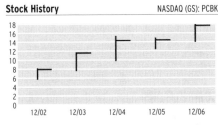

	STOCK PRICE ($) FY Close	P/E High/Low		PER SHARE ($)		
				Earnings	Dividends	Book Value
12/06	17.68	17	13	1.07	0.29	8.99
12/05	14.44	16	13	0.95	0.25	7.96
12/04	14.32	19	12	0.82	0.17	5.71
12/03	11.56	16	11	0.72	0.20	6.22
12/02	7.91	22	16	0.37	0.17	7.28
Annual Growth	22.3%	—	—	30.4%	14.3%	5.4%

Pacific Premier Bancorp

Like most Southern Californians, Pacific Premier Bancorp is getting on with its second act. Formerly Life Financial, the company is the parent of Pacific Premier Bank (previously Life Bank), which has a handful of branches and a Small Business Administration loan production office in Orange and San Bernardino counties in Southern California. After a stint during the 1990s in which the bank focused on subprime mortgages and nearly went under, it has reorganized as a commercial bank. The bank focuses on multifamily residential and commercial real estate loans (about 87% of its portfolio) and is seeking to diversify its book.

EXECUTIVES

Chairman, Pacific Premier Bancorp and Pacific Premier Bank: Ronald G. Skipper, age 67
President, CEO, and Director, Pacific Premier Bancorp and Pacific Premier Bank: Steven R. (Steve) Gardner, age 46, $600,000 pay
EVP, CFO, Treasurer, and Secretary, Pacific Premier Bancorp and Pacific Premier Bank: John Shindler, age 51, $200,000 pay
EVP and Chief Banking Officer, Pacific Premier Bank: Edward (Eddie) Wilcox, age 39, $225,000 pay
SVP and Director of Information Technology and Security Officer, Pacific Premier Bank: James (Jim) Sanchez
SVP and Manager, SBA Loan Department, Pacific Premier Bank: Lou Malesci
VP and Manager, Commercial Lending, Pacific Premier Bank: Ronald (Ron) Meyers
Chief Appraiser, Pacific Premier Bank: John Hagan
Auditors: Vavrinek, Trine, Day & Co., LLP

LOCATIONS

HQ: Pacific Premier Bancorp, Inc.
    1600 Sunflower Ave., 2nd Fl., Costa Mesa, CA 92626
Phone: 714-431-4000   **Fax:** 714-433-3000
Web: www.ppbi.net

PRODUCTS/OPERATIONS

2006 Sales

	$ mil.	% of total
Interest		
Loans	41.3	82
Other	2.8	5
Noninterest		
Gain on sale of loans	3.7	7
Loan servicing fee income	1.5	3
Other	1.3	3
Total	**50.6**	**100**

COMPETITORS

Bank of America
Citibank
City National
Comerica
Downey Financial
Washington Mutual
Wells Fargo
Zions Bancorporation

HISTORICAL FINANCIALS
Company Type: Public

Income Statement

FYE: December 31

	ASSETS ($ mil.)	NET INCOME ($ mil.)	INCOME AS % OF ASSETS	EMPLOYEES
12/06	730.9	7.4	1.0%	109
12/05	702.7	7.2	1.0%	88
12/04	543.1	6.7	1.2%	—
12/03	309.4	2.1	0.7%	—
12/02	238.3	2.9	1.2%	59
Annual Growth	**32.3%**	**26.4%**	**—**	**16.6%**

2006 Year-End Financials

Equity as % of assets: 7.9%
Return on assets: 1.0%
Return on equity: 13.6%
Long-term debt ($ mil.): 326.8
No. of shares (mil.): 5.2
Market value ($ mil.): 63.5
Dividends
    Yield: —
    Payout: —
Sales ($ mil.): 50.6
R&D as % of sales: —
Advertising as % of sales: —

Stock History

NASDAQ (CM): PPBI

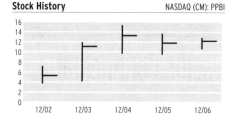

	STOCK PRICE ($) FY Close	P/E High/Low		PER SHARE ($) Earnings	Dividends	Book Value
12/06	12.18	11	10	1.11	—	11.13
12/05	11.80	13	9	1.08	—	9.67
12/04	13.26	15	10	1.02	—	8.37
12/03	11.09	19	7	0.61	—	7.10
12/02	5.31	3	2	2.16	—	8.71
Annual Growth	**23.1%**	**—**	**—**	**(15.3%)**	**—**	**6.3%**

Pacific State Bancorp

Farmers are more common than surfers in California's Long Valley, and serving their banking needs is Pacific State Bancorp, the holding company for Pacific State Bank. The bank offers deposit and loan products to individuals and small to midsized businesses from branches around Stockton and in San Joaquin County in California. Not surprising considering the region's dependence on agriculture, the bank takes pride in being a national leader in the underwriting of USDA business and industry loans. Commercial mortgages make up about 45% of the bank's loan portfolio, followed by commercial and agricultural loans which account for more than a quarter. The bank also originates construction and installment loans.

President, CEO, and director Steven Rosso owns about 7% of Pacific State Bancorp; director Maxwell Freeman owns just over 9%; chairman Harold Hand owns a little more than 8%.

EXECUTIVES

Chairman: Harold Hand, age 69
President, CEO, and Director, Pacific State Bancorp and Pacific State Bank: Steven A. Rosso, age 53, $335,770 pay

EVP, Chief Credit Officer, and Director, Pacific State Bancorp and Pacific State Bank: Gary A. Stewart, age 57, $212,933 pay
VP and CFO; SVP and CFO, Pacific State Bank: JoAnne C. Roberts, age 50, $122,500 pay
VP and Senior Operations Officer, Pacific State Bank: Sylvia Hanania
VP and MIS Director, Pacific State Bank: Glenn Scott
Auditors: Perry-Smith LLP

LOCATIONS

HQ: Pacific State Bancorp
    1899 W. March Ln., Stockton, CA 95207
Phone: 209-870-3200   **Fax:** 209-870-3250
Web: www.pacificstatebank.com

PRODUCTS/OPERATIONS

2006 Sales

	$ mil.	% of total
Interest		
Loans	24.9	86
Other	1.6	5
Noninterest		
Service charges	0.9	3
Sale of loans	0.3	1
Other	1.4	5
Total	**29.1**	**100**

COMPETITORS

1867 Western Financial
Bank of America
Capital Corp of the West
E. J. De La Rosa
Oak Valley Community Bank
Washington Mutual
Wells Fargo

HISTORICAL FINANCIALS
Company Type: Public

Income Statement

FYE: December 31

	ASSETS ($ mil.)	NET INCOME ($ mil.)	INCOME AS % OF ASSETS	EMPLOYEES
12/06	386.8	5.5	1.4%	84
12/05	309.6	4.3	1.4%	82
12/04	254.4	3.2	1.3%	—
12/03	200.9	2.0	1.0%	—
12/02	180.1	1.2	0.7%	—
Annual Growth	**21.1%**	**46.3%**	**—**	**2.4%**

2006 Year-End Financials

Equity as % of assets: 7.5%
Return on assets: 1.6%
Return on equity: 21.8%
Long-term debt ($ mil.): 13.7
No. of shares (mil.): 3.7
Market value ($ mil.): 79.6
Dividends
    Yield: —
    Payout: —
Sales ($ mil.): 29.1
R&D as % of sales: —
Advertising as % of sales: —

Stock History

NASDAQ (GM): PSBC

	STOCK PRICE ($) FY Close	P/E High/Low		PER SHARE ($) Earnings	Dividends	Book Value
12/06	21.74	17	12	1.41	—	7.94
12/05	18.50	20	13	1.10	—	6.08
12/04	20.50	25	9	0.84	—	4.88
12/03	8.07	14	7	0.59	—	7.97
12/02	4.00	14	11	0.34	—	13.71
Annual Growth	**52.7%**	**—**	**—**	**42.7%**	**—**	**(12.8%)**

Packeteer, Inc.

Packeteer is on a mission to improve the quality of Internet service. The company develops bandwidth management systems that enable businesses and Internet service providers to find and classify network traffic, analyze network performance, control traffic, and prioritize Web site access. Packeteer's PacketShaper systems help network managers reduce congestion that can result from such electronic traffic as file transfers, transactions, or multimedia transmissions. The company has some 7,000 customers worldwide in the areas of education, finance, health care, manufacturing, and retail, and has shipped more than 60,000 units.

Packeteer's sales are roughly split between the Americas and other regions. The company sells directly and through channel partners. Packeteer has more than 600 distributors, system integrators, and value-added resellers. Distributors Westcon Group and Alternative Technology together accounted for about 40% of Packeteer's sales in 2006. The company outsources its manufacturing and warranty repair to SMTC.

Packeteer acquired network service provider Mentat in December 2004 for about $17 million in cash. In 2006 the company acquired Tacit Networks, a developer of WAN file services software, for $78 million in cash.

EXECUTIVES

Chairman: Steven J. Campbell, age 66
President, CEO, and Director: David (Dave) Côté, age 53, $375,000 pay
CFO and Secretary: David C. Yntema, age 63, $272,500 pay
VP Business Development: Ajmal Noorani, age 44
VP Engineering: Nelu Mihai, age 52, $222,756 pay
VP Human Resources: Greg Pappas, age 45
VP Operations and Customer Support: Manuel R. (Manny) Freitas, age 59, $239,089 pay
VP Sales, Americas: Wayne M. Bergland
VP Sales, Asia Pacific: Alan Leong
VP Sales, EMEA: Bernard Girbal
VP Marketing: Alan Menezes, age 48
Auditors: KPMG LLP

LOCATIONS

HQ: Packeteer, Inc.
10201 N. De Anza Blvd., Cupertino, CA 95014
Phone: 408-873-4400   **Fax:** 408-873-4410
Web: www.packeteer.com

2006 Sales

	$ mil.	% of total
Americas	67.6	47
Europe, Middle East & Africa	42.2	29
Asia/Pacific	35.3	24
Total	**145.1**	**100**

PRODUCTS/OPERATIONS

2006 Sales

	$ mil.	% of total
Products	110.2	76
Services	34.9	24
Total	**145.1**	**100**

Selected Products

iShared (WAFS, WAN optimization)
Mobiliti (acceleration and file access for mobile users)
PacketShaper (traffic and bandwidth management)
PolicyCenter (policy management software)
ReportCenter (network metrics aggregation software)
Sky X (application and network acceleration)

COMPETITORS

Alacritech	Expand Networks
Allot Communications	F5 Networks
Blue Coat	Juniper Networks
Check Point Software	MPC Corp.
Cisco Systems	NetScout Systems
Citrix Systems	Riverbed Technology
Ellacoya Networks	TippingPoint

HISTORICAL FINANCIALS

Company Type: Public

Income Statement

FYE: December 31

	REVENUE ($ mil.)	NET INCOME ($ mil.)	NET PROFIT MARGIN	EMPLOYEES
12/06	145.1	4.9	3.4%	421
12/05	112.9	19.2	17.0%	304
12/04	92.4	14.5	15.7%	—
12/03	72.7	11.0	15.1%	—
12/02	55.0	3.7	6.7%	203
Annual Growth	**27.4%**	**7.3%**	**—**	**20.0%**

2006 Year-End Financials

Debt ratio: —
Return on equity: 3.4%
Cash ($ mil.): 65.3
Current ratio: 2.01
Long-term debt ($ mil.): —
No. of shares (mil.): 35.4
Dividends
  Yield: —
  Payout: —
Market value ($ mil.): 481.4
R&D as % of sales: —
Advertising as % of sales: —

Stock History

NASDAQ (GS): PKTR

	STOCK PRICE ($) FY Close	P/E High/Low	PER SHARE ($) Earnings	Dividends	Book Value
12/06	13.60	103 54	0.14	—	4.51
12/05	7.77	32 12	0.55	—	3.76
12/04	14.45	56 18	0.42	—	3.05
12/03	16.98	68 22	0.32	—	2.57
12/02	6.86	71 21	0.12	—	2.07
Annual Growth	**18.7%**	**— —**	**3.9%**	**—**	**21.4%**

Palomar Medical Technologies

Palomar Medical Technologies' laser light show is more functional than flashy. Palomar makes lasers, delivery systems, and related disposable products that are used in medical and aesthetic procedures. The company's products include the EsteLux, StarLux, and MediLux systems. The company's lasers are used for tattoo, hair, and wrinkle removal, as well as leg-vein, acne, and pigmented lesion treatment. It is developing products for both professional use (dermatologists, aestheticians, spas) and the consumer market for home use. Palomar Med-

ical markets its products through distributors in 45 countries as well as a direct-sales force.

Partnerships and contracts have allowed Palomar Medical Technologies more resources to develop new products. The company has an agreement with Johnson & Johnson Consumer Companies to develop devices for reducing body fat and for improving appearance of the skin. It also has a research contract for more than $3 million with the U.S. Department of the Army for the development of a self-treatment system for Pseudofolliculitis Barbae (also known as "razor bumps"). Another agreement with Global Gillette is allowing the company to further develop a home-use laser hair removal device.

To facilitate its international expansion, Palomar Medical Technologies is establishing operations in the Netherlands.

EXECUTIVES

Chairman: Louis P. (Dan) Valente, age 77, $377,153 pay
President, CEO, and Director: Joseph P. Caruso, age 48, $522,872 pay
SVP, CFO, and Treasurer: Paul S. Weiner, age 44, $360,010 pay
SVP, General Counsel, and Secretary: Patricia A. Davis
SVP Operations: Steven Armstrong
SVP Research: Gregory Altshuler
SVP Sales and Marketing: Paul F. Wiener
CTO: Michael H. Smotrich
Auditors: Ernst & Young LLP

LOCATIONS

HQ: Palomar Medical Technologies, Inc.
82 Cambridge St., Burlington, MA 01803
Phone: 781-993-2300   **Fax:** 781-993-2330
Web: www.palmed.com

2006 Sales

	% of total
US	75
Canada	8
Europe	6
Asia/Pacific	5
Japan	3
South & Central America	2
Australia	1
Total	**100**

PRODUCTS/OPERATIONS

2006 Sales

	$ mil.	% of total
Products	92.2	73
Royalties	30.5	24
Funded product development	3.8	3
Total	**126.5**	**100**

COMPETITORS

Candela Corporation	Lumenis
Cutera	Syneron
Cynosure	Thermage
IRIDEX	

HISTORICAL FINANCIALS

Company Type: Public

Income Statement

FYE: December 31

	REVENUE ($ mil.)	NET INCOME ($ mil.)	NET PROFIT MARGIN	EMPLOYEES
12/06	126.5	53.0	41.9%	225
12/05	76.2	17.5	23.0%	188
12/04	54.4	10.6	19.5%	—
12/03	34.8	3.4	9.8%	—
12/02	25.4	0.0	—	92
Annual Growth	**49.4%**	**—**	**—**	**25.1%**

2006 Year-End Financials

Debt ratio: —
Return on equity: 62.7%
Cash ($ mil.): 104.2
Current ratio: 5.82
Long-term debt ($ mil.): —
No. of shares (mil.): 18.1

Dividends
Yield: —
Payout: —
Market value ($ mil.): 915.3
R&D as % of sales: —
Advertising as % of sales: —

Stock History

NASDAQ (GS): PMTI

	STOCK PRICE ($) FY Close	P/E High/Low		PER SHARE ($) Earnings	Dividends	Book Value
12/06	50.67	22	12	2.62	—	6.48
12/05	35.04	43	23	0.91	—	3.03
12/04	26.07	46	16	0.60	—	1.80
12/03	10.52	52	5	0.21	—	0.99
12/02	1.05	—	—	—	—	0.41
Annual Growth	163.6%	—	—	131.9%	—	99.5%

Panera Bread

Panera Bread is ready for an epochal change in American eating habits. The company is a leader in the quick-casual restaurant business with more than 1,000 bakery-cafes in almost 40 states. Its locations, which operate under the Panera and Saint Louis Bread Company banners, offer made-to-order sandwiches built using a variety of artisan breads, including Asiago cheese bread, focaccia, and its classic sourdough bread. Its menu also features soups, salads, and gourmet coffees. In addition, Panera sells its bread, bagels, and pastries to go. Almost 400 of its locations are company-operated, while the rest are run by franchisees.

Panera (which is Latin for "time for bread") has built significant brand loyalty by concentrating on the quality of its fresh-baked breads and other ingredients. It targets suburban areas where real estate is less expensive and the competition is less intense.

One of the best-performing and fastest-growing restaurant companies, Panera opened about 150 new locations in 2006, including 70 new corporate-owned stores. It worked to increase those growth numbers slightly in 2007. The company has also been acquiring a small number of locations from its franchisees to increase its company-owned store count.

In 2006 Panera acquired 51% of Paradise Bakery & Café, which runs a chain of more than 40 bakery-cafes in the Southwest. The $21 million deal included the right to acquire the remaining stake in Paradise Bakery after 2008.

Chairman and CEO Ron Shaich controls more than 15% of Panera's voting stock.

HISTORY

Panera Bread traces its roots to a restaurant opened in Boston by French commercial oven manufacturer Pavailler. Au Bon Pain, opened in 1976, was intended as a showcase for Pavailler's ovens. The scent of hot croissants (and money) caught the attention of Louis Kane, who bought the business in 1978 and began expanding in Boston. Ron Shaich (pronounced "shake") joined Kane in 1981, and together they formed Au Bon Pain Co., Inc. The chain grew rapidly until the early 1990s, saturating the high-traffic areas in eastern US cities. After its IPO in 1991, Au Bon Pain began making acquisitions, including Saint Louis Bread in 1993.

Saint Louis Bread was founded in 1987 when Ken Rosenthal, spurred into the restaurant business by his brother, opened his first cafe in Kirkwood, Missouri. Based on sourdough bakeries in San Francisco, the concept eventually spread to five stores by 1990 and nearly 20 units two years later. In 1993 the company made *Inc.* magazine's list of the 500 fastest-growing companies. At the end of that year, Au Bon Pain paid $24 million for the company, franchising its new units outside of the St. Louis area as Panera Bread. Rosenthal stayed on with Au Bon Pain as chairman of its new chain before leaving to become a major franchisee.

By 1995 the company was facing new competition from coffee and bagel shops. Flat sales and sharp price increases for butter hurt the chain's bottom line. By 1997 the company had added bagels to its menu and was considering extensive renovations. It ultimately decided the chain had peaked in the US, and it limited expansion to countries with dense urban areas and emerging middle classes, such as Brazil and Indonesia.

During 1998 Au Bon Pain's Panera Bread unit perked up with new stores and growing sales. But that success was offset by the company's namesake chain, where sales continued to struggle. The company eventually sold the Au Bon Pain chain in 1999 to investment firm Bruckmann, Rosser, Sherrill, and Co. for $73 million. (Bruckmann, Rosser later sold the chain to UK-based Compass Group, which ran the eateries through its subsidiary ABP Corporation. ABP was next sold to a management group, with Compass maintaining a 25% stake.) Shaich remained with the company, which was renamed Panera Bread, as chairman and CEO. Panera Bread later moved its headquarters back to the St. Louis area.

In 2001 president and COO Rich Postle resigned to run a joint venture with Panera Bread to build and manage 40 bakery-cafes in the northern Virginia and central Pennsylvania regions.

In 2004 the company introduced its new upscale take-out program, Via Panera. With Via Panera, the company simplified the to-go ordering process while upgrading its customization, particularly for larger orders. Panera Bread also released its first cookbook that year, *The Panera Bread Cookbook: Breadmaking Essentials and Recipes from America's Favorite Bakery-Cafe*.

In 2006 the company acquired a 51% stake in Paradise Bakery & Café, the operator of a small bakery-cafe chain in the Southwest, for about $20 million.

EXECUTIVES

Chairman and CEO: Ronald M. (Ron) Shaich, age 53, $515,000 pay
EVP: John M. Maguire, age 41, $404,708 pay
SVP and CFO: Jeffrey W. (Jeff) Kip, age 39, $324,987 pay
SVP and Chief Brand Officer: Michael Markowitz, age 60
SVP and Chief Concept Officer: Scott G. Davis, age 43, $454,711 pay
SVP and Chief Development Officer: Michael J. Nolan, age 47
SVP, Chief Franchise Officer, and Assistant Secretary: Michael J. (Mike) Kupstas, age 50, $354,769 pay
SVP and Chief People Officer: Rebecca A. Fine, age 44
SVP and Chief Supply Chain Officer: Mark A. Borland, age 54, $364,795 pay
SVP and CIO: Thomas C. (Tom) Kish, age 41
SVP Company and Joint Venture Operations: William H. Simpson, age 44
VP and Controller: Amy L. Kuzdowicz, age 37
Head, Research and Development: John Taylor
Principal Accounting Officer: Mark D. Wooldridge, age 32
Auditors: PricewaterhouseCoopers LLP

LOCATIONS

HQ: Panera Bread Company
6710 Clayton Rd., Richmond Heights, MO 63117
Phone: 314-633-7100   **Fax:** 314-633-7200
Web: www.panerabread.com

Panera Bread operates about 20 dough manufacturing facilities in California, Colorado, Florida, Georgia, Illinois, Kansas, Massachusetts, Maryland, Michigan, Minnesota, Missouri, New Jersey, North Carolina, Ohio, Texas, and Washington.

2006 Locations

	No.
Illinois	95
Ohio	82
Florida	78
Missouri	62
Pennsylvania	55
Michigan	52
California	49
New York	46
Virginia	46
New Jersey	42
Maryland	34
North Carolina	34
Massachusetts	31
Indiana	29
Texas	26
Minnesota	25
Georgia	24
Colorado	22
Tennessee	21
Wisconsin	20
Kansas	18
Connecticut	17
Iowa	17
Oklahoma	17
Kentucky	13
South Carolina	11
Other states	61
Total	**1,027**

PRODUCTS/OPERATIONS

2006 Sales

	$ mil.	% of total
Bakery-cafe operations		
Company-owned	666.2	80
Franchising	61.5	8
Food supplies	101.3	12
Total	**829.0**	**100**

2006 Locations

	No.
Franchised	636
Company-owned	391
Total	**1,027**

COMPETITORS

ABP Corporation	Einstein Noah
Bruegger's	El Pollo Loco
California Pizza Kitchen	Fresh Enterprises
Caribou Coffee	Qdoba
CBC Restaurant	Starbucks
Chipotle	Subway

HISTORICAL FINANCIALS

Company Type: Public

Income Statement

FYE: Last Tuesday in December

	REVENUE ($ mil.)	NET INCOME ($ mil.)	NET PROFIT MARGIN	EMPLOYEES
12/06	829.0	58.8	7.1%	7,200
12/05	640.3	52.2	8.2%	5,100
12/04	479.1	38.6	8.1%	—
12/03	355.9	30.4	8.5%	—
12/02	277.8	21.8	7.8%	6,253
Annual Growth	31.4%	28.2%	—	3.6%

2006 Year-End Financials

Debt ratio: —
Return on equity: 16.5%
Cash ($ mil.): 72.1
Current ratio: 1.16
Long-term debt ($ mil.): —
No. of shares (mil.): 30.3

Dividends
  Yield: —
  Payout: —
Market value ($ mil.): 1,683.2
R&D as % of sales: —
Advertising as % of sales: —

Stock History

NASDAQ (GS): PNRA

	STOCK PRICE ($) FY Close	P/E High/Low		PER SHARE ($) Earnings	Dividends	Book Value
12/06	55.47	41	25	1.84	—	13.11
12/05	67.11	44	24	1.65	—	10.62
12/04	39.73	36	26	1.25	—	8.32
12/03	39.50	48	25	1.00	—	6.95
12/02	35.31	52	32	0.73	—	5.62
Annual Growth	12.0%	—	—	26.0%	—	23.6%

Parallel Petroleum

Parallel Petroleum seeks unparalleled success by exploring for and producing oil and natural gas. The company has estimated proved reserves of 58.9 billion cu. ft. of natural gas and 28.7 million barrels of oil. Parallel Petroleum operates primarily on the Gulf Coast of South Texas, in East Texas, and in the Permian Basin of West Texas. The company sells directly on a month-to-month basis to other oil and gas companies. Founded in 1979, Parallel Petroleum originally focused on acquiring relatively unproven high-risk, high-cost properties. However, heavy losses prompted the company to sell its First Permian oil and gas assets in 2002 for $31 million and shift its strategy to exploiting less risky properties.

Parallel Petroleum changed its business plan in 2002 to focus more on lower risk acquisition and development of producing properties and less on higher risk exploration.

In 2006 the company's Parallel L.P. subsidiary increased its interests in 16 wells in Parallel's Barnett Shale gas project in North Texas to about 36% through agreements with five unaffiliated third parties.

EXECUTIVES

President, CEO, and Director: Larry C. Oldham, age 53, $476,525 pay
COO: Donald E. (Don) Tiffin, age 49, $380,584 pay
CFO: Steven D. (Steve) Foster, age 51, $230,959 pay
VP Corporate Engineering: Eric A. Bayley, age 58, $205,084 pay
VP Land and Administration: John S. Rutherford, age 46, $205,084 pay
Secretary: Thomas Ortloff
Director Business Development: Jerry W. Nevans
Manager Operations: Brian W. McCurry
Manager Financial Reporting: Rebecca A. (Becky) Burrell
Manager Land Administration: Rita A. Ramirez
Manager Investor Relations: Cynthia D. (Cindy) Thomason
Controller: Tom Hanna
Auditors: BDO Seidman, LLP

LOCATIONS

HQ: Parallel Petroleum Corporation
  1004 N. Big Spring, Ste. 400, Midland, TX 79701
Phone: 432-684-3727   **Fax:** 432-684-3905
Web: www.parallel-petro.com

PRODUCTS/OPERATIONS

2006 Sales

	% of total
Oil	63
Natural gas	37
Total	**100**

2006 Sales

	% of total
Texland Petroleum	30
ConocoPhillips	20
Tri-C Resources	12
Dale Operating Company	10
Other customers	28
Total	**100**

COMPETITORS

Abraxas Petroleum
Anadarko Petroleum
BP
Brigham Exploration
Exxon Mobil
Forest Oil
Pioneer Natural Resources
Royal Dutch Shell

HISTORICAL FINANCIALS

Company Type: Public

Income Statement

FYE: December 31

	REVENUE ($ mil.)	NET INCOME ($ mil.)	NET PROFIT MARGIN	EMPLOYEES
12/06	97.0	26.2	27.0%	41
12/05	66.2	(1.6)	—	40
12/04	35.8	5.6	15.6%	—
12/03	33.9	7.6	22.4%	—
12/02	12.1	18.7	154.5%	17
Annual Growth	68.3%	8.8%	—	24.6%

2006 Year-End Financials

Debt ratio: 97.6%
Return on equity: 19.2%
Cash ($ mil.): 5.9
Current ratio: 0.83
Long-term debt ($ mil.): 179.4
No. of shares (mil.): 37.5

Dividends
  Yield: —
  Payout: —
Market value ($ mil.): 659.7
R&D as % of sales: —
Advertising as % of sales: —

Stock History

NASDAQ (GM): PLLL

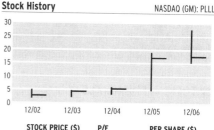

	STOCK PRICE ($) FY Close	P/E High/Low		PER SHARE ($) Earnings	Dividends	Book Value
12/06	17.57	39	22	0.71	—	4.89
12/05	17.01	—	—	(0.06)	—	2.58
12/04	5.39	29	17	0.20	—	2.36
12/03	4.35	14	8	0.31	—	2.43
12/02	2.74	6	2	0.79	—	2.15
Annual Growth	59.1%	—	—	(2.6%)	—	22.8%

Parke Bancorp

Community banking is a walk in the park for Parke Bancorp, holding company for Parke Bank, which has three bank branches in the New Jersey communities of Sewell and Northfield, as well as a loan production office in Philadelphia. The bank provides such traditional community-oriented products as checking and savings accounts, money market and individual retirement accounts, and certificates of deposit. In lending activities, Parke Bank has a strong focus on commercial real estate lending; commercial mortgages make up 60% of the bank's lending portfolio and commercial construction loans make up more than 25%. The bank also writes business and consumer loans, as well as residential construction and mortgage loans.

CEO Vito Pantilione and chairman Chuck Pennoni each own about 6% of Parke Bancorp; director Jeffrey Kripitz holds about 7%. Two limited partnerships, Banc Fund V and Banc Fund VI, together have an equity stake of more than 8%.

EXECUTIVES

Chairman, Parke Bankcorp and Parke Bank: Celestino R. (Chuck) Pennoni, age 69
Vice Chairman, Parke Bancorp and Parke Bank: Thomas E. Hedenberg, age 62
President, CEO, and Director, Parke Bancorp and Parke Bank: Vito S. Pantilione, age 55, $360,577 pay
SVP; SVP, Senior Loan Officer, and Secretary, Parke Bank: David O. Middlebrook, age 48, $137,654 pay
SVP and CFO, Parke Bancorp and Parke Bank: Robert A. Kuehl, age 59, $12,980 pay (prior to promotion)
SVP Branch Administration and Systems: Elizabeth A. Milavsky, age 55, $133,846 pay
SVP Philadelphia Region: Paul E. Palmieri, age 48, $128,769 pay
Auditors: McGladrey & Pullen, LLP

LOCATIONS

HQ: Parke Bancorp, Inc.
601 Delsea Dr., Sewell, NJ 08080
Phone: 856-256-2500   **Fax:** 856-256-2590
Web: www.parkebank.com

COMPETITORS

Bank of America
Commerce Bancorp
Hudson City Bancorp
Ocean Shore
PNC Financial
Susquehanna Bancshares
Wachovia

HISTORICAL FINANCIALS

Company Type: Public

Income Statement				FYE: December 31
	ASSETS ($ mil.)	NET INCOME ($ mil.)	INCOME AS % OF ASSETS	EMPLOYEES
12/06	360.0	4.6	1.3%	47
12/05	297.8	3.5	1.2%	40
12/04	224.3	2.7	1.2%	—
12/03	174.0	2.0	1.1%	—
Annual Growth	27.4%	32.0%	—	17.5%

2006 Year-End Financials

Equity as % of assets: 8.5%
Return on assets: 1.4%
Return on equity: 15.9%
Long-term debt ($ mil.): 10.4
No. of shares (mil.): 2.8
Market value ($ mil.): 44.8
Dividends
 Yield: 1.1%
 Payout: 14.2%
Sales ($ mil.): 26.3
R&D as % of sales: —
Advertising as % of sales: —

Stock History

NASDAQ (CM): PKBK

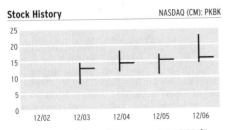

	STOCK PRICE ($) FY Close	P/E High/Low		PER SHARE ($) Earnings	Dividends	Book Value
12/06	15.85	18	11	1.27	0.18	10.88
12/05	15.30	17	11	1.00	—	11.75
12/04	14.38	23	15	0.80	0.91	10.49
12/03	12.84	22	13	0.64	0.83	11.19
Annual Growth	7.3%	—	—	25.7%	(39.9%)	(0.9%)

Patriot Capital Funding

Patriot Capital Funding is loyal to the companies in which it invests. The investment firm specializes in financing small to midsized companies in a variety of industries, including manufacturing, consumer goods, and defense. Target companies generally have revenues ranging between $10 million and $100 million. The company has designed itself to be a one-stop shop for revolving credit lines, senior loans, and subordinated debt investment. Patriot Capital oversees a portfolio worth some $260 million.

EXECUTIVES

Chairman: Mel P. Melsheimer, age 67
President, CEO, and Director: Richard P. Buckanavage, age 43, $339,583 pay
COO, Chief Compliance Officer, and Director: Timothy W. Hassler, age 38, $339,583 pay
EVP, CFO, and Secretary: William E. Alvarez Jr., age 53, $200,000 pay
EVP and Chief Investment Officer: Clifford L. Wells, age 51, $206,333 pay
EVP and Managing Director: Matthew R. Colucci, age 35, $196,875 pay
Auditors: Grant Thornton LLP

LOCATIONS

HQ: Patriot Capital Funding, Inc.
274 Riverside Ave., Westport, CT 06880
Phone: 203-429-2700   **Fax:** 203-227-5257
Web: www.patcapfunding.com

PRODUCTS/OPERATIONS

2006 Portfolio By Industry Sector

	% of total
Manufacturing	45
Consumer/retail goods	22
Distribution	18
Service	13
Defense & publishing	2
Total	**100**

Selected Portfolio Investments

Adapco, Inc. (products and services related to mosquito control)
Agent Media Corporation (database marketing and publications)
Allied Defense Group (diversified defense company)
Borga, Inc. (prefabricated metal building systems and components)
Cheese Works, Inc. (cheese and specialty food distribution)
Copperhead Chemical Company (bulk pharmaceuticals)
Dover Saddlery (equestrian supplies retailer)
Eight O'Clock Coffee Company (coffee marketer and distributor)
EXL Acquisition Corp. (lab testing supplies maker)
Fairchild Industrial Products Company (industrial control products maker)
Impact Products, LLC (supplier of commercial cleaning, maintenance & related products) Innovative Concepts in Entertainment, Inc. (coin-operated games
Keltner Enterprises LLC (automotive supplies distributor)
L.A. Spas, Inc. (above-ground spa maker)
Natural Products (personal care products maker)
Prince Mineral Company, Inc. (specialty minerals)
Quartermaster, Inc. (uniforms & equipment for law enforcement & security professionals)
Robert Rothschild Farm (specialty food products)
R-O-M Corporation (doors, ramps & bulkheads for the fire truck and food transportation markets)
Sidump'r Trailer Company (side-dump trailer manufacturer)

COMPETITORS

Allied Capital
CapitalSource
Main Street Resources
MCG Capital
Waud Capital Partners

HISTORICAL FINANCIALS

Company Type: Public

Income Statement				FYE: December 31
	REVENUE ($ mil.)	NET INCOME ($ mil.)	NET PROFIT MARGIN	EMPLOYEES
12/06	30.3	15.6	51.5%	11
12/05	13.4	(1.2)	—	9
12/04	4.9	(0.3)	—	6
12/03	0.3	(2.1)	—	5
Annual Growth	365.7%	—	—	30.1%

2006 Year-End Financials

Debt ratio: 59.9%
Return on equity: 10.7%
Cash ($ mil.): 9.3
Current ratio: —
Long-term debt ($ mil.): 98.4
No. of shares (mil.): 15.8
Dividends
 Yield: 8.3%
 Payout: 109.1%
Market value ($ mil.): 229.3
R&D as % of sales: —
Advertising as % of sales: —

Stock History

NASDAQ (GS): PCAP

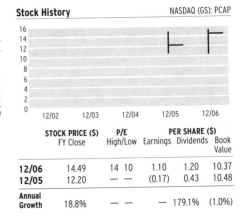

	STOCK PRICE ($) FY Close	P/E High/Low		PER SHARE ($) Earnings	Dividends	Book Value
12/06	14.49	14	10	1.10	1.20	10.37
12/05	12.20	—	—	(0.17)	0.43	10.48
Annual Growth	18.8%	—	—	—	179.1%	(1.0%)

Patriot National Bancorp

Patriot National Bancorp is the holding company for Patriot National Bank, which has about a dozen branches in southwestern Connecticut and two in New York, where it plans to open more branches. Serving consumers, professionals, and small and midsized businesses, the bank offers deposit products such as checking, savings, and money market accounts, as well as CDs, IRAs, and health savings accounts. Commercial real estate and construction loans make up the bulk of the company's loan portfolio, which also includes commercial, consumer installment, home equity, and residential real estate loans.

EXECUTIVES

Chairman and CEO; Chairman, Patriot National Bank: Angelo De Caro, age 64, $236,688 pay
Vice Chairman and President; Vice Chairman, President and CEO, Patriot National Bank: Charles F. (Charlie) Howell, age 58, $325,338 pay
SEVP, CFO, and Director, Patriot National Bancorp and Patriot National Bank: Robert F. O'Connell, age 58, $264,411 pay
SVP and Controller, Patriot National Bancorp and Patriot National Bank: Michael A. Capodanno, age 46

266

COO, Secretary, and Director, Patriot National Bancorp and Patriot National Bank: Philip W. (Phil) Wolford, age 59
EVP and Cashier, Patriot National Bank: John Kantzas, age 71
EVP and Sales Manager, Mortgage Brokerage: Marcus Zavattaro, age 42, $368,557 pay
EVP and Senior Loan Officer, Patriot National Bank: Martin G. Noble, age 57, $224,613 pay
Human Resources Manager: Judy Davidson
Auditors: McGladrey & Pullen, LLP

LOCATIONS

HQ: Patriot National Bancorp, Inc.
900 Bedford St., Stamford, CT 06901
Phone: 203-324-7500   **Fax:** 203-324-8877
Web: www.pnbdirect.com

Patriot National Bancorp has bank branches in Darien, Fairfield (2), Greenwich, Norwalk (2), Old Greenwich, Southport, Stamford (2), Trumbull, and Wilton (2), Connecticut, and in New York City.

PRODUCTS/OPERATIONS

2006 Sales

	$ mil.	% of total
Interest		
Loans, including fees	34.1	85
Investment securities, including dividends	3.4	8
Other	0.6	1
Noninterest		
Mortgage brokerage referral fees	1.2	3
Other	1.1	3
Total	**40.4**	**100**

COMPETITORS

Citigroup
Fairfield County Bank
HSBC Holdings
JPMorgan Chase
NewAlliance Bancshares
People's United Financial
U.S. Trust
Wachovia
Webster Financial

HISTORICAL FINANCIALS
Company Type: Public

Income Statement				FYE: December 31
	ASSETS ($ mil.)	NET INCOME ($ mil.)	INCOME AS % OF ASSETS	EMPLOYEES
12/06	646.0	2.4	0.4%	112
12/05	470.6	1.4	0.3%	104
12/04	405.0	0.9	0.2%	—
12/03	342.5	1.3	0.4%	—
12/02	248.5	1.0	0.4%	69
Annual Growth	27.0%	24.5%	—	12.9%

2006 Year-End Financials

Equity as % of assets: 10.0%
Return on assets: 0.4%
Return on equity: 5.0%
Long-term debt ($ mil.): 8.3
No. of shares (mil.): 4.7
Market value ($ mil.): 125.4
Dividends
Yield: 0.7%
Payout: 25.8%
Sales ($ mil.): 40.4
R&D as % of sales: —
Advertising as % of sales: —

Stock History   NASDAQ (GM): PNBK

	STOCK PRICE ($) FY Close	P/E High/Low		PER SHARE ($) Earnings	Dividends	Book Value
12/06	26.45	46	30	0.66	0.17	13.56
12/05	20.75	42	33	0.51	0.16	9.71
12/04	18.40	50	34	0.37	0.13	7.95
12/03	12.50	23	17	0.55	0.09	7.80
12/02	9.40	25	19	0.43	0.07	7.72
Annual Growth	29.5%	—	—	11.3%	24.8%	15.1%

Peet's Coffee & Tea

Peet's Coffee & Tea enjoys the daily grind. With about 135 coffee shops in six states, Peet's offers java lovers more than 30 types of whole bean and fresh ground coffee, including more than 20 blends. Its teas run the spectrum from India black to herbal blends. The stores also offer fresh brewed coffee, biscotti, and other pastries, along with mugs and brewing equipment. Most of the company's outlets are located in California. In addition to its retail operation, which accounts for about two-thirds of sales, Peet's sells coffee through specialty channels such as mail order and the Internet. The company also sells its coffee wares through national grocery chains, including Safeway and Whole Foods.

Peet's continues to expand its chain of retail stores in the western US, with the addition of 25 new stores last year. Another 30 stores were slated to open in 2007.

The company's new roasting facility in Alameda, California went into full production in April 2007. The sale of specialty coffee accounts for nearly 85% of the company's total sales. Non-coffee beverages, pastries, and other food items make up the rest.

Peet's namesake, Alfred Peet, founded the company in 1966. Starbucks' co-founders Gerald Baldwin and Gordon Bowker bought the company in 1984. (They sold their stakes in Starbucks in 1987.)

CEO Patrick O'Dea owns about 5% of Peet's.

EXECUTIVES

Chairman: Jean-Michel Valette, age 46
President, CEO, and Director: Patrick J. (Pat) O'Dea, age 44, $493,479 pay
Roastmaster Emeritus: James A. (Jim) Reynolds
Senior Master Roaster: John Weaver
VP, CFO, and Secretary: Thomas P. Cawley, age 46, $380,801 pay
VP Coffee: Doug Welsh, age 44
VP Operations and Information Systems: James E. (Jim) Grimes, age 51, $227,863 pay
VP Retail Operations: Kay Bogeajis

Chief Marketing Officer and General Manager Consumer Business: Christine P. (Chris) Lansing
Director, Tea: Eliot Jordan
Director, Coffee Purchasing: Shirin Moayyad
Auditors: Deloitte & Touche LLP

LOCATIONS

HQ: Peet's Coffee & Tea, Inc.
1400 Park Ave., Emeryville, CA 94608
Phone: 510-594-2100   **Fax:** 510-594-2180
Web: www.peets.com

2006 Locations

	No.
California	114
Oregon	7
Massachusetts	6
Colorado	4
Washington	3
Illinois	2
Total	**136**

PRODUCTS/OPERATIONS

2006 Sales

	$ mil.	% of total
Retail stores	141.4	67
Specialty sales	69.1	33
Total	**210.5**	**100**

2006 Sales

	$ mil.	% of total
Whole bean coffee & related products	117.6	56
Beverages & pastries	92.9	44
Total	**210.5**	**100**

COMPETITORS

Bruegger's
The Coffee Bean
Community Coffee
Diedrich Coffee
Einstein Noah Restaurant Group
Farmer Bros.
Fireside Coffee
Green Mountain Coffee
Hawaii Coffee
illy
Kraft Foods
Le Boulanger
Nestlé
Procter & Gamble
Republic of Tea
Starbucks
Tully's Coffee

HISTORICAL FINANCIALS
Company Type: Public

Income Statement			FYE: Sunday nearest December 31
	REVENUE ($ mil.)	NET INCOME ($ mil.)	NET PROFIT MARGIN	EMPLOYEES
12/06	210.5	7.8	3.7%	3,169
12/05	175.2	10.7	6.1%	2,813
12/04	145.7	8.8	6.0%	—
12/03	119.8	5.2	4.3%	—
12/02	104.1	4.7	4.5%	1,667
Annual Growth	19.2%	13.5%	—	17.4%

2006 Year-End Financials

Debt ratio: —
Return on equity: 6.2%
Cash ($ mil.): 27.2
Current ratio: 2.69
Long-term debt ($ mil.): —
No. of shares (mil.): 13.5
Dividends
Yield: —
Payout: —
Market value ($ mil.): 354.7
R&D as % of sales: —
Advertising as % of sales: —

Stock History

NASDAQ (GS): PEET

	STOCK PRICE ($) FY Close	P/E High/Low		PER SHARE ($) Earnings	Dividends	Book Value
12/06	26.24	60	44	0.55	—	9.43
12/05	30.35	50	31	0.74	—	9.07
12/04	26.47	44	26	0.63	—	8.08
12/03	17.09	60	32	0.39	—	7.24
12/02	14.82	48	27	0.40	—	6.65
Annual Growth	15.4%	—	—	8.3%	—	9.1%

Penn Virginia Corporation

Incorporated in Virginia and based in Pennsylvania, Penn Virginia is an oil and gas exploration and production company operating primarily in the Appalachian area of the US. It also explores in East Texas, Mississippi, and the Gulf Coast. The company, which has proved reserves of 457 billion cu. ft. of natural gas and 5 million barrels of oil, and holds working interests in more than 2,000 gross wells, sells mostly on the spot market. It also has interests in coal (which it leases to other operators) and timber properties through 44%-owned Penn Virginia Resource Partners, which it spun off in 2001. In 2006 the company acquired explorer Crow Creek Holding Corp. for $71.5 million.

Legendary corporate buyout artist T. Boone Pickens made an unsolicited offer to buy Penn Virginia, but abandoned the bid in 2002. The company holds some 765 million tons of proven and probable coal reserves in Kentucky, New Mexico, Virginia, and West Virginia.

In 2007 the company acquired $44.9 million of assets in the Cotton Valley in East Texas.

EXECUTIVES

Chairman: Robert (Rob) Garrett, age 71
President, CEO, and Director: A. James (Jim) Dearlove, age 59, $812,040 pay
EVP and CFO: Frank A. Pici, age 52, $533,040 pay
EVP; President, Penn Virginia Oil and Gas: H. Baird Whitehead, age 56, $554,200 pay
EVP and Director; President and COO, Penn Virginia Resource, and Co-President, Penn Virginia Operating Co., LLC: Keith D. Horton, age 54, $470,140 pay
EVP, General Counsel and Corporate Secretary: Nancy M. Snyder, age 53, $475,040 pay
VP, Business Planning: Dana G. Wright, age 51
VP, Corporate Development: Ronald K. (Ron) Page, age 57
Auditors: KPMG LLP

LOCATIONS

HQ: Penn Virginia Corporation
3 Radnor Corporate Center, Ste. 300,
100 Matsonford Rd., Radnor, PA 19087
Phone: 610-687-8900 **Fax:** 610-687-3688
Web: www.pennvirginia.com

Penn Virginia has offices in Charleston, West Virginia; Houston; Kingsport, Tennessee; and Radnor, Pennsylvania.

PRODUCTS/OPERATIONS

2006 Sales

	$ mil.	% of total
Midstream	404.9	54
Oil & gas	236.0	31
Coal	113.0	15
Total	**753.9**	**100**

COMPETITORS

Arch Coal
Cabot Oil & Gas
CONSOL Energy
Equitable Resources
Peabody Energy
Petroleum Development
PrimeEnergy
Range Resources

HISTORICAL FINANCIALS

Company Type: Public

Income Statement

FYE: December 31

	REVENUE ($ mil.)	NET INCOME ($ mil.)	NET PROFIT MARGIN	EMPLOYEES
12/06	753.9	75.9	10.1%	282
12/05	673.9	62.1	9.2%	229
12/04	228.4	33.4	14.6%	—
12/03	181.3	28.5	15.7%	—
12/02	111.0	12.1	10.9%	104
Annual Growth	61.4%	58.3%	—	28.3%

2006 Year-End Financials

Debt ratio: 113.8%	Dividends
Return on equity: 21.9%	Yield: 0.6%
Cash ($ mil.): 38.6	Payout: 10.9%
Current ratio: 1.11	Market value ($ mil.): 657.7
Long-term debt ($ mil.): 435.3	R&D as % of sales: —
No. of shares (mil.): 18.8	Advertising as % of sales: —

Stock History

NYSE: PVA

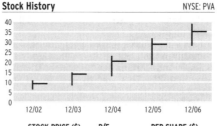

	STOCK PRICE ($) FY Close	P/E High/Low		PER SHARE ($) Earnings	Dividends	Book Value
12/06	35.02	19	14	2.01	0.22	20.36
12/05	28.70	19	11	1.65	0.17	16.64
12/04	20.28	25	15	0.90	0.23	13.69
12/03	13.91	18	11	0.79	0.22	23.38
12/02	9.09	31	19	0.34	0.22	21.01
Annual Growth	40.1%	—	—	55.9%	0.0%	(0.8%)

Penn Virginia Resource Partners

The motto for Penn Virginia Resource Partners (PVR) could be "Baby, it's *coal* outside." PVR was formed by energy company Penn Virginia Corporation to manage its coal properties. PVR leases mining rights on its properties to third-party mine operators, collecting royalties based on the amount of coal produced and the price at which it is sold. Its land contains about 765 million tons of proven or probable reserves (mostly low-sulfur bituminous coal). PVR also sells timber from its properties and charges fees to mine operators for use of its coal preparation and transportation facilities. Penn Virginia Corporation controls some 40% of the firm.

Although PVR will continue to expand its holdings in Appalachia, the company has made acquisitions in other regions of the US. A purchase in the Illinois Basin area has increased the company's coal reserves by nearly 15% over 2005. Eliminating the third party that had performed the task previously, PVR began marketing its natural gas production in Louisiana, Oklahoma, and Texas in 2006.

In 2007 PVR acquired roughly 62,000 acres of West Virginia forestland from packaging and paper manufacturer MeadWestvaco for approximately $93 million. The deal significantly expands PVR's timber operations.

EXECUTIVES

Chairman and CEO: A. James (Jim) Dearlove, age 59, $368,500 pay
President; Co-President and COO, Coal: Keith D. Horton, age 54, $442,000 pay
Co-President and COO, Midstream: Ronald K. (Ron) Page, age 57, $370,000 pay
VP, CFO, and Director: Frank A. Pici, age 52, $146,560 pay
VP and Principal Accounting Officer: Forrest W. McNair
VP, General Counsel, and Director: Nancy M. Snyder, age 53, $172,000 pay
Auditors: KPMG LLP

LOCATIONS

HQ: Penn Virginia Resource Partners, L.P.
3 Radnor Corporate Center, Ste. 300,
100 Matsonford Rd., Radnor, PA 19087
Phone: 610-687-8900 **Fax:** 610-687-3688
Web: www.pvresource.com

PRODUCTS/OPERATIONS

2006 Sales

	$ mil.	% of total
Natural gas	402.7	78
Coal royalties	98.2	19
Coal services	5.9	1
Other	11.1	2
Total	**517.9**	**100**

COMPETITORS

Alliance Resource
Arch Coal
Bridgeline
CONSOL Energy
Massey Energy
Peabody Energy
Westmoreland Coal

HISTORICAL FINANCIALS
Company Type: Public

Income Statement
FYE: December 31

	REVENUE ($ mil.)	NET INCOME ($ mil.)	NET PROFIT MARGIN	EMPLOYEES
12/06	517.9	73.9	14.3%	0
12/05	446.4	51.2	11.5%	0
12/04	75.6	34.3	45.4%	—
12/03	55.6	22.7	40.8%	—
12/02	38.6	24.7	64.0%	—
Annual Growth	91.4%	31.5%	—	—

2006 Year-End Financials
Debt ratio: 53.2%
Return on equity: 21.5%
Cash ($ mil.): 11.9
Current ratio: 0.92
Long-term debt ($ mil.): 213.8
No. of shares (mil.): 42.1
Dividends
Yield: 5.7%
Payout: 94.9%
Market value ($ mil.): 1,094.0
R&D as % of sales: —
Advertising as % of sales: —

Stock History
NYSE: PVR

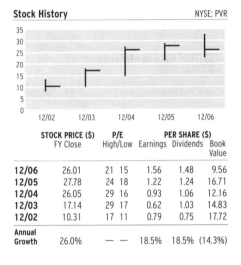

	STOCK PRICE ($) FY Close	P/E High/Low		PER SHARE ($) Earnings	Dividends	Book Value
12/06	26.01	21	15	1.56	1.48	9.56
12/05	27.78	24	18	1.22	1.24	16.71
12/04	26.05	29	16	0.93	1.06	12.16
12/03	17.14	29	17	0.62	1.03	14.83
12/02	10.31	17	11	0.79	0.75	17.72
Annual Growth	26.0%	—	—	18.5%	18.5%	(14.3%)

Pennsylvania Commerce Bancorp

Pennsylvania Commerce Bancorp brings "America's Most Convenient Bank" to Pennsylvania. A part of the Commerce Bancorp network, the company is the holding company for Commerce Bank/Harrisburg, which uses the larger company's logo and advertising in its service area. Through 30 branches, the bank provides community banking services, including checking, savings, and money market accounts, to customers in south central Pennsylvania. Commerce Bank offers commercial real estate (one-third of its loan portfolio), construction, and land development loans, as well as residential mortgage, commercial, and consumer loans. Commerce Bancorp owns about 11% of the company and supplies marketing and technical support.

Directors and executive officers collectively own about 25% of Pennsylvania Commerce Bancorp; of that, CEO Gary Nalbandian owns nearly 9%.

EXECUTIVES
Chairman, President, and CEO, Pennsylvania Commerce Bancorp and Commerce Bank: Gary L. Nalbandian, age 64, $355,000 pay
EVP and COO: Mark A. Ritter, age 48
EVP and CFO, Pennsylvania Commerce Bancorp and Commerce Bank: Mark A. Zody, age 43, $177,500 pay
EVP and Chief Lending Officer, Pennsylvania Commerce Bancorp and Commerce Bank: Rory G. Ritrievi, age 43, $207,500 pay
SVP and Chief Risk Officer, Pennsylvania Commerce Bancorp and Commerce Bank: D. Scott Huggins, age 57, $125,000 pay
Public Relations: Jason S. Kirsch
Investor Relations: Sherry Richart
Chief Credit Officer: James Ridd
Secretary and Counsel to the Board: Peter J. Ressler
Auditors: Beard Miller Company LLP

LOCATIONS
HQ: Pennsylvania Commerce Bancorp, Inc.
3801 Paxton St., Harrisburg, PA 17111
Phone: 717-412-6301   **Fax:** 717-412-6171
Web: www.commercepc.com

PRODUCTS/OPERATIONS

2006 Sales

	$ mil.	% of total
Interest		
Loans	65.6	53
Securities & other	39.0	32
Noninterest		
Service charges & fees	16.8	14
Other	1.9	1
Total	**123.3**	**100**

COMPETITORS
Abington Bancorp
Bryn Mawr Bank Corp.
Codorus Valley Bancorp
Fulton Financial
M&T Bank
PNC Financial
PSECU
Sovereign Bancorp
Stonebridge Financial
Wachovia

HISTORICAL FINANCIALS
Company Type: Public

Income Statement
FYE: December 31

	ASSETS ($ mil.)	NET INCOME ($ mil.)	INCOME AS % OF ASSETS	EMPLOYEES
12/06	1,866.5	7.3	0.4%	909
12/05	1,641.1	8.8	0.5%	787
12/04	1,277.4	8.6	0.7%	—
12/03	1,052.0	6.6	0.6%	—
12/02	786.6	5.7	0.7%	382
Annual Growth	24.1%	6.4%	—	24.2%

2006 Year-End Financials
Equity as % of assets: 5.4%
Return on assets: 0.4%
Return on equity: 7.6%
Long-term debt ($ mil.): 29.4
No. of shares (mil.): 6.1
Market value ($ mil.): 161.7
Dividends
Yield: —
Payout: —
Sales ($ mil.): 123.3
R&D as % of sales: —
Advertising as % of sales: —

Stock History
NASDAQ (GS): COBH

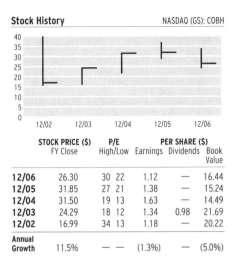

	STOCK PRICE ($) FY Close	P/E High/Low		PER SHARE ($) Earnings	Dividends	Book Value
12/06	26.30	30	22	1.12	—	16.44
12/05	31.85	27	21	1.38	—	15.24
12/04	31.50	19	13	1.63	—	14.49
12/03	24.29	18	12	1.34	0.98	21.69
12/02	16.99	34	13	1.18	—	20.22
Annual Growth	11.5%	—	—	(1.3%)	—	(5.0%)

Penson Worldwide

Penson Worldwide works behind the scenes to help brokers do their jobs. The company offers a range of independent securities clearing services to brokers, investment advisors, and market makers; services include integrated trade execution, clearing and custody services, customer account maintenance, and customized data processing. The company does business through such subsidiary units as NEXA Technologies (software for direct access to market data), Penson Financial Futures, Penson Financial Services (with Canadian and UK units), and futures commission merchant Penson GHCO.

The acquisitive company's buying spree has been bolstered by funds from its 2006 IPO. Some purchases boost the clients customer count, such as its acquisitions of Computer Clearing Service (CCS), Goldenberg Hehmeyer and Co. (GHCO), and the clearing business of a unit of Schonfeld Group. Others add services (the acquisition of Tick Data, which offered intraday securities trading data, including tick-by-tick trade and quote data on all US equities dating back to 1993) or broaden Penson Worldwide's geographic reach (acquisitions of the UK's Worldwide Settlements and Canada's ECE Electronic Clearing, both of which have been rebranded as Penson Financial Services). Penson Worldwide in 2007 launched a Hong Kong office to tap the vast Asian market. Penson Worldwide was founded by CEO Phil Pendergraft and president Dan Son as Service Asset Holdings in 1995. Following Penson Worldwide's IPO, major shareholders included director John Drew (about 15%) and chairman Roger Engemoen (11%). Altogether, the company's officers and directors control about 50% of the company. Penson Worldwide in 2006 split off its non-core SAMCO Financial Services, which provides investment and advisory services.

EXECUTIVES

Chairman: Roger J. Engemoen Jr., age 52,
  $1,069,758 pay
CEO and Director: Philip A. (Phil) Pendergraft, age 47,
  $1,743,863 pay
President and Director: Daniel P. (Dan) Son, age 68,
  $1,738,263 pay
SVP and CFO: Kevin W. McAleer, age 56, $787,200 pay
SVP and CTO: William McLemore
SVP Finance: Dave R. Henkel, age 54, $443,589 pay
  (prior to title change)
**SVP and Chief Administrative Officer, Penson
  Financial Services:** Bart McCain
SVP and General Counsel: Andrew B. Koslow, age 46,
  $787,200 pay
VP Human Resources: Dawn Gardner
President, Nexa Technologies: Eric Stoop
President and CEO, Penson GHCO: Chris Hehmeyer
President and CEO, Penson Financial Services:
  Alan Philpot
Director Client Services, Sales, and Marketing:
  Sharron Davey
Manager Corporate Communication:
  Amanda McCutcheon
Auditors: BDO Seidman, LLP

LOCATIONS

HQ: Penson Worldwide, Inc.
  1700 Pacific Ave., Ste. 1400, Dallas, TX 75201
Phone: 214-765-1100   **Fax:** 214-217-4978
Web: www.penson.com

Penson Worldwide and its subsidiaries have domestic
offices in Chicago; Dallas; Irvine, California; and New
York. Its international operations are in Hong Kong,
London, Montreal, and Toronto.

2006 Sales

	$ mil.	% of total
US	213.7	74
Canada	58.6	21
Other countries	15.3	5
Total	**287.6**	**100**

PRODUCTS/OPERATIONS

2006 Sales

	$ mil.	% of total
Interest	163.8	57
Revenues from clearing operations	76.2	27
Technology revenues	11.9	4
Other	35.7	12
Total	**287.6**	**100**

COMPETITORS

Banc of America Securities
Bank of New York Mellon
Bear, Stearns & Co.
eSpeed
FMR
GSEC
Knight Capital
Merrill Lynch
Pershing LLC
SWS Group

HISTORICAL FINANCIALS

Company Type: Public

Income Statement   FYE: December 31

	REVENUE ($ mil.)	NET INCOME ($ mil.)	NET PROFIT MARGIN	EMPLOYEES
12/06	287.6	24.5	8.5%	763
12/05	174.6	2.9	1.7%	—
12/04	116.1	7.8	6.7%	—
Annual Growth	**57.4%**	**77.2%**	**—**	**—**

2006 Year-End Financials

Debt ratio: 755.2%
Return on equity: 18.3%
Cash ($ mil.): 680.4
Current ratio: —
Long-term debt ($ mil.): 1,599.4
No. of shares (mil.): 25.1

Dividends
  Yield: —
  Payout: —
Market value ($ mil.): 687.4
R&D as % of sales: —
Advertising as % of sales: —

Stock History   NASDAQ (GM): PNSN

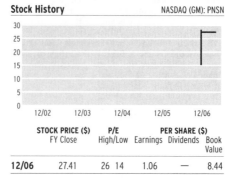

	STOCK PRICE ($) FY Close	P/E High/Low	Earnings	PER SHARE ($) Dividends	Book Value
12/06	27.41	26 14	1.06	—	8.44

Peoples Financial

Peoples Financial is helping people to help
themselves. The holding company for The Peoples Bank, which had five of its 16 branches in
southern Mississippi damaged or destroyed by
Hurricane Katrina, has been working to get personal and business customers badly needed
funds to help them move on with their lives.
Founded in Biloxi in 1896, the bank offers the
usual checking and savings products as well as
business, real estate, construction, and personal
loans. Other offerings include asset management
and trust services, safe deposit boxes, and online
banking services. Chairman and CEO Chevis
Swetman owns about 15% of Peoples Financial;
the Swetman family has had an interest in the
bank since its inception.

EXECUTIVES

**Chairman, President, and CEO, Peoples Financial and
  The Peoples Bank:** Chevis C. Swetman, age 58,
  $281,288 pay
Vice Chairman: Dan Magruder, age 59
EVP, Peoples Financial and The Peoples Bank:
  A. Wes Fulmer, age 47, $151,646 pay
**CFO and Controller; SVP and Cashier, The Peoples
  Bank:** Lauri A. Wood, age 45, $133,675 pay
First VP; SVP and CIO, The Peoples Bank:
  Thomas J. Sliman, age 70, $138,487 pay
**Second VP; SVP and Retail Banking Officer, The
  Peoples Bank:** Jeannette E. Romero, age 61
VP; SVP and Chief Credit Officer, The Peoples Bank:
  Robert M. Tucei, age 60, $137,307 pay
VP and Secretary; SVP, The Peoples Bank: Ann F. Guice
VP and Auditor, The Peoples Bank:
  Gregory M. (Greg) Batia
VP Business Development, The Peoples Bank:
  Dennis J. Burke
VP Human Resources, The Peoples Bank:
  Jackie L. Henson
Auditors: Piltz, Williams, LaRosa & Co.

LOCATIONS

HQ: Peoples Financial Corporation
  152 Lameuse St., Biloxi, MS 39530
Phone: 228-435-5511   **Fax:** 228-435-8418
Web: www.thepeoples.com

2006 Sales

		$ mil.	% of total
Interest			
	Loans, including fees	28.7	47
	Securities, including dividends	19.4	32
	Federal funds sold	0.8	1
Noninterest			
	Service charges on deposit accounts	5.4	9
	Trust department income & fees	1.7	3
	Other	5.2	8
Total		**61.2**	**100**

COMPETITORS

BancorpSouth
Hancock Holding
Regions Financial
Wachovia
Whitney Holding

HISTORICAL FINANCIALS

Company Type: Public

Income Statement   FYE: December 31

	ASSETS ($ mil.)	NET INCOME ($ mil.)	INCOME AS % OF ASSETS	EMPLOYEES
12/06	964.0	12.8	1.3%	227
12/05	845.3	5.9	0.7%	222
12/04	577.4	5.8	1.0%	—
12/03	575.4	5.0	0.9%	—
12/02	550.1	3.2	0.6%	—
Annual Growth	**15.1%**	**41.4%**	**—**	**2.3%**

2006 Year-End Financials

Equity as % of assets: 10.2%
Return on assets: 1.4%
Return on equity: 13.8%
Long-term debt ($ mil.): —
No. of shares (mil.): 5.5
Market value ($ mil.): 149.8

Dividends
  Yield: 1.5%
  Payout: 17.8%
Sales ($ mil.): 61.2
R&D as % of sales: —
Advertising as % of sales: —

Stock History   NASDAQ (CM): PFBX

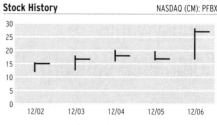

	STOCK PRICE ($) FY Close	P/E High/Low	Earnings	PER SHARE ($) Dividends	Book Value
12/06	27.00	12 7	2.30	0.41	17.70
12/05	16.85	18 16	1.06	0.38	15.77
12/04	17.99	19 16	1.04	0.32	15.44
12/03	16.70	20 14	0.90	0.26	15.03
12/02	15.00	27 21	0.57	0.24	14.64
Annual Growth	**15.8%**	**— —**	**41.7%**	**14.3%**	**4.9%**

Perficient, Inc.

Perficient is proficient in helping its customers use Internet-based technologies to their advantage. The information technology (IT) consulting firm's services include software development, systems integration, consulting, and support. The company specializes in developing middleware applications that are used to integrate and modernize legacy computer hardware and software. Perficient's Advanced Technology Services (ATS) group offers contracted services such as consulting, application development, and training through IBM, which is also a top customer. Other customers have included Anheuser-Busch, AT&T Mobility, EMC Corporation, and Wachovia.

Perficient has expanded its offerings through a string of acquisitions. In 2006 it bought San Francisco-based consulting firm Bay Street Solutions in a cash and stock deal valued at more than $9 million. The company also picked up the energy, government, and general business unit of Digital Consulting & Software Services, a private IT services provider that is focusing on its convenience store retail services business. The 2006 deal was valued at about $13 million.

In 2007 Perficient acquired IT consultancy E-Tech Solutions in a deal worth about $12 million, as well as ePairs. Addtional acquisitions made that year in order to expand its presence in the Denver area included Tier1 Innovation and Boldtech Systems.

EXECUTIVES

Chairman and CEO: John T. (Jack) McDonald, age 44, $588,359 pay
President and COO: Jeffrey S. (Jeff) Davis, age 43, $425,301 pay
CFO: Paul E. Martin, age 47
VP Finance and Administration and Controller: Richard (Dick) Kalbfleish, age 51, $172,227 pay
VP Client Development: Timothy J. (Tim) Thompson, age 47
VP Corporate Operations: Kathy Henely
VP Field Operations: Chris Gianattasio
VP Field Operations: John Jenkins
VP Field Operations: Thomas (Tom) Pash
Human Resources: Tracy Robinson
Marketing and Public Relations: Bill Davis
Auditors: BDO Seidman, LLP

LOCATIONS

HQ: Perficient, Inc.
1120 S. Capital of Texas Hwy., Bldg. III, Ste. 220, Austin, TX 78731
Phone: 512-531-6000 **Fax:** 512-531-6011
Web: www.perficient.com

2006 Sales

	% of total
US	99
Canada	1
Total	**100**

PRODUCTS/OPERATIONS

2006 Sales

	% of total
Services revenues	86
Software revenues	9
Reimbursed expenses	5
Total	**100**

Selected Services

Business intelligence
Custom applications development
eCommerce
Enterprise content management
Enterprise portals & collaborations
Mobile technology services
Online customer relationship management (CRM)
Service-oriented architectures and enterprise service bus services

COMPETITORS

Accenture
Answerthink
BearingPoint
CIBER
Cognizant Tech Solutions
EDS
Haverstick Consulting
Infosys
Quilogy
Sapient
Satyam
Wipro

HISTORICAL FINANCIALS

Company Type: Public

Income Statement

FYE: December 31

	REVENUE ($ mil.)	NET INCOME ($ mil.)	NET PROFIT MARGIN	EMPLOYEES
12/06	160.9	9.6	6.0%	972
12/05	97.0	7.2	7.4%	580
12/04	58.8	3.9	6.6%	—
12/03	30.2	1.0	3.3%	—
12/02	22.5	(2.4)	—	141
Annual Growth	**63.5%**	**—**	**—**	**62.0%**

2006 Year-End Financials

Debt ratio: 0.1%
Return on equity: 11.1%
Cash ($ mil.): 4.6
Current ratio: 2.12
Long-term debt ($ mil.): 0.1
No. of shares (mil.): 26.7
Dividends
Yield: —
Payout: —
Market value ($ mil.): 438.1
R&D as % of sales: —
Advertising as % of sales: —

Stock History

NASDAQ (GS): PRFT

	STOCK PRICE ($) FY Close	P/E High/Low		PER SHARE ($) Earnings	Dividends	Book Value
12/06	16.41	55	25	0.35	—	4.02
12/05	8.91	37	18	0.28	—	2.72
12/04	6.56	38	11	0.19	—	2.09
12/03	2.24	56	6	0.07	—	1.06
12/02	1.00	—	—	(0.53)	—	1.38
Annual Growth	**101.3%**	**—**	**—**	**—**	**—**	**30.7%**

PetMed Express

Convenience is king to PetMed Express. Through 1-800-PetMeds and 1800petmeds.com, as well as a catalog with hundreds of items, PetMed Express offers prescription and non-prescription medicines for your calico or collie. Founded in 1996 the company purchases its products at wholesale prices and ships directly to customers. Non-prescription items, such as flea and tick medications and health and nutritional supplements, account for 70% of PetMed's total sales. Tricon Holdings owns about 12% of PetMed and Dr. Marc Puleo, founder and chairman, owns some 5%.

The company makes 62% of its sales through its Web site. It also offers pet health information on a separate Web site, PetHealth101.com, which it began sponsoring in 2006. PetMeds also sells its products via catalog.

PetMeds has seen its customer base grow by about 8% from 2006 to 2007. Its customers base is primarily individual pet owners; wholesale business orders account for less than 1% of sales.

EXECUTIVES

CEO and Director: Menderes (Mendo) Akdag, age 47, $250,000 pay
CFO: Bruce S. Rosenbloom, age 38, $136,006 pay
Director of Information Systems: Richard Kirsch
Information Systems Manager: Chris Digiacomo
General Counsel and Corporate Secretary: Alison Berges
Attorney: Gregory Chaires
Auditors: McGladrey & Pullen, LLP

LOCATIONS

HQ: PetMed Express, Inc.
1441 SW 29th Ave., Pompano Beach, FL 33069
Phone: 954-979-5995 **Fax:** 954-971-0544
Web: www.1800petmeds.com

PRODUCTS/OPERATIONS

2007 Sales

	% of total
Non-prescription medications	70
Prescription medications	29
Shipping, handling & other	1
Total	**100**

COMPETITORS

Drs. Foster & Smith	PetSmart
KV Vet	Professional Veterinary
Medical Management	United Pharmacal
Pet Supermarket	VCA Antech
Pet Valu	Virbac Corporation
PetCareRx	Wal-Mart
PETCO	

HISTORICAL FINANCIALS

Company Type: Public

Income Statement

FYE: March 31

	REVENUE ($ mil.)	NET INCOME ($ mil.)	NET PROFIT MARGIN	EMPLOYEES
3/07	162.3	14.4	8.9%	216
3/06	137.6	12.1	8.8%	213
3/05	108.4	8.0	7.4%	180
3/04	94.0	5.8	6.2%	—
3/03	55.0	3.3	6.0%	—
Annual Growth	**31.1%**	**44.5%**	**—**	**9.5%**

2007 Year-End Financials

Debt ratio: —
Return on equity: 31.5%
Cash ($ mil.): 39.4
Current ratio: 7.89
Long-term debt ($ mil.): —
No. of shares (mil.): 24.3

Dividends
  Yield: —
  Payout: —
Market value ($ mil.): 288.1
R&D as % of sales: —
Advertising as % of sales: —

Stock History

NASDAQ (GS): PETS

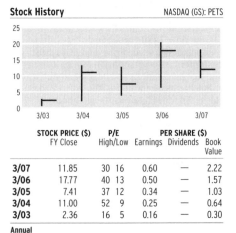

	STOCK PRICE ($) FY Close	P/E High/Low		PER SHARE ($) Earnings	Dividends	Book Value
3/07	11.85	30	16	0.60	—	2.22
3/06	17.77	40	13	0.50	—	1.57
3/05	7.41	37	12	0.34	—	1.03
3/04	11.00	52	9	0.25	—	0.64
3/03	2.36	16	5	0.16	—	0.30
Annual Growth	49.7%	—	—	39.2%	—	64.5%

Petrohawk Energy

Petrohawk Energy (formerly Beta Oil & Gas) is riding rising oil prices to higher profits. The independent company's activities include the exploration, development, and production of crude oil and natural gas in the Anadarko, Arkoma, East Texas/North Louisiana, Gulf Coast, Permian Basin, and South Texas regions. Petrohawk Energy has estimated proved reserves of 1.1 trillion cu. ft. of natural gas equivalent. In 2004 it participated in a reverse stock split with Petrohawk Energy, LLC and relocated to Houston. CEO Floyd Wilson controls 67% of the company. In 2006, in a move that greatly boosted its reserves, the company acquired KCS Energy for $1.9 billion.

In 2005 Petrohawk Energy acquired Proton Oil & Gas Corp., which has properties and related assets in South Louisiana and South Texas, for approximately $53 million. That year the company also acquired Mission Resources.

In 2006 Petrohawk Energy acquired North Louisiana gas properties for $262 million. It also sold its Gulf of Mexico assets for $52.5 million, and the next year it agreed to sell its Gulf Coast division for $825 million. Also in 2007 it acquired the assets of Fayetteville Shale for $343 million from Alta Resources, Contango Oil & Gas, and other companies.

In 2008 Petrohawk Energy agreed to acquire additional acreage in the Fayetteville Shale Trend from a private seller for $222.5 million.

EXECUTIVES

Chairman, President, and CEO: Floyd C. Wilson, age 60, $1,300,000 pay
Vice Chairman: James W. Christmas, age 59
COO: Richard K. (Dick) Stoneburner, age 53, $484,469 pay

EVP Finance and Administration: Larry L. Helm, age 60, $600,000 pay (prior to title change)
EVP Corporate Development: Stephen W. (Steve) Herod, age 48, $584,469 pay
EVP, CFO, and Treasurer: Mark J. Mize, age 35
EVP Mid-Continent Operations: Weldon Holcombe
VP Corporate Reserves: Tina Obut
Auditors: Deloitte & Touche LLP

LOCATIONS

HQ: Petrohawk Energy Corporation
  1000 Louisiana, Ste. 5600, Houston, TX 77002
Phone: 832-204-2700   **Fax:** 832-204-2800
Web: www.petrohawk.com

Petrohawk Energy has operations in the Anadarko, Arkoma, East Texas/North Louisiana, Gulf Coast, Permian Basin, and South Texas regions.

COMPETITORS

Anadarko Petroleum
Apache
BP
Chevron
Comstock Resources
El Paso
Exxon Mobil
Hunt Consolidated
McMoRan Exploration
Newfield Exploration
Nexen
Noble Energy
Royal Dutch Shell
Sunoco
Swift Energy

HISTORICAL FINANCIALS

Company Type: Public

Income Statement

FYE: December 31

	REVENUE ($ mil.)	NET INCOME ($ mil.)	NET PROFIT MARGIN	EMPLOYEES
12/06	587.8	116.6	19.8%	318
12/05	258.0	(16.6)	—	154
12/04	33.6	8.1	24.1%	—
12/03	12.9	1.0	7.8%	—
12/02	9.6	(6.9)	—	15
Annual Growth	179.7%	—	—	114.6%

2006 Year-End Financials

Debt ratio: 69.4%
Return on equity: 9.5%
Cash ($ mil.): 5.6
Current ratio: 0.74
Long-term debt ($ mil.): 1,338.0
No. of shares (mil.): 168.5

Dividends
  Yield: —
  Payout: —
Market value ($ mil.): 1,937.6
R&D as % of sales: —
Advertising as % of sales: —

Stock History

NYSE: HK

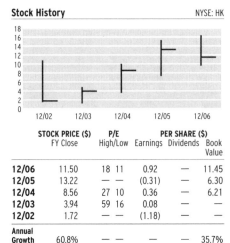

	STOCK PRICE ($) FY Close	P/E High/Low		PER SHARE ($) Earnings	Dividends	Book Value
12/06	11.50	18	11	0.92	—	11.45
12/05	13.22	—	—	(0.31)	—	6.30
12/04	8.56	27	10	0.36	—	6.21
12/03	3.94	59	16	0.08	—	—
12/02	1.72	—	—	(1.18)	—	—
Annual Growth	60.8%	—	—	—	—	35.7%

Pinnacle Entertainment

Pinnacle Entertainment knows most gamblers never know when they've reached their peak. The firm owns a handful of casinos in Indiana, Louisiana, Missouri, and Nevada, most of which operate under the Boomtown and Casino Magic banners. Pinnacle also owns an Embassy Suites hotel in St. Louis, Missouri. Outside the US, the company operates casinos in Argentina and the Bahamas. Once purely a racing concern, the company exited that business when it sold Turf Paradise, its racetrack in Phoenix. Most of the company's properties cater to locals or those who can easily drive there. Focused on expansion, Pinnacle is opening casinos in new markets and branching out overseas.

Pinnacle has been busy lately. The company purchased a riverboat casino near its hotel in St. Louis in 2006, and is planning to open two additional casinos in Missouri. In addition, that year it opened a casino adjoining the Four Seasons Resort Great Exuma at Emerald Bay in the Bahamas, the first and only casino on the island. Also that year Pinnacle purchased the site of the former Sands Hotel and Casino neighboring land along the Atlantic City Boardwalk for about $250 million. Its next gamble includes building a new $350 million casino resort in Lake Charles, Louisiana, adjacent to its L'Auberge du Lac Hotel & Casino property.

Pinnacle's proposed purchase of Aztar Corporation, which would have given the company a presence in Las Vegas and Atlantic City under the Tropicana name, was trumped by a higher offer from Columbia Sussex; as a result Aztar paid Pinnacle $78 million in breakup fees in 2006.

Its Boomtown properties along the Gulf Coast received varying degrees of damage as a result of Hurricane Katrina. Pinnacle reopened Boomtown New Orleans in Harvey, Louisiana, in 2005; the following year Pinnacle sold its Casino Magic Biloxi in Mississippi, which suffered substantial damage, to Harrah's Entertainment. As part of the deal, Pinnacle paid $25 million for two of Harrah's casino boats in Lake Charles, Louisiana.

HISTORY

The Hollywood Park Turf Club was founded in 1938 by a group of Hollywood entertainers, including producers Jack Warner (Warner Bros.) and Mervyn Leroy (*The Wizard of Oz*), and went public that year. Watching the horses went along with watching movie stars who frequented the track. Marje Everett became CEO in 1972, and during her two-decade reign, Hollywood Park hosted the first ever Breeder's Cup in 1984.

By the end of the 1980s, however, Hollywood Park was losing money. R. D. Hubbard ousted Everett in a bitter proxy battle in 1991, became CEO, and started renovating the track. The company began diversifying in 1994, opening a card casino adjacent to its racetrack; it acquired Turf Paradise racetrack and Sunflower Racing (the latter fared poorly; it went bankrupt in 1996 and was sold at auction in 1998).

Hollywood Park further diversified when it bought three casinos from Boomtown in 1997 and acquired Casino Magic in 1998. The company sold the Hollywood Park Race Track and casino to Churchill Downs in 1999 (promptly leasing back the casino) and sold its Turf Paradise racetrack to a private investor for $53 million. It also sold two of its Mississippi casinos (Casino Magic Bay St. Louis and Boomtown Biloxi) to Penn National gaming for $195 million.

In 2000 Hollywood Park changed its name to Pinnacle Entertainment to reflect its shift from horse racing to gaming. Later that year it agreed to be bought by Harveys Casino Resorts for about $675 million. The deal was cancelled in January 2001. The following year saw charges of prostitution at Pinnacle's Belterra casino in Indiana and an investigation by the Indiana Gaming Commission. Also in 2002 chairman Hubbard, CEO Paul Alanis, and director Robert Manfuso resigned. Daniel Lee, a hotel/casino developer and former Mirage Resorts executive, assumed chairman and CEO duties.

The company continued its race away from the track in 2004 when it signed contracts to open two casinos and hotels in Missouri and one in the Bahamas. It also began work on the 750-room L'Auberge du Lac Hotel & Casino in Lake Charles, Louisiana.

EXECUTIVES

Chairman and CEO: Daniel R. (Dan) Lee, age 50, $1,375,000 pay
President: Wade W. Hundley, age 41, $1,057,308 pay
COO: Alain Uboldi, age 60, $728,654 pay
EVP and CFO: Stephen H. Capp, age 45, $1,132,154 pay
EVP, Secretary, and General Counsel:
John A. (Jack) Godfrey, age 57, $818,500 pay
SVP Human Resources: Humberto (HT) Trueba Jr.
SVP Public Relations and Government:
James W. (Jim) Barich
SVP Risk Management and Benefits:
Arthur I. (Art) Goldberg
VP Corporate Accounting and Corporate Controller:
Linda A. Shaffer
VP Investor Relations and Treasurer:
Christopher K. Plant
VP Hotel Operations: John Durham
VP Operations: Sarah Lee Tucker
VP Relationship Marketing: Keith Henson
VP Real Estate Development: Arthur Schleifer
President, Pinnacle Design and Construction:
Clifford D. Kortman
President, Pinnacle-Atlantic City:
Kimberly C. (Kim) Townsend
President, Pinnacle-Atlantic City: Larry Buck
CIO: Carol F. Pride
Director Strategic Marketing: Kyle Eichman
Auditors: Deloitte & Touche LLP

LOCATIONS

HQ: Pinnacle Entertainment, Inc.
3800 Howard Hughes Pkwy., Las Vegas, NV 89109
Phone: 702-784-7777   **Fax:** 702-784-7778
Web: www.pnkinc.com

PRODUCTS/OPERATIONS

2006 Sales

	$ mil.	% of total
L'Auberge du Lac	312.3	34
Boomtown New Orleans	201.5	22
Belterra Casino Resort	172.7	19
Boomtown Bossier City	96.3	11
Boomtown Reno	87.1	10
International (Argentina & the Bahamas)	28.6	3
Embassy Suites	11.6	1
President Riverboat Casino	2.2	—
Other	0.1	—
Total	**912.4**	**100**

Select Operations

Belterra Casino Resort (casino and hotel; Vevay, IN)
Boomtown Bossier City (casino and hotel; Bossier City, LA)
Boomtown New Orleans (Harvey, LA)
Boomtown Reno (casino and hotel; Reno, NV)
The Casino at Emerald Bay, The Bahamas (casino; Great Exuma, the Bahamas)
Casino Magic Argentina (Neuquen and San Martin, Argentina)
Embassy Suites (hotel; St. Louis, MO)
L'Auberge du Lac (Lake Charles, LA)
President Riverboat Casino (casino; St. Louis, MO)

COMPETITORS

Argosy Gaming
Boyd Gaming
Harrah's Entertainment
Horseshoe Gaming
Hyatt
Isle of Capri Casinos
Lakes Entertainment
MGM MIRAGE
President Casinos

HISTORICAL FINANCIALS

Company Type: Public

Income Statement

FYE: December 31

	REVENUE ($ mil.)	NET INCOME ($ mil.)	NET PROFIT MARGIN	EMPLOYEES
12/06	912.4	76.9	8.4%	7,186
12/05	725.9	6.1	0.8%	6,716
12/04	553.3	9.2	1.7%	—
12/03	531.5	(28.2)	—	—
12/02	514.0	(69.6)	—	5,994
Annual Growth	**15.4%**	**—**	**—**	**4.6%**

2006 Year-End Financials

Debt ratio: 111.3%
Return on equity: 13.7%
Cash ($ mil.): 210.9
Current ratio: 1.51
Long-term debt ($ mil.): 773.2
No. of shares (mil.): 48.2
Dividends
  Yield: —
  Payout: —
Market value ($ mil.): 1,596.7
R&D as % of sales: —
Advertising as % of sales: —

Stock History

NYSE: PNK

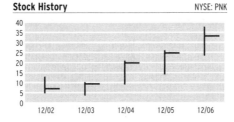

	STOCK PRICE ($) FY Close	P/E High/Low	PER SHARE ($) Earnings	Dividends	Book Value
12/06	33.14	24 15	1.56	—	14.42
12/05	24.71	183 103	0.14	—	10.44
12/04	19.78	82 37	0.25	—	10.25
12/03	9.32	— —	(1.09)	—	8.39
12/02	6.93	— —	(2.70)	—	9.58
Annual Growth	**47.9%**	**— —**	**—**	**—**	**10.8%**

Pinnacle Financial Partners

Pinnacle Financial Partners wants to be the pinnacle of community banking in central Tennessee. It is the holding company for Pinnacle National Bank, which operates more than 15 branches. The bank's deposit products include checking, money market, and savings accounts and CDs. Business loans, including commercial mortgage and construction loans, make up about 70% of its portfolio, which also includes residential real estate and consumer loans. The company provides brokerage services through its Pinnacle Asset Management division. It also offers investment, insurance, and trust services.

Pinnacle Financial Partners acquired Cavalry Bank in 2006. The following year it bought Mid-America Bancshares, the holding company for Nashville-area banks PrimeTrust Bank and Bank of the South, for nearly $200 million.

EXECUTIVES

Chairman: Robert A. (Rob) McCabe Jr., age 56, $389,500 pay
Vice Chairman: Ed C. Loughry Jr., age 64
President and CEO, Pinnacle Financial and Pinnacle Bank: M. Terry Turner, age 51, $410,000 pay
EVP and Chief Administrative Officer:
Hugh M. Queener, age 51, $234,000 pay
EVP and Client Services Group Manager:
Joanne B. Jackson, age 50, $140,400 pay
EVP and Senior Lending Officer, Pinnacle Bank:
J. Edward (Ed) White, age 54, $174,120 pay
EVP and Senior Credit Officer:
Charles B. (Charlie) McMahan, age 60, $175,000 pay
EVP and CFO: Harold R. Carpenter Jr., age 48, $175,000 pay
EVP and Manager, Pinnacle Asset Management:
Barry Moody
SVP, Marketing and Communications Director:
Victoria Lowe
SVP and Credit Officer: G. Glenn Layne
SVP and Mortgage Advisor: Scott Ractliffe
Chief People Officer: Martha B. Olsen
Auditors: KPMG LLP

LOCATIONS

HQ: Pinnacle Financial Partners, Inc.
211 Commerce St., Ste. 300, Nashville, TN 37201
Phone: 615-744-3700   **Fax:** 615-744-3861
Web: www.mypinnacle.com

Pinnacle Financial Partners has branches in Tennessee's Bedford, Davidson, Rutherford, Sumner, and Williamson counties.

PRODUCTS/OPERATIONS

2006 Sales

	$ mil.	% of total
Interest		
Loans, including fees	92.0	73
Securities	14.6	12
Federal funds sold & other	3.1	2
Noninterest		
Service charges on deposit accounts	4.6	4
Investment sales commissions	2.5	2
Insurance sales commissions	2.1	2
Gains on loans & loan participations sold	1.9	1
Trust fees	1.2	1
Other	3.5	3
Total	**125.5**	**100**

COMPETITORS

Bank of America
BB&T
First Horizon
SunTrust

HISTORICAL FINANCIALS

Company Type: Public

Income Statement

	ASSETS ($ mil.)	NET INCOME ($ mil.)	INCOME AS % OF ASSETS	EMPLOYEES
				FYE: December 31
12/06	2,142.2	17.9	0.8%	438
12/05	1,016.8	8.1	0.8%	159
12/04	727.1	5.3	0.7%	—
12/03	498.4	2.5	0.5%	—
12/02	305.3	0.6	0.2%	66
Annual Growth	62.8%	133.7%	—	60.5%

2006 Year-End Financials

Equity as % of assets: 12.0%
Return on assets: 1.1%
Return on equity: 11.2%
Long-term debt ($ mil.): 51.5
No. of shares (mil.): 15.4
Market value ($ mil.): 512.5

Dividends
  Yield: —
  Payout: —
Sales ($ mil.): 125.5
R&D as % of sales: —
Advertising as % of sales: —

Stock History

NASDAQ (GS): PNFP

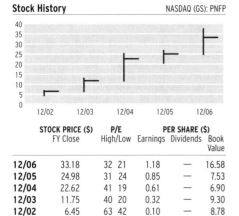

	STOCK PRICE ($) FY Close	P/E High/Low		PER SHARE ($) Earnings	Dividends	Book Value
12/06	33.18	32	21	1.18	—	16.58
12/05	24.98	31	24	0.85	—	7.53
12/04	22.62	41	19	0.61	—	6.90
12/03	11.75	40	20	0.32	—	9.30
12/02	6.45	63	42	0.10	—	8.78
Annual Growth	50.6%	—	—	85.3%	—	17.2%

Pioneer Drilling

Pioneer Drilling digs down deep to make money on the land where Texas pioneers used to roam. The company, formerly South Texas Drilling & Exploration, provides contract drilling and related services to oil and gas companies in Texas, and to a lesser degree in Oklahoma and the Rockies. Pioneer Drilling operates 66 land drilling rigs that can reach depths of 8,000-18,000 feet. The company moved into East Texas by acquiring privately owned Mustang Drilling. In 2004 the company acquired seven drilling rigs from Wolverine Drilling and five from Allen Drilling. It also acquired a land rig in 2007.

Texas is the geographic focus of Pioneer Drilling's business. In 2007 it had 20 drilling rigs operating in East Texas, 17 in South Texas, 13 in the Rocky Mountains, and 10 in North Texas.

EXECUTIVES

Chairman: C. Robert (Bob) Bunch, age 52
President, CEO, and Director: William S. (Stacy) Locke, age 50, $610,200 pay
EVP and COO: Franklin C. (Red) West, age 66, $473,800 pay
EVP, CFO, and Secretary: Joyce (Joy) Schuldt, age 42
SVP Marketing: Donald G. Lacombe, age 52, $244,800 pay
VP and Chief Accounting Officer: Kurt M. Forkheim
VP Operations: Willie Walker
VP and Manager, East Texas Division: Billy King
VP and Manager, South Texas Division: Buddy Shamblin
VP Operations: Blaine David
Senior Financial Manager: William D. Hibbetts, age 57, $275,400 pay
Auditors: KPMG LLP

LOCATIONS

HQ: Pioneer Drilling Company
1250 NE Loop 410, Ste. 1000,
San Antonio, TX 78209
Phone: 210-828-7689   **Fax:** 210-828-8228
Web: www.pioneerdrlg.com

PRODUCTS/OPERATIONS

2007 Sales

	$ mil.	% of total
Daywork contracts	399.2	96
Footage contracts	13.6	3
Turnkey contracts	3.4	1
Total	**416.2**	**100**

COMPETITORS

Grey Wolf
Helmerich & Payne
Nabors Industries
Parker Drilling
Patterson-UTI Energy
Rowan Companies
Unit Corporation

HISTORICAL FINANCIALS

Company Type: Public

Income Statement

	REVENUE ($ mil.)	NET INCOME ($ mil.)	NET PROFIT MARGIN	EMPLOYEES
				FYE: March 31
3/07	416.2	84.2	20.2%	1,700
3/06	284.1	50.6	17.8%	1,540
3/05	185.3	10.8	5.8%	—
3/04	107.9	(1.8)	—	—
3/03	80.2	(5.1)	—	—
Annual Growth	50.9%	—	—	10.4%

2007 Year-End Financials

Debt ratio: —
Return on equity: 21.9%
Cash ($ mil.): 84.9
Current ratio: 4.63
Long-term debt ($ mil.): —
No. of shares (mil.): 49.6

Dividends
  Yield: —
  Payout: —
Market value ($ mil.): 629.8
R&D as % of sales: —
Advertising as % of sales: —

Stock History

AMEX: PDC

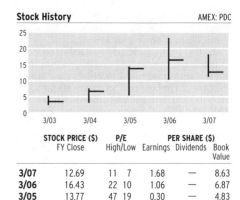

	STOCK PRICE ($) FY Close	P/E High/Low		PER SHARE ($) Earnings	Dividends	Book Value
3/07	12.69	11	7	1.68	—	8.63
3/06	16.43	22	10	1.06	—	6.87
3/05	13.77	47	19	0.30	—	4.83
3/04	6.65	—	—	(0.08)	—	2.59
3/03	3.49	—	—	(0.31)	—	2.20
Annual Growth	38.1%	—	—	—	—	40.8%

Pope Resources

More earthly than divine, Pope Resources owns some 115,000 acres of timberland and development property in Washington. The partnership annually harvests more than 60 million board ft. from its 71,000-acre Hood Canal and 44,000-acre Columbia tree farms in Washington. It sells its Douglas fir and other timber products mainly in the US and Japan: Weyerhaeuser is a major customer. Pope Resources also provides timberland management and consulting services to third-party timberland owners and managers in Washington, Oregon, and California. Its real estate unit acquires, develops, resells, and rents residential and commercial real estate. Investment advisor Private Capital Management owns 28% of Pope Resources.

Pope Resources' fee timber segment also gains revenue by selling gravel and by leasing cellular communication towers.

The partnership's Olympic Property Group real estate operations relate to its nearly 3,000-acre portfolio of higher-and-better-use properties that may be reforested, developed for sale as improved property, or sold in developed or undeveloped acreage tracts. The company's Rural Lifestyles projects allow it to resell fully logged plots that no longer have value for timber production. Its operations are focused on residential and commercial property in Port Gamble, Kingston, Bremerton, and Gig Harbor.

In 2004 the company acquired 3,300 acres of timberland in southwest Washington from Plum Creek Timber Company, Inc., for $8.5 million; it also paid about $12 million to a private party for 1,339 acres of timberland in western Washington. That year the company sold 426 acres in northern Kitsap County near Kingston, Washington, and agreed to extend to the county an option to acquire up to 360 additional acres of adjacent land (in one or two phases); the option will expire in July 2008.

In 2006 the company sold more than 200 acres of residential land for $12 million.

Pope Resources was spun off from Pope & Talbot in 1985, and the latter retains some control of the company through managing general partner Pope MGP, Inc. Pope MGP is owned by Emily Andrews and Peter Pope (former chairman of Pope & Talbot), who own 12% and 7%, respectively, of Pope Resources.

EXECUTIVES

President, CEO, and Director: David L. (Dave) Nunes, age 45, $565,096 pay
VP, CFO, and Secretary: Thomas M. (Tom) Ringo, age 53, $330,058 pay
Director Business Development, Olympic Resource Management: John T. Shea
Director Real Estate and President, Olympic Property Group: Jonathon P. (Jon) Rose
Director Timberland Operations, Olympic Resource Management: Thomas (Tom) Kametz
Auditors: KPMG LLP

LOCATIONS

HQ: Pope Resources, A Delaware Limited Partnership
19245 10th Ave. NE, Poulsbo, WA 98370
Phone: 360-697-6626   **Fax:** 360-697-1156
Web: www.poperesources.com

Pope Resources owns more than 115,000 acres of fee timberland in western Washington. It has real estate holdings in the state's Jefferson, Kitsap, and Pierce counties.

PRODUCTS/OPERATIONS

2006 Sales

	% of total
Fee timber	53
Real estate	42
Timberland Management & Consulting	5
Total	**100**

Species Distribution

	mil. board ft.	% of total
Conifers		
Douglas fir	320	75
Western hemlock	50	12
Western red cedar	14	3
Other conifer	13	3
Hardwoods		
Red alder	26	6
Other hardwood	4	1
Total	**427**	**100**

Selected Subsidiaries

Olympic Property Group
Olympic Resource Management

COMPETITORS

Alcan Baltek
Hampton Affiliates
International Paper
Plum Creek Timber
Potlatch
Simpson Investment
Weyerhaeuser

HISTORICAL FINANCIALS

Company Type: Public

Income Statement

	REVENUE ($ mil.)	NET INCOME ($ mil.)	NET PROFIT MARGIN	EMPLOYEES
12/06	66.3	24.9	37.6%	81
12/05	57.0	13.7	24.0%	81
12/04	39.7	10.2	25.7%	—
12/03	27.0	3.5	13.0%	—
12/02	32.2	3.3	10.2%	37
Annual Growth	19.8%	65.7%	—	21.6%

FYE: December 31

2006 Year-End Financials

Debt ratio: 35.2%
Return on equity: 32.3%
Cash ($ mil.): 32.2
Current ratio: 2.78
Long-term debt ($ mil.): 30.9
No. of shares (mil.): 4.7

Dividends
  Yield: 3.1%
  Payout: 20.3%
Market value ($ mil.): 161.9
R&D as % of sales: —
Advertising as % of sales: —

Stock History

NASDAQ (GM): POPEZ

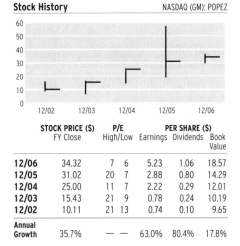

	STOCK PRICE ($) FY Close	P/E High/Low		PER SHARE ($) Earnings	Dividends	Book Value
12/06	34.32	7	6	5.23	1.06	18.57
12/05	31.02	20	7	2.88	0.80	14.29
12/04	25.00	11	7	2.22	0.29	12.01
12/03	15.43	21	9	0.78	0.24	10.19
12/02	10.11	21	13	0.74	0.10	9.65
Annual Growth	35.7%	—	—	63.0%	80.4%	17.8%

Portfolio Recovery Associates

When times get tough, some businesses find the going a little easier with Portfolio Recovery Associates. The firm makes its way in the world by collecting on defaulted consumer debt. It either collects on behalf of clients (including banks, credit unions, consumer and auto finance companies, and retail merchants) or buys charged-off debt portfolios from them and then collects the debts on its own behalf. Portfolio Recovery Associates was formed in 1996 by veterans of the consumer receivables unit of the former Household International (now HSBC Finance).

Portfolio Recovery Associates has broadened the scope of its service offerings through acquisitions. The company has subsidiaries or business units dedicated to government accounts receivable management (Revenue Discovery Systems); skip-tracing and asset location for auto finance companies (IGS Nevada); and contingency collections (Anchor Receivables Management).

EXECUTIVES

Chairman, President, and CEO:
  Steven D. (Steve) Fredrickson, age 47, $995,000 pay
EVP, CFO, Chief Administrative Officer, Treasurer, and Assistant Secretary: Kevin P. Stevenson, age 42, $665,000 pay
EVP Acquisitions: Craig A. Grube, age 46, $665,000 pay
EVP, General Counsel, and Secretary: Judith S. Scott, age 61, $285,000 pay
SVP and COO, Owned Portfolios: Neal Stern
SVP Operations: William F. O'Daire, $310,000 pay
SVP: Michael J. Petit, $462,298 pay
VP Portfolio Acquisitions: Chris Graves
VP Human Resources: James Donahoe
Auditors: KPMG LLP

LOCATIONS

HQ: Portfolio Recovery Associates, Inc.
  120 Corporate Blvd., Norfolk, VA 23502
Phone: 757-519-9300   **Fax:** 757-518-0901
Web: www.portfoliorecovery.com

Portfolio Recovery Associates has operations in Birmingham, Alabama; Hampton and Norfolk, Virginia; Hutchinson, Kansas; Jackson, Tennessee; and Las Vegas, Nevada.

PRODUCTS/OPERATIONS

2006 Sales

	% of total
Income on finance receivables	87
Commissions	13
Total	**100**

2006 Portfolio Composition

	% of total
Visa/Mastercard/Discover	47
Consumer finance	31
Private-label credit cards	19
Auto deficiency	3
Total	**100**

COMPETITORS

Asset Acceptance
Asta Funding
Encore Capital Group, Inc.
FirstCity Financial
iQor

Nationwide Recovery
NCO
Outsourcing Solutions
Rampart Capital

HISTORICAL FINANCIALS

Company Type: Public

Income Statement

	REVENUE ($ mil.)	NET INCOME ($ mil.)	NET PROFIT MARGIN	EMPLOYEES
12/06	188.3	44.5	23.6%	1,291
12/05	148.5	36.8	24.8%	1,110
12/04	113.4	27.5	24.3%	—
12/03	84.9	20.7	24.4%	—
12/02	55.8	17.1	30.6%	—
Annual Growth	35.5%	27.0%	—	16.3%

FYE: December 31

2006 Year-End Financials

Debt ratio: 0.4%
Return on equity: 20.1%
Cash ($ mil.): 25.1
Current ratio: 2.27
Long-term debt ($ mil.): 0.9
No. of shares (mil.): 16.0

Dividends
  Yield: —
  Payout: —
Market value ($ mil.): 746.5
R&D as % of sales: —
Advertising as % of sales: —

Stock History

NASDAQ (GS): PRAA

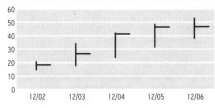

	STOCK PRICE ($) FY Close	P/E High/Low		PER SHARE ($) Earnings	Dividends	Book Value
12/06	46.69	19	14	2.77	—	15.47
12/05	46.44	21	14	2.28	—	12.39
12/04	41.22	24	14	1.73	—	9.77
12/03	26.55	26	13	1.32	—	7.79
12/02	18.25	—	—	—	—	5.95
Annual Growth	26.5%	—	—	28.0%	—	27.0%

Powell Industries

Powell Industries gets a charge out of making equipment and computer systems that monitor and control the flow of electricity in industrial, commercial, and government facilities. Products include switchgears (units that manage the flow of electricity to motors, transformers, and other equipment); bus ducts (insulated power conductors housed in a metal enclosure); process control systems for instrumentation, computer control, and communications; and data management. Powell sells to refineries, utilities, paper mills, offshore oil-and-gas drilling platforms, and transportation companies, among other customers. The company gets two-thirds of its sales in the US.

Powell is attempting to diversify through acquisitions in order to be less dependent on one range of products, though electrical power products such as switchgear and bus ducts account for more than 90% of sales. In 2005 the company acquired a UK firm, Switchgear & Instrumentation (S&I), for about $19 million in cash and notes.

In 2006 Powell acquired the medium-voltage switchgear product line of GE Consumer & Industrial, with related assets, for $32 million. The company paid $8.5 million in cash upfront, and will make four installment payments of between $5.5 million and $6.25 million through the end of 2009. Powell also signed a supply agreement with GE Consumer & Industrial as part of the deal.

The company is also looking to increase sales to oil and gas production facilities, such as the $7.5 million deal its Powell Electrical Manufacturing subsidiary has signed with ConocoPhillips for a deepwater development program in the Gulf of Mexico. Powell is generating significant revenues from a contract to provide intelligent transportation systems for the Port Authority of New York and New Jersey. The company is installing roadway sensors, electronic message boards, computers, and other equipment for the Holland and Lincoln tunnels, which run under the Hudson River, connecting Manhattan to northern New Jersey. Powell's Transdyn Controls subsidiary earlier installed a similar system on the George Washington Bridge, which spans the Hudson north of the two tunnels.

In 2004 Powell closed its bus duct manufacturing plant in Elyria, Ohio, and consolidated those operations with its Illinois facility. The company also closed its power electronics development operations in Watsonville, California, and moved those operations to its Houston facility. Powell retains plants in North Canton, Ohio, and Pleasanton, California.

Chairman, president, and CEO Thomas Powell, son of the founder, owns nearly 28% of the company. Royce & Associates owns almost 12% of Powell. Bonnie L. Powell holds more than 7% of the company. Tontine Capital Management has an equity stake of 6%. Wellington Management owns more than 5% of Powell. The company's employee stock ownership trust holds around 5%.

EXECUTIVES

Chairman and CEO: Thomas W. (Tom) Powell, age 66, $831,212 pay
President and COO: Patrick L. McDonald, age 53
EVP, CFO, Treasurer, Secretary, and Chief Administrative Officer: Don R. Madison, age 49

VP and Controller: Milburn Honeycutt, age 44, $239,955 pay
Director, Human Resources: Bob Murphy
Director, Corporate Communications: Gary King
Director, Supply Management: Tim Irons
Director, Internal Audit: Ernest Lopez
Director, Information Technology: Carolyn S. Davis
Director, International Sales and Marketing: Mark Williams
Auditors: PricewaterhouseCoopers LLP

LOCATIONS

HQ: Powell Industries, Inc.
  8550 Mosley Dr., Houston, TX 77075
Phone: 713-944-6900   **Fax:** 713-947-4435
Web: www.powellind.com

Powell Industries has plants in California, Georgia, Illinois, Ohio, and Texas, and overseas in Singapore and the UK.

2007 Sales

	$ mil.	% of total
Americas		
US	372.7	66
Other countries	77.0	14
Middle East & Africa	58.9	10
Europe	28.1	5
Asia	27.6	5
Total	**564.3**	**100**

PRODUCTS/OPERATIONS

2007 Sales

	$ mil.	% of total
Electrical power products	541.6	96
Process control systems	22.7	4
Total	**564.3**	**100**

Selected Products

Electrical power products
  Bus duct
  Cable bus
  Custom modules
  DC switchgear
  Grounding systems
  Isolated phase bus
  Metal-clad switchgear
  Powlsmart substations
  Rectifiers
  Traction substations
  Transfer switches
Process control systems
Service and parts
Training

COMPETITORS

ALSTOM	FKI
AREVA T&D	GE
AZZ	Kohler
Baldor Electric	Magnetek
Cooper Industries	S&C Electric
Eaton	SatCon Technology
Emerson Electric	Spirent

HISTORICAL FINANCIALS

Company Type: Public

Income Statement

FYE: September 30

	REVENUE ($ mil.)	NET INCOME ($ mil.)	NET PROFIT MARGIN	EMPLOYEES
9/07	564.3	9.9	1.8%	2,123
9/06*	374.5	9.8	2.6%	—
10/05	256.6	2.3	0.9%	—
10/04	206.1	1.7	0.8%	—
10/03	253.4	7.1	2.8%	—
Annual Growth	**22.2%**	**8.7%**	**—**	**—**

*Fiscal year change

2007 Year-End Financials

Debt ratio: 15.8%
Return on equity: 6.0%
Cash ($ mil.): 5.3
Current ratio: 1.75
Long-term debt ($ mil.): 27.4
No. of shares (mil.): 11.1
Dividends
  Yield: —
  Payout: —
Market value ($ mil.): 422.2
R&D as % of sales: —
Advertising as % of sales: —

Stock History

NASDAQ (GM): POWL

	STOCK PRICE ($) FY Close	P/E High	P/E Low	PER SHARE ($) Earnings	PER SHARE ($) Dividends	PER SHARE ($) Book Value
9/07	37.89	43	23	0.88	—	15.57
9/06*	22.13	31	20	0.89	—	14.53
10/05	20.97	114	76	0.21	—	13.31
10/04	16.12	137	97	0.15	—	13.03
10/03	19.38	31	18	0.67	—	12.84
Annual Growth	**18.2%**	**—**	**—**	**7.1%**	**—**	**4.9%**

*Fiscal year change

PowerSecure International

PowerSecure International (formerly Metretek Technologies) measures its success by the number of meters it monitors. The company's Southern Flow gas measurement services allow natural gas and pipeline companies to verify gas transfer volumes. Subsidiary PowerSecure offers distributed generation electricity systems to industrial and commercial users. PowerSecure International also supplies automated meter-reading (AMR) systems through its Metretek subsidiary. With these systems, utilities can monitor, record, and transmit data about its customers' gas and electricity consumption.

In 2004 Metretek Technologies sold its contract manufacturing operations, which operated under its Metretek Florida subsidiary, to Instrutech Florida.

In 2006 the company acquired the business of Reid's Trailer, Inc., which builds trailers for the transportation of goods and equipment.

In 2007 Metretek Technologies changed its corporate name to reflect the strength of its largest subsidiary, PowerSecure.

EXECUTIVES

Chairman: Basil M. Briggs, age 71
President, CEO, and Director: Sidney Hinton, age 44, $312,981 pay (prior to promotion)
CFO: Christopher T. (Chris) Hutter, age 41
VP Financial Reporting, Controller, and Principal Accounting Officer: Gary J. Zuiderveen, age 48
President and CEO, Southern Flow Companies: John D. Bernard, age 52, $219,231 pay
President and CEO, Metretek, Inc.: Joseph L. (Joe) Harley
VP Sales and Service, Metretek, Inc.: Danny MacDonald

LOCATIONS

HQ: PowerSecure International, Inc.
1609 Heritage Commerce Ct.,
Wake Forest, NC 27587
Phone: 919-556-3056 **Fax:** 919-556-3596
Web: www.powersecure.com

Metretek Technologies has offices in Colorado, Florida, Louisiana, Mississippi, New Mexico, North Carolina, Oklahoma, and Texas.

2006 Sales

	$ mil.	% of total
North America		
US	120.2	100
Canada	0.1	—
South America	0.1	—
Europe & other	0.1	—
Total	**120.5**	**100**

PRODUCTS/OPERATIONS

2006 Sales

	$ mil.	% of total
PowerSecure	99.5	83
Southern Flow	16.2	13
Metretek, Inc. (Metretek Florida)	3.7	3
Other	1.1	1
Total	**120.5**	**100**

Major Operations

PowerSecure
  Distributed generation of electricity to industrial and commercial users
  Project design and engineering
  Switch gear acquisition and installation

Southern Flow
  Chart processing operations
  Data collection and analysis
  Integrated natural gas measurement
  Laboratory analysis

Metretek Florida
  Application specific recording systems
  Electronic gas flow computers and volume correctors
  Remote data collectors

COMPETITORS

ABB
Badger Meter
Caterpillar
Comverge
Cummins
Duke Energy
Emerson Electric
Exterran
Honeywell International
Itron
Magellan Midstream
Schlumberger
Siemens Power Generation

HISTORICAL FINANCIALS

Company Type: Public

Income Statement

FYE: December 31

	REVENUE ($ mil.)	NET INCOME ($ mil.)	NET PROFIT MARGIN	EMPLOYEES
12/06	120.4	11.7	9.7%	335
12/05	47.3	2.3	4.9%	266
12/04	35.2	(3.2)	—	—
12/03	39.3	0.9	2.3%	—
12/02	27.0	(3.4)	—	—
Annual Growth	**45.3%**	**—**	**—**	**25.9%**

2006 Year-End Financials

Debt ratio: 0.0%
Return on equity: 31.5%
Cash ($ mil.): 15.9
Current ratio: 2.23
Long-term debt ($ mil.): 0.0
No. of shares (mil.): 15.8

Dividends
  Yield: —
  Payout: —
Market value ($ mil.): 194.8
R&D as % of sales: —
Advertising as % of sales: —

Stock History

NASDAQ (GS): POWR

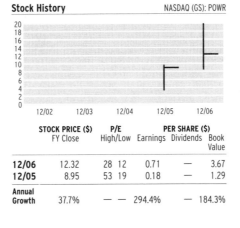

	STOCK PRICE ($) FY Close	P/E High/Low		PER SHARE ($) Earnings	Dividends	Book Value
12/06	12.32	28	12	0.71	—	3.67
12/05	8.95	53	19	0.18	—	1.29
Annual Growth	**37.7%**	**—**	**—**	**294.4%**	**—**	**184.3%**

PriceSmart, Inc.

PriceSmart is wise in the ways of members-only club retailing. The company runs about two dozen US-style membership stores under the PriceSmart names in Latin America and the Caribbean. It sells low-cost food, pharmacy, and basic consumer items. In each store, nearly half of the merchandise comes from the US, and the other half is sourced locally. In-store services include auto/tire centers, banking, and photo developing. PriceSmart stores are smaller than wholesale clubs in the US, averaging about 40,000-50,000 sq. ft., and the membership fees vary by market from around $20 up to $35. Together, chairman Robert Price, his father Sol, and directors Murray Galinson and Jack McGrory own nearly 50% of PriceSmart.

During fiscal 2005 the company closed stores in Mexico and Guam and terminated its licensing agreement in China. It also divested its interest in PSMT Philippines, its former subsidiary there. On the plus side, it opened a store in Costa Rica.

The firm opened a new store in Guatemala City in 2007 and plans to open a third location in Trinidad in late 2007. It also announced that year that it sold its 50% stake in PSMT Mexico to Grupo Gigante.

PriceSmart has been searching for a new CEO since April 2003, when Gilbert Partida left the company. (Jose Luis Laparte, a former Wal-Mart executive and consultant to PriceSmart, joined the company as president in late 2004.)

HISTORY

Sol Price created the members-only warehouse retail concept in the mid-1950s when he started Fedmart. In 1976 he and son Robert began Price Club. Facing pressure in the warehouse club niche, Price Club and competitor Costco merged in 1993, forming Price/Costco. But their managements disagreed over direction and policy, and the next year Price/Costco spun off Price Enterprises, Inc. (PEI). PEI assets included commercial real estate and international

development projects. Eventually, Price/Costco resumed its maiden name, Costco.

In mid-1997 PEI split into two companies, Price Enterprises (a real estate investment trust, now Price Legacy) and PriceSmart. PriceSmart was built from subsidiaries Price Quest, Price Global Trading, and Price Ventures. During a busy 1998 the company closed stores in Indonesia and Guam and opened locations in China and Panama. In addition, it formed a joint venture (60% owned by PriceSmart) with Panamanian firm PSC to open nine new warehouse clubs in Central America and the Caribbean. That year the company's joint venture with PSC opened warehouses in Costa Rica, the Dominican Republic, El Salvador, Guatemala, and Honduras.

PriceSmart entered an agreement in fiscal 1999 with investors from Trinidad and Tobago to open two warehouses in Trinidad. (One opened a year later.) The company sold its domestic auto referral program in 1999 and its travel program in 2000. Also in 2000, the company announced a joint-venture with Philippine investors to open five to 10 stores in the Philippines. In 2001 the company received more than $30 million in loans to build 13 stores in Central America and the Caribbean. PriceSmart opened six stores in 2001, including two in the Philippines.

In fiscal 2002 PriceSmart opened four new warehouse stores in Trinidad, Guam, and two outlets in the Philippines. In 2002 the company opened three locations in Mexico and one in the Philippines.

In April 2003 president and CEO Gilbert A. Partida resigned from the company and its board of directors. Chairman Robert E. Price took on the additional role of interim president and CEO during the search for Partida's replacement. In 2003, the company opened three warehouse stores (one each in Jamaica, Nicaragua, and the Philippines) and closed four clubs.

In October 2004 Jose Luis Laparte became president of the company, while chairman Robert E. Price remained interim CEO of PriceSmart. The company opened one new store in the Philippines and closed its warehouse club in Guam in 2004.

PriceSmart closed its Mexican operations and terminated its licensing agreement in China in 2005. In 2006 the retailer sold its interest in its PSMT Philippines subsidiary, the operator of four warehouse clubs there.

EXECUTIVES

Chairman and CEO: Robert E. Price, age 65, $59,952 pay
President and Director: Jose Luis Laparte, age 41, $467,200 pay
EVP and COO: William J. (Bill) Naylon, age 45, $272,517 pay
EVP and CFO: John M. Heffner, age 52, $258,390 pay
EVP, Central America Operations: John D. Hildebrandt, age 49
EVP Construction Management: Brud E. Drachman, age 52
EVP Information Technology and Logistics: A. Edward Oats, age 46
EVP Merchandising: Thomas D. Martin, age 51
EVP Real Estate and Development, and Director: Jack McGrory, age 58
EVP, Secretary, and General Counsel: Robert M. Gans, age 58, $293,625 pay
SVP and Controller: Michael McCleary
SVP Latin America and Caribbean Legal Affairs: Ernesto Grijalva
SVP Treasury: Atul Patel
Auditors: Ernst & Young LLP

LOCATIONS

HQ: PriceSmart, Inc.
9740 Scranton Rd., San Diego, CA 92121
Phone: 858-404-8800 **Fax:** 858-404-8848
Web: www.pricesmart.com

2007 Stores

	No.
Costa Rica	4
Panama	4
Dominican Republic	2
Guatemala	3
El Salvador	2
Honduras	2
Trinidad	3
Aruba	1
Barbados	1
Jamaica	1
Nicaragua	1
U.S. Virgin Islands	1
Total	**25**

COMPETITORS

Carrefour
Wal-Mart

HISTORICAL FINANCIALS

Company Type: Public

Income Statement — FYE: August 31

	REVENUE ($ mil.)	NET INCOME ($ mil.)	NET PROFIT MARGIN	EMPLOYEES
8/07	888.8	12.9	1.5%	3,434
8/06	734.7	11.9	1.6%	2,937
8/05	618.8	(42.3)	—	2,961
8/04	609.7	(30.0)	—	—
8/03	660.7	(30.2)	—	—
Annual Growth	7.7%	—	—	7.7%

2007 Year-End Financials

Debt ratio: 3.3%
Return on equity: 5.4%
Cash ($ mil.): 40.1
Current ratio: 1.18
Long-term debt ($ mil.): 8.0
No. of shares (mil.): 29.4
Dividends
 Yield: 0.7%
 Payout: 36.4%
Market value ($ mil.): 703.4
R&D as % of sales: —
Advertising as % of sales: —

Stock History — NASDAQ (GM): PSMT

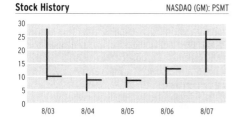

	STOCK PRICE ($) FY Close	P/E High/Low		PER SHARE ($) Earnings	Dividends	Book Value
8/07	23.96	61	27	0.44	0.16	8.36
8/06	12.92	31	18	0.43	—	7.97
8/05	8.60	—	—	(3.15)	—	6.85
8/04	8.75	—	—	(4.57)	—	7.30
8/03	10.10	—	—	(4.67)	—	21.88
Annual Growth	24.1%	—	—	—	—	(21.4%)

Princeton National Bancorp

Far from the Ivy League institution that shares its name, Princeton National Bancorp is the holding company for Citizens First National Bank. The bank provides community banking to businesses and residents in north-central Illinois with about 20 branches serving Bureau, DeKalb, Grundy, Kane, Kendall, LaSalle, Marshall, McHenry, and neighboring counties. Founded in 1865, the bank offers deposit products including checking and savings accounts and CDs. Commercial loans and commercial real estate mortgages each account for about 20% of the bank's loan portfolio. Through Citizens Financial Advisors, it offers trust and farm management, and investment services.

In early 2005 Princeton National Bancorp acquired Somonauk FSB Bancorp, holding company for Farmers State Bank of Somonauk, which has branches in Millbrook, Newark, Plano, Sandwich, and Somonauk, Illinois.

EXECUTIVES

Chairman, Princeton National Bancorp and Citizens First National Bank: Craig O. Wesner, age 65
President, CEO, and Director, Princeton National Bancorp and Citizens First National Bank: Tony J. Sorcic, age 53, $337,464 pay
SVP and CFO, Princeton National Bancorp and Citizens First National Bank: Todd D. Fanning, age 44, $132,563 pay
EVP; EVP and Commercial Banking Manager, Citizens First National Bank: James B. Miller, age 51, $178,687 pay
SVP, Human Resources, Citizens First National Bank: Jill Smith
SVP, Citizens Financial Advisors, Citizens Bank: Patrick B. Murray, $161,129 pay
SVP, Administrative Services, Citizens First National Bank: Joyce Roggy
SVP, Consumer Banking, Citizens First National Bank: Jacqualyn L. Karlosky, age 46, $108,614 pay
Auditors: BKD, LLP

LOCATIONS

HQ: Princeton National Bancorp, Inc.
606 S. Main St., Princeton, IL 61356
Phone: 815-875-4444 **Fax:** 815-872-0247
Web: www.pnbc-inc.com

PRODUCTS/OPERATIONS

2006 Sales

	$ mil.	% of total
Interest		
Loans	41.9	66
Securities & other	11.6	18
Noninterest		
Service charges on deposit accounts	4.2	7
Trust & farm management fees	1.5	2
Other service charges	1.8	3
Other	2.8	4
Total	**63.8**	**100**

COMPETITORS

ABN AMRO	Jacksonville Bancorp (IL)
AMCORE Financial	Old Second Bancorp
Associated Banc-Corp	Regions Financial
Banco Popular	UnionBancorp
Fifth Third	U.S. Bancorp
Harris Bankcorp	Wintrust Financial

HISTORICAL FINANCIALS

Company Type: Public

Income Statement — FYE: December 31

	ASSETS ($ mil.)	NET INCOME ($ mil.)	INCOME AS % OF ASSETS	EMPLOYEES
12/06	1,032.0	6.5	0.6%	336
12/05	945.3	7.6	0.8%	326
12/04	655.7	6.9	1.1%	—
12/03	609.7	6.6	1.1%	—
12/02	587.4	6.1	1.0%	241
Annual Growth	15.1%	1.6%	—	8.7%

2006 Year-End Financials

Equity as % of assets: 6.3%
Return on assets: 0.7%
Return on equity: 10.1%
Long-term debt ($ mil.): 35.8
No. of shares (mil.): 3.4
Market value ($ mil.): 109.1
Dividends
 Yield: 3.2%
 Payout: 55.0%
Sales ($ mil.): 63.8
R&D as % of sales: —
Advertising as % of sales: —

Stock History — NASDAQ (GM): PNBC

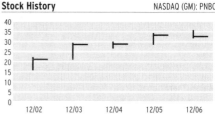

	STOCK PRICE ($) FY Close	P/E High/Low		PER SHARE ($) Earnings	Dividends	Book Value
12/06	32.55	19	17	1.91	1.05	19.50
12/05	33.25	14	12	2.37	1.03	18.87
12/04	28.80	13	12	2.21	0.96	17.13
12/03	28.55	14	10	2.05	0.89	16.29
12/02	21.15	12	9	1.86	0.85	15.79
Annual Growth	11.4%	—	—	0.7%	5.4%	5.4%

PrivateBancorp

It's your private banker, a banker for money, and any old teller won't do. PrivateBancorp's PrivateBank subsidiaries provide customized banking and money management services to wealthy individuals and their families, owners of closely-held businesses, and commercial real estate investors through eight offices in Chicago and its affluent suburbs, plus about ten more in the Detroit, Milwaukee, St. Louis, and Atlanta metropolitan areas. PrivateBancorp is opening a new branch in Kansas City, Missouri, and is considering expansion into selected Sun Belt cities in Arizona and Florida. The company is modeled after a traditional European private bank, placing emphasis on personal service.

PrivateBancorp lends mainly to businesses: Commercial mortgages account for about half of its loan portfolio; business operating loans add about 15%. The bank is increasing its focus on serving middle-market businesses. It also writes residential, consumer, and construction loans.

PrivateBancorp expanded into the affluent Detroit communities of Bloomfield Hills, Grosse Point, and Rochester with its 2005 acquisition of Bloomfield Hills Bancorp, the holding company for The Private Bank, which operates three branches, a trust and wealth management unit, and a mortgage banking subsidiary.

In 2006 the company acquired Piedmont Bancshares, the holding company for Piedmont Bank of Georgia, whose two branches in the Atlanta area have been renamed The PrivateBank.

Former LaSalle Bank CEO Larry Richman was named president and CEO of PrivateBancorp and PrivateBank in 2007, succeeding Ralph Mandell (who remained chairman).

EXECUTIVES

Chairman: Ralph B. Mandell, age 66, $1,265,000 pay
Co-Vice Chairman and Managing Director, The PrivateBank and Trust Company: Gary S. Collins, age 48, $530,000 pay
Co-Vice Chairman and Managing Director, The PrivateBank and Trust Company: Hugh H. McLean, age 48, $530,000 pay
President and CEO; President and CEO, The PrivateBank and Trust Company: Larry Richman
COO and Director; Chairman and CEO, The PrivateBank — Wisconsin: John B. (Jay) Williams, age 55
CFO and Corporate Secretary; CFO and Managing Director, The PrivateBank and Trust Company: Dennis L. Klaeser, age 49, $545,000 pay
General Counsel and Corporate Secretary; General Counsel, Corporate Secretary, and Managing Director, The PrivateBank and Trust Company: Christopher J. Zinski, age 44
Chief Credit Officer; Managing Director and Chief Credit Officer, The PrivateBank and Trust Company: James A. (Jim) Ruckstaetter, age 59
Chief Marketing Officer; Managing Director and Director of Marketing, The PrivateBank and Trust Company: Thomas N. (Tom) Castronovo, age 46
Director; President and CEO, Lodestar Investment Counsel; Managing Director, The PrivateBank and Trust Company: William A. Goldstein, age 67, $100,000 pay
Director; Chairman, CEO, and Managing Director, The PrivateBank — St. Louis: Richard C. Jensen, age 61
Chairman and CEO, The PrivateBank — Michigan: David T. Provost, age 53
CEO, Wealth Management; Managing Director and Senior Trust Officer, The PrivateBank and Trust Company: Wallace L. Head, age 56
Auditors: Ernst & Young LLP

LOCATIONS

HQ: PrivateBancorp, Inc.
70 West Madison, Chicago, IL 60602
Phone: 312-683-7100   **Fax:** 312-683-7111
Web: www.privatebancorp.com

PRODUCTS/OPERATIONS

2006 Sales

	$ mil.	% of total
Interest		
Loans, including fees	228.8	82
Securities	27.6	10
Other	0.7	—
Noninterest		
Wealth management	13.9	5
Other	9.7	3
Total	**280.7**	**100**

Selected Subsidiaries

The PrivateBank — Georgia
The PrivateBank Michigan
The PrivateBank and Trust Company
Lodestar Investment Counsel, LLC
The PrivateBank Mortgage Company, LLC
TrustCo, Company

COMPETITORS

CFS Bancorp	MB Financial
Citizens Republic Bancorp	Northern Trust
First Midwest Bancorp	Park Bancorp
Harris Bankcorp	Wintrust Financial

HISTORICAL FINANCIALS

Company Type: Public

Income Statement

FYE: December 31

	ASSETS ($ mil.)	NET INCOME ($ mil.)	INCOME AS % OF ASSETS	EMPLOYEES
12/06	4,261.4	37.8	0.9%	471
12/05	3,494.2	33.4	1.0%	386
12/04	2,535.8	27.0	1.1%	—
12/03	1,984.9	19.1	1.0%	—
12/02	1,543.4	11.0	0.7%	190
Annual Growth	28.9%	36.2%	—	25.5%

2006 Year-End Financials

Equity as % of assets: 7.0%
Return on assets: 1.0%
Return on equity: 14.2%
Long-term debt ($ mil.): 379.7
No. of shares (mil.): 22.0
Market value ($ mil.): 917.3
Dividends
  Yield: 0.6%
  Payout: 13.6%
Sales ($ mil.): 280.7
R&D as % of sales: —
Advertising as % of sales: —

Stock History

NASDAQ (GS): PVTB

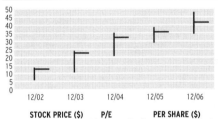

	STOCK PRICE ($) FY Close	P/E High/Low		PER SHARE ($) Earnings	Dividends	Book Value
12/06	41.63	27	20	1.76	0.24	13.48
12/05	35.57	24	19	1.58	0.14	11.22
12/04	32.23	27	16	1.30	0.09	9.51
12/03	22.65	22	10	1.06	0.08	16.94
12/02	12.62	19	9	0.71	0.05	11.56
Annual Growth	34.8%	—	—	25.5%	48.0%	3.9%

Prospect Capital

Prospect Capital (formerly Prospect Energy) is a business development concern focused on prospecting for riches in underperforming energy-related businesses. The corporation invests in companies that have annual revenues of less than $250 million, and in transaction sizes no greater than $100 million. These targeted middle-market companies are either privately held or thinly traded public companies. To protect its assets, Prospect Capital avoids directly investing in any energy companies exclusively engaged in oil and gas exploration, or in speculative development and trading in oil, gas, and/or other commodities. The company was formed in 1988 by former senior managers of Merrill Lynch.

EXECUTIVES

Chairman and CEO: John F. Barry III, age 55
President, COO, and Director: M. Grier Eliasek, age 34
CFO and Chief Compliance Officer: William E. Vastardis, age 52
SVP Administration: Robert F. Kleinman
SVP Administration: Samir Mohin
Managing Director and Head of Oil and Gas Investments: David L. Belzer
Operations, Finance, and Investor Relations: Daria Becker
Energy Finance: James A. Flores
Investment Banking: Bart J. de Bie
Investment Origination and Execution: W. Montgomery Cook
Investment Management and Research: Amir Friedman
Private Equity and Restructuring: Robert S. Everett, age 43
Private Equity and Investment Banking: Mark Hull
Attorney and Portfolio Manager: Kurt W. Rieke
Auditors: BDO Seidman, LLP

LOCATIONS

HQ: Prospect Capital Corporation
10 E. 40th St., Ste. 4400, New York, NY 10016
Phone: 212-448-0702   **Fax:** 212-448-9652
Web: www.prospectstreet.com

HISTORICAL FINANCIALS

Company Type: Public

Income Statement

FYE: June 30

	REVENUE ($ mil.)	NET INCOME ($ mil.)	NET PROFIT MARGIN	EMPLOYEES
6/07	40.7	16.7	41.0%	19
6/06	21.2	12.9	60.8%	12
6/05	8.1	8.8	108.6%	—
Annual Growth	124.2%	37.8%	—	58.3%

2007 Year-End Financials

Debt ratio: —
Return on equity: 8.2%
Cash ($ mil.): 41.8
Current ratio: —
Long-term debt ($ mil.): —
No. of shares (mil.): 19.9
Dividends
  Yield: 8.8%
  Payout: 145.3%
Market value ($ mil.): 348.5
R&D as % of sales: —
Advertising as % of sales: —

Stock History

NASDAQ (GM): PSEC

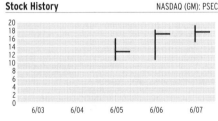

	STOCK PRICE ($) FY Close	P/E High/Low		PER SHARE ($) Earnings	Dividends	Book Value
6/07	17.47	18	14	1.06	1.54	15.04
6/06	16.99	10	6	1.83	0.64	15.31
6/05	12.60	13	9	1.24	—	14.60
Annual Growth	17.8%	—	—	(7.5%)	140.6%	1.5%

Prosperity Bancshares

Feeling prosperous? Prosperity Bancshares wants to help you manage your riches. The company operates about 90 Prosperity Bank branches in and around major Texas cities, as well as eastern and southern portions of the state. The bank offers traditional deposit and cash management services. Commercial mortgages make up the largest segment (more than 33%) of the company's loan portfolio, which also includes residential mortgage, construction, home equity, business, and agricultural loans. The acquisitive company has been buying up small banks in Texas. It bought Texas United Bancshares and the single-branch Bank of Novasota in 2007 after buying SNB Bancshares the year before.

In early 2008 Prosperity Bancshares acquired six branches in Houston from Banco Popular North America. Those deals came after the company purchased South Texas' FirstCapital Bankers and Grapeland Bancshares in 2005. All told, the company has bought more than 15 banks since 2000.

EXECUTIVES

Chairman and CEO: David Zalman, age 50, $514,600 pay
Vice Chairman: H. E. (Tim) Timanus Jr., age 62, $329,600 pay
Vice Chairman: D. Michael (Mike) Hunter, age 66
President, COO, and Director:
  James D. (Dan) Rollins III, age 48, $340,400 pay
CFO; EVP and CFO, Prosperity Bank: David Hollaway, age 51, $244,165 pay
Chairman, Austin Area Banking Centers:
  Edward Z. (Eddie) Safady
Chairman, South Texas Area Banking Centers:
  Steve Hipes
President, South Texas Area Banking Centers:
  Bob Kuhn
President, Waugh Drive Banking Center and Chief Credit Officer, Prosperity Bank: Chris Bagley
General Counsel; Vice Chairman and General Counsel, Prosperity Bank: Peter E. Fisher, age 60, $217,400 pay
Auditors: Deloitte & Touche LLP

LOCATIONS

HQ: Prosperity Bancshares, Inc.
  4295 San Felipe, Houston, TX 77027
Phone: 713-693-9300   **Fax:** 713-693-9360
Web: www.prosperitybanktx.com

PRODUCTS/OPERATIONS

2006 Sales

	$ mil.	% of total
Interest		
Loans, including fees	157.4	59
Securities	72.6	27
Other	1.7	1
Noninterest		
Service charges on deposit accounts	27.4	10
Other	6.6	3
Total	**265.7**	**100**

COMPETITORS

Amegy Corporation
Bank of America
Compass Bancshares
Cullen/Frost Bankers
JPMorgan Chase
Sterling Bancshares
Wells Fargo

HISTORICAL FINANCIALS

Company Type: Public

Income Statement

	ASSETS ($ mil.)	NET INCOME ($ mil.)	INCOME AS % OF ASSETS	EMPLOYEES
12/06	4,586.8	61.7	1.3%	908
12/05	3,586.0	47.9	1.3%	859
12/04	2,697.2	34.7	1.3%	—
12/03	2,398.7	26.5	1.1%	—
12/02	1,822.3	21.3	1.2%	457
Annual Growth	**26.0%**	**30.5%**	**—**	**18.7%**

FYE: December 31

2006 Year-End Financials

Equity as % of assets: 14.5%
Return on assets: 1.5%
Return on equity: 10.9%
Long-term debt ($ mil.): 126.9
No. of shares (mil.): 32.8
Market value ($ mil.): 1,131.7
Dividends
  Yield: 1.2%
  Payout: 21.1%
Sales ($ mil.): 265.7
R&D as % of sales: —
Advertising as % of sales: —

Stock History

NASDAQ (GS): PRSP

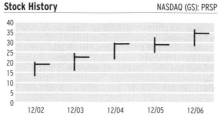

	STOCK PRICE ($) FY Close	P/E High/Low		PER SHARE ($) Earnings	Dividends	Book Value
12/06	34.51	19	15	1.94	0.41	20.26
12/05	28.74	18	14	1.77	0.35	16.70
12/04	29.21	19	14	1.59	0.15	12.32
12/03	22.64	18	12	1.36	0.25	10.49
12/02	19.00	16	11	1.22	0.22	8.19
Annual Growth	**16.1%**	**—**	**—**	**12.3%**	**16.8%**	**25.4%**

Providence Service

Providence Service Corporation contracts with state and local government agencies to manage social service programs throughout the US and in Canada. The company provides behavioral health and counseling services to individuals, families, and at-risk students. Providence Service Corporation is able to save its government clients money by providing care at the patient's home or school. The company also licenses family foster homes, recruits and trains prospective foster parents, and provides behavioral health services to foster children. In addition, Providence Service Corporation offers case management, benefit screening, correctional services, and administrative support.

Providence Service Corporation's Home and Community Based Services segment (behavioral health services) generates about 80% of the company's revenue.

The company has been growing by expanding its services and strategically acquiring businesses in new markets. With the acquisition of Maple Star Nevada and Maple Services LLC in 2005, Providence Service Corporation expanded into Colorado, Nevada, and Oregon. In 2006 the company purchased A to Z In-Home Tutoring. It

has also acquired the Correctional Services Business of MAXIMUS; the unit provides privatized probation services in five states.

Getting folks to the services it provides is another piece of Providence Service's expansion plan. In 2007 it acquired non-emergency transportation broker LogistiCare.

It also expanded into Canada with the acquisition of WCG International Consultants, a company that manages welfare-to-work training and employee placement initiatives throughout British Columbia.

EXECUTIVES

Chairman and CEO: Fletcher Jay McCusker, age 57, $210,000 pay
COO: Craig A. Norris, age 39, $195,833 pay
EVP and General Counsel: Fred D. Furman, age 58, $195,000 pay (prior to title change)
EVP Program Services: Mary J. Shea, age 51
VP, CFO, Secretary, and Treasurer: Michael N. Deitch, age 50, $179,167 pay
CIO: Mike Hill
COO Eastern Region: Michael Fidgeon
VP Clinical Services, Eastern Region: Tasha Walsh
VP Development, Eastern Region: Betty Dixon
Director Corporate Integrity and Communications:
  Michelle Pitot
Director Human Resources: Janet McGee
Director Investor and Public Relations: Kate Blute
Auditors: McGladrey & Pullen, LLP

LOCATIONS

HQ: The Providence Service Corporation
  5524 E. 4th St., Tucson, AZ 85711
Phone: 520-747-6600   **Fax:** 520-747-6605
Web: www.provcorp.com

PRODUCTS/OPERATIONS

2006 Sales

	$ mil.	% of total
Home & community-based services	152.1	79
Foster care services	21.9	11
Management fees	17.9	10
Total	**191.9**	**100**

COMPETITORS

Cornell Companies
Jewish Board of Family and Children's Services
MAXIMUS
Premier Behavioral Solutions
Psychiatric Solutions
Res-Care
Salvation Army

HISTORICAL FINANCIALS

Company Type: Public

Income Statement

	REVENUE ($ mil.)	NET INCOME ($ mil.)	NET PROFIT MARGIN	EMPLOYEES
12/06	191.9	9.4	4.9%	6,828
12/05	145.7	9.4	6.5%	4,930
12/04	97.0	7.1	7.3%	—
12/03	59.3	2.7	4.6%	—
12/02	41.8	(3.9)	—	—
Annual Growth	**46.4%**	**—**	**—**	**38.5%**

FYE: December 31

2006 Year-End Financials

Debt ratio: 0.4%
Return on equity: 7.8%
Cash ($ mil.): 43.0
Current ratio: 3.35
Long-term debt ($ mil.): 0.6
No. of shares (mil.): 12.2
Dividends
  Yield: —
  Payout: —
Market value ($ mil.): 305.9
R&D as % of sales: —
Advertising as % of sales: —

Stock History

NASDAQ (GS): PRSC

	STOCK PRICE ($) FY Close	P/E High/Low		PER SHARE ($) Earnings	Dividends	Book Value
12/06	25.13	43	28	0.80	—	13.07
12/05	28.79	35	20	0.95	—	8.27
12/04	20.98	29	20	0.76	—	6.81
12/03	16.33	—	—	(0.25)	—	5.24
Annual Growth	15.5%	—	—	23.0%	—	—

PSB Holdings

PSB Holdings thinks it offers Pretty Smart Banking for the businesses and individuals of Connecticut's Windham and New London counties. The holding company owns Putnam Savings Bank, a thrift with about a half-dozen banking locations. The bank offers standard deposit products and services, including checking and savings accounts, merchant and check cards, CDs, and IRAs. It largely uses funds from deposits to write real estate loans: Residential mortgages account for more than 70% of the company's loan portfolio; commercial mortgages account for nearly 25%. Mutual holding company Putnam Bancorp owns about 55% of PSB Holdings.

EXECUTIVES

Chairman and CEO, PSB Holdings and Putnam Savings Bank: Thomas A. Borner, age 53, $78,368 pay
President, CFO, and Director; President and CFO, Putnam Savings Bank: Robert J. Halloran Jr., age 53, $117,945 pay
SVP and Senior Retail Loan Officer, Putnam Savings Bank: John F. LaFountain
SVP and Senior Commercial Loan Officer, Putnam Savings Bank: Anthony J. (Tony) Serio
SVP and Branch Administrator, Putnam Savings Bank: Lynn K. Brodeur
VP and Controller, Putnam Savings Bank: Sandra J. (Sandy) Maciag
Auditors: Snyder & Haller, PC

LOCATIONS

HQ: PSB Holdings, Inc.
40 Main St., Putnam, CT 06260
Phone: 860-928-6501   **Fax:** 860-928-2147
Web: www.putnamsavings.com

PRODUCTS/OPERATIONS

2007 Sales

	$ mil.	% of total
Interest		
Loans	14.0	49
Investments	11.4	41
Noninterest		
Service fees	2.3	8
Other	0.5	2
Total	**28.2**	**100**

COMPETITORS

Bank of America
Citizens Financial Group
Liberty Bank
NewAlliance Bancshares
People's United Financial
SI Financial
TD Banknorth
Webster Financial

HISTORICAL FINANCIALS

Company Type: Public

Income Statement
FYE: June 30

	ASSETS ($ mil.)	NET INCOME ($ mil.)	INCOME AS % OF ASSETS	EMPLOYEES
6/07	491.2	1.9	0.4%	117
6/06	474.4	2.1	0.4%	116
6/05	337.6	1.3	0.4%	91
6/04	279.1	1.5	0.5%	—
Annual Growth	20.7%	8.2%	—	13.4%

2007 Year-End Financials

Equity as % of assets: 10.4%
Return on assets: 0.4%
Return on equity: 3.8%
Long-term debt ($ mil.): 143.1
No. of shares (mil.): 6.8
Market value ($ mil.): 71.7
Dividends
  Yield: 1.7%
  Payout: 64.3%
Sales ($ mil.): 28.2
R&D as % of sales: —
Advertising as % of sales: —

Stock History
NASDAQ (GM): PSBH

	STOCK PRICE ($) FY Close	P/E High/Low		PER SHARE ($) Earnings	Dividends	Book Value
6/07	10.58	41	36	0.28	0.18	7.56
6/06	10.63	38	33	0.30	0.22	7.18
6/05	10.25	—	—	—	0.10	7.64
Annual Growth	1.6%	—	—	(6.7%)	34.2%	(0.5%)

Pulaski Financial

Community-oriented banking is the push at Pulaski. Pulaski Financial is the holding company for Pulaski Bank, which provides financial services to residents and businesses throughout the St. Louis and Kansas City metropolitan areas through around 10 branches. Its deposit products include certificates of deposit, retirement savings plans, and checking, savings, NOW, and money market accounts. The bank's loan portfolio consisting of residential mortgages, construction and development loans, commercial real estate, commercial loans, and consumer and other loans. Through subsidiaries Pulaski offers title insurance, insurance and annuities, and fixed-income investment and trading.

EXECUTIVES

Chairman: Lee S. Wielansky, age 55
Chairman Emeritus: Walter A. Donius
President, CEO, and Director, Pulaski Financial and Pulaski Bank: William A. (Bill) Donius, age 49, $477,127 pay
CFO: Ramsey K. Hamadi, age 38, $207,150 pay
President, Commercial Lending and Banking, Pulaski Bank: Brian J. Björkman
President, Mortgage Lending Division: Matthew A. (Matt) Locke
President, Pulaski Financial and Pulaski Bank: W. Thomas Reeves, age 53, $118,459 pay
Regional President, Pulaski Bank: Paul Grosse
SVP Commercial Lending, Pulaski Bank: Mark A. Greenley, age 41
SVP and Director of Human Resources, Pulaski Bank: Lisa K. Simpson
SVP Commercial Lending, Pulaski Bank: Rita M. Kuster
SVP Mortgage Lending Operations, Pulaski Bank: Jerry W. Thompson
SVP Retail Banking, Pulaski Bank: Bret L. Mayberry
Corporate Secretary: Christine A. (Chris) Munro
Auditors: KPMG LLP

LOCATIONS

HQ: Pulaski Financial Corp.
12300 Olive Blvd., Creve Coeur, MO 63141
Phone: 314-878-2210   **Fax:** 314-878-7130
Web: www.pulaskibankstl.com

Pulaski Financial has offices in Chesterfield, Florissant, Kansas City, O'Fallon, St. Charles, and St. Louis, Missouri, and Overland Park, Kansas.

PRODUCTS/OPERATIONS

2006 Sales

	$ mil.	% of total
Interest		
Loans	52.6	79
Securities & other	1.3	2
Noninterest		
Mortgage revenues	4.0	6
Retail banking fees	3.0	4
Other	5.8	9
Total	**66.7**	**100**

COMPETITORS

Bank of America	Marshall & Ilsley
Central Bancompany	National City
Commerce Bancshares	Regions Financial
Enterprise Financial Services	Stupp Bros.
	UMB Financial
First Banks	U.S. Bancorp

HISTORICAL FINANCIALS

Company Type: Public

Income Statement
FYE: September 30

	ASSETS ($ mil.)	NET INCOME ($ mil.)	INCOME AS % OF ASSETS	EMPLOYEES
9/06	962.5	9.8	1.0%	361
9/05	789.9	7.5	0.9%	327
9/04	637.9	5.8	0.9%	258
9/03	401.4	5.8	1.4%	255
9/02	369.3	4.2	1.1%	175
Annual Growth	27.1%	23.6%	—	19.8%

2006 Year-End Financials

Equity as % of assets: 7.9%
Return on assets: 1.1%
Return on equity: 15.8%
Long-term debt ($ mil.): 22.9
No. of shares (mil.): 9.9
Market value ($ mil.): 164.4
Dividends
  Yield: 2.0%
  Payout: 31.7%
Sales ($ mil.): 66.7
R&D as % of sales: —
Advertising as % of sales: —

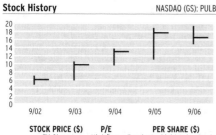

	STOCK PRICE ($) FY Close	P/E High/Low		Earnings	PER SHARE ($) Dividends	Book Value
9/06	16.53	19	15	1.01	0.32	7.62
9/05	17.70	22	13	0.85	0.20	5.72
9/04	13.03	20	15	0.67	0.18	7.47
9/03	9.76	15	9	0.67	0.09	6.51
9/02	6.00	14	10	0.49	0.10	11.83
Annual Growth	28.8%	—	—	19.8%	33.7%	(10.4%)

QCR Holdings

Quad City is muscling in on the community banking scene in the Midwest. QCR Holdings is the holding company for Quad City Bank and Trust, Cedar Rapids Bank and Trust, Rockford Bank and Trust, and First Wisconsin Bank and Trust. Together, the banks have about 10 offices serving the Quad City area of Illinois and Iowa, as well as the communities of Cedar Rapids, Iowa; Rockford, Illinois; and Milwaukee. The banks offer traditional deposit products and services and concentrate their lending activities on local businesses: Commercial loans and leases make up nearly half of the loan portfolio; commercial real estate loans add another 35%.

QCR Holdings' Quad City Bancard provides credit card processing services. Its M2 Lease Funds leases machinery and equipment to commercial and industrial businesses. QCR Holdings acquired its 80% stake in the leasing company in 2005 as part of a strategy to strengthen the banks' commercial product offerings. QCR Holdings has grown by launching operations in new geographic markets and then building upon them. In 2007 the company acquired a Wisconsin bank charter with three branches (two of which were sold) to enter the Milwaukee metro banking market; the company already had a loan production office there.

Jeffrey Gendell's Tontine Financial Partners owns more than 5% of QCR Holdings.

EXECUTIVES

Chairman: James J. Brownson, age 61
Vice Chairman: Michael A. Bauer, age 58, $220,500 pay (prior to title change)
President, CEO, and Director; Chairman, Quad City Bank and Trust: Douglas M. (Doug) Hultquist, age 52, $220,500 pay
EVP, CFO, and Secretary; President and CEO, Quad City Bancard: Todd A. Gipple, $212,236 pay (prior to promotion)
SVP and Senior Lending Officer: John Bradley
SVP and Human Resources Manager: Jill DeKeyser
SVP, IT: Kathy Francque
SVP, Marketing and Communications: Julie Carstensen
Director; Chief Lending Officer; President and CEO, Cedar Rapids Bank & Trust: Larry J. Helling, age 50

President and CEO, Quad City Bank & Trust: John H. Anderson
President and CEO, Rockford Bank and Trust: Thomas Budd
Director; Chairman, Quad City Bank & Trust: Mark C. Kilmer, age 48
Auditors: McGladrey & Pullen, LLP

LOCATIONS

HQ: QCR Holdings, Inc.
3551 7th St., Ste. 204, Moline, IL 61265
Phone: 309-736-3580 **Fax:** 309-743-7705
Web: www.qcbt.com

PRODUCTS/OPERATIONS

2006 Sales

	$ mil.	% of total
Interest		
Loans	60.1	74
Securities & other	8.7	11
Trust department fees	3.1	4
Merchant card fees	1.9	2
Deposit service fees	1.9	2
Investment advisory & management fees	1.2	2
Other	4.0	5
Total	**80.9**	**100**

2006 Sales By Segment

	% of total
Commercial banking	
Quad City Bank & Trust	57
Cedar Rapids Bank & Trust	25
Rockford Bank & Trust	6
Leasing	4
Trust management	4
Credit card processing	4
Total	**100**

COMPETITORS

AMCORE Financial
Bank of America
Blackhawk Bancorp
Corus Bankshares
First Business Financial
First Midwest Bancorp
First National of Nebraska
IndyMac Bancorp
MidWestOne
National City
U.S. Bancorp
Wachovia
Washington Mutual
Wells Fargo

HISTORICAL FINANCIALS

Company Type: Public

Income Statement				FYE: December 31
	ASSETS ($ mil.)	NET INCOME ($ mil.)	INCOME AS % OF ASSETS	EMPLOYEES
12/06	1,271.7	2.8	0.2%	351
12/05	1,042.6	4.8	0.5%	305
12/04	870.1	5.2	0.6%	—
12/03	710.0	5.5	0.8%	—
12/02	604.6	3.2	0.5%	—
Annual Growth	20.4%	(3.3%)	—	15.1%

2006 Year-End Financials

Equity as % of assets: 5.6%
Return on assets: 0.2%
Return on equity: 4.5%
Long-term debt ($ mil.): 39.8
No. of shares (mil.): 4.6
Market value ($ mil.): 80.5
Dividends
  Yield: 0.5%
  Payout: 14.0%
Sales ($ mil.): 80.9
R&D as % of sales: —
Advertising as % of sales: —

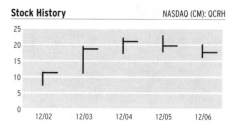

	STOCK PRICE ($) FY Close	P/E High/Low		Earnings	PER SHARE ($) Dividends	Book Value
12/06	17.66	35	28	0.57	0.08	15.54
12/05	19.70	22	17	1.04	0.08	12.02
12/04	21.00	18	14	1.20	0.04	11.29
12/03	18.67	15	9	1.27	0.07	14.92
12/02	11.27	15	10	0.75	0.03	13.24
Annual Growth	11.9%	—	—	(6.6%)	27.8%	4.1%

Quality Systems

Quality Systems raises doctors' IQs when it comes to health care information technology. The company provides information management software for medical and dental practices, ambulatory care centers, community health centers, and medical and dental schools. Its NextGen Healthcare Information Systems division, which focuses on medical practices, makes electronic medical records and practice management systems for managing patient information, appointments, billing, referrals, and insurance claims. Through its QSI division, the company offers practice management software for dental and niche medical practices.

While Quality Systems had its start as a provider of dental practice software, the company has been growing through its NextGen medical practice software division.

EXECUTIVES

Chairman: Sheldon Razin, age 70
President, CEO, and Director: Louis E. (Lou) Silverman, age 48, $656,817 pay
CFO and Secretary: Paul A. Holt, age 41, $249,154 pay
Director; President, NextGen Healthcare Information Systems Division: Patrick B. Cline, age 46, $665,224 pay
Auditors: Grant Thornton LLP

LOCATIONS

HQ: Quality Systems, Inc.
18191 Von Karman Ave., Ste. 450, Irvine, CA 92612
Phone: 949-255-2600 **Fax:** 949-255-2605
Web: www.qsii.com

PRODUCTS/OPERATIONS

2007 Sales

	% of total
System sales	52
Maintenance, EDI & other services	48
Total	**100**

2007 Sales

	% of total
NextGen division	89
QSI division	11
Total	**100**

Selected Products

Clinical data management software
Dental charting software
Dental practice management systems
Internet-based consumer health portal
Medical records storage software
Medical practice management systems

COMPETITORS

AMICAS
CareCentric
Cerner
CPSI
Eclipsys
GE Healthcare
Global Med
HLTH Corp.
McKesson
MEDITECH
Misys Healthcare
QuadraMed

HISTORICAL FINANCIALS

Company Type: Public

Income Statement

FYE: March 31

	REVENUE ($ mil.)	NET INCOME ($ mil.)	NET PROFIT MARGIN	EMPLOYEES
3/07	157.2	33.2	21.1%	661
3/06	119.3	23.3	19.5%	538
3/05	89.0	16.1	18.1%	418
3/04	70.9	10.4	14.7%	—
3/03	54.8	7.0	12.8%	—
Annual Growth	30.1%	47.6%	—	25.8%

2007 Year-End Financials

Debt ratio: —
Return on equity: 40.6%
Cash ($ mil.): 60.0
Current ratio: 2.36
Long-term debt ($ mil.): —
No. of shares (mil.): 27.1

Dividends
  Yield: 2.5%
  Payout: 82.6%
Market value ($ mil.): 1,084.9
R&D as % of sales: —
Advertising as % of sales: —

Stock History

NASDAQ (GS): QSII

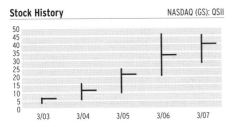

	STOCK PRICE ($) FY Close	P/E High/Low		PER SHARE ($) Earnings	Dividends	Book Value
3/07	40.00	38	23	1.21	1.00	3.36
3/06	33.10	54	24	0.85	0.88	2.71
3/05	21.17	40	16	0.61	0.75	4.78
3/04	11.36	38	14	0.40	—	9.64
3/03	6.38	24	13	0.28	—	7.73
Annual Growth	58.2%	—	—	44.2%	15.5%	(18.8%)

Quicksilver Gas Services

It may not be the fastest process ever but Quicksilver Gas Services does its best. The company gathers and processes natural gas and natural gas liquids from the Barnett Shale formation near Fort Worth, Texas, for Quicksilver Resources, its parent (which has proved reserves of 704 Bcfe and average production of 34.7 MMcf/d annually). The company's assets include a pipeline and a processing plant with 200 MMcf/d capacity; plans for the IPO proceeds include another processing unit at the existing plant, extensions to the existing pipeline, and pipelines in other drilling areas in Texas. Quicksilver Gas Services was founded in 2004; Quicksilver Resources owns about 75% of it.

EXECUTIVES

President and CEO: Thomas F. (Toby) Darden, age 53
EVP and COO: Paul J. Cook, age 50
SVP and General Counsel: John C. (Chris) Cirone, age 58
SVP, CFO, and Director: Philip W. Cook
Auditors: Deloitte & Touche LLP

LOCATIONS

HQ: Quicksilver Gas Services LP
  777 W. Rosedale St., Ste. 300, Fort Worth, TX 76104
Phone: 817-665-5000   **Fax:** 817-665-5004

PRODUCTS/OPERATIONS

2006 Sales

	$ mil.	% of total
Processing (for parent)	7.3	52
Processing	0.1	1
Gathering and transportation (for parent)	6.4	46
Gathering and transportation	0.1	1
Total	**13.9**	**100**

COMPETITORS

Crosstex Energy
DCP Midstream Partners
Energy Transfer Equity
Enterprise Products
Penn Virginia
Plains All American Pipeline
Regency Energy
Southern Natural Gas
Texas Gas Transmission

HISTORICAL FINANCIALS

Company Type: Public

Income Statement

FYE: December 31

	REVENUE ($ mil.)	NET INCOME ($ mil.)	NET PROFIT MARGIN	EMPLOYEES
12/06	13.9	2.4	17.3%	32
12/05	4.9	1.6	32.7%	—
12/04	0.0	0.0	—	—
Annual Growth	—	—	—	—

2006 Year-End Financials

Debt ratio: 0.0%
Return on equity: 2.7%
Cash ($ mil.): 2.8

Current ratio: 1.62
Long-term debt ($ mil.): 0.0

Net Income History

NYSE Arca: KGS

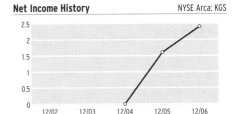

Quicksilver Resources

With mercurial speed, Quicksilver Resources seeks to turn oil and gas finds into profits, primarily through acquiring the assets of rival oil and gas firms. The independent exploration and production company owns assets in Indiana, Kentucky, Michigan, Montana, Texas, and Wyoming, and in Alberta, Canada. Quicksilver Resources has proved reserves (located primarily in Michigan and Alberta) of 1.6 trillion cu. ft. of natural gas equivalent. In 2007 BreitBurn Energy Partners acquired Quicksilver Resources' midstream assets for $750 million. Chairman Thomas Darden, CEO Glenn Darden, and other Darden family members control 31% of the company.

The company is recognized as a leading developer and producer of unconventional natural gas reserves, including shale gas, coal bed methane, and tight sand gas.

EXECUTIVES

Chairman: Thomas F. (Toby) Darden, age 53, $594,840 pay
President, CEO, and Director: Glenn M. Darden, age 51, $594,840 pay
EVP Operations: Paul Cook, age 51
SVP and CFO: Philip W. Cook
SVP General Counsel, and Secretary:
  John C. (Chris) Cirone, age 58
SVP and COO, MGV Energy: Dana W. Johnson, age 45
VP Finance: D. Wayne Blair, age 50
VP Human Resources and Director: Anne Darden Self, age 49
VP Engineering Technology: William S. (Bill) Buckler, age 46, $338,000 pay
VP Treasurer: MarLu Hiller, age 45
VP Investor Relations and Corporate Planning:
  Rick Buterbaugh
VP, Chief Accounting Officer, and Controller:
  John C. Regan, age 37
Director Investor Relations: Diane Weaver
Auditors: Deloitte & Touche LLP

LOCATIONS

HQ: Quicksilver Resources Inc.
  777 W. Rosedale St., Ste. 300, Fort Worth, TX 76104
Phone: 817-665-5000   **Fax:** 817-665-5004
Web: www.qrinc.com

Quicksilver Resources has operations in Indiana, Kentucky, Michigan, Montana, Texas, and Wyoming, and in Alberta, Canada.

2006 Sales

	$ mil.	% of total
US	273.7	70
Canada	116.7	30
Total	**390.4**	**100**

PRODUCTS/OPERATIONS

2006 Sales

	$ mil.	% of total
Natural gas	322.4	83
Oil	35.2	9
Natural gas liquids	30.0	8
Other	2.8	—
Total	**390.4**	**100**

Selected Subsidiaries and Affiliates

Beaver Creek Pipeline, L.L.C. (50%)
GTG Pipeline Corporation
Mercury Michigan, Inc.
Quicksilver Resources Canada Inc.
Terra Energy Ltd

COMPETITORS

Abraxas Petroleum
Anadarko Petroleum
BP
ConocoPhillips
Devon Energy
Exxon Mobil
Noble Energy
Royal Dutch Shell
Swift Energy

HISTORICAL FINANCIALS

Company Type: Public

Income Statement

FYE: December 31

	REVENUE ($ mil.)	NET INCOME ($ mil.)	NET PROFIT MARGIN	EMPLOYEES
12/06	390.4	93.7	24.0%	494
12/05	310.5	87.4	28.1%	400
12/04	179.7	31.3	17.4%	—
12/03	140.9	16.2	11.5%	—
12/02	122.2	13.8	11.3%	247
Annual Growth	**33.7%**	**61.4%**	**—**	**18.9%**

2006 Year-End Financials

Debt ratio: 159.7%
Return on equity: 19.5%
Cash ($ mil.): 69.4
Current ratio: 0.86
Long-term debt ($ mil.): 919.1
No. of shares (mil.): 77.6
Dividends
  Yield: —
  Payout: —
Market value ($ mil.): 2,839.5
R&D as % of sales: —
Advertising as % of sales: —

Stock History

NYSE: KWK

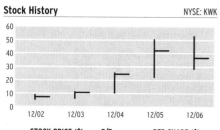

	STOCK PRICE ($) FY Close	P/E High/Low		PER SHARE ($) Earnings	Dividends	Book Value
12/06	36.59	46	25	1.15	—	7.42
12/05	42.01	46	21	1.08	—	5.04
12/04	24.52	41	17	0.62	—	6.07
12/03	10.77	47	28	0.24	—	9.78
12/02	7.48	39	25	0.23	—	6.11
Annual Growth	**48.7%**	**—**	**—**	**49.5%**	**—**	**5.0%**

Rackable Systems

Rackable Systems provides rack-mounted computer servers designed for large-scale data center deployments. Rackable aims its products at IT system administrators looking to replace servers running the UNIX operating system with new equipment operating under Linux or Windows. The company uses both AMD and Intel microprocessors in designing its servers. Rackable Systems relies on contract electronics manufacturers such as Sanmina-SCI and E-Cycle to produce its servers. The company targets enterprises in a wider range of sectors, including technology, Internet and e-commerce, financial services, government, and electronics.

Rackable counts Microsoft (34% of sales in 2006), Yahoo! (26%) Amazon.com, Deutsche Bank), Lawrence Livermore National Laboratory, and Toshiba America Electronic Components among its customers.

Rackable acquired Terrascale Technologies, a specialist in grid and cluster computing products, for $38 million in cash in 2006.

EXECUTIVES

Chairman: Ronald D. Verdoorn, age 55
President, CEO, and Director: Mark J. Barrenechea, age 42
CFO: Madhu Ranganathan, age 42
CTO: Giovanni Coglitore, age 39
EVP RapidScale: Gautham Sastri, age 41
EVP Worldwide Sales and Marketing: Carl E. Boisvert
SVP Corporate Development, General Counsel, and Secretary: Maurice Leibenstern
SVP and Chief Products Officer: Tony Gaughan
VP, Corporate Development, General Counsel, and Secretary: William P. (Bill) Garvey, age 42
VP, Engineering: Robert (Bob) Weisickle, age 54
VP, Human Resources: Jennifer L. Pratt
VP, Information Technology: Dominic Martinelli
VP, Marketing: Colette LaForce, age 33
Auditors: Deloitte & Touche LLP

LOCATIONS

HQ: Rackable Systems, Inc.
46600 Landing Pkwy., Fremont, CA 94538
Phone: 510-933-8300   **Fax:** 408-321-0293
Web: www.rackable.com

2006 Sales

	$ mil.	% of total
US	328.4	91
Other countries	32.0	9
Total	**360.4**	**100**

PRODUCTS/OPERATIONS

2006 Sales

	$ mil.	% of total
Computer servers	325.5	90
Storage systems	34.9	10
Total	**360.4**	**100**

2006 Sales

	$ mil.	% of total
Foundation computer servers	300.2	83
Foundation storage servers	34.9	10
Scale Out computer servers	25.3	7
Total	**360.4**	**100**

Selected Products

Foundation Series (computer servers, data storage systems)
Scale Out Series (general-purpose computer servers)

COMPETITORS

Dell	Linux Networx
Egenera	NetApp
EMC	Sun Microsystems
Hewlett-Packard	Super Micro Computer
Hitachi Data Systems	Verari Systems
IBM	

HISTORICAL FINANCIALS

Company Type: Public

Income Statement

FYE: December 31

	REVENUE ($ mil.)	NET INCOME ($ mil.)	NET PROFIT MARGIN	EMPLOYEES
12/06	360.4	11.5	3.2%	286
12/05	215.0	8.5	4.0%	174
12/04	109.7	(55.4)	—	—
12/03	52.9	(52.7)	—	—
12/02	27.6	(0.6)	—	31
Annual Growth	**90.1%**	**—**	**—**	**74.3%**

2006 Year-End Financials

Debt ratio: —
Return on equity: 5.2%
Cash ($ mil.): 160.5
Current ratio: 4.07
Long-term debt ($ mil.): —
No. of shares (mil.): 28.2
Dividends
  Yield: —
  Payout: —
Market value ($ mil.): 874.3
R&D as % of sales: —
Advertising as % of sales: —

Stock History

NASDAQ (GS): RACK

	STOCK PRICE ($) FY Close	P/E High/Low		PER SHARE ($) Earnings	Dividends	Book Value
12/06	30.97	140	47	0.40	—	11.18
12/05	28.48	63	24	0.47	—	5.35
Annual Growth	**8.7%**	**—**	**—**	**(14.9%)**	**—**	**109.0%**

Radiant Systems

Radiant Systems helps businesses provide shining service. Its touch-screen point-of-sale systems are used in cinemas, gas stations, and restaurants. The company's hardware and software link point-of-sale data with centralized merchandising functions like ordering and scheduling. Radiant also offers consulting and systems integration services. Radiant, which has traditionally charged one-time fees for its systems, has shifted toward a subscription-based model. Radiant Systems counts 7-Eleven, BP, ConocoPhillips, Exxon Mobil, Kroger, and The Home Depot among its customers.

The company acquired the assets of Synchronics, a developer of business management and point-of-sale software, for around $27 million in cash and stock in 2006.

The company bought E-Needs, which supplies software for running movie-theater chains, in 2004. It widened its offerings in the hospitality industry with the purchase of point-of-sale software provider Aloha Technologies in 2004, and back-office software developer MenuLink Computer Solutions in 2005.

EXECUTIVES

Chairman and CTO: Alon Goren, age 41, $382,500 pay
CEO and Director: John H. Heyman, age 45, $522,500 pay
COO: Andrew S. (Andy) Heyman, age 43, $476,153 pay
CFO: Mark E. Haidet, age 39, $312,330 pay
Chief Marketing Officer: Scott Kingsfield
VP International Sales: David Griffin
President Hardware: Carlyle M. Taylor, age 52
President Retail and Entertainment: Chris Lybeer
President Global Petroleum and Convenience Retail: Mark Schoen
President Hospitality: Paul Langenbahn
VP Human Resources: Keith Hicks
Controller: Robert R. Ellis
Investor Relations Manager: Sara Ford
Auditors: Deloitte & Touche LLP

LOCATIONS

HQ: Radiant Systems, Inc.
3925 Brookside Pkwy., Alpharetta, GA 30022
Phone: 770-576-6000   **Fax:** 770-754-7790
Web: www.radiantsystems.com

2006 Sales

	$ mil.	% of total
US	183.9	83
Other countries	38.4	17
Total	**222.3**	**100**

PRODUCTS/OPERATIONS

2006 Sales

	$ mil.	% of total
Systems	130.2	59
Services	92.1	41
Total	**222.3**	**100**

2006 Sales

	$ mil.	% of total
Hospitality	141.2	64
Retail	78.5	35
Other	2.6	1
Total	**222.3**	**100**

Selected Products

Kiosks
Point-of-sale terminals
Peripherals
Servers

COMPETITORS

Accenture	IBM Global Services
Alphameric	Ingenico
CAM Commerce Solutions	JDA Software
Capgemini	Matsushita Electric
Clarity Commerce	MICROS Systems
Danaher	NCR
Dell	PAR Technology
Diebold	Retalix
Dresser Wayne	VeriFone
EDS	WebRaiser
Hypercom	

HISTORICAL FINANCIALS

Company Type: Public

Income Statement

FYE: December 31

	REVENUE ($ mil.)	NET INCOME ($ mil.)	NET PROFIT MARGIN	EMPLOYEES
12/06	222.3	18.4	8.3%	1,032
12/05	172.0	5.6	3.3%	904
12/04	134.9	4.2	3.1%	—
12/03	111.8	(47.7)	—	—
12/02	146.2	6.5	4.4%	917
Annual Growth	11.0%	29.7%	—	3.0%

2006 Year-End Financials

Debt ratio: 18.0%
Return on equity: 18.4%
Cash ($ mil.): 15.7
Current ratio: 1.51
Long-term debt ($ mil.): 20.9
No. of shares (mil.): 30.9
Dividends
  Yield: —
  Payout: —
Market value ($ mil.): 323.0
R&D as % of sales: —
Advertising as % of sales: —

Stock History

NASDAQ (GM): RADS

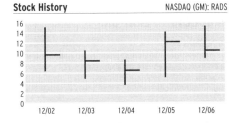

	STOCK PRICE ($) FY Close	P/E High/Low		PER SHARE ($) Earnings	Dividends	Book Value
12/06	10.44	27	16	0.56	—	3.75
12/05	12.16	78	29	0.18	—	2.81
12/04	6.51	61	27	0.14	—	2.51
12/03	8.40	—	—	(1.71)	—	2.35
12/02	9.63	65	28	0.23	—	4.09
Annual Growth	2.0%	—	—	24.9%	—	(2.1%)

Radiation Therapy Services

Radiation Therapy Services operates a network of about 75 freestanding and hospital-based radiation therapy centers in more than 15 states, with Florida its largest market. The company, which also does business as 21st Century Oncology, offers a wide variety of radiation therapy services, including linear accelerators for treatment of deep-seated tumors, brachytherapy for treatment directly into affected areas, seed implantation for prostate cancer, and stereotactic radiosurgery for treating brain tumors. The centers are equipped with treatment planning simulators and a computer-based system for treatment planning and verification.

Radiation Therapy Services plans to grow by building new radiation treatment centers in its existing markets, and by acquiring or developing centers in new markets. Its growth strategy for existing facilities includes increasing the number of doctor referrals and expanding its treatment options. Medicare accounts for more than 50% of sales. The company also owns The Radiation Therapy School for Radiation Therapy Technology, from which it has hired about 50% of the graduates for its facilities. CEO Daniel Dosoretz owns 16% of Radiation Therapy Services. Chairman Howard Sheridan and director Michael Katin each own 10% of the company, and secretary James Rubenstein holds 12%.

EXECUTIVES

Chairman: Howard M. Sheridan, age 62, $496,154 pay
President, CEO, and Director: Daniel E. Dosoretz, age 54, $1,871,425 pay
CFO: David N. T. Watson, age 40
SVP: Paul Wallner
Medical Director, Secretary, and Director: James H. Rubenstein, age 52, $1,424,576 pay
Treasurer: Jeffrey A. Pakrosnis
Corporate Controller and Chief Accounting Officer: Joseph Biscardi, age 38, $177,498 pay
Human Resources Director: Joyce White
Auditors: Ernst & Young LLP

LOCATIONS

HQ: Radiation Therapy Services, Inc.
2234 Colonial Blvd., Fort Myers, FL 33907
Phone: 239-931-7275   **Fax:** 239-931-7380
Web: www.rtsx.com

Radiation Therapy Services operates centers in Alabama, Arizona, California, Delaware, Florida, Kentucky, Maryland, Massachusetts, Michigan, Nevada, New Jersey, New York, North Carolina, Rhode Island, and West Virginia.

Treatment Centers by State

	No. of locations
Florida	24
Nevada	9
Michigan	7
North Carolina	7
New York	6
Maryland	5
California	3
Kentucky	3
New Jersey	3
Rhode Island	3
Alabama	2
Arizona	1
Delaware	1
Massachussetts	1
Pennsylvania	1
West Virginia	1
Total	**77**

PRODUCTS/OPERATIONS

2006 Sales

	$ mil.	% of total
Net patient revenues	284	97
Other revenues	10	3
Total	**294**	**100**

2006 Sales

	% of total
Medicare & Medicaid	52
Commercial	46
Self-pay	2
Total	**100**

COMPETITORS

Aptium Oncology
OnCure Medical
US Oncology

HISTORICAL FINANCIALS

Company Type: Public

Income Statement

FYE: December 31

	REVENUE ($ mil.)	NET INCOME ($ mil.)	NET PROFIT MARGIN	EMPLOYEES
12/06	294.0	30.3	10.3%	1,341
12/05	227.3	25.0	11.0%	980
12/04	171.4	9.2	5.4%	—
12/03	138.7	24.0	17.3%	—
12/02	111.1	19.3	17.4%	—
Annual Growth	27.5%	11.9%	—	36.8%

2006 Year-End Financials

Debt ratio: 143.1%
Return on equity: 26.3%
Cash ($ mil.): 15.4
Current ratio: 2.33
Long-term debt ($ mil.): 193.0
No. of shares (mil.): 23.4

Dividends
Yield: —
Payout: —
Market value ($ mil.): 736.5
R&D as % of sales: —
Advertising as % of sales: —

Stock History

NASDAQ (GS): RTSX

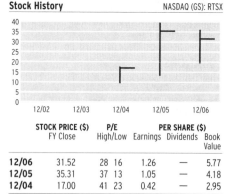

	STOCK PRICE ($) FY Close	P/E High/Low		PER SHARE ($) Earnings	Dividends	Book Value
12/06	31.52	28	16	1.26	—	5.77
12/05	35.31	37	13	1.05	—	4.18
12/04	17.00	41	23	0.42	—	2.95
Annual Growth	36.2%	—	—	73.2%	—	39.9%

Radyne Corp.

Radyne's satellite and cable television systems open the floodgates of information. Its satellite modems, frequency converters, and earth stations convert and transmit voice, video, or data across satellite systems. Radyne's digital audio and video broadcast equipment and modems are used by radio stations, retailers, and financial groups to distribute advertising, music, video, and images. The company also makes equipment used by cable television companies to broadcast digital video and high-definition TV across their terrestrial systems. Customers include the US Department of Defense.

Radyne acquired California-based Xicom Technology in 2005. Xicom, which operates as a subsidiary of the company, produces a line of satellite and microwave power amplifiers.

In 2007 Radyne purchased AeroAstro, a manufacturer of microsatellite systems, for about $18 million.

EXECUTIVES

President, CEO, and Director: Carl Myron Wagner, age 52
EVP and CTO: Steven W. Eymann, age 56, $403,406 pay
VP Finance, CFO, and Secretary: Malcolm C. Persen, age 54, $293,283 pay
VP, Corporate Controller, and Assistant Secretary: Garry D. Kline, age 59, $204,550 pay

President and General Manager, Tiernan HDTV:
Brian Duggan, age 66
President, Radyne Division: Louis Dubin
President and General Manager, Xicom Technologies:
Walter C. Wood, age 67
Auditors: KPMG LLP

LOCATIONS

HQ: Radyne Corp.
3138 E. Elwood St., Phoenix, AZ 85034
Phone: 602-437-9620   Fax: 602-437-4811
Web: www.radynecomstream.com

2006 Sales

	% of total
Americas	
US	58
Other countries	2
Asia	19
Europe	16
Africa & Middle East	5
Total	100

PRODUCTS/OPERATIONS

2006 Sales

	$ mil.	% of total
Satellite electronics & broadcast equipment	72.2	54
Amplifiers	62.0	46
Total	134.2	100

Selected Products

Cable and microwave modems
Communication systems integration and installation services
Data, audio, and video broadcast equipment
Digital TV ATM and network interface adapters
Digital video broadcast (DVB) and high-speed modems
Frequency converters
Internet via Satellite terminal equipment
Microwave and satellite power amplifiers
Satellite communication systems design services
Satellite modems and earth stations
Standard and High Definition digital television encoders and integrated receivers/decoders

COMPETITORS

Comtech Telecommunications
CPI International
Intelek
Scopus
TANDBERG Television

HISTORICAL FINANCIALS

Company Type: Public

Income Statement

FYE: December 31

	REVENUE ($ mil.)	NET INCOME ($ mil.)	NET PROFIT MARGIN	EMPLOYEES
12/06	134.2	11.9	8.9%	343
12/05	103.3	10.7	10.4%	320
12/04	56.6	13.5	23.9%	—
12/03	58.0	4.1	7.1%	—
12/02	57.7	(8.9)	—	205
Annual Growth	23.5%	—	—	13.7%

2006 Year-End Financials

Debt ratio: —
Return on equity: 13.3%
Cash ($ mil.): 27.5
Current ratio: 4.46
Long-term debt ($ mil.): —
No. of shares (mil.): 18.4

Dividends
Yield: —
Payout: —
Market value ($ mil.): 197.1
R&D as % of sales: —
Advertising as % of sales: —

Stock History

NASDAQ (GS): RADN

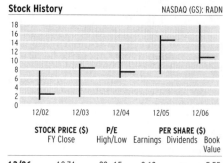

	STOCK PRICE ($) FY Close	P/E High/Low		PER SHARE ($) Earnings	Dividends	Book Value
12/06	10.74	28	15	0.63	—	5.55
12/05	14.57	26	12	0.60	—	4.48
12/04	7.48	17	8	0.79	—	3.50
12/03	8.29	35	7	0.26	—	2.70
12/02	2.40	—	—	(0.59)	—	2.44
Annual Growth	45.4%	—	—	—	—	22.9%

Rainmaker Systems

Rainmaker Systems wants to turn your revenue stream into a flood with its outsourced marketing services. The company generates the majority of its sales through its proprietary Contract Renewals Plus program, which focuses not only on contract renewals, but also on new contract sales, service upgrades, and license sales through direct marketing, telesales, and hosted e-commerce channels. Rainmaker also offers database enhancement, order management, and technology integration services, primarily to software and hardware companies. Top clients Dell and Hewlett-Packard collectively represent about 45% of the company's total revenues each year.

In 2006, the company bought ViewCentral, a provider of marketing and training software and related services, for $4.3 million. Keeping the buyouts rolling along, Rainmaker snatched up CAS Systems, a California-based telemarketing services company, in early 2007. Rainmaker plans for the acquisitions to significantly increase its lead generation operations while also bolstering its international presence, since CAS owns a facility in Canada.

Founded in 1991, Rainmaker Systems has cultivated relationships with a small number of large clients which account for a significant portion of the company's revenue. CEO Michael Silton owns 10% of the company.

EXECUTIVES

Chairman: Alok Mohan
President, CEO, and Director: Michael Silton, age 42, $275,000 pay
VP Finance, CFO, and Secretary: Steve Valenzuela, age 49, $225,000 pay
VP Marketing: Carmela Wong
VP Service Sales: Eric Anderson
VP and CTO: Kenneth (Ken) Forbes, age 58
General Manager, Service Sales: Ritch Haselden, age 41, $160,000 pay
General Manager, Lead Generation Business:
Larry Norris, age 42
General Manager, Contract Sales: Moe Bawa, age 44
Auditors: BDO Seidman, LLP

LOCATIONS

HQ: Rainmaker Systems, Inc.
900 E. Hamilton Ave., Ste. 400, Campbell, CA 95008
Phone: 408-626-3800   **Fax:** 408-369-0910
Web: www.rmkr.com

COMPETITORS

Acxiom Digital
APAC Customer Services
aQuantive
Convergys
Covente
Digital River
Encover, Inc.
Fulcrum Analytics
Harte-Hanks
Kana
Oracle
PointClear
Saba Software
Sales Direct
SAP
Sapient
Sykes Enterprises
TeleTech
Unica
ValueClick
West Corporation

HISTORICAL FINANCIALS

Company Type: Public

Income Statement
FYE: December 31

	REVENUE ($ mil.)	NET INCOME ($ mil.)	NET PROFIT MARGIN	EMPLOYEES
12/06	48.9	3.4	7.0%	415
12/05	32.1	(5.0)	—	336
12/04	15.3	(4.9)	—	—
12/03	41.3	(3.1)	—	—
12/02	39.3	(3.5)	—	94
Annual Growth	5.6%	—	—	45.0%

2006 Year-End Financials

Debt ratio: 1.9%
Return on equity: 24.4%
Cash ($ mil.): 22.3
Current ratio: 1.16
Long-term debt ($ mil.): 0.4
No. of shares (mil.): 15.1
Dividends
Yield: —
Payout: —
Market value ($ mil.): 112.7
R&D as % of sales: —
Advertising as % of sales: —

Stock History
NASDAQ (GM): RMKR

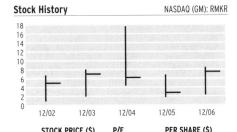

	STOCK PRICE ($) FY Close	P/E High/Low		PER SHARE ($) Earnings	Dividends	Book Value
12/06	7.47	36	10	0.23	—	1.44
12/05	2.83	—	—	(0.48)	—	0.54
12/04	6.20	—	—	(0.55)	—	0.13
12/03	7.00	—	—	(0.40)	—	0.10
12/02	5.00	—	—	(0.45)	—	0.18
Annual Growth	10.6%	—	—	—	—	69.3%

Range Resources

Range Resources is riding the range as an independent acquirer and developer of US oil and gas resources. The company's long-term strategy involves acquiring long-lived established properties and it has major development areas in the Appalachian, Gulf Coast, and Southwest (West Texas, western Oklahoma, and Texas Panhandle) regions. Natural gas accounts for about 82% of Range Resources' proved reserves of about 1.8 trillion cu. ft. of natural gas equivalent. The company holds about 2.5 million net acres of leasehold properties, and an inventory of almost 11,400 net drilling locations. In 2006 Range Resources acquired Stroud Energy for $450 million.

The company has grown through some 70 property acquisitions in its core areas. However, the oil slump of the late-1990s led to heavy debts, prompting Range Resources to sell some assets and cut back on exploration, production, and acquisitions.

Range Resources formed joint venture Great Lakes Energy Partners, L.L.C., with Ohio-based utility FirstEnergy in 1999 to jointly develop their Appalachian oil and gas resources. As part of its ongoing plans to reduce debt, Range Resources sold its Sterling gas processing plant the next year for about $20 million.

In 2004 Range Resources acquired the 50% of Great Lakes Energy Partners that it did not already own for $295 million.

In 2005 the company acquired Plantation Petroleum Holdings II, LLC, a company with Permian Basin oil and gas properties, for $116.5 million.

Range Resources sold its Gulf of Mexico properties to a private entity for $155 million in 2007. In 2008 it acquired producing and nonproducing Barnett Shale properties for $284 million.

HISTORY

Lomak Petroleum was a small gas drilling company with assets in Ohio and West Virginia when Snyder Oil Company (later part of Santa Fe Snyder) bought a 75% stake in 1988. Though Snyder soon started divesting its stake, Snyder VP John Pinkerton was appointed president of Lomak in 1990 (he became CEO in 1992). Pinkerton charted a 10-year mission: Acquire a critical mass of producing properties, operate the properties to establish cash flow, and then begin exploration where it had properties and operating experience.

In 1991 Lomak acquired properties in the Permian basin of West Texas. Acquisitions continued in 1993 and 1994 as the company beefed up its Appalachian business and established positions in the midcontinent and Gulf Coast areas.

Lomak launched exploration efforts in 1996. The next year the company acquired properties in Texas and the Gulf of Mexico from American Cometra. That year Lomak purchased natural gas properties in Appalachia and oil properties in West Texas. It sold $54 million in property in 1998, including all of its San Juan Basin, New Mexico, assets. Also that year the company changed its name to Range Resources after its purchase of Domain for $217 million.

EXECUTIVES

Chairman: Charles L. Blackburn, age 80
President, CEO, and Director: John H. Pinkerton, age 54, $480,000 pay
EVP, COO, and Director: Jeffrey L. (Jeff) Ventura, age 50, $360,000 pay
SVP and CFO: Roger S. Manny, age 50, $266,923 pay
SVP Appalachia: Steven L. Grose, age 59
SVP Corporate Development: Chad L. Stephens, age 53, $342,885 pay
SVP, Chief Compliance Officer, and Corporate Secretary: Rodney L. Waller, age 58, $234,712 pay
SVP Permian Business Unit and Engineering Technology: Mark D. Whitley, age 56, $248,077 pay
SVP Reservoir Engineering: Aklan W. Farquharson, age 61
Human Resources Director: Carol Culpepper
Investor Relations Specialist: Karen M. Giles
Auditors: Ernst & Young LLP

LOCATIONS

HQ: Range Resources Corporation
777 Main St., Ste. 800, Fort Worth, TX 76102
Phone: 817-870-2601   **Fax:** 817-870-2316
Web: www.rangeresources.com

2006 Proved Reserves

	% of total
Appalachia	55
Southwest	37
Gulf Coast	8
Total	**100**

PRODUCTS/OPERATIONS

2006 Sales

	$ mil.	% of total
Natural gas	497.5	64
Crude oil	149.4	19
Natural gas liquids (NGLs)	36.7	5
Transportation & gathering	2.5	—
Mark-to-market on oil & gas derivatives	86.5	11
Other	6.8	1
Adjustments	0.3	—
Total	**779.7**	**100**

COMPETITORS

Anadarko Petroleum
Apache
Belden & Blake
BP
Cabot Oil & Gas
Chesapeake Energy
Devon Energy
Dominion Resources
EOG
Equitable Resources
Exxon Mobil
Forest Oil
Murphy Oil
Noble Energy
Pioneer Natural Resources
Royal Dutch Shell
XTO Energy

HISTORICAL FINANCIALS

Company Type: Public

Income Statement
FYE: December 31

	REVENUE ($ mil.)	NET INCOME ($ mil.)	NET PROFIT MARGIN	EMPLOYEES
12/06	779.7	158.7	20.4%	644
12/05	536.0	111.0	20.7%	578
12/04	320.7	42.2	13.2%	—
12/03	249.2	35.4	14.2%	—
12/02	198.2	25.8	13.0%	145
Annual Growth	40.8%	57.5%	—	45.2%

2006 Year-End Financials

Debt ratio: 83.5%
Return on equity: 16.3%
Cash ($ mil.): 96.0
Current ratio: 1.38
Long-term debt ($ mil.): 1,048.8
No. of shares (mil.): 138.9
Dividends
Yield: 0.3%
Payout: 7.9%
Market value ($ mil.): 3,815.1
R&D as % of sales: —
Advertising as % of sales: —

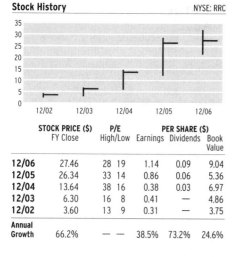

	STOCK PRICE ($) FY Close	P/E High/Low		PER SHARE ($) Earnings	Dividends	Book Value
12/06	27.46	28	19	1.14	0.09	9.04
12/05	26.34	33	14	0.86	0.06	5.36
12/04	13.64	38	16	0.38	0.03	6.97
12/03	6.30	16	8	0.41	—	4.86
12/02	3.60	13	9	0.31	—	3.75
Annual Growth	66.2%	—	—	38.5%	73.2%	24.6%

Red Hat, Inc.

Red Hat hopes that businesses are ready to try open-source operating systems on for size. The company dominates the market for Linux, the open-source computer operating system (OS) that is the chief rival to Microsoft's Windows operating systems. In addition to its Red Hat Enterprise Linux OS, the company's product line includes database, content, and collaboration management applications; server and embedded operating systems; and software development tools. Red Hat also provides consulting, custom software development, support, and training services.

Corporate use of Linux is Red Hat's primary focus. The company established the Fedora Project, an open-source software effort relying on the work of volunteer programmers, for support of its original Linux distribution.

Early in 2005 the company established a government business unit; Red Hat US government customers include the Department of Energy and the Federal Aviation Administration. In 2006 the company acquired open source middleware developer JBoss for about $350 million.

HISTORY

Finnish graduate student Linus Torvalds created the Linux operating system in 1991 as a hobby. When Torvalds released its programming code free over the Internet for anyone to revise, Linux quickly attracted a core base of devoted programmers — including Marc Ewing. A programmer for IBM by day, Ewing developed improvements to Linux in his spare bedroom. Soon he began selling the improved operating system as Red Hat — named after a red and white Cornell lacrosse cap Ewing's grandfather had given him.

In 1994 Ewing was contacted by Robert Young, who after selling typewriters and running a computer leasing company had started a

UNIX newsletter. But Young saw better profit margins in catalog sales. Young's ACC Corp. bought the rights to Ewing's creation and the two went into business together. ACC Corp. was renamed Red Hat Software, Inc.

The company compiled Linux's most significant improvements and distributed them on a CD-ROM and through the budding Internet. Their revenues actually came from manuals and technical support sold to new users and businesses who were challenged by the software's ever-changing source code.

By 1997 Linux — and Red Hat's package — were known only among the most militant programmers who sought alternatives to Microsoft's Windows. Hundreds of developers had continually doctored Linux online to create an operating system known for its speed and reliability.

Red Hat exploded in popularity in 1998 after Intel and Netscape both made minor investments in the company. In 1999 Compaq, IBM, Novell, Oracle, and SAP invested in Red Hat. The company went public later that year.

In 2000 Red Hat used its soaring stock as currency to acquire embedded programming specialist Cygnus Solutions for $674 million and Hell's Kitchen Systems (HKS), a maker of payment processing software. President Matthew Szulik replaced Young as CEO and Ewing stepped down as CTO.

Red Hat expanded its software products in 2001 to include database applications and an e-commerce software suite designed for midsize businesses. The following year Szulik assumed the additional role of chairman.

Red Hat in late 2003 acquired Sistina Software, a supplier of data storage infrastructure software for Linux operating systems, for about $31 million in stock.

EXECUTIVES

Chairman: Matthew J. (Matt) Szulik, age 51, $1,040,000 pay
President, CEO, and Director:
James F. (Jim) Whitehurst, age 40
EVP and CFO: Charles E. (Charlie) Peters Jr., age 54
EVP, Corporate Affairs: Tom Rabon
EVP, Engineering: Paul J. Cormier, age 50, $611,667 pay
EVP, Worldwide Sales: Alex Pinchev, age 57, $716,667 pay
EVP and General Counsel: Michael R. Cunningham, age 47
VP, Engineering and CTO: Brian Stevens
VP, Government Sales Operations: Paul Smith
VP, Marketing: John Young
VP, Human Capital: DeLisa Alexander
VP, North American Channel Sales: Mark Enzweiler
VP, Open Source Affairs: Michael (Mike) Tiemann, age 42
VP Global Operations and Senior Transformation Executive: Nicholas (Nick) Van Wyk
VP, Partner Development: Michael (Mike) Evans
VP, Product Management: Deb Woods
VP, Services: Kate Johnson
Deputy General Counsel and Secretary:
Mark H. Webbink, age 56
Public Relations: Kathryn Bishop
President and Managing Director, Red Hat India: Nandu Pradhan
President, Greater China: Andrew Hu
President, Red Hat Japan: Yuji Hirokawa
Auditors: PricewaterhouseCoopers

LOCATIONS

HQ: Red Hat, Inc.
1801 Varsity Dr., Raleigh, NC 27606
Phone: 919-754-3700   **Fax:** 919-754-3701
Web: www.redhat.com

2007 Sales

	$ mil.	% of total
US	256.0	64
Other countries	144.6	36
Total	**400.6**	**100**

PRODUCTS/OPERATIONS

2007 Sales

	$ mil.	% of total
Subscriptions	341.2	85
Training and services	59.4	15
Total	**400.6**	**100**

Software

Red Hat Enterprise
  Red Hat Enterprise Linux AS
  Red Hat Enterprise Linux ES
  Red Hat Enterprise Linux WS
  Red Hat Desktop
  Red Hat Professional Workstation
Red Hat Network
  Update
  Management
  Provisioning
Red Hat Applications
  Red Hat Cluster Suite
  Red Hat Developer Suite
  Red Hat Content Management System
  Red Hat Portal Server

Selected Services

Consulting
Custom development
Technical support
Training

COMPETITORS

Apple	MontaVista Software
BMC Software	Novell
CA, Inc.	SCO Group
Hewlett-Packard	SourceForge
IBM Global Services	Sun Microsystems
Linspire	Turbolinux
Microsoft	Unisys

HISTORICAL FINANCIALS

Company Type: Public

Income Statement				FYE: February 28
	REVENUE ($ mil.)	NET INCOME ($ mil.)	NET PROFIT MARGIN	EMPLOYEES
2/07	400.6	59.9	15.0%	1,800
2/06	278.3	79.7	28.6%	1,100
2/05	196.5	45.4	23.1%	—
2/04	124.7	13.7	11.0%	—
2/03	90.9	(6.6)	—	566
Annual Growth	44.9%	—	—	33.5%

2007 Year-End Financials

Debt ratio: 69.4%
Return on equity: 9.2%
Cash ($ mil.): 878.1
Current ratio: 3.35
Long-term debt ($ mil.): 570.0
No. of shares (mil.): 192.9

Dividends
  Yield: —
  Payout: —
Market value ($ mil.): 4,330.4
R&D as % of sales: —
Advertising as % of sales: —

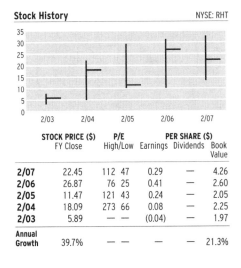

	STOCK PRICE ($) FY Close	P/E High/Low		PER SHARE ($) Earnings	Dividends	Book Value
2/07	22.45	112	47	0.29	—	4.26
2/06	26.87	76	25	0.41	—	2.60
2/05	11.47	121	43	0.24	—	2.05
2/04	18.09	273	66	0.08	—	2.25
2/03	5.89	—	—	(0.04)	—	1.97
Annual Growth	39.7%	—	—	—	—	21.3%

Red Robin Gourmet Burgers

Hamburger fans are chirping about Red Robin Gourmet Burgers. The company operates a chain of more than 340 casual-dining restaurants in almost 40 states and Canada that specialize in high-end hamburgers. Its menu features more than 20 different twists on the American classic, including the Pot Roast Burger, the Banzai Burger (marinated in teriyaki), and the jalapeño-charged 5 Alarm Burger. The signature Royal Red Robin Burger features bacon and a fried egg on top of the beef. Red Robin also serves chicken, seafood, and turkey burgers, as well as vegetarian alternatives. Non-burger entrées include salads, pasta, seafood, and fajitas. The company operates more than 200 of its locations and franchises the rest.

Red Robin's restaurants are typically freestanding units in retail areas and near entertainment centers. The company, which added more than 30 new restaurants to its chain in 2006, has slowed its expansion plans to focus on improving unit sales. It hopes to open about 25 locations in 2007, mostly in markets where it is already operating.

Former CEO Michael Snyder, who resigned in 2005 after questions were raised about corporate travel expenditures, owns more than 5% of the company.

EXECUTIVES

Chairman and CEO: Dennis B. Mullen, age 63, $608,105 pay (partial-year salary)
President and COO: Eric C. Houseman, age 39, $365,754 pay (prior to promotion)
SVP and CFO: Katherine L. (Katie) Scherping, age 47
SVP and Chief Development Officer: Todd A. Brighton, age 49, $234,673 pay (prior to promotion)
SVP and Chief Knowledge Officer:
Michael E. (Mike) Woods, age 57, $494,260 pay (prior to promotion)
SVP, Chief Legal Officer, and Secretary:
Annita M. Menogan, age 52
SVP and Chief Marketing Officer: Susan Lintonsmith

VP Management Information Systems and CIO:
Robert K. (Rob) Jakoby, age 41
VP Purchasing: Ray S. Masters, age 46
VP Team Member Resources: Wes Garnett
Director Of Communications: Kevin Caulfield
Auditors: Deloitte & Touche LLP

LOCATIONS

HQ: Red Robin Gourmet Burgers, Inc.
6312 S. Fiddler's Green Cir., Ste. 200N,
Greenwood Village, CO 80111
Phone: 303-846-6000   **Fax:** 303-846-6048
Web: www.redrobin.com

PRODUCTS/OPERATIONS

2006 Sales

	$ mil.	% of total
Restaurants	603.4	98
Franchising	15.1	2
Rents	0.2	—
Total	**618.7**	**100**

2006 Locations

	No.
Company-owned	208
Franchised	139
Total	**347**

COMPETITORS

Applebee's
Bob Evans
Brinker
California Pizza Kitchen
Carlson Restaurants
CBRL Group
Cheesecake Factory
Chipotle
Darden
Denny's
Fuddruckers
Hooters
Johnny Rockets
Max & Erma's Restaurants
Metromedia Restaurant Group
Ruby Tuesday
Steak n Shake

HISTORICAL FINANCIALS

Company Type: Public

Income Statement

FYE: December 31

	REVENUE ($ mil.)	NET INCOME ($ mil.)	NET PROFIT MARGIN	EMPLOYEES
12/06	618.7	29.4	4.8%	21,535
12/05	486.0	27.4	5.6%	16,545
12/04	409.1	23.4	5.7%	—
12/03	328.6	15.7	4.8%	—
12/02	274.4	8.3	3.0%	9,211
Annual Growth	22.5%	37.2%	—	23.7%

2006 Year-End Financials

Debt ratio: 46.1%	Dividends
Return on equity: 13.1%	Yield: —
Cash ($ mil.): 2.8	Payout: —
Current ratio: 0.42	Market value ($ mil.): 594.7
Long-term debt ($ mil.): 112.3	R&D as % of sales: —
No. of shares (mil.): 16.6	Advertising as % of sales: —

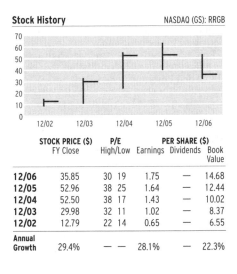

	STOCK PRICE ($) FY Close	P/E High/Low		PER SHARE ($) Earnings	Dividends	Book Value
12/06	35.85	30	19	1.75	—	14.68
12/05	52.96	38	25	1.64	—	12.44
12/04	52.50	38	17	1.43	—	10.02
12/03	29.98	32	11	1.02	—	8.37
12/02	12.79	22	14	0.65	—	6.55
Annual Growth	29.4%	—	—	28.1%	—	22.3%

RehabCare Group

RehabCare helps hospitals help you to get back on your feet. The company is a major provider of rehabilitation program management services to hospitals, nursing homes, and other long-term care facilities in the US. It operates both inpatient and outpatient rehab units for its hospital clients and offers contract therapy services to nursing homes and assisted living facilities. With the acquisition of Symphony Health Services and its subsidiary RehabWorks in 2006, the company counts some 1,400 health care facilities among its clients. In addition to its program management offerings, RehabCare owns several acute care and rehab hospitals of its own, and it provides health care management consulting services.

The acquisition of Symphony Health brought program management contracts for 500 skilled nursing facilities and expanded the company's operations into new geographic markets.

RehabCare derives the majority of its revenue from fees paid by health care providers as opposed to government or other parties. Its contract therapy is the fastest-growing segment, thanks largely to Symphony's RehabWorks segment.

The company is focused on growing its portfolio of freestanding hospitals, with plans to acquire Solara Hospital in New Orleans and Memorial Rehabilitation Hospital in Midland, Texas. It opened a new rehab hospital in Austin, Texas (with Seton Healthcare) in 2007 and is also developing another facility near St. Louis.

RehabCare previously held a 25% stake in health care staffing firm InteliStaf Healthcare (acquired when it sold Intelistaf its StarMed staffing subsidiary); however, the company decided in 2006 to abandon its interest in Intelistaf, due to that company's poor operating performance.

HISTORY

In 1982 chemical dependence treatment provider Comprehensive Care Corp. (CompCare) set up RehabCare to provide medical and rehabilitation services. By the late 1980s, CompCare's $1,000-a-day fees had health insurers pressuring the company to reduce patient stays. Low on cash, CompCare sold 52% of RehabCare to the public in 1991; RehabCare eventually bought CompCare's remaining 48%.

RehabCare's was to expand via acquisitions, including Advanced Rehabilitation Resources (1993) and Physical Therapy Resources (1994). Demand for the company's services grew as more hospitals outsourced rehabilitation services.

In 1996 RehabCare entered the lucrative medical staffing business by buying Healthcare Staffing Solutions, which staffs hospitals, nursing homes, and contract therapy companies. In 1997 RehabCare expanded its range of services by providing outpatient therapy to school systems in a joint venture with Allied Therapy Services.

In the late 1990s the company pointed its shopping cart toward staffing and contract therapy companies, acquiring StarMed (national nurse staffing) in 1998 and All Staff (nurse staffing in Iowa and western Illinois) in 1999. The strategy paid off in 2000, when the company's stock surged in popularity, boosted by better-than-expected results.

In 2001 RehabCare announced plans to collaborate with the American Stroke Association on an education and training program for acute stroke rehabilitation patients and their families

In 2004, the company sold its subsidiary (StarMed Staffing Group) to InteliStaf Healthcare. RehabCare Group acquired MeadowBrook Healthcare, which operates acute rehabilitation hospitals and long-term acute care hospitals the next year.

EXECUTIVES

Chairman: Harry E. Rich, age 68
President, CEO, and Director: John H. Short, age 63, $664,913 pay
EVP Operations: Patricia M. Henry, age 55, $350,026 pay
SVP and CFO: Jay W. Shreiner, age 57
SVP Operations: Susan Krall
SVP and Chief Human Resources Officer: John L. McWilliams
SVP Medical Affairs and Chief Medical Officer: Kenneth K. Adams
SVP Business Development: Peter Doerner
SVP Corporate Development: Vincent L. Germanese, age 53, $314,967 pay (prior to title change)
SVP Clinical Research and Development: Sean Maloney
SVP Market Development: Sharon Noe
SVP Corporate Marketing and Communications: David J. (Dave) Totaro
SVP and Chief Development Officer: Don Adam
SVP Target Markets: Alan Sauber
VP, General Counsel, and Secretary: Patricia S. (Patty) Williams
VP Chief Accounting Officer: Jeff A. Zadoks, age 42
CEO, Northland LTAC Hospital: Randy Hamilton
CIO: Richard S. (Dick) Escue
Chief Human Resources Officer: Michael R. Garcia
Director Investor Relations: Betty D. Cammarata
Auditors: KPMG LLP

LOCATIONS

HQ: RehabCare Group, Inc.
   7733 Forsyth Blvd., 23rd Fl., St. Louis, MO 63105
Phone: 314-863-7422   **Fax:** 314-863-0769
Web: www.rehabcare.com

RehabCare Group has operations in more than 40 US states, plus Washington, DC, and Puerto Rico.

PRODUCTS/OPERATIONS

2006 Sales

	$ mil.	% of total
Program management		
Contract therapy	331.6	54
Hospital rehabilitation services	179.8	29
Freestanding hospitals	77.1	13
Other health care services	26.9	4
Adjustments	(0.6)	—
Total	**614.8**	**100**

Selected Services

Contract therapy services for skilled nursing and long-term care facilities
Freestanding hospitals
   Arlington Rehabilitation Hospital (Arlington, Texas)
   Clear Lake Rehabilitation Hospital (Webster, Texas)
   Howard Regional Specialty Hospital (Kokomo, Indiana)
   Louisiana Specialty Hospital (Marrero, Louisiana)
   MeadowBrook Specialty Hospital of Lafayette (Lafayette, Louisiana)
   MeadowBrook Specialty Hospital of Tulsa (Tulsa, Oklahoma)
   Northwest Texas Rehabilitation Hospital (Amarillo, Texas)
   West Gables Rehabilitation Hospital (Miami, Florida)
Health care management consulting
Hospital rehabilitation unit staffing and management

Selected Subsidiaries

American VitalCare, Inc.
Clear Lake Rehabilitation Hospital, LLC
Lafayette Specialty Hospital, LLC
Managed Alternative Care, Inc.
RehabCare Group Management Services, Inc.
Salt Lake Physical Therapy Associates, Inc.
Tulsa Specialty Hospital, LLC

COMPETITORS

Continucare
HCA
HealthSouth
Horizon Health
Kindred Healthcare
Mariner Health Care
Paradigm Management Services
Select Medical
Tenet Healthcare

HISTORICAL FINANCIALS

Company Type: Public

Income Statement

	REVENUE ($ mil.)	NET INCOME ($ mil.)	NET PROFIT MARGIN	EMPLOYEES
12/06	614.8	7.3	1.2%	16,500
12/05	454.3	(17.0)	—	10,900
12/04	383.9	23.2	6.0%	—
12/03	539.3	(13.7)	—	—
12/02	562.6	24.4	4.3%	13,400
Annual Growth	**2.2%**	**(26.0%)**	**—**	**5.3%**

FYE: December 31

2006 Year-End Financials

Debt ratio: 54.6%
Return on equity: 3.6%
Cash ($ mil.): 9.4
Current ratio: 1.93
Long-term debt ($ mil.): 115.0
No. of shares (mil.): 17.1
Dividends
   Yield: —
   Payout: —
Market value ($ mil.): 254.4
R&D as % of sales: —
Advertising as % of sales: —

RELM Wireless

Stock History   NYSE: RHB

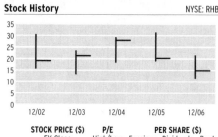

	STOCK PRICE ($) FY Close	P/E High/Low		PER SHARE ($) Earnings	Dividends	Book Value
12/06	14.85	51	28	0.42	—	12.31
12/05	20.20	—	—	(1.01)	—	11.78
12/04	27.99	21	13	1.38	—	12.51
12/03	21.26	—	—	(0.86)	—	11.02
12/02	19.08	22	11	1.38	—	11.90
Annual Growth	**(6.1%)**	—	—	**(25.7%)**	**—**	**0.8%**

The domain of RELM Wireless is populated by those who get around. The company makes portable land mobile radio (LMR) products, as well as base stations and related subsystems, used for mobile handheld and vehicle communications. It primarily serves the US government and public safety agencies; the US Forest Service and the Department of Interior are top clients. Products branded with the BK Radio brand are sold to these customers. RELM Wireless also sells private radio communications systems under the RELM/BK and RELM brands to customers in communications and industrial markets.

In 2006 the company introduced a portable repeater it calls the Rapid Deployment Portable Repeater (RDPR), nicknamed "The Go Box," for use by emergency responders.

Long-standing director Donald Goebert owns a nearly 12% stake in the company.

EXECUTIVES

Chairman: George N. Benjamin III, age 69
President, CEO, and Director: David P. Storey, age 54, $268,000 pay
EVP Finance, CFO, and Secretary: William P. Kelly, age 50, $160,000 pay
EVP Engineering: James W. Spence, age 51
EVP Operations: Harold B. Cook, age 61, $125,000 pay
VP Engineering: Theresa M. Zagaruyka, age 51
Auditors: BDO Seidman, LLP

LOCATIONS

HQ: RELM Wireless Corporation
   7100 Technology Dr., West Melbourne, FL 32904
Phone: 321-984-1414   **Fax:** 321-984-0168
Web: www.relm.com

2006 Sales

	% of total
US	98
Other countries	2
Total	**100**

PRODUCTS/OPERATIONS

2006 Sales

	% of total
Government and public safety	82
Business and industrial market	18
Total	**100**

Selected Products

Mobile vehicle-mounted radios
Portable handheld radios
Radio base stations and repeaters

COMPETITORS

BearCom
Cobra Electronics
Datamarine
EFJ
Ericsson
Harris Corp.
Kenwood
KVH Industries
Motorola, Inc.
Nokia
Sony
Uniden

HISTORICAL FINANCIALS

Company Type: Public

Income Statement				FYE: December 31
	REVENUE ($ mil.)	NET INCOME ($ mil.)	NET PROFIT MARGIN	EMPLOYEES
12/06	32.4	3.4	10.5%	92
12/05	28.5	10.3	36.1%	83
12/04	20.7	7.9	38.2%	—
12/03	19.7	0.9	4.6%	—
12/02	16.0	(3.6)	—	73
Annual Growth	19.3%	—	—	6.0%

2006 Year-End Financials

Debt ratio: —
Return on equity: 11.3%
Cash ($ mil.): 13.3
Current ratio: 9.53
Long-term debt ($ mil.): —
No. of shares (mil.): 13.3

Dividends
  Yield: —
  Payout: —
Market value ($ mil.): 80.0
R&D as % of sales: —
Advertising as % of sales: —

Stock History

AMEX: RWC

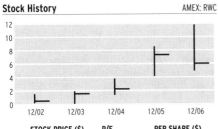

	STOCK PRICE ($) FY Close	P/E High/Low		PER SHARE ($) Earnings	Dividends	Book Value
12/06	6.00	49	21	0.24	—	2.42
12/05	7.31	11	6	0.75	—	2.12
12/04	2.25	6	2	0.65	—	1.36
12/03	1.55	20	2	0.09	—	0.66
12/02	0.49	—	—	(0.47)	—	0.57
Annual Growth	87.1%	—	—	—	—	43.5%

Renasant Corporation

Those who want to see their wealth reborn (or born, for that matter) might bank at Renasant Corporation. Formerly The Peoples Holding Company, Renasant is the parent of Renasant Bank and Renasant Insurance. Through about 70 branches in Alabama, Mississippi, and Tennessee, the bank provides a range of services to individuals and local businesses, including checking and savings accounts, loans, and investment products. Lending activities account for about 70% of the company's annual revenue; more than 60% of its loan portfolio consists of commercial, construction, and commercial real estate loans. Renasant Insurance offers personal and business insurance.

After entering the Tennessee market with its purchase of Renasant Bancshares in 2004, The Peoples Holding Company in mid-2005 adopted the Renasant name.

Renasant gained a foothold in northern and central Alabama through its 2005 acquisition of Heritage Financial Holding Corporation and its subsidiary Heritage Bank. In 2007 it expanded its presence in Tennessee with the acquisition of Nashville, Tennessee-based Capital Bancorp for about $135 million.

A group of some two dozen directors and executive officers controls nearly 10% of Renasant Corporation.

EXECUTIVES

Chairman, President, and CEO; President and CEO, Renasant Bank: E. Robinson (Robin) McGraw, age 60, $370,000 pay
Vice Chairman: J. Larry Young, age 68
EVP and Director; President, Renasant Bank Tennessee Division: Francis J. (Frank) Cianciola, age 56
EVP and General Counsel; SVP and General Counsel, Renasant Bank: Stephen M. Corban, age 51
EVP; President, Mississippi Division, Renasant Bank: C. Mitchell (Mitch) Waycaster, age 48, $225,000 pay
EVP; SEVP and CIO, Renasant Bank: James W. Gray, age 50, $230,000 pay
EVP; President, Alabama Division, Renasant Bank: Larry R. Mathews, age 54, $239,000 pay
EVP; SEVP and Chief Credit Officer, Renasant Bank Alabama Division: Harold H. Livingston, age 58
EVP and CFO; SEVP, CFO, and Cashier, Renasant Bank: Stuart R. Johnson, age 53, $230,000 pay
EVP; SEVP and Chief Credit Policy Officer, Renasant Bank: Claude H. Springfield III, age 59
EVP and Senior Credit Officer, Renasant Bank: Gregory L. Goldberg
EVP and Human Resources Director, Renasant Bank: Hollis R. (Ray) Smith Jr.
Auditors: Horne LLP

LOCATIONS

HQ: Renasant Corporation
  209 Troy St., Tupelo, MS 38802
Phone: 662-680-1001 **Fax:** 662-680-1234
Web: www.renasantbank.com

Renasant Bank has offices located in Mississippi, Tennessee, and Alabama. Renasant Insurance has offices in the Mississippi communities of Corinth, Louisville, and Tupelo.

PRODUCTS/OPERATIONS

2006 Sales

	$ mil.	% of total
Interest		
Loans	132.7	66
Securities & other	21.6	11
Noninterest		
Service charges on deposit accounts	18.4	9
Fees & commissions	13.9	7
Other	13.6	7
Total	**200.2**	**100**

COMPETITORS

BancorpSouth
Cadence Financial Corporation
Citizens Holding
Colonial BancGroup
Compass Bancshares
First Horizon
Hancock Holding
Regions Financial
Trustmark
United Tennessee Bankshares

HISTORICAL FINANCIALS

Company Type: Public

Income Statement				FYE: December 31
	ASSETS ($ mil.)	NET INCOME ($ mil.)	INCOME AS % OF ASSETS	EMPLOYEES
12/06	2,611.4	27.1	1.0%	813
12/05	2,397.7	24.2	1.0%	789
12/04	1,707.5	18.4	1.1%	703
12/03	1,415.2	18.2	1.3%	580
12/02	1,344.5	16.4	1.2%	587
Annual Growth	18.1%	13.4%	—	8.5%

2006 Year-End Financials

Equity as % of assets: 9.7%
Return on assets: 1.1%
Return on equity: 11.1%
Long-term debt ($ mil.): 72.2
No. of shares (mil.): 15.5
Market value ($ mil.): 475.9

Dividends
  Yield: 2.0%
  Payout: 36.8%
Sales ($ mil.): 200.2
R&D as % of sales: —
Advertising as % of sales: 1.8%

Stock History

NASDAQ (GS): RNST

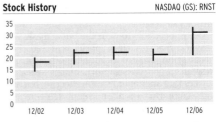

	STOCK PRICE ($) FY Close	P/E High/Low		PER SHARE ($) Earnings	Dividends	Book Value
12/06	30.63	19	12	1.71	0.63	16.26
12/05	21.09	15	12	1.54	0.29	22.74
12/04	22.07	17	13	1.43	—	19.79
12/03	22.00	16	12	1.46	—	16.79
12/02	18.11	15	11	1.30	—	23.82
Annual Growth	14.0%	—	—	7.1%	117.2%	(9.1%)

ResMed Inc.

Breathe easy, because you won't lose any sleep while using ResMed's products. ResMed makes and distributes medical equipment used to diagnose and treat respiratory disorders that occur during sleep, such as sleep apnea. Most of its products treat obstructive sleep apnea (OSA), a condition in which a patient's air flow is periodically obstructed, causing multiple disruptions during sleep that lead to daytime sleepiness and possibly conditions such as high blood pressure. Its products include air-flow generators, face masks, diagnostic products, and accessories. ResMed sells directly and through distributors worldwide to home health equipment dealers and sleep clinics.

ResMed manufactures its products primarily at its Australian facility, though it has additional production plants in France and the US. It sells them in nearly 70 countries through its own subsidiaries (mainly in the US, Europe, and Australia) and through independent distributors. The US and Germany account for nearly 70% of sales.

The company has been focused on expanding its geographic reach, acquiring a number of medical equipment makers and distributors in Europe and elsewhere. It bought its Dutch distributor Resprecare in 2004 and a Scandinavian distributor in 2005. It also shored up its European operations and expanded its product line with the 2005 purchase of Saime, a French maker of home ventilation products.

Building on research showing linkages between sleep-disordered breathing and conditions such as hypertension, stroke, heart disease, and even diabetes, ResMed is expanding its own research activities into other clinical areas. It is working on a device, for example, to treat Cheyne-Stokes breathing, a disorder associated with congestive heart failure.

ResMed also won FDA approval in 2006 for a device (called Adapt SV) used to treat central sleep apnea, a form of the disorder in which the brain temporarily fails to tell the appropriate muscles to breathe.

Getting patients to wear the bulky masks and headgear that treat sleep apnea has proved a barrier to selling the products, and another focus of ResMed's product development efforts is creating devices that are not only more effective, but also more comfortable and convenient. The company introduced two mask products in 2007 — dubbed Mirage Quattro and Mirage Liberty — that are designed for comfort and allow for greater movement during sleep.

Sales of the Quattro and Liberty masks have been brisk, but the company nevertheless saw a decline in profits in 2007, largely due to a voluntary safety recall of 300,000 units of a major line of flow generators. The company had determined that there was a slight risk of short circuiting in the products.

HISTORY

ResMed was founded as ResCare in 1989 after Peter Farrell led a management buyout of Baxter Healthcare's respiratory technology unit. ResCare initially developed the SULLIVAN nasal CPAP systems (named after inventor Colin Sullivan) in Australia. In 1991 it introduced the Bubble Mask and the APD2 portable CPAP device. Three years later ResCare began marketing its first VPAP, which applied different air pressures for inhalation and exhalation, in the US.

In 1995 the company went public, changing its name to ResMed (its former name was already taken by another medical company). Over the next two years, ResMed spent a lot of oxygen in court suing rival Respironics for patent infringements; judgments in 1997 and 1998 found in favor of Respironics, but ResMed made plans to appeal. In 1998 the firm received FDA approval to market its VPAP device as a critical-care treatment for lung diseases.

In 1999 the firm's listing was switched from the Nasdaq to the NYSE to stabilize stock prices after court losses against Respironics; it also listed on the Australian Stock Exchange. The introduction of two new products, the AutoSet CPAP unit and the Mirage face mask, boosted sales that year. In 2001 ResMed bought MAP Medizin-Technologie, a German manufacturer of sleep-disordered breathing treatment devices. The acquisition enhanced ResMed's position in Germany, which is the company's second-biggest market for its products.

EXECUTIVES

Chairman: Peter C. Farrell, age 64, $1,123,896 pay
CEO and Director: Kieran T. Gallahue, age 45, $776,965 pay
COO Americas: Keith M. Serzen, age 54, $529,455 pay
COO Europe: Lasse Beijer
COO Sydney: Robert Douglas, age 48
CFO: Brett Sandercock, age 40
SVP, General Counsel, and Corporate Secretary: David Pendarvis, age 48, $466,068 pay
SVP, Telemedicine and Occupational Health: Dana Voien
SVP, Asia Pacific: Paul Eisen, age 48
SVP, Strategic Marketing Initiatives, Americas: Ron F. Richard
VP and Director, Marketing, Americas: Michael J. Farrell
VP, Clinical Education and Training: Ann Tisthammer
VP, Global Customer Operations: Caroline Carr
VP, Global Tax: Holly Sepa
VP, USA Operations: Elliott Glick
VP, US Regulatory and Clinical Affairs: David D'Cruz
Director, Human Resources, Americas: Lenita Maljan
Manager, Investor Relations and Business Development: Matthew Borer
Auditors: KPMG LLP

LOCATIONS

HQ: ResMed Inc.
14040 Danielson St., Poway, CA 92064
Phone: 858-746-2400   **Fax:** 858-746-2900
Web: www.resmed.com

2007 Sales

	$ mil.	% of total
US	376.7	52
Germany	107.9	15
France	76.0	11
Australia	19.8	3
Other countries	135.9	19
Total	**716.3**	**100**

COMPETITORS

Allied Healthcare Products
CHAD Therapeutics
Covidien
Respironics
Restore Medical
Sunrise Medical
Vanda
Vital Signs

HISTORICAL FINANCIALS

Company Type: Public

Income Statement

FYE: June 30

	REVENUE ($ mil.)	NET INCOME ($ mil.)	NET PROFIT MARGIN	EMPLOYEES
6/07	716.3	66.3	9.3%	2,700
6/06	607.0	88.2	14.5%	2,500
6/05	425.5	64.8	15.2%	1,927
6/04	339.3	57.3	16.9%	—
6/03	273.6	45.7	16.7%	—
Annual Growth	27.2%	9.7%	—	18.4%

2007 Year-End Financials

Debt ratio: 9.4%
Return on equity: 7.9%
Cash ($ mil.): 277.7
Current ratio: 3.30
Long-term debt ($ mil.): 87.7
No. of shares (mil.): 77.6
Dividends
  Yield: —
  Payout: —
Market value ($ mil.): 3,202.5
R&D as % of sales: —
Advertising as % of sales: —

Stock History

NYSE: RMD

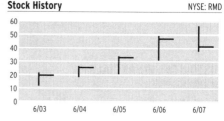

	STOCK PRICE ($) FY Close	P/E High/Low		PER SHARE ($) Earnings	Dividends	Book Value
6/07	41.26	66	45	0.85	—	12.00
6/06	46.95	42	27	1.16	—	9.75
6/05	32.99	37	23	0.91	—	13.54
6/04	25.48	32	23	0.81	—	10.68
6/03	19.60	32	18	0.67	—	8.58
Annual Growth	20.5%	—	—	6.1%	—	8.7%

Resource America

Resource America used to look underground for resources to exploit, but the company exited the natural gas business in favor of financial services. The company's fund management units include Apidos Capital Management, Ischus Capital Management, Trapeza Capital Management, and others, which invest in corporate credit, asset-backed securities, trust-preferred securities, mortgages, and private equity. Resource America and its affiliates have more than $17 billion of assets under management on behalf of individual and institutional clients. In 2005 the company spun off its 80% stake in natural gas producer Atlas America, along with its interest in Atlas Pipeline Partners, in order to focus on asset management.

Through its real estate finance business, Resource Real Estate, the company has amassed a portfolio of commercial properties and multifamily housing.

Resource America also operates an equipment leasing business, LEAF Financial; the parent company gave LEAF a lift in 2007, acquiring the commercial equipment leasing business of Pacific Capital Bancorp, the equipment financing business of Lehman Brothers Bancorp, and the $430 million leasing portfolio of failed Internet bank NetBank.

HISTORY

Resource Exploration was founded as a natural gas and oil exploration and production company in 1966, with operations focusing on the Appalachian region. Chairman and CEO Edward Cohen took the reins in 1988 and soon led Resource Exploration onto the path of developing niche businesses in the financial services markets. In 1989 Resource Exploration changed its name to Resource America to reflect its expanded operations.

The company began purchasing troubled commercial real estate loans in 1991, and entered the small equipment lease financing business in 1995 through the purchase of Fidelity Mutual Life Insurance Co. (now Fidelity Leasing). In 1997 it established Resource Asset Investment Trust (RAIT Investment Trust) to acquire and provide nonconforming mortgage financing. Also that year Resource America contracted with Frontier Systems to create billing and related customer software to serve deregulating energy markets.

It took the REIT public in 1998. That year Resource America's stock plunged after it was accused of shady accounting, but an independent auditor ratified its methods. Slow recovery on the stock market caused Resource America stockholders to push for reorganization.

As the decade wound down, the company returned to its roots, buying oil and gas company Atlas Group (now Atlas America) in 1998 and energy finance company Viking Resources in 1999. These two acquisitions more than doubled Resource America's gas and oil well and pipeline assets in the Appalachian Basin. It subsequently formed subsidiary Atlas Pipeline Partners in 1999 to manage all of its pipeline assets; in 2000 Resource America spun off 47% of Atlas Pipeline Partners to the public.

Also in 2000 Resource America formed 50%-owned Optiron, a merger of Frontier Systems and Atlas Technologies (a company created to license Frontier's software). Resource America also sold Fidelity Leasing to ABN AMRO subsidiary European American Bank, and discontinued Fidelity Mortgage Funding, its residential mortgage lending subsidiary.

EXECUTIVES

Chairman: Edward E. Cohen, age 68
President, CEO, and Director: Jonathan Z. Cohen, age 37
EVP and CFO: Steven J. Kessler, age 64, $564,808 pay
EVP: Jeffrey F. (Jeff) Brotman, age 44
SVP; President, Resource Real Estate, Inc.:
David E. Bloom, age 42
SVP; CEO, Resource Real Estate, Inc.:
Alan F. Feldman, age 43, $579,808 pay
SVP, Finance: Thomas Elliott, age 32, $320,932 pay
SVP, Chief Legal Officer, and Secretary:
Michael S. Yecies, age 39

Chairman and CEO, LEAF Financial: Crit S. DeMent, age 54
President and COO, LEAF Financial Corporation:
Miles Herman
President, Resource Banking Advisory & Management Company: Kent Carstater
President, Resources Financial Fund Management, Inc.: Jeffrey D. Bloomstrom
President and Chief Porfolio Manager, Apidos Capital Management, LLC: Gretchen L. Bergstresser, age 44
President, Chief Investment Officer and Senior Portfolio Manager, Ischus Capital Management, LLC:
Andrew P. Shook, age 37
Auditors: Grant Thornton LLP

LOCATIONS

HQ: Resource America, Inc.
1845 Walnut St., Ste. 1000, Philadelphia, PA 19103
Phone: 215-546-5005   **Fax:** 215-546-5388
Web: www.resourceamerica.com

PRODUCTS/OPERATIONS

2007 Sales

	$ mil.	% of total
Financial fund management	64.1	50
Commercial finance	40.7	32
Real estate	23.0	18
Total	**127.8**	**100**

Selected Subsidiaries

Resource Financial Fund Management, Inc.
  Apidos Capital Management, LLC
  Ischus Capital Management, LLC
  Resource Credit Partners G.P., Inc.
  Resource Financial Institutions Group, Inc.
  Trapeza Capital Management, LLC
LEAF Financial Corporation
Resource Capital Corp.
Resource Europe Limited
Resource Real Estate, Inc.

COMPETITORS

Allianz Global Investors of America
BlackRock
Equity Office Properties
Forest City Enterprises
Fortress Investment Group
KKR Financial
Old Mutual (US)

HISTORICAL FINANCIALS

Company Type: Public

Income Statement

FYE: September 30

	ASSETS ($ mil.)	NET INCOME ($ mil.)	INCOME AS % OF ASSETS	EMPLOYEES
9/07	969.7	4.3	0.4%	394
9/06	416.8	19.9	4.8%	224
9/05	456.8	16.5	3.6%	154
9/04	725.7	18.4	2.5%	—
9/03	670.8	(2.9)	—	—
Annual Growth	**9.7%**	**—**	**—**	**60.0%**

2007 Year-End Financials

Equity as % of assets: 19.0%
Return on assets: 0.6%
Return on equity: 2.3%
Long-term debt ($ mil.): 706.4
No. of shares (mil.): 17.6
Market value ($ mil.): 278.2
Dividends
Yield: 1.7%
Payout: 117.4%
Sales ($ mil.): 127.8
R&D as % of sales: —
Advertising as % of sales: —

	STOCK PRICE ($) FY Close	P/E High/Low		PER SHARE ($) Earnings	Dividends	Book Value
9/07	15.79	124	53	0.23	0.27	10.44
9/06	20.80	21	14	1.04	0.24	11.16
9/05	17.71	23	12	0.86	32.34	10.36
9/04	10.55	11	5	1.01	0.07	14.74
9/03	5.30	—	—	(0.17)	0.06	13.11
Annual Growth	**31.4%**	**—**	**—**	**—**	**45.6%**	**(5.5%)**

Rex Energy

Though it isn't exactly the T. rex of the oil and gas industry, Rex Energy is making its way in the world today. The oil and gas exploration and production company has estimated proved reserves of 14.5 million barrels of oil equivalent, primarily from three regions: the Illinois Basin (in Illinois and Indiana); the Appalachian Basin (Pennsylvania and West Virginia); and the southwestern US (New Mexico and Texas). The company's Lawrence Field ASP (alkaline-surfactant-polymer) Flood Project utilizes ASP technology, which washes residual oil from reservoir rock, thereby improving the existing waterflow's ability to sweep the residual oil and increasing ultimate oil recoveries. Lawrence Field is in Illinois.

Rex has completed more than a dozen acquisitions — including acquisitions of acreage in the Illinois Basin and of producing properties (which added 13.1 million barrels of oil equivalent to its portfolio) — since 2004.

EXECUTIVES

CEO: Benjamin W. Hulburt, age 33, $208,602 pay
CFO: Thomas C. Stabley, age 36, $147,600 pay
EVP, Secretary, and General Counsel:
Christopher K. Hulburt, age 36, $164,224 pay
SVP Reservoir Engineering, Rex Energy Corporation and Rex Energy Operating Corp: William L. Ottaviani, age 46
VP and Illinois Basin District Manager:
Jack S. Shawver, age 48, $229,427 pay
VP and Appalachian Basin District Manager:
Michael S. Carlson, age 50
VP and Permian Basin District Manager: Joe Clement, age 48

LOCATIONS

HQ: Rex Energy Corporation
1975 Waddle Rd., State College, PA 16803
Phone: 814-278-7267   **Fax:** 814-278-7286
Web: www.rexenergy.com

Rex Energy owns oil and gas properties in Illinois, Indiana, New Mexico, Pennsylvania, Texas, and West Virginia.

Income Statement				FYE: December 31
	REVENUE ($ mil.)	NET INCOME ($ mil.)	NET PROFIT MARGIN	EMPLOYEES
12/06	44.7	3.8	8.5%	105
12/05	16.3	(4.9)	—	—
12/04	12.5	0.4	3.2%	—
Annual Growth	89.1%	208.2%	—	—

2006 Year-End Financials

Debt ratio: (7,287.0%)
Return on equity: —
Cash ($ mil.): 0.6

Current ratio: 0.19
Long-term debt ($ mil.): 45.0

Net Income History

NASDAQ (GM): REXX

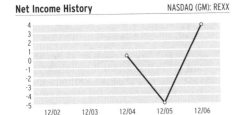

Rick's Cabaret

Far from Casablanca, these night clubs offer topless entertainment as part of the floor show. Rick's Cabaret International operates about 15 adult night clubs in Florida, Minnesota, New York, North Carolina, and Texas. Most of the gentlemen's clubs are run under the Rick's Cabaret name, while others operate under such banners as Club Onyx and XTC. Rick's caters to highbrow patrons with dough to blow: VIP memberships for individual and corporate clients can cost hundreds of dollars annually. In addition to its night clubs, Rick's operates adult Web sites and an auction site for adult entertainment products.

Rick's has been expanding its nightclub operations through a series of acquisitions, a strategy it plans to continue through 2009. During 2006 it purchased additional strip clubs in Austin, Houston, and San Antonio, Texas, and the following year the company acquired a club in Fort Worth, Texas. Also in 2007, Rick's expanded its brand internationally through a licensing agreement with Rick's Buenos Aires, a subsidiary of Latin Entertainment, to open adult clubs in Buenos Aires and other Latin American cities.

CEO Eric Langan owns about 20% of the company; Ralph McElroy, an early investing partner of Langan, owns about 10% of Rick's.

HISTORY

Dallas Fontenot and Salah Izzedin founded Trumps in 1982. The following year they bought a disco and turned it into a swank topless bar called Rick's Cabaret (the name came from an encounter with a drunk in a taxi who was looking for "Rick's"). Izzedin's attorney Robert Watters bought a 10% interest in Trumps in 1987, the same year that the company opened the first members-only VIP room in Houston. The partnership of Fontenot, Izzedin, and Watters soured in 1989 with allegations that Izzedin pocketed unreported money, supplied narcotics to waitresses and dancers, and forced some of them to have sex with him.

Watters took over as CEO in 1991 and became sole owner in 1993. He converted Trumps into Rick's Cabaret International the next year and made Rick's the first topless bar to go public in 1995. The company expanded to New Orleans the following year, opening a club on Bourbon Street. Rick's opened a new club in Minneapolis in 1998 and bought a 93% stake in Taurus Entertainment. Watters resigned in 1999, sold his stock in the company to new CEO Eric Langan and his investment partner, Ralph McElroy, and acquired the firm's New Orleans location, which operated as a Rick's Cabaret under a licensing agreement. (The company sold it the same year.) Later in 1999 Rick's launched its adult Web sites.

In 2000 the company bought a third topless bar in Houston, as well as another adult Web site, xxxPasswords.com. It also began selling pre-paid debit cards that allow customers to anonymously buy access to adult entertainment Web sites. Rick's purchased the Chesapeake Bay Cabaret, an upscale club, in Houston in November. Later that year the company inked a deal with adult Web site operator Entertainment Network to offer its content through CandidCam.com. In 2001 Rick's launched NaughtyBids.com, an auction site for adult products. It also began buying a number of porn auction sites, including Pornauction.com and XXXbids.com, in an effort to enhance the products available on NaughtyBids.com. Late that year it opened Encounters, an upscale club for swinging couples in Houston.

During 2003 Rick's acquired a 51% stake in Houston's Wild Horse Cabaret and opened a sports bar called Hummers (later renamed under the Club Onyx brand). It also acquired the XTC clubs outright from Taurus Entertainment and reorganized some of its other holdings, leaving it with a 51% stake in Encounters (sold in 2004).

The company in 2004 converted its original Rick's Cabaret nightclub in Houston into Club Onyx, an upscale venue that caters to urban professionals, businessmen, and professional athletes. It also bought a new location in Manhattan near Madison Square Garden. The following year the company closed on its acquisition of a three-in-one complex in North Carolina that included a men's club, a male review for women, and a traditional night club. Also in 2005 it bought swingers-oriented dating Web site CouplesClick.net.

During 2006 Rick's purchased four new nightclubs in Texas. The following year it inked a licensing deal with a subsidiary of Argentina-based Latin Entertainment to open adult clubs in Buenos Aires and other Latin American cities under the Rick's Cabaret name.

EXECUTIVES

Chairman, President, CEO, and CFO: Eric S. Langan, age 39, $395,300 pay
CFO: Phillip K. (Phil) Marshall, age 58
VP, Director of Technology, and Board Member: Travis Reese, age 38, $167,201 pay
Operations Director: Andy Studebaker
Operations Director, Club Onyx: Ed Anakar
Investor and Media Relations Manager: Allan Priaulx
Auditors: Whitley Penn

LOCATIONS

HQ: Rick's Cabaret International, Inc.
10959 Cutten Rd., Houston, TX 77066
Phone: 281-397-6730 **Fax:** 281-820-1445
Web: www.ricks.com

PRODUCTS/OPERATIONS

2007 Sales

	$ mil.	% of total
Nightclubs		
Services	14.9	47
Alcohol	12.1	38
Food & merchandise	3.2	10
Internet	0.7	2
Other	1.1	3
Total	**32.0**	**100**

Selected Operations

Night clubs
  Club Onyx (adult entertainment for urban professionals and professional athletes)
  Rick's Cabaret
  Rick's Sports Cabaret
  XTC
Internet
  CouplesClick.net (85%, adult content and online dating)
  CouplesTouch.com (85%, adult content and online dating)
  NaughtyBids.com (adult auction Web site)
  xxxPassword.com (adult content)

COMPETITORS

Galardi South
LFP
Million Dollar Saloon
New Frontier Media
Penthouse Media Group
Playboy.com
Private Media Group
Scores Holding
Vivid Entertainment

HISTORICAL FINANCIALS

Company Type: Public

Income Statement				FYE: September 30
	REVENUE ($ mil.)	NET INCOME ($ mil.)	NET PROFIT MARGIN	EMPLOYEES
9/07	32.0	3.0	9.4%	696
9/06	24.5	1.8	7.3%	—
9/05	14.8	(0.2)	—	443
9/04	16.0	0.8	5.0%	—
9/03	15.1	0.4	2.6%	—
Annual Growth	20.7%	65.5%	—	25.3%

2007 Year-End Financials

Debt ratio: 46.2%
Return on equity: 15.8%
Cash ($ mil.): 3.0
Current ratio: 0.81
Long-term debt ($ mil.): 11.1
No. of shares (mil.): 6.0

Dividends
  Yield: —
  Payout: —
Market value ($ mil.): 69.8
R&D as % of sales: —
Advertising as % of sales: —

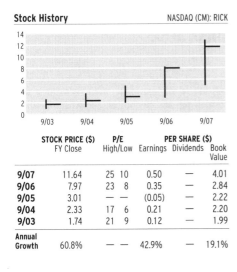

NASDAQ (CM): RICK

	STOCK PRICE ($) FY Close	P/E High/Low		PER SHARE ($) Earnings	Dividends	Book Value
9/07	11.64	25	10	0.50	—	4.01
9/06	7.97	23	8	0.35	—	2.84
9/05	3.01	—	—	(0.05)	—	2.22
9/04	2.33	17	6	0.21	—	2.20
9/03	1.74	21	9	0.12	—	1.99
Annual Growth	60.8%			42.9%	—	19.1%

Riverview Bancorp

Riverview Bancorp is the holding company for Riverview Community Bank, which has more than 15 branches in the Columbia River Gorge area of Washington State. Serving consumers and local businesses, the bank offers such standard retail banking services as checking and savings accounts, money market accounts, NOW accounts, and CDs. Commercial real estate loans account for about 65% of its loan portfolio. Other loans consist of one-to-four family residential mortgages, residential construction loans, and business and consumer loans. Trust and investment services are provided through 85%-owned subsidiary Riverview Asset Management.

Another subsidiary, RAM Corp, also provides asset management services. Riverview Bancorp bought Portland, Oregon-based American Pacific Bank in April 2005.

EXECUTIVES

Chairman and CEO; CEO, Riverview Community Bank: Patrick Sheaffer, age 66, $281,735 pay
President, COO, Interim CFO, and Director; President and COO, Riverview Community Bank: Ronald A. (Ron) Wysaske, age 53, $248,815 pay
EVP and Chief Credit Officer, Riverview Community Bank: David A. Dahlstrom, age 55, $209,216 pay
EVP; President and CEO, Reiverview Asset Management Corp.: John A. Karas, age 57, $226,596 pay
SVP, Business and Professional Banking, Riverview Community Bank: Jeff Donaldson
SVP, Lending, Riverview Community Bank: Karen M. Nelson
SVP, Operations and Information Technology, Riverview Community Bank: Terry Long, age 46
SVP, Retail Banking Division, Riverview Community Bank: James D. (Jim) Baldovin, age 46, $140,324 pay
Corporate Secretary: Phyllis Kreibich
Auditors: Deloitte & Touche LLP

LOCATIONS

HQ: Riverview Bancorp, Inc.
900 Washington St., Ste. 900, Vancouver, WA 98660
Phone: 360-693-6650   **Fax:** 360-693-6275
Web: www.riverviewbank.com

PRODUCTS/OPERATIONS

2007 Sales

	$ mil.	% of total
Interest		
Interest & fees on loans receivable	59.5	84
Interest on investment securities — taxable	0.8	1
Interest on investment securities — non taxable	0.2	—
Interest on mortgage-backed securities	0.4	1
Other interest & dividends	0.4	1
Noninterest		
Fees & service charges	5.7	8
Asset management fees	1.9	3
Net gain on sale of loans held for sale	0.4	1
Loan servicing income	0.2	—
Gain on sale of land & fixed assets	0.0	—
Gain of sale of credit card portfolio	0.1	—
Bank owned life insurance	0.5	1
Other	0.2	—
Total	**70.3**	**100**

COMPETITORS

Bank of America
Banner Corp
Columbia Bancorp (OR)
Commerce Bank of Oregon
Cowlitz Bancorporation
Heritage Financial
KeyCorp
Merchants Bancorp
Sterling Financial (WA)
Umpqua Holdings
U.S. Bancorp
Washington Mutual
Wells Fargo
West Coast Bancorp

HISTORICAL FINANCIALS

Company Type: Public

Income Statement

FYE: March 31

	ASSETS ($ mil.)	NET INCOME ($ mil.)	INCOME AS % OF ASSETS	EMPLOYEES
3/07	820.3	11.6	1.4%	255
3/06	763.8	9.7	1.3%	239
3/05	572.6	6.5	1.1%	—
3/04	520.5	6.6	1.3%	—
3/03	419.9	4.4	1.0%	—
Annual Growth	18.2%	27.4%	—	6.7%

2007 Year-End Financials

Equity as % of assets: 12.2%
Return on assets: 1.5%
Return on equity: 12.1%
Long-term debt ($ mil.): 9.9
No. of shares (mil.): 11.7
Market value ($ mil.): 186.6
Dividends
  Yield: 3.1%
  Payout: 49.5%
Sales ($ mil.): 70.3
R&D as % of sales: —
Advertising as % of sales: —

Stock History

NASDAQ (GS): RVSB

	STOCK PRICE ($) FY Close	P/E High/Low		PER SHARE ($) Earnings	Dividends	Book Value
3/07	15.94	18	12	1.01	0.50	8.56
3/06	13.38	16	12	0.86	0.34	15.88
3/05	10.63	17	14	0.67	0.16	11.98
3/04	10.10	16	12	0.69	0.28	13.64
3/03	8.49	17	13	0.50	0.25	12.51
Annual Growth	17.1%			19.2%	18.9%	(9.0%)

Rochester Medical

It's all about quality of life for Rochester Medical. The company focuses on urinary incontinence and urinary retention treatment products, including male external catheters and urethral inserts for women. The firm's RELEASE-NF catheter is designed to prevent urinary tract infections. Most of the company's products are made of silicone rather than latex to reduce the risk of allergic reactions. Rochester Medical makes a disposable device for women, the FemSoft Insert, for stress urinary incontinence. The company markets to hospitals and extended-care facilities.

In 2006 the company purchased assets from Coloplast and Mentor Medical, including sales offices and a warehouse facility in Lancing, England, through subsidiary Rochester Medical Limited. Rochester Medical also entered into a distribution agreement with Coloplast; the company will supply silicone male external catheters, which will be sold under Coloplast's brands around the globe.

In addition, that same year the company acquired assets from Mentor Corporation used in its silicon male external catheters business.

EXECUTIVES

Chairman, President, CEO, and Secretary: Anthony J. Conway, age 63, $238,496 pay
CFO and Treasurer: David A. (Dave) Jonas, age 43, $168,802 pay
Corporate VP: Martyn R. Sholtis, age 48, $172,189 pay
VP Marketing: Dara Lynn Horner, age 49, $154,970 pay
VP Production Technologies and Director: Philip J. Conway, age 51, $161,841 pay
Director of Human Resources: Elsa Maas
Director of Quality and Regulatory: Rob Anglin
Executive Secretary to CEO: Lonnie Boe
Director of International Sales: Mark Foote
National Sales Director: Brad Duffy
Quality Engineer: Prashanth Prabhakar
Auditors: McGladrey & Pullen, LLP

LOCATIONS

HQ: Rochester Medical Corporation
1 Rochester Medical Dr., Stewartville, MN 55976
Phone: 507-533-9600   **Fax:** 507-533-9740
Web: www.rocm.com

PRODUCTS/OPERATIONS

2007 Sales

	$ mil.	% of total
US	13.9	43
Europe	16.8	51
Other	2.0	6
Total	**32.7**	**100**

Selected Products

FemSoft (female urethral insert)
Personal Catheter (male and female catheter)
Pop-On (male external catheter)
RELEASE-NF (catheter for the prevention of urinary tract infection)
UltraFlex (male external catheter)
WideBand (male external catheter)

COMPETITORS

A.P. Møller - Mærsk
C. R. Bard
Hollister Incorporated
Johnson & Johnson
Kimberly-Clark
PhytoMedical Technologies
Procter & Gamble
Tyco

HISTORICAL FINANCIALS

Company Type: Public

Income Statement

FYE: September 30

	REVENUE ($ mil.)	NET INCOME ($ mil.)	NET PROFIT MARGIN	EMPLOYEES
9/07	32.7	34.0	104.0%	268
9/06	21.7	2.0	9.2%	—
9/05	15.9	0.9	5.7%	172
9/04	15.0	0.8	5.3%	—
9/03	14.7	0.3	2.0%	—
Annual Growth	22.1%	226.3%	—	24.8%

2007 Year-End Financials

Debt ratio: 9.4%
Return on equity: 77.6%
Cash ($ mil.): 37.1
Current ratio: 10.42
Long-term debt ($ mil.): 6.1
No. of shares (mil.): 11.7
Dividends
  Yield: —
  Payout: —
Market value ($ mil.): 212.2
R&D as % of sales: —
Advertising as % of sales: —

Stock History

NASDAQ (GM): ROCM

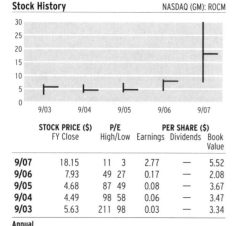

	STOCK PRICE ($) FY Close	P/E High	P/E Low	PER SHARE ($) Earnings	PER SHARE ($) Dividends	PER SHARE ($) Book Value
9/07	18.15	11	3	2.77	—	5.52
9/06	7.93	49	27	0.17	—	2.08
9/05	4.68	87	49	0.08	—	3.67
9/04	4.49	98	58	0.06	—	3.47
9/03	5.63	211	98	0.03	—	3.34
Annual Growth	34.0%	—	—	210.0%	—	13.3%

Rodman & Renshaw Capital Group

Investment bank Rodman & Renshaw provides private placements, underwriting, mergers & acquisitions support, equity research, and alternative financing techniques for its clients. The firm began as a Chicago-based partnership in the early 1950s, went public, was sold to Mexico's Abaco Casa de Bolsa, and ultimately was liquidated. A group of executives relaunched the firm, which focuses on emerging companies in the life sciences (biotech), technology (electronic communications), and mid-market industrial sectors. Former presidential candidate and retired general Wesley Clark is chairman of Rodman & Renshaw.

As part of a specialization strategy, the investment bank in 2006 launched its Acumen BioFin unit, specializing in serving clients in the biotechnology, medical device, and specialty pharmaceutical industries.

In 2007 the company completed a reverse merger with Enthrust Financial Services, allowing the company to be listed as a public company without the entanglements of an IPO.

EXECUTIVES

Chairman: Wesley K. Clark, age 62
Vice Chairman: Michael Vasinkevich, age 39
CEO and Director: Michael Lacovara, age 43
President and Director: Edward Rubin, age 39
CFO: Thomas Pinou, age 48
President Acumen BioFin Division and Senior Managing Director Investment Banking: John W. Chambers, age 45
Senior Managing Director Investment Banking: Matthew Geller, age 59
Senior Managing Director and Head Investment Banking: John J. Borer III, age 50
Managing Director, Director of Research, and Senior Biotechnology Analyst: Michael G. King Jr., age 46
Managing Director, Institutional Sales: Alger Boyer
Managing Director Institutional Sales and Director: F. Alger Boyer, age 38
Chief Compliance Officer and Director: William A. Iommi, age 57
Auditors: Marcum & Kliegman LLP

LOCATIONS

HQ: Rodman & Renshaw Capital Group, Inc.
  1270 Avenue of the Americas, 16th Floor, New York, NY 10020
Phone: 212-356-0500   **Fax:** 212-581-5690
Web: www.rodmanandrenshaw.com

COMPETITORS

Burrill & Company
Canaccord Adams
Cowen Group
Fox-Pitt
Friedman, Billings, Ramsey
Houlihan Lokey
Jefferies Group
KBW
Oppenheimer Holdings
Piper Jaffray
Raymond James Financial
Sandler O'Neill
Thomas Weisel Partners

HISTORICAL FINANCIALS

Company Type: Public

Income Statement

FYE: December 31

	REVENUE ($ mil.)	NET INCOME ($ mil.)	NET PROFIT MARGIN	EMPLOYEES
12/06	64.0	17.5	27.3%	105
12/05	29.3	4.5	15.4%	—
12/04	20.9	0.3	1.4%	—
Annual Growth	75.0%	663.8%	—	—

2006 Year-End Financials

Debt ratio: 0.0%
Return on equity: 115.4%
Cash ($ mil.): —
Current ratio: —
Long-term debt ($ mil.): 0.0

Net Income History

NASDAQ (GM): RODM

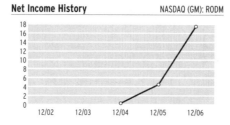

RPC, Inc.

RPC helps to grease the wheels of oil and gas production. Through its Cudd Pressure Control subsidiary, the company provides oil industry consulting and technical services including snubbing, coiled tubing, nitrogen services, and well control. Another subsidiary, Patterson Services, rents specialized tools and equipment such as drill pipe, tubing, and blowout preventers. RPC also provides maintenance, emergency services, and storage and inspection services for offshore and inland vessels. The company operates in most of the world's major oil producing regions. Chairman R. Randall Rollins and his brother Gary own 62% of RPC.

EXECUTIVES

Chairman: R. Randall Rollins, age 75, $400,000 pay
President, CEO, and Director: Richard A. Hubbell, age 63, $500,000 pay
VP, CFO, and Treasurer: Ben M. Palmer, age 47, $175,000 pay
VP, Secretary, and Director: Linda H. Graham, age 71, $135,000 pay
VP and General Manager, Cudd Pressure Control: Ray Saliba
VP and General Manager, Patterson Rental Tools: Jim Daniel
VP Corporate Finance: James C. (Jim) Landers
Investor Relations and Corporate Communication: Natasha Coleman
Auditors: Grant Thornton LLP

LOCATIONS

HQ: RPC, Inc.
  2170 Piedmont Rd. NE, Atlanta, GA 30324
Phone: 404-321-2140   **Fax:** 404-321-5483
Web: www.rpc.net

RPC has 85 facilities, including principal operations in Houma and Morgan City, Louisiana; Houston, and Kilgore, Texas; in Elk City and Seminole, Oklahoma; and in Rock Springs, Wyoming.

2006 Sales

	$ mil.	% of total
US	566.6	95
Other countries	30.0	5
Total	**596.6**	**100**

PRODUCTS/OPERATIONS

2006 Sales

	$ mil.	% of total
Technical services	495.1	83
Support services	101.5	17
Total	**596.6**	**100**

COMPETITORS

Baker Hughes
BJ Services
Boots & Coots
Ensign Energy Services
Exterran
Grant Prideco
Precision Drilling
Schlumberger
Transocean Inc.
Weatherford International

Income Statement				FYE: December 31
	REVENUE ($ mil.)	NET INCOME ($ mil.)	NET PROFIT MARGIN	EMPLOYEES
12/06	596.6	110.8	18.6%	2,000
12/05	427.6	66.5	15.6%	1,600
12/04	339.8	34.8	10.2%	—
12/03	270.5	10.9	4.0%	—
12/02	209.0	(5.3)	—	1,419
Annual Growth	30.0%	—	—	9.0%

2006 Year-End Financials

Debt ratio: 10.6%
Return on equity: 39.0%
Cash ($ mil.): 2.7
Current ratio: 2.57
Long-term debt ($ mil.): 35.6
No. of shares (mil.): 97.2

Dividends
 Yield: 1.0%
 Payout: 15.0%
Market value ($ mil.): 1,641.0
R&D as % of sales: —
Advertising as % of sales: —

Stock History — NYSE: RES

	STOCK PRICE ($) FY Close	P/E High/Low		PER SHARE ($) Earnings	Dividends	Book Value
12/06	16.88	21	10	1.13	0.17	3.45
12/05	17.56	27	9	0.67	0.07	3.61
12/04	7.44	24	9	0.36	0.04	4.20
12/03	3.26	35	24	0.11	0.03	5.28
12/02	3.44	—	—	(0.06)	0.03	5.07
Annual Growth	48.8%	—	—	—	54.3%	(9.2%)

RTI International Metals

RTI International Metals hopes manufacturers that seek a lightweight yet tougher-than-nails material will have titanium on the cranium. Through its subsidiaries, the company operates in two segments: titanium products and metals fabrication and distribution. The titanium group's products include ingots, bars, plates, sheets, strips, pipes, and welded tubing that are used by the aerospace industry to make aircraft bulkheads, tail sections, engine components, and wing supports. RTI's fabrication and distribution group operates through subsidiary RTI Energy Systems and makes pipe, tubing, and offshore riser systems for the oil, gas, and geothermal energy industries.

Other titanium products include bar used in medical implants and high-performance automotive engine parts.

It may sound odd at first but rising fuel prices are actually helping RTI International. As fuel prices go up, many commercial airlines are updating their fleets with new airplanes. Aircraft manufacturers Boeing and Airbus are building new planes designed to incur lower operating costs — partly through lower fuel consumption as a result of reduced aircraft weight. Boeing and Airbus between them have hefty aircraft order backlogs; this combined with a demand for lightweight components is great news for RTI International.

FMR Corp. owns about 12% of the company.

HISTORY

In 1964 Quantum Chemical (now a subsidiary of Millennium Chemical) and U.S. Steel (now United States Steel) formed Reactive Metals Inc. The company changed its name to RMI Titanium Company in 1971. It went public in 1990, with Quantum selling its shares and United States Steel retaining its interest.

The titanium industry is closely tied to the ups and downs of the aerospace industry, and just after RMI's IPO, the industry hit one of its cyclical slumps. RMI suffered years of losses even as it worked to cut costs and develop new markets. In 1992 it closed its titanium sponge (a porous metal used as raw material) facility and began buying lower-cost sponge from third parties. The next year it began providing seamless titanium pipe to California Energy Co. for use in that company's geothermal well. In 1995 RMI completed the world's first high-pressure titanium drilling riser for use in a Conoco North Sea oil rig.

In 1996 two events turned RMI's fortunes around. The aerospace industry took off once more, and golfers discovered titanium club heads. RMI formed a joint venture with Earthline Technologies in 1997 to offer soil-remediation services (perhaps relying on its experience as an owner of a Superfund site). In 1997 RMI bought Galt Alloys, a producer of ferrotitanium. The next year the company signed long-term supply agreements with Boeing, Northrop, and Aerospatiale. The company changed its name to RTI International Metals in 1998. USX sold off its 27% stake in 1999.

In 2000 RTI International Metals received a $6 million settlement from Boeing after the aerospace giant failed to meet the conditions of a 1999 long-term supply agreement between the two companies. Later in the year the company purchased the remaining shares of Reamet, S.A., a French-market distributor of titanium products. In 2001 RTI International Metals saw an increase in net income of about $12.1 million on sales of $285.9 million but noticed troubles ahead for its titanium group because of a weakening commercial aerospace industry.

In 2002 the company entered into agreements with Europe's largest aerospace group, European Aeronautic Defense and Space Company, to supply titanium products and parts. The following year, a work stoppage was held by the company's unionized employees at its Niles, Ohio plant. Non-union employees operated the plant until an agreement was hashed out between union representatives and the company's management.

EXECUTIVES

Chairman: Robert M. Hernandez, age 63
Vice Chairman and CEO: Dawne S. Hickton, age 49, $259,000 pay (prior to title change)
President, COO and Director: Michael C. Wellham, age 41, $158,000 pay (prior to title change)
EVP, RMI Titanium: Stephen R. Giangiordano, age 49
SVP and CFO: William T. Hull, age 49
SVP Strategic Planning and Finance:
 William F. Strome, age 53
Manager, Investor Relations: Richard E. Leone
Auditors: PricewaterhouseCoopers LLP

LOCATIONS

HQ: RTI International Metals, Inc.
 1000 Warren Ave., Niles, OH 44446
Phone: 330-544-7700 **Fax:** 330-544-7701
Web: www.rti-intl.com

RTI International Metals has titanium product manufacturing facilities in Ohio and Utah, and fabrication and distribution centers in California, Connecticut, Indiana, Missouri, Pennsylvania, and Texas, in the US, and in Canada, France, and the UK.

2006 Sales

	$ mil.	% of total
US	396.0	78
UK	38.1	8
France	32.6	6
Canada	14.6	3
Germany	8.6	2
South Korea	1.5	—
Other countries	14.0	3
Total	**505.4**	**100**

PRODUCTS/OPERATIONS

2006 Sales

	$ mil.	% of total
Fabrication & Distribution Group	300.5	59
Titanium Group	204.9	41
Total	**505.4**	**100**

Selected Products

Fabricated Products
 Cut shapes
 Drill pipe
 Engineered tubular products
 Engineering services
 Hot-formed parts
 Offshore riser systems
 Pipe
 Stress joints
Titanium Mill Products
 Billet
 Bloom
 Ingot
 Plate
 Sheet
 Slab
 Titanium powders
 Welded tubes

COMPETITORS

Allegheny Technologies
Carpenter Technology
Hurlen Corporation
Liquidmetal
Metals USA
Titanium Metals

HISTORICAL FINANCIALS
Company Type: Public

Income Statement				FYE: December 31
	REVENUE ($ mil.)	NET INCOME ($ mil.)	NET PROFIT MARGIN	EMPLOYEES
12/06	505.4	75.7	15.0%	1,362
12/05	346.9	38.9	11.2%	1,225
12/04	214.6	(3.0)	—	—
12/03	205.5	4.7	2.3%	—
12/02	270.9	15.1	5.6%	1,202
Annual Growth	16.9%	49.6%	—	3.2%

2006 Year-End Financials

Debt ratio: 2.9%
Return on equity: 18.0%
Cash ($ mil.): 125.1
Current ratio: 4.61
Long-term debt ($ mil.): 13.3
No. of shares (mil.): 23.0

Dividends
 Yield: —
 Payout: —
Market value ($ mil.): 1,796.5
R&D as % of sales: —
Advertising as % of sales: —

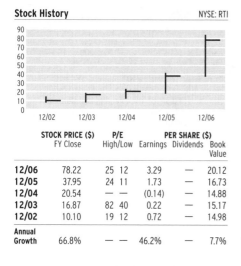

	STOCK PRICE ($) FY Close	P/E High/Low		PER SHARE ($) Earnings	Dividends	Book Value
12/06	78.22	25	12	3.29	—	20.12
12/05	37.95	24	11	1.73	—	16.73
12/04	20.54	—	—	(0.14)	—	14.88
12/03	16.87	82	40	0.22	—	15.17
12/02	10.10	19	12	0.72	—	14.98
Annual Growth	66.8%	—	—	46.2%	—	7.7%

Rudolph Technologies

Rudolph Technologies' inspection and metrology systems lead the way to better yields for chip makers. To create semiconductors, manufacturers deposit precise layers of conducting and insulating materials on silicon wafers. Rudolph makes process control metrology equipment (about one-third of sales) that monitors these layers to ensure that the material doesn't get too thick or too thin. Its inspection equipment (one-half of Rudolph's sales) looks for defects not obvious to the human eye, such as tiny scratches or gouges in the surface of a silicon wafer. The company sells to more than 70 semiconductor manufacturers worldwide; Intel accounts for about 23% of sales.

In 2006 Rudolph acquired August Technology, a supplier of semiconductor inspection and metrology tools, for about $193 million in cash and stock, beating out competing bids from rivals KLA-Tencor and Nanometrics.

The August Technology acquisition saga played out for more than a year, from Nanometrics' agreement to acquire August in early 2005 to Rudolph's winning bid in mid-2005. August then restated its financial results for fiscal 2004 and the first half of fiscal 2005, which delayed the consummation of Rudolph's acquisition offer until early 2006. August became Rudolph's Advanced Macro Defect Inspection business unit.

Late in 2007 Rudolph agreed to buy the semiconductor business of Applied Precision. Terms of the deal were not disclosed.

Rudolph also expanded its offerings with its 2002 purchase of ISOA, a privately held maker of defect control equipment.

The company, with more than 70% of its sales from customers outside the US, reduced its workforce in response to the dismal worldwide chip industry slump of the early 21st century.

Liberty Capital Partners owns more than 9% of Rudolph. FMR (Fidelity Investments) holds nearly 9% of the company. Mazama Capital Management has an equity stake of around 5%. Company insiders own nearly 19% of Rudolph Technologies.

EXECUTIVES

Chairman and CEO: Paul F. McLaughlin, age 61, $480,496 pay
COO: Alexander A. (Alex) Oscilowski, age 48
EVP, General Manager, Inspection: Nathan H. Little, age 55, $210,400 pay
SVP, Finance and Administration, CFO, and Secretary: Steven R. Roth, age 46, $236,389 pay
VP and General Manager, Data Analysis and Review: Michael P. Plisinski, age 37, $177,789 pay
VP, Corporate Marketing: Ardelle R. Johnson, age 52
VP, Manufacturing, Inspection: Jeffrey T. (Jeff) Nelson, age 51
VP, International Accounts: Ajay Khanna, age 47
VP and General Counsel: Robert A. Koch, age 45
VP, Global Customer Support: Robert DiCrosta, age 59
VP, Global Sales: D. Mayson Brooks, age 48
VP, New Business Development: George J. Collins, age 58
President, Japan KK: Yoshiro Ogaya
Auditors: KPMG LLP

LOCATIONS

HQ: Rudolph Technologies, Inc.
   1 Rudolph Rd., Flanders, NJ 07836
Phone: 973-691-1300   **Fax:** 973-691-4863
Web: www.rudolphtech.com

Rudolph Technologies has facilities in China, Japan, Singapore, South Korea, Taiwan, the UK, and the US.

2006 Sales

	$ mil.	% of total
Asia/Pacific	120.5	60
US	59.1	29
Europe	21.6	11
Total	**201.2**	**100**

PRODUCTS/OPERATIONS

2006 Sales

	% of total
Systems	
Inspection	50
Metrology	34
Parts	7
Services	6
Licensing	3
Total	**100**

Selected Products

3Di Inspection System (inspection for bumped devices)
AutoEL Series (ellipsometers for measuring film thickness, refractive index, and absorption)
AXi Series (defect inspection for various process steps)
MetaPULSE Systems (optical acoustic-based systems for opaque thin-film layers)
NSX Series (macro-defect inspection)
S3000 and S2000 Systems (transparent thin-film measurement systems)
WaferView (automated macro-defect lithography inspection systems)
YieldView (yield management and process control software)

COMPETITORS

Applied Materials	Metara
Camtek	Nanometrics
Carl Zeiss	Nikon
Dainippon Screen	Nova Measuring
FEI	PANalytical
Hexagon AB	PDF Solutions
Hitachi High-Technologies	Qcept
ICOS Vision Systems	Veeco Instruments
KLA-Tencor	Yield Dynamics

HISTORICAL FINANCIALS

Company Type: Public

Income Statement   FYE: December 31

	REVENUE ($ mil.)	NET INCOME ($ mil.)	NET PROFIT MARGIN	EMPLOYEES
12/06	201.2	12.7	6.3%	620
12/05	82.9	5.0	6.0%	312
12/04	84.3	6.8	8.1%	—
12/03	58.5	1.8	3.1%	—
12/02	57.4	(1.4)	—	333
Annual Growth	36.8%	—	—	16.8%

2006 Year-End Financials

Debt ratio: —	Dividends
Return on equity: 4.6%	Yield: —
Cash ($ mil.): 106.2	Payout: —
Current ratio: 6.52	Market value ($ mil.): 461.3
Long-term debt ($ mil.): —	R&D as % of sales: —
No. of shares (mil.): 29.0	Advertising as % of sales: —

Stock History   NASDAQ (GS): RTEC

	STOCK PRICE ($) FY Close	P/E High/Low		PER SHARE ($) Earnings	Dividends	Book Value
12/06	15.92	44	28	0.46	—	13.56
12/05	12.88	66	40	0.29	—	9.71
12/04	17.17	76	33	0.40	—	9.32
12/03	24.54	259	101	0.11	—	8.92
12/02	19.16	—	—	(0.09)	—	8.82
Annual Growth	(4.5%)	—	—	—	—	11.3%

St. Mary Land & Exploration

St. Mary Land & Exploration isn't afraid to travel. The oil and gas exploration and production company spreads its operations across the US: the midcontinent, the ArkLaTex region and Gulf Coast, the Williston Basin in North Dakota and Montana, and the Permian Basin in West Texas and New Mexico. In 2006 the company posted estimated proved reserves of 927.6 billion cu. ft. of natural gas equivalent. In the late 1990s St. Mary Land & Exploration sold its Russian oil and North American copper mining investments to focus on its core US oil and gas properties. The company has expanded its activities in the Rockies through the acquisition of coalbed methane assets in Wyoming and Montana.

In addition to growing through the drill bit, St. Mary Land & Exploration makes selective acquisitions. In 2004, it acquired Goldmark Engineering, and in 2005, Agate Petroleum.

In 2006 the company acquired oil and gas properties in the Sweetie Peck Field in the Permian Basin for $247.6 million.

In 2008 it sold oil and gas properties in the Rockies and Mid-Continent regions to Abraxas Petroleum's Abraxas Energy Partners for $131.6 million.

EXECUTIVES

Chairman: Mark A. Hellerstein, age 54, $435,240 pay (prior to title change)
President, CEO, and Director: Anthony J. (Tony) Best, age 57, $1,003,112 pay
EVP and COO: Javan D. (Jay) Ottoson, age 48
SVP, CFO, Treasurer, and Secretary: David W. Honeyfield, age 39, $219,240 pay
SVP and Regional Manager, Mid-Continent: Paul M. Veatch, age 39
SVP and Regional Manager ArkLaTex: Stephen Pugh
SVP and Regional Manager Rocky Mountain: Mark D. Mueller
VP Administration: Garry A. Wilkening, age 56
VP Land and Legal, and Assistant Secretary: Milam Randolph Pharo, age 54, $189,000 pay
Controller: Mark T. Solomon
Assistant VP and Director Marketing: David J. Whitcomb
Director Investor Relations: Brent A. Collins
Auditors: Deloitte & Touche LLP

LOCATIONS

HQ: St. Mary Land & Exploration Company
1776 Lincoln St., Ste. 700, Denver, CO 80203
Phone: 303-861-8140   **Fax:** 303-861-0934
Web: www.stmaryland.com

PRODUCTS/OPERATIONS

2006 Proved Reserves

	% of total
Rocky Mountains	46
Midcontinent	18
ArkLaTex	17
Permian Basin	15
Gulf Coast	4
Total	**100**

COMPETITORS

Abraxas Petroleum
Apache
BP
Devon Energy
Exxon Mobil
Pioneer Natural Resources
Range Resources
Royal Dutch Shell

HISTORICAL FINANCIALS

Company Type: Public

Income Statement

FYE: December 31

	REVENUE ($ mil.)	NET INCOME ($ mil.)	NET PROFIT MARGIN	EMPLOYEES
12/06	787.7	190.0	24.1%	359
12/05	739.6	151.9	20.5%	305
12/04	483.4	92.5	19.1%	—
12/03	393.9	95.6	24.3%	—
12/02	199.0	27.6	13.9%	185
Annual Growth	**41.1%**	**62.0%**	**—**	**18.0%**

2006 Year-End Financials

Debt ratio: 64.6%
Return on equity: 28.9%
Cash ($ mil.): 59.0
Current ratio: 1.11
Long-term debt ($ mil.): 480.4
No. of shares (mil.): 55.0
Dividends
  Yield: 0.3%
  Payout: 3.4%
Market value ($ mil.): 2,026.3
R&D as % of sales: —
Advertising as % of sales: —

Stock History

NYSE: SM

	STOCK PRICE ($) FY Close	P/E High	P/E Low	Earnings	Dividends	Book Value
12/06	36.84	16	11	2.94	0.10	13.52
12/05	36.81	18	8	2.33	0.10	10.03
12/04	20.87	15	10	1.44	0.05	17.01
12/03	14.25	11	8	1.40	0.05	13.83
12/02	12.50	28	19	0.49	0.05	10.71
Annual Growth	**31.0%**	**—**	**—**	**56.5%**	**18.9%**	**6.0%**

---

salesforce.com

salesforce.com knows the power of good customer relations. The company offers hosted applications that manage customer information for sales, marketing, and customer support, providing clients with a rapidly deployable alternative to buying and maintaining enterprise software. salesforce.com's applications are used for generating sales leads, maintaining customer information, and tracking customer interactions. The company's services can be accessed from devices including PCs, cellular phones, and personal digital assistants. CEO Marc Benioff owns about 26% of the company.

The company's nearly 30,000 customers come from a variety of industries, including financial services, telecommunications, manufacturing, and entertainment.

salesforce.com continues to bolster its offerings as part of a push to expand past its core market of small and midsized businesses. The company has also begun to encourage third parties (including customers and independent software vendors) to develop applications that run on salesforce.com's technology platform, but are sold separately as modules or add-ons.

In April 2006 the company acquired Sendia (a provider of wireless software delivery tools) for about $15 million in cash, marking the first acquisition in salesforce.com's history. It purchased Koral in March 2007. Koral provided the technology behind salesforce.com's content management service.

EXECUTIVES

Chairman and CEO: Marc Benioff, age 42, $10 pay
CFO: Steven M. (Steve) Cakebread, age 56, $476,100 pay
President, Worldwide Sales and Distribution: Jim Steele, age 51, $647,100 pay
President, Worldwide Corporate Sales and Services: Frank R. Van Veenendaal, age 47
EVP, Americas: Dave Orrico
EVP, Law, Policy, and Corporate Strategy: Kenneth I. (Ken) Juster, age 51, $634,800 pay
EVP, Technology: Parker Harris, age 40

SVP and General Counsel: David Schellhase, age 43
SVP, Corporate and Product Marketing: Kendall Collins
SVP, Global Integration/Technology Services: Cindy Warner
SVP, Marketing: Elizabeth Pinkham
SVP, Service Delivery and CIO: Jim Cavalieri, age 36, $419,250 pay
SVP, Worldwide Channel and Alliances: Bobby Napiltonia
SVP and Chief Accounting Officer: Bill Dewes, age 50
SVP Strategic Employee Services: Michael Kent
CTO: David (Dave) Moellenhoff, age 36, $369,709 pay
Auditors: Ernst & Young LLP

LOCATIONS

HQ: salesforce.com, inc.
1 Market St., Ste. 300, San Francisco, CA 94105
Phone: 415-901-7000   **Fax:** 415-901-7040
Web: www.salesforce.com

2007 Sales

	$ mil.	% of total
Americas	387.6	78
Europe	75.0	15
Asia/Pacific	34.5	7
Total	**497.1**	**100**

PRODUCTS/OPERATIONS

2007 Sales

	$ mil.	% of total
Subscription & support	451.7	91
Professional service & other	45.4	9
Total	**497.1**	**100**

COMPETITORS

Amdocs
BMC Software
Chordiant Software
Consona CRM
Epicor Software
FrontRange Solutions
IBM
Infor global
Kana
Microsoft Dynamics
NetSuite
Oracle
Pivotal
RightNow Technologies
Sage Software
SAP

HISTORICAL FINANCIALS

Company Type: Public

Income Statement

FYE: January 31

	REVENUE ($ mil.)	NET INCOME ($ mil.)	NET PROFIT MARGIN	EMPLOYEES
1/07	497.1	0.5	0.1%	2,070
1/06	309.9	28.5	9.2%	1,304
1/05	176.4	7.3	4.1%	—
1/04	96.0	3.5	3.6%	—
1/03	51.0	(9.7)	—	—
Annual Growth	**76.7%**	**—**	**—**	**58.7%**

2007 Year-End Financials

Debt ratio: 0.0%
Return on equity: 0.2%
Cash ($ mil.): 252.4
Current ratio: 1.11
Long-term debt ($ mil.): 0.0
No. of shares (mil.): 114.5
Dividends
  Yield: —
  Payout: —
Market value ($ mil.): 5,020.2
R&D as % of sales: —
Advertising as % of sales: —

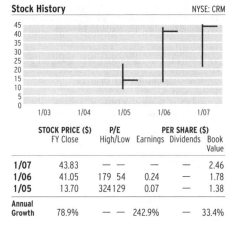

Stock History   NYSE: CRM

	STOCK PRICE ($) FY Close	P/E High/Low	Earnings	PER SHARE ($) Dividends	Book Value
1/07	43.83	— —	—	—	2.46
1/06	41.05	179 54	0.24	—	1.78
1/05	13.70	324 129	0.07	—	1.38
Annual Growth	78.9%	— —	242.9%	—	33.4%

Salix Pharmaceuticals

Salix Pharmaceuticals is a finishing school for tummy drugs. Focusing on drugs for gastrointestinal diseases, the company shops for drug products that are nearing commercial viability. It then takes them through the final development stages and brings them to market. The company's products already on the market include Colazal (for ulcerative colitis), Azasan (immune system suppressant), Proctocort (hydrocortisone suppositories and cream for hemorrhoids), and Xifaxan (an antibiotic to prevent travelers' diarrhea). Its string of drug candidates awaiting FDA approval include bowel purgatives and another treatment for ulcerative colitis. Salix' sales and marketing team primarily targets gastroenterologists.

Azasan was acquired from aaiPharma, and while it's only received approval for the treatment of severe arthritis and to prevent kidney transplant rejection, physicians are using it on patients with Crohn's disease and ulcerative colitis.

The company expanded its gastroenterology product line when it acquired InKine Pharmaceutical in 2005. InKine brought with it Visicol which is used to clear the bowels prior to colonoscopy. Salix received approval in 2006 for the use of Colazal to treat ulcerative colitis in children. The next year, the company acquired the US prescription rights to Pepcid and Diuril oral suspensions from Merck as part of its strategy to expand product lines.

Salix relies on third-party manufacturers to produce its materials and does not operate any manufacturing facilities.

EXECUTIVES

Chairman: John F. Chappell, age 70
President, CEO, and Director: Carolyn J. Logan, age 58, $688,000 pay
SVP Finance and Administration and CFO: Adam C. Derbyshire, age 41, $422,000 pay
VP Research and Development and Chief Development Officer: William P. Forbes, age 46, $380,000 pay
Director, Investor Relations and Corporate Communications: G. Michael Freeman
Auditors: PricewaterhouseCoopers LLP

LOCATIONS

HQ: Salix Pharmaceuticals, Ltd.
    1700 Perimeter Park Dr., Morrisville, NC 27560
Phone: 919-862-1000   **Fax:** 919-228-4265
Web: www.salix.com

Salix Pharmaceuticals has facilities in Morrisville, North Carolina and Palo Alto, California.

PRODUCTS/OPERATIONS

2006 Sales

	$ mil.	% of total
Colazal	103.5	49
Xifaxan	51.6	25
Purgatives	45.5	22
Other	7.9	4
Total	**208.5**	**100**

COMPETITORS

Axcan Pharma
Bayer AG
Bradley Pharmaceuticals
C.B. Fleet
Ferndale Laboratories
GlaxoSmithKline
Pfizer
Procter & Gamble
Prometheus Labs
Ranbaxy Pharmaceuticals
SCHWARZ PHARMA, Inc.
Shire
Solvay
Teva Pharmaceuticals USA

HISTORICAL FINANCIALS

Company Type: Public

Income Statement   FYE: December 31

	REVENUE ($ mil.)	NET INCOME ($ mil.)	NET PROFIT MARGIN	EMPLOYEES
12/06	208.5	31.5	15.1%	240
12/05	154.9	(60.6)	—	215
12/04	105.5	6.8	6.4%	—
12/03	55.8	(20.1)	—	—
12/02	33.5	(24.7)	—	135
Annual Growth	57.9%	—	—	15.5%

2006 Year-End Financials

Debt ratio: 0.2%	Dividends
Return on equity: 12.2%	Yield: —
Cash ($ mil.): 76.5	Payout: —
Current ratio: 3.78	Market value ($ mil.): 572.4
Long-term debt ($ mil.): 0.6	R&D as % of sales: —
No. of shares (mil.): 47.0	Advertising as % of sales: —

Stock History   NASDAQ (GM): SLXP

	STOCK PRICE ($) FY Close	P/E High/Low	Earnings	PER SHARE ($) Dividends	Book Value
12/06	12.17	29 15	0.65	—	5.90
12/05	17.58	— —	(1.55)	—	5.18
12/04	17.59	135 78	0.18	—	2.37
12/03	15.12	— —	(0.61)	—	3.12
12/02	4.66	— —	(0.81)	—	2.83
Annual Growth	27.1%	— —	—	—	20.2%

SandRidge Energy

This sand ridge reveals not a desert but a vista of future profits. SandRidge Energy explores for and produces oil and natural gas, mainly in West Texas. The company also owns and operates drilling rigs and a related oilfield services business. In addition it operates gas gathering, marketing, and processing subsidiaries. Its 87%-owned PetroSource subsidiary operates CO2-treating and transportation facilities and has tertiary oil recovery operations. SandRidge Energy also has oil and gas acreage in Oklahoma's Anadarko and Arkoma Basins, and in Colorado's Piceance Basin. It has estimated net proved reserves of 1 trillion cu. ft. equivalent. CEO Tom Ward holds 34% of the company.

SandRidge Energy's strategy for growth is to integrate its exploration and production operations with its drilling and oilfield services and CO2 flooding businesses. Additionally, it plans to pursue tertiary oil recovery operations and purchase more drilling rigs and related oilfield service equipment. The company plans to explore acquisition opportunities as well.

In 2006 the company acquired American Real Estate Partners' NEG Oil & Gas for $1.5 billion, greatly expanding its holdings in West Texas.

SandRidge Energy operates 32 drilling rigs. The company operates an oil and natural gas property base with 1,281 wells. It has CO2 transportation pipelines and interests in more than 541,787 net acres of leasehold properties.

The company's oilfield services mainly support its own operations. The services include pulling units, mud logging, trucking, tool rentals, location and road construction, and roustabout services. SandRidge Energy also provides services to third parties.

The company was founded (as Riata Energy) in 1984 and began exploration and production operations in 1986.

EXECUTIVES

Chairman, President, and CEO: Tom L. Ward, age 47
EVP, Exploration: Todd N. Tipton, age 51
EVP, Land: Larry K. Coshow, age 48
EVP and COO: Matthew K. Grubb, age 43
EVP and CFO: Dirk M. Van Doren, age 48
SVP, Information Technology and Chief Information Officer: Thomas L. Winton, age 60
SVP, Reservoir Engineering: Rodney E. Johnson, age 50
SVP, Legal and General Counsel: V. Bruce Thompson, age 60
SVP, Human Resources: Mary L. Whitson, age 46
SVP, Accounting: Randall D. Cooley, age 53
SVP Business Development: Kevin R. White, age 48
Auditors: PricewaterhouseCoopers LLP

LOCATIONS

HQ: SandRidge Energy, Inc.
    1601 NW Expwy., Ste. 1600,
    Oklahoma City, OK 73118
Phone: 405-753-5500   **Fax:** 405-753-5975
Web: www.sandridgeenergy.com

PRODUCTS/OPERATIONS

2006 Sales

	$ mil.	% of total
Drilling & oil field services	138.6	36
Midstream services	122.9	32
Exploration & production	106.4	27
Other	20.3	5
Total	**388.2**	**100**

COMPETITORS

Apache
Brigham Exploration
Chesapeake Energy
DCP Midstream Partners
Denbury Resources
El Paso
Martin Midstream Partners
Occidental Permian
TEPPCO Partners
Williams Companies

HISTORICAL FINANCIALS

Company Type: Public

Income Statement
FYE: December 31

	REVENUE ($ mil.)	NET INCOME ($ mil.)	NET PROFIT MARGIN	EMPLOYEES
12/06	388.2	15.6	4.0%	1,752
12/05	287.7	18.1	6.3%	664
12/04	173.3	21.3	12.3%	936
12/03	151.7	8.5	5.6%	—
12/02	58.7	1.6	2.7%	—
Annual Growth	60.4%	76.7%	—	36.8%

2006 Year-End Financials

Debt ratio: 160.1%
Return on equity: 3.3%
Cash ($ mil.): 38.9
Current ratio: 1.10
Long-term debt ($ mil.): 1,040.6

Net Income History
NYSE: SD

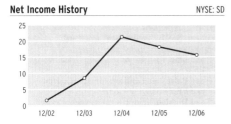

Sapient Corporation

Sapient is no sap when it comes to services. A provider of business and technology consulting services, Sapient targets information-based businesses in the financial services, communications and technology, automotive and industrial manufacturing, consumer, public services, health care, energy services, and transportation industries. Customers such as AT&T Mobility (formerly Cingular), Staples, Janus Capital, and agencies of the US government use Sapient's consulting, design, implementation, user experience research, and other services for e-commerce, customer relationship management, high-volume transaction processing, online supply chain development, learning and knowledge management, and other processes.

Sapient offers its services primarily on a fixed-price basis, targeting customers who want fast services at low costs. The company relies on its international facilities, which enable development teams to work on projects 24 hours a day, to ensure quick turnaround.

In mid-2005 the company acquired Miami-based Business Information Solutions, a provider of consulting services for companies using enterprise planning software developed by SAP.

In 2006 Sapient purchased Planning Group International. Later that year the company sold its stake in its HWT subsidiary for about $5.4 million.

Sapient founders Jerry Greenberg and Stuart Moore each own 17% of the company.

HISTORY

In 1991 information technology systems salesman Jerry Greenberg and software developer Stuart Moore saw a market for providing businesses with fixed-price software systems by a guaranteed delivery date. Greenberg and Moore charged more than $100,000 on their credit cards and used $60,000 of their personal savings to form Sapient.

As the company took off, Moore managed internal operations, such as creating software, and Greenberg handled sales and finance. The two worked closely together and helped establish teamwork as Sapient's most prized trait (as co-CEOs, they shared an office with only inches separating their desks, and they required the same of all senior managers).

The company began specializing in distinct areas such as telecommunications, manufacturing, and energy, and it found a third of its early clients in financial services. Specialization enabled the company to reuse software; coupling that with Sapient's proprietary team-based development process resulted in lower costs and shorter development times.

The company went public in 1996 and started expanding through acquisitions, buying systems integrators and Internet consultants. It opened offices in London in 1998, and in Italy and Australia the next year. Also in 1999 Sapient increased its staff by more than 40% and expanded its consulting services with the purchase of customer behavior specialist E.Lab.

In 2000 Sapient opened an office in India and acquired Human Code, a privately held developer of education, e-commerce, and entertainment software, for about $104 million. The next year, looking to cut costs, the company closed its Australian office, cut its workforce by about 35%, and exited the gaming business. It also began to shift more of its project workload to its office in India in order to take advantage of lower operating costs.

Citing decreased demand for its services in the troubled economic climate, Sapient posted a loss of nearly $190 million for 2001, followed by a loss of nearly $230 million for 2002. The company continued to reduce its workforce in 2002, cutting about 600 more jobs. The following year the company began to see its service revenues pick up, and its workforce size stabilized.

EXECUTIVES

Chairman: Jeffrey M. (Jeff) Cunningham, age 54
President, CEO, and Director: Alan J. Herrick, age 41
COO and Chief Administrative Officer:
Preston B. Bradford, age 50
SVP and CFO: Joseph S. (Joe) Tibbetts Jr., age 55
SVP and Chief Creative Officer: Gaston Legorburu
SVP, North American Operations: Alan M. Wexler
SVP, General Counsel, and Secretary: Jane E. Owens, age 53
SVP: Christopher R. (Chris) Davey
SVP: Amy B. Shah
SVP: Hank G. Summy
SVP: Bob Van Beber

VP and CIO: Changappa Kodendera
VP Corporate Controller and Chief Accounting Officer:
Stephen P. Sarno, age 40
VP Corporate Communications: Gail Scibelli
Managing Director and VP, European Operations:
Christian Oversohl
Leader, Global Trading and Risk Management:
Chip Register
Creative Director: Federico Montemurro
Director of Technology: Ravi Narla
Director Investor Relations: Mindy S. Kohl
Auditors: PricewaterhouseCoopers LLP

LOCATIONS

HQ: Sapient Corporation
25 1st St., Cambridge, MA 02141
Phone: 617-621-0200 **Fax:** 617-621-1300
Web: www.sapient.com

PRODUCTS/OPERATIONS

2006 Sales

	% of total
North America Commercial	63
UK	18
Germany	8
Experience Marketing	7
Government Services	4
Total	**100**

Selected Services

Business and operational consulting
Creative design
Internet consulting
Internet design
Software implementation
Systems design and integration
Technology development
User experience research

COMPETITORS

Accenture
Booz Allen
Boston Consulting
Capgemini
CIBER
Computer Sciences Corp.
Computer Task Group
Diamond Management & Technology Consultants
EDS
IBM
Inforte
Keane
Perot Systems
Sapiens
Technology Solutions
Unisys

HISTORICAL FINANCIALS

Company Type: Public

Income Statement
FYE: December 31

	REVENUE ($ mil.)	NET INCOME ($ mil.)	NET PROFIT MARGIN	EMPLOYEES
12/06	421.6	3.1	0.7%	4,952
12/05	333.0	25.7	7.7%	3,017
12/04	266.0	22.8	8.6%	—
12/03	194.4	(4.9)	—	—
12/02	182.4	(229.2)	—	1,491
Annual Growth	23.3%	—	—	35.0%

2006 Year-End Financials

Debt ratio: —
Return on equity: 1.5%
Cash ($ mil.): 127.4
Current ratio: 2.37
Long-term debt ($ mil.): —
No. of shares (mil.): 123.3
Dividends
  Yield: —
  Payout: —
Market value ($ mil.): 676.9
R&D as % of sales: —
Advertising as % of sales: —

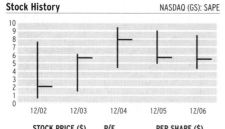

	STOCK PRICE ($) FY Close	P/E High/Low	PER SHARE ($) Earnings	Dividends	Book Value
12/06	5.49	279 145	0.03	—	1.74
12/05	5.69	45 25	0.20	—	1.64
12/04	7.91	52 25	0.18	—	1.50
12/03	5.64	— —	(0.04)	—	1.25
12/02	2.05	— —	(1.83)	—	1.28
Annual Growth	27.9%	— —	—	—	8.0%

Savannah Bancorp

Savannah Bancorp's "garden" grows green, rather than good and evil. The holding company owns Savannah Bank, Bryan Bank & Trust, and Harbourside Community Bank. The banks have more than a half-dozen offices in coastal Georgia and South Carolina. The banks offer a variety of retail services, including checking, savings, and money market accounts, and certificates of deposit. Real estate mortgage loans make up about two-thirds of the company's loan portfolio; the banks also make construction, business, and consumer loans. The banks serve metro Savannah, Georgia, and Hilton Head, South Carolina.

In 2006 Savannah Bancorp launched Harbourside Community Bank on Hilton Head; the company had previously operated a mortgage loan production office there.

The company acquired Minis & Co., Inc., a Savannah-based investment advisory firm, in 2007, adding to its trust and investment services.

EXECUTIVES

Chairman and General Counsel, Savannah Bancorp and The Savannah Bank: J. Wiley Ellis, age 66
Vice Chairman; Chairman and CEO, Bryan Bank & Trust: E. James (Jimmy) Burnsed, age 67, $125,000 pay
President, CEO, and Director; President and CEO, The Savannah Bank: John C. Helmken II, age 44, $175,000 pay
CFO; EVP and CFO, The Savannah Bank: Robert B. Briscoe, age 55, $125,000 pay
EVP, Lending, The Savannah Bancorp and The Savannah Bank: R. Stephen Stramm, age 57, $150,000 pay
SVP, Operations: Tommy E. Wyatt
SVP Credit and Risk Management: Robert T. Whelen Jr., age 45
VP, Accounting: Michael W. Harden Jr.
VP, Human Resources: James M. Joyce
Secretary and Director; Secretary, The Savannah Bank: J. Curtis Lewis III, age 54
Controller: Cynthia H. Rochefort
Director, Marketing and Training: Barbara R. Thureson
President, Bryan Bank & Trust: Jerry O'Dell (Dell) Keith
President and CEO, Harbourside Community Bank: Thomas W. (Tom) Lennox
Auditors: Mauldin & Jenkins, LLC

LOCATIONS

HQ: The Savannah Bancorp, Inc.
25 Bull St., Savannah, GA 31401
Phone: 912-629-6486 **Fax:** 912-232-3733
Web: www.savb.com

Savannah Bancorp operates in Georgia's Bryan and Chatham counties and in South Carolina's Beaufort County.

PRODUCTS/OPERATIONS

2006 Sales

	% of total
Interest income	
Loans	87
Securities & other	6
Service charges on deposit accounts	2
Other	5
Total	**100**

COMPETITORS

Bank of America
BB&T
Citizens Effingham
Delta Financial
Southeastern Banking
SunTrust
Synovus
Wachovia

HISTORICAL FINANCIALS

Company Type: Public

Income Statement

FYE: December 31

	ASSETS ($ mil.)	NET INCOME ($ mil.)	INCOME AS % OF ASSETS	EMPLOYEES
12/06	843.5	10.0	1.2%	207
12/05	717.9	9.0	1.3%	200
12/04	617.3	5.7	0.9%	—
12/03	476.9	4.6	1.0%	—
12/02	437.6	4.5	1.0%	139
Annual Growth	17.8%	22.1%	—	10.5%

2006 Year-End Financials

Equity as % of assets: 7.9%
Return on assets: 1.3%
Return on equity: 16.0%
Long-term debt ($ mil.): 23.6
No. of shares (mil.): 5.8
Market value ($ mil.): 157.5
Dividends
Yield: 1.6%
Payout: 26.5%
Sales ($ mil.): 59.5
R&D as % of sales: —
Advertising as % of sales: —

Stock History

NASDAQ (GM): SAVB

	STOCK PRICE ($) FY Close	P/E High/Low	PER SHARE ($) Earnings	Dividends	Book Value
12/06	27.25	18 16	1.70	0.45	11.52
12/05	28.38	19 12	1.63	0.43	12.75
12/04	21.64	20 15	1.09	0.21	9.74
12/03	18.56	21 14	0.89	1.65	11.20
12/02	12.20	17 13	0.86	0.29	11.65
Annual Growth	22.3%	— —	18.6%	11.6%	(0.3%)

SCBT Financial

SCBT Financial is the holding company for South Carolina Bank and Trust and South Carolina Bank and Trust of the Piedmont. The banks operate nearly 50 branches throughout the Palmetto state, providing deposit accounts and loans, as well as private banking, trust, and investment services. Nearly half of the company's loan portfolio is devoted to commercial mortgages; consumer real estate loans are almost 25%. The Mortgage Banc, a subsidiary of South Carolina Bank and Trust, provides mortgage products and services to other banks and mortgage companies.

The company is growing by opening new branches and loan production offices throughout South Carolina. SCBT Financial opened several new locations in 2006.

The company acquired New Commerce BanCorp and Sun Bancshares in 2005. Both financial institutions were merged into South Carolina Bank and Trust.

EXECUTIVES

Chairman, SCBT Financial and South Carolina Bank and Trust: Robert R. Horger, age 56
President, CEO, and Director; CEO, South Carolina Bank and Trust: Robert R. Hill Jr., age 40, $300,000 pay
COO and CFO: John C. Pollok, age 41, $204,212 pay (prior to promotion)
President, South Carolina Bank and Trust: John F. Windley, $190,962 pay
EVP and Chief Risk Officer: Richard C. Mathis, age 56, $264,870 pay
EVP and Chief Credit Officer: Joe Burns, age 52
EVP and CIO: Rodney W. Overby
EVP and Division Head, Lowcountry and Orangeburg Regions: Dane H. Murray
EVP and Regional President: James A. (Alex) Shuford III
EVP and Senior Credit Administrator: P. Hobson Busby
EVP, Support Division: Allen M. Hay Jr.
SVP and Director, Marketing: Frank G. Carter
SVP and Sales Executive: Marc J. Bogan
SVP, Human Resources: Leslie M. Dunn
VP and Public Relations Director: Donna Pullen
President and CEO, South Carolina Bank and Trust of the Piedmont: Thomas S. Camp, age 55, $185,402 pay
President, The Mortgage Banc: Thomas S. Ledbetter
President, Wealth Management Group: Todd Harward
Controller and Principal Accounting Officer, SCBT Financial, South Carolina Bank and Trust, and South Carolina Bank and Trust of Piedmont: Karen L. Dey
President, Midlands Region: John S. (Jack) Goettee
Corporate Secretary: Renee R. Brooks
Auditors: J. W. Hunt and Company, LLP

LOCATIONS

HQ: SCBT Financial Corporation
520 Gervais St., Columbia, SC 29201
Phone: 803-771-2265 **Fax:** 803-531-0524
Web: www.scbandt.com

PRODUCTS/OPERATIONS

2006 Sales

	$ mil.	% of total
Interest		
Loans, including fees	120.7	76
Investment securities	9.7	6
Other	1.3	1
Noninterest		
Service charges on deposit accounts	13.4	9
Other service charges & fees	13.3	8
Total	**158.4**	**100**

COMPETITORS

Bank of America	First Financial Holdings
Bank of South Carolina	Regions Financial
BB&T	Security Federal
Community Bankshares	South Financial
Comsouth Bankshares, Inc.	Wachovia
First Citizens Bancorporation	

HISTORICAL FINANCIALS

Company Type: Public

Income Statement

FYE: December 31

	ASSETS ($ mil.)	NET INCOME ($ mil.)	INCOME AS % OF ASSETS	EMPLOYEES
12/06	2,178.4	19.8	0.9%	634
12/05	1,925.9	16.7	0.9%	590
12/04	1,437.0	14.0	1.0%	—
12/03	1,197.7	14.8	1.2%	—
12/02	1,144.9	13.8	1.2%	480
Annual Growth	17.4%	9.4%	—	7.2%

2006 Year-End Financials

Equity as % of assets: 7.4%
Return on assets: 1.0%
Return on equity: 12.8%
Long-term debt ($ mil.): 90.4
No. of shares (mil.): 8.7
Market value ($ mil.): 346.5

Dividends
  Yield: 2.0%
  Payout: 37.7%
Sales ($ mil.): 158.4
R&D as % of sales: —
Advertising as % of sales: —

Stock History

NASDAQ (GS): SCBT

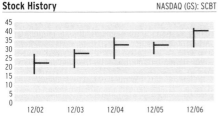

	STOCK PRICE ($) FY Close	P/E High/Low	PER SHARE ($) Earnings	Dividends	Book Value
12/06	39.74	19 14	2.15	0.81	18.57
12/05	31.83	17 14	1.93	0.65	17.17
12/04	31.97	22 15	1.64	1.31	14.75
12/03	27.22	17 11	1.73	—	14.61
12/02	21.77	16 10	1.62	—	13.49
Annual Growth	16.2%	— —	7.3%	(21.4%)	8.3%

Sciele Pharma

Sciele Pharma (formerly First Horizon Pharmaceutical) is keeping an eye on the hearts and the women of America. The company buys drugs from larger companies for cardiovascular health and women's health and sells them. Its prescription drug portfolio includes more than 15 products, such as Prenate prenatal vitamins, drugs for treating high blood pressure and menstrual pain, and a treatment for swimmer's ear. Sales are made directly to primary care doctors and specialists in the US through a network of sales representatives. Sciele Pharma does not make the products it sells; instead, it has manufacturing agreements with the companies whose products it acquires, including Pfizer, Bayer, and Andrx.

Major customers include pharmaceutical distributors McKesson (about one third of sales), Cardinal Health (about one quarter), and AmerisourceBergen (more than 10%).

In 2007 Sciele Pharma expanded into pediatrics with the acquisition of Alliant Pharmaceuticals, an Atlanta-based firm that sells branded remedies for childhood ailments, such as colds, asthma, head lice, and attention deficit hyperactivity disorder.

Also in 2007 it gained FDA approval for a formulation of fenofibrate, a cholesterol drug it developed with LifeCycle Pharma.

EXECUTIVES

Chairman: Pierre Lapalme, age 67, $139,329 pay
CEO, and Director: Patrick P. Fourteau, age 60, $325,000 pay
President and COO: Edward J. Schutter, age 55
EVP, CFO, Secretary, and Treasurer: Darrell E. Borne, age 45, $240,000 pay
EVP and Chief Medical Officer: Larry M. Dillaha, $179,352 pay
EVP, Global Business Development: Michael Mavrogordato, age 55
VP, Legal and Compliance: Leslie Zacks, $205,000 pay
VP, Sales: Sam F. Gibbons, $270,000 pay
VP, Sales: Ron Scalf
VP, Clinical Development: Edda Gomez-Panzani
Auditors: BDO Seidman, LLP

LOCATIONS

HQ: Sciele Pharma Inc.
  5 Concourse Pkwy., Ste. 1800, Atlanta, GA 30328
Phone: 770-442-9707   **Fax:** 678-341-1470
Web: www.horizonpharm.w1.com/Corp

PRODUCTS/OPERATIONS

2006 Sales

	% of total
Cardiovascular products	76
Women's health products	19
Non-promoted products	5
Total	**100**

Selected Products

Altoprev (high cholesterol)
Cognex (Alzheimer's disease)
Fortamet (type 2 diabetes)
Furadantin (urinary tract infections)
Nitrolingual Pumpspray (angina relief)
Prenate Elite (prenatal vitamins)
Sular (hypertension)
Triglide (high cholesterol)
Zebutal (headaches)
Zoto-HC (swimmer's ear)

COMPETITORS

Abbott Labs
AstraZeneca
Biovail
Bristol-Myers Squibb
Elan
Eli Lilly
Forest Labs
King Pharmaceuticals
Medicis Pharmaceutical
Merck
Pfizer
Reliant Pharmaceuticals
Shire
Teva Pharmaceuticals
Watson Pharmaceuticals

HISTORICAL FINANCIALS

Company Type: Public

Income Statement

FYE: December 31

	REVENUE ($ mil.)	NET INCOME ($ mil.)	NET PROFIT MARGIN	EMPLOYEES
12/06	293.2	45.2	15.4%	782
12/05	216.4	39.2	18.1%	568
12/04	152.0	26.5	17.4%	—
12/03	95.3	(1.7)	—	—
12/02	115.2	6.2	5.4%	249
Annual Growth	26.3%	64.3%	—	33.1%

2006 Year-End Financials

Debt ratio: 38.7%
Return on equity: 12.4%
Cash ($ mil.): 166.4
Current ratio: 7.11
Long-term debt ($ mil.): 150.0
No. of shares (mil.): 35.1

Dividends
  Yield: —
  Payout: —
Market value ($ mil.): 841.8
R&D as % of sales: —
Advertising as % of sales: —

Stock History

NASDAQ (GS): SCRX

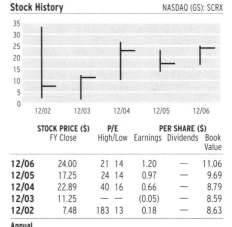

	STOCK PRICE ($) FY Close	P/E High/Low	PER SHARE ($) Earnings	Dividends	Book Value
12/06	24.00	21 14	1.20	—	11.06
12/05	17.25	24 14	0.97	—	9.69
12/04	22.89	40 16	0.66	—	8.79
12/03	11.25	— —	(0.05)	—	8.59
12/02	7.48	183 13	0.18	—	8.63
Annual Growth	33.8%	— —	60.7%	—	6.4%

SeaBright Insurance

SeaBright Insurance Holdings makes smooth sailing of the choppy waters of workers' compensation. Through its SeaBright Insurance subsidiary, the company provides a variety of specialty workers' compensation insurance to companies in niche industries, including maritime and construction. It also offers coverage to employers that participate in collectively bargained workers' compensation agreements, as well as traditional workers' compensation coverage in some markets. SeaBright sells its products through independent brokers and through wholesale subsidiary PointSure Insurance Services. The company was formed in 2003 to facilitate a management buyout of Eagle Pacific Insurance.

SeaBright specializes in providing workers' compensation insurance for customers who require complex, customized coverage or who operate in underserved markets. Its maritime customers include ship builders and companies involved in marine construction and stevedoring (ship loading and unloading). It does most of its business in the construction industry with California employers who are engaged in workers' compensation collective bargaining agreements, in which claims are handled through alternative dispute resolution (ADR). The company also sells traditional workers' compensation insurance in some underserved markets, such as Alaska, Arizona, California, Hawaii, and Illinois.

California brings in about half of SeaBright's premium revenue; other key markets for the company include Alaska, Illinois, Hawaii, and Lousiana. SeaBright is using money from its 2005 IPO to write more business in these markets, and is also planning to move into new states where it is already licensed to do business (it is licensed in 45 states). It opened an office in the Philadelphia area in 2006 and one in Atlanta the following year to launch expansion in the Northeast and Southeast, respectively. It also wants to take advantage of other states who have ADR laws similar to the ones in California.

The company strives to control the medical costs associated with workplace injuries by consulting with employers on workplace safety and accident prevention. It also offers a network of doctors and other health care providers that follow approved treatment guidelines to get injured or ill workers back on the job as quickly as possible.

EXECUTIVES

Chairman, President, and CEO: John G. Pasqualetto, age 65
EVP Operations: Richard J. Gergasko, age 49
SVP, CFO, and Assistant Secretary: Joseph S. De Vita, age 66
SVP and Chief Medical Officer: Marc B. Miller, age 51
SVP, General Counsel, and Secretary: D. Drue Wax, age 57
SVP Policyholder Services: Richard W. Seelinger, age 48
SVP Underwriting: Jeffrey C. Wanamaker, age 41
VP Finance, Principal Accounting Officer, and Assistant Secretary: M. Philip Romney, age 53
VP and CIO: James L. (Skip) Borland III, age 46
Assistant VP and National Marketing Director: Dean Rappleye
President, PointSure Insurance Services: Craig Pankow
Auditors: KPMG LLP

LOCATIONS

HQ: SeaBright Insurance Holdings, Inc.
2101 4th Ave., Ste. 1600, Seattle, WA 98121
Phone: 206-269-8500   **Fax:** 206-269-8903
Web: www.sbic.com

SeaBright Insurance has offices in Anchorage, Alaska; Atlanta; Camarillo, California; Chicago; Honolulu; Houston; Orange, California; Philadelphia; San Francisco; Seattle; and Tampa.

PRODUCTS/OPERATIONS

2006 Sales

	$ mil.	% of total
Premiums	185.6	90
Investment income	15.2	7
Claims services	2.0	1
Other services	0.1	—
Other	3.4	2
Adjustments	(0.4)	—
Total	**205.9**	**100**

COMPETITORS

ACE Limited	Louisiana Workers'
Acuity Mutual	Compensation
AIG	State Compensation
AMERISAFE	Insurance Fund
First Insurance Company	Texas Mutual
of Hawaii	Travelers Companies
Liberty Northwest	Zurich American

HISTORICAL FINANCIALS

Company Type: Public

Income Statement

FYE: December 31

	ASSETS ($ mil.)	NET INCOME ($ mil.)	INCOME AS % OF ASSETS	EMPLOYEES
12/06	614.3	33.2	5.4%	178
12/05	427.3	18.3	4.3%	152
12/04	226.1	7.2	3.2%	—
Annual Growth	**64.8%**	**114.7%**	**—**	**17.1%**

2006 Year-End Financials

Equity as % of assets: 40.6%
Return on assets: 6.4%
Return on equity: 16.4%
Long-term debt ($ mil.): 12.0
No. of shares (mil.): 20.6
Market value ($ mil.): 370.2

Dividends
  Yield: —
  Payout: —
Sales ($ mil.): 205.9
R&D as % of sales: —
Advertising as % of sales: —

Stock History

NASDAQ (GS): SEAB

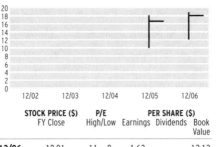

	STOCK PRICE ($) FY Close	P/E High/Low		PER SHARE ($) Earnings	Dividends	Book Value
12/06	18.01	11	8	1.63	—	12.12
12/05	16.63	16	9	1.13	—	9.49
Annual Growth	**8.3%**	**—**	**—**	**44.2%**	**—**	**27.8%**

Seacoast Banking

Seacoast Banking Corporation of Florida sees money on Florida's southeastern coast. Subsidiary First National Bank and Trust Company of the Treasure Coast has about 30 branches offering individuals and local businesses a comprehensive range of retail banking and trust services, as well as securities and annuities products. The company also provides brokerage services and fiduciary and investment services. Residential mortgages make up around 30% of the bank's loan portfolio, which also includes commercial, consumer, and marine loans. Vice chairman Dale Hudson, chairman and CEO Dennis Hudson III (the vice chairman's nephew), and their families together own more than 20% of Seacoast Banking.

A division of the bank, Seacoast Marine Finance, specializes in marine lending with an emphasis on loans of $200,000 and greater. Loans originated by the Seacoast Marine Finance Division outside of the bank's primary service area are typically sold.

In 2005 Seacoast acquired Orlando, Florida-based Century National Bank and merged it into First National Bank & Trust Company of the Treasure Coast.

The company acquired Big Lake Financial, adding about eight branches in six Florida counties, in 2006.

EXECUTIVES

Chairman and CEO; Chairman and CEO, First National Bank: Dennis S. (Denny) Hudson III, age 51, $580,650 pay
Vice Chairman: Dale M. Hudson, age 72
President, COO, and Director; Vice Chairman and Chief Credit Officer, First National Bank: A. Douglas Gilbert, age 66, $672,481 pay
President and CEO, Big Lake National Bank: Joe G. Mullins, age 63
SEVP; President and COO, First National Bank: O. Jean Strickland, age 47, $347,500 pay
SEVP and Chief Banking Officer, Seacoast Banking and First National Bank: C. William Curtis Jr., age 68, $302,250 pay
EVP, Finance Group and CFO, Seacoast Banking and First National Bank: William R. Hahl, age 58
SVP, Administrative Support Services and Human Resources Manager, First National Bank: Charles A. Olsson
Orlando Regional President: Michael Sheffey, $200,000 pay
Auditors: PricewaterhouseCoopers LLP

LOCATIONS

HQ: Seacoast Banking Corporation of Florida
815 Colorado Ave., Stuart, FL 34994
Phone: 772-287-4000   **Fax:** 772-288-6012
Web: www.seacoastcorp.com

PRODUCTS/OPERATIONS

2006 Sales

	$ mil.	% of total
Interest		
Interest on securities		
Taxable	21.9	13
Nontaxable	0.3	0
Interest & fees on loans	114.4	70
Interest on federal funds sold & interest bearing deposits	3.2	2
Noninterest	24.3	15
Total	**164.1**	**100**

COMPETITORS

Bank of America
BankAtlantic
National City
Regions Financial
SunTrust
TIB Financial
Wachovia
Wilmington Trust

HISTORICAL FINANCIALS

Company Type: Public

Income Statement

FYE: December 31

	ASSETS ($ mil.)	NET INCOME ($ mil.)	INCOME AS % OF ASSETS	EMPLOYEES
12/06	2,389.4	23.9	1.0%	534
12/05	2,132.2	20.8	1.0%	426
12/04	1,615.9	14.9	0.9%	—
12/03	1,353.8	14.0	1.0%	—
12/02	1,281.3	15.3	1.2%	335
Annual Growth	**16.9%**	**11.8%**	**—**	**12.4%**

2006 Year-End Financials

Equity as % of assets: 8.9%
Return on assets: 1.1%
Return on equity: 13.1%
Long-term debt ($ mil.): 67.8
No. of shares (mil.): 19.0
Market value ($ mil.): 470.6

Dividends
  Yield: 2.5%
  Payout: 47.7%
Sales ($ mil.): 164.1
R&D as % of sales: —
Advertising as % of sales: —

Stock History

NASDAQ (GS): SBCF

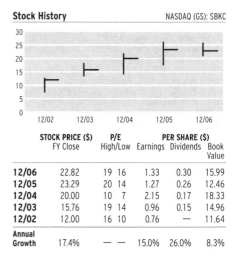

	STOCK PRICE ($) FY Close	P/E High/Low		PER SHARE ($) Earnings	Dividends	Book Value
12/06	24.80	25	18	1.28	0.61	11.20
12/05	22.95	21	15	1.24	0.44	8.93
12/04	22.25	25	18	0.97	0.54	7.01
12/03	17.35	20	16	0.91	0.46	6.78
12/02	17.13	20	15	0.97	0.28	7.25
Annual Growth	9.7%	—	—	7.2%	21.5%	11.5%

EXECUTIVES

Chairman: Alford C. Bridges, age 68
Vice Chairman: Edward M. Beckham II, age 68
President, CEO, and Director, Security Bank Corporation and Security Bank of Bibb County: H. Averett (Rett) Walker, age 53, $359,700 pay
EVP and COO; President, Security Bank of Bibb County: Richard A. Collinsworth, age 57, $237,600 pay
EVP and CFO, Security Bank Corporation and Security Bank of Bibb County: James R. McLemore, age 47, $189,000 pay
SVP Investor Relations: Lorraine D. Miller
VP, Human Resources, Security Bank of Bibb County: Betsy J. Baugham
President, Security Bank of Bibb County: Daniel M. Forrester
Secretary: Linda L. Cassidy
Auditors: McNair, McLemore, Middlebrooks & Co., LLP

LOCATIONS

HQ: Security Bank Corporation
4219 Forsyth Rd., Macon, GA 31210
Phone: 478-722-6200   **Fax:** 478-722-6229
Web: www.securitybank.net

Stock History

NASDAQ (GS): SBKC

	STOCK PRICE ($) FY Close	P/E High/Low		PER SHARE ($) Earnings	Dividends	Book Value
12/06	22.82	19	16	1.33	0.30	15.99
12/05	23.29	20	14	1.27	0.26	12.46
12/04	20.00	10	7	2.15	0.17	18.33
12/03	15.76	19	14	0.96	0.15	14.96
12/02	12.00	16	10	0.76	—	11.64
Annual Growth	17.4%	—	—	15.0%	26.0%	8.3%

Security Bank

Security Bank Corporation is the holding company for Security Bank of Bibb County, Security Bank of Houston County, Security Bank of Jones County, Security Bank of North Metro (acquired in 2005), and Security Bank of North Fulton and Security Bank of Gwinnett County (both acquired in 2006). The banks operate more than 20 locations in central and southeastern Georgia. Targeting individuals and small to midsized business customers, they offer checking and savings accounts, money market accounts, certificates of deposit, and individual retirement accounts.

Security Bank of Bibb County subsidiary Fairfield Financial Services issues residential mortgages and real estate development loans through more than 15 offices throughout Georgia. These types of loans represent nearly two-thirds of Security Bank Corporation's loan portfolio. The banks also originate commercial real estate, business, agricultural, and consumer loans.

Security Bank Corporation has been growing via small acquisitions. It bought one-branch Bank of Gray in 2003 and renamed it Security Bank of Jones County. In 2005 it purchased SouthBank (now Security Bank of North Metro) and early the following year the company acquired Rivoli BanCorp which was merged into Security Bank of Bibb County.

Also in 2006 Security Bank Corporation bought Neighbors Bank and Homestead Bank and changed their names to Security Bank of North Fulton and Security Bank of Gwinnett County, respectively.

The company acquired financial planning firm CFS Wealth Management in 2007. Also that year Security Bank Corporation announced plans to buy another Georgia bank holding company, First Commerce Community Bankshares, but the deal was later terminated by the boards of both companies.

PRODUCTS/OPERATIONS

2006 Sales

	$ mil.	% of total
Interest		
Loans, including fees	138.5	83
US government agency securities	6.5	4
Other	3.1	2
Noninterest		
Service charges on deposits	9.2	6
Mortgage banking income	4.9	3
Other	3.8	2
Total	**166.0**	**100**

COMPETITORS

Bank of America
BB&T
Colonial BancGroup
PAB Bankshares
Regions Financial
SunTrust
Synovus
Wachovia

HISTORICAL FINANCIALS

Company Type: Public

Income Statement

FYE: December 31

	ASSETS ($ mil.)	NET INCOME ($ mil.)	INCOME AS % OF ASSETS	EMPLOYEES
12/06	2,494.1	23.4	0.9%	501
12/05	1,662.4	16.2	1.0%	422
12/04	1,063.5	12.3	1.2%	—
12/03	911.3	8.6	0.9%	—
12/02	580.8	5.3	0.9%	250
Annual Growth	44.0%	45.0%	—	19.0%

2006 Year-End Financials

Equity as % of assets: 12.3%
Return on assets: 1.1%
Return on equity: 9.6%
Long-term debt ($ mil.): 124.7
No. of shares (mil.): 19.2
Market value ($ mil.): 437.4
Dividends
 Yield: 1.3%
 Payout: 22.6%
Sales ($ mil.): 166.0
R&D as % of sales: —
Advertising as % of sales: —

Select Comfort Corporation

Select Comfort Corporation has got your number. The firm's line of Sleep Number beds, which reach $4,000, use air-chamber technology to allow sleepers to adjust the firmness on each side of the mattress, providing better sleep quality and addressing sleep-related problems such as lower back pain. Select Comfort also offers foundations, frames, pillows, and a sofa bed. A leading bedding retailer, Select Comfort sells its products in more than 440 stores nationwide (under the banners Select Comfort and Sleep Number Store) and through leased sections in other retailers' stores. The company also sells through a company-operated call center, its own Web site, and on the QVC shopping channel.

Select Comfort has been aggressively expanding, adding about 40 stores in 2006. It has also signed an agreement with retail partners Sleepy's and Mattress Firm. The retailers agreed to increase the number of stores that carry the Sleep Number bed to more than 430 of their stores nationwide. The beds began ending sleepless nights in Canada in 2005 through a strategic alliance bringing Sleep Number products into Sleep Country Canada stores. Additionally, the company's mattresses are found in nearly all of Radisson's hotel rooms in the US, Canada, and the Caribbean.

The company expanded its office space in late 2007 by moving its executive offices, as well as its headquarters address, to a leased office nearby on 59th Avenue North in Minneapolis.

Investment groups Goldman Sachs and Lord, Abbett & Co. each own some 9% of the company's shares. Baron Capital Group owns 8%.

EXECUTIVES

Chairman, President, and CEO: William R. (Bill) McLaughlin, age 50, $1,244,596 pay
SVP and CFO: James C. (Jim) Raabe, age 46, $420,888 pay
SVP and CIO: Ernest (Ernie) Park, age 54
SVP and Chief Marketing Officer: Catherine Bur-Hall

SVP, Legal, General Counsel, and Secretary:
 Mark A. Kimball, age 48, $404,239 pay
SVP, Human Resources: Scott F. Peterson, age 47
SVP, Global Supply Chain: Kathryn V. Roedel, age 46,
 $370,476 pay (partial-year salary)
SVP and General Manager, New Channel Development
 and Strategy: Wendy L. Schoppert, age 40
SVP, Sales: Keith C. Spurgeon, age 52, $476,829 pay
VP, Investor Relations: Francis X. (Frank) Milano,
 age 45
Senior Director, Corporate Communications and Public
 Relations: Gabby Nelson
Auditors: KPMG LLP

LOCATIONS

HQ: Select Comfort Corporation
 9800 59th Ave., North, Minneapolis, MN 55442
Phone: 763-551-7000   Fax: 763-551-7826
Web: www.selectcomfort.com

PRODUCTS/OPERATIONS

2006 Sales

	% of total
Retail	76
Direct marketing	9
Wholesale	9
E-commerce	6
Total	**100**

Selected Products

Bed frames
Foundations
Mattress pads
Mattresses
Pillows
Pillowtops
Sleep Number SofaBed

COMPETITORS

1800mattress.com
DUX
Mattress Discounters
Mattress Giant
Mattress Holding
Sealy
Serta
Simmons Bedding
Spring Air
Tempur-Pedic

HISTORICAL FINANCIALS

Company Type: Public

Income Statement				FYE: Saturday nearest December 31
	REVENUE ($ mil.)	NET INCOME ($ mil.)	NET PROFIT MARGIN	EMPLOYEES
12/06	806.0	47.2	5.9%	3,053
12/05	691.1	43.8	6.3%	2,685
12/04	557.6	31.6	5.7%	—
12/03	458.5	27.2	5.9%	—
12/02	335.8	37.1	11.0%	1,805
Annual Growth	**24.5%**	**6.2%**	**—**	**14.0%**

2006 Year-End Financials

Debt ratio: —
Return on equity: 39.8%
Cash ($ mil.): 46.6
Current ratio: 1.06
Long-term debt ($ mil.): —
No. of shares (mil.): 51.5
Dividends
 Yield: —
 Payout: —
Market value ($ mil.): 896.4
R&D as % of sales: —
Advertising as % of sales: —

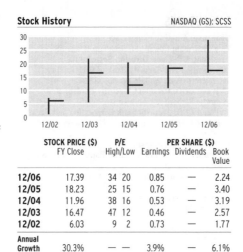

	STOCK PRICE ($) FY Close	P/E High/Low		PER SHARE ($) Earnings	Dividends	Book Value
12/06	17.39	34	20	0.85	—	2.24
12/05	18.23	25	15	0.76	—	3.40
12/04	11.96	38	16	0.53	—	3.19
12/03	16.47	47	12	0.46	—	2.57
12/02	6.03	9	2	0.73	—	1.77
Annual Growth	**30.3%**	**—**	**—**	**3.9%**	**—**	**6.1%**

Shoe Pavilion

The hunt for bargain quality footwear might end at Shoe Pavilion, a discount shoe retailer with 100-plus stores in California and half a dozen other western states. Its self-service style stores are typically located in outlet centers and strip malls. Shoe Pavilion sells brand-name shoes, such as Ralph Lauren, Steve Madden, and Nine West at discount (20% to 60% less than department store prices) by purchasing manufacturers' overruns; buying shoes directly from Italian and Chinese factories; and purchasing shoes during off-peak production periods. Shoe Pavilion discontinued its licensed shoe departments (in Gordman's stores) in 2002. Founder and CEO Dmitry Beinus owns about a third of Shoe Pavilion's shares.

Prior to founding Shoe Pavilion in 1979, Beinus worked in Nordstrom's shoe department.

Following its expansion into Texas and New Mexico in 2006, fast-growing Shoe Pavilion plans to open as many as 25 new stores this year and is selectively closing smaller stores and replacing them with larger ones in better locations.

Women's shoes account for nearly 60% of Shoe Pavilion's sales. The footwear chain also sells shoes online.

EXECUTIVES

Chairman, President, and CEO: Dmitry Beinus, age 55
EVP and CFO: Michael P. McHugh
VP and COO: Robert R. (Bob) Hall, age 54, $161,501 pay
Manager, Human Resources: Stephanie DaCosta
Controller and Interim Principal Accounting Officer:
 Richard Romay
Auditors: Grant Thornton LLP

LOCATIONS

HQ: Shoe Pavilion, Inc.
 13245 Riverside Dr., Ste. 450,
 Sherman Oaks, CA 91423
Phone: 818-907-9975   Fax: 818-907-8017
Web: www.shoepavilion.com

2006 Stores

	No.
Southern California	42
Northern California	33
Washington	10
Texas	8
Arizona	7
Oregon	4
Nevada	3
New Mexico	1
Total	**108**

PRODUCTS/OPERATIONS

2006 Sales

	% of total
Women's shoes	59
Men's shoes	29
Children's shoes	7
Accessories	5
Total	**100**

COMPETITORS

Collective Brands	Nine West
DSW	Nordstrom
J. C. Penney	Ross Stores
Kmart	Sears
Loehmann's	Target
Macy's	TJX Companies
Mervyns	Wal-Mart

HISTORICAL FINANCIALS

Company Type: Public

Income Statement			FYE: Saturday nearest December 31	
	REVENUE ($ mil.)	NET INCOME ($ mil.)	NET PROFIT MARGIN	EMPLOYEES
12/06	131.3	1.9	1.4%	1,141
12/05	102.5	2.6	2.5%	672
12/04	85.8	2.1	2.4%	—
12/03	83.6	(2.7)	—	—
12/02	83.8	0.2	0.2%	510
Annual Growth	**11.9%**	**75.6%**	**—**	**22.3%**

2006 Year-End Financials

Debt ratio: 0.9%
Return on equity: 5.6%
Cash ($ mil.): 0.7
Current ratio: 1.95
Long-term debt ($ mil.): 0.4
No. of shares (mil.): 9.5
Dividends
 Yield: —
 Payout: —
Market value ($ mil.): 70.4
R&D as % of sales: —
Advertising as % of sales: —

	STOCK PRICE ($) FY Close	P/E High/Low		PER SHARE ($) Earnings	Dividends	Book Value
12/06	7.38	55	26	0.20	—	4.32
12/05	7.84	25	8	0.36	—	3.78
12/04	3.03	12	3	0.30	—	3.02
12/03	1.21	—	—	(0.40)	—	2.81
12/02	1.14	97	50	0.02	—	3.21
Annual Growth	**59.5%**	**—**	**—**	**77.8%**	**—**	**7.7%**

ShoreTel, Inc.

ShoreTel's protocol demands utilizing the Internet for telecommunications. The company provides Internet Protocol (IP)-based telephony equipment for businesses, government agencies, and schools. Its products include phones and switches, as well as messaging and systems management software. The company outsources the manufacturing of its products. ShoreTel sells primarily through channel partners; the company's customers have included CNET Networks, the City of Oakland, California, Robert Half International, SEGA, and Wedbush Morgan Securities.

Almost all of ShoreTel's revenues in fiscal 2007 were generated in the US, but the company is expanding into Asia and Europe. Most of ShoreTel's revenues come from product sales (its channel partners typically handle installations), but the company does generate service revenue, primarily from software updates and technical support.

EXECUTIVES

Chairman, President, and CEO: John W. Combs, age 60
CFO: Michael E. (Mike) Healy, age 45
CTO and Director: Edwin J. (Ed) Basart, age 57, $200,000 pay
CIO: Rick Parkinson
VP Engineering: Dale Tonogai
VP Engineering and Operations: Pedro E. Rump, age 51
VP Marketing: Stephen G. (Steve) Timmerman, age 47
VP Sales: Joseph A. (Joe) Vitalone, age 45, $155,000 pay
VP Business Development: Mark Arman
VP Global Support Services: Walter (Walt) Weisner, age 50, $214,038 pay
Auditors: Deloitte & Touche LLP

LOCATIONS

HQ: ShoreTel, Inc.
   960 Stewart Dr., Sunnyvale, CA 94085
Phone: 408-331-3300   **Fax:** 408-331-3333
Web: www.shoretel.com

2007 Sales

	$ mil.	% of total
North America	95.4	97
Other regions	2.4	3
Total	**97.8**	**100**

PRODUCTS/OPERATIONS

2007 Sales

	$ mil.	% of total
Products	87.1	89
Services	10.7	11
Total	**97.8**	**100**

COMPETITORS

3Com
Alcatel-Lucent
Avaya
Cisco Systems
Inter-Tel
Mitel Networks
Nokia Siemens Networks
Nortel Networks

HISTORICAL FINANCIALS

Company Type: Public

Income Statement

FYE: June 30

	REVENUE ($ mil.)	NET INCOME ($ mil.)	NET PROFIT MARGIN	EMPLOYEES
6/07	97.8	6.1	6.2%	—
6/06	61.6	4.0	6.5%	174
6/05	35.5	(1.4)	—	118
6/04	18.8	(6.3)	—	—
Annual Growth	**73.3%**	**—**	**—**	**47.5%**

2007 Year-End Financials

Debt ratio: —
Return on equity: —
Cash ($ mil.): 17.3
Current ratio: 1.95
Long-term debt ($ mil.): —

Net Income History

NASDAQ (GM): SHOR

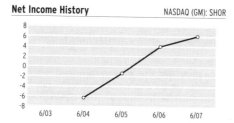

Shuffle Master

You might be good at rearranging a deck of cards, but are you a Shuffle Master? Shuffle Master is a leading supplier of single- and multi-deck automatic card shuffling devices. It has about 25,000 shufflers in use by casinos and other gaming businesses. The company also markets chip-sorting devices and information systems used to monitor gaming activity and security on the casino floor. In addition, Shuffle Master makes a number of table games and electronic gaming machines, as well as electronic table systems that allow operators to offer live action wagering in markets that do not permit live table games. About 5,000 of its table games are in use by its customers.

During 2007 the company shifted its emphasis towards leasing its gaming equipment under contracts that will result in recurring revenue rather than one-time sales. It also worked to integrate products acquired from video slot machine manufacturer Stargames Limited.

That same year Shuffle Master took steps to expand its gaming machine business, acquiring the table game manufacturing operations of Progressive Gaming International. The $20 million deal included such branded games as Caribbean Stud and Texas Hold 'Em Bonus Poker.

HISTORY

A former truck driver, John Breeding founded the company in 1983 to develop and market automatic card shufflers. Shuffle Master developed its first single-deck shuffling system in 1989 and installed its first automatic shuffling machine at Bally's Casino in Las Vegas in 1992, the year the company went public. Shuffle Master began licensing its Let It Ride table game the following year and became profitable by 1995. That year it

introduced a multi-deck shuffler and began selling its products in addition to leasing.

To bolster its presence in the higher-margin game business, Shuffle Master formed an agreement with master game designer Mark Yoseloff in 1996 (the developer of consumer versions of Pac Man and Donkey Kong) that included access to Yoseloff's personal game library. The alliance produced Five Deck Frenzy, a video poker game that Shuffle Master debuted in 1996. The company also formed a joint marketing agreement with International Game Technology (IGT) that year to market Five Deck Frenzy and the video version of Let It Ride.

Yoseloff joined the Shuffle Master staff in 1997 as head of the New Games division. Later that year Breeding retired for health reasons (he has diabetes) and was replaced by Joseph Lahti. The company developed four new casino video games using IGT machine technology in 1998. Shuffle Master also penned an agreement with Bally Gaming that year to create a casino video version of Let's Make a Deal, based on the Monty Hall game show. The company had trouble marketing its new Three Stooges slot machine in 1999 because of concerns that the game lures children. Shuffle Master introduced its King shuffler in 2000, which shuffles cards continuously, making card counting virtually impossible.

In 2002 Yoseloff added chairman to his CEO title when Lahti retired; EVP Mark Lipparelli was named president. The following year Lipparelli resigned and was replaced by Paul Meyer.

In 2004 the company began selling off its slot operations to focus on its core shuffler and table game businesses. In that vein, Shuffle Master purchased BET Technology (three table games) and CARD Casinos Austria Research & Development (card shufflers and chip sorters) the same year.

EXECUTIVES

Chairman and CEO: Mark L. Yoseloff, age 61, $711,000 pay
President, COO, and Acting CFO: Paul C. Meyer, age 60, $431,000 pay
SVP: R. Brooke Dunn, age 51, $332,000 pay
SVP and General Counsel: Jerome R. (Jerry) Smith, age 62
SVP Product Management: David Lopez
SVP and Chief Accounting Officer: Coreen Sawdon, age 40
VP Sales: Donald W. Bauer
President and Managing Director, Stargames: John Rouse
Managing Director, CARD: Ernest Blaha
Director Human Resources: Victoria Harper
Director Sales and Utility, Europe: Georg Fekete
Senior Sales Executive: Chris Costello
Senior Sales Executive: Steve Venuto
Media Relations: Kirsten Clark
Auditors: Deloitte & Touche LLP

LOCATIONS

HQ: Shuffle Master, Inc.
   1106 Palms Airport Dr., Las Vegas, NV 89119
Phone: 702-897-7150   **Fax:** 702-260-6691
Web: www.shufflemaster.com

Shuffle Master has operations in Nevada and Minnesota, as well as offices in Australia and Austria.

2007 Sales

	$ mil.	% of total
US	80.3	45
Australia	52.5	29
Asia	21.8	12
Europe	9.7	6
Canada	7.3	4
Other	7.3	4
Total	**178.9**	**100**

PRODUCTS/OPERATIONS

2007 Sales

	$ mil.	% of total
Utility products	78.5	44
Proprietary Table Games	33.1	18
Electronic Table Systems	27.9	16
Electronic Gaming Machines	39.3	22
Other	0.1	—
Total	**178.9**	**100**

Selected Products

Utility products (casino products)
  Card shufflers
  Casino information systems
  Chip-sorting products
Entertainment products
  Electronic multi-player table games
  Table games
    Casino War
    Fortune Pai Gow Poker
    Let It Ride
    Let It Ride Bonus
    Let It Ride The Tournament
    Royal Match 21
    Three Card Poker
  Video slot machines

COMPETITORS

Aristocrat Leisure
Aruze Gaming
Bally Technologies
elixir
Gaming Partners International
International Game Technology
Konami Gaming
PokerTek
Progressive Gaming
WMS Industries

HISTORICAL FINANCIALS

Company Type: Public

Income Statement   FYE: October 31

	REVENUE ($ mil.)	NET INCOME ($ mil.)	NET PROFIT MARGIN	EMPLOYEES
10/07	178.9	16.4	9.2%	570
10/06	163.0	5.1	3.1%	550
10/05	112.9	29.2	25.9%	320
10/04	84.8	24.1	28.4%	—
10/03	67.4	16.9	25.1%	—
Annual Growth	**27.6%**	**(0.7%)**	**—**	**33.5%**

2007 Year-End Financials

Debt ratio: 265.5%
Return on equity: 27.3%
Cash ($ mil.): 13.5
Current ratio: 2.62
Long-term debt ($ mil.): 232.7
No. of shares (mil.): 35.2

Dividends
  Yield: —
  Payout: —
Market value ($ mil.): 481.5
R&D as % of sales: —
Advertising as % of sales: —

Stock History   NASDAQ (GS): SHFL

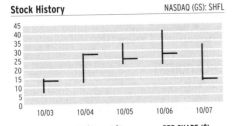

	STOCK PRICE ($) FY Close	P/E High/Low	PER SHARE ($) Earnings	PER SHARE ($) Dividends	PER SHARE ($) Book Value
10/07	13.68	71 29	0.46	—	2.49
10/06	27.98	291 161	0.14	—	0.93
10/05	25.36	42 28	0.80	—	0.39
10/04	28.06	44 20	0.65	—	0.63
10/03	13.56	33 17	0.44	—	2.90
Annual Growth	**0.2%**	**— —**	**1.1%**	**—**	**(3.7%)**

Shutterfly, Inc.

Whether or not you are the consummate shutterbug, you can rely on Shutterfly for digital prints. An e-commerce company specializing in digital photo products and services (enhanced by its VividPics technology) for the consumer and professional photography markets, the company offers customers the ability to upload, share, store, and edit digital photos through its Web site. In addition to traditional 4-inch by 6-inch prints, Shutterfly offers enlargements and photo novelty items including mugs, photo books, calendars, and T-shirts. Shutterfly users are not required to become members to view shared photos. James Clark, who resigned as chairman in 2007, owns about 30% of the firm through various affiliations.

Shutterfly makes about half its revenues during the fourth quarter of the year due to holiday sales.

In early 2008 the company acquired Nexo Systems for under $15 million in cash and stock. Nexo provides technology that allows users to create their own Web sites.

Shutterfly was founded in 1999, funded partly by Clark, a Silicon Valley investor and co-founder of Netscape Communications Corp. Shutterfly hired eBay veteran Jeff Housenbold as CEO in 2005 and went public in an IPO the following year. Board member Nancy Schoendorf represents investment firm Mohr, Davidow Ventures, which owns 17% of Shutterfly.

EXECUTIVES

Chairman: Philip A. (Phil) Marineau, age 60
President, CEO, and Director:
  Jeffrey T. (Jeff) Housenbold, age 37, $275,866 pay
CFO: Mark J. Rubash, age 50
SVP Business and Corporate Development:
  Douglas J. (Doug) Galen, age 45, $288,349 pay
SVP Technology: Stanford S. Au, age 46, $227,635 pay
  (partial-year salary)
SVP Operations: Dwayne A. Black, age 46
VP Client Engineering: Lou Montulli
VP Consumer Marketing: Janice Gaub
VP Finance: John A. Kaelle, age 38
VP Human Resources: Patricia (Pat) Schoof
VP Product Marketing: Peter Elarde
VP Web Engineering: Patrick Teo
VP Legal: Douglas (Doug) Appleton, age 40
VP Corporate Strategy: Dan McCormick
VP Product Engineering: Jerry Ko
VP Internet Operations and CIO: Jeffrey Whitehead
Chief Marketing Officer: Kathryn E. Olson, age 46
Director Corporate Communications: Bridgette Thomas
Director Investor Relations: Judith H. McGarry
Auditors: PricewaterhouseCoopers LLP

LOCATIONS

HQ: Shutterfly, Inc.
  2800 Bridge Pkwy., Ste. 101,
  Redwood City, CA 94065
Phone: 650-610-5200   **Fax:** 650-654-1299
Web: www.shutterfly.com

COMPETITORS

Costco Wholesale
CVS/Caremark
Kodak Imaging Network
PhotoWorks
Rite Aid
Ritz Camera Centers
Snapfish
Walgreen
Wal-Mart

HISTORICAL FINANCIALS

Company Type: Public

Income Statement   FYE: December 31

	REVENUE ($ mil.)	NET INCOME ($ mil.)	NET PROFIT MARGIN	EMPLOYEES
12/06	123.3	5.8	4.7%	275
12/05	83.9	28.9	34.4%	—
12/04	54.5	3.7	6.8%	—
12/03	31.4	2.0	6.4%	—
Annual Growth	**57.8%**	**42.6%**	**—**	**—**

2006 Year-End Financials

Debt ratio: 1.1%
Return on equity: 9.3%
Cash ($ mil.): 119.1
Current ratio: 4.87
Long-term debt ($ mil.): 1.7
No. of shares (mil.): 23.7

Dividends
  Yield: —
  Payout: —
Market value ($ mil.): 341.4
R&D as % of sales: —
Advertising as % of sales: —

Stock History   NASDAQ (GM): SFLY

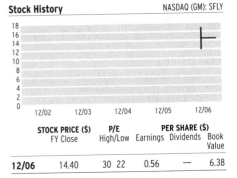

	STOCK PRICE ($) FY Close	P/E High/Low	PER SHARE ($) Earnings	PER SHARE ($) Dividends	PER SHARE ($) Book Value
12/06	14.40	30 22	0.56	—	6.38

SI International

Technology services? Yes! SI International provides information technology services, including application development, network design, systems engineering and integration, and business process outsourcing. SI also offers enterprise resource planning, training, and data security services. The company serves the US government, including the Department of Defense (more than half of sales), the Air Force Space Command, and the Department of State; commercial clients include GEICO and Hewlett-Packard. Chairman Ray Oleson and former vice-chairman Walter Culver founded SI International in 1998.

SI's IT services are primarily aimed at federal IT modernization, defense transformation, homeland defense, and mission-critical outsourcing (personnel shortages, operational efficiencies, etc.).

The company has expanded aggressively via acquisitions, including the purchases of Matcom International, Shenandoah Electronic Intelligence, Bridge Technology Corporation, and Zen Technology. In 2007 it acquired Logtec, a provider of logistics, acquisition, and IT support to the federal government, in a $59 million deal.

EXECUTIVES

Chairman: Ray J. Oleson, age 62, $839,077 pay
President, CEO, and Director: S. Bradford (Brad) Antle, age 51, $705,923 pay
EVP, CFO, and Treasurer: Thomas E. (Ted) Dunn, age 55, $573,000 pay
EVP and Chief Marketing Officer: Leslee Belluchie
EVP IT Solutions Group: Marylynn Stowers, age 46
EVP Mission Services Group: P. Michael (Mike) Becraft, age 62
EVP Strategic Programs Group: Harry D Gatanas, age 60, $195,346 pay
SVP Business Development: Patricia (Patty) Pickett
SVP Human Resources: Lee Stratton
SVP Networks and Telecom: Daniel (Dan) Cooley
SVP Outsourcing Business Unit: Steven (Steve) Hagan
SVP Finance and Accounting: Marc Tommer
SVP, General Counsel and Secretary: James E. (Jim) Daniel
VP and CIO: Stephen M. Hunt
VP and Controller: Nedra Engelson
VP Corporate Communications and Investor Relations: Alan Hill
VP Corporate Development: Thomas E. Lloyd, age 72, $254,423 pay
Auditors: Ernst & Young LLP

LOCATIONS

HQ: SI International, Inc.
   12012 Sunset Hills Rd., Ste. 800, Reston, VA 20190
Phone: 703-234-7000   **Fax:** 703-234-7500
Web: www.si-intl.com

PRODUCTS/OPERATIONS

2006 Sales

	% of total
Federal civilian agencies	52
Department of Defense	47
Commercial entities	1
Total	**100**

2006 Sales

	% of total
Prime contract revenue	80
Subcontract revenue	20
Total	**100**

Selected Services

Application development and integration
Business process outsourcing
Consulting
Network design and implementation
Security assessment and training
Software and systems testing and validation
Systems engineering, integration, and management
Telecommunications engineering
Training and support
Transaction management
Web-based application and portal development and management

COMPETITORS

Alion
Apptis
Boeing
CACI International
Computer Sciences Corp.
EDS
IBM
ITT Defense
Lockheed Martin
MTC Technologies
Northrop Grumman IT
Raytheon
RS Information Systems
SAIC
Unisys

HISTORICAL FINANCIALS

Company Type: Public

Income Statement
FYE: Saturday nearest December 31

	REVENUE ($ mil.)	NET INCOME ($ mil.)	NET PROFIT MARGIN	EMPLOYEES
12/06	462.0	20.1	4.4%	4,300
12/05	397.9	16.9	4.2%	4,000
12/04	262.3	10.9	4.2%	—
12/03	168.3	7.4	4.4%	—
12/02	149.4	2.5	1.7%	1,200
Annual Growth	**32.6%**	**68.4%**	**—**	**37.6%**

2006 Year-End Financials

Debt ratio: 29.0%
Return on equity: 9.9%
Cash ($ mil.): 19.5
Current ratio: 2.15
Long-term debt ($ mil.): 69.4
No. of shares (mil.): 13.0
Dividends
   Yield: —
   Payout: —
Market value ($ mil.): 420.4
R&D as % of sales: —
Advertising as % of sales: —

Stock History
NASDAQ (GS): SINT

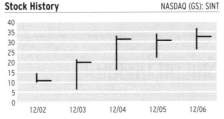

	STOCK PRICE ($) FY Close	P/E High/Low		PER SHARE ($) Earnings	Dividends	Book Value
12/06	32.42	23	17	1.56	—	18.45
12/05	30.57	23	15	1.45	—	14.80
12/04	31.25	29	14	1.14	—	13.13
12/03	19.83	24	8	0.87	—	9.65
12/02	10.75	—	—	(0.03)	—	8.77
Annual Growth	**31.8%**	**—**	**—**	**—**	**—**	**20.4%**

Sigma Designs

Sigma Designs can dress your PC like a TV star in streaming video. The company's REALmagic line of PC cards and chipsets enhances the realistic feel of DVD and other multimedia applications. Its MPEG-based products simulate the picture quality of television on PCs by turning computer screens into full-screen, full-motion video displays. Sigma Designs, which outsources the manufacturing of its products, also offers services such as custom development of MPEG decoding chips and software support. Customers include Freebox (20% of sales), Uniquest (17%), and Cisco Systems. More than half of Sigma Designs' sales comes from customers located in Asia.

The company is focusing its development efforts on the consumer appliance market — including DVD player and set-top box makers — to drive future growth in MPEG chipsets. Video and TV products account for more than 90% of sales. Sigma Designs has alliances with companies including Microsoft and Intel. Distributors and partners of Sigma Designs include Ingram Micro, Fujitsu Siemens, LG Electronics, Samsung, and Silicon Image.

The company nearly tripled its sales in fiscal 2007, selling more chipsets for applications in Internet protocol TV, Blu-ray and HD DVD systems, HDTV sets, and digital media players.

In early 2006 Sigma Designs acquired Blue7 Communications, a developer of advanced wireless technologies and ultra-wideband (UWB) semiconductors, for around $14 million in stock. Blue7 was founded in 2002.

The company has agreed to acquire the assets of the VXP Image Processing business from Gennum for about $18 million in cash and the assumption of certain liabilities. The VXP group develops single-chip image processors delivering broadcast-quality, artifact-free images for professional audio-visual processing, video projection, and digital TV applications. Sigma plans to hire the 46 employees of the VXP group, based in the Toronto area. The transaction is expected to close in February 2008.

Kingdon Capital Management owns more than 6% of Sigma Designs. CEO Thinh Tran holds nearly 6% of the company.

EXECUTIVES

Chairman, President, and CEO: Thinh Q. Tran, age 53
CFO and Secretary: Thomas E. (Tom) Gay III
SVP Worldwide Sales: Silvio Perich, age 59, $178,448 pay
VP Strategic Marketing: Kenneth (Ken) Lowe, age 51, $177,844 pay
VP Engineering: Jacques Martinella, age 51, $223,549 pay
VP Planning and Administration: Kit Tsui, age 57
Director Operations: Michael Lin
General Manager and VP Wireless Products Division: Hung Nguyen
Manager Investor Relations: Edward McGregor
Auditors: Grant Thornton LLP

LOCATIONS

HQ: Sigma Designs, Inc.
   1221 California Circle, Milpitas, CA 95035
Phone: 408-262-9003   **Fax:** 408-957-9740
Web: www.sigmadesigns.com

Sigma Designs has offices in China, France, Hong Kong, Japan, Taiwan, and the US.

2007 Sales

	$ mil.	% of total
Asia/Pacific		
South Korea	15.6	17
China	9.8	11
Singapore	7.4	8
Japan	7.3	8
Taiwan	4.4	5
Hong Kong	3.7	4
New Zealand & other countries	0.4	—
Europe		
France	26.8	29
Other countries	6.2	7
North America		
US	9.5	11
Canada	0.1	—
Total	**91.2**	**100**

PRODUCTS/OPERATIONS

2007 Sales

	$ mil.	% of total
Chipsets	87.0	95
Boards	2.9	3
Other	1.3	2
Total	**91.2**	**100**

2007 Sales by Market

	$ mil.	% of total
Internet protocol video applications	61.5	67
Advanced DVD/media players	24.7	27
HDTV products	1.6	2
PC add-ins & other products	3.4	4
Total	**91.2**	**100**

Products

Chipsets
  Analog multiplexer with digital-to-analog converter
  DVD decoder chips (converters, decoders, and
    multiplexers)
  Multimedia analog overlay

Boards
  REALmagic DVR (video and audio compression and
    decompression)
  REALmagic Hollywood Plus (PC-DVD playback card)
  REALmagic NetStream 2000 (decoder card for
    streaming video)
  REALmagic Remote Control (infrared controller for
    DVD appliances)
  REALmagic Xcard (decoder card for PC-to-TV output)

Other products
  Audio adapter cable
  Connector kit
  Remote controls
  VGA pass-through cable
  Video adapter cable

COMPETITORS

Alereon
AMD
Analog Devices
Artimi
Broadcom
Cirrus Logic
Conexant Systems
Creative Technology
ESS Technology
FOCUS Enhancements
Genesis Microchip
IBM
LSI Corp.
MediaTek
NVIDIA
NXP
Optibase
Pixelworks
STMicroelectronics
Texas Instruments
Time Domain
VIA Technologies
WiQuest
Wisair
Zoran

HISTORICAL FINANCIALS

Company Type: Public

Income Statement

FYE: Saturday nearest January 31

	REVENUE ($ mil.)	NET INCOME ($ mil.)	NET PROFIT MARGIN	EMPLOYEES
1/07	91.2	6.2	6.8%	180
1/06	33.3	1.9	5.7%	160
1/05	31.4	1.8	5.7%	—
1/04	30.5	1.5	4.9%	—
1/03	18.1	(6.1)	—	116
Annual Growth	**49.8%**	**—**	**—**	**11.6%**

2007 Year-End Financials

Debt ratio: 0.0%
Return on equity: 14.3%
Cash ($ mil.): 33.2
Current ratio: 2.70
Long-term debt ($ mil.): 0.0
No. of shares (mil.): 22.9

Dividends
  Yield: —
  Payout: —
Market value ($ mil.): 588.6
R&D as % of sales: 24.7%
Advertising as % of sales: —

Stock History

NASDAQ (GM): SIGM

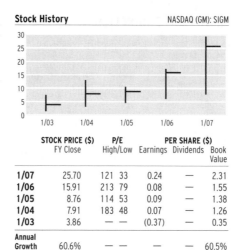

	STOCK PRICE ($) FY Close	P/E High	P/E Low	PER SHARE ($) Earnings	PER SHARE ($) Dividends	PER SHARE ($) Book Value
1/07	25.70	121	33	0.24	—	2.31
1/06	15.91	213	79	0.08	—	1.55
1/05	8.76	114	53	0.09	—	1.38
1/04	7.91	183	48	0.07	—	1.26
1/03	3.86	—	—	(0.37)	—	0.35
Annual Growth	**60.6%**	**—**	**—**	**—**	**—**	**60.5%**

Silicon Image

It would be silly to imagine that Silicon Image's chips only produce pretty pictures. Silicon Image designs and sells a variety of integrated circuits, including digital video controllers, receivers, transmitters, and processors that are built into personal computers, set-top boxes, and DVD players. Its chips also are found in video systems, such as flat-panel displays and cathode-ray tubes, as well as storage networking devices. Top customers of the fabless semiconductor company include big Asian distributors. Silicon Image primarily outsources production of its chips to Taiwan Semiconductor Manufacturing.

With a wide variety of consumer electronics manufacturers supporting the High Definition Multimedia Interface (HDMI) industry standard, Silicon Image has more than 500 companies licensing the technology from its HDMI Licensing subsidiary. It is also developing three sub-brands to increase its profile among consumers. They are PinnaClear, for presentation products; Steel-Vine, for data storage products; and VastLane, for Digital Visual Interface (DVI) and HDMI transmitters and receivers.

Silicon Image is expanding its HDMI licensing and testing services through a new subsidiary called Simplay Labs.

Customers located outside of the US account for around 80% of Silicon Image's sales. The company has added offices in Japan, South Korea, and Taiwan to expand its customer and support operations in the Asia/Pacific region. Silicon Image sells primarily to the personal computer, storage, and consumer electronics markets.

Silicon Image expanded its offerings in the storage components business through its 2003 acquisition of privately held TransWarp Networks (switching, CPU, and memory products for storage management). The company is also phasing out its storage subsystems products, opting to license the technology rather than develop new products.

A dispute over patent royalties due from rival Genesis Microchip was resolved in Silicon Image's favor in late 2006, with Genesis paying $4.5 million in one lump sum and a confidential amount in recalculated royalties to Silicon Image. Under a previous agreement between the competitors reached in 2002, Genesis had already paid a total of about $11 million in royalties to Silicon Image.

Barclays Global Investors owns about 6% of Silicon Image.

EXECUTIVES

Chairman: Peter G. Hanelt, age 61
President, CEO, and Director: Steve Tirado, age 52, $1,125,790 pay
COO: Paul Dal Santo, age 57
CFO: Harold L. (Hal) Covert, age 60
CTO: J. Duane Northcutt, age 49, $532,317 pay
VP, Worldwide Operations and Quality: Peter J. Rado
VP, Business Development and Intellectual Property Licensing: Eric C. Almgren
VP, Worldwide Marketing: Dale Zimmerman, age 48
VP, Strategic Business Development: Brett Gaines
VP, Human Resources: Doug Haslam
President, Silicon Image Japan: Youkichi Den
President, Simplay Labs: Joseph L. Lias, age 49
Chief Legal Officer: Edward Lopez
Manager, Public Relations: Sheryl M. Gulizia
Investor Relations: Gloria Lee
Auditors: Deloitte & Touche LLP

LOCATIONS

HQ: Silicon Image, Inc.
  1060 E. Arques Ave., Sunnyvale, CA 94085
Phone: 408-616-4000   **Fax:** 408-830-9530
Web: www.siimage.com

Silicon Image has offices in China, Germany, Japan, South Korea, Taiwan, Turkey, the UK, and the US.

2006 Sales

	$ mil.	% of total
Asia/Pacific		
Japan	103.1	35
Taiwan	59.9	20
South Korea	20.9	7
Hong Kong	11.3	4
US	63.3	22
Other countries	36.5	12
Total	**295.0**	**100**

PRODUCTS/OPERATIONS

2006 Sales

	$ mil.	% of total
Consumer electronics	167.9	57
Personal computers	49.4	17
Storage products	33.1	11
Development, licensing & royalties	44.6	15
Total	**295.0**	**100**

Selected Products

Communications integrated circuits
  Fibre Channel serializer/deserializers (SerDes)
  Receivers
  Transmitters
Controller integrated circuits for video displays
Digital video processors and processing systems

COMPETITORS

AMD
Analog Devices
Atmel
Avago Technologies
Broadcom
Chrontel
Conexant Systems
FOCUS Enhancements
Genesis Microchip
Hitachi
Intel Corporation
LSI Corp.
Macronix International
Marvell Technology
Matsushita Electric Works
Micronas Semiconductor
Mindspeed
National Semiconductor
NVIDIA
NXP
Philips Electronics
Pixelworks
PMC-Sierra
Promise Technology
QLogic
Silicon Integrated Systems
Silicon Optix
Sony
STMicroelectronics
Texas Instruments
THOMSON
Toshiba
Trident Microsystems
VIA Technologies
Vitesse Semiconductor

HISTORICAL FINANCIALS

Company Type: Public

Income Statement

FYE: December 31

	REVENUE ($ mil.)	NET INCOME ($ mil.)	NET PROFIT MARGIN	EMPLOYEES
12/06	295.0	42.5	14.4%	442
12/05	212.4	49.5	23.3%	384
12/04	173.2	(0.3)	—	—
12/03	103.5	(12.8)	—	—
12/02	81.5	(40.1)	—	249
Annual Growth	37.9%	—	—	15.4%

2006 Year-End Financials

Debt ratio: —
Return on equity: 17.6%
Cash ($ mil.): 250.6
Current ratio: 4.52
Long-term debt ($ mil.): —
No. of shares (mil.): 86.5
Dividends
Yield: —
Payout: —
Market value ($ mil.): 1,100.1
R&D as % of sales: —
Advertising as % of sales: —

Stock History

NASDAQ (GS): SIMG

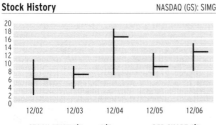

	STOCK PRICE ($) FY Close	P/E High/Low		Earnings	PER SHARE ($) Dividends	Book Value
12/06	12.72	30	17	0.49	—	3.53
12/05	9.07	21	12	0.59	—	2.18
12/04	16.46	—	—	—	—	1.56
12/03	7.16	—	—	(0.18)	—	0.86
12/02	6.00	—	—	(0.62)	—	0.72
Annual Growth	20.7%			—	—	48.6%

Simclar, Inc.

Simclar could be the name of a new superhero. Instead, the company provides contract manufacturing and services for equipment makers that serve the data processing, telecommunications, food preparation, military, and instrumentation markets. Simclar's products include printed circuit boards, custom electromechanical assemblies, cables, and wire harnesses. The company also provides product repair and refurbishment services. Simclar's customers include Illinois Tool Works. Contract manufacturer Simclar Group Limited (which is owned by CEO Samuel Russell and his wife, director Christina Russell) controls nearly three-quarters of the company.

Nearly all of Simclar's sales are to customers located in the US, with a small portion in Mexico. The company is focusing on value-added services for continued growth; it acquired AG Technologies, a small contract manufacturer with facilities in Mexico and the US, in 2003. In 2005 Simclar acquired Simclar (North America) from Simclar Group, adding sheet metal fabrication and higher-level assembly capabilities.

In 2006 the company acquired certain US assets of Litton Interconnect Technologies, a unit of Northrop Grumman, for $16 million. At the same time, Simclar's parent company acquired the Litton unit's assets in China and the UK for $12 million.

EXECUTIVES

Chairman and CEO: Samuel J. (Sam) Russell, age 63, $60,000 pay
President and Director: Barry J. Pardon, age 56, $130,000 pay
CFO, Treasurer, and Secretary: Marshall W. Griffin, age 50
VP Finance and Director: John I. Durie, age 51
General Manager, Northeast: Nathan Whipple
General Manager, West: David Garcia
General Manager, Interconnect Technologies: Ken Cleeton
General Manager, Simclar de Mexico: Ricardo Juarez
Plant Manager, North Carolina: Kevin Jamieson
Auditors: Battelle & Battelle LLP

LOCATIONS

HQ: Simclar, Inc.
2230 W. 77th St., Hialeah, FL 33016
Phone: 305-556-9210 **Fax:** 305-364-1350
Web: www.simclar.com

Simclar has operations in Florida, Massachusetts, Missouri, North Carolina, Ohio, and Texas, and also in Mexico.

2006 Sales

	$ mil.	% of total
US	115.9	100
Mexico	0.1	—
Total	116.0	100

PRODUCTS/OPERATIONS

2006 Sales

	% of total
Backplane interconnect systems	39
Printed circuit boards	26
Cable & harness assemblies	24
Refurbishing & other	11
Total	100

2006 Sales by Market

	% of total
Telecommunications	43
Contract manufacturing	12
Data processing	12
Power equipment	9
Food preparation equipment	8
Instrumentation	8
Electrical equipment & appliances	3
Military & government	2
Other	3
Total	100

Products

Backplane interconnect systems
Cable assemblies
Injection-molded and electronic assembly products
Printed circuit boards
Sheet metal
Subassemblies
Wire harnesses

Services

Contract manufacturing
Design and engineering
Reworking and refurbishing

COMPETITORS

Amphenol
Benchmark Electronics
Electronic Product Integration
Flextronics
Hon Hai
Jabil
Kimball International
Methode Electronics
Nortech Systems
Sanmina-SCI
Sparton
TTM Technologies
Viasystems
Volex

HISTORICAL FINANCIALS

Company Type: Public

Income Statement

FYE: December 31

	REVENUE ($ mil.)	NET INCOME ($ mil.)	NET PROFIT MARGIN	EMPLOYEES
12/06	116.0	2.9	2.5%	934
12/05	61.0	0.9	1.5%	837
12/04	53.6	2.3	4.3%	—
12/03	36.2	1.1	3.0%	—
12/02	33.7	1.4	4.2%	284
Annual Growth	36.2%	20.0%	—	34.7%

2006 Year-End Financials

Debt ratio: 92.2%
Return on equity: 17.6%
Cash ($ mil.): 0.1
Current ratio: 1.50
Long-term debt ($ mil.): 16.5
No. of shares (mil.): 6.5
Dividends
Yield: —
Payout: —
Market value ($ mil.): 38.7
R&D as % of sales: —
Advertising as % of sales: —

Stock History

NASDAQ (CM): SIMC

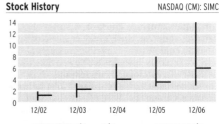

	STOCK PRICE ($) FY Close	P/E High/Low		Earnings	PER SHARE ($) Dividends	Book Value
12/06	5.98	31	7	0.44	—	2.77
12/05	3.57	53	20	0.15	—	2.33
12/04	4.06	18	6	0.36	—	2.18
12/03	2.30	19	6	0.17	—	1.82
12/02	1.25	9	2	0.21	—	1.58
Annual Growth	47.9%			20.3%	—	15.1%

SiRF Technology

Surf the seas, the highways, or the wireless Web — SiRF Technology's semiconductor designs and software will help you keep track of where you are. SiRF's products, which employ Global Positioning System (GPS) data, allow manufacturers to add navigation and mapping, lost person location, and fleet vehicle tracking functions into their own wireless devices. The fabless semiconductor company, which was founded in 1995, expanded its offerings through a 2002 agreement with Conexant Systems: Conexant contributed its own GPS technology to SiRF in return for an ownership stake in the company (which it sold in early 2006). Promate Electronic, Garmin, and Gateway are among the company's leading customers.

In the biggest acquisition in the company's history, SiRF has acquired Centrality Communications for $283 million in stock and cash. Centrality develops processors for mobile navigation devices. The firm was founded in 1999.

The Centrality acquisition added significantly to SiRF's headcount. Hiring Centrality's 190-plus employees increased SiRF's payroll by more than 40%.

SiRF has signed a license and joint development agreement with Intel, agreeing to collaborate with the chip giant on developing location and wireless connectivity product platforms for mobile electronics. SiRF licensed certain technologies to Intel under the deal and will cooperate with Intel in marketing and selling products resulting from those technologies.

In 2005 SiRF acquired Kisel Microelectronics, a Swedish design house specializing in radio-frequency integrated circuits (RFICs). Also in 2005 SiRF acquired the GPS chipset line of Motorola for $20 million in cash and will continue to provide those chipsets to the communications giant under a supply agreement between the companies. Motorola uses the chipsets in its automotive telematics equipment, cell phones, and GPS-enabled radios for public safety organizations. In late 2005 the company acquired Impulsesoft Pvt. Ltd., a developer of Bluetooth stereo products and embedded software.

In early 2006 SiRF acquired TrueSpan, a developer of silicon-based and software platforms for digital audio and video in mobile applications. The purchase brought in about 30 employees, most of them in Bangalore and some in Long Beach, California.

SiRF's chips are primarily manufactured by IBM Microelectronics, Samsung Electronics, STMicroelectronics, and Taiwan Semiconductor Manufacturing. Those companies also assemble and test SiRF's devices, along with STATS ChipPAC.

FMR (Fidelity Investments) owns about 10% of SiRF Technology. Founder and chairman Diosdado Banatao, along with his firm Tallwood Venture Capital, holds nearly 8% of the company. Janus Capital Management has an equity stake of nearly 7%. OppenheimerFunds owns more than 5%.

EXECUTIVES

Chairman: Diosdado P. (Dado) Banatao
President, CEO, and Director: Michael L. Canning, age 66, $375,000 pay
SVP, Finance and CFO: Geoffrey G. (Geoff) Ribar, age 48, $235,764 pay

VP, Marketing and Director: Kanwar Chadha, age 48, $240,133 pay
VP, Sales: Joseph M. (Joe) LaValle, age 58, $260,344 pay
VP, Engineering: Jamshid (Jim) Basiji, age 67
VP, Operations and Quality: Atul P. Shingal, age 47, $244,250 pay
VP, Human Resources: Jim Murphy
VP, Hardware Engineering: Jeff Hawkey
Auditors: Ernst & Young LLP

LOCATIONS

HQ: SiRF Technology Holdings, Inc.
217 Devcon Dr., San Jose, CA 95112
Phone: 408-467-0410   **Fax:** 408-467-0420
Web: www.sirf.com

SiRF Technology Holdings has offices in Belgium, China, Germany, India, Japan, South Korea, Sweden, Taiwan, the UK, and the US.

2006 Sales

	$ mil.	% of total
Asia/Pacific		
Taiwan	159.2	64
Singapore	20.8	8
China	6.3	3
Japan	5.0	2
New Zealand	2.7	1
North America		
US	37.2	15
Canada	4.3	2
Europe	7.7	3
Other regions	4.5	2
Total	**247.7**	**100**

PRODUCTS/OPERATIONS

Selected Products

Atlas (processors for navigation infotainment systems)
SiRFDRive (software for automotive applications)
SiRFLoc and SiRFXTrac (software for wireless devices)
SiRFstar semiconductors
  Embedded core software
  Enhanced digital signal processing circuit
  Internal processor and memory
  Radio-frequency integrated circuit
Titan (high-end navigation processors)

COMPETITORS

Analog Devices	NAVSYS
Andrew Corporation	NXP
Atmel	QUALCOMM
CEVA	RF Micro Devices
CSR	Sony
Freescale Semiconductor	STMicroelectronics
Hittite Microwave	Texas Instruments
Infineon Technologies	Trimble Navigation
MediaTek	TruePosition

HISTORICAL FINANCIALS

Company Type: Public

Income Statement

FYE: December 31

	REVENUE ($ mil.)	NET INCOME ($ mil.)	NET PROFIT MARGIN	EMPLOYEES
12/06	247.7	2.4	1.0%	445
12/05	165.1	30.0	18.2%	354
12/04	117.4	30.7	26.1%	202
12/03	73.2	3.6	4.9%	—
12/02	30.4	(12.5)	—	—
Annual Growth	**69.0%**	**—**	**—**	**48.4%**

2006 Year-End Financials

Debt ratio: 0.2%
Return on equity: 0.8%
Cash ($ mil.): 170.2
Current ratio: 5.83
Long-term debt ($ mil.): 0.5
No. of shares (mil.): 52.3

Dividends
  Yield: —
  Payout: —
Market value ($ mil.): 1,334.3
R&D as % of sales: —
Advertising as % of sales: —

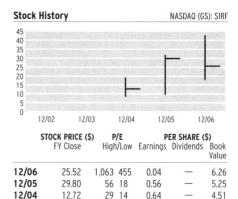
	STOCK PRICE ($) FY Close	P/E High/Low		Earnings	PER SHARE ($) Dividends	Book Value
12/06	25.52	1,063	455	0.04	—	6.26
12/05	29.80	56	18	0.56	—	5.25
12/04	12.72	29	14	0.64	—	4.51
Annual Growth	**41.6%**	**—**	**—**	**(75.0%)**	**—**	**17.8%**

Sirona Dental Systems

Smile pretty for the camera! Sirona Dental Systems (formerly Schick Technologies) makes imaging systems, dental restoration equipment, and a full line of other products and instruments for dentists and dental laboratories worldwide. Its CEREC system is a computer-aided contraption for making ceramic restorations (such as crowns and bridges) in the dentist's office rather than a lab. The firm also makes dental imaging systems, including traditional X-ray equipment and digital radiography systems that use less radiation. Other products include dental chairs that integrate diagnostic, hygiene, and other functions, as well as instruments for fixing cavities, performing root canals, and executing other procedures.

The company operates globally, with about 30% of its revenues coming from the US. Its top distributors are Patterson and Henry Schein, and it uses Patterson exclusively to distribute its CEREC products in North America.

Sirona has been growing both in the US and in international markets, adding a number of sales and service centers in Australia, China, Europe, and Japan since 2004.

The current version of the company was formed in 2006 through a reverse merger of private equity-backed Sirona Dental Systems (based in Germany) with the smaller US-based Schick Technologies, a publicly traded company. The deal happened only a few months after Madison Dearborn Partners and Beecken Petty O'Keefe had acquired Sirona from Swedish private equity firm EQT. (Sirona was formerly the dental division of Siemens AG but became independent from that company in 1997.)

Schick Technologies contributed to the match its strong North American presence in the digital radiography market, while Sirona contributed a worldwide presence in dental restoration, imaging, treatment centers (i.e. dentists' chairs), and dental instruments.

EXECUTIVES

Chairman, President, and CEO: Jost Fischer, age 52
EVP, CFO, and Director: Simone Blank, age 44
EVP and COO, US Operations; Director:
Jeffrey T. Slovin, age 43
EVP, Human Resources and Services: Theo Haar,
age 60
VP, Imaging Systems: Stefan Hehn
VP, Instruments: Jan Siefert
VP, Sales: Walter Petersohn
VP, Sales, Europe and Canada: Thomas Scherer
VP, Sales, Germany, Benelux, and Austria:
Regina Kuhnert
VP, Sales, World Markets: Jörg Vogel
VP, Treatment Centers: Michael Geil
President, Sirona Dental Systems, LLC, USA:
Michael Augins
President, Schick Technologies: Michael Stone, age 52
General Counsel and Secretary: Jonathan I Friedman,
age 37
Head, Corporate Communications: Stefan Kohl
Director, Investor Relations: John Sweeney
Auditors: Grant Thornton LLP

LOCATIONS

HQ: Sirona Dental Systems, Inc.
30-00 47th Ave., Long Island City, NY 11101
Phone: 718-937-5765   **Fax:** 718-937-5962
Web: www.sirona.de

Sirona Dental Systems has production facilities in
China, Denmark, Germany, Italy, and the US.

2007 Sales

	$ mil.	% of total
US	215.9	33
Germany	140.6	21
Other	303.5	46
Total	**660.0**	**100**

PRODUCTS/OPERATIONS

2007 Sales

	$ mil.	% of total
Imaging Systems	225.7	34
Dental CAD/CAM Systems	208.5	32
Treatment Centers	143.1	22
Instruments	82.7	12
Total	**660.0**	**100**

Selected Products

Dental CAD/CAM systems
  CEREC (in-office dental restoration system)
  inLab (laboratory dental restoration system)
  inEos (laboratory dental restoration system)
Imaging systems
  Computed digital radiography system (intra-oral
    digital imaging system)
  Orthophos XG (digital panoramic X-ray system)
Treatment centers
  Basic dentists chairs
  Integrated treatment centers
Instruments
  PerioScan (ultrasonic scaling unit)
  SIROEndo (root canal preparation unit)
  SIROLaser (diode laser used in endodontics,
    periodontology, and oral surgery)

COMPETITORS

AFP Imaging
Align Technology
Astra Tech
DENTSPLY
Eastman Kodak
GE Healthcare
National Dentex
Philips Electronics
Siemens Medical
Sybron Dental
Young Innovations

HISTORICAL FINANCIALS

Company Type: Public

Income Statement

FYE: September 30

	REVENUE ($ mil.)	NET INCOME ($ mil.)	NET PROFIT MARGIN	EMPLOYEES
9/07	660.0	56.5	8.6%	2,280
9/06*	520.6	0.8	0.2%	1,978
3/06	70.2	15.8	22.5%	1,978
3/05	52.4	12.1	23.1%	139
3/04	39.4	18.1	45.9%	—
Annual Growth	**102.3%**	**32.9%**	**—**	**154.1%**

*Fiscal year change

2007 Year-End Financials

Debt ratio: 88.7%
Return on equity: 10.3%
Cash ($ mil.): 100.8
Current ratio: 1.81
Long-term debt ($ mil.): 540.1
No. of shares (mil.): 54.8
Dividends
  Yield: —
  Payout: —
Market value ($ mil.): 1,953.5
R&D as % of sales: —
Advertising as % of sales: —

Stock History

NASDAQ (GS): SIRO

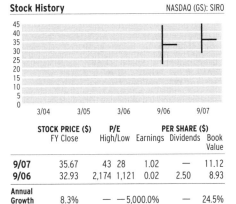

	STOCK PRICE ($) FY Close	P/E High/Low		PER SHARE ($) Earnings	Dividends	Book Value
9/07	35.67	43	28	1.02	—	11.12
9/06	32.93	2,174	1,121	0.02	2.50	8.93
Annual Growth	**8.3%**	**—**		**—5,000.0%**	**—**	**24.5%**

Smith Micro Software

Smith Micro Software links you to the world.
The company provides a variety of communication and utility software, including applications
for sending and receiving faxes, videoconferencing, roaming between wireless wide area networks and Wi-Fi hot spots, mobile music
distribution, and integrating voice, fax, and data
communications. Other products include personal firewall and system utility and diagnostic
software. Smith Micro sells its software directly,
as well as through distributors including Apple
and Verizon Wireless; Verizon accounts for about
75% of sales. Chairman William Smith and his
wife, co-founder Rhonda Smith, own about 55%
of the company.

Smith Micro offers wireless telephony software that enhances the performance and utiliza-
tion of various operating systems.

Smith Micro also has OEM relationships in
place with various wireless service providers and
manufacturers, including Audiovox, Cingular
Wireless, Kyocera, Samsung, and Verizon.

In July 2005 the company acquired Allume
Systems for about $13 million.

In early 2006 the company acquired PhoTags,
a developer of technology for managing digital
photos and music. Early the following year Smith
Micro purchased Ecutel for about $8 million.

EXECUTIVES

Chairman, President, and CEO: William W. Smith Jr.,
age 59, $337,500 pay
CFO and Secretary: Andrew C. (Andy) Schmidt, age 45,
$236,667 pay
**EVP and General Manager, Compression and
Consumer:** Jonathan Kahn, age 49, $200,000 pay
VP and CTO: David P. Sperling, age 38, $227,842 pay
VP Advanced Technology: Darryl Lovato
VP Business Development and Investor Relations:
Bruce T. Quigley
VP Channel Sales: Jeff Costello
VP Corporate Marketing: Robert E. Elliott
VP Operations: Christopher G. (Chris) Lippincott,
age 36
VP Wireless and OEM Sales: William R. (Rick) Wyand,
age 59, $190,833 pay
VP Registered In-House Counsel: David Przeracki
Auditors: Singer Lewak Greenbaum & Goldstein LLP

LOCATIONS

HQ: Smith Micro Software, Inc.
51 Columbia, Ste. 200, Aliso Viejo, CA 92656
Phone: 949-362-5800   **Fax:** 949-362-2300
Web: www.smithmicro.com

PRODUCTS/OPERATIONS

2006 Sales

	$ mil.	% of total
Products	53.8	99
Services	0.7	1
Total	**54.5**	**100**

Selected Software

Desktop fax (FAXstfX, FAXstfX Pro, QuickLink)
Desktop file management, Internet, and systems
  management (CheckIt NetOptimizer, CheckIt Utilities,
  QuickLink Mobile Phonebook)
Integrated voice, fax, and data applications (HotFax
  MessageCenter, VideoLink, VideoLink Mail, VideoLink
  Pro)
Electronic business software (WebDNA)
Web traffic monitoring and pop-up blocking (CheckIt
  86)
Wireless modem and fax (QuickLink Fax, QuickLink
  Mobile)

Selected Services

Consulting
Fulfillment (order fulfillment services for customer Web
  stores)
Web site design and hosting

COMPETITORS

CA, Inc.
Cisco Systems
Microsoft
Omtool
PCTEL
Polycom
Symantec
VocalTec

HISTORICAL FINANCIALS

Company Type: Public

Income Statement

FYE: December 31

	REVENUE ($ mil.)	NET INCOME ($ mil.)	NET PROFIT MARGIN	EMPLOYEES
12/06	54.5	9.0	16.5%	128
12/05	20.3	4.7	23.2%	91
12/04	13.3	3.4	25.6%	52
12/03	7.2	(0.9)	—	—
12/02	7.1	(0.7)	—	56
Annual Growth	**66.5%**	**—**	**—**	**23.0%**

2006 Year-End Financials

Debt ratio: —
Return on equity: 10.9%
Cash ($ mil.): 92.6
Current ratio: 20.88
Long-term debt ($ mil.): —
No. of shares (mil.): 28.4

Dividends
  Yield: —
  Payout: —
Market value ($ mil.): 403.6
R&D as % of sales: —
Advertising as % of sales: —

Stock History

NASDAQ (GM): SMSI

	STOCK PRICE ($) FY Close	P/E High/Low		PER SHARE ($) Earnings	Dividends	Book Value
12/06	14.19	54	17	0.35	—	4.43
12/05	5.85	46	16	0.21	—	1.76
12/04	8.95	59	7	0.19	—	0.62
12/03	1.99	—	—	(0.06)	—	0.33
12/02	0.46	—	—	(0.04)	—	0.35
Annual Growth	135.7%	—	—	—	—	89.2%

Smith & Wesson

When Dirty Harry said, "You've got to ask yourself one question: 'Do I feel lucky?' Well, do ya punk?", his .44-caliber Smith & Wesson revolver was really doing all the talking. Smith & Wesson Holding Corporation (operating through subsidiary Smith & Wesson Corp.) makes handguns and police accessories, as well as gun safety devices (Maximum Security Cable, Saf-T-Trigger, Versa Vault). It also sells mountain bikes outfitted for police officers and car, boat, and home alarm system packages. It licenses its brand name to apparel, watches, sunglasses, gift sets, and more. In 2001 Smith & Wesson Holding (formerly Saf-T-Hammer) purchased Smith & Wesson, which was founded in 1852.

It acquired Thompson/Center Arms in 2007 for $102 million. A 40-year-old firm based in New Hampshire, Thompson/Center Arms makes and markets premium hunting firearms. Smith & Wesson expects the acquisition to give it a strong foothold in the hunting rifle market and expand its reach into the long gun niche.

Smith & Wesson operates one retail store and commercial shooting range in its headquarters town of Springfield, and is the exclusive importer of Walther pistols with US production rights for the Walther PPK model.

Among its customers, the company estimates 14% of its products are sold to law enforcement agencies, 8% are sold internationally, and the other 78% are sold to domestic consumers through independent distributors and dealers.

Smith & Wesson has increased its sales under CEO Michael Golden. He started a company sales force, instead of relying on independent manufacturers' representatives, to sell its products, including its line of polymer pistols. In order to capitalize on its well-known brand, the company has branched out into new gun markets such as tactical rifles, hunting rifles, and shotguns.

The company relocated its Scottsdale, Arizona, headquarters to its subsidiary's Massachusetts location in early 2004. The move was designed to place executive operations near the manufacturing facility. In addition to its headquarters relocation, the company shut down its Crossings catalog business (home décor items), as well as its Smith & Wesson Advanced Technologies (SWAT) division, to re-focus on its core firearms operations.

James Minder resigned as chairman in February 2004 after news emerged of his time served in prison for armed robbery during the 1950s. He remains a member of the board of directors. In November of the same year president, CEO, and director Roy Cuny left the company (no reason was reported) and chairman G. Dennis Bingham resigned due to other professional and personal commitments; director Barry Monheit was then named chairman. Golden was appointed president and CEO.

Directors Colton Melby and Mitchell Saltz each own over 22% of the company's common stock. Vice chairman Robert Scott owns about 13%.

EXECUTIVES

Chairman: Barry M. Monheit, age 60
Vice Chairman: Robert L. (Bob) Scott, age 61
President, CEO, and Director: Michael L. Golden, age 53, $777,332 pay
CFO and Treasurer: John A. Kelly, age 48, $360,226 pay
VP, Sales; President and COO, Smith and Wesson Corp.: Leland A. Nichols, age 45, $350,760 pay (prior to promotion)
VP, Licensing: Barbara (Bobbie) Hunnicutt
VP, Marketing: Thomas L. (Tom) Taylor, age 46, $336,612 pay
VP, Operations: Kenneth W. Chandler, age 46, $332,026 pay
VP, Human Resources: Bill Lachenmeyer
VP, Investor Relations: Elizabeth A. (Liz) Sharp
Secretary and Corporate Counsel: Ann B. Makkiya, age 37, $106,236 pay
Director, Technical Support: Kurt J. Hindle
Director, Law Enforcement Sales: Bryan K. James
Director, Federal Law Enforcement and Military Sales: Ernest Langdon
Director, Sporting Goods Sales: Eoin B. Stafford
Auditors: PricewaterhouseCoopers LLP

LOCATIONS

HQ: Smith & Wesson Holding Corporation
  2100 Roosevelt Ave., Springfield, MA 01104
Phone: 413-781-8300   **Fax:** 413-747-3317
Web: www.smith-wesson.com

2007 Sales

	% of total
US	92
International	8
Total	**100**

PRODUCTS/OPERATIONS

2007 Sales

	% of total
Firearms	
Pistols	35
Revolvers	27
Walther	10
Hunting rifles	7
Tactical rifles	5
Performance Center	4
Engraving	4
Other	2
Handcuffs	3
Specialty services	2
Other	1
Total	**100**

Selected Products

Accessories
  Cases
  Fiber-optic sights
  Gloves
  Grips
  Holsters
  Locks
  Magazines
Apparel
Firearms
  Pistols
  Revolvers
  Rifles
Knives
Handcuffs and restraints
Personal security
  Racks
  Safes
  Vaults

COMPETITORS

American Derringer
Browning Arms
Colt Defense
Colt's
Fabbrica D'Armi Pietro Beretta
Glock
Ruger
SIG
Springfield Armory
Taurus
Taurus International

HISTORICAL FINANCIALS

Company Type: Public

Income Statement

FYE: April 30

	REVENUE ($ mil.)	NET INCOME ($ mil.)	NET PROFIT MARGIN	EMPLOYEES
4/07	236.6	13.0	5.5%	1,457
4/06	160.1	8.7	5.4%	—
4/05	125.8	5.3	4.2%	734
4/04	119.5	1.4	1.2%	—
4/03	100.0	15.7	15.7%	—
Annual Growth	24.0%	(4.6%)	—	40.9%

2007 Year-End Financials

Debt ratio: 203.9%
Return on equity: 25.9%
Cash ($ mil.): 4.1
Current ratio: 1.83
Long-term debt ($ mil.): 120.5
No. of shares (mil.): 39.8

Dividends
  Yield: —
  Payout: —
Market value ($ mil.): 545.8
R&D as % of sales: —
Advertising as % of sales: —

Stock History

NASDAQ (GS): SWHC

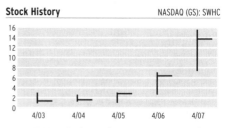

	STOCK PRICE ($) FY Close	P/E High/Low		PER SHARE ($) Earnings	Dividends	Book Value
4/07	13.72	50	24	0.31	—	1.49
4/06	6.39	32	13	0.22	—	1.05
4/05	2.84	21	8	0.14	—	0.84
4/04	1.61	63	34	0.04	—	0.54
4/03	1.35	7	2	0.44	—	0.49
Annual Growth	78.5%	—	—	(8.4%)	—	32.1%

Smithtown Bancorp

Regardless of its name, Smithtown Bancorp is on Long Island (or Paumanok if you're old school). The institution is the holding company for Bank of Smithtown, a community bank founded in 1910. The company touts its one-on-one customer service it offers through more than a dozen locations on Long Island, New York. Services include checking and savings accounts, IRAs, and CDs. Through its insurance subsidiary, Seigerman-Mulvey, the bank offers commercial and personal insurance products and financial services. Commercial mortgages make up more than half of Smithtown Bancorp's loan portfolio, which also includes residential mortgages, commercial and industrial loans, and real estate construction loans.

Director Augusta Kemper owns 6% of Smithtown Bancorp; directors and executive officers collectively control some 12% of the company.

EXECUTIVES

Chairman, President, and CEO, Smithtown Bancorp and Bank of Smithtown: Bradley E. Rock, age 54, $446,154 pay
EVP; EVP and Chief Retail Officer, Bank of Smithtown: John A. Romano, age 50, $189,923 pay
EVP and Treasurer; EVP and CFO, Bank of Smithtown: Anita M. Florek, age 56, $191,077 pay
EVP and Chief Commercial Lending Officer, Bank of Smithtown: Thomas J. Stevens, age 48, $163,230 pay
EVP and Chief Lending Officer, Bank of Smithtown: Robert J. Anrig, age 58, $191,077 pay
SVP, Operations, Bank of Smithtown: Patricia Guidi
SVP, Consumer Lending, Bank of Smithtown: Susan Ladone
VP, Human Resources, Bank of Smithtown: Deborah L. McElroy
Corporate Secretary; Corporate Secretary and Cashier, Bank of Smithtown: Judith Barber
General Counsel and Director: Patricia C. Delaney, age 48

LOCATIONS

HQ: Smithtown Bancorp, Inc.
100 Motor Pkwy., Ste. 160, Hauppauge, NY 11788
Phone: 631-360-9300   **Fax:** 631-360-9373
Web: www.bankofsmithtown.com

PRODUCTS/OPERATIONS

2006 Sales

	$ mil.	% of total
Interest		
Loans	62.0	80
Securities	4.6	6
Other	1.1	1
Noninterest		
Revenues from insurance agency	3.8	5
Service charges on deposits	1.9	3
Other	3.7	5
Total	**77.1**	**100**

COMPETITORS

Apple Bank	First of Long Island
Astoria Financial	HSBC USA
Bank of America	JPMorgan Chase
Bank of New York Mellon	New York Community
Bridge Bancorp	Bancorp
Brooklyn Federal Bancorp	State Bancorp
Citibank	Washington Mutual
Dime Community	
Bancshares	

HISTORICAL FINANCIALS

Company Type: Public

Income Statement

				FYE: December 31
	ASSETS ($ mil.)	NET INCOME ($ mil.)	INCOME AS % OF ASSETS	EMPLOYEES
12/06	1,048.2	14.0	1.3%	188
12/05	878.3	11.1	1.3%	179
12/04	677.0	10.0	1.5%	—
12/03	565.1	9.1	1.6%	—
12/02	451.8	8.0	1.8%	—
Annual Growth	**23.4%**	**15.0%**	**—**	**5.0%**

2006 Year-End Financials

Equity as % of assets: 6.4%
Return on assets: 1.5%
Return on equity: 22.8%
Long-term debt ($ mil.): 77.8
No. of shares (mil.): 8.9
Market value ($ mil.): 219.1
Dividends
 Yield: 0.6%
 Payout: 9.7%
Sales ($ mil.): 77.1
R&D as % of sales: —
Advertising as % of sales: —

Stock History

NASDAQ (GM): SMTB

	STOCK PRICE ($)	P/E		PER SHARE ($)		
	FY Close	High/Low		Earnings	Dividends	Book Value
12/06	24.66	19	12	1.44	0.14	7.52
12/05	18.06	18	11	1.14	0.14	9.43
12/04	19.24	25	12	1.02	0.09	7.92
12/03	13.14	65	9	0.92	0.11	13.17
12/02	8.14	11	7	0.79	0.09	22.27
Annual Growth	**31.9%**	**—**	**—**	**16.2%**	**11.7%**	**(23.8%)**

Somanetics Corporation

Somanetics sells the INVOS System, a noninvasive device that monitors blood-oxygen levels in the brain, primarily during surgery. Based on Somanetics' in vivo optical spectroscopy (INVOS) technology, the device's disposable SomaSensors attach to each side of the patient's forehead, and the firm's proprietary software displays oxygen levels on a computer screen. Somanetics also makes the CorRestore patch from cow's heart tissue, for use in cardiac repair and reconstruction. Somanetics markets through a direct sales staff and distributors such as Covidien and Fresenius. Customers include surgeons, anesthesiologists, and other health care providers in the US and in nearly 60 countries abroad.

Somanetics plans to continue to develop new applications for its INVOS System. The company also intends to interface its technology with other monitoring systems in hospitals. CEO Bruce Barrett owns about 7% of Somanetics.

EXECUTIVES

President, CEO, and Director: Bruce J. Barrett, age 48, $329,541 pay
SVP Sales and Marketing: Dominic J. Spadafore, age 47, $164,246 pay
VP, CFO, Controller, and Treasurer: William M. Iacona, age 37, $132,416 pay
VP Research and Development: Richard S. Scheuing, age 51
VP, Chief Administrative Officer, and Secretary: Mary Ann Victor, age 50, $146,651 pay
VP Medical Affairs: Ronald A. Widman, age 56
VP Operations: Pamela A. Winters, age 48
Auditors: Deloitte & Touche LLP

LOCATIONS

HQ: Somanetics Corporation
1653 E. Maple Rd., Troy, MI 48083
Phone: 248-689-3050   **Fax:** 248-689-4272
Web: www.somanetics.net

PRODUCTS/OPERATIONS

2006 Sales

	% of total
SomaSensors	75
INVOS System Monitors	24
CorRestore Systems	1
Total	**100**

Selected Products

CorRestore System (cardiac implant patch)
INVOS System (patient monitoring system)
SomaSensors (disposable sensors used with the INVOS System)

COMPETITORS

Aspect Medical Systems
Bio-logic
CAS
Covidien
Criticare
GE Healthcare
Masimo
OSI Systems
Philips Electronics
Siemens Medical
Welch Allyn

HISTORICAL FINANCIALS

Company Type: Public

Income Statement

				FYE: November 30
	REVENUE ($ mil.)	NET INCOME ($ mil.)	NET PROFIT MARGIN	EMPLOYEES
11/06	28.7	10.4	36.2%	89
11/05	20.5	7.8	38.0%	55
11/04	12.6	8.7	69.0%	—
11/03	9.4	0.1	1.1%	—
11/02	6.7	(1.2)	—	28
Annual Growth	**43.9%**	**—**	**—**	**33.5%**

2006 Year-End Financials

Debt ratio: —
Return on equity: 17.6%
Cash ($ mil.): 49.7
Current ratio: 27.23
Long-term debt ($ mil.): —
No. of shares (mil.): 13.2
Dividends
 Yield: —
 Payout: —
Market value ($ mil.): 255.4
R&D as % of sales: —
Advertising as % of sales: —

	STOCK PRICE ($)	P/E		PER SHARE ($)		
	FY Close	High/Low	Earnings	Dividends	Book Value
11/06	19.40	49 19	0.75	—	6.85
11/05	30.91	56 19	0.66	—	2.60
11/04	13.88	22 8	0.77	—	1.73
11/03	7.82	943 148	0.01	—	0.66
11/02	2.02	— —	(0.13)	—	0.61
Annual Growth	76.0%	— —	—	—	83.4%

Somerset Hills Bancorp

Somerset Hills Bancorp is on the *Razor's Edge* of the financial community. The institution is the holding company for Somerset Hills Bank (aka Bank of Somerset Hills), which has branches in the northern New Jersey communities of Bernardsville, Mendham, Morristown, and Summit. The bank focuses on lending to small and midsized companies: Commercial and industrial loans account for about 40% of the loan portfolio and commercial mortgages represent nearly 35%. The bank also serves consumer clients, offering private banking and wealth management services in addition to deposit products, residential mortgages, and personal loans.

Somerset Hills Bancorp provides securities and investment advice through a joint venture with Massachusetts Mutual (MassMutual). The bank also owns Sullivan Financial Services, a mortgage lender with an office in West Orange, New Jersey.

Executives and directors collectively own 22% of the company.

EXECUTIVES

Chairman, Somerset Hills Bancorp and Somerset Hills Bank: Edward B. Deutsch, age 60
Vice Chairman, President, CEO, and COO; CEO and COO, Somerset Hills Bank: Stewart E. McClure Jr., age 56, $261,539 pay
Vice Chairman, Business Development and Director: Thompson H. McDaniel, age 69
EVP, CFO, and Director, Somerset Hills Bancorp and Somerset Hills Bank: Gerard Riker, age 66, $184,769 pay
SVP and Senior Loan Officer, Somerset Hills Bank: James M. Nigro
SVP, Installment Lending, Somerset Hills Bank: Peter A. Longo
SVP, Operations, Somerset Hills Bank: Christopher J. Pribula
SVP, Operations, Sullivan Financial Services: Laura Lyons
SVP, Sales, Sullivan Financial Services: Judy Tobia
Corporate Secretary; VP, Corporate Secretary, and Human Resources, Somerset Hills Bank: Bette A. Schmitt
Director, Investor Relations: Melissa A. Elias

LOCATIONS

HQ: Somerset Hills Bancorp
155 Morristown Rd., Bernardsville, NJ 07924
Phone: 908-221-0100   **Fax:** 908-221-1514
Web: www.bankofsomersethills.com

PRODUCTS/OPERATIONS

2006 Sales

	% of total
Interest	
Loans, including fees	73
Federal funds sold	1
Investment securities	11
Cash & due from banks	0
Noninterest	
Service fees on deposit accounts	1
Gains on sales of mortgage loans & fees, net	11
Other income	3
Total	**100**

COMPETITORS

American Bancorp of New Jersey
Bank of America
Center Bancorp
Clifton Savings
Greater Community Bancorp
Investors Bancorp
Kearny Financial
Peapack-Gladstone Financial
Sussex Bancorp
Unity Bancorp
Wachovia

HISTORICAL FINANCIALS

Company Type: Public

Income Statement

				FYE: December 31
	ASSETS ($ mil.)	NET INCOME ($ mil.)	INCOME AS % OF ASSETS	EMPLOYEES
12/06	289.4	2.2	0.8%	88
12/05	245.9	2.1	0.9%	82
12/04	181.9	1.4	0.8%	—
12/03	169.7	1.2	0.7%	—
12/02	149.8	0.2	0.1%	—
Annual Growth	17.9%	82.1%	—	7.3%

2006 Year-End Financials

Equity as % of assets: 13.1%
Return on assets: 0.8%
Return on equity: 7.0%
Long-term debt ($ mil.): —
No. of shares (mil.): 4.8
Market value ($ mil.): 60.1
Dividends
  Yield: 1.0%
  Payout: 27.1%
Sales ($ mil.): 18.6
R&D as % of sales: —
Advertising as % of sales: —

	STOCK PRICE ($)	P/E		PER SHARE ($)		
	FY Close	High/Low	Earnings	Dividends	Book Value
12/06	12.62	29 24	0.48	0.13	7.96
12/05	11.50	23 18	0.51	0.02	7.60
12/04	11.12	35 29	0.33	1.77	7.56
12/03	9.82	31 18	0.33	1.69	7.50
12/02	6.24	120 76	0.08	0.82	7.50
Annual Growth	19.3%	— —	56.5%	(36.9%)	1.5%

Sonic Solutions

Sonic Solutions provides tools to capture the digital revolution. The company's products include applications for creating digital audio and video titles, recording data files, and backing up information stored on hard drives. Though its offerings are used primarily to create CDs and DVDs, Sonic has expanded the capability of its products to include Blu-ray Disc and HD-DVD formats. Sonic Solutions markets to consumers, as well as professional organizations such as movie studios. It also licenses its technology to third parties who incorporate it into their own products and it has product bundling partnerships with such companies as Adaptec, Dell, IBM, Iomega, Pioneer, Sony, and Toshiba.

Sonic's consumer division, which accounts for the bulk of its revenues, was gained from its 2004 acquisition of the consumer software division of Roxio for $80 million. The purchase provided Sonic with a new set of consumer software brands, access to distribution channels, and relationships with retail outlets.

In early 2004 the company acquired InterActual Technologies. With the $8.8 million purchase, Sonic Solutions further strengthened its position in the Hollywood-based DVD production market. InterActual's software lets studios add features to DVD-Video titles that are viewed on PCs.

EXECUTIVES

Chairman: Robert J. (Bob) Doris, age 54, $218,750 pay (prior to title change)
President and CEO: David C. (Dave) Habiger, age 37, $382,901 pay
EVP, Worldwide Operations and Finance and CFO: A. Clay Leighton, age 49, $255,730 pay
EVP, Strategy: Mark Ely, age 36, $275,560 pay
SVP, Asia Pacific Rim Operations: Koki Terui
SVP; General Manager, Advanced Technology Group: Jim Taylor
SVP; General Manager, Professional Products Group: Rolf Hartley
Managing Director, European Operations, Professional Products Group: Richard Linecar
General Manager, Roxio Division: Stan Wong
Secretary and Director: Mary C. Sauer, age 54, $158,917 pay (prior to title change)
Director, Marketing Communications: Chris Taylor
Auditors: BDO Seidman, LLP

LOCATIONS

HQ: Sonic Solutions
101 Rowland Way, Novato, CA 94945
Phone: 415-893-8000   **Fax:** 415-893-8008
Web: www.sonic.com

2007 Sales

	$ mil.	% of total
US	116.4	78
Japan	13.3	9
Other countries	18.9	13
Total	**148.6**	**100**

PRODUCTS/OPERATIONS

2007 Sales

	$ mil.	% of total
Consumer		
Roxio Division	122.3	82
Advanced Technology Group	18.1	12
Professional	8.2	6
Total	**148.6**	**100**

Selected Products

Backup and copy
  BackUp MyPC
  Easy DVD Copy
CD and DVD creation and playback
  Digital Media Network
  Digital Media Studio
  DVD for Photo Story
  DVDit
  Easy Media Creator
  MyDVD
  PhotoSuite
  PrimeTime Line
  RecordNow!
  VideoWave
Mac products
  Popcorn
  The Boom Box
  Toast
Professional products
  CineVision
  DVD-Audio Creator
  DVDit Pro
  eDVD
  ReelDVD
  Scenarist

COMPETITORS

Adobe	Pacific Research
Apple	& Engineering
ArcSoft	Panasonic of
Avid Technology	North America
Corel	Sony
Dolby	Toshiba
Massive Incorporated	ZOO Digital Group
Optibase	

HISTORICAL FINANCIALS

Company Type: Public

Income Statement

FYE: March 31

	REVENUE ($ mil.)	NET INCOME ($ mil.)	NET PROFIT MARGIN	EMPLOYEES
3/07	148.6	6.3	4.2%	734
3/06	148.7	19.9	13.4%	637
3/05	90.6	8.5	9.4%	—
3/04	56.8	11.1	19.5%	—
3/03	32.7	2.5	7.6%	—
Annual Growth	46.0%	26.0%	—	15.2%

2007 Year-End Financials

Debt ratio: —
Return on equity: 4.1%
Cash ($ mil.): 64.3
Current ratio: 1.58
Long-term debt ($ mil.): —
No. of shares (mil.): 26.2
Dividends
  Yield: —
  Payout: —
Market value ($ mil.): 369.4
R&D as % of sales: —
Advertising as % of sales: —

Stock History

NASDAQ (GS): SNIC

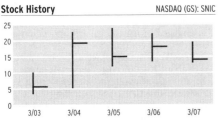

	STOCK PRICE ($) FY Close	P/E High/Low		Earnings	PER SHARE ($) Dividends	Book Value
3/07	14.10	84	58	0.23	—	5.76
3/06	18.11	30	19	0.73	—	5.38
3/05	15.05	74	38	0.32	—	4.09
3/04	19.25	49	12	0.46	—	2.55
3/03	5.70	77	28	0.13	—	1.07
Annual Growth	25.4%	—	—	15.3%	—	52.3%

Sonus Networks

Sonus Networks has found a sound place in the voice infrastructure market. The company makes hardware and software that public network providers — including long-distance carriers, ISPs, and cable operators — use to provide voice and data communications services to their subscribers. Its products include switches and related network software. Sonus also provides network installation, support, and training services. The company sells its products directly and through resellers, including Nissho Electronics and Samsung, to such customers as Qwest Communications, Global Crossing, and Deutsche Telekom.

Sonus Networks' largest customers — AT&T Wireless, KDDI, and Level 3 — together accounted for more than 40% of 2006 revenues.

EXECUTIVES

Chairman, President, and CEO: Hassan M. Ahmed, age 49, $454,688 pay
CFO: Richard J. Gaynor
CTO: Vikram Saksena
VP Internal Operations: Gale England
VP Global Services: Matt Dillon
VP Senior Advisor: Jeffrey (Jeff) Mayersohn
VP Worldwide Engineering: Chuba Udokwu
VP Corporate Marketing and Investor Relations: Jocelyn Philbrook
VP and General Counsel: Charles J. (Charlie) Gray
VP Worldwide Sales: Mohammed Shanableh
Managing Director, Sonus Bangalore: Shailin Sehgal
Auditors: Deloitte & Touche LLP

LOCATIONS

HQ: Sonus Networks, Inc.
  7 Technology Park Dr., Westford, MA 01886
Phone: 978-614-8100   **Fax:** 978-614-8101
Web: www.sonusnet.com

2006 Sales

	% of total
US	72
Asia/Pacific	
Japan	19
Other countries	2
Europe, Middle East & Africa	5
Other regions	2
Total	**100**

PRODUCTS/OPERATIONS

2006 Sales

	$ mil.	% of total
Products	203.6	73
Services	75.9	27
Total	**279.5**	**100**

Selected Products

Call routing servers
Network management software
Signaling gateways
Switches

COMPETITORS

Alcatel-Lucent
Cisco Systems
Ericsson
NEC Electronics
Nokia Siemens Networks
Nortel Networks
UTStarcom
Veraz
Verso Technologies

HISTORICAL FINANCIALS

Company Type: Public

Income Statement

FYE: December 31

	REVENUE ($ mil.)	NET INCOME ($ mil.)	NET PROFIT MARGIN	EMPLOYEES
12/06	279.5	102.8	36.8%	850
12/05	194.6	8.4	4.3%	719
12/04	170.7	24.5	14.4%	537
12/03	93.2	(15.1)	—	401
12/02	62.6	(68.5)	—	361
Annual Growth	45.4%	—	—	23.9%

2006 Year-End Financials

Debt ratio: —
Return on equity: 28.8%
Cash ($ mil.): 300.7
Current ratio: 3.56
Long-term debt ($ mil.): —
No. of shares (mil.): 259.8
Dividends
  Yield: —
  Payout: —
Market value ($ mil.): 1,711.9
R&D as % of sales: 19.8%
Advertising as % of sales: —

Stock History

NASDAQ (GS): SONS

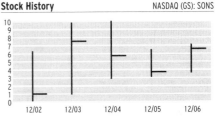

	STOCK PRICE ($) FY Close	P/E High/Low		Earnings	PER SHARE ($) Dividends	Book Value
12/06	6.59	18	9	0.40	—	1.67
12/05	3.72	214	105	0.03	—	1.12
12/04	5.73	100	29	0.10	—	1.07
12/03	7.54	—	—	(0.07)	—	0.96
12/02	1.00	—	—	(0.36)	—	0.28
Annual Growth	60.2%	—	—	—	—	56.5%

Southcoast Financial

Southcoast Financial Corporation pays a great deal of interest to the Palmetto State. The institution is the holding company for Southcoast Community Bank, which serves South Carolina's Berkeley, Charleston, and Dorchester counties. The bank, which targets local small businesses, offers savings, checking, NOW, IRA, and money market accounts, as well as CDs. Lending products include commercial, consumer, and real estate loans, and personal and business lines of credit. Southcoast Community Bank also offers insurance and investment products and services.

EXECUTIVES

Chairman, President, and CEO; President, Southcoast Community Bank: L. Wayne Pearson, age 59, $534,067 pay
EVP, COO, and Director: Paul D. Hollen III, age 58, $253,156 pay
EVP, CFO, and Director; EVP and CFO, Southcoast Community Bank: Robert M. (Bob) Scott, age 63
EVP and Chief Lending Officer: Robert A. Daniel Jr., age 56, $189,871 pay
EVP and Head of Retail Banking: William B. Seabrook, age 50, $220,659 pay
SVP and CFO: William C. (Clay) Heslop, age 31
Auditors: Clifton D. Bodiford

HQ: Southcoast Financial Corporation
530 Johnnie Dodds Blvd.,
Mount Pleasant, SC 29464
Phone: 843-884-0504 **Fax:** 843-884-2886
Web: www.southcoastbank.com

PRODUCTS/OPERATIONS

2006 Sales

	$ mil.	% of total
Interest		
Loans, including fees	28.1	80
Investment securities	2.9	8
Federal funds sold	0.5	1
Noninterest		
Service fees on deposit accounts	0.9	3
Gain on sale of property & equipment	0.4	1
Gain on sale of loans	0.3	1
Other	2.2	6
Total	**35.3**	**100**

COMPETITORS

Bank of South Carolina
First Financial Holdings
Regions Financial
SCBT Financial
SunTrust
Tidelands Bancshares

HISTORICAL FINANCIALS

Company Type: Public

Income Statement

FYE: December 31

	ASSETS ($ mil.)	NET INCOME ($ mil.)	INCOME AS % OF ASSETS	EMPLOYEES
12/06	481.9	4.8	1.0%	115
12/05	476.6	4.2	0.9%	96
12/04	366.1	3.0	0.8%	—
12/03	252.9	1.7	0.7%	—
12/02	181.2	1.1	0.6%	—
Annual Growth	**27.7%**	**44.5%**	**—**	**19.8%**

2006 Year-End Financials

Equity as % of assets: 16.4%
Return on assets: 1.0%
Return on equity: 6.3%
Long-term debt ($ mil.): 87.7
No. of shares (mil.): 5.5
Market value ($ mil.): 102.9
Dividends
  Yield: —
  Payout: —
Sales ($ mil.): 35.3
R&D as % of sales: —
Advertising as % of sales: —

Stock History

NASDAQ (GM): SOCB

	STOCK PRICE ($) FY Close	P/E High/Low	PER SHARE ($) Earnings	Dividends	Book Value
12/06	18.82	27 22	0.81	—	14.41
12/05	19.92	24 18	0.97	1.74	14.80
12/04	19.48	28 18	0.74	1.58	12.31
12/03	14.34	23 11	0.68	2.12	12.46
12/02	7.81	18 13	0.49	0.72	9.61
Annual Growth	**24.6%**	**— —**	**13.4%**	**34.2%**	**10.6%**

Southern First Bancshares

Southern First Bancshares wants the world to know it's expanding its horizons. Formerly Greenville First Bancshares, the bank operates in two markets — in Greenville, South Carolina (in which it will continue to operate under the Greenville moniker) and now in Columbia as Southern First. Opened in 2000, the bank targets individuals and small to midsized businesses, selling itself as a local alternative to larger institutions. It offers traditional deposit services and products, including checking accounts, savings accounts, and CDs. The bank uses funds from deposits to write mortgages and other real estate loans (more than 80% of its loan book), business loans, and consumer loans.

EXECUTIVES

Chairman: James B. Orders III, age 53
CEO and Director, Greenville First Bancshares and Greenville First Bank: R. Arthur (Art) Seaver Jr., age 43, $280,910 pay (prior to title change)
President, Greenville First Bancshares and Greenville First Bank: F. Justin Strickland
EVP, CFO, and Director, Greenville First Bancshares and Greenville First Bank: James M. (Jim) Austin III, age 49, $196,010 pay
SVP, Secretary, and Director, Greenville First Bancshares and Greenville First Bank: Frederick (Fred) Gilmer Jr., age 71
Director; EVP and Senior Lending Officer, Greenville First Bank: Frederick (Fred) Gilmer III, age 42, $211,535 pay
Director; EVP, Greenville First Bank: J. Edward (Eddie) Terrell, age 44, $169,235 pay
Auditors: Elliott Davis LLC

LOCATIONS

HQ: Southern First Bancshares Inc.
100 Verdae Blvd., Ste. 100, Greenville, SC 29607
Phone: 864-679-9000 **Fax:** 864-679-9099
Web: www.southernfirst.com

PRODUCTS/OPERATIONS

2006 Sales

	% of total
Interest	
Loans	87
Investment securities	9
Federal funds sold	2
Noninterest	
Service fees on deposit accounts	1
Other	1
Total	**100**

COMPETITORS

Bank of America
BB&T
First Citizens Bancorporation
Regions Financial
South Financial
Wachovia

HISTORICAL FINANCIALS

Company Type: Public

Income Statement

FYE: December 31

	ASSETS ($ mil.)	NET INCOME ($ mil.)	INCOME AS % OF ASSETS	EMPLOYEES
12/06	509.3	3.9	0.8%	70
12/05	405.3	2.5	0.6%	55
12/04	315.8	2.0	0.6%	—
12/03	230.7	1.0	0.4%	—
12/02	170.4	0.8	0.5%	—
Annual Growth	**31.5%**	**48.6%**	**—**	**27.3%**

2006 Year-End Financials

Equity as % of assets: 6.8%
Return on assets: 0.9%
Return on equity: 12.0%
Long-term debt ($ mil.): 13.4
No. of shares (mil.): 2.9
Market value ($ mil.): 63.0
Dividends
  Yield: —
  Payout: —
Sales ($ mil.): 31.7
R&D as % of sales: —
Advertising as % of sales: —

Stock History

NASDAQ (GM): SFST

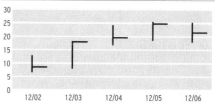

	STOCK PRICE ($) FY Close	P/E High/Low	PER SHARE ($) Earnings	Dividends	Book Value
12/06	21.47	21 15	1.20	—	11.79
12/05	24.75	32 24	0.78	—	11.46
12/04	19.61	29 21	0.82	—	10.60
12/03	18.00	37 17	0.48	—	6.49
12/02	8.57	33 18	0.39	—	8.90
Annual Growth	**25.8%**	**— —**	**32.4%**	**—**	**7.3%**

Southwestern Energy

Southwestern Energy is putting a lot of energy into gas and oil exploration and production in the Southwest. The company operates in Arkansas, Louisiana, New Mexico, Oklahoma, and Texas. In 2006 the oil and gas company reported estimated proved reserves of more than 1 trillion cu. ft. of natural gas equivalent, some 95% of which was natural gas. Southwestern Energy is also engaged in natural gas transportation and marketing. The company also operates subsidiary Arkansas Western Gas, which distributes natural gas to about 151,000 customers in Arkansas.

In 2004 Southwestern Energy formed subsidiary DeSoto Gathering Company, L.L.C., to engage in gathering activities related to its Fayetteville Shale play.

EXECUTIVES

Chairman, President, and CEO: Harold M. Korell, age 63, $1,272,375 pay
EVP Finance and CFO: Gregory D. (Greg) Kerley, age 52, $621,340 pay
EVP; President, Southwestern Energy Production and SEECO: Richard F. Lane, age 50, $606,772 pay
EVP, General Counsel, and Secretary: Mark K. Boling, age 50, $479,349 pay

President, Arkansas Western Gas: Alan N. Stewart, age 63
President, Southwestern Midstream Services: Gene A. Hammons, age 62
SVP, SEECO: John D. Thaeler, $568,600 pay
Chief Accounting Officer and Controller: Stanley T. Wilson
Manager, Investor Relations: Brad D. Sylvester
Auditors: PricewaterhouseCoopers LLP

LOCATIONS

HQ: Southwestern Energy Company
2350 N. Sam Houston Pkwy., East, Ste. 125, Houston, TX 77032
Phone: 281-618-4700 **Fax:** 281-618-4818
Web: www.swn.com

PRODUCTS/OPERATIONS

2006 Sales

	$ mil.	% of total
Exploration & production	491.5	43
Midstream services	475.2	42
Gas distribution & other	172.7	15
Adjustments	(376.3)	—
Total	**763.1**	**100**

Selected Subsidiaries

Arkansas Western Gas Company (natural gas utility)
DeSoto Drilling, Inc. (oil and gas drilling)
DeSoto Gathering Company, L.L.C (natural gas gathering)
SEECO, Inc. (exploration and production)
Southwestern Energy Pipeline Company (natural gas pipeline)
Southwestern Energy Production Company (exploration and production)
Southwestern Energy Services Company (natural gas marketing and transportation)

COMPETITORS

Alliant Energy
Apache
BP
CenterPoint Energy
Chesapeake Energy
Energen
Exxon Mobil
Hunt Consolidated
Murphy Oil
National Fuel Gas
Newfield Exploration
Pioneer Natural Resources
Royal Dutch Shell
Southern Union
Williams Companies

HISTORICAL FINANCIALS

Company Type: Public

Income Statement
FYE: December 31

	REVENUE ($ mil.)	NET INCOME ($ mil.)	NET PROFIT MARGIN	EMPLOYEES
12/06	763.1	162.6	21.3%	1,278
12/05	676.3	147.8	21.9%	784
12/04	477.1	103.6	21.7%	—
12/03	327.4	48.9	14.9%	—
12/02	261.5	14.3	5.5%	522
Annual Growth	**30.7%**	**83.6%**	**—**	**25.1%**

2006 Year-End Financials

Debt ratio: 9.9%
Return on equity: 12.8%
Cash ($ mil.): 107.0
Current ratio: 0.85
Long-term debt ($ mil.): 141.5
No. of shares (mil.): 169.0
Dividends
 Yield: —
 Payout: —
Market value ($ mil.): 5,921.8
R&D as % of sales: —
Advertising as % of sales: —

Stock History
NYSE: SWN

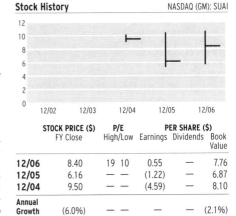

	STOCK PRICE ($) FY Close	P/E High/Low		PER SHARE ($) Earnings	Dividends	Book Value
12/06	35.05	47	25	0.95	—	8.49
12/05	35.94	44	12	0.95	—	6.64
12/04	12.67	20	7	0.70	—	12.30
12/03	5.97	18	8	0.36	—	9.51
12/02	2.86	28	17	0.14	—	6.84
Annual Growth	**87.1%**	**—**	**—**	**61.4%**	**—**	**5.6%**

Specialty Underwriters' Alliance

Specialty Underwriters' Alliance, through subsidiary SUA Insurance, offers specialty commercial property/casualty insurance to a number of niche customer groups, including general contractors, carpenters, tow-truck operators, professional employer organizations (PEOs), and public entities. It markets its products through non-exclusive partner agents, who may earn a share of underwriting profits in addition to up-front sales commissions.

The company acquired SUA Insurance (then named Potomac Insurance Company of Illinois) from OneBeacon Insurance Group in 2004. Specialty Underwriters' Alliance is licensed to do business in more than 40 states.

In 2006 the company partnered with American Patriot Insurance Agency to provide specialized coverage for roofing contractors.

EXECUTIVES

Chairman, President, and CEO: Courtney C. Smith, age 59, $525,000 pay
EVP, CFO, Treasurer, and Director: Peter E. Jokiel, age 59, $459,375 pay
SVP, Chief Underwriting Officer, and Secretary: William S. Loder, age 58, $328,125 pay
SVP and Chief Claims Officer: Gary J. Ferguson, age 63, $328,125 pay
SVP anf CIO: Barry G. Cordeiro
SVP, General Counsel, Administration, Corporate Relations and Secretary: Scott W. Goodreau, age 39
VP and Chief Actuary: Scott K. Charbonneau, age 47
VP and Controller: Daniel J. Rohan, age 50
VP and Chief Underwriting Officer: Daniel Cacchione
Auditors: PricewaterhouseCoopers LLP

LOCATIONS

HQ: Specialty Underwriters' Alliance, Inc.
222 S. Riverside Plaza, Chicago, IL 60606
Phone: 312-277-1600 **Fax:** 312-277-1800
Web: www.suainsurance.com

COMPETITORS

ACE Limited
AIG
Arch Insurance Group
CNA Financial
James River Group
Liberty Mutual
Markel
Meadowbrook Insurance
Navigators
RLI
State Compensation Insurance Fund
W. R. Berkley
Zurich Financial Services

HISTORICAL FINANCIALS

Company Type: Public

Income Statement
FYE: December 31

	ASSETS ($ mil.)	NET INCOME ($ mil.)	INCOME AS % OF ASSETS	EMPLOYEES
12/06	363.3	8.4	2.3%	83
12/05	277.2	(18.0)	—	60
12/04	217.2	(8.2)	—	—
Annual Growth	**29.3%**	**—**	**—**	**38.3%**

2006 Year-End Financials

Equity as % of assets: 31.4%
Return on assets: 2.6%
Return on equity: 7.8%
Long-term debt ($ mil.): —
No. of shares (mil.): 14.7
Market value ($ mil.): 123.3
Dividends
 Yield: —
 Payout: —
Sales ($ mil.): 117.3
R&D as % of sales: —
Advertising as % of sales: —

Stock History
NASDAQ (GM): SUAI

	STOCK PRICE ($) FY Close	P/E High/Low		PER SHARE ($) Earnings	Dividends	Book Value
12/06	8.40	19	10	0.55	—	7.76
12/05	6.16	—	—	(1.22)	—	6.87
12/04	9.50	—	—	(4.59)	—	8.10
Annual Growth	**(6.0%)**	**—**	**—**	**—**	**—**	**(2.1%)**

Sport Supply Group

Sport Supply Group (formerly Collegiate Pacific) knows how to play the game. Primarily through its catalogs, the company markets about 22,000 sports equipment products to some 200,000 customers, including balls of all types, tennis court nets, soccer goals, weight-lifting equipment, and other sporting and recreational equipment. It also sells through telemarketing programs and the Internet. Sport Supply Group (SSG) sells mostly to institutional customers like youth sports programs, YMCAs, schools, and municipal recreation departments. In late 2006 it acquired the shares of Texas-based Sport Supply Group that it didn't already own for about $24 million. In July 2007 Collegiate Pacific adopted the SSG name.

The company acquired Florida-based sporting goods distributor Orlando Team Sports in January 2005. It partnered with New Era Cap in mid-2006 in an exclusive marketing and distribution deal that creates the New Era Team Sports Division. The division will be run by SSG and serve as a single point of contact for customers who cater to the institutional and sporting goods markets and want marketing and order processing expertise.

SSG has been growing through acquisitions of sports equipment manufacturers and distributors. It bought a company owned by Blumenfeld, as well as a tennis court maintenance company, Equipmart. It also purchased California-based Tomark, maker of baseball and other sports equipment; Kesslers Team Sports, a leading team sporting goods distributor based in Richmond, Indiana; and Richmond, Virginia-based team sports distributor Dixie Sporting Goods.

Tomark Sports became the exclusive supplier of Porter Athletic gymnasium equipment in Southern California, covering 10 counties. More recently, the firm signed a multi-year agreement to become the exclusive supplier of sports equipment to Varsity Group.

About 3% of the company's sales are to US government agencies.

EXECUTIVES

Chairman and CEO: Adam Blumenfeld, age 37, $375,000 pay (prior to promotion)
President, COO, General Counsel and Secretary: Terrence M. (Terry) Babilla, age 45
CFO: John E. Pitts, age 42
EVP Sales and Marketing: Kurt Hagen, age 39, $80,000 pay (partial-year salary)
EVP, US Operations: Tevis Martin, age 51, $175,000 pay
VP Corporate Development: Chadd H. Edlein
VP Marketing: Harvey Rothenberg
General Manager, Team Sports Division: Bob Dickman
CFO: John E. Pitts, age 42
Auditors: Grant Thornton LLP

LOCATIONS

HQ: Sport Supply Group, Inc.
1901 Diplomat Dr., Farmers Branch, TX 75234
Phone: 972-484-9484 **Fax:** 972-406-3467
Web: www.sportsupplygroup.com

PRODUCTS/OPERATIONS

2007 Sales

	$ mil.	% of total
Sporting goods equipment	154.5	65
Athletic apparel & footwear	82.4	35
Total	236.9	100

Selected Products

Archery equipment
Baseball equipment
Basketball equipment
Boxing equipment
Camping equipment
Coaching equipment
Equipment carts
Field hockey
Floor covers
Football equipment
Goalpost pads
Goals and nets
Golf equipment
Inflatable balls
Lacrosse equipment
Protective equipment
Soccer equipment
Track and field equipment
Weight-lifting equipment

COMPETITORS

adidas	Rawlings
Amer Sports	SAM'S CLUB
NIKE	

HISTORICAL FINANCIALS

Company Type: Public

Income Statement

FYE: June 30

	REVENUE ($ mil.)	NET INCOME ($ mil.)	NET PROFIT MARGIN	EMPLOYEES
6/07	236.9	3.9	1.6%	776
6/06	224.2	1.9	0.8%	863
6/05	106.3	3.6	3.4%	570
6/04	39.6	1.9	4.8%	—
6/03	21.1	1.3	6.2%	—
Annual Growth	83.1%	31.6%	—	16.7%

2007 Year-End Financials

Debt ratio: 141.3%
Return on equity: 8.0%
Cash ($ mil.): 5.7
Current ratio: 2.52
Long-term debt ($ mil.): 71.4
No. of shares (mil.): 10.4

Dividends
Yield: —
Payout: —
Market value ($ mil.): 94.7
R&D as % of sales: —
Advertising as % of sales: —

Stock History

AMEX: RBI

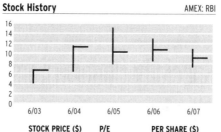

	STOCK PRICE ($) FY Close	P/E High/Low	PER SHARE ($) Earnings	Dividends	Book Value
6/07	9.15	29 20	0.37	—	4.88
6/06	10.75	71 48	0.18	—	4.62
6/05	10.30	43 23	0.35	—	4.46
6/04	11.30	46 26	0.25	—	3.29
6/03	6.65	25 15	0.27	—	1.42
Annual Growth	8.3%	— —	8.2%	—	36.1%

Stamps.com Inc.

Stamps.com hopes its customers keep putting letters in the mail. The company's PC Postage service lets 350,000 registered users who have downloaded Stamps.com software buy stamps online and print the postage directly onto envelopes and labels. Customers can also order US Postal Service options such as registered mail, certified mail, and delivery confirmation, as well as printing custom stamps using virtually any image. Stamps.com charges a monthly fee for its service, which is aimed mainly at consumers, home offices, and small businesses. In addition, customers can buy mailing labels, scales, and dedicated postage printers from Stamps.com. Postage fees are sent directly to the US Postal Service.

Stamps.com was founded as StampMaster in 1996. The company changed its name to Stamps.com in late-1998 and went public the following year.

The Internet postage firm has a new service called PhotoStamps, a form of postage that allows users to turn digital photos, designs or other images into valid US postage. Rival Envelope Manager Software (aka Endicia.com) has also launched a service called "PictureItPostage."

EXECUTIVES

CEO and Director: Kenneth (Ken) McBride, age 39, $536,667 pay
VP Finance, CFO, and Chief Accounting Officer: Kyle Huebner, age 36, $328,333 pay
VP, General Counsel, and Secretary: Seth Weisberg, age 37, $282,083 pay
VP Postal Affairs and Technology: J.P. Leon, age 50
VP Postal Affairs: Mike Boswell
VP Sales and Marketing: James M. Bortnak, age 38, $317,833 pay
VP Product and Service Operation: John Clem, age 36, $197,193 pay
Auditors: Ernst & Young LLP

LOCATIONS

HQ: Stamps.com Inc.
12959 Coral Tree Place, Los Angeles, CA 90066
Phone: 310-482-5800 **Fax:** 310-482-5900
Web: www.stamps.com

COMPETITORS

Envelope Manager Software
FedEx
Hasler, Inc.
Neopost
Pitney Bowes
UPS
US Postal Service

HISTORICAL FINANCIALS

Company Type: Public

Income Statement

FYE: December 31

	REVENUE ($ mil.)	NET INCOME ($ mil.)	NET PROFIT MARGIN	EMPLOYEES
12/06	84.6	16.5	19.5%	165
12/05	61.9	10.4	16.8%	155
12/04	38.1	(4.7)	—	—
12/03	21.2	(9.3)	—	—
12/02	16.3	(6.8)	—	84
Annual Growth	50.9%	—	—	18.4%

2006 Year-End Financials

Debt ratio: —
Return on equity: 15.0%
Cash ($ mil.): 33.6
Current ratio: 3.52
Long-term debt ($ mil.): —
No. of shares (mil.): 22.2

Dividends
Yield: —
Payout: —
Market value ($ mil.): 349.4
R&D as % of sales: —
Advertising as % of sales: —

Stock History

NASDAQ (GM): STMP

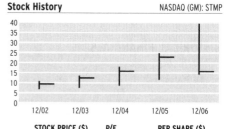

	STOCK PRICE ($) FY Close	P/E High/Low	PER SHARE ($) Earnings	Dividends	Book Value
12/06	15.75	57 21	0.69	—	4.98
12/05	22.96	56 27	0.44	—	4.77
12/04	15.84	— —	(0.21)	—	4.22
12/03	12.40	— —	(0.42)	—	3.95
12/02	9.34	— —	(0.28)	—	4.19
Annual Growth	14.0%	— —	—	—	4.4%

Standard Microsystems

Standard Microsystems Corporation (SMSC) hopes to set standards inside PCs. The company is a top supplier of input/output (I/O) chips, which perform basic control and interface functions inside of PCs or between PCs and peripherals such as keyboards and disk drives. Its I/O chips are used by leading computer makers, including Dell, Gateway, IBM, and Hewlett-Packard. SMSC, which outsources its manufacturing, also makes Universal Serial Bus (USB) interconnectivity products, as well as chips for embedded networking applications and LANs. The company also has long-term cross-licensing agreements with big chip makers, such as IBM, Intel, and Micron Technology.

SMSC continues to look for growth from customers outside the US; about two-thirds of sales are to customers in the Asia/Pacific region. Taiwan alone accounts for more than a third of the company's sales.

Unlike many chip makers, especially those closely associated with the PC market, SMSC is a consistently profitable company.

Chartered Semiconductor Manufacturing, STMicroelectronics, and Taiwan Semiconductor Manufacturing serve as the primary contractors for fabricating SMSC's chips. Assembly services are farmed out to Advanced Semiconductor Engineering, Amkor Technology, ChipMOS TECHNOLOGIES, and STATS ChipPAC. SMSC does some of the final testing of packaged devices.

Citigroup owns about 9% of Standard Microsystems. Barclays Global Investors holds nearly 6% of the company.

HISTORY

Standard Microsystems Corporation (SMSC) was founded in 1971 by a group that included Paul Richman and investor Herman Failkov. The company built its business around computer peripheral-related chips such as those used in IBM's original PCs. SMSC formed Toyo Microsystems in 1986 and later that year sold 20% of Toyo to Sumitomo Metal Industries. In 1991 SMSC doubled its size with the purchase of Western Digital's LAN business. The next year the company bought Sigma Network Systems, a high-end enterprise switching hub maker.

Networking products maker Cabletron Systems (later broken up into several smaller companies) bought SMSC's line of switches in 1996; difficulty selling and delivering the unit's products had hurt SMSC's bottom line. Also that year SMSC acquired EFAR Microsystems, a developer of core logic chipsets for use with microprocessors.

In 1997 SMSC sold 80% of its System Products division to Accton Technology, a Taiwanese maker of LAN products, to focus on its integrated circuit operations. Richman handed the CEO title over to Steven Bilodeau in 1999. That year SMSC combined its (money-losing) foundry unit with that of Inertia Optical Technology Applications to form Standard MEMS. (SMSC kept a minority stake in Standard MEMS, which filed for Chapter 11 bankruptcy protection in 2002.)

In 2000 Richman retired, and Bilodeau was named chairman. Late in 2001 SMSC announced that it would exit the highly competitive market for PC chipsets and would cut its workforce by more than a tenth in the process. Early the next year it changed the name of Toyo Microsystems to SMSC Japan. (In 2004 the company bought out Sumitomo's minority stake in SMSC Japan, making it a wholly owned subsidiary.) Also in 2002 the company acquired privately held Gain Technology, which designs analog and mixed-signal chips, for about $34 million in cash and stock.

SMSC settled patent litigation with Analog Devices in early 2005, with the company making a $6 million payment to ADI.

In 2005 the company acquired OASIS SiliconSystems Holding, which designs semiconductors for automotive applications, for nearly $119 million in cash and stock. OASIS SiliconSystems (not to be confused with Oasis Semiconductor) provides what it calls Media Oriented Systems Transport (MOST) technology, enabling transport of digital audio, video, and packet-based data within automobiles. OASIS is a supplier to many European car makers, providing chips for "infotainment" systems within models for such marques as Audi, BMW, Fiat, Jaguar, Land Rover, Mercedes-Benz, Porsche, PSA, Saab and Volvo.

William Shovers stepped aside as the company's CFO in June 2005, only three weeks after assuming the post. Shovers received a Wells notice from the SEC in connection with the commission's investigation of financial practices at Hayes Lemmerz International, where Shovers previously served as CFO. Andrew Caggia, who had retired as SMSC's CFO and was succeeded by Shovers, stepped in as interim CFO.

Caggia later retired again from management, after the company hired David Smith as CFO in 2005. Smith previously held CFO posts at Crane and Dover. Caggia remained on the board.

EXECUTIVES

Chairman, President, and CEO: Steven J. Bilodeau, age 48, $534,728 pay
SVP and CFO: David S. Smith, age 51, $325,000 pay
SVP and General Manager, Connectivity Solutions Group: Robert E. Hollingsworth, $276,271 pay
SVP Products and Technology: Aaron L. Fisher, age 49
VP and General Manager, Connected Media: Johnson Tan, $212,788 pay
VP: Christian Thiel
VP and CTO: Douglas L. (Doug) Smith
VP Operations: Peter S. Byrnes, age 49, $243,462 pay
VP, Corporate Controller: Joseph S. Durko, age 41, $209,327 pay
VP and Managing Director, Asia/Pacific Sales: Louis Lam
VP, General Counsel, and Secretary: Walter Siegel, age 47, $280,000 pay
VP Worldwide Sales: Mitchell A. Statham, age 47, $227,981 pay
Director Corporate Communications: Carolynne Borders
President, SMSC Japan: Yasuo Suzuki

LOCATIONS

HQ: Standard Microsystems Corporation
80 Arkay Dr., Hauppauge, NY 11788
Phone: 631-435-6000   **Fax:** 631-273-5550
Web: www.smsc.com

Standard Microsystems has offices in China, Germany, Hong Kong, Japan, Singapore, South Korea, Sweden, Taiwan, and the US.

2007 Sales

	$ mil.	% of total
Taiwan	133.0	36
Japan	70.7	19
China	52.1	14
Germany	46.7	13
US	35.0	9
Other countries	33.1	9
Total	**370.6**	**100**

PRODUCTS/OPERATIONS

Selected Semiconductor Products

Automotive infotainment system-on-chip devices
Ethernet physical layer (PHY) devices
Fan control devices
Hub controller devices
Input/output controllers
Temperature monitors
Universal Serial Bus (USB) controllers

COMPETITORS

Analog Devices
Cirrus Logic
ClariPhy
Cypress Semiconductor
Fairchild Semiconductor
Infineon Technologies
Micrel
National Semiconductor
NEC Electronics
NXP
Oxford Semiconductor
PLX Technology
QLogic
Renesas
Texas Instruments
VIA Technologies
Winbond Electronics

HISTORICAL FINANCIALS

Company Type: Public

Income Statement

FYE: February 28

	REVENUE ($ mil.)	NET INCOME ($ mil.)	NET PROFIT MARGIN	EMPLOYEES
2/07	370.6	27.0	7.3%	856
2/06	319.1	12.0	3.8%	767
2/05	208.8	1.6	0.8%	—
2/04	215.9	21.5	10.0%	—
2/03	155.5	(7.5)	—	499
Annual Growth	**24.2%**	**—**	**—**	**14.4%**

2007 Year-End Financials

Debt ratio: 0.9%
Return on equity: 7.4%
Cash ($ mil.): 160.0
Current ratio: 4.15
Long-term debt ($ mil.): 3.5
No. of shares (mil.): 22.9
Dividends
  Yield: —
  Payout: —
Market value ($ mil.): 653.3
R&D as % of sales: —
Advertising as % of sales: —

Stock History

NASDAQ (GS): SMSC

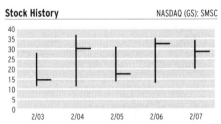

	STOCK PRICE ($) FY Close	P/E High/Low		PER SHARE ($) Earnings	Dividends	Book Value
2/07	28.57	29	18	1.16	—	17.14
2/06	32.52	64	24	0.55	—	15.18
2/05	17.53	384	177	0.08	—	14.44
2/04	30.13	24	8	1.53	—	14.27
2/03	14.62	—	—	(0.45)	—	12.17
Annual Growth	**18.2%**	**—**	**—**	**—**	**—**	**8.9%**

Starent Networks

Starent Networks makes infrastructure equipment used by wireless carriers to offer enhanced voice and data services like video, multimedia messaging, and Internet service. Its ST16 Intelligent Mobile Gateway helps cellular companies as they transition from second- to third-generation networks. Carriers that have deployed Starent's equipment include Verizon Wireless, Virgin Mobile, and China Unicom. Founded in 2000, the company has received funding from Matrix Partners, North Bridge Venture Partners, and Highland Capital Partners, among others. It has operations in Brazil, Canada, China, India, Japan, South Korea, Spain, the UK, and the US. Starent went public in 2007.

EXECUTIVES

Chairman, President, and CEO: Ashrof M. (Ash) Dahod, age 55, $301,153 pay
VP Finance and Administration: John P. Delea Jr., age 45, $258,406 pay
VP Worldwide Field Operations: Pierre G. Kahhale, age 49, $1,025,231 pay
VP and General Manager, India: Vijay Kathuria, age 46
VP Manufacturing Operations: Robert J. Kelly, age 50
VP Engineering: Anthony P. Schoener, age 45, $258,406 pay
VP Product Management: Gennedy H. Sirota, age 42, $258,406 pay
VP and General Counsel: Kevin F. Newman, age 46
VP Global Marketing and Business Development: Thierry Maupilé, age 48
VP Americas: Greg Alden
VP Operations and CFO: Paul J. Milbury, age 58
VP Marketing Communications: Andy Capener
President, Starent Networks Japan K.K.: Keisuke Sakamoto
Auditors: PricewaterhouseCoopers LLP

LOCATIONS

HQ: Starent Networks Corporation
30 International Place, Tewksbury, MA 01876
Phone: 978-851-1100   **Fax:** 978-640-6825
Web: www.starentnetworks.com

COMPETITORS

Alcatel-Lucent
Cisco Systems
Ericsson
Motorola, Inc.
Nokia
Nortel Networks
UTStarcom

HISTORICAL FINANCIALS

Company Type: Public

Income Statement

FYE: December 31

	REVENUE ($ mil.)	NET INCOME ($ mil.)	NET PROFIT MARGIN	EMPLOYEES
12/06	94.3	3.6	3.8%	441
12/05	59.7	0.9	1.5%	—
12/04	34.4	(14.0)	—	—
Annual Growth	**65.6%**	**—**	**—**	**—**

2006 Year-End Financials

Debt ratio: —
Return on equity: —
Cash ($ mil.): 60.2
Current ratio: 1.27
Long-term debt ($ mil.): —
No. of shares (mil.): 7.5

Dividends
  Yield: —
  Payout: —
Market value ($ mil.): 203.8
R&D as % of sales: —
Advertising as % of sales: —

	STOCK PRICE ($) FY Close	P/E High/Low	PER SHARE ($) Earnings	Dividends	Book Value
12/06	27.33	— —	(0.62)	—	(14.15)
12/05	23.74	— —	(0.97)	—	(15.40)
Annual Growth	**15.1%**	**— —**	**—**	**—**	**—**

Stericycle, Inc.

Bubble, bubble, toil and trouble, Stericycle treats medical rubble. A leading medical waste management company, Stericycle serves 351,700 customers in North America and the UK, including outpatient clinics, hospitals, dental offices, and blood banks. At 53 treatment centers in North America and 22 in the UK, the company treats medical waste through autoclaving (using high temperature and pressure to kill pathogens), incineration, and its electro-thermal-deactivation (ETD) process, which uses low-frequency radio waves to destroy pathogens so the waste can be recycled or used for fuel in waste-to-energy plants. Stericycle also has technology licensing agreements with companies in Australia, Brazil, and Japan.

Stericycle acquired rival Scherer Healthcare in early 2003, adding the handling of sharps to its mix of services, and in 2004 the company grew internationally by buying UK-based White Rose Environmental. Stericycle has indicated that it will consider further acquisitions that would enable the company to expand geographically or to broaden its service offerings, and in 2006 the company bought Sterile Technologies Group, a provider of medical waste management services in Ireland and the UK.

Along with its waste processing operations, Stericycle owns a controlling stake in 3CI Complete Compliance, a medical waste transporter. Stericycle took full ownership of 3CI in order to settle a lawsuit filed by 3CI and by minority shareholders of that company. The settlement, announced in November 2005 and approved in March 2006, called for Stericycle to pay $32.5 million.

Besides its operations in North America and the UK, Stericycle does business in the Asia/Pacific region, South Africa, and South America through joint ventures and licensing agreements.

EXECUTIVES

Chairman: Jack W. Schuler, age 66
President, CEO, and Director: Mark C. Miller, age 51, $809,467 pay
EVP and COO: Richard T. Kogler, age 47, $440,008 pay
EVP and CFO: Frank J. M. ten Brink, age 50, $440,008 pay

EVP International: Shan S. Sacranie, age 53, $332,500 pay
EVP Corporate Development: Richard L. Foss, age 52, $380,000 pay
President, Return Management Services Division: Michael J. Collins, age 50
Auditors: Ernst & Young LLP

LOCATIONS

HQ: Stericycle, Inc.
28161 N. Keith Dr., Lake Forest, IL 60045
Phone: 847-367-5910   **Fax:** 847-367-9493
Web: www.stericycle.com

2006 Sales

	$ mil.	% of total
North America		
US	616.4	78
Europe	128.7	16
Other regions	44.5	6
Total	**789.6**	**100**

PRODUCTS/OPERATIONS

2006 Sales

	$ mil.	% of total
US		
Medical waste management services	557.9	71
Pharmaceutical returns services	58.5	7
Other countries	173.2	22
Total	**789.6**	**100**

Selected Subsidiaries and Affiliates

American Medical Disposal, Inc.
BFI Medical Waste, Inc.
Biowaste Management Corp.
Bridgeview, Inc.
Enviromed, Inc.
Environmental Health Systems, Inc.
Ionization Research Co., Inc.
Medam S.A. de C.V. (Mexico)
Med-Tech Environmental, Inc.
Micro-Med Industries, Inc.
Scherer Laboratories, Inc.
Stericycle of Washington, Inc.
Sterile Technologies Group Limited (Ireland)
Stroud Properties, Inc.
Waste Systems, Inc.
  3CI Complete Compliance Corporation (80%)
White Rose Environmental, Ltd. (UK)

COMPETITORS

American Ecology
Ecolab UK
Waste Management

HISTORICAL FINANCIALS

Company Type: Public

Income Statement

FYE: December 31

	REVENUE ($ mil.)	NET INCOME ($ mil.)	NET PROFIT MARGIN	EMPLOYEES
12/06	789.6	105.3	13.3%	5,254
12/05	609.5	67.2	11.0%	4,431
12/04	516.2	78.2	15.1%	—
12/03	453.2	65.8	14.5%	—
12/02	401.5	45.7	11.4%	2,565
Annual Growth	**18.4%**	**23.2%**	**—**	**19.6%**

2006 Year-End Financials

Debt ratio: 70.9%
Return on equity: 18.4%
Cash ($ mil.): 16.0
Current ratio: 1.54
Long-term debt ($ mil.): 443.1
No. of shares (mil.): 44.3

Dividends
  Yield: —
  Payout: —
Market value ($ mil.): 1,670.5
R&D as % of sales: —
Advertising as % of sales: —

Stock History

NASDAQ (GS): SRCL

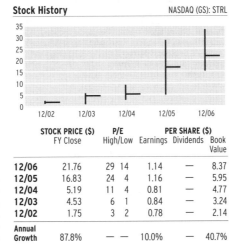

	STOCK PRICE ($) FY Close	P/E High/Low		PER SHARE ($) Earnings	Dividends	Book Value
12/06	37.75	33	24	1.16	—	14.13
12/05	29.44	43	29	0.74	—	11.82
12/04	22.98	31	25	0.85	—	11.07
12/03	23.35	36	22	0.71	—	9.74
12/02	16.19	40	25	0.50	—	8.08
Annual Growth	23.6%	—	—	23.4%	—	15.0%

Sterling Construction

Sterling Construction is a purely Texas operation. The heavy civil construction company builds sewers and water mains and works on highway paving, bridge, and light rail projects, primarily for the Texas Department of Transportation (TXDOT) and the Harris County MTA; work is concentrated not only in Houston but also in such metro areas as Austin, Dallas, Fort Worth, and San Antonio. TXDOT accounts for about two-thirds of Sterling Construction's business. Contracts with the City of Houston and Harris County contribute another 17%. The company is exploring growth outside of Texas, along the Gulf Coast and into the Southwest.

To better concentrate on its core business, Sterling Construction sold Pittsburgh-based subsidiary Steel City Products, which distributes automotive accessories, pet supplies, and lawn and garden products to supermarket chains and other retailers, mostly in the Northeast. Sterling Construction was awarded its largest contract to date, more than $90 million, with TXDOT, in 2006; the work is for the reconstruction of a section of highway outside Kingwood, Texas, that involves six bridges, a storm drainage system, and 630 sq. yds. of concrete paving.

EXECUTIVES

Chairman and CEO; President and CEO, Sterling Construction L.P.: Patrick T. (Pat) Manning, age 61, $240,000 pay
President, COO, Treasurer, and Director; Treasurer, Sterling Construction L.P.: Joseph P. (Joe) Harper Sr., age 61, $235,800 pay
EVP Business Development: Brian Manning
SVP, CFO, and Chief Accounting Officer: James H. (Jim) Allen Jr., age 66
SVP, Secretary, and General Counsel: Roger M. Barzun, age 65
VP and Corporate Controller: Karen A. Stempinski
Auditors: Grant Thornton LLP

LOCATIONS

HQ: Sterling Construction Company, Inc.
20810 Fernbush Ln., Houston, TX 77073
Phone: 281-821-9091 **Fax:** 281-821-2995
Web: www.sterlingconstructionco.com

COMPETITORS

Austin Industries	J.D. Abrams
Bechtel	McCarthy Building
Boh Bros Construction	Peter Kiewit Sons'
Fluor	Shaw Group
Holloman	Williams Brothers
InfrastruX	Zachry Construction
Insituform Technologies	

HISTORICAL FINANCIALS

Company Type: Public

Income Statement

FYE: December 31

	REVENUE ($ mil.)	NET INCOME ($ mil.)	NET PROFIT MARGIN	EMPLOYEES
12/06	249.4	13.3	5.3%	1,025
12/05	219.4	11.1	5.1%	800
12/04	154.2	5.7	3.7%	—
12/03	170.1	5.4	3.2%	—
12/02	134.6	4.7	3.5%	—
Annual Growth	16.7%	29.7%	—	28.1%

2006 Year-End Financials

Debt ratio: 33.7%
Return on equity: 19.1%
Cash ($ mil.): 54.6
Current ratio: 2.41
Long-term debt ($ mil.): 30.7
No. of shares (mil.): 10.9

Dividends
Yield: —
Payout: —
Market value ($ mil.): 236.6
R&D as % of sales: —
Advertising as % of sales: —

Stock History

NASDAQ (GS): STRL

	STOCK PRICE ($) FY Close	P/E High/Low		PER SHARE ($) Earnings	Dividends	Book Value
12/06	21.76	29	14	1.14	—	8.37
12/05	16.83	24	4	1.16	—	5.95
12/04	5.19	11	4	0.81	—	4.77
12/03	4.53	6	1	0.84	—	3.24
12/02	1.75	3	2	0.78	—	2.14
Annual Growth	87.8%	—	—	10.0%	—	40.7%

Sterling Financial

Sterling Financial has a reputation to uphold. The firm (unrelated to the Pennsylvania company of the same name) is the holding company for Sterling Savings Bank, which provides standard retail banking services through more than 160 branches in Washington, Oregon, Idaho, and Montana. Residential mortgages and construction loans make up about 40% of the bank's loan portfolio, which also includes commercial real estate, business, and consumer loans. Subsidiaries Action Mortgage and Golf Savings Bank originate residential mortgages in the bank's market states; INTERVEST originates commercial mortgages in the western US.

Sterling Financial makes no bones about its empire building. The company is racking up a string of acquisitions, including Montana's Empire Federal Bancorp (2003), Oregon's Klamath First Bancorp (2004), and Washington's Lynnwood Financial Group and its Golf Savings Bank (2006). The company also bought FirstBank NW, with branches in Idaho, Oregon, and Washington.

In keeping with its expanding realm, the company bought California bank holding company Northern Empire Bancshares for $335 million in cash and stock. It also arranged to buy North Valley Bancorp for nearly $200 million in cash and stock, but the deal stalled and was eventually terminated.

EXECUTIVES

Chairman and CEO: Harold B. Gilkey, age 67, $750,000 pay
President, COO, and Director: William W. Zuppe, age 66, $525,000 pay
EVP Finance, CFO, and Assistant Secretary, Sterling Financial and Sterling Savings Bank: Daniel G. Byrne, age 52
EVP Credit Management and Portfolio Manager: Stephen L. Page, age 58
SVP Human Resources: Debby J. Ogan
VP, Controller, and Principal Accounting Officer; VP and Controller, Sterling Savings Bank: Robert G. Butterfield, age 38
Assistant VP Investor Relations: E. Marie Hirsch
Vice Chairman, President and CEO, Sterling Savings Bank: Heidi B. Stanley, age 50, $360,000 pay
President, Harbor Financial Services: Jeffery D. Schlenker, age 39
EVP and Corporate Administrative Manager, Sterling Savings Bank: David A. Brukardt, age 50
EVP and Corporate Technical Services Manager, Sterling Savings: Ezra A. Eckhardt, age 35
EVP and Portfolio Manager, Sterling Savings Bank: Nancy R. McDaniel, age 46
SVP and CFO, Sterling Savings Bank: Thomas W. Colosimo, age 55
Secretary: Andrew J. Schultheis
Public Relations Specialist: Jennifer Lutz
Auditors: BDO Seidman, LLP

LOCATIONS

HQ: Sterling Financial Corporation
111 N. Wall St., Spokane, WA 99201
Phone: 509-458-3711 **Fax:** 509-358-6161
Web: www.sterlingsavingsbank.com

PRODUCTS/OPERATIONS

2006 Sales

	$ mil.	% of total
Interest income		
Loans	458.6	74
Mortgage-backed securities	88.4	14
Investments & cash equivalents	3.9	1
Non-interest income		
Fees & service charges	43.0	7
Mortgage banking operations	20.2	3
Other	7.0	1
Total	**621.1**	**100**

Selected Subsidiaries

Golf Savings Bank
Sterling Savings Bank
  Action Mortgage Company
  The Dime Service Corporation
  Evergreen Environmental Development Corporation
  Evergreen First Service Corporation
    Harbor Financial Services, Inc.
  Fidelity Service Corporation
  INTERVEST-Mortgage Investment Company
  Pacific Cascades Financial, Inc.
  Source Capital Corporation
    Peter W. Wong Associates, Inc.
    Source Capital Leasing Corporation
Tri-Cities Mortgage Corporation

COMPETITORS

AmericanWest	Glacier Bancorp
BancWest	U.S. Bancorp
Bank of America	Washington Federal
Banner Corp	Washington Mutual
Columbia Banking	Wells Fargo
First Mutual Bancshares	Zions Bancorporation

HISTORICAL FINANCIALS
Company Type: Public

Income Statement
FYE: December 31

	ASSETS ($ mil.)	NET INCOME ($ mil.)	INCOME AS % OF ASSETS	EMPLOYEES
12/06	9,828.7	73.9	0.8%	2,405
12/05	7,558.9	61.2	0.8%	1,789
12/04	6,942.2	56.3	0.8%	—
12/03	4,276.9	34.9	0.8%	—
12/02	3,506.1	25.6	0.7%	953
Annual Growth	29.4%	30.3%	—	26.0%

2006 Year-End Financials

Equity as % of assets: 8.0%	Dividends
Return on assets: 0.9%	Yield: 1.0%
Return on equity: 11.5%	Payout: 16.9%
Long-term debt ($ mil.): 240.2	Sales ($ mil.): 621.1
No. of shares (mil.): 42.0	R&D as % of sales: —
Market value ($ mil.): 1,421.5	Advertising as % of sales: —

Stock History
NASDAQ (GS): STSA

	STOCK PRICE ($) FY Close	P/E High/Low		PER SHARE ($) Earnings	Dividends	Book Value
12/06	33.81	17	12	2.01	0.34	18.63
12/05	24.98	16	12	1.75	0.10	14.54
12/04	26.17	17	12	1.62	1.40	20.48
12/03	20.74	14	7	1.56	1.27	16.84
12/02	10.37	11	6	1.15	1.16	17.03
Annual Growth	34.4%	—	—	15.0%	(26.4%)	2.3%

Stifel Financial

Stifel Financial doesn't repress investors. The company serves individual, corporate, municipal, and institutional investors through about 170 offices in the US, with a concentration in the Midwest and Mid-Atlantic regions. Through subsidiaries Stifel, Nicolaus & Company; Century Securities Associates (CSA); and others, the company provides securities brokerage, trading, and investment advisory services for more than 375,000 client accounts. Stifel also offers merger and acquisition advisory services for corporate clients, underwrites corporate and municipal securities, and provides research on more than 700 companies. It has three offices in Europe that conduct research on European equities.

Stifel Financial has been growing vigorously via acquisitions. In 2005 the company acquired

virtually all of the capital markets business of Legg Mason from Citigroup and purchased the retail brokerage business of Miller Johnson Steichen Kinnard the following year. In 2007 Stifel Financial bought St. Louis-based First Service Bank (now Stifel Bank and Trust), which allows it to offer banking services to its clients.

It purchased investment bank and brokerage Ryan Beck from BankAtlantic Bancorp in 2007; BankAtlantic now owns more than 15% of Stifel Financial. The Western and Southern Life Insurance Company holds a nearly 10% stake.

EXECUTIVES

Chairman, President, and CEO:
Ronald J. (Ron) Kruszewski, age 48, $1,407,500 pay
SVP and President; President and Co-COO, Stifel Nicolaus: Scott B. McCuaig, age 57, $1,025,000 pay
SVP, CFO, and Treasurer; EVP and Co-COO, Stifel Nicolaus: James M. Zemlyak, age 46, $857,500 pay
SVP and Director; EVP, Investment Banking, Stifel Nicolaus: Richard J. Himelfarb, age 66
SVP, Denver Public Finance, Stifel Nicolaus: Stephen H. Bell
SVP and Director; EVP, Equity Capital Markets, Stifel Nicolaus: Thomas P. Mulroy, age 46
SVP and Director; EVP, Fixed Income Capital Markets, Stifel Nicolaus: Joseph A. Sullivan, age 50
SVP and Managing Director, Denver Municipal Trading, Stifel Nicolaus: Michael F. Imhoff
SVP, General Counsel, and Secretary; SVP and General Counsel, Stifel Nicolaus: David M. Minnick, age 50, $252,500 pay
SVP, Operations and Technology; SVP, Stifel Nicolaus: David D. Sliney, age 37, $468,750 pay
Senior Human Resources Associate: Carrie Kramer
Corporate Secretary: Marcia Kellams
President, Stifel Bank & Trust: Christopher K. (Chris) Reichert, age 43
Auditors: Deloitte & Touche LLP

LOCATIONS

HQ: Stifel Financial Corp.
501 N. Broadway, St. Louis, MO 63102
Phone: 314-342-2000   **Fax:** 314-342-2151
Web: www.stifel.com

PRODUCTS/OPERATIONS

2006 Sales

	$ mil.	% of total
Commissions	199.0	42
Principal transactions	86.4	18
Investment banking	82.9	18
Asset management & service fees	57.7	12
Interest	35.8	8
Other	9.6	2
Total	**471.4**	**100**

Selected Subsidiaries

Century Securities Associates, Inc.
  CSA Insurance Agency, Incorporated
Hanifen, Imhoff Inc.
Ryan Beck Holdings, Inc.
  Ryan Beck & Co., Inc.
Stifel Asset Management Corp.
Stifel, Nicolaus & Company, Incorporated
  Stifel, Nicolaus Insurance Agency, Incorporated
Stifel Nicholas Limited (UK)
Stifel Venture Corp.

COMPETITORS

A.G. Edwards	Oppenheimer Holdings
Bear Stearns	Piper Jaffray
Edward Jones	Raymond James Financial
Morgan Stanley	Robert W. Baird & Co.
Newtek Business Services	

HISTORICAL FINANCIALS
Company Type: Public

Income Statement
FYE: December 31

	REVENUE ($ mil.)	NET INCOME ($ mil.)	NET PROFIT MARGIN	EMPLOYEES
12/06	471.4	15.4	3.3%	2,809
12/05	270.0	19.6	7.3%	1,659
12/04	251.2	23.1	9.2%	—
12/03	221.6	15.0	6.8%	—
12/02	194.1	2.8	1.4%	1,172
Annual Growth	24.8%	53.1%	—	24.4%

2006 Year-End Financials

Debt ratio: 31.6%	Dividends
Return on equity: 8.2%	Yield: —
Cash ($ mil.): 177.1	Payout: —
Current ratio: —	Market value ($ mil.): 471.8
Long-term debt ($ mil.): 69.5	R&D as % of sales: —
No. of shares (mil.): 12.0	Advertising as % of sales: —

Stock History
NYSE: SF

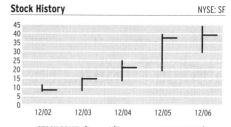

	STOCK PRICE ($) FY Close	P/E High/Low		PER SHARE ($) Earnings	Dividends	Book Value
12/06	39.23	40	27	1.11	—	18.32
12/05	37.59	25	12	1.56	—	15.07
12/04	20.95	13	7	1.88	—	13.27
12/03	14.63	11	6	1.37	—	14.16
12/02	8.35	43	31	0.25	0.02	11.52
Annual Growth	47.2%	—	—	45.2%	—	12.3%

Stratasys, Inc.

Stratasys doesn't make the LEGO pieces strewn across your kid's bedroom, but it does make rapid prototyping systems that designers and engineers — including the makers of LEGO toys — use to get products to market faster. The company's Insight software takes a conceptual model generated from a CAD workstation and creates a series of cross-sections to form a 3-D blueprint. Stratasys's fused deposition modeling (FDM) machines use the blueprint to create physical models by building up layers of wax and plastic polymers. Ford, Intel, NASA, and other customers use the company's products to build prototypes for cars, electronics, tools, and other products.

EXECUTIVES

Chairman, President, CEO, and Treasurer:
S. Scott Crump, age 53, $227,624 pay
COO and Secretary: Thomas W. (Tom) Stenoien, age 56, $202,837 pay
CFO: Robert F. Gallagher, age 51, $172,596 pay (partial-year salary)

VP and General Manager, Dimension:
Jonathan Lee (Jon) Cobb
VP FDM Sales, Marketing and Customer Service:
Woodrow J. (Woody) Frost
VP Operations: Kurt Hinrichsen
VP Process Improvement: Paul G. Grette
VP Research and Development: Paul Blake
Director, Human Resources: Cary Feik
Director, Investor Relations: Shane Glenn
Marketing Manager: Fred Fisher
Public Relations Manager: Joe Hiemenz
Auditors: Grant Thornton LLP

LOCATIONS

HQ: Stratasys, Inc.
　7665 Commerce Way, Eden Prairie, MN 55344
Phone: 952-937-3000　**Fax:** 952-937-0070
Web: www.stratasys.com

2006 Sales

	$ mil.	% of total
North America	64.7	62
Europe	21.5	21
Asia/Pacific	16.6	16
Other	1.0	1
Total	**103.8**	**100**

PRODUCTS/OPERATIONS

2006 Sales

	$ mil.	% of total
Products	83.4	80
Services	20.4	20
Total	**103.8**	**100**

Selected Products

Modeling equipment
　3-D printer (Dimension)
　Fused deposition modelers (FDM 3000, Quantum, and
　　Maxum)
　Prototyping system (Prodigy Plus)
　Prototyping system for durable materials (Titan)
Modeling materials
　Casting wax
　Elastomer materials
　Hard polymer materials
　Medical grade polymers
　Release materials
　Water-soluble materials
Software
　3-D printer model builder (AutoGen)
　Fused deposition pre-processing (Insight)

COMPETITORS

3D Systems	SOGECLAIR
Dassault	Solidscape
Delcam	Soligen 2006
EOS	Teijin
Mitsui	Vero International
Moldflow	Z Corp

HISTORICAL FINANCIALS

Company Type: Public

Income Statement　FYE: December 31

	REVENUE ($ mil.)	NET INCOME ($ mil.)	NET PROFIT MARGIN	EMPLOYEES
12/06	103.8	11.2	10.8%	360
12/05	82.8	10.6	12.8%	325
12/04	70.3	9.1	12.9%	—
12/03	50.9	6.2	12.2%	—
12/02	39.8	3.1	7.8%	196
Annual Growth	**27.1%**	**37.9%**	**—**	**16.4%**

2006 Year-End Financials

Debt ratio: —	Dividends
Return on equity: 12.2%	Yield: —
Cash ($ mil.): 36.7	Payout: —
Current ratio: 3.74	Market value ($ mil.): 159.3
Long-term debt ($ mil.): —	R&D as % of sales: —
No. of shares (mil.): 10.1	Advertising as % of sales: —

Stock History　NASDAQ (GS): SSYS

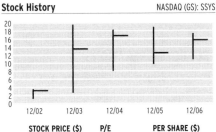

	STOCK PRICE ($) FY Close	P/E High/Low		PER SHARE ($) Earnings	Dividends	Book Value
12/06	15.70	32	20	0.54	—	9.64
12/05	12.51	38	20	0.50	—	7.02
12/04	16.78	43	19	0.43	—	8.13
12/03	13.52	61	9	0.32	—	7.20
12/02	3.18	18	7	0.19	—	6.14
Annual Growth	**49.1%**	**—**	**—**	**29.8%**	**—**	**11.9%**

Stratus Properties

Stratus Properties is on cloud nine over the prospect of real estate development in Austin, Texas. The company acquires, develops, manages, and sells commercial and residential real estate in Texas — primarily in the Austin area, where it has some 2,600 acres of developed and undeveloped land. The firm's most important developments include Austin's Barton Creek subdivision and portions of the metro area's Circle C Ranch. Stratus is developing two high-profile, mixed-use projects in Austin. The company also owns the land on which a 70-acre residential project in Plano (north of Dallas) is being developed, and owns a few scattered acres in San Antonio.

Stratus Properties is joining forces with Trammell Crow to develop an urban project called Crestview Station in Austin. The project, which is being built on the site of a former Huntsman facility, will include single- and multi-family homes, offices, and retail space.

The company is also spearheading Block 21, another mixed-use project in downtown Austin. Block 21 will include a new home for the *Austin City Limits* television program, as well as a W hotel (from Starwood Hotels & Resorts Worldwide), condominiums, a children's museum, restaurants, and retail spaces. Stratus has teamed with the Canyon-Johnson Urban Fund (a joint venture between basketball legend Earvin "Magic" Johnson and Canyon Capital Realty Advisors) for project funding.

Stratus Properties in 2006 sold 58 acres of its Lantana development in Austin to Advanced Micro Devices for that firm's new campus.

Stratus Properties' upscale developments have sometimes put the company at odds with Austin environmentalists over watershed protection and other issues, resulting in restrictions on some of its projects.

Stratus Properties in 2007 hired JPMorgan Chase & Co. to advise it on strategic alternatives, including a possible sale of the company. Later in the year, Stratus said it was taking itself off the market, but would continue to consider other methods of boosting shareholder value.

Real estate investor Carl Berg (also the CEO of Mission West Properties) owns nearly 20% of Stratus Properties.

EXECUTIVES

Chairman, President, and CEO:
　William H. (Beau) Armstrong III, age 43, $700,000 pay
SVP and CFO: John E. Baker, age 61, $425,000 pay
General Counsel and Secretary: Kenneth N. Jones, age 48
Engineering and Construction: Stephen A. Hay
Public Relations and Advertising: Belinda D. Wells
Auditors: PricewaterhouseCoopers LLP

LOCATIONS

HQ: Stratus Properties Inc.
　98 San Jacinto Blvd., Ste. 220, Austin, TX 78701
Phone: 512-478-5788　**Fax:** 512-482-0644
Web: www.stratusprop.com

PRODUCTS/OPERATIONS

2006 Sales

	$ mil.	% of total
Real estate		
Developed property sales	33.5	52
Undeveloped property sales	24.9	39
Rental income	3.8	6
Commissions, management fees & other	1.8	3
Total	**64.0**	**100**

COMPETITORS

A.G. Spanos
Choice Homes
Drees
Highland Homes
Meritage Homes
Morrison Homes
Pulte Homes
The Ryland Group
Standard Pacific
Trammell Crow Company

HISTORICAL FINANCIALS

Company Type: Public

Income Statement　FYE: December 31

	REVENUE ($ mil.)	NET INCOME ($ mil.)	NET PROFIT MARGIN	EMPLOYEES
12/06	64.0	40.3	63.0%	31
12/05	35.2	8.5	24.1%	27
12/04	20.9	0.7	3.3%	—
12/03	14.4	0.0	—	—
12/02	11.6	(0.5)	—	21
Annual Growth	**53.3%**	**—**	**—**	**10.2%**

2006 Year-End Financials

Debt ratio: 37.6%	Dividends
Return on equity: 35.3%	Yield: —
Cash ($ mil.): 5.7	Payout: —
Current ratio: 0.61	Market value ($ mil.): 241.0
Long-term debt ($ mil.): 50.4	R&D as % of sales: —
No. of shares (mil.): 7.5	Advertising as % of sales: —

Stock History

Stock History   NASDAQ (GM): STRS

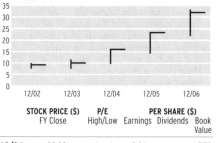

	STOCK PRICE ($) FY Close	P/E High/Low		PER SHARE ($) Earnings	Dividends	Book Value
12/06	32.00	6	4	5.26	—	17.79
12/05	23.33	21	13	1.11	—	13.05
12/04	16.03	178	110	0.09	—	12.21
12/03	10.05	—	—	—	—	12.17
12/02	9.20	39	31	0.25	—	12.17
Annual Growth	36.6%	—	—	114.2%	—	9.9%

Strayer Education

Students who wander from the traditional learning path can turn to Strayer Education. The company's Strayer University has nearly 50 campuses in 11 states in the eastern US and Washington, DC. Founded in 1892, the university serves more than 31,000 students, mostly working adults seeking associate's, bachelor's, and master's degrees in fields such as accounting, business administration, computer information systems, and computer networking. Strayer Education also offers Internet-based classes through its Strayer University Online, in which over 21,000 students are currently enrolled. Strayer Education is expanding, with eight new campuses planned for 2007.

Nearly half of the company is owned by a handful of investment firms, including Baron Capital Group (10%); AXA Financial and Morgan Stanley (8% each); Massachusetts Financial Services and Wasatch Advisors (more than 6% each); and Maverick Capital (nearly 6%). Strayer Education directors and executives as a group control more than 5% of the company.

EXECUTIVES

Chairman and CEO: Robert S. Silberman, age 49, $1,100,000 pay
President and COO: Karl McDonnell, age 40, $218,000 pay (partial-year salary)
SVP and CFO: Mark C. Brown, age 48, $401,000 pay
SVP Marketing and Administration: Lysa A. Hlavinka, age 39, $311,000 pay
SVP and General Counsel: Gregory Ferenbach, age 46, $256,000 pay
VP and CTO: Kevin P. O'Reagan, age 47, $294,000 pay
VP Operations, Strayer University: James F. McCoy, age 47
VP Corporate Communications: Sonya G. Udler, age 39
SVP Academic Administration, Strayer University: Randi S. Reich
Controller: Michael J. Fortunato, age 42
Auditors: PricewaterhouseCoopers LLP

LOCATIONS

HQ: Strayer Education, Inc.
1100 Wilson Blvd., Ste. 2500, Arlington, VA 22209
Phone: 703-247-2500   **Fax:** 703-527-0112
Web: www.strayereducation.com

Strayer Education has campuses in Alabama, Delaware, Florida, Georgia, Kentucky, Maryland, North Carolina, Pennsylvania, South Carolina, Tennessee, Virginia, and Washington, DC.

PRODUCTS/OPERATIONS

Selected Undergraduate Degree Programs

Associate in Arts Degrees
  Accounting
  Acquisition and Contract Management
  Business Administration
  Computer Information Systems
  Computer Networking
  Database Technology
  Economics
  General Studies
  Internetworking Technology
  Marketing
Bachelor of Business Administration Degree
Bachelor of Science Degrees
  Accounting
  Computer Information Systems
  Computer Networking
  Database Technology
  Economics
  International Business
  Internetworking Technology
Certificate Programs
  Accounting
  Business Administration
  Computer Information Systems
Diploma Programs
  Accounting
  Acquisition and Contract Management
  Computer Information Systems
  Internetworking Technology
  Network Security
  Web Development

Selected Graduate Degree Programs

Executive Graduate Certificate Programs
  Business Administration
  Computer Information Systems
  Professional Accounting
Master of Business Administration Degree
Master of Education Degree
Master of Health Services Administration Degree
Master of Public Administration Degree
Master of Science Degree
  Communications Technology
  Information Systems
  Management Information Systems
  Professional Accounting

COMPETITORS

Apollo Group	DeVry
Career Education	Education Management
Corinthian Colleges	ITT Educational

HISTORICAL FINANCIALS

Company Type: Public

Income Statement

	REVENUE ($ mil.)	NET INCOME ($ mil.)	NET PROFIT MARGIN	EMPLOYEES	FYE: December 31
12/06	263.6	52.3	19.8%	2,177	
12/05	220.5	48.1	21.8%	2,096	
12/04	183.2	41.2	22.5%	—	
12/03	147.0	33.7	22.9%	—	
12/02	116.7	25.8	22.1%	1,269	
Annual Growth	22.6%	19.3%	—	14.4%	

2006 Year-End Financials

Debt ratio: —
Return on equity: 32.3%
Cash ($ mil.): 128.4
Current ratio: 2.33
Long-term debt ($ mil.): —
No. of shares (mil.): 14.3
Dividends
  Yield: 1.0%
  Payout: 29.4%
Market value ($ mil.): 1,515.8
R&D as % of sales: —
Advertising as % of sales: —

Stock History   NASDAQ (GS): STRA

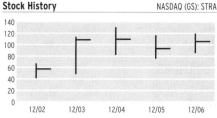

	STOCK PRICE ($) FY Close	P/E High/Low		PER SHARE ($) Earnings	Dividends	Book Value
12/06	106.05	33	24	3.61	1.06	12.00
12/05	93.70	36	24	3.26	0.63	10.62
12/04	109.79	47	30	2.74	0.41	10.15
12/03	108.83	50	22	2.27	0.26	3.08
12/02	57.50	37	24	1.78	0.26	0.60
Annual Growth	16.5%	—	—	19.3%	42.1%	111.6%

Sucampo Pharmaceuticals

Sucampo Pharmaceuticals works to alleviate some of life's more uncomfortable — and lesser uttered — conditions. Sucampo works with a group of compounds derived from functional fatty acids, called prostones; it uses prostones in the development of therapies for the treatment of age-related gastrointestinal, vascular, and central nervous system diseases and disorders. Its lead product AMITIZA (lubiprostone) received FDA approval in 2006 for the treatment of chronic idiopathic constipation. Other applications for AMITIZA, including treatment of irritable bowel syndrome, are in the works. The company's two founders, wife and husband Sachiko Kuno and Ryuji Ueno, own more than 70% of the company.

AMITIZA works by increasing fluid secretion into the intestines by activating specific chloride channels in cells lining the small intestine. The increased fluid level softens the stool, which causes bowel movements. AMITIZA is also in clinical trials to measure its effectiveness in alleviating opioid-induced bowel dysfunction, a common post-surgical complication. Sucampo collaborated with Takeda Pharmaceutical Company to develop and commercialize AMITIZA. Sucampo's sister company R-Tech holds the manufacturing rights to AMITIZA, and Takeda will market the product in the US.

A second product, SPI-8811, is under development for the treatment of cystic fibrosis, fatty liver disease, NSAID-induced ulcers, and chronic obstructive pulmonary disease. The company is also developing a treatment, SPI-017, for peripheral arterial and vascular disease, strokes, and nervous system disorders, including Alzheimer's.

Proceeds from Sucampo's initial public offering will be used to further develop its AMITIZA, SPI-8811, and SPI-017, including additional clinical trials and sales and marketing efforts in Europe and Asia. Following the IPO, Kuno and Ueno will control 95% of the company's voting power.

EXECUTIVES

Chairman, CEO, and Chief Scientific Officer: Ryuji Ueno, age 54
CFO: Mariam E. Morris, age 40, $156,512 pay
EVP Commercial Operations: Brad E. Fackler, age 54, $107,500 pay
SVP Research and Development: Gayle Robert Dolecek, age 65
VP Business Development and Company Operations and Secretary: Kei S. Tolliver, age 34, $123,945 pay
VP Marketing: Charles S. Hrushka, age 56
Auditors: PricewaterhouseCoopers LLP

LOCATIONS

HQ: Sucampo Pharmaceuticals, Inc.
4520 East-West Hwy, Ste. 300, Bethesda, MD 20814
Phone: 301-961-3400   **Fax:** 301-961-3440
Web: www.sucampo.com

COMPETITORS

Alizyme
Microbia
Novartis Corporation
Progenics Pharmaceuticals
Solvay Pharmaceuticals
Theravance

HISTORICAL FINANCIALS

Company Type: Public

Income Statement				FYE: December 31
	REVENUE ($ mil.)	NET INCOME ($ mil.)	NET PROFIT MARGIN	EMPLOYEES
12/06	59.3	21.8	36.8%	37
12/05	40.2	(0.3)	—	—
12/04	2.7	(19.7)	—	—
12/03	4.1	(22.0)	—	—
Annual Growth	143.6%	—	—	—

2006 Year-End Financials

Debt ratio: —   Current ratio: 3.10
Return on equity: —   Long-term debt ($ mil.): —
Cash ($ mil.): 51.9

Net Income History   NASDAQ (GM): SCMP

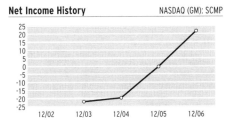

Sun American Bancorp

Here comes the Sun. Known as PanAmerican Bancorp until it changed its name in early 2006, Sun American Bancorp is the holding company for Sun American Bank (formerly PanAmerican Bank). The institution offers checking accounts, savings and money market accounts, and CDs, as well as individual retirement accounts. Concentrated in South Florida, the bank has more than a dozen offices in and around Miami. The bank concentrates on lending to area small and mid-sized businesses (commercial mortgages make up the bulk of its loan portfolio), but also writes residential real estate, home equity, and other consumer loans. Sun American acquired Tequesta, Florida-based Independent Community Bank in 2007.

Increasing its presence in Miami-Dade County, the company bought the assets and branches of Beach Bank in 2006.

Puerto Rico-based First BanCorp owns about 10% of Sun American Bancorp.

EXECUTIVES

Chairman: James F. Partridge, age 78
Vice Chairman: Nelson Famadas, age 58
President, CEO, and Director; Chairman, CEO, and President, Sun American Bank: Michael E. Golden, age 63, $337,500 pay (prior to title change)
COO; EVP and COO, Sun American Bank: Alfredo Barreiro, age 40, $110,000 pay (prior to title change)
CFO, Sun American Bancorp and Sun American Bank: Robert L. Nichols, age 48, $183,958 pay
EVP and Chief Lending Officer, Sun American Bank: Robert K. Garrett, age 45, $113,750 pay
EVP Sales and Service, Sun American Bank: William T. Ross, age 58
SVP Finance, Sun American Bank: Will Bermudez
SVP and Chief Compliance Officer, Sun American Bank: Eduardo Granda
SVP Wealth Management, Sun American Bank: David W. House

LOCATIONS

HQ: Sun American Bancorp
9293 Glades Rd., Boca Raton, FL 33434
Phone: 561-544-1960   **Fax:** 561-487-1632
Web: www.panamericanbank.com

PRODUCTS/OPERATIONS

2006 Sales

	$ mil.	% of total
Interest		
Loans, including fees	22.8	88
Other	2.3	9
Noninterest		
Service charges on deposit accounts & sale of securities	0.9	3
Total	**26.0**	**100**

COMPETITORS

AmTrust Bank
Bank of America
BankUnited
Citibank
EuroBancshares
Ocean Bankshares
Regions Financial

HISTORICAL FINANCIALS

Company Type: Public

Income Statement				FYE: December 31
	ASSETS ($ mil.)	NET INCOME ($ mil.)	INCOME AS % OF ASSETS	EMPLOYEES
12/06	503.9	3.2	0.6%	122
12/05	277.1	2.9	1.0%	74
12/04	191.5	(0.2)	—	—
12/03	94.1	(0.4)	—	—
12/02	90.2	(0.5)	—	—
Annual Growth	53.7%	—	—	64.9%

2006 Year-End Financials

Equity as % of assets: 16.8%   Dividends
Return on assets: 0.8%   Yield: —
Return on equity: 4.4%   Payout: —
Long-term debt ($ mil.): —   Sales ($ mil.): 26.0
No. of shares (mil.): 23.2   R&D as % of sales: —
Market value ($ mil.): 302.5   Advertising as % of sales: —

Stock History   AMEX: SBK

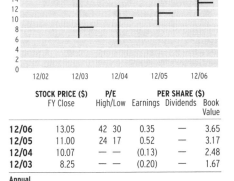

	STOCK PRICE ($)	P/E		PER SHARE ($)		
	FY Close	High/Low	Earnings	Dividends	Book Value
12/06	13.05	42 30	0.35	—	3.65
12/05	11.00	24 17	0.52	—	3.17
12/04	10.07	— —	(0.13)	—	2.48
12/03	8.25	— —	(0.20)	—	1.67
Annual Growth	16.5%	— —	—	—	85.0%

SunPower Corporation

As the name suggests, SunPower makes solar cells and panels, used to generate electrical power from that giant star the Earth revolves around. The company also sells imaging and infrared detector products that SunPower makes using its thin-wafer manufacturing process for solar cells. Conergy is a leading customer (about 25% of sales), along with Solon AG (25%), GE/Plexus, and Integration Associates. Cypress Semiconductor owns more than half of SunPower; the parent company retains control over SunPower by holding all of the Class B common shares in SunPower, giving Cypress voting rights of around 91%.

In early 2007 SunPower acquired PowerLight, a large customer (16% of 2006 sales), for up to $333 million in cash and stock. SunPower pursued the PowerLight acquisition in the expectation that it would also bring SunPower closer to end-users of its solar cells and panels and help drive down the cost of solar power, making it more competitive with electrical power from other sources, without government tax incentives or subsidies. PowerLight has specialized in installing large-scale solar power systems in California, Hawaii, Nevada, and New Jersey, and overseas in Germany, Italy, Portugal, South

Korea, and Spain. PowerLight also provides residential solar power systems to more than a dozen home builders in California.

SunPower is securing a source of polysilicon, the raw material used in making silicon-based solar cells, through a four-year supply agreement with DC Chemical. Beginning in 2008, SunPower will pay approximately $250 million over four years to purchase polysilicon from the Korean company, which is putting a new plant into service that can produce 3,000 metric tons of polysilicon a year. A worldwide polysilicon shortage is holding back some manufacturers of silicon-based solar cells, causing them to line up vendors with long-term supply agreements.

Cypress Semi became SunPower's majority shareholder in 2002 through an investment of nearly $9 million. In 2005 Cypress spent around $94 million to acquire the rest of SunPower. SunPower used Cypress Semi's investments to first set up a fabrication line in Round Rock, Texas, where Cypress makes some of its semiconductor products, and then to develop a new wafer fabrication facility in the Philippines, which began producing solar cells in late 2004.

SunPower claims that its method of manufacturing solar cells is more efficient than the fabrication technology of other solar cell suppliers, allowing its solar panels (assembled in China by contractors) to generate greater amounts of electricity, producing up to 50% more power per square foot than competing products.

SunPower's technology was originally developed at Stanford University by Richard Swanson (president/CTO) and his students, with funding from the Electric Power Research Institute (EPRI) and the US Department of Energy. SunPower was established in 1985 to commercialize the advanced solar cell technology.

Affiliates of Janus Capital Group own nearly 11% of SunPower's Class A common shares. Baron Capital Group and affiliates hold almost 10% of those shares. Affiliates of BlackRock have an equity stake of about 9%, as does investor Thomas L. Dinwoodie. FMR (Fidelity Investments) owns 6%.

EXECUTIVES

Chairman: T. J. Rodgers, age 59
CEO and Director: Thomas H. (Tom) Werner, age 46, $321,642 pay
President and CTO: Richard (Dick) Swanson, age 61, $204,231 pay
CFO: Emmanuel T. (Manny) Hernandez, age 52, $308,095 pay
VP, Public Policy and Corporate Communications: Julie Blunden
VP, Corporate Strategy: Peter C. Aschenbrenner, age 51, $211,869 pay
VP, Strategic Supply: Jon Whiteman
VP, Technology and Development: William P. Mulligan
VP, Global Business Units: Howard J. Wenger, age 47
VP, Global Quality and Customer Satisfaction: Surinder Bedi
VP, Human Resources: Douglas J. Richards
Chief Marketing Officer: J. Bradley (Brad) Davis
General Counsel: Bruce R. Ledesma, age 39
Chairman, CEO, and CTO, PowerLight: Thomas (Tom) Dinwoodie, age 52
Auditors: PricewaterhouseCoopers LLP

LOCATIONS

HQ: SunPower Corporation
3939 N. 1st Street, San Jose, CA 95134
Phone: 408-240-5500   **Fax:** 408-240-5400
Web: www.sunpowercorp.com

SunPower has facilities in Germany, the Philippines, South Korea, Switzerland, and the US.

2006 Sales

	% of total
Germany	49
US	32
Asia	7
Other regions	12
Total	**100**

PRODUCTS/OPERATIONS

2006 Sales

	% of total
Solar electric power products	94
Imaging & infrared detectors	6
Total	**100**

COMPETITORS

Avago Technologies
BP Solar
DayStar Technologies
Evergreen Solar
First Solar
GE Energy
Hamamatsu Photonics
Kyocera Solar
Mitsubishi Power Systems
Q-Cells
ROHM
SANYO
SCHOTT Solar
Sharp Corporation
Solarfun
Suntech Power
Vishay Intertechnology

HISTORICAL FINANCIALS

Company Type: Public

Income Statement

FYE: December 31

	REVENUE ($ mil.)	NET INCOME ($ mil.)	NET PROFIT MARGIN	EMPLOYEES
12/06	236.5	26.5	11.2%	1,572
12/05	78.7	(15.8)	—	788
12/04	10.9	(28.9)	—	416
12/03	5.0	(14.5)	—	—
12/02	4.1	(3.5)	—	—
Annual Growth	**175.6%**	**—**	**—**	**94.4%**

2006 Year-End Financials

Debt ratio: —
Return on equity: 7.1%
Cash ($ mil.): 182.1
Current ratio: 4.78
Long-term debt ($ mil.): —
No. of shares (mil.): 69.8
Dividends
  Yield: —
  Payout: —
Market value ($ mil.): 2,596.3
R&D as % of sales: —
Advertising as % of sales: —

Stock History

NASDAQ (GM): SPWR

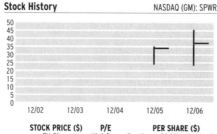

	STOCK PRICE ($) FY Close	P/E High/Low	PER SHARE ($) Earnings	Dividends	Book Value
12/06	37.17	122 64	0.37	—	7.00
12/05	33.99	— —	(0.68)	—	4.23
Annual Growth	**9.4%**	**— —**	**—**	**—**	**65.3%**

Super Micro Computer

Super Micro Computer strives for super macro computer sales. The company manufactures motherboards based on Intel's x86 architecture, plus complete server systems utilizing Intel's Itanium, Pentium, and Xeon microprocessors, as well as AMD's Opteron processors. Other products include chassis enclosures for rack-mounted servers and power supplies that feature redundant cooling systems. Super Micro also resells third-party cables, cooling fans, RAID (redundant array of independent disks) port cards, and other computer accessories. President and CEO Charles Liang and his wife own about a third of the company.

The company sells primarily through distributors and resellers (roughly 70% sales), but it also markets to manufacturers and directly to end users. About 40% of Super Micro's sales are to customers outside the US.

Super Micro Computer's SuperServers line is dominated by Intel microprocessors, but the company added AMD's Opteron MPU (a rival to Intel's Xeon processor) to its product line in 2005.

EXECUTIVES

Chairman, President, and CEO: Charles Liang, age 49, $285,457 pay
CFO: Howard Hideshima, age 47, $36,808 pay (partial-year salary)
VP Operations, Treasurer, and Director: Chiu-Chu Liu (Sara) Liang, age 45, $135,639 pay
VP International Sales, Corporate Secretary, and Director: Yih-Shyan (Wally) Liaw, age 52, $152,038 pay
Chief Sales and Marketing Officer: Alex Hsu, age 58
Corporate Marketing Program Manager: Angela Rosario
Auditors: Deloitte & Touche LLP

LOCATIONS

HQ: Super Micro Computer, Inc.
980 Rock Ave., San Jose, CA 95131
Phone: 408-503-8000   **Fax:** 408-503-8008
Web: www.supermicro.com

2007 Sales

	$ mil.	% of total
US	248.9	59
Europe		
Germany	28.8	7
UK	20.1	5
Other countries	48.6	12
Asia	64.9	15
Other regions	9.1	2
Total	**420.4**	**100**

PRODUCTS/OPERATIONS

2007 Sales

	$ mil.	% of total
Serverboards & other components	267.9	64
Server systems	152.5	36
Total	**420.4**	**100**

Selected Products

Chassis enclosures (pedestal, rack-mount, tower)
Motherboards (desktop, server, workstation)
Power supplies
Servers (rack-mount, tower)

COMPETITORS

Celestica
Dell
Egenera
Flextronics
Hewlett-Packard
Hon Hai

IBM
Intel Corporation
Quanta Computer
Rackable Systems
Sun Microsystems
Wistron

HISTORICAL FINANCIALS

Company Type: Public

Income Statement

FYE: June 30

	REVENUE ($ mil.)	NET INCOME ($ mil.)	NET PROFIT MARGIN	EMPLOYEES
6/07	420.4	19.3	4.6%	624
6/06	302.5	17.0	5.6%	—
6/05	211.8	7.1	3.4%	—
6/04	167.1	4.9	2.9%	—
6/03	137.2	5.7	4.2%	—
Annual Growth	32.3%	35.7%	—	—

2007 Year-End Financials

Debt ratio: 9.7%
Return on equity: 23.6%
Cash ($ mil.): 65.9
Current ratio: 2.21
Long-term debt ($ mil.): 11.3
No. of shares (mil.): 31.2

Dividends
  Yield: —
  Payout: —
Market value ($ mil.): 312.0
R&D as % of sales: —
Advertising as % of sales: —

Stock History

NASDAQ (GM): SMCI

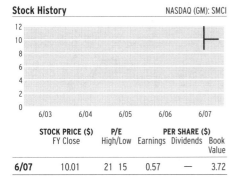

	STOCK PRICE ($) FY Close	P/E High/Low		PER SHARE ($) Earnings	Dividends	Book Value
6/07	10.01	21	15	0.57	—	3.72

Superior Well Services

It is superior well services, not a superior attitude, that lets Superior Well Services live up to its name. The oil service company provides technical pumping services (stimulation, nitrogen, and cementing) and down-hole surveying services (logging and perforating) that smaller rivals do not provide, and at competitive prices to those offered by the big oilfield services companies such as BJ Services and Schlumberger. The bulk of Superior Well Services' customers are regional independent oil and gas companies. The technical pumping services unit owns a fleet of 558 commercial vehicles. The down-hole surveying services unit owns a fleet of 81 trucks and cranes. Directors and executives own 33% of the company.

Superior Well Services was founded in 1997 by three former employees of Halliburton Energy

Services: David Wallace, Jacob Linaberger, and Rhys Reese.

The company has expanded from two service centers in the Appalachian region to 19 centers serving customers in 38 states. Its customer base has grown from 89 in 1999 to more than 1,200 in 2007.

EXECUTIVES

Chairman and CEO: David E. Wallace, age 53, $309,500 pay
President: Jacob B. Linaberger, age 59, $304,500 pay
EVP, COO, and Secretary: Rhys R. Reese, age 48, $304,500 pay
VP, CFO, and Principal Accounting Officer: Thomas W. Stoelk, age 52
VP: Fred E. Kistner, age 66
VP Sales and Marketing: Daniel (Dan) Arnold, age 48
Controller: Scott E. Whetsell
Auditors: Schneider Downs & Co., Inc.

LOCATIONS

HQ: Superior Well Services, Inc.
  1380 East, Ste. 121, Indiana, PA 15701
Phone: 724-465-8904   **Fax:** 724-465-8907
Web: www.superiorwells.com

Superior Well Services serves customers in several US oil and natural gas producing regions.

2006 Sales

	$ mil.	% of total
Appalachia	118.9	48
Southeast	58.5	24
Mid-Continent	43.6	18
Rocky Mountains	16.8	7
Southwest	6.8	3
Total	**244.6**	**100**

PRODUCTS/OPERATIONS

2006 Sales

	% of total
Technical pumping services	
Stimulation	59
Cementing	21
Nitrogen	10
Down-hole surveying services	10
Total	**100**

2006 Sales

	$ mil.	% of total
Technical pumping services	219.6	90
Down-hole surveying services	25.0	10
Total	**244.6**	**100**

COMPETITORS

Baker Hughes
BJ Services
Halliburton
Schlumberger
Smith International
Weatherford International

HISTORICAL FINANCIALS

Company Type: Public

Income Statement

FYE: December 31

	REVENUE ($ mil.)	NET INCOME ($ mil.)	NET PROFIT MARGIN	EMPLOYEES
12/06	244.6	31.9	13.0%	1,068
12/05	131.7	9.5	7.2%	646
12/04	76.0	9.8	12.9%	—
12/03	51.5	8.2	15.9%	—
12/02	34.2	5.3	15.5%	—
Annual Growth	63.5%	56.6%	—	65.3%

2006 Year-End Financials

Debt ratio: 0.7%
Return on equity: 20.9%
Cash ($ mil.): 56.8
Current ratio: 3.96
Long-term debt ($ mil.): 1.6
No. of shares (mil.): 23.4

Dividends
  Yield: —
  Payout: —
Market value ($ mil.): 596.9
R&D as % of sales: —
Advertising as % of sales: —

Stock History

NASDAQ (GS): SWSI

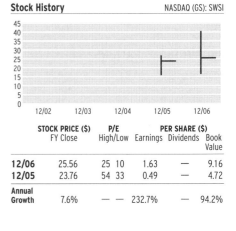

	STOCK PRICE ($) FY Close	P/E High/Low		PER SHARE ($) Earnings	Dividends	Book Value
12/06	25.56	25	10	1.63	—	9.16
12/05	23.76	54	33	0.49	—	4.72
Annual Growth	7.6%	—	—	232.7%	—	94.2%

Supertex, Inc.

Look! There in that electronic device! It's a chip from . . . Supertex! Supertex designs and manufactures high-voltage analog and mixed-signal integrated circuits (ICs) and transistors. Its ICs are used in a variety of applications, including flat-panel displays, printers, medical ultrasound imaging equipment, automatic test equipment, and telecommunications gear. Supertex touts its proprietary technologies as enabling it to combine low power consumption with high-voltage output on a single chip. Motorola accounts for approximately 24% of sales. Supertex gets 70% of its sales outside the US.

CEO Henry Pao and members of his family own nearly 13% of Supertex. FMR Corp. and Columbia Wanger Asset Management own about 15% and 11%, respectively.

EXECUTIVES

President, CEO, and Director: Henry C. Pao, age 69
SVP Technology Development, Secretary, and Director: Benedict C. K. Choy, age 61, $283,153 pay
VP Finance and CFO: Phillip A. Kagel, age 57
VP I.C. Design: Michael Lee, age 52, $246,228 pay
VP Process Technology: Franklin Gonzalez, age 57, $192,307 pay
VP Standard Products: Dilip Kapur, age 58, $214,867 pay
VP Wafer Fab Operations: William P. Ingram, age 60
VP Worldwide Sales: William (Pete) Petersen, age 54
VP Marketing: Ahmed Masood, age 46
VP Standard Products: Michael Tsang, age 48
Human Resources Manager: Carol Klemstein
Marketing Communications Manager: Ken Vickers
Auditors: PricewaterhouseCoopers LLP

LOCATIONS

HQ: Supertex, Inc.
  1235 Bordeaux Dr., Sunnyvale, CA 94089
Phone: 408-222-8888   **Fax:** 408-222-4800
Web: www.supertex.com

Supertex has operations in China, Hong Kong, Japan, South Korea, Taiwan, the UK, and the US.

2007 Sales

	$ mil.	% of total
Asia/Pacific		
China	32.4	33
Japan	6.9	7
Other countries	16.2	17
US	29.3	30
Europe	11.8	12
Other regions	1.4	1
Total	**98.0**	**100**

PRODUCTS/OPERATIONS

2007 Sales

	$ mil.	% of total
Imaging	41.1	42
Medical electronics	35.6	36
Telecommunications	14.9	15
Other	6.4	7
Total	**98.0**	**100**

Operations and Applications

Medical Electronics Group (ultrasound diagnostic imaging equipment circuits)

Telecommunications/Broadband Group (telephone interface equipment and military device circuits)

Imaging Group (flat-panel displays and nonimpact printers and plotters)

COMPETITORS

Analog Devices	National Semiconductor
Exar	ON Semiconductor
Hitachi	Pericom Semiconductor
International Rectifier	Rogers Corporation
Linear Technology	Siliconix
Maxim Integrated Products	Sipex
Microsemi	Texas Instruments

HISTORICAL FINANCIALS

Company Type: Public

Income Statement				FYE: Saturday nearest March 31
	REVENUE ($ mil.)	NET INCOME ($ mil.)	NET PROFIT MARGIN	EMPLOYEES
3/07	98.0	21.4	21.8%	401
3/06	80.1	15.9	19.9%	373
3/05	56.6	6.5	11.5%	349
3/04	51.4	2.2	4.3%	—
3/03	54.9	2.9	5.3%	—
Annual Growth	**15.6%**	**64.8%**	**—**	**7.2%**

2007 Year-End Financials

Debt ratio: —
Return on equity: 14.5%
Cash ($ mil.): 138.9
Current ratio: 7.14
Long-term debt ($ mil.): —
No. of shares (mil.): 13.8

Dividends
  Yield: —
  Payout: —
Market value ($ mil.): 458.1
R&D as % of sales: —
Advertising as % of sales: —

Stock History

NASDAQ (GS): SUPX

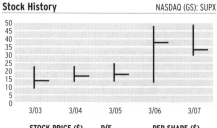

	STOCK PRICE ($) FY Close	P/E High/Low		PER SHARE ($) Earnings	Dividends	Book Value
3/07	33.21	32	20	1.53	—	11.69
3/06	37.62	41	11	1.15	—	9.80
3/05	17.76	50	28	0.49	—	8.18
3/04	16.68	133	79	0.17	—	7.59
3/03	13.75	102	42	0.22	—	7.31
Annual Growth	**24.7%**	**—**	**—**	**62.4%**	**—**	**12.5%**

Swift Energy

No laggard, oil and gas exploration and production company Swift Energy has interests in almost 1,100 producing wells, primarily in Louisiana and Texas. It also has two major exploration regions in New Zealand (but has announced plans to sell these). The company's core US production areas are the Lake Washington Field in Louisiana, and the AWP Olmos Field in Texas. Swift Energy aims to increase reserves and production by adjusting the balance between drilling and acquisition activities in response to market conditions. The company's proved reserves consist of 816.8 billion cu. ft. of natural gas equivalent. Swift Energy Company was founded in 1979.

At the end of 2005 Swift Energy restructured as a holding company. The change separates Swift Energy's US and international operations and provides greater administrative and organizational flexibility.

In 2006 the company began to explore several sites in the Cook Basin Inlet of Alaska through a participation agreement with Aurora Gas LLC.

That year it acquired stakes in five onshore South Louisiana properties from BP America Production Co. for $167.9 million.

In 2007 the company began selling its assets in New Zealand, and announced plans to sell all its New Zealand properties in 2008.

EXECUTIVES

Chairman and CEO; Chairman, Swift Energy International: Terry E. Swift, age 51
Vice Chairman: Raymond E. (Ray) Galvin, age 75
President and Director: Bruce H. Vincent, age 60
EVP and COO: Joseph A. (Joe) D'Amico, age 59
EVP and CFO: Alton D. Heckaman Jr., age 50
SVP Operations: James M. Kitterman, age 63
SVP Commercial Transactions and Land:
  James P. Mitchell, age 53
SVP and Chief Compliance Officer: Victor R. Moran, age 52
VP Exploration and Development:
  Edward A. (Ed) Duncan
Chief General Counsel: Laurent A. (Larry) Baillargeon
Director Corporate Development and Investor Relations: Scott Espenshade
President and COO, Swift Energy New Zealand:
  R. Alan Cunningham
President, Swift Energy International; Chairman, Swift Energy New Zealand: Donald L. Morgan
Auditors: Ernst & Young LLP

LOCATIONS

HQ: Swift Energy Company
  16825 Northchase Dr., Ste. 400, Houston, TX 77060
Phone: 281-874-2700　　**Fax:** 281-874-2726
Web: www.swiftenergy.com

2006 Sales

	$ mil.	% of total
US	537.5	89
New Zealand	64.0	11
Adjustments	13.9	—
Total	**615.4**	**100**

PRODUCTS/OPERATIONS

2006 Proved Reserves

	% of total
Crude oil	50
Natural gas	40
Natural gas liquids (NGLs)	10
Total	**100**

COMPETITORS

Adams Resources	Exxon Mobil
Apache	Forest Oil
BP	Frontier Oil
Chesapeake Energy	XTO Energy
Devon Energy	

HISTORICAL FINANCIALS

Company Type: Public

Income Statement				FYE: December 31
	REVENUE ($ mil.)	NET INCOME ($ mil.)	NET PROFIT MARGIN	EMPLOYEES
12/06	615.4	161.6	26.3%	345
12/05	423.2	115.8	27.4%	311
12/04	310.3	68.4	22.0%	—
12/03	208.9	29.9	14.3%	—
12/02	150.0	11.9	7.9%	234
Annual Growth	**42.3%**	**92.0%**	**—**	**10.2%**

2006 Year-End Financials

Debt ratio: 47.8%
Return on equity: 23.0%
Cash ($ mil.): 1.1
Current ratio: 0.63
Long-term debt ($ mil.): 381.4
No. of shares (mil.): 29.7

Dividends
  Yield: —
  Payout: —
Market value ($ mil.): 1,332.8
R&D as % of sales: —
Advertising as % of sales: —

Stock History

NYSE: SFY

	STOCK PRICE ($) FY Close	P/E High/Low		PER SHARE ($) Earnings	Dividends	Book Value
12/06	44.81	10	6	5.38	—	26.83
12/05	45.07	13	6	3.95	—	20.94
12/04	28.94	13	7	2.41	—	16.88
12/03	16.85	17	7	1.08	—	14.46
12/02	9.67	47	15	0.45	—	13.42
Annual Growth	**46.7%**	**—**	**—**	**85.9%**	**—**	**18.9%**

Sycamore Networks

The routes of Sycamore Networks flourish in light soil. The company makes optical switches used by communications service providers to build fiber-optic networks. Sycamore's switches and network management software enable phone service carriers to provide voice and high-speed data services. The company also serves ISPs and cable companies. It sells directly and through resellers and distributors. Major customers include Sprint Nextel (53% of sales in fiscal 2007) and Vodafone Group (16%). Chairman Gururaj Deshpande and CEO Daniel Smith each own about 16% of the company.

Sycamore acquired Allen Organ's Eastern Research subsidiary in 2006. Eastern Research developed access systems for fixed line and mobile network operators. In addition to expanding its product portfolio and customer base, the purchase contributed to Sycamore's efforts to expand its sales channels, particularly with resellers.

EXECUTIVES

Chairman: Gururaj (Desh) Deshpande, age 56
President, CEO, and Director:
 Daniel E. (Dan) Smith Jr., age 59
CFO, VP Finance and Administration, and Treasurer:
 Paul F. Brauneis, age 59
VP Operations: John E. Dowling, age 53
VP Systems and Technology: Kevin J. Oye, age 47
VP Worldwide Sales and Support: John B. Scully
Public Relations: Scott Larson
General Counsel and Secretary: Alan R. Cormier, age 49
Auditors: PricewaterhouseCoopers LLP

LOCATIONS

HQ: Sycamore Networks, Inc.
 220 Mill Rd., Chelmsford, MA 01824
Phone: 978-250-2900   **Fax:** 978-256-3434
Web: www.sycamorenet.com

2007 Sales

	% of total
US	73
The Netherlands	16
Other countries	11
Total	**100**

PRODUCTS/OPERATIONS

2007 Sales

	% of total
Products	85
Services	15
Total	**100**

Selected Products

Network access
 Access gateways
 Multiservices access and cross-connect
 Network management (ENvision)

Optical switching
 Network management software (SILVX)
 Switches

COMPETITORS

Alcatel-Lucent
Ciena
Cisco Systems
Ericsson
Huawei Technologies
Juniper Networks
Nortel Networks
Siemens AG
Tellabs
ZTE

HISTORICAL FINANCIALS

Company Type: Public

Income Statement

	REVENUE ($ mil.)	NET INCOME ($ mil.)	NET PROFIT MARGIN	EMPLOYEES
7/07	156.1	(13.2)	—	426
7/06	87.4	19.4	22.2%	246
7/05	65.4	(23.8)	—	276
7/04	44.5	(44.8)	—	—
7/03	38.3	(55.1)	—	—
Annual Growth	**42.1%**	**—**	**—**	**24.2%**

2007 Year-End Financials

Debt ratio: —	Dividends
Return on equity: —	Yield: —
Cash ($ mil.): 907.6	Payout: —
Current ratio: 17.95	Market value ($ mil.): 1,165.0
Long-term debt ($ mil.): —	R&D as % of sales: —
No. of shares (mil.): 280.0	Advertising as % of sales: —

Stock History

NASDAQ (GM): SCMR

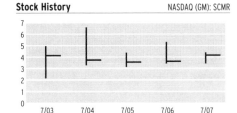

	STOCK PRICE ($) FY Close	P/E High/Low	PER SHARE ($) Earnings	Dividends	Book Value
7/07	4.16	— —	(0.05)	—	3.47
7/06	3.63	75 50	0.07	—	3.50
7/05	3.56	— —	(0.09)	—	3.40
7/04	3.74	— —	(0.17)	—	3.49
7/03	4.13	— —	(0.21)	—	3.65
Annual Growth	**0.2%**	**— —**	**—**	**—**	**(1.3%)**

Synchronoss Technologies

Synchronoss Technologies hopes to help you synch up a variety of customer service efforts. The company provides software and services that communications service providers use to manage tasks such as service activation and customer transactions including additions, subtractions, and changes to service plans. Synchronoss' customers include AT&T Mobility (formerly Cingular), Vonage, Cablevision, and Time Warner Cable. The company is targeting service providers in markets including wireless and wireline communications, as well as Voice over Internet Protocol (VoIP).

Primarily dependent on revenue from North America, Synchronoss has begun looking abroad for new opportunities, particularly in Europe, Asia/Pacific, and Latin America.

Director James McCormick controls a 20% stake in the company, while chairman, president, and CEO Stephen Waldis holds a 10% stake; other significant stakeholders include ABS Ventures (16%), Rosewood Capital (11%), and Vertek Corporation (8%).

Synchronoss was spun off from Vertek in 2000. AT&T Mobility is responsible for about 65% of Synchronoss' sales; Vonage accounts for about 10%.

EXECUTIVES

Chairman, President, and CEO: Stephen G. Waldis, age 39, $411,996 pay
COO: Robert (Bob) Garcia, age 39, $252,499 pay
CFO and Treasurer: Lawrence R. Irving, age 51, $255,000 pay
EVP Business Development and Marketing:
 Joy A. Nemitz
EVP Operations: Peter Halis, age 44, $431,709 pay
EVP Sales: Christopher (Chris) Putnam, age 39, $175,000 pay
VP and CTO: David E. Berry, age 40, $427,783 pay
VP, General Counsel, and Secretary: Ronald J. Prague, age 44
President, International Operations: Sean Parkinson
Chief Marketing Officer: Omar Téllez, age 39, $260,000 pay
CIO: S. Andrew Cox, age 42
Investor Relations: Tim Dolan
Media Relations: Stacie Hiras
Auditors: Ernst & Young LLP

LOCATIONS

HQ: Synchronoss Technologies, Inc.
 750 Rte. 202 South, Ste. 600,
 Bridgewater, NJ 08807
Phone: 908-547-1250   **Fax:** 908-547-1285
Web: www.synchronoss.com

COMPETITORS

Accenture
Motive, Inc.
NeuStar
VeriSign

HISTORICAL FINANCIALS

Company Type: Public

Income Statement

FYE: December 31

	REVENUE ($ mil.)	NET INCOME ($ mil.)	NET PROFIT MARGIN	EMPLOYEES
12/06	72.4	10.1	14.0%	170
12/05	54.2	12.4	22.9%	117
12/04	27.2	0.0	—	—
12/03	16.5	(1.0)	—	—
Annual Growth	**63.7%**	**—**	**—**	**45.3%**

2006 Year-End Financials

Debt ratio: —	Dividends
Return on equity: 22.3%	Yield: —
Cash ($ mil.): 77.7	Payout: —
Current ratio: 10.01	Market value ($ mil.): 441.2
Long-term debt ($ mil.): —	R&D as % of sales: —
No. of shares (mil.): 32.2	Advertising as % of sales: —

Stock History

NASDAQ (GM): SNCR

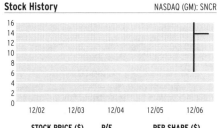

	STOCK PRICE ($) FY Close	P/E High/Low	PER SHARE ($) Earnings	Dividends	Book Value
12/06	13.72	45 18	0.35	—	2.96

Synergetics USA

Synergetics USA makes microsurgical instruments and electrosurgery systems used in minimally invasive surgeries, primarily in the fields of ophthalmology and neurology. Among its products are forceps, retractors, scissors, and illuminators used in vitreoretinal surgeries; precision neurosurgery instruments; and the Omni ultrasonic aspirator used to remove tumors. It also makes bipolar electrosurgical generators, which use electrical currents to cut tissue and seal blood vessels. The company sells some products in the pain management and dental markets, as well. It sells its products to hospitals, physicians, and clinics through direct sales and distributors in the US and abroad.

Synergetics USA was formed when Valley Forge Scientific Corp. (a maker of electrosurgical generators) and Synergetics, Inc. (which made microsurgical instruments) merged in 2005.

EXECUTIVES

Chairman, President, and CEO: Gregg D. Scheller, age 52, $382,000 pay
EVP, COO, and Director: Kurt W. Gampp Jr., age 47, $351,000 pay
EVP, CFO, Treasurer, and Secretary: Pamela G. Boone, age 44, $184,423 pay
EVP, Chief Scientific Officer, and Director:
  Jerry L. Malis, age 75, $235,000 pay
EVP Sales and Marketing: Dave Dallam
Auditors: UHY Advisors, Inc.

LOCATIONS

HQ: Synergetics USA, Inc.
  3845 Corporate Center Dr., O'Fallon, MO 63368
Phone: 636-939-5100   **Fax:** 636-939-6885
Web: www.synergeticsusa.com

2007 Sales

	$ mil.	% of total
US (including Valley Forge)	35.2	77
International	10.7	23
Total	**45.9**	**100**

PRODUCTS/OPERATIONS

Selected Products

Synergetics segment
  Ophthalmic
    Endoilluminators
    Laser probes
    Scrapers
    Vitreoretinal instruments
  Neurosurgery
    OMNI ultrasonic aspirator and disposables
    TruMicro instruments
  Dental
    Bident bipolar tissue management system
Valley Forge segment
  Malis Advantage bipolar electrosurgical generator

COMPETITORS

Aesculap, Inc. USA
Alcon
B. Braun Melsungen
Bausch & Lomb
BioLase Technology
Covidien
Integra LifeSciences
IRIDEX
Stryker

HISTORICAL FINANCIALS

Company Type: Public

Income Statement

FYE: July 31

	REVENUE ($ mil.)	NET INCOME ($ mil.)	NET PROFIT MARGIN	EMPLOYEES
7/07	45.9	0.8	1.7%	333
7/06	38.3	3.1	8.1%	—
7/05	21.8	1.5	6.9%	250
Annual Growth	**45.1%**	**(27.0%)**	**—**	**15.4%**

2007 Year-End Financials

Debt ratio: 26.6%
Return on equity: 2.4%
Cash ($ mil.): 0.2
Current ratio: 1.74
Long-term debt ($ mil.): 8.9
No. of shares (mil.): 24.3

Dividends
  Yield: —
  Payout: —
Market value ($ mil.): 87.8
R&D as % of sales: —
Advertising as % of sales: —

Stock History

NASDAQ (CM): SURG

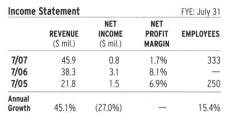

	STOCK PRICE ($) FY Close	P/E High/Low		PER SHARE ($) Earnings	Dividends	Book Value
7/07	3.62	198	112	0.03	—	1.38
7/06	4.52	59	21	0.15	—	1.33
7/05	5.37	14	3	0.42	—	2.93
Annual Growth	**(17.9%)**	**—**	**—**	**(73.3%)**	**—**	**(31.5%)**

Syntax-Brillian

I want my HDTV! That's music to the ears of Syntax-Brillian, which designs rear-projection, high-definition televisions (HDTVs) that use the company's liquid crystal on silicon (LCoS) microdisplay technology. LCoS microdisplays allow more content to be displayed in a smaller size and at a lower cost than traditional LCDs, and are also used in home theater projectors and near-to-eye displays, such as headsets. Syntax-Brillian also offers optical modules and light engines — including prisms, color separators, and lenses — for complete display systems. Through its Vivitar subsidiary, the company also makes a variety of cameras, binoculars, and photographic accessories. Asian customers provide half of sales.

In 2006 Syntax-Brillian exchanged 4,565,141 shares of its common stock for all of Vivitar's. Syntax-Brillian sees synergies between its digital imaging and LCD products and Vivitar's photographic, electronic, optical, and digital imaging products. The company especially sees Vivitar providing wider distribution for its LCD TV sets in Europe.

Publicly traded Brillian Corp. merged in 2005 with Syntax Groups, a privately held manufacturer of HDTV-ready LCD TVs.

In LCoS microdisplays, the liquid crystalline material is suspended between a glass plate and a silicon backplane, rather than between two glass plates as with LCDs. Syntax-Brillian primarily sells to OEMs for use in medical, military, industrial, and consumer applications.

While the HDTV sets the company is marketing grow larger in size, Syntax-Brillian is also targeting the near-to-eye market, where microdisplays are incorporated into industrial, medical, and military products. The small displays are being designed into headsets for video games, to provide a more three-dimensional presentation of game imagery.

The company has become a virtual manufacturer in many senses, outsourcing much of its production to a contractor, Taiwan Kolin. Syntax-Brillian has also established a joint venture with state-owned China South Industries Group to assemble LCoS light engines for Chinese HDTV manufacturers.

In 2007 the company sold its LCoS plant in Arizona to Compound Photonics, a UK-based firm. Syntax-Brillian will retain the patents and intellectual property associated with the LCoS technology, licensing the technology to Compound Photonics. The company took an equity stake of 10% in Compound Photonics as part of the transaction.

The company is the former microdisplay division of Three-Five Systems, which spun it off in 2003. Three-Five Systems, a contract electronics manufacturer, later went into Chapter 11 protection from creditors and ultimately liquidated its assets.

Taiwan Kolin Co. and its affiliates own around 12% of Syntax-Brillian. Including stock options, EVP Thomas Chow holds more than 7% of the company. All officers and directors as a group own about one-quarter of Syntax-Brillian. Investor Lily Lau has an equity stake of about 5%, as does Tony Tzu Ping Ho.

EXECUTIVES

Executive Chairman: Vincent F. Sollitto Jr., age 60
President and CEO and Director: James Ching Hua Li, age 41
EVP and Chief Procurement Officer and Director:
  Man Kit (Thomas) Chow, age 47
EVP LCD and Corporate Secretary: Michael Chan, age 39
EVP, CFO, Treasurer, and Director:
  John S. (Jack) Hodgson, age 55
SVP Operations and CIO: Paul Tearnen
Chief Marketing Officer: Hope S. Frank, age 48
CTO: Robert L. Melcher, age 67
Auditors: Grobstein, Horwath & Company LLP

LOCATIONS

HQ: Syntax-Brillian Corporation
  1600 N. Desert Dr., Tempe, AZ 85281
Phone: 602-389-8888   **Fax:** 602-389-8801
Web: www.brilliancorp.com

Syntax-Brillian has facilities in Arizona, California, and Colorado, with a warehouse in Canada.

2007 Sales

	$ mil.	% of total
Asia	351.0	50
North America	319.4	46
Europe	27.2	4
Total	**697.6**	**100**

PRODUCTS/OPERATIONS

2007 Sales

	$ mil.	% of total
LCD TVs	650.5	93
Digital cameras	41.5	6
Microdisplay products	5.6	1
Total	**697.6**	**100**

Selected Products

LCD TVs
  Brillian HDTVs
    6501 720p 3-megapixel HDTV
    6580iFB 1080p 6-megapixel HDTV
  Olevia HDTVs
    Olevia 3 Series HDTVs (23- to 42-inch LCD TVs)
    Olevia 5 Series HDTVs (27- to 42-inch LCD TVs)
    Olevia 7 Series HDTVs (42- to 47-inch LCD TVs)
Digital Imaging
  Auto-focus cameras
  Binoculars
  Camera accessories
  Digital still cameras
  Digital video cameras
  Multimedia players
  Point-and-shoot cameras
  Projectors
  Single-lens reflex cameras
Microdisplays
  Application-specific integrated circuit (ASIC) display drivers
  BR1080HC development kits
  Gen II liquid crystal on silicon (LCoS) microdisplays
  UltraContrast BLE1080 light engines

COMPETITORS

AU Optronics
Canon
CASIO COMPUTER
Chi Mei Optoelectronics
Cree
Dell
Displaytech
Document Capture Technologies
eMagin
Epson
Forth Dimension Displays
Gateway, Inc.
Hewlett-Packard
Hitachi
Konica Minolta
Kopin
LG Electronics
Microvision
Nokia
Olympus
Panasonic Shikoku
Philips Electronics
Samsung Electronics
SANYO
Sharp Corporation
Sony
Texas Instruments
THOMSON
Toshiba
UMC
Victor Company of Japan
ViewSonic

HISTORICAL FINANCIALS

Company Type: Public

Income Statement

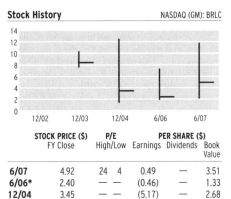

Stock History		NASDAQ (GM): BRLC

	STOCK PRICE ($) FY Close	P/E High/Low		Earnings	PER SHARE ($) Dividends	Book Value
6/07	4.92	24	4	0.49	—	3.51
6/06*	2.40	—	—	(0.46)	—	1.33
12/04	3.45	—	—	(5.17)	—	2.68
12/03	8.40	—	—	(3.51)	—	7.20
Annual Growth	(16.3%)	—	—	—	—	(21.3%)

*Fiscal year change

FYE: June 30

	REVENUE ($ mil.)	NET INCOME ($ mil.)	NET PROFIT MARGIN	EMPLOYEES
6/07	697.6	29.8	4.3%	293
6/06*	193.0	(18.9)	—	—
12/04	2.7	(32.9)	—	—
12/03	2.2	(18.7)	—	—
12/02	1.4	(23.2)	—	73
Annual Growth	372.5%	—	—	41.5%

*Fiscal year change

2007 Year-End Financials

Debt ratio: —
Return on equity: 15.7%
Cash ($ mil.): 172.2
Current ratio: 2.22
Long-term debt ($ mil.): —
No. of shares (mil.): 89.9

Dividends
  Yield: —
  Payout: —
Market value ($ mil.): 442.2
R&D as % of sales: —
Advertising as % of sales: —

Targacept, Inc.

Depressed because you can't smoke anymore? Targacept might be able to help as it researches how to put the nervous system's nicotinic receptors to good use. The biotechnology company is the result of nicotine research conducted by R.J. Reynolds Tobacco, which spun off the firm in 2000. Targacept's drug candidates address conditions related to cognitive impairment, depression, and pain by targeting neuronal nicotinic receptors (NNRs) in the nervous system using non-nicotine compounds. The firm hopes its drug candidates will reproduce the therapeutic effects of NNR interaction without the side effects of nicotine (but they may not offer that smooth, satisfying taste).

The company has partnered with drug giant AstraZeneca to further the development of its Alzheimer's treatment AZD3480. The agreement has already brought $30 million to Targacept's coffers and grants milestone payments that could total as much as $249 million.

The company bought the marketing rights to Inversine in 2002 from Layton BioScience, which acquired the rights from Merck & Co. Inversine has FDA approval to treat moderately severe to severe hypertension, but Targacept is investigating its use to treat neuropsychiatric disorders, including autism and bipolar disorder, in children and adolescents.

Targacept's investors include New Enterprise Associates (17%), Nomura (11%), and EuclidSR Partners (10%). R.J. Reynolds Tabacco no longer holds a stake in Targacept.

The company launched its initial public offering in April 2006 and has used the proceeds to fund development of its clinical and preclinical candidates and cover general operating expenses.

EXECUTIVES

Chairman: Mark B. Skaletsky, age 59
President, CEO, and Director:
  J. Donald (Don) deBethizy, age 57, $415,400 pay
VP, CFO, Treasurer, and Secretary: Alan A. Musso, age 45, $257,275 pay
VP Business and Commercial Development:
  Jeffrey P. (Jeff) Brennan, age 50, $293,670 pay

VP Clinical Development and Regulatory Affairs:
  Geoffrey C. Dunbar, age 60, $331,717 pay
VP Drug Discovery and Development:
  William S. Caldwell, age 53, $243,159 pay
VP Legal Affairs, General Counsel, and Assistant Secretary: Peter A. Zorn, age 37
VP Preclinical Research: Merouane Bencherif, age 52, $251,000 pay
Senior Director Finance and Controller:
  Mauri K. Hodges
Director Human Resources: Karen A. Hicks
Director Investor, Public Relations and Corporate Communications: Linda Gretton
Auditors: Ernst & Young LLP

LOCATIONS

HQ: Targacept, Inc.
  200 E. 1st St., Ste. 300, Winston-Salem, NC 27101
Phone: 336-480-2100   **Fax:** 336-480-2107
Web: www.targacept.com

PRODUCTS/OPERATIONS

COMPETITORS

Abbott Labs
AstraZeneca
Biovail
Critical Therapeutics
Eli Lilly
Forest Labs
GlaxoSmithKline
Johnson & Johnson
Memory Pharmaceuticals
Merck
Novartis
Pfizer
Purdue Pharma
Sanofi-Aventis
Wyeth

HISTORICAL FINANCIALS

Company Type: Public

Income Statement

FYE: December 31

	REVENUE ($ mil.)	NET INCOME ($ mil.)	NET PROFIT MARGIN	EMPLOYEES
12/06	27.5	2.1	7.6%	89
12/05	1.2	(29.0)	—	75
12/04	3.7	(24.0)	—	—
12/03	2.5	(19.4)	—	72
12/02	2.3	(21.1)	—	65
Annual Growth	86.0%	—	—	8.2%

2006 Year-End Financials

Debt ratio: 1.3%
Return on equity: —
Cash ($ mil.): 54.2
Current ratio: 8.81
Long-term debt ($ mil.): 0.8
No. of shares (mil.): 19.1

Dividends
  Yield: —
  Payout: —
Market value ($ mil.): 173.1
R&D as % of sales: —
Advertising as % of sales: —

Stock History		NASDAQ (GM): TRGT

	STOCK PRICE ($) FY Close	P/E High/Low		Earnings	PER SHARE ($) Dividends	Book Value
12/06	9.05	—	—	(0.09)	—	3.40

Technitrol, Inc.

Technitrol pulses with the desire to control electronic impulses. The company's Pulse electronic components segment makes a variety of passive magnetic components, including chokes, filters, transformers, and inductors. These items regulate electronic signals in devices such as telecommunications and computer networking equipment. Technitrol's AMI DODUCO electrical components division makes precisely engineered electrical contacts and contact assemblies used in a wide range of products, including circuit breakers, electrical switches and relays, consumer appliances, and thermostatic devices. More than 85% of the company's sales comes from customers outside the US.

Technitrol continues to troll for acquisitions to complement its core operations. While acquisitions have expanded the company's AMI DODUCO operations in Europe and China, Technitrol has also closed offices elsewhere to control costs.

The company has agreed to acquire Sonion A/S for about $385 million in cash. Sonion makes microacoustic transducers and micromechanical components, used in hearing aids, high-end earphones, medical devices, wireless handsets, and other mobile terminal equipment. Sonion employs around 4,900 people at operations in Asia and Europe, and it posted 2007 sales of approximately $180 million. Technitrol expects to close the transaction by the end of February 2008. Sonion will become part of the Electronic Components (Pulse) business.

In 2007 the company offered to acquire rival Bel Fuse, which has made its own unsolicited bids for other competitors in the past. Technitrol was offering $480 million in cash to buy Bel Fuse. The company made several private overtures to Bel Fuse regarding a possible acquisition in 2006, with Bel Fuse refusing to go beyond initial talks.

When Bel Fuse rebuffed the Technitrol bid as too low, Technitrol offered to increase its value to $514 million, if Bel Fuse representatives would engage in more substantive negotiations. Days after making the conditional higher offer (also rejected by Bel Fuse), Technitrol withdrew the offer, stating that Bel Fuse had refused to negotiate in good faith.

Royce & Associates owns nearly 6% of Technitrol. Barclays Global Investors, AXA Financial, and Boston Partners Asset Management each hold about 5% of the company.

HISTORY

Technitrol was founded in 1947 by Gordon Palmer and three other University of Pennsylvania engineering graduates, all of whom helped develop ENIAC, the world's first electronic computer. Technitrol held the first patent for a magnetic disk drive, the most widely licensed disk memory device during the 1960s and 1970s. The company's licensees included IBM and General Electric.

The company never made the drive, focusing instead on the development of its other breakthrough invention, the pulse transformer, and supplying this and other components to the emerging computer industry. But changes in core memory technology for mainframe computers in the 1970s nearly sank Technitrol's

pulse transformer business, prompting the company to diversify.

Technitrol began pursuing a strategy of buying troubled companies and folding them into existing operations to win market leadership in niche component areas. In 1972 it bought electrical contact maker Advanced Metallurgy and measuring instruments and scales specialist John Chatillon & Sons. By the end of the 1980s Technitrol had settled on three core lines — electronics, metallurgical, and test and measurement.

When sales began stagnating in the early 1990s, Technitrol turned to higher-margin products in the computer network and telecommunications realms. It bought Fil-Mag in 1994 and Pulse Engineering in 1995. That year longtime company executive Thomas Flakoll became CEO. In 1996 the company acquired Doduco, a Germany-based maker of electric contacts, and reshuffled its magnetic components business under the name Pulse. The company sold off its test and measurement business that year and the next.

Acquisitions continued, including purchases of Northern Telecom's (now Nortel Networks) magnetic components operations (1997), telecommunications and power conversion equipment component maker FEE Technology (1998), and computer network component specialist GTI (1998). Also in 1998, Technitrol unified its metallurgical components businesses under the name AMI DODUCO. When Flakoll resigned in 1999, he was succeeded by Technitrol chairman James Papada.

Both company units made major expansion pushes in 1999 and 2000. AMI DODUCO acquired businesses in China, Estonia, and Italy, while Pulse formed a new unit to develop off-the-shelf products for the fast-growing broadband cable market. In 2001 Technitrol further expanded AMI DODUCO when it acquired the France-based electrical contacts business of Engelhard-CLAL.

Early in 2003 the company acquired the consumer electronics components business of Italy-based Eldor Corporation.

In 2004 Technitrol acquired the controlling interest in Full Rise Electronic (FRE), a Taiwanese supplier of connector and cabling products. The company first took an equity stake in FRE in 2001.

The company acquired LK Products, a supplier of antennas and modules for mobile devices, for €67 million (about $83 million) in cash in 2005. Technitrol bought the company from Filtronic and made LK Products part of its antenna products division.

In early 2006 Technitrol acquired ERA Group for €49 million (approximately $58 million). ERA Group makes electronic coils and transformers, primarily for the European automotive market. Technitrol plans to form an automotive products division within the power products group of Pulse Engineering.

EXECUTIVES

Chairman, President, and CEO: James M. Papada III, age 58, $626,451 pay
COO, Product Divisions, Operations, Sales, Pulse:
  Alan Benjamin
SVP; CEO, Pulse: John L. Kowalski, age 63,
  $325,240 pay
SVP, Signal Product Group, Pulse: John Houston
SVP, Production Operations, Pulse:
  Roger Shahnazarian
SVP and CFO: Drew A. Moyer, age 42, $275,866 pay

VP, Human Resources: David W. Lacey, age 62,
  $205,110 pay
VP, Corporate Communications: David J. Stakun, age 51
VP and General Manager, Pulse LAN Division:
  Joe Ocampo
VP and General Manager, Pulse Power Division:
  Bruce Hamilton
VP, China Operations, Pulse: Colman Tso
VP, Consumer Division, Pulse: Mike McAuliffe
VP, Information Technology, Pulse: Steve Mentas
VP, Logistics, Pulse: Bill Fister
VP, Quality: Mark E. Jackson
Secretary: Ann Marie Janus
Chief Accounting Officer and Corporate Controller:
  Edward J. (Ed) Prajzner, age 40
Auditors: KPMG LLP

LOCATIONS

HQ: Technitrol, Inc.
  1210 Northbrook Dr., Ste. 470, Trevose, PA 19053
Phone: 215-355-2900   **Fax:** 215-355-7397
Web: www.technitrol.com

Technitrol has manufacturing facilities in China, Finland, Germany, Hungary, Mexico, Spain, Taiwan, Tunisia, and the US.

2006 Sales

	$ mil.	% of total
Europe		
Germany	168.5	18
Other countries	285.5	30
Asia/Pacific	315.3	33
US	124.7	13
Other regions	60.1	6
Total	**954.1**	**100**

PRODUCTS/OPERATIONS

2006 Sales

	$ mil.	% of total
Electronic components	627.5	66
Electrical contact products	326.6	34
Total	**954.1**	**100**

Selected Products

Electronic Components (Pulse Engineering)
  Chokes
  Delay lines
  Filters
  Inductors
  Transformers

Electrical Contact Products (AMI DODUCO)
  Contact assemblies
  Contact materials
  Electrical contacts
  Electroplating
  Stamped metal parts

COMPETITORS

Airpax
API Nanotronics
Bel Fuse
California Micro Devices
Cookson Group
Del Global
Espey Mfg.
Gowanda Electronics
Jaco Electronics
JDS Uniphase
Mitsubishi Materials
OECO
Omron Scientific Technologies
QTran
Sensata
SGL Carbon
Spang & Company
SWCC SHOWA HOLDINGS
Torotel
TTI Inc.
Vishay Intertechnology

HISTORICAL FINANCIALS

Company Type: Public

Income Statement — FYE: December 31

	REVENUE ($ mil.)	NET INCOME ($ mil.)	NET PROFIT MARGIN	EMPLOYEES
12/06	954.1	57.2	6.0%	28,100
12/05	616.4	(25.5)	—	29,500
12/04	582.3	6.9	1.2%	22,800
12/03	509.3	12.0	2.4%	18,600
12/02	406.4	(43.5)	—	19,000
Annual Growth	23.8%	—	—	10.3%

2006 Year-End Financials

Debt ratio: 11.9%
Return on equity: 12.7%
Cash ($ mil.): 87.2
Current ratio: 1.97
Long-term debt ($ mil.): 57.3
No. of shares (mil.): 40.8

Dividends
  Yield: 1.5%
  Payout: 24.8%
Market value ($ mil.): 973.5
R&D as % of sales: —
Advertising as % of sales: —

Stock History — NYSE: TNL

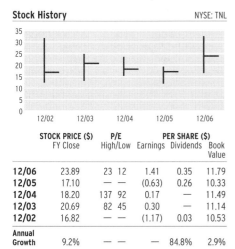

	STOCK PRICE ($) FY Close	P/E High/Low	PER SHARE ($) Earnings	Dividends	Book Value
12/06	23.89	23 12	1.41	0.35	11.79
12/05	17.10	— —	(0.63)	0.26	10.33
12/04	18.20	137 92	0.17	—	11.49
12/03	20.69	82 45	0.30	—	11.14
12/02	16.82	— —	(1.17)	0.03	10.53
Annual Growth	9.2%	— —	—	84.8%	2.9%

Techwell, Inc.

How goes tech? Well, thank you. Techwell designs decoder chips that convert analog video into digital form, and processors used to display digital video, high-definition television (HDTV), and PC data. Mixed-signal semiconductors, which blend analog and digital elements, are in high demand as popular consumer products, such as cell phones and Apple's iPod, are now capable of playing videos downloaded from the Web or from providers of wireless services. Techwell's OEM customers include Fujitsu, LG Electronics, Samsung Electronics, and Toshiba. Technology Crossover Ventures owns about 20% of Techwell.

Techwell's chips are finding their way not only into portable consumer electronics products, such as camcorders and DVD players, but also into automotive display systems and surveillance cameras. Other applications for the company's mixed-signal integrated circuits include advanced TV sets, DVD recorders, set-top boxes, video game consoles, and VCRs.

Almost all of Techwell's sales are to customers in Asia.

The company's auditor found material weaknesses in Techwell's internal financial controls, leading the company to restate its financial results for 2002, 2003, and 2004. Techwell started turning a profit in 2005, but has an accumulated deficit of about $25 million.

As a fabless semiconductor company, Techwell relies on contractors to produce its devices. Taiwan Semiconductor Manufacturing Co. (TSMC), the world's largest silicon foundry, makes Techwell's chips, which are then assembled, packaged, and tested by Advanced Semiconductor Engineering (ASE), one of the biggest contractors in that field.

Techwell counted Credit Suisse, Genesis Microchip, Mitsubishi, Panasonic, and Sanyo among its investors. The company raised $43 million in private equity funding.

CEO Hiro Kozato owns nearly 7% of Techwell. Sanyo Semiconductor holds around 4% of the company.

EXECUTIVES

President, CEO, and Director: Fumihiro (Hiro) Kozato, age 47, $198,087 pay
VP, Finance and Administration and CFO: Mark Voll, age 52, $192,773 pay
VP, Sales and Marketing: Dong Wook (David) Nam, age 39, $137,814 pay
CTO: Feng Kuo, age 49, $198,127 pay
Director, Business Development: Tom Krause, age 28
Director, Manufacturing: Joe Kamei, age 49
Auditors: Deloitte & Touche LLP

LOCATIONS

HQ: Techwell, Inc.
  408 E. Plumeria Dr., San Jose, CA 95134
Phone: 408-435-3888   **Fax:** 408-435-0588
Web: www.techwellinc.com

Techwell has offices in China, South Korea, Taiwan, and the US.

2006 Sales

	% of total
Taiwan	43
South Korea	31
China & Hong Kong	21
Japan	3
US	1
Other countries	1
Total	**100**

PRODUCTS/OPERATIONS

2006 Sales

	$ mil.	% of total
Security surveillance	27.7	51
Video decoders	18.2	34
LCD displays	6.9	13
Other	0.9	2
Total	**53.7**	**100**

COMPETITORS

Cirrus Logic
Genesis Microchip
Micronas Semiconductor
NVIDIA
NXP
Pixelworks
Texas Instruments
Trident Microsystems
Zoran

HISTORICAL FINANCIALS

Company Type: Public

Income Statement — FYE: December 31

	REVENUE ($ mil.)	NET INCOME ($ mil.)	NET PROFIT MARGIN	EMPLOYEES
12/06	53.7	13.2	24.6%	96
12/05	36.0	4.5	12.5%	—
12/04	17.3	(1.7)	—	—
12/03	11.1	(5.2)	—	—
12/02	4.8	(6.0)	—	—
Annual Growth	82.9%	—	—	—

2006 Year-End Financials

Debt ratio: —
Return on equity: 69.6%
Cash ($ mil.): 49.6
Current ratio: 8.51
Long-term debt ($ mil.): —
No. of shares (mil.): 20.5

Dividends
  Yield: —
  Payout: —
Market value ($ mil.): 329.7
R&D as % of sales: —
Advertising as % of sales: —

Stock History — NASDAQ (GM): TWLL

	STOCK PRICE ($) FY Close	P/E High/Low	PER SHARE ($) Earnings	Dividends	Book Value
12/06	16.06	30 14	0.64	—	2.78

Temecula Valley Bancorp

Temecula wants to protect your money from bloodsuckers. Temecula Valley Bancorp is the holding company for Temecula Valley Bank, which operates more than a dozen branches and loan and mortgage origination offices north of San Diego. A Small Business Administration (SBA) preferred lender, the company has SBA loan production offices in towns throughout California as well as one in Florida. More than 90% of its loan portfolio is secured by real estate, mainly in the form of commercial mortgages and construction and land development loans.

As part of its business strategy, the bank has closed all of its SBA lending offices on the East Coast, with the exception of one facility in Florida, to concentrate on the Western US.

Chairman, president, and CEO Stephen Wacknitz owns more than 8% of Temecula Valley Bancorp; while director Luther Mohr owns more than 5%.

EXECUTIVES

Chairman, President, and CEO, Temecula Valley Bancorp and Temecula Valley Bank:
  Stephen H. Wacknitz, age 67, $1,923,000 pay
SEVP and Director Finance and SBA:
  William H. (Bill) McGaughey, age 50

EVP and COO: Martin E. (Marty) Plourd, age 48
EVP, CFO, and Secretary: Donald A. Pitcher, age 57
EVP and Chief Administrative Officer, Temecula Valley Bank: Frank Basirico Jr., age 52
EVP and Senior Loan Officer, Temecula Valley Bank: Scott J. Word, age 52, $275,000 pay
EVP and East County Regional Manager, Temecula Valley Bank: Thomas P. Ivory, age 53, $282,661 pay
EVP and North San Diego County Regional Manager, and Carlsbad Branch Manager, Temecula Valley Bank: Donald L. (Don) Schempp, age 58
EVP and North County Regional Manager, Temecula Valley Bank: Gerald W. (Jerry) Van Dyke
EVP and Real Estate Manager, Temecula Valley Bank: James W. Andrews, age 57
President, SBA Division: David H. (Dave) Bartram
Auditors: Crowe Chizek and Company LLP

LOCATIONS

HQ: Temecula Valley Bancorp Inc.
27710 Jefferson Ave., Ste. A100,
Temecula, CA 92590
Phone: 951-694-9940   **Fax:** 951-694-9194
Web: www.temvalbank.com

PRODUCTS/OPERATIONS

2006 Sales

	% of total
Interest	
Loans	82
Securities & other	1
Noninterest	
Gain on sales of loans	11
Loan broker income	4
Other	2
Total	**100**

COMPETITORS

Bank of America
California Bank & Trust
Downey Financial
First PacTrust
UnionBanCal
Washington Mutual
Wells Fargo

HISTORICAL FINANCIALS

Company Type: Public

Income Statement

FYE: December 31

	ASSETS ($ mil.)	NET INCOME ($ mil.)	INCOME AS % OF ASSETS	EMPLOYEES
12/06	1,238.2	16.9	1.4%	317
12/05	869.0	13.9	1.6%	281
12/04	606.8	10.6	1.7%	229
12/03	431.2	7.8	1.8%	194
12/02	310.3	4.2	1.4%	194
Annual Growth	**41.3%**	**41.6%**	**—**	**13.1%**

2006 Year-End Financials

Equity as % of assets: 8.3%
Return on assets: 1.6%
Return on equity: 20.9%
Long-term debt ($ mil.): 41.2
No. of shares (mil.): 10.6
Market value ($ mil.): 248.8
Dividends
  Yield: —
  Payout: —
Sales ($ mil.): 116.3
R&D as % of sales: —
Advertising as % of sales: —

Stock History

NASDAQ (GS): TMCV

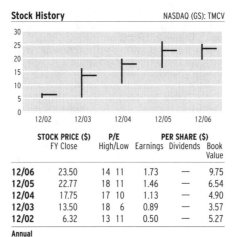

	STOCK PRICE ($) FY Close	P/E High/Low		PER SHARE ($) Earnings	Dividends	Book Value
12/06	23.50	14	11	1.73	—	9.75
12/05	22.77	18	11	1.46	—	6.54
12/04	17.75	17	10	1.13	—	4.90
12/03	13.50	18	6	0.89	—	3.57
12/02	6.32	13	11	0.50	—	5.27
Annual Growth	**38.9%**	**—**	**—**	**36.4%**	**—**	**16.6%**

Tennessee Commerce Bancorp

You might say that Tennessee Commerce Bancorp has a genuine *interest* in Music City USA. Founded in 2000, the financial institution is the holding company for Tennessee Commerce Bank. Concentrating on the Greater Nashville area, Tennessee Commerce Bank caters primarily to consumers and members of the service and manufacturing industries but avoids retail establishments as customers. Instead of creating a network of branch locations, the bank utilizes Internet options and provides free courier services for deposits. Commercial, financial, and agricultural loans account for more than 60% of the bank's lending portfolio.

EXECUTIVES

Chairman and CEO, Tennessee Commerce Bancorp and Tennessee Commerce Bank: Arthur F. Helf, age 69, $332,500 pay
President and Director; President and Chief Lending Officer, Tennessee Commerce Bank: Michael R. Sapp, age 54, $332,500 pay
CFO, Tennessee Commerce Bancorp and Tennessee Commerce Bank: George W. Fort, age 49, $212,672 pay
Chief Administrative Officer, Secretary, and Director; Chief Administrative Officer and Secretary, Tennessee Commerce Bank: H. Lamar Cox, age 64, $315,000 pay
Auditors: KraftCPAs PLLC

LOCATIONS

HQ: Tennessee Commerce Bancorp, Inc.
381 Mallory Station Rd., Ste 207,
Franklin, TN 37067
Phone: 615-599-2274   **Fax:** 615-599-2275
Web: www.tncommercebank.com

PRODUCTS/OPERATIONS

2006 Sales

	% of total
Interest	
Loans, including fees	89
Securities	5
Federal funds sold	1
Noninterest	
Gain on sale of loans	5
Total	**100**

COMPETITORS

CFB Bancshares	First Security Group
Cornerstone Bancshares	Green Bankshares
First Horizon	Pinnacle Financial
First Pulaski National	Tennessee Valley Financial

HISTORICAL FINANCIALS

Company Type: Public

Income Statement

FYE: December 31

	ASSETS ($ mil.)	NET INCOME ($ mil.)	INCOME AS % OF ASSETS	EMPLOYEES
12/06	623.5	4.8	0.8%	50
12/05	404.0	3.1	0.8%	41
12/04	245.9	1.7	0.7%	—
Annual Growth	**59.2%**	**68.0%**	**—**	**22.0%**

2006 Year-End Financials

Equity as % of assets: 8.2%
Return on assets: 0.9%
Return on equity: 12.4%
Long-term debt ($ mil.): 8.3
No. of shares (mil.): 4.5
Market value ($ mil.): 139.1
Dividends
  Yield: —
  Payout: —
Sales ($ mil.): 43.6
R&D as % of sales: —
Advertising as % of sales: —

Stock History

NASDAQ (GM): TNCC

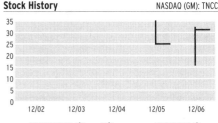

	STOCK PRICE ($) FY Close	P/E High/Low		PER SHARE ($) Earnings	Dividends	Book Value
12/06	31.25	28	14	1.14	—	11.51
12/05	25.00	40	29	0.87	—	8.16
Annual Growth	**25.0%**	**—**	**—**	**31.0%**	**—**	**41.0%**

Tessera Technologies

Tessera doesn't have to put nutritional labels on its packages. The company licenses a portfolio of patented semiconductor packaging technologies; these designs enable semiconductor makers to produce high-performance packages for use in mobile phones, PDAs, PCs, and other electronic products. Licensees include big chip makers, such as Hitachi, Intel, and Toshiba, as well as leading semiconductor assemblers, such as ASE and Amkor. Tessera has taken on the likes of Micron Technology (15% of sales), Qimonda (21%), Sharp, and Texas Instruments in lawsuits defending its patents and won settlements from them. The company gets nearly two-thirds of its sales from outside of the US.

Tessera also offers prototype design, assembly line consulting, and related services.

In mid-2006 Tessera acquired Digital Optics Corp., a supplier of micro-optical components, for nearly $60 million in cash.

In 2005 Tessera acquired certain assets of Shellcase, a supplier of wafer-level chip size packaging. The acquisition, for around $33 million in cash, took Tessera into the new markets of wafer-level packaging for image sensors, which go into camera phones and other applications, and for microelectromechanical systems (MEMS). Tessera hired the majority of Shellcase's employees following the purchase.

Tessera sees the Digital Optics acquisition building on the wafer-level image sensor packaging technology assets acquired from Shellcase.

Flextronics, the giant multinational electronics manufacturing services provider, has licensed the Shellcase CF wafer-level assembly technology from Tessera for use in making camera modules.

In early 2007 Tessera acquired Eyesquad for about $20 million in cash. Eyesquad develops digital auto-focus and optical zoom technology for camera phones and other electronic products that integrate cameras, without using moving parts. The acquisition advances the strategic direction taken by the company in buying Digital Optics and Shellcase.

In early 2008 the company agreed to acquire FotoNation, a developer of embedded imaging products for digital still cameras and mobile phones, for $29 million in net cash, plus up to another $10 million in an earnout payment, depending on certain milestones over a year. FotoNation's products correct "red eyes" in photos, track faces, and detect blinks and smiles, among other functions.

In 2005 Tessera organized itself into five operating groups: the Advanced Semiconductor Packaging Group; the Emerging Markets and Technologies Group; Tessera Interconnect Materials, Inc.; the Wafer Level Technologies Division; and the Product Miniaturization Division. All but the Product Miniaturization Division are gathered under the company's intellectual property segment, while Product Miniaturization falls under services.

Goldman Sachs Asset Management owns nearly 13% of Tessera, while Morgan Stanley holds around 10% of the company. Fred Alger Management has an equity stake of about 5%, as does Wells Fargo.

EXECUTIVES

Chairman, President, and CEO: Bruce M. McWilliams, age 50, $374,039 pay
EVP and CFO: Charles A. Webster, age 44, $91,538 pay (partial-year salary)
EVP and COO: Michael (Mike) Bereziuk, age 55, $278,212 pay (partial-year salary)
EVP and Director: Al S. Joseph, age 74
SVP and CTO: David B. Tuckerman, age 49
SVP, Business Development and Sales: Steven T. Chen
SVP, Emerging Markets and Technologies Group: Liam Goudge, age 39, $244,942 pay
SVP and General Counsel: Scot A. Griffin, age 39
VP, Finance and Corporate Secretary: Michael A. (Mike) Forman, age 49, $208,769 pay
Auditors: PricewaterhouseCoopers LLP

LOCATIONS

HQ: Tessera Technologies, Inc.
3099 Orchard Dr., San Jose, CA 95134
Phone: 408-894-0700   **Fax:** 408-894-0768
Web: www.tessera.com

Tessera has facilities in Israel, Japan, Taiwan, and the US.

2006 Sales

	$ mil.	% of total
US	75.0	36
Asia/Pacific		
Japan	30.9	15
Other countries	36.3	17
Europe	66.3	32
Other regions	0.2	—
Total	**208.7**	**100**

PRODUCTS/OPERATIONS

2006 Sales

	$ mil.	% of total
Intellectual property	182.8	88
Services	25.9	12
Total	**208.7**	**100**

Services

Assembly line consulting
Prototype design
Test and failure analysis
Training

COMPETITORS

Advanced Semiconductor Engineering
Amkor
ASAT Holdings
FlipChip International
Freescale Semiconductor
Fujitsu Microelectronics
Hynix
IBIDEN
IBM Microelectronics
Infineon Technologies
Intel Corporation
Irvine Sensors
Marubeni
Micron Technology
NEC Electronics
Oki Electric
OmniVision Technologies
Renesas
Samsung Electronics
Sharp Corporation
STATS ChipPAC
STMicroelectronics
Sumitomo Electric
Texas Instruments
Toshiba Semiconductor

HISTORICAL FINANCIALS

Company Type: Public

Income Statement

FYE: December 31

	REVENUE ($ mil.)	NET INCOME ($ mil.)	NET PROFIT MARGIN	EMPLOYEES
12/06	208.7	61.3	29.4%	271
12/05	94.7	31.5	33.3%	162
12/04	72.7	59.1	81.3%	—
12/03	37.3	9.4	25.2%	—
12/02	28.3	6.5	23.0%	—
Annual Growth	**64.8%**	**75.2%**	**—**	**67.3%**

2006 Year-End Financials

Debt ratio: —
Return on equity: 25.2%
Cash ($ mil.): 194.1
Current ratio: 14.30
Long-term debt ($ mil.): —
No. of shares (mil.): 47.2

Dividends
Yield: —
Payout: —
Market value ($ mil.): 1,904.6
R&D as % of sales: —
Advertising as % of sales: —

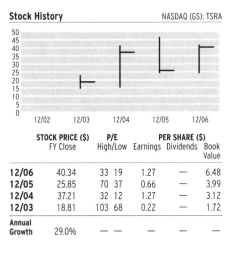

Stock History

NASDAQ (GS): TSRA

	STOCK PRICE ($) FY Close	P/E High/Low	PER SHARE ($) Earnings	Dividends	Book Value
12/06	40.34	33 19	1.27	—	6.48
12/05	25.85	70 37	0.66	—	3.99
12/04	37.21	32 12	1.27	—	3.12
12/03	18.81	103 68	0.22	—	1.72
Annual Growth	**29.0%**	**— —**	**—**	**—**	**—**

TETRA Technologies

TETRA Technologies is a smooth operator when it comes to discarded oil wells. The company is composed of three divisions: fluids, well abandonment and decommissioning, and product enhancement. The fluids unit makes clear brine fluids as well as dry calcium chloride that aid in drilling for the oil and gas industry. Its well abandonment segment decommissions offshore platforms and pipelines. In addition to production testing services for oil and gas operations, the product enhancement division also recycles oily residuals that are a byproduct of refining and exploration. TETRA Technologies owns producing properties and has proved reserves of 8.8 million barrels of oil and 39.7 billion cu. ft. of natural gas.

In 2006 TETRA Technologies acquired Beacon Resources LLC, an onshore production testing company, for $15 million coupled with a potential earn-out payment. It also acquired Epic Divers Inc. for $50 million.

EXECUTIVES

Chairman: Ralph S. Cunningham, age 66
President, CEO, and Director: Geoffrey M. Hertel, age 62, $770,000 pay
EVP and COO: Stuart M. Brightman, age 50, $393,885 pay (partial-year salary)
EVP Strategic Initiatives and Director: Paul D. Coombs, age 51, $600,000 pay (prior to title change)
SVP and CFO: Joseph M. (Joe) Abell III, age 52
SVP: Dennis R. Matthews, age 48
SVP: Raymond D. Symens, age 56, $298,339 pay
VP Administration and Director Human Resources: Linden H. Price, age 61
President, Maritech Resources: G. Matt McCarroll, age 47, $397,512 pay
Manager Investor Relations: Eileen Price
Auditors: Ernst & Young LLP

LOCATIONS

HQ: TETRA Technologies, Inc.
25025 I-45 North, Ste. 600,
The Woodlands, TX 77380
Phone: 281-367-1983   **Fax:** 281-364-4346
Web: www.tetratec.com

TETRA Technologies has operations in Brazil, Canada, Finland, Mexico, the Netherlands, Nigeria, Norway, Saudi Arabia, Sweden, the UK, and the US.

2006 Sales

	$ mil.	% of total
North America		
US	663.3	84
Canada & Mexico	22.0	3
Europe	74.3	10
South America	12.9	2
Africa	3.4	—
Asia & other regions	9.0	1
Total	**784.9**	**100**

PRODUCTS/OPERATIONS

2006 Sales

	$ mil.	% of total
Well abandonment & decommissioning	392.1	50
Fluids	244.6	31
Product enhancement	148.9	19
Adjustments	(0.7)	—
Total	**784.9**	**100**

COMPETITORS

Baker Hughes
BJ Services
Global Industries
Halliburton
Helix Energy Solutions
Key Energy
Schlumberger
Smith International
Superior Energy

HISTORICAL FINANCIALS

Company Type: Public

Income Statement				FYE: December 31
	REVENUE ($ mil.)	**NET INCOME** ($ mil.)	**NET PROFIT MARGIN**	**EMPLOYEES**
12/06	784.9	101.9	13.0%	2,536
12/05	531.0	38.1	7.2%	1,668
12/04	353.2	17.7	5.0%	—
12/03	318.7	21.7	6.8%	—
12/02	242.6	8.9	3.7%	1,391
Annual Growth	34.1%	83.9%	—	16.2%

2006 Year-End Financials

Debt ratio: 80.0%
Return on equity: 28.9%
Cash ($ mil.): 6.1
Current ratio: 2.52
Long-term debt ($ mil.): 336.4
No. of shares (mil.): 71.9
Dividends
  Yield: —
  Payout: —
Market value ($ mil.): 1,840.0
R&D as % of sales: —
Advertising as % of sales: —

Stock History

NYSE: TTI

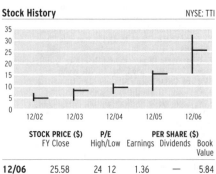

	STOCK PRICE ($) FY Close	P/E High/Low		PER SHARE ($) Earnings	Dividends	Book Value
12/06	25.58	24	12	1.36	—	5.84
12/05	15.26	31	16	0.52	—	8.17
12/04	9.43	43	28	0.25	—	10.49
12/03	8.08	28	13	0.31	—	9.53
12/02	4.75	50	28	0.13	—	12.77
Annual Growth	52.3%	—	—	79.8%	—	(17.7%)

Texas Capital Bancshares

Texas Capital Bancshares is the holding company for Texas Capital Bank, which has about 10 branches in Austin, Dallas, Fort Worth, Houston, Plano, and San Antonio. Targeting individuals and small and midsized businesses (with a focus on the energy industry), the bank offers personal and commercial deposit accounts, mortgages, business and construction loans, Visa credit cards, equipment leasing, insurance products, wealth management, and trust services. Online banking is offered through its BankDirect division. Texas Capital Bancshares was formed in 1998 with a Texas-sized bankroll of $80 million.

EXECUTIVES

Chairman and CEO: Joseph M. (Jody) Grant, age 68, $422,000 pay
Director; President and CEO, Texas Capital Bank: George F. Jones Jr., age 63, $400,000 pay
CFO and Director; CFO, Texas Capital Bank: Peter B. Bartholow, age 58, $367,500 pay
EVP and Chief Lending Officer, Texas Capital Bank: C. Keith Cargill, age 54, $301,600 pay
EVP, Business Banking, Texas Capital Bank: David L. Cargill
EVP, Wealth Management and Trust Services, Texas Capital Bank: David Folz
EVP, Corporate Banking, Texas Capital Bank: Russell Hartsfield
EVP, Energy Banking, Texas Capital Bank: Terry Owen McCarter
EVP and Manager of Cash Management, Texas Capital Bank: Robert T. McDaniel
EVP, Real Estate Services, Texas Capital Bank: James R. Reynolds
Chief Credit Officer: John Hudgens
Controller: Julie Anderson
Director of Finance: Dwain Howard
Director of Human Resources: Lynette Rogers
Director of Investor Relations: Myrna Vance
Marketing and Communications: Tricia Linderman
Auditors: Ernst & Young LLP

LOCATIONS

HQ: Texas Capital Bancshares, Inc.
  2100 McKinney Ave., Ste. 900, Dallas, TX 75201
Phone: 214-932-6600   **Fax:** 214-932-6604
Web: www.texascapitalbank.com

PRODUCTS/OPERATIONS

2006 Sales

	$ mil.	% of total
Interest		
Loans, including fees	211.1	82
Securities	26.3	10
Other	0.1	—
Noninterest		
Insurance commissions	4.2	2
Equipment rental income	3.9	2
Trust fee income	3.8	1
Service charges on deposit accounts	3.3	1
Other	5.7	2
Total	**258.4**	**100**

COMPETITORS

Amegy Corporation
Bank of America
BOK Financial
Comerica
Compass Bancshares
Cullen/Frost Bankers
Guaranty Financial
JPMorgan Chase
Prosperity Bancshares
State National Bancshares
Washington Mutual
Wells Fargo

HISTORICAL FINANCIALS

Company Type: Public

Income Statement				FYE: December 31
	ASSETS ($ mil.)	**NET INCOME** ($ mil.)	**INCOME AS % OF ASSETS**	**EMPLOYEES**
12/06	3,675.4	28.9	0.8%	503
12/05	3,042.2	27.2	0.9%	709
12/04	2,611.2	19.6	0.8%	—
12/03	2,192.9	13.8	0.6%	—
12/02	1,793.3	7.3	0.4%	—
Annual Growth	19.7%	41.1%	—	(29.1%)

2006 Year-End Financials

Equity as % of assets: 6.9%
Return on assets: 0.9%
Return on equity: 12.3%
Long-term debt ($ mil.): 115.7
No. of shares (mil.): 26.0
Market value ($ mil.): 516.5
Dividends
  Yield: —
  Payout: —
Sales ($ mil.): 258.4
R&D as % of sales: —
Advertising as % of sales: —

Stock History

NASDAQ (GS): TCBI

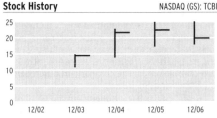

	STOCK PRICE ($) FY Close	P/E High/Low		PER SHARE ($) Earnings	Dividends	Book Value
12/06	19.88	23	17	1.09	—	9.76
12/05	22.38	24	17	1.02	—	8.39
12/04	21.62	30	19	0.75	—	7.70
12/03	14.48	24	18	0.60	—	6.97
Annual Growth	11.1%	—	—	35.9%	—	9.5%

Texas Roadhouse

You might not find Patrick Swayze at this roadhouse, but you will find plenty of ribs and steaks. Texas Roadhouse operates and franchises more than 250 of its signature steak restaurants in more than 40 states. The Southwest-themed eateries serve a variety of hand-cut steaks, ribs, chicken, and seafood, as well as freshly baked bread and other sides — but only for dinner because most locations are closed on weekday afternoons. About 160 Texas Roadhouse locations are company-owned, while the rest are franchised. Chairman Kent Taylor, a veteran of the restaurant business who has served with such chains as Metromedia Restaurant Group's Bennigan's, Hooters, and KFC, controls about 55% of the voting stock.

The company has followed a vigorous expansion strategy that is heavy on building new corporate-owned locations. In 2006 Texas Roadhouse added about 30 new eateries, 25 of which were company-operated. It also acquired about a dozen locations from franchisees. It plans to open about 30 new restaurants in 2007.

EXECUTIVES

Chairman: W. Kent Taylor, age 52, $64,615 pay
President, CEO, and Director: G. J. Hart, age 50, $759,790 pay
COO: Steven L. Ortiz, age 50, $573,260 pay
CFO: Scott M. Colosi, age 43, $309,659 pay
Director Public Relations: Juli Hart
General Counsel and Corporate Secretary: Sheila C. Brown, age 55, $191,733 pay
Auditors: KPMG LLP

LOCATIONS

HQ: Texas Roadhouse, Inc.
6040 Dutchmans Ln., Ste. 400, Louisville, KY 40205
Phone: 502-426-9984   **Fax:** 502-426-3274
Web: www.texasroadhouse.com

2006 Locations

	No.
Texas	38
Indiana	18
Ohio	18
Pennsylvania	14
Colorado	12
Tennessee	12
North Carolina	10
Georgia	9
Kentucky	9
Wisconsin	8
Illinois	7
Michigan	7
Virginia	7
Arizona	6
Florida	6
Louisiana	6
South Carolina	6
Maryland	5
Massachusetts	5
Iowa	4
Missouri	4
Oklahoma	4
Other states	36
Total	**251**

PRODUCTS/OPERATIONS

2006 Sales

	$ mil.	% of total
Restaurants	586.5	98
Franchising	10.6	2
Total	**597.1**	**100**

2006 Locations

	No.
Company-owned	163
Franchised	88
Total	**251**

COMPETITORS

Applebee's	Logan's Roadhouse
Avado Brands	Lone Star Steakhouse
Bill Miller Bar-B-Q	Metromedia
Brinker	O'Charley's
Carlson Restaurants	OSI Restaurant Partners
CBRL Group	P.F. Chang's
Cheesecake Factory	RARE Hospitality
Darden	Roadhouse Grill
Hooters	Romacorp
Houlihan's	Ruby Tuesday
Johnny Carino's	Stuart Anderson's
Landry's	

HISTORICAL FINANCIALS

Company Type: Public

Income Statement

FYE: Last Tuesday in December

	REVENUE ($ mil.)	NET INCOME ($ mil.)	NET PROFIT MARGIN	EMPLOYEES
12/06	597.1	34.0	5.7%	19,000
12/05	458.8	30.3	6.6%	14,900
12/04	363.0	21.7	6.0%	—
12/03	286.5	23.1	8.1%	—
12/02	232.8	17.0	7.3%	—
Annual Growth	**26.6%**	**18.9%**	**—**	**27.5%**

2006 Year-End Financials

Debt ratio: 11.1%
Return on equity: 12.3%
Cash ($ mil.): 33.8
Current ratio: 0.67
Long-term debt ($ mil.): 35.4
No. of shares (mil.): 69.0
Dividends
  Yield: —
  Payout: —
Market value ($ mil.): 915.7
R&D as % of sales: —
Advertising as % of sales: —

Stock History

NASDAQ (GS): TXRH

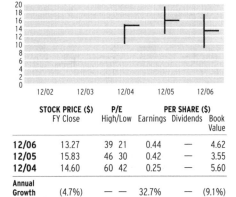

	STOCK PRICE ($) FY Close	P/E High	P/E Low	PER SHARE ($) Earnings	PER SHARE ($) Dividends	PER SHARE ($) Book Value
12/06	13.27	39	21	0.44	—	4.62
12/05	15.83	46	30	0.42	—	3.55
12/04	14.60	60	42	0.25	—	5.60
Annual Growth	**(4.7%)**	**—**	**—**	**32.7%**	**—**	**(9.1%)**

TGC Industries

It might have flopped in the movie theaters, but 3-D technology works in the oil patch, and for TGC Industries. From its inception, TGC Industries has conducted seismic surveys for oil exploration companies in the US. The company principally employs land surveys using Sercel/Opseis Eagle seismic systems, which obtain 3-D seismic data related to subsurface geological features. Employing radio-frequency telemetry and multichannel recorders, the system enables the exploration of rivers, swamps, and inaccessible terrain. TGC Industries also sells gravity information from its data bank to oil and gas exploration companies.

Tidelands Geophysical was founded in 1967 to conduct seismic, gravity, and magnetic surveys for oil and gas companies. It was acquired by Supreme Industries (formerly ESI Industries) in 1980. Tidelands changed its name to TGC Industries in 1986, and the company was spun off that year.

EXECUTIVES

President, CEO, and Director: Wayne A. Whitener, age 55, $350,000 pay
CFO, Treasurer, and Secretary: Kenneth W. (Ken) Uselton, age 64, $96,751 pay
VP: Daniel G. Winn, age 56, $143,521 pay
Auditors: Lane Gorman Trubitt, L.L.P.

LOCATIONS

HQ: TGC Industries, Inc.
101 E. Park Blvd., Ste. 955, Plano, TX 75074
Phone: 972-881-1099   **Fax:** 972-424-3943
Web: www.tgcseismic.com

TGC Industries operates from its facility in Plano, Texas.

COMPETITORS

Dawson Geophysical
ION Geophysical
Landmark Graphics
Seitel
WesternGeco

HISTORICAL FINANCIALS

Company Type: Public

Income Statement

FYE: December 31

	REVENUE ($ mil.)	NET INCOME ($ mil.)	NET PROFIT MARGIN	EMPLOYEES
12/06	67.8	8.1	11.9%	481
12/05	30.9	6.2	20.1%	152
12/04	20.1	2.9	14.4%	—
12/03	8.5	0.6	7.1%	—
12/02	6.3	(1.7)	—	—
Annual Growth	**81.1%**	**—**	**—**	**216.4%**

2006 Year-End Financials

Debt ratio: 8.7%
Return on equity: 26.3%
Cash ($ mil.): 9.4
Current ratio: 1.07
Long-term debt ($ mil.): 3.1
No. of shares (mil.): 15.7
Dividends
  Yield: —
  Payout: —
Market value ($ mil.): 118.4
R&D as % of sales: —
Advertising as % of sales: —

Stock History

AMEX: TGE

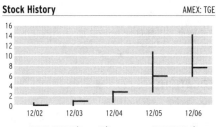

	STOCK PRICE ($) FY Close	P/E High	P/E Low	PER SHARE ($) Earnings	PER SHARE ($) Dividends	PER SHARE ($) Book Value
12/06	7.54	29	12	0.49	—	2.23
12/05	5.87	24	6	0.44	—	1.79
12/04	2.67	13	3	0.22	—	0.75
12/03	0.86	25	2	0.04	—	0.34
12/02	0.06	—	—	(0.34)	—	0.25
Annual Growth	**234.8%**	**—**	**—**	**—**	**—**	**73.4%**

Theragenics Corporation

Theragenics helped former New York City Mayor Rudolph Giuliani win a fight against cancer, but it couldn't win him a Senate seat. The firm's TheraSeed product, used to treat Giuliani's prostate cancer, is a radioactive implant about the size of a grain of rice. The seeds are implanted in early stage prostate tumors and release radiation that kills cancerous cells with minimal damage to surrounding healthy tissue. Palladium-103, produced by Theragenics, is the radiation source. Theragenics also provides a variety of vascular and wound care products, including sutures, needles, and guidewires, used in surgery. C. R. Bard distributes TheraSeed.

Theragenics expanded its surgical product business through the acquisition of Galt Medical, which develops devices used in radiology and cardiology, in 2006.

In April 2005 the company bought CP Medical, a medical device maker, as part of a plan to focus on its brachytherapy (radiation treatment) offerings and its medical device products. Later that year Theragenics restructured its operations, including closing two facilities, discontinuing radiochemical and plasma separation technology development, and halting its vascular, macular degeneration (eye disease leading to loss of vision), and breast cancer research.

EXECUTIVES

Chairman, President, and CEO: M. Christine Jacobs, age 56, $525,175 pay (prior to promotion)
CFO and Treasurer: Frank J. Tarallo, age 47, $265,000 pay
EVP, Organizational Development: R. Michael O'Bannon, age 57, $196,000 pay
EVP, Strategy and Business Development: Bruce W. Smith, age 54, $275,000 pay
President, CP Medical: Patrick J. Ferguson, age 50, $230,000 pay
President, Galt Medical: James Eddings
Chief Medical Director: Peter J. Fitzgerald
Auditors: Grant Thornton LLP

LOCATIONS

HQ: Theragenics Corporation
5203 Bristol Industrial Way, Buford, GA 30518
Phone: 770-271-0233   **Fax:** 770-831-5294
Web: www.theragenics.com

Theragenics has facilities in Georgia and Oregon.

PRODUCTS/OPERATIONS

2006 Sales

	$ mil.	% of total
Brachytherapy	34.9	64
Surgical products	19.4	36
Adjustment	(0.2)	—
Total	**54.1**	**100**

COMPETITORS

AngioDynamics	Mentor Corporation
Boston Scientific	Merit Medical Systems
C. R. Bard	North American Scientific
Endocare	TAP Pharmaceutical
Enpath Medical	Terumo Medical
Ethicon	Varian Medical Systems
LabCorp	

HISTORICAL FINANCIALS
Company Type: Public

Income Statement
FYE: December 31

	REVENUE ($ mil.)	NET INCOME ($ mil.)	NET PROFIT MARGIN	EMPLOYEES
12/06	54.1	6.9	12.8%	315
12/05	44.3	(29.0)	—	219
12/04	33.3	(4.3)	—	—
12/03	35.6	(0.3)	—	—
12/02	41.9	5.6	13.4%	167
Annual Growth	**6.6%**	**5.4%**	**—**	**17.2%**

2006 Year-End Financials

Debt ratio: 5.9%	Dividends	
Return on equity: 5.7%	Yield: —	
Cash ($ mil.): 33.0	Payout: —	
Current ratio: 14.30	Market value ($ mil.): 102.6	
Long-term debt ($ mil.): 7.5	R&D as % of sales: —	
No. of shares (mil.): 33.1	Advertising as % of sales: —	

Stock History
NYSE: TGX

	STOCK PRICE ($) FY Close	P/E High/Low	Earnings	PER SHARE ($) Dividends	Book Value
12/06	3.10	19 12	0.21	—	3.81
12/05	3.02	— —	(0.93)	—	3.61
12/04	4.06	— —	(0.14)	—	4.60
12/03	5.47	— —	(0.01)	—	4.75
12/02	4.03	55 18	0.19	—	4.76
Annual Growth	**(6.3%)**	**— —**	**2.5%**	**—**	**(5.4%)**

Thomas Group

At consulting firm Thomas Group, watching the clock is encouraged. Thomas Group aims to help its clients reduce manufacturing time, streamline product development, and generally improve performance. Customers have included automotive manufacturers, financial services firms, technology companies, and government agencies. Contracts involving the US Navy accounted for more than 90% of the company's sales in 2006. Thomas Group operates from offices in Dallas, Detroit, and Hong Kong; nearly all of its sales come from the US. Director Edward Evans owns about 36% of Thomas Group; chairman John Chain, a retired Air Force general, owns about 30%.

EXECUTIVES

Chairman: John T. Chain Jr., age 72
President, CEO, and Director: James T. (Jim) Taylor, age 60
SVP Healthcare: Gary B. Morrison
SVP Sales: Trent Humphries
SVP Sales: Sam Callesen
SVP Transportation Business: John Nussrallah

VP, CFO, Secretary, and Treasurer: Michael J. Barhydt
VP Marketing: P. J. Hoke
VP Human Resources: Kerry Shaughnessy
VP Strategy and Alliances: Josh R. Ridker
VP; President, North America, Government: James C. (Jimmy) Houlditch, age 69, $2,958,808 pay
President, Government and Air Force: Thad Wolfe
President, Government Operations: Tom Zych

LOCATIONS

HQ: Thomas Group, Inc.
5221 N. O'Connor Blvd., Ste. 500, Irving, TX 75039
Phone: 972-869-3400   **Fax:** 972-443-1742
Web: www.thomasgroup.com

COMPETITORS

Accenture
A.T. Kearney
Bain & Company
BearingPoint
Booz Allen
Boston Consulting
Capgemini
Celerant Consulting
Deloitte Consulting
FTI Consulting
Huron Consulting
Management Network Group
McKinsey & Company

HISTORICAL FINANCIALS
Company Type: Public

Income Statement
FYE: December 31

	REVENUE ($ mil.)	NET INCOME ($ mil.)	NET PROFIT MARGIN	EMPLOYEES
12/06	59.5	11.5	19.3%	155
12/05	43.1	6.8	15.8%	147
12/04	30.0	1.5	5.0%	108
12/03	30.4	0.7	2.3%	—
12/02	33.2	(7.7)	—	—
Annual Growth	**15.7%**	**—**	**—**	**19.8%**

2006 Year-End Financials

Debt ratio: 0.5%	Dividends	
Return on equity: 84.9%	Yield: 2.0%	
Cash ($ mil.): 8.5	Payout: 28.8%	
Current ratio: 4.57	Market value ($ mil.): 164.5	
Long-term debt ($ mil.): 0.1	R&D as % of sales: —	
No. of shares (mil.): 10.9	Advertising as % of sales: —	

Stock History
NASDAQ (GM): TGIS

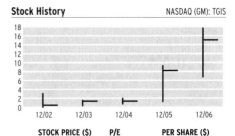

	STOCK PRICE ($) FY Close	P/E High/Low	Earnings	PER SHARE ($) Dividends	Book Value
12/06	15.04	17 7	1.04	0.30	1.71
12/05	8.20	15 2	0.63	0.05	0.79
12/04	1.35	14 5	0.14	—	0.25
12/03	1.35	21 5	0.07	—	0.07
12/02	0.45	— —	(1.39)	—	0.00
Annual Growth	**140.4%**	**— —**	**—**	**500.0%**	**—**

TIB Financial

TIB Financial is the holding company for TIB Bank, which operates more than 15 branches in South Florida's Collier, Dade, Highlands, Lee, and Monroe counties. In 2007 TIB Financial bought the The Bank of Venice, which has two locations in Venice, Florida, and kept its name after the acquisition. Serving individuals and local businesses, the banks offer checking and savings accounts, NOW accounts, CDs, and IRAs. Commercial real estate loans make up slightly more than half of the company's loan portfolio, which also includes commercial, residential mortgage, business, consumer, construction, and land loans. TIB Bank also originates government-guaranteed loans and indirect loans through automobile dealerships.

EXECUTIVES

Chairman: Thomas J. Longe, age 44
President, CEO, and Director; President and CEO, TIB Bank: Edward V. Lett, age 61
EVP, CFO, and Treasurer; CFO, TIB Bank: Stephen J. (Steve) Gilhooly, age 54
President and CEO, TIB Bank: Michael D. Carrigan, age 55
EVP and COO, TIB Bank: Andrew D. (Andy) Wallace
EVP and Treasurer, TIB Bank: David P. Johnson, age 51, $201,500 pay (prior to title change)
EVP, TIB Bank and Southwest Florida Relationship Executive: Millard J. Younkers Jr., age 63, $230,500 pay
EVP and Chief Administration Officer, TIB Bank: Edward J. (Ed) Crann
EVP, TIB Bank; CEO Southwest Florida Market: Alma R. Shuckhart, age 57
Investor Relations: Connie Miller
President, TIB Investment Center: John Scott
Director; Chairman and CEO, The Bank of Venice: David F. Voigt, age 66
President and CEO, The Bank of Venice: Mack R. Wilcox Jr.
Human Resources Officer, TIB Bank of the Keys: Connie Dixon

LOCATIONS

HQ: TIB Financial Corp.
599 9th St. North, Ste. 101, Naples, FL 34102
Phone: 239-263-3344 **Fax:** 305-451-6241
Web: www.tibbank.com

PRODUCTS/OPERATIONS

2006 Sales

	$ mil.	% of total
Interest		
Loans, including fees	78.4	86
Investment securities	5.8	6
Other	1.0	1
Noninterest		
Service charges on deposit accounts	2.5	3
Fees on mortgage loans sold	1.6	2
Other	2.2	2
Total	**91.5**	**100**

COMPETITORS

Bank of America
Colonial BancGroup
Fifth Third
Home BancShares
Regions Financial
SunTrust
Wachovia

HISTORICAL FINANCIALS
Company Type: Public

Income Statement
FYE: December 31

	ASSETS ($ mil.)	NET INCOME ($ mil.)	INCOME AS % OF ASSETS	EMPLOYEES
12/06	1,319.1	9.3	0.7%	348
12/05	1,076.1	11.8	1.1%	344
12/04	829.3	5.2	0.6%	—
12/03	669.3	5.1	0.8%	—
12/02	567.0	4.7	0.8%	269
Annual Growth	**23.5%**	**18.6%**	**—**	**6.6%**

2006 Year-End Financials

Equity as % of assets: 6.5%	Dividends
Return on assets: 0.8%	Yield: 1.3%
Return on equity: 11.4%	Payout: 30.8%
Long-term debt ($ mil.): 37.0	Sales ($ mil.): 91.5
No. of shares (mil.): 11.7	R&D as % of sales: —
Market value ($ mil.): 205.0	Advertising as % of sales: —

Stock History
NASDAQ (GM): TIBB

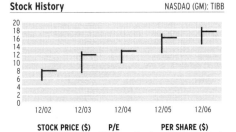

	STOCK PRICE ($) FY Close	P/E High/Low	PER SHARE ($) Earnings	Dividends	Book Value
12/06	17.49	24 19	0.78	0.24	7.33
12/05	15.99	17 12	1.00	0.23	13.38
12/04	12.69	27 21	0.47	0.17	11.99
12/03	11.80	22 13	0.57	0.22	9.31
12/02	7.89	14 10	0.57	0.16	8.30
Annual Growth	**22.0%**	**— —**	**8.2%**	**10.7%**	**(3.1%)**

Tidelands Bancshares

Tidelands Bancshares has got its feet wet while wading out into the sea of regional banking. Tidelands Bancshares is the holding company for Tidelands Bank, which opened in October 2003 with an office in Mount Pleasant, South Carolina. The bank offers traditional retail services and products such as checking and savings accounts, money market accounts, and commercial and consumer loans. Tidelands Bank also operates loan production offices in Summerville and Myrtle Beach, South Carolina. The company plans to expand with new stores in the tri-state area.

Company executives and directors collectively own nearly one-quarter of Tidelands Bancshares. A branch in the West Park section of Mount Pleasant, South Carolina has been opened and plans for another full-service branch in West Ashley have been made.

EXECUTIVES

Chairman: Barry I. Kalinsky, age 46
President, CEO, and Director, Tidelands Bancshares and Tidelands Bank: Robert E. (Chip) Coffee Jr., age 59, $319,500 pay
EVP and CFO, Tidelands Bancshares and Tidelands Bank: Alan W. Jackson, age 45, $237,996 pay
EVP; EVP and Chief Administrative Officer, Tidelands Bank: Thomas H. Lyles
EVP and Chief Credit Officer, Tidelands Bancshares and Tidelands Bank: Milon C. Smith, age 56
EVP and Senior Commercial Lender, Tidelands Bank: Robert H. (Bobby) Mathewes Jr., age 40, $237,996 pay
SVP and Mid-Coast Executive, Tidelands Bank: Kenneth M. (Ken) Pickens
SVP, Commercial Lending, and North Coast Executive, Tidelands Bank: James A. (Jimmy) Kimbell III
VP Human Resources and Legal Administration, Tidelands Bank: Pamela Dada
Auditors: Elliott Davis LLC

LOCATIONS

HQ: Tidelands Bancshares, Inc.
875 Lowcountry Blvd., Mt. Pleasant, SC 29464
Phone: 843-388-8433 **Fax:** 843-388-8081
Web: www.tidelandsbank.com

COMPETITORS

Bank of South Carolina
Coastal Banking Company
Community Bankshares
First Financial Holdings
Regions Financial
Southcoast Financial
Synovus

HISTORICAL FINANCIALS
Company Type: Public

Income Statement
FYE: December 31

	ASSETS ($ mil.)	NET INCOME ($ mil.)	INCOME AS % OF ASSETS	EMPLOYEES
12/06	336.6	1.5	0.4%	68
12/05	206.4	0.0	—	—
12/04	75.6	(0.8)	—	—
12/03	28.7	(0.5)	—	—
12/02	0.3	(0.6)	—	1
Annual Growth	**478.8%**	**—**	**—**	**187.2%**

2006 Year-End Financials

Equity as % of assets: 12.4%	Dividends
Return on assets: 0.6%	Yield: —
Return on equity: 4.6%	Payout: —
Long-term debt ($ mil.): 8.3	Sales ($ mil.): 22.7
No. of shares (mil.): 4.3	R&D as % of sales: —
Market value ($ mil.): 65.8	Advertising as % of sales: —

Stock History
NASDAQ (GM): TDBK

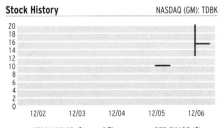

	STOCK PRICE ($) FY Close	P/E High/Low	PER SHARE ($) Earnings	Dividends	Book Value
12/06	15.39	45 28	0.44	—	9.79
12/05	9.98	499 499	0.02	—	7.59
Annual Growth	**54.2%**	**— —**	**2,100.0%**	**—**	**29.0%**

TierOne Corporation

TierOne Corporation is the holding company for TierOne Bank, which operates approximately 70 branches throughout Nebraska, northern Kansas, and southwestern Iowa. It also has about 10 loan production offices in Arizona, Colorado, Florida, Minnesota, and North Carolina. Serving consumers and businesses, the bank offers a variety of deposit products, including different checking options, savings and retirement accounts, and CDs. Funds gathered are generally used to originate real estate loans, with residential construction loans comprising some 20% of the company's loan portfolio. TierOne also issues consumer and business loans. Maryland-based lender CapitalSource is buying the company.

EXECUTIVES

Chairman and CEO, TierOne Corporation and TierOne Bank: Gilbert G. Lundstrom, age 65, $581,715 pay
President, COO, and Director, TierOne Corporation and TierOne Bank: James A. Laphen, age 58, $396,923 pay
EVP, CFO, Corporate Secretary, and Treasurer: Eugene B. Witkowicz, age 59, $183,068 pay
EVP and Director Lending, TierOne Bank: Gale R. Furnas, age 53, $200,883 pay
EVP and Director Retail Banking, TierOne Bank: Roger R. Ludemann, age 58
EVP and Director Administration, TierOne Bank: Larry L. Pfeil, age 64, $164,096 pay
SVP and Human Resources Officer, TierOne Bank: Paula J. Luther
Auditors: KPMG LLP

LOCATIONS

HQ: TierOne Corporation
1235 N St., Lincoln, NE 68508
Phone: 402-475-0521   **Fax:** 402-435-0427
Web: www.tieronebank.com

PRODUCTS/OPERATIONS

2006 Sales

	% of total
Interest	
Loans receivable	85
Investment securities & other	3
Noninterest	
Fees & service charges	9
Debit card fees	1
Other	2
Total	**100**

COMPETITORS

Great Western	Union Bank & Trust
Lincoln Bancorp	U.S. Bancorp
Pinnacle Bancorp	Wells Fargo

HISTORICAL FINANCIALS

Company Type: Public

Income Statement

FYE: December 31

	ASSETS ($ mil.)	NET INCOME ($ mil.)	INCOME AS % OF ASSETS	EMPLOYEES
12/06	3,431.2	41.3	1.2%	850
12/05	3,222.3	32.8	1.0%	772
12/04	3,048.1	23.9	0.8%	—
12/03	2,207.9	23.8	1.1%	—
12/02	1,945.5	15.0	0.8%	—
Annual Growth	**15.2%**	**28.8%**	**—**	**10.1%**

2006 Year-End Financials

Equity as % of assets: 10.3%	Dividends
Return on assets: 1.2%	Yield: 0.9%
Return on equity: 12.5%	Payout: 11.2%
Long-term debt ($ mil.): —	Sales ($ mil.): 253.4
No. of shares (mil.): 18.0	R&D as % of sales: —
Market value ($ mil.): 570.3	Advertising as % of sales: —

Stock History

NASDAQ (GS): TONE

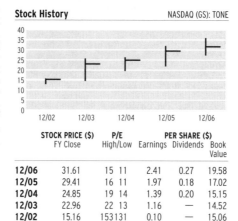

	STOCK PRICE ($) FY Close	P/E High/Low	PER SHARE ($) Earnings	Dividends	Book Value
12/06	31.61	15 11	2.41	0.27	19.58
12/05	29.41	16 11	1.97	0.18	17.02
12/04	24.85	19 14	1.39	0.20	15.15
12/03	22.96	22 13	1.16	—	14.52
12/02	15.16	153 131	0.10	—	15.06
Annual Growth	**20.2%**	**— —**	**121.6%**	**16.2%**	**6.8%**

Titan Machinery

Titan Machinery is a big dealer to farmers and builders in the Midwest. It sells and rents new and used agricultural and construction equipment through its 33 retail locations located in North Dakota, South Dakota, Minnesota, and Iowa. Farming equipment includes excavators, seeders, tillers, and tractors; it offers such construction machinery as earthmoving equipment and cranes.

Titan primarily deals in products manufactured by CNH which are sold under the Case and New Holland brands; other brands on offer include K-Tec and Grove. The company also sells parts and provides maintenance and repair services.

Titan has fueled its growth, in part, through acquisitions. The company has bought 13 rival dealerships since 2003 and added 29 retail locations in the process. It has said that it will continue to seek out new candidates for purchase in the future.

Chairman and CEO David Meyer owns 55% of the company.

EXECUTIVES

Chairman and CEO: David J. Meyer, age 54
President, CFO, and Director: Peter Christianson, age 50
VP, Finance and Treasurer: Ted Christianson, age 48
Human Resources: Josh Koehnen
Auditors: Eide Bailly LLP

LOCATIONS

HQ: Titan Machinery Inc.
4876 Rocking Horse Cr., Fargo, ND 58104
Phone: 701-356-0130   **Fax:** 701-356-0139
Web: titanmachinery.com

PRODUCTS/OPERATIONS

2007 Sales

	$ mil.	% of total
Equipment	220.9	76
Parts	42.6	15
Service	22.0	7
Other	7.1	2
Total	**292.6**	**100**

COMPETITORS

Caterpillar
Deere
RDO Equipment

HISTORICAL FINANCIALS

Company Type: Public

Income Statement

FYE: January 31

	REVENUE ($ mil.)	NET INCOME ($ mil.)	NET PROFIT MARGIN	EMPLOYEES
1/07	292.6	3.7	1.3%	555
1/06	228.5	2.7	1.2%	—
1/05	162.2	1.3	0.8%	—
Annual Growth	**34.3%**	**68.7%**	**—**	**—**

2007 Year-End Financials

Debt ratio: 53.8%	Current ratio: 1.27
Return on equity: 28.2%	Long-term debt ($ mil.): 8.0
Cash ($ mil.): 7.6	

Net Income History

NASDAQ (GM): TITN

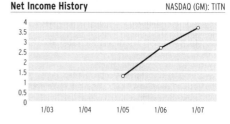

Toreador Resources

Toreador Resources is looking to the bull market in oil prices to lift its revenues. The oil and gas explorer, which focuses on exploration opportunities in the international arena, owns royalty and mineral interests in properties located in France, Hungary, Romania, and Turkey. In 2004 the company sold its active US hydrocarbon properties, but owns 5.5 million gross acres (4.2 million net) of undeveloped land in Kansas, Louisiana, New Mexico, Oklahoma, and Texas. Toreador, which in 2006 had proved reserves of 16 million barrels of oil equivalent, sells its oil and gas to refiners and pipeline companies.

Toreador owns 35% of property auction Web site EnergyNet.com and has partial stakes in 3-D seismic projects. In 2005 Toreador reported a natural gas strike at its 37%-owned Akkaya-1 well in Turkey. In 2005 the company acquired Pogo Hungary from Pogo Producing for approximately $9 million.

EXECUTIVES

Chairman: John M. McLaughlin, age 76
President, CEO, and Director: Nigel J. B. Lovett, age 61
EVP Exploration and Operations: Michael J. FitzGerald, age 56, $270,000 pay
SVP Exploration and Production: Edward Ramirez, age 56
VP Finance and Accounting and Chief Accounting Officer: Charles J. Campise, age 56
VP Investor Relations: Stewart P. Yee
VP Technical: William J. Moulton, age 48
Corporate Secretary: Shirley Anderson
Auditors: Grant Thornton LLP

LOCATIONS

HQ: Toreador Resources Corporation
4809 Cole Ave., Ste. 108, Dallas, TX 75205
Phone: 214-559-3933　　**Fax:** 214-559-3945
Web: www.toreador.net

2006 Sales

	$ mil.	% of total
France	27.3	68
US	7.1	18
Turkey	3.8	9
Romania	2.2	5
Total	**40.4**	**100**

COMPETITORS

Avenue Group
Koç
Regal Petroleum
Sabanci
TOTAL
Tullow Oil

HISTORICAL FINANCIALS

Company Type: Public

Income Statement

FYE: December 31

	REVENUE ($ mil.)	NET INCOME ($ mil.)	NET PROFIT MARGIN	EMPLOYEES
12/06	40.4	2.6	6.4%	96
12/05	31.1	10.6	34.1%	67
12/04	21.0	25.0	119.0%	—
12/03	17.9	2.4	13.4%	—
12/02	23.9	(6.1)	—	40
Annual Growth	**14.0%**	**—**	**—**	**24.5%**

2006 Year-End Financials

Debt ratio: 73.3%
Return on equity: 1.9%
Cash ($ mil.): 33.2
Current ratio: 1.32
Long-term debt ($ mil.): 107.8
No. of shares (mil.): 15.9
Dividends
　Yield: —
　Payout: —
Market value ($ mil.): 410.6
R&D as % of sales: —
Advertising as % of sales: —

Stock History

NASDAQ (GM): TRGL

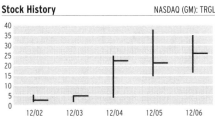

	STOCK PRICE ($) FY Close	P/E High/Low		PER SHARE ($) Earnings	Dividends	Book Value
12/06	25.77	230	110	0.15	—	9.23
12/05	21.07	57	23	0.65	—	8.58
12/04	22.19	12	2	1.97	—	5.75
12/03	4.65	23	10	0.20	—	4.00
12/02	2.51	—	—	(0.69)	—	3.21
Annual Growth	**79.0%**	**—**	**—**	**—**	**—**	**30.2%**

Tower Financial

This tower aims to be a power in Indiana. Tower Financial is the holding company for Tower Bank & Trust, which was formed in 1999 to fill the void in community banking services left in the wake of the consolidation of local banks into national banking companies. Targeting individuals and small to midsized businesses, the bank has nearly ten branches and loan production offices, mainly in and around Fort Wayne. It focuses mainly on commercial lending, with business mortgages and operating loans making up around three-quarters of its loan portfolio. It also issues residential mortgages and personal loans. Deposit products include checking, savings, and money market accounts, and CDs.

Formed in 2006, Tower Trust Company offers investment management and trust services. Also that year Tower Financial announced plans to form Tower Bank of Central Indiana. The company will own 51% of the new bank, which will be based in Indianapolis.

EXECUTIVES

Chairman, President, and CEO, Tower Financial and Tower Bank: Donald F. Schenkel, age 66, $376,299 pay
COO and Director; CEO, Tower Financial and Tower Bank & Trust: Michael D. Cahill, age 47, $220,769 pay (prior to promotion)
CFO and Secretary: Richard R. Sawyer, age 42
EVP; President and CEO, Tower Trust Company: Gary D. Shearer, age 43, $179,860 pay
EVP and Chief Lending Officer: Darrell L. Jaggers, age 60, $145,923 pay (prior to title change)
SVP, Business Services, Tower Bank & Trust: James E. Underwood
SVP: William Olds Jr.
First VP and CIO, Tower Bank & Trust: Michael A. Rice
VP, Marketing and Public Relations, Tower Bank & Trust: Trois K. Hart
Human Resources Officer, Tower Bank & Trust: Tina DeMeritt

LOCATIONS

HQ: Tower Financial Corporation
116 E. Berry St., Fort Wayne, IN 46802
Phone: 260-427-7000　　**Fax:** 260-427-7180
Web: www.towerbank.net

PRODUCTS/OPERATIONS

2006 Sales

	$ mil.	% of total
Interest		
Loans, including fees	37.7	82
Securities	2.8	6
Other	0.6	1
Noninterest		
Trust & brokerage fees	2.8	6
Other	2.3	5
Total	**46.2**	**100**

COMPETITORS

1st Source
Fifth Third
National City
STAR Financial Group
Wells Fargo

HISTORICAL FINANCIALS

Company Type: Public

Income Statement

FYE: December 31

	ASSETS ($ mil.)	NET INCOME ($ mil.)	INCOME AS % OF ASSETS	EMPLOYEES
12/06	671.2	3.7	0.6%	192
12/05	557.8	3.4	0.6%	158
12/04	481.1	2.5	0.5%	—
12/03	436.5	1.8	0.4%	—
12/02	377.3	1.7	0.5%	98
Annual Growth	**15.5%**	**21.5%**	**—**	**18.3%**

2006 Year-End Financials

Equity as % of assets: 7.6%
Return on assets: 0.6%
Return on equity: 7.5%
Long-term debt ($ mil.): 17.5
No. of shares (mil.): 4.0
Market value ($ mil.): 72.1
Dividends
　Yield: 0.9%
　Payout: 18.0%
Sales ($ mil.): 46.2
R&D as % of sales: —
Advertising as % of sales: —

Stock History

NASDAQ (GM): TOFC

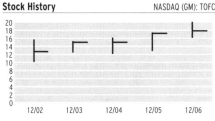

	STOCK PRICE ($) FY Close	P/E High/Low		PER SHARE ($) Earnings	Dividends	Book Value
12/06	17.82	22	18	0.89	0.16	12.60
12/05	17.20	21	15	0.84	—	11.79
12/04	15.00	26	20	0.61	—	10.99
12/03	15.00	34	28	0.45	—	10.38
12/02	12.69	28	18	0.56	—	9.96
Annual Growth	**8.9%**	**—**	**—**	**12.3%**	**—**	**6.0%**

Tower Group

Tower Group is hoping to rise high in the insurance business. Through subsidiaries Tower Insurance Company of New York and Tower National Insurance Company, the firm sells specialty commercial and personal property/casualty insurance to individuals and small to midsized businesses in New York, New Jersey, and Massachusetts; it also sells commercial lines in several other northeastern states. Its commercial products include auto, general liability, and workers' compensation coverage in the retail, wholesale, service, real estate, and construction industries. Its personal insurance lines focus on homeowners policies for modestly priced homes, primarily in the New York City area.

Tower Group has been expanding its operations into New Jersey and other eastern seaboard states; it acquired Preserver Group, which sells commercial and personal lines in eight northeastern states, in 2007. In addition to increasing Tower's premium volume, the Preserver acquisition expands its distribution network of retail agencies in the region.

The previous year Tower Group had bought shell insurance company North American Lumber Insurance (since renamed Tower National

Insurance Company, or TNIC), acquiring licenses in 11 northeastern states. The company has increased TNIC's licensing to include more than two dozen states.

Through its general agency subsidiary Tower Risk Management, Tower Group earns commissions on policies it sells for other providers. Tower Risk Management also provides underwriting, claims administration, and reinsurance intermediary services.

Tower Group plans to cede nearly half of its written premiums to Bermuda-based reinsurer CastlePoint Holdings, whose formation it sponsored. It owns about 10% of CastlePoint, and its CEO Michael Lee also helms the reinsurance provider. Lee owns 14% of Tower Group.

EXECUTIVES

Chairman, President, and CEO: Michael H. Lee, age 49, $875,000 pay
SVP and COO: Patrick J. Haveron
SVP, CFO, Treasurer, and Director: Francis M. (Frank) Colalucci, age 62, $321,911 pay
SVP and CIO: Jerome (Jerry) Kaiser, age 50
SVP and Chief Underwriting Officer: Gary S. Maier, age 42
SVP Branch Management: Eugene B. Kelly, age 54
SVP Operations: Laurie Ranegar, age 45
SVP Marketing and Distribution: Christian K. Pechmann, age 57, $280,000 pay
SVP and General Counsel: Stephen L. Kibblehouse, age 51
Managing VP and Controller: Brian Finkelstein
Managing VP Human Resources: Catherine M. Wragg
Managing VP and Chief Accounting Officer: Michael Haines
Marketing and Corporate Communications: Eugenie M. McKay

LOCATIONS

HQ: Tower Group, Inc.
120 Broadway, 14th Fl., New York, NY 10271
Phone: 212-655-2000   **Fax:** 212-655-2199
Web: www.twrgrp.com

PRODUCTS/OPERATIONS

2006 Sales

	$ mil.	% of total
Net premiums earned	224.0	75
Ceding commission revenue	43.1	14
Net investment income	23.0	8
Insurance services revenue	8.0	3
Policy billing fees	1.2	0
Total	**299.3**	**100**

COMPETITORS

ACE Limited
AIG
Allstate
CNA Financial
Erie Insurance Group
GNY Insurance Companies
Hanover Insurance
The Hartford
Magna Carta Companies
Middlesex Mutual
Nationwide
OneBeacon
Preferred Mutual
Safeco
Selective Insurance
State Farm
Travelers Companies
Utica Mutual Insurance

HISTORICAL FINANCIALS

Company Type: Public

Income Statement

FYE: December 31

	ASSETS ($ mil.)	NET INCOME ($ mil.)	INCOME AS % OF ASSETS	EMPLOYEES
12/06	954.1	36.8	3.9%	403
12/05	657.5	20.8	3.2%	360
12/04	494.1	9.0	1.8%	—
12/03	286.0	6.3	2.2%	—
12/02	186.1	5.6	3.0%	—
Annual Growth	**50.5%**	**60.1%**	**—**	**11.9%**

2006 Year-End Financials

Equity as % of assets: 19.3%
Return on assets: 4.6%
Return on equity: 22.4%
Long-term debt ($ mil.): 68.0
No. of shares (mil.): 23.1
Market value ($ mil.): 717.8
Dividends
　Yield: 0.3%
　Payout: 5.5%
Sales ($ mil.): 299.3
R&D as % of sales: —
Advertising as % of sales: —

Stock History

NASDAQ (GS): TWGP

	STOCK PRICE ($) FY Close	P/E High/Low	Earnings	PER SHARE ($) Dividends	Book Value
12/06	31.07	20　9	1.82	0.10	9.69
12/05	21.98	23　10	1.03	0.10	7.29
12/04	12.00	12　8	1.06	0.03	6.56
Annual Growth	**60.9%**	**— —**	**31.0%**	**82.6%**	**21.6%**

TradeStation Group

TradeStation is chugging along two tracks in the financial services and software markets. The company offers an electronic trading platform to provide commission-based, direct-access online brokerage services. The platform helps investors develop custom trading strategies and executes orders for equities and futures. Subsidiary TradeStation Technologies offers the TradeStation platform as either a hosted subscription-based service or a licensed software package, and it operates an online trading strategy community site. Brothers, co-founders, and co-CEOs William and Ralph Cruz collectively control just under 50% of the company.

EXECUTIVES

Co-Chairman: William R. (Bill) Cruz, age 46
Co-Chairman; Director, TradeStation Securities: Ralph L. Cruz, age 43
President and CEO: Salomon Sredni, age 39

VP Finance, CFO, Treasurer and Principal Accounting Officer: David H. Fleischman, age 61, $330,000 pay
VP Corporate Development, General Counsel, and Secretary; Director, TradeStation Securities and TradeStation Technologies: Marc J. Stone, age 46, $330,000 pay
VP Strategic Relations: Janette Perez
VP Product Development, TradeStation Technologies: T. Keith Black, age 44
Chief Marketing Officer: John Roberts
Chief Growth Officer; President, TradeStation Securities: Joseph (Joe) Nikolson, age 39
Director, Human Resources: Lenia Echemendia
Auditors: Ernst & Young LLP

LOCATIONS

HQ: TradeStation Group, Inc.
8050 SW 10th St., Ste. 4000, Plantation, FL 33324
Phone: 954-652-7000   **Fax:** 954-652-7300
Web: www.tradestation.com

COMPETITORS

Bank of America
Charles Schwab
E*TRADE Financial
Interactive Brokers
JPMorgan Chase
Merrill Lynch
TD Ameritrade
Terra Nova Gold
UBS Financial Services

HISTORICAL FINANCIALS

Company Type: Public

Income Statement

FYE: December 31

	REVENUE ($ mil.)	NET INCOME ($ mil.)	NET PROFIT MARGIN	EMPLOYEES
12/06	128.6	31.0	24.1%	302
12/05	100.5	21.1	21.0%	266
12/04	71.8	14.7	20.5%	—
12/03	60.2	11.6	19.3%	—
12/02	48.4	1.8	3.7%	230
Annual Growth	**27.7%**	**103.7%**	**—**	**7.0%**

2006 Year-End Financials

Debt ratio: —
Return on equity: 30.9%
Cash ($ mil.): 492.0
Current ratio: —
Long-term debt ($ mil.): —
No. of shares (mil.): 44.7
Dividends
　Yield: —
　Payout: —
Market value ($ mil.): 614.4
R&D as % of sales: —
Advertising as % of sales: —

Stock History

NASDAQ (GS): TRAD

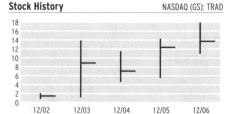

	STOCK PRICE ($) FY Close	P/E High/Low	Earnings	PER SHARE ($) Dividends	Book Value
12/06	13.75	27　17	0.67	—	2.65
12/05	12.38	30　12	0.48	—	1.87
12/04	7.03	35　14	0.33	—	1.18
12/03	8.86	51　5	0.27	—	0.72
12/02	1.44	48　23	0.04	—	0.31
Annual Growth	**75.8%**	**— —**	**102.3%**	**—**	**70.5%**

Transcend Services

Transcend Services helps make sense of doctors' gibberish. The company uses Internet-based technology to turn doctors' audio patient records into manageable electronic records. The physicians' audio notes are digitized at the firm's Atlanta hub, and transcribers access them over the Internet. Transcend also provides transcription services using the client's transcription technology system. In addition, the company offers editing and consulting services. Transcend Services' medical transcription customers include hospitals, clinics, and physician provider groups. Chairman and CEO Larry Gerdes and director Walter Huff Jr. together own about a quarter of Transcend Services.

The company plans to grow by acquiring medical transcription businesses. Transcend bought medical transcription firm OTP Technologies in 2007; it purchased Medical Dictation and the medical transcription unit of PracticeXpert in 2005.

EXECUTIVES

President, CEO and Chairman: Larry G. Gerdes, age 58, $235,000 pay (prior to title change)
COO: Sue McGrogan, age 41
CFO: Lance T. Cornell, age 42
SVP Sales and Marketing: Jeffrey (Jeff) McKee, age 49
Director Human Resources and Payroll:
Kathy Stevenson
Director Staffing and Employee Development:
Tara Goehring
Auditors: Miller Ray & Houser LLP

LOCATIONS

HQ: Transcend Services, Inc.
1 Glenlake Pkwy., Ste. 1325, Atlanta, GA 30328
Phone: 678-808-0600   **Fax:** 678-808-0601
Web: www.transcendservices.com

Transcend Services operates through its offices in Florida, Georgia, Oregon, and Texas.

COMPETITORS

MedQuist
Precyse Solutions
QuadraMed
Sandata Technologies
Spheris

HISTORICAL FINANCIALS

Company Type: Public

Income Statement   FYE: December 31

	REVENUE ($ mil.)	NET INCOME ($ mil.)	NET PROFIT MARGIN	EMPLOYEES
12/06	32.9	1.5	4.6%	877
12/05	25.8	(1.2)	—	916
12/04	15.2	0.3	2.0%	—
12/03	14.7	1.0	6.8%	—
12/02	12.2	0.9	7.4%	282
Annual Growth	28.1%	13.6%	—	32.8%

2006 Year-End Financials

Debt ratio: 71.5%
Return on equity: 43.3%
Cash ($ mil.): 0.2
Current ratio: 1.52
Long-term debt ($ mil.): 3.1
No. of shares (mil.): 7.8
Dividends
  Yield: —
  Payout: —
Market value ($ mil.): 28.2
R&D as % of sales: —
Advertising as % of sales: —

Stock History

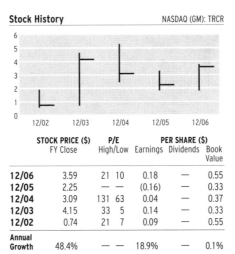

NASDAQ (GM): TRCR

	STOCK PRICE ($) FY Close	P/E High/Low		PER SHARE ($) Earnings	Dividends	Book Value
12/06	3.59	21	10	0.18	—	0.55
12/05	2.25	—	—	(0.16)	—	0.33
12/04	3.09	131	63	0.04	—	0.37
12/03	4.15	33	5	0.14	—	0.33
12/02	0.74	21	7	0.09	—	0.55
Annual Growth	48.4%	—	—	18.9%	—	0.1%

TransDigm Group

Through its subsidiaries, TransDigm Group manufactures and distributes a wide range of components for commercial and military aircraft. TransDigm operates through 11 subsidiaries: AeroControlex (mechanical controls, pumps, valves) and Adel Wiggins (clamps, connectors), Adams Rite Aerospace (cockpit security products, electromechanical controls, latches and locks), ADS/Transcoil (LCDs, motors), Avionic Instruments (power conversion equipment), Avtech (flight deck audio), Bruce Aerospace (aircraft lighting), Champion Aerospace (ignition systems and components), CDA InterCorp (actuators, motors, and gears), Marathon Norco Aerospace (batteries and related products), and Skurka Aerospace (electric motors).

Investment firm Warburg Pincus controls a 30% stake in TransDigm.

Components made by TransDigm companies are used in a variety of aircraft, including models produced by many of the world's leading manufacturers. Commercial aviation-related customers account for about 73% of the company's sales; military users, about 24%. Boeing (including Aviall, Inc.) accounts for about 16% of the company's sales; Honeywell accounts for about 11%.

TransDigm focuses on specialized products rather than commodities. Most of the company's sales come from proprietary products for which TransDigm owns the design and/or is the sole-source provider for a particular aircraft.

The company is growing by continuing to acquire manufacturers of proprietary components. Late in 2006 TransDigm bought CDA InterCorp for about $45 million. CDA is a provider of drive actuators, motors, transducers, and gears that are found on such military aircraft as the F-22, F-18, and C-130, as well as the Cessna Citation X.

Early in 2007 TransDigm paid $430 million to acquire Aviation Technologies from Odyssey Investment Partners. The acquisition of Aviation Technologies gave TransDigm two new divisions — Avtech (flight deck and passenger audio systems, cabin lighting, and power control products) and ADS/Transicoil (displays,

---

clocks, and brushless motors). Avtech and ADS/Transicoil count Boeing, Airbus, and Embraer among their customers.

TransDigm added its eleventh division later in 2007 when it acquired Bruce Aerospace for about $35 million. Bruce Aerospace is a provider of specialized fluorescent lighting products, primarily to the commercial aircraft market. Customers include Airbus, Boeing, Gulfstream, and Bombardier; the company also has significant aftermarket sales to commercial airlines.

The company isn't reliant solely on acquisitions for growth. TransDigm is growing organically through contracts for work on next-generation aircraft such as the Airbus A380 and the Boeing 787.

EXECUTIVES

Chairman and CEO: W. Nicholas (Nick) Howley, age 55, $855,000 pay
President and COO, TD Holding, Holdings and TransDigm: Raymond F. Laubenthal, age 46, $425,000 pay
EVP, CFO, and Secretary: Gregory Rufus, age 51, $352,994 pay
EVP, TD Group, and President; Adel Wiggins Group: Robert S. Henderson, age 51, $325,000 pay
EVP, Mergers and Acquisitions: Albert J. Rodriguez, age 47, $261,865 pay
President, Adams Rite Aerospace: John F. Leary, age 60
President, AeroControlex Group: James Riley, age 41
President, Champion Aerospace: Brent G. Iversen II, age 50
President, Skurka Aerospace: Howard A. Skurka, age 56
President, MarathonNorco Aerospace:
Ralph McClelland, age 49
President, Avtech Corporation: Christopher Anderson, age 45
Investor Relations: Sean Maroney
Auditors: Ernst & Young LLP

LOCATIONS

HQ: TransDigm Group Incorporated
1301 E. 9th St., Ste. 3710, Cleveland, OH 44114
Phone: 216-706-2960   **Fax:** 216-706-2937
Web: www.transdigm.com

PRODUCTS/OPERATIONS

2007 Sales

	$ mil.	% of total
Ignition systems & components	78.7	13
Mechanical/electro-mechanical actuators & controls	73.9	12
Gear pumps	63.3	10
Engineered connectors	48.8	8
Specialized valves	47.4	8
Power conditioning devices	42.0	7
Engineered latching & locking devices	39.3	6
AC/DC electric motors	34.0	6
Lavatory hardware	30.6	5
Rods & locking devices	27.9	5
Audio systems	24.9	4
NiCad batteries/chargers	23.6	4
Power, lighting & control	22.5	3
Elastomers	19.1	3
Specialized cockpit displays	16.8	3
Total	**592.8**	**100**

Selected Products

Cockpit security devices
Engineered connectors
Engineered latches
Gear pumps
Hold-open rods and locking devices
Ignition systems and components
Lavatory hardware and components
Mechanical/electromechanical controls and actuators
NiCad batteries/chargers
Power conditioning devices
Specialized AC/DC electric motors
Specialized valving

COMPETITORS

Goodrich Corporation
Honeywell International
United Technologies

HISTORICAL FINANCIALS

Company Type: Public

Income Statement
FYE: September 30

	REVENUE ($ mil.)	NET INCOME ($ mil.)	NET PROFIT MARGIN	EMPLOYEES
9/07	592.8	88.6	14.9%	2,100
9/06	435.2	25.1	5.8%	—
9/05	374.3	34.7	9.3%	1,300
9/04	300.7	13.6	4.5%	—
9/03	293.3	(72.8)	—	—
Annual Growth	19.2%	—	—	27.1%

2007 Year-End Financials

Debt ratio: 278.5%
Return on equity: 20.8%
Cash ($ mil.): 105.9
Current ratio: 5.44
Long-term debt ($ mil.): 1,357.8
No. of shares (mil.): 47.0
Dividends
  Yield: —
  Payout: —
Market value ($ mil.): 2,150.3
R&D as % of sales: —
Advertising as % of sales: —

Stock History
NYSE: TDG

	STOCK PRICE ($) FY Close	P/E High/Low	Earnings	PER SHARE ($) Dividends	Book Value
9/07	45.71	26 13	1.83	—	10.36
9/06	24.42	52 40	0.53	—	8.13
Annual Growth	87.2%	— —	245.3%	—	27.5%

Travelzoo Inc.

Travelzoo displays travel deals and specials and related information on its Web sites. Travel companies, such as airlines, cruise lines, hotels, and travel agencies, pay Travelzoo to publicize fares and promotions on Travelzoo's eponymous Web site, through its *Travelzoo Top 20* newsletter, and across its *Newsflash* e-mail alert service. Travelzoo also operates *SuperSearch*, a pay-per-click search engine specializing in travel content. Clients Expedia and Travelport collectively accounted for 30% of the company's revenues in 2006. Travelzoo commenced its UK operations in mid-2005, looking to expand even further into the European market. CEO Ralph Bartel owns 50% of the company, which was founded in 1998.

EXECUTIVES

Chairman, President, and CEO: Ralph Bartel, age 41
CFO: Wayne Lee, age 35
EVP, Asia: Raymond Ng, age 45
EVP, Europe: Christopher (Chris) Loughlin, age 33

SVP, Sales: Shirley Tafoya, age 43
CTO: Steven M. Ledwith, age 49
CIO: Max Rayner, age 47
Controller: Lisa Su, age 31
Commercial Director, UK: Stephen Dunk
Marketing Director, Europe: Seema Kotecha
Media Contact: Amanda Lee
Director: Holger Bartel, age 40
President, North America: C. J. Kettler
Auditors: KPMG LLP

LOCATIONS

HQ: Travelzoo Inc.
  590 Madison Ave., 21st Fl., New York, NY 10022
Phone: 212-521-4200   **Fax:** 212-521-4230
Web: www.travelzoo.com

Travelzoo maintains offices in Chicago, Las Vegas, Miami, Toronto, and the Silicon Valley.

2006 Sales

	$ mil.	% of total
North America	66.3	95
Europe	3.2	5
Total	**69.5**	**100**

PRODUCTS/OPERATIONS

Selected Clients

American Airlines
ATA
Avis Rent A Car
British Airways
Budget Rent A Car
Caesars Entertainment
Expedia
Fairmont Hotels and Resorts
Interstate Hotels & Resorts
JetBlue Airways
Kimpton Hotels
Liberty Travel
Lufthansa
Marriott Hotels
Royal Caribbean
Spirit Airlines
Starwood Hotels & Resorts Worldwide
United Airlines
Vanguard Rent-A-Car

COMPETITORS

AOL
Google
MSN
Yahoo!

HISTORICAL FINANCIALS

Company Type: Public

Income Statement
FYE: December 31

	REVENUE ($ mil.)	NET INCOME ($ mil.)	NET PROFIT MARGIN	EMPLOYEES
12/06	69.5	16.8	24.2%	82
12/05	50.8	8.0	15.7%	70
12/04	33.7	6.0	17.8%	49
12/03	18.0	2.0	11.1%	—
12/02	9.9	0.9	9.1%	—
Annual Growth	62.8%	107.9%	—	29.4%

2006 Year-End Financials

Debt ratio: —
Return on equity: 39.4%
Cash ($ mil.): 33.6
Current ratio: 6.30
Long-term debt ($ mil.): —
No. of shares (mil.): 15.3
Dividends
  Yield: —
  Payout: —
Market value ($ mil.): 456.7
R&D as % of sales: —
Advertising as % of sales: —

Stock History
NASDAQ (GS): TZOO

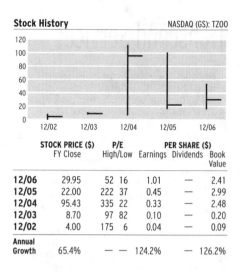

	STOCK PRICE ($) FY Close	P/E High/Low	Earnings	PER SHARE ($) Dividends	Book Value
12/06	29.95	52 16	1.01	—	2.41
12/05	22.00	222 37	0.45	—	2.99
12/04	95.43	335 22	0.33	—	2.48
12/03	8.70	97 82	0.10	—	0.20
12/02	4.00	175 6	0.04	—	0.09
Annual Growth	65.4%	— —	124.2%	—	126.2%

Trico Marine Services

Yes, it's ocean-going, but Trico Marine Services is a workhorse, not a seahorse. The company's support vessels haul mobile drilling rigs and materials, construction and production equipment, oil workers, and supplies to and from offshore oil rigs. Its supply fleet is #2 in the Gulf of Mexico (behind Tidewater); it also plies the waters in the North Sea and offshore Brazil, Mexico, and West Africa. Trico Marine's diversified 68-vessel fleet includes 44 supply boats, seven crew boats, and 10 platform supply vessels, as well as six towing boats, and one line-handling vessel. The majority of its revenues come from chartering vessels on a day rate basis.

The company filed for Chapter 11 bankruptcy protection in December 2004. It exited Chapter 11 in March 2005.

EXECUTIVES

Chairman and CEO: Joseph S. (Joe) Compofelice, $173,488 pay
SVP Business and Strategic Development: Robert V. O'Connor
VP and CFO: Geoff A. Jones, $404,584 pay (prior to promotion)
VP, General Counsel, Corporate Secretary and Director: Rishi A. Varma, $253,334 pay (partial-year salary)
VP Human Resources: Michael D. (Mike) Danford
Global Director of Sales and Marketing: Tomas Salazar
Global Director of Technical Services: Ray Hoover
Chief Accounting Officer: Jim Katosic
CEO Eastern Marine Services Limited: D. Michael Wallace, $396,666 pay (prior to promotion)
Auditors: PricewaterhouseCoopers LLP

LOCATIONS

HQ: Trico Marine Services, Inc.
  3200 Southwest Fwy., Ste. 2950,
  Houston, TX 77027
Phone: 713-780-9926   **Fax:** 713-780-0062
Web: www.tricomarine.com

Trico Marine Services operates in the Gulf of Mexico, the North Sea, offshore Mexico, offshore West Africa, offshore Brazil, and offshore China.

2006 Sales

	$ mil.	% of total
North Sea	106.5	43
US	102.8	41
West Africa	27.7	11
Other regions	11.7	5
Total	**248.7**	**100**

PRODUCTS/OPERATIONS

2006 Sales

	$ mil.	% of total
Charter hire	243.4	98
Other	5.3	2
Total	**248.7**	**100**

COMPETITORS

Global Industries
GulfMark Offshore
Oceaneering International
Schlumberger
SEACOR
Tidewater Inc.

HISTORICAL FINANCIALS

Company Type: Public

Income Statement

FYE: December 31

	REVENUE ($ mil.)	NET INCOME ($ mil.)	NET PROFIT MARGIN	EMPLOYEES
12/06	248.7	58.7	23.6%	834
12/05	182.3	(41.3)	—	836
12/04	112.5	(95.9)	—	—
12/03	123.5	(164.4)	—	—
12/02	133.9	(68.0)	—	1,076
Annual Growth	**16.7%**	**—**	**—**	**(6.2%)**

2006 Year-End Financials

Debt ratio: 2.8%
Return on equity: 22.0%
Cash ($ mil.): 117.4
Current ratio: 5.70
Long-term debt ($ mil.): 8.6
No. of shares (mil.): 14.8

Dividends
  Yield: —
  Payout: —
Market value ($ mil.): 567.6
R&D as % of sales: —
Advertising as % of sales: —

Stock History

NASDAQ (GM): TRMA

	STOCK PRICE ($) FY Close	P/E High/Low	PER SHARE ($) Earnings	Dividends	Book Value
12/06	38.31	10 7	3.86	—	21.08
12/05	26.00	16 9	1.74	—	15.20
Annual Growth	**47.3%**	**— —**	**121.8%**	**—**	**38.7%**

Trident Microsystems

This Trident can't stir up the oceans or shatter rocks like Poseidon's model, but its chips are behind some pretty powerful displays. Trident Microsystems offers integrated circuits (ICs) for digital television, LCD TV, and digital set-top box applications. The company's video processors enhance the quality of both analog and digital TV outputs, while its encoder chips optimize the display of computer images on TV. Trident outsources its manufacturing (mainly to United Microelectronics) and sells primarily to OEMs located in Asia. The company's top customers are Samsung Electronics (about 41% of sales) and Sony (25%).

After years of focusing on chips for notebook computers and desktop PCs, Trident set its sights on the digital TV market. Trident restructured its remaining operations by combining its digital media division with its Trident Technologies, Inc. (TTI) subsidiary. Trident owns nearly all of TTI. Trident's board has decided against spinning off TTI through an IPO in Taiwan or the US, a move that had been under consideration.

The company is facing investigations by the SEC and the US Department of Justice regarding its past practices in granting stock options. Trident is cooperating with both inquiries. An internal inquiry by a special board committee led to Trident founder Frank Lin resigning as chairman and CEO in 2006. Trident is also facing an audit of its 401(k) plan by the US Department of Labor following the internal inquiry.

D. E. Shaw & Co. owns about 7% of Trident Microsystems. Veredus Asset Management holds nearly 6% of the company. Next Century Growth Investors has an equity stake of around 5%.

HISTORY

Frank Lin, co-founder of graphics products maker Genoa Systems, started Trident Microsystems in 1987. The company shipped its first graphics-standard controller the next year. It opened a Taiwan office in 1989 and another in Hong Kong in 1992. That year Trident went public, introduced a chip for non-alphanumeric alphabets such as Chinese and Korean, and shipped a chipset for PC-based video production.

In 1995 Trident invested $60 million in a Taiwanese joint venture fabrication plant, which later became part of Taiwanese chip foundry United Microelectronics Corporation (UMC). Two years later the company beefed up its marketing efforts in the US by opening new sales offices and R&D centers.

In fiscal 1998 Trident posted its first annual loss, thanks in part to the Asian economic crisis of that year; a 10% workforce reduction followed. The company continued to introduce new product lines, including digital television video processors, in 1999 and 2000, and fared much better than many chip companies as it weathered dismal market conditions in fiscal 2001 and 2002.

In 2003 Trident transferred its graphics division to XGI Technology, a Silicon Integrated Systems spinoff, in order to focus on chips for digital television applications. Trident restructured its remaining operations by combining its digital media division with its Trident Technologies, Inc. (TTI) subsidiary.

Following an internal investigation by a special board committee into the company's past practices in granting stock options, founder Frank Lin resigned as chairman and CEO in late 2006. While leaving the board, he agreed to serve as a consultant to Trident during a transition period, helping smooth over relationships with key customers and suppliers. Glen Antle, a director of Trident since 1992, was named chairman and acting CEO to succeed Lin.

Among other measures adopted following the stock-options probe, which found that the company used incorrect measurement dates in granting options to officers and employees from 1994 to 2006, the Trident board voted to separate the positions of chairman and CEO in the future.

The board's probe apparently cleared other Trident officers of responsibility in the stock-options problems, which resulted in the company taking non-cash charges for stock-based compensation expenses of nearly $56 million; a non-executive employee who reported to Lin also resigned as the probe committee wrapped up its work. The board also relieved Peter Jen, the chief accounting officer, from his position, and determined that he would have no responsibilities or oversight in finance, human resources, or information systems.

Sylvia Summers, an EVP of Spansion and a former AMD executive, was named CEO in late 2007. Summers was also named to a seat on the Trident board.

EXECUTIVES

Chairman: Glen M. Antle, age 68
CEO and Director: Sylvia D. Summers, age 55
President: Jung-Herng Chang, $538,630 pay
  (prior to title change)
SVP Asia Operations: Peter Jen
VP Worldwide Business Development and Corporate Marketing, Trident Technologies: Peter Wicher
VP Human Resources, General Counsel, and Corporate Secretary: David L. Teichmann, age 51
VP Finance and Interim CFO: Pete J. Mangan, age 48
VP Human Resources: Donna M. Hamlin, age 53
Director Finance and Chief Accounting Officer: Chris P. Siu
Auditors: PricewaterhouseCoopers LLP

LOCATIONS

HQ: Trident Microsystems, Inc.
  3408 Garrett Dr., Santa Clara, CA 95054
Phone: 408-764-8808
Web: www.tridentmicro.com

Trident Microsystems has facilities in China, Hong Kong, Japan, Taiwan, and the US.

2007 Sales

	$ mil.	% of total
Asia/Pacific		
South Korea	115.5	43
Japan	91.7	34
China	31.4	12
Taiwan	14.4	5
Europe	17.4	6
Other regions	0.4	—
Total	**270.8**	**100**

PRODUCTS/OPERATIONS

Selected Products

TV encoders
TV video processors

COMPETITORS

3Dlabs	NXP
AMD	Pixelworks
Cirrus Logic	Silicon Image
ESS Technology	STMicroelectronics
Genesis Microchip	Techwell
Imagination Technologies	Toshiba Semiconductor
LSI Corp.	Tvia
Matrox Electronic Systems	VIA Technologies
MediaTek	Zoran
Micronas Semiconductor	

HISTORICAL FINANCIALS

Company Type: Public

Income Statement

FYE: June 30

	REVENUE ($ mil.)	NET INCOME ($ mil.)	NET PROFIT MARGIN	EMPLOYEES
6/07	270.8	30.1	11.1%	520
6/06	171.4	26.2	15.3%	—
6/05	69.0	(10.5)	—	—
6/04	52.5	9.6	18.3%	—
6/03	52.8	(24.8)	—	—
Annual Growth	50.5%	—	—	—

2007 Year-End Financials

Debt ratio: —
Return on equity: 16.9%
Cash ($ mil.): 199.3
Long-term debt ($ mil.): —
No. of shares (mil.): 57.7

Dividends
  Yield: —
  Payout: —
Market value ($ mil.): 1,059.7
R&D as % of sales: —
Advertising as % of sales: —

Stock History

NASDAQ (GM): TRID

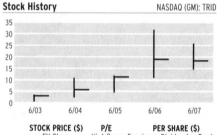

	STOCK PRICE ($) FY Close	P/E High/Low		Earnings	PER SHARE ($) Dividends	Book Value
6/07	18.35	53	31	0.48	—	3.50
6/06	18.98	75	27	0.42	—	2.66
6/05	11.35	—	—	(0.22)	—	4.22
6/04	5.68	56	14	0.19	—	3.22
6/03	2.99	—	—	(0.60)	—	3.73
Annual Growth	57.4%	—	—	—	—	(1.6%)

Trimeris, Inc.

Trimeris hopes to safeguard cells from viral invaders. The company develops fusion inhibitor drugs that prevent viruses from attaching to a host cell. Its first product, Fuzeon, approved in the US and the European Union, can stop HIV from fusing with human cells in HIV patients for whom other antiretroviral therapies have failed. Development partner Roche markets Fuzeon worldwide. Trimeris is working to develop next-generation fusion inhibitor drugs that it hopes will prove more effective and require less frequent dosing than Fuzeon.

Fuzeon is an injectable drug taken twice a day. Through its collaboration with Roche, the com-

pany is working on improved delivery systems for the drug, including needle-free injection using Bioject's Biojector 2000 device.

A 2006 restructuring reduced the company's marketing workforce and shifted more of Fuzeon's commercialization activities to Roche. Trimeris also amended its collaboration with Roche that year, obtaining all the intellectual property rights related to its next-generation fusion inhibitor research programs.

Board members and brothers Julian and Felix Baker own 16% of Trimeris, while the Tisch family, which heads diversified giant Loews, owns 10%. Other investors include T. Rowe Price (13%), Franklin Advisers (10%), Mazama Capital Management (8%), and Perry Corp. (7%).

Two New York-based investment firms bought up sizable stakes in Trimeris in 2007. Bridger Management acquired about 10%, and HealthCor Management owns nearly 17%, making it Trimeris' largest shareholder. HealthCor has been advising Trimeris to consider strategic alternatives, such as a sale of the company.

EXECUTIVES

CEO: Martin A. Mattingly, age 50
Secretary and CFO: Andrew L. Graham, age 37, $163,000 pay
EVP Scientific Operations: George (Barney) Koszalka, age 56
SVP Clinical Development and Medical Affairs and Chief Medical Officer: Neil Graham
VP Project Planning: Carol-Ann Olmstede, age 51
Manager, IT: Joe Rutledge
General Counsel: Michael A. Alrutz, age 39
Auditors: KPMG LLP

LOCATIONS

HQ: Trimeris, Inc.
  3500 Paramount Pkwy., Morrisville, NC 27560
Phone: 919-419-6050   **Fax:** 919-419-1816
Web: www.trimeris.com

PRODUCTS/OPERATIONS

2006 Sales

	$ mil.	% of total
Collaborations	21.8	59
Royalties	11.8	32
Milestone payments	3.4	9
Total	**37.0**	**100**

COMPETITORS

Abbott Labs	Merck
Achillion	Panacos
Boehringer Ingelheim	Pfizer
Bristol-Myers Squibb	Progenics Pharmaceuticals
Gilead Sciences	Schering-Plough
GlaxoSmithKline	Valeant
Hollis-Eden	Vertex Pharmaceuticals

HISTORICAL FINANCIALS

Company Type: Public

Income Statement

FYE: December 31

	REVENUE ($ mil.)	NET INCOME ($ mil.)	NET PROFIT MARGIN	EMPLOYEES
12/06	37.0	7.4	20.0%	103
12/05	19.1	(8.1)	—	90
12/04	6.7	(40.1)	—	—
12/03	3.7	(65.7)	—	—
12/02	1.1	(75.7)	—	129
Annual Growth	140.8%	—	—	(5.5%)

2006 Year-End Financials

Debt ratio: —
Return on equity: 23.8%
Cash ($ mil.): 48.0
Current ratio: 7.01
Long-term debt ($ mil.): —
No. of shares (mil.): 22.1

Dividends
  Yield: —
  Payout: —
Market value ($ mil.): 281.4
R&D as % of sales: —
Advertising as % of sales: —

Stock History

NASDAQ (GM): TRMS

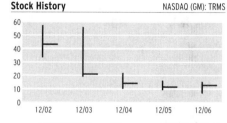

	STOCK PRICE ($) FY Close	P/E High/Low		Earnings	PER SHARE ($) Dividends	Book Value
12/06	12.71	44	21	0.34	—	1.71
12/05	11.49	—	—	(0.37)	—	1.10
12/04	14.17	—	—	(1.86)	—	1.38
12/03	20.94	—	—	(3.06)	—	3.14
12/02	43.17	—	—	(3.93)	—	6.09
Annual Growth	(26.3%)	—	—	—	—	(27.3%)

Trio-Tech International

Three's certainly company, if the company is Trio-Tech. Performing a trio of functions related to semiconductor manufacturing and testing, Trio-Tech International lives up to its name. First, the company makes its own chip manufacturing and test equipment; its front- and back-end testing products include temperature-controlled chucks, centrifuges, leak detectors, and burn-in equipment. Second, Trio-Tech provides outsourced testing services for chip manufacturers. Third, it distributes semiconductor manufacturing and testing equipment made by other companies. Trio-Tech's top customers are Advanced Micro Devices (60% of sales), Freescale Semiconductor (15%), and Catalyst Semiconductor.

In 2006 Trio-Tech International acquired a burn-in testing facility in China to accommodate business in that country. The company closed its testing facility in Ireland in 2005.

Company insiders own more than one-quarter of Trio-Tech's equity. CEO Siew Yong holds around 10% of Trio-Tech, while chairman Charles Wilson owns about 6%, as does director Richard Horowitz.

EXECUTIVES

Chairman: A. Charles Wilson, age 83
President, CEO, and Director: Siew Wai Yong, age 54, $700,186 pay
VP and CFO: Victor H. M. Ting, age 53, $213,982 pay
VP Testing: Hwee Poh (Richard) Lim, age 48, $110,137 pay
Sales Manager: Jon Easterson
Auditors: BDO International

LOCATIONS

HQ: Trio-Tech International
14731 Califa St., Van Nuys, CA 91411
Phone: 818-787-7000
Web: www.triotech.com

Trio-Tech International has operations in China, Malaysia, Singapore, Thailand, and the US.

2007 Sales

	$ mil.	% of total
Singapore	25.6	55
Malaysia	6.9	15
US	6.4	13
China	4.8	10
Thailand	2.4	5
Other countries	0.8	2
Adjustments	(0.1)	—
Total	**46.8**	**100**

PRODUCTS/OPERATIONS

2007 Sales

	$ mil.	% of total
Manufacturing	24.1	51
Testing services	20.9	45
Distribution	1.8	4
Total	**46.8**	**100**

Testing Services

Component reclaim
Constant acceleration
Electrical testing
Gross and fine leak tests
Highly accelerated stress testing (HAST)
Lead conditioning
Programming
Stabilization bake
Static and dynamic burn-in tests
Tape and reel
Temperature cycling

Manufactured Products

Autoclave systems
Burn-in board testers
Burn-in systems
Centrifuge systems
Component leak detection systems
HAST (highly accelerated stress testing) equipment
Rate/position tables
Temperature-controlled wafer chucks
Wet-process stations

COMPETITORS

Aehr Test Systems	LTX
Aetrium	Mirae
Agilent Technologies	Reliability Incorporated
Amkor	Rockwood Holdings
ASE Test	STATS ChipPAC
Credence Systems	Teradyne
Hitachi	Tokyo Electron
inTEST	UTAC
KLA-Tencor	

HISTORICAL FINANCIALS

Company Type: Public

Income Statement			FYE: Last Friday in June
	REVENUE ($ mil.)	NET INCOME ($ mil.)	NET PROFIT MARGIN	EMPLOYEES
6/07	46.8	3.3	7.1%	658
6/06	29.1	9.1	31.3%	—
6/05	25.7	0.2	0.8%	—
6/04	19.1	0.2	1.0%	—
6/03	21.3	(0.1)	—	—
Annual Growth	**21.7%**	**—**	**—**	**—**

2007 Year-End Financials

Debt ratio: 1.4%	Dividends
Return on equity: 17.0%	Yield: 0.5%
Cash ($ mil.): 14.9	Payout: 9.8%
Current ratio: 3.00	Market value ($ mil.): 64.4
Long-term debt ($ mil.): 0.3	R&D as % of sales: —
No. of shares (mil.): 3.2	Advertising as % of sales: —

Stock History

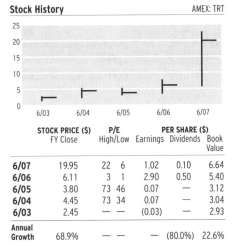

AMEX: TRT

	STOCK PRICE ($) FY Close	P/E High/Low		PER SHARE ($) Earnings	Dividends	Book Value
6/07	19.95	22	6	1.02	0.10	6.64
6/06	6.11	3	1	2.90	0.50	5.40
6/05	3.80	73	46	0.07	—	3.12
6/04	4.45	73	34	0.07	—	3.04
6/03	2.45	—	—	(0.03)	—	2.93
Annual Growth	**68.9%**	**—**	**—**	**—**	**(80.0%)**	**22.6%**

True Religion Apparel

Who knew you could find religion just by throwing open the doors to your closet? True Religion Apparel designs, makes, and markets upscale denimwear through its wholly owned subsidiary, Guru Denim. Its apparel offerings (jeans, skirts, denim jackets, and tops) are sold under the True Religion Brand Jeans label in 50 countries including Australia, Canada, China, Europe, Japan, the Middle East, the UK, and the US. Upscale retailers, such as Barneys New York, Bergdorf Goodman, Neiman Marcus, Nordstrom, Saks Fifth Avenue, and about 650 high-end boutiques nationwide sell True Religion's merchandise. It got into scents in late 2007. The firm has hired Goldman Sachs to advise it on ways to boost shareholder value.

The pricey jeans maker has been considering going private to maintain its double-digit sales and earnings gains, as well as expand its store operations. It then would like to re-emerge by taking the company public again. In the interim True Religion enlisted the expertise of InGroup Licensing to expand the brand into a lifestyle collection.

The company intends to maintain its brand image by limiting distribution of its apparel to the more exclusive boutiques, specialty stores, and department stores while expanding its retail presence. A licensing deal with Pash Industries, inked in January 2007, gave True Religion its own branded outerwear and its foot in the door at many exclusive shops where Pash already sells. It opened its first retail store in California in December 2005 and its first East Coast shop in New York's Soho district in mid-2006. Expanding its retail footprint on the East Coast, the company is concentrating on store openings in Short Hills, New Jersey, in 2007 and Oyster Bay, New York, in 2008. A licensing deal with Selective Fragrances, inked in mid-2007, allows True Religion to add scents for men and women by fall 2008 to its products portfolio. The fragrances

---

will be sold in its own stores, as well as in Neiman Marcus, Nordstrom, and Barneys, among others.

It's looking overseas for growth, as well. To peddle its pricey pants in Asia, True Religion has enlisted Hong Kong-based Bright Unity International to distribute its apparel in Hong Kong, Macao, and China.

To control costs and market its apparel as "Made in the USA," True Religion employs contract manufacturers in the US and a one-off supplier in Mexico.

EXECUTIVES

Chairman and CEO: Jeffrey (Jeff) Lubell, age 51, $1,325,212 pay (prior to promotion)
President: Michael F. Buckley, age 43, $462,836 pay (partial-year salary)
CFO: Peter F. (Pete) Collins, age 42
SVP, Merchandising: Rodney Hutton
VP, Real Estate: Marc J. Klein, age 41
Senior Designer, Women's Sportswear: Caius Olowu
Design Director: Zihaad Wells, age 31
Director, Marketing and Public Relations: Emilio Fields
Auditors: Deloitte & Touche LLP

LOCATIONS

HQ: True Religion Apparel Inc.
2263 E. Vernon Ave., Vernon, CA 90058
Phone: 323-266-3072   **Fax:** 323-266-8060
Web: www.truereligionbrandjeans.com

PRODUCTS/OPERATIONS

2006 Sales

	$ mil.	% of total
Wholesale	134.1	96
Retail	5.0	4
Total	**139.1**	**100**

COMPETITORS

Abercrombie & Fitch
Armani
Berkshire Partners
Calvin Klein
Diesel SpA
Joe's Jeans
Levi Strauss
Phat
Polo Ralph Lauren
Sean John

HISTORICAL FINANCIALS

Company Type: Public

Income Statement			FYE: December 31
	REVENUE ($ mil.)	NET INCOME ($ mil.)	NET PROFIT MARGIN	EMPLOYEES
12/06	139.1	24.4	17.5%	163
12/05	102.6	19.5	19.0%	95
12/04	27.7	4.2	15.2%	—
12/03	2.4	0.0	—	—
12/02	9.2	0.0	—	—
Annual Growth	**97.2%**	**—**	**—**	**71.6%**

2006 Year-End Financials

Debt ratio: —	Dividends
Return on equity: 47.5%	Yield: —
Cash ($ mil.): 44.9	Payout: —
Current ratio: 6.11	Market value ($ mil.): 352.2
Long-term debt ($ mil.): —	R&D as % of sales: —
No. of shares (mil.): 23.0	Advertising as % of sales: —

NASDAQ (GM): TRLG

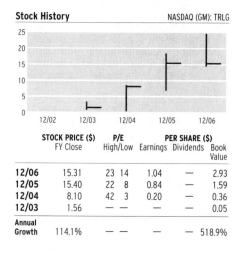

	STOCK PRICE ($) FY Close	P/E High/Low		PER SHARE ($) Earnings	Dividends	Book Value
12/06	15.31	23	14	1.04	—	2.93
12/05	15.40	22	8	0.84	—	1.59
12/04	8.10	42	3	0.20	—	0.36
12/03	1.56	—	—	—	—	0.05
Annual Growth	114.1%		—	—	—	518.9%

UCBH Holdings

UCBH Holdings is the holding company for United Commercial Bank, which caters to the Asian-American community through about 50 branches in California, plus locations in the Atlanta, Boston, Houston, New York, and Seattle areas. It also has offices in China, Hong Kong, and Taiwan. Offering services in English, Mandarin, and Cantonese, the bank markets to small and midsized businesses and individuals, providing deposit accounts, cash management services, and online banking. UCBH also offers international trade finance for goods shipped between California and the Pacific Rim. Subsidiaries provide brokerage and asset management services. The acquisitive firm bought Business Development Bank in Shanghai in 2007.

UCBH changed the name of Business Development Bank to United Commercial Bank (China) Limited.

The groundbreaking deal is the first outright acquisition of a bank in China by a US firm. UCBH scored a major coup by beating out much larger competitors like Citigroup and Bank of America, which own minority stakes in Chinese banks.

In late 2005 UCBH Holdings acquired Pacifica Bancorp, the holding company for Pacifica Bank, giving UCBH Holdings entrée into the Pacific Northwest's Chinese market. Not long after, UCBH Holdings got a toehold in New England when it completed its acquisition of Asian American Bank & Trust Company and its three branches in the Greater Boston area.

UCBH Holdings had planned to acquire Great Eastern Bank, a privately held commercial bank with five branches in New York City. However, in early 2006 Great Eastern Bank terminated the agreement with UCBH, accepting what it considered a "superior proposal" from Cathay General Bancorp instead.

Undaunted, the company acquired Summit Bank Corporation. The deal gave it a presence in Atlanta and Houston, added an office in Shanghai, and expanded its footprint in San Francisco.

Commercial real estate loans make up around 35% of UCBH's loan portfolio; business loans are

more than 20%. The bank also offers mortgages secured by multifamily properties, as well as business, construction, consumer, and one- to four-family residential mortgage loans.

EXECUTIVES

Chairman, President, and CEO, UCBH Holdings and United Commercial Bank: Thomas S. Wu, age 49, $1,200,000 pay
EVP and COO, UCBH Holdings and United Commercial Bank: Ebrahim Shabudin, age 59, $273,750 pay (prior to promotion)
EVP, CFO, and Director, UCBH Holdings and United Commercial Bank: Dennis Wu, age 66, $196,314 pay (partial-year salary)
EVP and Director, Corporate Development and Investor Relations, UCBH Holdings and United Commercial Bank: Jonathan H. Downing, age 55, $242,500 pay
EVP and Chief Lending Officer, UCBH Holdings and United Commercial Bank: Sylvia Loh, age 52, $247,916 pay (prior to promotion)
EVP and Chief Risk and Compliance Officer: Daniel M. Gautsch, age 59
EVP and Director New York Region: William J. Laraia, age 71
EVP and Director Southeast Region: David Yu, age 55
EVP and Regional Director Southern California, UCBH Holdings and United Commercial Bank: Alan Thian, age 54, $220,000 pay
EVP and General Manager, Greater China Region, UCBH Holdings and United Commercial Bank: Ka Wah (Tony) Tsui, age 54
SVP and Director of Human Resources, UCBH Holdings and United Commercial Bank: Carol F. Zoner, age 46
SVP, Corporate Counsel, and Assistant Corporate Secretary, UCBH Holdings and United Commercial Bank: Dennis A. Lee, age 64
SVP and Director of Marketing, United Commercial Bank: Eleanor Chang
President and CEO, UCB Investment Services: Joseph Lee
CEO and Chief Investment Officer, UCB Asset Management: John Lui
Auditors: PricewaterhouseCoopers LLP

LOCATIONS

HQ: UCBH Holdings, Inc.
555 Montgomery St., San Francisco, CA 94111
Phone: 415-315-2800   **Fax:** 415-986-3878
Web: www.ibankunited.com

2006 Branch Locations

	No.
Northern California	28
Southern California	22
Atlanta	5
New York	5
Asia/Pacific	4
Boston	3
Seattle	2
Houston	1
Total	**70**

PRODUCTS/OPERATIONS

2006 Sales

	$ mil.	% of total
Interest		
Loans	448.7	77
Investment & mortgage-backed securities	77.7	13
Other	8.7	1
Noninterest		
Net gain on sale of multifamily & commercial mortgages	17.8	3
Commercial banking fees	15.4	3
Other	15.0	3
Total	**583.3**	**100**

COMPETITORS

BancWest	East West Bancorp
Bank of America	UnionBanCal
Cathay General Bancorp	U.S. Bancorp
City National	Wells Fargo
Downey Financial	

HISTORICAL FINANCIALS

Company Type: Public

Income Statement

FYE: December 31

	ASSETS ($ mil.)	NET INCOME ($ mil.)	INCOME AS % OF ASSETS	EMPLOYEES
12/06	10,346.4	100.9	1.0%	1,318
12/05	7,961.1	97.8	1.2%	1,098
12/04	6,315.7	85.6	1.4%	—
12/03	5,585.2	64.6	1.2%	—
12/02	4,853.6	38.9	0.8%	597
Annual Growth	20.8%	26.9%	—	21.9%

2006 Year-End Financials

Equity as % of assets: 7.6%
Return on assets: 1.1%
Return on equity: 14.5%
Long-term debt ($ mil.): 1,147.2
No. of shares (mil.): 99.4
Market value ($ mil.): 1,746.3
Dividends
  Yield: 0.7%
  Payout: 11.7%
Sales ($ mil.): 583.3
R&D as % of sales: —
Advertising as % of sales: —

Stock History

NASDAQ (GS): UCBH

	STOCK PRICE ($) FY Close	P/E High/Low		PER SHARE ($) Earnings	Dividends	Book Value
12/06	17.56	19	15	1.03	0.12	7.90
12/05	17.88	23	15	1.02	0.08	6.42
12/04	22.91	27	19	0.90	0.08	10.62
12/03	19.49	28	14	0.70	0.05	9.20
12/02	10.61	23	14	0.47	0.05	13.44
Annual Growth	13.4%		—	21.7%	24.5%	(12.4%)

Ulta Salon

Ulta Salon, Cosmetics & Fragrance wants to be every woman's ultimate beauty stop. Ulta operates about 235 stores in about 30 states. More than a third of its stores are located in Illinois, Texas, and California. Ulta sells cosmetics, fragrances, skin and hair care products and appliances, and accessories. Ulta stores also offer hair salon services, as well as manicures, pedicures, massages, and other beauty and spa treatments. The company's Web site ULTA.com is being upgraded to offer about 9,000 products and more than 400 brand names. The company, which was founded in 1990 by director Terry Hanson and Dick George, went public in 2007.

Ulta exceeded its expectations with its IPO, raising more than $153 million. Proceeds in part will be used to pay about $92 million in dividends owed to holders of Ulta's preferred stock.

Investment firms Global Retail Partners and Netherlands-based Doublemousse B.V. own nearly 23% and 20% of the company's shares, respectively. Oak Investment Partners owns about 11% of Ulta's shares.

Ultimately, Ulta hopes to grow to more than 1,000 stores throughout the US. The company also aims to expand its product selection and brand offerings, particularly its range of higher-priced "prestige" products, such as Estée Lauder fragrances, Frédéric Fekkai haircare products, and Smashbox cosmetics. To that end, Ulta added boutique areas to about 90 of its stores in 2007 to highlight high-end products. Eventually, most Ulta stores will house boutiques.

EXECUTIVES

President, CEO, and Director: Lyn P. Kirby, age 53
COO and Secretary: Bruce E. Barkus, age 54
CFO and Assistant Secretary: Gregg R. Bodnar, age 42
SVP, Human Resources: Wayne L' Heureux
SVP, Operations: Melissa Whitehead
SVP, Private Label: Mary Bolyard
SVP, Real Estate: Alex Lelli
SVP, Systems: Greg Smolarek
VP, Construction: Doron Sacham
VP, Finance: Joe Addante
VP, Distribution: Matthew Strall
VP Marketing: Nancy Altman
VP, Market Research: Bruce Haynes
Controller: Chris Lialios
Auditors: Ernst & Young LLP

LOCATIONS

HQ: Ulta Salon, Cosmetics & Fragrance, Inc.
1135 Arbor Dr., Romeoville, IL 60446
Phone: 630-226-0020   **Fax:** 630-226-8367
Web: www.ulta.com

2007 Stores

	No.
Illinois	27
Texas	27
California	25
Arizona	19
Georgia	11
Pennsylvania	11
Colorado	9
Florida	9
New Jersey	9
North Carolina	8
Virginia	7
Minnesota	6
New York	6
Nevada	5
Indiana	4
Michigan	4
Oklahoma	4
Maryland	3
South Carolina	3
Washington	3
Other states	7
Total	**207**

PRODUCTS/OPERATIONS

Selected Products

Accessories
  Brush sets
  Eyelash curlers
  Flip-flops
  Hair accessories
  Manicure sets
  Yoga accessories
Appliances
  Curling irons
  Flat irons
  Hair dryers
  Microdermabrasion systems
  Shavers

Bath & Body
  Aromatherapy
  Body butter
  Body souffle
  Deodorants
  Exfoliators
  Scrubs
  Soaps
Cosmetics
  Blush
  Concealer
  Eye liner
  Eyeshadow
  Lipstick
Fragrance
  Candles
  Cologne
  Perfume
  Potpourri
Haircare
  Coloring
  Conditioner
  Masks
  Shampoo
  Styling creams
Skincare
  Cellulite cream
  De-aging cream
  Face wash
  Gloves
  Lotions
  Nail strengthening cream
  Sunscreens

COMPETITORS

Bath & Body Works	Macy's
Bed Bath & Beyond	Merle Norman
Body Shop	Nordstrom
CVS/Caremark	Regis Corporation
Dillard's	Sally Beauty
drugstore.com	Sephora USA
Intimate Brands	Supercuts
J. C. Penney	Target
L'Oréal USA	Walgreen
Lush Ltd.	Wal-Mart

HISTORICAL FINANCIALS

Company Type: Public

Income Statement

FYE: Saturday nearest January 31

	REVENUE ($ mil.)	NET INCOME ($ mil.)	NET PROFIT MARGIN	EMPLOYEES
1/07	755.1	22.5	3.0%	7,100
1/06	579.1	16.0	2.8%	—
1/05	491.2	9.5	1.9%	—
Annual Growth	**24.0%**	**53.9%**	**—**	**—**

2007 Year-End Financials

Debt ratio: (68.3%)   Current ratio: 2.05
Return on equity: —   Long-term debt ($ mil.): 50.7
Cash ($ mil.): 3.6

Net Income History

NASDAQ (GS): ULTA

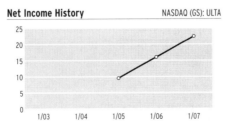

Ultimate Software

The Ultimate Software Group isn't shy about the benefits of its workforce management products. The company is a provider of Web-based payroll and employee management software that helps businesses manage their workforces more efficiently. Its UltiPro Workforce Management application, which is geared toward midsized companies in a variety of industries, manages employee communications, benefits, payroll, and staffing functions. Ultimate Software offers similar human resources management applications targeted to the health care and professional employer organization industries. The company also offers a hosted version of its software.

More than half of Ultimate Software's sales in 2006 were recurring revenues. The company boasts more than 1,400 customers, which have included Omni Hotels, The Container Store, and Elizabeth Arden.

Ultimate Software primarily markets the licensed version of its software to companies with more than 500 employees, and it markets the hosted version to smaller companies that can't spend as much on implementing and maintaining their technology systems. The company has a licensing agreement with human resources services provider Ceridian, allowing Ceridian to market the UltiPro software as part of an online workforce management offering for companies with fewer than 500 employees. Ultimate Software has also extended its alliances to use business service providers to market its software to larger companies with more than 10,000 employees.

EXECUTIVES

Chairman, President, and CEO: Scott Scherr, age 54
Vice Chairman and COO: Marc D. Scherr, age 49
EVP, CFO, and Treasurer:
  Mitchell K. (Mitch) Dauerman, age 49
SVP and General Counsel: Robert Manne, age 53
SVP and CTO: Adam Rogers, age 32
SVP, Marketing: Linda Miller, age 62
SVP, People and Secretary: Vivian Maza, age 45
SVP, Product Strategy: Laura Johnson, age 42
SVP and Chief Sales Officer: Greg Swick, age 43
SVP and Chief Services Officer: Jon Harris, age 42
SVP and CIO: William (Bill) Hicks, age 42
SVP, Talent Management Systems: Daniel Taylor, age 38
Media Contact: Darlene Marcroft
Auditors: KPMG LLP

LOCATIONS

HQ: The Ultimate Software Group, Inc.
2000 Ultimate Way, Weston, FL 33326
Phone: 954-331-7000   **Fax:** 954-331-7300
Web: www.ultimatesoftware.com

PRODUCTS/OPERATIONS

2006 Sales

	$ mil.	% of total
Recurring	63.9	55
Services	38.6	34
Licenses	12.3	11
Total	**114.8**	**100**

Selected Products and Services

Software
  Health care industry-based human resources and
    payroll (UltiPro Healthcare)
  Human resources, benefits administration, and payroll
    (UltiPro Workforce Management)
  Staffing business-based human resources and payroll
    (UltiPro PEO)

Services
  Implementation
  Product support
  Technical support
  Training

COMPETITORS

ADP
Authoria
Ceridian
Kronos Inc.
Lawson Software
Oracle
Peopleclick
Sage Software
SAP
Synygy
Workscape

HISTORICAL FINANCIALS

Company Type: Public

Income Statement

FYE: December 31

	REVENUE ($ mil.)	NET INCOME ($ mil.)	NET PROFIT MARGIN	EMPLOYEES
12/06	114.8	4.1	3.6%	623
12/05	88.6	3.4	3.8%	512
12/04	72.0	(5.0)	—	—
12/03	60.4	(9.2)	—	—
12/02	55.2	(14.6)	—	415
Annual Growth	20.1%	—	—	10.7%

2006 Year-End Financials

Debt ratio: 5.2%
Return on equity: 15.0%
Cash ($ mil.): 31.0
Current ratio: 1.27
Long-term debt ($ mil.): 1.6
No. of shares (mil.): 24.4
Dividends
  Yield: —
  Payout: —
Market value ($ mil.): 567.4
R&D as % of sales: —
Advertising as % of sales: —

Stock History

NASDAQ (GM): ULTI

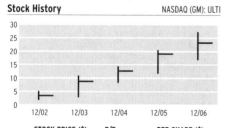

	STOCK PRICE ($) FY Close	P/E High/Low		PER SHARE ($) Earnings	Dividends	Book Value
12/06	23.26	180	114	0.15	—	1.27
12/05	19.07	156	92	0.13	—	1.00
12/04	12.68	—	—	(0.23)	—	0.60
12/03	8.77	—	—	(0.49)	—	0.08
12/02	3.45	—	—	(0.90)	—	(0.45)
Annual Growth	61.1%	—	—	—	—	—

Ultra Clean Technology

Ultra Clean Holdings helps chip makers handle gases under ultraclean conditions. The company, which does business as Ultra Clean Technology (UCT), makes customized gas delivery systems used in the production of semiconductors. It has also developed a catalytic steam generator designed for use in several chip production steps that call for high-purity steam. UCT, which was founded as a subsidiary of Mitsubishi Corporation in 1991, draws most of its sales from Applied Materials (40% of sales), Lam Research (32%), and Novellus (14%). Venture capital firm Francisco Partners owns around 23% of the company.

In 2006 Ultra Clean Technology acquired Sieger Engineering for about $50 million in cash, stock, and assumed debt. Sieger makes subsystems for capital equipment used in the flat-panel display, medical, and semiconductor industries. UCT paid $32 million in cash and issued around 2.47 million common shares. There is no overlap between the two companies' product lines, and Sieger (now UCT-Sieger) will also leverage UCT's operations in China by adding more outsourced manufacturing.

Mazama Capital Management owns nearly 9% of Ultra Clean Technology, while Discovery Group I holds around 6% of the company. Including stock options, CEO Clarence Granger has an equity stake of about 3%.

EXECUTIVES

CEO: Clarence L. Granger, age 59, $350,000 pay
President and COO: David Savage, age 46
VP and CFO: Jack Sexton, age 43, $208,333 pay
VP Technology and CTO: Sowmya Krishnan, age 39
SVP Engineering: Bruce Wier, age 59
SVP Sales: Deborah Hayward, age 46
Director: Leonid Mezhvinsky, age 53
Auditors: Deloitte & Touche LLP

LOCATIONS

HQ: Ultra Clean Holdings, Inc.
  150 Independence Dr., Menlo Park, CA 94025
Phone: 650-323-4100   **Fax:** 650-326-0929
Web: www.uct.com

Ultra Clean Holdings has manufacturing operations in California, Oregon, and Texas, and also in Shanghai, China.

2006 Sales

	$ mil.	% of total
US	320.6	95
Asia & Europe	16.6	5
Total	**337.2**	**100**

COMPETITORS

Air Products
Allegro MicroSystems
ATMI
Celerity
Ebara
Flextronics
L'Air Liquide
Matheson Tri-Gas
Praxair
Sanmina-SCI
Wolfe Engineering

HISTORICAL FINANCIALS

Company Type: Public

Income Statement

FYE: December 31

	REVENUE ($ mil.)	NET INCOME ($ mil.)	NET PROFIT MARGIN	EMPLOYEES
12/06	337.2	16.3	4.8%	1,005
12/05	147.5	2.0	1.4%	—
12/04	184.2	8.6	4.7%	—
12/03	77.5	0.1	0.1%	—
12/02	84.3	(2.2)	—	—
Annual Growth	41.4%	—	—	—

2006 Year-End Financials

Debt ratio: 25.8%
Return on equity: 20.1%
Cash ($ mil.): 23.3
Current ratio: 2.44
Long-term debt ($ mil.): 27.7
No. of shares (mil.): 21.1
Dividends
  Yield: —
  Payout: —
Market value ($ mil.): 260.3
R&D as % of sales: —
Advertising as % of sales: —

Stock History

NASDAQ (GS): UCTT

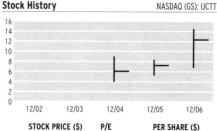

	STOCK PRICE ($) FY Close	P/E High/Low		PER SHARE ($) Earnings	Dividends	Book Value
12/06	12.35	17	8	0.83	—	5.08
12/05	7.24	69	45	0.12	—	3.35
12/04	6.06	16	7	0.55	—	3.21
Annual Growth	42.8%	—	—	22.8%	—	25.9%

Ultra Petroleum

Ultra Petroleum is ultrakeen in its search for petroleum products. The independent exploration and production company recovers natural gas from Cretaceous sandstone deposits in the Green River Basin of southwestern Wyoming. The company also has assets in Pennsylvania and Texas. The oil and gas company expanded into China though the acquisition of Pendaries Petroleum, a Houston-based oil and gas exploration company that had large oil assets in Bohai Bay. Ultra Petroleum has proved reserves of 2.4 trillion cu. ft. of natural gas equivalent in the US and China. In 2007 the company sold its assets in China for $223 million.

EXECUTIVES

Chairman, President, and CEO: Michael D. Watford, age 53, $993,750 pay
CFO: Marshal D. (Mark) Smith, age 47, $482,500 pay
VP Operations: William B. (Bill) Picquet, age 55, $462,500 pay
VP Marketing: Stuart E. Nance
Corporate Secretary and Manager Investor Relations: Kelly L. Whitley
Corporate Controller and Principal Accounting Officer: Garland Shaw
Auditors: Ernst & Young LLP

LOCATIONS

HQ: Ultra Petroleum Corp.
363 N. Sam Houston Pkwy. East, Ste. 1200,
Houston, TX 77060
Phone: 281-876-0120   **Fax:** 281-876-2831
Web: www.ultrapetroleum.com

Ultra Petroleum Corporation operates in Pennsylvania, Texas, and Wyoming in the US, and in Bohai Bay, China.

2006 Sales

	$ mil.	% of total
US	508.7	86
China	84.0	14
Total	**592.7**	**100**

PRODUCTS/OPERATIONS

2006 Sales

	$ mil.	% of total
Natural gas	470.3	79
Oil	122.4	21
Total	**592.7**	**100**

COMPETITORS

Apache
BP
Cabot Oil & Gas
ConocoPhillips
EOG
Exxon Mobil
Royal Dutch Shell
Samson Oil
XTO Energy

HISTORICAL FINANCIALS

Company Type: Public

Income Statement				FYE: December 31
	REVENUE ($ mil.)	NET INCOME ($ mil.)	NET PROFIT MARGIN	EMPLOYEES
12/06	592.7	231.2	39.0%	57
12/05	516.5	228.3	44.2%	57
12/04	258.0	109.2	42.3%	—
12/03	121.6	45.3	37.3%	—
12/02	42.3	8.1	19.1%	22
Annual Growth	**93.5%**	**131.1%**	**—**	**26.9%**

2006 Year-End Financials

Debt ratio: 30.5%
Return on equity: 38.5%
Cash ($ mil.): 15.4
Current ratio: 0.77
Long-term debt ($ mil.): 191.6
No. of shares (mil.): 151.8
Dividends
  Yield: —
  Payout: —
Market value ($ mil.): 7,246.7
R&D as % of sales: —
Advertising as % of sales: —

Stock History

NYSE: UPL

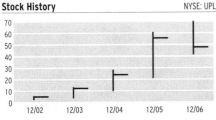

	STOCK PRICE ($) FY Close	P/E High/Low	PER SHARE ($) Earnings	Dividends	Book Value
12/06	47.74	49 29	1.43	—	4.14
12/05	55.80	43 15	1.41	—	3.68
12/04	24.07	41 15	0.68	—	3.55
12/03	12.31	44 14	0.29	—	2.00
12/02	4.95	101 56	0.05	—	1.40
Annual Growth	**76.2%**	**— —**	**131.3%**	**—**	**31.1%**

Umpqua Holdings

Umpqua Holdings thinks of itself not so much as a bank but as a retailer that sells financial products. Consequently, many of the company's more than 130 Umpqua Bank "stores" in Oregon, southwestern Washington, and northern California feature coffee bars and computer cafes. While customers sip Umpqua Bank-brand coffee, read the morning paper, pay bills online, or check out local bands at the bank's online music store, bank staff pitches checking and savings accounts, mortgages, business and consumer loans, investments, and more. Subsidiary Strand, Atkinson, Williams & York provides retail brokerage services through more than a dozen locations; most are inside Umpqua Bank branches.

As the largest bank headquartered in Oregon, Umpqua Holdings has branches scattered across the state, in addition to two branches in Clark County, Washington. It entered the Northern California market with its 2004 purchase of Humboldt Bancorp.

As part of its strategy to continue expanding along the Interstate 5 corridor from Seattle to Sacramento, California, Umpqua Holdings in 2007 acquired Northern California-based North Bay Bancorp; the branches of North Bay Bancorp's Vintage Bank and its Solano Bank division were rebranded to reflect the new ownership. The previous year, the company acquired another Northern California bank holding company, Western Sierra Bancorp, and merged principal subsidiaries Western Sierra Bank, Central California Bank, Lake Community Bank, and Auburn Community Bank into Umpqua Bank.

EXECUTIVES

Chairman: Allyn C. Ford, age 65
Vice Chairman: Dan Giustina, age 57
President, CEO, and Director, Umpqua Holdings and Umpqua Bank: Raymond P. (Ray) Davis, age 57, $1,121,000 pay
SEVP and Chief Credit Officer, Umpqua Holdings and Umpqua Bank: Brad F. Copeland, age 58, $431,000 pay
EVP and CIO: Mark J. Tarmy
EVP; President, Umpqua Bank NW Region: David M. Edson, age 57, $437,500 pay
EVP; President, Umpqua Bank California: William T. (Bill) Fike, age 59, $333,076 pay
SVP and Principal Financial Officer: Ronald L. (Ron) Farnsworth Jr., age 36
SVP, Principal Accounting Officer, and Controller: Neal McLaughlin
Auditors: Moss Adams, LLP

LOCATIONS

HQ: Umpqua Holdings Corporation
1 SW Columbia St., Ste. 1200, Portland, OR 97258
Phone: 866-486-7782   **Fax:** 503-546-2498
Web: www.umpquabank.com

PRODUCTS/OPERATIONS

2006 Sales

	$ mil.	% of total
Interest		
Loans, including fees	372.2	81
Investment securities	31.3	7
Other	2.4	—
Noninterest		
Service charges on deposit accounts	27.0	6
Brokerage commissions & fees	9.7	2
Net mortgage banking revenue	7.6	2
Other	9.4	2
Total	**459.6**	**100**

COMPETITORS

Bank of America
Bank of the West
KeyCorp
U.S. Bancorp
Washington Federal
Washington Mutual
Wells Fargo
West Coast Bancorp

HISTORICAL FINANCIALS

Company Type: Public

Income Statement				FYE: December 31
	ASSETS ($ mil.)	NET INCOME ($ mil.)	INCOME AS % OF ASSETS	EMPLOYEES
12/06	7,344.2	84.4	1.1%	1,530
12/05	5,360.6	69.7	1.3%	1,396
12/04	4,873.0	47.2	1.0%	—
12/03	2,963.8	34.1	1.2%	—
12/02	2,556.0	22.0	0.9%	987
Annual Growth	**30.2%**	**40.0%**	**—**	**11.6%**

2006 Year-End Financials

Equity as % of assets: 15.7%
Return on assets: 1.3%
Return on equity: 8.9%
Long-term debt ($ mil.): 213.2
No. of shares (mil.): 58.1
Market value ($ mil.): 1,709.3
Dividends
  Yield: 2.0%
  Payout: 37.7%
Sales ($ mil.): 459.6
R&D as % of sales: —
Advertising as % of sales: —

Stock History

NASDAQ (GS): UMPQ

	STOCK PRICE ($) FY Close	P/E High/Low	PER SHARE ($) Earnings	Dividends	Book Value
12/06	29.43	19 15	1.59	0.60	19.91
12/05	28.53	19 13	1.55	0.32	16.57
12/04	25.21	20 14	1.30	0.16	15.55
12/03	20.79	19 14	1.19	0.16	11.23
12/02	18.25	18 12	1.03	0.16	10.30
Annual Growth	**12.7%**	**— —**	**11.5%**	**39.2%**	**17.9%**

Under Armour

Under Armour is proving its mettle as an apparel warrior. Since its foray into the sporting goods market, the maker of performance athletic undies and apparel has risen to the top of the industry pack, boasting more than 90% of the compression garment market. It is gaining a foothold in footwear, too. Under Armour is the official supplier of MLB and the NHL. Specializing in sport-specific garments, the company dresses its consumers from head (Cold Weather Hood) to toe (Team Sock). Most products are made from its moisture-wicking and heat-dispersing fabrics, able to keep athletes dry during workouts. Under Armour sells its products via the Internet, catalogs, and 12,000 sporting goods stores worldwide.

Its customers include the likes of Cabela's, Dick's Sporting Goods, and the Army and Air Force Exchange.

Under Armour has dipped its toes into the footwear niche of the industry with its introduction of football cleats in mid-2006 for the fall season. In 2007 it expanded its footwear with baseball and softball cleats.

Nearly all of the company's products are manufactured by third parties. Under Armour's four largest suppliers are located in Mexico, China, and Colombia.

Thus far, Under Armour's primary consumer segment has been men, but it is actively working to expand its apparel offerings for women and children. Under Armour sells its product lines to almost 400 women's sports teams at NCAA Division I-A colleges.

EXECUTIVES

Chairman, President, and CEO: Kevin A. Plank, age 35, $500,000 pay
EVP and CFO: Wayne A. Marino, age 46, $300,000 pay (prior to promotion)
SVP, Marketing: William J. Kraus, age 43, $268,750 pay (prior to promotion)
SVP, Retail: J. Scott Plank, age 41, $333,591 pay
SVP, Sourcing, Quality Assurance, and Product Development: Kip J. Fulks, age 34
SVP, Apparel: Suzanne J. Karkus
VP, House Counsel, and Secretary: Kevin M. Haley, age 38
VP, North American Sales: Matthew C. Mirchin, age 47, $240,000 pay
VP, Operations: Michael F. Fafaul Sr., age 48
VP, Product Creation and Merchandising: Raphael J. Peck, age 35
VP, Human Resources: Melissa Wallace, age 48
CIO: Joseph D. Giles, age 42
President and Managing Director, Under Armour Europe: Peter Mahrer
Auditors: PricewaterhouseCoopers LLP

LOCATIONS

HQ: Under Armour, Inc.
1020 Hull St., 3rd Fl., Baltimore, MD 21230
Phone: 410-454-6428   **Fax:** 410-468-2516
Web: www.underarmour.com

2006 Sales

	$ mil.	% of total
US	403.7	94
Canada	16.5	4
Other countries	10.5	2
Total	**430.7**	**100**

PRODUCTS/OPERATIONS

2006 Sales

	$ mil.	% of total
Men's	255.7	60
Women's	85.7	20
Youth	31.8	7
Footwear	26.9	6
Licensing	15.7	4
Accessories	14.9	3
Total	**430.7**	**100**

COMPETITORS

adidas
Calvin Klein
Columbia Sportswear
Fruit of the Loom
Hanesbrands
Jockey International
K2
L.L. Bean
NIKE
North Face
Patagonia, Inc.
Victoria's Secret Stores
Warnaco Swimwear

HISTORICAL FINANCIALS

Company Type: Public

Income Statement

FYE: December 31

	REVENUE ($ mil.)	NET INCOME ($ mil.)	NET PROFIT MARGIN	EMPLOYEES
12/06	430.7	39.0	9.1%	979
12/05	281.0	19.7	7.0%	610
12/04	205.2	16.3	7.9%	—
12/03	115.4	5.8	5.0%	—
12/02	49.5	2.8	5.7%	175
Annual Growth	**71.7%**	**93.2%**	**—**	**53.8%**

2006 Year-End Financials

Debt ratio: 1.3%
Return on equity: 21.4%
Cash ($ mil.): 70.7
Current ratio: 3.42
Long-term debt ($ mil.): 2.8
No. of shares (mil.): 34.6
Dividends
  Yield: —
  Payout: —
Market value ($ mil.): 1,743.3
R&D as % of sales: —
Advertising as % of sales: —

Stock History

NYSE: UA

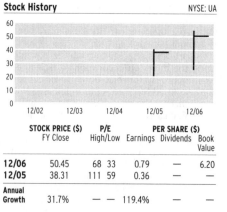

	STOCK PRICE ($) FY Close	P/E High/Low	PER SHARE ($) Earnings	Dividends	Book Value
12/06	50.45	68 33	0.79	—	6.20
12/05	38.31	111 59	0.36	—	—
Annual Growth	**31.7%**	**— —**	**119.4%**	**—**	**—**

Unica Corporation

Unica can help your company predict the behavior of even the most unique clients. The company's enterprise marketing software helps businesses identify, measure, and predict customer behaviors and preferences. Its software suite enables users to conduct large-scale, personalized marketing campaigns, incorporate enterprise data, and analyze the effectiveness of marketing efforts. Unica also offers consulting, installation, integration, and training services.

The company's customers come from a variety of fields, including financial services, health care, manufacturing, retail, and telecommunications.

In 2005 the company acquired MarketSoft for $7.25 million. Unica also purchased marketing resource management software developer MarketingCentral in 2007.

Chairman, president, and CEO Yuchun Lee owns about 24% of the company.

EXECUTIVES

Chairman, President, and CEO: Yuchun Lee, age 42, $519,167 pay
SVP and CFO: Ralph A. Goldwasser, age 60, $214,902 pay (partial-year salary)
SVP and Chief Marketing Officer: Paul McNulty
SVP Worldwide Sales: Eric Schnadig, age 41, $376,667 pay

SVP Professional Services: Richard B. (Rick) Welch, age 50
SVP Corporate Development: David Sweet, age 48
VP Business Development: Kevin Keane
VP Engineering: John Hogan, age 43, $226,667 pay
VP, Corporate Controller, and Chief Accouting Officer: Kevin Thimble
VP, General Counsel, and Corporate Secretary: Jason W. Joseph, age 37
Senior Director, Marketing Communications: Carol Wolicki
Auditors: PricewaterhouseCoopers LLP

LOCATIONS

HQ: Unica Corporation
Reservoir Place North, 170 Tracer Ln., Waltham, MA 02451
Phone: 781-839-8000   **Fax:** 781-890-0012
Web: www.unica.com

PRODUCTS/OPERATIONS

2007 Sales

	$ mil.	% of total
Maintenance & services	54.3	53
License	39.0	38
Subscription	8.9	9
Total	**102.2**	**100**

Selected Products

Affinium Campaign (customer interaction and campaign management)
Affinium eMessage (creates, personalizes, optimizes, and tracks e-mail marketing)
Affinium Interact (online customer personalization)
Affinium Model (predictive modeling software)
Affinium Report (monitors, measures, and reports marketing status and results)

Selected Services

Consulting
Design recommendation
Implementation
Installation
Operational assessment
Training

COMPETITORS

Applix
Art Technology Group
CA, Inc.
Consona CRM
Kana
Oracle
Pivotal
SAP

HISTORICAL FINANCIALS

Company Type: Public

Income Statement

FYE: September 30

	REVENUE ($ mil.)	NET INCOME ($ mil.)	NET PROFIT MARGIN	EMPLOYEES
9/06	82.4	0.7	0.8%	395
9/05	63.5	4.5	7.1%	—
9/04	48.7	3.5	7.2%	—
9/03	31.3	2.5	8.0%	—
Annual Growth	**38.1%**	**(34.6%)**	**—**	**—**

2006 Year-End Financials

Debt ratio: —
Return on equity: 1.4%
Cash ($ mil.): 40.3
Current ratio: 1.53
Long-term debt ($ mil.): —
No. of shares (mil.): 19.6
Dividends
  Yield: —
  Payout: —
Market value ($ mil.): 201.9
R&D as % of sales: —
Advertising as % of sales: —

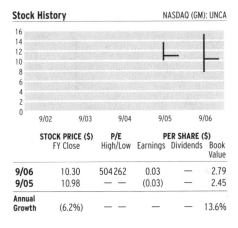

| | 9/02 | 9/03 | 9/04 | 9/05 | 9/06 |

	STOCK PRICE ($) FY Close	P/E High/Low	PER SHARE ($) Earnings	Dividends	Book Value
9/06	10.30	504 262	0.03	—	2.79
9/05	10.98	— —	(0.03)	—	2.45
Annual Growth	(6.2%)	— —	—	—	13.6%

Union Drilling

A leading independent US drilling contractor, Union Drilling unifies hydrocarbons and pipelines via the drill bit. With 76 drilling rigs (70 operating, and six in reserve), the company provides contract land drilling services, primarily in the Appalachian Basin, where 36 of its rigs are located. Union Drilling operates in Arkansas, Colorado, Kentucky, New York, Ohio, Oklahoma, Pennsylvania, Texas, Virginia, and West Virginia. The company's primary customers include XTO Energy, CONSOL, and Fortuna. Union Drilling is controlled by a unit of Morgan Stanley.

Union Drilling was formed in 1997 to acquire the drilling equipment assets of Equitable Resources Energy. In 2005 the company acquired drilling contractors Thornton Drilling Company and SPA Drilling, LP.

EXECUTIVES

Chairman: Thomas H. O'Neill Jr., age 65
President and CEO: Christopher D. (Chris) Strong, age 48
VP, CFO, and Treasurer: A. J. Verdecchia
VP, General Counsel, and Corporate Secretary: David S. Goldberg, age 44
Director Environment, Health, and Safety: Rick Waltemire
Director Human Resources: Lee Spangler
Operations Manager, Central: Charlie S. Hull
Operations Manager, Texas: Jim Mayfield
Operations Manager, Oklahoma: Darwin Hale
Auditors: Ernst & Young LLP

LOCATIONS

HQ: Union Drilling, Inc.
4055 International Plaza, Ste. 610,
Fort Worth, TX 76109
Phone: 817-735-8793   **Fax:** 817-735-9226
Web: www.uniond.com

COMPETITORS

Grey Wolf
Helmerich & Payne
Nabors Industries
Patterson-UTI Energy
Petroleum Development
Pride International
Resource America
Unit Corporation

HISTORICAL FINANCIALS
Company Type: Public

Income Statement   FYE: December 31

	REVENUE ($ mil.)	NET INCOME ($ mil.)	NET PROFIT MARGIN	EMPLOYEES
12/06	256.9	31.9	12.4%	1,515
12/05	141.6	5.6	4.0%	1,300
12/04	67.8	3.5	5.2%	1,060
12/03	58.1	(2.6)	—	—
12/02	47.0	(3.4)	—	—
Annual Growth	52.9%	—	—	19.6%

2006 Year-End Financials

Debt ratio: 19.7%
Return on equity: 21.3%
Cash ($ mil.): 0.0
Current ratio: 1.83
Long-term debt ($ mil.): 33.1
No. of shares (mil.): 21.5

Dividends
  Yield: —
  Payout: —
Market value ($ mil.): 303.1
R&D as % of sales: —
Advertising as % of sales: —

Stock History   NASDAQ (GS): UDRL

| | 12/02 | 12/03 | 12/04 | 12/05 | 12/06 |

	STOCK PRICE ($) FY Close	P/E High/Low	PER SHARE ($) Earnings	Dividends	Book Value
12/06	14.08	13 7	1.47	—	7.79
12/05	14.53	46 40	0.34	—	6.26
Annual Growth	(3.1%)	— —	332.4%	—	24.4%

United Community Banks

United Community Banks is the holding company for about 25 community banks united in their quest to provide consumer and business banking services in Georgia, western North Carolina, and eastern Tennessee. Operating mainly under the United Community Bank or UCB banners, the banks collectively have more than 100 branches offering deposit products, mortgages, and other services. Construction and land development loans account for the largest segment of United Community Banks' loan portfolio (more than 40%); commercial and residential mortgages each make up about 25% apiece. Growing through acquisitions, the company announced plans to buy Gwinnett Commercial Group, the parent of First Bank of the South, in 2007.

The pending deal will add five branches in the Atlanta area.

United Community Banks purchased Georgia-based Southern Bancorp, the holding company for Southern National Bank, in 2006. That deal followed the acquisitions of five other community banks in 2004 and 2003.

United Community Banks provides insurance through its United Community Insurance Services subsidiary, which does business as United Community Advisory Services. Another subsidiary, Brintech, acts as a consultant to financial services firms.

EXECUTIVES

Chairman: Robert L. Head Jr., age 67
Vice Chairman: W. C. Nelson Jr., age 63
President, CEO, and Director: Jimmy C. Tallent, age 54, $897,500 pay
EVP, Secretary, General Counsel, and Director: Thomas C. Gilliland, age 59, $382,700 pay
EVP and CFO: Rex S. Schuette, age 56, $435,600 pay
EVP and COO: Guy W. Freeman, age 70, $490,000 pay
EVP Marketing: Craig Metz, age 49
SVP Banking: Robert L. Cochran
SVP Technology and Operations: Jim Stewart
SVP Human Resources: Susan L. (Susie) Hooper
SVP Chief Compliance Officer: Carol A. Chastain
SVP Retail Banking: William M. Gilbert, age 52
SVP Controller: Alan H. Kumler
Chief Operating Officer, United Community Bank, Brunswick: Gene Haskins
Auditors: Porter Keadle Moore, LLP

LOCATIONS

HQ: United Community Banks, Inc.
63 Hwy. 515, Blairsville, GA 30512
Phone: 706-781-2265   **Fax:** 706-745-8960
Web: www.ucbi.com

PRODUCTS/OPERATIONS

2006 Sales

	$ mil.	% of total
Interest		
Loans, including fees	394.9	80
Securities	49.1	10
Other	0.8	—
Noninterest		
Service charges & fees	27.2	6
Mortgage loans & related fees	7.3	1
Consulting fees	7.3	1
Other	8.0	2
Total	**494.6**	**100**

COMPETITORS

Bank of America
BB&T
Fidelity Southern
First Citizens BancShares
Main Street Banks
RBC Centura Banks
Regions Financial
SunTrust
Synovus
Wachovia
Washington Mutual

HISTORICAL FINANCIALS
Company Type: Public

Income Statement   FYE: December 31

	ASSETS ($ mil.)	NET INCOME ($ mil.)	INCOME AS % OF ASSETS	EMPLOYEES
12/06	7,101.3	68.8	1.0%	1,866
12/05	5,865.8	56.7	1.0%	1,643
12/04	5,087.7	46.6	0.9%	—
12/03	4,068.8	38.1	0.9%	—
12/02	3,211.3	32.8	1.0%	1,097
Annual Growth	21.9%	20.3%	—	14.2%

2006 Year-End Financials

Equity as % of assets: 8.7%
Return on assets: 1.1%
Return on equity: 12.6%
Long-term debt ($ mil.): 113.2
No. of shares (mil.): 44.5
Market value ($ mil.): 1,436.8

Dividends
  Yield: 1.0%
  Payout: 19.3%
Sales ($ mil.): 494.6
R&D as % of sales: —
Advertising as % of sales: —

Stock History

NASDAQ (GS): UCBI

	STOCK PRICE ($) FY Close	P/E High/Low		PER SHARE ($) Earnings	Dividends	Book Value
12/06	32.32	20	16	1.66	0.32	13.87
12/05	26.66	21	15	1.43	0.28	11.79
12/04	26.93	24	17	1.25	0.18	10.39
12/03	21.91	22	14	1.08	0.10	12.73
12/02	16.25	20	14	0.99	—	10.42
Annual Growth	18.8%	—	—	13.8%	47.4%	7.4%

United States Lime & Minerals

Don't be crushed there's no tequila; it's not that kind of lime. Instead, United States Lime & Minerals operates limestone and lime plants in Arkansas, Colorado, Louisiana, Oklahoma, and Texas. It sells pulverized limestone, quicklime, and hydrated lime for making roof shingles, agriculture feeds, sanitation filtering systems, soil enhancers, and asphalt. Customers, primarily in the southwestern and south-central US, include highway, street, and parking lot contractors; steel producers; poultry and cattle feed producers; roofing shingle manufacturers; municipal sanitation and water treatment facilities; and steel producers. Investor George Doumet owns nearly 60% of the company through Inberdon Enterprises.

The company also has natural gas interests in Johnson County, Texas.

United States Lime & Minerals acquired O-N Minerals (St. Clair) Company from an Oglebay Norton Company subsidiary for $14 million in cash and transaction costs at the close of 2005. St. Clair extracts limestone from an underground quarry in Oklahoma.

In 2002 United States Lime & Minerals discovered that its former CFO Larry Ohms had embezzled more than $2 million from the company over four years. Ohms was sentenced to prison and ordered to repay the company.

Investor Robert Beall owns nearly 11% of United States Lime & Minerals.

EXECUTIVES

Chairman: Antoine M. Doumet, age 47
Vice Chairman: Edward A. Odishaw, age 71
President, CEO, and Director: Timothy W. Bryne, age 49, $425,000 pay
SVP Sales and Marketing: Billy R. Hughes, age 68, $207,114 pay
VP, CFO, Secretary, and Treasurer: M. Michael Owens, age 53, $159,083 pay
VP and and Plant Manager, Texas Lime: Richard D. Murray, age 66
VP Manufacturing: Johnney G. Bowers, age 60, $153,633 pay
VP Production: Russell W. Riggs, age 49, $179,013 pay
Auditors: Grant Thornton LLP

LOCATIONS

HQ: United States Lime & Minerals, Inc.
5429 LBJ Fwy., Ste. 230, Dallas, TX 75240
Phone: 972-991-8400   **Fax:** 972-385-1340
Web: www.uslm.com

United States Lime & Minerals has quarries in Batesville, Arkansas; Cleburne, Texas; Marble City, Oklahoma; and Salida, Colorado. The company sells its products primarily in Arkansas, Colorado, Indiana, Kansas, Louisiana, Mississippi, Missouri, New Mexico, Oklahoma, Pennsylvania, Tennessee, Texas, and West Virginia.

PRODUCTS/OPERATIONS

Selected Products

Limestone
  Hydrated lime (calcium hydroxide)
  Pulverized limestone (ground calcium carbonate)
  Quicklime (calcium oxide)

COMPETITORS

Cementos de Chihuahua
Chemical Lime
Edw. C. Levy
Florida Rock
Giant Cement
Hanson Limited
Lafarge North America
Martin Marietta Materials
Monarch Cement
Oglebay Norton
Vulcan Materials

HISTORICAL FINANCIALS

Company Type: Public

Income Statement

FYE: December 31

	REVENUE ($ mil.)	NET INCOME ($ mil.)	NET PROFIT MARGIN	EMPLOYEES
12/06	118.7	12.7	10.7%	—
12/05	81.1	7.9	9.7%	292
12/04	55.7	6.3	11.3%	—
12/03	45.3	3.9	8.6%	—
12/02	39.2	0.6	1.5%	192
Annual Growth	31.9%	114.5%	—	15.0%

2006 Year-End Financials

Debt ratio: 82.3%
Return on equity: 19.4%
Cash ($ mil.): 0.3
Current ratio: 1.22
Long-term debt ($ mil.): 59.6
No. of shares (mil.): 6.2

Dividends
  Yield: —
  Payout: —
Market value ($ mil.): 187.2
R&D as % of sales: —
Advertising as % of sales: —

Stock History

NASDAQ (GM): USLM

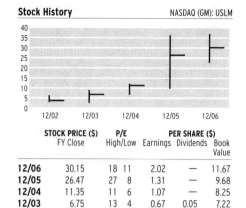

	STOCK PRICE ($) FY Close	P/E High/Low		PER SHARE ($) Earnings	Dividends	Book Value
12/06	30.15	18	11	2.02	—	11.67
12/05	26.47	27	8	1.31	—	9.68
12/04	11.35	11	6	1.07	—	8.25
12/03	6.75	13	4	0.67	0.05	7.22
12/02	3.70	55	29	0.11	0.10	6.61
Annual Growth	69.0%	—	—	107.0%	(50.0%)	15.3%

United Therapeutics

United Therapeutics hopes its products will be in vein. Its Remodulin treats pulmonary hypertension, which affects the blood vessels between the heart and lungs; the firm is investigating Remodulin as a treatment for peripheral vascular disease, which affects blood vessels in the legs. Other products in the biotech's pipeline aim to treat cardiovascular disease, as well as various cancers and infectious diseases. In addition to its drug development activities, United Therapeutics' Medicomp unit provides cardiac monitoring services over the phone and Internet using its CardioPAL event monitors, which detect heart arrhythmias. The company also sells arginine nutritional supplements for cardiovascular health.

EXECUTIVES

Chairman and CEO: Martine A. Rothblatt, age 52, $840,000 pay
President, COO, and Director: Roger Jeffs, age 45, $720,000 pay
CFO and Treasurer: John M. Ferrari, age 52
CIO: Shola Oyewole
EVP Strategic Planning, General Counsel, and Secretary: Paul A. Mahon, age 43, $595,000 pay
COO, Unither Pharmaceuticals: Peter C. Gonze
Chief Medical Officer, United Therapeutics and Lung Rx: Eugene Sullivan
EVP and COO, Production: David Walsh
CEO, Medicomp: Daniel (Dan) Balda
Corporate Communications: Andrew (Andy) Fisher
Auditors: Ernst & Young LLP

LOCATIONS

HQ: United Therapeutics Corporation
1110 Spring St., Silver Spring, MD 20910
Phone: 301-608-9292   **Fax:** 301-608-9291
Web: www.unither.com

PRODUCTS/OPERATIONS

2006 Sales

	$ mil.	% of total
Remodulin	152.5	96
Telemedicine services & products	6.6	4
Other products	0.5	—
Total	**159.6**	**100**

Selected Products

Marketed
 CardioPAL (arrhythmia and angina monitoring
  system)
 Remodulin (hypertension)
In Development
 Beraprost (cardiovascular disease)
 OvaRex (ovarian cancer)
 Viveta (hypertension)

COMPETITORS

Abbott Labs
Actelion
American HealthChoice
AstraZeneca
Bayer Schering Pharma
Encysive Pharmaceuticals
Gilead Sciences
GlaxoSmithKline
Merck
Novartis
Pfizer
Raytel

HISTORICAL FINANCIALS

Company Type: Public

Income Statement — FYE: December 31

	REVENUE ($ mil.)	NET INCOME ($ mil.)	NET PROFIT MARGIN	EMPLOYEES
12/06	159.6	74.0	46.4%	285
12/05	115.9	65.0	56.1%	210
12/04	73.6	15.4	20.9%	—
12/03	53.3	(10.0)	—	—
12/02	30.1	(23.6)	—	150
Annual Growth	**51.7%**	**—**	**—**	**17.4%**

2006 Year-End Financials

Debt ratio: 122.2%
Return on equity: 30.9%
Cash ($ mil.): 227.8
Current ratio: 14.41
Long-term debt ($ mil.): 250.0
No. of shares (mil.): 21.5
Dividends
 Yield: —
 Payout: —
Market value ($ mil.): 1,167.6
R&D as % of sales: —
Advertising as % of sales: —

Stock History

NASDAQ (GS): UTHR

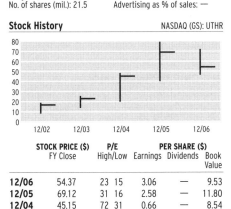

	STOCK PRICE ($) FY Close	P/E High/Low		PER SHARE ($) Earnings	Dividends	Book Value
12/06	54.37	23	15	3.06	—	9.53
12/05	69.12	31	16	2.58	—	11.80
12/04	45.15	72	31	0.66	—	8.54
12/03	22.95	—	—	(0.47)	—	7.87
12/02	16.70	—	—	(1.15)	—	8.20
Annual Growth	**34.3%**	**—**	**—**	**—**	**—**	**3.8%**

Universal Stainless

At Universal Stainless & Alloy Products, even if something is just semi-finished, that's OK. The company makes both semifinished and finished specialty steels, including stainless, tool, and alloyed steels. Universal Stainless' stainless steel products are used in end products made by the automotive, aerospace, and medical industries; its high-temperature steel is produced mainly for the aerospace industry. Before the products get there, however, Universal Stainless sells them to service centers, rerollers, forgers, and wire redrawers. Three customers — Carpenter Technology, Reliance Steel, and Fry Steel — account for more than 30% of Universal Stainless' sales.

The company's finished bar, rod, and wire specialty steel products complement its semifinished products. Universal Stainless also makes specialty steel in the form of long products (ingots, blooms, billets, and bars) and flat-rolled products (slabs and plates).

EXECUTIVES

Chairman: Clarence M. (Mac) McAninch, age 71,
 $245,000 pay (prior to title change)
President, CEO, and Director: Dennis M. Oates, age 56
VP Finance, CFO, and Treasurer: Richard M. Ubinger,
 age 47, $161,923 pay
VP Administration, General Counsel, and Secretary:
 Paul A. McGrath, age 55, $165,077 pay
VP Sales and Marketing: Richard J. Hack
Director Purchasing and Production Planning:
 Bruce A. Kramer
Auditors: Schneider Downs & Co., Inc.

LOCATIONS

HQ: Universal Stainless & Alloy Products, Inc.
 600 Mayer St., Bridgeville, PA 15017
Phone: 412-257-7600 **Fax:** 412-257-7640
Web: www.univstainless.com

Universal Stainless & Alloy Products operates facilities in Bridgeville and Titusville, Pennsylvania, and Dunkirk, New York.

PRODUCTS/OPERATIONS

2006 Sales by Product

	$ mil.	% of total
Steel products		
Stainless steel	151.7	74
Tool steel	23.4	12
High-strength low-alloy steel	16.5	8
High-temperature alloy steel	9.8	5
Conversion services	2.1	1
Other	0.4	—
Total	**203.9**	**100**

2006 Sales by Customer

	$ mil.	% of total
Service centers	101.5	50
Forgers	38.5	19
Rerollers	33.3	16
OEMs	18.4	9
Wire redrawers	9.7	5
Conversion services	2.1	1
Other	0.4	—
Total	**203.9**	**100**

Selected Products

Flat-rolled products (plate, slab)
Long products (bars, blooms, billets, bars, ingots)
Special shapes (precision-rolled shapes from strip or
 bars)

COMPETITORS

Allegheny Technologies
Carpenter Technology
Copper and Brass Sales
Dofasco
PAV Republic
Thomas Steel Strip
ThyssenKrupp Stainless
Timken

HISTORICAL FINANCIALS

Company Type: Public

Income Statement — FYE: December 31

	REVENUE ($ mil.)	NET INCOME ($ mil.)	NET PROFIT MARGIN	EMPLOYEES
12/06	203.9	20.6	10.1%	527
12/05	170.0	13.1	7.7%	482
12/04	120.6	7.1	5.9%	—
12/03	69.0	(1.4)	—	—
12/02	70.9	2.1	3.0%	393
Annual Growth	**30.2%**	**77.0%**	**—**	**7.6%**

2006 Year-End Financials

Debt ratio: 16.5%
Return on equity: 22.2%
Cash ($ mil.): 2.9
Current ratio: 4.22
Long-term debt ($ mil.): 17.2
No. of shares (mil.): 6.6
Dividends
 Yield: —
 Payout: —
Market value ($ mil.): 219.9
R&D as % of sales: —
Advertising as % of sales: —

Stock History

NASDAQ (GM): USAP

	STOCK PRICE ($) FY Close	P/E High/Low		PER SHARE ($) Earnings	Dividends	Book Value
12/06	33.48	12	5	3.12	—	15.92
12/05	15.00	9	6	2.02	—	12.62
12/04	14.85	14	8	1.12	—	10.57
12/03	10.80	—	—	(0.23)	—	9.44
12/02	6.05	48	14	0.34	—	9.67
Annual Growth	**53.4%**	**—**	**—**	**74.0%**	**—**	**13.3%**

Universal Truckload Services

Universal Truckload Services hasn't hauled freight beyond its own galaxy yet, but the company does offer comprehensive coverage of the US and Canada. Universal Truckload Services is an "asset-light" provider of truckload freight transportation. Rather than employing drivers and investing heavily in equipment, the company operates through a network of truck owner-operators. The company can call upon a fleet of some 3,800 tractors and 4,400 trailers, including both standard dry vans and flatbeds. Universal Truckload Services generates business primarily through sales agents. Trucking magnates Matthew Moroun and his father, Manuel Moroun, control a 62% stake in Universal Truckload Services.

In addition to freight transportation, Universal Truckload Services provides freight brokerage services, matching customers' freight with carriers' capacity. The company also offers intermodal support services, which involve picking up shipping containers at ports and railheads and delivering them by truck to customers.

Universal Truckload Services sees its freight brokerage services as a key source of growth, and the company is encouraging its agents to promote that business line. In addition, the company will continue to pursue acquisitions. It expanded in 2006 by buying Alabama-based truckload carrier and freight broker Noble & Pitts, which posted sales of about $33 million in 2005.

Along with Universal Truckload Services, the Morouns control diversified transportation company CenTra, and Matthew Moroun owns a significant stake in truckload carrier P.A.M. Transportation Services.

EXECUTIVES

Chairman: Matthew T. Moroun, age 33
President, CEO, and Director: Donald B. Cochran, age 56, $636,965 pay
VP, CFO, Secretary, and Treasurer:
Robert E. (Bob) Sigler, age 62, $565,448 pay
President, Universal Am-Can: Mark Limback
Auditors: KPMG LLP

LOCATIONS

HQ: Universal Truckload Services, Inc.
12755 E. Nine Mile Rd., Warren, MI 48089
Phone: 586-920-0100   **Fax:** 586-920-0258
Web: www.goutsi.com

PRODUCTS/OPERATIONS

2006 Sales

	$ mil.	% of total
Truckload	375.2	58
Brokerage	170.6	27
Intermodal	95.8	15
Total	**641.6**	**100**

COMPETITORS

C.H. Robinson Worldwide
Crete Carrier
Hub Group
J.B. Hunt
Landstar System
Pacer Global Logistics
Schneider National
Swift Transportation
U.S. Xpress
Werner Enterprises

HISTORICAL FINANCIALS

Company Type: Public

Income Statement				FYE: December 31
	REVENUE ($ mil.)	NET INCOME ($ mil.)	NET PROFIT MARGIN	EMPLOYEES
12/06	641.6	21.0	3.3%	644
12/05	531.3	17.2	3.2%	494
12/04	362.0	11.1	3.1%	—
12/03	277.7	8.7	3.1%	—
12/02	252.8	7.5	3.0%	—
Annual Growth	**26.2%**	**29.4%**	**—**	**30.4%**

2006 Year-End Financials

Debt ratio: 0.7%	Dividends
Return on equity: 17.0%	Yield: —
Cash ($ mil.): 20.3	Payout: —
Current ratio: 2.24	Market value ($ mil.): 382.8
Long-term debt ($ mil.): 1.0	R&D as % of sales: —
No. of shares (mil.): 16.1	Advertising as % of sales: —

Stock History

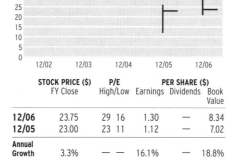

NASDAQ (GM): UACL

	STOCK PRICE ($) FY Close	P/E High/Low	PER SHARE ($) Earnings	Dividends	Book Value
12/06	23.75	29 16	1.30	—	8.34
12/05	23.00	23 11	1.12	—	7.02
Annual Growth	**3.3%**	**— —**	**16.1%**	**—**	**18.8%**

U.S. Auto Parts Network

Your next trip to the auto parts store may be as close as the nearest computer, thanks to U.S. Auto Parts Network. The company offers more than 550,000 after-market auto parts through its partstrain.com and autopartswarehouse.com Web sites, allowing customers to order and then have delivered the various body, engine, and performance parts used by shade tree mechanics nationwide. In 2006 the company acquired rival online auto parts retailer Partsbin, expanding its product lines, particularly in engine parts and performance accessories. In early 2007 cofounders Sol Khazani and Mehran Nia (both directors) took the company public. Former Blockbuster general manager Shane Evangelist was named CEO in late 2007.

Evangelist headed up the launch of Blockbuster's online movie-rental service. Nia stepped down as president and CEO as part of the move but remains on the board.

U.S. Auto Parts Network intends to use $100 million raised in the February IPO to repay debt, expand its infrastructure and sales and marketing activities, and possibly for acquisitions. Prior to the IPO, Nia and Khazani each owned about 25% of the company's shares. Their post-IPO holdings total nearly 16% for Nia and about 13% for Khazani.

Although the company primarily serves individual consumers (the average online order is about $120) it also sells products wholesale to auto body shops in Southern California and sells its Kool-Vue mirror line nationally to auto parts wholesale distributors.

EXECUTIVES

Chairman: Robert J. Majteles, age 42
President, CEO, and Director: Shane Evangelist
EVP Finance, CFO, Treasurer, and Secretary:
Michael J. McClane, age 38, $519,770 pay
VP Marketing: Houman Akhavan, age 29, $293,788 pay
CIO: Alexander Adegan, age 37
Director, Perfectfit: Ben Elyashar, age 36
Auditors: Ernst & Young LLP

LOCATIONS

HQ: U.S. Auto Parts Network, Inc.
17150 S. Margay Ave., Carson, CA 90746
Phone: 310-719-8666   **Fax:** 310-632-1681
Web: www.usautoparts.net

PRODUCTS/OPERATIONS

Selected Product Categories

Body Parts
  Bumpers
  Fenders
  Grills
  Hoods
  Lights
  Mirrors
  Wheels
  Window regulators
Engine Parts
  Air filters
  Brakes
  Catalytic converters
  Clutch parts
  Cold air intake
  Condensers
  Exhaust systems
  Radiators
Accessories
  Bike racks
  Car covers
  Floor mats and carpeting
  Gauges
  Headers
  Navigation systems
  Nerf bars
  Spoilers

COMPETITORS

Advance Auto Parts
Amazon.com
AutoZone
CSK Auto
eBay
Genuine Parts
Keystone Automotive
LKQ
O'Reilly Automotive
Pep Boys

HISTORICAL FINANCIALS

Company Type: Public

Income Statement				FYE: December 31
	REVENUE ($ mil.)	NET INCOME ($ mil.)	NET PROFIT MARGIN	EMPLOYEES
12/06	120.1	3.5	2.9%	451
12/05	59.7	6.8	11.4%	—
12/04	40.7	7.1	17.4%	—
12/03	31.7	3.8	12.0%	—
Annual Growth	**55.9%**	**(2.7%)**	**—**	**—**

2006 Year-End Financials

Debt ratio: 107.0% Current ratio: 0.59
Return on equity: 27.1% Long-term debt ($ mil.): 22.0
Cash ($ mil.): 2.4

Net Income History

NASDAQ (GM): PRTS

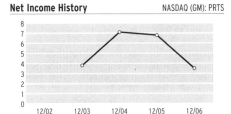

US Global Investors

It may be a small world, but U.S. Global Investors wants to make it a little greener, after all. Along with its U.S. Global Accolade Funds, the company is an investment manager and adviser that offers no-load mutual funds generally geared toward long-term investing. Other subsidiaries of U.S. Global Investors provide transfer agent, brokerage, and mailing services. The company also engages in corporate investment, providing initial financing to start-ups and supplying capital to established businesses for expansion, acquisitions, management buyouts, or restructuring. It has more than $4.5 billion in assets under management.

EXECUTIVES

Chairman: Jerold H. (Jerry) Rubinstein, age 70
Vice Chairman: Roy D. Terracina, age 62
CEO and Chief Investment Officer: Frank E. Holmes, age 53, $2,106,152 pay
President and General Counsel: Susan B. McGee, age 47, $756,610 pay
CFO: Catherine A. Rademacher, age 46, $214,990 pay
Director, Institutional Services: Michael S. Dunn, age 44
Director, Research: John Derrick
Director Marketing: Susan K. Filyk
Portfolio Manager, Charlemagne Capital: Stefan Böttcher
Portfolio Manager, U.S. Global Accolade Eastern European Fund: Andrew Wiles
Chief Compliance Officer and Associate General Counsel: James L. Love
Auditors: BDO Seidman, LLP

LOCATIONS

HQ: U.S. Global Investors, Inc.
7900 Callaghan Rd., San Antonio, TX 78229
Phone: 210-308-1234 **Fax:** 210-308-1223
Web: www.usfunds.com

PRODUCTS/OPERATIONS

2007 Sales

	$ mil.	% of total
Investment Management Services	58.2	99
Corporate Investments	0.4	1
Total	**58.6**	**100**

Selected Mutual Funds

All American Equity Fund
China Region Opportunity Fund
Eastern European Fund
Global Resources Fund
Gold Shares Fund
Holmes Growth Fund
Megatrends Fund
Near-Term Tax Free Fund
Tax Free Fund
U.S. Government Securities Savings Fund
U.S. Treasury Securities Cash Fund
World Precious Minerals Fund

COMPETITORS

AGF Management
AIM Funds
Atalanta Sosnoff
Eaton Vance
FMR
Franklin Resources
Janus Capital
MFS
Nuveen
Oak Associates
PIMCO
Putnam
T. Rowe Price
TIAA-CREF
Van Kampen Investments
The Vanguard Group
Westwood Holdings

HISTORICAL FINANCIALS

Company Type: Public

Income Statement

FYE: June 30

	ASSETS ($ mil.)	NET INCOME ($ mil.)	INCOME AS % OF ASSETS	EMPLOYEES
6/07	39.8	13.8	34.7%	82
6/06	29.0	10.4	35.9%	78
6/05	12.1	1.5	12.4%	67
6/04	9.5	2.2	23.2%	—
6/03	7.4	0.0	—	—
Annual Growth	**52.3%**	**—**	**—**	**10.6%**

2007 Year-End Financials

Equity as % of assets: 78.1%
Return on assets: 40.1%
Return on equity: 53.4%
Long-term debt ($ mil.): —
No. of shares (mil.): 12.9
Market value ($ mil.): 293.5

Dividends
  Yield: 0.6%
  Payout: 15.6%
Sales ($ mil.): 58.6
R&D as % of sales: —
Advertising as % of sales: —

Stock History

NASDAQ (CM): GROW

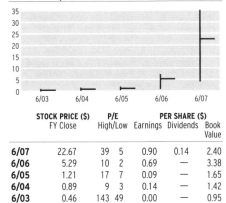

	STOCK PRICE ($) FY Close	P/E High	P/E Low	PER SHARE ($) Earnings	PER SHARE ($) Dividends	PER SHARE ($) Book Value
6/07	22.67	39	5	0.90	0.14	2.40
6/06	5.29	10	2	0.69	—	3.38
6/05	1.21	17	7	0.09	—	1.65
6/04	0.89	9	3	0.14	—	1.42
6/03	0.46	143	49	0.00	—	0.95
Annual Growth	**165.0%**	**—**	**—**	**—**	**—**	**26.0%**

VAALCO Energy

VAALCO Energy has boldly gone where bigger players are sure to follow. The small independent, which merged with the 1818 Oil Corp. in a reverse acquisition in 1998, is engaged in the acquisition, exploration, development, and production of oil and gas. Its strategy is to balance its lower-risk domestic drilling with higher-potential international prospects. VAALCO holds exploration assets in Angola and Gabon, and has interests in the Texas Gulf Coast. It has proved reserves of 6 million barrels of oil and 17 million cu. ft. of gas. The company sold its Philippine holdings in 2004. The 1818 Fund, managed by Brown Brothers Harriman & Co. of New York, controlled 65% of VAALCO, but sold this stake in 2005.

EXECUTIVES

Chairman and CEO: Robert L. Gerry III, age 69, $370,700 pay
President, CFO, and Director: W. Russell Scheirman, age 51, $264,000 pay
VP and Corporate Secretary: Gayla M. Cutrer, $131,112 pay
Auditors: Deloitte & Touche LLP

LOCATIONS

HQ: VAALCO Energy, Inc.
4600 Post Oak Place, Ste. 309, Houston, TX 77027
Phone: 713-623-0801 **Fax:** 713-623-0982
Web: www.vaalco.com

VAALCO Energy has oil and gas exploration interests in Angola, Gabon, and the US.

PRODUCTS/OPERATIONS

Selected Subsidiaries

VAALCO Energy (Gabon), Inc.
VAALCO Energy (USA), Inc.
VAALCO Garbon (Etame), Inc. (90%)
VAALCO Production (Gabon), Inc.

COMPETITORS

Exxon Mobil
Hess Corporation
Imperial Oil
Pioneer Natural Resources
Royal Dutch Shell
TOTAL

HISTORICAL FINANCIALS

Company Type: Public

Income Statement

FYE: December 31

	REVENUE ($ mil.)	NET INCOME ($ mil.)	NET PROFIT MARGIN	EMPLOYEES
12/06	98.3	40.3	41.0%	16
12/05	84.9	29.2	34.4%	16
12/04	56.5	22.9	40.5%	12
12/03	36.0	8.9	24.7%	28
12/02	10.0	0.4	4.0%	29
Annual Growth	**77.1%**	**216.8%**	**—**	**(13.8%)**

2006 Year-End Financials

Debt ratio: 4.1%
Return on equity: 40.2%
Cash ($ mil.): 65.7
Current ratio: 3.15
Long-term debt ($ mil.): 5.0
No. of shares (mil.): 59.0

Dividends
  Yield: —
  Payout: —
Market value ($ mil.): 398.2
R&D as % of sales: —
Advertising as % of sales: —

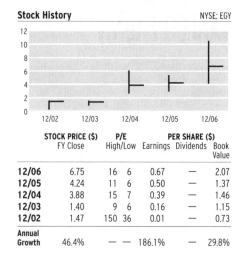

	STOCK PRICE ($) FY Close	P/E High/Low		PER SHARE ($) Earnings	Dividends	Book Value
12/06	6.75	16	6	0.67	—	2.07
12/05	4.24	11	6	0.50	—	1.37
12/04	3.88	15	7	0.39	—	1.46
12/03	1.40	9	6	0.16	—	1.15
12/02	1.47	150	36	0.01	—	0.73
Annual Growth	46.4%	—	—	186.1%	—	29.8%

Valley Financial

Down in the valley, valley so low ... Valley Financial has a banking business, dontcha know? The financial institution is the holding company for Valley Bank, which has locations in and around Roanoke, Virginia. Valley Bank offers traditional banking products and services to individuals and small to midsized businesses in its market area. Deposit products include checking and savings accounts, NOW accounts, and CDs. Commercial real estate loans account for more than 35% of its loan portfolio, while residential real estate makes up nearly a quarter.

Chairman George Logan owns about 10% of Valley Financial; as a group, executive officers and directors own more than 35%.

EXECUTIVES

Chairman, Valley Financial and Valley Bank:
George W. Logan, age 62
President, CEO, and Director; President and CEO, Valley Bank: Ellis L. Gutshall, age 56, $268,000 pay
EVP and CFO, Valley Financial and Valley Bank:
Kimberly B. Snyder, age 36, $120,000 pay
EVP and COO, Valley Financial and Valley Bank:
J. Randall (Randy) Woodson, age 45, $175,000 pay
SVP and Chief Strategic Planning Officer:
Penny Y. Goodwin
SVP and Chief Risk Officer: Mary P. (Gill) Hundley, age 47
SVP and CIO: JoAnn M Lloyd, age 53
SVP and Chief Lending Officer: John T. McCaleb, age 45, $121,000 pay
SVP and Chief Retail Banking Officer:
Connie W. Stanley, age 53
SVP and Senior Real Estate Officer: Andrew B. Agee, age 45, $110,240 pay
SVP and Chief Credit Officer: Edward C. Martin
Director: A. Wayne Lewis, age 63
Auditors: Elliott Davis LLC

LOCATIONS

HQ: Valley Financial Corporation
36 Church Ave. SW, Roanoke, VA 24011
Phone: 540-342-2265　　**Fax:** 540-342-4514
Web: www.myvalleybank.com

PRODUCTS/OPERATIONS

2006 Sales

	$ mil.	% of total
Interest		
Interest and fees on loans	32.0	87
Interest on securities taxable	2.3	6
Interest on securities nontaxable	0.5	1
Interest on deposits in banks	0.1	0
Noninterest		
Service charges on deposit accounts	1.0	3
Income earned on bank owned life insurance	0.5	1
Other income on real estate loans	0.1	0
Other income	0.6	2
Total	**37.1**	**100**

COMPETITORS

Bank of America
Bank of the James
BB&T
First National Bankshares
FNB Corporation (VA)
MainStreet BankShares
National Bankshares
Pinnacle Bankshares
SunTrust
Wachovia

HISTORICAL FINANCIALS
Company Type: Public

Income Statement
FYE: December 31

	ASSETS ($ mil.)	NET INCOME ($ mil.)	INCOME AS % OF ASSETS	EMPLOYEES
12/06	591.9	2.9	0.5%	120
12/05	499.0	3.4	0.7%	111
12/04	374.0	2.8	0.7%	—
12/03	309.0	2.6	0.8%	—
12/02	248.9	2.3	0.9%	—
Annual Growth	24.2%	6.0%	—	8.1%

2006 Year-End Financials

Equity as % of assets: 5.6%
Return on assets: 0.5%
Return on equity: 9.0%
Long-term debt ($ mil.): 64.5
No. of shares (mil.): 4.1
Market value ($ mil.): 53.9
Dividends
　Yield: 1.1%
　Payout: 20.6%
Sales ($ mil.): 37.1
R&D as % of sales: —
Advertising as % of sales: —

Stock History
NASDAQ (CM): VYFC

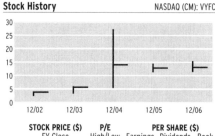

	STOCK PRICE ($) FY Close	P/E High/Low		PER SHARE ($) Earnings	Dividends	Book Value
12/06	13.10	22	17	0.68	0.14	8.12
12/05	12.85	18	14	0.80	0.13	7.53
12/04	14.00	39	8	0.70	0.06	6.95
12/03	5.65	9	5	0.67	—	11.76
12/02	3.78	6	4	0.60	—	10.40
Annual Growth	36.4%	—	—	3.2%	52.8%	(6.0%)

ValueClick, Inc.

If you think that banner ad is worth a look, ValueClick will put a price on it. The company brings Web publishers together with advertisers providing the technology necessary for each side to manage online advertising. ValueClick's media services segment offers e-mail marketing, search marketing, and ad placement services throughout a network of more than 14,000 Web sites in the US. The company's affiliate marketing tools track and analyze online marketing programs through its Commission Junction subsidiary, while its Mediaplex unit provides online ad serving and management tools. Pricerunner and Shopping.net allow consumers to compare and research products online.

ValueClick has been expanding through several acquisitions. The 2005 acquisition of Webclients expanded ValueClick's online marketing services with the addition of more than 100 promotional Web sites. That same year, ValueClick bought Fastclick, owner of more than 9,000 third-party publisher Web sites. The buyout significantly boosted ValueClick's own advertising network capabilities. (By the end of 2006, the company boasted 16,000 online publishing partnerships worldwide.)

In addition, ValueClick acquired Shopping.net, an operator of 27 comparison shopping Web sites, for $13 million in cash in 2006. Shopping.net is being integrated into the company's European operations, ValueClick Europe. The following year, ValueClick agreed to buy another comparison shopping site, MeziMedia, for $100 million in cash. The deal will give ValueClick a leg up in the coveted online Chinese market since MeziMedia owns an engineering and operations center in Shanghai, in addition to comparison shopping Web sites in China.

EXECUTIVES

Executive Chairman: James R. Zarley, age 62
CEO and Director: Thomas A. (Tom) Vadnais, age 59
CFO: John Pitstick
VP, General Counsel, and Secretary: Scott P. Barlow, age 38
CTO: Peter J. Wolfert, age 43
Chief Administrative Officer: Samuel J. (Sam) Paisley, age 57
Director, Corporate Communications: Gary J. Fuges
CEO, ValueClick Europe: Carl White, age 42
COO, US Media: David Yovanno
VP Product Management, ValueClick Media: John Ellis
VP Eastern Sales, ValueClick Media: Bill Todd
VP Western Sales, ValueClick Media: Matthew Boyd
VP Media Development, ValueClick Media:
Chad Peplinski
VP Operations, ValueClick Media: Barbara Jennings
Director Marketing, ValueClick Media: Tony Winders
Auditors: PricewaterhouseCoopers LLP

LOCATIONS

HQ: ValueClick, Inc.
30699 Russell Ranch Rd., Ste. 250,
Westlake Village, CA 91362
Phone: 818-575-4500　　**Fax:** 818-575-4501
Web: valueclick.com

ValueClick operates in France, Germany, Sweden, the UK, and the US.

2006 Sales

	$ mil.	% of total
US	486.8	87
Europe	69.7	13
Adjustments	(10.9)	—
Total	**545.6**	**100**

PRODUCTS/OPERATIONS

2006 Sales

	$ mil.	% of total
Media	383.0	70
Affiliate marketing	112.1	20
Comparison shopping	26.2	5
Technology	25.7	5
Adjustments	(1.4)	—
Total	**545.6**	**100**

Selected Subsidiaries and Services

ValueClick Media
  Brand marketing
  Direct marketing
  Pay Per Click Search Marketing

Commission Junction
  Affiliate marketing
  Search marketing
  Program management

Mediaplex
  Ad serving
  Publisher ad management
  E-mail management and delivery

Pricerunner
  Comparison shopping
  Consumer reviews
  Mobile services

COMPETITORS

24/7 Real Media
Acxiom Digital
Advertising.com
Agency.com
aQuantive
BURST! Media
Digital River
DoubleClick
Kelkoo
LinkShare
MIVA
NexTag
Performics
PriceGrabber.com
Publicis Modem
Shopzilla
Yahoo! Search Marketing

HISTORICAL FINANCIALS

Company Type: Public

Income Statement — FYE: December 31

	REVENUE ($ mil.)	NET INCOME ($ mil.)	NET PROFIT MARGIN	EMPLOYEES
12/06	545.6	62.6	11.5%	1,072
12/05	304.0	40.6	13.4%	1,014
12/04	169.2	87.9	52.0%	—
12/03	92.5	9.8	10.6%	—
12/02	62.5	(10.6)	—	419
Annual Growth	**71.9%**	**—**	**—**	**26.5%**

2006 Year-End Financials

Debt ratio: 6.9%
Return on equity: 9.9%
Cash ($ mil.): 281.6
Current ratio: 4.61
Long-term debt ($ mil.): 44.5
No. of shares (mil.): 99.4

Dividends
  Yield: —
  Payout: —
Market value ($ mil.): 2,349.1
R&D as % of sales: —
Advertising as % of sales: —

Stock History — NASDAQ (GS): VCLK

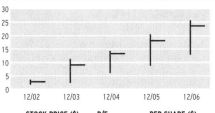

	STOCK PRICE ($) FY Close	P/E High/Low		PER SHARE ($) Earnings	Dividends	Book Value
12/06	23.63	41	21	0.62	—	6.48
12/05	18.11	45	20	0.45	—	6.06
12/04	13.33	13	6	1.05	—	4.69
12/03	9.07	86	20	0.13	—	3.52
12/02	2.79	—	—	(0.14)	—	3.04
Annual Growth	**70.6%**	**—**	**—**	**—**	**—**	**20.8%**

Vanguard Natural Resources

Vanguard Natural Resources is at the forefront of oil and gas exploration in the hills of the Appalachian Basin. Focusing its efforts in southeastern Kentucky and northeastern Tennessee, the company acquires and develops oil and gas properties in the region. Vanguard Natural Resources has an estimated proved reserve of 66 billion cu. ft. of natural gas equivalent. The company also owns an interest in nearly 790 net and about 850 gross wells and a 40% working interest in some 107,000 acres in the area. Vinland owns the remaining 60% working interest of the acreage. The company plans to use IPO funds to pay off debt.

EXECUTIVES

President and CEO: Scott W. Smith, age 49
EVP and CFO: Richard A. Robert, age 41
Auditors: UHY LLP

LOCATIONS

HQ: Vanguard Natural Resources, LLC
  7700 San Felipe, Ste. 485, Houston, TX 77063
Phone: 832-327-2255

COMPETITORS

Cabot Oil & Gas
Quicksilver Resources
Royal Dutch Shell

HISTORICAL FINANCIALS

Company Type: Public

Income Statement — FYE: December 31

	REVENUE ($ mil.)	NET INCOME ($ mil.)	NET PROFIT MARGIN	EMPLOYEES
12/06	54.4	26.6	48.9%	29
12/05	11.9	(10.6)	—	—
12/04	17.0	5.3	31.2%	—
Annual Growth	**78.9%**	**124.0%**	**—**	**—**

2006 Year-End Financials

Debt ratio: 306.3%
Return on equity: 146.8%
Cash ($ mil.): 1.7
Current ratio: 1.64
Long-term debt ($ mil.): 94.1

Net Income History — NYSE Arca: VNR

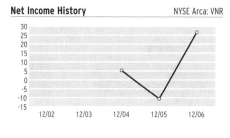

VASCO Data Security International

VASCO Data Security International holds the key to electronic banking. Its Digipass product line features security tokens, handheld devices, and related software used for authenticating a person's identity to computer networks. The company's products incorporate authentication and digital signature security technologies, and can be used to secure intranets and extranets, as well as local area networks (LANs). In addition to banking, VASCO's products are used to provide remote workers with secure access to corporate networks; other applications include e-commerce transactions. Chairman and CEO Kendall Hunt owns more than a quarter of the company.

The company has customers in more than 100 countries. Clients have included HSBC, Rabobank, Volvo, and Wachovia.

VASCO acquired Able, a provider of unified threat management software, in 2006.

EXECUTIVES

Chairman and CEO: T. Kendall (Ken) Hunt, age 63, $350,000 pay
President and COO: Jan Valcke, age 51, $432,852 pay
EVP, CFO, and Secretary: Clifford K. Bown, age 54, $260,000 pay
VP Asia Pacific: Daren Leong
CIO: Victor Hoogland
Director Corporate Communications: Jochem Binst
Director Worldwide Human Resources: Bernhard Kolb
Director Contracts and Compliance: Alexandra Spirig
Auditors: KPMG LLP

LOCATIONS

HQ: VASCO Data Security International, Inc.
  1901 S. Meyers Rd., Ste. 210,
  Oakbrook Terrace, IL 60180
Phone: 630-932-8844   **Fax:** 630-932-8852
Web: www.vasco.com

2006 Sales

	$ mil.	% of total
Europe	47.5	62
US	7.4	10
Other regions	21.2	28
Total	**76.1**	**100**

PRODUCTS/OPERATIONS

2006 Sales by Market

	$ mil.	% of total
Banking	65.0	85
Enterprise Security	11.1	15
Total	**76.1**	**100**

Selected Products

Authentication devices and software (Digipass)
Authentication utilities (VACMAN)

COMPETITORS

ActivIdentity
Aladdin Knowledge Systems
CA, Inc.
Check Point Software
Entrust
McAfee
NTRU
RSA Security
SafeNet
Secure Computing
Symantec
WatchGuard Technologies

HISTORICAL FINANCIALS

Company Type: Public

Income Statement

FYE: December 31

	REVENUE ($ mil.)	NET INCOME ($ mil.)	NET PROFIT MARGIN	EMPLOYEES
12/06	76.1	12.6	16.6%	184
12/05	54.6	7.7	14.1%	128
12/04	29.9	3.3	11.0%	—
12/03	22.9	2.8	12.2%	—
12/02	18.9	(4.5)	—	77
Annual Growth	**41.7%**	**—**	**—**	**24.3%**

2006 Year-End Financials

Debt ratio: —
Return on equity: 37.3%
Cash ($ mil.): 14.8
Current ratio: 2.15
Long-term debt ($ mil.): —
No. of shares (mil.): 36.5
Dividends
Yield: —
Payout: —
Market value ($ mil.): 433.1
R&D as % of sales: —
Advertising as % of sales: —

Stock History

NASDAQ (GM): VDSI

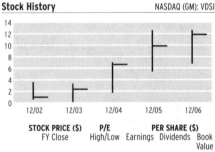

	STOCK PRICE ($) FY Close	P/E High/Low	PER SHARE ($) Earnings	Dividends	Book Value
12/06	11.85	38 21	0.33	—	1.15
12/05	9.86	59 26	0.21	—	0.70
12/04	6.62	77 20	0.09	—	0.39
12/03	2.34	— —	(0.06)	—	0.29
12/02	0.97	— —	(0.20)	—	0.10
Annual Growth	**87.0%**	**— —**	**—**	**—**	**84.8%**

Venoco, Inc.

Santa Barbara's pristine beaches and Venoco's oil and gas exploration and production activities make for a volatile mix. Although Venoco has traditionally operated in the environmentally sensitive Santa Barbara Channel, it has been expanding its geographic reach and diversifying its operations. It also owns interests in 298 producing wells in Southern and Northern California. Venoco has estimated proved reserves of 87.9 million barrels of oil equivalent. In 2006 the company acquired TexCal Energy (LP) LLC, an independent exploration and production firm with assets in Texas and California. Chairman and CEO Tim Marquez controls Venoco.

Marquez founded Venoco in 1992. The company sold its former oil and gas exploration and production assets in Texas in 2004 in order to focus on the California market, but subsequently moved back into Texas in 2006.

EXECUTIVES

Chairman and CEO: Timothy (Tim) Marquez, age 48, $366,000 pay
President: William (Bill) Schneider, age 45, $280,952 pay
SVP and COO: Mark DePuy, age 52
SVP: Jeff Janik
CFO: Timothy A. Ficker, age 40
VP Asset Development: Gregory B. Schrage, age 50, $185,079 pay
VP Investor Relations: Michael G. Edwards, age 48
VP, Coastal Operations: Roger K. Hamson, age 49
VP, Acquisitions: T Terry Sherban
VP, Sac Basin Operations: Kevin Morrato
VP Texas Operations: Brady McConaty
Chief Accounting Officer: Douglas Griggs, age 48
Secretary and General Counsel: Terry L. Anderson, age 60, $212,853 pay
Chief Human Resources Officer: Carla J. Wolin, age 50
Auditors: Deloitte & Touche LLP

LOCATIONS

HQ: Venoco, Inc.
370 17th St., Ste. 3900, Denver, CO 80202
Phone: 303-626-8300 **Fax:** 303-626-8315
Web: www.venocoinc.com

COMPETITORS

Berry Petroleum
Chevron
Delta Petroleum
Plains Exploration
Provident Energy
Pyramid Oil

HISTORICAL FINANCIALS

Company Type: Public

Income Statement

FYE: December 31

	REVENUE ($ mil.)	NET INCOME ($ mil.)	NET PROFIT MARGIN	EMPLOYEES
12/06	280.3	24.0	8.6%	250
12/05	137.9	16.1	11.7%	—
12/04	125.3	23.5	18.8%	171
12/03	103.2	11.2	10.9%	—
12/02	85.1	1.0	1.2%	—
Annual Growth	**34.7%**	**121.3%**	**—**	**20.9%**

2006 Year-End Financials

Debt ratio: 281.9%
Return on equity: 24.7%
Cash ($ mil.): 18.7
Current ratio: 0.99
Long-term debt ($ mil.): 536.5
No. of shares (mil.): 42.8
Dividends
Yield: —
Payout: —
Market value ($ mil.): 751.3
R&D as % of sales: —
Advertising as % of sales: —

Stock History

NYSE: VQ

	STOCK PRICE ($) FY Close	P/E High/Low	PER SHARE ($) Earnings	Dividends	Book Value
12/06	17.56	26 24	0.69	—	4.45

VeraSun Energy

VeraSun Energy hopes its profits rise with the progress of the US quest for energy independence. The company is one of the nation's leading producers of ethanol, a type of alcohol that can be blended with gasoline and used to fuel motor vehicles. In the US, ethanol is made primarily from corn, and VeraSun maintains five production facilities in the Midwest; four more facilities are under construction and scheduled to begin production in 2008. The company sells a branded fuel, VE85, at service stations in the Midwest. VeraSun agreed to buy fellow ethanol producer US BioEnergy for $685 million in 2007. CEO Don Endres owns just over 50% of VeraSun Energy; South Dakota investment firm Bluestem Funds owns 33%.

VE85 is a branded version of E85, a fuel blend that can contain as much as 85% ethanol. Automakers Ford and General Motors are helping VeraSun Energy promote VE85.

In 2007 the company acquired three facilities from ASAlliances Biofuels for $725 million. Only one is currently in production, but when all three get going, VeraSun will have 1 billion gallons of production capacity.

EXECUTIVES

Chairman: Gordon Ommen, age 48
CEO: Donald L. (Don) Endres, age 46, $468,586 pay
President and CFO: Danny C. Herron, age 52, $183,419 pay
SVP and General Counsel: John M. Schweitzer, age 62, $295,886 pay
SVP, Corporate Development and Director: Paul A. Schock, age 49
SVP, Operations: Paul J. Caudill, age 53
SVP, Sales and Marketing: William L. (Bill) Honnef, age 40, $301,567 pay
SVP, Logistics: Barry P. Schaps, age 54
SVP, Human Resources: Robert Antoine
VP, Finance: Ginja R. Collins, age 32
VP, Ethanol Sales: Paul Kreter
VP, Plant Operations: Kevin T. Biehle, age 42
VP, Technology: Matthew K.R. (Matt) Janes, age 50
VP, Mergers and Acquisitions: Peter A. Atkins, age 47
Director Investor Relations: Patty Dickerson
Auditors: McGladrey & Pullen, LLP

LOCATIONS

HQ: VeraSun Energy Corporation
100 22nd Ave., Brookings, SD 57006
Phone: 605-696-7200 **Fax:** 605-696-7250
Web: www.verasun.com

VeraSun operates plants in Indiana, Iowa, Nebraska, and South Dakota and has commenced construction on others in Iowa, Minnesota, and Ohio.

PRODUCTS/OPERATIONS

2006 Sales

	$ mil.	% of total
Ethanol	488.1	87
Distillers grains	58.3	11
E85	7.6	1
Other	3.8	1
Total	**557.8**	**100**

COMPETITORS

Abengoa Bioenergy
ADM
Aventine
Badger State Ethanol
Cargill
Hawkeye Holdings
US BioEnergy
Xethanol Corporation

HISTORICAL FINANCIALS

Company Type: Public

Income Statement

FYE: December 31

	REVENUE ($ mil.)	NET INCOME ($ mil.)	NET PROFIT MARGIN	EMPLOYEES
12/06	557.8	75.7	13.6%	195
12/05	236.4	0.3	0.1%	145
12/04	193.8	14.8	7.6%	—
12/03	12.7	0.6	4.7%	—
Annual Growth	252.8%	401.6%	—	34.5%

2006 Year-End Financials

Debt ratio: 41.2%
Return on equity: 23.2%
Cash ($ mil.): 330.4
Current ratio: 8.36
Long-term debt ($ mil.): 208.9
No. of shares (mil.): 75.5
Dividends
Yield: —
Payout: —
Market value ($ mil.): 1,490.4
R&D as % of sales: —
Advertising as % of sales: —

Stock History

NYSE: VSE

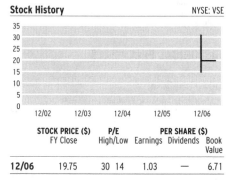

	STOCK PRICE ($) FY Close	P/E High/Low	PER SHARE ($) Earnings	Dividends	Book Value
12/06	19.75	30 14	1.03	—	6.71

Versar, Inc.

Environmental engineering company Versar is well-versed in keeping the homeland clean and secure. The company's infrastructure and management services business, which accounts for most of Versar's sales, helps clients with six main tasks: compliance with environmental regulations, conservation of natural resources, construction oversight, engineering and design, pollution prevention, and restoration of contaminated sites. Major customers include the US Department of Defense and the US Environmental Protection Agency. Subsidiary GEOMET Technologies, which constitutes Versar's national defense business segment, makes biohazard suits for agencies involved in emergency response and counterterrorism efforts.

Versar merged its former engineering and construction business segment into its infrastructure and management services business segment in fiscal 2005.

In 2006 the company was awarded a contract to provide personal services support to the U.S. Army Corps of Engineers and to manage an associated Iraqi workforce that provides quality control on Army projects.

In 2007 Versar created international subsidiary VIAP, Inc. (Versar International Assistance Programs) and opened an office in Manila, in the Philippines. Chairman emeritus Michael Markels owns 9.4% of Versar. Director Robert Durfee owns 9.7%.

EXECUTIVES

Chairman Emeritus: Michael Markels Jr., age 82
Chairman: Paul J. Hoeper, age 62
President, CEO, and Director:
Theodore M. (Ted) Prociv, age 60, $285,413 pay
EVP, COO, CFO, and Treasurer: Lawrence W. Sinnott, age 46, $173,000 pay
SVP Corporate Development: Jerome B. Strauss, age 59, $172,000 pay
SVP General Counsel, and Secretary: James C. Dobbs, age 63, $168,000 pay
SVP Professional Services Group: Gina L. Foringer, age 39
SVP Global Marketing and Planning: Paul W. Kendall, age 55, $151,000 pay
SVP Program Management Business Segment:
Jeffrey A. Wagonhurst, age 60
SVP Compliance and Environmental Programs:
Michael J. Abram, age 52
President, Versar International Assistance Programs:
Bill Johnson
Auditors: Grant Thornton LLP

LOCATIONS

HQ: Versar, Inc.
6850 Versar Center, Springfield, VA 22151
Phone: 703-750-3000 **Fax:** 703-642-6807
Web: www.versar.com

Versar has offices in Arizona, California, Colorado, Illinois, Maryland, Ohio, Oklahoma, Pennsylvania, Texas, and Virginia.

PRODUCTS/OPERATIONS

2007 Sales

	$ mil.	% of total
Program management	58.8	57
Compliance & environmental programs	29.8	29
Professional services	7.3	7
National security	6.8	7
Total	**102.7**	**100**

Selected Services

Air-quality management
Architecture
Biohazard suits
Construction management
Counterterrorism programs
Energy
Engineering
Environmental assessments
Hazardous waste management
Information technology
Management consulting
Pollution prevention
Remedial action

COMPETITORS

AECOM
ATC Associates
Bechtel National
Ecology and Environment
Environmental Resources Management Ltd
KBR
Lakeland Industries
Mine Safety Appliances
Shaw Group
Sperian Protection
Tetra Tech
TRC Companies
URS
Washington Division

HISTORICAL FINANCIALS

Company Type: Public

Income Statement

FYE: June 30

	REVENUE ($ mil.)	NET INCOME ($ mil.)	NET PROFIT MARGIN	EMPLOYEES
6/07	102.7	5.3	5.2%	364
6/06	34.3	1.4	4.1%	—
6/05	35.6	0.2	0.6%	379
6/04	60.5	1.2	2.0%	—
6/03	57.1	(1.0)	—	—
Annual Growth	15.8%	—	—	(2.0%)

2007 Year-End Financials

Debt ratio: —
Return on equity: 33.1%
Cash ($ mil.): 6.3
Current ratio: 2.01
Long-term debt ($ mil.): —
No. of shares (mil.): 8.7
Dividends
Yield: —
Payout: —
Market value ($ mil.): 72.8
R&D as % of sales: —
Advertising as % of sales: —

Stock History

AMEX: VSR

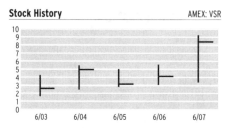

	STOCK PRICE ($) FY Close	P/E High/Low	PER SHARE ($) Earnings	Dividends	Book Value
6/07	8.41	15 6	0.62	—	2.24
6/06	4.12	34 20	0.16	—	1.55
6/05	3.16	247 145	0.02	—	1.33
6/04	4.95	34 16	0.16	—	1.29
6/03	2.61	— —	(0.14)	—	1.02
Annual Growth	34.0%	— —	—	—	21.8%

Village Bank & Trust

Does it take a village to raise a bank? Village Bank & Trust is the holding company for Village Bank, which has about 10 branches in such suburbs of Richmond, Virginia as Midlothian and Chester. It offers such standard services as deposit accounts, loans, and credit cards. Deposit funds are used to write loans for consumers and small businesses in the area; commercial real estate loans account for more than 40% of the bank's lending portfolio, which also includes construction, residential mortgage, and other loans. Village Bank & Trust subsidiaries provide property/casualty insurance, mortgages, and other financial services.

Village Bank & Trust focuses its business in Virginia's Chesterton County; it also has branches in nearby Henrico and Powhatan counties. Village Bank & Trust plans to continue launching new branch banking offices in its service area.

EXECUTIVES

Chairman: Craig D. Bell, age 49
Vice Chairman: Donald J. Balzer Jr., age 51
President, CEO, and Director; President and CEO, Village Bank: Thomas W. Winfree, age 61, $172,500 pay
SVP, Lending, Village Bank: Jack M. Robeson Jr., age 58, $104,963 pay
SVP and CFO, Village Bank and Trust Financial and Village Bank: C. Harrill Whitehurst, age 56, $109,313 pay
SVP; SVP and COO, Village Bank: Raymond E. Sanders, age 53, $109,313 pay
SVP, Commercial Banking: Dennis J. Falk, age 48, $90,000 pay
VP, Financial Services, Village Bank: Robert G. Astrop
VP, Mortgage and Consumer Lending, Village Bank: Diane C. Canada
VP and Director, Human Resources: Robert R. Staples
Auditors: BDO Seidman, LLP

LOCATIONS

HQ: Village Bank & Trust Financial Corp.
1231 Alverser Dr., Midlothian, VA 23113
Phone: 804-897-3900   **Fax:** 804-897-4750
Web: www.villagebank.com

PRODUCTS/OPERATIONS

2006 Sales

	$ mil.	% of total
Interest		
Loans	18.0	84
Securities & other	1.0	4
Gain on sale of loans	1.5	7
Service charges & fees	0.6	3
Other operating income	0.4	2
Total	**21.5**	**100**

COMPETITORS

Bank of America
Bank of McKenney
Bank of Virginia
BB&T
C&F Financial
Central Virginia Bankshares
F & M Bank
First Capital Bancorp
SunTrust
TransCommunity Financial
Union Bankshares Corp.
Wachovia

HISTORICAL FINANCIALS

Company Type: Public

Income Statement

FYE: December 31

	ASSETS ($ mil.)	NET INCOME ($ mil.)	INCOME AS % OF ASSETS	EMPLOYEES
12/06	291.2	1.4	0.5%	120
12/05	215.0	1.2	0.6%	101
12/04	160.3	0.9	0.6%	—
12/03	115.1	0.1	0.1%	—
12/02	80.3	(0.3)	—	—
Annual Growth	**38.0%**	**—**	**—**	**18.8%**

2006 Year-End Financials

Equity as % of assets: 8.8%
Return on assets: 0.6%
Return on equity: 6.5%
Long-term debt ($ mil.): 5.9
No. of shares (mil.): 2.6
Market value ($ mil.): 36.4
Dividends
  Yield: —
  Payout: —
Sales ($ mil.): 21.5
R&D as % of sales: —
Advertising as % of sales: —

Stock History

NASDAQ (CM): VBFC

	STOCK PRICE ($) FY Close	P/E High/Low	PER SHARE ($) Earnings	Dividends	Book Value
12/06	14.20	25 20	0.59	—	10.01
12/05	12.85	23 20	0.61	—	9.25
12/04	11.60	31 24	0.45	—	8.51
12/03	12.40	321 190	0.04	—	7.94
12/02	7.70	— —	(0.32)	—	7.94
Annual Growth	**16.5%**	**— —**	**—**	**—**	**6.0%**

Vineyard National Bancorp

Red, white, or savings? Vineyard National Bancorp is the holding company for Vineyard Bank which operates about 15 branches in Southern California. It also has a location in the San Francisco Bay area. The bank operates five loan production offices that specialize in Small Business Administration (SBA) loans and loans for the construction of luxury homes; the latter account for more than a quarter of the company's loan portfolio, as do commercial mortgages. To a lesser extent, Vineyard Bank writes consumer and land loans and loans for tract housing. Deposit products include CDs, and checking, savings, money market, and NOW accounts.

EXECUTIVES

Chairman and Interim CEO: James G. LeSieur III, age 66
EVP and CFO, Vineyard National Bancorp and Vineyard Bank: Gordon Fong, age 40, $210,000 pay
Secretary; EVP, COO, Chief Credit Officer, and Secretary, Vineyard Bank: Richard S. Hagan, age 57, $220,000 pay

EVP and Chief Administrative Officer, Vineyard National Bancorp and Vineyard Bank: Donald H. Pelgrim Jr., age 46, $167,500 pay (prior to promotion)
EVP and Chief Banking Officer, Vineyard National Bancorp and Vineyard Bank: J. Christopher (Chris) Walsh, age 49
EVP and Chief Banking Officer, Vineyard Bank: Elizabeth (Liz) Reno, age 45
EVP and Chief Lending Officer, Vineyard National Bancorp and Vineyard Bank: Michael Cain, age 50
SVP and Manager, Credit Portfolio Management: Jacqueline Calhoun Schaefgen, age 37, $175,000 pay
EVP and Managing Director, Northern California Operations, Vineyard Bank: Mariano (Marty) Rubino
SVP and Chief Culture Officer, Vineyard National Bancorp and Vineyard Bank: Tina Sandoval, age 35, $137,842 pay
SVP and Executive Director, Community Banking: Tom Rosa
SVP and CIO: Maureen C. Clark, age 47
Auditors: KPMG LLP

LOCATIONS

HQ: Vineyard National Bancorp
1260 Corona Pointe Court, Corona, CA 92879
Phone: 951-893-2979   **Fax:** 951-278-0047
Web: www.vineyardbank.com

PRODUCTS/OPERATIONS

2006 Sales

	$ mil.	% of total
Interest		
Loans, including fees	146.2	89
Investment securities	11.7	7
Federal funds sold	0.4	—
Noninterest		
Sale of SBA loans & SBA broker fees	2.8	2
Other fees & service charges	1.8	1
Other	1.0	1
Total	**163.9**	**100**

COMPETITORS

Bank of America
Bank of the West
Comerica
CVB Financial
Downey Financial
First Community Bancorp
PFF Bancorp
Provident Financial Holdings
UnionBanCal
Washington Mutual
Wells Fargo

HISTORICAL FINANCIALS

Company Type: Public

Income Statement

FYE: December 31

	ASSETS ($ mil.)	NET INCOME ($ mil.)	INCOME AS % OF ASSETS	EMPLOYEES
12/06	2,257.7	19.7	0.9%	349
12/05	1,713.6	18.9	1.1%	293
12/04	1,311.5	14.0	1.1%	—
12/03	887.8	8.0	0.9%	—
12/02	385.3	3.0	0.8%	116
Annual Growth	**55.6%**	**60.1%**	**—**	**31.7%**

2006 Year-End Financials

Equity as % of assets: 5.9%
Return on assets: 1.0%
Return on equity: 17.6%
Long-term debt ($ mil.): 160.5
No. of shares (mil.): 10.4
Market value ($ mil.): 228.7
Dividends
  Yield: 1.4%
  Payout: 17.2%
Sales ($ mil.): 163.9
R&D as % of sales: —
Advertising as % of sales: —

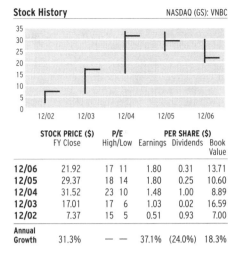

	STOCK PRICE ($) FY Close	P/E High/Low		PER SHARE ($) Earnings	Dividends	Book Value
12/06	21.92	17	11	1.80	0.31	13.71
12/05	29.37	18	14	1.80	0.25	10.60
12/04	31.52	23	10	1.48	1.00	8.89
12/03	17.01	17	6	1.03	0.02	16.59
12/02	7.37	15	5	0.51	0.93	7.00
Annual Growth	31.3%	—	—	37.1%	(24.0%)	18.3%

Virginia Commerce Bancorp

Virginia Commerce Bancorp is the holding company for Virginia Commerce Bank, which has about 20 offices serving metropolitan Washington, DC's northern Virginia suburbs. The bank's customer base includes consumers and small to midsized businesses, particularly those that have contracts with the US government. It primarily originates commercial mortgages, which account for approximately 40% of its portfolio, and construction loans, which make up more than 30%. Other offerings include checking, savings, money market, and retirement accounts; CDs; residential mortgages; business and consumer loans; mutual funds and bonds; and asset management services.

EXECUTIVES

Chairman: W. Douglas Fisher, age 69
Vice Chairman: David M. Guernsey, age 59
Vice Chairman: Arthur L. Walters, age 87
CEO and Director; President and CEO, Virginia Commerce Bank: Peter A. Converse, age 56, $625,000 pay
President and Director: Michael G. Anzilotti, age 57, $210,000 pay
Secretary and Director: Robert H. L'Hommedieu, age 80
Treasurer and CFO; EVP and CFO, Virginia Commerce Bank: William K. Beauchesne, age 50, $240,000 pay
EVP and Chief Lending Officer, Virginia Commerce Bank: Richard B. Anderson Jr., age 52, $330,000 pay
EVP, Human Resources, Virginia Commerce Bank: Patricia M. Ostrander, age 40, $140,000 pay
EVP Operations and Technology: John P. Perseo Jr., age 61
EVP, Retail Banking, Virginia Commerce Bank: Steven A. Reeder, age 40, $175,000 pay
SVP and Senior Credit Officer, Virginia Commerce Bank: George L. Greco
Auditors: Yount, Hyde & Barbour, P.C.

LOCATIONS

HQ: Virginia Commerce Bancorp, Inc.
5350 Lee Hwy., Arlington, VA 22207
Phone: 703-534-0700   **Fax:** 703-534-1782
Web: www.vcbonline.com

PRODUCTS/OPERATIONS

2006 Sales

	$ mil.	% of total
Interest		
Loans, including fees	115.4	87
Investment securities, including dividends	8.7	7
Other	1.1	1
Noninterest		
Service charges & other fees	3.2	2
Fees & net gains on loans held for sale	3.1	2
Other	1.1	1
Total	**132.6**	**100**

COMPETITORS

Abigail Adams
Bank of America
BB&T
Burke & Herbert Bank
Chevy Chase Bank
SunTrust
United Bankshares
Wachovia

HISTORICAL FINANCIALS
Company Type: Public

Income Statement   FYE: December 31

	ASSETS ($ mil.)	NET INCOME ($ mil.)	INCOME AS % OF ASSETS	EMPLOYEES
12/06	1,949.1	24.5	1.3%	275
12/05	1,518.4	19.7	1.3%	219
12/04	1,139.3	14.2	1.2%	—
12/03	881.1	11.6	1.3%	—
12/02	662.9	7.7	1.2%	160
Annual Growth	30.9%	33.6%	—	14.5%

2006 Year-End Financials

Equity as % of assets: 7.2%
Return on assets: 1.4%
Return on equity: 19.5%
Long-term debt ($ mil.): 44.3
No. of shares (mil.): 21.6
Market value ($ mil.): 389.7
Dividends
  Yield: —
  Payout: —
Sales ($ mil.): 132.6
R&D as % of sales: —
Advertising as % of sales: —

Stock History   NASDAQ (GS): VCBI

	STOCK PRICE ($) FY Close	P/E High/Low		PER SHARE ($) Earnings	Dividends	Book Value
12/06	18.07	24	18	0.98	—	6.49
12/05	17.63	23	16	0.79	—	7.96
12/04	13.73	24	16	0.60	—	8.27
12/03	12.34	25	9	0.53	—	7.01
12/02	4.59	16	9	0.37	—	11.19
Annual Growth	40.9%	—	—	27.6%	—	(12.7%)

ViroPharma Incorporated

ViroPharma didn't want to wait until its drugs were approved to start making money, so it bought one that was already approved. The development-stage firm discovers drugs to combat RNA viruses, a category that includes cytomegalovirus (CMV) and hepatitis C. To finance its development, however, the company acquired the antibiotic Vancocin from Eli Lilly. The company is also developing Maribavir, which it acquired from GlaxoSmithKline, for the treatment of CMV, and HCV-796 for the treatment of hepatitis C. The company ceased developing Pleconaril, an intranasal formulation that could treat the common cold, and sold the development rights to Schering-Plough.

EXECUTIVES

Chairman, President, and CEO: Michel de Rosen, age 56, $560,149 pay
VP, CFO, and COO: Vincent J. (Vinnie) Milano, age 43, $338,250 pay (prior to promotion)
VP and Chief Commercial Officer: Daniel B. (Dan) Soland, age 48
VP and Chief Scientific Officer: Colin Broom, age 51, $469,706 pay
VP Strategic Initiatives: Thomas F. Doyle, age 46, $399,159 pay
VP Clinical Research and Development: Stephen (Steve) Villano
VP Human Resources: Carolyn Vanderweghe
VP Information Technology: Thomas Lembck
VP Regulatory Affairs and Quality: Robert (Bob) Pietrusko
VP Clinical Development and Medical Affairs, ViroPharma Europe: Richard Bax
VP and General Manager, ViroPharma Europe: Thierry Darcis
VP, General Counsel, and Secretary: J. Peter Wolf
Director, Corporate Communications and Investor Relations: William C. (Will) Roberts
Auditors: KPMG LLP

LOCATIONS

HQ: ViroPharma Incorporated
397 Eagleview Blvd., Exton, PA 19341
Phone: 610-458-7300   **Fax:** 610-458-7380
Web: www.viropharma.com

PRODUCTS/OPERATIONS

Selected Products

Approved
  Vancocin (antibiotic)
In development
  HCV-796 (hepatitis C)
  Maribavir (cytomegalovirus)

COMPETITORS

Amgen
AstraZeneca
Genzyme
Gilead Sciences
GlaxoSmithKline
Idenix Pharmaceuticals
MedImmune
Optimer

Oscient Pharmaceuticals
Roche
Salix Pharmaceuticals
Schering-Plough
Valeant
Vertex Pharmaceuticals
Vical

HISTORICAL FINANCIALS

Company Type: Public

Income Statement

FYE: December 31

	REVENUE ($ mil.)	NET INCOME ($ mil.)	NET PROFIT MARGIN	EMPLOYEES
12/06	167.2	66.7	39.9%	67
12/05	132.4	113.7	85.9%	48
12/04	22.4	(19.5)	—	—
12/03	1.6	(36.9)	—	—
12/02	5.5	(15.8)	—	139
Annual Growth	134.8%	—	—	(16.7%)

2006 Year-End Financials

Debt ratio: —
Return on equity: 18.1%
Cash ($ mil.): 255.4
Current ratio: 15.97
Long-term debt ($ mil.): —
No. of shares (mil.): 69.8

Dividends
  Yield: —
  Payout: —
Market value ($ mil.): 1,021.4
R&D as % of sales: —
Advertising as % of sales: —

Stock History

NASDAQ (GS): VPHM

	STOCK PRICE ($) FY Close	P/E High/Low	PER SHARE ($) Earnings	Dividends	Book Value
12/06	14.64	25 7	0.95	—	5.90
12/05	18.50	12 1	2.02	—	4.77
12/04	3.25	— —	(0.73)	—	(0.98)
12/03	2.77	— —	(1.43)	—	(0.28)
12/02	1.46	— —	(0.66)	—	1.07
Annual Growth	77.9%	— —	—	—	53.2%

Vital Images

Vital Images knows that everything is better in 3-D. The company develops 3-D medical visualization and analysis software used primarily in clinical diagnosis, disease screening, and therapy planning. The firm's software applies computer graphics and image-processing technologies to data supplied by diagnostic imaging equipment including computed tomography (CT) scanners and magnetic resonance imaging (MRI) devices. Vital Images' flagship product Vitrea creates two-, three-, and four-dimensional views of the human body, enabling physicians and surgeons to see internal structures and recognize potential abnormalities. The company markets its products to radiologists, surgeons, and other medical practitioners.

The company has relationships with major medical distributors including McKesson, but more than one-third of company sales come through its partnership with Toshiba Medical Systems (part of electronics giant Toshiba). Diagnostic imaging equipment manufacturers including Emageon sell Vital Images' software in conjunction with their products.

EXECUTIVES

Chairman: Douglas M. (Doug) Pihl, age 67
Director: Jay D. Miller, age 47, $465,038 pay
President and CEO: Michael H. Carrel, age 36, $389,615 pay
CFO: Peter Goepfrich
EVP Corporate Development: Philip I. (Phil) Smith, age 39, $321,964 pay (prior to title change)
EVP Global Sales: Steven P. (Steve) Canakes, age 51, $302,245 pay (prior to title change)
EVP Marketing and Clinical Development: Susan A. Wood, age 44
VP Quality and Customer Satisfaction: Jeremy A. Abbs, age 43, $265,752 pay
VP Europe: Stephen S. Andersen, age 37
Auditors: PricewaterhouseCoopers LLP

LOCATIONS

HQ: Vital Images, Inc.
  5850 Opus Pkwy., Ste. 300, Minnetonka, MN 55343
Phone: 952-487-9500   **Fax:** 952-487-9510
Web: www.vitalimages.com

PRODUCTS/OPERATIONS

2006 Sales

	$ mil.	% of total
License fees	46.3	66
Maintenance & services	22.6	32
Hardware	1.6	2
Total	70.5	100

COMPETITORS

GE Healthcare
Metrx
MGT Capital Investments
Philips Medical Systems
Siemens Medical
VirtualScopics

HISTORICAL FINANCIALS

Company Type: Public

Income Statement

FYE: December 31

	REVENUE ($ mil.)	NET INCOME ($ mil.)	NET PROFIT MARGIN	EMPLOYEES
12/06	70.5	6.6	9.4%	283
12/05	51.7	5.8	11.2%	200
12/04	36.1	0.3	0.8%	—
12/03	27.3	8.5	31.1%	—
12/02	21.1	0.8	3.8%	105
Annual Growth	35.2%	69.5%	—	28.1%

2006 Year-End Financials

Debt ratio: —
Return on equity: 5.1%
Cash ($ mil.): 165.2
Current ratio: 7.20
Long-term debt ($ mil.): —
No. of shares (mil.): 16.9

Dividends
  Yield: —
  Payout: —
Market value ($ mil.): 588.4
R&D as % of sales: —
Advertising as % of sales: —

Stock History

NASDAQ (GM): VTAL

	STOCK PRICE ($) FY Close	P/E High/Low	PER SHARE ($) Earnings	Dividends	Book Value
12/06	34.80	79 42	0.46	—	11.29
12/05	26.15	64 30	0.44	—	5.35
12/04	16.75	850 764	0.02	—	4.53
12/03	17.86	35 12	0.71	—	4.00
12/02	8.97	144 56	0.08	—	1.30
Annual Growth	40.3%	— —	54.9%	—	71.5%

VMware, Inc.

VMware develops software that creates and manages virtual machines — computer functions spread across multiple systems that act as one. Companies use VMware's software to more efficiently integrate and manage server, storage, and networking functions, thereby lowering the operating costs of their computing resources. VMware also provides consulting, support, and training services. The company has marketing relationships with computer hardware vendors including Dell, Hewlett-Packard, and IBM. Founded in 1998, VMware was acquired by EMC for about $625 million in cash in 2004. Looking to unlock some of the value in its subsidiary, EMC sold about 10% of VMware via an IPO in 2007. Cisco Systems and Intel purchased small stakes in the company.

EMC's acquisition of VMware was a key component of a major push to grow its software portfolio. The company has maintained some independence since being acquired by EMC, operating as a separate subsidiary.

Early in 2006 VMware began offering a free version of its virtualization software, with the aim of attracting new customers that might eventually upgrade to its enterprise-class product.

EMC augmented VMware's operations in mid-2006 with the acquisition of Akimbi Systems, a provider of application configuration testing software. VMware announced two acquisitions at the beginning of 2008: assets of virtualization services specialist Foedus, and application virtualization software developer Thinstall.

EXECUTIVES

Chairman: Joseph M. (Joe) Tucci, age 60
President, CEO, and Director: Diane B. Greene, age 52
CFO: Mark S. Peek, age 50
EVP Worldwide Field Operations: Carl M. Eschenbach, age 41, $467,500 pay
VP and General Counsel: Rashmi Garde, age 42, $250,000 pay
VP Corporate and Field Marketing: Yael Zheng

VP Global Support Services: Debra Hagan
VP Finance: Thomas (Tom) Jurewicz, age 43,
  $207,500 pay
VP Product Development: Paul Chan
VP Technology Development: Stephen Herrod
VP Emerging Products and Markets: Dan Chu
VP Human Resources: Betsy Sutter
Chief Scientist: Mendel Rosenblum
Group Manager, Corporate Communications:
  Amber Rowland
Auditors: PricewaterhouseCoopers LLP

LOCATIONS

HQ: VMware, Inc.
  3145 Porter Dr., Palo Alto, CA 94304
Phone: 650-475-5000   Fax: 650-475-5005
Web: www.vmware.com

2006 Sales

	$ mil.	% of total
US	391.6	56
Other countries	312.3	44
Total	**703.9**	**100**

PRODUCTS/OPERATIONS

2006 Sales

	$ mil.	% of total
Licenses	491.9	70
Services	212.0	30
Total	**703.9**	**100**

Selected Products

Accelerators (VMware Converter)
Data center optimization and management (VMware
  Infrastructure, ESX Server, VirtualCenter)
Development and test (VMware Lab Manager)
Enterprise desktop management (VMware ACE)

COMPETITORS

IBM
Levanta
Microsoft
Novell
Oracle
Parallels
Sun Microsystems
Symantec
Virtual Iron

HISTORICAL FINANCIALS

Company Type: Public

Income Statement

FYE: December 31

	REVENUE ($ mil.)	NET INCOME ($ mil.)	NET PROFIT MARGIN	EMPLOYEES
12/06	703.9	85.9	12.2%	3,000
12/05	387.1	66.8	17.3%	—
12/04	218.8	16.8	7.7%	—
Annual Growth	**79.4%**	**126.1%**	**—**	**—**

2006 Year-End Financials

Debt ratio: —   Current ratio: 0.88
Return on equity: 77.0%   Long-term debt ($ mil.): 804.5
Cash ($ mil.): 176.1

Net Income History

NYSE: VMW

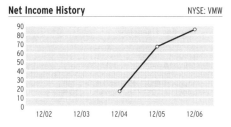

Vocus, Inc.

Vocus' focus is simplifying public and government relations processes. Vocus produces software that helps automate some public relations duties; it organizes media contacts, manages news collection, and analyzes public relations effectiveness. Its government relations software offers a state and federal legislative contact list and project management tracking and lobbying analysis tools. Users vary from not-for-profits and the government to corporations and public relations professionals. The company acquired privately held Gnossos Software in 2004, boosting its government relations software business.

EXECUTIVES

Chairman, President, and CEO:
  Richard (Rick) Rudman, age 46, $433,313 pay
CFO, Secretary, and Treasurer: Stephen (Steve) Vintz,
  age 38, $253,563 pay
VP North American Sales: Norman Weissberg, age 45
VP Client Services: Darren Stewart, age 38
VP Business Development: Matthew (Matt) Siegal,
  age 43
Chief Marketing Officer: William R. (Bill) Wagner,
  age 39
Managing Director, Vocus International: Andrew Muir,
  age 51
Media Relations: Robin Lane
Auditors: Ernst & Young LLP

LOCATIONS

HQ: Vocus, Inc.
  4296 Forbes Blvd., Lanham, MD 20706
Phone: 301-459-2590   Fax: 301-459-2827
Web: www.vocus.com

COMPETITORS

Biz360
Factiva
Medialink
PR Newswire
United Business Media

HISTORICAL FINANCIALS

Company Type: Public

Income Statement

FYE: December 31

	REVENUE ($ mil.)	NET INCOME ($ mil.)	NET PROFIT MARGIN	EMPLOYEES
12/06	40.3	0.4	1.0%	317
12/05	28.1	(5.1)	—	220
12/04	20.4	(2.6)	—	170
12/03	15.4	(2.7)	—	—
12/02	11.5	(3.4)	—	115
Annual Growth	**36.8%**	**—**	**—**	**28.9%**

2006 Year-End Financials

Debt ratio: 0.8%   Dividends
Return on equity: 1.1%   Yield: —
Cash ($ mil.): 29.9   Payout: —
Current ratio: 1.26   Market value ($ mil.): 269.2
Long-term debt ($ mil.): 0.3   R&D as % of sales: —
No. of shares (mil.): 16.0   Advertising as % of sales: —

Stock History   NASDAQ (GM): VOCS

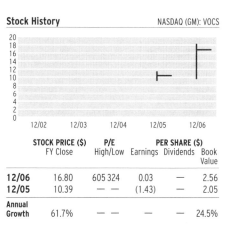

	STOCK PRICE ($) FY Close	P/E High/Low	PER SHARE ($)		
			Earnings	Dividends	Book Value
12/06	16.80	605 324	0.03	—	2.56
12/05	10.39	— —	(1.43)	—	2.05
Annual Growth	**61.7%**	**— —**	**—**	**—**	**24.5%**

Volcom, Inc.

Volcom says it's "youth against establishment" and this establishment comes down firmly on the side of youth — skateboarding, surfing, and snowboarding youth in Mongoose hoodies and Friggin Chinos. Volcom designs and makes apparel and accessories for board sports and offers its wares through stores in Southern California and youth-focused retailers like Zumiez and Pac Sun across the US, Canada, and Puerto Rico. The company sells to distributors in Asia Pacific and Latin America while licensing its brand in other parts of the world. Sponsorship of various concerts, riders, and sports events, along with film and music divisions, keep Volcom's logo front and center with anti-establishment youth.

The company used proceeds from its 2005 IPO to expand the brand in Europe and develop proprietary in-store marketing displays for retailers to properly show off those trucker caps, board shorts, belts, and bags sporting the Volcom gray triangular stone logo. Volcom opened several Volcom stores in the US in 2006 and plans four more in Hawaii and California in 2007.

Retailer Pacific Sunwear accounts for about a quarter of sales while the company's five largest customers account for about 45%.

The company has extended its brand into kids' clothing, as well as sandals and slip-on footwear. Volcom branched out further in 2008 when it acquired Electric Visual Evolution, a maker of eyewear and apparel, for $25 million.

Longtime surfer and former marketer for surfwear giant and rival Quiksilver, Richard Woolcott (president and CEO) founded the company in 1991 and owns 16% of the company shares. Chairman René Woolcott and independent investor Stephanie Kwock each own 13%.

EXECUTIVES

Chairman: René R. Woolcott, age 75
President, CEO, and Director: Richard R. Woolcott,
  age 41, $375,000 pay
COO: Jason W. Steris, age 37, $300,000 pay
CFO, Secretary, and Treasurer: Douglas P. Collier,
  age 44, $300,000 pay
VP, Marketing: Troy C. Eckert, age 34, $281,250 pay
VP, Sales: Tom D. Ruiz, age 46, $300,000 pay
VP Strategic Development and General Counsel:
  S. Hoby Darling
Auditors: Deloitte & Touche LLP

LOCATIONS

HQ: Volcom, Inc.
  1740 Monrovia Ave., Costa Mesa, CA 92627
Phone: 949-646-2175   **Fax:** 949-646-5247
Web: www.volcom.com

Volcom has licensing agreements with companies in Australia, Brazil, South Africa, and Indonesia as well as across Europe. The company operates three stores in California; licensees operate retail stores in Bali, Indonesia and Hossegor, France.

PRODUCTS/OPERATIONS

2006 Sales

	$ mil.	% of total
Products	201.2	98
Licensing	4.1	2
Total	**205.3**	**100**

Selected Sponsored Athletes

Skateboarding
  Mark Appleyard
  Lauren Perkins
  Geoff Rowley
  Ryan Sheckler

Snowboarding
  Terje Haakonsen
  Elena Hight
  Jana Meyen
  Shaun White

Surfing
  Randy Bonds
  Dean Morrison

COMPETITORS

Abercrombie & Fitch
Apple
Billabong
Burton Snowboards
Columbia Sportswear
K2
Lost International
Napster
Pacific Sunwear
Patagonia, Inc.
Quiksilver
Rusty, Inc.
Skechers U.S.A.
Sony BMG
Sony USA
Stüssy
Vans
Vivendi

HISTORICAL FINANCIALS

Company Type: Public

Income Statement

FYE: December 31

	REVENUE ($ mil.)	NET INCOME ($ mil.)	NET PROFIT MARGIN	EMPLOYEES
12/06	205.3	28.8	14.0%	259
12/05	159.9	29.3	18.3%	181
12/04	113.2	24.6	21.7%	—
12/03	76.3	14.3	18.7%	—
Annual Growth	**39.1%**	**26.3%**	**—**	**43.1%**

2006 Year-End Financials

Debt ratio: 0.1%
Return on equity: 24.3%
Cash ($ mil.): 85.4
Current ratio: 8.84
Long-term debt ($ mil.): 0.1
No. of shares (mil.): 24.3

Dividends
  Yield: —
  Payout: —
Market value ($ mil.): 718.4
R&D as % of sales: —
Advertising as % of sales: —

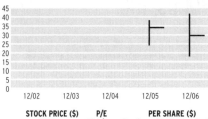

	STOCK PRICE ($) FY Close	P/E High/Low	PER SHARE ($) Earnings	Dividends	Book Value
12/06	29.57	35 15	1.18	—	5.52
12/05	34.01	28 18	1.34	—	4.24
Annual Growth	(13.1%)	— —	(11.9%)	—	30.1%

Volterra Semiconductor

Volterra Semiconductor aims to usher in a new era in voltage control for semiconductors. The fabless company designs and markets low-voltage power supply chips, including switching regulators for communications and networking applications. Its products are designed to replace several power management components with a single device. IBM, distributor Metatech, and Sabre are top customers of the company, which was founded by a group including former CFO Greg Hildebrand, former CTO Anthony Stratakos, and VP Craig Teuscher. Stratakos and other company insiders own around one-fifth of Volterra Semi.

Volterra outsources fabrication of its products, primarily to Chartered Semiconductor Manufacturing, Samsung Electronics, and Taiwan Semiconductor Manufacturing.

A former Volterra employee was arrested in early 2005 by federal agents and charged with illegally e-mailing proprietary data sheets to CMSC, a semiconductor company in Taiwan. The former employee may also have transferred files of proprietary company information to his personal computers. The man, Shin-Guo Tsai, pleaded guilty later that year to a federal felony charge.

The company takes its name from Italian mathematician Vito Volterra. There is also a Tuscan town named Volterra.

Entities affiliated with Waddell & Reed Investment Management own nearly 12% of Volterra Semi, while William Blair & Company holds about 11%. Schroder Investment Management North America, part of Schroders, has an equity stake of nearly 8% in the company. FMR (Fidelity Investments) and persons affiliated with RS Investment Management each own 5% of Volterra.

EXECUTIVES

Chairman: Christopher B. Paisley, age 55
President, CEO, and Director: Jeffrey (Jeff) Staszak, age 54, $298,138 pay
VP and CFO: Mike Burns, age 41
VP, Advanced Circuit Design: Andrew Burstein
VP Design Engineering: David Lidsky, age 40, $195,420 pay
VP, IC Technology and Process Development: Marco Zuniga
VP Marketing: William (Bill) Numann, age 49, $188,133 pay
VP Sales and Applications Engineering: Craig Teuscher, age 39, $194,546 pay
VP World Wide Operations: David Ng
Investor Relations: Heidi Flannery
Auditors: KPMG LLP

LOCATIONS

HQ: Volterra Semiconductor Corporation
  47467 Fremont Blvd., Fremont, CA 94538
Phone: 510-743-1200   **Fax:** 510-743-1600
Web: www.volterra.com

Volterra Semiconductor has offices in Singapore and the US.

2006 Sales

	% of total
Singapore	49
China	26
Taiwan	8
US	7
Japan	4
Other countries	6
Total	**100**

PRODUCTS/OPERATIONS

Selected Products

Voltage regulator chipsets (VT1000)
Voltage regulator semiconductors (VT100, VT200)

COMPETITORS

Analog Devices
Analogic Technologies
International Rectifier
Intersil
Linear Technology
Marvell Technology
Maxim Integrated Products
Microsemi
National Semiconductor
ON Semiconductor
Semtech
Texas Instruments

HISTORICAL FINANCIALS

Company Type: Public

Income Statement

FYE: December 31

	REVENUE ($ mil.)	NET INCOME ($ mil.)	NET PROFIT MARGIN	EMPLOYEES
12/06	74.6	6.9	9.2%	151
12/05	53.9	5.4	10.0%	121
12/04	43.9	5.1	11.6%	—
Annual Growth	**30.4%**	**16.3%**	**—**	**24.8%**

2006 Year-End Financials

Debt ratio: —
Return on equity: 10.6%
Cash ($ mil.): 51.8
Current ratio: 6.66
Long-term debt ($ mil.): —
No. of shares (mil.): 24.4

Dividends
  Yield: —
  Payout: —
Market value ($ mil.): 365.8
R&D as % of sales: —
Advertising as % of sales: —

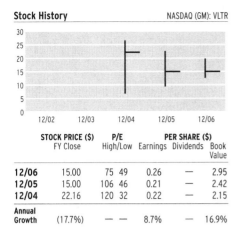

	STOCK PRICE ($)	P/E		PER SHARE ($)		
	FY Close	High/Low	Earnings	Dividends	Book Value	
12/06	15.00	75 49	0.26	—	2.95	
12/05	15.00	106 46	0.21	—	2.42	
12/04	22.16	120 32	0.22	—	2.15	
Annual Growth	(17.7%)	— —	8.7%	—	16.9%	

VSE Corporation

VSE brings military hand-me-downs back into fashion. The company provides engineering, testing, and logistics services for the US ARMY and Navy (each account for about 45% of sales) and other government agencies on a contract basis. VSE's BAV division (formed in cooperation with management and technology consultant Booz Allen Hamilton) helps reactivate old Navy ships and transfer them to other countries. Nearly all of VSE's revenues are derived from the US government (including the Navy, the Army, the Air Force, the Coast Guard, and the Department of Energy) and its prime contractors. Employees own about 10% of VSE.

VSE depends heavily on just a few large contracts. Its largest, the ship transfer contract between BAV and the Navy, accounts for almost one third of VSE's sales. In 2004 VSE landed a share of a separate contract to provide maintenance and engineering services for the Navy that is expected to be worth as much as $1.3 billion a year for 15 years.

In 2007 VSE acquired Integrated Concepts and Research Corporation for about $11.6 in cash (ICRC). ICRC is a provider of diversified technical and management services, primarily to the US government.

Investor Calvin Koonce, a member of VSE's board, controls a 23% stake in the company.

EXECUTIVES

Chairman, President, CEO, and COO:
Donald M. Ervine, age 70, $325,000 pay
EVP, Chief Administrative Officer, and Secretary:
Craig S. Weber, age 62, $170,000 pay
EVP and Director, International Group:
James M. Knowlton, age 64, $200,000 pay
EVP and CFO: Thomas R. Loftus, age 51, $175,000 pay
EVP; President, Federal Group: Thomas G. Dacus, age 61, $200,000 pay
EVP, International Group: Michael E. (Mike) Hamerly, age 61
EVP Strategic Initiatives and Business Development:
James W. Lexo
VP and Director, Contracts/Procurement:
James S. Fallon
President, Energetics Incorporated: James E. Reed
Director, Human Resources: Elizabeth M. (Liz) Price
Security Officer: Paul W. Duncan
Auditors: Ernst & Young LLP

LOCATIONS

HQ: VSE Corporation
2550 Huntington Ave., Alexandria, VA 22303
Phone: 703-960-4600   **Fax:** 703-960-2688
Web: www.vsecorp.com

PRODUCTS/OPERATIONS

2006 Sales

	$ mil.	% of total
Government		
US Army	174.4	48
US Navy	164.8	45
Department of Energy	9.4	3
US Air Force	4.6	1
US Treasury	2.4	1
US Coast Guard	0.9	—
Other government	4.8	1
Commercial & other	2.4	1
Total	**363.7**	**100**

Selected Operating Units

BAV Division (ship reactivation and life cycle support services)
Coast Guard Division
Communications and Engineering Division
Engineering and Logistics Division
Fleet Maintenance Division
Management Sciences Division
Systems Engineering Division

COMPETITORS

Boeing
General Dynamics
Lockheed Martin
Northrop Grumman
Todd Shipyards

HISTORICAL FINANCIALS

Company Type: Public

Income Statement

	REVENUE ($ mil.)	NET INCOME ($ mil.)	NET PROFIT MARGIN	EMPLOYEES
				FYE: December 31
12/06	363.7	7.8	2.1%	857
12/05	280.1	6.2	2.2%	716
12/04	216.0	3.4	1.6%	—
12/03	134.5	2.0	1.5%	—
12/02	134.4	0.6	0.4%	450
Annual Growth	**28.3%**	**89.9%**	**—**	**17.5%**

2006 Year-End Financials

Debt ratio: —   Dividends
Return on equity: 22.8%   Yield: 0.8%
Cash ($ mil.): 8.7   Payout: 8.1%
Current ratio: 1.44   Market value ($ mil.): 40.6
Long-term debt ($ mil.): —   R&D as % of sales: —
No. of shares (mil.): 2.4   Advertising as % of sales: —

Stock History   NASDAQ (GM): VSEC

	STOCK PRICE ($)	P/E		PER SHARE ($)		
	FY Close	High/Low	Earnings	Dividends	Book Value	
12/06	16.95	16 6	1.61	0.13	15.97	
12/05	21.05	16 8	1.29	0.11	12.78	
12/04	12.59	23 8	0.75	0.09	10.11	
12/03	6.63	16 9	0.45	0.08	8.61	
12/02	5.38	38 17	0.15	0.06	7.80	
Annual Growth	33.2%	— —	81.0%	21.3%	19.6%	

Waccamaw Bankshares

Waccamaw Bancshares is the holding company for, surprise, the Waccamaw Bank. The community bank, which has about a dozen branches in North Carolina as well as South Carolina, provides traditional services, such as checking and savings accounts and IRAs. The bank's loan portfolio is largely made up of commercial and real estate loans, including business operating loans, commercial mortgages, residential mortgages, and construction and land development loans. The financial institution also offers investment services and insurance brokerage through Waccamaw Financial Services.

Waccamaw Bank opened its Southport and Elizabethtown offices in 2005, and acquired Lancaster County, South Carolina-based Bank of Heath Springs the following year. (South Carolina banking laws only permit out-of-state banks to operate in South Carolina through acquisitions.)

EXECUTIVES

Chairman: Alan W. Thompson, age 43
President, CEO, and Director; President and CEO, Waccamaw Bank: James G. Graham, age 56, $231,500 pay
SVP and COO, Waccamaw Bank: Freda H. Gore, age 45
SVP and CFO, Waccamaw Bank: David A. Godwin, age 49
SVP and Senior Credit Officer, Waccamaw Bank: Richard C. Norris, age 41
SVP and Chief Administrative Officer: Kim T. Hutchens, age 51
SVP and Chief Lending Officer: J. Daniel Hardy Jr., age 52
VP and Compliance/Security Officer: Gracie B. McClary
VP Credit Administration Officer, Waccamaw Bank: Pamela Simmons
VP and Investments and Insurance Advisor, Waccamaw Financial Services: John Hensley
Auditors: Elliott Davis LLC

LOCATIONS

HQ: Waccamaw Bankshares, Inc.
110 N. J.K. Powell Blvd., Whiteville, NC 28472
Phone: 910-641-0044   **Fax:** 910-641-0978
Web: www.waccamawbank.com

PRODUCTS/OPERATIONS

2006 Sales

	$ mil.	% of total
Interest		
Loans, including fees	22.6	81
Securities & other	2.8	10
Noninterest		
Service charges on deposits	1.1	4
Other	1.5	5
Total	**28.0**	**100**

COMPETITORS

Bank of America
BB&T
Community Bankshares
Cooperative Bankshares
First Bancorp (NC)
First Citizens Bancorporation
First Citizens BancShares
HCSB Financial
New Century Bancorp
RBC Centura Banks
SCBT Financial
Wachovia

HISTORICAL FINANCIALS

Company Type: Public

Income Statement

FYE: December 31

	ASSETS ($ mil.)	NET INCOME ($ mil.)	INCOME AS % OF ASSETS	EMPLOYEES
12/06	399.6	3.7	0.9%	116
12/05	322.8	3.0	0.9%	85
12/04	258.4	2.4	0.9%	—
12/03	193.2	2.0	1.0%	—
12/02	161.3	1.6	1.0%	—
Annual Growth	25.5%	23.3%	—	36.5%

2006 Year-End Financials

Equity as % of assets: 7.7%
Return on assets: 1.0%
Return on equity: 13.9%
Long-term debt ($ mil.): 31.8
No. of shares (mil.): 4.8
Market value ($ mil.): 72.0
Dividends
Yield: —
Payout: —
Sales ($ mil.): 28.0
R&D as % of sales: —
Advertising as % of sales: —

Stock History

NASDAQ (CM): WBNK

	STOCK PRICE ($) FY Close	P/E High/Low		PER SHARE ($) Earnings	Dividends	Book Value
12/06	14.88	25	20	0.69	—	6.55
12/05	16.14	33	27	0.58	—	4.93
12/04	16.36	53	20	0.47	1.00	4.39
12/03	10.32	28	14	0.39	0.83	9.12
Annual Growth	13.0%	—	—	22.1%	20.5%	(9.0%)

Wayside Technology Group

Wayside is far from falling by the wayside to programmers and tech-head execs. The company, formerly Programmer's Paradise, markets technical software, hardware, and related products to technology professionals through direct sales, the Internet, and catalogs such as *Programmer's Paradise* (for software developers) and *Corporate Developer's Paradise* (for corporate information technology professionals). Its thousands of tech tools include discounted software and hardware, as well as training and reference manuals. The company's Lifeboat Distribution subsidiary handles distribution to dealers and resellers. CDW Corporation accounts for nearly 16% of sales.

The company announced in 2006 that it would change its corporate name in an effort to pursue different market segments that operate under a variety of names. Its business segments — Programmer's Paradise and Lifeboat — continue under their current names, while the company launched a third unit under the moniker TechXtend. TechXtend offers corporations and organizations onsite IT services such as server consolidation, disaster recovery, and development.

EXECUTIVES

Chairman, President, and CEO: Simon F. Nynens, age 35
VP and Chief Accounting Officer: Kevin T. Scull, age 41
VP and General Manager, Lifeboat:
 Daniel T. (Dan) Jamieson, age 49, $195,025 pay
VP Information Systems: Vito Legrottaglie, age 43, $176,637 pay
Human Resources Manager: MaryBeth Auleta
Auditors: Amper, Politziner & Mattia, P.C.

LOCATIONS

HQ: Wayside Technology Group, Inc.
 1157 Shrewsbury Ave., Shrewsbury, NJ 07702
Phone: 732-389-0932 **Fax:** 732-389-1207
Web: www.waysidetechnology.com

2006 Sales

	$ mil.	% of total
US	159.3	87
Canada	23.0	13
Total	182.3	100

PRODUCTS/OPERATIONS

2006 Sales

	$ mil.	% of total
Lifeboat	128.6	71
Programmer's Paradise	53.7	29
Total	182.3	100

COMPETITORS

Best Buy
CDW
CompUSA
Dell
Insight Enterprises
Newegg
PC Connection
PC Mall
Systemax
Zones

HISTORICAL FINANCIALS

Company Type: Public

Income Statement

FYE: December 31

	REVENUE ($ mil.)	NET INCOME ($ mil.)	NET PROFIT MARGIN	EMPLOYEES
12/06	182.3	3.3	1.8%	99
12/05	137.7	2.7	2.0%	116
12/04	103.6	6.3	6.1%	—
12/03	69.6	1.0	1.4%	—
12/02	65.2	0.0	—	86
Annual Growth	29.3%	—	—	3.6%

2006 Year-End Financials

Debt ratio: —
Return on equity: 16.8%
Cash ($ mil.): 20.9
Current ratio: 1.46
Long-term debt ($ mil.): —
No. of shares (mil.): 4.6
Dividends
Yield: 1.9%
Payout: 38.9%
Market value ($ mil.): 69.5
R&D as % of sales: —
Advertising as % of sales: —

Stock History

NASDAQ (GM): WSTG

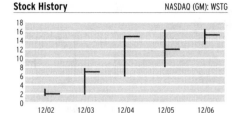

	STOCK PRICE ($) FY Close	P/E High/Low		PER SHARE ($) Earnings	Dividends	Book Value
12/06	15.12	23	18	0.72	0.28	4.63
12/05	11.93	26	13	0.61	—	4.51
12/04	14.78	10	4	1.51	—	4.27
12/03	6.89	30	8	0.25	—	2.99
12/02	1.97	295	166	0.01	—	3.05
Annual Growth	66.4%	—	—	191.3%	—	11.1%

WCA Waste

Some might see a garbage dump, but WCA Waste sees a pile of money. WCA Waste provides collection, transfer, and disposal of nonhazardous solid waste for about 250,000 commercial, industrial, and residential customers in Alabama, Arkansas, Florida, Kansas, Missouri, North Carolina, South Carolina, Tennessee, and Texas. Through its subsidiaries, the company operates some 24 collection businesses, 24 transfer stations, and 20 landfills, including eight separate landfills that are devoted to handling municipal solid waste and 12 for construction and demolition debris. Former company director William Esping and his family own about 13% of WCA Waste.

WCA Waste has grown through a series of acquisitions. The company's plan for growth calls for more acquisitions — specifically, acquisitions of collection businesses that can use the company's existing landfills. WCA Waste also will pursue geographic expansion as opportunities arise. The company entered the Florida and North Carolina markets in 2005; it moved into Colorado and New Mexico in 2006. In 2007 it acquired Southwest Dumpster, Inc. (Fort Myers, Florida) and Sunrise Disposal (Springfield, Missouri).

A former subsidiary of Waste Corporation of America, WCA Waste began operating in 2000, when it acquired assets from industry giant Waste Management. In connection with its IPO in 2004, WCA Waste briefly became the parent of Waste Corporation of America, which was then spun off. Waste Corporation of America wound up with solid waste management operations in Colorado, Florida, and New Mexico.

EXECUTIVES

Chairman and CEO: Tom J. Fatjo Jr., age 66, $608,122 pay
President, COO, and Director: Jerome M. Kruszka, age 58, $608,122 pay
SVP and CFO: Charles A. (Chuck) Casalinova, age 48, $418,571 pay
SVP Finance and Secretary: Tom J. (Tommy) Fatjo III, age 42, $348,676 pay
Auditors: KPMG LLP

LOCATIONS

HQ: WCA Waste Corporation
  1 Riverway, Ste. 1400, Houston, TX 77056
Phone: 713-292-2400   **Fax:** 713-292-2455
Web: www.wcawaste.com

WCA Waste has operations in Alabama, Arkansas, Colorado, Florida, Kansas, Missouri, New Mexico, North Carolina, South Carolina, Tennessee, and Texas.

2006 Sales

	$ mil.	% of total
Kansas & Missouri	48.9	33
Texas	30.9	21
Florida	21.1	14
Arkansas	13.4	9
North Carolina	10.9	7
Other states	24.3	16
Total	**149.5**	**100**

PRODUCTS/OPERATIONS

2006 Sales

	$ mil.	% of total
Collection	85.8	57
Disposal	39.1	26
Transfer & other	24.6	17
Total	**149.5**	**100**

COMPETITORS

Allied Waste
IESI
Republic Services
Veolia ES Solid Waste
Waste Connections
Waste Management

HISTORICAL FINANCIALS

Company Type: Public

Income Statement

FYE: December 31

	REVENUE ($ mil.)	NET INCOME ($ mil.)	NET PROFIT MARGIN	EMPLOYEES
12/06	149.5	3.0	2.0%	850
12/05	114.1	3.5	3.1%	800
12/04	73.5	(4.4)	—	—
12/03	64.2	5.1	7.9%	—
12/02	62.2	1.2	1.9%	—
Annual Growth	**24.5%**	**25.7%**	**—**	**6.3%**

2006 Year-End Financials

Debt ratio: 98.9%
Return on equity: 2.3%
Cash ($ mil.): 52.6
Current ratio: 3.27
Long-term debt ($ mil.): 166.0
No. of shares (mil.): 17.0

Dividends
  Yield: —
  Payout: —
Market value ($ mil.): 136.3
R&D as % of sales: —
Advertising as % of sales: —

Stock History

NASDAQ (GM): WCAA

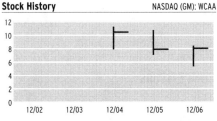

	STOCK PRICE ($) FY Close	P/E High/Low	PER SHARE ($) Earnings	Dividends	Book Value
12/06	8.03	93 61	0.09	—	9.88
12/05	7.90	48 33	0.22	—	5.46
12/04	10.45	— —	(0.38)	—	5.02
Annual Growth	**(12.3%)**	**— —**	**—**	**—**	**40.3%**

WebMD Health

House calls are a browser click away thanks to this online doctor. WebMD Health is a leading Internet publisher of health information for both consumers and health care professionals. Its flagship consumer site, WebMD.com, offers a portal where users can get information on common health ailments, as well as articles and features on staying healthy through diet and exercise. Doctors and other professionals can access clinical information through the company's Medscape from WebMD service. The WebMD Health Network attracts more than 30 million users. Medical practice services provider HLTH Corporation controls nearly 97% of WebMD Health.

The company generates the lion's share of its revenue through online advertising, as well as marketing sponsorships and licensing. It produces custom versions of its Web content through private portals used by corporations (American Airlines, Microsoft) and health plans (Cigna, WellPoint). Additionally, WebMD distributes content through the AOL portal.

Beyond digital media, WebMD Health publishes traditional magazines and other print publications including *WebMD the Magazine* and such textbooks as *ACP Medicine* and *ACS Surgery: Principles of Practice*. It also publishes *The Little Blue Book*, a directory of physician information. Traditional publishing accounts for about 10% of sales.

In 2006 WebMD Health acquired privately held Summex Corp., a provider of health and wellness programs, for $30 million. Later that year WebMD Health further expanded its marketing and sales offerings with the acquisition of fellow Web-based medical information company Medsite. It next purchased online health applications provider Subimo LLC for $60 million.

HLTH Corp, previously known as Emdeon, spun off the content business in 2005 in an effort to focus on its core health care support services operations. Founded by Silicon Valley entrepreneur Jim Clark as Healthscape, the company merged with Web portal operator WebMD in 1999 following its IPO.

EXECUTIVES

Chairman: Martin J. Wygod, age 67, $4,505,000 pay
President, CEO, and Director: Wayne T. Gattinella, age 55, $900,000 pay
COO: Anthony (Tony) Vuolo, age 49, $1,150,000 pay
EVP and CFO: Mark D. Funston, age 47
EVP, General Counsel, and Secretary: Douglas W. Wamsley, age 48
EVP Consumer Services: Nan-Kirsten Forte, age 45, $462,500 pay
EVP Health Services: Craig Froude, age 40
EVP Professional Services: Steven L. Zatz, age 50
SVP and COO, WebMD Health Services: Ray Herschman
SVP and General Manager: Clare A. Martorana
VP Community and Members: Hope Dlugozima
Investor Relations: Risa Fisher
Public Relations: Jennifer Newman
Auditors: Ernst & Young LLP

LOCATIONS

HQ: WebMD Health Corp.
  111 8th Ave., New York, NY 10011
Phone: 212-624-3700   **Fax:** 212-624-3800
Web: www.wbmd.com

WebMD Health has US offices in California, Connecticut, Georgia, Massachusetts, Nebraska, New York, and Oregon. It also has an office in Canada.

PRODUCTS/OPERATIONS

2006 Sales

	$ mil.	% of total
Online services		
Advertising & promotion	170.7	67
Licensing	55.6	22
Content syndication & other	3.5	1
Publishing services & other	24.1	10
Total	**253.9**	**100**

COMPETITORS

A.D.A.M.
Caremark Pharmacy Services
EBSCO
HealthStream
Hewitt Associates
iVillage
Mayo Foundation
Medline Industries
Medsite
Merck
New York Academy of Medicine
Reed Elsevier Group
Yahoo!

HISTORICAL FINANCIALS

Company Type: Public

Income Statement

FYE: December 31

	REVENUE ($ mil.)	NET INCOME ($ mil.)	NET PROFIT MARGIN	EMPLOYEES
12/06	253.9	2.5	1.0%	1,025
12/05	168.9	7.7	4.6%	720
12/04	134.1	6.5	4.8%	—
12/03	110.2	(7.4)	—	—
12/02	84.2	(24.4)	—	—
Annual Growth	**31.8%**	**—**	**—**	**42.4%**

2006 Year-End Financials

Debt ratio: —
Return on equity: 0.6%
Cash ($ mil.): 54.2
Current ratio: 2.67
Long-term debt ($ mil.): —
No. of shares (mil.): 8.3

Dividends
  Yield: —
  Payout: —
Market value ($ mil.): 333.7
R&D as % of sales: —
Advertising as % of sales: —

Stock History

NASDAQ (GS): WBMD

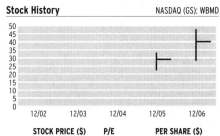

	STOCK PRICE ($) FY Close	P/E High/Low	PER SHARE ($) Earnings	Dividends	Book Value
12/06	40.02	1,183 714	0.04	—	59.50
12/05	29.05	219 151	0.15	—	37.63
Annual Growth	**37.8%**	**— —**	**(73.3%)**	**—**	**58.1%**

Websense, Inc.

That strange feeling someone is looking over your shoulder might just be true, thanks to Websense. The company offers employee Internet management, Web filtering, and security software designed to help businesses monitor and improve employee productivity, control what content employees can access, and reduce network bandwidth and storage usage. Companies use the Websense Enterprise software to monitor and report employee Internet usage, block access to certain content, and set time periods for when access is available. Clients such as McDonald's and the US Army subscribe to the hosted service, which checks for compliance against a proprietary database of more than 20 million Web sites in about 90 categories.

Websense's customers range from small companies to multinational corporations and government agencies. The company derives about 85% of its revenues from indirect channels such as value-added resellers in the US and overseas distributors and resellers, with the remaining 15% coming from its direct sales team. Websense is working to expand its international business, targeting clients in Europe, Latin America, and the Asia/Pacific region. Customers outside the US accounted for more than a third of Websense's sales in fiscal 2006.

Late in 2006 Websense agreed to acquire data protection specialist PortAuthority Technologies for $90 million in cash; the deal closed early in 2007. Websense also acquired rival SurfControl in 2007.

EXECUTIVES

Chairman: John B. Carrington, age 64
CEO: Gene Hodges
President and Secretary: Douglas C. (Doug) Wride, age 54
SVP Product Development: John McCormack
SVP and CFO: Dudley W. Mendenhall, age 52
SVP Americas Sales: David Roberts
VP and General Counsel: Michael A. Newman, age 39, $280,474 pay
VP Finance and Accounting: Mike Bouchard
VP Business Development: Ramon J. Peypoch
VP; General Manager of Websense Wireless Division: Kian Saneii, age 41
VP Human Resources and Administration: Susan Brown
VP Investor Relations: Kate Patterson
VP Marketing: Leo J. Cole, age 50, $317,658 pay
CIO: Jim Haskin
Senior Manager Public Relations: Cas Purdy
Investor Relations Manager: Becky Wheeler
Auditors: Ernst & Young LLP

LOCATIONS

HQ: Websense, Inc.
10240 Sorrento Valley Rd., San Diego, CA 92121
Phone: 858-320-8000   **Fax:** 858-458-2950
Web: ww2.websense.com

2006 Sales

	$ mil.	% of total
US	113.9	64
Europe, Middle East & Africa	44.4	25
Canada & Latin America	12.8	7
Asia/Pacific	7.7	4
Total	**178.8**	**100**

COMPETITORS

8e6 Technologies	Microsoft
Blue Coat	NetIQ
CA, Inc.	Secure Computing
Check Point Software	SonicWALL
Cisco Systems	St. Bernard Software
Internet Security Systems	Symantec
McAfee	Trend Micro

HISTORICAL FINANCIALS

Company Type: Public

Income Statement

FYE: December 31

	REVENUE ($ mil.)	NET INCOME ($ mil.)	NET PROFIT MARGIN	EMPLOYEES
12/06	178.8	32.1	18.0%	728
12/05	148.6	38.8	26.1%	635
12/04	111.9	26.2	23.4%	—
12/03	81.7	16.7	20.4%	—
12/02	61.0	16.7	27.4%	329
Annual Growth	**30.8%**	**17.7%**	**—**	**22.0%**

2006 Year-End Financials

Debt ratio: —
Return on equity: 16.6%
Cash ($ mil.): 326.9
Current ratio: 2.34
Long-term debt ($ mil.): —
No. of shares (mil.): 44.8
Dividends
  Yield: —
  Payout: —
Market value ($ mil.): 1,022.4
R&D as % of sales: —
Advertising as % of sales: —

Stock History

NASDAQ (GS): WBSN

	STOCK PRICE ($) FY Close	P/E High/Low	PER SHARE ($) Earnings	PER SHARE ($) Dividends	PER SHARE ($) Book Value
12/06	22.83	51 26	0.68	—	4.04
12/05	32.82	44 28	0.79	—	8.59
12/04	25.36	49 24	0.55	—	7.14
12/03	14.64	41 16	0.37	—	5.74
12/02	10.68	48 14	0.36	—	4.91
Annual Growth	**20.9%**	**— —**	**17.2%**	**—**	**(4.8%)**

Website Pros

Website Pros has everything a growing business needs to get on the Internet. The company provides Web site building software, custom design consulting, and Web hosting. Its eWorks! XL program also helps companies improve their visibility online through search engine optimization and Internet advertising. Website Pros' desktop Web design software is branded under its NetObjects Fusion label and helps customers to design their own Web site. The company sells to more than 50,000 small and midsized businesses in the US, mostly on a subscription basis. Hoping to cement itself as a heavy hitter in the Web services industry, Website Pros in October 2007 acquired Web hosting services provider Web.com.

The acquisition of Web.com augments the company's subscriber count to more than 245,000 and gives it access to about 20 patents.

The Web.com deal is just the tail end of a recent string of buyouts for Website Pros. In 2005 the company acquired E.B.O.Z. and Leads.com, expanding its lead generation and Internet marketing offerings. The buyouts continued in 2006 when the company acquired Renovation Experts.com (Renex), an online lead generation business catering to homeowners and contractors, and 1ShoppingCart.com, a designer of online shopping cart software and services. In 2007, Website Pros acquired Submitawebsite, Inc., a search engine optimization firm.

Through the company's eWorks! XL program, Website Pros' goal is to have a Web site visible on the Internet for the customer within 72 hours of receiving the customer's initial information. The program includes a wide assortment of services and products including initial site design setup, the purchase and registration of the domain name, online marketing applications, Web mail, and hosting and technical support.

EXECUTIVES

President, CEO, and Director: David Brown, age 53, $400,706 pay
EVP Leads.com: Tobias Dengel, age 34
EVP Leads.com: Todd Walrath, age 38
SVP Business Development: Darin Brannan, age 39, $171,969 pay
SVP Marketing: Roseann Duran, age 55, $147,379 pay
SVP Web Services: Lisa Anteau, age 33
VP Finance and CFO: Kevin Carney, age 43, $252,706 pay
VP Operations: Joel Williamson, age 57
VP NetObjects Fusion Group: Steve Raubenstine, age 38
Auditors: Ernst & Young LLP

LOCATIONS

HQ: Website Pros, Inc.
12735 Gran Bay Pkwy. West, Bldg. 200, Jacksonville, FL 32258
Phone: 904-680-6600   **Fax:** 904-880-0350
Web: www.websitepros.com

Website Pros has offices in California, Florida, Virginia, and Washington.

PRODUCTS/OPERATIONS

2006 Sales

	$ mil.	% of total
Subscription	46.8	90
License	3.5	7
Professional services	1.7	3
Total	**52.0**	**100**

COMPETITORS

Adobe
AOL
EarthLink
Equinix
Microsoft Dynamics
Verio

HISTORICAL FINANCIALS

Company Type: Public

Income Statement

	REVENUE ($ mil.)	NET INCOME ($ mil.)	NET PROFIT MARGIN	EMPLOYEES
12/06	52.0	8.6	16.5%	639
12/05	37.8	0.8	2.1%	163
12/04	23.4	0.9	3.8%	—
12/03	17.0	(1.5)	—	—
12/02	13.7	(6.3)	—	—
Annual Growth	39.6%	—	—	292.0%

FYE: December 31

2006 Year-End Financials

Debt ratio: 0.2%
Return on equity: 11.3%
Cash ($ mil.): 42.2
Current ratio: 5.38
Long-term debt ($ mil.): 0.2
No. of shares (mil.): 17.3
Dividends
  Yield: —
  Payout: —
Market value ($ mil.): 156.9
R&D as % of sales: —
Advertising as % of sales: —

Stock History

NASDAQ (GM): WSPI

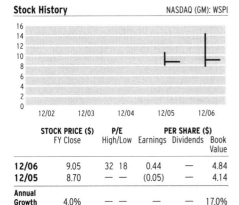

	STOCK PRICE ($) FY Close	P/E High/Low	PER SHARE ($) Earnings	Dividends	Book Value
12/06	9.05	32 18	0.44	—	4.84
12/05	8.70	— —	(0.05)	—	4.14
Annual Growth	4.0%	— —	—	—	17.0%

West Pharmaceutical Services

West Pharmaceutical Services makes products for drug packaging and plastic components used in the health care and consumer products industries. Its products include metal, elastomeric, and plastic stoppers, containers, closures, and medical device components. Among its customers are biotechnology and pharmaceutical companies, as well as medical device makers and hospital suppliers.

EXECUTIVES

Chairman and CEO: Donald E. Morel Jr., age 50, $905,352 pay (prior to title change)
President and COO: Steven A. Ellers, age 57, $515,066 pay (prior to title change)
VP and CFO: William J. Federici, age 48, $555,632 pay
VP General Counsel and Secretary: John R. Gailey III
VP and Controller: Joseph E. Abbott, age 55
VP and Treasurer: Michael A. (Mike) Anderson, age 52
VP Human Resources: Richard D. Luzzi, age 57
President, Europe and Asia Pacific, Pharmaceutical Systems Division: Robert J. Keating, age 59, $491,131 pay
President, North America, Pharmaceutical Systems Division: Donald A. (Don) McMillan, age 49
President, The Tech Group: Robert S. Hargesheimer
Auditors: PricewaterhouseCoopers LLP

LOCATIONS

HQ: West Pharmaceutical Services, Inc.
101 Gordon Dr., Lionville, PA 19341
Phone: 610-594-2900   **Fax:** 610-594-3000
Web: www.westpharma.com

West Pharmaceutical Services has facilities in the Americas, Europe, and the Asia/Pacific.

2006 Sales

	$ mil.	% of total
US	464.5	51
Europe		
Germany	97.7	11
France	73.7	9
Other countries	174.4	19
Other regions	103.0	10
Total	**913.3**	**100**

PRODUCTS/OPERATIONS

2006 Sales

	$ mil.	% of total
Pharmaceutical systems	538.3	59
Tech Group	375.0	41
Total	**913.3**	**100**

COMPETITORS

Cardinal Supply Chain Medical
Kerr Group
Owens-Illinois
Tekni-Plex

HISTORICAL FINANCIALS

Company Type: Public

Income Statement

	REVENUE ($ mil.)	NET INCOME ($ mil.)	NET PROFIT MARGIN	EMPLOYEES
12/06	913.3	67.1	7.3%	6,323
12/05	699.7	45.6	6.5%	5,570
12/04	541.6	19.4	3.6%	—
12/03	490.7	31.9	6.5%	—
12/02	419.7	18.4	4.4%	4,140
Annual Growth	21.5%	38.2%	—	11.2%

FYE: December 31

2006 Year-End Financials

Debt ratio: 56.9%
Return on equity: 17.9%
Cash ($ mil.): 47.1
Current ratio: 1.80
Long-term debt ($ mil.): 235.8
No. of shares (mil.): 32.9
Dividends
  Yield: 1.0%
  Payout: 24.5%
Market value ($ mil.): 1,685.5
R&D as % of sales: —
Advertising as % of sales: —

Stock History

NYSE: WST

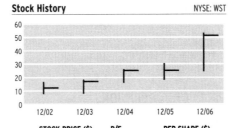

	STOCK PRICE ($) FY Close	P/E High/Low	PER SHARE ($) Earnings	Dividends	Book Value
12/06	51.23	26 12	2.00	0.49	12.60
12/05	25.03	21 13	1.40	0.45	10.50
12/04	25.03	40 26	0.63	0.43	9.80
12/03	16.95	16 8	1.10	0.41	17.61
12/02	12.20	25 13	0.64	0.38	13.92
Annual Growth	43.1%	— —	33.0%	6.6%	(2.5%)

Western Alliance Bancorporation

The allies behind Western Alliance Bancorporation are Alliance Bank of Arizona, Alta Alliance Bank, Bank of Nevada (formerly BankWest of Nevada), and Torrey Pines Bank, which together operate about 30 branches in Nevada, Arizona, and California. The banks provide local businesses and individuals with standard deposit products, such as checking and money market accounts and CDs. Commercial real estate and construction loans dominate the banks' lending (about 40% and 25% of the company's loan portfolio, respectively). Subsidiaries Miller/Russell & Associates and Premier Trust offer financial planning and trust services. Director Marianne Boyd Johnson owns about 15% of Western Alliance.

CEO Robert Sarver (also majority owner of the Phoenix Suns) holds about 15% of the company, which serves the Nevada metro areas of Las Vegas and Reno; the Phoenix, Tucson, and Flagstaff metro areas in Arizona; and the Bay Area and the San Diego metro in California. The company has been busily expanding its operations through acquisitions. In 2006 it acquired Intermountain First Bancorp (parent of Nevada First Bank) and Bank of Nevada, effectively tripling Western Alliance's size. With the latter acquisition, Western Alliance changed the name of its Nevada banking operations to Bank of Nevada. The subsidiary banks are also growing organically, with plans to add de novo branches for each bank. Western Alliance in 2006 moved into the San Francisco Bay area, joining forces with an investor group to launch Alta Alliance Bank in Oakland, California.

EXECUTIVES

Chairman, President, and CEO: Robert G. Sarver, age 45, $536,539 pay
EVP, Arizona Administration; President and CEO, Alliance Bank of Arizona: James Lundy, age 57, $225,000 pay
EVP, Southern California Administration: Gary Cady, age 52
EVP and Chief Administrative Officer: Merrill S. Wall, age 59, $257,308 pay
EVP and Chief Credit Officer: Duane Froeschle, age 54, $200,000 pay
EVP and CFO: Dale M. Gibbons, age 46, $260,000 pay
EVP Operations: Linda Mahan, age 49
EVP Northern Nevada Administration: Grant Markham, age 49
EVP Northern California Administration: Arnold Grisham, age 60
President, Premier Trust of Nevada: Mark Dreschler
President, Miller/Russell & Associates: Dennis Miller
Secretary: Robert E. Clark
Auditors: McGladrey & Pullen, LLP

LOCATIONS

HQ: Western Alliance Bancorporation
2700 W. Sahara Ave., Las Vegas, NV 89102
Phone: 702-248-4200   **Fax:** 702-362-2026
Web: www.westernalliancebancorp.com

Western Alliance Bancorporation's subsidiary banks have about 15 branches in Nevada, about 10 in Arizona, and about five in California.

PRODUCTS/OPERATIONS

2006 Sales

	% of total
Interest income	
Loans	81
Securities	11
Other	1
Trust & investment advisory services	3
Service charges	1
Other	3
Total	**100**

COMPETITORS

Bank of America
Bank of the West
Community Bancorp (NV)
Desert Schools FCU
First Banks
First Community Bancorp
Nevada State Bank
Silver State Bancorp
UCBH Holdings
UnionBanCal
U.S. Bancorp
Washington Mutual
Wells Fargo
Westamerica
Zions Bancorporation

HISTORICAL FINANCIALS

Company Type: Public

Income Statement   FYE: December 31

	ASSETS ($ mil.)	NET INCOME ($ mil.)	INCOME AS % OF ASSETS	EMPLOYEES
12/06	4,169.6	39.9	1.0%	785
12/05	2,857.3	28.1	1.0%	537
12/04	2,176.9	20.1	0.9%	—
12/03	1,576.8	8.7	0.6%	—
Annual Growth	**38.3%**	**47.6%**	**—**	**46.2%**

2006 Year-End Financials

Equity as % of assets: 9.8%
Return on assets: 1.1%
Return on equity: 12.2%
Long-term debt ($ mil.): 159.9
No. of shares (mil.): 27.1
Market value ($ mil.): 941.7

Dividends
  Yield: —
  Payout: —
Sales ($ mil.): 251.0
R&D as % of sales: —
Advertising as % of sales: —

Stock History   NYSE: WAL

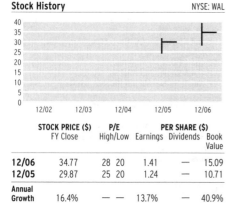

	STOCK PRICE ($) FY Close	P/E High/Low	PER SHARE ($) Earnings	Dividends	Book Value
12/06	34.77	28 20	1.41	—	15.09
12/05	29.87	25 20	1.24	—	10.71
Annual Growth	**16.4%**	**— —**	**13.7%**	**—**	**40.9%**

W-H Energy Services

W-h-a-t is W-H? W-H Energy Services offers diversified oil field services both onshore and off — from completion and workover related products and services to drilling related products and services. Products include specialty chemicals, drilling motors and fluids, wireline logging and perforating, and measurement-while-drilling systems. Founded in 1989, W-H Energy Services serves oil and gas firms, petrochemical companies, and other oil field service companies, primarily on the US Gulf Coast and in the Gulf of Mexico and the North Sea. The company, which has grown through acquisitions, is pursuing international expansion.

In order to focus on its core operations, in 2004 the company sold its maintenance and safety related products and services units, including Charles Holston, Inc. and Well Safe, Inc.

EXECUTIVES

Chairman, President, and CEO: Kenneth T. White Jr., age 66, $1,350,000 pay
VP COO: Jeffrey L. (Jeff) Tepera, age 42
VP and CFO: Ernesto Bautista III, age 36
VP; President and CEO of W-H Drilling Solutions, and President, Thomas Energy Services: William J. (Mac) Thomas III, age 55, $680,000 pay
VP: Glen J. Ritter, age 54, $680,000 pay (partial-year salary)
VP and Intellectual Property Counsel: Stuart J. Ford, age 50, $460,000 pay
President, Agri-Empresa: Stephen T. Goree
President, Drill Motor Services: Daniel M. (Dan) Spiller
President, Dyna Drill Technologies: Leif Syverson
President, Grinding and Sizing: Ronald A. Rose
President, Integrity Industries: William M. (Max) Duncan Jr.
Auditors: Grant Thornton LLP

LOCATIONS

HQ: W-H Energy Services, Inc.
  2000 W. Sam Houston Pky, South, Ste. 500, Houston, TX 77042
Phone: 713-974-9071   **Fax:** 713-974-7029
Web: www.whes.com

W-H Energy Services has onshore operations in the US and in Brazil, Canada, Europe, the Middle East, and North Africa. It has offshore operations off the coast of Brazil and in the Gulf of Mexico, the Gulf of Suez, the Mediterranean Sea, and the North Sea.

2006 Sales

	$ mil.	% of total
US	806.5	90
North Sea	39.3	4
Other countries & regions	49.0	6
Total	**894.8**	**100**

PRODUCTS/OPERATIONS

2006 Sales

	$ mil.	% of total
Drilling	564.0	63
Completion	330.8	37
Total	**894.8**	**100**

Selected Subsidiaries

Agri-Empresa, Inc. (specialty chemicals)
Boyd's Bit Service, Inc. (drilling equipment)
Coil Tubing Services, L.L.C. (oilfield services)
Drill Motor Services, Inc.
Dyna Drill Technologies, Inc. (drilling motor services and rentals)
Grinding and Sizing Company, Inc. (drilling mud products)
Integrity Industries, Inc. (specialty chemicals)
PathFinder Energy Services AS (Norway, logging-while-drilling and measurement-while-drilling services)
PathFinder Energy Services, Inc. (logging-while-drilling and measurement-while-drilling services)
PathFinder Energy Services Limited (UK, logging-while-drilling and measurement-while-drilling services)
Perf-O-Log, Inc. (completion and workover related products and services)
Thomas Energy Services, Inc. (rental tools)

COMPETITORS

Baker Hughes
BJ Services
Dailey International Inc.
Dril-Quip
Halliburton
National Oilwell Varco
Newpark Resources
Oil States International
Schlumberger
Smith International
Weatherford International

HISTORICAL FINANCIALS

Company Type: Public

Income Statement   FYE: December 31

	REVENUE ($ mil.)	NET INCOME ($ mil.)	NET PROFIT MARGIN	EMPLOYEES
12/06	894.8	115.0	12.9%	2,959
12/05	634.4	49.0	7.7%	2,333
12/04	462.4	17.9	3.9%	—
12/03	398.4	19.3	4.8%	—
12/02	313.4	16.3	5.2%	1,618
Annual Growth	**30.0%**	**63.0%**	**—**	**16.3%**

2006 Year-End Financials

Debt ratio: 30.6%
Return on equity: 27.7%
Cash ($ mil.): 36.3
Current ratio: 2.75
Long-term debt ($ mil.): 151.0
No. of shares (mil.): 30.2

Dividends
  Yield: —
  Payout: —
Market value ($ mil.): 1,468.4
R&D as % of sales: —
Advertising as % of sales: —

Stock History   NYSE: WHQ

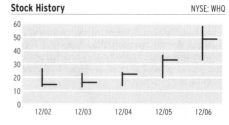

	STOCK PRICE ($) FY Close	P/E High/Low	PER SHARE ($) Earnings	Dividends	Book Value
12/06	48.69	15 9	3.76	—	16.34
12/05	33.08	22 12	1.68	—	11.76
12/04	22.36	37 22	0.64	—	9.66
12/03	16.20	33 19	0.69	—	9.03
12/02	14.59	44 23	0.59	—	8.20
Annual Growth	**35.2%**	**— —**	**58.9%**	**—**	**18.8%**

Whiting Petroleum

There's nothing fishy about what Whiting Petroleum is about. The company engages in oil and natural gas exploration and production activities, mainly in California, the Gulf Coast, Michigan, and the mid-continent, Permian Basin, and Rocky Mountains regions. It has estimated proved reserves of 248.1 million barrels of oil equivalent. Whiting Petroleum had 3,659 net productive wells in 2006. The company expanded in 2004 by acquiring stakes in 17 oil and gas fields in Texas and New Mexico for $345 million. It also bought Equity Oil for $76 million. In 2005 the company acquired oil and gas assets in Mississippi, Oklahoma, and Texas.

In 2005 Whiting Petroleum acquired three institutional partnerships managed by subsidiary, Whiting Programs, for about $30.5 million. The partnership properties (with reserves of 17.4 billion cu. ft. of natural gas equivalent) are located primarily in Arkansas, Louisiana, Oklahoma, Texas, and Wyoming.

EXECUTIVES

Chairman, President, and CEO: James J. Volker, age 60, $487,500 pay
VP and CFO: Michael J. Stevens, age 41, $205,000 pay
VP Exploration and Development: Mark R. Williams, age 50, $190,000 pay
VP General Counsel and Secretary: Bruce R. DeBoer, age 54
VP Human Resources: Patricia J. Miller, age 69
VP Information Technology: Gale Keithline
VP Land: David M. (Dave) Seery, age 52
VP Operations: James T. Brown, age 54, $185,000 pay
VP Reservoir Engineering and Acquisitions: J. Douglas Lang, age 57, $146,250 pay
VP Human Resources: Heather Duncan
Director Investor Relations: John Kelso
Controller and Treasurer: Brent P. Jensen, age 37
Auditors: Deloitte & Touche LLP

LOCATIONS

HQ: Whiting Petroleum Corporation
1700 Broadway, Ste. 2300, Denver, CO 80290
Phone: 303-837-1661   **Fax:** 303-861-4023
Web: www.whiting.com

2006 Proved Reserves

	% of total
Permian Basin	48
Mid-continent	21
Rocky Mountains	21
Michigan	5
Gulf Coast	5
Total	**100**

PRODUCTS/OPERATIONS

2006 Proved Reserves

	% of total
Oil	79
Natural gas	21
Total	**100**

COMPETITORS

Anadarko Petroleum
Black Hills
Cabot Oil & Gas
Frontier Oil
Newfield Exploration
Stone Energy

HISTORICAL FINANCIALS

Company Type: Public

Income Statement

FYE: December 31

	REVENUE ($ mil.)	NET INCOME ($ mil.)	NET PROFIT MARGIN	EMPLOYEES
12/06	786.3	156.4	19.9%	359
12/05	540.5	121.9	22.6%	309
12/04	287.0	70.1	24.4%	—
12/03	167.4	18.3	10.9%	—
12/02	120.5	7.7	6.4%	—
Annual Growth	**59.8%**	**112.3%**	**—**	**16.2%**

2006 Year-End Financials

Debt ratio: 84.3%
Return on equity: 14.3%
Cash ($ mil.): 10.4
Current ratio: 0.85
Long-term debt ($ mil.): 1,000.6
No. of shares (mil.): 36.9

Dividends
  Yield: —
  Payout: —
Market value ($ mil.): 1,721.8
R&D as % of sales: —
Advertising as % of sales: —

Stock History

NYSE: WLL

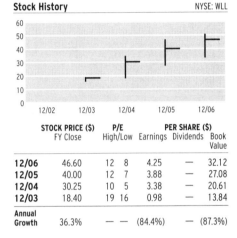

	STOCK PRICE ($) FY Close	P/E High/Low		PER SHARE ($) Earnings	Dividends	Book Value
12/06	46.60	12	8	4.25	—	32.12
12/05	40.00	12	7	3.88	—	27.08
12/04	30.25	10	5	3.38	—	20.61
12/03	18.40	19	16	0.98	—	13.84
Annual Growth	**36.3%**	**—**	**—**	**(84.4%)**	**—**	**(87.3%)**

Willamette Valley Vineyards

In the heart of Oregon's Willamette Valley, far from California's wine country, you'll find Willamette Valley Vineyards. The company makes premium varietal wines, including pinot noir (its flagship varietal), chardonnay, dry Riesling, and pinot gris under the Willamette Valley Vineyards, Tualatin Estates, and Griffin Creek labels. Its wines are sold to visitors at its winery, in restaurants and at retail outlets, and through wine distributors across the US. Retail prices for the company's wines range from $7 to $50 a bottle. Willamette Valley Vineyards owns, leases, and contracts for about 770 acres of vineyards.

Willamette Valley Vineyards produces as many as 124,000 cases of wine per year, making it one of the largest wineries in the state. Like many small and midsized wineries, Willamette Valley Vineyards looks to capitalize on a 2005 Supreme Court decision that opened up interstate sales of wine in those states that allow wine to ship directly to consumers without first passing through a wholesaler.

Founder and CEO Jim Bernau owns 16% of the company.

EXECUTIVES

Chairman and President: James W. (Jim) Bernau, age 53, $196,158 pay
CFO and Controller: Jeffrey J. Fox
VP Corporate, Secretary, Director HR, and Board Member: James L. Ellis, age 62
National Sales Manager: Cara Pepper
Communications Coordinator: Shelby Zadow
Winemaker: Forrest Klaffke
Vineyard Manager: Efren Loeza
Auditors: Moss Adams, LLP

LOCATIONS

HQ: Willamette Valley Vineyards, Inc.
8800 Enchanted Way SE, Turner, OR 97392
Phone: 503-588-9463   **Fax:** 503-588-8894
Web: www.wvv.com

PRODUCTS/OPERATIONS

COMPETITORS

Constellation Wines
E. & J. Gallo
Foster's Americas
Kendall-Jackson
Newton Vineyard
Ravenswood Winery
R.H. Phillips
Scheid Vineyards
Sebastiani Vineyards
Terlato Wine
Trinchero Family Estates
Yamhill Valley Vineyards

HISTORICAL FINANCIALS

Company Type: Public

Income Statement

FYE: December 31

	REVENUE ($ mil.)	NET INCOME ($ mil.)	NET PROFIT MARGIN	EMPLOYEES
12/06	14.9	1.3	8.7%	102
12/05	13.7	1.2	8.8%	86
12/04	9.4	0.5	5.3%	—
12/03	7.4	0.2	2.7%	—
12/02	6.0	0.1	1.7%	60
Annual Growth	**25.5%**	**89.9%**	**—**	**14.2%**

2006 Year-End Financials

Debt ratio: 10.9%
Return on equity: 12.3%
Cash ($ mil.): 1.6
Current ratio: 4.28
Long-term debt ($ mil.): 1.2
No. of shares (mil.): 4.8

Dividends
  Yield: —
  Payout: —
Market value ($ mil.): 32.7
R&D as % of sales: —
Advertising as % of sales: —

Stock History

NASDAQ (CM): WVVI

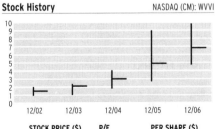

	STOCK PRICE ($) FY Close	P/E High/Low		PER SHARE ($) Earnings	Dividends	Book Value
12/06	6.82	38	18	0.26	—	2.37
12/05	4.90	36	11	0.25	—	2.09
12/04	2.99	40	19	0.10	—	1.81
12/03	2.12	58	27	0.04	—	1.71
12/02	1.50	65	33	0.03	—	1.68
Annual Growth	**46.0%**	**—**	**—**	**71.6%**	**—**	**8.9%**

Williams Partners

Fractionating natural gas liquids is only a small fraction of what Williams Partners does. The company is engaged in gathering, transporting, and processing natural gas and the fractionating and storing of natural gas liquids. Its assets include a 3,500-mile natural gas gathering system in the San Juan Basin; 40% of Discovery Producer Services (a gas gathering and transportation pipeline system running from the Gulf of Mexico to a processing facility in Louisiana); the Carbonate Trend gas gathering pipeline off the coast of Alabama; and three integrated NGL storage facilities and a 50%-owned fractionator in Kansas. The Williams Companies spun off Williams Partners in 2005, but retains a 21% stake in the firm.

NGLs, the result of natural gas processing and crude oil refining, are used in a number of industry applications, including gasoline additives, heating fuels, and petrochemical feedstocks.

Williams Partners intends to pursue a growth strategy that includes acquisitions. In 2006 the company spent $360 million for a 25% interest in the Williams Companies' Four Corners natural gas gathering subsidiary, and subsequently bought the remainder for $1.2 billion.

EXECUTIVES

Chairman, President, and CEO; Chairman and CEO, Williams Partners GP LLC: Steven J. (Steve) Malcolm, age 59
SVP; COO and Director, Williams Partners GP LLC: Alan S. Armstrong, age 45
SVP and CFO; CFO and Director, Williams Partners GP LLC: Donald R. (Don) Chappel, age 56
SVP and General Counsel; General Counsel, Williams Partners GP LLC: James J. Bender, age 51
Auditors: Ernst & Young LLP

LOCATIONS

HQ: Williams Partners L.P.
1 Williams Ctr., Tulsa, OK 74172
Phone: 918-573-2000
Web: www.williamslp.com

PRODUCTS/OPERATIONS

2006 Sales

	$ mil.	% of total
Product sales	272.0	48
Gathering & processing	248.7	44
Storage	25.2	5
Fractionation	11.7	2
Other	5.8	1
Total	**563.4**	**100**

COMPETITORS

Dynegy
Enterprise Products
TEPPCO Partners

HISTORICAL FINANCIALS

Company Type: Public

Income Statement
FYE: December 31

	REVENUE ($ mil.)	NET INCOME ($ mil.)	NET PROFIT MARGIN	EMPLOYEES
12/06	563.4	146.9	26.1%	304
12/05	51.8	4.8	9.3%	66
12/04	41.0	(13.4)	—	120
12/03	28.3	5.2	18.4%	—
12/02	25.7	7.8	30.4%	—
Annual Growth	**116.4%**	**108.3%**	**—**	**59.2%**

2006 Year-End Financials

Debt ratio: 553.9%
Return on equity: 82.3%
Cash ($ mil.): 57.5
Current ratio: 2.58
Long-term debt ($ mil.): 750.0
No. of shares (mil.): 25.6
Dividends
Yield: 4.1%
Payout: 99.4%
Market value ($ mil.): 988.9
R&D as % of sales: —
Advertising as % of sales: —

Stock History
NYSE: WPZ

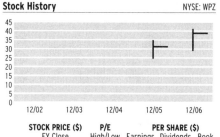

	STOCK PRICE ($) FY Close	P/E High/Low	PER SHARE ($) Earnings	Dividends	Book Value
12/06	38.70	25 18	1.62	1.61	5.30
12/05	31.15	78 57	0.44	0.15	31.64
Annual Growth	**24.2%**	**— —**	**268.2%**	**973.3%**	**(83.3%)**

Willow Financial Bancorp

Willow Financial Bancorp (formerly Willow Grove Bancorp) is the holding company for Willow Financial Bank (previously Willow Grove Bank), which operates nearly 30 branches in Philadelphia and its suburbs. Founded in 1909, the bank uses funds collected from deposit accounts mainly to invest in securities and originate loans.

Mortgages, including residential, commercial real estate, construction, and home equity loans, make up more than 90% of the company's lending portfolio. The bank also writes business and consumer loans. It provides investments and brokerage services through an agreement with UVEST.

The company acquired Chester Valley Bancorp in 2005; former Chester Valley CEO Donna Coughey took the helm of the combined firm.

In 2007 it bought Philadelphia-area employee benefits consulting firm BeneServ to expand its offerings for small businesses.

EXECUTIVES

Chairman: Rosemary C. Loring, age 55
President, CEO, and Director, Willow Grove Bancorp and Willow Grove Bank: Donna M. Coughey, age 56, $453,310 pay
COO: Christopher E. Bell, age 47, $171,713 pay
CFO and Treasurer, Willow Grove Bancorp and Willow Grove Bank; Secretary: Joseph T. Crowley, age 44, $242,797 pay
Regional President, First Financial Division, Willow Grove Bank: Colin N. Maropis, age 54
Regional President, Bucks and Montgomery Counties: John T. Powers, age 56
SVP and Chief Retail Officer: Richard Hymanson
Chief Administrative Officer and Risk Manager: Patrick Killeen
Chief Accounting Officer: Neelesh (Neil) Kalani, age 31
Chief Wealth Management Officer, Willow Grove Bank: Matthew D. Kelly, age 42, $170,500 pay
Chief Credit Officer: Ammon J. Baus, age 57, $203,115 pay
Chief Human Development Officer: Allen Wagner
Treasurer: Jerome P. Arrison, age 53, $151,381 pay
Auditors: KPMG LLP

LOCATIONS

HQ: Willow Financial Bancorp, Inc.
170 S. Warner Rd., Ste. 300, Wayne, PA 19087
Phone: 610-995-1700
Web: www.willowgrovebank.com

PRODUCTS/OPERATIONS

2007 Sales

	$ mil.	% of total
Interest		
Loans	69.6	70
Investment securities & other	16.7	17
Noninterest		
Service charges & fees	5.4	6
Investment services	3.3	3
Other	3.8	4
Total	**98.8**	**100**

COMPETITORS

Citizens Financial Group
Harleysville National
M&T Bank
National Penn Bancshares
PNC Financial
Sovereign Bancorp
Wachovia

HISTORICAL FINANCIALS

Company Type: Public

Income Statement
FYE: June 30

	ASSETS ($ mil.)	NET INCOME ($ mil.)	INCOME AS % OF ASSETS	EMPLOYEES
6/07	1,550.3	8.4	0.5%	418
6/06	1,576.7	11.1	0.7%	372
6/05	959.3	6.7	0.7%	220
6/04	921.6	6.1	0.7%	—
6/03	845.1	7.5	0.9%	—
Annual Growth	**16.4%**	**2.9%**	**—**	**37.8%**

2007 Year-End Financials

Equity as % of assets: 13.2%
Return on assets: 0.5%
Return on equity: 4.1%
Long-term debt ($ mil.): 25.5
No. of shares (mil.): 15.5
Market value ($ mil.): 201.5
Dividends
Yield: 4.4%
Payout: 107.4%
Sales ($ mil.): 98.8
R&D as % of sales: —
Advertising as % of sales: —

Stock History

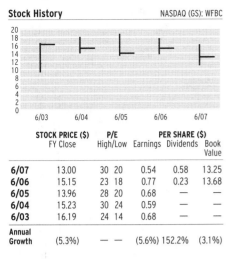

	STOCK PRICE ($) FY Close	P/E High/Low		PER SHARE ($) Earnings	Dividends	Book Value
6/07	13.00	30	20	0.54	0.58	13.25
6/06	15.15	23	18	0.77	0.23	13.68
6/05	13.96	28	20	0.68	—	—
6/04	15.23	30	24	0.59	—	—
6/03	16.19	24	14	0.68	—	—
Annual Growth	(5.3%)	—	—	(5.6%)	152.2%	(3.1%)

Wilshire Bancorp

Wilshire Bancorp is the holding company for Wilshire State Bank, where ethnic minorities are the banking majority. Based in the Koreatown section of Los Angeles, the bank has more than 15 branches mainly in Southern California but also in Dallas and New York City. It also has nearly 10 lending offices that specialize in Small Business Administration (SBA) loans in those markets and other large US cities. Wilshire State Bank targets small to midsized minority-owned businesses and ethnic groups underserved by most national banking institutions. In addition to offering standard deposit services (including checking and savings accounts, CDs, and IRAs), the bank also offers mortgages and import/export financing.

Expanding beyond its traditional Korean-American customer base, Wilshire State Bank also serves Hispanic and Vietnamese communities. In 2006 the company acquired Liberty Bank of New York and its two locations in the New York metropolitan area give it an East Coast presence.

As a group, board members and executive officers of Wilshire Bancorp control around 40% of the company, led by chairman Steven Koh's nearly 20% stake.

EXECUTIVES

Chairman: Steven Koh, age 62
Interim President and Interim CEO: Joanne Kim, age 53, $281,353 pay
Interim CFO, First VP, Controller, and Accounting Manager: Elaine Jeon
EVP and Manager, SBA Department: Sung Soo Han, age 50, $312,612 pay
SVP and Chief Compliance Officer: Jean Lim
SVP and Chief Information Officer: Jake Seo
SVP and Manager, Home Loan Center: Gene Sheen
SVP and Manager, Trade Finance Department: Radu M. Spiridon
SVP and Branch Manager, Valley Office: Susan Magidow
SVP, Dallas Branch BDO: J. P. Park
Auditors: Deloitte & Touche LLP

LOCATIONS

HQ: Wilshire Bancorp, Inc.
3200 Wilshire Blvd., Los Angeles, CA 90010
Phone: 213-387-3200   **Fax:** 213-427-6562
Web: www.wilshirebank.com

PRODUCTS/OPERATIONS

2006 Sales

	$ mil.	% of total
Interest		
Loans, including fees	127.8	76
Investment securities & deposits in other financial institutions	8.7	5
Federal funds sold & other cash equivalents	4.9	3
Noninterest		
Gain on sale of loans	11.6	7
Service charges on deposit accounts	9.6	6
Loan-related servicing income	2.1	1
Other	3.1	2
Total	**167.8**	**100**

COMPETITORS

Bank of America	East West Bancorp
Bank of the West	FirstFed Financial
Broadway Financial	Fremont Investment & Loan
California Bank & Trust	Hanmi Financial
California National Bank	Nara Bancorp
Cathay General Bancorp	UnionBanCal
Center Financial	U.S. Bancorp
Citibank	Washington Mutual
Citigroup	Wells Fargo
City National	
Comerica	

HISTORICAL FINANCIALS

Company Type: Public

Income Statement

FYE: December 31

	ASSETS ($ mil.)	NET INCOME ($ mil.)	INCOME AS % OF ASSETS	EMPLOYEES
12/06	2,008.5	33.9	1.7%	335
12/05	1,666.3	27.8	1.7%	278
12/04	1,265.6	19.5	1.5%	—
12/03	983.3	12.8	1.3%	—
12/02	692.8	8.6	1.2%	—
Annual Growth	30.5%	40.9%	—	20.5%

2006 Year-End Financials

Equity as % of assets: 7.5%	Dividends
Return on assets: 1.8%	Yield: 1.1%
Return on equity: 25.8%	Payout: 17.2%
Long-term debt ($ mil.): 61.5	Sales ($ mil.): 167.8
No. of shares (mil.): 29.2	R&D as % of sales: —
Market value ($ mil.): 553.9	Advertising as % of sales: —

Stock History

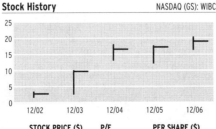

	STOCK PRICE ($) FY Close	P/E High/Low		PER SHARE ($) Earnings	Dividends	Book Value
12/06	18.97	17	14	1.16	0.20	5.13
12/05	17.19	18	13	0.96	0.12	3.95
12/04	16.54	26	19	0.68	—	3.14
12/03	9.71	22	6	0.44	—	4.54
12/02	2.70	10	5	0.32	—	7.80
Annual Growth	62.8%	—	—	38.0%	66.7%	(10.0%)

Wintrust Financial

Put yer hands up . . . we're buying you out! That seems to be the battle cry for ever-acquisitive Wintrust Financial, a multibank holding company engaged in banking and specialty financial services in several affluent Chicago suburbs. Through about 15 community banks (all of which retain a local identity) and some 75 branches, Wintrust Financial offers a range of traditional banking products. It emphasizes business and commercial real estate loans (more than 60% of the company's loan portfolio); the company also provides commercial insurance premium financing (more than 15% of the portfolio), indirect auto loans, and residential mortgages. Other company offerings include wealth management and mortgage banking.

Although Wintrust Financial's growth has been primarily fueled by acquisition in the past few years, the company has also launched several new banks and branches since 1991, targeting communities with high incomes and focusing on building a reputation for service.

Wintrust Financial also operates several non-bank subsidiaries. First Insurance Funding serves commercial customers throughout the country, providing financing for insurance premiums. Milwaukee-based Tricom offers the temporary staffing industry financing and administrative services. Wintrust Financial's Wayne Hummer Companies family of subsidiaries offers a variety of wealth management services, including brokerage. Other subsidiaries, including WestAmerica Mortgage Company, provide real estate mortgage loan origination, purchase, and related services.

EXECUTIVES

Chairman: John S. Lillard, age 77
President, CEO, and Director; Chairman, Wayne Hummer Investments, Wayne Hummer Trust, Wayne Hummer Asset Management, and First Insurance Funding: Edward J. Wehmer, age 54, $672,917 pay
SEVP, COO, and Secretary; Chairman, State Bank of the Lakes: David A. Dykstra, age 44, $486,667 pay
EVP and CFO: David L. Stoehr, $232,533 pay
EVP and Chief Credit Officer; Vice Chairman, Hinsdale Bank & Trust: Richard B. Murphy, age 46, $287,750 pay
EVP Marketing: Robert F. Key, age 51
EVP Risk Management: John S. Fleshood, age 44
EVP Technology; President and CEO, Wintrust Information Technology Services: Lloyd M. Bowden
EVP Wealth Management; President and CEO, Wayne Hummer Investments, Wayne Hummer Asset Management, and Focused Investments: James F. Duca II, age 47
SVP Corporate Real Estate: John S. Reagan, age 55
SVP Investments: David J. Galvan, age 45
VP Niche Marketing; SVP Marketing, First Insurance Funding: Matthew E. Doubleday
VP Human Resources: Michael A. Cherwin
Auditors: Ernst & Young LLP

LOCATIONS

HQ: Wintrust Financial Corporation
727 N. Bank Ln., Lake Forest, IL 60045
Phone: 847-615-4096   **Fax:** 847-615-4076
Web: www.wintrust.com

PRODUCTS/OPERATIONS

2006 Sales

	$ mil.	% of total
Interest		
Loans	456.4	70
Securities & other	101.6	16
Noninterest		
Wealth management fees	31.7	5
Mortgage banking	22.3	3
Other	37.2	6
Total	**649.2**	**100**

COMPETITORS

ABN AMRO
Citigroup
Citizens Financial Group
Citizens Republic Bancorp
Corus Bankshares
Cummins-American
Fifth Third
First Midwest Bancorp
Harris Bankcorp
JPMorgan Chase
MB Financial
Midwest Banc Holdings
National City
Northern States Financial
Northern Trust
Princeton National Bancorp
PrivateBancorp
U.S. Bancorp

HISTORICAL FINANCIALS

Company Type: Public

Income Statement   FYE: December 31

	ASSETS ($ mil.)	NET INCOME ($ mil.)	INCOME AS % OF ASSETS	EMPLOYEES
12/06	9,571.8	66.5	0.7%	1,897
12/05	8,177.0	67.0	0.8%	1,678
12/04	6,419.0	51.3	0.8%	—
12/03	4,747.4	38.1	0.8%	—
12/02	3,721.6	27.9	0.7%	822
Annual Growth	**26.6%**	**24.3%**	**—**	**23.3%**

2006 Year-End Financials

Equity as % of assets: 8.1%
Return on assets: 0.7%
Return on equity: 9.5%
Long-term debt ($ mil.): 499.6
No. of shares (mil.): 25.8
Market value ($ mil.): 1,239.0
Dividends
Yield: 0.6%
Payout: 10.9%
Sales ($ mil.): 649.2
R&D as % of sales: —
Advertising as % of sales: —

Stock History   NASDAQ (GS): WTFC

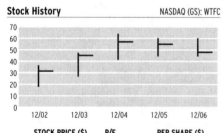

	STOCK PRICE ($) FY Close	P/E High/Low	PER SHARE ($) Earnings	Dividends	Book Value
12/06	48.02	23 18	2.56	0.28	29.97
12/05	54.90	22 16	2.75	0.24	26.23
12/04	56.96	27 18	2.34	0.20	21.81
12/03	45.10	24 14	1.98	0.16	17.43
12/02	31.32	22 11	1.60	0.06	13.19
Annual Growth	**11.3%**	**— —**	**12.5%**	**47.0%**	**22.8%**

Wireless Telecom

In an industry that abhors noise, Wireless Telecom Group sure makes a lot of it. The company, which markets its products under the brand name Noise Com, makes electronic noise generators for wireless telecommunications systems. Its products are used to test whether such systems can receive transmitted information. Its noise emulator products also operate in radar and satellite systems to continually monitor and test receivers or to jam signals. Wireless Telecom's Boonton Electronics subsidiary makes radio-frequency (RF) and microwave test equipment. Its Microlab/FXR subsidiary makes high-power, passive microwave components. Investcorp Technology Ventures owns one-quarter of Wireless Telecom.

Wireless Telecom Group markets its products through in-house representatives and manufacturer representatives, primarily to commercial customers (87% of sales); the remaining revenue comes from government and military clients. The company has expanded its line of products in an effort to reach a wider range of customers.

FMR (Fidelity Investments) owns nearly 7% of Wireless Telecom Group. Damany Holding holds about 5% of the company.

HISTORY

Founded in Paramus, New Jersey, in 1985 by Karabet (Gary) Simonyan, Noise Com began providing noise sources and systems testing for the military. Its products determined whether sophisticated communications devices were receiving and understanding the information being transmitted. Until 1992, the majority of sales continued to come from government and military contracts.

In the wake of defense cutbacks, in 1993 the company expanded its commercial product lines to include signal testing devices for the commercial telecommunications market, which by 1997 accounted for 95% of sales. In 1994 the company changed its name to Wireless Telecom; it continued to market its noise source products under the name of Noise Com, and distributed test systems under its new name. Simonyan stepped away from day-to-day responsibilities in 1996, and was replaced by president Dale Sydnor.

In 1997 the company began providing test systems for ICO Global Communications' satellite network. Lowered sales in its wireless and satellite test emulator line caused a drop in profits for 1998. In 1999 longtime Wireless Telecom employee Edward Garcia replaced Sydnor as chairman and CEO. As part of a reorganization around noise generators, the company that year sold its wireless and satellite communications test equipment business to Telecom Analysis Systems (TAS), a subsidiary of electronics company Bowthorpe (now Spirent Communications). As part of the deal, Wireless Telecom gained TAS's noise generation product line.

In 2000 the company acquired test equipment maker Boonton Electronics to expand its line of products for measuring wireless signal power. The next year Wireless Telecom added passive components to its catalog in 2002 with the purchase of Microlab/FXR.

Later in 2002 Wireless Telecom relocated its corporate headquarters and other offices in the former HQ of Boonton Electronics in Parsippany, New Jersey. Boonton Electronics took its name from the New Jersey town just north of Parsippany, where it was located for many years. Boonton Electronics was established in nearby Morris Plains in 1947.

Edward Garcia resigned as president and CEO in early 2004, becoming an engineering consultant to the company. Terence McCoy, a Reed Elsevier executive, was named to succeed Garcia as CEO, while CFO Paul Genova took on the additional post of president. McCoy quit after just three months as CEO, however. Founder and chairman Gary Simonyan stepped in as interim CEO.

Wireless Telecom greatly grew in size with its 2005 acquisition of Willtek Communications, a German test and measurement firm. Sales increased in all geographic regions of the world, especially in Europe, as a result of the acquisition. The acquisition more than doubled Wireless Telecom's headcount.

Cyrille Damany, the CEO and GM of Willtek Communications, took over as CEO of Wireless Telecom following the acquisition. He lasted only two months before resigning. Paul Genova, the president and CFO, became interim CEO.

Gary Simonyan became vice chairman of the board upon closing of the Willtek transaction in mid-2005; Savio Tung was appointed chairman. Simonyan resigned from the board three months later, finally leaving the company he founded 20 years earlier.

In early 2006 Wireless Telecom named Tekelec executive James (Monty) Johnson Jr. as vice chairman and CEO of the company.

EXECUTIVES

Chairman: Savio W. Tung, age 57
Vice Chairman and CEO: James M. (Monty) Johnson Jr., age 52, $335,000 pay
President and CFO: Paul Genova, age 51, $244,000 pay
EVP, Marketing: Bent Hessen-Schmidt, age 42, $151,463 pay
SVP, Global Customer Operations: Lawrence D. (Larry) Henderson
Controller: Reed E. DuBow
Auditors: PKF

LOCATIONS

HQ: Wireless Telecom Group, Inc.
25 Eastmans Rd., Parsippany, NJ 07054
Phone: 973-386-9696   **Fax:** 973-386-9191
Web: www.wirelesstelecomgroup.com

Wireless Telecom Group has facilities in Germany and the US.

2006 Sales

	$ mil.	% of total
Americas	24.2	45
Europe	16.5	31
Asia	7.7	14
Other regions	5.4	10
Total	**53.8**	**100**

PRODUCTS/OPERATIONS

2006 Sales

	% of total
Commercial	87
Government & military contractors	13
Total	**100**

Selected Products

Broadband test equipment
Electronic testing and measuring instruments
Noise figure measurement devices
Noise generators
Passive components
    Directional couplers
    Filters
    Power splitters
Wireless communications network test equipment
    Air interface testing
    Terminal testing

COMPETITORS

Aeroflex
Agilent Technologies
Anaren
Anritsu
COM DEV
KATHREIN-Werke
M/A-Com
Merrimac Industries
Micronetics
Murata Manufacturing
ORBIT/FR
Rohde & Schwarz
STC Microwave Systems
Tektronix
telent
Tyco Electronics
Vishay Intertechnology
Wavelink

HISTORICAL FINANCIALS

Company Type: Public

Income Statement

FYE: December 31

	REVENUE ($ mil.)	NET INCOME ($ mil.)	NET PROFIT MARGIN	EMPLOYEES
12/06	53.8	3.5	6.5%	233
12/05	38.8	3.5	9.0%	229
12/04	22.1	2.3	10.4%	—
12/03	19.7	1.8	9.1%	—
12/02	20.8	1.8	8.7%	110
Annual Growth	26.8%	18.1%	—	20.6%

2006 Year-End Financials

Debt ratio: 8.8%
Return on equity: 6.4%
Cash ($ mil.): 15.7
Current ratio: 2.55
Long-term debt ($ mil.): 5.0
No. of shares (mil.): 25.9
Dividends
  Yield: —
  Payout: —
Market value ($ mil.): 65.9
R&D as % of sales: —
Advertising as % of sales: —

Stock History

AMEX: WTT

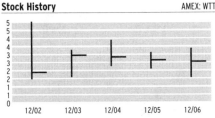

	STOCK PRICE ($) FY Close	P/E High/Low	PER SHARE ($) Earnings	Dividends	Book Value
12/06	2.55	24 11	0.14	—	2.20
12/05	2.65	19 13	0.16	0.12	2.06
12/04	2.84	30 18	0.13	0.12	1.69
12/03	2.95	32 16	0.10	0.09	1.67
12/02	1.89	50 15	0.10	0.06	1.65
Annual Growth	7.8%	— —	8.8%	26.0%	7.4%

WPCS International

WPCS International designs, installs, and maintains broadband wireless and specialty communications systems. Serving customers in the enterprise, government, and education sectors, the company builds Wi-Fi and mobile wireless networks, video security systems, and other communications systems. Its services include product integration, fiber-optic cabling, project management, and technical support. The company also provides engineering services to support wireless networks. Its specialty communication systems division offers support for telematics and telemetry systems, as well as networks designed for asset tracking.

WPCS International has served such diverse customers as Amtrak, Caesers Entertainment, the Jacksonville Jaguars, Wake Forest University Baptist Medical Center, and Sprint Nextel.

Since its founding in late 2001 the company has expanded rapidly through growth in operations and through acquisitions, including its 2004 purchase of Lakewood, New Jersey-based Quality Communications & Alarm Company, a wireless infrastructure provider serving the public safety and gaming markets. In 2007 it purchased communications infrastructure engineering company Taian AGS Pipeline Construction, opening the door to a Chinese expansion. The $1.6 million deal landed WPCS a 60% interest in AGS.

The company also agreed to acquire ATC International Holdings, a wireless and security systems services company with operations in the US and Central America. It additionally pursued the purchase of Voacolo Electric, a Mid-Atlantic electrical contractor specializing in high- and low-voltage applications. In the Pacific Northwest, WPCS closed a $3 million deal to acquire wireless contractor Major Electric, and acquired wireless infrastructure firm Max Engineering for $600,000.

EXECUTIVES

Chairman and CEO: Andrew (Andy) Hidalgo, age 50, $168,000 pay
CFO: Joseph Heater, age 42, $139,333 pay
EVP: James Heinz, age 44, $171,990 pay
EVP: Richard Schubiger, age 40, $213,658 pay
EVP: Donald Walker, age 43, $177,215 pay
EVP: Charles Madenford
President, WPCS International and Director: Gary Walker, age 51, $177,215 pay
Executive Administration: Carol Lindley
Senior Accountant: Paula Nussbaumer
Auditors: J.H. Cohn LLP

LOCATIONS

HQ: WPCS International Incorporated
    1 East Uwchlan Ave., Ste. 301, Exton, PA 19341
Phone: 610-903-0400   **Fax:** 610-903-0401
Web: www.wpcs.com

WPCS International has offices in California, Connecticut, Florida, Missouri, New Jersey, and Pennsylvania.

PRODUCTS/OPERATIONS

2007 Sales

	$ mil.	% of total
Specialty communication	56.8	81
Wireless infrastructure	13.2	19
Total	**70.0**	**100**

Selected Subsidiaries

Clayborn Contracting Group, Inc.
Heinz Corporation
Invisinet Inc.
New England Communication Systems, Inc.
Quality Communications & Alarm Company
Southeastern Communication Service, Inc.
Walker Comm Inc.
WPCS Incorporated

COMPETITORS

ARC Wireless Solutions
Dycom
EarthLink
EMCOR
Kratos Defense & Security Solutions
LCC International
MasTec
Proxim
Quanta Services
Tetra Tech
T-Mobile USA

HISTORICAL FINANCIALS

Company Type: Public

Income Statement

FYE: April 30

	REVENUE ($ mil.)	NET INCOME ($ mil.)	NET PROFIT MARGIN	EMPLOYEES
4/07	70.0	4.6	6.6%	361
4/06	52.1	(1.6)	—	204
4/05	40.2	1.3	3.2%	300
4/04	22.1	(0.1)	—	—
4/03	5.4	(0.4)	—	—
Annual Growth	89.7%	—	—	9.7%

2007 Year-End Financials

Debt ratio: 9.2%
Return on equity: 10.9%
Cash ($ mil.): 21.6
Current ratio: 3.27
Long-term debt ($ mil.): 4.7
No. of shares (mil.): 7.0
Dividends
  Yield: —
  Payout: —
Market value ($ mil.): 93.8
R&D as % of sales: —
Advertising as % of sales: —

Stock History

NASDAQ (GM): WPCS

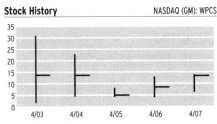

	STOCK PRICE ($) FY Close	P/E High/Low	PER SHARE ($) Earnings	Dividends	Book Value
4/07	13.45	19 9	0.72	—	7.39
4/06	8.43	— —	(0.40)	—	6.19
4/05	4.95	16 9	0.49	—	7.27
4/04	13.68	— —	—	—	0.54
4/03	13.80	— —	0.00	—	0.57
Annual Growth	(0.6%)	— —	—	—	89.7%

WPT Enterprises

This company is betting the house on televised poker. WPT Enterprises produces the *World Poker Tour* TV series that airs on the Travel Channel (owned by Cox Communications). The series highlights players taking part in 18 high-stakes poker tournaments hosted by casinos around the world. The tournaments are open to anyone able to pay the entry fee, which can range from $5,000 to $25,000. Member casinos operate the games and pay WPT Enterprises fees to film the tournaments. WPT Enterprises also licenses the WPT brand for consumer products, sells branded merchandise, and operates an online gaming site. Casino management firm Lakes Entertainment owns more than 60% of the company.

WPT Enterprises inked a licensing deal in 2007 with the Game Show Network (jointly owned by Sony Pictures Entertainment and Liberty Media) to broadcast a sixth season *World Poker Tour* after the Travel Channel decided not to renew. That leaves the company still shopping its new *Professional Poker Tour* show, which debuted on the Travel Channel in 2006 but was also not renewed. The company gets about 60% of its revenue through its broadcasting agreements with the Travel Channel.

WPT Enterprises and the rest of the poker industry got a shock that same year when the Federal government passed the Unlawful Internet Gambling Enforcement Act (UIGEA) designed to strengthen measures to keep US players from gambling online. Some in the industry feel this tough stance by the government could hurt the popularity of poker in the US.

The UIGEA has also made WPT Enterprises' own online gaming activities a bit dicey. While its WPTonline site, launched in 2005, does not accept wagers from US players, a further crackdown by the government could mean the company might have to shutter or modify that operation. In 2007 the company launched real money gaming site WorldPokerTour.com in partnership with gaming software maker CryptoLogic. (The site doesn't take US bets.) Online gaming accounts for about 10% of WPT Enterprises' business.

President and CEO Steve Lipscomb has a 10% stake in the company.

EXECUTIVES

Executive Chairman: Lyle Berman, age 65
President, CEO, and Director: Steven Lipscomb, age 45, $850,981 pay
COO: Peter Hughes, age 46, $280,769 pay
CFO: Scott A. Friedman, age 34, $198,500 pay (partial-year salary)
EVP WPT Studios; Supervising Producer, World Poker Tour: Robyn Moder, age 32, $300,000 pay
General Counsel and Secretary: Adam Pliska
Auditors: Piercy Bowler Taylor & Kern

LOCATIONS

HQ: WPT Enterprises, Inc.
5700 Wilshire Blvd., Ste. 350,
Los Angeles, CA 90036
Phone: 323-330-9900   **Fax:** 323-330-9902
Web: www.worldpokertour.com

PRODUCTS/OPERATIONS

2006 Sales

	$ mil.	% of total
WPT Studios	21.0	72
WPT Consumer Products	3.6	12
WPT Online Gaming	3.2	11
WPT Corporate Alliances	1.5	5
Total	**29.3**	**100**

Selected Operations

WPT Studios
 World Poker Tour
 WPT Bad Boys of Poker
 WPT Battle of Champions
 WPT Ladies Night
 WPT Young Guns of Poker
WPT Consumer Products
 Branded merchandise
 Licensed consumer products
WPT Online Gaming
 WPTonline.com
WPT Corporate Alliances
 Corporate events
 Marketing sponsorships

COMPETITORS

Bravo Company
FOX Sports
Harrah's Entertainment
NBC

HISTORICAL FINANCIALS

Company Type: Public

Income Statement

FYE: December 31

	REVENUE ($ mil.)	NET INCOME ($ mil.)	NET PROFIT MARGIN	EMPLOYEES
12/06	29.3	7.8	26.6%	88
12/05	18.1	(5.0)	—	83
12/04	17.6	0.8	4.5%	57
12/03	4.3	(0.5)	—	—
Annual Growth	**89.6%**	**—**	**—**	**24.3%**

2006 Year-End Financials

Debt ratio: —
Return on equity: 19.1%
Cash ($ mil.): 39.6
Current ratio: 5.49
Long-term debt ($ mil.): —
No. of shares (mil.): 20.4
Dividends
 Yield: —
 Payout: —
Market value ($ mil.): 78.9
R&D as % of sales: —
Advertising as % of sales: —

Stock History

NASDAQ (GM): WPTE

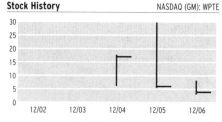

	STOCK PRICE ($) FY Close	P/E High/Low	PER SHARE ($) Earnings	Dividends	Book Value
12/06	3.87	21 9	0.38	—	2.12
12/05	5.94	— —	(0.26)	—	1.90
12/04	17.00	437 158	0.04	—	1.62
Annual Growth	**(52.3%)**	**— —**	**208.2%**	**—**	**14.4%**

WSB Financial Group

WSB Financial Group is the holding company for Westsound Bank, which has been serving the Puget Sound area of Washington State since 1999. Through eight branches and two loan production offices, the bank offers checking and savings accounts, CDs, IRAs, and credit cards. Its lending activities center on real estate construction (more than half of the company's loan portfolio), loans to small to medium-sized businesses, and residential mortgages. WSB Financial plans to continue its growth strategy of opening about three bank branches and loan offices per year throughout its market area.

EXECUTIVES

Chairman, WSB Financial Group and Westsound Bank: Louis J. Weir, age 66
President, CEO, and Director, WSB Financial Group and Westsound Bank: David K. Johnson, age 42, $475,000 pay
EVP, Finance and Operations and CFO, WSB Financial Group and Westsound Bank: Mark D. Freeman, age 54, $226,667 pay
EVP, Sales and Lending, Westsound Bank: Brett T. Green, age 44, $650,000 pay
SVP and Chief Lending Officer, Westsound Bank: Brent A. Stenman, age 42, $145,875 pay
SVP, Operations, Westsound Bank: Robin A. Seelye, age 36, $62,538 pay (partial-year salary)
SVP and Chief Lending Officer, Westsound Bank: Charles Turner
SVP, Chief Risk Officer, and Secretary, WSB Financial Group and Westsound Bank: Veronica R. Colburn, age 44, $135,000 pay
Auditors: Moss Adams, LLP

LOCATIONS

HQ: WSB Financial Group, Inc.
607 Pacific Ave., Bremerton, WA 98337
Phone: 360-405-1200   **Fax:** 360-405-1206
Web: www.westsoundbank.com

WSB Financial Group has locations in Washington's Clallam, Jefferson, Kitsap, and Pierce counties.

PRODUCTS/OPERATIONS

2006 Sales

	$ mil.	% of total
Interest		
Loans, including fees	27.6	83
Investments	0.3	1
Federal funds sold & other	0.4	1
Noninterest		
Net gain on sale of loans	3.5	11
Service charges on deposit accounts	0.3	1
Other	0.9	3
Total	**33.0**	**100**

COMPETITORS

Bank of America
Cascade Financial
KeyCorp
Sterling Financial (WA)
Timberland Bancorp
U.S. Bancorp
Washington Mutual
Wells Fargo

HISTORICAL FINANCIALS

Company Type: Public

Income Statement				FYE: December 31
	ASSETS ($ mil.)	NET INCOME ($ mil.)	INCOME AS % OF ASSETS	EMPLOYEES
12/06	386.8	3.9	1.0%	130
12/05	250.0	2.4	1.0%	—
12/04	137.4	1.3	0.9%	—
Annual Growth	67.8%	73.2%	—	—

2006 Year-End Financials

Equity as % of assets: 15.9%	Dividends
Return on assets: 1.2%	Yield: —
Return on equity: 10.0%	Payout: —
Long-term debt ($ mil.): 8.3	Sales ($ mil.): 33.0
No. of shares (mil.): 5.6	R&D as % of sales: —
Market value ($ mil.): 106.7	Advertising as % of sales: —

Stock History

NASDAQ (GM): WSFG

	STOCK PRICE ($) FY Close	P/E High/Low		PER SHARE ($) Earnings	Dividends	Book Value
12/06	19.20	18	16	1.18	—	11.10

Zumiez Inc.

Zumiez's customers like to zoom. The online and mall-based retailer offers swank swag-like clothing, shoes, accessories, and gear to 12- to 24-year-olds who enjoy such action sports as snowboarding, BMX, skateboarding, and surfing. From 235 stores in nearly 25 states, Zumiez sells popular youth brands like Billabong, Burton, Hurley, Quiksilver, Vans, and Spy Optic, as well as private-label goods. Besides the usual hoodies, T-shirts, puffy skater shoes, and snowboarding goggles, stores also sport couches, video games, and sales clerks who really use the gear — all designed to encourage the kids to hang out. Zumiez was founded in 1978 by its chairman Thomas Campion, who owns 25% of the company's stock.

The fast-growing sporting goods retailer opened more than 40 stores in 2006, during which it acquired the Action Concepts Fast Forward sporting goods chain of 20 stores, mostly in Texas. (The company plans to convert all of its Fast Forward stores to the Zumiez nameplate by 2008.) This year Zumiez plans to open another 50 shops in new and existing markets. Zumiez is also increasing the size of its stores.

President and CEO Richard Brooks owns some 15% of the company. Director William Barnam Jr. owns about 6% through Brentwood-Zumiez Investors LLC, which is controlled by Brentwood Associates.

EXECUTIVES

Chairman: Thomas D. Campion, age 58, $231,000 pay
President, CEO, and Director: Richard M. Brooks, age 47
CFO: Trevor Lang, age 36
General Merchandising Manager: Lynn K. Kilbourne, age 44, $226,620 pay
Auditors: Moss Adams, LLP

LOCATIONS

HQ: Zumiez Inc.
6300 Merrill Creek Pkwy., Ste. B, Everett, WA 98203
Phone: 425-551-1500   **Fax:** 425-551-1555
Web: www.zumiez.com

2007 Stores

	No.
California	45
New York	24
Texas	22
Washington	22
Colorado	16
Illinois	11
Oregon	11
Utah	11
Arizona	10
Minnesota	10
New Jersey	10
Pennsylvania	7
Wisconsin	6
Florida	5
Idaho	5
Nevada	5
Other states	15
Total	**235**

PRODUCTS/OPERATIONS

2007 Sales

	% of total
Accessories & other	53
Men's apparel	32
Women's apparel	15
Total	**100**

COMPETITORS

Abercrombie & Fitch
Aéropostale
American Eagle Outfitters
Big 5
The Buckle
Charlotte Russe Holding
Claire's Stores
Dick's Sporting Goods
Forever 21
Hot Topic
Old Navy
Pacific Sunwear
Sport Chalet
Sports Authority
Urban Outfitters
Wet Seal

HISTORICAL FINANCIALS

Company Type: Public

Income Statement				FYE: Saturday nearest January 31
	REVENUE ($ mil.)	NET INCOME ($ mil.)	NET PROFIT MARGIN	EMPLOYEES
1/07	298.2	20.9	7.0%	3,006
1/06	205.6	12.9	6.3%	2,273
1/05	153.6	7.3	4.8%	—
1/04	117.9	4.5	3.8%	—
Annual Growth	36.2%	66.8%	—	32.2%

2007 Year-End Financials

Debt ratio: —	Dividends
Return on equity: 23.4%	Yield: —
Cash ($ mil.): 52.0	Payout: —
Current ratio: 2.11	Market value ($ mil.): 939.0
Long-term debt ($ mil.): —	R&D as % of sales: —
No. of shares (mil.): 27.9	Advertising as % of sales: —

Stock History

NASDAQ (GS): ZUMZ

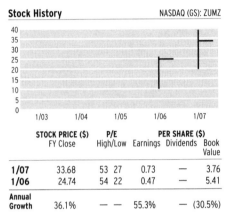

	STOCK PRICE ($) FY Close	P/E High/Low		PER SHARE ($) Earnings	Dividends	Book Value
1/07	33.68	53	27	0.73	—	3.76
1/06	24.74	54	22	0.47	—	5.41
Annual Growth	36.1%	—	—	55.3%	—	(30.5%)

Hoover's Handbook of

Emerging Companies

Master Index for all
2008 Hoover's Handbooks

Index by Industry

AEROSPACE & DEFENSE

SPARTA, Inc. P449

Aerospace & Defense Maintenance & Service
Limco-Piedmont Inc. E218
VSE Corporation E369

Aerospace & Defense Parts Manufacturing
Astronics Corporation E39
Axsys Technologies E45
BAE SYSTEMS W55
Ceradyne, Inc. E87
DRS Technologies A295
Goodrich Corporation A392
HEICO Corporation E177
Honeywell International A434
ITT Corporation A461
Kreisler Manufacturing E210
L-3 Communications A500
Ladish Co. E212
LMI Aerospace E221
Lockheed Martin A524
Northrop Grumman A614
Rolls-Royce W276
Sequa Corporation A748
TransDigm Group E345
Vought Aircraft Industries P518

Aircraft Leasing
AeroCentury Corp. E19
Aircastle Limited E20

Aircraft Manufacturing
AeroVironment, Inc. E20
Airbus S.A.S. W31
The Boeing Company A153
Bombardier Inc. W72
EADS (European Aeronautic Defence and Space Company EADS N.V.) W119
Textron Inc. A813

Weaponry & Related Product Manufacturing
Alliant Techsystems A62
Force Protection E150
General Dynamics A379
Raytheon Company A699

AGRICULTURE

Agricultural Support Activities & Products
Ag Processing P30
Alabama Farmers Cooperative P31
Cargill, Incorporated A182, P108
CHS Inc. A210
DeBruce Grain P154
Dunavant Enterprises P168
The Scoular Company P431

Wilbur-Ellis Company P530

Animal Production
King Ranch A490

Crop Production
Archer Daniels Midland A105
Blue Diamond Growers P89
Chiquita Brands International A207
Dole Food A286, P161
National Grape Cooperative P335
Staple Cotton Cooperative P454
Sunkist Growers P461

AUTOMOTIVE & TRANSPORT

Auto Manufacturing
BMW (Bayerische Motoren Werke AG) W69
Chrysler LLC A209
Daimler AG W105
Fiat S.p.A. W130
Ford Motor A357
General Motors A384
Honda Motor Co. W151
Hyundai Motor W156
Koç Holding W180
Mazda W208
New United Motor Manufacturing P346
Nissan Motor Co. W228
Peugeot Citroën (PSA Peugeot Citroën S.A.) W248
Porsche AG (Dr. Ing. h.c. F. Porsche AG) W253
Renault S.A. W267
Suzuki Motor W315
Toyota Motor W344
Volkswagen AG W357

Auto Parts Manufacturing
Affinia Group P28
ArvinMeritor A108
Autocam Corporation P66
The Boler Company P92
BorgWarner Inc. A156
Commercial Vehicle Group E96
Cooper-Standard Automotive P138
Cummins, Inc. A260
Delphi Corporation A274
DENSO CORPORATION W109
Hayes Lemmerz International A410
J.B. Poindexter & Co. P250
Johnson Controls A474
Key Safety Systems P262
Lear Corporation A504
LKQ Corporation E221
Magna International W202
Mark IV Industries P297
Metaldyne Corporation P314
Remy International P407
Robert Bosch W272
TA Delaware P465

Tenneco Inc. A805
Tomkins plc W339
Tower Automotive A830
United Components P493

Container Leasing
GATX Corporation A374
TTX Company P489

Motorcycle & Other Small Engine Vehicle Manufacturing
Harley-Davidson A403
Polaris Industries A668

Pleasure Boat Manufacturing
Brunswick Corporation A170
Genmar Holdings P196

Rail & Trucking Equipment Manufacturing
American Railcar Industries E32
Carlisle Companies A183
Trinity Industries A835

Recreational Vehicle Manufacturing
Fleetwood Enterprises A350
Thor Industries A817

Truck, Bus & Other Vehicle Manufacturing
AB Volvo W358
Isuzu Motors W167
MAN W203
Miller Industries E234
Obsidian Enterprises P361
Oshkosh Truck A634
PACCAR Inc A638

Truck Leasing
Ryder System A719

BANKING

Automated Teller Machine Operators
Euronet Worldwide E134

Banking – Asia & Australia
Bank of China W57
Commonwealth Bank of Australia W98
Mitsubishi UFJ Financial Group W213
National Australia Bank W219

Banking – Canada
Bank of Montreal W57
Canadian Imperial Bank of Commerce W84
Royal Bank of Canada W278
Toronto-Dominion Bank W340

Banking – Europe
Allied Irish Banks W39
BBVA (Banco Bilbao Vizcaya Argentaria, S.A.) W64
Crédit Agricole W101

GSI Commerce E169
HireRight, Inc. E180
Huron Consulting E186
ICF International E187
LECG Corporation E214
McKinsey & Company A561, P307
Thomas Group E340
Towers Perrin P480
Website Pros E372

Information & Records Management Services

Iron Mountain A460

Legal Services

Baker & McKenzie A121, P69
Baker Botts P70
Baker, Donelson P70
Dewey & LeBoeuf P158
Foley & Lardner P188
Jones Day P257
Kirkland & Ellis P265
Latham & Watkins P275
O'Melveny & Myers P365
Paul, Hastings, Janofsky & Walker P375
Sidley Austin P438
Skadden, Arps, Slate, Meagher & Flom A758, P442
Weil, Gotshal & Manges P526
White & Case P529
Wilson Sonsini Goodrich & Rosati P531

Parking Facility Management

Central Parking P119

Staffing

Adecco S.A. W24
Allegis Group P35
Automatic Data Processing A112
CareerBuilder LLC P108
CHG Healthcare Services P122
COMSYS IT Partners E100
Express Personnel Services P181
Hewitt Associates A423
Kelly Services A484
Kenexa Corporation E208
Manpower Inc. A538
MPS Group A583
On Assignment E255
Paychex, Inc. A644
Robert Half International A710
Spherion Corporation A772
Volt Information Sciences A876

Technical & Scientific Research Services

Aerospace Corporation P28
Battelle Memorial Institute P74
Midwest Research Institute P322
MITRE Corporation P325
Research Triangle Institute P408
SRI International P452
Wyle Laboratories P536

Uniform Rental & Laundry Services

Alsco, Inc. P38
Cintas Corporation A215

CHARITABLE ORGANIZATIONS

American Cancer Society P39
Feed The Children P184
Goodwill Industries P205
Heifer Project P229
Red Cross P404
Salvation Army P421
United Way P495
Volunteers of America P518
YMCA P538

CHEMICALS

Agricultural Chemicals

Agrium Inc. W28
Koor Industries W182
Monsanto Company A578
Phibro Animal Health P382
Scotts Miracle-Gro A741
Terra Industries A808

Basic and Intermediate Chemical & Petrochemical Manufacturing

Air Products and Chemicals A49
Ampacet Corporation P45
Arizona Chemical P55
Badger State Ethanol P68
BASF AG (BASF Aktiengesellschaft) W60
Chevron Phillips Chemical P121
FMC Corporation A354
J.M. Huber P254
Lake Area Corn Processors P272
Old World Industries P365
Praxair, Inc. A674
Sinopec Shanghai Petrochemical W304
VeraSun Energy E362
W. R. Grace A915

Chemical Distribution

Airgas, Inc. A50
Ashland Inc. A109
ICC Industries P238

Paints, Coatings & Other Finishing Product Manufacturing

Akzo Nobel W32
Daubert Industries P150
PPG Industries A671
Rohm and Haas A713
RPM International A717
Sherwin-Williams A753
The Valspar Corporation A867

Plastic & Fiber Manufacturing

Carpenter Co. P112
Dow Chemical A291
Dow Corning P164
E. I. duPont de Nemours A313
Formosa Plastics W132
Momentive Performance Materials P326
Teknor Apex P470

Specialty Chemical Manufacturing

3M Company A26
American Pacific E31
Avery Dennison A116
Cabot Corporation A175
Cytec Industries A263
Day International Group P153
Eastman Chemical A304
Ecolab Inc. A311
Flotek Industries E149
Hercules Incorporated A417
Hexion Specialty Chemicals P231
International Flavors & Fragrances A454
International Specialty Products P246
The Lubrizol Corporation A531
MacDermid, Incorporated P293
Nalco Holding A585
Sigma-Aldrich A755

COMPUTER HARDWARE

NEC Corporation W220
Toshiba Corporation W342

Computer Networking Equipment

Cisco Systems A218
NETGEAR, Inc. E243

Novatel Wireless E249
Numerex Corp. E250
Packeteer, Inc. E263

Computer Peripherals

Apple Inc. A98
Canon Inc. W85
Lexmark International A514
Oki Electric W238
Pitney Bowes A665
Ricoh Company W269
Seiko Epson W297
SmartDisk Corporation P443
ViewSonic Corporation P516
Western Digital A902
Xerox Corporation A919

Handheld Computers & Accessories

Palm, Inc. A639

Mass Storage Systems

EMC Corporation A320
Network Appliance A597
Seagate Technology A743

Personal Computers

Acer Inc. W23
Dell Inc. A272
Gateway, Inc. A373
Hewlett-Packard A424

Servers & Mainframes

Rackable Systems E284
Silicon Graphics A756
Stratus Technologies P458
Sun Microsystems A784
Super Micro Computer E328

Specialized Computer Systems

Diebold, Incorporated A282
Kronos Incorporated P270
NCR Corporation A596
Radiant Systems E284
Stratasys, Inc. E324

COMPUTER SERVICES

Akamai Technologies E21
The Go Daddy Group P203

Computer Products Distribution & Support

ASI Corp. P58
Bell Microproducts A139
D&H Distributing P148
Ingram Micro A449
Intcomex, Inc. P245
MA Laboratories P291
Software House International P445
Tech Data A797

Information Technology Services

Atos Origin W49
CACI International A176
Capgemini W86
Computer Sciences A235
Derive Technologies P157
Edgewater Technology E125
Electronic Data Systems A317
Forsythe Technology P191
Fujitsu Limited W138
Infosys Technologies W162
International Business Machines A452
INX Inc. E198
Perficient, Inc. E271
Perot Systems A653
SAIC, Inc. A726
Sapient Corporation E301
SI International E308
Synchronoss Technologies E331
Unisys Corporation A844
Wipro Limited W363

World Wide Technology P536

COMPUTER SOFTWARE

Accounting & Finance Software

Concur Technologies E101
Intuit Inc. A459
TradeStation Group E344

Billing & Service Provisioning Software

Gelco Information Network P195

Business Intelligence Software

SAS Institute P423

Collaborative Software

Deltek, Inc. E115

Content & Document Management Software

GlobalSCAPE, Inc. E162
Perceptive Software P380

Customer Relationship Management, Marketing & Sales Software

LivePerson, Inc. E220
NetSuite Inc. P344
salesforce.com E299
Unica Corporation E354
Varolii Corporation P514
Vocus, Inc. E367

Database & File Management Software

Oracle Corporation A633

Development Tools, Operating Systems & Utilities Software

Microsoft Corporation A573
Red Hat, Inc. E288

E-commerce Software

CyberSource Corporation E109

Education & Training Software

Datatel, Inc. P149

Engineering, Scientific & CAD/CAM Software

ANSYS, Inc. E34
Autodesk, Inc. A111

Enterprise Resource Planning Software

Activant Solutions P22
Epicor Software E132
Infor Global Solutions P242
SAP W292

Entertainment & Games Software

Electronic Arts A316

Financial Services, Legal & Government Software

BancTec, Inc. P71
DealerTrack Holdings E112
DST Systems A296
EPIQ Systems E133
SunGard Data Systems P460

Health Care Management Software

Allscripts Healthcare Solutions E26
Medical Information Technology P310
Quality Systems E282
Vital Images E366

Human Resources & Workforce Management Software

Plateau Systems P386
Ultimate Software E351
Vurv Technology P520

GSC Enterprises P214
H.T. Hackney Company P237
ITOCHU Corporation W168
Nash-Finch A588
Purity Wholesale Grocers P395
Spartan Stores A769
Topco Associates P479
Unified Western Grocers P491
United Natural Foods A846
Vistar Corporation P517
Wakefern Food A879, P521
Western Family Foods P527

Foodservice

ARAMARK Corporation A103, P53
Ben E. Keith P80
Centric Group P119
Compass Group W99
Delaware North P155
Dot Foods P164
Golden State Foods P203
Gordon Food Service P206
Keystone Foods P263
MAINES Paper & Food Service P294
MBM Corporation P305
Performance Food Group A652
Reyes Holdings P409
Services Group of America P435
Shamrock Foods P435
Sodexho Alliance W307
SYSCO Corporation A792

Fresh Prepared Foods

Pierre Foods P384

Grains

Dakota Growers Pasta Company P147
Dawn Food Products P152
Flowers Foods A351
General Mills A382
Kellogg Company A482
McKee Foods P307
Pinnacle Foods Group P384
Ralcorp Holdings A698
Riceland Foods P409

Meat Products

ContiGroup Companies A245, P137
Hormel Foods A435
Koch Foods P266
OSI Group P367
Perdue Farms P380
Pilgrim's Pride A662
San Miguel Corporation W287
Sara Lee A732
Seaboard Corporation A742
Smithfield Foods A760
Tyson Foods A840

Sauces & Condiments

Goya Foods P207
H. J. Heinz A429
J. M. Smucker A469

Sugar & Sweeteners

American Crystal Sugar P40
Merisant Worldwide P313
Minn-Dak Farmers Cooperative P324
Tate & Lyle W320

FOUNDATIONS

Bill & Melinda Gates Foundation P83
The David and Lucile Packard
  Foundation P151
The Ford Foundation P190
MacArthur Foundation P293
Robert Wood Johnson
  Foundation P412
Rockefeller Foundation P413
W.K. Kellogg Foundation P533

GOVERNMENT

Fannie Mae (Federal National
  Mortgage Association) A341
Federal Reserve P183
National Rural Utilities
  Cooperative P338
Tennessee Valley Authority A806,
  P472
United States Postal Service A849,
  P494

US Federal

Freddie Mac (Federal Home Loan
  Mortgage Corporation) A365

US Local/County/City

New York City Health and
  Hospitals P346

US State/Regional

Lower Colorado River Authority P289

HEALTH CARE

Health Care Products

Angeion Corporation E34
Arrhythmia Research Technology E36
ArthroCare Corporation E37
Aspect Medical Systems E38
Baxter International A129
Becton, Dickinson A136
Boston Scientific A158
C. R. Bard A256
Cardiac Science E75
CAS Medical Systems E77
Cutera, Inc. E108
DENTSPLY International A279
Henry Schein A417
Hillenbrand Industries A427
Hologic, Inc. E182
ICU Medical E188
Integra LifeSciences E192
Intuitive Surgical E196
LifeCell Corporation E216
Masimo Corporation E228
Medline Industries P310
Medtronic, Inc. A564
NeuroMetrix, Inc. E244
Owens & Minor A635
Palomar Medical Technologies E263
Patterson Companies A643
ResMed Inc. E292
Rochester Medical E295
Sirona Dental Systems E312
Somanetics Corporation E315
St. Jude Medical A727
Synergetics USA E332
Theragenics Corporation E340
Universal Hospital Services P496
West Pharmaceutical Services E373

Health Care Services

Adventist Health System P27
Advocate Health Care P27
Aetna Inc. A42
Amedisys, Inc. E28
Ardent Health Services P54
Ascension Health P56
BJC HealthCare P85
Blue Cross and Blue Shield
  Association P87
Blue Cross (MA) (Blue Cross and Blue
  Shield of Massachusetts, Inc.) P88
Blue Cross (MI) (Blue Cross Blue
  Shield of Michigan) P88
Blue Shield Of California P89
Catholic Health East P112
Catholic Health Initiatives P113
Catholic Healthcare Partners P115
Catholic Healthcare West P115

Children's Medical Center of
  Dallas P124
CIGNA Corporation A213
Concentra Inc. P132
Continucare Corporation E102
Dartmouth-Hitchcock Alliance P149
DaVita Inc. A266
Dialysis Corporation E116
Duke University Health System P168
Express Scripts A337
FHC Health Systems P185
Genesis HealthCare P196
HCA Inc. A411, P223
Health Care Service
  Corporation P224
Health Grades E174
Health Insurance of New York P225
Health Management Associates A412
Health Net A413
HealthMarkets, Inc. P226
HealthSouth A414
Healthways, Inc. E176
Henry Ford Health System P230
Highmark Inc. A426, P232
Horizon Healthcare P235
Humana Inc. A438
IASIS Healthcare P238
InSight Health P245
I-trax, Inc. E201
Kaiser Foundation Health Plan A480,
  P260
Kaiser Permanente P260
Kaleida Health P261
Kindred Healthcare A488
LCA-Vision Inc. E214
LHC Group E215
Life Care Centers P282
Magellan Health Services A535
Manor Care A537
Mayo Foundation P304
MedAssets, Inc. E228
Medco Health Solutions A563
Mount Sinai Hospital P327
NewYork-Presbyterian Healthcare
  System P354
Northwest Community
  Healthcare P357
NovaMed, Inc. E248
Omnicare, Inc. A629
Pediatric Services of America P376
Providence Health System P394
Providence Service P280
Quest Diagnostics A693
Radiation Therapy Services E285
RehabCare Group E289
Saint Barnabas Health Care
  System P420
SavaSeniorCare P424
Select Medical P432
Sentara Healthcare P434
Sisters of Mercy Health System P441
Spectrum Health P450
Sutter Health P463
Team Health P468
Tenet Healthcare A803
Transcend Services E345
Trinity Health P485
Triple-S Management P485
Tufts Associated Health Plans P489
UnitedHealth Group A854
University of Iowa Hospitals and
  Clinics P499
US Oncology P509
Vanderbilt University Medical
  Center P512
Vanguard Health Systems P514
WellPoint, Inc. A895
Wheaton Franciscan Services P528

INDUSTRIAL MANUFACTURING

Ingersoll-Rand A447
Marmon Group P297

Agricultural Machinery Manufacturing

AGCO Corporation A46
Deere & Company A269
Kubota Corporation W185
Lindsay Corporation E219

**Construction, Mining & Other Heavy
Equipment Manufacturing**

Bucyrus International E68
Caterpillar Inc. A189
Joy Global A477
Komatsu Ltd. W181
The Manitowoc Company A536
Terex Corporation A807

**Fluid Control Equipment, Pump, Seal
& Valve Manufacturing**

Crane Co. A257
Dresser, Inc. P166
Graham Corporation E165
McWane, Inc. P308
Parker Hannifin A642
SPX Corporation A774
Swagelok Company P463

**Foodservice & Food Retail Equipment
Manufacturing**

The Middleby Corporation E233

Glass & Clay Product Manufacturing

Guardian Industries P215

**Industrial Automation & Industrial
Control Products Manufacturing**

ABB W20
Danaher Corporation A264
Emerson Electric A322
Invensys plc W166
Rockwell Automation A711
Siemens AG W300

Industrial Contract Manufacturing

Federal Prison Industries P182
Mitsubishi Corporation W212

Industrial Equipment Leasing

Penhall International P377

**Industrial Machinery & Equipment
Distribution**

Applied Industrial Technologies A100
DXP Enterprises E122
Gould Paper P207
H&E Equipment Services E172
Hillman Companies P233
Houston Wire & Cable E185
McJunkin Corporation P306
Titan Machinery E342
W.W. Grainger A916

**Industrial Machinery & Equipment
Manufacturing**

Advanced Technology Services P25
Amsted Industries P46
Briggs & Stratton A160
Chart Industries E88
Connell Limited Partnership P134
Dover Corporation A290
Electro-Motive Diesel P173
Goss International P206
Hitachi, Ltd. W149
Illinois Tool Works A445
Kadant Inc. E206
Kennametal Inc. A485
Lincoln Electric Holdings A519
RBS Global P400
Tecumseh Products A799
The Timken Company A823
United Technologies A852

Index by Headquarters

A = AMERICAN BUSINESS
E = EMERGING COMPANIES
P = PRIVATE COMPANIES
W = WORLD BUSINESS

Hiram
Great Lakes Cheese P212

Hudson
Jo-Ann Stores A471

Jackson Center
Thor Industries A817

Kent
Davey Tree P151

Marysville
Scotts Miracle-Gro A741

Mayfield Village
Anthony & Sylvan Pools P50
The Progressive Corporation A683

Medina
RPM International A717

Miamisburg
NewPage Holding P353

Middletown
AK Steel Holding A52

New Albany
Abercrombie & Fitch A32
Commercial Vehicle Group E96

New Bremen
Crown Equipment P143

Niles
RTI International Metals E297

North Canton
Diebold, Incorporated A282

Orrville
J. M. Smucker A469

Perrysburg
Owens-Illinois A636

Sandusky
Cedar Fair E81

Sharonville
Multi-Color Corporation E238

Solon
Advanced Lighting Technologies P25
Swagelok Company P463

Toledo
Manor Care A537

Valley City
MTD Products P328

West Chester
CONTECH Construction
Products P137

Wickliffe
The Lubrizol Corporation A531

OKLAHOMA

Edmond
Bronco Drilling E64

Enid
Hiland Partners E179

Oklahoma City
Chesapeake Energy A205
Devon Energy A280
Express Personnel Services P181
Feed The Children P184
GMX Resources E163

Gulfport Energy E171
Hobby Lobby P234
Love's Travel Stops & Country
  Stores P288
SandRidge Energy E300

Tulsa
Arena Resources E35
Limco-Piedmont Inc. E218
North American Galvanizing E248
ONEOK, Inc. A632
QuikTrip Corporation P396
SemGroup, L.P. P433
Williams Companies A909
Williams Partners E376

OREGON

Beaverton
NIKE, Inc. A606

Bend
Cascade Bancorp E78

Corvallis
Citizens Bancorp P125

Dillard
Roseburg Forest Products P415

Eugene
Pacific Continental E261

Klamath Falls
JELD-WEN, inc. P252

McMinnville
Evergreen Holdings P180

Portland
Bonneville Power Administration P92
Columbia Forest Products P130
Hampton Affiliates P220
North Pacific Group P357
Portland Trail Blazers (Trail Blazers,
  Inc.) P389
Precision Castparts A675
Schnitzer Steel Industries A738
Umpqua Holdings E353

Prineville
Les Schwab Tire Centers P278

Tigard
Western Family Foods P527

Tillamook
Tillamook County Creamery
  Association P477

Turner
Willamette Valley Vineyards E375

PENNSYLVANIA

Allentown
Air Products and Chemicals A49
PPL Corporation A673

Altoona
Sheetz, Inc. P436

Bala Cynwyd
Central European Distribution E84

Bensalem
Charming Shoppes A203

Blue Bell
Unisys Corporation A844

Bridgeville
Universal Stainless E357

Bristol
Jones Apparel Group A475

Camp Hill
Rite Aid A708

Canonsburg
ANSYS, Inc. E34

Chadds Ford
I-trax, Inc. E201

Chesterbrook
AmerisourceBergen A82

Eighty Four
84 Lumber P16

Exton
ViroPharma Incorporated E365
WPCS International E379

Frazer
Cephalon, Inc. A198

Greensburg
Allegheny Energy A57

Harrisburg
American Education Services
  (Pennsylvania Higher Education
  Assistance Agency) P41
D&H Distributing P148
Pennsylvania Commerce
  Bancorp E269

Hershey
The Hershey Company A420

Horsham
NutriSystem, Inc. E251
Penn Mutual Life Insurance P377
Toll Brothers A825

Indiana
Superior Well Services E329

Kennett Square
Genesis HealthCare P196

King of Prussia
AmeriGas Partners A81
GSI Commerce E169
InterDigital, Inc. E193
UGI Corporation A842

Lancaster
Eastern Insurance Holdings E124

Latrobe
Kennametal Inc. A485

Lionville
West Pharmaceutical Services E373

Malvern
IKON Office Solutions A444
The Vanguard Group A868, P512
Vishay Intertechnology A875

Mechanicsburg
Select Medical P432

Middletown
Pennsylvania Lottery P378

Moon Township
Atlas America E42
Atlas Energy Resources E42
Atlas Pipeline Partners E43

Newtown Square
Catholic Health East P112

Philadelphia
ARAMARK Corporation A103, P53
Berwind Group P81
CIGNA Corporation A213
Comcast Corporation A231
Crown Holdings A258
Day & Zimmermann Group P153
FMC Corporation A354
Lincoln National A520

The Pep Boys A646
Resource America E292
Rohm and Haas A713
Sunoco, Inc. A785
Temple University P471
The University of Pennsylvania P502

Pittsburgh
Allegheny Technologies A58
CONSOL Energy A240
Education Management P172
Giant Eagle P198
GNC Corporation P202
H. J. Heinz A429
HFF, Inc. E179
Highmark Inc. A426, P232
Pittsburgh Penguins P385
Pittsburgh Steelers P385
PNC Financial Services Group A667
PPG Industries A671
United States Steel A850
WESCO International A900

Radnor
Airgas, Inc. A50
Penn Virginia Corporation E268
Penn Virginia Resource
  Partners E268

Reading
Boscov's Department Store P93

State College
Rex Energy E293

Trevose
Broder Bros. P99
Technitrol, Inc. E334

Warrendale
American Eagle Outfitters A71

Wawa
Wawa, Inc. P524

Wayne
Kenexa Corporation E208
Safeguard Scientifics A723
SunGard Data Systems P460
Willow Financial Bancorp E376

West Conshohocken
Keystone Foods P263

Willow Grove
Asplundh Tree Expert P58

York
The Bon-Ton Stores A154
DENTSPLY International A279
Graham Packaging P208

PUERTO RICO

San Juan
Triple-S Management P485

RHODE ISLAND

Johnston
Factory Mutual Insurance P181

Pawtucket
Hasbro, Inc. A408
Teknor Apex P470

Providence
Gilbane, Inc. P200
NTK Holdings P359
Textron Inc. A813
Warren Equities P522

Woonsocket
CVS/Caremark A261

Index of Executives

A = AMERICAN BUSINESS
E = EMERGING COMPANIES
P = PRIVATE COMPANIES
W = WORLD BUSINESS

Baker, Emily E134
Baker, Glen A. P62
Baker, James (Flying J) P187
Baker, James A. IV (Baker Botts) P70
Baker, Janet A46
Baker, Jeffrey B. E133
Baker, John E. (Stratus Properties) E325
Baker, John J. (National Wine & Spirits) P339
Baker, Jonathan B. (Sealed Air Corporation) A745
Baker, Kathy W366
Baker, Larry V. A427
Baker, Mari J. A473
Baker, Mark A. A783
Baker, Maxine B. A366
Baker, Michael A. (ArthroCare) E37
Baker, Michael F. (Forest Labs) A359
Baker, Nick W266
Baker, Phillips S. Jr. E176
Baker, Reginald P297
Baker, Richard A885
Baker, Robert J. (Intel) A452
Baker, Robert W. (El Paso) A315
Baker, Sheryl A306
Baker, Tod (Health Grades) E175
Baker, Todd (Gordon Food Service) P206
Baker, Todd H. (Washington Mutual) A889
Baker, Tom A730
Baker, Vernon G. II A108
Baker, W. Kirk P238
Baker, W. Randolph A90
Baker, Wendy W193
Baker, William P129
Baker-Oliver, Debbie A788
Bakewell, Michael D. A325
Bakhshi, Nandita A889
Bakken, Eric A. A703
Bakos, Tony P16
Balagna, Jeffrey A. P110
Balakrishnan, V. W163
Balan, Rosabel Socorro T. W287
Balbinot, Sergio W47
Balboni, John N. A457
Balcells, Esteban Levin W247
Balch, Richard P182
Balcom, Robert A. W142, W196
Balda, Daniel E356
Baldi, Alessandro W131
Baldino, Frank Jr. A199
Baldovin, James D. E295
Baldridge, Sally P250
Balduino, Michael J. A457
Baldwin, Christopher J. A420
Baldwin, H. Furlong A587
Baldwin, Maire A. A326
Baldwin, Paul A630
Baldwin, Randi E30
Baldwin, Robert H. A571
Bales, Brian A. A705
Bales, Bruce M. E131
Balfour, Don P521
Balfour, Fergus W349
Bali, S. Ashish A274
Balian, John P308
Balisle, Phillip M. A296
Ball, Benny P192
Ball, C. Lowell A133
Ball, F. Michael A60
Ball, Garry L. A47
Ball, J. Fred P61
Ball, Jim A921
Ball, Jon W. P231
Ball, Russell D. A602
Ball, Susan M. P145
Ballard, Ernesta A904

Ballard, James C. A653
Ballard, Rand A. E228
Ballard, Robert P440
Ballard, Shari L. A144
Ballas, Nicholas P. A175
Ballentine, Anne P528
Ballhaus, William F. Jr. P28
Ballin, Robert A. E261
Ballinger, Dean P237
Ballmer, Steven A. A574
Ballot, Alissa E. A363
Ballotti, Geoffrey A. A780
Ballou, Ernie E105
Ballou, Rebecca W. A115
Balmuth, Michael A. A715
Balogh, Aristotle N. A869
Balser, Jeffrey R. P512
Balster, Donald E. A908
Baltazar, Miguel W360
Balte, Mark A. E222
Baltes, Kelly A266
Balthasar, Norman J. A349
Baltz, Jeffrey D. P51
Balzer, Donald J. Jr. E364
Bambara, Jay A846
Bamforth, Mark R. A387
Banaszak, David P167
Banatao, Diosdado P. E312
Banbury, Gary W. E94
Bancroft, Joan E. P216
Bandi, Anne M. P98
Bando, Aihiko W46
Bandrowczak, Steven J. W234
Bandy, Jo Etta A347
Banerjee, Gautam A677, W258
Banerjee, Sudip W363
Banerjee, Suparno A318
Banga, Ajay A221
Banga, Manvinder Singh W349
Bangle, Chris W70
Bangs, Nelson A. P343
Banholzer, William F. A292
Banikarim, Maryam P507
Banis, William J. P359
Banker, John G. E123
Banks, Britt D. A602
Banks, David D. A186
Banks, Donna J. A483
Banks, Glen B. P191
Banks, Hunter P310
Banks, Jim E209
Banks, Lee C. A642
Banks, W. Michael E157
Banner, Roderick W368
Bannister, C. C. R. W155
Bannister, David G. E153
Bannister, Michael E. A357
Banos, Leonard C. P68
Banta, Vivian L. A686
Banu, John E. A562
Banwart, Sidney C. A189
Banziger, Hugo W113
Bar, Roselyn R. A547
Baraga, Anthony R P501
Baranko, David J. E98
Baranowski, Carl E65
Barat, Jean-Paul W171
Baraya, Donna P435
Barba, Glenn P. A226
Barbagello, John A. A683
Barbaroux, Olivier W120, W352
Barbassa, Almir G. W245
Barbato, Anthony L. P115, P289
Barbee, J. Ray P416
Barber, Alison E P319
Barber, Barry P210
Barber, Bradley W. E172
Barber, Douglas E. A192
Barber, Hal P263
Barber, Judith E315
Barber, Mike P381
Barber, Patrick P50
Barber, R. G. W155
Barber, Roger L. P431
Barber, Sam P152

Barber, Timothy C. A336
Barber, Walter C. A465
Barberio, Mark G. P297
Barberis, Joe W98
Barberot, Olivier W136
Barbet, Alain W244
Barbier, Jean-Michel W23
Barbosa, Fabio C. W22
Barbosa, Flavio P452
Barbosa, Geraldo Q. A137
Barby, George E109
Barceló, Nancy P501
Barckley, Becky A528
Barclay, Betsy A332
Barclay, David A. (Republic Services) A705
Barclay, David L. (Centex) A197
Barclay, Kathleen S. A385
Bardgett, Edward R. P540
Bardis, John A. E228
Bardowell, L. Scott P424
Bareksten, Jim A210
Barer, Sol J. E82
Baresich, Michael A220
Bareuther, James L. A169
Barge, James W. A822
Barge, Peter A. A477
Barger, Donald G. Jr. A924
Bargeron, Gary A879
Bargmann, Mike P525
Barham, Thomas P75
Barhydt, Michael J. E340
Barich, James W. E273
Baril, Thierry W81
Barkauskas, Steven E60
Barker, Clarence W. P248
Barker, Debra E163
Barker, Jake P283
Barker, John D. (Wendy's) A898
Barker, John R. (ONEOK) A632
Barker, Lori A730
Barker, Michael H. E100
Barker, Myra O. P300
Barker, Paul A400, P220
Barker, Phil P84
Barker, Robert P. A642
Barker, Ros W188
Barkley, James M. A757
Barkley, Michael T. A638
Barkov, Anatoly A. W200
Barkus, Bruce E. E351
Barlett, Todd A. A100
Barley, Susan E. A661
Bärlocher, Urs W235
Barlow, Charles P440
Barlow, James F. A60
Barlow, Jon P523
Barlow, Ron P212
Barlow, Scott P. E360
Barna, Bruce P206
Barna, Jeff A335
Barna, Kenneth G. A697
Barnard, Mark P235
Barnavon, Erez P138
Barndt, Natalie A199
Barner, Karen E52
Barner, Marianne W158
Barnes, Arthur H. P225
Barnes, Brenda C. A732
Barnes, David A. A847
Barnes, Eric E. E18
Barnes, Gerald P343
Barnes, Jamey A528
Barnes, Joscie P182
Barnes, Lou P438
Barnes, Mark P182
Barnes, Michael E195
Barnes, R. E. A543
Barnes, Terry R. A441
Barnes, Warren W. A402
Barnes, William P144
Barneson, Dale P58
Barnett, Blake T. E27
Barnett, Dennis P539
Barnett, Evan E140

Barnett, Hoyt R. A688
Barnett, J. Mark P340
Barnett, John P. A768
Barnett, Lee W40
Barnett, Lilli P263
Barnett, Preston B. A255, P142
Barnett, Steve P447
Barnett, Tammy D. E184
Barnette, W. E. A276
Barney, James W. A379
Barney, Thomas W. E55
Barnhardt, Candice R. P340
Barnhill, Mark P387
Barnholt, Edward W. A492
Barnum, Michael P. A487
Barnwell, Charles M. E254
Baron, Jessica E178
Baron, Joseph M. A204
Barone, Bob P99
Barone, Daniel E75
Barone, Tony P312
Barone, Tony Jr. P312
Baroni, Greg J. A845
Barpoulis, John C. A863
Barr, D. Scott A602
Barr, David (SGI) A756
Barr, David H. (Baker Hughes) A123
Barr, Jonathan S. E17
Barr, Kevin A. A808
Barr, William G. III (NGAS Resources) E247
Barr, William P. (Verizon) A871
Barra, Joe A113
Barraclough, Bill E19
Barranca, Nicholas F. A850
Barrat, Sherry S. A613
Barratt, Craig H. E40
Barratt, Simon W362
Barrault, François W81
Barre, Steven C. P250
Barreiro, Alfredo E327
Barreiro, José W65
Barrenechea, Mark J. E284
Barrera-Moses, Sylvia P20
Barrett, Bruce J. E315
Barrett, Colleen C. A769
Barrett, Craig R. A452
Barrett, Dandy A186
Barrett, David J. A416, P227
Barrett, Dean A558
Barrett, Fredrick J. E57
Barrett, Kelly H. A433
Barrett, L.C. A323
Barrett, Philip A. P124
Barrett, Richard A201
Barrett, Scott P254
Barrett, Terry R. E57
Barretta, Jacquelyn A248
Barrie, Sidney W132
Barrier, Frederick P454
Barrigan, Ian W77
Barrineau, Don A798
Barrington, Mark P153
Barrington, Mark R. P154
Barris, Marcia A. A587
Barron, Arnold S. A825
Barron, Francis B. E57
Barron, Gregory J. A734, P426
Barron, Hal A377
Barron, Henry B. Jr. A299
Barron, Mark P99
Barros, Colleen P337
Barrows, Charles W51
Barrows, John A118
Barrows, Paul W. P506
Barrs, W. Craig A767
Barry, Alan H. A548
Barry, Clifford P130
Barry, Coral E200
Barry, David P. A752
Barry, G. C. A423
Barry, John F. III E279
Barry, Kevin P98
Barry, Lisa (Advanced Lighting Technologies) P25

Borst, Walter G. A385
Bortnak, James M. E320
Bortolussi, David W135
Bortolussi, Pierluigi W66
Boruff, Chris E237
Bosbous, John F. E68
Bosch, Joseph A. A197
Boschulte, R. D. P42
Bosco, Anthony J. Jr. P153
Bosco, Harry L. E258
Bosco, M. Jeffrey P42
Bose, Amar G. P94
Bosgang, Jeremiah P447
Bosman, Cees P. W184
Bosman, Ruud H. P181
Bosowski, Edward M. A864
Bosscher, James W. P485
Bossi, Giorgio W165
Bossick, Jerry A552
Bossidy, Lawrence A. E55
Bossmann, Lori L. A37, P21
Bosson, Laurent W313
Bost, Glenn E. II A672
Bostick, Russell M. A239
Bostjancic, John E192
Bostock, Kate W205
Boston, Bradford J. A219
Boston, Dennis H. P256
Boston, Terry A807, P472
Boston, Wallace E. Jr. E31
Bostrom, Robert A366
Bostrom, Susan L. A219
Boswell, Caroline W. P70
Boswell, Gina R. A121
Boswell, John P423
Boswell, Justin C. A776
Boswell, Mike E320
Boswood, Mike W335
Botch, Jim P458
Botham, Lydia A503, P273
Botín, Ana Patricia W290
Botín-Sanz de Sautuola, Emilio W290
Botman, Selma P126
Bott, Kevin A720
Bott, Sara W75
Böttcher, Stefan E359
Bottenhagen, Cindy P90
Botter, Jennifer L. P166
Botterbusch, Fred E217
Bottini, Mark (Barnes & Noble) A128
Bottini, Mark (IKON) A444
Bottle, Lisa A393
Bottoms, Michael A239
Bottorff, Dennis C. P512
Bottorff, Thomas E. A659
Botz, Janet M. P164
Bouayad, Hassan E173
Boublil, Robert W117
Bouchard, Gilles E258
Bouchard, Mike E372
Bouchee, William L. E161
Boucher, David P530
Boucher, Jonathan F. P258
Boucher, Mark E. P205
Boucher, Peter P185
Boucher, Robert C. Jr. P465
Bouchey, Keith E65
Bouchut, Pierre B. W295
Bouckaert, Carl M. P76
Boudier, Marc (Air France) W29
Boudier, Marc (Electricité de France) W120
Boudreau, Thomas M. A337
Boudreaux, Gail K. P225
Bougon, Philippe W295
Bouknight, J.A. Jr. A312
Bouknight, Joseph C. A735
Boulanger, Rodney E. P321
Boulet-Gercourt, Jill A546
Boulis, Paul S. P225
Boulton, Richard E214
Boulware, Bruce A. P365
Bourdais de Charbonnière, Éric W164, W211
Bourdeau, Joseph P. E47

Bourgeois, Mary P75
Bourgeois, Michel W355
Bourgeois, Richard D. A549, P303
Bourke, Murphy A. E170
Bourke, Peter E164
Bourlon, Michel A204
Bousbib, Ari A853
Bousquet-Chavanne, Patrick A331
Boustridge, Michael W81
Boutilier, Warren F. E53
Bouton, Daniel W306
Bouton, Garrett F. E214
Boutte, Dalton A738
Bouvier, Robert P470
Bouyer, Bryony A409
Bouygues, Martin W73
Bouygues, Olivier W73
Bovender, Jack O. Jr. A411, P223
Bøving, Jesper W236
Bow, Susan E. A254
Bowden, Curtis P139
Bowden, Lloyd M. E377
Bowden, Michael E101
Bowe, William J. P175
Bowen, Anne P. E143
Bowen, Christopher K. E252
Bowen, Jim C. A764
Bowen, Lane M. A489
Bowen, Tim P447
Bower, Curtis A. P374
Bower, Kevin P241
Bowers, Brian P428
Bowers, Cynthia S. A762
Bowers, Dave E250
Bowers, Elizabeth W. A620
Bowers, G. Thomas E145
Bowers, Johnney G. E356
Bowers, Kim A866
Bowers, Mary Ellen A536
Bowers, Thomas W113
Bowie, Arvelia A827
Bowker, Robert E186
Bowler, Jeffrey W. A504
Bowler, Peter M. A86
Bowles, Howard D. P151
Bowlin, David L. A702
Bowman, Charles A126
Bowman, Mark J. W283
Bowman, Michael L. A296
Bowman, Robert A. P296
Bowman, Steven P. A81
Bown, Clifford K. E361
Bownes, Michael A. P497
Bowyer, Christopher J. P164
Boxall, Lyn A874
Boxer, Charlotte A. E261
Boxer, Jason A526
Boxer, Mark L. A896
Boxer, Michael E. P226
Boxer, Scott J. A511
Boyan, Craig P228
Boyance, Michel W329
Boyanovsky, Harold D. W131
Boyce, Kevin T. A577
Boyce, Richard W. P482
Boycott, William A. W28
Boyd, Calvin R. A690
Boyd, Chris P531
Boyd, Daniel M. IV E92
Boyd, Deborah A409
Boyd, James K. (SkyWest) A759
Boyd, James W. (Toll Brothers) A826
Boyd, John (SUPERVALU) A789
Boyd, John F. (Albertsons) P32
Boyd, Larry C. A449
Boyd, Lois A806
Boyd, Madeline J. E252
Boyd, Matthew E360
Boyd, Norman L. A47
Boyd, Pamela S. A464
Boyd, Ralph F. Jr. A366
Boyd, Wendell E250
Boyd, William B. (Rotary) P416
Boyd, William Gordon (Commercial Vehicle) E96

Boyd, William R. (Boyd Gaming) A159
Boyd, William S. (Boyd Gaming) A159
Boyd Johnson, Marianne A159
Boydston, Cory J. A133
Boydstun, J. Herbert A180
Boyer, Alger E296
Boyer, Andrew A894
Boyer, Aurelia G. P354
Boyer, Blake E98
Boyer, F. Alger E296
Boyer, Herbert W. A60
Boyer, John W. P498
Boyer, Paul (Meijer) P311
Boyer, Paul (National Semiconductor) A592
Boyer, Raymond C. P293
Boyer de la Giroday, Eric W164
Boyette, John G. A255, P142
Boyette, Judith P497
Boykin, Frank H. A575
Boyko, Alan A740
Boylan, Christopher P. P317
Boyle, Alexander R.M. P122
Boyle, Jack H. (Kohl's) A496
Boyle, Joe P200
Boyle, John W. (Roundy's Supermarkets) P417
Boyle, Marsilia P277
Boyle, Patrick (Loyola University) P289
Boyle, Patrick F. (NYSE Euronext) A623
Boyle, Richard J. Jr. E223
Boyle, Robert W77
Boyle, Scott C. E142
Boylson, Michael J. A468
Boynton, Peter W321
Boynton, Robert D. P278
Boys, Jack A. A606
Boysan, Hasan Ferit E34
Boyum, Keith O. P104
Bozard, Richard F. A636
Bozer, Ömer W180
Bozick, Nicholas L P462
Bozotti, Carlo W313
Bozsum, Bruce S. P325
Bozzelli, Richard L. P170
Bozzuto, Michael A. P96
Brabeck-Letmathe, Peter W222
Brabender, Todd P. A427
Bracchi, Giampio W165
Bracco, Gustavo Emanuele W324
Brace, Frederic F. A842
Brace, Philip G. A531
Bracher, Peter W334
Bracken, Richard M. A411, P223
Brackenbury, James A505
Bracker, Mark A173
Bradeen, Richard C. W72
Bradford, Charlie P333
Bradford, Douglas K. A124
Bradford, Earle L. Jr. P113
Bradford, Guy A72
Bradford, Marlon D. A527
Bradford, Patricia A. A845
Bradford, Preston B. E301
Bradford, William R. A368
Bradley, Charles E. Jr. E101
Bradley, Dan P433
Bradley, David P139
Bradley, Donald E. P531
Bradley, James H. A484
Bradley, Joann A60
Bradley, John (QCR Holdings) E282
Bradley, John F. (JPMorgan Chase) A479
Bradley, John J. (TVA) A807, P472
Bradley, Keith A449
Bradley, Mark J. P506
Bradley, Mike Sr. W166
Bradley, R. Bruce P274
Bradley, R. Todd A425
Bradley, Rickford D. P63
Bradley, Steve W367
Bradley, Tom A796
Bradshaw, Chris A112

Bradshaw, Mark P228
Bradshaw, Tracy A797
Brady, Cliff P477
Brady, David J. E182
Brady, Patricia A. P506
Brady, Sharon M. A445
Brady, Shawn P221
Brady, Sheri A. P533
Brady, Stephen P. E153
Brady, Thomas F. A244
Brady, William J. A175
Brafford, H. Wayne A457
Bragg, David K. W196
Bragg, Frank G. P462
Braham, Elizabeth M. E133
Brahms, Hero W44
Brailer, Daniel A. A901
Braithwait, Austin P508
Brake, John P251
Brakensiek, Nancy P40
Braly, Angela F. A896
Bram, Stephen B. A242
Brame, Kenneth L. A115
Bramlage, Stephen P. Jr. A637
Bramlett, Ken R. Jr. E100
Bramwell, Phillip W56
Bramwell, Richard P150
Branch, Bill P157
Branch, David P26
Branch, Zelma A399
Brancheau, Joan M. A484
Branco, L. P96
Branco, Roberto C. W350
Brand, Patrick A666
Brandecker, John A. P499
Brandenberg, Frank G. A615
Brandenburger, Larry B. A867
Brandgaard, Jesper W236
Branding, Elaine A337
Brandjes, Michiel W281
Brandman, Andrew T. A623
Brandon, David A. A289
Brandorff, Perry O. A424
Brandreth, Jacky W63
Brandt, Andrew A397, P213
Brandt, Donald E. A663
Brandt, Linda P373
Brandt, Michael A867
Brandt, Peter C. A657
Brandt, Ron P246
Brandt, Werner W292
Brandtzæg, Svein Richard W232
Brannagan, Douglas T. P209
Brannan, Darin E372
Brannock, Kirk R. A111
Brannon, Christy P92
Branson, Mark W347
Branson, Richard W354
Brantley, Leland W. Jr. E106
Brantley, Mitch P305
Brantley, Sherry P409
Brantner, Doug A700
Brashear, James F. P419
Brashear, Mark S. A610
Brasher, Richard W. P. W334
Brasier, Barbara L. A448
Brasuell, Thomas C. P296
Braswell, Harvey V. A44
Braswell, Robert T. E76
Bratches, Sean H. R. P178
Bratz, Mike P117
Brauchli, Marcus A293
Brauer, Rhonda L. A600
Braught, Elaine E123
Braun, Chris (Jordan Industries) P258
Braun, Christopher J. (Fleetwood Enterprises) A350
Braun, Hartmut A815
Braun, J. Eric P60
Braun, Karl A657
Brauneis, Paul F. E331
Brauner, Susan P89
Brause, Kenneth A. A127
Braverman, Alan N. A884
Bravman, John P454

A = AMERICAN BUSINESS
E = EMERGING COMPANIES
P = PRIVATE COMPANIES
W = WORLD BUSINESS

Bravo, Charles E. A850, P495
Bravo, Norka Ruiz P337
Bravo Collao, Isabel Margarita W326
Brawley, Otis W. P40
Bray, Eric P208
Braz Ferro, Claudio W162
Brazeau, Perry R. P181
Brazeman, Cary E223
Brazier, Graham R. A165
Bready, Richard L. P359
Breakiron-Evans, Maureen P480
Breakspear, Drew J. A782
Brearton, David A498
Brebberman, Mark A. A410
Brecher, Elliot P244
Bredenkoetter, William P428
Breed, John S. A609
Breeden, Kenneth R. A807, P472
Breeden, Mimi A787
Breedlove, James T. A674
Breedon, Tim W191
Breen, Bant A458
Breene, John P60
Breene, R. Timothy S. A35
Breffort, Jean-Claude W285
Brégier, Fabrice W31
Bregman, Mark A790
Bregman, Mitchell S. A335
Brehm, Eric J. E115
Breier, Alan A319
Breier, Benjamin A. A489
Breig, Geralyn R. A121
Breiing, Burkhard W357
Breinholt, Garin P191
Breisinger, James R. A486
Breitbard, Mark A514, P280
Breitbart, Gary L. A204
Breitenbach, Randall H. E63
Brekhus, Melvin G. A811
Bremer, Charles A. A71
Bremer, John M. A617, P358
Bremner, Joseph P101
Bren, Donald L. P248
Brenchley, Lynn C. P239
Brender, Mark E. E159
Brendle, Jim A138
Brenholt, John P517
Brenkert, Karl III E207
Brenn, James E. A161
Brennan, Daniel J. A158
Brennan, David R. W48
Brennan, Donald A. A496
Brennan, Edward W201
Brennan, Fran A250
Brennan, Jack (Southern Wine & Spirits) P449
Brennan, Jeffrey A. (Grande Communications) P209
Brennan, Jeffrey P. (Targacept) E333
Brennan, John D. (Adobe) A38
Brennan, John J. (The Vanguard Group) A868, P513
Brennan, Joseph P. A284
Brennan, Michael A. P401
Brennan, Robert A. (Lefrak Organization) P277
Brennan, Robert T. (Iron Mountain) A460
Brennan, Troyen A. A43
Brennan, William P. P191
Brenneman, Rodney K. A742
Brenner, Harry J. P144
Brenner, James H. E214
Brenner, Kenneth D. E64
Brennet, Marc E108
Brent, John A. A148
Brentan, Andrea W123
Breon, Richard C. P450
Brereton, Michael P296

Bresciani, Dean P473
Bresciani, Richard L. P95
Bresky, Steven J. A742
Breslawski, James P. A417
Bresler, Charles A566
Breslin, Brian P311
Breslow, Stuart A580
Bresnehan, Scott P437
Bress, Joseph M. P47
Bresten, Theresa M. P237
Brestle, Daniel J. A331
Bretas, Nancy A705
Breton, Lionel W244
Brett, Ellen A657
Brettingen, Thomas R. P60
Bretz, Darcy E233
Breu, Raymond W235
Breuche, Rob W82
Breuer, Jurgen E161
Breunig, Joseph W61
Brevard, Mary E. A157
Brewer, David E233
Brewer, Jane A596
Brewer, Larry K. A296
Brewer, Murray A794
Brewer, Robert A626
Brezina, Michael P152
Brezovec, Daniel T. A100
Brian, James S. A195
Brick, Kathryn P508
Brickey, Gerald L. E105
Bridenbaker, Mark P460
Bridge, Anthony R. A851
Bridge, Gary A219
Bridgeford, Gregory M. A530
Bridger, Dickson B. E102
Bridgers, David P475
Bridges, Alford C. E305
Bridges, Gary P453
Bridges, Jonathan B. P124
Bridges, Michael O. A87
Bridges, Terry A178, P106
Bridgman, Peter A. A651
Brierwood, David C. E238
Brigden, John F. A790
Briggs, Basil M. E276
Briggs, C. John A703
Briggs, David W188
Briggs, Gary S. A309
Briggs, Gordon E248
Briggs, Mary E207
Briggs, Timothy W. A115
Brigham, Steven P. P100
Bright, Alan E161
Bright, Kimberly P370
Bright, Mary Ann P195
Brightman, Stuart M. E337
Brighton, Todd A. E289
Brill, James L. E255
Brill, John D. P389
Brill, Tony G. A827
Brimhall, Reed N. A858
Brimont, Stéphane W139
Brin, Sergey A396
Brind'Amour, Yvon W189
Brinded, Malcom W281
Brink, Calvin C. P430
Brinker, Daniel J. P314
Brinker, Norman E. A163
Brinkley, Alan P131
Brinkley, Amy W. A126
Brinkman, Dale T. A914
Brinson, Vance B. Jr. E92
Brisco, John P425
Briscoe, Bill P340
Briscoe, John H. A833
Briscoe, Robert B. E302
Briskman, Louis J. A193
Brisky, Lauren J. P512
Brisson, Bill P103
Brito, Carlos W161
Britt, Glenn A. A822
Britt, Timothy C. E149
Brittain, Max Jr. P357
Brittan, Kent L. A853

Britton, Lynn P441
Brizel, Michael A. A729
Brlas, Laurie A223
Broad, Matthew R. A627
Broadbent, Dave A525
Broaddrick, William Randall E36
Broadhurst, Daniel P. E187
Broadhurst, Mariane E. E54
Broadley, Philip W259
Broatch, Robert E. P216
Brobst, Lawrence S. E106
Brockman, Nicholas P. E101
Brockman, Robert D. E79
Brockway, Larry T. A851
Brockway, Robert P235
Brocoum, Chris A492
Broder, Matthew A666
Broderick, Dennis J. A534
Brodeur, Lynn K. E281
Brodnax, Jennifer B. E139
Brodsky, Howard P117
Brodsky, Julian A. A232
Brody, Alan A686
Brody, Jeffrey P235
Brody, John S. P295
Brody, Wayne A107
Broecker, David A. E22
Broeders, Henk W. W87
Broeker, Helmut W254
Broeksmit, Robert D. P122
Broerman, Robert A. P434
Brogan, Cynthia D. A754
Brogan, Michael P. A585
Brogan, Stephen J. P257
Broger, Armin A514, P280
Brogna, Sal E196
Brohm, Fred P264
Broiles, Randy L. W159
Brok, Martin A172
Brokatzky-Geiger, Juergen W235
Brolick, Emil J. A925
Broman, Donald E. A763
Bromell, Simon P299
Bromley, C. Corwin E227
Bromley, Michael A222
Bronczek, David J. A343
Brondeau, Pierre R. A713
Bronfin, Kenneth A. A416, P227
Bronfman, Edgar M. Jr. A886
Bronner, Judith L. P497
Bronstein, Andrew P. P461
Bronzo, Neal A. A648
Brooke, Beth A. A329, P177
Brooke, F. Dixon Jr. P170
Brooker, Brian P72
Brooker, Thomas G. A719
Brooklier, John L. A445
Brookman, Robert S. P471
Brooks, Alfred R. A889
Brooks, Bruce W. A149
Brooks, Carolynn A627
Brooks, Clint D. A454
Brooks, Craig L. A84
Brooks, D. Mayson A298
Brooks, Douglas H. A163
Brooks, Dwaine R. P154
Brooks, Gary J. P178
Brooks, H. Joseph P103
Brooks, J. Douglas E18
Brooks, Jerry M. E121
Brooks, Joe G. E18

Brooks, Kathryn S. E167
Brooks, Lynne M. A199
Brooks, Marjorie S. E18
Brooks, Michael (CVR) P145
Brooks, Michael (Foster's Group) W135
Brooks, Paul P331
Brooks, Renee R. E302
Brooks, Richard E. (Alion) P34
Brooks, Richard M. (Zumiez) E381
Brooks, Rodney A. E200
Brooks, Stephen W. E18
Brooks, Thomas V. A244
Brooks, Vonda P241
Brookshire, Brad P99
Brookshire, Britt P99
Brookshire, Jane T. A662
Brookshire, Mark P99
Brookshire, Tim P99
Broom, Colin E365
Broom, Joe A752
Broome, Anne C. P497
Broome, J. Tol Jr. A131
Brophy, Daniel P. E113
Brophy, R. Gregory A415
Broshy, Eran E196
Brosnahan, Michael P. P527
Brosnan, Shawn P383
Brosnan, Timothy J. P295
Bross, Richard A. A436
Brostowitz, James M. A404
Brothers, Ellen L. A552
Brothers, Gary P148
Brothers, Jeffrey J. P35
Brotman, Adam B. P139
Brotman, Jeffrey F. (Resource America) E293
Brotman, Jeffrey H. (Costco Wholesale) A253
Brots, John M. A802
Brough, M. Joseph P239
Broughton, Martin F. W77
Brous, Maria A688
Brouse, Mark S. E255
Broussard, Bruce D. P509
Broussard, Eric A67
Broussard, Susan E93
Brousse, François W29
Brouwer, Aart E82
Brova, Jacquelin J. A212
Brower, David B. P319
Brower, Robert Keith P134
Brown, Adriane M. A435
Brown, Allen P26
Brown, Andrew J. A640
Brown, Bart R. A374
Brown, Beverly A423
Brown, Bob (Goss International) P206
Brown, Brad P405
Brown, Carolyn A128
Brown, Charles E. A626
Brown, Christopher A. (Nash-Finch) A588
Brown, Christopher M. G. (Jones Lang LaSalle) A477
Brown, Colin P254
Brown, Cristopher P154
Brown, Dan (The Hartford) A406
Brown, Daniel K. (American Tire) P44
Brown, Danny (CalPERS) A178, P106
Brown, David (Website Pros) E372
Brown, David A. B. (Layne Christensen) E213
Brown, Dennis (Interstate Batteries) P247
Brown, Dennis L. (Pinnacle West) A663
Brown, Elizabeth P101
Brown, Eric B. (Transocean) A832
Brown, Erika (Golden State Warriors) P204
Brown, Francis (Celgene) E82
Brown, Frank (Colonial Group) P129
Brown, Gary N. E76
Brown, George W. Jr. P50
Brown, Gregory C. (BreitBurn) E63

Brown, Gregory Q. (Motorola, Inc.) A581
Brown, Hal D. (Casey's General Stores) A188
Brown, Hal M. (Pacific Continental) E261
Brown, Jack H. P457
Brown, James T. (Whiting Petroleum) E375
Brown, Janice A. P297
Brown, Jeff A316
Brown, Jim (Capital Group) P107
Brown, Jim (Halliburton) A399
Brown, Jody (kowabunga) E209
Brown, Jody A. (CACI International) A176
Brown, Joseph W. A723
Brown, Julie Nguyen P386
Brown, Kathleen J. (American Financial) A76
Brown, Kathryn (Imperial Tobacco) W160
Brown, Kathryn F. (University of Minnesota) P501
Brown, Ken (Keystone Foods) P263
Brown, Kent W. (Rent-A-Center) A704
Brown, Kevin (Jo-Ann Stores) A471
Brown, Kevin (Qantas) W261
Brown, Kevin (Sinclair Oil) P440
Brown, LaRay P347
Brown, Lolanda Butler E215
Brown, Loren A185
Brown, Lynn C. (Waste Management) A892
Brown, Lynne P. (NYU) P351
Brown, Marc (Del Monte Foods) A271
Brown, Marc P. (State Street) A782
Brown, Mark C. (Strayer Education) E326
Brown, Mark E. (Whirlpool) A905
Brown, Martin (Tesco) W334
Brown, Mary Rose A866
Brown, Michael J. (Euronet) E134
Brown, Michael K. (Lowe's) A530
Brown, Michael W. (InSight Health Corp.) P245
Brown, Mike (Cavaliers) P117
Brown, Mike (Life Time Fitness) E216
Brown, Nathaniel T. P519
Brown, Neil L. E241
Brown, Patrick E134
Brown, Paul F. P87
Brown, Pauline J. A121
Brown, Peter D. (Foot Locker) A356
Brown, Peter S. (Arrow Electronics) A107
Brown, Philippa A631
Brown, Randal L. A896
Brown, Richard C. A915
Brown, Robert (New York Yankees) P352
Brown, Robert A. (Boston University) P96
Brown, Robert B. (Corning) A251
Brown, Robin D. E142
Brown, Ronald L. A398
Brown, Russell W75
Brown, Sam A621
Brown, Scott D. A463
Brown, Sheila C. E339
Brown, Shona L. A396
Brown, Stephanie L. (Linsco/Private Ledger) P285
Brown, Stephen F. (Tenet Healthcare) A804
Brown, Stephen M. (True Temper Sports) P486
Brown, Stephen R. (IDT) A442
Brown, Susan E372
Brown, Thaddeus B. P236
Brown, Thomas K. (Ford) A357
Brown, Thomas W. (GlobalSCAPE) E162
Brown, Tonya M. P504
Brown, Treg S. A386

Brown, W. Douglas A50
Brown, William E. Jr. (Toro) A828
Brown, William M. (United Technologies) A853
Browne, Donald A594
Browne, Joe P334
Browne, John P383
Browne, Julian P111
Browne, Paul P485
Browne, Rick A210
Browne, Sherry L. P57
Brownell, Thomas H. P338
Browning, Candace A569
Browning, Carol P84
Browning, Douglas E. A412
Browning, Jay D. A866
Browning, Keith D. A186
Browning, Michael P483
Brownson, James J. E282
Brozek, Duane P516
Brubaker, William W. P445
Bruce, Brian A482
Bruce, Colin W149
Bruce, David A720
Bruce, Jessica P60
Bruce, Lori P524
Bruce, Misty E98
Bruce, Peter W. A617, P358
Bruce, Robert W. W275
Bruce, Thomas W. P140
Bruch, Ruth E. A483
Bruder, John F. P432
Bruder, Scott P. A137
Brudermüller, Martin W61
Brudzynski, Daniel G. A298
Brueckman, Robert C. P387
Brueckner, Richard F. A127
Brueckner, Stefen F. A438
Bruegenhemke, Kathleen L. E174
Bruening, Rebecca J. A718
Brufau Niubó, Antonio W269, W370
Brugge, Richard A. A201
Bruininks, Robert H. P501
Brukardt, David A. E323
Brumley, I. Jon E128
Brumley, Jon S. E128
Brummel, Lisa A574
Brundage, Jeffery J. A86
Brundage, Maureen A. A211
Brune, Catherine S. A65
Bruneel, Dirk W117
Brunel, Jérôme W102
Brunelle, David P82
Bruner, Eric S. A829
Bruner, Judy A730
Brunet, Alexandre W295
Brunet, Claude W52
Brunger, William P239
Brungess, Barbara A. A83
Brunn, Robert A720
Brunner, James E. A226
Brunner, Kim M. A781, P455
Brunner, Robert E. A445
Brunnworth, Kristin L. A536
Bruno, Angelo P99
Bruno, Casey P265
Bruno, Gabriel A520
Bruno, Joe P470
Bruno, Melanie A. E207
Bruno-Carbone, Melanie E58
Brunot, Edward L. A588
Bruns, Klaus W209
Brunson, Curtis A501
Brunt, Benjamin P355
Brunton, Patty E203
Bruscato, Jay A216
Bruse, Anders W330
Brush, Sue A. A780
Bruton, Stephen F. A731
Bruton, William S. E149
Brutosky, Martin P189
Bruzdzinski, Andrew E185
Bruzelius, Peggy W121
Bryan, David K. E26
Bryan, Dick P535

Bryan, James P365
Bryan, Karry E132
Bryant, Andy D. A452
Bryant, Bill P242
Bryant, Del R. P99
Bryant, Dick P532
Bryant, Gregory T. A61
Bryant, James E. A174
Bryant, John A. A483
Bryant, Karen P432
Bryant, Leah S. W. A482
Bryant, R. Bruce A881
Bryant, Stephen H. A608
Bryant, Terry P141
Bryant, Warren F. A527
Brymer, Charles A631
Bryne, Timothy W. E356
Bryson, John E. A312
Bsirske, Frank W282
BuAbbud, George H. E199
Bubolz, Kerry P117
Bucci, David A283
Bucci, Laura P45
Bucciarelli, Edward A518
Buccina, Anthony J. A155
Bucek, Mike P383
Buchan, John R. P66
Buchanan, Alan (British Airways) W77
Buchanan, Alasdair I. (BJ Services) A147
Buchanan, Greg P272
Buchanan, John (O'Melveny & Myers) P365
Buchanan, John G. S. (Vodafone) W356
Buchanan, Lisa Manget E70
Buchanan, Paul W. A437
Buchanan, R. Kent A405
Buchanan, Richard P332
Buchanan, Robert Gerald E158
Buchanan, Sally Knapp P192
Buchbinder, Darrell P389
Buchen, David A. A894
Bucher, Nancy E205
Buchheim, Jim P144
Buchholz, Karen Dougherty A232
Buchi, J. Kevin A199
Buchman, Kathleen P528
Buchold, Jack B. E47
Buchschacher, Paul W. A294
Buck, Carl N. E19
Buck, Helen W171
Buck, Kenneth D. A676
Buck, Larry E273
Buck, Michele B. A420
Buck, Nancy P484
Buckaloo, G.W. Jr. P393
Buckanavage, Richard P. E266
Buckelew, Alan B. A187
Buckey, Alan H. E214
Buckingham, Peter W365
Buckland, William C. P290
Buckler, Robert J. A298
Buckler, William S. E283
Buckley, George W. A26
Buckley, Jean P163
Buckley, Jerry S. A179
Buckley, Michael (Hanover Insurance) A402
Buckley, Michael C. (Robert Half) A710
Buckley, Michael F. (True Religion Apparel) E349
Buckley, Mike (Dot Foods) P163
Buckley, Mortimer J. A868, P513
Buckley, Richard C. A766
Buckley, Rose M. E54
Buckley, Stephen P415
Buckman, Kurt P84
Buckman, Michael A. P75
Buckman, Paul R. A727
Buckminster, Douglas E. A75
Bucknall, Chris D. W100
Bucknall, William L. Jr. A853
Bucknam, Ted P133
Buckner, Lindsay P484
Buckwalter, M. Melissa A675

Buda, James B. A189
Budd, Thomas E282
Budde, Florian A561, P308
Budde, Tom L. P188
Budejen, Oscar A103
Budzulyak, Bogdan Vladimirovich W141
Buehler, Marc A. P286
Buell, Erik F. A404
Buenrostro, Fred R. Jr. A178, P106
Buensuceso, Maria Belen C. W287
Buer, Pete E104
Buese, Nancy K. E227
Buettgen, James A266
Buettner, Anne A884
Bufacchi, Alessandro W123
Buffenbarger, R. Thomas P30
Buffett, Warren E. A143
Buford, R. C. P422
Buhler, David P465
Buhr, James P73
Buhrmaster, Mindy E49
Buitenhuis, André W277
Bujack, Denise A. P225
Bukaty, Raymond M. A903
Buker, Edwin L. A799
Bukowski, Gerard T. P103
Bular, Edward W. A859
Bulcke, Paul W222
Buley, Beryl J. P163
Bulger, Richard A. A42
Bulgurlu, Bülent W180
Bulkley, Benjamin E26
Bull, Julie J. A284
Bulla, L. Thomas A345
Bullerdick, Michael J. E142
Bullinger, Philip W. A531
Bullington, Michael W. A764
Bullock, Galen F. A647
Bullock, Robert P120
Bulluck, Vicangelo P330
Bullukian, Jean-Manuel W25
Bullwinkel, George J. Jr. A735
Bulmahn, T. Paul E43
Bulman, Lyn P184
Bulman, Neil Jr. A72
Bulus, Domingos H. G. A675
Bulzis, James T. A356
Bumgardner, Eunice Lin P101
Bummer, Raymond L. A58
Bumpers, Bennie W. A877
Bumstead, Matt E495
Bumstead, R. Gantt P495
Bunce, David A497, P270, W183
Bunce, Jode P171
Bunch, C. Robert E274
Bunch, Charles E. A672
Bunch, John A796
Bundonis, Paul E69
Bundy, Steve P171
Bunge, Gene E. E212
Bunger, Steven G. E236
Bunn, Kevin S. E246
Bunn, Susanne W118
Bunn, Thomas W. A487
Bunnell, David A. P430
Bunsick, Robert P207
Bunt, Diane C. A748
Bunte, Alan G. E99
Bunting, Clark P160
Buonaiuto, Joseph M. A73
Buoncontri, Gregory E. A665
Buonocore, Angela A. A462
Buonomo, James R. P360
Bur, Eric J. P380
Burbage, Charles T. A525
Burbatsky, Alexander B. A598
Burcar, Alison D. E188
Burch, Robert P440
Burch, Sarena D. A735
Burch, Stephen P. (OSI Group LLC) P367
Burch, Steven A. (Pulte Homes) A690
Burchard, Jacquie P152
Burchill, Jeffrey A. P181

A = AMERICAN BUSINESS
E = EMERGING COMPANIES
P = PRIVATE COMPANIES
W = WORLD BUSINESS

Cohen, Cory F. A482
Cohen, Daniel G. E47
Cohen, David (AMP Limited) W40
Cohen, David L. (Comcast) A232
Cohen, Debbie E86
Cohen, Edward (Plateau Systems) P387
Cohen, Edward E. (Atlas America, Atlas Energy Resources, Atlas Pipeline Partners, Resource America) E42, E43, E293
Cohen, Eran A646
Cohen, Eric I. A808
Cohen, Ilyse P102
Cohen, Joan K. A401
Cohen, Jonathan Z. E42, E43, E293
Cohen, K. P. A338
Cohen, Lawrence H. P36
Cohen, Lyor A887
Cohen, Margaret Kirch E237
Cohen, Maryjo E241
Cohen, Michael (Och-Ziff Capital Management) P362
Cohen, Michael H. (NYSE Euronext) A623
Cohen, Mitchell M. E39
Cohen, Neal S. A616
Cohen, Oren P397
Cohen, Raanan W182
Cohen, Raymond W. E75
Cohen, Richard B. P107
Cohen, Robert (Bozzuto's) P96
Cohen, Robert L. (Scarborough Research) P427
Cohen, Roger J. P529
Cohen, Shai E229
Cohen, Tracey P301
Cohen, Yossi A167
Cohn, Gary D. A392
Cohn, John D. A712
Cohn, Mary A528
Cohorn, Lisa P300
Cohrs, Michael W113
Coia, Angelo P360
Coia, Anne W162
Coiner, George R. A667
Cojuangco, Eduardo M. Jr. W287
Coker, Susan W. A255, P142
Colalillo, Claudia J. A605
Colalillo, Joseph A880, P522
Colalucci, Francis M. E344
Colangelo, Jerry J. P383
Colao, Vittorio A. W356
Colarossi, John R. P515
Colatriano, David P. P515
Colatriano, Vince P264
Colbert, Celia A. A567
Colbert, Daniel L. A257
Colbert, Kevin P385
Colbourne, William P87
Colburn, Cordis A380
Colburn, J. Brian W203
Colburn, Veronica R. E380
Colby, David C. A896
Colby, Janice M. A113
Cole, Albert D. P489
Cole, Calisa A621
Cole, Chip P32
Cole, Christopher A. A392
Cole, Dan (Denbury Resources) E115
Cole, Daniel F. (Ameren) A70
Cole, David A. (ABN AMRO) W22
Cole, David D. (CenturyTel) A198
Cole, David L. (Aon) A95
Cole, David W. (Coinstar) E95
Cole, Don P217
Cole, Ellen E141
Cole, G. Marcus P454
Cole, Jon C. (ENSCO) A324
Cole, Jonathan W. (Merisant Worldwide) P313
Cole, Kenneth W. A385
Cole, Kit M. E132
Cole, Leo J. E372
Cole, M. Mark A201
Cole, M. Ray Jr. E141

Cole, Martin I. A35
Cole, Michael H. (Smithfield Foods) A760
Cole, Michael J. (A. O. Smith) A93
Cole, Thomas A. (Sidley Austin) P438
Cole, Thomas L. (Macy's) A534
Cole, Timothy A. A271
Cole, Tom (Ceradyne) E87
Cole, Vincent J. A515
Coleman, Amy A350
Coleman, Elizabeth A. P183
Coleman, Gary L. A827
Coleman, Gordon A. E231
Coleman, Gregory G. A922
Coleman, J. Edward A374
Coleman, James E. A303, P169
Coleman, Leroy A404
Coleman, Mary Sue P500
Coleman, Natasha E296
Coleman, Rob P290
Coleman, Steven B. A326
Coleman, Wesley A. A884
Colen, Fredericus A. A158
Coles, Martin A779
Coles, Pamela W264
Coletta, John A. P413
Coley, James W. Jr. A890
Colf, Richard W. A655, P382
Colin, Jean-François W29
Colina, Julius P524
Coll, Mario M. III A87
Collar, Gary L. A47
Collas, Philippe W306
Collat, Charles A. Sr. P304
Collat Goedecke, Nancy P304
Collazo, José A. W81
Colleran, Lisa N. E216
Collette, Chris A616
Colley, E. Lee III A895
Colley, Gerald R. A326
Colley, James P92
Colley, M. David A895
Colli, Bart J. A103, P53
Collier, Brice P345
Collier, Doug (La-Z-Boy) A504
Collier, Douglas P. (Volcom) E367
Collier, Earl M. Jr. A387
Collier, Kevin P. A652
Collier, Samantha E175
Collier, Sharon P38
Collier, William L. III A367
Colliflower, Michael A. P226
Colligan, Edward T. A640
Collignon, Randy S. P243
Collin, Dirk A626
Collin, Jean-Philippe W248
Collins, Arthur D. Jr. A565
Collins, Brent A. E299
Collins, Charles F. E71
Collins, Christopher D. W240
Collins, Gary S. E279
Collins, George J. E298
Collins, Ginja R. E362
Collins, J. Barclay II A423
Collins, Jim A443, P240
Collins, John (IGA) A443, P240
Collins, John (NHL) P337
Collins, John R. (Constellation Energy Group) A244
Collins, John S. (Bitstream) E58
Collins, Kathleen M. A347
Collins, Keith R. (Phibro Animal Health) P383
Collins, Keith V. (SAS Institute) P423
Collins, Kendall E299
Collins, Malcolm Kelvin A596
Collins, Michael (REI) P405
Collins, Michael J. (Stericycle) E322
Collins, Patrick T. A852
Collins, Paul (Bell Microproducts) A139
Collins, Paul (Gould Paper) P207
Collins, Peter F. E349
Collins, Staci R. P256
Collins, Steven E26

Collins, Thomas J. E170
Collins, Timothy R. P171
Collins, Valerie K. A266
Collinsworth, Richard A. E305
Colliou, Yves W139
Collis, Steven H. A82
Colliver, Mary Margaret P500
Collombert, Marie-Tatiana W49
Collum, Don A836
Collupy, Ed A641
Colm, Rudolf W272
Colo, David J. A237
Colombi, Paolo E. E159
Colon, Conrad O. P208
Colon, Margaret A. A366
Colony, Sandy D. P244
Colosi, Scott M. E339
Colosimo, Thomas W. E323
Colotti, Raymond L. A113
Colpo, Charles C. A636
Colson, Rick P250
Colucci, Matthew R. E266
Colvin, Dwain S. P239
Comas, Daniel L. A264
Combes, Philippe A107
Combs, John W. E307
Combs, Samuel III A632
Combs, Sean P67
Combs, Stephen R. A893
Comer, Jeffrey L. A149
Comey, James B. A525
Comey, Paul E167
Comfort, Stephanie Georges A696
Comin, Gianluca W123
Cominelli, Massimiliano W252
Commiskey, James K. A119
Comneno, Maurizia A. W348
Compagno, Robert P184
Companion, Lydia P70
Company, Jean-Claude W343
Competti, Eileen M. A556
Compofelice, Joseph S. E346
Compton, James A246
Compton, John C. A651
Compton, Paul P477
Compton, Ronnie D. P56
Comstock, Elizabeth J. P341
Conant, Douglas R. A179, P133
Conaway, Doug A104
Conaway, Thomas M. A845
Concannon, Christopher R. A587
Concannon, William F. A190
Concina, Antonio W324
Conda, Joseph V. A637
Conde, Cesar P507
Conde, Cristóbal I. P461
Condon, James E. P470
Condon, John A416, P227
Condon, Kenneth G. P96
Condos, George M. P193
Condrin, J. Paul III P282
Condron, Christopher M. W52
Congrove, Chad A152
Conish, Mark G. A212
Conklyn, Elizabeth D. A862, P510
Conley, Don P518
Conley, E. Renae A325
Conley, Forrest M. Jr. E169
Conley, Gregory R. E179
Conley, James E. Jr. P355
Conley, Michael P. P192
Conley, Stephen C. E179
Conliffe, Roy R. W142, W196
Conlon, John (Amscan) P45
Conlon, John K. (Infosys) W163
Conlon, Michael W. A566
Conlon, Richard P99
Conn, Iain C. W75
Conn, Michael R. E169
Connealy, Paul J. A705
Connell, B. Allen E77
Connell, Margot P134
Connell, Sharon P40
Connell, Tara J. A371
Connell, Thomas A. A394

Connelly, Beth A686
Connelly, James M. P231
Connelly, John J. A851
Connelly, Kevin P81
Connelly, Michael D. P115
Connelly, Thomas M. Jr. A314
Conner, Marjorie L. P151
Conner, Penelope M. A619
Conner, Scott B. E46
Conner, Wayne J. P173
Connerty, Thomas F. E251
Connery, Bruce L. A315
Conniff, Will P449
Connolly, Brian C. A121
Connolly, C. Lawrence III A424
Connolly, Christine P163
Connolly, John P. P156, W109
Connolly, Michael J. (Aetna) A43
Connolly, Mike (Legal & General Group) W191
Connolly, Patrick J. A910
Connolly, Timothy P. A852
Connor, Charles Dean P404
Connor, Christopher M. A754
Connor, P. Eric P320
Connor, Rick W244
Connors, Brendan E229
Connors, Greg P397
Connors, John J. (Cutera) E109
Connors, John J. (Iron Mountain) A461
Connors, Kevin P. E109
Connors, Robert P450
Conover, Donna D. A769
Conover, Pamela C. A187
Conrad, Joel P338
Conrades, George H. E22
Conroy, J. Patrick P379
Conroy, John J. Jr. A122, P69
Consaul, Sheila P496
Consedine, Stephen W271
Considine, John R. A137
Considine, Tim A443, P240
Constans, Jordi W107
Constantine, Clem W205
Constantine, Jim P437
Constantinides, Ellen A660
Constantino, Ferdinand K. W287
Contamine, Jérôme W352
Conte, David P345
Conte, Kathleen E178
Conti, Corrado A872
Conti, Fulvio W123
Conti, Vittorio W165
Continelli, Richard M. A208
Contino, Francis A. A555
Contreras, Mark G. A333
Conver, Timothy E. E20
Converse, Peter A. E365
Conway, Anthony J. E295
Conway, John W. A259
Conway, Michael A. (Aon) A94
Conway, Mike (Sherwin-Williams) A754
Conway, Philip J. E295
Conway, Timothy C. A44
Conway, William A. (Henry Ford Health System) P231
Conway, William E. Jr. (The Carlyle Group) P111
Conway, William S. (Mutual of America) P328
Conway-Welch, Colleen P512
Conyers, Doug E162
Conyers, James W79
Conzemius, Peter A. P291
Coogan, William J. A336
Cook, Brian J. A864
Cook, Chuck A302
Cook, Colin A497, P270, W183
Cook, E. Gary A528
Cook, Harold B. E290
Cook, Ian M. A231
Cook, Jeffrey L. A369
Cook, Jill A261
Cook, John S. E185
Cook, Julie P51

Dill, Kent S. E144
Dillabough, Gary A309
Dillaha, Larry M. E303
Dillard, Alex A284
Dillard, James E. III A865
Dillard, Mike A284
Dillard, Richard P323
Dillard, Steve P61
Dillard, William II A284
Dillard, William III A284
Diller, Barry A441
Diller, Kathleen L. A585
Dilley, Timothy P344
Dillman, Frederick A845
Dillman, Linda Marie A882
Dillon, Adrian T. A48
Dillon, Daniel P. P336
Dillon, David B. A500
Dillon, Donald F. A349
Dillon, Eva P401
Dillon, John (Houston Rockets) P236
Dillon, John T. (Evercore
   Partners) E135
Dillon, Kris E152
Dillon, Mary A558
Dillon, Matt E317
Dillon, Michael A. A784
Dillon, Ricky T. A161
Dillon, Roderick H. Jr. E116
Dillon, Timothy J. P408
Dillon, Veronica A890
Dilotsotlhe, Mokaedi W240
Dilsaver, Evelyn S. A202
Dimanche, Conrad P67
DiMaria, Edward J. E50
DiMicco, Daniel R. A620
Dimich, Daniel L. A817
Dimitrelis, Dimitrios E243
Dimon, James A479
Dimond, Randall P393
Dimond, Robert B. A588
Dinan, Curtis L. A632
DiNapoli, Dominic E153
DiNapoli, Mark L. P460
DiNardo, Sheila S. E34
Dineen, Robert W. A521
DiNello, Michele P460
Diner, Steven J. P418
Dinesh, Krishnaswamy W163
Dingle, David K. A187
Dingle, Robert L. Jr. E124
Dingus, David H. E46
DiNicola, Robert J. P203, P284
Dinkel, Richard A495, P267
Dintino, Daniel A. Jr. E145
Dinwoodie, Jason S. P158
Dinwoodie, Thomas E328
Dion, Gregory R. E252
Dion, N. Michael P384
Dion, Pierre W262
Diorio, Marianne A331
DiPalma, Dino E17
DiPaola, Paul P68
DiPiazza, Samuel A. Jr. A677, P133,
   P391, W258
DiPietrantonio, Cynthia A476
Diracles, John M. Jr. P110
Diraddo, Geno A422
Diradoorian, Raymond A60
Dirks, Bob A429
Dirks, Thorsten W184
DiRusso, Lonny R. A717
Discepolo, Michaelanne C. A678
Disch, Joanne P19
Disclafani, Mary A852
DiSilvestro, Anthony P. A179
Disken, Kenneth J. A525
Diskin, Eileen P394
Diskin, Jeffrey A429
Disney, Anthea A376, A604
Dissinger, Anthony A471
Ditkoff, James H. A264
Ditore, Melanie P167
Dittberner, Chad R. A900
Dittemore, Ronald D. A62

Dittmann, Jay A400, P220
Dittmer, Jerald K. A431
Divers, Jim P38
DiVittorio, Thomas P196
Dixon, Betty E280
Dixon, Bradley O. A632
Dixon, Connie E341
Dixon, Diane B. A117
Dixon, Geoff W261
Dixon, John L. P371
Dixon, Leslie H. P411
Dixon, Robert P337
Dixon, Simon W175
Dixon, Steven C. A206
Dixon, Thomas H. E256
Dixon, Tim P157
Dixon, Wendy L. A165
Djurklou, Nils W331
Dlugopolski, Stephanie P268
Dlugozima, Hope E371
Dobashi, Akio W309
Dobashi, Satoshi W152
Dobbelaere, Rik W72
Dobbins, James W. P356
Dobbs, James C. E363
Dobbs, Janice A. A281
Dobbs, Johnnie C. A882
Dobbs, Kelley J. A54
Dobbs, Randy E. P509
Dobelbower, Peter P234
Dobkin, David P. P392
Dobrin, Allan H. P126
Dobson, Thomas E. P528
Doby, Winston C. P497
Dodd, Martin W194
Dodd, Patrick A303
Dodd, Timothy J. P147
Dodds, Hamish W264
Dodds, William R. Jr. A613
Dodge, Allen E175
Dodge, Colin W229
Dodge, Daniel R. A605
Dodge, Jeffrey L. A327
Dodge, Karen P481
Dodson, Tim W312
Doeppe, Pamela P422
Doerfler, Ronald J. A416, P227
Doerig, Hans-Ulrich W103
Doering Meshke, Sheryl P60
Doerner, Peter E290
Doerr, Kurt D. A326
Dogan, Dedra N. A912
Doheny, Daniel P. P409
Doheny, Jim P27
Doherty, Colm E. W39
Doherty, Ged P447
Dohle, Ulrich W272
Doh-Seok, Choi W286
Doi, Yoshihiro W369
Doise, Daryl J. E215
Doke, Timothy J. A368
Dokoozlian, Nick A303, P169
Dolan, D. Kevin A569
Dolan, David M. P166
Dolan, Gregory J. P529
Dolan, Michael J. (Exxon Mobil) A338
Dolan, Michael K. (CarMax) A186
Dolan, Patrick A802
Dolan, Scott J. A842
Dolan, Terrance R. A860
Dolan, Thomas (j2 Global) E203
Dolan, Thomas J. (Xerox) A920
Dolan, Tim E331
Dolan, Tom (Amedisys) E28
Dolan, Vincent M. A682
Dolara, Peter J. A86
Dolby, Michael B. A62
Dolby, Ray M. E119
Dolceamore, Gwen P235
Dolch, Gary D. A181
Dolecek, Gayle Robert E327
Dolich, Andy P312
Doll, Carie P50
Doll, Robert C. A569
Dollins, Mark D. A651

Dollive, James P. A498
Dolloff, Wilton W. A440
Dolney, Andy A847
Dombek, Gerard M. A748
Dombroski, Harry P238
Dombrowski, Dave P117
Domeck, Brian A683
Domeyer, Diane A710
Domingue, Charles S. A471
Domino, Joseph F. A325
Domowitz, Ian E197
Don, Diana A180
Donaghy, Brian M. P459
Donaghy, James K. P459
Donaho, Jerry P214
Donahoe, James E275
Donahoe, John J. A309
Donahue, John J. A536
Donahue, Joseph A867
Donahue, Michael P248
Donahue, Patrick R. A850, P495
Donahue, Thomas P179
Donahue, Timothy J. A259
Donald, James L. A779
Donaldson, Jeff E295
Donaldson, Philip A49
Donaldson, Rich P286
Donargo, Vincent A162
Donatelli, David A. A321
Donatello, Susan L. P430
Donati, Carlo Maria W222
Donavan, Pat P148
Donbaugh, Chuck P197
Donche-Gay, Philippe W87
Donegan, Mark A676
Donelson, John M.A. A863
Donenberg, Phillip B. E57
Donius, Walter A. E281
Donius, William A. E281
Donley, Douglas A709
Donley, Patrick M. P522
Donlon, James D. III A108
Donna, James M. P60
Donnalley, Joseph A476
Donnell, Curtis R. E171
Donnellan, Kevin P19
Donnelly, Christopher J. A430
Donnelly, Eugene A677, P391, W258
Donnelly, Gloria G. P133
Donnelly, Jeff P119
Donnelly, Kevin W. P359
Donnelly, Nicky W78
Donnelly, Peter P22
Donnelly, Robert M. A572
Donnelly, Thomas M. E117
Donnet, Philippe W53
D'Onofrio, Anthony B. P284
Donofrio, Nicholas M. A453
Donoghue, Craig W. E68
Donoghue, Kenneth L. P458
Donohue, Mark J. A293
Donohue, Sean P. A842
Donohue, Stephen J. A555
Donovan, Donna M. E204
Donovan, Joan W. P481
Donovan, John M. (VeriSign) A869
Donovan, John N. (Bank Holdings) E47
Donovan, Paul (Boston Scientific) A158
Donovan, Paul (Vodafone) W356
Donovan, Robert S. (Blue Diamond
   Growers) P89
Donovan, Robert V. (CACI
   International) A176
Donovan, Timothy R. A63
Donovan, William J. W234
Donzeaud, Alain W87
Doody, James L. P52
Doody, Joseph G. A777
Doogan, Declan A657
Dooley, Barbara M. P197
Dooling, Larry E258
Dooner, John J. Jr. A458
Dooner, Marlene S. A232
Döpfner, Mathias W54
Dopychai, Martin W114

Doran, Howard E182
Doran, Mark E. A647
Doran, Mary Ann A926
Doran, Shelly J. A757
Dordell, Timothy P. A828
Dore, James P. E58
Dore-Falcone, Carol E160
Dorer, Benno A225
Dorer, Lori E207
Dorey, Gérard W89
Dorgan, David M. A712
Doria, Joseph G. A520
Doria, Kelly P431
Doris, Robert J. E316
Dorland-Clauzel, Claire W53
Dorman, Courtney Chiang P531
Dormann, Jürgen W288
Dorph, Martin P351, P471
Dorr, Marjorie W. A896
Dorrance, Robert J. W341
Dorsey, Dana P. P536
Dorsey, Jim P202
Dorsey, John A397, P214
Dorsey, Patrick (Morningstar) E237
Dorsey, Patrick B. (Tiffany) A819
Dorsey, Paul P301
Dorsman, Peter A. A596
D'Orso, Chris P367
Dorval, Bernard T. W341
Dorvilien, Nixon P422
Dosch, Ted A. A905
Dosoretz, Daniel E. E285
Doss, Christine A763
Döss, Manfred W282
Dossani, Nazir G. A366
Doswell, Mary C. A288
Dotson, Connie M. A332
Dotta, Jim P58
Dotterer, Herbert T. P82
Dotti, Jim P45
Dotts, Kevin M. A304
Doty, Debbie P350
Doty, Douglas C. A123
Doty, Elmer L. P518
Doubinine, Andrei W51
Doubleday, Matthew E. E377
Doucet-Sillano, Dorothy E120
Doucette, John J. A853
Dougan, Brady W. W103
Douget, Susan E. A147
Dougherty, Dennis F. P504
Dougherty, Jim A438
Dougherty, Kevin R. E153
Dougherty, Lynne A780
Dougherty, Michael D. A669
Dougherty, Robert A. A51
Doughty, Dennis O. P93
Doughty, Peggy P136
Douglas, Charles W. A438
Douglas, David C. E189
Douglas, Dianne A552
Douglas, Elyse A422
Douglas, George A. Jr. P372
Douglas, Gustaf W296
Douglas, Iain A303, P169
Douglas, James A445
Douglas, Lee P63
Douglas, Paul C. W341
Douglas, Richard H. A387
Douglas, Robert E292
Douglas, William W. III A230
Douglass, Elizabeth A845
Douglass, Scott R. P502
Doumet, Antoine M. E356
Dout, A. Jacqueline P377
Douville, Jean A386
Douville, Richard A. P178
Dove, Timothy L. A664
Dovenberg, David E. P496
Dow, Bill P138
Dow, H. Allan E222
Dow, James E. P275
Dow, John A. S. A602
Dow, Tom (Carnival) A187

Durkee, Robert K. P392
Durkin, G. Michael Jr. A650
Durko, Joseph S. E321
Duroc-Danner, Bernard J. A895
Durose, Peter W334
Durovich, Christopher J. P124
Dürr, Thomas W317
Durrani, Faisel A522
Durski, Michael S. E150
Durso, Ed P178
Durso, Joseph E132
Durzy, Hani A309
Dussart, Marc A140
Dussault, Nancy E200
Dussert, Bertrand P520
Dutheil, Alain W313
Dutiné, Gottfried W250
Dutkowsky, Robert M. A797
Dutra, Felipe W161
Dutta, Rajiv A309
Duvall, William R. E223
Duverne, Denis W52
Duvillet, Christian W102
Duzan, Jean-Baptiste W268
Duzy, Stanley B. Jr. A485
Dvorak, Robert D. P192
Dvoroznak, Mark J. A754
Dworak, Cathy P214
Dworken, Jeffrey H. A329, P177, W129
Dworkin, Philippa A243
Dwyer, Bill P285
Dwyer, Brian J. P98
Dwyer, Carrie E. A202
Dwyer, Edward M. A165
Dwyer, John M. Jr. P407
Dwyer, Joseph P. P58
Dwyer, Kathleen M. A648
Dwyer, Laurence J. A117
Dwyer, Michael P150
Dwyer, Stacey H. A294
Dwyer, Steven F. (Rolls-Royce) W276
Dwyer, Steven M. (Ryland) A722
Dyapaiah, Shruthi E134
Dyck, Jeffrey A739
Dyck, Robert G. E141
Dye, Justin P32
Dye, Molly A47
Dye, Robert J. A96
Dye, Tim A872
Dyer, Colin A477
Dyer, John L. P450
Dyer, Joseph W. E200
Dyer, Mark P331
Dyer, Rick A730
Dyer, Stephen G. W28
Dyer-Bruggeman, Dianne A167
Dyke, Jonathan N. E104
Dykema, Scot P410
Dykhouse, Elaine P89
Dykstra, David A. E377
Dykstra, Paul B. A873
Dynes, Robert C. P497
Dyott, Stephen M. P22
Dyrbus, Robert W160
Dyrek, Gerri E117
Dyrvik, Harold W55
Dyson, Ian W205
Dzau, Victor J. P168
Dziak, Jack A773
Dziedzic, John T. P523
Dziesinski, Ray P124
Dzura, Michael D. A163
Dzuryachko, Thomas A. A426

E

Eades, Mike P187
Eads, Emanuel J. P119
Eagle, A. Rae A620
Eagle, J. Breckenridge E38
Eagle, Jevin S. A777
Eaker, Norman L. P258
Ealy, C. Cato A457
Eames, Edward J. E137

Earhart, Cindy C. A611
Earhart, Stephen P. P242
Earl, James F. A375
Earley, Anthony F. Jr. A298
Early, Richard E97
Earner, William P340
Earnest, Tawn P163
Easley, Robert J. A709
Easter, James R. A556
Easter, William H. III A299
Easterday, Adam P185
Easterling, Barbara P496
Easterson, Jon E348
Eastland, Woods E. P454
Eastman, David A631
Eastman, Karen E. P389
Eastman, Lynne E. P245
Easton, R. Lee A900
Easton, Robin E59
Eaton, Jonathan P285
Eaton, Michael P301
Eaton, Robin E. A638
Eaton, Thomas E. Jr. P108
Eaves, John W. A104
Eayrs, Mike A397, P214
Ebbighausen, Harold E. A461
Ebe, Tsutomu W228
Ebeid, Russell J. P215
Ebeling, Thomas W235
Eberhard, Douglas D. P373
Eberhard, Michael L. E101
Eberhart, H. Paulett W166
Eberle, Dave P255
Ebersman, David A. A377
Ebersol, Dick A594, P341
Ebersole, Tony E94
Ebert, Charles D. A894
Eberwein, Elise R. A859
Ebeyan, Gary W163
Ebihara, Minoru A48
Ebrard, Alberto W360
Ebrom, Charles P540
Eby, Rob P148
Eby, Thomas E151
Ebzery, James P. A618
Eceles, Jeff P468
Echemendia, Lenia E344
Eck, Franklin P24
Eckel, John R. Jr. E103
Ecker, Elissa P364
Eckert, Bruce M. E124
Eckert, James C. E253
Eckert, Robert A. A552
Eckert, Troy C. E367
Eckhardt, B. N. A323
Eckhardt, Ezra A. E323
Eckhardt, Mark H. A734, P426
Eckhart, Brian D. E103
Eckmann, Jeffrey A. A708
Eckrote, Douglas E. A194
Eckroth, Joseph F. Jr. A422
Eckstein, Catherine W. A450
Eckstein, Frank O. A912
Eckstein, Marie N. P164
Ecton, Virgil E. E236
Eddings, James E340
Eddy, Jeanne H. P294
Edelman, Daniel J. P172
Edelman, Harriet A121
Edelman, John D. P172
Edelman, Richard W. P172
Edelman, Robert J. M. A454
Edelson, David B. A526
Edelson, James I. E260
Eden, Doug P294
Edenborg, Mats W359
Edenfield, J. Michael E222
Edenfield, James C. E222
Edens, Wesley R. E21
Edge, Jayne W. P149
Edgemond, James E104
Edgley, Erin A388
Edgley, Kevin E149
Edgren, Roger C. A857
Edholm, Phil W234

Edig, Thomas W254
Edington, Randall K. A663
Edison, Stewart I. P483
Edl, John P. P173
Edlein, Chadd H. E320
Edman, Jeff P246
Edmonds, David B. A702
Edmonds, Paul A592
Edmonds, Stan W. E98
Edmondson, Charles A. E35
Edmondson, Ralph W78
Edmunds, Alan P101
Edson, David M. E353
Edwab, David H. A566
Edwards, Brady P289
Edwards, Brian D. A444
Edwards, Bruce A. W114
Edwards, Bryce P. P411
Edwards, Carol P427
Edwards, Darryl W234
Edwards, David M. (TIAA-CREF) A818, P476
Edwards, David N. (Avery Dennison) A117
Edwards, Dewitt H. E62
Edwards, Dirk E238
Edwards, Doug (Google) A396
Edwards, Douglas J. (Eastman Kodak) A306
Edwards, G. Douglas A702
Edwards, Gary E26
Edwards, Jeffrey L. (Allergan) A60
Edwards, Jeffrey N. (Merrill Lynch) A569
Edwards, Jon S. E32
Edwards, Joseph S. E20
Edwards, Kristin G. P257
Edwards, Mark V. E150
Edwards, Michael G. E362
Edwards, Nancy A. A538
Edwards, Patricia L. A326
Edwards, Robert L. A725
Edwards, S. Eugene A866
Edwards, Steven B. P532
Edwards, Tom P288
Edwards, Wesley B. A463
Edwards, William T. A40
Edwardson, John A. A194
Egan, Cynthia L. A794
Egan, Jack A876
Egan, Kathy W127
Egan, Martin F. E47
Egan, Peter P192
Egan, Rob (Tufts Health Plan) P489
Egan, Robert (Boise Cascade) P91
Egerton, Anthony W193
Eggemeyer, John M. III E141
Egger, Richard A201
Egidi, Kenneth A. P379
Egnotovich, Cynthia M. A393
Ehinger, Kenneth R. P338
Ehlers, Albrecht W151
Ehlers, Karen C. A848
Ehmann, Thomas R. P192
Ehrhardt, Paul D. E231
Ehrhart, Christof W119
Ehrich, Elliot W. E22
Ehrline, Leo P345
Ehrling, Anders W294
Ehrman, Daniel S. Jr. A371
Ehrmann, Jacques W91
Eichenlaub, Brian A275
Eichiner, Friedrich W70
Eichler, Edwin W336
Eichler, Rodney J. A96
Eichman, Kyle E273
Eichner, Kevin G. E130
Eick, Karl-Gerhard W116
Eidson, Dennis A770
Eidson, Thomas E. A355, P188
Eigen, Steven P119
Eiges, Peter P360
Eikenboom, Marnix W107
Eimer, Rich A302
Einhorn, Margaret H. P412

Einstein, James L. A711
Eisele, Charles R. A844
Eisele, Mark O. A100
Eisen, James A471
Eisen, Paul E292
Eisenberg, Barbara K. A92
Eisenberg, Bruce J. A831
Eisenberg, Glenn A. A823
Eisenberg, Mark P295
Eisenberg, Mitchell S. E205
Eisenberg, Warren A138
Eisenhart, Jo A657
Eisenhaur, Patricia A894
Eisenreich, Ted P214
Eisgruber, Christopher L. P392
Eisman, Robert B. A68
Eisner, Dean H. A255, P142
Eitel, Charles R. P440
Eitel, J. Timothy A699
Eitel, Maria S. A606
Ekdahl, Jon P43
Ekelschot, Paul P. M. W277
Ekey, Jacqueline P463
Eklof, Carl Jr. E210
Ekman, Mary A779
Ekman, Ulrika W168
El, Pam A781, P455
Elam, Mickey P247
Elarde, Peter E308
Elbers, Peter W179
Elcano, Mary S. P404
Elder, Bruce W. E106
Elder, Clay E201
Elder, Darlene E69
Elder, Eric E. A722
Elder, Renwyck A896
Elder, Richard M. E144
Eldridge, Benjamin N. E151
Eldridge, James F. P42
Elflein, Catherine B. E82
Elg, Annette P259
Elger, Jess A. A53
Elges, Matthew K. P133
El-Hibri, Fuad E127
El-Hillow, Jennifer P286
Elias, Howard D. A320
Elias, Melissa A. E316
Elías Ayub, Arturo W328
Eliasek, M. Grier E279
Eliasson, Karin W331
Elicker, John A165
Eline, William G. A643
Elisburg, Andy P318
Elise, Lori P65
Elix, Douglas T. A453
Elizondo, Raúl Alejandro Livas W247
Elkann, John Philip W131
Elkins, John A874
Elko, Ed P94
Ell, Susan P27
Elledge, Pam A276
Ellekrog, Henriette Fenger W294
Ellen, Martin M. A763
Eller, Timothy R. A197
Ellers, Steven A. E373
Ellingen, David R. A763
Ellinghausen, James R. A690
Ellingsen, Catharine D. A63
Elliot, Guy R. W271
Elliott, Anita C. P163
Elliott, Brian W. A745
Elliott, Dale F. A80
Elliott, Eric C. E215
Elliott, Gary W336
Elliott, Greg E236
Elliott, Jeff A253
Elliott, Kelley A337
Elliott, Robert E. (Smith Micro) E313
Elliott, Robert N. (Irvine Company) P248
Elliott, Thomas E293
Ellis, Andrew C. (Greenfield Online) E167
Ellis, Andy (Akamai) E22
Ellis, Bob (Wyle Laboratories) P536

Ewing, Anna M. A587
Ewing, Gary P298
Ewing, Joe A. A809
Ewing, R. Stewart Jr. A198
Exon, Charles S. A694
Exum, James F. Jr. P271
Eyerly, Mark P471
Eylar, Paula A159
Eylott, Malcolm W85
Eymann, Steven W. E286
Eymard, Benoît W136
Eynon, Richard R. A843
Eyre, William Jr. P480
Eyrich, Keith P248
Eytchison, Brian R. A192
Eyuboglu, Vedat M. E21

F

Faas, Charles P423
Faber, Emmanuel W107
Faber, Joachim W38
Faber, Terrance A. A91
Faber, Timothy J. A518
Fabian, Jerry R. P450
Fabius, Raymond J. E201
Fabrico, Michael P99
Fabritiis, Edward A186
Fabrizio, Joseph M. P94
Fabrizio, R. W. A81
Fabry, John J. A397, P213
Facchetti, Katia A. A808
Faccini, M. A185
Faciane, E. Leo A811
Fackler, Brad E. E327
Fadel, Mitchell E. A704
Fadell, Anthony A98
Fafaul, Michael F. Sr. E354
Fagan, Charles E. A670
Fagan, Mark W. A612
Fagundes, Heather L. A554
Faherty, Gregory T. P64
Fahey, James K. A852
Fahey, John M. Jr. P335
Fahour, Ahmed W219
Fahy, Chris W114
Fahy, Dennis J. W75
Fahy, William J. Jr. E256
Faigin, Larry B. E56
Fain, Eric S. A727
Fain, Jonathan D. P471
Fain, Richard D. A716
Fain, T. Scott A32
Fainé Casas, Isidro W327
Fairbairn, Kevin E195
Fairbank, Richard D. A180
Fairbanks, Joseph C. Jr. E34
Fairbanks, Valerie P384
Fairbrass, Nigel W283
Fairchild, Mark D. P71
Fairey, Michael E. W194
Fairhead, Rona A. W243
Fairhurst, David W334
Fairl, William M. A176
Faith, Brian A341
Faith, David M. P431
Faith, Marshall E. P431
Faivre-Duboz, Michel W268
Fakahany, Ahmass L. A568
Falcinelli, Richard P. E210
Falck, David P. A687
Falco, Fabián W370
Falco, Randel A. A822
Falcon, Michael F. E243
Falcone, Joseph C. P336
Faldyn, Rod P20
Falfas, Jacob T. E81
Falgoust, Dean T. A367
Falick, Paul P239
Falk, Dennis J. E364
Falk, Susan G. A407
Falk, Thomas J. A488
Falkenberg, Morten W122
Fall, Amadou Gallo P148

Falle, Jim W51
Fallin, Michael D. P71
Falline, Brian A867
Fallon, Charles M. Jr. A172
Fallon, James M. (ONEOK) A632
Fallon, James S. (VSE) E369
Fallon, John A. P88
Fallon, Patrick W260
Fallon, William C. A553
Fallowfield, Tim W171
Falque-Pierrotin, Thierry W256
Falvey, Joe P492
Falvey, Michael E38
Famadas, Nelson E327
Fanelli, Germano A107
Fanger, Michael J. E66
Fangzheng, Jiao W95
Fanning, Bridie A. A349
Fanning, Michael R. A549, P303
Fanning, Thomas A. A767
Fanning, Todd D. E278
Fannon, Diane P410
Fanska, Jerry W. E213
Fant, Paul V. A735
Fantazzini, Marco W348
Fantom, Lynn A458
Fanton, Jonathan F. P293
Faraci, John V. Jr. A457
Faraci, Philip J. A306
Farage, Christopher M. A643
Farah, John M. Jr. A199
Farah, Roger N. A670
Farandou, Jean-Pierre W306
Farbacher, Elizabeth A. A426, P233
Farber, Jeffrey M. A132
Farber, John J. P239
Farber, Sandra P239
Faremo, Grete W232
Farese, Michael R. A640
Farewell, Thomas A286
Farhat, Jamal M. A157
Farias, Edward J. E194
Faridi, Hamed A555
Farley, Edward I. P493
Farley, Stephen E537
Farley, Thomas W. E192
Farmer, Ian P. W197
Farmer, Jeff P470
Farmer, Jeremy G.O. A94
Farmer, Peter P206
Farmer, Richard T. A216
Farmer, Scott D. A216
Farnan, Joseph A303
Farnham, Robert E. A412
Farnsworth, Bradley P. E240
Farnsworth, Bryan D. A436
Farnsworth, Ronald L. Jr. E353
Farnsworth, Susan E. A915
Farquharson, Aklan W. E287
Farr, David A. (Stewart's Shops) P458
Farr, David N. (Emerson Electric) A323
Farr, Kevin M. A552
Farr, Paul A. A673
Farrant, Guy W205
Farrar, Eileen C. A857
Farrell, Anne V. P405
Farrell, Anthony A751
Farrell, Christopher B. E252
Farrell, David A825
Farrell, Diana A561, P308
Farrell, Edward J. P36
Farrell, Gretchen A520
Farrell, John T. A90
Farrell, June A542
Farrell, Liam A271
Farrell, Matthew T. A212
Farrell, Michael J. E292
Farrell, Pat (Enterprise Rent-A-Car) P176
Farrell, Patricia A. (Aetna) A43
Farrell, Paul E133
Farrell, Peter C. E292
Farrell, Philip P506
Farrell, Shannon B. A294

Farrell, Thomas F. II (Dominion Resources) A288
Farrell, Thomas G. (Lafarge) W189
Farrelly, John P277
Farrelly, Joseph W. A458
Farris, G. Steven A96
Farrow, Stephen R. A859
Faruolo, Edward A. A214
Farver, Charles P377
Farwell, David L. A34
Farwerck, J. F. E. W184
Fasano, Philip A481, P260
Fasold, Mark P286
Fasone Holder, Julie A292
Fassati, Ariberto W102
Fassbind, Renato W103
Fassino, J.C. P217
Fassino, Rob E209
Fast, Eric C. A257
Fast, Larry E. A379
Fatemizadeh, Ebrahim A752
Fatjo, Tom J. III E370
Fatjo, Tom J. Jr. E370
Fato, Lucy A544
Fatovic, Robert A720
Fattori, Ruth A. A581
Fau, Jean-Francois A812
Faubel, William P. A123
Faugère, Mireille W305
Faulk, William F. P124
Faulkner, Duane H. P215
Faulkner, Glenn C. A587
Faulkner, Kenneth G. P465
Faulkner, Susan A126
Fauser, Chad A835
Fauss, Ronnie P148
Faust, Drew Gilpin P222
Favaro, Paul F. A610
Favey, Alain W248
Favorite, Melissa M. E151
Favorule, Denise E209
Fawaz, Marwan A205
Fawcett, Dan A362
Fawcett, Gayle P. E55
Fawcett, Gerald A. P261
Fawcett, Jayne G. P325
Fawkes, Kurt A773
Fawley, Daniel A. A708
Fay, George R. A227
Fay, Roger L. P408
Fayard, Gary P. A228
Fayyad, Usama A922
Fazio, George J. A727
Fazio, Peter V. Jr. A607
Feagin, Susan K. P131
Feagles, Louis P254
Fealing, Burt A789
Fealy, Robert L. P167
Fearon, Mark W365
Fearon, Richard H. A307
Featherstone, Diane L. A312
Fechter, Jürgen H. W336
Feckner, Rob A178, P106
Feczko, Joseph M. A657
Feder, Benjamin P540
Feder, Philip N. P375
Federici, William J. E373
Federle, Louis A. A234
Federle, Mark P526
Federman, Irwin A730
Fedewa, Scott A522
Fedotov, Gennady W200
Fedun, Leonid A. W200
Fedyna, Michael W. A438
Fee, Troy E. A647
Feehan, Daniel R. E79
Feeler, Jeffrey R. E29
Feener, Maxwell P421
Feeney, Kevin P493
Feeney, Michael P18
Fees, John A. A556
Feeser, Robert A. A562
Fegan, Mike W170
Feher, Darren P341
Feher, William A322

Fehrenbach, Franz W272
Fehrman, William J. P320
Feiger, George M. A927
Feik, Cary E325
Feilmeier, Steve A495, P267
Feinberg, David M. A58
Feingold, David P174
Feinstein, Leonard A138
Feinstein, Richard S. A138
Feir, Hank E151
Feitel, Tom A563
Fekete, Georg E307
Felago, Richard T. A892
Felch, Donna E140
Feld, Alana P184
Feld, Charles S. A317
Feld, Joseph E130
Feld, Karen A. A299
Feld, Kenneth J. P184
Feld, Nicole P184
Feldberg, Harley M. A119
Feldeisen, Ronald Jr. P262
Felder, Helmut P429
Felder, Stephanie E65
Feldman, Alan (MGM MIRAGE) A571
Feldman, Alan F. (Resource America) E293
Feldman, Arlene C. A148
Feldman, Greg S. P150
Feldman, Margaret P. P118
Feldman, Sally J. A758, P442
Feldman, Sheila B. A104
Feldman, Steve P333
Feldman, Tamara S. A431
Feldser, Michael W. A124
Feldstein, Eric A. A384
Felice, Stephen J. A277
Felicetti, James R. P354
Felicetty, James F. E152
Felix, Sonny P73
Fell, Anthony S. W279
Fell, Greg A808
Fell, Nick W283
Feller, Lloyd H. A469
Feller, Martha R. E207
Feller, Nancy P. P190
Fellin, Paolo A189
Fellinger, Bob P180
Fellman, Lars W88
Fellon, Andrew R. A244
Fellowes, James P184
Fellowes, John P184
Fells Davis, Cheryl A745
Fels, Jonathan E44
Felsinger, Donald E. A747
Feltrin, Tony P348
Fenaroli, Paul A646
Fencl, Eric R. P369
Fender, Jeff A652
Fendrich, Stephen G. P440
Fendrock, Charles E244
Fenech, Ronald J. A817
Fenech, William C. A817
Fenn, Grant W261
Fennell, Joseph E. E201
Fennell, Laura A. A459
Fennell, Michael P390
Fenner, John H. P490
Fenner, Thomas D. A635
Fennessy, Richard A. A450
Fenton, Charles E. A149
Fenton, Dave A28
Fenton, Ken P51
Fenton, Stuart A. A450
Fenton, Timothy J. A558
Fentress, Camilla P356
Fenwick, Katherine A227
Fenwick, Lex P86
Feragen, Jody H. A436
Ferber, Alan D. A848
Ferber, Norman A. A715
Ferchau, Mark E. E164
Ferdinandi, V. Michael A262
Ferenbach, Gregory E326
Ferencz, Szabolcs W217

G

Gaasche, Theodore J. P461
Gabbe, Steven G. P512
Gabel, Theresa A. E147
Gaberino, John A. Jr. A632
Gabetti, Gianluigi W167
Gable, Greg A202
Gabriel, John L. Jr. A282
Gabriel, Nicholas M. P190
Gabriel, Yves W74
Gabrielli de Azevedo, José Sérgio W245
Gaburo, Michael P. A216
Gaddis, Betty B. E92
Gaddis, Byron J. A676
Gadek, Stanley J. A52
Gadiesh, Orit P68
Gadonneix, Pierre W120
Gadre, Anil P. A784
Gaemperle, Chantal W201
Gaer, Samuel H. E252
Gaertner, Deborah E154
Gaeta, Tony E258
Gaffney, John T. E147
Gaffney, Karmela P82
Gaffney, Steven F. A462
Gafford, Ronald J. P65
Gafvert, Rolf A. E60
Gage Lofgren, Diane A481, P260
Gagelmann, Diethard W242
Gagey, Frederic W179
Gagliardi, Veda E125
Gagliardo, Jean P388
Gagnon, Dave A172
Gagnon, Michael O. A677, P391, W258
Gahlon, Dan E. A26
Gaier, Elizabeth A. P309
Gailey, John R. III E373
Gaines, Adrienne P539
Gaines, Bennett L. A348
Gaines, Brett E310
Gaines, Gay Hart P141
Gaitanzis, Denise P195
Gaither, Eva D. P421
Gaither, Israel L. P421
Gaither, J. Michael P44
Gaither, John F. Jr. P466
Galaev, Magomed A392
Galang, Faustino F. W287
Galanko, William A. A611
Galante, Joe P447
Galanti, Richard A. A253
Galarce, Carlos E. P242
Galassi, Nicholas J. E191
Galateri, Gabriele W324
Galateri di Genola, Gabriele W47
Galaz, Santiago W296
Galbato, Chan W. W166
Galbo, Philip C. A262
Galbraith, Caroline E148
Galdon, Rafael W240
Gale, Brent E. P320
Gale, Nick W278
Gale, Robert G. P310
Gale, William C. A216
Galen, Douglas J. E308
Galgano, Brenda M. A29
Galifi, Vincent J. W203
Galin, Tomi P238
Gallagher, Brian A. P496
Gallagher, Catherine R. P134
Gallagher, Dan E224
Gallagher, Donald J. A223
Gallagher, Everett E. Jr. A898
Gallagher, John P301
Gallagher, Kevin C. A801, A848
Gallagher, Lisa A. E180
Gallagher, Maurice J. Jr. E23
Gallagher, Michael P. P143
Gallagher, Robert F. E324
Gallagher, Simon L. P228
Gallagher, Thomas A. A386
Gallagher, Timothy J. E158
Gallagher, William T. A259

Gallahue, Kieran T. E292
Galland, Benoit P162
Gallant, Mark P64
Gallardo, Luis P156, W109
Gallaway, Katherine E236
Gallegos, James H. A173
Gallegos, José Angel W360
Gallegos, Lisa A365
Gallen, Robert M. A858
Gallentine, Michael L. A304
Gallet, Patrick W102
Galligan, William P. A850, P495
Gallina, Bennett R. A121
Gallini, Pete P365
Gallo, A. C. A907
Gallo, David J. E125
Gallo, Dominic P217
Gallo, Joseph E. A303, P169
Gallo, Lorien O. A719
Gallo, Robert J. A303, P169
Gallo, Stephanie A303, P170
Gallogly, James L. A238
Gallois, Louis W119, W190
Galloway, David A. W58
Gallup, Ross W. A609
Galluzzo, Jay A. A885
Galow, Geoffrey G. A692
Galvan, David J. E377
Galvin, Peggie P50
Galvin, Raymond E. E330
Galvin, Walter J. A323
Galyean, Angela E159
Gamache, David P. E21
Gamba, Philippe W268
Gambelli, Marianne P341
Gambill, Harry P483
Gambill, Mark A194
Gamble, John W. Jr. A515
Gamble, Mark A75
Gambrell, George P452
Gambrell, Michael R. A292
Gamgort, Bob A543, P299
Gammage, Kennedy E118
Gamoran, Reuben A908
Gampp, Kurt W. Jr. E332
Gams, Edward A581
Gamsin, Sharon A551
Gamson, Peter P210
Ganal, Michael W70
Gander, Fred P158
Gandhi, Arunkumar R. W319
Gandhi, Kaushikkumar E75
Gandolfo, Thomas J. A68
Ganek, Jeffrey E. E245
Gang, Xiao W57
Gangwani, Kishore E237
Gannaway, Michael T. A872
Gannett, Benjamin H. A127
Gannon, John Timothy P368
Gannon, Michael J. A577
Gannon, Richard B. P136
Gannon, Thomas A. P428
Gans, Robert M. E277
Gant, Douglas W. A53
Gant, Tony A. A37
Gantert, Thomas J. P330
Gantt, Michael P73
Ganz, Peter J. A361
Ganzi, Victor F. A416, P227
Gao, Jinping W304
Gapontsev, Denis E199
Gapontsev, Valentin P. E199
Garafolo, Paulette A407
Garagiola, Joe Jr. P295
Garanzini, Michael J. P289
Garber, Stefan W112
Garceau, Mary L. A152
Garcia, Angel L. A37
Garcia, Anthony M. P226
Garcia, Art A. A720
Garcia, Carlos M. A254
Garcia, Claudio W162
Garcia, David E311
Garcia, Edwin A488
Garcia, Elisa D. A626

Garcia, Guillermo R. E194
Garcia, John A. A773
García, Jorge Segrelles W269
Garcia, Jose M. E102
Garcia, Lillian D. A839
Garcia, Linda P415
Garcia, Lorisse P367
Garcia, Michael R. E290
Garcia, Ray P402
Garcia, Robert E331
Garcia C., Elisa D. A289
García Meyer-Dohner, José M. W65
García Naranjo, Guillermo P270, W183
Garcia Sanz, Francisco Javier W357
Garcia-Hill, Leny J. A352
Garcia-Ovies, Ramiro Sanchez de Lerin W327
Gard, Greg E. P387
Garde, Rashmi E366
Gardet, Michel W235
Gardi, Paul A441
Gardies, Philippe W365
Gardiner, Bill A490
Garding, Edward P186
Gardner, Brian (D.R. Horton) A294
Gardner, Brian E. (Hallmark) A400, P220
Gardner, Chester S. P499
Gardner, David P. A316
Gardner, Dawn E270
Gardner, H. McIntyre A569
Gardner, John P195
Gardner, Julie A496
Gardner, Marilyn A133
Gardner, Max L. P248
Gardner, Roy A. W100
Gardner, Simon A409
Gardner, Stephen (Credit Suisse) W103
Gardner, Steven R. (Pacific Premier) E262
Gardner, Thomas D. (Reader's Digest) P401
Gardner, Thomas R. (Allegheny Energy) A58
Gardner, Timothy S. W103
Gardynik, John A527
Garfinkel, Jodie R. A758, P442
Garg, Neeraj E134
Gargano, Charles A. P389
Gargaro, Eugene A. Jr. A548
Gargaro, Salvatore E66
Garguilo, William R. Jr. E140
Garland, Greg C. P121
Garland, Jerry P61
Garland, Karla P30
Garland, Kim A723
Garland, Linda B. E102
Garland, Trish P179
Garlinghouse, Brad A922
Garman, M. Lawrence P150
Garman, Scott P173
Garner, David E. P441
Garner, John E62
Garner, Karen P463
Garnero, Patrick P465
Garnett, Wes E289
Garnick, Robert L. A377
Garnier, Jean-Pierre W143
Garnier, Thierry W89
Garofalo, Donald L. P49
Garrabrants, Gregory E61
Garrambone, Peter L. Jr. P406
Garrard, V. Jane A839
Garraux, James D. A851
Garren, Ruth P307
Garrett, Caroline A262
Garrett, J. Patrick E93
Garrett, Joseph K. P297
Garrett, Kenneth R. A354
Garrett, Mark (McKinsey & Company) P308
Garrett, Mark S. (Adobe) A38
Garrett, Melanie P75
Garrett, Michael D. A767
Garrett, Robert (Penn Virginia) E268

Garrett, Robert K. (Sun American Bancorp) E327
Garrett, Scott A135
Garrett, Thomas A. (Triarc) A835
Garrett, Tom (Brasfield & Gorrie) P97
Garrick, Ronald W144
Garrison, Carol Z. P497
Garrison, David A. E36
Garrison, J. Daniel A749
Garrison, Robert K. A326
Garrison, Wayne A467
Garrity, James A879
Garrity, Laurine M. A796
Garrity, Thomas J. E85
Garrow, Daniel W. P325
Garson, Gary W. A526
Garthwaite, Thomas L. P113
Gartland, Thomas M. P256
Gartman, John A. A423
Garton, Daniel P. A86
Gartshore, H. Anthony E145
Gartzke, David G. P23
Garvett, Donald S. A54
Garvey, Michelle A885
Garvey, William P. E284
Garvin, Martin J. A272
Garwood, Amber P354
Garwood, Mark E132
Garwood, Stephen C. E138
Gary, Christian W23
Gary, Sally D. E234
Garza, Debra B. A881
Garza, Sam P147
Gase, Matthew P17
Gaska, Carrie A347
Gasparovic, John J. A157
Gaspin, Jeff A594, P341
Gasquet, Denis W352
Gass, John D. A207
Gass, Michelle A777
Gasser, Michael J. A398
Gasser, Robert C. E197
Gast, Steven D. A924
Gaster, R. Scott P35
Gastfriend, David R. E22
Gaston, Dwight E59
Gaston, Michael D. E79
Gaston, Steve P439
Gatanas, Harry D E309
Gatch, Christopher C. E80
Gately, James H. A868, P513
Gates, Jamie P482
Gates, Marshall M. A254
Gates, Melinda F. P83
Gates, R. Jordan A336
Gates, Stephen F. A238
Gates, William H. III (Microsoft, Bill & Melinda Gates Foundation, Corbis) A574, P83, P139
Gates, William H. Sr. (Bill & Melinda Gates Foundation) P83
Gatfield, Stephen J. A458
Gathers, Patricia P113
Gatling, James Michael A129
Gats, Michael P145
Gatta, Lawrence J. Jr. A527
Gatta, Louis A. P357
Gattai, Bruno P158
Gatti, Rosa P178
Gattinella, Wayne T. E371
Gatto, Christopher S. P508
Gatto, Domenic P64
Gatto, Michele S. P338
Gatzke, Carla S. E110
Gaub, Janice E308
Gaube, Frank W254
Gaudino, Alberto W36
Gaudiosi, Monica M. A768
Gaufin, Shirley P85
Gaughan, Tony E284
Gaul, Hans Michael W126
Gauld, William B. A448
Gault, Polly L. A312
Gaunt, Ian J. A187
Gaut, C. Christopher A399

Green, Steven (Hobby Lobby) P234
Green, Steven J. (Pitney Bowes) A666
Green, William D. A35
Greenberg, Alan C. A132
Greenberg, David I. A66
Greenberg, Hinda F. P412
Greenberg, Lon R. A81, A843
Greenberg, Mark S. W175
Greenblatt, Jason A838, P488
Greene, Alan (A.D.A.M.) E18
Greene, Alan D. (State Street) A782
Greene, Charles J. A405
Greene, Dale E. A233
Greene, David A. (University of Chicago) P498
Greene, David M. (Dreams, Inc.) E120
Greene, Diane B. A320, E366
Greene, Edward A. A192
Greene, Ellen P420
Greene, Gregory F. A720
Greene, Harold P191
Greene, Jeff (Invensys) W166
Greene, Jeffrey M. (Consolidated Container) P134
Greene, Jesse J. Jr. A453
Greene, Melissa P520
Greene, Richard S. A277
Greene, Robert E. A131
Greene, Ronald G. E115
Greene, Stephen S. A863
Greener, Charles V. A341
Greenfield, David W. A485
Greenfield, Moray P20
Greenhill, Robert F. E168
Greenlee, Al P89
Greenlee, David P80
Greenley, Mark A. E281
Greenman, Jason E223
Greenough, Linda W. E97
Greenstein, Ira A. A442
Greenwald, Jerry P173
Greenwell, Claire P40
Greenwell, Daniel D. A809
Greenwood, Bruce A. A253
Greenwood, Don P103
Greenwood, James M. P133
Greenwood, Loren A409
Greer, Demetrius P375
Greer, G. Bruce Jr. A629
Greer, Mar-D P197
Greer, Raymond B. P213
Gregg, Kirk P. A251
Gregg, Mary Hall A693
Gregg, Peter W261
Gregoire, Daniel N. A536
Gregoire, Eric P95
Gregory, Gary L. E244
Gregory, Gerard E120
Gregory, James P337
Gregory, Joseph M. A509
Gregory, Michael J. A585
Gregory, Robert B. E144
Gregson, Terry P337
Greifeld, Robert A587
Greig, Andy P77
Greig, Jeff P103
Grein, Thomas W. A319
Greiner, Bob P79
Greiner, Fred R. P181
Greiner, Helen E200
Greiner, Mark T. A783
Greisch, John J. A129
Greiter, Karl L. II E26
Grendys, Joseph C. P266
Grenner, Lawrence P246
Grenolds, Richard L. P297
Gress, Felix W61
Gress, Robin Roy P241
Gress, William J. A171
Gressett, Scott E. E228
Gretenhart, Keith P191
Grether, John M. P462
Gretlein, Raymond C. P450
Grette, Paul G. E325
Gretton, Linda E333

Gretzema, Chad P355
Gretzky, Wayne P383
Greub, Linda M. A100
Greubel, Richard A. Jr. A579, A840
Greving, Robert C. A857
Grevious, Jarvio A. A178, P106
Grewcock, Bruce E. A655, P382
Grewe, Wolfgang P156
Grey, Chris P174
Grey, Robert J. A673
Grey, Robin A512
Grezo, Charlotte W356
Gri, Françoise A539
Grider, D. Lynn W321
Grief, Gary P474
Grier, Anne A288
Grier, Mark B. A686
Grier, Robin A. A792
Griesbach, Staci W311
Grieshaber, Joseph A. Jr. A500
Grieve, Tom W. A497
Griffin, Brian T. A564
Griffin, David E285
Griffin, Denise C. E144
Griffin, J. Timothy A616
Griffin, Jim A443, P240
Griffin, John Q. P335
Griffin, Joseph L. E180
Griffin, Kristy P430
Griffin, Marshall W. E311
Griffin, R. J. Jr. P251
Griffin, Robert G. A507
Griffin, Scot A. E337
Griffin, Thomas J. A848
Griffin, Tricia P116
Griffith, Dennis M. E76
Griffith, G. Sanders III A791, A829
Griffith, Geoffrey L. A37
Griffith, James W. A823
Griffith, Maxine P131
Griffith, Ray A. A36, P21
Griffith, Susan Patricia A683
Griffith, Terry P311
Griffith, Timothy P138
Griffith-Jones, John A497, P270, W183
Griffiths, Andrew M. A350
Griffiths, Gary P173
Griffiths, Jill A43
Griffiths, Sheena E161
Griffiths, William C. A201
Griffon, Lester J. Jr. P490
Grifonetti, John A796
Grigaliunas, Ben P27
Grigg, Christopher W59
Grigg, Richard R. A348
Griggs, Douglas E362
Griggs, Kathleen M. E203
Griggs, Steve P324
Grigioni, Carlo W347
Grignon, Perianne A746
Grigsby, Frederick J. Jr. A312
Grigsby, Jennifer M. A206
Grijalva, Ernesto E277
Grilk, Thomas S. E67
Grill, John P536
Grill, Michael E87
Grillet, Robert J. A457
Grillo, Jeffrey A. A538
Grimà, Joan-David W290
Grimes, Bruce E221
Grimes, David W. E156
Grimes, F. Virginia E76
Grimes, James E. E267
Grimes, Jonathan D. P469
Grimes, Suzanne P401
Grimestad, Dwight E. A106
Grimme, Paul E. A368
Grimmelikhuizen, Paul W32
Grimmer, Ralph P327
Grimmett, Gail A276
Grimshaw, Eric A632
Grimshaw, Stuart I. W99
Grinnell, Charles W. E153
Grinney, Jay A415
Grinrød, Mads W312

Grinstead, Dan P327
Grinstein, Gerald A276
Grinstein, Keith D. E95
Grinsteiner, Dennis E148
Griot, Denis A368
Grippo, Michael J. A427
Grisé, Cheryl W. A612
Grisham, Arnold E373
Grisoni-Bachelier, Nicole W285
Grissinger, Dick P452
Griswell, J. Barry A680
Griswold, Scott A. A286, P162
Gritton, Susan P242
Gritzmahn, Ulli W26
Grizzle, Charles P97
Grizzle, J. David A246
Große-Loheide, Dirk W357
Grob, Kellie P137
Groeneveld, Oscar Y. L. W271
Groff, Dave P383
Groh, François W343
Groll, Tony P206
Grollier, Jean-François W198
Groman, Sandra L. P435
Gromek, Joseph R. A885
Gronbach, Tyler A696
Gronda, John D. A405
Grondin, Tom M. P. W27
Gronfein, Hal P272
Gronksi, Claudette M. P158
Groobey, Carolyn A341
Groom, Gary L. A817
Groom, Jeff P416
Groomes, David P395
Grooms, Sharon P236
Groppi, George E212
Groscost, Dan P31
Grose, Douglas A40
Grose, Steven L. E287
Gross, Alan A296
Gross, Arthur P231
Gross, Bruce E. A510
Gross, Edmund S. P145
Gross, Lawrence A. A492
Gross, Lynne A896
Gross, Marc W146
Gross, Peter W317
Gross, Sanford M. E118
Gross, Siegfried A48
Gross, Thomas S. A307
Grosse, Paul E281
Grossenbacher, John J. P74
Grossett, James M. W28
Grossman, Blake R. W59
Grossman, David P507
Grossman, Edward E205
Grossman, Jeffrey W. A607
Grossman, Kevin L. E178
Grossman, Marc A. A429
Grossman, Mindy F. A441
Grossman, Paul D. A100
Grossman, Robert E158
Grosvenor, Gilbert M. P335
Grotbeck, Eugene P289
Grote, Byron E. W75
Groth, Edward P136
Grothues, Timothy E198
Grotto, Daniel P. P527
Grove, Janet E. A534
Grover, Fredrick W. A72
Grover, Steven F. A172
Growcock, Terry D. A536
Grubb, Matthew K. E300
Grubb, Richard N. A875
Grubbs, Robert W. Jr. A91
Grube, Craig A. E275
Grube, John P. A613
Grube, Rüdiger W106
Gruber, Steven B. E136
Gruberg, Amy P315
Grubman, Eric P. P334
Gruen, Frank P217
Gruen, Robert P. A156
Grueneich, Lynn P468
Gruener, Jeffery A746

Grüger, Günther W67
Gruhn, Jerzy W237
Grumbacher, M. Thomas A155
Grumski, J.T. A727
Grundhofer, Jerry A. A860
Grundke, Manfred W272
Grundy, Leslie A821
Grunstein, Leonard P424
Gruosso, Gerard P18
Grupinski, Raymond S. P360
Grupp, Robert W. A199
Grups, John M. A764
Gruzen, Alexander A272
Gryska, David W. E82
Grzelak, David W. W181
Grzybowski, Edward J. A818, P476
Guarascio, Phil P334
Guariglia, Richard P425
Guarino, Gilbert B. A176
Guarino, Ludwig M. A876
Guarrero, Elaine P327
Guay, Phill P130
Gubanich, Kathleen C. A868, P513
Gubert, Walter A. A479
Gudbranson, Robert K. A520
Gude, Atish A773
Gudenas, Mark P464
Guedry, Donald J. Jr. E169
Guennewig, Victoria B. A249
Guennouni, Tajeddine W50
Guenther, Cynthia S. A117
Guenthner, Kevin P186
Guerber, Jacques W117
Guerin, Ray P409
Guerini, Bernard A50
Guerini, L. Renato A497, P270, W183
Guernsey, David M. E365
Guerra, R. David E194
Guest, James A. (Consumers Union) P136
Guest, Jim (84 Lumber) P16
Guest, Walter R. P306
Guge, Brett P104
Guglielmo, Frank A458
Gugliermina, Pierre W45
Guice, Ann F. E270
Guidara, Frank W. P508
Guidi, Patricia E315
Guido, Jeffry P516
Guidoni-Tarissi, Bernard-Franck W117
Guidroz, Stan P249
Guifarro, Jan A231
Guiffre, Craig A214
Guilbaud, Jean-Jacques W343
Guild, Howard A738
Guiles, Edwin A. A747
Guilhou, Eric W49
Guillard, Stephen L. A538
Guillaumin, Caroline W34
Guillebeau, David C. E98
Guillemin, Jean-François W74
Guillermo, Tessie P116
Guimarães, Alberto W245
Guimarães, Marcus Vinicius W245
Guindani, Pietro W356
Guinn, Patricia L. P480
Guion, Kathleen R. P163
Guiony, Jean-Jacques W201
Guise, Sue P525
Guitard, Juan W290
Guitreau, Joseph W. P490
Gulden, Neil P60
Guldig, John F. A110
Guldimann, Till M. P461
Gulizia, Sheryl M. E310
Gullang, Douglas P367
Gulling, Mark V. A562
Gulliver, Stuart T. W155
Gulyas, Diane H. A314
Gum, Barry E. A742
Gum, Randy P117
Gummeson, Göran W359
Günak, Murat W357
Gunby, Steven H. P95
Gundermann, Peter J. E39

Hohmann, James E. A65
Hoiberg, Dale P175
Høiland, Jesper W236
Hoke, P. J. E340
Hoker, Richard A. A732
Holba, Carolyn A706
Holbrook, Karen A. P364
Holbrook, Tom A694
Holcomb, Luther C. E141
Holcombe, Weldon E272
Holden, Arthur E. E189
Holden, Mark A495, P267
Holden, Tim E236
Holdener, Eduard E. W274
Holder, Thomas E. Jr. E106
Holder, William L. Jr. A284
Holderness, Darin G. A664
Holding, R. Earl P440
Holdren, Gary E. E187
Holewinski, Paul P. P159
Holgate, Randy L. P498
Holian, Robert R. P33
Holifield, Mark A433
Holl, David B. P300
Holladay, Mark G. A791
Holland, Alan E71
Holland, Beverly J. P440
Holland, Christopher S. A103, P53
Holland, Cindy E242
Holland, Deborah P395
Holland, Erin P172
Holland, G. Edison Jr. A767
Holland, Gregory D. A584
Holland, J. Bradley W142
Holland, James M. E44
Holland, John A804
Holland, Kevin R. A208
Hollander, Ellie P19
Hollander, Gilbert P. A926
Hollander, Jacob P51
Hollaway, David E280
Holle, Oliver A869
Hollen, Paul D. III E317
Hollenbeck, John M. A347
Holleran, Charles B. A357
Holleran, John W. E202, P91
Hollerbach, Michael D. P445
Hollern, Michael P. P220
Holley, Charles M. Jr. A882
Holley, Jean K. A802
Holley, Jeffrey D. P144
Holley, Rodger B. E146
Holliday, Charles O. Jr. A314
Hollidge, Vernon R. Jr. P149
Hollifield, Matthew V. A530
Holliman, Wilbert G. A369
Hollinger, Mark (Discovery
   Communications) P160
Hollinger, Mark R. (MacDermid) P293
Hollinger, William R. A482
Hollingshead, Kevin P319
Hollingsworth, Richard A. P364
Hollingsworth, Robert E. E321
Hollinrake, David A. P446
Hollis, Chris W201
Hollis, James E. E199
Holloway, Janet M. A579
Holm, Claes P314
Holm, George L. P517
Holman, Bob P159
Holman, Brad L. A694
Holman, Darcy E241
Holman, Gene E50
Holman, William E. E61
Holmes, Beverly A. A549, P303
Holmes, Donald N. P119
Holmes, Frank E. E359
Holmes, Jack A847
Holmes, Tod C. A705
Holmes, Tom P254
Holmes, Walter P247
Holmes, William R. P153
Holmkvist, Lars A100
Holschuh, Laurel A. A897
Holsclaw, Lisa E. A500

Holsenbeck, G. Penn A66
Holstad, Kathy P477
Holstein, Michael P516
Holstein, Steven S. A549, P303
Holsten, Joseph M. E221
Holston, Michael J. A425
Holt, Bradford R. A759
Holt, Jack A. A240
Holt, Paul A. E282
Holt, Peter M. P422
Holt, Thomas E243
Holt, Timothy A. A43
Holt, Victoria M. A672
Holt, Wayne P31
Holt, William M. A452
Holton, Lisa A740
Holtrop, Thomas W199
Holtsberg, Warren A581
Holveck, David P. A473
Holwill, Richard P38
Holyfield, Jeff A226
Holz, Kelli J. E184
Hölzle, Urs A396
Holzwart, Stanley H. P517
Homan, Matt A669
Hombach, Robert J. A129
Homfray, Chris A259
Homler, Robert P284
Homlish, Martin W292
Hommen, Jan H. M. W164, W266,
   W277
Hommer, Carolyn E224
Hommert, Douglas D. P51
Honce, Tom P60
Honda, Haruhisa W86
Honda, Takeshi W92
Honeycutt, John P160
Honeycutt, Milburn E276
Honeyfield, David W. E299
Hong, Jin E257
Hong, Julie A725
Hong, Peter A56
Hong, Simon A98
Hongler, Markus W372
Honickman, Harold A. P235
Honickman, Jeffrey A. P235
Honma, Mitsuru W291
Honnef, William L. E362
Honoway, Rachel E209
Honsawa, Yoshio W46
Hood, Beth B. E248
Hood, Henry J. A206
Hood, Lynn M. A538
Hood, Mark E. A168
Hooda, Sheila A818
Hoogasian, Seth H. A815
Hoogenboom, Jeffery L. A531
Hoogenboom, Paul G. P. A717
Hoogerwerf, Glenn A876
Hooghiemstra, Coen E258
Hooghiemstra, Roland E258
Hooghiemstra, Tjerk W250
Hoogland, Victor E361
Hoogterp, Daniel P. E50
Hook, Lisa A. E245
Hooker, E. Stanton III P321
Hooks, Brian P234
Hooley, Joseph L. A782
Hoon, Je-Jin W286
Hooper, Anthony C. A165
Hooper, John (Weyerhaeuser) A904
Hooper, John E. (National Australia
   Bank) W219
Hooper, Max A51
Hooper, Ned A219
Hooper, Patrick P252
Hooper, Sandy A32
Hooper, Susan (Royal Caribbean
   Cruises) A716
Hooper, Susan L. (United Community
   Banks) E355
Hoopes, Jeffrey C. P464
Hootkin, Pamela N. A660
Hooton, James G. P473
Hoover, Dennis A. A253

Hoover, J. D. P454
Hoover, Joan A98
Hoover, Julie A32
Hoover, Nancy P271
Hoover, R. David A124
Hoover, Ray E346
Hope, Barclay A846
Hope, James D. A793
Hopf, C. Joseph Jr. A673
Hopkey, Andrea P76
Hopkins, Frank A664
Hopkins, Henry H. A794
Hopkins, Lynn M. E141
Hopkins, Paul N. W372
Hopkins, Sally A753
Hopkins, Sandra L. P471
Hopkins, Stephen W175
Hopkins, Thomas E. A754
Hoplamazian, Mark S. A391, P202
Hopp, Anthony J. A458
Hopp, Daniel F. A905
Hoppel, James H. Jr. E88
Hopper, James T. A100
Hopper, Sidney P495
Hopson, Kenneth R. A865
Hopwood, T. A185
Horan, Anthony J. A479
Horan, Carolyn B. E132
Horan, Douglas S. A619
Horcajo Aguirre, Alberto M. W327
Horder-Koop, Robin P38
Horger, Robert R. E302
Hori, Yoshikazu A306
Horn, Alan D. W275
Horn, Andrew P20
Horn, David C. A53
Horn, Kimberly K. P450
Horn, Randall C. A857
Horn, Stephen P169
Hornaday, Bill P526
Hornbeck, Todd M. E185
Hornbuckle, Mertroe B. A270
Hornby, Andy W144
Horncastle, Britt C. P108
Horne, Chuck E251
Horne, Ed P337
Horne, Greg E175
Horne, J. Frank E157
Horne, Skip P275
Horner, Dara Lynn E295
Hornfeck, Daniel D. E76
Horning, Roxanne V. A371
Hornsby, Claude A. S. III W365
Hornung, Karlheinz W204
Horowitz, Alison M. E226
Horowitz, Peter A677, P391, W258
Horowitz, Steven L. E50
Horrell, Tony A477
Horrocks, Michael G. W85
Horsch, James A302
Horta-Osório, António W290
Hortman, Edwin W. Jr. E32
Horton, Bill A702
Horton, Chandler P263
Horton, D. Vernon E260
Horton, Donald R. A294
Horton, Eustace M. P134
Horton, Gary B. A69
Horton, Keith D. E268
Horton, Peter W367
Horton, Rick A294
Horton, Thomas W. A86
Horvath, Albert G. P131
Horvath, Debora M. A889
Horváth, Ferenc W217
Horwitch, Matthew A94
Horwood, Graeme P486
Horzepa, Joseph E. E198
Hosaka, Shigetsutoshi W339
Hoshino, Toshio W176
Hoskins, Gary F. E92
Hoskins, John M. P472
Hoskins, Richard W240
Hoskyn, Thomas C. P409
Hosoi, Hideki A596

Hosokawa, Koichi P264
Hostetter, Jerry A760
Hotarek, Brian W. P84
Hotchkin, Nicholas P. A777
Hotta, Takao W173
Höttges, Timotheus W116
Hotz, Peter (Briggs & Stratton) A161
Hotz, Peter M. (I-trax) E201
Hou, Andy E233
Houël, Patrick W201
Hough, Christine P459
Houghton, Robert P319
Houhanisin, George L. P72
Houk, Keith D. A859
Houlditch, James C. E340
Houle, Patricia S. P96
Hounslow, Simon E97
Houri, Olivier A845
Hourihan, Seamus E17
Hours, Bernard W107
House, Andrew W311
House, Beverly A33
House, David W. E327
House, Garvey E71
House, Roger P387
House, Todd A186
Housego, David P536
Householder, Joseph A. A747
Houseman, Eric C. E289
Housenbold, Jeffrey T. E308
Houser, Mark A. P78
Houssin, Pascal A498
Houston, Frederick W. P508
Houston, J. Wayne A877
Houston, John E334
Hove, Robert C. A270
Hovnanian, Ara K. A437
Hovnanian, Kevork S. A437
Hovsepian, Ronald W. A92, A618
Howald, Beatrice W317
Howard, Bonnie A221
Howard, Christian P287
Howard, D. Wayne (International
   Flavors) A454
Howard, Deborah P214
Howard, Dwain (Texas Capital
   Bancshares) E338
Howard, Frank M. A386
Howard, Graeme A706
Howard, James M. II (C. R. Bard) A256
Howard, James W. (Axsys) E46
Howard, Jeffrey G. A852
Howard, Jerry A540
Howard, John L. (W.W. Grainger) A916
Howard, John V. Jr. (Vertis Inc) P515
Howard, Kay L. A510
Howard, Kevin D. A205
Howard, Lynn E228
Howard, Mark G. P144
Howard, Norman P533
Howard, Tim J. A817
Howard-Allen, Flic W205
Howard-Anderson, Robert L. E252
Howard-Dunn, Eileen A262
Howe, Douglas T. P128
Howe, James E. P75
Howe, Jörg W44
Howe, Keith B. P518
Howe, Paul P406
Howe, Steve W129
Howell, Bruce I. E106
Howell, Charles F. E266
Howell, Dennis A697
Howell, Edward R. P286
Howell, Elizabeth E201
Howell, Eva (Crescent Banking) E106
Howell, Eve (Apache) A96
Howell, J. Mark A162
Howell, James A151
Howell, Janice M. E114
Howell, Jeffrey F. P484
Howell, Joseph M. III A512
Howell, Josh A512
Howell, Mary L. A813
Howells, Jeffery P. A797

A = AMERICAN BUSINESS
E = EMERGING COMPANIES
P = PRIVATE COMPANIES
W = WORLD BUSINESS

Manning, Sylvia P499
Manning, Timothy R. A619
Manning, Wendy P87
Mannino, Daniel P244
Mannion, John A692
Mannix, Kevin A880, P522
Manny, Roger S. E287
Manoogian, Richard A. A548
Manos, Kristen L. A419
Manoushagian, Ralph P. E35
Mansbart, Johannes A375
Mansell, Kevin B. A496
Mansfield, Christopher C. A517, P282
Mansfield, Dean P344
Mansfield, Rick E140
Mansfield, William L. A867
Manske, Susan E. P293
Manson, Sherlyn P380
Mansoor, Leah P175
Mansour, James M. P209
Manspeizer, David A. A917
Mansueto, Joseph E237
Mansur, Bernadette P337
Mante, Charles P236
Mantovani, Massimo W125
Manuel, Mark A. P143
Manupella, Mary T. A586
Manzardo, Claudio W365
Manze, Vince A594
Manzi, Jim P. A815
Manzini, Aldo A571
Manzolillo, Barbara A. P310
Maortua, Jorge W290
Mapes, Chris (Commercial
  Vehicle) E96
Mapes, Christopher L. (A. O.
  Smith) A93
Maples, Ken E180
Maquet, Alain A449
Mara, Chris P347
Mara, John K. P347
Mara, Shaun A908
Marabeti, Dean P207
Maranell, Michael L. P30
Marantette, Thomas M. Jr. P143
Marantz, Alan P. A509
Marasco, Kevin P520
Maraver Sánchez-Valdepeñas,
  Óscar W327
Marbach, Paula J. A138
Marberry, Michael P254
Marcarelli, Dean P117
Marcelissen, Staci L. E253
Marcelle, Dawn P47
Marcello, Richard A845
March, Kevin P. A812
March, Stanley W313
Marchal, Sylvie P257
Marchbank, Robert W365
Marchetti, Michael A316
Marchioli, Nelson J. A278
Marchionne, Sergio W131
Marcial, Edwin D. E192
Marcinelli, James A. P237
Marcinelli, Ronald P. A233
Marcinowski, Stefan W61
Marcogliese, Richard J. A866
Marcos, Ann Takiguchi E86
Marcotte, Gary A114
Marcotte, Michael E75
Marcroft, Darlene E351
Marcucci, Mark A. A692
Marcuccili, J. Brink P489
Marcum, R. Alan A280
Marcus, Bruce D. A559
Marcus, Lawrence P157
Marcus, Richard C. A926
Marcuzzi, Andres P383
Marczak, Kathryn H. A404

Marder, Steven E181
Mardrus, Christian W268
Marek, Mary-Irene A306
Marek, Tracy P117
Marembeaud, Olivier W306
Marengo, Ana P347
Marentette, Charles A144
Maresca, Bob (Bose) P94
Maresca, Robert A. (Metromedia) P316
Maresh, Richard E129
Marett, Michael A. E250
Marey-Semper, Isabel W248
Marfatia, Noshirwan P478
Margetts, Rob J. W191
Margolin, Stephen M. A904
Margolis, John D. P359
Margolis, Lawrence A. E37
Margolis, Michael C. E107
Margolis, Robert E89
Margulis, Bill E217
Margulis, Heidi S. A438
Mariani, Frank P288
Mariani, Kenneth P78
Mariani, Pierre W71
Mariano, Robert A. P417
Mariette, Bernard A694
Marilley, Leanne D. A611
Marin, Lori P. P256
Marinangeli, Daniel A. W341
Marineau, Philip A. E308
Marinelli, Joseph V. P37
Mariner, Jonathan D. P295
Marini, Alex P. P250
Marini-Mir, Luis A. P485
Marinko, Mark P483
Marino, Anthony S. A510
Marino, Frederick M. P393
Marino, John E47
Marino, Robert A. P235
Marino, Robin A546
Marino, V. James A55
Marino, Wayne A. E354
Marino, William J. P235
Marino D'Arienzo, Annette P90
Marinos, E. P. E36
Mariola, Melissa E209
Marion-Bouchacourt, Anne W306
Maritz, W. Stephen P296
Mark, Reuben A231
Mark, William P453
Markel, Anthony F. A540
Markel, Steven A. A540
Markels, Michael Jr. E363
Marker, Andy P474
Markert, Norbert P251
Markey, Edward W. A394
Markfield, Roger S. A72
Markham, Grant E373
Markham, Jackie P518
Markley, H. J. A270
Markley, William C. III A465
Markmann, Melanie W333
Markovich, Paul P90
Markowitz, Michael E264
Marks, Ann A293
Marks, David P144
Marks, Gordon W. P464
Marks, Gretchen J. E95
Marks, Judy F. A525
Marks, Peter W272
Marks, Rebecca P514
Marks, Terrance M. A230
Markus, John A415
Markus, Julie E41
Marlett, Wendy A482
Marley, Brian T. P79
Marlow, Carol A187
Marmer, Lynn A500
Marohn, William D. A601
Maroney, Sean E345
Maroni, Alice Collier P445
Maroone, Michael E. A114
Maropis, Colin N. E376
Marosits, Joseph E. A263
Marotta, Daniel A. A167

Marotta, Dean L. A927
Marquez, Timothy E362
Marquie, Serge W113
Marr, Ann W. P536
Marra, Thomas M. A406
Marrazzo, Nancy A. A437
Marren, Elizabeth T. A865
Marrero, Jose E. A115
Marrett, Cora B. P506
Marrett, Phillip E. P44
Marrinan, Susan F. A763
Marriott, Daniel C. A441
Marriott, J. W. Jr. A542
Marriott, John W. III A542
Marrone, Virgilio W167
Mars, Dale W. E184
Mars, John Franklyn A543, P299
Mars, Paul A324
Mars, Thomas A. A882
Marsan, Richard J. Jr. A146
Marschke, Brett E121
Marsden, Bill P157
Marsden, George P169
Marsden, Robert A. E51
Marsh, Brenda A128
Marsh, Carol W. E74
Marsh, Jim W82
Marsh, Kevin B. A735
Marsh, Richard H. A348
Marsh, Stephen P. E130
Marshall, Barbara W. E54
Marshall, Brian E184
Marshall, Bruce P127
Marshall, Charles N. E158
Marshall, Christopher G. A345
Marshall, Fran P335
Marshall, Geoffrey A185
Marshall, Jan A769
Marshall, Jane W170
Marshall, John L. III (MPS) A584
Marshall, Jonathan (Bechtel) P77
Marshall, Kenneth P29, P192
Marshall, Phillip K. E294
Marshall, Richard N. A768
Marshall, Robert B. A89
Marshall, Siri S. A383
Marshall, Steven A. P151
Marshi, Marwan W113
Marsiello, Lawrence A. A220
Marsland, John W. A50
Marsocci, Robert A. A285
Marston, James G. III E164
Martegani, Franco W250
Martel, Roger W262
Martel, Roland M. A445
Martell, Kenneth R. P356
Martens, Carol Lynn P17
Martens, Jim A895
Martens, Philip R. A108
Martens, Robert E. A895
Marterer, Gerald C. P55
Martin, Amanda P355
Martin, Andrew (Compass
  Group) W100
Martin, Andrew (Protective Life) A684
Martin, Bernadette P76
Martin, Brian M. A492
Martin, Bruce A626
Martin, Burt M. A895
Martin, Carolyn A. P140
Martin, Charles N. Jr. P514
Martin, Christopher J. P489
Martin, Craig L. A465
Martin, D. Pruitt P372
Martin, Darla E227
Martin, Dave P86
Martin, Dezora M. A611
Martin, Donna K. A70
Martin, Doug P492
Martin, Edward C. (Valley
  Financial) E360
Martin, Edward L. (Atheros) E40
Martin, Edward N. (Green Bay
  Packers) A397
Martin, Felix W107

Martin, Frank A. E201
Martin, Gary L. E73, E177
Martin, Gemma W109
Martin, George P. P354
Martin, Greg T. E61
Martin, Harry P272
Martin, J. Chandler A126
Martin, Jana M. P471
Martin, Jay (CyberSource) E109
Martin, Jay G. (Baker Hughes) A123
Martin, Jennifer H. P475
Martin, John C. (Big Lots) A146
Martin, John C. (Gilead Sciences) A388
Martin, Joseph R. E67
Martin, Lauralee E. A477
Martin, Lois M. E71
Martin, Mark (Fellowes) P184
Martin, Mark A. (Swift
  Transportation) P464
Martin, Marshall G. (First State
  Bancorporation) E147
Martin, Maureen E167
Martin, Melvin W. P247
Martin, Michael A. (Constellation
  Brands) A243
Martin, Michael D. (Pilgrim's
  Pride) A662
Martin, Murray D. A665
Martin, Patricia A. E109
Martin, Paul C. (Darwin Professional
  Underwriters) E111
Martin, Paul E. (Perficient) E271
Martin, Peggy Ann P114
Martin, Raymond A. E102
Martin, Richard J. P492
Martin, Robert V. E134
Martin, Rodney J. (Whataburger) P528
Martin, Rodney O. Jr. (AIG) A78
Martin, Roger W353
Martin, Roy M. Jr. W335
Martin, Ruben S. III E227
Martin, Scott D. E227
Martin, Stanley J. D. A366
Martin, Sue Ann A609
Martin, Tevis E320
Martin, Thomas D. (PriceSmart) E277
Martin, Thomas P. (Royal Caribbean
  Cruises) A716
Martin, Thomas R. (ITT Corp.) A462
Martin, Tom (knight inc) P266
Martin, William E. (Zions
  Bancorporation) A927
Martin, Willie C. (DuPont) A314
Martincich, Carl P288
Martiné, Kate P489
Martineau, Jean P129
Martinella, Jacques E309
Martinelli, Andrea F. W209
Martinelli, Dominic E284
Martinetto, Joseph A202
Martinez, Alberto R. P466
Martinez, Angel R. E114
Martinez, Arthur C. W22
Martinez, Dalia F. E194
Martinez, Erwin V. E132
Martínez, Georgina Kessel W247
Martínez, Josep M. A379
Martinez, Martha P104
Martinez, Mitch P157
Martinez, R. Eric Jr. A723
Martinez, Randy J. P535
Martinez, Rich A741
Martínez, Robert E. A611
Martinez Saiz, Juan Carlos W31
Martinez San Martin, Miguel W269
Martínez-Caro, Diego W326
Martin-Flickinger, Gerri A38
Martini, Jeffrey R. P458
Martinides, R. Douglas A103
Martins, Alex P367
Martins, Tito Botelho Jr. W350
Martling, Len P526
Marton, Steven G. A601
Martone, S. Michael A113
Martorana, Adrian W134

A = AMERICAN BUSINESS
E = EMERGING COMPANIES
P = PRIVATE COMPANIES
W = WORLD BUSINESS

Mirbagheri, Mike A432
Mirchandani, Sanjay A321
Mirchin, Matthew C. E354
Mirdamadi, Susan L. A278
Mirzayantz, Nicolas A454
Mischell, Thomas E. A76
Mischler, Elaine H. A349
Misener, Paul A67
Misenhimer, Holly P103
Misericordia, Lynne M. P384
Mish, J. Vincent E235
Misheff, Michael A245
Mishek, Pete P30
Mishkin, Sandy P117
Miskimins, Lisa J. P290
Misner, Jeffrey A. A246
Misra, Alka E136
Missano, Anthony J. P425
Missett, Judi Sheppard P250
Missett, Kathy P250
Missey, Jennifer E185
Mitachi, Takashi P95
Mitarai, Fujio W86
Mitau, Lee R. A860
Mitcham, Billy F. Jr. E236
Mitchell, Clarence D. P363
Mitchell, Dan P444
Mitchell, Dick P410
Mitchell, George P147
Mitchell, Gregg P201
Mitchell, H. Thomas P101
Mitchell, J. Barry A334
Mitchell, James G. (Steelcase) A783
Mitchell, James P. (Swift Energy) E330
Mitchell, Jim (Corbis) P139
Mitchell, Joanne P252
Mitchell, John (Pep Boys) A647
Mitchell, John R. (Panda Restaurant Group) P373
Mitchell, John W. (Aavid) P19
Mitchell, Max H. A257
Mitchell, Michael A208
Mitchell, Patrick A908
Mitchell, Paul P143
Mitchell, Roger N. A632
Mitchell, Samuel J. Jr. A110
Mitchell, Scott P. E209
Mitchell, Thomas H. (Dollar General) P163
Mitchell, Thomas L. (Noble) A609
Mitchell, Tony P27
Mitchell, William E. A107
Mitsch, George P492
Mitscherlich, Matthias W204
Mitsuda, Minoru W208
Mitsuhashi, Yasuo W86
Mitsunaga, Hiroshi W212
Mittag, Andrew K. W28
Mittal, Lakshmi N. W45
Mittal, Vinay E136
Mittelstadt, Alison A332
Mittler, Gilbert W134
Miura, Satoshi W228
Miura, Zenji W270
Miwa, Sal E18
Mix, James P. A745
Mixon, Peter H. A178, P106
Mixon, William C. P509
Miyake, Senji W178
Miyamoto, Masao W213
Miyamoto, Seiki W226
Miyamoto, Shigeru W224
Miyashita, Masao W239
Miyazaki, Shunichi W215
Miyazawa, Kaname W297
Miyoshi, Takashi W149
Mize, Mark J. E272
Mizell, Steven C. A579
Mizell, Will P521

Mizokuchi, Makoto W339
Mizuno, Ichiro W213
Mizuno, Toshihide W214
Mizuochi, Shoji W76
Mizushima, Shigeaki W298
Mizutani, Katsumi W337
Mlotek, Mark E. A417
Moad, Martin O. A697
Moag, Anthony P530
Moake, James P238
Moayyad, Shirin E267
Moberg, Karin W330
Moberg, Lars-Göran W359
Mobius, Painer W35
Mobley, Jeffrey L. A206
Mobley, Stacey A. A526
Mobriant, Joanne W. E256
Mobsby, Timothy P. A483
Moch, Carmen A795
Mochizuki, Eiji W316
Mock, Danny A397, P214
Mock, Thomas E90
Moder, Robyn E380
Modi, David A80
Modi, Pradeep P386
Modise, Jeanett W240
Modjtabai, Avid A897
Modrzynski, Chris P345
Mody, Apurva S. A271
Moehle, Mary Jo A205
Moellenhoff, David E299
Moeller, Eric A866
Moeller, Jeff P287
Moeller, Joseph W. A495, P267
Moeller, Kate W96
Moeller, Pam A139
Moeller, Tom A908
Moeller, William E. A855
Moen, Timothy P. A613
Moens, Dirk W162
Moerdyk, Carol B. A627
Moerk, Hallstein W230
Moffat, Brian W155
Moffat, Robert W. Jr. A453
Moffatt, David W332
Moffatt, Donald E. W275
Moffett, James R. A367
Mog, Steve P49
Mogel, Ronald D. E253
Moghadam, Hossein M. A903
Moglia, Joseph H. A796
Mogren, Håkan W48
Mogulescu, John P126
Mohamed, Datuk Syed Tamin Syed W302
Mohamed, Nadir H. W275
Mohan, Alok E286
Mohan, J. Patrick W321
Mohapatra, Surya N. A693
Mohin, Samir E279
Mohler, David W. A299
Mohler, Hugh W. E53
Mohler, Lucy E53
Mohler, Max P533
Mohn, Johannes W67
Mohn, Liz W67
Mohn, Reinhard W67
Mohney, Ralph W. Jr. A857
Mohr, James G. P318
Mohr, Marshall L. E196
Mohr, Ronnie A502, P273
Moine, Véronique W295
Mok, Barry C. T. W153
Mok, Wilbur W. A50
Moksnes, Mark A. P154
Mola-Davis, Fernando P414
Molay, Hilary A926
Molendorp, Dayton H. P44
Moler, Elizabeth Ann A334
Moler, Spencer C. A538
Moles Valenzuela, José W326
Molina, Geof P294
Molinaro, Samuel L. Jr. A132
Molinaroli, Alex A. A474
Moline, Jennifer A626

Molinié, Arnaud W190
Molinini, Michael L. A51
Moll, Curtis E. P328
Moll, Magdalena W61
Moll, Theodore S. P328
Mollen, John T. A321
Mollenkopf, John C. E227
Möller, Peter W294
Mollering, Matt P180
Mollien, Jerry W. A548
Molnar, Attila W62
Molnár, József W217
Molohon, Richard A. E226
Moloney, Chris X. P431
Moloney, Daniel M. A581
Molson, Eric H. A577
Momeyer, Alan A526
Mon, Antonio B. A798
Mon, Hector A159
Monaghan, Carey M. A81
Monagle, Ed A740
Monahan, Bonnie M. P169
Monahan, Michael A665
Monahan, Thomas L. III E104
Moncrief, Herman E222
Mondello, Mark T. A463
Mondics, Ben J. A100
Mondragón, Manuel A745
Mondragón Alarcón, Javier W328
Mondschein, Warren H. E99
Monet, Laurent W71
Monette, Scott A698
Monetti, Marta P390
Money, David R. P186
Money, Marti P487
Monferino, Paolo W131
Monfried, David M. A723
Monheit, Barry M. E314
Monico, Timmy D. E191
Monié, Alain A449
Monitto, Vincent P350
Monk, John H. Jr. E98
Monko, Cezary P178
Monnet, Beverly C. A632
Monney, Janelle S. A368
Monribot, Joël A482
Monroe, Bryan P256
Monroe, James III E163
Monroe, Joseph M. A810
Monroe, Michael J. A487
Monroe, Paul P148
Monroe, Thad A369
Monser, Edward L. A323
Montaglione, Christopher J. P297
Montagna, Julia P254
Montagner, Philippe W74
Montague, Christopher A. W341
Montague, William P. P297
Montanaro, Carl L. P189
Monte, Paul A. E163
Monteiro, Chris A551
Monteiro, Frank J. P293
Monteiro de Castro, Antonio W78
Monteith, Timothy J. A548
Montemore, Mitzi P470
Montemurro, Federico E301
Montero, Ernesto Rios W247
Montero, Sylvia M. A657
Montero-Luque, Carlos A618
Monterossi, Gina P252
Montes Pérez, Eduardo W301
Montgomery, A. Bruce A388
Montgomery, Dan T. P127
Montgomery, Dirk A. P368
Montgomery, Lloyd L. III E146
Montgomery, R. Lawrence A496
Montgomery, Robert G. P84
Montgomery, Robin A735
Montgomery, W. Swope Jr. E60
Montgomery-Talley, La June P533
Monti, Kathleen P. E145
Monticelli, Dennis A592
Monticelli, S. Mark A176
Montie, Jeffrey W. A483
Montreuil, Charles P110

Montulli, Lou E308
Monty, Richard L. P232
Mood, Francis P. Jr. A735
Moody, Barry E273
Moody, Brent P29, P192
Moody, David A98
Moody, Debra A151
Moody, Dennis P. A536
Moody, Howard W280
Moody, Michael E150
Moody, Richard F. A668
Moody-Stuart, Mark W41
Moomjian, Cary A. Jr. A324
Moon, Christine E212
Moon, Craig A. A371
Moon, Dale F. A684
Moon, David W. A511
Moon, Harry K. E48
Moon, Marian J. A280
Mooney, Beth E. A487
Mooney, John P223
Mooney, Ken P75
Mooney, Michael M. E78
Mooney, Stephen M. A804
Moonves, Leslie A193
Moor, Deborah W193
Moor, Kristian P. A78
Moor, Rob P324
Moore, A. Bruce Jr. A411
Moore, Allan A335
Moore, Andrew W205
Moore, Ann S. A822
Moore, Ben A144
Moore, Bob (Freeman Decorating Services) P193
Moore, Brian A821
Moore, C. Bradley P359
Moore, Cheryl R. A652
Moore, Christopher P. P458
Moore, Colin A779
Moore, D. C. A856
Moore, Diane E27
Moore, Donald L. Jr. A625
Moore, E. Kevin A736
Moore, George C. (RBS Global) P400
Moore, George E. (Temple University) P471
Moore, Gordon E. A452
Moore, Ian (Momentive Performance Materials) P326
Moore, Ian (News Corp.) A604
Moore, Jackson W. (Regions Financial) A702
Moore, James Brock III (Adams Resources) A37
Moore, Jim (Guardian Industries) P215
Moore, John II (ABM Industries) A34
Moore, Joseph D. P514
Moore, Kevin P. P415
Moore, Kirk P366
Moore, Lori W237
Moore, Lynn E91
Moore, Maureen P184
Moore, Michael (Capital Bank) E72
Moore, Michael (MGM) P315
Moore, Michael G. (Gulfport Energy) E171
Moore, Milton E. A366
Moore, Morris L. A708
Moore, Nathan P. P300
Moore, Patrick J. A762
Moore, Paul E50
Moore, Peter A316
Moore, Randy E46
Moore, Richard (Dillard's) A284
Moore, Rick E. (Gould Paper) P207
Moore, Robert J. (ABN AMRO) W22
Moore, Robert R. (Whataburger) P528
Moore, Ronald L. P500
Moore, Rosemary A842
Moore, Sam P474
Moore, Steve (HealthStream) E175
Moore, Steven B. (Texas A&M) P473
Moore, Terrill R. P186
Moore, Thomas M. P462

Moore, Tim (Plains All American Pipeline) A667
Moore, Timothy L. (Genentech) A377
Moore, William B. (Westar Energy) A902
Moore, William F. (Red Cross) P404
Moores, Peter A699
Moorkamp, Mary P428
Moorman, Charles W. IV A611
Moos, Walter H. P453
Moosally, Fred P. A525
Moose, James A. P466
Mooy, Tom P277
Moquin, Patrick J. P270
Mora, Elizabeth P222
Mora, Tricia E27
Mora, Vivian L. P236
Morales, Colin E196
Morales, Jeff P373
Morales, Vince A672
Morales Gil, Carlos A. W247
Morales-Tirado, Roberto O. P485
Moran, Allison P398
Moran, Charles E. Jr. P155
Moran, David C. A430
Moran, Eileen A. A687
Moran, Janice P31
Moran, John J. E247
Moran, Joseph A662
Moran, Mark J. A246
Moran, Michael P. E25
Moran, Montgomery F. E90
Moran, Paul A627
Moran, Robert F. A656
Moran, Thomas J. P328
Moran, Victor R. E330
Moran, Wally P173
Morander, Jeff P419
Morange, William A. P317
Morant, Sébastien W353
Morante, Tony P352
Morawski, Andrew W332
Mordovskoi, Yuri E56
Morean, William D. A463
Moreau, Emilie W49
Moreau, Jean W211
Moreau, Nicolas W53
Moreci, Stephen F. A158
Morecroft, Michael J. A585
Morefield, Michael T. P390
Morehouse, David P385
Morehouse, Ted P174
Morel, Donald E. Jr. E373
Moreland, Kenneth V. A794
Moreland, Mark H. A228
Morelli, Dan P261
Morena, Christine A. A729
Moreno, Glen W243
Moreno, Jeanne M. A763
Moreno, Manuel M. W287
Moret, Pamela J. P475
Moreton, Christopher J. P388
Moreton, Mary A134, P77
Moretti, Albert V. A660
Moretti, George A762
Moretti, Richard D. P204
Moretz, Lawrence P421
Morey, Daryl P236
Morey, Katie P362
Morgan, Allen B. Jr. A702
Morgan, Andrew W118
Morgan, Bennett J. A669
Morgan, Cristina W47
Morgan, David (Air New Zealand) W30
Morgan, David (Capital Bank) E72
Morgan, David (Euronet) E134
Morgan, David (Stanley Works) A776
Morgan, David H. (Quiksilver) A694
Morgan, David L. (Mayer Electric) P304
Morgan, Donald L. E330
Morgan, Eileen P155
Morgan, Gary P439
Morgan, George D. P509
Morgan, Glenn R. A407

Morgan, James B. (Daktronics) E110
Morgan, James C. (Applied Materials) A102
Morgan, Jeffrey D. A671
Morgan, Jim (Insight Communications) P244
Morgan, Jim (Pennsylvania Lottery) P378
Morgan, John (Legal & General Group) W191
Morgan, John W. (Occidental Petroleum) A624
Morgan, Jon M. (AMEN Properties) E29
Morgan, Marsha K. A173
Morgan, Melody E205
Morgan, Michael D. (Elecsys) E126
Morgan, Michael P. (Raytheon) A700
Morgan, Mike (Sempra Energy) A747
Morgan, Randy N. P449
Morgan, Roger J. E131
Morgan, Stanley J. E224
Morgan, Steven R. A370
Morgan, Tara E209
Morgan, Wayne P204
Morgan-Prager, Karole A554
Morgensen, Jerry L. P231
Morgridge, John P. A219
Mori, Akio W297
Mori, Kosaku W104
Mori, Ryuichi W111
Mori, Simone W123
Mori, Taizo W137
Mori, Yoshihiro W224
Moriarty, Dennis M. A283
Moriarty, Rowland T. E105
Morikis, John G. A754
Morimoto, Mitsuo W37
Morishita, Shunzo W228
Morisie, Debbie P427
Morita, Naoyuki W187
Morita, Tsuneo W216
Moritz, Edward P. A248
Moriyasu, Toshinori W342
Morizono, Hideto W239
Morley, Cheryl P. A579
Morley, Keith R. A895
Morley, Norah P443
Morling, Scott P354
Morlock, Jim P348
Morman, Louise M. P349
Mornet, Joël Luc Albert W91
Moro, Richard D. P465
Moroe, Akiyoshi W86
Morof, Benjamin E259
Moroi, Ken W172
Moroun, Matthew T. E358
Morozumi, Masayuki W297
Morphy, John M. A645
Morra, Marion E. P40
Morrato, Kevin E362
Morreau, Jane C. A169
Morrice, Robert R. E80
Morris, Bret A, A414
Morris, Bruce E205
Morris, Clifton H. Jr. A81
Morris, Cynthia L. P342
Morris, Daniel T. W208
Morris, Darren P370
Morris, Diana P474
Morris, Douglas W355
Morris, George (Northwest Community Healthcare) P357
Morris, George R. (ATP Oil & Gas) E43
Morris, Henry A760
Morris, Holly J. P475
Morris, Iain M. A921
Morris, Jeff P318
Morris, John L. P73
Morris, Kenneth C. (Duke University Health System) P168
Morris, Kenneth R. (Ceradyne) E87
Morris, Les A757
Morris, M. Catherine A107
Morris, Mariam E. E327

Morris, Michael G. A73
Morris, R. Steven P26
Morris, Robert L. A487
Morris, Tracy L. E73
Morrish, David J. A144
Morrison, Alex G. A602
Morrison, Andrew P297
Morrison, Angela W171
Morrison, Bill (Associated Wholesale Grocers) P61
Morrison, Craig O. P232
Morrison, David G. A873
Morrison, Denise M. A179
Morrison, Gary B. E340
Morrison, Gregory B. A255, P142
Morrison, James E. (Kennametal) A485
Morrison, James E. (Teknor Apex) P471
Morrison, Mark (AnnTaylor) A92
Morrison, Mark J. (Hallmark Financial) E171
Morrison, Michael (Davidson Companies) P152
Morrison, Michael L. (ION Geophysical) E199
Morrison, Patricia B. A581
Morrison, Richard P27
Morrison, Scott C. (Ball Corporation) A124
Morrison, Scott D. (Day International) P153
Morrison, Vanessa A362
Morrison, William L. (Northern Trust) A613
Morriss, Frances C. P124
Morris-Tyndall, Lucille P464
Morrow, David A318
Morrow, George J. A84
Morrow, Joseph J. E248
Morrow, Ken (Milan Express Co.) P322
Morrow, Ken (New York Islanders) P348
Morrow, Michael S. A484
Morrow, William A. (Crain Communications) P143
Morrow, William T. (PG&E) A659
Mörsdorf, Wolfram W336
Morse, Arnold D. A176
Morse, David (FARO Technologies) E138
Morse, David J. (Robert Wood Johnson Foundation) P412
Morse, John (Encyclopædia Britannica) P175
Morse, John B. Jr. (Washington Post) A890
Morse, Lawrence J. A777
Morse, Paul E. P48
Morse, Phillip H. P95
Morse, Robert J. P355
Morse, Rosemarie P197
Mortazavi, Diane E258
Mortensen, Eric J. A512
Mortensen, Steve P539
Mortenson, M. A. Jr. P291
Mortenson, Mark A. P291
Mortimer, Mike P397
Morton, C. Hugh P232
Morton, John D. P450
Morton, Margaret L. A612
Morton, Mike P237
Morton, Steven D. P478
Morton, William H. E63
Morway, David P241
Mosbacher, Tim P355
Mosch, James G. A279
Moschella, Frank A639
Moscicki, Richard A. A387
Mosconi, Piero W313
Moseley, Colin P440
Moseley, Ellis P193
Moser, Bobby D. P364
Moser, Richard P. P357
Moser, Sara P27
Moser, Wayne D. A486
Moses, Alan C. W237

Mosey, Ed P92
Mosey, Roger W63
Mosher, Timothy C. A73
Moshiashvili, Shabtai E218
Moshier, Arnold P424
Moskalenko, Anatoly W200
Moskowitz, David K. A310
Moskowitz, Joel P. E87
Moskowitz, Paul A268
Mosonyi, György W217
Moss, Andrew W51
Moss, Derrick E17
Moss, Diane P183
Moss, Douglas P383
Moss, Edward R. P309
Moss, Jay L. A482
Moss, Marcia K. P445
Moss, Patricia L. E78
Moss, Ralph L. A742
Moss, Sara E. A331
Moss, Steve P139
Moss, Susan E. A489
Moss, William J. A29
Mossbeck, Sheri L. A507
Mossé, David I. A835
Mossman, Frances W361
Mosteller, Richard G. A548
Mostrom, Michael P45
Mostyn, William J. III A126
Motafram, Feroze D. E75
Motamed, Thomas F. A211
Motel, George P96
Motenko, Paul A. E58
Mothe, Gérard W256
Motheral, Brenda A337, E176
Motroni, Hector J. A920
Mott, Daniel C. P40
Mott, Randall D. A425
Moty, Patrick J. E48
Motzenbecker, Kenneth C. A582
Mougin, Franck W107
Mouillon, Christian A329, P177, W129
Moullet, Barry B. A266
Moulonguet, Thierry W268
Moulton, Michael E. E132
Moulton, Paul G. A253
Moulton, William J. E343
Mountcastle, Laura L. A226
Mountford, Adrian W171
Mounts, L. David A289
Mouton, Philippe W244
Movens, Daniel H. E75
Moya, Steven O. A438
Moyer, Drew A. E334
Moyer, J. Keith A554
Moyer, Matthew G. A197
Moyers, K. Douglass A186
Moyes, Jerry C. P383, P464
Moylan, James E. Jr. E90
Moynihan, Brian T. A126
Moynihan, Dave A243
Mozdean, Robert R. E260
Mozilo, Angelo R. A254
Mraz, Robert L. P366
Mroczkowski, Marek W253
Mrozek, Ernest J. P435
Mruz, Robert J. P355
Mucci, Martin A645
Mucci, Paul L. P393
Mucha, Zenia A884
Muchnick, Ed P117
Muckian, William M. A375
Mudd, Daniel H. A341
Mudd, John O. P57
Mudge, Robert A871
Mudry, Ronald J. A682
Muehlbauer, James L. A144
Muehlberg, Brent P324
Muehlhaeuser, Hubertus A47
Mueller, Brian A97
Mueller, Cody P306
Mueller, Donald S. A864
Mueller, Edward A. A696, A869
Mueller, Gene W. P386
Mueller, Mark D. E299

Shih, Elizabeth P116
Shikanai, Masatoshi W323
Shilgalis, Joseph A802
Shilling, Jack W. A59
Shilston, Andrew B. W276
Shilts, Steve P148
Shim, Maria A396
Shimada, Tadao W291
Shimazu, Takeshi W178
Shimizu, Koichi W251
Shimizu, Masakazu (Japan
  Tobacco) W174
Shimizu, Masataka (Tokyo
  Electric) W337
Shimizu, Shinobu W172
Shimizu, Yasuaki W168
Shimomitsu, Hidejiro W342
Shimomura, Ryuichi W173
Shin, Hak Cheol A26
Shindler, John E262
Shine, Cathleen A469
Shine, Kenneth I. P504
Shine, Robert J. Jr. E109
Shing, Steve P214
Shingal, Atul P. E312
Shingleton, Jonathan W368
Shinmachi, Toshiyuki W172
Shinn, Chad P345
Shinn, George P345
Shinn, Millie P460
Shinohara, Akira W168
Shinohara, Eisaku W186
Shinozuka, Katsumasa W239
Shinto, Yutaka W308
Shioji, Nobuyo W186
Shiomi, Takao W169
Shipley, Craig P95
Shipley, Zachary K. P369
Shipp, Lawrence A760
Shipway, John F. A380
Shiraishi, Motoatsu W152
Shirakawa, Susumu W337
Shires, Mark F. A667
Shirk, Brent L. E124
Shirk, Gary M. P70
Shirley, Brian A572
Shirley, Edward D. A681
Shirley, Rob A684
Shirtliff, Bryan A709
Shisler, Arden L. A593, P340
Shivers, Robert M. III E43
Shivery, Charles W. A612
Shives, Paula J. A266
Shivinsky, Stephen M. P485
Shkurti, William J. P364
Shmavonian, Nadia P414
Shmuger, Marc P341
Shoaf, N.B. Forrest A192
Shoback, Robert G. A68
Shockro, Dennis P537
Shoemaker, Allen E99
Shoemaker, Rodney A. A91
Shoen, Edward J. A69
Shoen, James P. A69
Shoen, Mark V. A69
Sholkin, Howard P246
Sholtis, Martyn R. E295
Shon, Warren P449
Shonkoff, Fredi P88
Shontere, James G. P253
Shook, Andrew P. E293
Shook, Kevin M. E124
Shoop, Randall A. A612
Shore, Brian K. A909
Shore, Paul A729
Shorland-Ball, Alexandra W197
Shorris, Anthony E. P389
Short, John (Sigma-Aldrich) A755
Short, John H. (RehabCare) E290
Short, Jonathan H.
  (IntercontinentalExchange) E192
Short, Michael J. A114
Short, William S. A704
Shortt, Thomas H. P493
Shoshani, Ziv A875

Shott, Al E105
Shoulak, Judith A. E68
Showalter, Linda G. P464
Showalter, Richard P149
Shoyama, Etsuhiko W149
Shoylekov, Richard W365
Shrader, Patricia B. A137
Shrader, Ralph W. P93
Shrager, Gail M. A322
Shreiner, Jay W. E290
Shriver, Bryce L. A673
Shroads, John P. Jr. E16
Shroder, Robert W. P115
Shroyer, John L. A62
Shuart, David A370
Shubic, Michael T. P249
Shuckhart, Alma R. E341
Shufeldt, R. Charles A787
Shuford, James A. III E302
Shull, Dan A156
Shull, Mark W. P25
Shulman, Becky S. A401
Shulman, Steven J. A536
Shuman, Jeffrey S. A405
Shumway, Jeff P383
Shurney, Dexter E176
Shurtleff, Mark E69
Shusterich, Fred L. A298
Shute, William H. P505
Shuttleworth, William P115
Shutzberg, Larry S. A711
Shyer, Terry L. A281
Siamsiis, Andreas N. W147
Sibigtroth, Scott P310
Sibley, Nigel W365
Sibrel, Lisa E210
Sicard, Daniel W91
Sicilia, Mark E212
Siciliano, Daniel R. A455
Siciliano, Frank E252
Sickels, Linda S. A836
Siclare, Chris A587
Sicree, Joseph R. A826
Siddeek, Mohamed A621
Siddiqui, Ohmar P194
Siddons, Mary Beth A763
Sidel, Steve P160
Sidhu, Inder A219
Sidwell, David H. A580
Siefert, Jan E313
Siegal, Matthew E367
Siegel, Clifford A. A469
Siegel, Frederic S. E30
Siegel, Howard (Cherokee, Inc.) E89
Siegel, Howard M. (American Medical
  Alert) E30
Siegel, Jason P345
Siegel, Jay P. A473
Siegel, Jeffrey E217
Siegel, Kenneth S. A780
Siegel, Stephen B. A191
Siegel, Susan A201
Siegel, Walter E321
Sieger, Marc J. A217
Siegler, Scott P540
Siegmund, Jan A113
Siekierka, Nathan A236
Siemek, Alan G. P342
Siemik, Suzanne C. P133
Sienko, Ray E87
Sieracki, Eric P. A254
Sieron, Mark A. E233
Sievers, Terry P165
Sievert, Barry A268
Sievertsen, Jennifer A504
Sievewright, Mark A349
Siewert, Richard L. A56
Sifferlin, Mark P45
Sifton, Michael W262
Sigafus, Cindy P68
Sigal, Elliott A165
Sigler, Robert E. E358
Signorelli, Ivan A398
Siguier, Bertrand W260
Sih, Chang Loo A175

Sihilling, Calvin S. A588
Sihler, Helmut W254
Sihota, Bhupinder S. A149
Sikka, Vishal W292
Sikora, Scott P514
Silber, Irene E71
Silberman, Mitch A442
Silberman, Robert S. E326
Silbey, Victoria E. P461
Silcock, Raymond P. A865
Siler, Ginni P63
Siliakus, Richard P. A340
Silk, Arthur T. Jr. A148
Silkin, Allen E175
Sillerman, Robert F. X. E92
Silletto, Richard P51
Sills, Stephen J. E111
Silten, Roberta H. A373
Silton, Michael E286
Siluk, Linda M. A92
Silva, Brian A. A683
Silva, D. Gary A386
Silva, Ken A869
Silva, Kevin D. A553
Silva, Roger B. P213
Silva Coutinho, António J. W124
Silva Rosa, Sérgio Ricardo W350
Silveira, Jean E132
Silveira, Kenneth B. E64
Silveira, Mike P425
Silveira, William C. A566
Silver, Adam P332
Silver, Scott P284
Silverman, Barry J. A548
Silverman, Ben A594, P341
Silverman, Bruce A907
Silverman, Burt E250
Silverman, Henry R. P402
Silverman, Jacob E121
Silverman, Jan C. A756
Silverman, Josh A309
Silverman, Kenneth P49
Silverman, Louis E. E282
Silverman, Mark S. P520
Silverman, Nat P107
Silverman, Richard H. P420
Silvers, Laurie S. E181
Silverstein, Larry A. P351
Silverstein, Michael P95
Silverstein, Stanley P. A885
Silvestri, Scott P268
Silvey, Lou P300
Sim, Judith A634
Sim, Wong Hoo W101
Sim Chye Hock, Ron P100
Siman, Leila A780
Simcic, Christian A. A117
Simek, Jeffrey A563
Simes, Stephen M. E57
Simkins, Lawrence R. P523
Simm, Daryl D. A631
Simmer, Thomas L. P89
Simmonds, Malcolm P447
Simmons, Charles H. A165
Simmons, Harris H. A927
Simmons, Irina A321
Simmons, Jeffrey C. E42
Simmons, Jerry Matthews Jr. A673
Simmons, Juanita G. A37
Simmons, Kelly E. E162
Simmons, Lisa E253
Simmons, Pamela E369
Simmons, Patricia S. P501
Simmons, Robert J. A332
Simmons, Sabrina A373
Simmons, Tedd C. A379
Simmons, Wayne R. A693
Simola, József W217
Simon, Adam P318
Simon, David A757
Simon, Herbert A757, P241
Simon, J. Stephen A338
Simon, Lou Anna K. P319
Simon, Melvin A757, P241
Simon, Ron P66

Simon, William S. A882
Simoncini, Matthew J. A505
Simone, Joseph J. P478
Simone, Thomas B. A846
Simoneau, Marie-Claire W72
Simonelli, John P19
Simons, Doyle R. A803
Simonsen, Charlotte W192
Simonsen, Knut A298
Simonson, Eric A. A65
Simonson, Richard A. W230
Simpkin, Michael W188
Simpkins, Frank P. A485
Simplot, Scott R. P259
Simpson, David E131
Simpson, Debbie P95
Simpson, Elbert C. A687
Simpson, Jack A294
Simpson, Lisa K. E281
Simpson, Peter F. A401
Simpson, Robert G. A892
Simpson, William H. E264
Sims, Arthur P. P152
Sims, C. Randall P183
Sims, Carol M. E185
Sims, Ed W30
Sims, Frank L. A182, P109
Sims, Gregory P20
Sims, Julie A710
Sims, Kerry M. P450
Sims, Mike A528
Sims, Paula J. A682
Sims, Sid J. E157
Simson, Claudine A531
Sinclair, Ron P44
Sindoni, Edward J. E207
Sinegal, James D. A253
Singer, Brian W347
Singer, David M. A222
Singer, Jeffrey H. (Nasdaq Stock
  Market) A587
Singer, Jeffrey L. (Universal
  Hospital) P496
Singer, Mark P97
Singer, Paula R. P275
Singer, Richard D. E99
Singer, Steve P96
Singh, Basant E261
Singh, Bedi A. A376
Singh, Devinder A303, P169
Singh, Gurpartap E75
Singh, J. J. P187
Singh, Jillian P526
Singh, Kanwalinder A691
Singh, Manoj P. A274, P156, W109
Singh, Piyush K. A76
Singh, Rajeev E101
Singh, S. Steven E101
Singh, Sanjay W319
Singh, Vijay A673
Singleton, Shirley E125
Singleton, William D. P60, P309
Sinha, Ajay P173
Sinha, Arun W372
Sinicropi, Joseph P161
Siniscalchi, Patric A118
Sinkley, Jeffrey A33
Sinn, Jerry L. A296
Sinni, Paolo E199
Sinnott, Lawrence W. E363
Siodlowski, Bob P378
Siong, Chong Tze P67
Sipes, Larry P197
Sipia, Joseph A. Jr. A212
Sipling, Philip J. A547
Siracusa, Paul A. (Church &
  Dwight) A212
Siracusa, Paul J. (Hertz) A422
Sirisena, Mervyn W303
Sirkin, Allen E. A660
Sirkis, Ronald B. W58
Sirota, Gennedy H. E322
Sirpilla, John A. P192
Sisco, Robby D. A175
Siskind, Arthur M. A604

Swenson, Michael L. (Xcel
  Energy) A919
Swenson, Mike (Barkley) P72
Swenson, Scott A. A669
Swent, James W. III A324
Swetman, Chevis C. E270
Swette, Brian Thomas A172
Swick, Greg E351
Swidarski, Thomas W. A283
Swiech, Randal P444
Swienton, Gregory T. A720
Swier, Ryan P58
Swift, Alicia P403
Swift, Charles W. E52
Swift, Randy P520
Swift, Terry E. E330
Swiger, Andrew P. A338
Swiller, Ari P539
Swinburn, Peter A577
Swindel, Jim P200
Swire, Lawrence J. A462
Swist, Bob P104
Switzer, James D. A323
Swope, Jack P367
Swope, William A. A452
Swoyer, Jeffrey P390
Swyers, Philip P421
Swygert, H. Patrick P236
Sykes, Dan P274
Sykes, Rebecca P115
Sykes, Russell P444
Sylvan, Audrey E. P98
Sylvester, Brad D. E319
Sylvester, David C. A783
Sylvester, Debra A. E48
Sylvester, Pat A443
Symens, Raymond D. E337
Symons, John P84
Symons, Robert A. A673
Synowicki, Robert E. Jr. A900
Sypolt, Gary L. A288
Syrjamaki, Maxine A469
Syron, Richard F. A366
Syron, Robert P530
Syverson, Leif E374
Szalay, Maria A. E206
Szczech, Lawrence A796
Szczesny, Jeffrey D. P398
Szefc, Richard E209
Szews, Charles L. A635
Szilagyi, Gary L. E40
Szilagyi, Stephen J. A530
Szkutak, Thomas J. A67
Sznewajs, John G. A548
Szulik, Matthew J. E288
Szwed, Stanley F. A348
Szwedowski, Krzysztof W253
Szygenda, Ralph J. A384
Szymanczyk, Michael E. A66
Szymanski, Pawel W253

T

Taaffe, Paul W368
Tabak, James W. P196
Tabak, Natan A880, P522
Tabata, Teruo W291
Tabata, Yoshihiko W186
Tabb, Robert P. A311
Tabinowski, Dale P241
Tabolt, David A122, P69
Tabor, Jim A52
Tabor, Tom A426
Taborelli, Marco W103
Tacas, Sandy P204
Tacchetti, Gregory A723
Taccini, Cindy P362
Tacconi, Leonard J. P160
Tachner, Adam H. E40
Tacka, David W. A421
Tacker, Carol L. P63
Tada, Hiroshi W215
Tada, Hitoshi W231
Taddonio, Francesco W244

Tae-Seon, Hwang W286
Taff, Michael S. A556
Tafoya, Shirley E346
Taft, Terry P366
Tagli, Hugo Jr. P225
Tagliaferro, Maria A89
Tague, John P. A842
Taheripour, Mori P404
Tahernia, Omid A921
Tai, David E233
Tai, Ichiro W342
Tainaka, Kunihiko W111
Tait, Duncan A845
Tait, Steven A401
Tajima, Akio W110
Takabe, Toyohiko W228
Takada, Osamu W251
Takagi, Akinori W92
Takagi, Norihiko W176
Takahashi, Haruyuki W111
Takahashi, Hideyuki W231
Takahashi, Kazuo W105
Takahashi, Minoru W323
Takahashi, Naoya E258, W149
Takahashi, Shoji W300
Takahashi, Tadao W229
Takahashi, Tatsuo W176
Takahashi, Toshio W137
Takahashi, Tsuneo A368
Takahashi, Yoshiaki W105
Takamori, Kohichi W299
Takamori, Tatsuomi W300
Takanami, Koichi W104
Takano, Akira W152
Takashige, Mitsuo W300
Takashima, Akira W138
Takashima, Tatsuyoshi W111
Takashino, Shizuo W310
Takasu, Tadashi W92
Takasuka, Tsutomu W214
Takayama, Toshio W176
Takayanagi, Koji W169
Takebuchi, Hiroki W339
Takeda, Genyo W224
Takeda, Yoshikazu W225
Takei, Masaru W337
Takeichi, Kouichi W92
Takekuro, Ichiro W337
Takemura, Kaoru W224
Takenaka, Tetsuya W172
Taker, Bryan W188
Takeuchi, Hideshi W213
Taki, Tetsuro W225
Takimoto, Masatami W345
Takizawa, Saburo W221
Talalai, James J. P433
Talamantes, Patrick J. A554
Talbert, Harry E124
Talbert, Robin P19
Talbert, Stephen R. E49
Talbi, Stanley J. A570
Taliaferro, Elizabeth W. A379
Tallent, Jimmy C. E355
Tallett-Williams, Michael A521
Talley, Bruce A921
Talley, Emet C. P44
Talley, Joseph J. P40
Talwalkar, Abhijit Y. A531
Talwar, Vikram E136
Tam, Michael A. A156
Tamaddon, Sina A98
Tamai, Tashiyuki P104
Tamakoshi, Ryosuke W214
Tamar, Mark P523
Tamaru, Takuya W369
Tamba, Toshihito W169
Tamburo, Steven T. E258
Tamer, Ford G. A167
Tamke, George W. P435
Tamplen, Brian A302
Tamura, Jun W178
Tamura, Minoru W316
Tamura, Shigemi W337
Tan, Benjamin P483
Tan, Bian Ee P67

Tan, Ethel M. L. W303
Tan, Hock E. P67
Tan, Holly A887
Tan, Johnson E321
Tan, Larry A812
Tan, Pee Teck W303
Tan, Peter A172
Tan, Poh Lee A122, P69
Tan, William S. K. W303
Tanabe, Charles Y. A516, P281
Tanabe, Hiroyuki W309
Tanaka, Kazuo W239
Tanaka, Nobuyoshi W86
Tanaka, Seiichi (Mitsui) W215
Tanaka, Seiji (NTT DoCoMo) W238
Tanaka, Shigeharu W169
Tanaka, Takashi W238
Tanaka, Toshizo W86
Tanbourgi, Gabriel W61
Tancer, Edward F. A363
Tandowsky, Keith R. A225
Taneja, Jugal K. E160
Taneja, Mandeep K. E160
Taneja, Mihir K. E160
Taner, Marla P312
Tang, Anthony M. E79
Tang, Chengjian W304
Tang, Cyrus P467
Tang, Edmund E117
Tang, Francis E117
Tang, Paul C. P102
Tangeman, Amy J. A336
Tangen, Terrance J. E233
Tangney, Michael J. A231
Tangry, Mark J. E238
Tanigawa, Kazuo W342
Taniguchi, Nobuyuki W299
Taniguchi, Shinichi W309
Tanji, Erin E100
Tank, Andrew P133
Tank Uzun, Ali W180
Tannenbaum, Richard P107
Tannenbaum, Ross E120
Tanner, Gregg A. A420
Tanner, Harold P140
Tanner, R. Michael P499
Tanner, Ronald R. P471
Tanner, Steve P402
Tanous, Will A886
Tanski, Ronald J. A591
Tansky, Burton M. P343
Tanzberger, Eric D. A749
Tanzer, Martin S. A858
Tapia, Andrés A424
Tapp, Charles P23
Tarallo, Frank J. E340
Tarantini, Riccardo W131
Tarbox, Richard C. P461
Tarczy, Stephen C. E113
Tardanico, Susan M. A813
Tarde, Merv P247
Targhetta, Javier A367
Taride, Michel A422
Tarkoff, Robert M. A38
Tarmy, Mark J. E353
Tarola, Robert M. A915
Taron, Florence W244
Tarr, Mark J. A415
Tarr, Peter B. E143
Tarrant, Thomas E. A469
Tarry, Jason W334
Tart, C. Lee Jr. E246
Tartaglione, Bruce P494
Tarver, Van A500
Tarvin, Michael E. P433
Taschetta, James E52
Tasher, Steven A. A917
Tashjian, Lee C. A353
Tashma, Lauren S. A360
Tasooji, Michael B. A373
Tasooji, Nick P539
Tassinari, Florence P193
Tassler, Nina A193
Tassopoulos, Timothy P. P124
Tata, Ratan N. W319

Tataseo, Frank A. A225
Tate, Brenda R. A875
Tate, Christian E120
Tate, G. Truett W194
Tate, James Donald A745
Tate, John E. P143
Tate, Leland E. E43
Tate, Michael T. E243
Tate, Nicola W160
Tate, Stanley P449
Tate, William S. E68
Tatham, Alex A139
Tatlock, Anne M. P133
Tatom, Patrick G. P408
Tatton-Brown, Duncan W177
Tattrie, Amy P89
Taub, Robert E254
Taub, Stephen G. E226
Taubman, Paul J. A580
Tauke, Thomas J. A871
Taurel, Sidney A319
Taussig, Timothy T. E134
Tavakoli, Hassan Alex A581
Tavares, Carlos W229
Tavares, Silvio P186
Tavernier, Jacques W353
Tawada, Etsuji W178
Taylor, Andrew C. P176
Taylor, Bernard E135
Taylor, Beth A. P22
Taylor, Carlyle E. E285
Taylor, Charlotte P397
Taylor, Chris (Sonic Solutions) E316
Taylor, Christine (MacAndrews &
  Forbes) A533, P292
Taylor, Christine M. (M & F
  Worldwide) E226
Taylor, Chuck A236
Taylor, Colin A274
Taylor, Craig G. A888
Taylor, Dan (Brightpoint Inc.) A162
Taylor, Daniel (Ultimate
  Software) E351
Taylor, Daphne E75
Taylor, David (Ingram Industries) P243
Taylor, David L. (Ball
  Corporation) A124
Taylor, David W. (Bank of Florida) E48
Taylor, Don P381
Taylor, Douglas A. E219
Taylor, Elinor Z. P41
Taylor, Gary J. A325
Taylor, Glen A. (Minnesota
  Timberwolves, Taylor
  Corporation) P324, P468
Taylor, Glenn C. (Medco Health
  Solutions) A564
Taylor, Gregory D. (Lubrizol) A532
Taylor, Gregory T. (UAL) A842
Taylor, Harold E215
Taylor, Jack T. (KPMG) W183
Taylor, James H. (NACCO
  Industries) A585
Taylor, James T. (Thomas Group) E340
Taylor, Jean M. P468
Taylor, Jessica Gorman A580
Taylor, Jim (Sonic Solutions) E316
Taylor, John (Panera Bread) E264
Taylor, Jonathan H. (Crescent
  Financial) E106
Taylor, Joseph G. A163
Taylor, Julie A. A284
Taylor, Karl A262
Taylor, Kelvin P296
Taylor, L. Edward P180
Taylor, Lance B. (ABC) A32
Taylor, Landon V. (First
  American) A347
Taylor, Lyndon C. A280
Taylor, Mark P103
Taylor, Michael A. (FHC Health
  Systems) P185
Taylor, Michael V. (Sentara
  Healthcare) P434

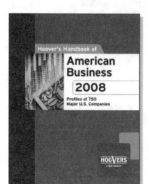

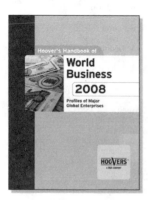